Rick Atkinson is the bestselling author of *An Army at Dawn* (winner of the Pulitzer Prize for history), *The Day of Battle*, *The Long Gray Line*, *In the Company of Soldiers*, and *Crusade*. His many other awards include two Pulitzer Prizes for journalism, the George Polk award, and the Pritzker Military Library Literature Award. He is a former staff writer and senior editor at the Washington Post.

By Rick Atkinson

The Long Gray Line

Crusade

An Army at Dawn

In the Company of Soldiers

The Day of Battle

The Guns at Last Light

The Guns at Last Light

THE WAR IN WESTERN EUROPE, 1944–1945

VOLUME THREE OF THE LIBERATION TRILOGY

Rick Atkinson

Little, Brown

LITTLE, BROWN
First published in the USA in 2013 by Henry Holt and Company, LLC
First published in Great Britain in 2013 by Little, Brown
This paperback edition published in 2014

A CIP catalogue record for this book
is available from the British Library.

ISBN 978-0-349-14009-4

Maps by Gene Thorp

Printed and bound in Great Britain by
Clays Ltd, St Ives plc

Papers used by Little, Brown are from well-managed forests
and other responsible sources.

MIX
Paper from
responsible sources
FSC® C104740

Little, Brown
An imprint of
Little, Brown Book Group
100 Victoria Embankment
London EC4Y 0DY

An Hachette UK Company
www.hachette.co.uk

www.littlebrown.co.uk

To those who knew neither thee nor me,
yet suffered for us anyway

But pardon, gentles all,
The flat unraisèd spirits that hath dared
On this unworthy scaffold to bring forth
So great an object. Can this cockpit hold
The vasty fields of France?

Shakespeare, *Henry V*, Prologue

CONTENTS

PART TWO

PART THREE

PART FOUR

Maps

Map Legend

		AXIS		ALLIED
∿	River/stream			
∿	HIGHWAY		Front line	
∿	MAJOR ROAD		Airborne drop	
∙∙∙	MINOR ROAD /TRAIL		Advance	
∿	RAILROAD		Retreat	
	WOODED		Infantry	
	SWAMP		Armor	
			Mechanized	
	TERRAIN		Armored cavalry	
△	HILL/MOUNTAIN		Airborne	
•	City/town/village with urban area		Engineers	
✿	**Capital city**		Glider	
○	Airfield			
▪	Landmark			
✸	Clash	I	Company	
		II	Battalion	
		III	Regiment	
	UNITED STATES	X	Brigade	
	UNITED KINGDOM	XX	Division	
		XXX	Corps	
	CANADA	XXXX	Army	
	GERMANY	XXXXX	Army Group	
	FRANCE			
	USSR			

ALLIED CHAIN OF COMMAND

ASSAULT FORCES, OPERATION OVERLORD, JUNE 6, 1944

Supreme Allied Commander: *Eisenhower*
Deputy Supreme Commander: *Tedder*
SHAEF Chief of Staff: *Smith*

Allied Strategic Air Forces

U.S. Strategic Air Forces Europe: *Spaatz*   RAF Bomber Command: *Harris*

U.S. Eighth Air Force: *Doolittle*
U.S. Fifteenth Air Force: *Twining*

Allied Naval Forces
Ramsay

Western Naval Task Force: *Kirk*
Eastern Naval Task Force: *Vian*

Allied Expeditionary Air Force
Leigh-Mallory

RAF Second Tactical Air Force:
Coningham
U.S. Ninth Air Force: *Brereton*

Allied Ground Forces, 21st Army Group
Montgomery

U.S. First Army: *Bradley*   British Second Army: *Dempsey*

VII Corps: *Collins*   V Corps: *Gerow*   XXX Corps: *Bucknall*   I Corps: *Crocker*

The Guns at
Last Light

PROLOGUE

A KILLING frost struck England in the middle of May 1944, stunting the plum trees and the berry crops. Stranger still was a persistent drought. Hotels posted admonitions above their bathtubs: "The Eighth Army crossed the desert on a pint a day. Three inches only, please." British newspapers reported that even the king kept "quite clean with one bath a week in a tub filled only to a line which he had painted on it." Gale winds from the north grounded most Allied bombers flying from East Anglia and the Midlands, although occasional fleets of Flying Fortresses still could be seen sweeping toward the Continent, their contrails spreading like ostrich plumes.

Nearly five years of war had left British cities as "bedraggled, unkempt and neglected as rotten teeth," according to an American visitor, who found that "people referred to 'before the war' as if it were a place, not a time." The country was steeped in heavy smells, of old smoke and cheap coal and fatigue. Wildflowers took root in bombed-out lots from Birmingham to Plymouth—sow-whistle, Oxford ragwort, and rosebay willow herb, a tall flower with purple petals that seemed partial to catastrophe. Less bucolic were the millions of rats swarming through three thousand miles of London sewers; exterminators scattered sixty tons of sausage poisoned with zinc phosphate, and stale bread dipped in barium carbonate.

Privation lay on the land like another odor. British men could buy a new shirt every twenty months. Housewives twisted pipe cleaners into hair clips. Iron railings and grillwork had long been scrapped for the war effort; even cemeteries stood unfenced. Few shoppers could find a fountain pen or a wedding ring, or bedsheets, vegetable peelers, shoelaces. Posters discouraged profligacy with depictions of the "Squander Bug," a cartoon rodent with swastika pockmarks. Classified advertisements included pleas in the *Times* of London for "unwanted artificial teeth" and cash donations to help wounded Russian war horses. An ad for Chez-Vous household services promised "bombed upholstery and carpets cleaned."

Other government placards advised, "Food is a munition. Don't waste it." Rationing had begun in June 1940 and would not end completely until 1954. The monthly cheese allowance now stood at two ounces per citizen.

Many children had never seen a lemon; vitamin C came from "turnip water." The Ministry of Food promoted "austerity bread," with a whisper of sawdust, and "victory coffee," brewed from acorns. "Woolton pie," a concoction of carrots, potatoes, onions, and flour, was said to lie "like cement upon the chest." For those with strong palates, no ration limits applied to sheep's head, or to eels caught in local reservoirs, or to roast cormorant, a stringy substitute for poultry.

More than fifty thousand British civilians had died in German air raids since 1940, including many in the resurgent "Baby Blitz" begun in January 1944 and just now petering out. Luftwaffe spotter planes illuminated their targets with clusters of parachute flares, bathing buildings and low clouds in rusty light before the bombs fell. A diarist on May 10 noted "the great steady swords of searchlights" probing for enemy aircraft as flak fragments spattered across rooftops like hailstones. Even the Wimbledon tennis club had been assaulted in a recent raid that pitted center court; a groundskeeper patched the shredded nets with string. Tens of thousands sheltered at night in the Tube, and the cots standing in tiers along the platforms of seventy-nine designated stations were so fetid that the sculptor Henry Moore likened wartime life in these underground rookeries to "the hold of a slave ship." It was said that some young children—perhaps those also unacquainted with lemon—had never spent a night in their own beds.

Even during these short summer nights, the mandatory blackout, which in London in mid-May lasted from 10:30 P.M. to 5:22 A.M., was so intense that one writer found the city "profoundly dark, like a mental condition." Darkness also cloaked an end-of-days concupiscence, fueled by some 3.5 million soldiers now crammed into a country smaller than Oregon. Hyde and Green Parks at dusk were said by a Canadian soldier to resemble "a vast battlefield of sex." A chaplain reported that GIs and streetwalkers often copulated standing up after wrapping themselves in a trench coat, a position known as "Marble Arch style." "Piccadilly Circus is a madhouse after dark," an American lieutenant wrote his mother, "and a man can't walk without being attacked by dozens of women." Prostitutes— "Piccadilly Commandos"—sidled up to men in the blackout and felt for their rank insignia on shoulders and sleeves before tendering a price: ten shillings (two dollars) for enlisted men, a pound for officers. Or so it was said.

Proud Britain soldiered on, a bastion of civilization even amid war's indignities. A hurdy-gurdy outside the Cumberland Hotel played "You Would Not Dare Insult Me, Sir, If Jack Were Only Here," as large crowds in Oxford Street sang along with gusto. London's West End cinemas this month screened *For Whom the Bell Tolls*, starring Gary Cooper and Ingrid

Bergman, and *Destination Tokyo,* with Cary Grant. Theater patrons could see John Gielgud play Hamlet, or Noël Coward's *Blithe Spirit,* now in its third year at the Duchess. At Ascot on Sunday, May 14, thousands pedaled their bicycles to the track to watch Kingsway, "a colt of the first class," gallop past Merchant Navy and Gone. Apropos of the current cold snap, the Royal Geographical Society sponsored a lecture on "the formation of ice in lakes and rivers."

Yet nothing brightened the drab wartime landscape more than the brilliant uniforms now seen in every pub and on every street corner, the exotic military plumage of Norwegians and Indians, Belgians and Czechs, Yorkshiremen and Welshmen and more Yanks than lived in all of Nebraska. One observer in London described the panoply:

> French sailors with their red pompoms and striped shirts, Dutch police in black uniforms and grey-silver braid, the dragoon-like mortar boards of Polish officers, the smart grey of nursing units from Canada, the cerise berets and sky-blue trimmings of the new parachute regiments . . . gaily colored field caps of all the other regiments, the scarlet linings of our own nurses' cloaks, the electric blue of Dominion air forces, sand bush hats and lion-colored turbans, the prevalent Royal Air Force blue, a few greenish-tinted Russian uniforms.

Savile Row tailors offered specialists for every article of a bespoke uniform, from tunic to trousers, and the well-heeled officer could still buy an English military raincoat at Burberry or a silver pocket flask at Dunhill. Even soldiers recently arrived from the Mediterranean theater added a poignant splash of color, thanks to the antimalaria pills that turned their skin a pumpkin hue.

Nowhere were the uniforms more impressive on Monday morning, May 15, than along Hammersmith Road in west London. Here the greatest Anglo-American military conclave of World War II gathered on the war's 1,720th day to rehearse the death blow intended to destroy Adolf Hitler's Third Reich. Admirals, generals, field marshals, logisticians, and staff wizards by the score climbed from their limousines and marched into a Gothic building of red brick and terra-cotta, where American military policemen—known as Snowdrops for their white helmets, pistol belts, leggings, and gloves—scrutinized the 146 engraved invitations and security passes distributed a month earlier. Then six uniformed ushers escorted the guests, later described as "big men with the air of fame about them," into the Model Room, a cold and crepuscular auditorium with black columns and hard, narrow benches reputedly designed to keep young schoolboys awake. The students of St. Paul's School had long been evacuated to rural Berkshire—German bombs had shattered seven hundred windows across the school's campus—but many ghosts lingered in this tabernacle of upper-class England: exalted Old Paulines included the poet John Milton; the astronomer Edmond Halley; the first Duke of Marlborough, John Churchill, who supposedly learned the rudiments of military strategy from a school library book; and the diarist Samuel Pepys, who played hooky to watch the beheading of Charles I in 1649.

Top secret charts and maps now lined the Model Room. Since January, the school had served as headquarters for the British 21st Army Group, and here the detailed planning for Operation OVERLORD, the Allied invasion of France, had gelled. As more senior officers found their benches in rows B through J, some spread blankets across their laps or cinched their greatcoats against the chill. Row A, fourteen armchairs arranged elbow to elbow, was reserved for the highest of the mighty, and now these men began to take their seats. The prime minister, Winston Churchill, dressed in a black frock coat and wielding his usual Havana cigar, entered with the supreme Allied commander, General Dwight D. Eisenhower. Neither cheers nor applause greeted them, but the assembly stood as one when King George VI strolled down the aisle to sit on Eisenhower's right. Churchill bowed to his monarch, then resumed puffing his cigar.

As they waited to begin at the stroke of ten A.M., these big men with their air of eminence had reason to rejoice in their joint victories and to hope for greater victories still to come. Nearly all the senior commanders had served together in the Mediterranean—they called themselves "Mediterraneanites"—and they shared Eisenhower's sentiment that "the Mediterranean theater will always be in my blood." There they had indeed been blooded, beginning with the invasion of North Africa in November 1942, when Anglo-American forces had swept aside feeble Vichy French defenders, then pivoted east through the wintry Atlas Mountains into Tunisia. Joined by the British Eighth Army, which had pushed west from Egypt after a signal victory at El Alamein, together they battled German and Italian legions for five months before a quarter million Axis prisoners surrendered in mid-May 1943.

The Anglo-Americans pounced on Sicily two months later, overrunning the island in six weeks before invading the Italian mainland in early September. The Fascist regime of Benito Mussolini collapsed, and the new government in Rome renounced the Axis Pact of Steel to make common cause with the Allies. But a death struggle at Salerno, south of Naples, foreshadowed another awful winter campaign as Allied troops struggled up the Italian boot for two hundred miles in one sanguinary brawl after another with entrenched, recalcitrant Germans at places like San Pietro, Ortona, the Rapido River, Cassino, and Anzio. Led by Eisenhower, many of the Mediterraneanites had left for England in mid-campaign to begin planning OVERLORD, and they could only hope that the spring offensive—launched on May 11 and code-named DIADEM—would break the stalemate along the Gustav Line in central Italy and carry the long-suffering Allied ranks into Rome and beyond.

Elsewhere in this global conflagration, Allied ascendancy in 1944 gave confidence of eventual victory, although no one doubted that future battles would be even more horrific than those now finished. Command of the seas had been largely secured by Allied navies and air forces. A double American thrust across the central and southwest Pacific had steadily reversed Japanese gains; with the Gilbert and Marshall Islands recouped, summer would bring assaults on the Marianas—Saipan, Tinian, Guam—as the American lines of advance converged on the Philippines, and captured airfields provided bases for the new long-range B-29 Superfortress to bomb Japan's home islands. A successful Japanese offensive in China had been offset by a failed thrust from Burma across the Indian border into southern Assam. With most of the U.S. Navy committed to the Pacific, along with almost one-quarter of the Army's divisions and all six Marine Corps divisions, the collapse of Tokyo's vast empire had begun.

The collapse of Berlin's vast empire in eastern Europe was well advanced. Germany had invaded the Soviet Union in 1941 with more than 3 million men, but by the beginning of 1944, German casualties exceeded 3.5 million even as Soviet losses quadrupled that figure. The tide had turned, red in all senses, and Soviet campaigns to recapture the Crimea, the western Ukraine, and the territory between Leningrad and Estonia chewed up German strength. The Third Reich now had 193 divisions on the Eastern Front and in southeastern Europe, compared to 28 in Italy, 18 in Norway and Denmark, and 59 in France and the Low Countries. Nearly two-thirds of German combat strength remained tied up in the east, although the Wehrmacht still mustered almost two thousand tanks and other armored vehicles in northwestern Europe. Yet the Reich was ever more vulnerable to air assault: Allied planes flying from Britain in May 1944 would drop seventy thousand tons of high explosives on Axis targets, more than four times the monthly tonnage of a year earlier. Though they paid a staggering cost in airplanes and aircrews, the Royal Air Force and U.S. Army Air Forces had won mastery of the European skies. At last, after wresting air and naval superiority from the Germans, the Allies could make a plausible case for a successful invasion of the Continent by the ground forces currently gathering in England.

In 1941, when Britain, the United States, and the Soviet Union first formed their grand alliance against the Axis, "the only plan was to perse-vere," as Churchill put it. Perseverance had brought them to this brink: a chance to close with the enemy and destroy him in his European citadel, four years after Germany overran France and the Low Countries. The Americans had long advocated confronting the main German armies as soon as possible, a muscle-bound pugnacity decried as "iron-mongering" by British strategists, whose preference for reducing the enemy gradually by attacking the Axis periphery had led to eighteen months of Mediterra-nean fighting. Now, as the great hour approached, the arena would shift north, and the British and Americans would monger iron together.

Cometh the hour, cometh the man: at ten A.M. that Monday, Eisen-hower rose to greet the 145 comrades who would lead the assault on For-tress Europe. Behind him in the cockpit of the Model Room lay an immense plaster relief map of the Normandy coast where the river Seine spilled into the Atlantic. Thirty feet wide and set on a tilted platform visible from the back benches, this apparition depicted, in bright colors and on a scale of six inches to the mile, the rivers, villages, beaches, and uplands of what would become the world's most famous battlefield. A brigadier wear-ing skid-proof socks and armed with a pointer stood at port arms, ready to indicate locales soon to achieve household notoriety: Cherbourg, St.-Lô, Caen, Omaha Beach.

With only a hint of the famous grin, Eisenhower spoke briefly, a man "at peace with his soul," in the estimate of an American admiral. He hailed king and comrades alike "on the eve of a great battle," welcoming them to the final vetting of an invasion blueprint two years in the making. A week earlier he had chosen June 5 as D-Day. "I consider it to be the duty of any-one who sees a flaw in the plan *not* to hesitate to say so," Eisenhower said, his voice booming. "I have no sympathy with anyone, whatever his sta-tion, who will not brook criticism. We are here to get the best possible results." The supreme commander would remain preoccupied for some weeks with the sea and air demands of OVERLORD, as well as with sundry political distractions, so he had delegated the planning and conduct of this titanic land battle in Normandy to the soldier who would now review his battle scheme.

A wiry, elfin figure in immaculate battle dress and padded shoes popped to his feet, pointer in hand. The narrow vulpine face was among the empire's most recognizable, a visage to be gawked at in Claridge's or huz-zahed on the Strand. But before General Bernard L. Montgomery could utter a syllable, a sharp rap sounded. The rap grew bolder; a Snowdrop flung open the Model Room door, and in swaggered Lieutenant General George

S. Patton, Jr., a ruddy, truculent American Mars, newly outfitted by those Savile Row artisans in bespoke overcoat, bespoke trousers, and bespoke boots. Never reluctant to stage an entrance, Patton had swept through London in a huge black Packard, bedizened with three-star insignia and sporting dual Greyhound bus horns. Ignoring Montgomery's scowl, he found his bench in the second row and sat down, eager to take part in a war he condemned, without conviction, as "goddamned son-of-bitchery." "It is quite pleasant to be famous," Patton had written his wife, Beatrice. "Probably bad for the soul."

With a curt swish of his pointer, Montgomery stepped to the great floor map. He had just returned from a hiking and fishing holiday in the Highlands, sleeping each night on his personal train, the *Rapier,* then angling for salmon in the Spey without catching a single fish. Even so, he was said by one admirer to be "as sharpened and as ready for combat as a pointed flint." Like Milton and Marlborough, he had been schooled here at St. Paul's, albeit without distinction other than as a soccer and rugby player, and without ascending above the rank of private in the cadet corps. Every morning for four years he had come to this hall to hear prayers in Latin; his office now occupied the High Master's suite, to which he claimed never to have been invited as a boy.

Glancing at his notes—twenty brief items, written in his tidy cursive on unlined stationery—Montgomery began in his reedy voice, each syllable as sharply creased as his trousers. "There are four armies under my command," he said, two comprising the assault force into Normandy and two more to follow in exploiting the beachhead.

> We must blast our way on shore and get a good lodgement before the enemy can bring sufficient reserves to turn us out. Armored columns must penetrate deep inland, and quickly, on D-Day. This will upset the enemy plans and tend to hold him off while we build up strength. We must gain space rapidly, and peg out claims well inland.

The Bay of the Seine, which lay within range of almost two hundred fighter airfields in England, had been designated as the invasion site more than a year earlier for both its flat, sandy beaches and its proximity to Cherbourg, a critical port needed to supply the invading hordes. True, the Pas de Calais coastline was closer, but it had been deemed "strategically unsound" because the small beaches there were not only exposed to Channel storms but also had become the most heavily defended strands in France. Planners under the capable British lieutenant general Frederick E. Morgan scrutinized other possible landing sites from Brittany to Holland

and found them wanting. Secret missions to inspect the OVERLORD beaches, launched from tiny submarines during the dark of the moon in what the Royal Navy called "impudent reconnaissance," dispelled anxieties about quicksand bogs and other perils. As proof, commandos brought back Norman sand samples in buckets, test tubes, and Durex condoms.

Upon returning from Italy five months earlier, Montgomery had widened the OVERLORD assault zone from the twenty-five miles proposed in an earlier plan to fifty miles. Instead of three seaborne divisions, five would lead the assault—two American divisions in the west, two British and one Canadian in the east—preceded seven hours earlier by three airborne divisions to secure the beachhead flanks and help the mechanized forces thrust inland. This grander OVERLORD required 230 additional support ships and landing vessels such as the big LSTs—"landing ship, tank"— that had proved invaluable during the assaults at Sicily, Salerno, and Anzio. Assembling that larger fleet had in turn meant postponing the Normandy invasion from May until early June, and delaying indefinitely an invasion of southern France originally scheduled to occur at the same moment.

As he unfolded his plan, Montgomery meandered across the plaster beaches and the tiny Norman villages, head bowed, eyes darting, hands clasped behind his back except when he pinched his left cheek in a characteristic gesture of contemplation, or when he stressed a particular point with a flat stroke of his palm. Often he repeated himself for emphasis, voice rising in the second iteration. He was, one staff officer observed, "essentially didactic by temperament and liked a captive audience." No audience had ever been more rapt, the officers perched on those unforgiving benches, bundled in their blankets and craning their necks. Only Churchill interrupted with mutterings about too many vehicles in the invasion brigades at the expense of too few cutthroat foot soldiers. And was it true, he subsequently demanded, that the great force would include two thousand clerks to keep records?

Montgomery pressed ahead. Hitler's so-called Atlantic Wall now fell under the command of an old adversary, Field Marshal Erwin Rommel. German divisions in western Europe had nearly doubled since October, from thirty-seven to almost sixty, one reason that Montgomery had insisted on a heftier invasion force. He continued:

> Last February, Rommel took command from Holland to the Loire. It is now clear that his intention is to deny any penetration. OVERLORD is to be defeated on the beaches. . . . Rommel is an energetic and determined commander. He has made a world of difference since he took over. He is best at the spoiling attack; his forte is disruption. . . . He will do his level best to "Dunkirk" us—*not* to fight the armored battle on

ground of his own choosing, but to avoid it altogether by preventing our tanks landing, by using his own tanks well forward.

Some officers in SHAEF—Eisenhower's Supreme Headquarters Allied Expeditionary Force—believed that German resistance might collapse from internal weaknesses, with the result that OVERLORD would quickly become an occupation force. Montgomery disagreed, and he ticked off the expected enemy counterpunch. Five German divisions, including the 21st Panzer Division, would oppose the invaders on D-Day; by dusk, two other panzer divisions could join the fight, reinforced by two more at the end of D+1, the second day of the invasion, for a total of nine German divisions battling eight Allied divisions ashore. "After a sea voyage and a landing on a strange coast, there is always some loss of cohesion," Montgomery said, swatting away the understatement with his palm. A death struggle to amass combat power would determine the battle: OVERLORD's plan called for Allied reinforcements to land at the rate of one and one-third divisions each day, but a bit more than a week into the fight, two dozen German divisions could well try to fling eighteen Allied divisions back into the sea.

Montgomery envisioned a battle beyond the beaches in which the British and Canadian Second Army on the left grappled with the main force of German defenders, while the American First Army on the right invested Cherbourg. Three weeks or so after the initial landings, Patton's Third Army would thunder into France, swing through Brittany to capture more ports, and then wheel to the river Seine around D+90, three months into the operation. Paris likely would be liberated in mid-fall, giving the Allies a lodgement between the Seine and the river Loire to stage for the fateful drive on Germany.

Precisely how that titanic final battle would unfold was difficult to predict even for the clairvoyants at SHAEF. The Combined Chiefs of Staff—Eisenhower's superiors in Washington and London, whom he privately called the Charlie-Charlies—had instructed him to aim northeast from Normandy toward the Ruhr valley, the German industrial heartland. SHAEF believed that loss of the Ruhr "would be fatal to Germany"; thus, an assault directed there would set up a decisive battle of annihilation by forcing the enemy to defend the region. Eisenhower also favored an Allied thrust toward the Saar valley, a subsidiary industrial zone farther south; as he had cabled the War Department in early May, a two-pronged attack "would oblige the enemy to extend his forces." To agglomerate power for that ultimate war-winning drive into central Germany, some forty-five Allied divisions and eleven major supply depots would marshal along a front south of Antwerp through Belgium and eastern France by D+270, or roughly early March 1945.

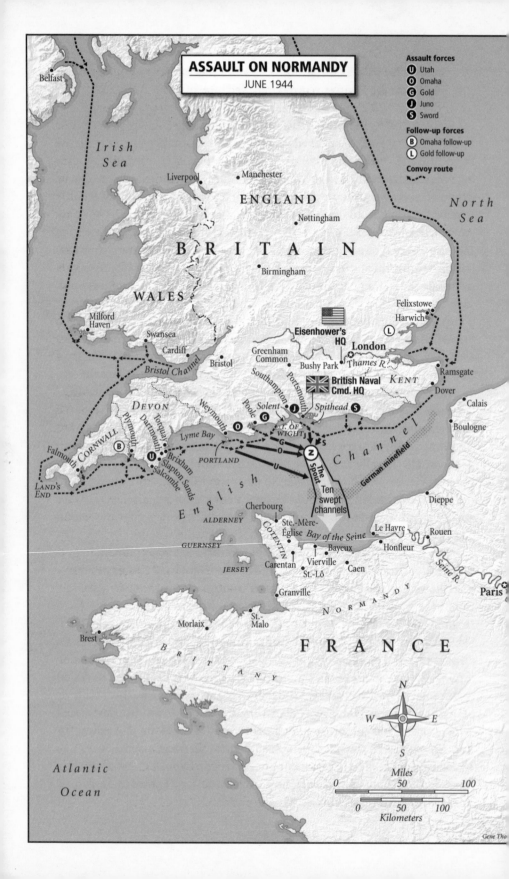

ASSAULT ON NORMANDY
JUNE 1944

Assault forces
U Utah
O Omaha
G Gold
J Juno
S Sword

Follow-up forces
B Omaha follow-up
L Gold follow-up

Convoy route

Irish Sea

Belfast

North Sea

Liverpool • Manchester •

ENGLAND

Nottingham •

B R I T A I N

Birmingham •

WALES

Felixstowe •
Harwich •

Milford Haven •

Swansea •
Cardiff •

Greenham Common

Eisenhower's HQ

L

Bristol •

London
✪
Bushy Park • Thames R.

KENT

Ramsgate •
Dover •

Bristol Channel

DEVON

Southampton •
Portsmouth

British Naval Cmd. HQ

Calais •

Weymouth •

Poole •
Solent •

J

Spithead **S**

Boulogne •

Plymouth
Torquay
Dartmouth
B

Lyme Bay

O

G
I. OF WIGHT

Z

Falmouth

CORNWALL

U

Brixham
PORTLAND

G

O

S

The Spout

C h a n n e l

German minefield

Slapton Sands
Salcombe

LAND'S END

U

Ten swept channels

E n g l i s h

Dieppe •

Cherbourg •
ALDERNEY

Ste.-Mère-Église •

Bay of the Seine

Le Havre •
Rouen •

GUERNSEY

COTENTIN

Bayeux •
Vierville •

Honfleur •

JERSEY

Carentan •
St.-Lô •

Caen •

Seine R.

Granville •

N O R M A N D Y

Paris

Morlaix •

St.-Malo •

F R A N C E

Brest •

B R I T T A N Y

N
W ✦ E
S

Atlantic Ocean

Miles
0   50   100

0   50   100
Kilometers

Gene Tho

But that lay in the distant future; the immediate task required reaching the far shore. If OVERLORD succeeded, the Normandy assault would dwindle to a mere episode in the larger saga of Europe's liberation. If OVERLORD failed, the entire Allied enterprise faced abject collapse. It must begin with "an ugly piece of water called the Channel," as the official U.S. Army history would describe it. Known to Ptolemy as Oceanus Britannicus and to sixteenth-century Dutch cartographers as the Engelse Kanaal, this watery sleeve—only twenty-one miles wide at its narrowest—had first been crossed by balloon in 1785, by passenger paddle steamer in 1821, and by swimmer in 1875. Yet for nearly a thousand years invading armies facing a hostile shore across the English Channel had found more grief than glory. "The only solution," one British planner had quipped, "is to tow the beaches over already assaulted." The U.S. War Department had even pondered tunneling beneath the seabed: a detailed study deemed the project "feasible," requiring one year and 15,000 men to excavate 55,000 tons of spoil. Wiser heads questioned "the strategic and functional" complexities, such as the inconvenience of the entire German Seventh Army waiting for the first tunneler to emerge. The study was shelved.

Montgomery closed with his twentieth and final point, eyes aglint. "We shall have to send the soldiers in to this party seeing red," he declared. "Nothing must stop them. If we send them in to battle this way, then we shall succeed." The bravado reminded Churchill's chief of staff, Lieutenant General Hastings Ismay, of the eve of Agincourt as depicted in *Henry V*: "He which hath no stomach to this fight, / Let him depart."

None departed. In quick succession other senior commanders laid out the naval plan for the invasion; the air plans in both the battle zone and across the Reich; the logistics plan; and the civil affairs scheme for governing Normandy. Staff officers scurried about after each presentation, unfurling new maps and swapping out charts. At 1:30 P.M. the assembly broke for lunch in the St. Paul's mess. Patton sat across from Churchill, who asked if he remembered their last meeting in the Mediterranean. When Patton nodded, the prime minister ordered him a tumbler of whiskey to commemorate their reunion. Of Patton a comrade noted, "He gives the impression of a man biding his time." In fact, he had revealed his anxiety in a recent note to his wife: "I fear the war will be over before I get loose, but who can say? Fate and the hand of God still run most shows."

At 2:30 the warlords reconvened in the Model Room for more briefings, more charts, more striding across the painted Norman terrain, this time by the commanders who would oversee the landings, including the senior tactical U.S. Army officer in OVERLORD, Lieutenant General Omar N. Bradley. Then they were done. Eisenhower stood for a few words of thanks, noting that Hitler had "missed his one and only chance of destroying with a single well-aimed bomb the entire high command of the Allied forces." Churchill gave a brief valedictory, grasping his coat lapels in both hands. "Let us not expect all to go according to plan. Flexibility of mind will be one of the decisive factors," he said. "Risks must be taken." He bade them all Godspeed. "I am hardening on this enterprise. I repeat, I am now hardening toward this enterprise."

Never would they be more unified, never more resolved. They came to their feet, shoulders squared, tramping from the hall to the limousines waiting on Hammersmith Road to carry them to command posts across England. Ahead lay the most prodigious undertaking in the history of warfare.

Shortly after six P.M., Eisenhower sped southwest through London in his chauffeured Cadillac, drawing deeply on a cigarette. In these fraught times he often smoked eighty Camels a day, aggravating the throat and respiratory infections that plagued him all spring. He also suffered from high blood pressure, headaches, and ringing in one ear; he had even begun placing hot compresses on his inflamed eyes. "Ike looks worn and tired," his naval aide, Commander Harry C. Butcher, noted in mid-May. "The strain is telling on him. He looks older now than at any time since I have been with him." The supreme commander was fifty-three.

As the drear suburbs rolled past, the prime minister's final confession at St. Paul's gnawed at Eisenhower. *I am now hardening toward this enterprise.* The tentative commitment and implicit doubt seemed vexing, although Churchill had never concealed either his reluctance to risk calamity in a cross-Channel attack or his dismay at the cautionary experience of Anzio, where four months after that invasion a large Anglo-American force remained bottled up and shelled daily in a pinched beachhead. Yet for OVERLORD the die was cast, spelled out in a thirty-word order to Eisenhower from the Charlie-Charlies: "You will enter the continent of Europe and, in conjunction with the other united nations, undertake operations aimed at the heart of Germany and the destruction of her armed forces." Now was the time, as Eisenhower put it, for "ramming our feet in the stirrups."

For years he had pondered just how to successfully enter the continent of Europe—first as a War Department planner, next as the senior American soldier in London in the spring and summer of 1942, then as the general superintending those other invasions in North Africa, Sicily, and mainland Italy, and now as SHAEF commander. No one knew the risks better. No one was more keenly aware that three times the Germans had nearly driven Allied landings back into the sea—on Sicily, at Salerno, and at Anzio.

Planners had even coined an acronym for the task at hand: PINWE, "Problems of the Invasion of Northwest Europe." Many PINWE issues had been aired at St. Paul's, but countless others required resolution. Some were petty—"folderol," Eisenhower said—yet still demanded the supreme commander's attention: for instance, a recent complaint from the U.S. Army chief of staff, General George C. Marshall, that motion picture coverage of the invasion could unfairly favor the British under a proposed "Joint Anglo-American Film Planning Commission." Of greater weight on the long PINWE list: a plan code-named CIRCON that ordered military and civilian police to arrest hundreds of absent-without-leave troops wandering across Britain. Also: a "fog dispeller," inspected by Eisenhower personally, that blew flames into the air to burn off mist from British airstrips, though it required sixty thousand gallons of gasoline an hour. Also: military replacements for civilian workers hired to assemble military gliders, which were critical to the invasion plan. The civilians had so botched the job that fifty-one of the first sixty-two gliders were deemed "unflyable"; another hundred, improperly lashed down, had been badly damaged by high winds.

For every PINWE item resolved, another arose. At Oxford, officers now studied Norman town construction to determine "what parts would burn best," a knowledge useful in dispensing scarce firefighting equipment. Intelligence officers were compiling a list of eighteen "leading German military personalities now in France [and] particularly ripe for assassination," Rommel among them. Given the stout security protecting such eminences, a top secret SHAEF edict instead gave priority to disrupting enemy transportation networks through the "liquidation of senior German civilian railway officials." A suitable target list, with addresses and phone numbers, would be smuggled to Resistance groups, with instructions "to concentrate on this particular class of person."

As the invasion drew nearer, anxieties multiplied. One intelligence source warned that German pilots planned to drop thousands of rats infected with bubonic plague on English cities; Allied authorities now offered a bounty on rat carcasses to test for signs of infection. Another agent, in France, claimed that German scientists were producing botulinum toxin in a converted Norman sugar-beet plant, as part of a biological warfare plot. An officer recently sent to London by General Marshall informed Eisenhower of both the top secret Manhattan Project to build an atomic bomb and of new fears that Germany could use "radioactive poisons" against OVERLORD. SHAEF consequently stockpiled Geiger counters in London; earlier in May, military doctors were told to report "photographic or X-ray film fogged or blackened without apparent cause" and to watch for "an epidemic disease . . . of unknown etiology," with symptoms that included nausea and a sharp drop in white blood cell counts.

Perhaps less far-fetched were concerns that Hitler might use poison gas when Allied troops were most vulnerable: in embarkation ports or on the Normandy beaches. Although a SHAEF consensus held that "Germany is unlikely to begin chemical warfare," never far from mind was the grim experience of World War I, when the warring powers—beginning with a German chlorine attack at Ypres in April 1915—used more than two dozen kinds of gas to inflict more than a million casualties.

Fifteen hundred British civilians had been trained in decontamination procedures. The United States alone stockpiled 160,000 tons of chemical munitions for potential use in Europe and the Mediterranean. A secret SHAEF plan, to be enacted only with Eisenhower's approval, called for retaliatory air strikes by Allied planes that would drop phosgene and mustard gas bombs. One target list, described as "involving risk to civilians," included telephone exchanges from St.-Lô to Le Mans, as well as fortified French villages used as German garrisons and rail junctions at Versailles, Avranches, and elsewhere. A second list, intended to minimize civilian casualties, targeted half a dozen German headquarters and many bridges across northwest Europe. Storage bunkers at two British airfields now held a thousand mustard bombs and five hundred more filled with phosgene.

"Everybody gets more and more on edge," Eisenhower had recently written a friend in Washington. "A sense of humor and a great faith, or else a complete lack of imagination, are essential to the project." He could only ram his feet deeper into the stirrups.

Thirty minutes after leaving St. Paul's, the supreme commander's Cadillac eased past a sentry box and through a gate in the ten-foot stone wall girdling Bushy Park, an ancient royal preserve tucked into a Thames oxbow. Majestic chestnut trees swept toward nearby Hampton Court Palace in a landscape designed by Christopher Wren, with rule-Britannia charms that included the Deer Pen, the Pheasantry, and Leg-of-Mutton Pond. An entire camouflage battalion ministered to this site with garnished nets and green paint, but the shabby, tin-roof hutments on brick piers and a warren of slit-trench air raid shelters proved difficult to hide. Code-named WIDEWING, the compound served as SHAEF's central headquarters.

Here hundreds of staff officers, including countless colonels wearing World War I service ribbons and described by one observer as "fat, gray, and oldish," puzzled over PINWE issues great and small. Plastic window sheeting, cracked linoleum, and potbelly stoves proved no match for the river-bottom damp; most officers wore long underwear and double socks.

A general officers' mess in Block C provided amenities to major generals and above. For others, French language classes at a nearby night school offered hope for a better day in a warmer clime.

Eisenhower's office, designated C-1 and guarded by more Snowdrops, featured a fireplace, a pair of leather easy chairs on a brown carpet, and a walnut desk with framed photos of his mother, his wife, Mamie, and his son, John. His four-star flag stood against one wall, along with a Union Jack and the Stars and Stripes. Visitors sometimes found him putting an imaginary golf ball across the floor, but now he sat in his swivel chair at the desk. A brimming in-basket and the maroon leather logbook of cables and intelligence digests occupied him into the evening as the furrows deepened on his brow and the mound of butts grew higher in the ashtray.

Vernal twilight lingered in the west when at last he let himself be driven down Kingston Road to a slate-roofed five-room Tudor bungalow. The ten-acre property came with a bomb shelter near the front gate, where a one-armed Great War veteran stood vigil. This, Telegraph Cottage, was the only place in the United Kingdom where Ike Eisenhower could relax, slipping on the straw sandals he had worn as a young officer in Manila under Douglas MacArthur. Here he played bridge and badminton, or thumbed through his Abilene High School yearbook, class of 1909. In nearby Richmond Park, amid purple rhododendrons and the cuckoo's cry, he occasionally rode horseback with Kay Summersby, his beautiful Irish driver and correspondence clerk. Such outings fueled so much salacious gossip about them that she sardonically referred to herself as "a Bad Woman." In the cottage this evening a stack of cowboy pulp novels awaited Eisenhower; stories of gunslinging desperadoes entranced him, he told Summersby, because "I don't have to think."

But how hard *not* to think, particularly in the late hours after a very long day. "How many youngsters are gone forever," Eisenhower had written Mamie in April. "A man must develop a veneer of callousness." British Empire casualties in the war now exceeded half a million; the sixteen divisions to be committed under Montgomery, including Canadians and Poles, amounted to Churchill's last troop reserves. British casualty forecasts, calculated under a formula known as Evetts' Rates, projected three levels of combat: Quiet, Normal, and Intense. But the anticipated carnage in Normandy had led planners to add a new level: Double Intense. According to a British study, enemy fire sweeping a two hundred–by–four hundred–yard swatch of beach for two minutes would inflict casualties above 40 percent on an assault battalion, a bloodletting comparable to the Somme in 1916.

American casualties, projected with an elaborate formula called Love's

Tables, would likely reach 12 percent of the assault force on D-Day, or higher if gas warfare erupted. The 1st Infantry Division, the point of the spear on Omaha Beach, estimated that under "maximum" conditions, casualties would reach 25 percent, of whom almost a third would be killed, captured, or missing. The admiral commanding bombardment forces at Utah Beach told his captains that "we might expect to lose one-third to one-half of our ships." Projected U.S. combat drownings in June, exclusive of paratroopers, had been calculated at a grimly precise 16,726. To track the dead, wounded, and missing, the casualty section under SHAEF's adjutant general would grow to three hundred strong; so complex were the calculations that an early incarnation of the computer, using punch cards, would be put to the task.

Recent exercises and rehearsals hardly gave Eisenhower cause for optimism. Since January, in coves and firths around Britain, troops were decanted into the shallows, "hopping about trying to keep our more vulnerable parts out of the water," one captain explained. A British officer named Evelyn Waugh later wrote, "Sometimes they stood on the beach and biffed imaginary defenders into the hills; sometimes they biffed imaginary invaders from the hills into the sea. . . . Sometimes they merely collided with imaginary rivals for the use of the main road and biffed them out of the way." Too often, in exercises with names like DUCK, OTTER, and MALLARD, the biffing proved clumsy and inept. "Exercise BEAVER was a disappointment to all who participated," a secret assessment noted. "The navy and the army and the airborne all got confused." When 529 paratroopers in 28 planes returned to their airfields without jumping during one rehearsal, courts-martial were threatened for "misbehavior in the presence of the enemy," even though the enemy had yet to be met.

The imaginary biffing turned all too real in Exercise TIGER on April 28. Through a "series of mistakes and misunderstandings," as investigators later concluded, troop convoy T-4 was left virtually unprotected as it steamed toward Slapton Sands on the south coast of Devon, chosen for its resemblance to Normandy. At two A.M., nine German E-boats eluded a British escort twelve miles offshore and torpedoed three U.S. Navy LSTs with such violence that sailors on undamaged vessels nearby believed they had been hit. Fire "spread instantly from stem to stern," a witness reported. Two ships sank, one in seven minutes, disproving latrine scuttlebutt that torpedoes would pass beneath a shallow-draft LST.

Survivors on rafts sang "Oh, What a Beautiful Mornin'" at first light, but sunrise belied that too. Hundreds of corpses in GI battle gear drifted on the tide until salvage crews with boat hooks could hoist them from the sea. Forty trucks hauled the dead to a cemetery near London, where all twenty-three licensed British embalmers—their practice was not widespread in the United Kingdom—agreed to help prepare the bodies for burial behind a tarpaulin curtain in a cedar grove. Drowned men continued to wash ashore for weeks; the final death toll approached seven hundred, and divers searched the wrecks until they could confirm the deaths of a dozen missing officers deemed "bigoted," which meant they had been privy to OVERLORD's top secret destination. For now the Slapton Sands calamity also remained secret.

Eisenhower grieved for the lost men, and no less for the lost LSTs: his reserve of the vital transports now stood at zero. "Not a restful thought," he wrote Marshall.

The supreme commander often quoted Napoléon's definition of a military genius as "the man who can do the average thing when all those around him are going crazy." Less than eighteen months earlier, even before the debacle at Kasserine Pass in Tunisia, Eisenhower had expected to be relieved of command, perhaps even reduced to his permanent rank of lieutenant colonel. Equanimity had helped preserve him then and since. Growing in stature and confidence, he had become the indispensable man, so renowned that a Hollywood agent had recently offered $150,000 for the rights to his life (plus $7,500 each to Mamie, his mother, and his in-laws). "He has a generous and lovable character," Montgomery would tell his diary before the invasion, "and I would trust him to the last gasp." Other comrades considered him clubbable, articulate, and profoundly fair; his senior naval subordinate, Admiral Sir Bertram H. Ramsay, asserted simply, "He is a very great man." Franklin D. Roosevelt had chosen him to command OVERLORD as "the best politician among the military men. He is a natural leader who can convince other men to follow him."

Yet he had not convinced everyone that he was a Great Captain, a commander with the ability to see the field both spatially and temporally, intuiting the enemy's intent and subordinating all resistance to an iron will. Montgomery, whose sense of personal infallibility and ambivalence toward Eisenhower's generalship would only intensify, offered private complaints as well as praise: "When it comes to war, Ike doesn't know the difference between Christmas and Easter." And on the same evening that Eisenhower thumbed absently through his pulp westerns at Telegraph Cottage, Field Marshal Sir Alan Brooke, chief of the Imperial General Staff, confided to his diary an assessment of the supreme commander's role at St. Paul's:

> No real director of thought, plans, energy or direction! Just a coordinator—a good mixer, a champion of inter-allied cooperation, and in those respects few can hold a candle to him. But is that enough? Or can we not find all the qualities of a commander in one man?

Eisenhower sensed such doubts, and perhaps harbored a few himself. In his own diary he lamented the depiction of him in British newspapers as an administrator rather than a battlefield commander. "They dislike to believe that I had anything particularly to do with campaigns. They don't use the words 'initiative' and 'boldness' in talking of me," he wrote. "It wearies me to be thought of as timid, when I've had to do things that were so risky as to be almost crazy. Oh, hum."

He needed sleep. Tomorrow would be hectic, beginning with morning meetings at Bushy Park; later he would decamp for another inspection trip aboard *Bayonet,* the armored rail coach he used for extended journeys. (Two adjoining boxcars, known as Monsters, carried five sedans, two jeeps, and a small arsenal of tommy and Bren guns, while the dining car could seat thirty-two.) By the end of the month he intended to visit more than two dozen divisions, a like number of airfields, and countless warships, depots, and hospitals. With luck, he would encounter another soldier from Kansas—such meetings always made him smile.

He had indeed taken risks, crazy risks, but more lay dead ahead. Eisenhower was neither philosopher nor military theorist. But he believed that too few commanders grappled with what he called "subjects that touch the human soul—aspirations, ideals, inner beliefs, affection, hatreds." On such broken ground during the coming weeks and months his captaincy and his cause would be assayed. For more than any other human enterprise, war revealed the mettle of men's souls.

By the tens of thousands, souls in olive drab continued to pour into Britain. Since January the number of GIs had doubled, to 1.5 million, a far cry from the first paltry tranche of four thousand in early 1942. Of the U.S. Army's eighty-nine divisions, twenty now could be found in the United Kingdom, with thirty-seven more either en route or earmarked for the European theater. Through Liverpool they arrived, and through Swansea, Cardiff, Belfast, Avonmouth, Newport. But most came into Glasgow and adjacent Greenock, more than 100,000 in April alone, 15,000 at a time on the two *Queens*—*Elizabeth* and *Mary*—each of which could haul an entire division and outrun German U-boats to make the crossing from New York in five days.

Down the gangplanks they tromped, names checked from a clipboard, each soldier wearing his helmet, his field jacket, and a large celluloid button color-coded by the section of the ship to which he had been confined during the passage. Troops carried four blankets apiece to save cargo space, while deluded officers could be seen lugging folding chairs, pillowcases, and tennis rackets. A brass band and Highland pipers greeted them on the dock; Scottish children raised their arms in a V for Victory. Combat pilots who had fulfilled their mission quotas, and were waiting to board ship for the return voyage, bellowed, "Go back before it's too late!" or "What's your wife's telephone number?" Each arriving unit was listed in a master log called the Iron Book, and another manifest, the Forecast of Destination, showed where every company would bivouac, momentarily, in Britain. As the men fell four abreast into columns and marched from the dock to nearby troop trains, no one needed a forecast to know that they were headed for trouble.

"You are something there are millions of," the poet Randall Jarrell had written without exaggeration. Just over eight million men had been inducted into the U.S. Army and Navy during the past two years—eleven thousand every day. The average GI was twenty-six, born the year that the war to end all wars ended, but manpower demands in this global struggle meant the force was growing younger: henceforth nearly half of all American troops arriving to fight in Europe in 1944 would be teenagers. One in three GIs had only a grade school education, one in four held a high school diploma, and slightly more than one in ten had attended college for at least a semester. War Department Pamphlet 21-13 would assure them that they were "the world's best paid soldiers." A private earned $50 a month, a staff sergeant $96. Any valiant GI awarded the Medal of Honor would receive an extra $2 each month.

The typical soldier stood five feet eight inches tall and weighed 144 pounds, but physical standards had been lowered to accept defects that once would have kept many young men out of uniform. A man with 20/400 vision could now be conscripted if his sight was correctable to at least 20/40 in one eye; toward that end, the armed forces would make 2.3 million pairs of eyeglasses for the troops. The old jest that the Army no longer examined eyes but instead just counted them had come true. A man could be drafted if he had only one eye, or was completely deaf in one ear, or had lost both external ears, or was missing a thumb or three fingers on either hand, including a trigger finger. Earlier in the war, a draftee had had to possess at least twelve of his original thirty-two teeth, but now he could be utterly toothless. After all, the government had drafted a third of all the civilian dentists in the United States; collectively they would extract 15 million teeth, fill 68 million more, and make 2.5 million sets of dentures, enabling each GI to meet the minimum requirement of "masticating the Army ration."

A revision of mental and personality standards also was under way. In April 1944, the War Department decreed that inductees need have only a "reasonable chance" of adjusting to military life, although psychiatric examiners were advised to watch for two dozen "personality deviations," including silly laughter, sulkiness, resentfulness of discipline, and other traits that would seemingly disqualify every teenager in the United States. In addition, the Army began drafting "moderate" obsessive-compulsives, as well as stutterers. Men with malignant tumors, leprosy, or certifiable psychosis still were deemed "nonacceptable," but by early 1944, twelve thousand venereal disease patients, most of them syphilitic, were inducted each month and rendered fit for service with a new miracle drug called penicillin.

But what of their souls? What of those ideals and inner beliefs that intrigued Eisenhower? Few professed to be warriors, or even natural soldiers. Most were "amateurs whose approach to soldiering was aggressively temporary," one officer observed. An April survey in Britain polled enlisted men about what they would ask Eisenhower if given the chance; at least half wanted to know what even the supreme commander could not tell them: When can we go home? A paratrooper in the 101st Airborne Division wrote, "I never will get used to having some other person do my thinking for me. All of these months and I am still a civilian at heart." And thus would he die, a few months hence, in Holland.

Skepticism and irony, those twin lenses of modern consciousness, helped to parse military life. A GI who saw *As You Like It* at Stratford-on-Avon pasted a quotation from Act II into his scrapbook—"Sweet are the uses of adversity, / Which, like the toad . . . / Wears yet a precious jewel in his head"—along with an annotation: "Sums up my attitude to the Army." Soldier slang, always revealing, grew richer and more profane by the week. "SOL" meant "shit out of luck"; the U.S. military had become "Sam's circus"; infantrymen were simply "feet"; and "SFA"—borrowed from the Australians—stood for "sweet fuck-all." The amphibious force was the "ambiguous farce." As one officer wrote, "If it's not ironic, it's not war." Most tried to keep their cynicism in check. "I expected the Army to be corrupt, inefficient, cruel, wasteful, and it turned out to be all those things, just like all armies, only much less so than I thought before I got into it," wrote a Signal Corps soldier and novelist named Irwin Shaw. Another novelist-soldier, Vernon Scannell, found that among those who had fought in North Africa or Sicily, "a kind of wild hilarity would explode in the ranks of the veterans . . . so irrational as to verge on madness."

"War is all foreground when you're in it," the fighter pilot Samuel Hynes observed. Even soldiers who sensed that "history grew near and large," in the phrase of the glider infantryman and poet Louis Simpson, would undoubtedly share Simpson's feeling that "no more than a hod-carrying Egyptian slave do I see the pyramids of which my bricks will be part." Few voiced enthusiasm for yet another American intervention in northwestern Europe—"that quarrelsome continent," as one GI called it in a letter home. A recent Army survey in Britain found that more than one-third of all troops doubted at times whether the war was worth fighting, a figure that had doubled since July 1943 but would rise no higher.

Certainly they believed in one another. Camaraderie offered a bulwark against what Scannell called "this drab khaki world" with its "boredom, cold, exhaustion, squalor, lack of privacy, monotony, ugliness and a constant teasing anxiety about the future." Like those at Kasserine and Cassino—or, for that matter, at Gettysburg and the Meuse-Argonne—they would risk all to be considered worthy of their comrades. A Japanese-American soldier who had fought in Italy and would fight again in France told his brother, "I have been greatly affected by the forces of love, hate, prejudice, death, life, destruction, reconstruction, treachery, bravery, comradeship, kindness, and by the unseen powers of God." Here indeed was the stuff of the soul.

And so four by four by four they boarded those troop trains on the docks to be hauled to 1,200 camps and 133 airfields across the British Isles. "This country reminds one constantly of Thomas Hardy," an over-educated lieutenant wrote his mother, but in truth it *was* a land of white swans and country folk who bicycled to ancient churches "in the old steady manner and unsmilingly touched their caps," as the journalist Eric Sevareid reported. Prayers tacked to parish doors in 1940 still pleaded, "Save our beloved land from invasion, O God," but no longer did the Home Guard expect to battle the Hun at Dover with decrepit rifles or with the pikes issued to those without firearms. Even some road signs, removed early in the war to confound enemy parachutists, had been put back after complaints that lost American truck drivers were using too much gasoline.

Nearly 400,000 prefabricated huts and 279,000 tents had been erected to accommodate the Yank horde, supplementing 112,000 borrowed British buildings and 20 million square feet of storage space. GIs called this new world "Spamland," but the prevailing odor came from burning feces in U.S. Army School of Hygiene coal-fired incinerators. Despite improving logistics, confusion and error abounded: the American juggernaut included 23 million tons of matériel, most of it carried across the Atlantic in cargo ships that arrived days if not months after the troops on their fast *Queens*. Truck drivers were separated from their trucks, drummers from their drums, chaplains from their chalices. Thousands of items arrived with indecipherable bills of lading or without shipping addresses other than GLUE (the code for southern England), or BANG (Northern Ireland), or UGLY (unknown). The Ministry of Transport allocated 120 berths for U.S. Army ships in May, but an extra 38 had arrived. Despite negotiations that reached the White House and Whitehall, almost half the cargo from these orphan vessels eventually was dumped outside various ports—including five thousand tons of peanuts and fifty thousand portable radios—and was subsequently lost "due to exposure to weather." Wags asserted that the Army was cutting red tape, lengthwise.

No alliance in the war proved more vital or enduring than that of the English-speaking peoples, but this vast American encampment strained the fraternal bond. "You may think of them as enemy Redcoats," each arriving GI was advised in a War Department brochure, "but there is no time today to fight old wars over again or bring up old grievances." Detailed glossaries translated English into English: chemist/druggist, geyser/hot water heater, tyre/tire. Disparities in pay caused resentment; a GI private earned triple what his Tommy counterpart drew, and the American staff sergeant's $96 was equivalent to a British captain's monthly salary. The Army tried to blur the difference by paying GIs twice a month. But British penury was as obvious as the pubs that required patrons to bring their own beer glasses, or the soap shortage that caused GIs to call unwashed Britain Goatland, or the fact that British quartermasters stocked only 18 shoe sizes compared to 105 provided by the U.S. Army. American authorities urged tolerance and gratitude. "It is always impolite to criticize your hosts," *A Short Guide to Great Britain* advised. "It is militarily stupid to insult your allies." Not least important, British producers stocked the American larder and supply depot with 240 million pounds of potatoes, 1,000 cake pans, 2.4 million tent pegs, 15 million condoms, 260,000 grave markers, 80 million packets of cookies, and 54 million gallons of beer.

The British displayed forbearance despite surveys revealing that less than half viewed the Americans favorably. "They irritate me beyond words," one housewife complained. "Loud, bombastic, bragging, self-righteous, morals of the barnyard, hypocrites." *Meet the Americans,* a manual published in London, included chapters titled "Drink, Sex and Swearing" and "Are They Our Cousins?" An essay written for the British Army by the anthropologist Margaret Mead sought to explain "Why Americans Seem Childish." George Orwell groused in a newspaper column that "Britain is now Occupied Territory."

Occasional bad behavior reinforced the stereotype of boorish Yanks. GIs near Newcastle ate the royal swans at the king's summer palace, Thomas Hardy be damned. Paratroopers from the 101st Airborne used grenades to fish in a private pond, and bored soldiers sometimes set haystacks ablaze with tracer bullets. Despite War Department assurances that "men who refrain from sexual acts are frequently stronger, owing to their conservation of energy," so many GIs impregnated British women that the U.S. government agreed to give local courts jurisdiction in "bastardy proceedings"; child support was fixed at £1 per week until the little Anglo-American turned thirteen, and 5 to 20 shillings weekly for teenagers.

Road signs cautioned, "To all GIs: please drive carefully, that child may be yours."

Both on the battlefield and in the rear, the transatlantic relationship would remain, in one British general's description, "a delicate hothouse growth that must be carefully tended lest it wither away." Nothing less than Western civilization depended on it. As American soldiers by the boatload continued to swarm into their Spamland camps, a British major spoke for many of his countrymen: "They were the chaps that mattered. . . . We couldn't possibly win the war without them."

The loading of invasion vessels bound for the Far Shore had begun on May 4 and intensified as the month wore away. Seven thousand kinds of combat necessities had to reach the Norman beaches in the first four hours, from surgical scissors to bazooka rockets, followed by tens of thousands of tons in the days following. Responsibility for embarkation fell to three military bureaucracies with acronyms evocative of the Marx Brothers: MOVCO, TURCO, and EMBARCO. Merchant marine captains sequestered in a London basement near Selfridges department store prepared loading plans with the blueprints of deck and cargo spaces spread on huge tables; wooden blocks scaled to every jeep, howitzer, and shipping container were pushed around like chess pieces to ensure a fit. Soldiers in their camps laid out full-sized deck replicas on the ground and practiced wheeling trucks and guns in and out.

In twenty-two British ports, stevedores slung pallets and cargo nets into holds and onto decks, loading radios from Pennsylvania, grease from Texas, rifles from Massachusetts. For OVERLORD, the U.S. Army had accumulated 301,000 vehicles, 1,800 train locomotives, 20,000 rail cars, 2.6 million small arms, 2,700 artillery pieces, 300,000 telephone poles, and 7 million tons of gasoline, oil, and lubricants. SHAEF had calculated daily combat consumption, from fuel to bullets to chewing gum, at 41.298 pounds per soldier. Sixty million K rations, enough to feed the invaders for a month, were packed in 500-ton bales. Huge U.S. Army railcars known as war flats hauled tanks and bulldozers to the docks, while mountains of ammunition were stacked on car ferries requisitioned from Boston, New York, and Baltimore. The photographer Robert Capa, who would land with the second wave at Omaha Beach, watched as the "giant toys" were hoisted aboard. "Everything looked like a new secret weapon," he wrote, "especially from a distance."

Armed guards from ten cartography depots escorted 3,000 tons of maps for D-Day alone, the first of 210 million maps that would be distributed in Europe, most of them printed in five colors. Also into the holds went 280,000 hydrographic charts; town plats for the likes of Cherbourg and St.-Lô; many of the one million aerial photos of German defenses, snapped from reconnaissance planes flying at twenty-five feet; and water-colors depicting the view that landing-craft coxswains would have of their beaches. Copies of a French atlas pinpointed monuments and cultural treasures, with an attached order from Eisenhower calling for "restraint and discipline" in wreaking havoc. The U.S. First Army battle plan for OVERLORD contained more words than *Gone with the Wind*. For the 1st Infantry Division alone, Field Order No. 35 had fifteen annexes and eigh-teen appendices, including a reminder to "drive on right side of road." Thick sheaves of code words began with the Pink List, valid from H-hour to two A.M. on D+1, when the Blue List would succeed it. Should the Blue List be compromised, the White List would be used, but only if the word "swallow" was broadcast on the radio. A soldier could only sigh.

Day after night after day, war matériel cascaded onto the wharves and quays, a catalogue Homeric in magnitude and variety: radio crystals by the thousands, carrier pigeons by the hundreds, one hundred Silver Stars and three hundred Purple Hearts—dubbed "the German marksmanship medal"—for each major general to award as warranted, and ten thousand "Hagensen packs," canvas bags sewn by sailmakers in lofts across England and stuffed with plastic explosive. A company contracted to deliver ten thousand metal crosses had missed its deadline; instead, Graves Registra-tion units would improvise with wooden markers. Cotton mattress covers used as shrouds had been purchased on the basis of one for every 375 man-days in France, a formula that proved far too optimistic. In July, with supplies dwindling, quartermasters would be forced to ship another fifty thousand.

Four hospital ships made ready, "snowy white . . . with many bright new red crosses painted on the hull and painted flat on the boat deck," the reporter Martha Gellhorn noted. Each LST also would carry at least two physicians and twenty Navy corpsmen to evacuate casualties, with oper-ating rooms built on the open tank decks—a "cold, dirty trap," in one officer's estimation—and steam tables used to heat twenty-gallon steriliza-tion cans. All told, OVERLORD would muster 8,000 doctors, 600,000 doses of penicillin, fifty tons of sulfa, and 800,000 pints of plasma meticulously segregated by black and white donors. Sixteen hundred pallets weighing half a ton each and designed to be dragged across the beaches were packed with enough medical supplies to last a fortnight.

A new *Manual of Therapy* incorporated hard-won lessons about com-bat medicine learned in the Mediterranean. Other lessons had still to be absorbed, such as how to avoid both the morphine poisoning too com-mon in Italy and the fatal confusion by anesthesiologists of British carbon dioxide tanks with American oxygen tanks—both painted green—which had killed at least eight patients. Especially salutary was the recognition that whole blood complemented plasma in reviving the grievously wounded; medical planners intended to stockpile three thousand pints for OVER-LORD's initial phase, one pint for every 2.2 wounded soldiers, almost a fourfold increase over the ratio used in Italy.

But whole blood would keep for two weeks at most. As the last week of May arrived, there could be little doubt that D-Day was near. The blood—in large, clearly marked canisters—had landed.

On Tuesday, May 23, a great migration of assault troops swept toward the English seaside and into a dozen marshaling areas—Americans on the southwest coast, British and Canadians in the south—where the final staging began. March rates called for each convoy to travel twenty-five miles in two hours, vehicles sixty yards apart, with a ten-minute halt before every even hour. Military policemen wearing brassards specially treated to detect poison gas waved traffic through intersections and thatched-roof villages. Soldiers snickered nervously at the new road signs reading "One Way." "We sat on a hilltop and saw a dozen roads in the valleys below jammed with thousands of vehicles, men, and equipment moving toward the south," wrote Sergeant Forrest C. Pogue, an Army historian. Pogue was reminded of Arthur Conan Doyle's description of soldiers bound for bat-tle: a "throng which set the old road smoking in the haze of white dust from Winchester to the narrow sea."

Mothers held their children aloft from the curb to watch the armies pass. An old man "bent like a boomerang" and pushing a cart outside London yelled, "Good luck to yer all, me lads," a British captain reported. On tanks and trucks, the captain added, men chalked the names of sweet-hearts left behind so that nearly every vehicle had a "patron girl-saint," or perhaps a patron girl-sinner. Almost overnight the bright plumage of military uniforms in London dimmed as the capital thinned out. "Restau-rants and night clubs were half empty, taxis became miraculously easier to find," one account noted. A pub previously used by American officers for assignations was rechristened the Whore's Lament.

By late in the week all marshaling camps were sealed, with sentries ordered to shoot absconders. "Do not loiter," signs on perimeter fences warned. "Civilians must not talk to army personnel." GIs wearing captured German uniforms and carrying enemy weapons wandered through the bivouacs so troops grew familiar with the enemy's aspect. The invasion had begun to resemble "an overrehearsed play," complained the correspon-dent Alan Moorehead. Fantastic rumors swirled: that British Commandos had taken Cherbourg; that Berlin intended to sue for peace; that a partic-ular unit would be sacrificed in a diversionary attack; that the German

Wehrmacht possessed both a death beam capable of incinerating many acres instantly and a vast refrigerating apparatus to create big icebergs in the English Channel. The military newspaper *Stars and Stripes* tried to calm jumpy soldiers with an article promising that "shock kept the wounded from feeling much pain." Another column advised, "Don't be surprised if a Frenchman steps up to you and kisses you. That doesn't mean he's queer. It just means he's emotional."

Security remained paramount. SHAEF concluded that OVERLORD had scant chance of success if the enemy received even forty-eight hours' advance notice, and "any longer warning spells certain defeat." As part of Churchill's demand that security measures be "high, wide, and handsome," the British government in early April imposed a ban that kept the usual 600,000 monthly visitors from approaching coastal stretches along the North Sea, Bristol Channel, and English Channel. Two thousand Army counterintelligence agents sniffed about for leaks. Censors fluent in twenty-two languages, including Ukrainian and Slovak, and armed with X-acto knives scrutinized soldier letters for indiscretions until, on May 25, all outgoing mail was impounded for ten days as an extra precaution.

Camouflage inspectors roamed through southern England to ensure that the invasion assembly remained invisible to German surveillance planes. Thousands of tons of cinders and sludge oil darkened new road cuts. Garnished nets concealed tents and huts—the British alone used one million square yards—while even medical stretchers and surgical hampers were slathered with "tone-down paint," either Standard Camouflage Color 1A (dark brown) or SCC 15 (olive drab). Any vehicle stopped for more than ten minutes was to be draped with a net "propped away from the contours of the vehicle."

Deception complemented the camouflage. The greatest prevarication of the war, originally known as "Appendix Y" until given the code name FORTITUDE, tried "to induce the enemy to make faulty strategic dispositions of forces," as the Combined Chiefs requested. Fifteen hundred Allied deceivers used phony radio traffic to suggest that a fictional army with eight divisions in Scotland would attack Norway in league with the Soviets, followed by a larger invasion of France in mid-July through the Pas de Calais, 150 miles northeast of the actual OVERLORD beaches. More than two hundred eight-ton "Bigbobs"—decoy landing craft fashioned from canvas and oil drums—had been conspicuously deployed beginning May 20 around the Thames estuary. Dummy transmitters now broadcast the radio hubbub of a spectral, 150,000-man U.S. 1st Army Group, notionally poised to pounce on the wrong coast in the wrong month.

The British genius for cozenage furthered the ruse by passing misinformation through more than a dozen German agents, all discovered, all arrested, and all flipped by British intelligence officers. A network of British double agents with code names like GARBO and TRICYCLE embellished the deception, and some five hundred deceitful radio reports were sent from London to enemy spymasters in Madrid and thence to Berlin. The FORTITUDE deception had spawned a German hallucination: enemy analysts now detected seventy-nine Allied divisions staging in Britain, when in fact there were but fifty-two. By late May, Allied intelligence, including Ultra, the British ability to intercept and decipher most coded German radio traffic, had uncovered no evidence suggesting "that the enemy has accurately assessed the area in which our main assault is to be made," as Eisenhower learned to his relief. In a final preinvasion fraud, Lieutenant Clifton James of the Royal Army Pay Corps—after spending time studying the many tics of General Montgomery, whom he strikingly resembled—flew to Gibraltar on May 26 and then to Algiers. Fitted with a black beret, he strutted about in public for days in hopes that Berlin would conclude that no attack across the Channel was imminent if Monty was swanning through the Mediterranean.

As May slid toward June, invasion preparations grew febrile. Every vehicle to be shoved onto the French coast required waterproofing to a depth of fifty-four inches with a gooey compound of grease, lime, and asbestos fibers; a vertical funnel from the exhaust pipe "stuck up like a wren's tail" to keep the engine from flooding. A single Sherman tank took three hundred man-hours to waterproof, occupying the five-man crew for a week. SHAEF on May 29 also ordered all eleven thousand Allied planes to display three broad white stripes on each wing as recognition symbols. A frantic search for 100,000 gallons of whitewash and 20,000 brushes required mobilizing the British paint industry, and workers toiled through Whitsun weekend. Some aircrews slathered on the white stripes with push brooms.

Soldiers drew seasickness pills, vomit bags, and life belts, incidentals that brought the average rifleman's combat load to 68.4 pounds, far beyond the 43 pounds recommended for assault troops. A company commander in Dorset with the 116th Infantry, bound for Omaha Beach, reported that his men were "loping and braying about the camp under their packs, saying that as long as they were loaded like jackasses they may as well sound like them." On June 2, the men donned "skunk suits," stiff and malodorous uniforms heavily impregnated against poison gas.

"We're ready now—as ready as we'll ever be," Brigadier General Theodore Roosevelt, Jr., of the 4th Infantry Division, wrote on May 30 to his wife, Eleanor. "The black bird says to his brother, if this be the last song ye shall sing, sing well, for you may not sing another." Each soldier placed his personal effects into a quartermaster box twelve inches long, eight inches wide, and four inches deep, for storage at a depot in Liverpool. Like shedding an old skin or a past life, troops bound for France would fill five hundred rail boxcars with such accoutrements of peace every week for the rest of the summer.

"I am a free man, so I pull no punches," a British gunner in a Sherman tank crew told his diary. "I've earned my place." The warriors began to sing, and they sang well: one soldier whose song would cease in Normandy wrote his family, "If I don't come out of this thing, I want my people (especially my father) to know I gave every ounce of my strength and energy for what I believe I am fighting for." Another young captain, who would instead survive to reach old age, told his parents back in Waco: "The destiny of life is an elusive thing."

Eisenhower left Bushy Park on Friday, June 2, for his war camp, code-named SHARPENER. Trailers and tents filled Sawyer's Wood, a sylvan tract of partridge brakes, dog roses, and foxglove five miles northwest of Portsmouth harbor. Eisenhower's personal "circus wagon" featured a bunk and a desk, with the usual stack of pulp westerns and three telephones, including a red one to Washington and a green one to Churchill's underground Map Room in Whitehall. A mile distant down a cinder path stood a three-story Georgian mansion with a bowed façade and Ionic columns. Originally requisitioned by the Royal Navy for a navigation school—nautical almanacs still stood in the bookcases—Southwick House now served as Admiral Ramsay's headquarters and a convenient redoubt from which the supreme commander could watch OVERLORD unspool.

"The intensity of the burdens," as Eisenhower conceded in his diary, had only grown in the past week. Harry Butcher on June 3 noted that his boss had "the pre-D-Day jitters." There was much to be jittery about. Each morning, intelligence officers scrutinized new reconnaissance photos and sent to Southwick House revised assessments of the beach obstacles sprouting along the Norman littoral, with every bunker and minefield plotted on a large-scale map. More alarming was intelligence from Ultra that another enemy division had reinforced the western rim of the invasion zone. A May 26 memo from the SHAEF operations staff noted that three German divisions now occupied this vital Cotentin Peninsula, plus sixty tanks and a parachute regiment, with perhaps a full additional division entrenched at Cherbourg.

Such a robust force, positioned to ambush the two lightly armed American airborne divisions planning to float into the peninsula, in turn spooked the senior air commander for OVERLORD, Air Chief Marshal Sir Trafford Leigh-Mallory. Described by one British officer as "a pompous nincompoop" and by another as a man with "a peculiar knack for rubbing everybody up the wrong way," Leigh-Mallory petitioned Eisenhower on May 29 to cancel the combat jumps of the 82nd and 101st Airborne Divisions or risk losing at least half the paratroopers and one-third of the accompanying gliders. A day later, in an appeal tête-à-tête, the air marshal upped the ante by warning the supreme commander that "this very speculative operation" could cost 70 percent of the glider force in a "futile slaughter." Leigh-Mallory added, "If you do this operation, you are throwing away two airborne divisions."

Here was the sort of crazy risk for which Eisenhower felt unappreciated. Alone he retired to chain-smoke in a tent and ponder what he called a "soul-racking problem." Canceling the airborne drop would require either scrubbing the seaborne landings at Utah Beach as well, or condemning that assault force to possible evisceration, since the paratroopers were intended to disrupt German counterattacks against the beaches of the eastern Cotentin on D-Day. Airborne calamities in North Africa and Sicily had left some officers skeptical of war by parachute, but Eisenhower still believed in the shock power of vertical envelopment, particularly if the troopers could be better concentrated. In recent days the 82nd Airborne drop zones had been shifted a dozen miles eastward, cheek-by-jowl with the sector to be occupied by the 101st. This consolidation would amass thirteen thousand men in six parachute regiments closer to Utah Beach.

Emerging from his canvas hideaway, Eisenhower issued orders worthy of a battle captain. After phoning Leigh-Mallory, he dictated his decision: there was "nothing for it" but to proceed with a plan two years in the making, even as commanders were told to review "to the last detail every single thing that may diminish the hazards.

"A strong airborne attack in the region indicated is essential to the whole operation," Eisenhower added. "It must go on."

A leafy hilltop near Southwick House offered a stunning panorama of the thousand-ship fleet now ready for launching from Spithead and the Solent, a sheltered strait separating the Isle of Wight from the English mainland. Thousands more—the OVERLORD armada numbered nearly seven thousand, including landing craft and barges—filled every berth in every port from Felixstowe on the North Sea to Milford Haven in Wales, with others moored in the Humber, the Clyde, and Belfast Lough. Late spring warmth had returned, and fleecy clouds drifted above the gray seawalls and church steeples. The scent of brine and timber creosote carried on a brisk breeze that straightened naval pennants and tossed quayside poppies, reminding the veterans of Tunisia. Semaphore lights winked from ship to shore and back to ship. Silver barrage balloons floated over the anchorages, sixty-five in Falmouth alone, and destroyers knifed hither and yon across the placid sea in an ecstatic rush of white water.

Soldiers still braying and bleating under their combat loads tramped up gangplanks or through the yawning bow doors of LSTs grounded on concrete pads at the water's edge. "Have a good go at it, mates," the leathery stevedores called. Others crammed into lighters for a short, wet ride out to troopships turning on their chains. "If any of you fellows get any closer," one soldier warned, "you will have to marry me." Tommies heated cocoa and oxtail soup on the decks; a British platoon commander marveled at being served "real white bread, which we hadn't seen in years." In Plymouth, where Drake played bowls before embarking to fight the Spanish Grande y Felicísima Armada and whence the *Mayflower* beat for the New World, so many vessels stood lashed gunwale to gunwale that "a man could have jumped from one deck to another and walked a half-mile up the Tamar River," an American lieutenant reported. Aboard the S.S. *Clara Barton*, swabs finished painting several buxom figureheads on the prow; an artillery officer scribbled in his diary, "I didn't ask which was Clara."

As always where land met sea, the U.S. Army and the U.S. Navy found reason to bicker. Each service had different numbers for the LSTs, so a perplexed GI could board both *LST 516* and *LST 487*, which were one and the same. A sixty-one-page booklet, "Preparation for Overseas Movement: Short Sea Voyage," instructed every unit to furnish forty copies of embarkation rosters, a requirement honored more in the breach than in the observance. Eighteen LCTs—landing craft, tank—were so overloaded that at the eleventh hour Navy officers demanded cargo be shifted. Sailors laboriously explained to soldiers that an LST had an immersion rate of one inch per thirty-three tons of weight; to load eight hundred tons rather than the maximum five hundred would force the crews to off-load vehicles in the surf through ten extra inches of water, drowning engines if not men. The ships were overloaded anyway. VII Corps, bound for Utah Beach, tried to board six hundred men on LSTs built to carry four hundred.

The deadweight included forty war correspondents, "an annoying and mysterious band of roving gypsies," as the reporter Don Whitehead described his tribe, summoned in great secrecy from various London alehouses. The most celebrated among them was Ernie Pyle, "sparse and gray of hair, kind and tired of face, dressed in coveralls that threatened to engulf him," in Forrest Pogue's description, "a short scarecrow with too much feet." His kit bag carried eleven liquor bottles, assorted good-luck trinkets, a Remington portable, and notice of the Pulitzer Prize he had won a month earlier for brilliant reporting in the Mediterranean. "All I do is drink and work and wait," he had written a friend. Now the wait was almost over. Omar Bradley, whom Pyle had made famous in Sicily, had offered him a berth on the headquarters ship U.S.S. *Augusta*; Pyle, wary of "too much brass," chose instead to wade onto *LST 353* in Falmouth harbor, endearing himself to the aft gun crew by autographing an antiaircraft barrel with a paintbrush.

"I'm no longer content unless I am with soldiers in the field," he confessed, but added, "If I hear another fucking GI say 'fucking' once more, I'll cut my fucking throat." Already plagued by hideous nightmares and given to signing his letters "the Unhappy Warrior," Pyle listened to a briefing on the OVERLORD attack plan and then lay awake, wide-eyed, until four A.M. "Now you were committed," he later wrote. "It was too late to back out now, even if your heart failed you."

In claustrophobic holds and on weather decks the troops made do, wedged like sprats in a tin. "I love my fellow man," one miserable soldier informed his diary, "but not in the mass." The click of dice and the slap of playing cards could be heard across the fleet, including "a long session of a wild, distant derivative of poker called 'high low rollem' using five-franc invasion scrip for chips," the correspondent A. J. Liebling reported. On *Augusta*, sailors sang "When Irish Eyes Are Smiling" around a piano, while the junior officers' mess watched, improbably, Alfred Hitchcock's *Lifeboat*. Without fanfare beyond an extra twinkling stutter of semaphore signals, convoys that had farthest to travel cast off and made for the open sea. For those who had sailed to Africa, or Salerno, or Anzio, the deep gnaw of ships' screws stirred what one veteran called "the old uneasiness."

More than five hundred weather stations were scattered across the United Kingdom, most reporting hourly. Eight U.S. Navy ships also took meteorological readings in the western Atlantic, and reconnaissance planes packed with instruments flew every day from Scotland, Cornwall, and Gibraltar. British beach watchers at fifty-eight wave observation stations thrice daily noted the height of every breaker during a three-minute interval, then sent their reports to a Swell Forecast Section. Six esteemed forecasters in England conferred twice each day by phone to discuss, often fractiously, the mysteries of wind, cloud, surf, and swell.

Each Allied invasion constituent had particular weather demands. Amphibious forces needed offshore surface winds not greater than Force 4—thirteen to eighteen miles per hour—for three consecutive days, as well as apposite tides. Pilots wanted a cloud ceiling of at least 2,500 feet for transport planes, with visibility of no less than three miles, and, for heavy bombers, no overcast thicker than the partly cloudy condition designated 5/10. Paratroopers required surface winds below twenty miles an hour, without gusts, and illumination of not less than a half moon at a thirty-degree altitude. The odds against such conditions aligning on the Norman coast for seventy-two hours in June were placed at thirteen to one.

Eisenhower had never been fortunate with his weather, despite ardently rubbing the seven lucky coins he had long kept in his pocket. Storms bedeviled the invasions of both Morocco and Sicily, and another now threatened OVERLORD. Cyclonic disturbances stretched as far back as the Rocky Mountains. Four low-pressure centers—roughly fourteen hundred miles apart and said by forecasters to be "full of menace"—had begun to drift east across the Atlantic. A great high-pressure collar around the Arctic Circle extruded cold air from the north. "The weather forecast is bad," Kay Summersby wrote in her diary on Saturday, June 3. "E. is very depressed."

At 4:30 A.M. on Sunday, June 4, in the high-ceilinged Southwick House library, a somber E. sat with Montgomery, Ramsay, Leigh-Mallory, and half a dozen other senior officers on two couches and a clutch of easy chairs. Beyond a set of French doors blanketed in blackout drapes, an immense map of southern England and Normandy covered one wall, with convoys and divisions depicted by pushpins and cabalistic symbols, which two uniformed clerks periodically adjusted from a stepladder. Standing ill at ease before the supreme commander was a tall, pigeon-breasted officer with a long face descending from his widow's peak to his cleft chin. Group Captain J. M. Stagg, a specialist in terrestrial magnetism and solar radiation, regretted to say that as SHAEF's chief meteorologist he was altering his grim forecast for the worse.

"A series of depressions across the Atlantic is moving rapidly eastward," Stagg reported. "These depressions will produce disturbed conditions in the Channel and assault area." Weather charts resembled conditions typical of midwinter rather than early summer; depression L5, now skulking toward the Shetland Islands, would produce the lowest atmospheric pressure recorded in the British Isles during June in the twentieth century. In a few hours complete overcast would blanket southern England, with a ceiling as low as five hundred feet and westerly winds up to thirty miles an hour at Force 6. Conditions for D-Day on June 5 had deteriorated from "most unpromising" to "quite impossible."

Eisenhower polled his lieutenants. "No part of the air support plan would be practicable," Leigh-Mallory told him. Even Ramsay, his mariner's face carved by gales, concurred; at Force 6, waves could be six feet or higher. Eisenhower nodded. "We need every help our air superiority can give us," he said. "If the air cannot operate, we must postpone." Only Montgomery disagreed. Conditions would be severe, but *not* impossible. He for one was willing to gamble.

At that moment the lights failed. Aides hurried in with guttering candles that limned the exasperation in Eisenhower's face. "Jesus!" he snapped at Montgomery, according to a subsequent account by Air Vice Marshal E. J. Kingston McCloughry. "Here you have been telling us for the past three or four months that you must have adequate air cover and that the airborne operations are essential to the assault, and now you say you will do without them. No, we will postpone OVERLORD twenty-four hours." The conference dissolved. Eisenhower stalked back to his caravan to read the Sunday papers between fitful naps.

Banks of gray cloud blustered in by midmorning, with pelting rain and gusts that tossed treetops and barrage balloons alike. At Southampton "the spindrift was flying scuds across the roadstead," a medical officer on the *Princess Astrid* reported, and the Portland Race was described as "a chaos of pyramidical waters leaping up suddenly." The coded radio message for a one-day postponement—HORNPIPE BOWSPRIT—reached many British troop convoys before they weighed anchor. Forces out of Falmouth had traveled only half a mile beyond the antisubmarine nets when frantic blinkering from shore brought them back.

But bombardment squadrons from Belfast and the Clyde were forced to countermarch up the black, squally Irish Sea. Worse off yet were the ships from Force U—Utah—that had put out from Cornwall and Devon the previous night to sail east down the Channel. Word passed from deck to deck that a "three-quarter gale" was blowing, a term foreign to landlubbers but quickly elucidated when the convoys came about into the teeth of a short, steep sea on the port bow. Miserable as men felt on the cold weather decks, they were fortunate compared to those below, who suffered in a green miasma of vomit and clogged toilets. Convoy U-2A, steaming at six knots with 247 vessels, failed to hear the recall signal and turned back only when apprehended halfway to France by two destroyers dispatched from Plymouth. Not until nine P.M. would the last stragglers punch through the head sea to find shelter in Weymouth Bay. Force U, the Navy reported, was "scattered and somewhat out of hand."

As anchors dropped and engines died, taut nerves led to bickering and a few fistfights. Officers tried to keep their men occupied by distributing *A Pocket Guide to France,* a War Department tract that explained the worthiness of the nation to be liberated. Soldiers also learned that "Normandy looks rather like Ohio," that a hectoliter equaled twenty-two gallons, and that the French were "good talkers and magnificent cooks." Troops studying an Army phrase book murmured the hopeful *"Encore une verre du vin rouge, s'il vous plaît, mademoiselle,"* that last often being pronounced *"mama-oiselle."* Many GIs attended Sunday church services belowdecks. In the main mess aboard U.S.S. *Bayfield,* soldiers and sailors bellowed out "Holy God, We Praise Thy Name," while a chaplain in Weymouth took his text from Romans 8: "If God be for us, who can be against us?"—an unsettling theological presumption at the moment. Dice and cards reappeared. A combat surgeon described playing "blackjack for twenty dollars a card with officers from headquarters company. I either go into this fight loaded or broke. What's the difference?" A 1st Division soldier reading *Candide* complained, "Voltaire used the same gag too often. The characters are always getting killed and then turning out not to have been killed at all." British paratroopers watched *Stormy Weather,* with Lena Horne and Fats Waller, while an American airborne artillery unit saw the bandleader Ted Lewis in *Is Everybody Happy?* Combat engineers debated whether the "D" in D-Day stood for "death."

The strange, tempestuous Sunday grew stranger and stormier. At 4:30 P.M., the Royal Marine sentry at the Southwick House gate snapped to attention upon being confronted by the prime minister, who stomped into the mansion flushed with rage at General Charles A. J. M. de Gaulle, whom he denounced as an "obstructionist saboteur." Churchill's color was also deepened by the "large number of whiskeys" he had tossed down in a bootless effort to calm himself.

The sad story was this: De Gaulle, head of the self-proclaimed provisional French government-in-exile, had recently arrived in London from Algiers and this morning had been driven to Droxford, north of Portsmouth, where Churchill had parked his personal train on a siding to be close to the great events unfolding. Although he greeted De Gaulle on the tracks with open arms and then offered him an elegant lunch in his coach, the prime minister found the Frenchman resentful at various snubs from the Anglo-Americans, notably his exclusion from the invasion planning and the refusal by Washington to recognize De Gaulle's regime. The conversation took a choleric turn: Churchill, who was said to speak French "remarkably well, but understands very little," subsequently proposed sending De Gaulle "back to Algiers, in chains if necessary." De Gaulle, who at six feet, six inches towered over the prime minister even when they were sitting, pronounced his host a "gangster."

No sooner had Churchill stormed across the Southwick House foyer than he was followed by De Gaulle himself. Deux Mètres, as the Americans called him for his metric height, was "balancing a chip like an epaulette on each martial shoulder." Only vaguely aware of their contretemps, Eisenhower received his visitors in the war room, where he revealed to De Gaulle for the first time the OVERLORD locale, battle plan, and date, now postponed for at least twenty-four hours. De Gaulle grew even huffier upon recognizing that most Gallic phenomenon, the fait accompli. He objected to "your forged notes"—the Allied invasion scrip, now being gambled away on many a troop deck—which he decried as "counterfeit money" and "a violation of national sovereignty, a humiliation to which not even the Germans had subjected France." He also declined to allow several hundred French liaison officers to embark with the Allied invaders until their duties and a chain of command were clarified. Nor did he care to record a radio broadcast urging Frenchmen to obey their liberators, particularly upon learning that Eisenhower had already recorded his liberation message—in Dutch, Flemish, Norwegian, and Danish as well as in French and English—without acknowledging De Gaulle's sovereign legitimacy. After declaring, "I cannot follow Eisenhower," he stamped from the mansion to motor back to London, *deux mètres* of umbrage folded into the backseat.

Churchill, ignoring his own maxim that "there is no room in war for pique, spite, or rancor," returned to his train outraged by such "treason at the height of battle" and mentally composing black notes for what he called his "Frog File." One British wit observed that a staple of De Gaulle's diet had long been the hand that fed him. "Remember that there is not a scrap of generosity about this man," the prime minister would write to his Foreign Office. Eisenhower in his diary lamented the "rather sorry mess." He had hoped De Gaulle would shed his "Joan of Arc complex," but now he told his staff, "To hell with him and if he doesn't come through, we'll deal with someone else."

At 9:30 P.M., the supreme commander again repaired with his lieutenants to the library, where a fire crackled in the hearth and momentous news from Stagg brightened the day's gloom. "There have been some rapid and unexpected developments," the meteorologist reported. H.M.S. *Hoste,* a weather frigate cruising seven hundred miles west of Ireland, reported in secret dispatches that atmospheric surface pressure was rising steadily. The offending Atlantic depressions, including the lugubrious L5, had moved quicker than expected, suggesting that a brief spell of better weather would arrive the following day and last into Tuesday. "I am quite confident that a fair interval will follow tonight's front," Stagg added.

Eisenhower polled his subordinates once more. Further postponement would likely delay the invasion for nearly two weeks, when the tides next aligned properly. Leigh-Mallory remained skeptical. Bombing would be "chancy," and spotting for naval gunfire difficult. Ramsay reported "no misgivings at all." The SHAEF chief of staff, Lieutenant General Walter Bedell "Beetle" Smith, said, "It's a helluva gamble, but it's the best possible gamble." Eisenhower turned to Montgomery, alert and lean in corduroy trousers and thick sweater.

"Do you see any reason for not going Tuesday?"

Montgomery answered instantly. "I would say go."

For a long minute the room fell silent but for rain lashing the French doors. Eisenhower stared vacantly, rubbing his head. "The question is, how long can you hang this operation on the end of a limb and let it hang there?" The tension seemed to drain from his face. "I'm quite positive we must give the order," he said. "I don't like it, but there it is. I don't see how we can possibly do anything else." They would reconvene before dawn on Monday, June 5, to hear Stagg's latest forecast, but the order would stand. "Okay," Eisenhower declared. "We'll go."

Outside the library, he turned to Stagg and said with a broad smile, "Don't bring any more bad news."

Across the fleet majestical the war cry sounded: "Up anchor!" In the murky, fretful dawn, from every English harbor and estuary spilled the great effluent of liberation, from Salcombe and Poole, Dartmouth and Wey-mouth, in tangled wakes from the Thames past the Black Deep and the Whalebone Marshes, all converging on the white-capped Channel: nearly 200,000 seamen and merchant mariners crewing 59 convoys carrying 130,000 soldiers, 2,000 tanks, and 12,000 vehicles. "Ships were heaving in the gray waves," wrote Alan Moorehead. Monday's early light revealed cutters, corvettes, frigates, freighters, ferries, trawlers, tankers, subchasers; ships for channel-marking, for cable-laying, for smoke-making; ships for refrigerating, towing, victualing. From the Irish Sea the bombardment squadrons rounded Land's End in pugnacious columns of cruisers, battleships, destroyers, and even some dreadnoughts given a second life, like the U.S.S. *Nevada*, raised and remade after Pearl Harbor, and the ancient monitor H.M.S. *Erebus*, built to shell German fortifications in the Great War with two 15-inch guns of dubious reliability. From the *Erebus* mast flew the signal Nelson had hoisted at Trafalgar: "England expects every man to do his duty." The heavy cruiser U.S.S. *Tuscaloosa* replied, "We are full of ginger," and swabs on *Bayfield* huzzahed Royal Navy tars on *Hawkins* and *Enterprise*, passing close aboard near Eddystone Light.

By midmorning the heavy skies lightened and the wind ebbed, recoloring the sea from pewter to sapphire. A luminous rainbow, said to be "tropical in its colors," arced above the wet green English fields, and dappled sun lit the chalk cliffs of Kent, turning them into white curtains. A naval officer on U.S.S. *Quincy* wrote, "War, I think, would tend to increase one's eye for beauty, just as it should tend to make peace more endurable." Braced against a bowsprit, a piper skirled "The Road to the Isles" down the river Hamble as soldiers lining ship rails in the Solent cheered him on. Nothing brightened the mood more than reports from the BBC, broadcast throughout the armada, that Rome had fallen at last, at long last.

Leading the fleet was the largest minesweeping operation in naval history. Some 255 vessels began by clearing Area Z, a circular swatch of sea below the Isle of Wight that was ten miles in diameter and soon dubbed Piccadilly Circus. From here the minesweepers sailed through eight corridors that angled to a German minefield in mid-Channel, where a week earlier Royal Navy launches had secretly planted underwater sonic beacons in thirty fathoms. Electronically dormant until Sunday, the beacons now summoned the sweepers to the entrances of ten channels, each of which was four hundred to twelve hundred yards wide; these channels would be cleared for thirty-five miles to five beaches on the Bay of the Seine in Normandy. Seven-foot waves and a cross-tidal current of nearly three knots bedeviled helmsmen who fought their wheels, the wind, and the sea to keep station. As the sweepers swept, more boats followed to lay a lighted dan buoy every mile on either side of each channel, red to starboard, white to port. The effect, one reporter observed, was "like street lamps across to France."

As the invasion convoys swung toward Area Z, the churlish open Channel tested the seaworthiness of every landing vessel. Flat-bottomed LSTs showed "a capacity for rolling all ways at once," and the smaller LCI— landing craft, infantry—revealed why it was widely derided as a Lousy Civilian Idea. Worse yet was the LCT, capable of only six knots in a millpond and half that into a head sea. Even the Navy acknowledged that "the LCT is not an ocean-going craft due to poor sea-keeping facilities, low speed, and structural weakness"; the latter quality included being bolted together in three sections so that the vessel "gave an ominous impression of being liable to buckle in the middle." Miserable passengers traded seasickness nostrums, such as one sailor's advice to "swallow a pork chop with a string, then pull it up again."

For those who could eat, pork chops were in fact served to the 16th Infantry, with ice cream. Aboard the *Thomas Jefferson*, 116th Infantry troops—also headed for Omaha Beach—ate what one officer described as "bacon and eggs on the edge of eternity." Soldiers primed grenades, sharpened blades, and field-stripped their rifles, again; a Navy physician recommended a good washing to sponge away skin bacteria, "in case you stop one." Some Yanks sang "Happy D-Day, dear Adolf, happy D-Day to you," but Tommies preferred "Jerusalem," based on William Blake's bitter poem set to music: "Bring me my bow of burning gold." Sailors broke out their battle ensigns, stripped each bridge to fighting trim, and converted mess tables into operating theaters. In watertight compartments belowdecks, crewmen aboard the resurrected *Nevada* stowed "dress blues, china, glassware, library books, tablecloths, office files, brooms, mirrors." A Coast Guard lieutenant noted in his diary, "Orders screeched over the PA system for Mr. Whozits to report to Mr. Whatzits in Mr. Wherezits' stateroom." Rear Admiral Morton L. Deyo, aboard U.S.S. *Tuscaloosa* as commander of the Utah bombardment squadron, hammered a punching bag in his cabin.

To inspirit the men, officers read stand-tall messages from Eisenhower and Montgomery, then offered their own prognostications and advice. "The first six hours will be the toughest," Colonel George A. Taylor of the 16th Infantry told reporters on the *Samuel Chase*. "They'll just keep throwing stuff onto the beaches until something breaks. That is the plan." Brigadier General Norman D. Cota, who would be the senior officer on Omaha Tuesday morning, told officers aboard the U.S.S. *Charles Carroll*:

> You're going to find confusion. The landing craft aren't going in on schedule and people are going to be landed in the wrong place. Some won't be landed at all. . . . We must improvise, carry on, not lose our heads. Nor must we add to the confusion.

A tank battalion commander was more succinct: "The government paid $5 billion for this hour. Get to hell in there and start fighting." Standing on the forecastle of *Augusta*, Omar Bradley, described by one colonel as "alone and conspicuous," flashed a V-for-victory to each wallowing LST before retiring to an armchair in his cabin to read *A Bell for Adano*.

"We are starting on the great venture of this war," Ted Roosevelt wrote Eleanor from the U.S.S. *Barnett*. "The men are crowded below or lounging on deck. Very few have seen action." Roosevelt, who at fifty-six would be the senior officer on Utah Beach for the first hours in both age and rank, had seen enough—in France during the last war, and in the landings at Oran and Gela during this one—to have premonitions:

> We've had a grand life and I hope there'll be more. Should it chance that there's not, at least we can say that in our years together we've packed enough for ten ordinary lives. We've known joy and sorrow, triumph and disaster, all that goes to fill the pattern of human existence. . . . Our feet were placed in a large room, and we did not bury our talent in a napkin.

Back on deck he told men from the 8th Infantry, "I'll see you tomorrow morning, 6:30, on the beach."

Far inland, at more than a dozen airfields scattered across England, some twenty thousand parachutists and glider troops also made ready. Soldiers from the British 6th Airborne Division blackened their faces with teakettle soot, then chalked bosomy girls and other graffiti on aircraft fuselages while awaiting the order to emplane. "I gave the earth by the runway a good stamp," one private reported.

American paratroopers smeared their skin with cocoa and linseed oil or with charcoal raked from campfires along the taxiways. A few company clowns imitated Al Jolson's minstrel act and joked about the imminent "$10,000 jump"—the maximum death benefit paid by government insurance policies. When a chaplain in the 101st Airborne began to pray aloud, one GI snapped, "I'm not going to die. Cut that crap out." Every man was overburdened, from the burlap strips woven in the helmet net to the knife with a brass-knuckle grip tucked into the jump boots. Also: parachute, reserve chute, Mae West, entrenching tool, rations, fragmentation and smoke grenades, blasting caps, TNT blocks, brass pocket compass, dime-store cricket, raincoat, blanket, bandoliers, rifle, cigarette carton, and morphine syrettes ("one for pain and two for eternity"). Carrier pigeons were stuffed into extra GI socks—their heads poking out of little holes cut in the toe—and fastened to jump smocks with blanket pins. Some officers trimmed the margins from their maps in order to carry a few more rounds of ammunition.

"We look all pockets, pockets and baggy pants. The only visible human parts are two hands," wrote Louis Simpson, the poet-gliderman. "The letter writers are at it again," he continued, "heads bowed over their pens and sheets of paper." Among the scribblers and the map trimmers was the thirty-seven-year-old assistant commander of the 82nd Airborne, Brigadier General James M. Gavin, who confessed in a note to his young daughter, "I have tried to get some sleep this afternoon but to no avail." The impending jump likely would be "about the toughest thing we have tackled," added Gavin, whose exploits on Sicily were among the most storied in the Mediterranean. In his diary, he was more explicit: "Either this 82nd Division job will be the most glorious and spectacular episode in our history or it will be another Little Big Horn. There is no way to tell now. . . . It will be a very mean and nasty fight."

The prospect of "another Little Big Horn," particularly for the two American airborne divisions ordered to France despite Leigh-Mallory's dire warning, gnawed at Eisenhower in these final hours. After watching British troops board their LCIs from South Parade Pier in Portsmouth, he had returned to SHARPENER to pass the time playing fox-and-hounds on a checkerboard with Butcher, then sat down to compose a contrite note of responsibility, just in case. "Our landings in the Cherbourg-Havre area have failed to gain a satisfactory foothold and I have withdrawn the troops," he wrote. "If any blame or fault attaches to the attempt it is mine alone." Misdating the paper "July 5"—symptomatic of exhaustion and anxiety—he slipped it into his wallet, for use as needed.

Just after six P.M., Eisenhower climbed into his Cadillac with Kay Summersby behind the wheel and the four-star bumper insignia hooded. Leading a three-car convoy, the supreme commander rolled north for ninety minutes on narrow roads clogged with military trucks. "It's very hard really to look a soldier in the eye when you fear that you are sending him to his death," he told Summersby. At Greenham Common airfield in the Berkshire Downs, outside the eleventh-century town of Newbury, he bolted down a quick supper in the headquarters mess of the 101st Airborne, then drove to the flight line. Hands in his pockets, he strolled among the C-47s, newly striped with white paint. Troopers with blackened faces and heads shaved or clipped Mohawk-style wiggled into their parachute harnesses and sipped a final cup of coffee. "The trick is to keep moving. If you stop, if you start thinking, you lose your focus," Eisenhower told a young soldier from Kansas. "The idea, the perfect idea, is to keep moving."

At aircraft number 2716, he shook hands with the division commander, Major General Maxwell D. Taylor, who was careful to conceal a bad limp from the tendon he had injured playing squash the previous day. Eisenhower wished him Godspeed, then returned to the headquarters manor house and climbed to the roof for a final glimpse of his men. "The light of battle," he would write George Marshall, "was in their eyes." To Summersby he confessed, "I hope to God I know what I'm doing."

Red and green navigation lights twinkled across the downs as the sun set at 10:06 P.M. Singing voices drifted in the gloaming—"Give me some men who are stout-hearted men / Who will fight for the right they adore"— punctuated by a guttural roar from paratroopers holding their knives aloft in homicidal resolve. Into the airplane bays they heaved themselves, with a helpful shove from behind. Many knelt on the floor to rest their cumbersome gear and chutes on a seat, faces bathed by the soft glow of cigarette embers and red cabin lights. "Give me guts," one trooper prayed. "Give me guts." Engines coughed and caught, the feathered propellers popping as crew chiefs slammed the doors. "Flap your wings, you big-assed bird," a soldier yelled.

From the west the last gleam of a dying day glinted off the aluminum fuselages. "Stay, light," a young soldier murmured, "stay on forever, and we'll never get to Normandy."

The light faded and was gone. Deep into the Channel, fifty-nine darkened convoys went to battle stations as they pushed past the parallel rows of dim buoys, red to starboard, white to port. "Our flag bridge is dead quiet," Admiral Deyo wrote on *Tuscaloosa*. An officer on *Quincy* noted, "This is like trying to slip into a room where everyone is asleep."

Small craft struggled in the wind and lop. "Men sick, waves washed over deck," an LCT log recorded. "Stove went out, nothing to eat, explosives wet and could not be dried out." Short seas snapped tow ropes, flooded engine rooms, and sloshed through troop compartments. Some helmsmen held their wheels thirty degrees off true to keep course. Several heaving vessels blinkered a one-word message: "Seasick. Seasick. Seasick."

Down the ten channels they plunged, two designated for each of the five forces steaming toward five beaches: Utah, Omaha, Gold, Juno, Sword. Wakes braided and rebraided. The amber orb of a full moon rose through a thinning overcast off the port bow, and the sea sang as swells slipped along every hull bound for a better world. Hallelujah, sang the sea. Hallelujah. Hallelujah.

Part One

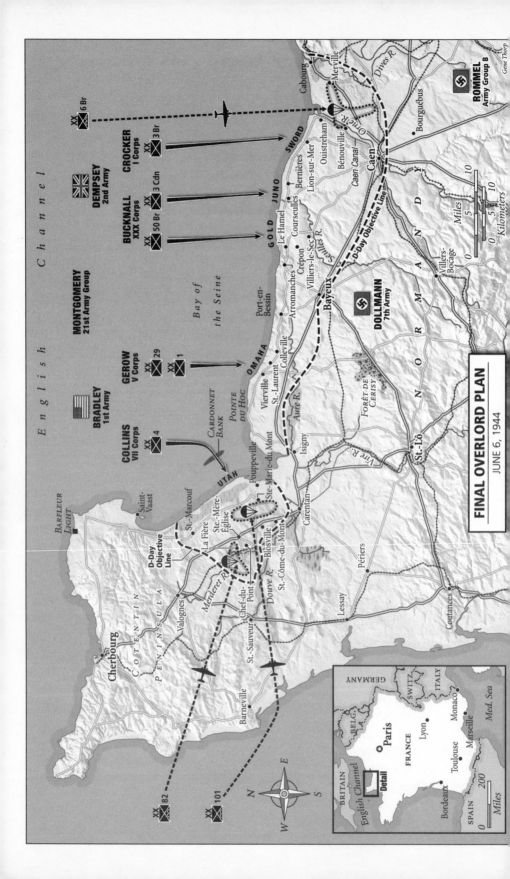

FINAL OVERLORD PLAN

JUNE 6, 1944

1. INVASION

The Far Shore

THE singing stopped as the Norman coast drew near. Stars threw down their silver spears on a long column of eight hundred airplanes ferrying thirteen thousand American paratroopers to battle. South they flew and low, skimming the inky Channel, then turning sharply east to climb between the islands of Guernsey and Alderney. Dead ahead in the moonlight lay the Cotentin Peninsula, famed for cattle and stiff with Germans. Jumpmasters barked above the engine drone, ordering the men to their feet. With a portentous *click* the sixteen or seventeen jumpers in each bay snapped their parachutes to static lines running overhead. Shortly after one A.M. on Tuesday, June 6, 1944, a captain standing in the slipstream of an open doorway peered down at the white surf beating against a beach. "Say hello to France!" he shouted. Red lights flashed to warn that four minutes ahead lay the drop zones—three tight ovals for the 101st Airborne Division in the lead, three more for the 82nd Airborne close behind.

Then France vanished. A gray cloud bank, unsuspected and so thick that pilots could barely see their own wingtips, swallowed planes, then groups of planes. Formations disintegrated as the C-47 Dakotas climbed and dove to avoid colliding. Dark patches of earth swam up through the murk only to disappear, and now German antiaircraft fire—like "so many lighted tennis balls," in one witness's description—began to rip into the clouds. Searchlight beams and magnesium flares drenched the cockpits in molten light, dazzling callow pilots who lurched left and right despite orders forbidding evasive jinking. Enemy tracers "thick enough to walk on" stitched the flak-spangled sky, one paratrooper reported, and shells blew through aluminum skins as if "someone threw a keg of nails against the side of the airplane." Three GIs died when a smoking two-foot hole opened in a fuselage; a dozen others became so entangled after slipping on the vomit-slick floor that they would return to England without jumping.

Even as the cloud bank thinned to the east, bewildered crewmen mistook one French village for another. Some of the pathfinders who had parachuted an hour earlier either missed the drop zones they were supposed to illuminate—using electronic transmitters and seven signal lamps arranged in a beckoning T—or else found enemy troops infesting the ground. Green jump lights began to flash in the aircraft bays anyway. Some flashed too soon or too late, dumping howling paratroopers into the sea. Cargo bundles got stuck in aircraft doors, delaying the queued troopers for two miles or more. Other planes failed to descend to the specified jump height of 500 feet, or to slow to 110 miles an hour; chutes ripped open with such G-force violence that "anything in my jump pants pockets simply burst through the reinforced bottom seams," a trooper recalled. Rations, grenades, underwear, and cooing pigeons spilled into the night. Gunfire thickened "like a wall of flame." Rather than half a minute, "the trip down took a thousand years," a private later told his family. One chute snagged on a vertical stabilizer, dragging the flailing jumper into the night; another soldier hurtled earthward beneath burning shreds of silk. Men in parachutes that failed to open hit the ground with a sound likened by one soldier to "watermelons falling off the back of a truck."

"I pulled up my knees to make myself as small a target as possible," a trooper in the 507th Parachute Infantry wrote. "I pulled on my risers to try to slip away from the fire." Flames licked through the cabin of a gut-shot C-47 as frantic soldiers dove out the door before the plane heeled onto its left wing, then stalled and crashed. Most of the jumpers survived; the crew did not. A burning building near St.-Côme-du-Mont gave German defenders enough illumination to fatally shoot a battalion commander, his executive officer, and a company commander before they touched France. Three other company commanders were captured.

Operation ALBANY, the 101st Airborne mission, was intended to seize four elevated causeways, each roughly a mile apart, leading from Utah Beach to the Cotentin interior. American planners knew that marshlands behind the sea dunes had been flooded with two to four feet of water by German engineers, who dammed eight small streams with boulders and tree branches to isolate any invaders arriving on the coastline. Planners did *not* know that the enemy inundations were in fact far more ambitious. Canals, dams, and locks in the southeast Cotentin, some dating to Napóleon's day, drained the watershed of the Douve and Merderet Rivers, creating pasture for those famous cows. Beginning in late 1942, German occupiers closed some floodgates and opened others, allowing tidal surges to create an inland sea ten miles long and up to ten feet deep. Reeds and marsh grass now grew so dense that not even the one million aerial photographs snapped by Allied reconnaissance planes had revealed the extensive flooding. No one was more surprised than the many flailing paratroopers who upon arriving over the coast of France had removed their life vests in the airplane bays only to be pulled to brackish graves by their heavy kit.

At four A.M., as thousands of lost and scattered parachutists blundered about in the dark, the first fifty-two gliders arrived "like a swarm of ravens," in one German description. Most were fifty-foot Wacos, each so flimsy "you could shoot an arrow through it," as a captain admitted, and without the hardened nose caps ordered in February but yet to arrive. Cut loose from their tow planes, they drifted to earth; pilots who had rarely if ever flown at night felt for the unseen ground while bullets punctured the gliders' fabric skins with a sound likened by a flight officer to "typewriter keys banging on loose paper." Some found the landing zone near Blosville, others found stone walls, tree trunks, dozing livestock, or the pernicious antiglider stakes known as Rommel's asparagus. All eight men in a 101st Airborne surgical team were injured in a crash. A Waco with a large "1" painted on the nose skipped downhill on wet grass for eight hundred feet before smashing into a stout sycamore, breaking both legs of the pilot and killing the copilot; in the cargo bay, as if napping in his jeep, sat the 101st assistant division commander, Brigadier General Don F. Pratt, dead from a broken neck. Survivors kicked through the glider fabric—"like bees out of a hive they came from that hole," a witness reported—and began to salvage the small bulldozer, antitank guns, and medical supplies now on Norman soil.

Of more than six thousand jumpers from the 101st Airborne, barely one thousand had landed on or near the H-hour objectives on this Tuesday morning. Most of the fifteen hundred–odd who had drifted far beyond the eight-mile square enclosing the division drop zones would be killed or captured; a few made their way to safety with maps torn from local telephone books by French farmers. More than half of all supply bundles lay beyond retrieval at the bottom of various water meadows, with a devastating loss of radios, mortars, and eleven of twelve 75mm pack howitzers. A sergeant peering into a barn found "men lying in the straw, wrapped in bloody soiled parachutes, their faces darkened and bandages stained."

Yet stalwart men, those stout-hearts celebrated in song, gathered themselves to press on. An officer pounding on a farmhouse door to ask directions announced in his best French, *"L'invasion est arrivé"*; a voice from the second-floor window replied, *"Très bien."* The 101st's commander, Major General Taylor, wandered in the dark on his gimpy leg with a drawn pistol and a dime-store cricket, collecting lost paratroopers and politely declining the ancient rifle offered by a French farmer who said, *"Allez me tuer un Boche."* Go kill me a German. In the first apricot glow of dawn, Taylor recognized the silhouette of Ste.-Marie-du-Mont's eleventh-century church with gargoyle drainpipes protruding from the soaring stone tower. While paratroopers and Germans exchanged gunfire in the belfry and around the confessional, Taylor sent a small force east to Pouppeville to rout the enemy garrison house by house and seize the southernmost causeway exit from Utah Beach. Three miles north, the 3rd Battalion of the 502nd Parachute Infantry did the same with the two northern causeways.

Five hours after leaping into Normandy, paratroopers lined the sandy ridge overlooking the flooded marshes behind the dunes, waiting for Force U to emerge from the sea.

In June 1940, led by officers on horseback, the first German troops had arrived in the village of Ste.-Mère-Église singing *"Wir fahren gegen England."* If they had never quite journeyed on to England, life as a Norman occupier proved pleasant enough. Clocks were set to Berlin time and ration cards issued to the locals, guaranteeing ample butter and cream for the master race. A huge swastika flag flew outside the town hall, near a spring once believed by pilgrims to have healing powers. Four years after the invasion, farmers still arrived on market day to weigh their wool and grain beneath chestnut and lime trees across from the ancient church, with its paired Gothic windows and its handrail of sculpted four-leaf clovers. A small garrison of Austrian antiaircraft gunners bivouacked nearby. They drove wood-burning trucks, and it was said that their elderly commander had once been the music critic for a Vienna newspaper; now his greatest interest seemed to lie in the bottom of a wineglass. Yet growing German anxiety about an impending invasion could be seen in the feverish construction this spring of Rommel's asparagus, and in the severe penalties levied for listening to the BBC.

No objective was more important than Ste.-Mère-Église for the 82nd Airborne as the division's six thousand men swooped over Normandy an hour behind the 101st. Roads from all compass points converged here, and the trunk cable linking Cherbourg in the north with Carentan in the south passed through Ste.-Mère. Unless it held the town, the 82nd had "almost no chance to sustain offensive operations across the Merderet River and to the westward," a regimental study concluded. Thus, when the division drop zones were abruptly shifted in late May, they tended to cluster around this drowsy medieval crossroads of a thousand souls.

Alas, the drops in Operation BOSTON proved even more deranged than those of ALBANY. Paratroopers sifted to earth as far as fifteen miles north of their intended zones, and twenty-five miles south; those too far afield east and west plunged into the Atlantic and vanished. Less than half of the following gliders landed within a mile of the landing zone, and many were demolished, with dire losses of antitank guns and other heavy gear. Brigadier General Jim Gavin, who had fretted over another Little Bighorn, floated into an apple orchard and spent the small hours of June 6 with M-1 rifle in hand, shoving scratch forces toward the critical Merderet bridges at La Fière and Chef-du-Pont. Soldiers stripped naked in the moonlight to dive for equipment bundles in the fens. A German train bushwhacked in the Chef-du-Pont station yielded only Norman cheese and empty bottles. One gunfight along the Merderet grew so frenzied that paratroopers not only shot down enemy soldiers but also slaughtered livestock in a barn. A lieutenant leading a patrol bayoneted three wounded Germans on a dirt road; he "felt that he could not take any prisoners," a unit report explained, "so he dispatched them." The wolf had risen in the heart, already.

Of the division's three parachute infantry regiments, only the 505th made a credible drop northwest of Ste.-Mère. A fire, perhaps ignited by a hissing flare, had awakened both the town and its German garrison. As a sexton hauled on the bell-tower ropes, villagers passed canvas buckets hand over hand from the cattle-market pump to a blazing villa across the church square. Then without warning C-47s roared just overhead, wingtip to wingtip, spitting out paratroopers who frantically tugged on their risers to sheer away from both the flames and aroused German gunners.

A few GIs were butchered in their harnesses, including one young trooper who dangled from a tree bough "with eyes open, as though looking down at his own bullet holes," as the Ste.-Mère mayor recorded. But hundreds more landed unmolested after pilots circled back through the gunfire to find the correct drop zone. The 3rd Battalion commander, Lieutenant Colonel Edward C. Krause, known as Cannonball, managed to round up a quarter of his men. Led through hedgerow shadows by a drunk Frenchman impressed as a guide, they crept into Ste.-Mère from the northwest, bounding between doorways with orders to avoid telltale muzzle flashes by using only knives, bayonets, and grenades. Ten Germans died defending the town they had held for four years, but most fled and a few hard sleepers were captured in their bunks. Four hundred yards from the church square, Krause personally severed the cable to Cherbourg. Patrols built roadblocks outside town with antitank mines and plastic explosive Gammon grenades. A burial detail cut down a half-dozen dead paratroopers still dangling from the chestnut trees.

In front of the town hall, Krause from his haversack pulled the same American flag raised over Naples when the battalion first entered that city on October 1, 1943. He hoisted it on a wobbly pole, then at five A.M. sent a runner—few radios had survived the drop—with a message that reached the division commander, Major General Matthew B. Ridgway: "I am in Ste. Mère Église." An hour later a second runner carried a postscript: "I have secured Ste. Mère Église." The Americans had liberated their first town in France.

By dawn, 816 planes and 100 gliders had inserted more than 13,000 GIs onto the Continent; only 21 planes had been shot down, far less than the carnage predicted by Air Marshal Leigh-Mallory. Yet only one of six regiments had been delivered where intended, and it was the sole regiment able to fight as a cohesive, three-battalion force, albeit at only half strength. Air commanders had not sent an advance weather plane to warn of the low cloud banks so common over Normandy in June; in this failure, they were remiss if not derelict. Dispersion thinned the combat power of a force armed with little more than rifles and grenades. But, as in Sicily, the haphazard scattering was "not an unmixed evil," as the official Army history would put it: dispersion confused the enemy as well as the dispersed. Across the Cotentin could be heard the metallic *thwang* of phone and telegraph wires snipped by paratroopers. Captured Germans were ordered to lie on their backs in a radial pattern, feet touching, awaiting evacuation to prisoner cages. Many others, gunned down in ambushes, simply lay dead.

Shortly before dawn, an American light bomber flew the first night photo-reconnaissance mission over Europe, illuminating the Norman landscape from 8,000 feet with a 200-million-candlepower electric lamp carried in the open bomb bay like a tiny sun. After shooting 180 exposures, the plane circled back to England, where analysts would study the film, frame by frame, looking for panzers trundling toward the Cotentin in the inevitable German counterattack.

Fifty miles to the east, the British 6th Airborne Division had crossed the coast of France, keen to settle scores after half a decade of war. Tommies hoping to bop a sleeping German heaved miscellaneous objects out the open doors of their transport planes: bricks inscribed with vulgarisms, a soccer ball painted to resemble Hitler's face, and a stuffed moose head purloined from an Exeter pub. Almost five thousand paratroopers and glidermen followed.

Two parachute brigades were to secure OVERLORD's left flank by seizing bridges over the river Orne and its attendant canal northeast of Caen while blowing up spans across the river Dives, which flowed roughly parallel five miles farther east. Many of the vicissitudes plaguing their American comrades in the Cotentin Peninsula bedeviled the British too: more than half the pathfinders landed in the wrong place, their electronic beacons and signal lamps damaged, missing, or invisible from the air after being ill-sited amid tall wheat. Evasive maneuvering knocked some paratroopers off balance and delayed their jumps; in one flock of ninety-one planes, only seventeen dropped in the correct spot. An antiaircraft shell blew a major from the 3rd Brigade through a hole in his plane's fuselage. With a static line wrapped around his legs, he dangled beneath the aircraft for half an hour until he was reeled back into the bay. He returned to England and then, later on June 6, made France by glider, mussed but unharmed.

Less fortunate were the men dumped into the Atlantic or the flooded Dives valley. One sodden brigadier took four hours to wade to the riverbank near Cabourg, steeping in the sixty tea bags he had sewn into his battle dress. "We could see where parachute canopies had collapsed in silken circles on the water," an officer reported. Bodies would be discovered in the Dives muck for the next half century.

Amid calamity came a celebrated success. Half a dozen large Horsa gliders, a craft named for the wife of a Saxon king but known as the "Flying Morgue" for its tendency to disintegrate in hard landings, carried 181 men under Major John Howard, a former Oxford policeman. Cheered by urns of tea spiked with rum, they too had sung—"Cow Cow Boogie" and "It's a Long Way to Tipperary"—until the pilots shouted, "Casting off!," and tow ropes parted from the Halifax bombers ahead. For three minutes Howard and his men sat in silence but for wind shrieking over the barndoor flaps, their arms linked and fingers locked in a butcher's grip. Three Horsas led by *Lady Irene* corkscrewed to the west until a pilot spotted their target and abruptly yelped, "Christ, there's the bridge!" Then: "Brace for impact!" With a sound likened by one private to "a giant sheet being ripped apart," the gliders clipped France at one hundred miles an hour, the wheels torn away as the Horsas bounded into the air, then settled on their skids in an orange spray of sparks so intense the glidermen mistook them for German tracers. Stunned but uninjured, Howard and his men wiggled headfirst through jagged holes in the glider fabric, lugging their Sten guns and canvas buckets brimming with grenades.

There, hardly fifty yards from *Lady Irene*'s battered nose, stood the squat Bénouville bridge over the Caen canal. An astonished sentry turned and fled, bellowing in alarm. A Very flare floated overhead, silvering the dark water, and fifty enemy soldiers—mostly *Osttruppen* conscripts from eastern Europe—stumbled toward the western bridge ramp as gunfire pinged from girders and rails. Too late: Howard's men shot and grenaded their way across, shouting "Able," "Baker," and "Charlie" to keep the three platoons intact. "Anything that moved," a British soldier later acknowledged, "we shot."

One platoon commander fell dead from enemy fire, but within a quarter hour the span belonged to the British. The German bridge commander was captured when his car, laden with lingerie and perfume, skittered into a ditch; to atone for the loss of his honor, he asked in vain to be shot. Three rickety French tanks crewed by Germans lumbered toward the bridge only to be smacked with Piat antiarmor fire. Two fled and the third burned for an hour after a crewman crawled from his hatch with both legs missing. Major Howard soon got word that the other half of his command had captured the nearby Orne River bridge at Ranville. He ordered the heartening news to be broadcast in a coded radio message, then dug in to await both reinforcement and a more resolute enemy counterstroke.

Across the Orne and Dives floodplains additional gliders plummeted after midair collisions caused by treacherous crosswinds, or crash-landed with the usual mangled undercarriages. One Horsa skidded through a cottage and emerged, it was said, bearing a double bed with a French couple still under the duvet. Hunting horns and bugles tooted in the night as officers rallied their scattered companies. After one vicious burst of gunfire, an unhinged young paratrooper cried, "They got my mate! They got my mate!" Mates fell, but so did bridges: those over the Orne were captured, and four across the Dives were blown.

Perhaps the most perilous mission fell to the 9th Battalion of the Parachute Regiment, ordered to destroy a coastal battery at Merville believed capable of ranging Sword Beach, easternmost of the OVERLORD quintet. Surrounded by a cattle fence, minefields, barbed-wire thickets, and machine-gun pits, the big guns and two hundred gunners were protected by steel doors and concrete six feet thick, with twelve feet of dirt overhead. Of 750 paratroopers dropped to do the deed, only 150 landed near the assembly area. Instead of sixty lengths of bangalore torpedo—metal tubes packed with explosive to breach barbed wire—just sixteen could be found by three A.M.

No matter. The bangalores blew two gaps rather than the planned four. Creeping paratroopers defused mines and trip-wire booby traps with their fingers. While a diversionary attack forced the main gate, assault teams slaughtered Germans by the score and spiked the guns by removing their breechblocks. A signal officer dispatched the news to England by banded pigeon. Though the guns proved both smaller and fewer than expected—only 75mm, and two rather than four—the menacing Merville battery had fallen. The price had been high: "I went in with 150," the battalion commander reported, "and came out with only 65 on their feet."

The butcher's bill had indeed been high for airborne forces on both flanks of the invasion crescent. Fewer than half of the 4,800 British troops now in France were either sufficiently near or sufficiently alive to join the fight in coherent units on June 6; still, the fraction exceeded that of American forces to the west. Yet this day would be famous even before it dawned, in no small measure because of the gutful men who had come to war by air. Beset by mischance, confounded by disorder, they had mostly done what they were asked to do. Now the battle would hang on those who came by sea.

First Tide

S HIP by ship, convoy by convoy, the OVERLORD fleets slid into the broad, black Bay of the Seine. A vanguard of minesweepers carved an intricate maze of swept channels, demarcated by dan buoys agleam in the phosphorescent sea. Sailors and soldiers alike were astonished to find the Barfleur lighthouse still burning east of Cherbourg; among the world's tallest and most conspicuous beacons, the rotating double flash was visible for thirty miles. Ahead lay the dark coastline where it was said that Norman pirates once paraded lanterns on the horns of oxen to imitate ships' lights, pulling rings from the fingers of drowned passengers on vessels lured onto the reefs. Glints of gold and crimson could be seen far to starboard over the Cotentin and far to port above the Orne—airborne troops had apparently found the fight they were seeking. A pilot in a P-51 Mustang, peering down at the armada spread across the teeming sea, would recognize an ancient, filthy secret: "War in these conditions is, for a short span, magnificent."

On the pitching decks below, grandeur remained elusive. Riflemen on the bridge wings of two old Channel steamers, H.M.S. *Prince Baudouin* and H.M.S. *Prince Leopold,* watched for mines beyond the bow waves. "Fear," a Coast Guardsman on *LCI-88* mused, "is a passion like any other passion." A ship's doctor on *Bayfield* confessed to drinking "so much coffee that I was having extra systoles every fourth or fifth beat." A veteran sergeant from Virginia aboard the *Samuel Chase* recorded, "The waiting is always the worst. The mind can wander." Waiting for battle induced the philosopher in every man. "Mac," a young soldier in the 16th Infantry asked a comrade, "when a bullet hits you, does it go all the way through?" A chaplain peering over the shoulder of a Royal Navy officer found him reading Horace's *Satires: "Si quid forte jocosius hoc mihi juris cum venia dabis dixero."* If I perchance have spoken too facetiously, indulge me.

At two A.M. the ship's loudspeaker on U.S.S. *Samuel Chase* broke up a poker game and summoned GIs to breakfast, where mess boys in white jackets served pancakes and sausage. In lesser messes, troops picked at cold sandwiches or tinned beef from Uruguay. On the bridge of H.M.S. *Danae*, an officer shared out drams of "the most superb 1812 brandy from a bottle laid down by my great-grandfather in 1821." A British Army officer aboard the *Empire Broadsword* told Royal Naval Commandos: "Do not worry if you do not survive the assault, as we have plenty of backup troops who will just go in over you."

Precisely what the enemy knew about the approaching flotillas remained uncertain. The German radar network—it stretched from Norway to Spain, with a major site every ten miles on the North Sea and Channel coasts— had been bombed for the past month. In recent days, 120 installations at forty-seven sites between Calais and Cherbourg had received particular attention from fighter-bombers and the most intense electronic jamming ever unleashed; the German early warning system had now been whittled to an estimated 5 percent of capacity. Various deceptions also played out, including the deployment of three dozen balloons with radar reflectors to simulate invasion ships where none sailed. Near Calais, where a German radar site had deliberately been left functioning, Allied planes dumped metal confetti, known as Window, into the airstream to mimic the electronic signature of bomber formations sweeping toward northern France. West of Le Havre and Boulogne, planes flying meticulously calibrated oblong courses also scattered enough Window to simulate two large naval fleets, each covering two hundred square miles, steaming toward the coast at eight knots.

The actual OVERLORD fleets deployed an unprecedented level of electronic sophistication that foreshadowed twenty-first-century warfare. Six hundred and three jammers had been distributed to disrupt the search and fire-control radars in enemy shore batteries, including 240 transmitters carried aboard LCTs and other small craft headed for the beaches, and 120 high-powered jammers to protect large warships. Jamming had begun at 9:30 P.M., when the first ships drew within fifteen miles of that brilliant Barfleur light.

Of particular concern were glide bombs, dropped from aircraft and guided by German pilots using a joystick and a radio transmitter. First used by the Luftwaffe in August 1943, glide bombs—notably a model called the Fritz-X—had sunk the Italian battleship *Roma* and nearly sank the cruiser U.S.S. *Savannah* off Salerno. Hitler had stockpiled Fritz-Xs and the similar Hs-293 to attack any invasion; Ultra revealed that 145 radio-control bombers now flew from French airdromes. But Allied ships were no longer as defenseless as they had been in the Mediterranean, where skippers had ordered electric razors switched on in the desperate hope of disrupting Luftwaffe radio signals. Now the dozen different jammer variants humming in the Bay of the Seine included devices designed against glide bombs specifically. In cramped forecastles on U.S.S. *Bayfield* and other ships, oscilloscope operators stared at their screens for the telltale electronic signature of a glide bomb—"a fixed pip, one that will stick straight up like a man's erect penis," in one sailor's inimitable description. After pinpointing the precise enemy frequency, a good countermeasures team could begin jamming within ten seconds. Or so it was hoped.

Allied bombing had intensified at midnight. "Each time they woke us up in the night somebody would say, 'It's D-Day.' But it never was," wrote Bert Stiles, an American B-17 pilot. "And then on the sixth of June it was." More than a thousand British heavy bombers struck coastal batteries and inland targets in the small hours, gouging gaping craters along the Norman seaboard. Antiaircraft fire rose like a pearl curtain, and flame licked from damaged Allied planes laboring back toward the Channel. A Canadian pilot radioed that he was losing altitude, then sent a final transmission before plowing into France: "Order me a late tea." Transfixed men aboard *Augusta* watched a stricken bomber with all four engines streaming fire plunge directly at the ship before swerving to starboard to crash amid the waves a mile astern.

Behind the British came virtually the entire American bomber fleet of 1,635 planes. B-26 Marauder crews, aware that paratroopers in the Cotentin were pressing toward the causeways on the peninsula's eastern lip, flew parallel to the shoreline below six thousand feet to drop 4,414 bombs with commendable accuracy along Utah Beach.

Less precise was the main American force, the 1,350 B-17 Flying Fortresses and B-24 Liberators of the Eighth Air Force, funneled from England in a roaring corridor ten miles wide and led by pathfinder planes flipping out flares at one-mile intervals like burning bread crumbs. Their targets included forty-five coastal fortifications, mostly within rifle range of the high-water mark from Sword Beach in the east to Omaha in the west. Given the imprecision of heavy bombers at sixteen thousand feet—under perfect conditions, less than half their bombs were likely to fall within a quarter mile of an aim point—the primary intent was not to pulverize enemy defenses but to demoralize German defenders beneath the weight of metal.

Conditions were far from perfect. Overcast shrouded the coast as the formations made landfall, six squadrons abreast on a course perpendicular to the beaches. Eisenhower a week earlier had agreed to permit clumsy "blind bombing" if necessary, using H2X radar to pick out the shoreline and approximate target locations. On the night of June 5, he authorized another abrupt change requested by Eighth Air Force: to avoid accidentally hitting the approaching invasion flotillas, bombardiers would delay dumping their payloads for an additional five to thirty seconds beyond the normal release point.

For an hour and a half, three thousand tons of bombs gouged the Norman landscape in a paroxysm of hellfire and turned earth. Minefields, phone wires, and rocket pits inland were obliterated, but less than 2 percent of all bombs fell in the assault areas, and virtually none hit the shoreline or beach fortifications. Repeated warnings against fratricide "had the effect of producing an overcautious attitude in the minds of most of the bombardiers," an Eighth Air Force analysis later concluded; some added "many seconds" to the half-minute "bombs away" delay already imposed. Nearly all payloads tumbled a mile or two from the coast, and some fell farther. Many thousands of bombs were wasted: no defenders had been ejected from their concrete lairs. Whether they felt demoralized by the flame and apocalyptic noise behind them would only be discerned when the first invasion troops touched shore.

Heavy chains rattled through hawse pipes across the bay, followed by splash after mighty splash as anchors slapped the sea and sank from sight. An anguished voice cried from a darkened deck, "For Chrissake, why in the hell don't we send the Krauts a telegram and let them know we're here?" Another voice called out: "Anchor holding, sir, in seventeen fathoms."

Aboard *Princess Astrid*, six miles from Sword Beach, a loudspeaker summons—"Troops to parade, troops to parade"—brought assault platoons to the mess deck. On ships eleven miles off Omaha, GIs in the 116th Infantry pushed single file through double blackout curtains to climb to the weather decks. Landing craft, described as "oversized metal shoeboxes," swung from davits, waiting to be loaded with soldiers; others would be lowered empty, smacking against the steel hulls, to be boarded by GIs creeping down the cargo nets that sailors now spread over the sides. A Coast Guard lieutenant on *Bayfield* watched troops "adjusting their packs, fitting bayonets to their rifles and puffing on cigarettes as if that would be their last. There was complete silence." Scribbling in his diary he added, "One has the feeling of approaching a great abyss."

Nautical twilight arrived in Normandy on June 6 at 5:16 A.M., when the ascending sun was twelve degrees below the eastern horizon. For the next forty-two minutes, until sunrise at 5:58, the dawning day revealed what enemy radar had not. To a German soldier near Vierville, the fleet materialized "like a gigantic town" afloat, while a French boy peering from his window in Grandcamp saw "more ships than sea."

Minesweepers nosed close to shore, clearing bombardment lanes for 140 warships preparing to drench the coast with gunfire. Blinkered messages from sweeps just two miles off the British beaches reported no hint of enemy stirrings, and Omaha too appeared placid. But at 5:30 A.M., on the approaches to Utah, black splashes abruptly leaped mast-high fore and aft of the cruisers H.M.S. *Black Prince* and U.S.S. *Quincy*, followed by the distant bark of shore guns. Two destroyers also took fire three miles from the shingle, and a minesweeper fled seaward, chased by large shells thrown from St.-Vaast. At 5:36 A.M., after allowing Mustang and Spitfire spotter planes time to pinpoint German muzzle flashes, Admiral Deyo ordered, "Commence counterbattery bombardment."

Soon enough eight hundred naval guns thundered along a fifty-mile firing line. Sailors packed cotton in their ears; concussion ghosts rippled their dungarees. "The air vibrated," wrote the reporter Don Whitehead. Ammunition cars sped upward from magazines with an ascending hum, followed by the heavy thump of shells dropped into loading trays before being rammed into the breech. Turrets slewed landward with theatrical menace. Two sharp buzzes signaled *Stand by*, then a single buzz for *Fire!* "Clouds of yellow cordite smoke billowed up," wrote A. J. Liebling as he watched the battleship *Arkansas* from *LCI-88*. "There was something leonine in their tint as well as in the roar that followed." The 12- and 14-inch shells from the murderous queens *Arkansas* and *Texas* sounded "like railway trains thrown skyward," wrote Ernest Hemingway, watching through Zeiss binoculars as a war correspondent aboard H.M.S. *Empire Anvil*. Paint peeled from *Nevada*'s scorched gun barrels, baring blue steel, and sailors swept cork shell casings and the burned silk from powder bags into the sea. David K. E. Bruce, an Office of Strategic Services operative who would later serve as U.S. ambassador in three European capitals, wrote in his diary aboard U.S.S. *Tuscaloosa*:

> There is cannonading on all sides as well as from the shore.... The air is acrid with powder, and a fine spray of disintegrated wadding comes down on us like lava ash.... The deck trembles under our feet, and the joints of the ship seem to creak and stretch.... Repeated concussions have driven the screws out of their sockets [and] shattered light bulbs.

German shells soared over the bay in crimson parabolas. "The arc at its zenith looks as if it would end up on the *Quincy*," wrote an officer eyeing an approaching round. "I am wrong, happily wrong." Ships zigged, zagged, and zigged some more, their battle ensigns snapping and their wakes boiling white. Seasoned tars could gauge the size of an enemy shell from the height of the splash, including the 210mm ship-killers thrown from the three-gun battery at St.-Marcouf. "It is a terrible and monstrous thing to have to fire on our homeland," an admiral on the French cruiser *Montcalm* advised his crew, "but I want you to do it this day." A French woman ashore wrote in her diary, "It is raining iron. The windows are exploding, the floor is shaking, we are choking in the smell of gunpowder." She piled her children and mattresses onto a horse cart and fled inland.

Allied planes swaddled the bombardment lanes with white smoke to blind German gunners. The destroyer U.S.S. *Corry*, which had fired four hundred rounds in an hour, slowed momentarily as sailors hosed down her sizzling 5-inch barrels. At that moment, the breeze tugged away the smoke screen long enough for St.-Marcouf to lay four shells in a neat line 150 yards to port. *Corry*'s skipper had just ordered twenty-five knots at hard right rudder when a stupefying explosion knocked the ship's company to the deck if not overboard.

"We seemed to jump clear of the water," a sailor later recalled. "A large fissure crossed the main deck and around through the hull." The blast cracked the destroyer like an eggshell, opening a foot-wide gap across the keel and between her stacks, flooding the engine and fire rooms, and scalding sailors to death with steam from a ruptured boiler. Crushed bulkheads and debris trapped other men belowdecks. With power and light gone, the rudder jammed. Both the fantail and bow levitated above *Corry*'s broken back. Crewmen hoisted a signal: "This ship needs help."

Most sailors on the destroyer believed that a salvo from German shore guns had struck the mortal blow, but subsequent reports blamed a sea mine. Eighty sweepers would trawl the Utah approaches, eventually finding two hundred mines; none, however, had yet discovered the enemy field across the boat lanes on Cardonnet Bank. An Ultra warning of the minefield had been sent to senior U.S. Navy commanders, "who appeared to have overlooked it," a British intelligence study later concluded.

Eight minutes after the first explosion, with the main deck awash knee-deep, *Corry*'s captain ordered her abandoned. Radio codes were slung overboard in weighted bags. For two hours, until rescue vessels pulled close, survivors thrashed about in fifty-four-degree water; an ensign dying of exposure tried to lash himself to a raft with his uniform necktie. German shells pummeled the wreckage, rupturing *Corry*'s smoke generator, detonating 40mm shells, and killing more men. She sank in six fathoms, with her prow and mainmast—an American flag still flying—visible at low water three miles from shore. The mishap killed twenty-two and injured thirty-three. Five more vessels were sunk and two dozen damaged near Cardonnet Bank in the next ten days.

Experience from the Pacific suggested that naval bombardment against stout coastal defenses should last days, even weeks. But profound differences existed between battering an isolated island and shelling, from the shallow, cramped English Channel, a long coastline with interior lines that permitted quick enemy reinforcement. The job was the tougher because German gun casemates had concrete walls and ceilings up to twelve feet thick. Consequently the preparatory bombardment for the American beaches in OVERLORD lasted barely half an hour in order to get on with the landings. Allied ships on June 6 fired 140,000 shells, but few enemy casemates were destroyed. Of 218 huge shells and almost 1,000 6-inch rounds flung at the Houlgate battery, for example, only one direct hit was recorded. Of 28 batteries capable of ranging Utah Beach with 111 guns, none were completely knocked out in the dawn barrage. And despite being hammered by three battleships, a heavy cruiser, and sundry lesser vessels, that pesky St.-Marcouf battery would hold out until June 12. As with the air bombardment, the extent to which German defenders were unmanned by the naval pummeling would be revealed only by making land.

Brigadier General Roosevelt intended to see with his own congenitally weak, vaguely crossed eyes just how stout the enemy defenses remained.

The Channel's idiosyncratic tidal flow required staggering the five beach landings over the space of an hour; Utah, the westernmost, would be first, and Roosevelt would be first among the first, landing with the initial twenty assault boats of the 4th Infantry Division. After a peevish colloquy aboard U.S.S. *Barnett* over his missing life belt—"I've already given you three," an exasperated aide complained—he stumped to the ship's wet rail, patting his shoulder holster. "I've got my pistol, one clip of ammunition, and my walking cane," he announced in his foghorn bass. "That's all I expect to need." When a soldier leaned across from the dangling landing craft to offer a hand, Roosevelt swatted it aside. "Get the hell out of my way. I can jump in there by myself. You know I can take it as well as any of you." Springing five feet into the boat, he steadied himself with his cane as whirring windlasses lowered the craft into the heaving chop. Sailors cast off the shackles as Roosevelt bantered with the pale, wide-eyed men around him because, as he had written Eleanor, "there are shadows when they stop to think."

"Away all boats," a voice called from above. Icy water sloshed around the ankles of thirty soldiers, already shivering and vomiting, packed like herring in the thirty-six-foot hull. A coxswain gunned the diesel engine, swinging the blunt bow into the swell, and Ted Roosevelt headed back to the war.

He was an unlikely vanguard, even if he had stormed ashore with the assault waves at Oran and Gela, even if he had won Distinguished Service Crosses in the Great War and for heroics against German panzers at El

Guettar, and even if, as A. J. Liebling warranted, he was "as nearly fearless as it is given to man to be." Short, gnarled, and bandy-legged, he reminded one GI of "some frazzle-assed old sergeant." Gassed in the eyes and lungs at Cantigny in 1918, then left with a permanent limp after being shot at Soissons, Roosevelt more recently had been hospitalized in England for three weeks after returning from the Mediterranean with pneumonia. He liked to quote from *The Pilgrim's Progress,* always tucked into his kit bag: "My marks and scars I carry with me." To no one had he disclosed the chest pains gnawing beneath his service ribbons.

His greatest ambition, according to his mother, was "to achieve the same heights as his father," the twenty-sixth president, whose famous crowded hour in combat—he had charged off to San Juan Hill in a Brooks Brothers cavalry uniform with a dozen spare pairs of steel-rimmed spectacles— seemed to haunt his son's own crowded hours. If Ted was unlikely to join Theodore on Mount Rushmore, his achievements were impressive enough given that he had nearly flunked out of Harvard before working as a mill hand in a Connecticut carpet factory. A wealthy investment banker by age thirty, he had served as assistant secretary of the Navy, chairman of American Express, governor-general of the Philippines, and governor of Puerto Rico, where he learned Spanish, attacked the island's health problems, and helped forestall a run on the banks by ponying up $100,000 of his own money. His many books included *Three Kingdoms of Indo-China,* and Hemingway included one of his World War I yarns in *Men at War: Best War Stories of All Time.* His correspondents ranged from Irving Berlin and Robert Frost to Orville Wright, Rudyard Kipling, and Babe Ruth. Roosevelt's political career stalled when he lost the 1924 New York gubernatorial election to Al Smith; the other Eleanor in the family, the wife of his distant cousin Franklin, had campaigned against him by touring the state in a truck shaped like a huge steaming teapot, implicating him in the Teapot Dome scandal. He was in fact guiltless.

"What man of spirit does not envy you?" Theodore had written to his son in France in 1917. Military life, then as now, proved Ted's "first, best destiny all along," one admirer wrote. Returning to uniform in 1941, he became assistant commander of the 1st Infantry Division, but his tolerance of rowdy indiscipline in a unit given to rampages ran afoul of Omar Bradley: Roosevelt and the division commander, Terry de la Mesa Allen, were sacked toward the end of the Sicilian campaign. Roosevelt wept at this "great grief," then promptly campaigned for another combat billet. "As long as I can fight in the front lines," he wrote, "I've still got manhood." After pestering Eisenhower's chief of staff, Beetle Smith, he asked his wife to petition George Marshall, reasoning that it was "all right to pull strings . . . if what you wanted was a more dangerous job than the one you had." Failing to move Marshall in a personal visit, Eleanor persisted with a note: "Is the matter considered so serious that he is not to be given another chance to command troops?"

The Army's chief capitulated. Roosevelt joined the 4th Division in early spring and immediately agitated to lead the Utah assault. Twice refused by the division commander, Major General Raymond O. "Tubby" Barton, Roosevelt on May 26 tried again with a six-point memorandum, arguing that "the behavior pattern of all is apt to be set by those first engaged." He added, "They'll figure that if a general is with them, it can't be that rough." Barton relented as well, and now, at 6:30 A.M., the boat ramp dropped one hundred yards from shore. Drenched, cold, and exhilarated, Roosevelt waded waist-deep through the surf and onto France.

He was on the wrong beach. Billowing dust from the air and naval bombardment hid what few landmarks existed on the flat coastline, and the two guide boats leading the cockleshell flotilla had fallen back, one with a fouled propeller, the other sunk with a hole in the port bow from a Cardonnet Bank mine. Rather than landing opposite beach Exit 3 and its adjacent causeway over the flooded marshlands, Roosevelt and his spearhead of six hundred men had come ashore almost two thousand yards south, near Exit 2. Worse still, eight LCTs carrying thirty-two Sherman tanks, outfitted with propellers and inflatable canvas bloomers allowing them to putter to shore, had been delayed when one vessel tripped another mine. "Higher than her length she rises," wrote Admiral Deyo on *Tuscaloosa*, "turns slowly, stern downward and crashes back into the bay." Four tanks went to the bottom and some twenty men to their graves. Rather than beaching just behind the assault infantry as intended, the remaining Shermans would arrive twenty minutes late.

Weak eyes or no, Roosevelt recognized his plight. Hobbling into the dunes, he spied a windmill and other structures far to the north. "We're not where we're supposed to be," he told the 8th Infantry commander, Colonel James A. Van Fleet, who arrived at seven A.M. "You see that brick building over there to our right front? It always showed up in those aerial photographs, and it was always on the left. . . . I'm sure we're about a mile or two miles farther south."

The accidental beach proved pleasingly benign, with few fortifications, fewer beach obstacles, and little enemy artillery; German defenders did indeed seem dazed by the air and naval pummeling. Wave followed wave of landing craft, jammed with standing troops who reminded Hemingway of "medieval pikemen." Roosevelt worked the waterline "with a cane in one hand, a map in the other, walking around as if he was looking over some real estate," as one sergeant recalled. Occasional enemy shells detonated in the dunes with a concussion likened by Hemingway to "a punch with a heavy, dry glove." Few of the shells fell with precision.

"How do you boys like the beach?" Roosevelt roared at arriving 12th Infantry troops. "It's a great day for hunting. Glad you made it!" Engineers swarmed ashore, blowing beach obstacles and gaps in the masonry seawall with "Hell Box" charges and cries of "Fire in the hole!" Demolition teams had hoped to clear the beaches in twelve hours; instead, ninety minutes after Roosevelt first sloshed ashore the fleet was advised that all boats could land with "no fear of impaling themselves on the obstacles."

Through the dunes and across the beach road, several thousand GIs— the first of 32,000 in Force U—cleared resistance nests with grenades, tommy guns, and tank fire. A German corpse crushed beneath a Sherman's tracks lay "ironed flat like a figure in a comic book," according to a staff officer's description, with "the arms of its gray uniform at right angles to its pressed and flattened coat, [and] black boots and the legs that were in them just as flat and thin as if they had been cut from a sheet of dirty cardboard." Four causeways leading to the Cotentin interior would be seized and exploited on June 6, including one under a foot of water. To avoid clogging the narrow roads, swimmers and nonswimmers from the 12th Infantry paired off to cross the flooded fields. "I gave an arm signal," the regimental commander reported, "and three thousand heavily burdened infantrymen walked into the man-made lake."

The mutter of gunfire sounded along a three-mile front, scarlet tracers skipping like hot stones across the water. Soldiers waggled swatches of orange cloth, peering westward through the haze for answering waggles from the 101st Airborne. Near Exit 1, in the far south, a tank lieutenant hopped down from his Sherman to help a wounded paratrooper only to trip a mine, blowing off both feet; his crew dragged both damaged men to safety with ropes. A dead German soldier was found stripped to the waist, shaving cream still on his chin. Others were mowed down or captured, including fifty gunners with three horse-drawn 88mm guns. An enemy soldier burned by a flamethrower was evacuated to the beach, charred, blistered, but still breathing. "It sure takes a lot to kill a German," a Coast Guard lieutenant told his diary. GIs snipped the unit flashes from enemy sleeves and gave the patches to intelligence analysts.

East of Pouppeville, a 101st Airborne squad cautiously summoned scouts from the 4th Division across the causeway. "Where's the war?" an 8th Infantry soldier asked, rifle slung on his shoulder. A paratrooper gestured vaguely inland. "Anywhere from here on back." Soon enough Roosevelt raced up in his newly landed jeep, *Rough Rider*. Hearing the slap of artillery ahead he shouted to an officer, "Hey, boy, they're shooting up there," then cackled with laughter as he drove off to the sound of the guns.

Eleven miles offshore, aboard U.S.S. *Bayfield*, the naval commander of Force U, Rear Admiral Don P. Moon, sent a heartening battle report at 9:45 A.M.: fifteen of twenty-six waves landed; obstacles cleared; vehicles moving inland. Moon's buoyant dispatch belied a fretful anxiety: the loss of *Corry* and other vessels on the Cardonnet Bank had already led him to delay seven assault waves, and now he had all but decided to halt the landings completely until minesweepers could carefully comb the shallows.

At age fifty, Admiral Moon was given to perturbations. The son of an Indiana lawyer, he had graduated from Annapolis in 1916 at the top of his class in ordnance, gunnery, and engineering; his graduate studies of ballistics at the University of Chicago led to successful field tests aboard the battleships *Maryland* and *Nevada*. He wrote short stories, secured a patent for a "razor blade holder," and commanded a destroyer squadron during the invasion of Morocco with "exemplary conduct and leadership under fire." After a year as a staff officer in Washington and promotion to flag rank, he took command of Force U when OVERLORD expanded from three beaches to five. Subordinates considered him "hardworking, hard-driving, and humorless," sometimes demanding of junior officers, "What are you famous for? What do you do?" The deaths of seven hundred men on his watch during Exercise TIGER in late April nearly unhinged him— "Moon really broke down," a staff officer reported—and he was determined that no such calamity would occur in the Bay of the Seine.

In his spare office aboard *Bayfield*, Moon abruptly revealed his plan to halt the landings to the Army's VII Corps commander. This was Major General J. Lawton Collins, a boyish towhead and Guadalcanal veteran known as Lightning Joe; he would oversee all operations in the Cotentin once Force U reached shore. Collins was appalled if unsurprised, having detected in Moon "a tendency to be overly cautious"; to his wife, the general wrote in mid-May, "He is the first admiral I've ever met who wears rubbers on a mere rainy day." Both forceful and charming, Collins ticked off the reasons to continue to press ahead: light resistance on Utah, with fewer than two hundred casualties in the 4th Division; troops boring inland; naval losses painful but moderate. More to the point, the 101st Airborne needed urgent reinforcement, and nothing had been heard from the 82nd Airborne. "I had to put my foot down hard to persuade the admiral," Collins later said.

Persuade him he did. Moon relented, with misgivings, then assumed a brave face in a brief, stilted statement to reporters on his flagship. "It is our good fortune, which always goes with parties who plan well, that Force U has made a successful landing," he told them, then added, "The initial action has been won."

Hell's Beach

FIFTEEN miles southeast of Utah, the flat Norman littoral lifted briefly to form a sea-chewed plateau named La Côte du Calvados after a reef on which legend held the Spanish galleon *Salvador* came to grief in 1588 as part of the Armada's larger mischance. In various Allied plans the crescent *plage* below the bluffs had been labeled Beach 46, Beach 313, and X Beach; now it was known, and would forever be known, as Omaha. Five miles long, composed of packed sand yielding to shingle sorted in size by a thousand storms, the beach offered but five exits up the hundred-foot escarpment, each following a narrow watercourse to four villages of thick-walled farmhouses a mile or so inland. June airs usually wafted out of the south, but on this fraught morning the wind whistled from the northwest at almost twenty knots, raising the offshore lop to six feet and accelerating the current from two knots to three, running easterly or westerly depending on the tide.

That Norman tide was a primordial force unseen in any previous amphibious landing. Rising twenty-three feet, twice daily it inundated the beach and everything on it at a rate of a vertical foot every eight minutes, then ebbed at almost an inch per second. Low tide typically revealed four hundred yards of open strand, but six hours later that low-tide mark would lie more than twenty feet deep. To finesse this phenomenon in landing the 30,000 assault troops of Task Force O, followed by 26,000 more in Force B, planners chose to attack on a rising tide the morning of June 6. This would permit landing craft to ferry the assault force as far up the exposed beach as possible, but without stranding the boats on falling water as the tide retreated. Ten thousand combat engineers would land with the infantry on June 6, as the historian Joseph Balkoski has written, yet the first sappers would have only half an hour to blow open lanes among the beach obstacles for landing craft before the rising sea swallowed them.

OVERLORD's plan called for nine infantry companies to attack simultaneously on a beach divided into segments: Dog, Easy, Charlie, and Fox. But three mistakes had already given Omaha an ineluctable tragic cast— one error attributable mostly to the Navy, two to the Army. To minimize the risk of German shore fire, naval captains had anchored their transport ships eleven miles distant, guaranteeing derangement of the landing echelons by wind, current, and confusion. In a bid for tactical surprise, Army commanders had insisted on truncating the naval bombardment to barely thirty-five minutes—enough to scare the defenders but not enough, given the clean miss by Allied air forces, to subdue them. The Army also had chosen to storm the narrow beach exits where fortifications were sturdiest, rather than stressing infiltration up the bluffs to outflank enemy strong points.

The German defenses were fearsome. Eighty-five machine-gun nests, soon known to GIs as "murder holes," covered Omaha, more than all three British beaches combined. Unlike the obstacles at Utah, many of the 3,700 wood pilings and iron barriers embedded in the tidal flat at Omaha were festooned with mines—"like huckleberries," as a Navy officer described them. Unique among the five beaches, the escarpment allowed plunging as well as grazing fire. Thirty-five pillboxes and eight massive bunkers—some "as big as a New England town hall," in one reporter's description—defended the beach's five exits, while eighteen antitank sites, six Nebelwerfer rocket-launcher pits, and four artillery positions covered the balance of the beach. Guns enfiladed nearly every grain of sand on Omaha, concealed from the sea by concrete and earthen blast shields that aerial photos had failed to find. Thanks to smokeless, flashless powder and a German ban on tracer bullets here, gun pits remained, as a Navy analysis conceded, "exceedingly difficult to detect."

Also undetected and unexpected by the assault troops were German reinforcements. Rommel in mid-March had shifted the 352nd Infantry Division to the coast from St.-Lô, twenty miles inland, placing two regiments behind Omaha and Gold Beaches alongside two regiments from the feebler 716th Infantry Division, while a third 352nd regiment bivouacked in reserve at Bayeux. Neither Ultra nor conventional intelligence sniffed out the move; belated suspicions of reinforcement reached Omar Bradley's First Army headquarters on June 4, too late to alert the scattered fleets under a radio blackout. The thirteen thousand troops from the 352nd—mobile, dangerous, and so young that Wehrmacht officers requisitioned milk from French farmers to build their bones—had spent much of their time in recent weeks hauling timber in dray carts from the Forêt de Cerisy to buttress the Atlantic Wall. Nearly half the division's infantry strength, including two battalions on bicycles, had been dispatched before dawn to the southern Cotentin with orders to confront reported paratroopers. Some of those invaders proved to be "exploding puppets," hundreds of airborne dummies with noisemakers, accompanied by a few British tricksters popping flares and playing gramophone recordings of gunfire.

If the Omaha defenses had been thinned to three weak battalions by such dupery, they remained far more lethal than the single immobile regiment scattered over a fifty-mile front that most GIs had expected to biff aside. Rather than the three-to-one ratio favored by attackers in storming an entrenched foe, some units now sweeping toward land would meet odds of three to five. The foreshore that had first warranted only a succession of code numbers, and then a homely code name, now would earn other enduring epithets, including Bloody Omaha and Hell's Beach.

For those who outlived the day, who survived this high thing, this bright honor, this destiny, the memories would remain as shot-torn as the beach itself. They remembered waves slapping the steel hulls, and bilge pumps choked with vomit from seasick men making "utterly inhuman noises" into their gas capes. Green water curled over the gunwales as coxswains waited for a tidal surge to lift them past the bars before dropping the ramps with a heavy clank and a shouted benediction: "It's yours, take it away!"

They remembered the red splash of shell bursts plumping the shallows, and machine-gun bullets puckering the sea "like wind-driven hail" before tearing through the grounded boats so that, as one sergeant recalled, "men were tumbling out just like corn cobs off a conveyor belt." Mortar fragments said to be the size of shovel blades skimmed the shore, trimming away arms, legs, heads. The murder holes murdered. Steel-jacketed rounds kicked up sand "like wicked living things," as a reporter wrote, or swarmed overhead in what the novelist-soldier Vernon Scannell called an "insectile whine." Soldiers who had sung "Happy D-Day, dear Adolf" now cowered like frightened animals. They desperately gouged out shallow holes in the shingle with mess kit spoons and barked knuckles, mouths agape in a rictus of astonishment intended to prevent artillery concussions from rupturing their eardrums.

They remembered brave men advancing as if "walking in the face of a real strong wind," in Forrest Pogue's image, all affecting the same tight grimace until whipcrack bullets cut them down. Above the battle din they remembered the cries of comrades ripped open, merging at moments into a single ululation described by the BBC reporter David Howarth as "a long terrible dying scream which seemed to express not only fear and pain, but amazement, consternation, and disbelief." And they remembered the shapeless dead, sprawled on the strand like smears of divine clay, or as flotsam on the making tide, weltering, with their life belts still cinched. All this they would remember, from the beaten zone called Omaha.

Army and Navy engineers, lugging twenty-eight tons of explosives, were supposed to land three minutes behind the infantry spearhead to blow sixteen gaps, each fifty yards wide, through tidal-zone obstacles emplaced in three belts. Little went right: some engineers landed early and alone, some landed late, nearly all drifted left—east—of their assigned beaches by up to a mile because of the current and navigation error. An

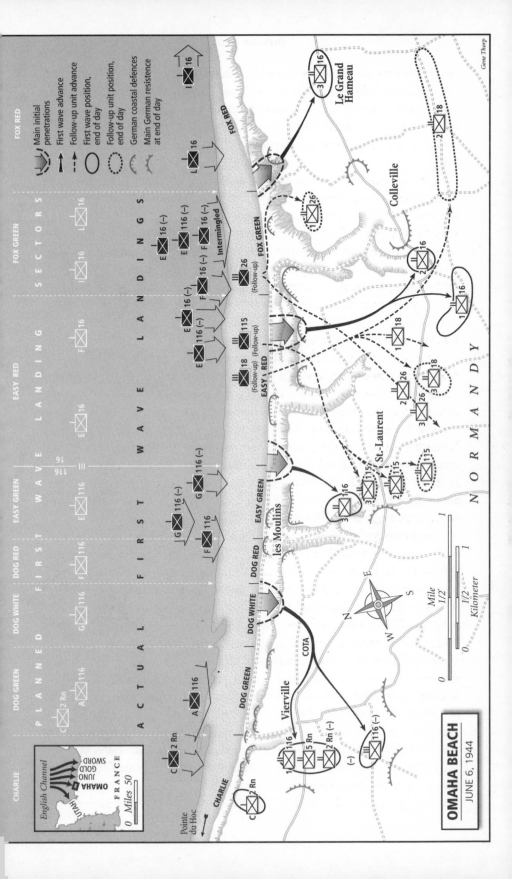

OMAHA BEACH
JUNE 6, 1944

Main initial penetrations
First wave advance
Follow-up unit advance
First wave position, end of day
Follow-up unit position, end of day
German coastal defences
Main German resistance at end of day

SECTORS

CHARLIE | DOG GREEN | DOG WHITE | DOG RED | EASY GREEN | EASY RED | FOX GREEN | FOX RED

PLANNED FIRST WAVE LANDINGS

ACTUAL FIRST WAVE LANDINGS

Pointe du Hoc

Vierville

les Moulins

St-Laurent

Colleville

Le Grand Hameau

NORMANDY

CHARLIE

DOG GREEN

DOG WHITE

COTA

DOG RED

EASY GREEN

EASY RED

FOX GREEN

FOX RED

Intermingled

(Follow-up)

Gene Thorp

English Channel

FRANCE

UTAH
OMAHA
GOLD
JUNO
SWORD

0   Miles   50

N
W   E
S

Mile 1/2
Kilometer 1/2
0

88mm shell hit Team 14's landing craft, blowing the coxswain overboard and slaughtering the vessel's entire Navy demolition squad; one man's lower trunk and severed legs were described by a seaman as "sticking up in the water like a pitiful V for victory." Seven died in Team 11 when shellfire hit their rubber boat; of forty men in Team 15, only four eluded death or injury. A mortar round caught Team 12, tripping the TNT primacord and explosive charges, and killing or wounding nineteen engineers in an explosion so violent that three-legged steel hedgehogs rained down "like fence posts falling," a survivor reported.

Demolitionists shinnied up pilings or stood on one another's shoulders to pluck off mines and place their charges, popping violet smoke grenades to signal an imminent detonation. Gunfire shot away fuses as fast as engineers could rig them, including one burst that also carried off the fuse man's fingers. Terrified infantrymen sheltered behind the German obstacles "like a cluster of bees," even as engineers screamed, kicked, and threatened to blow their charges anyway. By seven A.M., as the floodtide began to swallow the obstacles, only six of sixteen gaps had been cleared through all three belts, and at a fell cost: more than half of the engineers would be dead, wounded, or missing by midmorning.

The fiascos multiplied. Sherman amphibious tanks, ostensibly seagoing with their inflatable canvas skirts and twin propellers, began plopping into the waves from LCT ramps "like toads from the lip of an ornamental pond," as the historian John Keegan later wrote. Yet the tanks had only nine inches of freeboard in a pond with six-foot seas; of thirty-two Shermans in one battalion, twenty-seven sank trying to cross six thousand yards of open water, with a loss of 9 officers and 137 men. "There was a certain gallantry," the BBC's Howarth noted. "Commanders of the second, third, and fourth tanks in each [LCT] could see the leaders founder; but the order had been given to launch, and they launched." Farther west, a Navy lieutenant sensibly recognized the rough sea as unfit for a thirty-three-ton swimming tank, and LCTs carrying most of another armor battalion made for shore instead. Eight Shermans went under when their vessels took direct hits, but twenty-four others clanked ashore.

Artillerymen also struggled to land their guns. A dozen 105mm howitzers from the 111th Field Artillery Battalion had been loaded onto DUKW amphibious trucks, each of which also carried fourteen men, fifty shells, and a protective rampart of eighteen sandbags, enough to make the DUKW "altogether unseaworthy," as the Army belatedly recognized. Eight quickly shipped water and capsized, and three others were lost to waves or shellfire before reaching shore. "I can still hear those men calling for help over the noise," a master sergeant later recalled.

Two infantry regiments washed onto Hell's Beach early that morning, from the two assault divisions that formed V Corps. To the west, the 116th Infantry—rural Virginians marinated in Confederate glory and descended from the Stonewall Brigade of 1861—had trained in Britain for twenty months as part of the 29th Infantry Division, long enough to earn a derisive nickname: "England's Own." Officers ordered men in landing craft approaching the shore to keep their heads down, as one lieutenant explained, "so they wouldn't see it and lose heart." They saw soon enough. On the right flank of the invasion zone, German gunners abruptly turned beach Dog Green into an abattoir. Without firing a shot, Company A was reportedly "inert and leaderless" in ten minutes; after half an hour, two-thirds of the company had been destroyed, including Sergeant Frank Draper, Jr., killed when an antitank round tore away his left shoulder to expose a heart that beat until he bled to death. Among twenty-two men from tiny Bedford, Virginia, who would die in Normandy, Draper "didn't get to kill anybody," his sister later lamented. A surviving officer reported that his men fell "like hay dropping before the scythe."

German machine guns—with a sound one GI compared to "a venetian blind being lifted up rapidly"—perforated the beach, killing the wounded and rekilling the dead. All thirty-two soldiers in one boat, *LCA-1015*, were slaughtered, including their captain. A lieutenant shot in the brain continued to direct his troops until, a survivor recounted, "he sat down and held his head in the palm of his hand before falling over dead." Wounded men jabbed themselves with morphine or shrieked for medics, one of whom used safety pins to close a gaping leg wound. "A guy in front of me got it through the throat. Another guy in front of me got it through the heart. I run on," a survivor later recalled. An unhinged soldier sat in the sand, weeping softly and tossing stones into the water. "This," an officer declared, "is a debacle."

More than a mile to the east, the 16th Infantry Regiment—veterans of landings in Africa and Sicily with the 1st Infantry Division—had its own debacle. The entire first wave carried east of its intended beaches. Simply reaching the waterline reduced Company L from 187 men to 123. Medics found that "the greater portion of the dead had died of bullet wounds through the head"; officers and sergeants alike began slapping wet sand over the rank insignia on their helmets to confound snipers. "Fire was coming from everywhere, big and little stuff," a soldier in Company E recalled. Moved to computation by the demented shooting, one sergeant calculated that the beach was swept with "at least twenty thousand bullets and shells per minute." Robert Capa, who had removed his Contax camera from its waterproof oilskin to snap the most memorable photographs of the Second World War, crouched behind a burned-out Sherman on Easy Red and murmured a phrase he recalled from the Spanish Civil War: *"Es una cosa muy seria."* This is a very serious business.

The four-hundred-ton *LCI 85,* grounding ashore on the seam between Easy Red and Fox Green, had begun dispensing men down the left ramp when enemy 47mm and 88mm shells blew through the front hold, killing fifteen and wounding forty-seven. The Coast Guard crew backed off and steamed west several hundred yards only to face scorching fire upon putting in again. More than two dozen shells ripped into the ship, igniting troop compartments and leaving the decks slick with blood. White bandages from a shot-up medical company fluttered down through the smoke. On the bridge, the skipper reported, "we could hear the screams of the men through the voice tube." Listing, burning, bleeding, *LCI 85* steamed for the horizon, where the wounded and the dead were extracted before she capsized and sank.

By 8:30 A.M. the Omaha assault had stalled. The rising tide quickly reclaimed the thin strip of liberated beach, drowning those immobilized by wounds or fear. With no room to land more vehicles, a Navy beachmaster halted further unloading on much of the shoreline. "Face downwards, as far as eyes could see in either direction," a 16th Infantry surgeon later wrote, "were the huddled bodies of men living, wounded, and dead, as tightly packed together as layers of cigars in a box."

Two large boats burned furiously in the shallows of Dog White. *LCI 91,* carrying two hundred soldiers, had caught a shell in her fuel tanks, engulfing the well deck in flames. At least two dozen men were incinerated as others leaped into the sea, including one bright torch who dove in with even the soles of his boots blazing. Moments later, *LCI 92,* seeking cover in her sister's smoke, struck a mine on the port bow. The explosion blew two soldiers from a hatch like champagne corks and trapped more than forty others belowdecks. "A sheet of flame shot up thirty feet in the air through the number one hold directly forward of the conning tower," a yeoman reported. "Terror seized me." German gunners then found the range to finish off the boat. A survivor dog-paddled to the beach not as an infantry officer ready for combat, as he later acknowledged, but as the "helpless unarmed survivor of a shipwreck."

Only where escarpment turned to cliff, four miles west of Omaha, did the early-morning assault show promise. Three companies from the 2nd Ranger Battalion scaled the headland at Pointe du Hoc, first climbing freehand despite a rain of grenades, then using grapnels and braided ropes fired from mortar tubes. Comrades gave covering fire from ladders loaned by the London fire department and carried in DUKWs. As windswept as Troy, the promontory had been reduced to what one officer called "ripped-open dirt" by 250 shells from *Texas*'s 14-inch barrels. Rangers hauled themselves over the lip of the cliff, then used thermite grenades to wreck five shore guns that had been removed from their casemates and secreted in an apple orchard. The triumph was short-lived: they soon found themselves trapped by rallying Germans who spent the next thirty-six hours trying to sweep them from the scarp to the rocks below.

Back on Hell's Beach, several thousand shivering soldiers also found defilade where they could and waited for a counterattack from the bluffs to bowl them back into the sea. "They'll come swarming down on us," murmured Don Whitehead. A lieutenant, who watched sodden bodies advance on the creeping tide, later wrote, "After a couple of looks back, we decided we couldn't look back anymore." Among those huddled on the beach was Captain Joseph T. Dawson, a lanky, dark-eyed veteran of Company G in the 16th Infantry. An hour earlier, Dawson had leaped from his landing craft onto Easy Red just as an artillery shell struck the boat, exterminating the thirty-three men behind him. "The limitations of life come into sharp relief," he would write his family in Texas. "No one is indispensable in this world."

From the gray deck of the command ship U.S.S. *Augusta* none of this was clear. A brown miasma of dust and smoke draped the French coast to the south, mysterious and impenetrable except by the cherry-red battleship shells soaring toward inland targets. A cramped First Army war room had been built on the cruiser's afterdeck, ten feet by twenty, with a tarpaulin door, a Michelin map of France fastened to a sheet-metal wall, and a clock whose glass face had been taped against concussion. Other maps displayed the suspected location of enemy units, marked in red, and the range of German shore guns, delineated with concentric circles. Signalmen wearing headphones listened for radio messages, which they pounded out on a bank of typewriters. From Omaha only incoherent fragments had been heard, of sinkings, swampings, heavy fire. One dispatch picked up by another ship nearby advised, "We are being butchered like a bunch of hogs."

At a plotting table in the center of the war room sat a tall, bespectacled man in a helmet, Mae West, and three-star field jacket. Again he asked— "What's going on?"—and again got little more than an apologetic shrug. On several occasions as a young officer, Omar Bradley had studied Gallipoli, the disastrous British effort to capture Constantinople in 1915, and more recently he had scrutinized reports from Anzio. The preeminent lesson from both amphibious attacks, he concluded, was "to get ground quickly." Was that happening at Omaha? Another shrug. He had expected the two assault regiments to be a mile inland by 8:30 A.M., but now he was unsure whether they had even reached France. Bradley had begun contemplating his course if the troops failed to get off the strand. He felt not only alarmed but also a bit ridiculous: this morning the army commander sported an immense bandage on his nose to cover a boil that had been lanced in the ship's dispensary. Photographers were forbidden to take his picture.

After successfully commanding a corps in Africa and Sicily, Bradley had benefitted from hagiographic press coverage, including a recent *Time* cover story that called him "Lincolnesque . . . a plain, homely, steady man with brains and character." Ernie Pyle wrote that "he spoke so gently a person couldn't hear him very far," while Liebling described "the high cranium, bare on top except for a lattice of gray hairs; the heavy, almost undershot jaw; and the deeply emplaced presbytic eyes, peering out from under the dark brows with an expression of omnivorous but benevolent curiosity." That he still wore a cap with "Lieut. Col. O. N. Bradley" inked in the lining was considered emblematic of his humility; in fact, lieutenant colonel was his permanent rank.

Few could resist the biography. Son of a schoolteaching Missouri farmer who made $40 a month, married one of his pupils, and died when Omar was thirteen, Bradley had played football on an undefeated Army team that earned unlikely headlines, such as "West Point Finds Notre Dame Easy." He also befriended a classmate who was now his boss and greatest admirer: "*Ice*-in-hower," as Bradley pronounced the name in his sodbuster twang. As a lieutenant, he had been sent to Montana to keep the copper mines open with fixed bayonets against labor agitators; later he taught mathematics at West Point while moonlighting as a construction worker, stringing cable for the Bear Mountain Bridge over the Hudson. He skipped the rank of colonel and was the first of fifty-nine men in the Military Academy class of 1915 to win a general's stars. A teetotaler until the age of thirty-three, Bradley rarely drank; he had added the pint of whiskey and two flasks of brandy issued when he boarded *Augusta* to his unopened allotment from Sicily. Vain about his marksmanship—"If there's a bird anywhere in shootin' distance, I won't miss it," he once told a reporter—he had also nursed a sense of divine anointment ever since, in Tunisia, he drove his jeep over a mine that failed to explode. "I think I had some guidance from God," he later said. "I felt that I must be destined to play an important part in the war. . . . I was saved by a miracle."

Perhaps. But a few wondered if he was out of his depth, if he had been promoted beyond his natural level of competence, if some part of him remained "Lieut. Col. O. N. Bradley." Patton, who had been his commander in the Mediterranean and would be his subordinate in France, had rated Bradley "superior" in all categories of generalship in September

1943, while privately calling him "a man of great mediocrity." In his diary Patton added, with typical ambivalence: "Has a strong jaw, talks profoundly and says little. I consider him among our better generals." The Omaha plan had been largely Bradley's design, including the limited fire support from the Navy, and he had dismissed predictions of stiff losses as "tommyrot."

Now he was not so sure. Messages from the beachhead remained fragmentary, including: "Obstacles mined, progress slow." An aide dispatched by PT boat returned drenched and discouraged an hour later to report that troops were pinned down; a naval officer came back with a more vivid assessment: "My God, this is carnage!" Told that Admiral Moon was jittery over ship losses, Bradley advised Collins, his VII Corps commander, "We've got to get the buildup ashore even if it means paving the whole damned Channel bottom with ships." Another 25,000 troops and 4,000 vehicles were scheduled to land at Omaha on the second tide. Should those waves be diverted to Utah or to the British beaches? Would that consign those now ashore to annihilation?

The man described in his high school yearbook as "calculative" pushed through the canvas war-room door and climbed to *Augusta's* bridge, squinting at the opaque shore and mulling his odds.

Not for some hours would Bradley learn that by late morning his prospects on Omaha had brightened considerably, beginning at beach Dog White. There Brigadier General Norman Cota, known as Dutch and the son of a French-Canadian railroad telegrapher who emigrated to New England, had reached the five-foot timber seawall half a mile east of the beach exit leading to Vierville. Soldiers who could outcrawl the tide lay clustered like barnacles on the banked littoral, hugging wooden groins that jutted from the seawall.

We must improvise, carry on, not lose our heads, Cota had told officers from the 116th Infantry as they sailed for Normandy. Now he improvised. Chewing an unlit cigar, jut-jawed with pale eyes and a hooked nose, Cota scrabbled west along the groins. Pistol in hand, he sang tuneless, ad-libbed lyrics under his breath. Encountering a cluster of troops, he demanded, "What outfit is this? Goddamn it, if you're Rangers get up and lead the way. . . . I know you won't let me down. . . . We've got to get these men off this goddamned beach." A bangalore torpedo threaded through a double apron of barbed wire blew a gap across the beach road beyond the seawall. Machine-gun fire cut down the first GI into the breach—"Medico, I'm hit," he cried, then sobbed for his mother until he died—but others, including Cota, scampered across the blacktop and through the burning marsh grass beyond.

Up the bluff they climbed, single file, marking mines with white engineer tape, cigarettes, and scraps from a ration box. Smoke hid them from German marksmen but made them weep until they strapped on gas masks. Mortar rounds killed a trio of soldiers next to Cota and wounded his radioman; knocked flat but unscratched, the general regained his feet and followed the snaking column toward the hillcrest, past captured Germans spread-eagled on the ground. Then over the lip of the ridge they ran, past stunted pines and through uncut wheat as Cota yelled, "Now let's see what you're made of!" GIs hauling a captured MG-42 machine gun with ammunition belts draped around their necks poured fire into enemy trenches and at the broken ranks pelting inland.

By ten A.M. tiny Vierville had fallen but for snipers. Outside a cobbler's shop dead horses lay in their traces, still harnessed to a Wehrmacht supply wagon. Terrified civilians peeked from their window casements onto a road clogged with rubble. Another rifle company scuffing into the village found Cota twirling his pistol on his finger. "Where the hell have you been, boys?" he asked.

Elsewhere along Omaha, in what one witness called "a final stubborn reserve of human courage," more desperate men found additional seams up the escarpment. "I walked slowly," a 29th Division soldier recalled, "dragging my unwilling soul with me." Halfway up the slope, a soldier missing a lower leg sat smoking a cigarette and fiddling with the tourniquet tied at his knee. "Watch it," he warned. "There are some personnel mines here." Captain Joe Dawson's G Company used GI corpses as stepping stones through a minefield. "Fire everywhere it seems," a major scribbled on an envelope used as a diary. "Prayed several times." When a German feigned surrender and threw a grenade from his raised hand, disemboweling a Ranger lieutenant, the dead officer's enraged men not only killed the killer but each man reportedly "shot the corpse six or eight times" as they filed past.

A dozen destroyers—some so close to the beach that their keels scraped bottom—plied the inshore stations to fire onto targets marked by Army tracer and tank rounds. One soldier watching shells arc across the bluff reported that "a man standing there felt as if he could reach up and pick them out of the air." When a German artillery observer was spotted in the eleventh-century Colleville church tower, U.S.S. *Emmons* took a dozen rounds to find the range, then with the thirteenth knocked the tower into the nave and adjacent graveyard below. A similar call for fire against the church of St.-Laurent shattered the steeple with the first shell. After one shuddering broadside from *Texas,* an RAF pilot spotting for the battleship cried from his Spitfire cockpit, "Oh, simply champion!"

By noon the enemy line had been broken by half a dozen penetrations "coagulating haphazardly," as the official Army history later noted. Two fresh regiments, the 115th Infantry and the 18th Infantry, swarmed over Easy Red before the ebb tide despite the loss of many landing craft to mines and misadventure. Later the 26th Infantry also was ordered to shore, putting the entire infantry complement of the 1st Division back in France for the first time since 1918. By midafternoon, some five thousand infantrymen had scaled the bluff, finally free of plunging fire although still tormented by fires flanking and grazing, direct and indirect. Scraps of news reached the fleet, including a message dispatched from a colonel in a DUKW: "Men believed ours on skyline. . . . Things look better." But only after one P.M. did Omar Bradley, pacing on *Augusta*'s flag bridge, learn in a message from V Corps that the day was saved, if not won: "Troops formerly pinned down on beaches Easy Red, Easy Green, Fox Red advancing up heights behind beaches."

Cota continued his charmed day by hiking from Vierville down the narrow ravine toward Dog Green, forcing five prisoners yanked from foxholes to guide him through a minefield. "Come on down here, you sons of bitches," he yelled at snipers plinking away from the hillside. In a great geyser of masonry, engineers on the beach flats used a thousand pounds of dynamite to demolish a long antitank wall nine feet high and six feet thick. Armored bulldozers scraped debris from the Vierville draw, thus opening another portal for tanks, trucks, and the mechanized juggernaut that would be needed to liberate first Normandy, then France, then the continent beyond.

That left the British and Canadians, beating for three beaches to the east. Several tactical modifications aided the trio of assault divisions in Second Army: landing craft were launched seven miles from shore rather than the eleven typical in the American sector; the Royal Navy's bombardment lasted four times longer than that of the U.S. Navy; and half a dozen gadgets eschewed by the Yanks as either too newfangled or unsuited to the American beaches—such as an armored flamethrower and a mine flail bolted to the nose of a tank—proved useful at several points during the battle.

In other respects, "the bitches," as Tommies called Gold, Juno, and Sword, were of a piece with Utah and Omaha, if less benign than the former and less harrowing than the latter. Some amphibious Shermans, another British brainstorm, foundered in the chop, and many LCT engine rooms flooded from leaks and the low freeboard. Landing craft ferrying Centaur tanks proved no more seaworthy than the DUKWs overloaded with American howitzers; scores capsized. OVERLORD's eastern flank was considered especially vulnerable, so two battleships and a monitor pounded the landscape with 15-inch guns from twenty thousand yards, buttressed by five cruisers and fifteen destroyers. Thousands of rockets launched from modified landing craft soared inland "like large packs of grouse going for the next parish with a strong wind under their tails," as one brigadier reported. This twenty-eight-mile stretch of coast was defended by ninety shore guns and eight German battalions whose ranks included many conscripted Poles, Czechs, and Ukrainians of doubtful fealty to the Reich. British naval and air bombardments later were found to have demolished one in ten enemy mortars, one in five machine guns, and one in three larger guns, in addition to those abandoned by their affrighted crews. Still, British assault infantrymen were said to be disappointed, having "expected to find the Germans dead and not just disorganized."

During the run to shore, inevitable recitations from *Henry V* were bellowed above the roar of diesel engines and booming guns. More than a few men felt themselves accursed for swilling proffered tots of rum, "thick as syrup and as dark," in a Royal Engineer's description; thousands of expended "spew bags" bobbed on the boat wakes. Heartfelt snatches of "Jerusalem" could be heard in wallowing landing craft, and "The Beer Barrel Polka" blared from a motor launch loudspeaker.

On, on, you noble English! Closest to Omaha lay Gold, barricaded with 2,500 obstacles along its 3.5-mile length. Engineers managed to clear only two boat lanes on the rising tide, and stout fortifications at Le Hamel would hold out until reduced by petard bombs and grenades later in the day. "Perhaps we're intruding," one soldier mused. "This seems to be a private beach." Royal Marines storming the fishing village of Port-en-Bessin, on the Omaha boundary, suffered over two hundred casualties during the forty-eight hours needed to finally rout enemy diehards there. But by early afternoon on June 6, all four brigades of the 50th Division made shore, scuttling inland and threatening to turn the German flank.

On the eastern lip of the Allied beachhead, the British 3rd Division hit Sword on a narrow front in hopes of quickly knifing through to Caen, nine miles inland. "Ramp down! All out!" the boat crews cried, echoed by sergeants barking, "Bash on! Bash on!" Enemy mortar and machine-gun fire bashed back, and Royal Engineers cleared no beach obstacles on the first tide. Tommies "with shoulders hunched like boxers ready for in-fighting" found themselves in the surf, as a *Daily Mail* reporter wrote, "treading on an invisible carpet of squirming men." A Commando sergeant reported that the crimson-tinted seawater "made it look as though men were drowning in their own blood," and a lieutenant in the King's Liverpool Regiment told his diary: "Beach a shambles. Bodies everywhere. . . . Phil killed." The northwest wind shoved the high-tide line to within thirty feet of the dunes, leaving the narrow beach utterly clogged and so disrupting landing schedules that a reserve brigade remained at sea until midafternoon. Even so a kilted piper with a dirk strapped to his leg, Sergeant Bill Millin, waded through the shallows playing "Highland Laddie" despite cries of "Get down, you mad bastard, you're attracting attention to us!" Skirling "Blue Bonnets over the Border," Millin then marched off with Commandos "in parade-ground style" to search for British glidermen holding the Orne bridges.

The wind-whipped tide and a bullying current also played hob with the Canadian 3rd Division on Juno, wedged between the two British beaches. Almost one-third of three hundred landing craft were lost or damaged, and only six of forty tanks made shore. Street fighting raged along the Courseulles harbor, and fortified houses behind the twelve-foot seawall at Bernières kept Canadian artillery and vehicles jammed on the beaches. Pigeons carrying Reuters dispatches from Juno flew south rather than across the Channel, provoking outraged cries of "Traitors! Damned traitors!"

Despite such setbacks and a thousand Canadian casualties—about half the number expected—the Royal Winnipeg Rifles and Regina Rifles by midmorning had pushed two miles inland. Across the Anglo-Canadian bridgehead, once troops punched through the coastal defenses few German units remained to block village crossroads. At two P.M., Piper Millin and the Commandos led by their brigadier, Lord Lovat—wearing a green beret and white sweater, and swinging his shillelagh—tramped across the Bénouville bridge held by Major John Howard and his glider force; now the seaborne and airborne forces were linked on both invasion flanks. Fifteen miles to the west, Allied fighter-bombers at noon pounced on a counterattacking regiment of 2,500 Germans with twenty-two assault guns near Villiers-le-Sec. British troops hieing from Gold finished the rout at three P.M., killing the German commander and shattering the enemy column.

Reporters were told to expect a briefing by British officers at four P.M. in Caen. No such briefing transpired: the 3rd Division spearhead, harassed by mines and heavy gunfire, stalled three miles north of the city. Troops from the Royal Warwickshire Regiment who were issued bicycles and told to "cycle like mad behind the Sherman tanks into Caen" found bikes "not at all the ideal accessory" for crawling under mortar fire. The city and the road linking it to Bayeux remained in German hands, an inconvenience both vexing and consequential.

Yet the day seemed undimmed. Canadian troops had pressed six miles or more into France, and British soldiers reported reaching Bayeux's outskirts. Despite sniper fire nagging from a copse nearby, engineers by day's end began building a refueling airstrip at Crépon with a twelve-hundred-foot packed-earth runway. Prisoners trudged to cages on the beach, holding up trousers from which the buttons had been snipped to discourage flight. French women who emerged from cellars to kiss their liberators found themselves happily smudged with camouflage kettle soot and linseed oil. Inquiries by officers in their public-school French—"*Ou sont les Boches?*"—often provoked wild pointing and an incomprehensible torrent of Norman dialect. But there was no misunderstanding the scratchy strains of "La Marseillaise" played over and over by a young girl outside her cottage on an antique gramophone with a tin horn. *Allons enfants de la Patrie, / Le jour de gloire est arrivé!*

A Conqueror's Paradise

As if in pursuit of the sinking sun, a black Horch convertible raced west across France from the German frontier, threading the Marne valley from Reims, then swinging to the right bank of the Seine north of Paris. Since early May, Allied fighter-bombers had demolished all twenty-six bridges spanning the river from the French capital to the sea, converting the bucolic drive to Normandy into a circuitous annoyance. The sleek Horch, with its winged chrome ornament on the radiator grille and twin spare tires mounted behind the front fenders, provoked stares as the car sped through drowsy villages and farm communes. But it was the German officer in a leather coat in the front seat with a map spread across his knees who drew the eye: the familiar flat face with a narrow, sloping forehead and incipient jowls belonged to Hitler's youngest but most celebrated field marshal. Even French peasants recognized him, and as the convertible raced past they called aloud to one another: "*C'est Rommel!*"

Yes, Rommel. He had driven home to Herrlingen in southwest Germany the previous day with a pair of gray suede shoes from Paris as a surprise fiftieth-birthday present for his wife, Lucie-Maria. He had meant to confer afterward with the Führer in his Alpine retreat at Berchtesgaden and to complain about shortages of men and matériel for the Atlantic Wall, but had instead been summoned back to France by grave reports of Allied landings in Normandy on Tuesday morning. "*Tempo!*" he urged the driver. "*Tempo!*" Turning to an aide in the rear seat, he added, "If I was commander of the Allied forces right now, I could finish off the war in fourteen days."

At 9:30 P.M., with little left of the long summer day, sentries in camouflage capes waved the Horch into the red-roofed river village of La Roche-

Guyon, forty miles west of Paris. Past the church of St.-Samson and sixteen square-cut linden trees, the car turned right through a spiked wrought-iron gate to stop with a screech in a stone courtyard. The Château de La Roche–Guyon had presided above this great loop of the Seine since the twelfth century and had served since early March as Rommel's Army Group B headquarters. Clutching his silver-capped baton, the field marshal climbed a flight of steps to the main door, determined to salvage what he could from the day's catastrophe.

"How peaceful the world seems," he had told his diary in late April, "yet what hatred there is against us." If France proved "a conqueror's paradise," as one German general claimed, La Roche–Guyon was Rommel's secluded corner of that heaven. Brilliant fields of poppies and irises hugged the Seine near the nineteenth-century suspension bridge, now sitting cockeyed on the river bottom. Cézanne and Renoir had painted here together in the summer of 1885, following Camille Pissarro and preceding Georges Braque, who in 1909 made angular studies of the castle in buff and blue. Two hundred and fifty steep steps led to a battlement atop the circular medieval keep, where Rommel, after a hare shoot or a stroll with his dachshunds, sometimes watched barges loaded with fuel and ammunition glide past in the evening.

On the chalk cliffs overhanging the river's north bank and the castle's peppermill roofs stood a bristling array of antiaircraft batteries; deep tunnels had been blasted to house German troops without damaging the ducal orangery or the crypt crowded with dead seigneurs. The current duke, a spindly Nazi sympathizer, remained in residence without evident discomfort, and the duchess had donated four bottles of a luscious 1900 claret to commemorate the Führer's birthday on April 20. The chateau's timber-ceilinged Hall of the Ancestors, hung with family oils, had been consigned to Rommel's staff as a table-tennis room. From the field marshal's bedroom, with its canopied four-poster, fifteen-foot windows gave onto a fragrant rose terrace and another river vista.

Clacking typewriters and snatches of Wagner from a phonograph could be heard as Rommel ascended the grand staircase and hurried through the billiards room to the salon that now served as his office. Pegged parquet floors creaked beneath his boots. Four magnificent tapestries depicting the Jewish queen Esther had recently been shunted into storage, but fleecy painted clouds still drifted across the twenty-five-foot ceiling, and the inlaid desk on which the revocation of the Edict of Nantes had been signed in 1685 remained for Rommel's personal use. He stood instead, hands clasped behind his back, listening as staff officers sought to make sense of the sixth of June. "He's very calm and collected," an artillery officer wrote. "Grim-faced, as is to be expected."

There was much to be grim about. Thanks to Allied jamming and downed phone lines, little was known with certainty. Somehow thousands of ships had crossed the Channel undetected. No Luftwaffe reconnaissance planes had flown for the first five days of June, and naval patrols on June 5 were scrubbed because of the nasty weather. A decoded radio message—intercepted about the time the 101st Airborne launched from England—suggested a possible invasion within forty-eight hours. But an advisory on Monday evening from OB West, the German headquarters for western Europe, declared, "There are no signs yet of an imminent invasion." Besides Rommel, two of the top four German commanders in the west had been away from their posts on Tuesday morning, and several senior field officers in Normandy had driven to Rennes, in Brittany, for a map exercise. The Fifteenth Army, near the Pas de Calais, was placed on full alert before midnight, but the other major component of Rommel's Army Group B, the Seventh Army occupying Normandy, sounded no general alarm until 1:30 A.M. despite reports of paratroopers near Caen and in the Cotentin. Even then, OB West insisted at 2:40 A.M.: "It is not a major action."

Not until that fantastic armada materialized from the mist had the truth struck home. In subsequent hours the German navy remained supine; so too the air force. Luftwaffe pilots were supposed to fly up to five daily sorties each to disrupt any invasion, but German aircraft losses in the past five months exceeded thirteen thousand planes, more than half from accidents and other noncombat causes. Air Fleet Three, responsible for western France, had just 319 serviceable planes facing nearly 13,000 Allied aircraft; on D-Day, they would fly one sortie for every thirty-seven flown by their adversaries. Of the mere dozen fighter-bombers that reached the invasion zone, ten dropped their bombs prematurely. German soldiers now bitterly joked that American planes were gray, British planes black, and Luftwaffe planes invisible.

Still, Seventh Army asserted through much of the day that at least part of the Allied landing had been halted at the water's edge. "The enemy, penetrating our positions, was thrown back into the sea," the 352nd Infantry Division reported at 1:35 P.M. That soap-bubble delusion soon popped: at six P.M. the division acknowledged "unfavorable developments," including Allied troops infiltrating inland and armored spearheads nosing toward Bayeux.

Rommel's grim face grew grimmer. Here, in Normandy, he had first made his name as "the fighting animal," in one biographer's phrase, driving his 7th Panzer Division more than two hundred miles in four days to trap the French garrison at Cherbourg in June 1940. Soon after, in Africa, the fighting animal took vulpine form as the audacious Desert Fox, although even he could not forestall the Allied triumph in Tunisia. Now, he told a comrade, he hoped "to re-win great fame in the West."

Hitler's decision in November 1943 to reinforce the Atlantic Wall against "an Anglo-Saxon landing" offered him that chance. As commander of half a million men in Army Group B, with responsibility for the coast from Holland to the Loire, the field marshal had flung himself into building the "Rommel Belt." All told, 20,000 coastal fortifications had been constructed, 500,000 foreshore obstacles emplaced, and 6.5 million mines planted in what he called "the zone of death." To Lucie he wrote on May 19, "The enemy will have a rough time of it when he attacks, and ultimately achieve no success." Hitler agreed, declaring, "Once defeated, the enemy will never try to invade again."

If confident enough to travel home for his wife's birthday, Rommel harbored few illusions. He had never forgotten the endless acres of high-quality American war matériel he had inspected at Kasserine Pass; the battered U.S. Army was reeling then, but he knew it would be back in killing strength. Two years of campaigning in Africa gave him great faith in land mines, but he wanted 200 million of them, not 6 million. Some divisions were composed of overage troops, as well as many non-Germans—paybooks had been issued in eight different languages just for former Soviet citizens now serving the Wehrmacht. Army Group B relied on 67,000 horses for locomotion; across the entire front, fewer than 15,000 trucks could be found. A corps commander in Normandy complained, "Emplacements without guns, ammunition depots without ammunition, minefields without mines, and a large number of men in uniform with hardly a soldier among them."

Worse yet was the Anglo-American advantage in airpower and seapower, a frightful imbalance that Rommel knew firsthand from the Mediterranean. German officers with battle experience only against the Soviets misjudged the enemy edge in the west. "Our friends from the East cannot imagine what they're in for here," Rommel had warned in mid-May; battling a foe with air superiority was like "being nailed to the ground." Moreover, 71,000 tons of Allied bombs had already eviscerated the German transportation system in the west. Train traffic in France had declined 60 percent since March—a testimony to those spavined Seine bridges, almost half of which were rail spans—and even more in northern France. Allied fighter sweeps proved so murderous that German daytime rail movement in France was banned after May 26. Beyond the 45,000 armed railwaymen already transferred from Germany to forestall saboteurs, almost 30,000 workers were seconded from the Atlantic Wall to rail repair duties. Some field commanders, Rommel grumbled, "do not seem to have recognized the graveness of the hour." Six weeks earlier he had warned subordinates:

> The enemy will most likely try to land at night and by fog, after a tremendous shelling by artillery and bombers. They will employ hundreds of boats and ships unloading amphibious vehicles and waterproof submersible tanks. We must stop him in the water, not only delay him. . . . The enemy must be annihilated before he reaches our main battlefield.

In this injunction lay what one German general called "a cock-fight controversy." For months the high command had bickered over how best to thwart an Allied invasion. Rommel argued that "the main battle line must be the beach," with armored reserves poised near the coast. "If we can't throw the enemy into the sea within twenty-four hours," he told officers in Normandy, "then that will be the beginning of the end." In March he had proposed that all armored, mechanized, and artillery units in the west be bundled under his command, and that he assume some control over the First and Nineteenth Armies in southern France.

This impertinence found little favor in Berlin or Paris. The OB West commander, Field Marshal Gerd von Rundstedt, who called his brash subordinate "an unlicked cub" and "the Marshal Laddie," argued that to disperse counterattack forces along seventeen hundred miles of exposed Atlantic and Mediterranean coastline would be foolhardy. Better to concentrate a central mobile reserve near Paris, able to strike as a clenched fist whenever the invaders committed themselves. Better to follow Napoléon's dictum, as one panzer commander urged: *"S'engager, puis voir."* Engage the enemy, and then we shall see.

Hitler dithered, then ordered a compromise that pleased no one. Frontline forces on the coast were to fight "to the last man"—that phrase so easily uttered by those far from the trenches—and Army Group B would command three armored divisions among the ten on the Western Front. Three others went to southern France. The remaining four, controlled by Berlin, were clustered near Paris in a strategic ensemble called Panzer Group West. Neither Rundstedt nor Rommel could issue orders to air or naval forces, who were vaguely advised to cooperate with ground commanders. "In the East there is *one* enemy," an officer in Paris complained. *"Here* everything is so complicated." Just a few days earlier, Hitler had shifted troops from OB West to Italy and the Eastern Front. Perhaps predictably, when frantic pleas to release the armored reserves had arrived in Berlin and Berchtesgaden this morning, more than eight hours passed before the panzers were ordered to begin the long, tortuous journey toward

Normandy. Rommel denounced the delay as "madness," adding, "Of course now they will arrive too late." *S'engager, puis voir.*

Dusk sifted over the Seine valley. Swallows trawled the river bottoms, and the day's last light faded from the chalk cliffs above the château, where antiaircraft gunners strained for the drone of approaching bombers. Telephones jangled in the salon war room, and orderlies bustled across the parquet with the latest scraps of news.

In Berlin it had been whispered that Rommel suffered from "African sickness"—pessimism—to which he answered, *"Der Führer vertraut mir, und das genügt mir auch."* The Führer trusts me, and that's enough for me. He remained "the Führer's marshal," in one colleague's phrase, loyal in his own fashion and as beguiled by Hitler as steel filings by a magnet. War and the Nazis had been good to him: he was a stamp collector not above adding looted issues to his album, and the handsome villa in leafy Herrlingen where he delivered Lucie's shoes had been confiscated from Jews after the occupants were sent to Theresienstadt. Hitler was a bulwark against bolshevism, he had told staff officers; if the invasion was repelled, perhaps the West would "come round to the idea of fighting side by side with a new Germany in the East." The onslaught against the Atlantic Wall would be "the most decisive battle of the war," he had predicted a few weeks earlier. "The fate of the German people itself is at stake." His fate, too.

The struggle in Normandy would depend in large measure on the only armored unit within quick striking distance of the invasion beaches, the 21st Panzer Division. A stalwart from Africa, the division had been obliterated in Tunisia, then rebuilt with sixteen thousand men—some still wearing oddments of tropical uniforms—and 127 tanks. Even while racing back to France this afternoon, Rommel had stopped midway to confirm by phone that the unit was hurrying into action. Now the harsh truth came clear: orders, counterorders, and disorder had plagued the division almost as much as marauding Allied planes and scorching field-gun fire. Not least among the 21st's troubles was the temporary absence of the commanding general, who reportedly had spent the small hours of June 6 in a Parisian fleshpot. The division's antiaircraft battalion had been pulverized by naval gunfire north of Caen, and the tank regiment gutted from the air and by British gunners. This evening a panzer grenadier regiment knifing toward Sword Beach in the two-mile gap between Canadian and British troops had nearly reached the strand. Then, just before nine P.M., almost 250 more British gliders escorted by fighters swept into the Orne valley, doubling British airborne combat power in France and threatening to pin the grenadiers against the sea.

At 10:40 P.M., General Friedrich Dollmann, who had commanded Seventh Army since 1939, phoned La Roche–Guyon with baleful news. The "strong attack by the 21st Panzer Division has been smothered by new airborne landings," Dollmann reported. The counterattack had failed. Nearly two-thirds of the 21st Panzer's tanks were lost. Swarming enemy aircraft impeded movement, even at night. Grenadiers skulked back from the coast to blocking positions with two dozen 88mm guns in the hills around Caen.

Rommel returned the receiver to its cradle. Hands again clasped behind his back, he studied the wall map. The critical crossroads city of Caen remained in German hands, and nowhere did the Anglo-American penetration appear deeper than a few kilometers. The 12th SS Panzer and the Panzer Lehr Divisions were finally moving toward Normandy despite fighter-bombers flocking to the telltale dust clouds like raptors to prey. "We cannot hold everything," he would tell his chief of staff. The first critical twenty-four hours was nearly spent, yet perhaps the coastal battle could still be saved. He turned to an aide and said, as if reminding himself, "I've nearly always succeeded up to now." He was, as ever, the Führer's marshal.

A monstrous full moon rose over the beachhead, where 156,000 Allied soldiers burrowed in as best they could to snatch an hour of sleep. Rommel was right: the invader's grip on France was tenuous, ranging from six miles beyond Gold and Juno to barely two thousand yards beyond Omaha. A crude sod airstrip had opened alongside Utah at 9:15 P.M., the first of 241 airdromes the Americans would build across Western Europe in the next eleven months. Yet only 100 tons of supplies made shore by midnight, rather than the 2,400 tons planned for Omaha dumps. Paratroopers, particularly among the nineteen airborne battalions on the American western flank, fought as scattered gangs in a score or more of muddled, desperate gunfights. Every man who survived the day now knew in his bones, as one paratrooper wrote, that "we were there for one purpose, to kill each other."

If the 21st Panzer had failed to fulfill Rommel's imperative by cudgeling the enemy into the sea within twenty-four hours, the division *had* blocked the capture of Caen, gateway to the rolling terrain leading toward Paris. "I must have Caen," the British Second Army commander, Lieutenant General Miles Dempsey, had declared at St. Paul's School three weeks earlier. But he would not have it today, or any day soon, in part because his landing force was unprepared to fight enemy armor so quickly. Even so, a British captain wrote, "We were not unpleased with ourselves."

The failure of this truncated drive fell hardest on civilians in Caen.

Gestapo killers hurried to the city jail and murdered eighty-seven French-men in batches of six, including one victim who cried, "My wife, my children!" as he was gunned down in a courtyard. Caen was among seventeen Norman towns warned in leaflets dropped from Allied planes on June 6 that bomber fleets would follow, often in little more than an hour. Beginning at 1:30 P.M., high explosives and incendiaries, aimed at rail yards and other targets intended to impede German reinforcements, also shattered Caen's medieval heart, igniting fires that would burn for eleven days. Thousands sought refuge in the quarries south of town, whose stone had been used by Norman kings to build Westminster Abbey and the Tower of London. Amid the ruination, five hundred coffins stockpiled in a funeral home were reduced to ashes. "We won't have a single coffin to bury the dead," the deputy mayor told his diary.

All told, three thousand Normans would be killed on June 6 and 7 by bombs, naval shells, and other insults to mortality; they joined fifteen thousand French civilians already dead from months of bombardment before the invasion. Some injured citizens were reduced to disinfecting their wounds with calvados, the local brandy fermented from apples. "Liberation," wrote the journalist Alan Moorehead, "usually meant excessive hardship for the first few months."

As for the liberators, the eight assault divisions now ashore had suffered 12,000 killed, wounded, and missing, with thousands more unaccounted for, most of whom had simply gotten lost in the chaos. Allied aircraft losses in the invasion totaled 127. The 8,230 U.S. casualties on D-Day included the first of almost 400,000 men who would be wounded in the European theater, the first of 7,000 amputations, the first of 89,000 fractures. Many were felled by 9.6-gram bullets moving at 2,000 to 4,000 feet per second, or by shell fragments traveling even faster; such specks of steel could destroy a world, cell by cell. Aboard U.S.S. *Samuel Chase*, mess boys who that morning had served breakfast in white jackets were now as blood-smeared as slaughterhouse toughs from sewing corpses into burial sacks. A British doctor who spent Tuesday evening on Sword Beach reported that for most of the wounded "nothing was being done for them as there was no plasma or blood, and they lay there being bombed and machine-gunned all night long." On Utah, handkerchiefs draped the faces of the dead because, as a Navy lieutenant said, "They do not seem to matter as much with faces covered."

Omaha was the worst, of course. Stretcher bearers with blistered hands carried broken boys down the bluff to Easy Red—now dubbed Dark Red—only to find that a medical battalion had come ashore with typewriters and office files but no surgical equipment or morphine. Blankets were stripped from the dead or salvaged in the tidal wrack between petulant outbursts of German artillery. Fearful of mines and rough surf, most landing craft refused to pick up casualties from the beach after dark. A single ambulance with cat's-eye headlights crept along the dunes, delivering the wounded to collection-point trenches where medics plucked scraps of GI boot leather from mine wounds. Listening for the telltale crackle of gas gangrene, they hushed sufferers who asked only for a bullet in the brain. A soldier returning to Omaha for ammunition found many comrades "out of their heads. There were men crying, men moaning, and there were men screaming."

Others were beyond screams. Dead men lay in windrows like "swollen grayish sacks," in one reporter's image. "I walked along slowly, counting bodies," wrote the correspondent Gordon Gaskill, who prowled the beach on Tuesday evening. "Within 400 paces I counted 221 of them." More than double that number—487—would be gathered on Omaha, toes sticking up in a line as if at parade drill. "One came up on them rather too suddenly and wanted to stare hard," a Navy lieutenant wrote, "but there was that feeling that staring was rude."

Graves Registration teams tied Emergency Medical Tag #52B to each corpse for identification, then shrouded them in mattress covers fastened with safety pins. Two inland sites had been chosen for cemeteries but both remained under fire, so temporary graves were scooped out below the escarpment. Shovel details fortified with brandy buried their comrades in haste.

So ended the day, epochal and soon legendary, and perhaps indeed, as in the judgment of a Royal Air Force history, "the most momentous in the history of war since Alexander set out from Macedon." In southern England, "the first of the Master Race" arrived as prisoners on an LST, Martha Gellhorn reported. She studied the "small shabby men in field gray . . . trying to see in those faces what had happened in the world." A badly wounded American lieutenant, evacuated on a surgical litter next to a German shot in the chest and legs, murmured, "I'd kill him if I could move."

Such sanguinary purpose would be needed in the weeks and months ahead. For the moment, the Allies savored their triumph. "We will never again have to land under fire," a Navy officer wrote his wife on June 7. "This is the end of Germany and Japan." If too optimistic—assault landings were still to come in southern France and on various god-awful Pacific islands—the core sentiment obtained. For four years Hitler had fortified this coast, most recently entrusting the task to his most charismatic general, yet Allied assault troops had needed less than three hours to crack the Atlantic Wall and burst into Fortress Europe. Though far from over, the battle was won.

"We have come to the hour for which we were born," a *New York Times* editorial declared on Wednesday morning. "We go forth to meet the supreme test of our arms and of our souls." Company clerks already had begun sorting stacks of mail, scribbling "deceased," "wounded," and "missing" on letters and packages. Those killed in action would appear on personnel lists as "dead stock." Yet even as they still lay on the Norman sand, silvered by the rising moon, toes pointing toward the stars, the living would carry them along. "I shall never forget that beach," Corporal William Preston, who had come ashore at dawn in an amphibious tank, wrote to his family in New York. Nor would he forget one dead soldier in particular who caught his eye. "I wonder about him," Preston added. "What were his plans never to be fulfilled, what fate brought him to that spot at that moment? Who was waiting for him at home?" Destiny had also sorted them, and would sort them again and again, until that hour for which they were born had passed.

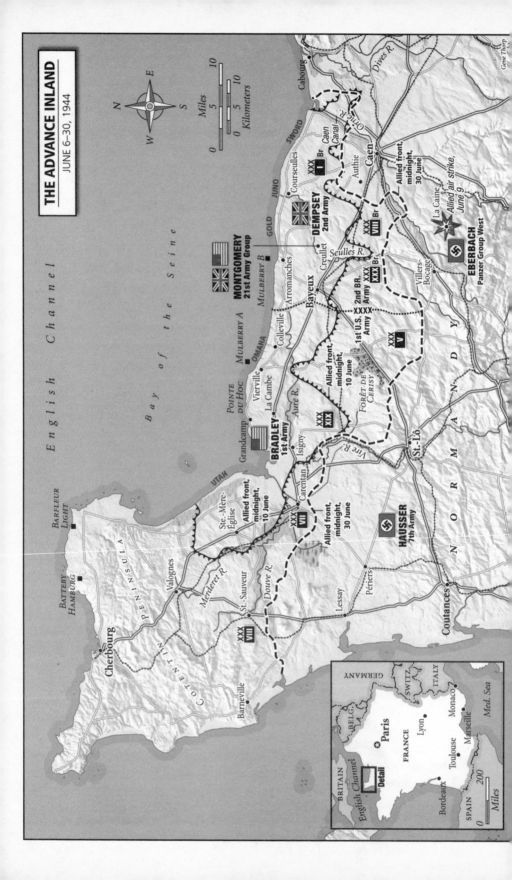

THE ADVANCE INLAND
JUNE 6–30, 1944

N
E
S
W

Miles
0 5 10
Kilometers
0 5 10

Gene Thorp

English Channel

Bay of the Seine

BARFLEUR LIGHT

BATTERY HAMBURG

Cherbourg

Barneville

C O T E N T I N   P E N I N S U L A

Valognes

St.-Sauveur

Merderet R.

Douve R.

Ste.-Mère-Église

XXX VIII

Lessay

Périers

Coutances

St.-Lô

HAUSSER
7th Army

Allied front,
midnight,
30 June

Vire R.

Carentan

Allied front,
midnight,
10 June

XXX VII

BRADLEY
1st Army

Grandcamp

Isigny

Aure R.

La Cambe

Vierville

POINTE DU HOC

UTAH

OMAHA

MULBERRY A

Colleville

Arromanches

MULBERRY B

Bayeux

Creullet

Seulles R.

Allied front,
midnight,
10 June

XXX XIX

FORÊT DE CERISY

1st U.S.
Army

XXXX

2nd BR.
Army

XXX V

MONTGOMERY
21st Army Group

Courseulles

SWORD

JUNO

GOLD

Authie

Caen Canal

Orne R.

Caen

XXX 1 Br

DEMPSEY
2nd Army

XXX VIII Br

XXX XXX Br

Villers-Bocage

La Caine

Allied front,
midnight,
30 June

Allied air strike,
June 9

EBERBACH
Panzer Group West

Cabourg

Dives R.

N O R M A N D Y

Detail

BRITAIN
English Channel
BELG.
LUX.
GERMANY
SWITZ.
ITALY
Paris
FRANCE
Lyon
Monaco
Marseille
Med. Sea
Toulouse
Bordeaux
SPAIN

Miles
0 200

2. LODGEMENT

"This Long Thin Line of Personal Anguish"

L IGHT rain fell in Portsmouth on Wednesday morning, June 7, as Eisenhower strode through a stone sally port to the dockyard below Broad Street. In the anchorage across from King's Stairs, where over the centuries many an English sea dog had sortied to battle, the fast minelayer H.M.S. *Apollo* awaited him, steam up in her triple stacks and a red pennant with four white stars already hoisted. No sooner had he boarded, at eight A.M., than the crew weighed anchor. The supreme commander knew little more about D-Day than did Corporal Preston in his tank, and he was keen to see for himself what D+1 would bring to the Norman coast.

Swinging east of the Isle of Wight, *Apollo* skipped across the Channel in three hours. The ship passed convoys returning, and convoys going out, and an alarming number of barges, boats, and landing craft, either foundering or abandoned, going nowhere. "A scene of great confusion met the eye," Admiral Ramsay, who accompanied Eisenhower, told his diary. "An anxious situation."

Mines continued to bedevil the roadstead. The lethal field on Cardonnet Bank claimed the sweeper U.S.S. *Tide* at midmorning, tossing her five feet into the air, killing the captain, and sending the vessel to the bottom in pieces. Not far away, the transport U.S.S. *Susan B. Anthony* had just arrived on station with 2,300 troops when a blast detonated beneath the number 4 hold. "The ship lifted and hogged, and then settled and sagged," a passenger reported. Troops were ordered to the port rails to counterballast an eight-degree starboard list, but nothing could check a snarling fire and ten feet of water in the engine room. By nine A.M., seas washed the main deck as rescue ships played hoses on the flames and took frightened men off the prow. An hour later, *Susan B.*'s skipper plunged into the water and swam from his dying ship. At 10:10 A.M., she "put her nose in the air and slipped backward calmly," wrote A. J. Liebling, "like a lady lowering herself into an armchair. In twenty minutes she was gone." Remarkably, all aboard were saved.

Dreadnoughts barked and bellowed, gray smoke rings drifting from their gun muzzles. Shortly before noon, *Apollo* pulled abreast of the *Augusta* off Omaha Beach as Eisenhower stood at the rail watching a Higgins boat wallow through the chop to a ladder lowered down the minelayer's hull. Omar Bradley, nose still bandaged, climbed to the deck and extended his hand, only to find the supreme commander in a red fury at the meager reporting from the beachhead. "Why in the devil didn't you let us know what was going on?" he snapped. "Nothing came through until late afternoon—not a damned word. I didn't know what had happened to you." Bradley sputtered in protest—"We radioed you every scrap of information we had"—then followed Eisenhower to Ramsay's flag cabin, seething at the rebuke. Only later did he learn that his hourly dispatches had piled up in Montgomery's radio room, where overwhelmed code clerks had fallen twelve hours behind in deciphering messages.

Swallowing his anger, Bradley tried to make amends by telling Eisenhower in detail what he knew. OVERLORD was "firmly rooted in France"—he had waded onto Dark Red earlier this morning to see for himself, even riding up the escarpment on a truck's running board. Fire on the beaches had dwindled. Captured enemy prisoners, particularly Poles and Russians, were helping to build their own cages. More than one-third of all shore obstacles would be cleared by low tide this evening, and nearly all would be gone in another day. Reinforcements continued to arrive: with the help of smoke screens and electronic jamming, nine troop transports sailing from the Thames late Tuesday were the first large Allied ships through the Straits of Dover in four years. A map found on a captured German artillery observer pinpointed not only enemy gun batteries near the invasion beaches but also every battalion, regimental, and division command post, all of which were now being pummeled by Allied fighter-bombers, naval guns, and artillery.

Yet First Army still had not reached most of its D-Day objectives. Only a quarter of the planned supplies and barely half of the fourteen thousand vehicles waiting offshore had been unloaded. V Corps's narrow purchase beyond Omaha expanded by the hour, but the 29th Division remained well short of the Aure River, six miles inland, which Bradley had hoped to reach on Tuesday. The 1st Division had not gotten much farther. On Pointe du Hoc, fewer than one hundred Rangers still fought in a perimeter hardly two hundred yards from the cliff's edge; only destroyer fire and Ranger pluck had kept the enemy at bay.

Beyond Utah Beach, confusion remained the order of the day. The 101st Airborne was churning south toward the Douve River and the vital crossroads town of Carentan. After going missing for twenty-four hours, the 82nd Airborne early on Wednesday morning sent an officer pumped full of Benzedrine to make contact with 4th Division commanders pushing inland; light tanks and tank destroyers had then been dispatched to stiffen the paratroopers. General Roosevelt subsequently rolled into the apple orchard that served as the 82nd's command post, helmet pushed back and waving his cane from *Rough Rider* "as if the bullet that could kill him had not been made," one witness reported. "Fellows," Roosevelt bellowed, "where's the picnic?"

The 82nd now occupied a triangular swatch of the Cotentin Peninsula, each embattled leg roughly six miles long. Two battalions held Ste.-Mère-Église, fighting off piecemeal German counterattacks from north and south, but several thousand other paratroopers remained badly scattered, and no real bridgehead existed west of the Merderet River. General Collins, the VII Corps commander, had gone ashore in the morning to take charge of a beachhead seven miles deep. A ten-mile gap remained between his VII Corps and the V Corps troops at Omaha; another gap of five miles also persisted between American and British forces. Closing those seams before Rommel could rip through them would be paramount in the coming days.

Eisenhower said little in response to Bradley's report, apparently lost in thought as he studied a map. "Bradley came over & discussed situation & did nothing to relieve my anxiety," Ramsay noted in his diary. "Bridgehead still very shallow. No guns to speak of ashore." After a flurry of salutes on deck, Bradley scrambled down the sea ladder and puttered back to *Augusta,* smoldering over what he deemed "a pointless interruption and annoyance."

Skies faired in the afternoon and *Apollo* steamed to the east for a distant look at the British beaches—but not distant enough. A lurch, and Eisenhower and others were flung to the deck; the vessel had struck a sandbar. "With the mast swaying violently, the entire ship jerking, grinding, and even bouncing . . . we eventually swung off the bar and floated free," wrote Harry Butcher. But the damage was done, the propellers and drive shafts bent badly enough to put the minelayer into dry dock for four months. Ramsay, who had first gone to sea in 1898 at the age of fifteen and was said to exude "an aura of vinegar," was mortified at this display of Royal Navy seamanship, although Eisenhower took responsibility for urging haste over caution. *Apollo* limped across the bay at six knots until a British destroyer picked up the supreme commander and whisked him back to Portsmouth.

"We've started," he scribbled in a quick, fretful note to Mamie. "Only time will tell how great our success will be."

Even war could not dim the radiance of a June morning in Normandy. Two battalions from the British 50th Division pushed into Bayeux on

Wednesday, led by French boys cadging cigarettes. White blossoms rioted in the orchards and geraniums spilled from window boxes. Roses climbed fence posts beneath painted wall advertisements for "Dubo ... Dubonn ... Dubonnet." Unmilked cows lowed in their stalls. Peasants in blue smocks and wooden clogs welcomed the Tommies, some with fascist salutes. Wine carts rolled down the Rue St. Jean, where shops offered goods long unseen in London: porcelain and plastic tableware, new furniture, forty thousand Camembert cheeses. (The priceless Bayeux tapestry, an embroidered eleventh-century record of that earlier invasion across the English Channel, had long been removed for safekeeping near Le Mans.) The last German in this town of seven thousand was said to have killed himself, and a widow living nearby recorded in her diary how others had fled through the rapeseed fields "without overcoats, without underwear, without razors."

Sherman tanks still wearing amphibious skirts clanked into town— "huge, dusty, belted with gigantic floats," a witness reported. Crews dismounted to brew the thick tea known as "gunfire." A civil affairs detachment arrived to impose a curfew and arrest collaborators. "At first sight," an exasperated officer lamented, "impossible to differentiate between pro-Nazis, Vichy, and patriot Frenchmen." Another report acknowledged, "Looting by troops pretty general." Journalists set up a press camp in the Lion d'Or, a ramshackle hotel with colored canvas awnings. The Lion served stewed lamb, gritty brown bread, and, Alan Moorehead reported, "a dry Sauterne, fifteen shillings a bottle.... The woman who ran the brothel above the hotel brought her girls down to eat." Thirty-six thousand French communes remained to be liberated, and few would enjoy as benign an emancipation as lovely Bayeux.

Devastation was but a mortar round away, of course. After seeing nearby villas and farmhouses reduced to "only shells with their insides blown out," Moorehead wrote, "one had the impression that the battle had been going on a long time, for weeks, even for months." Closer to Caen the gunplay was unremitting. A British major in the 50th Division recorded his daily prayer for June 7: "Oh, God, please stop the shells. If you stop them, I'll be good for always." A soldier cowering under German machine-gun fire complained, "What I can never understand is how those fuckers never run out of fucking ammunition." When artillery rounds began to fall, he added, "You curl up into the fetal position except that your hands go down to protect your genitalia. This instinct to defend the place of generation against the forces of annihilation [is] universal." For good measure he added: "Montgomery doesn't protect his privates, but by Christ, I protect mine." In Périers-sur-le-Dan, between Sword Beach and Caen, a French woman wrote, "Overhead the hisses and whines make you bend even lower. . . . Where is safety? Probably nowhere, or in the imponderables that save you."

Twenty-five miles to the west, the self-described "Unhappy Warrior" from Indiana also pondered the imponderables. Ernie Pyle had come ashore on Omaha early Wednesday, as Bradley's aide wrote, "looking helpless and insignificant . . . shading his emotions as he always does." For several hours he combed the high-water line, compiling an inventory:

> Socks and shoe polish, sewing kits, diaries, Bibles, hand grenades. Here are the latest letters from home, with the address on each one neatly razored out—one of the security precautions enforced before the boys embarked. Here are toothbrushes and razors, and snapshots of families staring up at you from the sand. Here are pocketbooks, metal mirrors, extra trousers, and bloody, abandoned shoes. . . . I picked up a pocket Bible with a soldier's name in it, and put it in my jacket. I carried it half a mile or so and then put it back down on the beach. I don't know why.

Pistol belts, canvas water buckets, stationery on which love letters would never be written, oranges, a tennis racket still clamped in its press with "not a string broken"—all formed what Pyle called "this long thin line of personal anguish." He returned to *LST-353* for the night and more nightmares, looking "very tired and very sad," an officer noted. To another reporter, Pyle confessed, "I become less used to it as the years go by."

A Gunman's World

E NEMY soldiers by the tens of thousands converged on Normandy, sweating through their field-gray blouses and black tunics, singing sentimental ballads of the kind beloved by German armies on the march since the Seven Years' War. By train and by truck they surged west and north, on foot and on bicycle and in ancient French buses upholstered with tree boughs. Dray carts, wagons, and horse-drawn caissons followed in snaking processions moving at a slow clop.

There was not a moment to lose, as Rommel repeatedly urged, yet moments, minutes, hours, and days were lost to disorder, indecision, and marauding Allied airplanes. Traveling by five dusty routes from Chartres, a hundred miles east of the invasion zone, the fifteen-thousand-man Panzer Lehr Division had been harassed from above since Tuesday evening. The burning town of Argentan was described by a German officer as a "fiery cage," with streets blocked by flaming debris and "bombers hovering above the roads." Ordered to travel by daylight on June 7 and averaging only six miles per hour—a third of the usual march speed—the division commander reported losses of forty fuel trucks, ninety other lorries, five tanks, and eighty-four half-tracks and self-propelled guns. Not until June 9 would Panzer Lehr join the battle in earnest, piecemeal and already wounded.

Half a dozen flak battalions moving toward the beachhead were mauled, suffering two hundred casualties before firing a shot. No anabasis would be more infamous than that of the 2nd SS Panzer Division, known as Das Reich, ordered north from Toulouse on June 7. To move a German tank division typically required at least sixty trains, but the only surviving rail bridge over the Loire proved so fragile that boxcars were nudged across one at a time. Das Reich matériel and troops traveling by rail would take seventeen days to cover 450 miles, normally a three-day journey.

Troops aboard the division's trucks moved somewhat faster, even as they were diverted for killing sprees against the maquis of the French Resistance. In Tulle, west of Lyon, ninety-nine men randomly chosen in reprisal for several SS deaths were told by the local abbé, "My friends, you are going to appear before God." They were hanged from lampposts and balconies, their bodies tossed into the town dump. On June 10 SS troops drove into Oradour-sur-Glane, a village bustling with farmworkers and children receiving vaccinations; the town crier beat his drum to summon one and all to a central square. Women and children were herded into a church, which was set ablaze with grenades and gunfire. Howling soldiers then shot dead the men in barns and garages before burning the town with straw, brush, and saddlery as kindling. More than 640 innocents died in Oradour. Das Reich, as an official British historian wrote, had "carved out for itself a private niche in the book of iniquity."

Evil also shadowed the 12th SS Panzer Division, crawling the seventy miles from Évreux to the coast at four miles per hour. Nicknamed Hitlerjugend—Hitler Youth—and composed of teenage fanatics led by Eastern Front veterans, the division's Panther tank battalion arrived near Caen on June 7 too low on fuel to give battle. That fell to the accompanying panzer grenadier regiment, led by Colonel Kurt Meyer, a broad-shouldered former miner and policeman who had joined the Nazi Party in 1930 at age nineteen. Highly decorated in Poland, Greece, and Russia, a motorcycle daredevil who had broken nineteen bones in various spills, "Panzermeyer" had been known to encourage timid troops to advance by tossing live hand grenades behind them. Climbing a spiral staircase in a corner turret of the twelfth-century Abbaye d'Ardenne, two miles northwest of Caen, Meyer on Wednesday afternoon spied Canadian troops from Juno Beach tramping south through the wheat fields and apple trees to nearby Authie.

Like hornets the grenadiers swarmed across almost a mile of open ground before naval guns and field artillery could range them; Canadian forward observers were trapped in traffic near the beach. Orange sheets of gunfire ripped through the North Nova Scotia Highlanders, and at 5:30 P.M. a white flare signaled German possession of Authie. Survivors scuttled away under a drifting loom of battle smoke while panzer crews rooted through twenty-one demolished Canadian tanks for chocolate, peanuts, and corned beef.

Belated salvos from the warships offshore and an armored counterattack took a toll on Meyer's men, who would lose more than thirty panzers on Wednesday. But the Canadians had been smacked back more than two miles, losing ground not to be recouped for a month. "Mortar and artillery fire almost continuous day and night. Noise so great we can only communicate with hand signals," a Cameron Highlander recorded. "No one dares to stand up, we crawl." Artillery spotters in trees or on roofs "last a couple days, couple hours, couple minutes." Platoons nipped from jugs of Jamaican rum while officers fortified themselves with gin or Teacher's Highland Cream. Caen burned, still in German hands.

Yet Panzermeyer lacked the strength to exploit his winnings. By nightfall, his troops remained six miles from the sea, and more than one hundred SS casualties in Authie made his regiment splenetic. The first murder may have been that of a wounded Canadian private, bayoneted by an SS trooper who shouted curses at his victim as he impaled him. Eight more prisoners were told to remove their helmets in Authie, then shot. Their bodies were dragged into the road and crushed beneath tank tracks; a French villager collected the remains with a shovel. Six others were frog-marched through a kitchen and shot in the head. The Sherbrooke Fusiliers chaplain was stabbed through the heart.

Other Canadian prisoners were herded to the Abbaye d'Ardenne. "Why do you bring prisoners to the rear? They only eat up our rations," Meyer was quoted as saying. "In the future no more prisoners are to be taken." Prisoners surrendered their paybooks, then were bludgeoned to death or dispatched by a bullet to the brain. On Thursday, June 8, the killings continued. Summoned one by one from a stable used as a jail, each condemned man shook hands with his mates before trudging up a flight of stairs and turning left into the pretty garden, where he was shot. Forty prisoners assembled in a field near the Caen–Bayeux road were ordered to sit facing east; SS troops brandishing Schmeisser machine pistols advanced in a skirmish line and opened fire, killing nearly three dozen. Several who bolted were soon recaptured and sent to prison camps. Now known as the Murder Division, the 12th SS Panzer would be accused of killing 156 defenseless men, nearly all Canadian, in little more than a week, igniting a cycle of atrocity and reprisal that persisted all summer. "Any German who tries to surrender nowadays is a brave man," said a Scottish soldier. "We just shoot them there and then, with their hands up." A British platoon commander jotted down his daily orders with a closing notation, "NPT below rank major": no prisoners to be taken below the rank of major.

Canadian battle casualties approached three thousand during the first week of OVERLORD, with more than a thousand dead. A witticism inspired by hard experience in Italy held that if "fuck" and "frontal" were removed from the military vocabulary, the Canadian army would have been both speechless and unable to attack. In less than five years that expeditionary army had expanded to more than fiftyfold its prewar strength but still evidenced little professional depth.

Yet the Canadian 3rd Division, carrying more than double its usual artillery complement, now displayed mettle in a battle described by one corporal as "just a straight shootout, both sides blasting at each other day and night. . . . They went at it like hockey players." Beaten back by firepower, the Hitlerjugend found the success at Authie impossible to replicate, even when reinforced by the 21st Panzer and Panzer Lehr Divisions. Clumsy, improvised attacks by the Murder Division were repelled with great gusts of howitzer, tank, and antitank fire; at noon on June 9, a single Sherman Firefly destroyed five Panthers with five 17-pounder antitank rounds. "I could have screamed from rage and grief," an SS officer wrote. Demonstrating the enduring utility of the fricative, a Canadian artillery commander later commented, "The Germans thought we were fucking Russians. They did stupid things, and we killed those bastards in large numbers."

Among the bastards watching from Panzermeyer's perch in the Abbaye turret on June 9 was General Leo Freiherr Geyr von Schweppenburg, commander of the Führer's armored reserve, Panzer Group West. A tall, cosmopolitan cavalryman who had previously served as Germany's military attaché in London, Brussels, and the Hague, Geyr more than most had embraced the Napoleonic *S'engager, puis voir.* Having dutifully engaged and then seen as Allied planes and artillery chewed up SS formations, he muttered, "My dear Meyer, the war can only now be won through political means." The next evening, after conferring with Rommel, Geyr postponed an attack against British troops north of Caen and ordered his tanks to regroup.

A few minutes later, at 8:30 P.M., Geyr stepped outside his château command post in La Caine, twelve miles southwest of Caen. Trailers, tents, and four large radio trucks filled an adjacent orchard; the destruction of phone lines across Normandy had forced German commanders to rely increasingly on the radio, despite the vulnerability of transmissions to decryption or direction finding. British eavesdroppers alone now intercepted seventeen thousand messages a day, including detailed information on supply levels and troop movements. Twice that morning, in fact, Ultra decrypts had identified La Caine as the Panzer Group West headquarters. The second intercept pinpointed the location precisely.

Geyr now cocked an ear to the drone of approaching aircraft. Other officers joined their commander, raking the heavens with field glasses as the sound grew louder. Suddenly, forty Typhoons from the RAF Second Tactical Air Force roared over the treetops in three waves, spitting rockets. Moments later, seventy-one Mitchell bombers pummeled the orchard with 436 500-pound bombs, turning La Caine into an inferno.

Geyr escaped with minor wounds, but the headquarters had been disemboweled. His chief of staff and more than thirty others were dead, the entire operations staff wiped out, the signal equipment wrecked. Those killed were interred in a bomb crater beneath a huge cross of polished oak, adorned with a swastika and an eagle. Geyr and other survivors fled to Paris for a fortnight's recuperation, crippling the armored strike force in Normandy.

Similar decapitations further impaired German battle leadership. Several days later, a British battleship shell exploded in the branches of a shade tree in the Odon River valley, instantly killing the 12th SS Panzer Division commanding general with a steel splinter through the face; Kurt Meyer would succeed him as leader of the Murder Division. Three other division commanders and a corps commander, General Erich Marcks, also were killed by mid-June. Slender and ascetic—he had banned whipped cream from his mess "as long as our country is starving"—Marcks had been disfigured in World War I, losing an eye, a leg, and the use of his right hand. In this war he had lost two sons. Now he lost all. Cautioned against driving in daylight, Marcks told a staff officer, "You people are always worried about your little piece of life." His wooden leg kept him from scrambling into a ditch when the staff car was strafed near Carentan on June 12. Marcks and the others were among 675 World War II German generals to die, including 223 killed in action, 64 suicides, and 53 who were executed, either by the Reich or by the Allies postwar.

"The Seventh Army is everywhere forced on the defensive," the OB West war diary recorded on June 10. Field Marshal von Rundstedt the same day ordered the "thorough destruction of Cherbourg harbor to begin forthwith," a scorched-earth decree intercepted by Ultra. Before leaving for Paris, Geyr recommended converting one-third of all panzers to antiaircraft gun carriers. Rail traffic had grown so sclerotic that of the 2,300 tons of food, fuel, and ammunition needed daily for Seventh Army, only 400 reached the front. A quartermaster had to borrow fifteen machine guns from the military governor of France for Cherbourg's defense.

Rommel too was unnerved. In an assessment for Rundstedt written June 10, even before the calamity at Panzer Group West's headquarters, he described the "paralyzing and destructive effect" of Allied air dominance from an estimated 27,000 sorties each day. (This was nearly triple the actual number.) He also feared another, bigger Allied landing in the Pas de Calais, and warned that the "material equipment of the Americans . . . is far and away superior." During a two-hour stroll through the La Roche–Guyon gardens, he told a subordinate that the best solution would be "to stop the war while Germany still held some territory for bargaining." Hitler disagreed, demanding of Seventh Army that "every man shall fight or fall where he stands."

"The battle is not going at all well for us," Rommel wrote Lucie on June 13, "mainly because of the enemy's air superiority and heavy naval guns." Almost as an afterthought he added, "I often think of you at home."

Rommel's lament would have delighted General Montgomery had he been privy to it. The 21st Army Group commander often tried to infiltrate the minds of his adversaries, to see the fight as they saw it. On the walls of his personal caravan, confiscated from a captured Italian field marshal in Tunisia, Montgomery had tacked up not only an invocation from *Henry V*—"O God of battles! Steel my soldiers' hearts!"—but photos of prominent battle captains. A visitor to Montgomery's encampment later counted "three of Rommel, one of Rundstedt, and about thirty of Monty."

On D+2 he had come home to Normandy, ancestral seat of the Montgomerys, including one forebear who accidentally killed King Henri II with a lance through the eye during a joust in 1559. His command post was tucked into the grounds of an imposing manor house with a hip roof and six chimneys at Creullet, four miles inland of Gold Beach. A sign on the twenty-foot iron gate advised "All traffic keep left"—a bit of England imported to France. Montgomery had also brought his beloved "betting book," a leather-bound volume in which innumerable small-stakes wagers—when Rome would fall, or the war end—had been entered in his tidy hand over the years; those resolved were marked "settled." And his pets: "I now have 6 canaries, 1 love bird, 2 dogs," he subsequently wrote, the latter a fox terrier named Hitler and a cocker spaniel named Rommel, both of whom "get beaten when necessary." The menagerie soon included a cow, ten chickens, and four geese; the fowl gave omelet eggs for his mess. Church services from the Creullet garden were broadcast to Britain, with Montgomery—"slender, hard, hawk-like, energetic," in an RAF officer's description—reading scripture to officers sitting in the flower beds.

"The way to fame is a hard one," he would write soon after the war.

"You must suffer and be the butt of jealousy and ill-informed criticism. It is a lonely matter." Lonely he was, but fame's fruits pleased him: the newborns named Bernard, the marriage proposals from strange women, the beret craze in New York, and the fact that his Eighth Army flag from the Mediterranean had brought 275 guineas at auction, proceeds to the Red Cross. He was "Master" to his aides, "this Cromwellian figure" to Churchill, "God Almonty" to the Canadians, "the little monkey" to Patton, and, to a fellow British general, "an efficient little shit." Churchill's wife considered him "a thrilling and interesting personage . . . with the same sort of conceit which we read Nelson had," while the prime minister's physician concluded that "Monty wants to be a king." Eisenhower came to believe that "Monty is a good man to serve under, a difficult man to serve with, and an impossible man to serve over." That maxim would tidily sum up the Allied high command in Europe.

He had arrived for the second time in this war to direct a battle that simply *had* to be won—Alamein was the first—and as leader of what one historian called "the last great field army imperial Britain would send into battle," a force officially anointed as the British Liberation Army. His command included an equal measure of Americans, but parity would soon yield to a threefold Yankee preponderance on the Continent; the imbalance was fraught with tension and grievance.

Few could gainsay his virtues: "the power of commanding affection while communicating energy," a quality also attributed to Marlborough; a conviction that gratuitous casualties were unpardonable; a sense that he knew the way home. Omar Bradley, who would later grow to detest him, believed Montgomery in Normandy to be "tolerant and judicious," a model of "wisdom, forbearance, and restraint." If "tense as a mousetrap," in Moorehead's image, he could be charming, generous, and buoyant. George Bernard Shaw admired how "he concentrates all space into a small spot like a burning glass."

"I keep clear of all details, indeed I must," Montgomery told his staff. "I see no papers, no files. I send for senior staff officers; they must tell me their problems in ten minutes." When pressing for a decision, he leaned in with jaws snapping: "Do you agree, do you agree, do you agree?" His shrewd intelligence officer, Brigadier Edgar T. Williams, later wrote, "One was impressed by his sheer competence, his economy, his clarity, above all his decisiveness." A man of habit and discipline, Montgomery had been awakened after his usual bedtime of 9:30 P.M. only twice during the war, both occasions in Africa, and he did not intend to be roused again. He had not come to France to lose the battle, to lose the war, or even to lose sleep. Certainly he had not come to lose a reputation earned at the cannon's mouth, a reputation to which he was now chained.

Alas, "too many of his best qualities were matched by folly or misjudgment," as his biographer Ronald Lewin would write. He was "a man made to be misunderstood," one of those "whose qualities intensify rather than expand during the course of their lives. . . . Like Bottom, he could play the ass while unaware of his metamorphosis." His bumptious, cocksure solipsism already had infuriated sundry generals in the Mediterranean, both American and British. If, as Churchill posited, a gentleman was "someone who is only rude intentionally," then Montgomery was disqualified. Knowing and unknowing, he could offend, rankle, enrage. Hardly a fatal flaw for a subaltern brawling in the trenches, this defect proved near mortal in coalition warfare, when political nuance and national sensitivities could be as combustible as gunpowder.

He remained "very small-boyish," in the phrase of the military historian B. H. Liddell Hart, scarred by the cold, shrewish mother who was forever saying, "Find out what Bernard is doing and tell him to stop." (He would refuse to attend her funeral.) A bully boy at St. Paul's and Sandhurst, he never quite outgrew the athlete who could be disruptive and fractious unless he was made team captain. "As long as 51 percent of your decisions are right," he had recently told Shaw, "you'll succeed." In truth his generalship reaped a far higher winning percentage, but by his account all too often the brilliant plan was his, the brilliant victory was his, the golden laurels were his, his, his. Brigadier Williams proposed a motto for Montgomery: "Alone I done it."

"Enjoying life greatly," he wrote to his rear headquarters in Portsmouth on June 13, "and it is great fun fighting battles again after five months in England." Several thousand men were dead, and thousands more had been maimed. Here was a man made to be misunderstood.

The OVERLORD plan *was* largely his, and now he sought to make it work. Since early May, Montgomery had intended to lure as much of the enemy's weight as possible to the British and Canadian divisions on his left wing, allowing the American right to capture Cherbourg and then thrust south of the Cotentin Peninsula. He reiterated the scheme to Field Marshal Brooke in London on June 11: "My general policy is to pull the enemy on to Second Army so as to make it easier for First Army to expand and extend the quicker." To gain maneuver room in the beachhead, he had called for "powerful armored force thrusts" on both left and right, beginning on D-Day afternoon, and he had been ready to sacrifice four tank brigades in an exchange of metal and men for space.

Yet after a week the beachhead remained pinched and crowded. Thirty-four Allied armored battalions and more than 300,000 troops had landed, with two thousand tanks, but they had nowhere to go. On the left, Second

Army had blunted the German counterattack without building momentum or gaining elbow room. The feeble direct assault on Caen had failed, and a proposal to drop British airborne troops behind the city found no favor with Eisenhower's air chief, Leigh-Mallory, who feared heavy aircraft losses. "He is a gutless bugger who refuses to take a chance," Montgomery fumed to his chief of staff on June 12. "I have no use for him."

A flanking attack from west of Caen began with promise on June 13 when the British 7th Armored Division—the famed Desert Rats from Africa—captured Villers-Bocage, guided through the village streets by gendarmes and baying civilians. Then calamity: on the far side of town, Tiger tank fire raked the lead column; within fifteen minutes, more than a dozen British tanks and as many trucks had been gutted, most by a single audacious panzer commander, SS captain Michael Wittmann. Winkled out of Villers-Bocage, with losses exceeding fifty armored vehicles, the clumsy British attack collapsed. The chastened Desert Rats drew back behind the massed fires of 160 Anglo-American guns and 1,700 tons of RAF bombs that turned the village into a smoking hole.

"The whole show on land is bogged up," Leigh-Mallory told his diary on June 14. "The Hun has kicked us out of Villers-Bocage and there is no sign of any forward movement, or a chance of it." With the front lines static—Tommies would not tramp the rubbled streets of Villers-Bocage again until August—the battle soon turned into an attritional struggle of snipers and artillery barrages in what Moorehead called "a gunman's world." "Bloody murder, people dropping dead," a company commander wrote. "One of my platoons ran away and was brought back at pistol-point. . . . The same platoon ran away again." A British corporal's diary entries for three consecutive days in mid-June:

June 18: Day of Hell. Counter-attack.
June 19: Day of Hell. Counter-attack.
June 20: Day of Hell. Advanced. Counter-attacked.

For the Americans in the west, progress was a bit more heartening. The V and VII Corps, heaving inland from Omaha and Utah respectively, merged into a single front after the capture of Carentan and the repulse of a ragged counterattack by the 17th SS Panzer Grenadier Division on June 13. "Lousy & undersized & scurvy & dirty," a combat engineer wrote in describing a gaggle of prisoners, "with greasy hair & flat mouths & short necks." A four-day struggle by the 82nd Airborne to secure a bridgehead over the Merderet finally won through, although more than one thousand paratroopers remained missing, and the 101st Airborne could not account for nearly three thousand more. Here too the landscape was wrecked—"When I first saw Isigny, with walls toppling and every-thing afire," an officer reported, "I thought of Carthage"—but most civil-ians seemed agreeable even amid the ruins. "The people are friendly & called us Libirators," a sergeant from the 18th Infantry wrote in his diary.

Bradley late on June 13 halted V Corps's drive toward St.-Lô; with the British stalled around Caen, he feared vulnerable flanks if the American salient grew too frisky. He also amended his original plan to simply bash on toward Cherbourg. Instead, he chose to first cut the Cotentin Peninsula by shoving three divisions west to the sea, blocking German reinforce-ments and sealing escape routes. The 4th Division, with Ted Roosevelt, would continue hammering northward toward the port.

"I'm sitting in a little gray stone Normandy château," Roosevelt wrote Eleanor from a grim encampment fifteen miles southeast of Cherbourg. *Rough Rider* stood outside beneath a camouflage net, a sunburst hole in the windshield from a shell fragment.

> I don't suppose there's a man here who's thirty but they look old. . . .
> Behind me lies a hard fought field. . . . The dead lie sprawled in every
> attitude. Their uniforms are dirty and torn, their faces are like yellow
> clay, and unshaven. Brown, dried blood stains them. . . . Today's been
> one of those days in battle when the heebie jeebies are in order.

No one took a greater proprietary interest in the Norman battlefield than the dour Frenchman known as Deux Mètres. At 5:40 A.M. on Wednes-day, June 14, Charles de Gaulle and fifteen companions left London's Con-naught Hotel in six automobiles, including a luggage car carrying 25 million francs. Escorted by two motorcycle policemen, the convoy drove to Kings Stairs in Portsmouth. Just before nine A.M. the French destroyer *La Combattante,* flying a tricolor embroidered with De Gaulle's initials—"not altogether in accordance with regulations," as a petty officer conceded—singled up her lines and made for France.

In his own fashion, De Gaulle had mended fences with Churchill after their railcar tiff ten days earlier. He rescinded his ban on placing French liaison officers in Allied units and, he reported, "I wrote to Mr. Churchill to salve the wounds he had inflicted on himself." Now, in his belted uniform, leather tunic, and two-star kepi, he scanned the horizon with field glasses for a first glimpse of the country he had fled in 1940 under a Vichy death sen-tence. "Has it occurred to you, General," an aide asked aboard *Combattante,* "that four years ago to the day the Germans marched into Paris?" With a lift of his great beak, De Gaulle replied, "They made a mistake."

Montgomery had authorized a visit by De Gaulle and two minions; instead, a platoon of nineteen came ashore by DUKW at Courseulles on

Juno Beach just before two P.M. Declining an invitation to dine—"We have not come to France to have luncheon with Montgomery," De Gaulle told an emissary from 21st Army Group—he instead drove by jeep to Creullet for a brief, awkward conference. The French general "clearly believed small talk to be a vice," a British diplomat observed, and conversation often "flowed like glue." A British officer in Creullet reported that De Gaulle, "forgetting no doubt General Montgomery's dislike of smoking... smoked cigarettes all over his famous caravan." Montgomery was reduced to discussing his wall photos of Rommel. "I missed him in Africa," he told De Gaulle, "but I hope to get him this time."

Then it was off to Bayeux, where a loudspeaker truck announced, "General de Gaulle will speak at four o'clock at the Place de Château." Down the Rue Saint-Jean he walked, "a stiff, lugubrious figure," in Moorehead's description, preceded by saluting gendarmes on wobbly bicycles, and greeted with tossed peonies and cries of *"Vive De Gaulle. À bas les boches, à bas les collaborateurs."* Several thousand people awaited him beneath the regimented lime trees in the grassy square. "At the sight of General de Gaulle," he later wrote in his memoirs—as usual referring to himself in the third person—"the inhabitants stood in a kind of daze, then burst into bravos or else into tears. . . . The women smiled and sobbed." Beneath the blue Cross of Lorraine, he proclaimed the resurrection of the French Republic, here in what he would call "our glorious and mutilated Normandy." His delegates—and the steamer trunk containing 25 million in banknotes—would remain to rebuild a government, with Bayeux as capital until Paris was unshackled. "The path of war is also the road to liberty and to honor," he told the cheering throng. "This is the voice of the mother country."

After belting out "La Marseillaise," he pressed on to Isigny and Grandcamp. But when Montgomery learned that the Frenchman had reserved fourteen hotel rooms in Bayeux, he furiously ordered him back to England, threatening to arrest and deport him personally. At 8:30 P.M. De Gaulle reluctantly reboarded *La Combattante*, convinced that "France would live, for she was equal to her suffering," while privately wondering, "How can one be expected to govern a country that has two hundred and forty-six different kinds of cheese?"

Montgomery wrote Churchill that De Gaulle's reception "was definitely lukewarm and there was no real enthusiasm." That was false. In fact, De Gaulle had stolen a march on the Anglo-Americans, demonstrating both his popular legitimacy and his principle that liberated France could be governed by Frenchmen rather than by another military occupation. "Blessed be he," the author André Gide would write, "through whom our dignity was restored."

Terror Is Broken by Terror

I N happier days, when the Reich was ascendant and the conquest of Britain seemed inevitable, Hitler had ordered construction of an elaborate command post for the German invasion of England in 1940. Tucked into a sheltered valley outside Margival, seventy-five miles northeast of Paris, Wolfsschlucht II, or W-II, was among more than a dozen elaborate Führer headquarters built in occupied Europe by a force of 28,000 workers pouring a million cubic meters of concrete. W-II rambled across ten square kilometers, with hundreds of offices, garrison rooms, and guest quarters appointed with thick rugs and new maple furniture. Engravings looted from Parisian art shops hung on the walls, and a bootjack could be found in every wardrobe. Larders held tons of canned meat and cherries, sugar, and tinned asparagus. Camouflage netting by the acre concealed the complex; rails leading into a train tunnel were painted rust-red to simulate disuse. Potemkin farmhouses, barns, and pig pens, and a grove of fake trees hid gun batteries on an adjacent ridge. An inconspicuous teahouse atop the Führer's personal bunker offered a fine view of Soissons Cathedral, five miles south.

Although W-II had never been used, locals deemed it "the most forbidden place in France," and it was here that Hitler ordered Rundstedt and Rommel to meet him for a secret conference on Normandy. The Führer and his entourage flew from Berchtesgaden in four Focke-Wulf Condors to Metz, then drove 175 miles in armored cars to Margival. (Venturing farther west by air seemed foolhardy when even SS soldiers had begun referring to predatory Allied fighter-bombers as "meat flies.") At nine A.M. on Saturday, June 17, Hitler received the two field marshals in an entry hall with cyclopean walls and a green tile fireplace.

This was Hitler's first return to France since 1940, and he looked like a man who was losing a world war: eyes bloodshot and puffy from insomnia, skin sallow, the toothbrush mustache a bit bedraggled. Aides reported that even his passion for music had waned. "It is tragic that the Führer has so cut himself off from life and is leading an excessively unhealthy life," wrote his propaganda minister, Joseph Goebbels. Often he checked his own pulse, as if fingering mortality; a quack dubbed the Reich Injection Master frequently administered sedatives or shots of a glandular concoction. He shunned bright lights and wore a cap with an enlarged visor to shield his eyes. "I always have the feeling of tipping to the right," he complained. He spoke of retirement, of a life devoted to reading, or meditating, or running a museum. His battle captains disappointed him, and of eighteen German field marshals and forty full generals, he would quarrel with more than half before the calamity ended. In Berlin it was rumored that he intended to take personal command in the west.

Hitler sat hunched on a wooden stool, fiddling with his spectacles and a fistful of colored pencils as Rommel opened the session with a glum progress report. The Allies had landed at least twenty divisions in Normandy—half a million men with 77,000 vehicles. The German Seventh Army opposed them with the equivalent of fourteen divisions, and those depleted units averaged under 11,000 men, compared with almost 17,000 a few years earlier. German casualties had reached 26,000, including more than 50 senior commanders. Allied naval guns could hit panzers more than twenty-five kilometers inland, while the enemy's superiority in matériel was at least as profound as it had been in Africa.

Anglo-American warplanes harried the battlefield to a depth of 150 kilometers or more; day marches in fair weather were suicidal. Rail traffic could get no closer to the beachhead than two hundred kilometers. Air attacks now immobilized nearly three hundred trains a day. German aircraft reinforcements were shot down at a rate of three dozen each day, while others lost their way, ran out of fuel, or were destroyed by their own antiaircraft guns; of fifty-seven fighters that left Wiesbaden for Évreux, only three arrived. At dusk on Wednesday, British planes had dropped twelve hundred tons of explosives on Le Havre port, including six-ton "Tallboy" bombs, and more attacks followed on Thursday. Seven hundred French houses had been destroyed in Le Havre, but so too sixty-three German vessels, including attack boats and minesweepers.

Rommel pointed to a large map. Just this morning American tanks had crossed the Cherbourg–Coutances road; soon the Cotentin Peninsula would be severed, trapping forty thousand troops and dooming Cherbourg. If the Anglo-Americans broke free of the beachhead, either south of Caen or below the Cotentin, the road to Paris lay open and Brittany could be cut off.

Hitler stirred on his stool. "Don't call it a beachhead, but the last piece of French soil held by the enemy," he said calmly, adding, "Cherbourg is to be held at all costs."

Rundstedt said little, taciturn as usual in his trim gray uniform with the carmine trouser stripe that marked a general staff officer. If Rommel was an unlicked cub, then Rundstedt—at sixty-eight, the oldest German field marshal, he had been a Prussian soldier for half a century—was known as both *der alte Herr,* the old gent, and *der schwarze Ritter,* the black knight. The scion of Junker gentry and eight centuries of soldiering ancestors, he had served as an army group commander and then military governor in Poland. After receiving his marshal's baton in 1940, Rundstedt arrived in France to help plan SEA LION, the aborted invasion of England. During the subsequent attack on the Soviet Union, he commanded six field armies, captured the Ukraine, and then retired in late 1941 after a spat with Hitler, only to return in uniform as commander-in-chief for the west.

Beset by rheumatism, an ailing heart, and what one general called "psychic resignation," Rundstedt lived in the Parisian suburb of St.-Germain-en-Laye, where he slept late, read Karl May westerns, and addressed visitors in credible French or English. He disdained both the telephone and the "brown dirt" of Nazi thuggery; although loyal to Hitler, he was not above deriding him as "the Bohemian corporal," or denouncing the Führer's orders with his favorite epithet, *"Quatsch!"* Nonsense! He "would have been most happy if Prussia had remained alone," his chief of staff later observed, "just as before 1866." Rarely did he visit the front, considering the Atlantic Wall "a bit of cheap bluff." He preferred to command from a one–to–one million scale map on which the beachhead—or rather, that last bit of France held by the enemy—was hardly bigger than a playing card. His pessimism ran deep, and the past ten days had only deepened his gloom.

Now Rundstedt stepped forward to support the Marshal Laddie. A rigid defense of the Cotentin was doomed, he warned. Better to pull exposed German forces back inside Cherbourg's bristling fortifications. Hitler nodded in agreement, but believed southern approaches to the port should also be defended. "The fortress is to hold out as long as possible," he said, "if possible until about mid-July." He had earlier drawn a line with a red pencil across the peninsula below Cherbourg, declaring, "They must hold here."

What about further Allied landings? the Führer asked. Rundstedt thought another invasion was likely. Intelligence from Britain suggested that fifty more divisions had coiled for a second, larger blow. For this reason the German Fifteenth Army had diverted but a single division to Normandy; twenty-one others remained in the Pas de Calais, peering seaward. Yet even if the Allied force in Normandy had been bottled up for the time being, Rundstedt agreed with Marshal Rommel that it was "impossible to hold everything." Both men advocated evacuating southern France to the Loire River, shortening German lines and forming a mobile reserve of some sixteen divisions to safeguard the line of the Seine.

Hitler waved away the proposal—"You must stay where you are"—then changed the subject. Great things were afoot, he said, magical things. New jet-propelled aircraft would soon dominate the skies. New sea mines, triggered by pressure waves from passing ships and almost impossible to sweep, had already holed a number of Allied ships. But the greatest secret weapon had just come into play. Until now, the Reich had no answer for the Anglo-American bombers devastating the Fatherland; a single German city might absorb more bombs in twenty-four hours than had fallen on Britain in all of 1943. That was about to change.

Hitler had once dismissed rocketry as "imagination run wild," but in September 1943 his scientists had begun production of a self-propelled bomb in a Volkswagen factory. Technical glitches and thirty-six thousand tons of Allied explosives dropped on suspected launch sites had delayed the program, but German engineers found that simple mobile equipment using little more than a flimsy metal ramp would suffice to get the bomb off the ground. The weapon was a flying torpedo, twenty-five feet long with stubby wings, a crude jet engine, and a one-ton warhead. It could cross the English coast twenty minutes after launch; when the fuel ran dry, the engine quit and the bomb fell. Hitler called them "cherry stones."

The first salvo, launched from western France early Tuesday morning, had flopped: in Operation RUMPELKAMMER—JUNKROOM—just four of the initial ten bombs even reached England, and only one caused any casualties. But subsequent volleys showed greater promise. By noon on June 16, of 244 launches, 73 cherry stones had reached "Target 42," also known as London. This very morning the nameless weapon had been anointed the *Vergeltungswaffe*—reprisal weapon—or V-1. "Terror is broken by terror," the Führer liked to say. "Everything else is nonsense."

Rundstedt suggested that the V-1 be used against those half million enemy soldiers now massed in the beachhead. Rommel agreed. Hitler summoned a military expert who explained that the flying bomb's inaccuracy made any target smaller than London difficult to hit: the V-1s were aimed at Tower Bridge on the Thames, but the margin of error might be fifteen kilometers or more. Relentless pummeling of Target 42, Hitler told the field marshals, would "make it easier for peace." Panic would paralyze Britain, with psychological and political chaos.

They broke for lunch, a joyless repast taken in silence. Two SS guards stood behind the Führer's chair as he wolfed down a plate of rice and vegetables—first sampled by a taster—garnished with pills and three liqueur glasses of colored medicines. A sudden warning of sixty Allied planes approaching sent Hitler and the field marshals scuttling into a cramped bomb shelter for another leaden hour until the all-clear sounded.

Hitler walked Rommel to his car at four P.M., promising to visit him at La Roche–Guyon the next morning. "What do you really think of our chances of continuing the war?" Rommel asked with his habitual effrontery. Was it not time to consider coming to terms with the West, perhaps in common cause against the Bolsheviks? "That is a question which is not your responsibility. You will have to leave that to me," Hitler snapped. "Attend to your invasion front."

A laconic Rundstedt later summarized the conference with concision: "The discussion had no success." Rather than press on to Rommel's headquarters, Hitler would abruptly bolt for Bavaria after an errant V-1 flew east rather than west and detonated near the Margival bunker; it did little damage but brought court-martial investigators sniffing for possible assassins. Back in Berchtesgaden, the Führer bemoaned Rommel's gloom. Had the Desert Fox lost his strut? "Only optimists can pull anything off today," Hitler told his courtiers.

In fact, Rommel felt buoyant, having been beguiled once again by the master he served. He "cannot escape the Führer's influence," an aide wrote home. After supper on Saturday he walked the château grounds with his chief naval adviser, Vice Admiral Friedrich Ruge, to discuss the day while admiring the mother-of-pearl vistas along the Seine. Movies often were projected on a cave wall behind the castle, and the sound of laughter from staff officers watching a light comedy carried on the evening air. Ruge was reading *Gone with the Wind,* and Rommel enjoyed hearing the latest plot twists. In Scarlett, Rhett, and the doomed Confederacy, the admiral detected "endless parallels with our time" and an affirmation that "rebuilding after a total defeat was possible."

Rommel retired to his chambers, beyond the ancient portcullis slot and the curiosity room with its glass cases of mounted insects and its stuffed hawk. In the morning he would dash off a "dearest Lu" note about Margival and the new V-1 campaign. "The long-range action has brought us a lot of relief," he told her. "The Führer was very cordial and in a good humor. He realizes the gravity of the situation."

Even on the Sabbath morn, antiaircraft crews across Target 42 manned their guns and scanned the southeastern sky for the apparition soon called Doodlebug, Hell Hound, Buzz Bomb, Rocket Gun, Headless Horseman, or, simply, It. Earlier in the week some gunners had crowed in jubilation at shooting down what they believed were German bombers but were now known to be pilotless bombs designed to fall from the sky. This Sunday, June 18, was Waterloo Day, and worshippers packed London churches to commemorate the British Army's victory over Napoléon in 1815, and to petition for divine help again.

In the Guards Chapel at Wellington Barracks on Birdcage Walk, across from the former pig meadow and leper colony currently known as St. James's Park, a full-throated congregation belted out the "Te Deum" and prepared to take communion from the bishop of Maidstone. "To Thee all angels cry aloud," they sang, "the heavens and all the powers therein." At 11:10 A.M. an annoying growl from those same heavens grew louder. Ernest Hemingway heard it in his Dorchester Hotel suite, where he was making pancakes with buckwheat flour and bourbon; from the window he looked for the telltale "white-hot bunghole" of a jet engine. Pedestrians in Parliament Square heard it and fell flat, covering their heads. Clementine Churchill, the prime minister's wife, heard it in Hyde Park, where she was visiting the gun battery in which her daughter Mary volunteered. The Guards Chapel congregation heard it and kept singing.

Then they heard nothing—that most terrifying of all sounds—as the engine quit, the bunghole winked out, and the black cruciform fell. Through the chapel's reinforced concrete roof It plummeted before detonating in a white blast that blew out walls, blew down support pillars, and stripped the leaves from St. James's plane trees. A funnel of smoke curled fifteen hundred feet above the wrecked nave; rubble ten feet deep buried the pews even as six candles still guttered on the altar and the bishop stood unharmed. One hundred and twenty-one others were dead and as many more injured. Two thousand memorial plaques accumulated by Guards regiments during eons of war lay pulverized, although a mosaic donated by Queen Victoria remained intact: "Be thou faithful unto death and I will give thee a crown of life."

Clementine Churchill hastened home to alert the prime minister, who was still reviewing papers in his bed at 10 Downing Street. "The Guards Chapel," she told him, "is destroyed." He hurried to Birdcage Walk and watched salvage teams lift out the dead. Among others, several musicians from the Coldstream Guards band were found in a side gallery, still holding their instruments as if in a wax tableau, surely faithful unto death. Churchill wept.

That afternoon he motored to Bushy Park and asked Eisenhower to redouble efforts against the flying bomb. In a memo on Sunday evening, the supreme commander ordered that the targets code-named CROSSBOW, comprising V-1 launch areas, supply dumps, and related sites, "are to take first priority over everything except the urgent requirements of the battle." Yet more than thirty thousand attack sorties already had flown in the past six months, dropping the tonnage equivalent of four Eiffel Towers on CROSSBOW in an effort to eviscerate a program Allied intelligence knew was in development. Some launch sites were hit forty or more times before analysts realized that the V-1 could be fired from elusive mobile launchers. Ideas for defeating the flying bombs poured in from the public: harpoons fired from tethered Zeppelins; huge butterfly nets; projectiles filled with carbolic acid. One patriot offered to put a curse on German launch crews.

CROSSBOW countermeasures in the coming weeks were more conventional but fitfully efficacious. Two thousand barrage balloons were deployed on approaches to London in hopes that their tethering cables would bring down the bombs in flight; German engineers responded by fitting V-1 wings with *Kuto-Nasen,* sharp blades to cut the cables. Fighter pilots grew adept at shooting down the bombs with 20mm cannons—at 380 miles per hour, the RAF Tempest could overtake the V-1—and some even learned to use their wings to create enough turbulence to send a bomb spiraling out of control. Although a V-1 was considered eight times more difficult to bring down with ground fire than a German bomber, more than a thousand antiaircraft guns were shifted from greater London to the southeast coast for better fields of fire, along with 23,000 gunners and 60,000 tons of ammunition and radar equipment. Sussex and Kent in the southeast became known as Bomb Alley.

Eisenhower's "first priority" edict dismayed his air force chieftains, who favored the uninterrupted smashing of German cities, oil facilities, and other strategic targets. The order stood: one-quarter of all combat sorties in the next two months would be flown against CROSSBOW targets, and crews would drop 73,000 tons of bombs—another eight Eiffel Towers. This enormous diversion of bombers had little impact on German launches; typically, one hundred V-1s were still fired at Target 42 each day. Few could doubt that the best solution was for Allied armies to overrun what was now dubbed the Rocket Gun Coast of northwestern France. "We must give the enemy full credit for developing one of the finer weapons of the war," the war diary for the U.S. Strategic Air Forces acknowledged. "People are beginning to get a bit jittery and jump when a door slams."

A British study calculated that "the average Londoner" could expect to be within a half mile of a V-1 detonation once a month, odds that did "not appear unduly alarming." Few Londoners saw it that way. V-1 explosions sucked workers from office windows, incinerated mothers in grocery stores, and butchered pensioners on park benches. A lieutenant who was recuperating in a hospital hit by a flying bomb wrote his wife that the blast "pushed through the walls and surrounded us, gripped us, entered us, and tossed us aside." He confessed to being "more afraid than I have ever been of anything in my life."

Soon not a pane of glass remained in city buses. Tens of thousands of houses were smashed. "The most horrible thing was the sound of burning timber," a witness reported, "the crackling, malicious sound, like little devilish laughs." Eisenhower complained in a note to Mamie that he had been forced into a Bushy Park air raid shelter nineteen times one morning. When a V-1 was heard during a performance at the St. James Theatre, one patron muttered, "How squalid to be killed at this disgusting little farce."

Fewer and fewer were willing to accept the risks. By August, 1.5 million Londoners would evacuate the city, more than during the Blitz. Of 10,492 V-1s ultimately fired at Britain, about 4,000 were destroyed by fighters, balloons, and antiaircraft guns, while others veered off course or crashed prematurely. But about 2,400 hit greater London, killing 6,000 and badly injuring 18,000. (Not one struck Tower Bridge.) It was, an official British history concluded, "an ordeal perhaps as trying to Londoners as any they had endured throughout the war."

How Easy It Is to Make a Ghost

W EST of Bayeux, the Norman uplands displayed the gnarled visage that had been familiar to Celtic farmers even before the Romans marched across Gaul. Over the centuries ten thousand tiny pastures had emerged from the limestone and pre-Cambrian schist, girdled by sunken lanes the width of an oxcart and enclosed with man-high hedgerows of thatched hawthorn roots, raspberry bushes, lupine, violets, and greasy mud. The sylvan noun for this terrain—"bocage," defined as a grove, or "an agreeably shady wood"—belied the claustrophobic reality of what one infantryman would call "the Gethsemane of the hedgerows." To Pacific veterans like General Collins, this jungly corner of France resembled Guadalcanal.

"I couldn't imagine the bocage until I saw it," Omar Bradley would say after the war. That failure of imagination was in fact a failure of command: Allied generals had been amply forewarned, and even Caesar had written of hedgerows that "present a fortification like a wall through which it was not only impossible to enter but even to penetrate with the eye." More recently, an August 1943 military study on French topography included two dozen photographs of "Norman bocage"; in mid-April, a First Army report described "embanked fields interspersed with thickets" and advised that tactics for fighting "through bocage country should be given considerable study." Aerial photos of an eight-square-mile swatch revealed some four thousand hedged enclosures. Yet, as in the amphibious assaults on North Africa and Sicily, planners preoccupied with gaining the hostile shore devoted little thought to combat beyond the dunes. "We were rehearsed endlessly for attacking beach defenses," a battalion commander later wrote, "but not one day was given to the terrain behind the beaches, which was no less difficult and deadly."

Now that difficult, deadly terrain played hob with First Army's timetable. As Rommel had predicted, American troops cut the Cotentin Peninsula early on June 18, after two regiments from the 9th Infantry Division lunged west to the sea near Barneville. Three divisions abreast in Collins's VII Corps then began clawing north toward Cherbourg, thirteen miles distant. In the south, the 29th Division commander on June 17 reported, "I feel we'll be getting to St. Lô before long." Alas, no: although barely five miles from the American line, that linchpin town would remain out of reach for another month.

Tank companies now reported that to advance 2,500 yards typically required seventeen tons of explosives to blow holes through nearly three dozen hedgerows, each defended like a citadel parapet. "Each one of them was a wall of fire," a soldier in the 30th Infantry Division wrote, "and the open fields between were plains of fire." An officer noted that "the enemy can be ten feet away and be undetected. He can fight up to spitting range." That intimacy neutralized Allied air and artillery advantages. "There were snipers everywhere," Ernie Pyle reported, "in trees, in buildings, in piles of wreckage, in the grass. But mainly they were in the high, bushy hedgerows." A sliding scale of rewards awaited the proficient German sniper, according to a SHAEF document: "10 corpses—100 cigarettes; 20 corpses—20 days' leave; 50 corpses—Iron Cross 1st Class and wristwatch from Himmler."

Enemy panzers, artillery, and savage small-arms fire made western Normandy ever more lethal. The poet-infantryman Louis Simpson described the "short, velvet bursts" of German machine pistols, and added: "The purr of the bullets is wicked." A soldier hesitant to cross an open pasture to a farmhouse wrote, "I lie in the grass pondering whether to take the chance. Yes-no-yes-no." In this "land of great danger," as Pyle called it, no weapon was more feared than the mortar—described by one soldier as "a soft siffle, high in the air, like a distant lark, or a small penny whistle, faint and elf-like, falling." Mortar fragments caused 70 percent of the battle casualties among four U.S. infantry divisions in Normandy; radar that could backtrack the parabolic flight of rounds to the firing tubes would not be battle-ready for months. Close combat heightened the animal senses; like many riflemen, Simpson sniffed for a smell "we have come to recognize as Germany—a compound of sausage and cheese, mildewed cloth, and ideas. Some ideas stink. Every German hole . . . exudes the smell of their philosophy."

French civilians waving white strips of don't-shoot cloth scurried to their chicken coops during lulls, gathering eggs that they sold to GIs for the equivalent of eight cents apiece. Soon even the henhouses were blown to smithereens, birds "plastered to the walls like pats of mud." Almost 400,000 buildings in Normandy would be demolished or badly damaged. Livestock casualties included 100,000 cows; bulldozers buried them by the herd, as stiff-legged as wooden toys. Many towns were beaten to death— "as if somebody had pulled them down with a gigantic rake," in one description; pilots reported smoke tinted red from pulverized brick. In St.-Sauveur "there was not a building standing whole," Don Whitehead reported. A medic told his family in Indiana of a smashed village "deserted and silent. Not the silence that you know, but a more profound and depressing silence."

Each contested town, like each hedgerow, added more dead, wounded, and missing to a tally that in OVERLORD's first fortnight exceeded eighteen hundred each day for the U.S. First Army alone, or one casualty every forty-seven seconds. A French nurse told her diary of wounded men "white as sheets, their nostrils tight, their eyes rolled back. Wide bleeding lacerations, shattered limbs, internal injuries, faces in shreds." Sharp spikes in combat exhaustion—a term coined in Tunisia to supplant the misnomer "shell shock"—reflected the stress of bocage combat; by mid-July, such neuropsychiatric cases would account for one of every four infantry casualties in 21st Army Group, with the worst of them "crouched down like hunted animals" in battalion aid stations. First Army by early August would also investigate more than five hundred cases of suspected "S.I.W."—self-inflicted wounds—typically a gunshot to the heel, toe, or finger. "A fine division was burned up taking the village of La Haye–du–Puits," one lieutenant colonel wrote. "There are 100 such villages between here and Paris. Have we 100 divisions to expend on them?"

There was nothing for it but to pound away. "Things are always confusing and mysterious in war," Pyle wrote. "I squatted there, just a bewildered guy in brown, part of a thin line of other bewildered guys." Captain Keith Douglas, a British veteran of North Africa and perhaps the most poignant poetic voice of the Second World War, had written of killing the enemy, "How easy it is to make a ghost."

And how easy to become one: Douglas died south of Bayeux, slain by a mortar splinter so fine that his body appeared unblemished. "I buried him close beside the hedge near where he was killed," a chaplain wrote. "Being quite alone and reading the brief Order of Service over the grave affected me deeply."

Only the sharpest weather eye could have noticed a faint tremor in the barometer glass on Sunday night, June 18. Despite a cold front descending from Iceland and a restless Mediterranean depression, SHAEF forecasters predicted fair skies and calm seas along the invasion coast for several days, in keeping with the benign season. *Channel Pilot,* a bible for mariners sailing the Norman coast, put the chance of a June gale near zero. Another analysis of storm records since the 1870s rated the odds at three hundred to one.

More than two hundred ships now plied the invasion anchorage each day. Though men and machines blackened the beaches, the 218,000 tons of supplies landed since D-Day amounted to 30 percent less than planned. Confusion reigned, both in jammed British ports and on the Far Shore, where ship captains often anchored off the wrong strand, manifests went missing, and petulant officers in small boats puttered from ship to ship demanding to know the contents of each bottom. Surfeits piled up: one quartermaster depot would report receiving 11,000 brooms, 13,000 mops, 5,000 garbage cans, and 33,000 reams of mimeograph paper. An officer was heard pleading, "Please, oh, please, stop sending me stuff I don't need."

But shortages were more common, ranging from compasses and helmet nets to shovels. Bradley's units desperately needed another six thousand M-7 grenade launchers. Thousands of tons of jumbled cargo was unloaded from nineteen ships in an urgent search for a few hundred bundles of maps. No need was more pressing in the bocage than 81mm mortar ammunition. The failure to find enough rounds in the anchorage led to a desperate requisition for nearly all of the ammo, of every sort, in the United Kingdom. Soon 145,000 tons lay offshore; troops rummaged through every hold for the right type, but strict firing limits would be imposed on eight divisions anyway. First Army on June 15 had also placed severe restrictions on artillery fire missions after some batteries, expected to shoot 125 rounds per gun daily, fired four times as much in only twelve hours.

Salvation appeared to be rising from the sea off beaches Omaha and Gold, where a pair of gigantic "synthetic harbors" took shape after two years of planning under excruciating secrecy. In one of the most ambitious construction projects ever essayed in Britain, twenty thousand workers at a cost of $100 million had labored on the components; another ten thousand now bullied the pieces across the Channel and into position with huge tow bridles, hawsers, and 160 tugs. Each artificial harbor, Mulberry A and Mulberry B—American and British, respectively—would have the port capacity of Gibraltar or Dover. Among other novelties, seventy-five derelict ships ballasted with sand had sortied from Scottish ports for Normandy in what was described as a "final journey of self-immolation"; they included superannuated merchantmen, antique side-wheelers, and ancient battleships like the British *Centurion* and the French *Courbet,* flying an enormous tricolor. Scuttled in three fathoms parallel to the shore, the vessels formed long breakwaters called Gooseberries.

To this suicide fleet were added 146 immense concrete caissons, each weighing up to six thousand tons. Towed like floating apartment buildings across the Channel, the caissons were then sunk near the Gooseberries to form additional breakwaters. Also shipped to the Norman coast were ten miles of floating piers and pierheads, with telescoping legs to rise and subside with the tide. In all, two million tons of construction materials went into the Mulberries, including seventeen times more concrete than had been poured for Yankee Stadium in the 1920s. Skeptics yawped—

"One storm will wash them all away," warned Rear Admiral John L. Hall, the senior salt at Omaha—but unloading had begun at Mulberry A on the night of June 16. Liberty ships and the like could now unburden more than half a mile from shore, and LSTs could be emptied in under an hour. At last, the OVERLORD beaches seemed rational and right.

And then, as if to rebuke those intent on taming the sea, the old gods objected. That trembling barometer abruptly plummeted, gray squalls and a rising wind piled seas against the lee shore, and one of the worst June gales in eighty years began to blow. By midmorning on Monday, June 19, unloading had halted; by noon, H.M.S. *Despatch* logged winds at Force 8—almost forty miles per hour—and seas exceeding five feet. Anchors dragged and fouled, tethers snapped, antiaircraft crews were evacuated from the Mulberry gun platforms after waves carried off handrails and catwalks. Tuesday was fiercer, with seas over nine feet racing down the Channel. Oil spread along the Gooseberries calmed neither sea nor nerves. "Storm continues if anything worse than before," a British lieutenant wrote. "In considerable danger of being swept away."

Swept away they were, pier by pier, and pierhead after pierhead, with the sound of steel grinding steel above the howling wind. Runaway vessels smashed into the pontoon piers despite shouted curses and even gunshots from sailors manning Mulberry A. Of three dozen steel floats—each two hundred feet long and twelve feet wide—twenty-five broke loose to rampage through the anchorage off Omaha. Pounding waves broke the backs of seven ships in the Omaha Gooseberry, including the venerable *Centurion*, and many concrete caissons fractured. Distress calls jammed all radio channels and the plaintive hooting of a hundred boat whistles added to the din. "This is a damnable spell we are going through," Admiral Ramsay told his diary on Wednesday, June 21.

After eighty hours, the spell broke. "The shriek dropped to a long-drawn sigh," a witness wrote. "In the west a rent in the sky revealed blue." Force 7 gusts continued through midafternoon Wednesday, but the Great Storm was spent, the havoc wreaked. "Not even a thousand-bomber raid could have done as much damage," a Navy salvage officer concluded. Eight hundred craft of all sizes had been tossed ashore, including a small tanker deep in the dunes, and dozens more were sunk. From Fox Red to Dog Green, every exit off Omaha was blocked by sea wrack. More than two miles of articulated steel pier, under tow from England when the blow began, were lost at sea.

Mulberry A was a total loss, washed ashore or bobbing as flotsam around the Bay of the Seine. Some scraps would be salvaged for Mulberry B, which had been less grievously injured because it was shielded by shoals and—the British believed—because the Gooseberries were positioned with greater care than the Yanks had exercised. Regardless, Ramsay decried the Mulberries as "an even more formidable abortion than I had antici-pated," while Admiral Hall called them "the greatest waste of manpower and steel and equipment . . . for any operation in World War II."

Mulberry B ultimately did prove useful: by summer's end nearly half of Britain's supply tonnage was arriving in France through the artificial harbor, which was completed in mid-July and came to be known as Port Winston. But for the moment the calamity had prevented 140,000 tons of stores and 20,000 vehicles from reaching France. Montgomery estimated on the evening of June 22 that the Allied buildup was "at least six days behind," a deficit that would not be overcome until late July. Second Army had three divisions fewer ashore than planned, delaying a renewed attack on Caen, and Rommel had exploited the bad weather to reinforce the beachhead. So sharp was the cry for ammunition that hand grenades were flown across the Channel, and Bradley ordered eight coasters deliberately beached so that holes could be slashed in their hulls for quick unloading.

With the beaches again in disarray, the capture of Cherbourg loomed ever more urgent. A First Army study had warned that if the port was not seized quickly, no more than eighteen Allied divisions could be supported, a shortfall that would allow the enemy to "overwhelm us." Cherbourg alone was believed capable of supplying up to thirty divisions in combat. Small wonder that Eisenhower's headquarters now described it as "the most important port in the world."

Great misfortune had befallen Cherbourg over the centuries. Proxim-ity to England brought pillage by the hereditary enemy in 1295, 1346, and 1418. In 1758, an English fleet burned every French ship in the harbor and demolished the fortifications. The town's stature and prosperity slowly rebounded. Bonaparte's mortal remains had arrived in Cherbourg en route to Paris from St. Helena in 1840, inspiring a movement to rename the town Napoléonville. Nothing came of it but an equestrian statue. Winter gales frustrated even the great military engineer Vauban in his efforts to enlarge the port with a breakwater; only on the third try did he succeed, using gigantic granite blocks fitted together with hydraulic cement. In April 1912, R.M.S. *Titanic* sailed from Cherbourg on her star-crossed maiden voyage. A further port expansion, financed with German reparations after World War I, had built the berths used by other great transatlantic liners between the wars. With vengeful pleasure, Rommel and his division seized these docks and the rest of the seaport in 1940.

Now Cherbourg was again besieged. By the night of June 21, three divisions of Collins's VII Corps were chewing at the concrete and field fortifications embedded in a collar of steep hills around the city. French farmers tossed roses at GIs wearing a two-week growth of beard and uniforms stiff with dirt. The troops "seemed terribly pathetic to me," wrote Ernie Pyle, "with guns in their hands, sneaking up a death-laden street in a strange and shattered city in a faraway country in a driving rain." U.S. Army sound trucks played Strauss waltzes to encourage nostalgia in enemy ranks while broadcasting surrender appeals, a tactic known as hog calling. Give-up leaflets called "bumf," for "bum fodder"—toilet paper—promised ample food and included pronunciation aides such as *"Ei sörrender," "Wen ken ai tek a bahs?," "Sam mor koffi, plies,"* and *"Senks for se siggarets."*

An American ultimatum expired without reply at nine A.M. on Thursday, June 22, just as the Great Storm ebbed. Shortly after noon, five hundred Allied fighter-bombers strafed and skip-bombed the town from three hundred feet, followed by an hour's pummeling by four hundred medium bombers. Sherman tanks crushed recalcitrant enemy riflemen, and by Friday all three U.S. divisions had penetrated the city from east, west, and south behind white phosphorus, satchel charges, and flame throwers. A horse was shooed into the city carrying a German corpse lashed across the saddle with a note: "All you sons-a-bitches are going to end up this way."

In radio messages decrypted by Ultra, the garrison commanding general, a heel-clicker named Karl-Wilhelm von Schlieben, advised Rommel that his 21,000 defenders were burdened with two thousand wounded suffering from "bunker paralysis" and "greatly worn out." Although Cherbourg still had a two-month supply of food, including five thousand cows that had been rustled into the city, a scheme to ferry eighty tons of ammunition aboard four U-boats fell apart. Rommel's reply, at one P.M. on Sunday, June 25, offered no solace: "You will continue to fight until the last cartridge in accordance with the order from the Führer."

Schlieben's miseries multiplied. Just as Rommel's command arrived, three Allied battleships, four cruisers, and eleven destroyers led by a minesweeper flotilla appeared on the horizon. On a glassy sea under light airs, the bombardment force split into two squadrons. Then, for the first time since the battle of Casablanca in November 1942, the Allied fleet commenced what swabs called a fire-away-Flanagan against enemy guns of comparable weight and range. Approaching west to east with destroyers laying smoke, the cruiser *Quincy* steamed to within seven miles of shore in the misbegotten belief that most enemy batteries had already been silenced. The bright wink of a muzzle flash suggested otherwise, and thirty seconds later a 150mm shell plumped the sea close aboard to prove the point.

Great salvos soon arced back and forth, "more concentrated firing toward and from the beach than I had ever expected to see," one officer reported. Fifteen rounds or more straddled *Quincy,* splashing green water across the forecastle as she and her sisters violently zigged and zagged in a boil of white wakes and bow waves. Some twenty German shells also straddled *Nevada,* that angry specter from Pearl Harbor; two clipped her superstructure yet hardly scratched the paint. A Spitfire spotting for H.M.S. *Glasgow* had trouble finding an offending battery through clouds of dust and smoke, but German gunners saw the cruiser clearly enough to lob shells into her port hangar and upper works, causing her to retire for a brief licking of wounds. More sound and fury than destruction resulted from three hours of hard shooting, although both the skipper and the executive officer of H.M.S. *Enterprise* were wounded by shell fragments. Some three hundred 6-inch shells finally quieted the most pugnacious German battery west of the port, but without killing it.

Six miles east of Cherbourg, a quartet of 11-inch guns in Battery Hamburg comprised the most powerful enemy strongpoint on the Cotentin, with a range of twenty-five miles. The second bombardment squadron had steamed to within eleven miles of the coast when shells abruptly smacked the American destroyers *Barton* and *Laffey,* in the engine room and port bow, respectively; both projectiles were duds. Less fortunate was U.S.S. *O'Brien,* hit just before one P.M. by a Hamburg shell that detonated in her command center, killing or wounding thirty-two men. Firing became general, with the battleship *Texas* straddled across the bow, then straddled across the stern, then hit in the conning tower by an 11-inch killer that mortally wounded the helmsman and hurt eleven others. *Texas* spat back more than two hundred 14-inch shells, among the eight hundred rounds dumped on Battery Hamburg by three P.M.

Yet by the time the Allied fleet swaggered back across the Channel, only one of the four enemy guns had been disabled. Despite "a naval bombardment of a hitherto unequalled fierceness," as a German war diary described the shelling, Fortress Cherbourg could not be reduced from the sea. The port would have to be taken by a land assault.

In this General Collins was ready to oblige. With Ted Roosevelt at his elbow, he watched the naval action on Sunday afternoon from a captured redoubt east of town, four hundred feet above the church steeples and gray stone houses with red roofs. "The view of Cherbourg from this point is magnificent," Collins wrote his wife a day later:

> We could see smoke from fires being directed into Fort du Roule,
> which is the central bastion of the German defenses, on a high bluff
> overlooking the city. Over to the right were the inner and outer break-
> waters with their old French forts guarding the entrance from the
> sea.... [Cherbourg] lay in a bowl from which billows of smoke poured

up in spots where the Germans were demolishing stores of oil and ammunition.

Joe Collins was where he always wanted to be: on the high ground. From the heights, he often told subordinates, "you can make the other fellow conform." With a slicked-down cowlick, a gift for persuasion, and a nonchalance about casualties, he was at forty-eight the youngest of the thirty-four men who would command a U.S. Army corps in World War II. Gavin considered him "runty, cocky, confident, almost to the point of being a bore"; to First Army staff officers, he was "Hot Mustard." The tenth of eleven children born to an Irish émigré who peddled nails, buckshot, and animal feed from a New Orleans emporium, Collins had graduated as an infantryman from West Point in 1917, commanded a battalion in France after the Great War at age twenty-two, and made his name in the South Pacific, whence he still suffered malarial shakes. "All the tactics you will ever need," he insisted, could be learned by studying General Winfield Scott's campaign from Veracruz to Mexico City. Self-improvement remained a lifelong impulse, and in the coming months he would place orders with a Washington bookstore for *Moby-Dick, Moll Flanders,* William Faulkner's *Sanctuary,* Émile Zola's *Nana,* and a stack of other novels. He also collected a kit bag of aphorisms, notably "An order is but an aspiration, a hope that what has been directed will come true." The virtues attributed to him by the West Point yearbook a quarter century earlier aptly described his command style: "first, concentration and decision; second, rapid and hearty action."

Now Cherbourg was nearly his—the high ground, the low ground, and the ground in between. Fort du Roule fell as he watched, although engineers would spend another day coaxing bitter-enders from the basements with white phosphorus down ventilation shafts and TNT lowered by wire to blast gun embrasures. GIs fought to the docks with grenades, bayonets, and 155mm rounds fired point-blank down the Boulevard Maritime.

General von Schlieben had by now retreated into a subterranean warren cut from a rock quarry just west of Fort du Roule. More than eight hundred comrades jammed the fetid chambers, leaving "hardly room enough to swing a cat." At three P.M. on June 26 Schlieben radioed Rommel a final message: "Documents burned, codes destroyed." Less than two hours later, an Army tank destroyer platoon fired twenty-two rounds at the tunnel entrance from three hundred yards. "It was good," a gunner murmured after the last shot.

Within minutes a German soldier bearing a white flag the size of a bedsheet emerged, followed by a staggering column of troops with hands raised and a tall, gray-faced Schlieben, his greatcoat flecked with mud and powdered masonry. In his pocket was found a printed menu from a dinner honoring him in Cherbourg a few weeks earlier: lobster and hollandaise, pâté de foie gras, roast lamb, peaches, champagne. Now, at the 9th Division command post, he was offered K-ration cheese and brandy as Robert Capa and other photographers circled round. When Schlieben complained, *auf Deutsch*, "I am tired of this picture-taking," Capa lowered his camera with a histrionic sigh and replied, also *auf Deutsch*, "I too am tired. I have to take pictures of so many captured German generals."

Cherbourg, a SHAEF officer reported, proved a "looter's heaven." Vast stores of "everything from shaving cream to torpedoes" were found in Fort du Roule, along with silks, cigars, radios, and soap in unmailed packages to families in Germany. The Hôtel Atlantique held great stocks of carbon paper, envelopes, and shoes, both wooden and leather, while Schlieben's cupboard in the Villa Meurice proffered beef tongue, bacon, artichokes, and canned octopus. Soldiers also found ten thousand barrels of cement—used for V-1 sites—a million board feet of lumber, and, most important, intact storage tanks for over 600,000 barrels of oil. MPs quickly secured warehouses stacked with thousands of cases of champagne, cognac, wine, and American whiskey. Bradley decreed that every soldier in Normandy would eventually receive two bottles of wine and three of liquor, but many chose not to wait for their allotment—VII Corps toasted the capture of Cherbourg with countless bottles of Hennessy and Benedictine. "The U.S. Army went on one big drunk," a Navy captain recorded. "There were drunken voices singing, rifle shooting all night ... with frequent detonation of hand grenades."

Those who had inspected the port felt less celebratory. SHAEF planners initially hoped to capture Cherbourg on D+7 and to reopen the harbor three days later; in the event, the city fell on D+20, the first port operations took three weeks to begin, and Allied engineers would spend months repairing a facility proudly described by Berlin as "completely wrecked." The German genius for destruction, honed with practice at Bizerte and Naples, produced what an American colonel called "a masterful job, beyond a doubt the most complete, intensive, and best-planned demolition in history." Trainloads of explosives had wreaked damage far beyond even the darkest Allied expectations. Electrical and heating plants were demolished, along with the port rail station and every bridge, every building, every submarine pen. Each ship basin and dry dock was blocked with toppled cranes and more than a hundred scuttled vessels, ranging from fishing smacks to a 550-foot whaler. Twenty thousand cubic yards of masonry rubble choked the Darse Transatlantique, where once the *Queen Mary* and the *Normandie* had docked. One jetty was punctured with nine holes fifty feet in diameter, while craters measuring one hundred feet by seventy feet had been blown in the great quays.

Countless booby traps seeded the ruins, and more than four hundred mines of half a dozen varieties would be lifted or triggered in the roadstead. Some mines remained dormant for nearly three months before arming, so eight magnetic and eight acoustical sweeps of the port had to be completed each morning for the rest of the summer. A tedious, dangerous reconstruction began within hours of Schlieben's surrender, despite delays in getting divers, tugs, and engineering gear from Britain. Eventually Cherbourg would shoulder over fifteen thousand tons of matériel a day, double an early SHAEF projection and more, but not until mid-July would the first barge enter the port, not until mid-August would the first Liberty ship dock, and not until mid-October would the deepwater basins be in good enough repair to berth big cargo carriers. "One cannot avoid noticing," an Army study acknowledged, "that things did not go according to plan." Cherbourg kept the Allied armies in France from wasting away, but the paramount task of enlarging and provisioning that host would bedevil Eisenhower for the rest of 1944.

For the moment the conquerors savored what Churchill called "this most pregnant victory": the capture of OVERLORD's first big objective, at the price of 22,000 VII Corps casualties. Before the Hôtel de Ville, near the statue of Bonaparte on his prancing charger, Collins on June 27 made a brief speech in ill-pronounced French and presented the mayor with a tricolor sewn from American parachutes. Civilians were instructed to surrender both firearms and pigeons—to prevent messages to the enemy—and to stay indoors after sunset. A band played various national anthems in dirge time before the Army brass strolled through the Place Napoléon to congratulate their filthy, hollow-eyed soldiers, one of whom muttered, "Make way for the fucking generals."

Prisoners by the acre dumped their effects—knives, lighters, dispatch cases—and shuffled past jeering, spitting Frenchmen "thinking up new lines of invective" to bellow, as Alan Moorehead reported. From nearby cages they would be herded onto LSTs and any other floatable conveyance for transport to British camps, still singing ballads from the Seven Years' War. Hitler was so enraged at the fall of Cherbourg that he threatened to court-martial the Seventh Army commander, who abruptly died on June 29, ostensibly from a heart attack, although many suspected poison, self-administered.

GIs also sorted through effects, including a low mountain of bedrolls stenciled with the names of soldiers killed in action and stacked along a stone wall near the Louis Pasteur Hospital. Quartermasters separated government gear from personal items, filling cardboard boxes with photos of smiling girls, harmonicas, and half-read paperbacks. A pocket Bible carried a flyleaf inscription: "To Alton C. Bright from Mother. Read it and be good." Staff Sergeant Bright, from Tennessee, could no longer be good because he was dead.

In a nearby nineteenth-century French naval hospital, bereft of both water and electricity for the past week, doctors found a morgue jammed with decomposing German, French, and American corpses. Amputated limbs filled buckets and trash cans in the corridors and underground surgeries. "There were dirty instruments everywhere, dirty linens," wrote a nurse from the 12th Field Hospital. Patients lay "stinking in their blood-soaked dressings and excreta." A *Life* magazine reporter wrote, "Perhaps more men should know the expense of war, for it is neither a fit way to live nor to die." He added, "The war in the West had barely begun."

Two bordellos promptly opened in Cherbourg, both operating from two P.M. to nine P.M. and one designated "whites-only." MPs kept order among long queues of soldiers. *Les tondues,* women shorn for *collaboration sentimentale* during the German occupation, were paraded on a truck labeled "The Collaborators' Wagon." They were the first of some twenty thousand who would be barbered in France this summer; their tresses burned in piles that could be smelled for miles.

Such stenches lingered in the nostril, to be carried beyond Cherbourg and beyond the war: the stink of diesel exhaust, of cordite, of broken plaster exposed to rain, of manure piles and the carcasses of the animals that shat them before being slaughtered by shellfire. An infantryman named John B. Babcock later catalogued the scents wafting around him: "cosmoline gun-metal preservative, oil used to clean weapons, chlorine in the drinking water, flea powder, pine pitch from freshly severed branches, fresh-dug earth." Also: "GI yellow soap and the flour-grease fumes" from field kitchens, as well as those pungent German smells, of cabbage and sour rye, of "stale-sweat wool [and] harsh tobacco." Even if the war in the west had barely begun, here was the precise odor of liberation.

3. LIBERATION

A Monstrous Blood-Mill

ONE million Allied soldiers had come ashore at Normandy by early July, yet the invasion increasingly resembled the deadlock at Anzio or, worse, the static trench warfare of World War I. Tentage vanished, replaced by labyrinthine burrows roofed with double layers of pine logs and sandbags. "They keep lobbing mortars at us," Lieutenant Orval E. Faubus informed his diary. "It is a world no civilian can ever know." Though Cherbourg had been taken, the beachhead on July 1 was only six miles deep in places. Caen and St.-Lô remained in German custody, and daily casualties in Normandy exceeded those of the 1917 British force in Flanders during the third battle of Ypres, which included the hellish struggle at Passchendaele. A German general who had fought in both world wars now described the Normandy struggle as "a monstrous blood-mill, the likes of which I have not seen in eleven years of war." Omar Bradley lamented, "I can't afford to stay here. I lose all my best boys. They're the ones who stick their heads through hedges and then have them blown off."

Eisenhower's planners had given little thought to the Allied recourse if OVERLORD led to stalemate. A few options were considered, including another airborne and amphibious assault outside the Normandy lodgement. But the only credible solution, a SHAEF study concluded, was to bash on: to "concentrate all available air and land forces for a breakout from within the captured area."

The supreme commander's jitters grew with each new casualty list. He switched cigarette brands to Chesterfields, but still smoked several score a day, contributing to an ominous blood pressure reading of 176/110. An Army doctor prescribed "slow-up medicine"; his ears rang anyway. He ate poorly and slept badly, not least because V-1 attacks often forced him into a renovated shelter at Bushy Park where paint fumes gave him headaches. A flying bomb on July 1 detonated two hundred yards from Eisenhower's office, sucking panes out of the windows and peeling off a swatch of WIDE-WING's roof. In a red leather journal, the supreme commander jotted brief, unhappy notes: "Bradley's attack to south now postponed to July 3. How I suffer! ... Tried to play bridge. Awful." During a visit to the beachhead in early July, he stayed at Bradley's command post, padding about at night in red pajamas and slippers; one afternoon he squeezed into the back of a P-51 Mustang from which the radio had been removed and for forty-five minutes flew west, then south, then east toward Paris for an aerial view of the battlefield. "Marshall would raise hell if he knew about this," he admitted. Upon being told that a German officer captured at Cherbourg refused to disclose where mines had been laid, Eisenhower said, "Shoot the bastard"—an order neither intended nor enforced.

Montgomery had long envisioned an attritional battle, which he called "the Dogfight," between the invasion assault and a breakout from the beachhead. Eisenhower chafed anyway. In a "dear Monty" note on July 7, he wrote:

> I am familiar with your plan for generally holding firmly with your left, attracting thereto all of the enemy armor, while your right pushes down the peninsula and threatens the rear and flank of the forces facing the Second British Army. ... We must use all possible energy in a determined effort to prevent a stalemate. ... I will back you up to the limit in any effort you may decide upon to prevent a deadlock.

Montgomery's reply a day later affected a bluff insouciance, despite 1,200 casualties that day in the Canadian 3rd Division alone, including 330 killed. "I am, myself, quite happy about the situation. ... I now begin to see daylight," he wrote, adding:

> I think the battle is going very well. The enemy is being heavily attacked all along the line, and we are killing a lot of Germans. Of one thing you can be quite sure—there will be no stalemate.

So it had begun. This direct, professional exchange concealed an enmity that already infected the Allied high command and would grow more toxic. In his diary, Montgomery complained that Eisenhower "cannot stop 'butting in' and talking—always at the top of his voice!! ... I like him very much but I could never live in the same house with him; he cannot talk calmly and quietly." Montgomery professed to spend one-third of his day "making sure I'm not sacked" and another third inspiriting the troops, which "leaves one-third of my time to defeat the enemy."

At SHAEF, the insistence by "Chief Big Wind"—as Montgomery was privately nicknamed—that the battle was unfolding as planned fed a seething disgruntlement, particularly among British air commanders. Montgomery had become "something of a dictator, something of a mystic," wrote one. "It was difficult to track him down and to get an audience with him." Eisenhower's deputy, Air Chief Marshal Sir Arthur W. Tedder, told Churchill in late June that fewer than half of the planned eighty-one squadrons were flying from Normandy because only thirteen airstrips had been built. "The problem is Monty, who can be neither removed nor moved to action," Tedder advised his diary. Persistent rain added to the gloom. A scowling Leigh-Mallory compulsively tapped his portable barometer, which always seemed to be falling. "Things are now egg-bound," he complained, "and they may become glacial."

Churchill too grew waspish. Fearful that Britain's contribution was undervalued even as the American preponderance grew, the prime minister demanded that Canadian dead and wounded be "included in the British publication of casualties, otherwise they will be very readily assumed to be part of the American casualties. The point is of Imperial consequence." The V-1s pummeling London made him bloody-minded, and he seemed to consider countering either with biological weapons—anthrax looked promising—or with a more conventional campaign that publicly listed one hundred small, lightly defended German towns, which would be obliterated "one by one by bombing attack."

Neither idea found favor with the British high command, mostly for pragmatic reasons, but Churchill on July 6 insisted that "a cold-blooded calculation" be made about whether Allied poison gas would shorten the war while also retaliating against CROSSBOW targets. "It would be absurd to consider morality on this topic when everybody used it in the last war without a word of complaint from the moralists or the church," Churchill argued. He also noted that bombing cities had been proscribed in the Great War but "now everybody does it. . . . It is simply a question of fashion changing as she does between long and short skirts for women." Strategic planners in London replied that gas "would not be likely to have more than a harassing effect" on the Third Reich, while it would provoke widespread chemical warfare, including attacks on London. When Eisenhower learned of the discussion he ended it—for the moment—with a tart note to Beetle Smith, his chief of staff: "I will *not* be party to so-called retaliation or use of gas. Let's for God's sake keep our eye on the ball and use some sense."

Montgomery's battle plan required a great lunge by the U.S. First Army to deepen the bridgehead, and in this he was disappointed. With high hopes but little imagination, Bradley ordered three corps abreast to attack south down three macadam roads beginning July 3. On the western edge of the Allied line, VIII Corps—with three divisions on a fifteen-mile front—took ten thousand casualties in twelve days while advancing only seven miles through swamp and bocage. Bitten witless by mosquitoes, "everyone was more or less confused," one unit reported.

Beyond Omaha Beach, on the left flank of the American sector, XIX Corps managed to cross the steep-banked Vire River and an adjacent canal in rubber boats. But a push for the high ground west of St.-Lô was thwarted by congestion, fratricide, and panzers counterattacking with sirens screaming. In the American center, VII Corps fared no better—"That is exactly what I *don't* want," Joe Collins said after one ill-fated action. Casualties included fourteen hundred men from the 83rd Division during its first day in combat. One regiment ripped through five colonels in a week, and more Norman fields were upholstered with what Hemingway called "the deads." An officer describing war in Normandy wrote simply, "The sadness of it is always with me." Combat skills proved suspect across First Army, from map reading to armor-infantry collaboration. Senior leadership seemed especially thin: in the space of two months, Bradley would relieve nine generals, including two division commanders from the 90th Division alone.

The hapless 90th was about to be assigned a new commander, although he did not know it yet. During the Sicilian campaign, Bradley had deemed Ted Roosevelt "too softhearted to take a division," but now he reconsidered and so recommended to Eisenhower. Roosevelt had been frantically busy as the military governor of Cherbourg; he had also been helping the 4th Division manage the five thousand casualties it had suffered since D-Day. The rifle company with which he had landed on Utah Beach had lost more than 80 percent of its men, he wrote Eleanor, and five of the original six officers. "Our best young men are being killed," he told her. "Let us hope the sacrifice will be to some purpose." With his fifty-seventh birthday approaching, he confessed to "a desperate weariness," and in a July 10 letter home complained that it had been "raining for God knows how long. It still is, for that matter." But, he added, "now I've got a little home in a truck. It was captured from the Germans . . . and I've got a desk and a bed in it. The inside is painted white." As always, he drew solace from *The Pilgrim's Progress:* "Maybe my feet hurt and the way is hard, but I must go on. . . . My soul's peace depends on it."

After a conference with Collins on Wednesday afternoon, July 12, Roosevelt was delighted by the arrival at 7:30 P.M. of his son, Quentin, an officer in the 1st Division. For more than two hours in the spiffed-up German lorry "we talked about everything," Quentin wrote, "home, the family, my plans, the war." Hardly an hour after his son left, Roosevelt suffered a severe coronary thrombosis. The 4th Division commander, Tubby Barton, was summoned at 11:30 P.M. "He was breathing but unconscious when I entered his truck," he wrote Eleanor a few hours later. "I sat helpless and saw the most gallant soldier and finest gentleman I have ever known expire. . . . The show goes on. He would have it so and we shall make it so."

An Army half-track bore Roosevelt to his grave on Friday, Bastille Day, past homemade American flags hanging from cottage sills and a sign declaring, *"Merci à Nos Libérateurs."* The division band played "The Son of God Goes Forth to War" before two buglers, one echoing the other, followed with "Taps." *Rough Rider* was returned to the motor pool for reissue with the name painted over. The show went on.

Roosevelt never knew of the division command assignment sitting on Eisenhower's desk, nor did he know of the Medal of Honor that would be awarded for his valor on Utah Beach. Eisenhower and Bradley favored reducing Barton's recommendation to a Distinguished Service Cross, but George Marshall made certain that his old World War I comrade received the higher honor. "He had the Elizabethan quality," a family friend wrote Eleanor. "A range of mountains, a fine line of poetry, a nobility of act all caught an answering fire in his spirit. I don't believe there are many people in the world like that." And now, one less.

The German travel writer Karl Baedeker had once described St.-Lô as "a very ancient place," fortified by Charlemagne and "picturesquely situated on a slope on the right bank of the Vire." Although sacked by Vikings, by Plantagenet kings, and, in 1574, by Catholic reactionaries who put Calvinist apostates to the sword, St.-Lô had always recovered its charm— until June 6, 1944, when Allied planes turned the town to powder. By dawn of D+1, eight hundred citizens were dead, and the bombers returned every day for a week, further pulverizing chokepoints to discomfit enemy convoys bound for the beachhead. Entire families lay buried beneath the rubble; others fled, and now no more than ten living inhabitants remained where there had been eleven thousand.

Eight roads and a rail line still radiated from St.-Lô, making it the most vital terrain in First Army's zone and the most ardently defended segment on a fifty-mile front. Artillery and "big-stuff bombs," in one reporter's phrase, turned the encircling hills into a "moth-eaten white blanket." Smoke draping the stone-ribbed fields reminded an Army observer of woodcut illustrations of Civil War battlefields. For more than a week GIs struggled to advance five hundred yards a day, through splintered apple orchards and across charred ridgelines defended by German paratroopers in baggy gray smocks. Bradley on July 11 had posited that enemy defenders were "on their last legs," and a final killing blow was ordered across a ten-mile sector. The 29th Infantry Division, martyrs of Omaha Beach, would aim for St.-Lô itself under the command of a pugnacious, bullet-headed major general named Charles Hunter Gerhardt, Jr.

"Everything about him was explosive: speech, movements, temper," one major wrote. "He was a detector and eradicator of lethargy." A classmate of Collins and Ridgway's at West Point, Gerhardt was known both as "Loose Reins," for his riding style as a polo player, and as "General Chickenshit," for his fussbudget ways. Even senior officers were required in training to answer five questions, including "describe the resuscitation of a man from drowning." While commanding a division in the United States, Gerhardt had required a suntan for all soldiers through shirtless daily exposure (7.5 minutes each for chest and back), and he still offered a ten-shilling bounty to any deadeye who could outshoot him with pistol or carbine. One subordinate described him as "hard, exacting, aggressive, percolating in his own vitality," while another considered him "completely off the beam. He would make a dashing Indian fighter." He had coined the division motto—"Twenty-nine, let's go!"—but even admirers would later joke that Charlie Gerhardt really commanded a corps of three divisions: one in the field, one in the hospital, and one in the cemetery.

By late afternoon on July 15, attacking from north and east, the 29th spearheads closed to within two miles of St.-Lô. Fire teams snaked through the bocage, one infantry squad in each field with a single Sherman tank creeping in first gear as a gesture toward stealth. Engineers then blew gaps in the hedgerows with slabs of TNT and ammonium nitrate as riflemen rushed forward. Sudden bursts of German fire knocked men "backward as though jerked with a rope," an officer wrote, to be answered with artillery that chopped enemy paratroopers into pieces "difficult to reconcile" with a whole man. Tracers stabbed the woodlot thickets like hot needles, and the roar of gunfire built until it "seemed like the end of everything," a private first class wrote. "There was no memory of any time before being here, under fire." A trooper with three days in the line was now deemed a veteran.

Before dawn on Monday, July 17, Gerhardt ordered all nine rifle battalions to attack. The 3rd Battalion of the 116th Infantry—at less than half strength, with barely four hundred men, but still the strongest of the nine—slipped through the fog in a column of companies to the hamlet of La Madeleine, a mile east of St.-Lô. Just after eight A.M. the Germans lashed back with mortar fire, killing the new commander, Major Thomas D. Howie, and his two radiomen. Only artillery and dive-bombing P-47 Thunderbolts prevented panzers from overrunning the battalion; GIs marked the front line with undershirts and yellow smoke, then rummaged through hedges for plasma bags dropped from Piper Cubs. Replacement troops in new olive-drab uniforms hurried forward carrying rifles with quartermaster tags still fluttering from the trigger guards—"an unbearably sorry scene," a young officer later recalled.

But German defenses were melting away. General Dutch Cota, that stalwart of Omaha Beach, led a task force into St.-Lô from the northeast at six P.M. on July 18, storming through a cemetery where the Famille Blanchet crypt became a command post, with eighteen-inch marble walls and a stone sarcophagus suitable for a map table. "Here among the dead," wrote Don Whitehead, "was the safest place in all St. Lô." After weeks in the bocage, troops capered into town up the Rue de Bayeux "with all the joy of a band of claustrophobes released from a maze," A. J. Liebling added. German artillery still dropped from the southern heights—Cota's fingertips dripped blood after a shell fragment slashed his arm—but GIs soon secured seventeen strongpoints. On Gerhardt's order, Howie's body arrived by jeep at dusk. Draped with a flag, the corpse was laid on a rubble bier that once had been the abbey church of Ste.-Croix.

Hardly a trace of sidewalk or street pavement remained in St.-Lô. "You couldn't identify anything any more," the poet Jean Follain wrote. "The persistence of durable objects had been solidly defeated." Fragments of stone houses with painted shutters now dammed the Vire, the correspondent Iris Carpenter reported. "On this lake floated planks from floors, timber from roofs, furniture, mattresses . . . and an assortment of dead horses, cows, cats, and dogs. Everything was gray." A GI added, "We sure liberated the hell out of this place." The Irish writer Samuel Beckett, who would arrive as a Red Cross volunteer, estimated that 2,000 of 2,600 buildings had been "completely wiped out" in what he described as "the capital of ruins." An Army list of booby-trapped items included "fence posts, teacups, doorbells, jackknives, purses, drawers, light switches, automobile starters, window curtains, inkwells." Added to that were the first booby-trapped German bodies, often with a grenade pin tied to a souvenir Luger or a fountain pen. GIs were warned that "bodies being picked up on the battlefield should be jerked by a rope at least 200 feet long."

The capture of St.-Lô ended Bradley's mid-July offensive. All in all, it was a disappointment: at a cost of forty thousand casualties, a dozen divisions had advanced between three and seven miles. "If there was a world beyond this tangle of hedgerows," a survivor wrote, "you never expected to live to see it." Most discovered, as a battalion commander put it, "a sinking feeling that the German army would take much more destroying."

But St.-Lô was no Pyrrhic victory. The offensive, in Montgomery's phrase, had "eaten the guts out of the German defense" and deprived Rommel of a road network critical to maneuvering east and west. An unfinished letter found on a dead German from the 9th Parachute Regiment described comrades chewing cigarettes and gnawing the ground in terror. "We thought the world was coming to an end."

In a green Norman meadow at La Cambe, Gerhardt would lead the living in singing "Nearer, My God, to Thee," as nearly two thousand division dead were honored beneath whitewashed wooden crosses and stars of David. An adjutant called the roster of those killed, each name answered in turn by a surviving comrade: "Here!" Then as the division band played "Beer Barrel Polka," the men gave a great roar—*Twenty-nine, let's go!*—and turned back to the battle.

Rommel rose with the sun as usual on Monday, July 17. As a precaution against Allied bombers he now often slept with the rest of his staff in paneled rooms tunneled into the chalk cliffs behind La Roche–Guyon. A dachshund, Elbo, dozed under the luggage stand; a good dog, Rommel told Lucie, "can take your mind off your troubles." After a quick breakfast in the château, he clattered down the fifteen stone steps to the courtyard and climbed into the front seat of the Horch. His aide, a sergeant, and another officer sat in back, peering up for enemy fighters as the big convertible pulled through the gate and swung west past Giverny, where, in a calmer age, Claude Monet had painted his water lilies. The field marshal planned to inspect two divisions at Falaise, then visit two of his corps command posts near Caen.

Troubles he had, and neither a dog nor the Brahms radio concert he had listened to the previous evening could take them away. For a field marshal who often drove two hundred miles or more each day to visit his battle commanders, simply venturing beyond La Roche–Guyon had become perilous. All German road convoys and most single vehicles now moved only during the brief midsummer nights; from Normandy to Holland, roadsides were excavated with "funk holes," slit trenches every sixty yards into which drivers and their passengers could dive whenever strafing planes appeared.

"Militarily things aren't at all good," he had written Lucie. "We must be prepared for grave events." Caen finally had fallen on July 9, after British planes gutted the city with six thousand half-ton bombs in forty minutes. "There was nothing more to see," a witness reported, "only more dust." Eight thousand French refugees now jammed a lycée and the reeking Abbaye-aux-Hommes, founded by William the Conqueror as penance for marrying his cousin Matilda. German troops still held Caen's southern outskirts, but the infantry strength of the 12th SS Panzer Division equaled a single battalion. The Murder Division had been murdered, at least a bit.

On any given day now, Army Group B might suffer as many losses as Rommel's Afrika Korps had in the entire summer of 1942. Only 10,000 replacements had arrived to compensate for 100,000 German casualties in Normandy over the past six weeks. A British cannonade of 80,000 artillery rounds at Caen on July 10 had been answered with 4,500 German shells, all that were available. Rommel had seen a battalion commander riding horseback for want of a car or of fuel. "The divisions are bleeding white," his war diary recorded. Berlin anticipated 1.6 million German casualties on all fronts from June through October, far more than the Fatherland could sustain.

That bloodletting had intensified with a Soviet summer offensive, launched on June 22 with close to two million Red Army troops, 2,700 tanks, and 24,000 field guns. In less than two weeks, an enormous pincer attack had obliterated twenty-five German divisions, ripping a hole 250 miles wide in the front. On this very Monday, tens of thousands of German prisoners would shuffle through Moscow in a winding column led by captured Wehrmacht generals.

Rommel's disaffection grew day by day. Hitler "will fight without the least regard for the German people until there isn't a house left standing in Germany," he told his confidant Admiral Ruge. The field marshal was aware of talk, dangerous talk, of a separate peace on the Western Front, and perhaps a coup; he opposed making Hitler a martyr but would consider taking command of the armed forces if necessary. In early July, Rundstedt had been removed as commander in the west, ostensibly after pleading age and infirmity, but in fact because he had advised Berlin to "make an end to the whole war." Hitler gave him a medal and a 250,000-mark gratuity to go take the cure at Bad Tölz. "I will be next," Rommel predicted.

Rundstedt's successor, Field Marshal Günther von Kluge, known as Cunning Hans, had commanded an army group in the east for two years and brought to France a reputation as a fearless and tenacious innovator. In their first meeting at La Roche–Guyon, he accused Rommel of "obstinate self-will," but within a week concurred that "the situation couldn't be grimmer." On July 15, Rommel composed a three-page report for the high command, in which he wrote: "The situation on the Normandy front is growing worse every day and is now approaching a grave crisis. The unequal struggle is approaching its end." Kluge endorsed the assessment in a cover note to Berlin.

Fried eggs and brandy awaited Rommel at midafternoon on Monday when the Horch pulled beneath a camouflage net at the I SS Panzer Corps command post in St.-Pierre-sur-Dives, twenty miles southeast of Caen. Nothing he had seen during the day's travels had lifted his gloom, including strafed Wehrmacht trucks smoldering on the road shoulders. When Kurt Meyer, commander of the 12th SS Panzer, pleaded for Luftwaffe support, Rommel snapped in frustration, "Who do you think you're talking to? Do you think I drive with my eyes closed through the country?"

During a conference at St.-Pierre with General Sepp Dietrich, the onetime butcher's apprentice and beer-hall brawler who commanded the panzer corps, Rommel warned that a "large-scale attack" might come as early as that night. British armor and bridging equipment had been seen and heard massing in the Orne valley despite efforts to conceal the noise with artillery barrages. Rommel suggested that layered antitank defenses ten miles deep could blunt the attack and prevent the Allied bridgehead from merging with a second invasion force, still expected in the Pas de Calais.

Dietrich agreed that an attack seemed imminent: limestone under the Caen plain acted as a sounding board, amplifying enemy tank sounds for any ear pressed to the ground. "You're the boss, Herr Feldmarschall," he said in his Bavarian twang. "I obey only you—whatever it is you're planning."

Just after four P.M., Rommel climbed back into the Horch, spreading a map over his knees. Bad news from St.-Lô required him back at La Roche–Guyon. "I've won Dietrich over," he murmured to his aide.

The car raced east on Route D-4, past cap-doffing peasants and oxcarts flying white flags. Outside Livarot the driver detoured onto a farm track, then rejoined the main road three miles north of Vimoutiers. On the northern horizon, half a dozen enemy planes could be seen darting like dragonflies.

Abruptly the sergeant in the rear seat cried out: two Spitfires had spotted the Horch and were closing from behind, streaking just above the treetops. Flooring the accelerator, the driver had nearly reached a narrow lane behind a screen of poplar trees when the first gun burst flashed from the lead fighter's wings at five hundred yards. Slugs stitched the left side of the Horch, mortally wounding the driver in the shoulder and arm. The car careered downhill, slamming against a tree stump before flipping into a ditch. Flung against the windshield and then from the car, Rommel lay in the roadbed twenty yards behind the wrecked Horch.

He was grievously hurt, bleeding from the ears with a fracture at the base of his skull, two more fractures at his left temple, a shattered cheekbone, a damaged left eye, and lacerations of face and scalp. Carried to a nearby gatekeeper's lodge, he was driven to Livarot after a forty-five-minute search for another car. The local pharmacist, found sipping his evening calvados in a café on the town square, dressed the field marshal's wounds, injected him with etherated camphor for shock, and pronounced him hopeless. Still unconscious, Rommel was loaded into another staff car and driven to the Luftwaffe hospital in Bernay, twenty-five miles distant.

There he would in fact survive, slowly recuperating in room 9 until stable enough to go home to Lucie in Herrlingen. Not for weeks would Reich propagandists announce that he had been injured in a car wreck, omitting the role of enemy fighters. For Erwin Rommel, the Führer's marshal, the war was over.

Rommel was right about the Allied attack: at five A.M. on Tuesday, July 18, a morning fine and bright, 1,000 Lancaster bombers swept across the glistening Channel at three thousand feet, the first of 4,500 planes that were to smash a narrow corridor southeast of Caen that Tuesday. "Aircraft were spread out in a great fan in the red dawn, coming in over the sea," Leigh-Mallory told his diary after watching from the cockpit of a small plane. "Soon there was nothing but a pall of dust and smoke." A German panzer crewman "saw little dots detach themselves from the planes, so many of them that the crazy thought occurred to us: are those leaflets? . . . Then began the most terrifying hours of our lives."

The first bombing wave alone dropped six thousand tons, with some targets calibrated to receive twenty-five pounds of high explosives per square yard in what one captain described as "a canopy of noise" that left German survivors stone deaf. The "little dots" fell and fell, and a few flaming aircraft fell too, but at length the formations made for home with what a Tommy called "a dreadful, unalterable dignity." At 7:45 A.M. the shrill cry went out among the armored ranks massed along the Orne—"Move now!"—and the biggest tank battle fought by Britain in World War II had begun.

Operation GOODWOOD massed three British and Canadian corps—some 76,000 troops and 1,370 tanks—for a southward dagger thrust into five German divisions with 230 tanks plus 600 guns and heavy mortars. The iron-plated British VIII Corps would lead the attack with 700 tanks in three armored divisions. Montgomery, who had ample tanks but ever dwindling British infantry reserves, told subordinates that he intended "to draw the main enemy forces into the battle on our eastern flank . . . so that our affairs on the western flank may proceed the easier."

That modest, credible battle plan—entangle Rommel with the British Second Army so the U.S. First Army could burst from the beachhead—was beset with tactical and conceptual complications. Flinging tanks insufficiently protected by infantrymen against entrenched antitank defenses had long proved perilous if not ruinous. Montgomery also told General Miles Dempsey, the Second Army commander, "to engage the German armor in battle and 'write it down' to such an extent that it is of no further value to the Germans as a basis of the battle"—that is, to attrit the enemy unto annihilation. British armored spearheads "should push far to the south towards Falaise," some twenty miles from Caen, while spreading "alarm and despondency." To Field Marshal Brooke in London,

Montgomery predicted "a real 'show down' on the eastern flank. . . . With 700 tanks loosed to the S.E. of Caen, and armored cars operating far ahead, anything may happen." War correspondents believed that a "Russian style" breakthrough could carry Second Army one hundred miles or more, nigh unto Paris.

Montgomery had overegged the pudding. Many subordinates and at least some of his superiors anticipated a titanic battle of exploitation and pursuit. Eisenhower, told by Montgomery that the "whole eastern flank will burst into flames," promised in return that the Yanks would continue "fighting like the very devil, twenty-four hours a day, to provide the opportunity your armored corps will need." The supreme commander added in a cable: "I am viewing the prospects with the most tremendous optimism and enthusiasm. I would not be at all surprised to see you gaining a victory that will make some of the 'old classics' look like a skirmish between patrols. . . . Forgive me if I grow a bit exuberant."

To wheedle those four thousand warplanes out of skeptical air commanders, Montgomery felt compelled "to paint his canvas in rather glowing colors, and to magnify or even over-emphasize the result to be gained," Dempsey said after the war. "In doing this he did not take Eisenhower into his confidence." Brigadier Williams, the British intelligence chief, added that Montgomery "had to be overconfident all the time in order to get people willing to be killed."

Move now! Willing or not, the tanks trundled forward "like a fleet raising anchor," prow to stern, debouching from minefield gaps marked with white tape. The 11th Armored Division led, followed by the Guards and 7th Armored Divisions, crossing three Orne bridges at a rate of one vehicle every twenty seconds: a grinding choreography that soon frayed. Through burning, breast-high wheat they rolled, in a hole-and-corner terrain of fruit trees and stone villages, on ground that inclined south and allowed the hidden enemy perfect observation with long fields of fire. Some 760 Royal Artillery guns howled and stamped, and "shells roared through the air like angry women swishing out of a room," as one captain wrote. The rolling barrage swept forward three hundred yards every two minutes in what a tank crewman described as "a solid grey wall of shellbursts. . . . It was hard to believe that anything could live in it." But soon the barrage outran the tank squadrons, slowed by a rail embankment two miles from the start line, and the Germans, rattled but not unhinged by an air bombardment less apocalyptic than Montgomery had hoped, recovered their wits.

Torrid orange sheaves of flanking fire came from Cagny, a battered hamlet on the left edge of the attack corridor. Here, at ten A.M., Lieutenant Colonel Hans von Luck, a Rommel acolyte still wearing his dress uniform

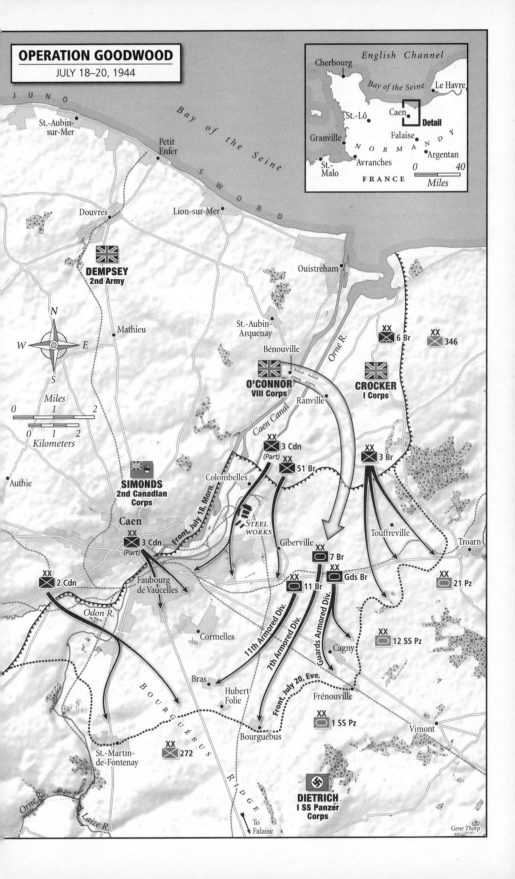

OPERATION GOODWOOD
JULY 18–20, 1944

English Channel

Cherbourg

Bay of the Seine   Le Havre

St.-Lô   Caen ☐ Detail

Granville   Falaise

N O R M A N D Y

St.-Malo   Avranches   Argentan

FRANCE   0   40   Miles

JUNO

Bay of the Seine

SWORD

St.-Aubin-sur-Mer

Petit Enfer

Douvres   Lion-sur-Mer

DEMPSEY
2nd Army

Ouistreham

Mathieu

N
W   E
S

St.-Aubin-Arquenay

Bénouville

6 Br   346

Orne R.

O'CONNOR
VIII Corps

CROCKER
I Corps

Miles
0   1   2

Ranville

Caen Canal

Kilometers
0   1   2

Authie

SIMONDS
2nd Canadian Corps

3 Cdn
(Part)

51 Br

3 Br

Colombelles

Front, July 18, Morn.

STEEL
WORKS

Touffreville

Troarn

Caen

Giberville

3 Cdn
(Part)

7 Br

2 Cdn

Faubourg de Vaucelles

11 Br   Gds Br   21 Pz

Odon R.

Cormelles

11th Armored Div.

7th Armored Div.

Guards Armored Div.

Cagny   12 SS Pz

Bras

Hubert Folie

Frénouville

Front, July 20, Eve.

B O U R G U É B U S

Bourguébus

1 SS Pz

Vimont

St.-Martin-de-Fontenay

272

R I D G E

Orne R.

Laize R.

To Falaise

DIETRICH
I SS Panzer Corps

Gene Thorp

after three days' leave in Paris, found an intact Luftwaffe battery of four 88mm antiaircraft guns. With drawn pistol, Luck forced the reluctant battery commander to shift his tubes into an apple orchard—"You are going to fight the tanks"—and rounds began zipping through the wheat stalks "like torpedoes." The 11th Armored Division reported "great difficulty in locating where the fire came from," and before long sixteen Shermans stood burning in the grain. Cagny would hold out until early evening, a wicked nuisance.

Many more tanks soon burned farther south, past a second rail embankment that gave onto the main enemy gun line along the Bourguébus Ridge, inevitably pronounced Buggersbus. Carpet bombing had left both the ridge and SS reinforcements mostly unscathed, and fighter-bomber pilots found that camouflaged gun pits using flashless, smokeless powder were almost invisible. German defenders lay low when British scouts nosed forward, and "as a result the reports of no opposition in the Bourguébus area sent by scout cars were erroneous," the 11th Armored Division commander later explained. "Violent, impassable fire" subsequently swept the tank fleet, and soon "the horizon was blazing with Shermans," a Coldstream Guards lieutenant recalled.

"Some tank crews are on fire and rolling about on the ground trying to put their clothes out," the gunner John M. Thorpe informed his diary. "Now all the tanks in front of us are burning fiercely. . . . Huge smoke rings leave their turrets, rising high into the windless sky." Another Tommy wrote that "burnt and injured men kept coming back through the corn. We gave them a drink of water, and told them to keep going." A corporal described the scorched Bourguébus slope as "a horrible graveyard of burning tanks."

Montgomery took a different view. "Operations this morning a complete success," he cabled Field Marshal Brooke just after four P.M. "Situation very promising and it is difficult to see what the enemy can do at present." To Eisenhower he added, "Am very well satisfied with today's fighting on eastern flank. We definitely caught the enemy off balance. . . . Second Army has three armored divisions now operating in the open country." He gave locations for those divisions that were pure fantasy: VIII Corps had scratched out six miles on a front hardly wider than a knife's edge, at a cost of two hundred tanks. Perhaps misled by blithe early dispatches from the field, he also issued a public statement in time for the BBC news at nine P.M.: "Second Army attacked and broke through. General Montgomery is well satisfied." The London *Times'* banner headline on Wednesday morning, July 19—"Second Army Breaks Through"—was outdone only by the *Daily Mail'*s: "Armor Now Swarming into Open Country."

Montgomery's cheery assurance sparked jubilation at Bushy Park, but that turned to ashes in the mouth when the true battle map came clear. On Wednesday, Kay Summersby wrote in her desk diary: "E worried because Monty has stopped going. E does not feel well, high blood pressure." The day's events would only make E feel worse. Bourguébus Ridge was reported "groaning with enemy," including antitank reinforcements that ignited more Sherman pyres on the Caen plain. Dempsey's two flanking corps, the British I to the east and the Canadian II to the west, found hardly more success: repeated attacks by the former on Troarn failed, and the latter seized the southern skirts of Caen before fighting off a ferocious counterattack. In one trapped brigade, according to a Canadian account, "men who were still alive lay hiding in the wheat" until they could creep to safety. At first light on Thursday, Tommies finally occupied the village of Bourguébus but advanced no farther. At four P.M. a thunderstorm broke "with tropical violence," the advent of a two-day downpour that put paid to Operation GOODWOOD. Sergeants passed around the rum rations as soldiers crept across the battlefield to collect the dead.

The offensive had liberated another thirty-four square miles of France, plus the rest of Caen; this enlarged the beachhead sufficiently to bring the Canadian First Army vanguard to Normandy but hardly constituted the breakthrough hoped for by SHAEF. More than two thousand Germans had been captured, and, as Montgomery envisioned, additional panzer forces were lured to the Allies' eastern wing. Yet Sepp Dietrich lost only seventy-five tanks and assault guns, by no means the evisceration of German armor that Montgomery also desired. The so-called death ride of the armored divisions cost more than four thousand Second Army casualties and more than four hundred tanks, about a third of the British armored force on the Continent. Airmen grumbled about "seven thousand tons of bombs for seven miles."

After nearly seven weeks, OVERLORD had inserted thirty-three Allied divisions along an eighty-mile front but penetrated no deeper into Normandy than thirty miles, at a cost of 122,000 casualties. "We are up against a tougher proposition than the worst pessimist had in mind during the planning stages," Major General Everett S. Hughes, a close confidant of Eisenhower's, wrote his wife on July 22. Wits invented mock headlines—"Montgomery Sitting on His Caen"—but the *New York Herald Tribune* captured the prevailing gloom: "Allies in France Bogged Down on Entire Front." The *Times* of London corrected its GOODWOOD zeal: "The word 'break-through' used in early reports can only be said to have a limited meaning." Leigh-Mallory told his diary, "The fault with us is, basically, generalship."

Grumbling and backbiting intensified within the Allied high command. Would Montgomery be sacked? Rumors flew, agitators agitated. Informed that V-1 launch sites would not soon be overrun, Air Marshal Tedder informed Beetle Smith, "Then we must change our leaders for men who will get us there." He, Eisenhower, and others "had been had for suckers," Tedder complained. "I do not believe there was the slightest intention to make a clean breakthrough." Worse yet, he told Eisenhower, was the failure to exploit an attempt by the German military to kill Hitler with a bomb on July 20; with the Norman battlefield still deadlocked, Hitler could attend to reprisals and to shoring up his regime. The failed assassin, Colonel Claus von Stauffenberg, and at least two hundred others would be executed—shot, hanged, beheaded, poisoned, or garroted, sometimes on film—and thousands more were jailed. Before the month ended, Wehrmacht officers would be required to demonstrate fealty by giving the stiff-armed Nazi *Heil* rather than the traditional military salute.

"E is not pleased at progress being made," Summersby noted. If displeased, he was also determined not to panic or to act rashly. Instead he would pressure his field commanders, directly and indirectly. Awakened one night by a phone call from Churchill, Eisenhower asked, "What do your people think about the slowness of the situation over there?" Perhaps the prime minister could "persuade Monty to get on his bicycle and start moving."

To Montgomery, the supreme commander sent a sober, fourteen-paragraph note. "Time is vital," Eisenhower wrote. "We must hit with everything."

> I thought that at last we had him and were going to roll him up. That did not come about. . . . Eventually the American ground strength will necessarily be much greater than the British. But while we have equality in size we must go forward shoulder to shoulder, with honors and sacrifices equally shared.

He would keep faith—with the battle plan, with his commanders, and with their common cause. Perhaps only to his mother could he reveal how weary he was. "If I could get home," he wrote Ida Eisenhower in Kansas on July 23, "I could lie down on the front lawn and stay there for a week without moving."

The Bright Day Grew Dark

W EARING the West Point bathrobe he had carried through Tunisia and Sicily, Omar Bradley often stood before dawn at the eight-foot map board that now filled an olive-drab tent in Vouilly, four miles southeast of Isigny-sur-Mer. He too slept badly, despite sedatives at bedtime. Nearly every night he could be found in the small hours pacing the wooden floor of the map tent next to his trailer, contemplating what he had called "the frightful country ahead." A wet moon drifted over the First Army headquarters encampment, and the nauseating stink of dead cows carried on the night air. Eventually the cock would crow as pearl-gray light leaked from the east, and still Bradley attended his map, sketching boundary lines or penciling in roads. Then, wielding a long beech twig as a pointer, he again rehearsed in his mind's eye the coming attack that must end the stalemate and win the battle of Normandy. "I want it to be the biggest thing in the world," he told his staff.

Operation COBRA, that biggest thing, was Bradley's plan, although not his plan alone. Montgomery for one had encouraged a sledgehammer blow on a narrower front than the Americans commonly preferred; this was sound advice, deftly delivered. "Take all the time you need, Brad," the British commander had urged, pressing two slender fingers together against a map. "If I were you, I think I should concentrate my forces a little more." Joe Collins, whose VII Corps would serve as the point of the spear, had chosen the precise spot to attack: a bocage copse just west of St.-Lô, on the old Roman road to Périers. Fifteen U.S. divisions—six in Collins's corps alone—would blow through the battlefront to eventually reach Avranches, thirty miles south, opening the route to Brittany and the vital Breton ports. "Pursue every advantage," Eisenhower had urged, "with an ardor verging on recklessness."

That advantage lay mainly in airpower, particularly since artillery ammunition continued in short supply. A single heavy bomber carried the explosive punch of more than one hundred howitzers firing simultaneously, and Bradley wanted fifteen hundred heavies dropping sixty thousand 100-pound bombs within an hour on a rectangular swatch five miles wide and a mile deep—one bomb every sixteen feet. For a week he had made his case to his air brethren, even traveling to Leigh-Mallory's headquarters at Stanmore in Middlesex on July 19, as GOODWOOD was coming unstitched. The use of small bombs with instant fuzes would prevent the deep cratering that had bedeviled tanks crossing the carpet-bombed terrain at Cassino and at Caen, Bradley argued. To forestall fratricide, the bomber fleets should fly parallel to the front, using the perfectly straight

St.-Lô–Périers road for guidance. Army assault battalions would pull back eight hundred yards as a precaution against errant bombs, yet this would leave them near enough to rush forward before the enemy recovered his wits, as apparently had happened in GOODWOOD.

Very little in Bradley's vision appealed to airmen. The Army Air Forces' "Handbook for Bombardiers" included 125 pages on—among other arcane topics—ballistic coefficients, dropping angles, and Williamson's probability, all of which suggested that the general's proposed attack route was impossible. Fifteen hundred planes could not funnel into a one-mile corridor in the single hour that First Army allotted before the ground attack began; such a bombardment would take closer to three hours. Other technical problems also obtained, including the difficulties of dropping in the prevailing crosswind and of flying over intense antiaircraft defenses. Only if the planes attacked perpendicular to the front line—approaching from the north, over the heads of American troops—could they drop several thousand tons of bombs in an hour. Moreover, even in daylight and good weather, the margin of safety for dug-in troops was three thousand yards from the bomb line, almost two miles. Anything closer amounted to what one air commander called "bombing between the Army's legs."

Bradley agreed to pull his assault battalions back twelve hundred yards rather than eight hundred, but he balked at further concessions. Warned that 3 percent of the munitions would likely fall awry—some 1,800 bombs in the proposed COBRA payload—he accepted the risk. If GIs died, they were "nothing more than tools to be used in the accomplishment of the mission," he later wrote. "War has neither the time nor heart to concern itself with the individual and the dignity of man." As he had once told Ernie Pyle, "I've spent thirty years preparing a frame of mind for accepting such a thing."

Pyle spent Monday night, July 24, in an apple orchard near Pont-Hébert, wrapped in a blanket among tree trunks gashed white with bullet scars. After the Cherbourg campaign he had felt hollow and lethargic, like someone using up "your own small quota of chances for survival." He drifted to the back of the beachhead, writing about ordnance troops who refurbished rusty M-1 rifles with sandpaper and gasoline solvent. To combat veterans, those in the rear were known as "they" and their world was the "they area." Pyle felt guilty at lingering in the they area.

Now he had returned to the front, his inevitable province, and on Tuesday morning he stood behind a stone house in a farmyard lacerated with slit trenches. Officers from the 4th Infantry Division studied mimeographed sketches of the COBRA bombing sequence that showed where the heavy B-17s and B-24s would dump their loads, complemented by medium

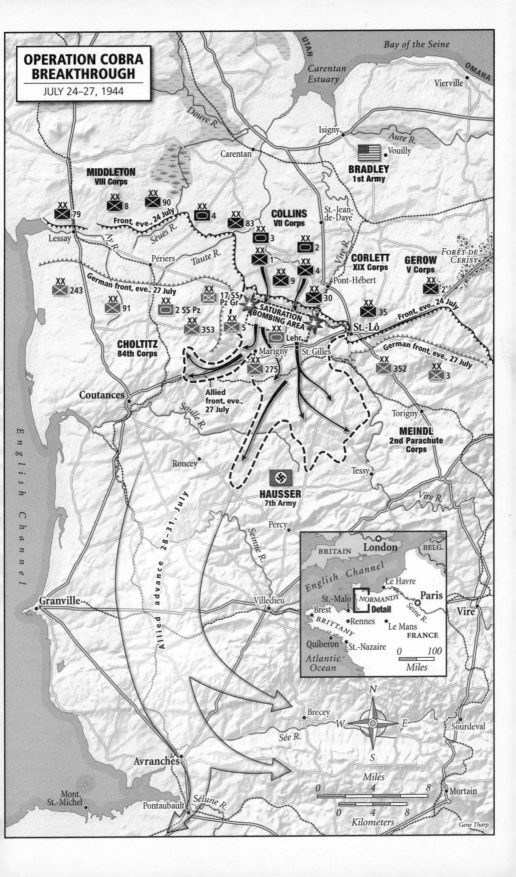

OPERATION COBRA BREAKTHROUGH

JULY 24–27, 1944

Bay of the Seine

UTAH

OMAHA

Carentan
Estuary

Douve R.

Vierville

Isigny

Aure R.

Carentan

BRADLEY
1st Army

Vouilly

MIDDLETON
VIII Corps

Front, eve., 24 July

St.-Jean-
de-Daye

XX 79

XX 8

XX 90

XX 4

XX 83

COLLINS
VII Corps

FORÊT-DE
CERISY

Lessay

Ay R.

Sèues R.

XX 3

XX 2

GEROW
V Corps

Vire R.

Périers

Taute R.

XX 1

XX 9

XX 4

CORLETT
XIX Corps

XX 2

German front, eve., 27 July

XX 243

XX 91

XX 17 SS
Pz Gr

2 SS Pz

XX 30

Pont-Hébert

XX 35

Front, eve., 24 July

CHOLTITZ
84th Corps

XX 353

XX 5

SATURATION
BOMBING
AREA

XX Lehr.

St.-Lô

German front, eve., 27 July

XX 352

XX 3

Coutances

Marigny

St. Gilles

XX 275

Allied
front, eve.,
27 July

Souelle R.

Torigny

MEINDL
2nd Parachute
Corps

Roncey

Tessy

Vire R.

HAUSSER
7th Army

English Channel

Seinne R.

Percy

Allied advance 28-31, July

Granville

Villedieu

BRITAIN

London

BELG.

English Channel

Le Havre

St.-Malo

NORMANDY

Detail

Paris

Brest

Rennes

Seine R.

Vire

BRITTANY

Le Mans

FRANCE

Quiberon

St.-Nazaire

Atlantic
Ocean

0   100

Miles

N

Brecey

W   E

Sourdeval

Sée R.

S

Avranches

Miles

0   4   8

Mortain

Mont.
St.-Michel

Pontaubault

Sélune R.

0   4   8

Kilometers

Gene Thorp

bombers and by fighter-bombers. Hardly half a mile to the south, red pillars of smoke from artillery canisters fired every thirty seconds rose at one-mile intervals along the St.-Lô–Périers road to delineate the bomb line. Cerise recognition panels covered the ground like flaming throw rugs, and every vehicle had been repainted with the Allied white-star insignia, first adopted two years earlier after tests to determine the geometric design most clearly visible from air and ground.

At 9:38 A.M., the first of 350 fighter-bombers began raking German positions along a three-hundred-yard corridor parallel to the road. From GIs tucked beneath the trees a throaty roar built to the echo, "like kids at a football game," a lieutenant noted. Pyle squinted at the sky, hands cupped around his eyes to block the glare, listening to "the heavy rip of the planes' machine guns and the splitting screams of diving wings."

Not much had gone right with COBRA thus far. Originally scheduled to follow hard on the heels of GOODWOOD, the operation had been delayed by rain and cloud for days while Bradley glumly studied the three barometers he kept in his command post. Leigh-Mallory then ordered the attack for noon on Monday, July 24, rejecting a U.S. Eighth Air Force request to wait another day, or at least until midafternoon, when skies were expected to clear.

Flying from Stanmore to Bradley's headquarters at Vouilly, Leigh-Mallory arrived on Monday at 11:20 A.M. to find clouds still smothering Normandy, bombers already on the wing, and no way to contact the pilots except by a frantic cancellation order radioed to England. Too late. Although many pilots chose to abort their drops because of poor visibility and explicit orders "not to bomb short as the penetration route is directly over friendly troops," some bombed by mistake—one startled bombardier accidentally tripped the toggle switch when a chaff bundle smacked the nose of his plane—and others took a chance on dropping through the thinning overcast. Of 350 heavies disgorging nearly a thousand tons, only 15 percent hit the target; several medium bombers also missed by as much as seven miles, and P-47s attacked misidentified targets four miles short of the bomb line. Twenty-five GIs were killed and 131 wounded, nearly all in the 30th Infantry Division, whose assistant commander told First Army, "As a fiasco this operation was a brilliant achievement."

Bradley's fury knew no bounds: Leigh-Mallory flew back to England with accusations of duplicity and bad faith ringing in his ears. At 10:30 P.M. he phoned Bradley to confirm that the attackers had flown perpendicular to the target box rather than parallel, and that many bombs heavier than 100-pounders had been dropped. Bradley had evidently misconstrued what had been agreed to at the Stanmore conference on July 19, and Leigh-Mallory had left that meeting early for another appointment before all details of the mission were clarified. A full COBRA bombardment could be launched again on Tuesday morning, Leigh-Mallory now added, but only by flying the same perpendicular route from the north. With more marginal weather predicted, Bradley agreed, grumbling bitterly, and Collins worked all night to get his bewildered corps repositioned to try again.

From his farmyard redoubt, Pyle watched for half an hour as fighter-bombers dipped and darted. The black blossoms of German antiaircraft shells spattered the sky. Then a new noise intruded, "a sound deep and all-encompassing with no notes in it—just a gigantic faraway surge of doomlike sound." From the north the B-17s and B-24s drew near, roofing the heavens with a stately procession of tiny silver cruciforms three miles up, "plowing their way forward as if there was no turmoil in the world." Gawking soldiers leaned back until their helmets fell off.

The first detonations to the south reminded Pyle of "the crackle of popcorn." Smoke and dust rolled back through the orchards, and "the bright day grew slowly dark." Then, inexplicably, the bomb loads drew ever closer, with a terrifying rattle of wind over tail fins, and the ponderous footfall of explosions stomped through the trees. Pyle dove beneath a heavy wagon behind the stone house, "waiting for darkness" as concussion waves hammered his chest and eyes in what he would describe as "the most sustained horrible thing I've ever gone through." At length the howling passed and a colonel staggered through the swirling dust, snapping his fingers and muttering "Goddammit, goddammit, goddammit."

For others it was worse. The star-crossed 30th Division took more casualties from the Army Air Forces (AAF) on this Tuesday forenoon than from the enemy on any day in the war. "Then came that awful rush of wind," a regimental history recorded, "that awful sound like the rattling of seeds in a dry gourd." Bombs entombed men in their trenches or split them open like deer carcasses. Bombs obliterated command posts, tossed cows into trees, and raised the dead from local cemeteries. The concussion "felt as if someone was beating you with a club," one officer reported, while another was whacked in the buttocks by what proved to be a body part. Men screamed for medics and raged against the "American Luftwaffe."

Just over fifteen hundred heavies dropped two thousand tons of high explosives and an even larger payload of fragmentation bombs; of those aircraft, three dozen bombed American troops, joined in the fratricide by forty-two medium bombers. High clouds had forced some planes to descend several thousand feet, loosening the formations and requiring crews to hurriedly recalculate data for their bombsights. Red marking smoke was easily confused with artillery muzzle flashes, and the St.-Lô–Périers road was soon hidden by dense bomb smoke carried on a five-knot southerly breeze. Two percent of all bombs had fallen short by a mile or more, killing

111 soldiers and wounding 490, this in addition to the casualties from the previous day. Among the dead was Lieutenant General Lesley J. McNair, the commander of Army Ground Forces, who was visiting from Washington and had rashly inserted himself into an assault battalion of the 30th Division; a search detail with picks and shovels combed the crater where he was last seen without finding a trace. Eventually his corpse was spotted sixty-five feet away, beyond recognition but for his dog tags, shoulder flash, and rank insignia. "I warned him time and again about unnecessary risk," Eisenhower cabled Marshall. A manifest listed all the personal effects left for his widow: "6 Lt. Gen. stars, tarnished, and clasp missing from 2 stars."

By the time the last medium bomber flew off at 12:23 P.M., nearly 2,500 planes had dropped five thousand tons of bombs plus heaps of white phosphorus and a new jellied-gasoline agent called napalm. In the pinched target box, where the Army's armored breakout was to burst forth, each square mile absorbed more than eleven thousand bombs, among the greatest concentrations of killing power in the history of warfare. As for the dead and dying GIs on the wrong side of the line, Pyle wrote with the laconic fatalism that now bleached his bones, "Anybody makes mistakes."

Eisenhower flew to see Bradley at Vouilly for a few hours on Tuesday afternoon, then returned to England, dejected and vowing never again to use heavy bombers in a tactical attack. "That's a job for artillery," he snapped. "I gave them a green light this time. But I promise you it's the last." Bradley continued to fume, at Leigh-Mallory and others, obfuscating his own role in putting troops danger close.

By early that afternoon the COBRA ground attack was well under way. Assault columns initially made meager progress: a 30th Division column butted into enemy resistance after only four hundred yards, including Panther tanks. "Good God," a GI in a light tank cried over the radio, "I fired three rounds and they all bounced off." Panzer return fire dismasted a platoon sergeant. "Just his legs and hips were there," a comrade wrote. "One arm, with the wrist watch on it, lay near the house." By nightfall, VII Corps had gained no more than a mile beyond the St.-Lô–Périers road and fewer than three hundred prisoners had been bagged. German shells rained down, leading an intelligence officer to conclude that "enemy artillery was not touched by our bombing."

Africa veterans like Eisenhower and Bradley should have recalled two lines of Kipling popular in Tunisia: *"Man cannot tell, but Allah knows / How much the other side was hurt."* In truth, German defenses had been blown to smithereens: the enemy was profoundly hurt, mortally hurt. The main opponent confronting VII Corps, the Panzer Lehr Division, had earlier been described as "worn out" by the German high command after six weeks of fighting; Tuesday's "conveyor belt bombing" had devastated the weakened division, flipping tanks, smashing radios, and obliterating headquarters. The division commander, General Fritz Bayerlein, former chief of staff for Rommel's Afrika Korps, described "half-crazed soldiers jumping out of the craters of a lunar landscape, running in circles. . . . Everything was burned and blasted." He calculated that 70 percent of his men were dead, wounded, or inert with "a feeling of helplessness, weakness, and inferiority." Orders could be transmitted only by motorcycle couriers nosing a path through drifted debris. When Field Marshal Kluge passed word that the St.-Lô–Périers corridor must hold, Bayerlein replied, "Tell the field marshal that the Panzer Lehr is destroyed. Only the dead can still hold."

Unaware of the size of the American host and lulled into complacency by Monday's aborted attack, German commanders had been caught out. As Montgomery intended, two-thirds or more of Seventh Army's panzers still faced the British in the east, and reserves in the German Fifteenth Army remained pinned to the Pas de Calais, awaiting the thirty Allied divisions still believed to be assembling in England for a second invasion. Seventh Army failed to keep a sufficient armored reserve to plug any breach in the Cotentin, and battlefield leadership proved wanting. Kluge's headquarters informed Berlin late Tuesday night: "The front has, so to speak, burst. There is a penetration of two to five kilometers deep on a front seven to eight kilometers wide. It has not yet been possible to seal this off."

Nor would it be possible. Collins had massed 120,000 troops on a five-mile front along the St.-Lô–Périers road, plus fifteen thousand engineers to lift mines and bury dead livestock. His six hundred artillery tubes, with 140,000 rounds stockpiled, exceeded the firepower of the other three First Army corps combined. Most Sherman tanks were now fitted with hedge cutters for slashing through the bocage—rugged tusks designed by GIs and fabricated with angle-iron salvaged from German beach obstacles. Welders and virtually all of the oxygen acetylene cylinders in England had been flown to Normandy, where an assembly line in St.-Jean-de-Daye turned out three hundred cutters in two days, all kept secret before COBRA. No less innovative was a decision by Major General Elwood "Pete" Quesada, the tactical air commander, to position liaison officers with VHF radios in each tank column for direct communication with fighter-bombers overhead, a collaboration that proved priceless in what airmen called "hazing the Hun."

Collins had not planned to launch his exploitation force—the 1st Infantry Division and two armored divisions, the 2nd and 3rd—until a clear hole had been drilled through enemy defenses by shock battalions from the 4th, 9th, and 30th Infantry Divisions. But the absence of the usual German counterattack on Tuesday afternoon suggested disarray and debility in the opposing ranks, even if the lead U.S. echelons had yet to break into the enemy's rear. At 5:45 P.M. on Tuesday, Collins ordered the follow-on forces to attack the next morning, July 26. Riflemen crept forward through the night, feeling for booby traps, removing mines, and listening for the growl of panzer engines.

With the new day, the American onslaught built momentum, as if both opposing armies had begun to slide across a landscape tilting south. GIs rode into battle "Russian style" on tank hulls, leaping off to spray every swale and thicket with blistering fire. On average, 1st Division troops required under three minutes to clear each hedgerow, a task that had taken hours just a few weeks earlier. On the eastern lip of the breach, forcing a narrow sunken road to St.-Gilles cost seven hundred 30th Division casualties, but by midafternoon tanks were churning through the village against little opposition. Marigny fell to the 1st Division, the 9th Division lunged nearly three miles beyond the Périers road, and at four P.M. the German Seventh Army reported Americans leaking through seven punctures in the narrow front. Enemy efforts to fling two divisions west across the Vire River to cork the bottle came to naught after the U.S. XIX Corps blocked the move. Fuel shortages forced abandonment of two Panther companies from the 2nd SS Panzer Division and an American patrol killed the Das Reich commander, a small but satisfying measure of vengeance for the massacres at Tulle and Oradour. Kluge told subordinates to expect no further reinforcements for at least a week.

By nightfall on Thursday, 100,000 Americans were pouring through the five-mile breach, armored columns had closed on Coutances, and Bradley's map board showed ever more enemy positions with unit icons marked "Rem"—remnants. "This thing has busted wide open," the 30th Division commander told Collins.

French farmers flitted across the battlefield, stripping shoes and tunics from German corpses. GIs found white tablecloths and wilting flowers on a mess table in a captured bivouac, along with well-thumbed pornography, copies of *Life* magazine, and checkers on a board abandoned in midgame. A tank lieutenant saw a German drop his rifle and scamper away. "Then I caught sight of holes in his head, and he crashed full tilt into an apple tree," he wrote. "He was running dead, like a chicken."

On Friday enemy forces scuffed to the rear across a twenty-mile front, pressed by both Collins's VII Corps and Major General Troy Middleton's VIII Corps, clattering down a corridor along the Cotentin coast. German ambuscades, local counterattacks, and confusion permitted substantial enemy forces to escape entrapment in the Cotentin. Even so, sheets of marching fire took a heavy toll. Pilots over Roncey reported a "fighter-bomber's paradise," with German traffic triple-banked and crawling bumper to bumper. For six hours Allied planes lashed the column, eventually joined by artillery, tanks, and tank destroyers until more than 100 panzers and 250 other vehicles stood wrecked if not burning; survivors pelted away on foot, silhouetted against the flames. The Hun had been hazed.

Coutances fell on Saturday morning, July 29. German naval crews at Granville spiked their shore guns before fleeing. "Things on our front really look good," an elated Bradley wrote Eisenhower. Ahead lay Avranches, among the oldest towns in Normandy, where the English monarch Henry II had arrived, barefoot and hatless, to make public penance on his knees for the murder of Thomas Becket in 1170. Built on a high bluff overlooking holy Mont-St.-Michel, eight miles to the west, Avranches gave onto Brittany and the Breton ports coveted by Allied logisticians. On Sunday evening, a spearhead from the 4th Armored Division lunged into the town only to find it undefended. Jubilant Frenchmen greeted them with waving tricolors.

Belatedly alive to their peril, German troops hurried toward Avranches in trucks and horse-drawn wagons. Counterattacking at dawn, they were thrown back with white phosphorus, strafing P-47s, and gouts of Sherman fire. American tankers and riflemen soon seized the vital bridge over the Sélune River at Pontaubault, four miles south of town and unaccountably still intact. Within hours, three more crossing sites over the Sélune had been secured. Here the roads radiated to all points of the compass, including the Brittany ports. Seven thousand German prisoners shambled into VIII Corps cages on July 31 alone; many had been simply disarmed and waved to the rear unescorted. "We face a defeated enemy," General Barton told subordinates in the 4th Infantry Division, "an enemy terribly low in morale, terribly confused."

In a phone call from Le Mans to his chief of staff in Paris at 10:30 that Monday morning, Kluge scoffed when told of Berlin's demand that another defensive line be thrown up in Normandy.

> It's a madhouse here. You can't imagine what it's like. . . . All you can do is laugh out loud. Don't they read our dispatches? Haven't they been oriented? They must be living on the moon. . . . Someone has to tell the Führer that if the Americans get through at Avranches they will be out of the woods and they'll be able to do what they want.

The Führer would learn the truth of Kluge's assessment soon enough. With agility and celerity, and bolstered by ten thousand tactical air sorties,

First Army had driven thirty miles in less than a week to outflank the German left and pivot into Brittany. This thing had indeed busted wide open. The war of movement had begun, at last.

Ministers of Thy Chastisement

D OWN metalled roads and farm lanes they pounded, columns of jeeps and tanks and deuce-and-a-half trucks snaking through the shot-threshed fields and the orchards heavy with fruit. MP motorcyclists weaved among the ranks, scolding dawdlers. Grenades hung from uniform lapels "like Cartier clips." Chalky dust powdered their faces and grayed their hair. "War was their business," wrote the photojournalist Lee Miller, "and they went on in a sloping march."

On they marched, south, east, and west: past stone barns and mules hauling milk in copper urns, past shops that still peddled perfume and silk scarves, past collaborators with crude swastikas swabbed onto their shaved heads. When the trucks halted for a moment and GIs tumbled out to urinate in squirming echelons on the road shoulders, civilians rushed up to plead for cigarettes with two fingers pressed to the lips, a gesture described by Forrest Pogue as the French national salute. Others offered tricolor nosegays made from blue hydrangeas, red roses, and white asters. "Heep, heep, whoo-ray!" the Frenchmen yelled, repeating phrases learned from doughboys a generation earlier. "I speeg Engless. Jees-Christ, cot-dam!" Soldiers replied in schoolboy French or with handy phrases published in *Stars and Stripes,* among which was the French for "My wife doesn't understand me." A GI shout of *"Vive la France!"* often elicited jugs of calvados and toasts to the spirit of Lafayette or hissing denunciations of the Boche, also known to the Yanks as Krauts, Jerries, Graybacks, Lice, Huns, and Squareheads.

German tourist posters still hung from schoolhouse walls, and German-language lessons—all umlauts and uppercase nouns—could be seen chalked on blackboards. But for mile after mile the only enemy encountered were prisoners, encouraged to surrender with the GI dialect known as Milwaukee German, or dead men, often buried beneath a makeshift marker with an epitaph reduced to a naked noun, also upper case: "A German." The Wehrmacht retreat had "a Napoleonic aspect," an officer in Army Group B conceded. Kluge in early August told his superiors, "No matter how many orders are issued, the troops cannot, are not able to, are not strong enough to defeat the enemy."

In hasty bivouacs the surging columns halted for the night, choking down cold K rations or heating soup in their helmets over a Sterno flame—

the charred crown, with steel burned to a blue sheen, marked veteran troops as surely as a Purple Heart. Evening also was the time for brief memorial services. "One's life is held in balance by a little piece of metal smaller than a man's finger," one soldier wrote. A chaplain who offered a prayer for the dead invoked the Irish poet Charles Wolfe: "We buried him darkly at dead of night. . . . we left him alone with his glory."

SHAEF planners in late July estimated that Germany could be defeated quickly if nine more divisions were added to the seventy-five already allocated to OVERLORD. Unfortunately, with fewer than three dozen divisions now in France, almost no additional British units remaining, and U.S. reinforcements reaching France at a rate of less than one division per week, that war-winning tally of eighty-four would not be available on the Continent until August 1945. Instead, the Allies would have to settle for the arrival on stage of a man described by a reporter as "a warring, roaring comet" and by a West Point classmate as a "pure-bred gamecock with brains."

The first glimpse of Lieutenant General George S. Patton, Jr., for many soldiers came in Avranches, where he leaped from his jeep into an umbrella-covered police box and directed convoy traffic through a congested roundabout for ninety minutes. Assigned by Bradley to oversee VIII Corps's drive south, Patton had helped shove seven divisions past Avranches in seventy-two hours, cigar smoldering as he snarled at occasional Luftwaffe marauders, "Those goddamned bastards, those rotten sons-of-bitches! We'll get them." When a subordinate called to report his position, Patton bellowed, "Hang up and keep going." In a Norman landscape of smashed vehicles, grass fires, and charred German bodies, he added, "Could anything be more magnificent? Compared to war, all other forms of human endeavor shrink to insignificance. God, how I love it."

At noon on Tuesday, August 1, his U.S. Third Army officially came into being, with nine divisions under three corps. At the same instant, Bradley ascended to command the new 12th Army Group, complementing 21st Army Group while still subordinate to Montgomery. Bradley's former deputy, Lieutenant General Courtney H. Hodges, succeeded him as First Army commander. "We are advancing constantly," Patton told his staff. "From here on out, until we win or die in the attempt, we will always be audacious." To his diary he confided, "I am very happy."

"There are apparently two types of successful soldiers," Patton had recently written his son. "Those who get on by being unobtrusive and those who get on by being obtrusive. I am of the latter type." True enough, but for nearly a year he had been consigned to near anonymity. Slapping two hospitalized soldiers in Sicily, ostensibly for malingering, nearly cost Patton his stars; he was denied an early role in OVERLORD and a chance to command the army group now led by Bradley, his junior and former subordinate. A minor but foolish indiscretion in April, when he told a British social club that "undoubtedly it is our destiny to rule the world—the Americans, the British, and of course the Russians," almost lost him Third Army. "Patton has broken out again," Eisenhower wrote Marshall after that incident. "Apparently he is unable to use reasonably good sense."

Narrowly pardoned, Patton spent the spring and early summer as a conspicuous decoy to confuse German intelligence about a second Allied landing. He shopped in Britain for hunting guns and saddles, wrote atrocious poetry, played badminton and golf, bought a white bull terrier named Willie, and offered Eisenhower $1,000 for every week in advance he was permitted to leave England for France. A reporter found him "neurotic and bloodthirsty." To his wife, Bea, who was not only his confidante but a kindred spirit—she once bribed an Egyptian boatman to smuggle her into a tattoo parlor in a failed effort to have a full-rigged clipper ship needled across her chest—Patton had written in early July, "Can't stand the times between wars."

He also reflected deeply on generalship and the exploitation juggernaut he would now command. His kit included Edward Augustus Freeman's six-volume *History of the Norman Conquest of England,* which Patton studied to understand William the Conqueror's use of road networks in France. He arrived in France determined not only to redeem his reputation but to find glory. "I'm in the doghouse," he told Joe Collins. "I've got to do something spectacular." Bradley had bluntly warned him: "You know, George, I didn't ask for you." But Bradley soon found himself impressed by a man who seemed more "judicious, reasonable, and likeable than in the Mediterranean." To his soldiers, Patton promised that the enemy would "raise up on their hind legs and howl, 'Jesus Christ, it's the goddamn Third Army and that son-of-a-bitch Patton again.'"

Now here they were, sluicing into Brittany with open flanks and a vulnerable rear. "I had to keep repeating to myself, 'Do not take counsel of your fears,'" Patton told his diary on August 1. To Bea he wrote that combat "always scares and lures me, like steeple-chasing." He ordered laminated battle maps of the sort he had carried in Tunisia and Sicily—ten by twenty inches each, with a scale of eight miles to the inch. When the set was delivered, he scowled. "It only goes as far east as Paris," he complained. "I'm going to Berlin."

First he was going to Brest, and no special map was needed to see that Brest lay west while Paris and Berlin lay east. Only the seizure of a Normandy beachhead ranked higher in importance for OVERLORD planners than the capture of Brittany and its ports: St.-Malo, St.-Nazaire, Lorient,

Brest, and Quiberon Bay, for which another grandiose artificial harbor was envisioned. Delays in shaking free of Normandy, as well as the cautionary tales of Mulberry A and scorched-earth demolitions at Cherbourg, failed to dampen the ardor of Eisenhower and his logisticians. Patton's army was to take Brittany.

But the collapse of the German left wing gave Montgomery pause, and as early as July 27 he had suggested that the campaign in Brittany might require only a single corps. Neither Bradley nor Patton took the hint. Patton, whose doghouse status made him leery of challenging Eisenhower's master plan, wagered Montgomery £5 that GIs would be in Brest by Saturday night, August 5. Claiming "a sixth sense by which I can always know to a moral certainty what the enemy is going to do," Patton insisted that "there aren't more than ten thousand Krauts in the entire [Brittany] peninsula." That was wrong by a factor of at least six. But to his 6th Armored Division, then 150 miles from the objective, he issued a two-word order on August 1: "Take Brest."

On the same day, Third Army's other spearhead, the 4th Armored Division, raced forty miles south from Avranches to the outskirts of Rennes, the Breton capital and a nexus for ten trunk roads. Here an epiphany struck Major General John S. Wood, the beetle-browed division commander. Known as P.—for "Professor," because he had tutored his classmates at West Point—Wood had attended the academy to play football after graduating from the University of Arkansas, where he studied chemistry. A devoted rose gardener and a linguist who had read both De Gaulle and the German panzer mastermind Heinz Guderian in the original, Wood often buzzed above the battlefield in a Piper Cub with red streamers flapping from the wingtips so that his men below could recognize him.

"We're winning this war the wrong way," Wood declared. "We ought to be going toward Paris." The French capital was only sixty miles farther from Rennes than Brest; Brittany was a cul-de-sac, while Paris led to the Reich. Wood ordered two 4th Armored columns to outflank Rennes and cut seven of those ten roads; the city fell on August 4. Proposing to reach Chartres—150 miles east—in two days, Wood radioed Patton, "Dear George . . . Trust we can turn around and get headed in right direction soon." Instead he was dispatched west into Brittany for a bloody siege at Lorient.

Bradley belatedly had come around to Montgomery's view that "the main business lies to the east." On August 3, he told Patton to clear Brittany with "a minimum of forces." Patton chose to pivot east with his XV and XX Corps while leaving VIII Corps behind, a splintering of the army that took time and consigned two cutthroat armored divisions, the 4th and 6th, to static siege warfare rather than freeing them to lead the charge across France.

The Brittany campaign soon proved bootless. None of the ports would be especially useful, in part because of their distance from the main battlefield—five hundred miles separated Brest from the German frontier—and in part because Hitler ordered various coastal fortresses held "to the last man, to the last cartridge." That recalcitrance soon neutered 280,000 German defenders along the European littoral, but it also denied several important ports to Allied logisticians for weeks, if not for the duration. The siege of St.-Malo ensnared twenty thousand GIs for a fortnight and wrecked the harbor; Brest, with seventy-five strongpoints, and walls up to twenty-five-feet thick, proved a particularly hard nut, costing ten thousand casualties among the seventy thousand Americans who would invest the citadel for more than a month in a medieval affair of scaling ladders and grappling hooks. Though Bradley later insisted that the Brest garrison was too dangerous to leave unchallenged in his rear, the diversion of five divisions to Brittany reflected an inflexible adherence to the OVERLORD plan. "We must take Brest in order to maintain the illusion of the fact that the U.S. Army cannot be beaten," Bradley told Patton, who agreed.

The war ended with not a single cargo ship or troopship having berthed at Brest, which bombs and a half million American shells knocked to rubble. The synthetic harbor at Quiberon Bay was never built. P. Wood, whose 4th Armored Division finally was released from siege duty at Lorient in mid-August to hie toward Nantes and far beyond, considered the Brittany sidestep "one of the colossally stupid decisions of the war." But with most of Patton's legions finally baying eastward by mid-August, both the initial swivel to the west and the failure to fulfill the strategic ambitions of the Brittany campaign seemed like small beer. "We have unloosed the shackles that were holding us down," Montgomery told his lieutenants:

> Whatever the enemy may want to do will make no difference to us. We will proceed relentlessly, and rapidly, with our plans for his destruction. . . . Our general situation is very good; the enemy situation is far from good. . . . Now is the time to press on boldly and to take great risks.

Montgomery's plan was a simple, handsome thing: three armies would clobber the Germans straight on while a fourth—Patton's Third—swung far to the right, toward Paris, to trap the reeling enemy against the Seine before the river bridges could be repaired. As Patton sent his XV Corps toward Le Mans, headquarters of the German Seventh Army, Montgomery heaved the bulk of Allied forces forward on a sixty-mile front from Avranches to Caen. The Canadian First Army on the left and the British

Second Army in the center made modest progress against the preponderance of German armor, including two SS panzer corps. Tommies at last overran ruined Villers-Bocage on August 4 and bulled toward Vire, cheek by jowl with the U.S. V Corps of First Army. But here there were no thirty-miles-before-lunch sprints: the 28th Infantry Division, formerly part of the Pennsylvania National Guard, took 750 casualties on its first day in combat, while Loose Reins Gerhardt's 29th Division suffered another thousand in struggling ten miles toward Vire.

War, as the historian Bruce Catton once wrote, sometimes "went by a queer script of its own," putting a jackboot down on some anonymous, unlikely place like Shiloh Church or Kasserine or Anzio or Ste.-Mère-Église. Such a place was Mortain, a village of 1,300, twenty miles east of Avranches amid broken terrain dubbed the Norman Switzerland in a triumph of tourist-bureau ebullience over geography. The town's name was said to derive from *Maurus,* a reference to Moors in the Roman army; renowned for cutlery, first of pewter and then of stainless steel, Mortain in recent times also had become a mining and market hub, linking inland communes with the coast. Since June 6, thousands of refugees from the invasion zone had shuffled through, among them children wearing tags with the addresses of relatives to contact should their mothers fall dead.

The last German occupier in Mortain had been gunned down on August 3 by a French policeman armed with a nineteenth-century rifle and one bullet. Hours later, the 1st Infantry Division arrived, only to move along on August 6, supplanted on that warm, luminous Sunday by the 30th Division. Cheering civilians tossed flowers at the newcomers in their grinding trucks as they rumbled past busy cafés and hotels. Known as Old Hickory for its National Guard roots in Tennessee and the Carolinas, the 30th Division still was licking wounds from COBRA, including the fratricidal bombing. Two of the division's nine infantry battalions had been dispatched elsewhere; the rest now burrowed in across a seven-mile front.

Of keen interest was stony, steep Montjoie, looming over Mortain to the east and so named because from here joyful pilgrims first caught sight of Mont-St.-Michel, twenty-seven miles distant. To GIs the mile-long escarpment was simply Hill 314, after its height in meters; seven hundred men from the 2nd Battalion of the 120th Infantry chuffed to the crest before scratching at the skimpy fieldworks left by the 1st Division. With them was Lieutenant Robert L. Weiss, a short, lean, twenty-one-year-old artillery forward observer who wore the same wool serge shirt his father, a Hungarian immigrant, had worn in World War I. In addition to binoculars on a tripod, Weiss lugged a thirty-five-pound SCR-610 radio in a saddle-soaped leather case; the FM set had a five-mile range, just far

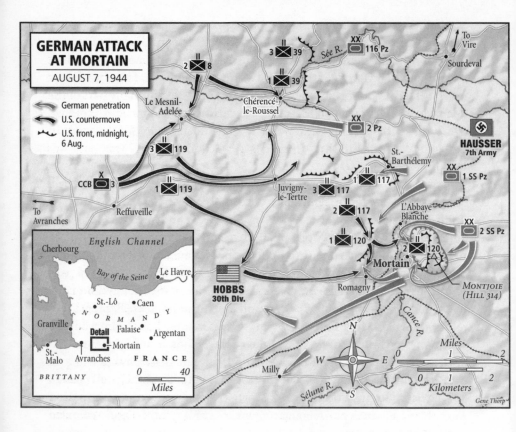

GERMAN ATTACK AT MORTAIN
AUGUST 7, 1944

German penetration
U.S. countermove
U.S. front, midnight, 6 Aug.

To Vire
Sourdeval
3 — 39   Sée R.   116 Pz
2 — 8
1 — 39
Le Mesnil-Adelée   Chérencé-le-Roussel
2 Pz
HAUSSER
7th Army
St.-Barthélemy
3 — 119
1 SS Pz
CCB — 3
1 — 119
Juvigny-le-Tertre   3 — 117   1 — 117
2 — 117   L'Abbaye Blanche
To Avranches   Reffuveille
2 SS Pz
1 — 120
English Channel
Cherbourg
2 — 120
Bay of the Seine   Le Havre
Mortain
HOBBS
30th Div.
Romagny   MONTJOIE (HILL 314)
St.-Lô   Caen
NORMANDY
Granville   Detail   Falaise   Argentan
N
Miles
Mortain
St.-Malo   Avranches   FRANCE
W   E   0   1   2
BRITTANY   0   40
Milly   0   1   2
Miles   Kilometers
Cance R.
Sélune R.   S
Gene Thorp

enough to reach the howitzer batteries dug in to the west. Recently he had written his mother in Indiana, "I hope I get a chance to do a little shooting on my own the next few days." His weary comrades hoped only for a little rest.

This they would not get. Montgomery's assessment that "the enemy situation is far from good" was unarguable, and that very vulnerability made the Germans desperate. From his East Prussian headquarters a thousand miles to the east, Hitler detected "a unique opportunity, which will never return . . . to drive into an extremely exposed enemy area." At his direction, a counterattack spearheaded by four panzer divisions was to blast through Mortain to Avranches, cleaving Patton's Third Army from Hodges's First Army and, if not cudgeling the invaders back to their ships, at least reimposing the static war of early summer. "Tell Kluge," Hitler added in a message sent through high command, "that he should keep his eyes riveted to the front and on the enemy without ever looking backward."

Field Marshal Kluge replied that "such an attack if not immediately successful" would risk envelopment and annihilation. Even if the spearhead reached Avranches, the force would be too weak to hold its gains against Allied air, artillery, and armor. Eight German divisions had already been obliterated during July fighting in and below the Cotentin, plus others written off in Brittany and the isolated Channel Islands. Six replacement divisions had recently arrived on the Norman front from southern France and the Pas de Calais, permitting a reorganization of sorts: Panzer Group West was rechristened Fifth Panzer Army, with a dozen divisions in four corps, and Seventh Army counted sixteen divisions. Yet this host was fragile and dispirited.

Hitler waved away all caviling. The attack would go forward, as ordered, "recklessly to the sea, regardless of the risk."

Swirling fog lifted and descended with stage-curtain melodrama in the balmy small hours of August 7. Shortly after one A.M., American pickets reported a spatter of rifle fire, followed by the distinctive growl of panzers on the hunt. Then the attack slammed against the 30th Division front in scalding, scarlet gusts: 26,000 Germans in the first echelon, with 120 tanks crewed by men in black uniforms evocative of the old imperial cavalry. Machine guns cackled, and the percussive boom of tank main guns rippled up and down the line. American howitzers barked back, firing by earshot at bent shadows barely a thousand yards ahead. GIs scrambled among firing positions to simulate greater numbers; pockets here and there were cut off in what one soldier described as "an all-gone feeling." Wounded men mewed in the night.

Almost nothing went right in the German attack. A stricken Allied fighter-bomber smashed into the lead tank of the 1st SS Panzer Division, blocking the column for hours. Only three of six enemy spearheads surged forward on time. The right wing, anchored by the 116th Panzer Division, hardly budged; the commander would be sacked for "uninspired and negative" leadership. Of three hundred Luftwaffe fighters promised for the battle, not one reached the front.

The German weight fell heaviest on St.-Barthélemy, a crossroads two miles north of Mortain. Aiming at muzzle flashes, U.S. tank destroyer crews here demolished a Panther with a 3-inch slug at fifty yards, then another at thirty yards; both slewed across the road, burning with white fury. GIs at one roadblock let the panzers roll through, then butchered the grenadiers trailing behind. The 1st Battalion of the 117th Infantry suffered 350 casualties and retired to a hillside a thousand yards west of St.-Barthélemy, but the German offensive had been delayed six hours, with forty panzers soon crippled. Meanwhile, at the Abbaye Blanche, a twelfth-century stone heap just north of Mortain, a platoon of sixty-six men with bazookas and artillery repelled an SS regiment. GIs stood fast against tanks, flamethrowers, and grenades. More than sixty enemy vehicles would be knocked out hub-to-hub-to-hub.

Dawn, that pitiless revealer of exigencies, unmasked the German predicament. Four armored divisions—from north to south, the 116th Panzer, the 2nd Panzer, and the 1st and 2nd SS Panzer—stood exposed and blinking in the brilliant sunshine once the fog burned off. "First really large concentration of enemy tanks seen since D-Day," an RAF patrol reported. Typhoon fighter-bombers soon scalded the German ranks with two thousand 60-pound rockets and 20mm cannon rounds the size of tent pegs. Joined by cab ranks of Thunderbolts and Hurricanes, the planes attacked until dusk in a shark-feed frenzy.

"Hundreds of German troops began spilling out into the road to spring for the open fields and hedgerows," a Typhoon pilot reported. Only a few dozen tanks and trucks were actually demolished from the air, and more than a few sorties mistakenly hit American revetments. But scores of other vehicles were abandoned under the onslaught or were wrecked by field artillery: a dozen battalions—144 tubes—raked the two roads leading west from St.-Barthélemy. A panzer corps headquarters described the attacks as "well-nigh unendurable," and Seventh Army on August 7 conceded that "the actual attack has been at a standstill since 1300 hours."

The only exception to the "exceptionally poor start," as Seventh Army described the offensive, was a narrow advance of four miles by the 2nd Panzer Division in the north, and the successful seizure of Mortain by the 2nd SS Panzer Division. Das Reich had struck at three A.M. on Monday in three columns, overrunning a roadblock to the south, capturing antitank guns to the north, and infiltrating through the 120th Infantry with help from two traitorous French guides. Wraiths in coal-scuttle helmets darted down the village streets, kicking in doors and poking through cellars. Thirty officers and men from the 2nd Battalion command post tiptoed out a back exit of the Hôtel de la Poste to hide in a house four hundred yards away. Most, including the battalion commander and a soldier armed only with an ax, would later be captured by the Germans while trying to creep off, though half a dozen escaped detection for a week, living on garden vegetables and food pilfered from the local hospital larder. A radioed query from the 30th Division headquarters six miles to the west—"What does your situation look like down there?"—drew a spare reply: "Looks like hell."

It also looked like hell from Hill 314, but at least the view was majestic. Lieutenant Weiss, with his field glasses and Signal Corps radio, had called in his first fire mission at six A.M., shooting only by sound and by map coordinates after sentries reported four hundred enemy troops scrabbling up the east slope. From a stone outcropping on the hill's southern lip, among scrub pines and the animal fragrance of summer pastures, Weiss soon saw columns of German soldiers threading the plain below, including bicycle troops with rifles slung across their shoulders. Again he murmured incantations into the radio handset. Moments later, rushing shells fell in splashes of fire and the singing fragments that gunners called Big Iron. German mortar and 88mm shells answered, pummeling Montjoie's rocky shoulders. Late in the afternoon Weiss radioed, "Enemy N, S, E, W." During a rare lull, one GI later wrote, "No birds were singing. No leaves were moving. No wind was blowing."

Nor were the Germans advancing. Artillery curtains directed from Hill 314 paralyzed Das Reich, kept the 17th SS Panzer Grenadier Division from scaling the hill, and prevented a collapse of the 30th Division's southern flank. White phosphorus forced enemy troops into the open, where they frantically brushed the burning flakes from skin and uniform; high-explosive shells then cut them to scraps. By nightfall, the German offensive had stalled completely; five divisions had been unable to punch through a single American division with fewer than six thousand infantrymen. "If only the Germans will go on attacking at Mortain for a few more days," Montgomery cabled Brooke that evening, "it seems that they might not be able to get away."

In this the enemy complied. Positions changed little on Tuesday, August 8, another pellucid day for killing, both on the wing and by observed artillery fire. Guns crashed and heaved around the clock. "Bruised them badly," Weiss radioed after one fire mission left spiraling smoke columns visible for miles. Although convinced that the offensive had failed, Kluge told his lieutenants, "We have to risk everything."

For four more days, Hill 314 remained what a German officer called a "thorn in the flesh." Hitler on August 9 again demanded that "the Allied invasion front be rolled up" with a renewed lunge toward Avranches by an improvised strike force under the Fifth Panzer Army commander, General Heinrich Eberbach. Arriving on the battlefield with little more than a radio truck, Eberbach told Kluge that the task was both impossible and "very unpleasant." At 6:20 P.M. that Wednesday, an SS officer scrambled up Montjoie under a white flag to demand the Americans capitulate within ninety minutes or be "blown to bits." Wounded GIs in slit trenches yelled, "No, no, don't surrender," and the senior officer on the hill, 1st Lieutenant Ralph A. Kerley, a lanky Texan, sent the envoy packing with a string of profanities. Five artillery battalions shattered a subsequent attack by bellowing Germans who fired machine guns and flicked grenades. Kerley called down one fire mission on his own command post. The field-gray tide receded.

Each night more slain soldiers on Hill 314 were tucked into makeshift morgues among the rocks after their bodies were searched for food and ammunition. Officers hoped that in removing the dead from sight they would bolster morale, but Montjoie reeked of men transformed into carrion. Each day Lieutenant Weiss set his precious radio batteries on a rocky shelf and let the sun recharge them a bit. Foragers filled canteens from a scummy cistern and found turnips, cabbages, and a few rabbits in a hutch. An effort to shoot medical supplies to the hilltop garrison in empty artillery smoke shells failed: G-forces shattered morphine syrettes and plasma bottles, and even crushed surgical tape into flat disks. A dozen C-47s using blue and orange parachutes sprinkled rations and other supplies over the hillcrest at 4:30 P.M. on August 10, but half the bundles drifted beyond the American perimeter into no-man's-land. On the night of August 11, the frustrated 30th Division chief of staff declared, "I want Mortain demolished. . . . Burn it up so nothing can live there." Artillery scourged the village like brimstone.

And then the battle ended. Even Hitler acknowledged futility. "The attack failed," he said ominously, "because Field Marshal von Kluge wanted it to fail." Sitting at a table in La Roche–Guyon with a map spread before him, Kluge tapped Avranches with his finger and said, "This is where I lose my reputation as a soldier." Before dawn on August 12, German columns skulked off to the north and east. A relief regiment from the 35th Division hiked up Hill 314 to carry off 300 dead and wounded; another 370 men walked down, including Lieutenants Weiss and Kerley. The 30th Division alone had suffered 1,800 casualties in the six-day brawl for Mortain, and other units together tallied almost as many.

Survivors would be fed, decorated, and returned to the fight. American artillery had once again displayed the killing prowess that had made it the king of battle since the Boston bookseller Henry Knox turned to gunnery in the Revolution. Here too the U.S. Army had asserted a dominance on the battlefield—with firepower, tenacity, and a credible display of combined arms competence—that would only intensify over the next eight months, as the European campaign grew ever more feverish.

French civilians returning to wrecked Mortain "stood crying and rocking back and forth, as though in prayer," a witness reported. GIs made puns about whether yet another town had been liberated or "ob-liberated." Lieutenant Weiss, a dutiful son, sat down and scribbled his mother a letter on August 13. "Not much to write home about from here," he told her. "You know more about what goes on than we do."

Ultra's big ears had given the Allied high command a clear sense of German intentions since before the onset of the Mortain offensive on August 7. Decrypted enemy radio transmissions were neither timely nor detailed enough to forewarn the 30th Division, but intercepted messages soon disclosed both Kluge's battle plan and the obstacles to executing it. A decrypt on August 10 revealed that a renewed attack toward Avranches likely would begin the next day. Kluge's order had carried a plaintive ring: the "decisive thrust *must* lead to success."

Encouraged by Eisenhower, Bradley kept most of Third Army galloping east toward Le Mans, convinced that airpower and Collins's VII Corps could blunt the German offensive even if the "decisive thrust" squeezed past Mortain. During a press briefing near Colombières, Ernest Hemingway asked Bradley about a rumor that he had wagered Patton $100 on who would reach Paris first. A startled Bradley replied, "I am General Patton's commanding officer and I don't think it would be very sporting for me to make such a bet. Besides you can surely understand that we are not talking in terms of Paris yet."

Certainly they were thinking of it. Allied forces now occupied one-tenth of France's landmass and straddled the main roads to the French capital from the west. The longer the Germans "obstinated" at Mortain, in Churchill's expression, the greater the chance to encircle two German field armies comprising more than 100,000 troops. From his left wing on August 7, Montgomery had launched the Canadian First Army in a drive southeast toward Falaise with a strike force that included fifteen hundred bombers and half as many tanks. Bofors gun tracers marked the axis of attack through dust and smoke, and searchlights bouncing off the low clouds created artificial moonlight. The attack purchased nine miles before stalling in confusion halfway to Falaise—"the blind leading the blind," in one colonel's assessment. Fifty 88mm antitank guns punished the attacking tanks; more air fratricide inflicted three hundred Allied casualties, many in the new Polish 1st Armored Division. SS troops encouraged German defenders at pistol point with cries of, "Push on, you dogs!"

As this unspooled, Bradley was once again poring over the maps in his trailer, now with mounting excitement. On August 8, during a roadside K-ration lunch near Coutances with Eisenhower, who was touring the battlefield in a Packard Clipper driven by Kay Summersby, Bradley proposed curtailing Patton's wide envelopment. Instead, both First and Third Armies would wheel to the north; Patton would make a sharp left turn at Le Mans, driving sixty miles through Alençon to Sées. The Canadians would press on for twenty-two miles through Falaise and Argentan to meet their American cousins, cinch the sack, and trap more than twenty German divisions.

An exuberant Eisenhower followed Bradley back to his command post, where a quick telephone call enlisted Montgomery's support. Patton was dubious, halfheartedly arguing on the phone for continuing east in a more audacious envelopment that would bag the enemy between the rivers Seine at Paris and Loire at Orléans. When Bradley persisted, Patton capitulated, ordering his XV Corps to pivot north from Le Mans. "If I were on my own," he wrote Bea, "I would take bigger chances than I am now permitted to take."

Montgomery issued a formal directive, ordering the Canadians to secure Falaise. "This is a first priority, and it should be done quickly." In a message to inspirit "the United Armies in France," he asked that the Almighty "make us ministers of Thy chastisement."

Bradley continued to chortle at German obduracy in Mortain, the "greatest tactical blunder I've heard of." To a visitor he said: "This is an opportunity that comes to a commander not more than once in a century. We're about to destroy an entire hostile army."

Rarely does a battle follow the tidy arrows that have been sketched on a map or limned in a commander's imagination. The mighty struggle for the Falaise Pocket was no exception. Several factors prevented the enemy annihilation envisioned by the Allied high command, including miscalculation, confusion, and dull generalship. Not least among the variables was a German reluctance to be annihilated.

In the south, Third Army's drive began well enough under Major General Wade Haislip's XV Corps. Two armored divisions abreast led two infantry divisions against fitful resistance. The French 2nd Armored Division, kitted out with U.S. Army tanks, captured intact the bridges at Alençon on August 12. With Argentan as the day's objective, although it lay a dozen miles inside the British 21st Army Group sector, Haislip ordered the French commander, Major General Jacques Philippe Leclerc, to bend west. That would free the highway north from Sées for the U.S. 5th Armored Division, giving greater heft to the Allied attack. Evincing an attitude of *je m'en foutisme*—I don't give a fuck—Leclerc instead fanned out on all available roads, blocking passage of 5th Armored fuel trucks and giving the Germans six hours to rally sixty panzers from Mortain into a sector previously held by a rearguard bakery company.

Patton was peeved but undeterred. With XV Corps sporting three hundred tanks, twenty-two artillery battalions, and complete air domination, he ordered Haislip to bowl through the German blockade, then "push on slowly until you contact our allies" near Falaise. Patton phoned Bradley early Sunday afternoon, August 13, to report his progress. "Shall we continue," he said with coarse humor, "and drive the British into the sea for another Dunkirk?"

But Bradley had heard things go bump in the night. He now issued the most controversial order of his long career. "Nothing doing," he told

Patton. "Don't go beyond Argentan. Stop where you are and build up on that shoulder." The Canadian pincer from the north had made no headway, and Bradley wrongly believed—on the basis of sketchy Ultra reports and faulty intuition—that at least nineteen German divisions had begun stampeding eastward to escape the Allied trap. If that was true, then Haislip's corps risked destruction by pushing north with an exposed left flank. Montgomery also felt perturbations at the American vulnerability, but as Bradley later wrote, "I did not consult with Montgomery. The decision to stop Patton was mine alone." Patton argued to no avail, then told his diary that Haislip could "easily advance to Falaise and completely close the gap. . . . This halt is a great mistake." A Third Army staff officer noted, "The General is beside himself."

Canadian difficulties further unstitched the Allied master plan. Not until August 14 did the Canadian First Army finally gather its four divisions for an attack toward Falaise. Montgomery's contempt for the Canadian army commander, General Harry D. G. Crerar, a chain-smoker with a hacking cough and recurrent dysentery, had only intensified in recent weeks. "I fear he thinks he is a great soldier," Montgomery had recently written Brooke. "He took over command at 1200 hours on 23 July. He made his first mistake at 1205 hours, and his second after lunch."

Worse yet, the Germans on August 13 had found detailed battle plans on the body of a Canadian officer killed after blundering into their lines; forewarned, the enemy shifted dozens of antitank guns to the avenue of attack. By Tuesday afternoon, August 15, the assault on Falaise had become "a molten fire bath of battle," as the Canadian Scottish Regiment war diary recorded. Fratricide once again shredded the ranks: only belatedly did anyone realize that the yellow smoke used by Canadian soldiers to signify friendly positions was the same color used by British Bomber Command to mark targets. "The more the troops burnt yellow flares to show their positions," the British official history recorded, "the more the errant aircraft bombed them." The consequent four hundred casualties, plus washboard terrain and "dust like I've never seen before," as one commander lamented, meant the Canadians would not reach Falaise until Wednesday. Even then, thirteen miles separated them from the Americans.

Bradley now made another momentous decision. Perhaps to mollify the restless, sulking Patton, and without consulting Montgomery, he agreed to dispatch more than half of Haislip's combat power—two divisions and fifteen artillery battalions—toward Dreux, sixty-five miles to the east. In his August 15 order, Bradley wrote:

> Due to the delay in closing the gap between Argentan and Falaise, it
> is believed that many of the German divisions which were in the pocket

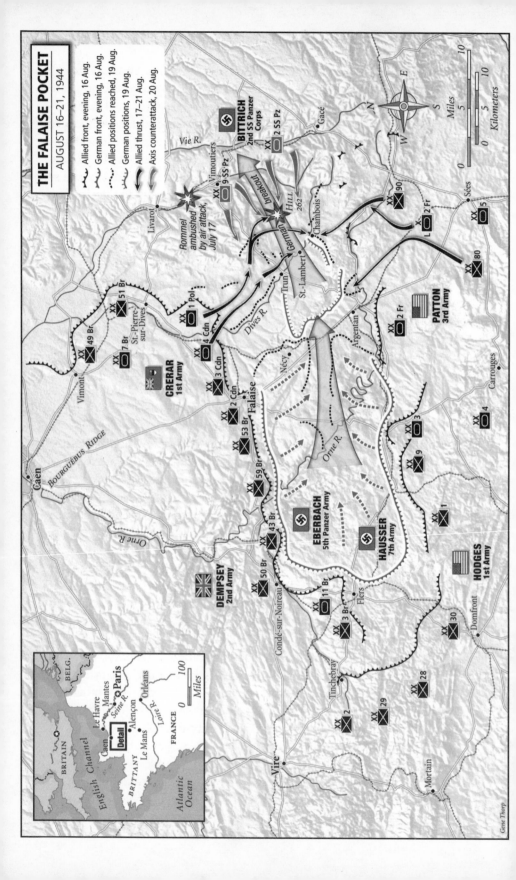

THE FALAISE POCKET

AUGUST 16–21, 1944

- ⌒⌒⌒ Allied front, evening, 16 Aug.
- ⌒⌒⌒ German front, evening, 16 Aug.
- ····· Allied positions reached, 19 Aug.
- ⌒⌒⌒ German positions, 19 Aug.
- → Allied thrust, 17–21 Aug.
- ⇒ Axis counterattack, 20 Aug.

BITTRICH
2nd SS Panzer Corps

2 SS Pz

9 SS Pz

Rommel ambushed
by air attack,
July 17

breakout

HILL
262

German

Chambois

St.-Lambert

Trun

Vimoutiers

Gacé

Sées

90

2 Fr

L

80

PATTON
3rd Army

2 Fr

Argentan

Vie R.

Livarot

Dives R.

Nécy

Orne R.

5

5

4

3

9

1

CRERAR
1st Army

51 Br

49 Br

7 Br

St.-Pierre-
sur-Dives

1 Pol.

4 Cdn

3 Cdn

2 Cdn

Falaise

53 Br

59 Br

43 Br

50 Br

11 Br

3 Br

Vimont

BOURGUÉBUS RIDGE

Caen

Orne R.

DEMPSEY
2nd Army

Condé-sur-Noireau

EBERBACH
5th Panzer Army

HAUSSER
7th Army

Flers

HODGES
1st Army

Domfront

Carrouges

30

1

28

29

2

Tinchebray

Vire

Mortain

N
E
S
W

Miles

Kilometers

10
10
5
5
0
0

Detail

FRANCE

BRITAIN

English Channel

BELG.

Le Havre
Mantes
Caen
Paris
Seine R.
Alençon
Orléans
Le Mans
Loire R.

BRITTANY

Atlantic
Ocean

Miles

0   100

Gene Thorp

have now escaped. . . . In order to take advantage of the confusion existing, the Third Army will now initiate a movement towards the east.

In fact, no German divisions had yet tried to escape; Hitler still would not permit it. To reinforce a wide envelopment toward Paris—Patton's original proposal—Bradley weakened the shorter envelopment that he personally had designed. Nor was he confident in his course. "For the first and only time during the war," he later confessed, "I went to bed that evening worrying over a decision I had already made."

The two most senior Allied field commanders, Montgomery and Bradley, had made a hash of things. Neither recognized that German forces facing the callow Canadians and Poles were more formidable than those facing the Americans, because the latter had been weakened by COBRA and at Mortain. Montgomery failed to reinforce Crerar with the veteran British legions at his disposal; he also made little effort to confirm that he and Bradley fully understood each other. From his command-post menagerie near Vire, atwitter with "squeaking and scuffling" canaries in their cages, Montgomery evinced his usual sangfroid without imparting either urgency or command omniscience. "These are great days," he wrote a friend on August 14. "Some [Germans] will of course escape, but I do not see how they can stand and fight seriously again this side of the Seine."

Bradley was quick to fault Montgomery for various sins, including failure to move the army group boundary north of Argentan, as well as neglect in requesting American help to seal the pocket. Yet he had been niggardly in offering that help and slippery in not disclosing his diversion of XV Corps to the east. Having recently read Douglas Southall Freeman's masterful *Lee's Lieutenants*, Bradley professed that "the one quality all the great generals had in common was their understanding." But such battlefield clairvoyance, which he had occasionally displayed as a corps commander in Tunisia and Sicily, often eluded him as an army group commander. The historian Russell F. Weigley later would lament "the absence of sustained operational forethought and planning on the part of both the principal allies."

Nor was Eisenhower much help. The supreme commander had proved an indifferent field marshal in Tunisia, on Sicily, and during the planning for Anzio; now at Falaise he continued in that deficiency, watching passively for more than a week without recognizing or rectifying the command shortcomings of his two chief lieutenants. Four armies—British Second, Canadian First, and U.S. First and Third—seemed only loosely hinged together. "Ike [was] fashionably garbed in suntans with Egyptian suede shoes and Kay was similarly dressed, making the rest of us look dull and dirty in comparison," an officer in Bradley's headquarters wrote after one mid-August visit. A British general later concluded, with more regret than censure, "He never really got the feel of the battle."

Whatever shortcomings vexed the Allied high command, they paled when stacked against the German fiasco. Dozens of tanks, assault guns, and artillery pieces stood immobile for lack of fuel. General Eberbach told Kluge on August 14 that three of his panzer divisions totaled only seventy tanks and that the 9th Panzer Division "has the strength of a company." Even SS troops were straggling. "Such tiredness," a German commander said later. "It caused hallucinations." For every five German casualties in the west since June 6, only one replacement had arrived. Kluge's headquarters warned the high command: "It is five minutes before midnight."

Then Kluge vanished. After a conference with Sepp Dietrich near Bernay, the field marshal left in his Horch at ten A.M. on August 15 to meet Eberbach and other field commanders at Nécy, six miles south of Falaise. He never arrived. "Ascertain whereabouts Kluge," Hitler's headquarters demanded. "Report results hourly." Berlin indelicately asked whether the field marshal might have defected.

Shortly before midnight he appeared at Eberbach's command post west of Argentan, disheveled and filthy. Fighter-bombers had strafed the Horch and two radio cars that morning, leaving him to cower in a ditch until sunset, then wend his way through snarled traffic. Eberbach told him that Hitler wanted another counterattack, a preposterous pipe dream. "The people there live in another world without any idea of the actual situation," Kluge said, gesturing vaguely toward Berlin. He returned to La Roche–Guyon in a borrowed car and at 2:40 P.M. on Wednesday, August 16, directed Army Group B to begin the retreat from Normandy. Hitler affirmed the decision two hours later.

The order would be Kluge's last. On Thursday, without warning, a short, jowly officer with a keen tactical eye framed by a monocle arrived at La Roche–Guyon with a letter from Hitler authorizing him to replace Kluge. Field Marshal Walter Model, son of a Royal Prussian music director, fancied himself "Hitler's fireman": during three years of service on the Eastern Front he had built a reputation as a soldier who could stabilize the field after defeats and retreats. A caustic, devout Lutheran with an adhesive memory, a taste for French red wine, and a belief in the prodigal use of firing squads for shirkers, Model was bold enough to have once asked a meddler from Berlin, "Who commands the Ninth Army, my Führer, you or I?" His bullying of subordinates led Rundstedt to observe that he had "the makings of a good sergeant." Even Hitler had muttered, "Did you see those eyes? I wouldn't like to serve under him."

Now Model was in command, and no Wehrmacht officer doubted it.

His favorite maxims were: "Can't that be done faster?" and a line from Goethe's *Faust*: *"Den lieb' ich, der Unmögliches begehrt"*—I love the one who craves the impossible. In a conference at Fifth Panzer Army headquarters in Fontaine-l'Abbé, Model told his commanders, "My intention is to withdraw behind the Seine." As the retreat accelerated across the Norman front, two SS panzer divisions would swing southwest from the river to shore up an escape corridor near Trun for forces threatened with encirclement at Falaise. Already under blistering artillery and air attack, much of the German host in the west was at risk. For those who craved the impossible, the hour was ripe.

Legend had it that upon returning from the hunt on a fateful morning in 1027, the seventeen-year-old heir to the Norman duchy, Robert the Magnificent, also known as Robert the Devil, spied a tanner's beautiful daughter with her skirts hiked as she washed linen in a creek below the castle wall at Falaise. The subsequent assignation produced a son, William the Bastard, who survived various assassination plots to rule Normandy for more than half a century, to extend his reign into England in 1066, and to earn a new sobriquet.

By August 17, 1944, nearly a millennium later, the Conqueror's hometown had been so roughly handled that Canadian troops could no longer discern where the streets were laid; bulldozers simply carved a strip four meters wide through the drifted rubble. Bullet holes dinged the hoary castle keep, although the equestrian bronze of William stood intact. The last Tigers had rumbled from the cathedral ruins out the southwest corner of town the previous evening, but not until Friday morning, August 18, would sixty 12th SS diehards be exterminated in the École Supérieure. The only survivors were two teenagers, chosen by lot, who crept away to report that the town had fallen.

The eponymous Falaise Pocket by this time extended twenty miles from west to east and was roughly ten miles wide. Ultra had decrypted Kluge's withdrawal order, correcting Bradley's delusion that the enemy had already fled, and prompting Montgomery at last to ask the Americans to lunge eight miles northeast from Argentan toward Chambois and Trun, where the Poles and Canadians were bound from the northwest in hopes of severing the two roads remaining to the Germans.

Bradley now confessed that he had sent most of XV Corps gamboling far to the east. He ordered Major General Leonard T. Gerow, commander of V Corps within First Army, to cobble together an attack using divisions left behind by Haislip, who was now racing toward Dreux. With three jeeps, nine officers, and a broken radio, Gerow drove sixty miles through teeming rain to arrive after daybreak on August 17 at his new command post in the Hôtel de France in Alençon. Here he found Major General Hugh J. Gaffey, the Third Army chief of staff, poised to attack in an hour under orders from Patton to form a provisional corps with the precise forces Gerow expected to command. After much confused palaver, Major General Gerow rejected Major General Gaffey's battle plan and postponed the attack until Friday morning to await more artillery.

Napoleonic it was not. Montgomery told Brooke at eleven P.M. on August 17 that "the gap has now been closed." That was untrue. He told Churchill, "The enemy cannot escape us." That too was untrue. To a friend he wrote, "I have some 100,000 Germans almost surrounded in the pocket." That was truer, but *almost* would not win the battle, much less the war. Fortunately, even as Allied commanders stumbled about, the reduction of the pocket by soldiers and airmen had begun in earnest. Spitfires, Typhoons, Mustangs, Lightnings, and Thunderbolts flew fifteen hundred to three thousand sorties each day in sanguinary relays from first light to last light. "Since the transports were sometimes jammed together four abreast," an RAF group captain explained, "it made the subsequent rocket and cannon attacks a comparatively easy business." A captured Canadian officer who later escaped described what he had seen on August 18: "Everywhere there were vehicle trains, tanks and vehicles towing what they could. The damage was immense, and flaming transport and dead horses were left in the road while the occupants pressed on, afoot."

Canadian troops on Friday won through to Trun, subsequently described as "an inferno of incandescent ruins." "Shoot *everything*," Montgomery urged them. The next day GIs from the 359th Infantry crept into flaming Chambois, soon dubbed Shambles. An officer reported blood "running in sizeable streams in the gutters." Fleeing Germans had been transformed into "nothing but charcoal in the forms of men" or "vertebrae attended by flies"; a dead driver perched on an artillery caisson still held reins attached to four horses, also dead. Then the Yanks spied Poles from the 10th Dragoons. "An American captain ran towards me," a Polish soldier later recalled, "and still running caught hold of me and lifted me in the air as if I had been a child." Cigarettes and chocolate were shared out, toasts drunk.

With eastbound roads now cut, remnants from nineteen German divisions were largely reduced to cart paths or to slinking cross-country by compass course. Three thousand Allied guns ranged the kill zone, and an artillery battalion commander from the 90th Division told his diary:

> The pocket surrounding the Germans is in the shape of a bowl and from the hills our observers have a perfect view of the valley below. . . . Every living thing or moving vehicle is under constant observation. I

can understand why our forward observers have been hysterical. There is so much to shoot at.

With guidance from aerial spotters, gunners walked white phosphorus and high explosives up and down the enemy ranks. "We always hit something," said one pilot. A German general reported that many of his men were "without headgear, belts, or footwear. Many go barefoot." A staff officer added, "Heavy firing into the sunken road. A tank immediately reversed and ran over some of our men. . . . Someone at the rear started to wave a white flag on a stick. We shot him." That which the gun batteries overlooked, the fighter-bombers found, as pilots squinted for raised dust or the telltale glint of glass beneath the beeches and hornbeams. "I saw a truck crew, sitting on the steps of a farmhouse, dejectedly looking at the burning wreckage of their vehicles in the road," a Spitfire pilot said. "So I shot them up as well." A French farmer escaped the carnage to report, "It seemed as though I was on the stage of the last act of the Valkyrie. We were surrounded by fire."

Two death struggles within the larger apocalypse bore on the battle. At St.-Lambert, a village straddling the river Dives between Trun and Shambles, savage counterattacks by "shouting, grey-clad men" against gutful troops from the Canadian 4th Armored Division raged through Saturday and Sunday, August 19 and 20. Pillars of fire from burning gasoline trucks smudged the heavens; corpses, carcasses, and charred equipment dammed the Dives in "an awful heap" beneath one bitterly contested bridge. "We fired till the machine gun boiled away," a Canadian gunner reported. Improvised German battle groups shot their way through the cordon southeast of St.-Lambert, extracting not only panzers—with grenadiers clinging to the hulls "like burrs"—but also the Fifth Panzer Army command group and assorted generals, including Eberbach, who soon would be given command of Seventh Army.

Three miles northeast, eighteen hundred men from the Polish 1st Armored Division on Friday afternoon had scaled a looming scarp known as Hill 262 but which they named Maczuga—Mace—for its contours on a map. On Sunday morning, after a productive evening disemboweling a surprised German column plodding toward Vimoutiers on the road below, the Poles caught the brunt of an assault by the 2nd and 9th SS Panzer Divisions, summoned by Model from the Seine as his "break-in" force to extricate survivors from the pocket. With low clouds grounding Allied planes for part of the day, Germans swarmed up the wooded slopes "from all the sides in the world," one Pole recalled. Panthers and Shermans traded fire point-blank as the hereditary enemies slaughtered each other with bayonets and grenades into the night and through the next morning; all the while, escaping Germans streamed past the hill mass. A French-Canadian artillery observer, perched on Maczuga with two radios and two hundred guns in range, built a ring of massed fires around the redoubt, just as Lieutenant Weiss had done at Mortain. By the time the Canadian 4th Armored Division broke through on Monday afternoon, 325 Poles lay dead on Maczuga and more than a thousand others had been wounded. Panzers burned like haystacks across the hill, and SS bodies roasted in the grass fires ignited by tracer rounds.

For another day German stragglers died trying to ford the Dives or sneak through the shadows. Others surrendered, shouting *"Merde pour la guerre"*—Shit on the war. "It was more of an execution than a battle," a Canadian gunner said. Several hundred Germans with armored cars and blazing 20mm guns charged through the wheat toward Trun on Monday; a Canadian line of eight Vickers machine guns "shot them down in droves," one soldier recorded. "It lasts a half hour or so." The dead were picked clean of Lugers, daggers, watches, and bloody francs, spread in the sun to dry. An old Frenchman pushing a cart poked a dead German with his foot, the reporter Iris Carpenter wrote, then chortled as he urinated on the body "with the greatest care and deliberation, subjecting each feature in the gray face to equally timed proportions of debasement." Yes, *merde pour la guerre.*

At last the guns fell silent, leaving the battlefield to resemble "one of those paintings of Waterloo or Borodino," wrote Alan Moorehead, who cabled the *Daily Express,* "I think I see the end of Germany from here."

Distances may deceive in war, and the German demise was farther off than he and others realized. The pursuit and annihilation of a beaten foe is among the most difficult military skills to master, as demonstrated from Gettysburg to Alamein; and defeats in Russia, North Africa, and Italy had taught the Wehrmacht how to retreat. Precisely a year earlier, 110,000 Germans and Italians had escaped seemingly sure destruction at Messina.

"All German formations that cross the Seine will be incapable of combat during the months to come," Montgomery promised London. That too was optimistic, and more enemy troops crossed than should have. Alas, no *corps de chasse* nipped at German heels for the forty miles from Vimoutiers to the river.

After liberating Orléans and Chartres on August 16 and 18, respectively, Third Army was ordered to swing below Paris and cross the Seine east of the capital en route to the German frontier. Fuel shortages already required daily emergency airlifts from England, but Eisenhower had ordered his lieutenants to outrun the enemy as he made for home. Of Patton's legions, only XV Corps had swiveled north, crossing the Seine on August 20 by boat, raft, treadway bridge, and a narrow footpath atop a dam near Mantes, thirty miles west of Paris. German blocking forces thwarted efforts to sweep downstream along the riverbank, but GIs managed to overrun La Roche–Guyon after firing mortars and rifle grenades into the courtyard; Model and his staff scurried off to Margival, where Rommel, Rundstedt, and Hitler had met two months earlier.

The Allied victory, though extraordinary, was incomplete. Despite "inextricable confusion," in one German general's phrase, as well as "shootings, threats, and violent measures" by SS toughs who controlled many of the sixty Seine crossing sites, those who escaped the Falaise Pocket mostly escaped Normandy. Two dozen improvised ferries, hidden by day along the oxbow glades, shuttled 25,000 vehicles to the east bank from August 20 to 24. Soldiers unable to book passage nailed together rafts from cider barrels, or pried doors from their hinges and floated them with empty fuel cans. Others lashed saplings with phone wire or clung to the bloated carcass of a dead cow drifting downstream. British intelligence estimated that 95 percent of German troops who reached the river also made the far bank. Estimates of the number escaping the Falaise trap ranged from thirty thousand to more than a hundred thousand; those who got away included four of five corps commanders, twelve of fifteen division commanders, and many capable staff officers. Tens of thousands more who were never within the pocket now joined the retreat across France.

Yet by any measure the defeat at Falaise was profound. Perhaps ten thousand Germans lay dead and fifty thousand more had been captured. Thunderbolts buzzed the roads, herding men waving white flags into prisoner columns. "Life in the cages is pretty crude," an American officer told his diary on August 24. "I heard one soldier tell another that water is being sold at 300 francs per canteen." Among the dead was Marshal Kluge: en route to Berlin after his displacement by Model, he stopped outside Verdun, spread a blanket in the underbrush, and swallowed a cyanide capsule. "When you receive these lines, I shall be no more," he told Hitler in a valedictory note. "The German people have suffered so unspeakably that it is time to bring the horror to a close." The Führer composed his epitaph: "Perhaps he couldn't see any way out. . . . It's like a western thriller."

Allied investigators counted nearly seven hundred tanks and self-propelled guns wrecked or abandoned from Falaise to the river. No Seine ferry could carry a Tiger, and panzers stood scuttled and charred on the docks at Rouen and elsewhere. The tally also included a thousand artillery pieces and twenty-five hundred trucks and cars. Model told Hitler that his panzer and panzer grenadier divisions averaged "five to ten tanks each." Divisions in the Fifth Panzer Army averaged only three thousand men, with barely one-third of their equipment. Army Group B had been demolished, complementing the destruction of Army Group Center in White Russia in June, although many divisions would display a knack for resurrection. As the historian Raymond Callahan later wrote, "The remarkable resurgence of the German army in the autumn obviously owes something forever unquantifiable to the imperfect Allied victory of Falaise."

Eisenhower took a quick tour of the pocket, swinging from Falaise to Trun and as far northeast as Vimoutiers. Two miles from Chambois, he climbed from the staff car and walked through the carnage wrought by his armies. "Indescribable horror and destruction," wrote a lieutenant colonel in his entourage. "German guns and trucks and wagons, bloated dead by the score scattered everywhere." Some were buried on the road verges, their paybooks tacked to crude crosses. A Canadian chaplain reported five thousand others tossed into a bulldozed mass grave at St.-Lambert. Charred corpses in burned-out panzers were dubbed "coal monuments" by Polish troops. British soldiers fired Sten rounds to evacuate gases from still more corpses before they were burned in a pyre. A German officer sat in the rear of a limousine next to his stylish mistress, both dead from cannon shells through the chest. "It was as if," one officer wrote, "an avenging angel had swept the area bent on destroying all things German."

Troops cleansing the pocket wore gas masks to cope with what became known as the "Falaise smell." Corruption even seeped into Spitfire cockpits at fifteen hundred feet. "Everything is dead," wrote Ernie Pyle, who had arrived on August 21. "The men, the machines, the animals—and you alone are left alive." A Canadian executioner with a pistol hiked along a stream bank where dozens of wounded horses "stood patiently waiting to die in the water." The labor of clearing eight thousand slaughtered horses and countless cows would keep the bulldozers busy until November; Allied administrators declared the Dives an "unhealthy zone," and drinking water was trucked in for months. Not until 1961 would scrap-metal collectors remove the last battle detritus from the orchards and grain fields.

Norman schoolchildren sang in English to Canadian soldiers, "Thank you for liberating us." The U.S. stock market tumbled in anticipation of peace and falling corporate profits. Reports from southern France suggested that a Franco-American invasion on the Mediterranean coast had pushed the enemy back on his heels. Many recalled November 1918, when the German army had abruptly disintegrated. "It is," Montgomery declared, "the beginning of the end of the war."

That much was true.

The Loveliest Story of Our Time

WARM summer rain drenched the motley legions of liberation at dawn on Thursday, August 24, as three columns from the French 2nd Armored Division made ready for battle twenty miles southwest of Paris. Village women scurried through the bivouacs carrying urns of coffee and platters heaped with fried eggs and breakfast rolls. Soldiers finished shaving with ritualistic precision, then shouldered their weapons and swaggered into formation, "booming like bitterns throughout the wood," as an American colonel later wrote, "pounding their chests and screaming, *'En avant!'*"

Tricolor pennants flew from three thousand vehicles named for Napoleonic triumphs or for French towns now unshackled, like *Caen* and *Cherbourg*. Each tank and scout car bore a white silhouette of France with the cross of Lorraine superimposed. The twelve thousand troops comprised not only French regulars, but sailors far from the sea, Lebanese Christian engineers, and Senegalese riflemen who until three weeks earlier had never set foot on European France. Also in the ranks could be found Spanish Republicans, Gaullists, monarchists, Jews, Muslims, Catholic reactionaries, animists, anarchists, antipapists, communists, socialists, freethinkers, and militant Quakers.

Scores of frisky "warcos"—war correspondents—buzzed about swapping rumors, including a ludicrous report that any procession into Paris must await the arrival of Franklin Roosevelt. Among the scribes was Pyle, wearing a beret that made him resemble Montgomery; also Hemingway, credentialed to *Collier's* magazine but commanding various French cutthroats whom he had ostensibly supplied with tommy guns and pistols and who called him Colonel or *"le grand capitaine."* These irregulars, wrote Robert Capa, could be seen "copying his sailor bear walk, spitting short sentences from the corners of their mouths," while Papa nipped from a canteen of calvados and patted the grenade tucked inside his field jacket, "just in case." Hundreds of other Resistance fighters fell in, including a circus truck of sharpshooters who hissed the day's challenge and parole to one another—"Paris" and "Orléans"—and daydreamed of unfurling a tricolor on the Arc de Triomphe after four years of the stinking swastika.

Astride the road outside Limours, with tank goggles perched on his kepi and clutching the malacca cane he had carried through the war, stood the commander of this unorthodox cavalcade, Philippe François Marie, vicomte de Hauteclocque, who had concocted the nom de guerre of Jacques Philippe Leclerc to prevent reprisals against his wife and six children. Scion of minor gentry from Picardy, lithe and avian with azure eyes and a deep voice, Leclerc cultivated an air of mystery: "Like the Scarlet

Pimpernel [he] is said to have been seen here, there, and everywhere," wrote the OSS operative David Bruce, who was among Leclerc's oddball lieutenants that Thursday morning. Leclerc had been a cavalry captain in June 1940 when he was wounded; he narrowly eluded German capture, escaping by bicycle to southwestern France, then slipping through Spain and Portugal on a forged passport amended with a child's toy printing set. Sent by De Gaulle from London to rally anti-Vichy resistance in central Africa, he reclaimed the Cameroons and Chad for Free France, routed the Italian garrison at Koufra in southern Libya, then marched across the continent with four thousand men and a camel corps in a Kiplingesque anabasis to tender his services to Montgomery at Tripoli in January 1943. He subsequently organized the 2nd Armored Division in Morocco before landing over Utah Beach on August 1, the vanguard of a reborn French army in France. A devout Catholic who received the Eucharist every day, gunplay permitting, Leclerc also evinced a mulish streak that discomfited his ostensible superiors, as when he had snarled the roads at Argentan. Now informed that U.S. intelligence detected five thousand SS troops ready to die for Paris, Leclerc pointed an index finger at heaven and said, "Have no fear, we shall smash them."

En avant, then, *en avant.* Bumper to bumper the columns surged forward at seven A.M., escorted by "a weird assortment of private cars, trucks, motorcycles, and bicycles," Don Whitehead reported. Veterans of the Franco-Prussian War stood at attention on the sidewalks, snapping stiff salutes. Cheering civilians tossed flowers, apples, and tomatoes, and offered tankards of "beer, cider, white and red Bordeaux, white and red Burgundy, champagne, rum, whiskey, cognac, Armagnac, and calvados," David Bruce recorded, "enough to wreck one's constitution."

Or perhaps enough to dull one's martial edge. Ignoring General Gerow's order to enter Paris from the west through Versailles, Leclerc shifted his weight to attack from the south past Arpajon, outrunning his artillery support and inadvertently stumbling into the thickest German perimeter defenses. The lesser, leftmost column punched through St.-Cyr to the intact Pont de Sèvres on the Seine, a few miles from the Eiffel Tower; the Arpajon force, after briefly sprinting at fifty miles an hour, soon battled roadblocks and street ambushes in suburban Massy and Fresnes. By Thursday evening the spearhead remained five miles from the Porte d'Orléans and eight miles from the city's heart. Leclerc had suffered more than 300 casualties, with 35 tanks and 117 other vehicles destroyed.

An irate Gerow complained to Bradley by radio about Leclerc "dancing to Paris" and "advancing on a one-tank front." Equally irked, Bradley ordered the U.S. 4th Infantry Division to outflank the French and "slam on in" to the city from the southeast. Leclerc had a note dropped by spotter plane over central Paris: *"Tenez bon. Nous arrivons."* Hold on. We're coming.

Eisenhower had long planned to bypass Paris to avoid street brawling and because SHAEF logisticians warned that victualing the city would be "equivalent to the maintenance of eight divisions" in combat. But events had forced his hand. Labor strikes began on August 11, first by rail and subway workers, then by the police, three thousand of whom seized the *préfecture* on August 18. Wehrmacht patrols were bushwhacked across the city; ration convoys were hijacked while traveling from train depots. Shootouts left 125 Parisians dead on August 19. The last train carrying Jewish deportees had left Paris for the east on August 15.

De Gaulle, who arrived in Cherbourg on August 20, feared another Warsaw: after a Polish uprising there began on August 1, in errant anticipation of the Red Army's arrival, the Germans had methodically razed the city. Some 35,000 Resistance fighters infested greater Paris as part of a loose organization known as the French Forces of the Interior, or FFI, but their arsenal included only 570 rifles and 820 revolvers. De Gaulle moreover believed an insurrection would strengthen French communists, one of whom, a sheet-metal worker known as Colonel Rol, thundered that "Paris is worth 200,000 dead." Eisenhower had consistently promised De Gaulle that French troops would free the city when the moment ripened; Deux Mètres now not only invoked that pledge but also displayed his genius for "tantrums, sulks, insults, postures, silence, Olympian detachment, political self-righteousness, [and] moral holier-than-thouery," as the historian John Keegan later wrote.

The moment grew riper. As the insurrection intensified, messengers had slipped from the capital, foretelling catastrophe if the Allies did not step in, quickly. Hundreds of skirmishes broke out before a fitful truce took hold, widely ignored by both the SS and the communists. Isolated in enclaves, German defenders built strongpoints and deployed 88mm anti-tank guns on approaches to the city. Parisians resurrected the nineteenth-century art of barricade building, using street cobblestones, manhole covers, upended German trucks, and even a five-hole *pissotière*. Soon more than four hundred such redoubts stippled the city, including barricades with portraits of Hitler propped up like targets. "The pictures of Delacroix and Daumier had been studied not in vain," a postwar account noted, "and some [Parisians] affected the loose neckerchief and shirt unbuttoned to bare the chest." Insurgents stitched FFI armbands and mass-produced Molotov cocktails with champagne bottles; the lightly wounded wore arm slings fashioned from Hermès scarves. "For every Parisian, a Boche," communist placards urged. A clandestine radio station

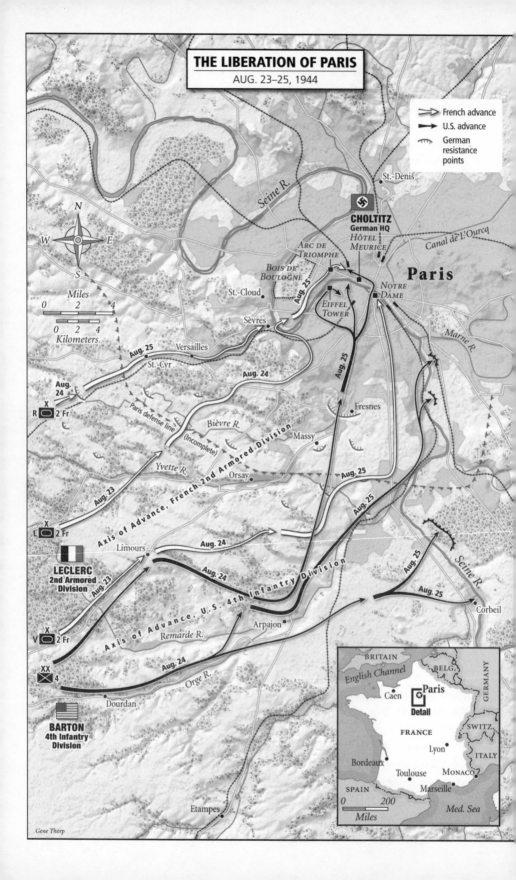

THE LIBERATION OF PARIS

AUG. 23–25, 1944

French advance
U.S. advance
German resistance points

St.-Denis

Seine R.

✡ CHOLTITZ
German HQ

HÔTEL
MEURICE

ARC DE
TRIOMPHE

Canal de L'Ourcq

BOIS DE
BOULOGNE

St.-Cloud

Paris

NOTRE
DAME

Aug. 25

Sèvres

EIFFEL
TOWER

Marne R.

Miles
0   2   4

Kilometers
0   2   4

Versailles

St.-Cyr

Aug. 25

Aug. 24

Aug. 25

Aug.
24

X
R ◼ 2 Fr

Paris defense line

Bièvre R.

(Incomplete)

Fresnes

Yvette R.

Massy

Orsay

Aug. 25

Aug. 23

Axis of Advance, French 2nd Armored Division

Aug. 25

X
L ◼ 2 Fr

Seine R.

LECLERC
2nd Armored
Division

Limours

Aug. 24

Aug. 24

Aug. 25

Axis of Advance, U.S. 4th Infantry Division

Aug. 23

Aug. 25

X
V ◼ 2 Fr

Aug. 24

Remarde R.

Arpajon

Corbeil

XX
◼ 4

Aug. 24

Orge R.

BARTON
4th Infantry
Division

Dourdan

Etampes

Gene Thorp

BRITAIN

English Channel

BELG.

GERMANY

Caen

Paris
Detail

FRANCE

SWITZ.

Bordeaux

Lyon

ITALY

Toulouse

MONACO

SPAIN

Marseille

0   200

Miles

Med. Sea

played "La Marseillaise," banned for four years; Parisians turned up the volume and opened their windows. "I have the feeling," a German sergeant wrote his wife, "things are going to get bad here fast." Another envoy, a plump Swedish ball-bearing factory manager named Raoul Nordling, told Bradley that at least some German authorities hoped for an Allied intervention before scorched-earth reprisals became inevitable.

By Tuesday, August 22, Eisenhower had relented. "If the enemy tries to hold Paris with any real strength," the supreme commander told the Combined Chiefs, "he would be a constant menace to our flank." Ambiguous intelligence suggested a German withdrawal. "It looks now as if we'd be compelled to go into Paris," Eisenhower wrote Beetle Smith. "Bradley and his G-2 think we can and *must* walk in."

Some Germans were indeed decamping. Hitler authorized the departure of clerks and police apparatchiks. One journalist described how "Gestapo small fry in gabardine raincoats" crowded the train stations along with "gray mice," uniformed German females. Ash from burning documents drifted around the Hôtel de Talleyrand and the Bois de Boulogne. Vindictive soldiers smashed hospital elevators and clogged the plumbing with concrete, then stripped foliage from boulevard trees to camouflage trucks piled high with bidets, carpets, and other loot. "We'll be back for Christmas," they shouted. Parisians, who for four years had so painstakingly avoided eye contact that Germans joked about "*la ville sans regard*"—the city that never looks at you—now jeered and flourished toilet brushes at their departing occupiers.

With his main thrust delayed by skirmishers, General Leclerc dispatched a force with three Shermans and sixteen half-tracks through the back streets of southern Paris at dusk on August 24. Up the Avenue d'Italie the detachment darted, through spattering picket fire near the Gare d'Austerlitz. Seeing the five-pointed white star on the Sherman hulls, Parisians shrieked, "*Les Américains!*" Soon the truth would out: these troops were France's own. Citizens opened barricades along the Seine and a radio broadcast from the Hôtel de Ville announced, "Rejoice! The Leclerc Division has entered Paris! . . . Tell all the priests to ring their church bells."

From a balcony of the Hôtel Meurice, on the Rue de la Rivoli overlooking the Tuileries gardens, a chubby elf in a German general's uniform stood listening to the consequent pealing, punctuated by a deep, fatidic toll from Notre Dame. Thick of body and short of leg, with a dimpled cowcatcher chin and hocks for cheeks, General Dietrich von Choltitz was considered a *ganz Harter*—a tough guy—for his role in obliterating Rotterdam in 1940 and Sevastopol two years later; for those actions he was nicknamed "the Smasher of Cities." As a corps commander in Normandy, Choltitz had seen his force routed in COBRA before he was assigned to Paris under Hitler's edict that the city "must not fall into the hands of the enemy except as a field of ruins." A Saxon whose forebears had soldiered for eight centuries, he had told the Swede Nordling, "It has been my fate to cover the retreat of our armies and to destroy the cities behind them." On Sunday he sent a note to his wife in Germany, along with coffee requisitioned from the Meurice kitchen: "Our task is hard and our days grow difficult."

With only twenty thousand men to hold a city of three million, Choltitz had no illusions about the outcome of the imminent battle. "The enemy has now recognized our weakness," he told Model. But reducing the City of Light to Hitler's field of ruins held little appeal even for the *ganz Harter,* and he had temporized with skill, guile, and perhaps conscience. "Ever since our enemies have refused to listen to and obey our Führer," he told his staff with a sardonic glint, "the whole war has gone badly." While encouraging Nordling and others to put spurs to the Allies, Choltitz played for time by concocting elaborate, largely imaginary plans to destroy bridges, utilities, and two hundred factories. He told superiors of placing explosives by the ton in Les Invalides, the Opéra, and other public buildings; demolitionists would level the Arc de Triomphe for enhanced fields of fire and dynamite the Eiffel Tower "as a wire entanglement to block the Seine." All the while he urged "a prudent and intelligent attitude" from his troops while trying to play Resistance factions off against one another and hoping for reinforcements. Now, in a phone call to Army Group B headquarters, he held the receiver overhead. "Will you listen, please?" Choltitz said. "Do you hear that? It is bells. . . . What they are telling this city is that the Allies are here."

Just so. By ten on Friday morning, August 25, Leclerc managed to slide his entire division into town, tank tracks shedding sparks as they clipped across the cobbles. Two hours later, the 4th Division's 12th Infantry reached Notre Dame, then clattered through the eastern precincts. Despite vicious firefights at the Quai d'Orsay and elsewhere, crowds lined the sidewalk twenty deep, baying *"Vive la France"* in a hallucinatory admixture of celebration and gunfire. Anticipating something wondrous, women curled their hair and pressed their finest dresses. At 12:30 the national colors flew from the Eiffel Tower for the first time since June 1940; ninety minutes later, firemen unfurled the tricolor from the Arc de Triomphe. Animals set loose from a local circus scampered down the Champs-Élysées. So many Parisians pulled uniforms from storage in a rush to join the FFI that they were dubbed *Naphtalinés,* for their strong scent of mothballs.

"The rip tide of courage," in one GI's phrase, proved stirring and strong. Volunteer nurses in white smocks darted through bullet-swept streets to carry bloody litters to safety. At a traffic circle, where artillery fire splintered a chestnut tree and snipers took potshots, French half-tracks and tanks raced round and round, pumping "not less than five thousand bullets" into adjacent buildings. Resistance fighters in automobiles combed Parisian parks, firing at enemy bivouacs from the rumble seats. Police watched subway exits for fleeing Germans; "those who come out," a U.S. Army report noted, "are massacred or made prisoners." Five hundred Germans at the Chamber of Deputies surrendered to a Signal Corps photographer, and negotiations at some strongholds were conducted in Yiddish, the closest common language. Wehrmacht troops emerging with hands raised from the Hôtel Continental had the Iron Crosses ripped from their necks, while GIs ordered those captured in the Crillon to check their weapons in the cloakroom. On this feast day of St. Louis, who died in Tunis while crusading in 1270, most Parisians ate lunch at the usual hour.

Choltitz dined too, on Sèvres china with silver candlesticks in the elegant Meurice dining room. "Germany's lost the war," he told his staff, "and we have lost it with her." Upstairs his orderly packed a valise with three shirts, underwear, socks. At table, a lieutenant recalled, the general and his staff were "silent from the effort of showing no emotions." When asked to move away from the window to avoid stray bullets fired from the Louvre across the street, Choltitz replied, "No, particularly not today." But as the gunfire intensified he at last pushed away his plate. "Gentlemen, our last combat has begun." He stood to go wash and don a fresh uniform.

Just down the street, fighting swept through the Place de la Concorde, where the guillotine had removed more than a thousand heads during the Revolution, including those of Louis XVI, Marie Antoinette, and Robespierre. Five Sherman tanks sent to assault the Meurice were soon knocked out, but two hundred French infantrymen trotted under the arcade fronting the Rue de la Rivoli. Lieutenant Henri Karcher bolted into the Meurice lobby, flinging a smoke grenade from behind the reception desk, while a soldier scorched the elevator cage with a flamethrower. Upstairs an FFI fighter burst into an office and demanded of the portly figure sitting behind a table, "*Sprechen deutsch?*" "Yes," Choltitz replied, "probably better than you do." Karcher arrived to declare, "You are my prisoner."

A furious mob punched and spat at the Germans, snatching spectacles, watches, and shoulder boards as the erstwhile occupiers were herded through the street. At three P.M. Choltitz arrived at the Préfecture, where Leclerc also had been dining on china and a white tablecloth. They retired to the billiard room; Choltitz adjusted his monocle, then signed the formal surrender of Paris. Bundled into an armored car, he sat bowed and silent in the rear while a triumphant Leclerc stood in front like a centurion in his chariot. At the 2nd Armored command post, abutting platform No. 3 in the Gare Montparnasse, Choltitz signed another document ordering his remaining strongpoints to cease fire. He then requested a glass of water. Asked whether he intended to swallow poison, he replied, "Oh, no. We don't do things like that."

Teams of French and German officers carried white flags and copies of the cease-fire through the city. In a final redoubt at the Palais du Luxembourg, 700 Wehrmacht soldiers each received a pint of cognac and a pack of cigarettes; then, at 7:35 P.M., the gates swung open and their commander marched out beneath a huge white flag, followed by his troops and ten panzers. All told, 15,000 German soldiers were bagged in Paris—many would be confined for days in the Louvre courtyard—with another 4,200 killed or wounded.

"German spoken" signs vanished from shop fronts, sometimes replaced by Resistance placards that warned, "Supplier of the Boche." Collaborators were pelted with eggs, tomatoes, and sacks of excrement; shorn women, stripped to the waist, had swastikas painted on their breasts and placards hung around their necks: "I whored with the Boches." An American sergeant barked at a mob shearing yet another wretch, "Leave her alone, goddamn you. You're all collaborationists." *Le Figaro* resumed publication of a daily feature called "Arrests and Purges." Rough justice flourished, the equivalent of that guillotine in the Place de la Concorde. The historian Robert Aron later calculated that as many as forty thousand summary executions of collaborators and other miscreants took place across France, "a figure sufficiently high to create a psychosis that will remain forever in the memories of the survivors." Some 900,000 French men and women would be arrested in the *épuration*—the purge—of whom 125,000 were forced to answer in court for their behavior during the occupation. Those guilty of *indignité nationale* served prison terms, while those convicted of *dégradation nationale* were banned from government jobs.

At ten P.M., the first of an eventual eighteen hundred Allied counterintelligence agents set up a command post in the Petit Palais. "T Force," mimicking a similar unit in Rome, had amassed the names of eighty thousand suspected spies, saboteurs, and villains in France, as well as thick dossiers on Gestapo and SS facilities. Eighty-four of those listed were collared that very day. Among the more wrenching discoveries would be three windowless torture cells in a German barracks, where condemned prisoners had scratched messages in charcoal or pencil. "Gaston Meaux, my time is up, leaves five children, may God have pity on them," read one; another, simply: "Revenge me." Alan Moorehead quoted a Parisian as saying, "I'll tell you what liberation is. It's hearing a knock on my door at six o'clock in the morning and knowing it's the milkman."

Such sobriety could not suppress "a great city where everybody is happy," in A. J. Liebling's judgment. "I never in my life been kissed so much," a sergeant wrote his parents in Minnesota. Another GI climbed three flights of stairs to visit a bedridden Frenchwoman who had pleaded to see an American before she died. "The cobblestones, the flapping signs in red and gold over the pavement cafés . . . three golden horse heads over the horse butcher, the *flics* with their flat blue kepis," Moorehead wrote. "Had we ever been away?" Leclerc's men seized a train before it departed for Germany with treasures from the Jeu de Paume in 148 packing cases: 64 Picassos, 29 Braques, 24 Dufys, 11 Vlamincks, 10 Utrillos, and works by Degas, Cézanne, Gauguin, and Renoir. The Bank of France cellars were found to hold 400,000 bottles of cognac, 3 million cigars, and 235 tons of sugar.

An American patrol arrived at the Claridge to be told by the manager, "This hotel is under lease to the officer corps of the German army." A colonel drew his .45 and said, "You've got just thirty seconds to get it unleased. We're moving in." Hemingway, pulling up to the Ritz with two truckloads of his French irregulars, told the bartender, "How about seventy-three dry martinis?" Later, after he and several companions had dined on soup, creamed spinach, raspberries in liqueur, and Perrier-Jouët champagne, the waiter added the Vichy tax to the bill, explaining, "It's the law." No matter: "We drank. We ate. We glowed," one of Hemingway's comrades reported. Private Irwin Shaw of the 12th Infantry, who later won fame as a writer, believed that August 25 was "the day the war should have ended."

To Ernie Pyle, ensconced in a hotel room with a soft bed though no hot water or electricity, "Paris seems to have all the beautiful girls we have always heard it had. . . . They dress in riotous colors." The liberation, he concluded, was "the loveliest, brightest story of our time."

De Gaulle entered the city late Friday afternoon by car down the Avenue d'Orléans, "gripped by emotion and filled with serenity," in his words. At five P.M. he made his way to the War Ministry in the Rue St.-Dominique, whence he had fled on June 10, 1940. All was unchanged— the heavy furniture, the ushers, the names on the phone extension buttons, even the blotting paper. "Nothing was missing except the state," De Gaulle later wrote. From a balcony at the Hôtel de Ville he proclaimed, "Paris outraged, Paris broken, Paris martyred, but Paris liberated. Liberated by herself, liberated by her people, with the help of the whole of France." He uttered hardly a word about the Americans, British, Canadians, or Poles, who together since June 6 had sacrificed more than fifty thousand lives for this moment. A U.S. Army captain assigned as De Gaulle's aide spent the evening scrounging rations, Coleman lanterns, and Players cigarettes for him.

"City is scarcely damaged. Great enthusiasm," 12th Army Group reported to SHAEF. Sufficient coal remained to fire the waterworks and to provide electricity for two hours a day until mid-September. A few buses with charcoal burners still ran, but they were far outnumbered by horse carts, antique carriages, and bicycles. The Dôme, the Rotonde, and other cafés in Montparnasse did a lively business beneath striped awnings. About two thousand Resistance fighters and twenty-five hundred civilians had been killed or wounded in the battle of Paris, and Hitler continued to kill more. Upon learning in answer to his infamous question—*"Brennt Paris?"*—that, no, the city was not burning, he ordered V-1 and Luftwaffe onslaughts. Bombers would inflict twelve hundred casualties in the eastern suburbs within a day after Choltitz's surrender. Parisians fired at the sky with every firearm at hand, including ancient pistols. "After a noisy hour," a witness reported, "the wheezy 'all clear' sounded." Eisenhower cabled Marshall, "We should not blame the French for growing a bit hysterical."

At three P.M. on Saturday, August 26, De Gaulle appeared at the Arc de Triomphe in an unadorned khaki uniform, as Moorehead reported, "stiff, ungainly, a heavy lugubrious face under his kepi . . . an imposing and unattractive figure." A police band played as he laid a cross of Lorraine fashioned from pink gladioli and relit the memorial flame that had gone cold four years earlier. Much palaver had been devoted to whether *le général* should ride a white horse or a black one down the Champs-Élysées; he chose instead to walk, preceded by four Leclerc tanks. A loudspeaker truck blared, "General de Gaulle confides his safety to the people of Paris." Behind him trailed an arm-in-arm, curb-to-curb phalanx of police, soldiers, and FFI fighters. They were followed by a procession of jeeps and armored vehicles teeming, it was said, "with girls whose destiny does not seem likely to be a nunnery."

A million people or more lined the boulevard, a prancing, dancing human herd, cheering to the echo the unsmiling man who strode a head taller than the rest. Across the Place de la Concorde, near the smoke-stained Hôtel Meurice, De Gaulle had just climbed into an open car when shots rang out. Thousands fell flat on the pavement. "It was like a field of wheat suddenly struck by a strong gust of wind," Moorehead wrote. "Everyone who had a gun began blazing away at the housetops." Armored cars rushed "up and down the streets at fifty miles an hour, firing wildly with machine guns at roofs and high windows," David Bruce told his diary. Thirty GIs standing on supply trucks fired "to beat hell," an officer reported. Nary a marksman seemed sure of his target.

Undeterred, De Gaulle and his entourage crossed the Pont d'Arcole, FFI men with bandoliers strapped across their chests astride the running boards. At 4:15 P.M., as the convoy arrived at Notre Dame, the clap of a revolver and then automatic weapons fire seemed to come from overhead, perhaps from behind a gargoyle, sparking another wild spray of return fire that brought stone chips sprinkling down. As Leclerc barked for a cease-fire and whacked at soldiers' rifles with his malacca, De Gaulle strolled through the Portal of the Last Judgment, head high and shoulders back. He marched down the aisle to the north transept, kepi in hand, when more shots reverberated through the nave. "The huge congregation, who had all been standing, suddenly fell flat on their faces," a British intelligence officer reported. Worshippers crouched behind columns and beneath wooden stalls as policemen and FFI fighters fired at the organ pipes and clerestory. Ricochets pinged off the ceiling. Through it all De Gaulle stood unflinching, "the most extraordinary example of courage that I've ever seen," a BBC reporter declared. Hymnal in hand, he honked through the *Magnificat*—a canticle to the Virgin—while an aide shouted at the cowering congregation, "Have you no pride? Stand up!"

Praise to God Himself would have to wait for a more pacific moment. The "Te Deum" was omitted, the service curtailed, and the great cathedral evacuated posthaste. Precisely who had started the gunfight would never be known. No sniper was shot, captured, or even spotted. "The first shots started a wild fusillade," De Gaulle would write a day later. "We shall fix this too." He returned to his car and drove off to begin the hard work of rebuilding France.

* * *

So ended the great struggle for Normandy. For Germany the defeat was monumental, comparable to Stalingrad, Tunis, and the recent debacle in White Russia. Fritz Bayerlein, commander of the Panzer Lehr Division and Rommel's erstwhile chief of staff, later concluded that among history's memorable battlefield drubbings, including Cannae and Tannenberg, none "can approach the battle of annihilation in France in 1944 in the magnitude of planning, the logic of execution, the collaboration of sea, air, and ground forces, the bulk of the booty, or the hordes of prisoners." The "greatest strategic effect," Bayerlein added, was to lay "the foundation for the subsequent final and complete annihilation of the greatest military state on earth." That was true, though it badly undersold Moscow's role in destroying the Reich.

German casualties in the west since June 6 exceeded 400,000, half of them now prisoners. More than four thousand panzers and assault guns were lost on all fronts during the summer, nearly half in Normandy. SHAEF would tell the Charlie-Charlies in Washington and London that the equivalent of eleven panzer or panzer grenadier divisions had been obliterated or "severely mauled," although some still mustered ten thousand men, even if bereft of tanks. Thirty-six infantry divisions had been eliminated, "very badly cut up," or isolated in coastal enclaves. Several thousand Luftwaffe planes were destroyed; as well, Berlin lost its early-warning network along the Atlantic and its access to French coal, bauxite, farm bounty, and horses. An OSS analysis concluded that Germany now averaged monthly casualties of a quarter million, while only 45,000 young men turned eighteen each month. A study of obituaries in seventy German newspapers over three years would find "a noticeable increase" in the proportion of war dead both eighteen or younger and thirty-eight or older. The Reich was bleeding to death.

The number of Americans killed, wounded, missing, or captured since June 6 topped 134,000; casualties among the British, Canadians, and Poles totaled 91,000. In half a million sorties flown during the summer, more than four thousand planes were lost, evenly divided between the RAF and the AAF. Some units had been eviscerated. The 82nd Airborne had given battle in Normandy with four regimental and sixteen battalion commanders, as well as several spare senior officers; of these, fifteen were killed, wounded, or captured. Normandy paid a fell price for her freedom: by one tally, of 3,400 Norman villages and towns, 586 required complete reconstruction. Throughout France, 24,000 FFI fighters would ultimately be slain or executed by the Germans; the 600,000 tons of Allied bombs dropped on occupied France—the weight of sixty-four Eiffel Towers—would be blamed for between 50,000 and 67,000 French deaths.

Most prominent among the German dead was Erwin Rommel, albeit his was a death delayed. For two months he recuperated from the strafing attack at home in Herrlingen, reminiscing about Africa and fingering his marshal's baton. Insomnia, headaches, and his injured left eye troubled him; merely lifting the eyelid proved difficult. Despite an unctuous letter to Hitler—"Just one thought possessed me constantly, to fight and win for your new Germany"—he was implicated in the July 20 assassination plot as a man who had known too much for his own good.

The killers would come to Herrlingen in a green car with Berlin plates on October 14. After a brief private meeting with them in his study, Rommel told his son, "I shall be dead in a quarter of an hour. . . . Hitler is charging me with high treason." Dressed in an open-collar Africa tunic, he emptied his wallet, petted the family dachshund, and climbed into the rear seat of the car with his marshal's baton under his left arm. To spare his family he swallowed cyanide, permitting the regime to claim he had died of his injuries. Hitler, who sent a six-foot floral wreath even before Rommel's death was confirmed, said of the news, "Yet another of the old ones." In a funeral oration at the Ulm town hall, Rundstedt would declare,

"A pitiless destiny has snatched him from us. His heart belonged to the Führer." That was another lie: not his heart, but certainly his soul.

Among the Allied casualties was Ernie Pyle. "If I ever was brave, I ain't any more," he wrote a friend. "I'm so indifferent to everything I don't even give a damn that I'm in Paris." The war had become "a flat, black depression without highlights, a revulsion of the mind and an exhaustion of the spirit." In a final column from Europe, he told his readers, "I have had all I can take for a while. I've been twenty-nine months overseas since this war started; have written around seven hundred thousand words about it. . . . The hurt has finally become too great." Arriving at Bradley's headquarters on September 2—"worn out, thin, and badly in need of a shave," one officer reported—he said goodbye, then sailed home on the *Queen Elizabeth*, her decks crowded with other wounded. "I feel like I'm running out," he confessed to another writer. Eight months later, while covering the Pacific war, he would be killed by a Japanese bullet in the head.

For many rank-and-file troops a wild optimism took hold, "spreading like a disease," as one SHAEF officer wrote home. PX officials announced that holiday gifts already in the mail from the home front to soldiers in Europe would be returned because the war was likely to end before Christmas. But others recognized, as an officer told his family, that "Hitler can trade space for a long time." Eisenhower advised reporters, "Anyone who measures this war in terms of weeks is just a damn fool."

Yet surely things looked brighter than ever for the Allies. Berlin had again demonstrated a "fundamental inability to make sound strategic judgments," as the historian Geoffrey P. Megargee later wrote, with profound weaknesses in intelligence, personnel, and logistical systems. The tactical edge long possessed by Wehrmacht troops now seemed much diminished as GIs gained competence and confidence. The Luftwaffe had fled to the Fatherland, whereas the U.S. Army Air Forces had built thirty-one airfields in France by August 25 and in the next three weeks would begin sixty-one more. The U.S. Army had displayed not only devastating firepower—a method as effective as any in killing an adversary—but also an impressive ability to adapt under the gun. And Montgomery's strategy had won through, even if he resisted acknowledging necessary deviations from the plan. He had fought perhaps his most skilled battle, in the estimation of the historians Allan R. Millett and Williamson Murray, and the swift liberation of Paris lifted spirits throughout the Allied ranks. A British major wrote his mother, "The war is much more amusing now we are on the move."

The European war also could be seen ever more clearly to "possess a vivid moral structure," in the phrase of the writer Paul Fussell, who fought as an infantry lieutenant. Just when Allied soldiers reached Paris, Soviet troops in Poland overran the concentration camp at Majdanek, where tens of thousands had been murdered. "I have just seen the most terrible place on the face of the earth," a *New York Times* reporter wrote. Other journalists accompanying the Red Army described machines for grinding bones into fertilizer. "This is German food production," a Soviet officer explained. "Kill people, fertilize cabbages." Photos of Zyklon B, the poison used in gas chambers, appeared in *Life,* and *Time* published a vivid account of a warehouse containing 820,000 pairs of shoes taken from inmates: "Boots. Rubbers. Leggings. Slippers. Children's shoes, soldiers' shoes, old shoes, new shoes. . . . In a corner there was a stock of artificial limbs." Other storerooms contained piled spectacles, razors, suitcases, toys. The evidence gave weight to Roosevelt's recent accusations of deportations and "the wholesale systematic murder of the Jews of Europe," although not until the camps in Germany were uncovered in 1945 would the full horror come clear to the civilized world.

In truth, a soldier need not look far to know what he was fighting for: markers on Allied graves all over Normandy contained that most stirring of epitaphs, *"Mort pour la liberté."* After viewing a military cemetery near Ste.-Mère-Église, a soldier on August 28 scribbled lines from A. E. Housman in his diary: "The saviors come not home tonight: Themselves they could not save." At the La Cambe cemetery, Don Whitehead listened as a French girl read a letter to a dead soldier from his mother: "My dearest and unfortunate son, on June 16, 1944, like a lamb you died and left me alone without hope. . . . Your last words to me were, 'Mother, like the wind I came and like the wind I shall go.'"

The death of Conrad J. Nutting III, whose P-51 clipped a tree as he attacked an enemy truck convoy on June 10, also prompted his pregnant wife, Katherine, to write to him beyond the grave:

> It will be my cross, my curse, and my joy forever, that in my mind you shall always be vibrantly alive. . . . I hope God will let me be happy, not wildly, consumingly happy as I was with you. . . . I will miss you so much—your hands, your kiss, your body.

Another pilot, Bert Stiles, who at age twenty-three had but three months of his own life left, wrote, "It is summer and there is war all over the world. . . . There is hope as bright as the sun that it will end soon. I hope it does. I hope the hell it does."

A final gesture of American arms played out in Paris three days after the Notre Dame shootout. De Gaulle had pleaded for two U.S. divisions as a "show of force" against communists and other troublemakers. A bemused Eisenhower agreed to a half measure, diverting the 28th Infantry Division through the capital en route to the front. The 28th's ancestry reached back to units first organized by Benjamin Franklin before the Revolution; its forebears had fought in every American war since. Once commanded by Omar Bradley, now the division was led by the paladin of Omaha Beach and St.-Lô, Dutch Cota, recently promoted to major general.

Hurriedly trucked to Versailles on Monday, August 28, then assembled in the Bois de Boulogne, the men toiled through a rainy night to clean uniforms and polish brass. On Tuesday morning, as skies cleared and the Seine bridges gleamed in the summer sun, Cota and the division band led the ranks in battle dress as they marched twenty-eight abreast to the strains of "Khaki Bill" beneath the Arc de Triomphe and down the Champs-Élysées, a sight so grand that its image soon appeared on a three-cent postage stamp. With weapons loaded and antiaircraft guns poised, the troops tramped past cheering Parisians and an improvised reviewing stand packed with generals in the Place de la Concorde.

Beyond Paris to St.-Denis they marched, through the rolling meadows of Ile-de-France, past stone churches and beetroot fields, marching as the blue shadows grew long, marching in pursuit of the foeman fleeing east, marching, marching, marching toward the sound of the guns.

Part Two

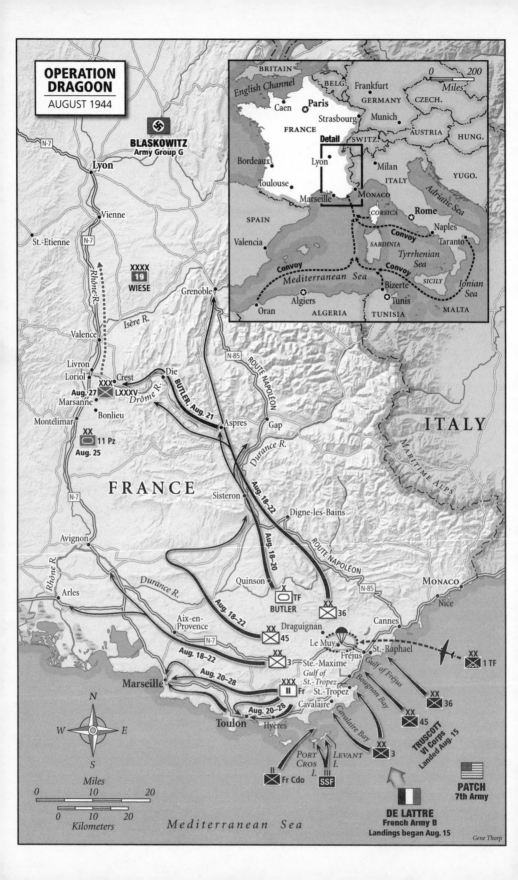

OPERATION DRAGOON

AUGUST 1944

BLASKOWITZ
Army Group G

Lyon

BRITAIN
English Channel
BELG.
Caen
Paris
Frankfurt
GERMANY
CZECH.
FRANCE
Strasbourg
Munich
AUSTRIA
HUNG.
Detail
SWITZ.
Bordeaux
Lyon
Milan
ITALY
YUGO.
Toulouse
Marseille
Monaco
CORSICA
Rome
Adriatic Sea
Naples
SPAIN
Convoy
SARDINIA
Tyrrhenian
Sea
Taranto
Valencia
Convoy
Mediterranean Sea
Convoy
SICILY
Ionian
Sea
Oran
Algiers
Bizerte
MALTA
ALGERIA
Tunis
TUNISIA

Vienne

St.-Etienne
N-7

XXXX
19
WIESE

Rhône R.

Grenoble

Valence
Isère R.

Livron
Loriol
Crest
Die
N-85
ROUTE NAPOLÉON
Aug. 27
XXX
LXXXV
Marsanne
Drôme R.
BUTLER Aug. 21
Bonlieu
Aspres
Gap
Montélimar
XX
11 Pz
Aug. 25
Durance R.
ITALY

FRANCE
Aug. 18–22
Sisteron
Digne-les-Bains

N-7
Aug. 18–20
ROUTE NAPOLÉON

Avignon
Quinson
N-85
MONACO

Rhône R.
Durance R.
Aug. 18–22
X
TF
BUTLER
XX
36
Nice

Arles
Aix-en-
Provence
Draguignan
Cannes

N-7
Aug. 18–22
XX
45
Le Muy
Fréjus
St.-Raphael
XX
1 TF

Aug. 18–22
XX
3
Ste.-Maxime
Gulf of Fréjus
XX
36

Marseille
Aug. 20–28
XXX
II
Fr
Gulf of
St.-Tropez
St.-Tropez
Bougnon Bay
XX
45

Aug. 20–28
Cavalaire
Toulon
Hyères
Cavalaire Bay
TRUSCOTT
VI Corps
Landed Aug. 15

N
W   E
S

Aug. 20–28
XX
3
Cavalaire Bay

PORT
CROS
I.
LEVANT
I.
SSF

Miles
0   10   20

II
Fr Cdo

PATCH
7th Army

0   10   20
Kilometers

DE LATTRE
French Army B
Landings began Aug. 15

Mediterranean Sea

Gene Thorp

4. Pursuit

"The Huntsman Is Hungry"

NAPLES in August 1944 still carried scars from the city's liberation ten months earlier and the hard winter that followed. A typhus epidemic had been suppressed by dusting a million citizens with DDT, but hungry Neapolitans rummaged for scraps in garbage bins along the piers, and black market C-ration hash sold for a quarter a can. Italian matrons struggling to make ends meet hawked their jewelry and old books "in a shamefaced and surreptitious way," wrote the British intelligence officer Norman Lewis; he described priests peddling umbrella handles and candlesticks supposedly carved from the bones of saints filched from the catacombs. The damage caused by German demolitions had been largely repaired, and the port was once again among the world's busiest; but a British study estimated that thieves pilfered one-third of all arriving cargo. American uniforms and GI blankets often reappeared on the street tailored as civilian suits after being unstitched, dyed, and recut. A sign above stolen footwear displayed on the Via Forcella promised, "You can march to kingdom come on these beautiful imported boots."

The city was "colorful, noisily poor, filthy, musical," wrote Lieutenant Douglas Fairbanks, Jr., a matinee idol now serving in the Navy. He might also have added baroque, sybaritic, and deeply odd. Superstitious men warded off the evil eye by reaching into a pocket to touch their testicles whenever strangers approached. Streetcorner troubadours sold freshly penned ballads, Lewis observed, all "dedicated to romantic frustration." Prostitutes' prices had jumped thirtyfold since the previous October, despite rumors that the Germans had smuggled in trollops with especially virulent strains of venereal disease. "Hey, Joe," adolescent pimps yelled at soldiers along the waterfront. "Piece ass! Gal nice!" Smoke and steam leaked from Vesuvius day and night, although most of the ash and vitrified clinkers from the eleven-day eruption in March had been swept up.

More than ever, Naples was a military town, sustaining two Allied armies that for a year had clawed their way up the Italian Peninsula. Although since June 6 the campaign seemed to have been reduced to a dismal backwater, two dozen divisions kept punching north of Rome, under the American Fifth Army in the west and the British Eighth Army in the east. German troops had abandoned Florence on August 7, and Allied forces now planned to assault the Gothic Line, yet another of those heart-breaking barriers built across the spiny Apennines. Troops poured into Naples for a final respite before the battle resumed, not just for "I&I"—intercourse and intoxication—but also for more sedate pastimes, like watching Dorothy Lamour in *Riding High* at the big open-air theater, or sipping a gin fizz at the Orange Club, or splashing about in the huge swimming pool with statuary nudes built for an antebellum world's fair.

But it was not the Allied armies preparing to breach the Gothic Line that now preoccupied military Naples. Rather, it was the quarter-million men seconded to Operation DRAGOON, who under Plan 4-44 had begun slipping inconspicuously from the port on August 9 for the invasion of southern France. Day by day more convoys left Naples, joined by ships from Malta and Palermo, Brindisi and Taranto, Bizerte and Oran, until nearly nine hundred vessels plied ten arterial routes across the Mediterranean, converging within striking distance of Provence along the west coast of Corsica. Making up the great fleet were attack transports and Liberty ships, LSTs and LCTs, twenty-one cruisers and eighty-seven destroyers and five battleships, including *Texas, Nevada,* and *Arkansas,* those smoke-stained veterans of Normandy.

By August 13, the 36th and 45th Infantry Divisions had finished their last rehearsals at Salerno, where wrecked Higgins boats and moldering corpses could still be found from the divisions' death struggle there the previous September. Now troops sat beneath tarpaulins on the transport decks, sewing shoulder flashes to uniform sleeves or thumbing through *A Pocket Guide to France.* The last tanks, trucks, and rubber terrain models were bullied into the holds. From the docks, cranes hoisted ten L-4 Piper Grasshoppers onto *LST-906,* which had been overlaid with a flight deck to serve as a makeshift aircraft carrier for artillery spotter planes. "Many a New Day" from *Oklahoma!* blared from loudspeakers on U.S.S. *Henrico,* while 3rd Division soldiers tuned a small radio to Axis Sally, a propaganda doxy in Berlin, who boasted that she was well acquainted with Allied designs on southern France. Unimpressed, the troops never glanced up from their poker game.

Pacing the bridge of the flagship, U.S.S. *Catoctin,* was a portly seafarer with cascading chins and as much experience at seizing a hostile shore as any American in uniform: Vice Admiral H. Kent Hewitt, who would command the invasion until ground forces were well inland. A native of Hackensack, New Jersey, Hewitt as a young Naval Academy ensign had circled the globe aboard U.S.S. *Missouri* with Theodore Roosevelt's Great

White Fleet, and in the four decades since, he had sailed the wettest corners of the remotest seas. Thirty years ago, he had been in Naples harbor as a navigator aboard U.S.S. *Idaho* when Archduke Franz Ferdinand was shot dead in Sarajevo; he recalled vividly the battleship lowering her flag to half mast, as if to salute a dying world. Hewitt had won the Navy Cross for valor in the ensuing war, and many decorations subsequently. In this war, too, he had distinguished himself by putting Patton's forces on the strand in both Morocco and Sicily despite ferocious storms. He was lucky, skilled, and unflappable. Now, as his crew prepared to cast off, Hewitt took a seat on the flag bridge and with a pencil stub began working a double-crostic. The puzzles lifted him above his troubles.

Troubles he had. DRAGOON had begun dreadfully. On August 4, Rear Admiral Don Moon, who had commanded the naval force at Utah Beach and would oversee the right wing of the DRAGOON landings, had begged Hewitt to postpone the invasion. For hours he argued that forces had arrived in Naples too late to prepare properly, that assault training had been too skimpy, that the forewarned Germans would butcher the landing teams. Hewitt had known Moon as an Annapolis midshipman, knew him to be intense, overworked, and reluctant to delegate authority; he evidently did not know that Moon on June 6 had tried to persuade Joe Collins to suspend the Utah landings, or that the ship's doctor aboard Moon's *Catoctin* had treated him for acute depression, or that the fleet medical officer also had interviewed Moon about his mental balance. "I don't think it's as bad as you think it is," Hewitt told him. He promised to consider Moon's plea.

At seven the next morning, Moon rang from his cabin to ask for orange juice. Fifteen minutes later, a steward entered the stateroom, opened the blackout curtain, and found the admiral, dressed in shorts and undershirt, sitting on the sofa with a .45 in his right hand, his eyes open, and a red worm of blood trickling from his ear. The spent bullet was found in the shower. A note in neat cursive on a ruled pad explained: "The mind is gone. . . . My mind is running cycles with occasional nearly lucid periods and then others the complete reverse. . . . What am I doing to you my wife and dear children? I am sick, *so* sick." An inquest before noon ruled death had come "during a period of insanity." The certificate read: "Cause: suicide, gunshot wound, head. Combat fatigue." He was buried at five P.M., ten hours after his passing, in the Naples military cemetery. To his widow and four children, Collins later wrote, "He was a casualty of this war just as much as if he had been killed in action." Hewitt sent his own chief of staff to take Moon's command.

At two P.M. on August 13, under clear skies on a calm sea, *Catoctin*, *Bayfield*, and more than two dozen transports eased away from the docks and built to twelve knots. An escort of sixteen warships joined this final convoy as it steamed from the Naples anchorage. A witness thought of John Masefield's lines from Gallipoli: "All that they felt was a gladness of exultation that their young courage was to be used."

Vesuvius had begun to recede in the distance when a commotion on deck caught Hewitt's attention. A British admiral's barge, making for the port from the island of Ischia, could be seen weaving among the outbound ships. A stubby figure with pink cheeks stood in the forepeak, disdaining a handhold and wearing a light tropical suit beneath an enormous sun helmet. Abruptly from soldiers and sailors crowding *Catoctin's* rails a cry went up: "It's Churchill!" So it was: with a smile he doffed his ten-gallon helmet, wispy hair tossing in the breeze, then raised his right hand to flash the famous V with his fingers. The men huzzahed until he slid from sight in their wake.

He was traveling under the improbable nom de guerre of Colonel Kent, as if a phony name and a big hat could render him inconspicuous. Ostensibly Churchill was on a fortnight's bathing holiday in southern Italy, wallowing "like a benevolent hippo" at Capri's Blue Grotto and in various Tyrrhenian coves around Naples while following the heartening news from Normandy in his portable map room. Yet he also had come to keep a pale eye on an enterprise he still bitterly opposed, and which had churned up as much enmity within the Anglo-American alliance as any episode of the war.

DRAGOON, originally called ANVIL, had first been intended as a diversion during OVERLORD to occupy eighteen German divisions south of the Loire in Army Group G. Shipping shortages and delays in capturing Rome forced a postponement until long after the Normandy landings, yet the Americans remained keen on the operation. Marseille and Toulon would provide ports at a time when dozens of U.S. Army divisions were stuck at home for lack of dockage in Normandy. DRAGOON could discomfit the enemy with a thrust up the Rhône valley, an invasion route since Caesar's wars, and it would profitably employ several veteran French divisions now fighting in Italy; with a mother country still to liberate, De Gaulle had forbidden those forces to venture beyond the river Arno. "France," Eisenhower told the British, "is the decisive theater."

The British disagreed, politely at first, then adamantly. Churchill warned Roosevelt of a "bleak and sterile" invasion through Provence, followed by "very great hazards, difficulties, and delays" in slogging up the Rhône. Marseille lay four hundred miles from Paris, and a battle there was unlikely to influence the fight for northern France; simply reaching Lyon, he predicted, would take three months. Pulling the U.S. VI Corps and the

French divisions from Italy "is unacceptable to us," the British military chiefs added. Instead, why not blast across the Po valley in northern Italy, swing east with help from an amphibious landing at Trieste, and drive through the so-called Ljubljana Gap in Slovenia to reach Austria and the Danube valley? The Allied commander in Italy, Field Marshal Sir Harold Alexander, promised Churchill that he intended to "eliminate the German forces in Italy. I shall then have nothing to prevent me from marching on Vienna." This thrust of "a dagger under the armpit," as the prime minister called it, might even force Hitler to abandon France in order to shore up his southeastern front.

Back and forth the argument flew like a shuttlecock. In an exasperated message to Marshall, Eisenhower decried the project of "wandering off overland via Trieste to Ljubljana. . . . We must concentrate our forces. . . . We need big ports." Even if the Germans in Italy collapsed, and heavily fortified Trieste fell, threading the gap meant traversing a high col only thirty miles wide, followed by six-thousand-foot mountains with poor roads, worse rails, and more narrow valleys. Pentagon studies, noting that "the Austrians held off the Italians [in this region] for four years in World War I," concluded that "not more than seven divisions at the outside could be pushed through" to Austria. Churchill advised Alexander to be ready to dash to Vienna with armored cars, even though British planners reckoned a need for at least fifteen divisions. ("Winston is a gambler," his physician later explained, "and gamblers do not count the coins in their pockets.") Brooke privately decried "Winston's strategic ravings" about campaigning "through the Alps in winter." While also skeptical of DRAGOON, Brooke advised telling Washington, "If you insist on being damned fools, sooner than falling out with you, which would be fatal, we shall be damned fools with you."

The prime minister would have none of it. Later he portrayed his scheme as a way to forestall Soviet domination of eastern Europe, but in the summer of 1944 no such argument was advanced. In a windy message to Roosevelt marked "strictly private, personal, and top secret," he warned of "the complete ruin of all our great affairs in the Mediterranean. . . . This has sunk very deeply into my mind." The president rebuffed him with election-year logic another politician could understand: "I would never survive even a slight setback in OVERLORD if it were known that fairly large forces had been diverted to the Balkans."

Still Churchill persisted, flying to Normandy with an escort of six Spitfires as Mortain and Falaise began to unfold, hectoring Eisenhower, Bradley, and others with, as an Army staff officer described, "beautifully colored speech, hunched forward on his chair, his eyes slightly red and beady, scattering cigar ashes on the floor and hiding his burnt match under the seat." After directing British commanders to examine "in the greatest secrecy" whether DRAGOON forces could be diverted to Brittany, the prime minister urged Eisenhower to do just that. This was a loony caprice, so "extremely unwise" that it would "cause the utmost confusion everywhere," as the Pentagon advised. Not least, tens of thousands of troops were already boarding vessels insufficiently seaworthy to venture beyond the Straits of Gibraltar, and no major Breton port would open for weeks. "Ike said no, continued saying no all afternoon, and ended up saying no in every form of the English language at his command," Harry Butcher wrote. In a subsequent session in London, Churchill wept copiously and threatened to "lay down the mantle of my high office." "I have never seen him so obviously stirred, upset, and even despondent," Eisenhower cabled Marshall on August 11, after a taxing confrontation at 10 Downing Street. Roosevelt put paid to the wrangling in nine words: "There is no more to be done about it."

Unable to move the president or his lieutenants, Churchill raged with the ineffectual petulance of a declining power. Denouncing the "sheer folly" of his "strong and dominating partner," he slipped into first-person royal: "We have been ill-treated and are furious. Do not let any smoothings or smirchings cover up this fact. . . . If we take this lying down, there will be no end to what will be put upon us." Even the king's equerry told his diary, "Winston is very bitter about it, and not so sure that he really likes FDR." As for Marshall and the other American chiefs, Churchill now derided them to Brooke as "one of the stupidest strategic teams ever seen. They are good fellows and there is no need to tell them this." To Clementine he later wrote, "The only times I ever quarrel with the Americans are when they fail to give us a fair share of the opportunity to win glory."

And so he had come to Naples to take the waters. Britain would win the war while losing this battle and most other battles waged against the Americans henceforth. More than two years of bickering over strategy—with London usually prevailing—had made Marshall truculent and inclined to agree with the State Department adage that "an Englishman's idea of cooperation is to persuade someone to do what he wants him to do." Even Roosevelt would later declare, "Churchill is always a disperser." This contretemps was indeed the final gasp of the prime minister's cherished peripheral strategy for winning World War II; it had become incoherent, in the judgment of the historian Michael Howard. The fabled soft underbelly was "a slogan not a strategy," another British historian concluded, a hodgepodge of improvisations. While the Americans were wary of British imperial interests in the Mediterranean and eastern Europe, the project of stealing a march on the Russians was both impractical—the Red Army already was poised to spread through Romania, Bulgaria, Poland, and

Hungary, and communist partisans were ascendant in Yugoslavia—and strategically suspect. Why antagonize Moscow when Soviet forces continued to do "the main work of tearing the guts out of the German army," as Churchill himself told the House of Commons in early August?

Certainly the fraught imperatives of national interest and national pride also were playing out. Britain's stature and influence seemed to diminish with each new arrival of a Liberty ship jammed with GIs; the empire's future was uncertain at best, and that insecurity would inform the Anglo-American brotherhood for the duration. Moreover, as Brooke wrote in August, the Americans "now look upon themselves no longer as the apprentices at war, but on the contrary as full-blown professionals." The U.S. Army this month would exceed eight million soldiers; more than one in every ten was in the Mediterranean, and the American high command was bent on putting them to good use quickly.

Churchill played a poor second fiddle. "The trouble is the P.M. can never give way gracefully," a British admiral observed. "He must always be right." As the war churned into its sixth year, some found the prime minister increasingly erratic. "He is becoming more and more unbalanced!" Brooke told his diary in late summer. "He was literally frothing at the corners of his mouth with rage." He was much given to "corrective sneering," his secretary reported, and obsessed with inconsequential details, such as the black bristles of the hairbrushes in the Cabinet War Room lavatory, which he complained hid the dirt. "Churchill is preoccupied by his own vivid world," the philosopher Isaiah Berlin wrote. "He does not react, he acts; he does not mirror, he affects others and alters them to his own powerful measure." The prime minister acknowledged his mulish nature: "Of course I am an egotist. Where do you get if you aren't?"

Without doubt, "that unresting genius," in the phrase of one contemporary, needed rest. "The P.M. is very tired," an aide complained. "He insists on everything being boiled down to half a sheet of notepaper. It simply can't be done." He had described himself in midsummer as "an old and weary man," and he advocated "economy of effort. Never stand up when you can sit down, and never sit down when you can lie down."

Already this Mediterranean sojourn had revivified him, as the Middle Sea always did. Champagne lunches were followed by brandy, an hour's nap, a bath, then a whiskey and soda, and more champagne and brandy at dinner before working until three A.M. (Churchill was no alcoholic, C. P. Snow once observed, because no alcoholic could drink that much.) Now, after passing the outbound fleet, he would return to the Villa Rivalta, his hostel above Naples Bay, and pack for a C-47 flight to Corsica, his own staging area for the invasion. The U.S. Joint Chiefs, that "stupidest strategic team," had cabled London a week earlier: "We are convinced that DRAGOON will be successful in its landing phase, and we anticipate a rapid advance up the Rhône valley." Churchill intended to see for himself.

In the smallest hours of Tuesday, August 15—Napoléon's birthday—the invasion force crept toward sixteen narrow beaches along a forty-five-mile stretch of the Côte d'Azur. The coast here was steep-to, plunging to one hundred fathoms only three miles from shore, with a negligible eight-inch tide. Allied bombers since late April had dumped twenty thousand tons on German fortifications, and on more than a few French towns. Much of the population already had fled to the hills, hiding in streambeds and hollows from what one refugee described as "a deluge of metal." Coded phrases broadcast from Algiers and London on Monday night had alerted the FFI and OSS teams of the imminent assault: "Nancy has a stiff neck. The huntsman is hungry. Gaby is going to lie down in the grass." Each soldier aboard the combat loaders received an American flag armband and two packs of Lucky Strikes. "Swilled coffee and chain-smoked, flicking our Zippos with trembling, nicotined fingers," a soldier in the 45th Division told his journal. Some lay thrashing in the sickbays with recurrent malaria contracted in Italy—"pure fire, sunstorms flaring from inside outward," as a victim described his symptoms. Yet for most, another GI wrote in his diary, "it hardly seems that an invasion is on, things are so quiet."

Catoctin's malfunctioning ventilation system had forced sweltering passengers belowdecks to strip to their undershirts for much of the passage. But as the French coast drew near, Major General Lucian K. Truscott, Jr., commander of the U.S. Army's VI Corps—the main assault force in DRAGOON—carefully dressed for combat: enameled two-star helmet, breeches, lucky cavalry boots, and the white scarf, fashioned from a paratrooper's silk map found on Sicily, that had become his trademark. This was Truscott's third invasion. Previously he had commanded the left flank of Patton's force in both TORCH and HUSKY, before taking command during the darkest hours at Anzio and rallying VI Corps to be in on the kill at Rome. Truscott possessed what one staff officer called a "predatory" face, with protruding gray eyes and gapped incisors set in a jut jaw built to scowl. But the "beaten-up foghorn" voice, scarred from carbolic acid swallowed as a child, had softened a bit in recent months after repeated paintings of his vocal cords with silver nitrate. Partial though he was to violets on his desk and to lively discussions of poetry, history, and the rationalist edition of the New Testament edited by Thomas Jefferson, at heart Truscott remained "one of the really tough generals," as the cartoonist and infantryman Bill Mauldin described him. From an enlisted iconoclast, that was staunch praise.

Truscott's was an unorthodox path to high command. His father, originally a cowboy on the Chisholm Trail, had abandoned the range to become both the physician and the pharmacist in Chatfield, Texas; an unlucky dabbler in racehorse and farmland investments, he later moved the family to Oklahoma. Lucian at sixteen claimed he was eighteen to win a teaching job in a hinterland schoolhouse, walking six miles to and fro each day. A voracious reader who renounced strong drink, tobacco, and profanity, he eventually was promoted to principal. Yet not until he joined the Army and won a cavalry officer's commission in 1917, at age twenty-two, did he find his true calling. Slowly ascending through the ranks between the wars, Truscott won admirers for both his professional competence and his skills as a polo player. Army life also put rough edges on the former teacher, who soon drank, smoked, and swore profusely. For the past two years in Africa and Italy, he had had few peers as a combat commander, demonstrating what one high-ranking comrade described as "willpower, decision, and drive"; Eisenhower still lamented his inability to get Truscott released from Anzio for OVERLORD. Truscott's generalship stressed speed, vigor, violence, and clarity; staff papers that displeased him provoked the blunt, scrawled epithet "Bullshit." Convinced that American soldiers were "hunters by instinct," he urged his officers to "make every soldier go into every fight feeling like a hunter."

To his wife, Sarah, waiting in Virginia, Truscott had confessed in recent letters how "horribly lonesome" he felt. He regretted being so "far removed from the softening touch of women and home." Before leaving his quarters on *Catoctin* he took a moment to write her again, beginning, as he always began, "Beloved wife":

> On the eve of every major undertaking in this war I have always written to you so that you would know that if anything should happen to me you were in my mind and in my heart. . . . I would live no part of my life over if I had the opportunity. My only real regret is that I have not made you happier and your life easier.

He stalked from the cabin to join Hewitt on the bridge, jaw set, thick shoulders slightly hunched, the hunter looking for prey.

The enemy never had a chance. In rubber boats and kayaks, and on surfboards with electric motors, three thousand American and French commandos swept onto coastal fortifications and two offshore islands. Much of the littoral was sparsely defended; some hilltop pillboxes were found to brandish only Quaker guns made from streetlight poles. Allied deceivers dropped hundreds of rubber "paradummies" with noisemakers and colored lights far from the actual assault, and electronic simulators created ghost convoys where no ships sailed. So befuddled were the Germans that for days defenders braced against an expected attack at Genoa, two hundred miles northeast.

The usual anarchy and intrepidity attended the airborne assault. From ten Italian airfields, nine thousand paratroopers and glidermen made for the Riviera. Thick inland fog caused six of nine pathfinder teams to miss their drop zones; more than half of the main jump force in predawn drops also drifted wide. Some sticks fell ten miles or more from their targets, landing on rooftops and in vineyards around St.-Tropez. Despite the muddle, airborne casualties were light—only 230, or under 3 percent—and the Germans were further discomposed.

At eight A.M., eleven American assault battalions swept ashore in a flat calm, hidden from enemy gunners by summer haze and six thousand tons of smoke spewed from special landing craft fitted with airplane propellers to spread the miasma. At Bougnon Bay, in the center of the assault, discouraged *Osttruppen* and superannuated Germans facing the 45th Division folded quickly. On the left, the 3rd Division also clattered through the dunes at Cavalaire Bay and across the St.-Tropez Peninsula.

Among those at the point of the spear with the 3rd Division's 15th Infantry Regiment was a short and skinny—5'7", 138 pounds—staff sergeant who on Sicily and at Anzio had already earned a reputation for élan, and would soon be deemed "the greatest folk hero of Texas since Davy Crockett." Audie Leon Murphy, Army Serial Number 18093707, was the seventh child of an itinerant farmer who owned a milk cow and little else. A fifth-grade dropout who at one point during the Depression lived in a rail boxcar, Murphy later said, "I can't remember ever being young in my life." He had learned to shoot by plinking squirrels—"little greys," he called them—and became proficient enough to hit a darting rabbit from a moving car. His sister forged his enlistment papers in 1942, falsely attesting that he was eighteen rather than seventeen. He had fainted during the induction immunizations.

Sharpshooting now served him well. Murphy and his rifle platoon were making for St.-Tropez at ten A.M., when German machine-gun fire rattled down a rocky draw, stopping the advance with the incivility of a slammed door. Murphy scampered back to the beach, grabbed a light machine gun from a dawdling gunner, and dragged it back uphill to his men. With his commandeered gun, grenades, and a carbine, he killed two enemy gunners atop a knoll and enticed a white flag from a second nest. But when Private First Class Lattie Tipton stood to take the surrender, a sniper shot him dead. Enraged, Murphy killed the surrendering Germans with grenades before seizing an enemy machine gun; firing from the hip, he exterminated two more enemy fighting positions. "My whole being," he later wrote, "is concentrated on killing." Here surely was Truscott's instinctive hunter. When the shooting finally ceased, Murphy slipped a pack under Tipton's head as a pillow, then sat down and wept. The Army would award ASN 18093707 the Distinguished Service Cross.

Only on the invasion right flank did the enemy stiffen, particularly along the Gulf of Fréjus. Napoléon had landed on this shore after returning from Egypt in 1799, and fifteen years later embarked from the same beach for his exile on Elba, complaining that the French mob was as "fickle as a weathercock." Now, thick mines, barbed-wire tangles, and strongpoints hidden in villas and seaside gazebos proved irksome, although hardly as lethal as Admiral Moon had feared. Secret Navy drone boats—radio-controlled landing craft packed with four tons of explosives to blow holes in beach obstacles—failed abjectly, possibly because German radios used the same frequencies. The boats "milled around at high speed in crazy directions, completely on their own," a witness reported; some reversed course toward the offshore fleet and had to be sunk by destroyers. "As a general proposition," a Navy demolition officer reported, "the drone boats did not function."

The American weight of metal soon carried the day. Bombers and naval gunfire raked the coast, leaving the piney hills charred and smoking. Boats carrying a regiment from the 36th Division pulled back from Fréjus, momentarily infuriating Truscott, who squinted through the haze from *Catoctin;* sensibly, officers orchestrating the landing chose to put in on an easier beach farther east. Hewitt's dispatch that afternoon was only slightly exaggerated in reporting unqualified success:

> All ships and craft reached their final assault destination as per plan.... Airborne landings were on schedule and successful.... No losses of own aircraft reported.... Bombardment reported excellent.... Landings on all beaches successful with good timing.

A naval officer aboard *LCI-233* was more succinct in his diary: "Frankly, this has been the quietest beachhead I have ever seen."

By the close of this D-Day, 66,000 troops were ashore with fewer than 400 casualties, including 95 dead. Some 2,300 German prisoners had been captured—many preferred to surrender rather than risk the vengeance of the maquis roaming the coastal uplands—and Hitler would declare August 15 "the worst day of my life." DRAGOON had fallen on an attenuated Army Group G: the German commander in southern France, General Johannes Blaskowitz, already in bad odor for objecting to SS atrocities in Poland, had been forced to give one-quarter of his infantry divisions and two-thirds of his armor to the struggle in Normandy. He was left with a hollow force of less than 300,000, including Armenians, Azerbaijanis, and four battalions of "Russians in France Fighting for Germany Against America." Within Blaskowitz's far-flung Nineteenth Army, the 11th Panzer Division, his only mobile reserve, was stuck west of the Rhône after the Army Air Forces destroyed every bridge on the river's lower reaches. Ferrying the entire division across took nearly a week; even then some panzers would be stalled for lack of fuel, which had to be floated down from Lyon.

By twilight on Tuesday, many defenders were scrambling north in disorder, jamming hijacked buses and even dray carts. American patrols snaked into the steep red-rock hills, thick with maritime pines and cork oaks. The coastal roads were "already choked with traffic, and bands of prisoners, their hands in the air, were marching toward the water line," wrote the reporter Eric Sevareid, ashore with the 45th Division. To oversee both Truscott's corps and follow-on French forces, the U.S. Seventh Army command post moved into Hôtel Latitude 43, an Art Deco complex on the lip of St.-Tropez; the army war diary noted that "resistance by German forces has been weak at most points." Sevareid described "the Cinzano signs, the powder-blue denim of the workmen, the faintly sourish smell of wine as one passed the *zincs,* the dusty plane trees, the little formal gardens, the soft, translucent air." A French admiral aboard *Catoctin* declared, "What happiness to recover this coast of France, the most fair, the most amiable, and the most smiling of our country." Truscott and his staff motored ashore to dine in a nearby château on white linen with the VI Corps crystal and silver service. Bill Mauldin declared DRAGOON to be "the best invasion I ever attended."

Within the Allied high command, perhaps only the prime minister was disgruntled. Wearing his blue, brass-buttoned Trinity House uniform, he had sailed for five hours from Corsica aboard H.M.S. *Kimberly* to join the bombardment fleet nine miles from the Riviera. Although Churchill was particularly keen to see French colonials in action—he described them as "frog blackmoors, whose bravery I do not doubt"—the *Kimberly* ventured no closer than seven thousand yards for fear of sea mines. St.-Tropez remained swaddled in haze and smoke, all but invisible. Out of cigars and "in a querulous mood," as his physician noted, the prime minister retired below to read *Grand Hotel,* a novel he had found in the captain's cabin. On the flyleaf he scratched an inscription: "This is a lot more exciting than the invasion of Southern France."

The Avenue of Stenches

T HE immediate objective of DRAGOON were the ports of Toulon and Marseille, respectively code-named ASTORIA and CYRIL. Seventh Army had little capacity for unloading supplies over the beach, so trucks, gasoline, ammunition, and other matériel needed to sustain Truscott's lunge to the north could come only through the twin anchorages, the capture of which was assigned to the French. On Wednesday evening, August 16, four divisions from the French II Corps began landing in the Gulf of St.-Tropez, a day ahead of schedule owing to feeble German resistance. They eventually would be joined by three more divisions in I Corps, giving France a quarter-million men under arms in the south.

Known for now as Army B, it was a vivid soldiery, as picturesque as Leclerc's division then capering toward Paris. Nearly half were from North Africa or the sub-Sahara, complemented by Somalis, New Caledonians, Tahitians, Indochines, Syrians, Lebanese, and Legionnaires. Africans composed almost three-quarters of the infantry regiments, including six thousand ferocious Berber *goumiers* wearing sandals and striped djellabas, with boots tied around their necks as they led their mules across the beaches. With little capacity for modern military logistics, the French relied on the U.S. Army for everything from pork-free rations for Muslim soldiers to French-English dictionaries. This summer alone the Americans had provided 1,100 tanks, 215,000 rifles, 17,000 tons of corned and frozen beef, 20 million Atabrine antimalaria tablets, 7 million packets of pipe tobacco, and 7,000 extra canteens. (Senegalese soldiers were said to require four liters of water each day, double the normal ration.) Extra tanker trucks also were needed because of French reluctance to convert cherished wine transports into gasoline carriers.

The gimlet-eyed commander of this force stepped ashore at six P.M. Wednesday after a voyage from Taranto aboard the former Polish cruise ship S.S. *Batory:* General Jean Joseph Marie Gabriel de Lattre de Tassigny, whose impeccable ensemble included kepi, yellow gloves, and a swagger stick tucked beneath his left arm. Described by French colleagues as "an animal of action" and "*jupiterien*," De Lattre impressed Hewitt as "very pleasant, very volatile," while Truscott saw "thin hair graying around the temples, a square open face with cold eyes, medium height, trim, neat, and very soldierly." Given to abrupt dead-of-night appearances in the ranks, roaring, "What have you done for France?," De Lattre would be acclaimed by one biographer as "the greatest soldier to serve France since the age of Napoleon I."

De Lattre sprang from minor gentry in the Vendée on the Atlantic coast and graduated near the bottom of his St.-Cyr class in 1909. During the Great War, he twice gathered intelligence by slipping through the lines disguised as a factory worker to dine in a Metz restaurant packed with German officers. In a skirmish in 1914, he killed two enemy soldiers with a sword his grandfather had carried in the Napoleonic Wars, but was impaled by a German lance; a sergeant had to stand on his chest to yank it out. He was to suffer three more wounds before the Armistice and be mentioned in dispatches eight times. A fervent Catholic—in peacetime he routinely helped, barefoot, to carry the sick at Lourdes—he had insisted that chaplains accompany his assault troops in order to give quick absolution to the dying. His personal motto, adopted in the 1930s, was *Ne Pas Subir:* Do not give up.

Loyal to Vichy for more than two years after the German invasion, he had finally refused to countenance Hitler's occupation of southern France following the Allied seizure of North Africa in November 1942. Charged by a Vichy court-martial with abandoning his post, he was sentenced to ten years in prison. His son Bernard, then fifteen, aided his escape by smuggling tools and a rope into his father's cell. In September 1943, De Lattre loosened a window frame, shinnied down to a courtyard, scaled an outer wall, and fled to Algiers by way of London. There De Gaulle gave him command of the French army in exile. Known as *le Roi Jean* for his imperial airs, De Lattre stationed an imposing *sénégalais* outside his office door to sound a clarion on a trumpet whenever the double doors flew open and the general stepped out. He "lived on stage," the historian Douglas Porch later wrote, "as gracious to dignitaries, whom he received with Bourbon *éclat,* as he was severe with subordinates, whom he slaved to exhaustion." Often dining at midnight, he worked until five A.M., then signed orders in bed at dawn; visitors to his headquarters might sit for days on the outer stairs, awaiting an audience. "The General," an aide explained, "is a nocturnal."

The DRAGOON landing plan for Army B had been redrafted seventeen times at De Lattre's insistence. While conceding that "we Frenchmen are not the masters" and that subordination "is the price we must pay to be able to participate in the liberation of France," he resented being under American command and beholden to American supply. Storming into a U.S. Army headquarters, aflame with grievances, De Lattre would let loose a torrent of French as an interpreter struggled to keep pace, then stalk out, always saluting smartly before slamming the door. He was "ardent to the point of effervescence," said De Gaulle, who believed that De Lattre's faults derived from "the excesses of his virtues." Now accompanied by Bernard, the youngest soldier in the French army, he collared a subordinate in St.-Tropez and with eyes bright told him, "Toulon awaits you."

The Germans waited, too. Here and in Marseille, thirty miles farther west, 35,000 defenders had been ordered by Hitler to stand "to the last man." General Blaskowitz reported that his fortifications at Toulon were 75 percent complete, with Marseille a bit more advanced; water and ammunition had been stockpiled, and both garrisons reinforced. Port demolitions began soon after the first Americans crossed the beaches to the east.

Toulon was the greatest naval base in France and the tougher nut. Three craggy fortresses dominated the landward approaches, and nearby mountainsides were rigged with dynamite to trigger rockslides. Seventy or more guns ranged the roadstead, among them "Big Willie," a turret with two 340mm barrels plucked from the scuttled French battleship *Provence* and installed in armor plate and thick concrete at St.-Mandrier, commanding the harbor mouth; with a range of twenty-two miles, the guns were more than a match for any weapon in the Allied fleet. Even so, Admiral Hewitt ordered the hornet's nest poked. On Saturday, August 19, after the fortifications had been pummeled from the air, *Nevada, Augusta, Quincy,* and the French battleship *Lorraine* paraded along the horizon, lobbing two hundred shells like so many playground taunts. Not until Sunday did Big Willie reply, chasing the interlopers back into their smoke banks at flank speed with a splashy fall of shot that quickly closed from a two-mile miss to a thirty-yard miss. Big Willie was "too much for us," an officer aboard *Quincy* confessed; Allied shells striking the turret's concrete casements "just bounced off like us spitting against the wall." The naval brawl would last more than a week, but Toulon—like Cherbourg—clearly would not fall from the sea.

De Lattre had assumed as much and so cleaved his army into five battle groups, with orders to outflank and encircle both Toulon and Marseille. This scheme began badly when German gunners demolished the lead French tank in a convoy on Highway 57, then cut down trees behind the rear tank to trap the column and pick off eight more. In Hyères, ten miles east of Toulon, defenders who included stranded submariners made a fortress of the Golf Hotel and adjacent links; three French artillery battalions fired a thousand rounds point-blank, augmented by two hundred naval shells. A sunset bayonet charge by Tahitian troops through the dining room and cellars ended resistance, with 140 Germans captured and many more slain.

By last light on Monday, August 21, Toulon was surrounded. Monks from a local monastery guided French detachments across the stony, pathless terrain to the north. A battalion commander led his men through the night by marking the trail with toilet paper provided, as De Lattre acknowledged, by U.S. Army quartermasters. A company commander scouted the city in a borrowed policeman's uniform while gunners shouldered a dozen battalions of artillery onto the frowning heights. One by one the battered strongpoints fell: defenders were flushed from their lairs with white phosphorus and flamethrowers, "like rabbits driven out by a terrier," in De Lattre's phrase. To diehards in the Arsenal Maritime, a French colonel on August 25 warned that at seven P.M. "my Senegalese will receive the order to massacre you all"; the last defenders blew up their remaining ammunition, roused themselves with a shout of "Heil Hitler!," and marched into captivity. Not until dawn on August 28 did the last two thousand sailors manning Big Willie and other guns on St.-Mandrier capitulate; Hewitt's ships had fired more than a thousand shells from as near as five miles. When the captured garrison commander declined to provide a map of German minefields, De Lattre vowed to shoot him. "Three hours later," he reported, "I had the plans."

Marseille fell almost at the same moment. Founded as a Greek trading post in the sixth century B.C., the storied port had become France's second largest city, with half a million citizens and the most vital anchorage in the Mediterranean, comprising thirteen miles of quays. On August 21, as De Lattre's columns approached from the east, northeast, and north, the Marseillais had rebelled, building barricades with paving stones and shooting up isolated German patrols. Oily smoke from burning refineries in the suburbs drifted over the city as *goumiers,* described by one Frenchman as "figures from another world," scrambled over goat paths and through olive groves to cut escape routes leading north. In the early hours of August 23, Algerian infantrymen accompanied by Sherman tanks hurried through the streets to the old port, cheered on by civilians in nightclothes who threw open their shutters to bray with delight. Although the German garrison bristled with at least two hundred guns in a double defensive line, the city soon grew indefensible. While *Nevada* and other warships pounded away, De Lattre spread his maps in a nearby hotel courtyard where vacationing guests, including pretty girls in sundresses, continued to sip iced apéritifs under umbrellas on the terrace.

When a tricolor rose over the captured redoubt at Fort St.-Nicolas, the garrison commander, General Hans Schaeffer, composed a message: "It would be purposeless to continue a battle which could lead only to the total annihilation of my remaining troops." French soldiers found him at dawn on August 28 in an underground burrow with two telephones and a plate of Gruyère cheese; he emerged pale and haggard to sign the surrender with a borrowed pen. Church bells rang in jubilation. Marseille had fallen nearly a month ahead of the DRAGOON timetable.

Thirty-seven thousand prisoners would be taken in the two port cities, at a cost of four thousand French casualties, including eight hundred dead.

Toulon had been so thoroughly dismembered by German demolitions that the Allies forsook it as a major port. Marseille was devastated even beyond Allied fears, "the German masterpiece" of ruination, according to American port officials who had rebuilt Naples. Of 121 piers, not one could be used; dynamite and two thousand large mines had transformed every quay and warehouse into "a chaos of steel, concrete, and cables." Eleven large ships, including transatlantic liners, had been wrecked to block the harbor entrance, and 257 cranes had been pitched into the water. Scores of other sunken vessels blocked each berth with scuttling techniques "not previously encountered." As in Cherbourg, booby traps seeded the ruins, and more than five thousand mines of seventeen different types would be lifted from the water with the help of blimps used to spot them.

Yet the Allies had their port. Almost miraculously, the first Liberty ship would berth in Marseille on September 15, and Hewitt reported that ten days later the docks could handle 12,500 tons of cargo each day. For now, French regiments hurried west, to the mouth of the Rhône. De Lattre cabled De Gaulle, newly installed in Paris: "In Army B's sector there is no German not dead or captive."

Following his abdication and removal to Elba in 1814, Napoléon threw himself into a life of exile while waiting for the restored Bourbon regime to make itself intolerable. Joined by his mother, his sister, and his Polish mistress with their illegitimate son, he built roads and bridges, organized balls, banquets, and theatricals, and played countless hands of cards, at which he cheated without scruple. Bored to tears after nine months, and burning with what the historian Norwood Young would call "the Corsican spirit of vendetta," he surreptitiously had the brig *Inconstant* painted, recoppered, and provisioned with biscuit, rice, brandy, and salt meat. Accompanied by a flotilla of six other vessels and determined to again become "the man of Austerlitz," Napoléon in February 1815 gave a British man-of-war the slip and beat for the French coast with twelve hundred retainers and old imperial guardsmen. "I was so unhappy that I was not risking much," the once and future emperor later explained, "only my life." He stepped ashore near Antibes to begin the fateful Hundred Days; in making for Paris, he avoided the royalist Rhône valley and chose a route along the western flank of the Alps, through Digne, Sisteron, and Grenoble.

The Route Napoléon led, indirectly, to Waterloo three months later, but that failed to discourage American planners: they had chosen this very path for a possible quick lunge toward Lyon, two hundred miles northwest of St.-Tropez. Since De Gaulle had demanded that the Americans immediately return to De Lattre's command a French armored brigade after just three days' employment in the initial DRAGOON landings, Truscott was forced to cobble together an all-American mechanized exploitation force. To command this scratch assemblage he appointed his deputy, Brigadier General Frederic Bates Butler, a West Point engineer from California who had once managed Herbert Hoover's White House for the War Department and more recently had seen much combat in Tunisia and Italy. Two days after the U.S. landings, as Army B began to pivot west toward Toulon, the most exhilarating Ultra messages ever intercepted in the Mediterranean galvanized Task Force Butler into an avenging instrument of pursuit.

An order radioed from the German high command at 9:40 A.M. on August 17 and deciphered by British cryptologists less than five hours later—even before General Blaskowitz received it—revealed that Hitler had directed Army Group G to retreat from southern and southwestern France, except for forces consigned to defend the ports. Other intercepts confirmed that the Germans intended to flee rather than fight. Blaskowitz would try to merge his forces with Army Group B, which had begun retreating eastward from Normandy. Now the U.S. Seventh Army could speed north without fear of counterattack from the east by enemy units in the Maritime Alps; airborne troops would screen that right flank, aided by the French maquis and commando teams code-named CHLOROFORM, NOVOCAINE, and EPHEDRINE. Unloading priorities on the beaches were immediately revised to emphasize vehicles and fuel, and Task Force Butler would be reinforced eventually by the 36th Infantry Division—formed from the Texas National Guard—with orders to intercept and destroy the fleeing Germans.

Truscott put the spurs to Butler, who galloped north from Le Muy before dawn on Friday, August 18. "No-man's land," he declared, "is our land." The force had traveled less than seven miles, choosing to avoid the easily barricaded Route Napoléon in this sector, when the column was stopped cold in Draguignan by a stupendous roadblock built by unwitting 36th Division engineers. While this barrow of boulders, mines, and cables was muscled aside, cavalry scouts captured a German corps commander who was found sitting on a park bench with pistol and brandy at hand, "having a nice quiet dignified weep," as Butler reported, while his orderly stood near holding the general's suitcase and eyeing a vengeful French mob.

And then they were off. Task Force Butler covered forty-five miles on Friday and the same on Saturday and Sunday, using Michelin maps and a Cub plane overhead to spot downed bridges, most of which had been blown by the maquis. In Quinson, when jeeps mired in a creek bed, civilians formed a fire brigade to pass flagstones and build a ford. A thousand prisoners were taken in Digne-les-Bains, many of them just arrived from

Grenoble with vague, useless orders to block the Route Napoléon. Sisteron fell without a fight on August 19.

Across folded limestone hills they sped, through stands of chestnut and Aleppo pine, slowed only by nagging gasoline shortages and by road signs that locals had jumbled to confuse the Boche. Frenchmen in thread-bare Great War uniforms held their salutes on the roadsides, and mildewed tricolors were retrieved from cellar hiding holes. Eric Sevareid described the chase

> through civilized, settled Provence, through the sun fields of Van Gogh and the green-and-purple patchwork of Cézanne. . . . The sun was warm and the air like crystal. The fruits were ripening, and the girls were lovely. . . . This was war as it ought to be, the war of pageantry and story.

In Gap, nearly a hundred miles from the sea, a cavalry troop of 130 men and ten armored cars fired a few dozen rounds from their assault guns, toppling a radio tower. An Army captain warned the German garrison that sixty B-17s were prepared to flatten the town; the bluff worked, or perhaps it was fear of maquis reprisals that caused another eleven hundred enemy soldiers to appear in the town plaza, wearing full packs and ready for the cages. They were frog-marched to the rear by captured Poles deputized as prison guards.

At four A.M. on Monday, August 21, an envoy appeared in Butler's command post at Aspres with a message from Truscott: "You will move at first light 21 August with all possible speed to Montélimar. Block all routes of withdrawal up the Rhône valley." Ultra and air reconnaissance had shown four retreating German divisions concentrated along the Rhône, with a rear guard provided by the 11th Panzer Division. The U.S. 3rd Division, Truscott's former command, would act as a hammer in striking from the south, while Task Force Butler and the 36th Division provided the anvil across the Rhône gorge at Montélimar, a town long celebrated for its nougat. Leaving a small blocking force at Gap to protect his rear, Butler and his wayworn column made a sharp turn to the west and at daybreak began a sixty-mile dash toward the river.

By now supply shortages threatened to undermine Truscott's master plan. Thousands of tons of ammunition had been loaded on top of other cargo in ships on the presumption that it would be required for fighting through the beachhead. Now stevedores stacked mountains of ammunition above the waterline so they could burrow deeper into the holds for desperately needed gasoline and food. The audacious sprint north—some scouts were almost to Grenoble—required supply trucks to make a three-hundred-mile round-trip, but the Seventh Army motor pool on August 21 comprised just sixty-two vehicles. Three U.S. infantry divisions together were burning 100,000 gallons of gasoline every day, but beach depots on this Monday held only 11,000 gallons. In the haste to turn ships around, thousands of artillery rounds had been inadvertently sent back to the United States, and a thousand mortar shells somehow ended up in Sardinia. French supply units proved particularly feeble, with severe shortages of even simple items such as tire patches. Artillery firing at night was reduced to conserve ammunition, and GIs in the battle zone were placed on two-thirds rations.

Even so, by late Monday afternoon the vanguard of Task Force Butler reached the wooded high ground north of Montélimar with armored cars, tank destroyers, and Stuart light tanks. An artillery battery unlimbered, and soon the crash of guns echoed across the riverbanks. German convoys nosing north on Highway 7 along the Rhône's eastern shore swerved in panic as exploding shells heaved up geysers of dirt and smoke. A cavalry troop pushed down the Drôme, a narrow, west-flowing tributary of the Rhône; they blew a road bridge and ripped up a truck convoy. Fifty Wehrmacht vehicles soon burned like pitch.

VI Corps had severed the enemy escape route, and they had done it with just a few platoons overlooking the river and gunners reduced to twenty-five rounds per howitzer. From his new command post in Marsanne, eight miles northeast of Montélimar, Butler advised Truscott in a message shortly before midnight that with reinforcement, resupply, and more artillery he would launch a full-throated attack the next day.

"Everything has gone better than we dared hope," Truscott told Sarah in a note scribbled on Monday night, subsequently adding, "Georgie P. is not the only one who can cover ground." He was cheerful enough to tell her about camp life, of eating Gruyère, "which of course delights my soul," and swapping a pound and a half of coffee for three bottles of vermouth. Although he had seen few wildflowers, "this country is too beautiful to fight over, or should be at any rate." He asked her to send him soda crackers, witch hazel, four bottles of hot sauce to spice his rations, and a dozen Benzedrine inhalers.

"I am having my troubles and think I need a lot of things I do not have," he told her. "But think of how my opponent must feel."

His opponent felt dreadful. Blaskowitz, trying to hustle two corps from the Nineteenth Army up the Rhône after receiving Hitler's withdrawal order, was so unsure of battlefield dispositions that he described himself as commanding in "pre-technical days." A sharp debate had unfolded within Army Group G over whether the 11th Panzer Division—the most mobile and lethal unit in southern France—should save itself by fleeing, or be sacrificed to help other divisions escape. For now, as ferries finished lugging panzers to the river's eastern shore near Avignon, the division feinted toward the beachhead, then fell in behind her retreating sisters as a rear guard, bounding north between successive positions eleven kilometers apart to remain beyond American 105mm howitzer range. Trucks and troop carriers dangled ropes to tow bicycle troops, and engineers blew holes in the Rhône cliffsides as shelters against Allied strafing attacks.

Truscott took the German feint. The 3rd Division had traveled more than thirty easy miles from the beachhead before encountering modest resistance and blown bridges on August 20 at Aix-en-Provence; the next morning, Truscott got wind of a battlefield rumor suggesting that 150 panzers had sortied southeast from Avignon. The division commander, Major General John W. "Iron Mike" O'Daniel, was ever eager to do battle. (De Lattre once said that his face "might have been carved out with an axe.") But at noon on August 21, Truscott phoned his command post. "Tell General O'Daniel that I want him to halt the bulk of his command," Truscott told a staff officer. "The 11th Panzer is out in front of you and there is a possibility you might get a counterattack." For two days, the 3rd Division inched along before creeping into Arles at midday on August 24 and into Avignon a day later, tormented by mines, felled trees, and dropped bridges, but by few Germans. Most enemy troops were scurrying north up the Rhône.

At Montélimar, Task Force Butler struggled to hold sway over a 250-square-mile sector east of the river, across terrain ranging from flat farmland to looming hills almost two thousand feet high. Now confronted by two German corps frantic to escape, Butler's little command included thirty Shermans, a dozen tank destroyers, an infantry battalion, and twelve self-propelled guns. Few American fighter-bombers appeared overhead; the first airstrip in southern France had been completed only late on the twentieth, and the Army's swift advance had outrun P-47s flying from Corsica, which often forsook bomb payloads in order to carry extra fuel in wing tanks. Reinforcements from the 36th Division were nowhere to be seen, except for a single infantry battalion and two VI Corps artillery battalions that arrived on August 22.

This pleased Truscott not at all. At eleven that morning he flew by Piper Cub to the 36th Division command post in Aspres to find an infantry regiment and various gunners still in bivouac. The division commander, Major General John E. Dahlquist, was out in the field, so Truscott wheeled on the staff, his carbolic growl restored:

Don't you understand? This is the opportunity of a lifetime. We can
trap the entire German corps and 11th Panzer Division with a few men
and guns. Every minute is precious. Now get moving.

For Dahlquist, he left a scorching note, describing himself as "considerably upset" that artillery and other corps units attached to the 36th were
meandering toward Grenoble rather than besieging Montélimar. "Apparently I failed to make your mission clear to you," Truscott wrote. "Make
no mistake about it—I expect you to command . . . and will hold you
responsible."

In truth, Dahlquist was out of his depth. A large, fleshy Minnesotan who
had worked as a haberdasher and college thespian in Swedish-language dramas before enlisting in 1917, he was humorless, blunt, and given to brooding. The campaign would quickly wear him down. "I must admit I get
winded going up the hills," he wrote his wife. "Too many cigarettes." After
receiving his commander's note, Dahlquist called Truscott to explain that
his division was scattered from St.-Tropez to Grenoble. Half his transport
had yet to be unloaded from the ships; his men had even commandeered a
Spanish consul's car, and a small truck towing an antitank gun had been
seen carrying three dozen men, including one astride the tube. "There is
absolutely no gas available at the beaches," Dahlquist added. "I have less
than five thousand gallons." Truscott waved away the excuses. "Your primary mission is to block the Rhône valley and I expect you to do it," he
said. "And when you run out of gas, you park your trucks and move on
foot."

Tough talk would not win the day. A battalion from the 141st Infantry
cut Highway 7 before dawn on Thursday, August 24, but by early afternoon enemy forces had breached both flanks. A grim unit history later
described Panthers "so close you could feel the heat from the motor." The
battalion withdrew "at night from a hill covered with burning, exploding
tanks, knocked out guns, and dead men."

The German capture of a 36th Division battle plan that same day
revealed a weak seam in the American line, along a segment held by a single engineer company at Bonlieu, several miles east of the Rhône. Six German battle groups attacked there and at other points on Friday, in fighting
so intense that a U.S. battalion commander called artillery onto his own
post to avoid being overrun. A chaotic midnight cavalry charge led personally by the 11th Panzer commander bowled aside another roadblock
on Highway 7—"Come on, you bastards, give up," the Germans demanded
in English—and enemy convoys continued leaking through to the north.

Truscott again flew to Dahlquist's command post, now south of Crest
on the Drôme. "John, I have come here with the full intention of relieving

you from command," the corps commander said. "You have failed to carry out my orders. You have just five minutes in which to convince me you are not at fault." Dahlquist used the time well; Truscott left persuaded the division had finally come to fight.

Surely the artillery had. More than eight battalions—some one hundred guns—ranged the highway, the town, and the narrow river gorge known as the Gate of Montélimar. Shellfire grew so furious that the road asphalt caught fire, and gunners aiming at nearby rail lines smashed several German trains trying to force the gate on the Rhône's east bank. A single infantry company fired 2,500 mortar rounds on Sunday, August 27, in beating off successive counterattacks. The weather gods also helped, with heavy downpours that put the Drôme in spate, inundating the fords German engineers had built of railroad sleepers laid on crushed stone; for several hours, until the water subsided, the fleeing columns were stalled on the south bank under scorching artillery. By midday Sunday, three German infantry divisions had splashed across the Drôme, herded by the 11th Panzer, while a fourth division struggled up Highway 7. Blaskowitz urged speed in messages carried through the screaming shellfire by couriers with dispatch cases.

In a confused mêlée after midnight on Monday, August 28, two columns from the German 198th Division collided northeast of Montélimar with Dahlquist's 143rd Infantry; enemy corpses carpeted the roadbed, and most of those not killed were captured. Savage gunfights raged through the orchards and scrub woods along the Drôme, where the 132nd Field Artillery Battalion opened fire at eight thousand yards on German columns stacked bumper to bumper and three abreast at river fords. Horse-drawn wagons unable to scale the muddy embankment slid back into the water, animals and men shrieking in terror as the singing shell fragments chopped them to pieces.

Task Force Butler, reduced to hardly more than a battalion, soon pushed into Loriol on Highway 7 just below the Drôme; GIs severed the road for a final time. At Livron, on the north bank, they counted five hundred dead horses and one hundred vehicles destroyed within a hundred-yard radius. Truckloads of cognac and cigarettes were abandoned by Germans pelting north toward Lyon, and riflemen pulled looted Bank of France notes by the fistful from the wreckage.

The 3rd Division's 15th Infantry pushed into Montélimar from the south at 2:30 P.M. on Monday, clearing the town of snipers and booby traps through the night and the next morning. Audie Murphy was among those creeping from house to house. As his eyes adjusted to the dim light, behind one creaking door he glimpsed what he later described as "a terrible looking creature with a tommy gun. His face is black; his eyes are red and glaring." Murphy saw a muzzle flash just as he fired; then came the sound of shattering glass. He had shot his own reflection in a mirror, prompting one comrade to observe, "That's the first time I ever saw a Texan beat himself to the draw."

The battle of Montélimar was over, but once again a chance to annihilate a fleeing enemy had gone begging. "Although the concept was daring," a VI Corps colonel concluded, "the execution left much to be desired." Task Force Butler had been too weak, the 36th Division too slow, the 3rd Division too cautious, the Army Air Forces too late to the game. Some sixty thousand U.S. artillery shells had scourged but not obliterated the enemy. "I fumbled it badly," Dahlquist wrote his wife on August 29, "and should have done a great deal better." In exchange for sixteen hundred American casualties, Blaskowitz's losses exceeded ten thousand, including six thousand captured, but half were laborers, railway workers, and other noncombatants. About 80 percent of those fleeing up the Rhône's east bank would reach Lyon, although Blaskowitz reported that the 338th Division mustered barely one thousand men. The 11th Panzer lost half its armor and a quarter of its artillery, but stolen French vehicles kept the division mobile. A German commander considered the escape "almost a miracle."

Truscott was disappointed—perhaps not least in his own generalship. Even the best battle captain may be outmaneuvered by war's caprice and a wily, desperate opponent. But a view of the battlefield from a Cub cockpit soon lifted his spirits: an aide described the scene as "carnage compounded." For fifteen miles along the river, the detritus of eight days' fighting stretched like a black mourning ribbon: two thousand charred vehicles; at least a thousand dead horses, many still harnessed to caissons and gun carriages; and "fire-blackened" Germans said to be such "an affront to the nose" that this grisly segment of highway became known as the Avenue of Stenches. As at Falaise, bulldozer operators wore gas masks.

All in all, Truscott allowed himself what he described as "some degree of satisfaction." In two weeks, another ten thousand square miles of France had been liberated, while VI Corps had captured 23,000 Germans to complement the even larger throng bagged by the French. The DRAGOON death struggle was over, and a race to the German frontier had begun.

Two field-gray torrents streamed toward the Fatherland from southern France. The German First Army—half of Blaskowitz's Army Group G—beat its slow way, mostly on foot, from the nether reaches of the southwest and the Atlantic coast. Though they were 88,000 strong, only a fraction were combat troops, and few of those were armed with more than rifles. Hitler had ordered them to "carry away or destroy during the retreat everything of economic or military value," including bridges, locomotives, and power stations; to this list the high command added horses, cattle, timber, coal, furniture, and even underwear, all of which was plundered or put to the torch. Frenchmen of military age were to be kidnapped whenever possible. Civilians were murdered for petty offenses, such as "improper remarks" about the shrinking Reich.

Allied air strikes and FFI marauders punished this retreating horde, and only sixty thousand or so would reach Germany. "Foot March Group South," one of three columns within First Army, found itself isolated and cut off near Beaugency, southwest of Orléans, despite giving 8 million francs to local officials to buy goodwill and to pay for scorched-earth inconveniences. After making bonfires of their weapons, twenty thousand Germans in Foot March Group South would surrender to one of Patton's divisions along the Loire.

The other retreating gaggle in what Berlin now called "the trekking Wehrmacht" included the 138,000 men of Nineteenth Army tramping up the Rhône with horses so heavily camouflaged that "from above they look like moving bushes," a VI Corps intelligence officer wrote. It was this force that drew most of Seventh Army's attention. Field Order No. 4, issued on August 28, demanded that every effort be exerted to overtake and destroy the Germans, if not in the eighty-four miles between Montélimar and Lyon, then in the two hundred miles between Lyon and the Rhine. Stalin the previous November had declared the Swiss to be "swine" and urged the Allies to disregard Switzerland's neutrality if necessary; that suggestion found no favor in Washington or London, and American and French pursuers were told to swing wide of Geneva and the adjacent cantons. The anxious Swiss mobilized their militia anyway as fighting drew near, and bitterly objected to repeated American violations of Swiss airspace. On a single September day thirty intrusions would be logged, including some by errant P-47s that shot up a train chuffing from Zurich to Basel, mistaking it for German.

By early September, almost 200,000 Allied soldiers had come ashore in Provence. Up the Rhône and along the Route Napoléon, a GI described scenes "of liberation, libation, osculation, gesticulation, and celebration." A BBC reporter found his jeep "festooned with humanity" as he tried to drive north; a British liaison officer accompanying VI Corps admitted that his job was "to get into towns we liberate with the first troops and hand out British flags to be put up, although we have no British fighting units with us." French farm wives filled the helmets of passing soldiers with eggs, or handed out cakes of butter rolled in clean wet leaves.

"Sometimes the sheets on the hotel beds don't get changed between German and American occupation," wrote J. Glenn Gray, a Seventh Army counterintelligence officer. A French officer pointed to a dead German lying on the roadside with his hands folded across his chest and said, *auf Deutsch, "So möchte ich sie alle sehen"*—I'd like to see them all like this. A dignified American woman with close-cropped gray hair, whose living room in Culoz was dominated by a large portrait of her painted by Picasso, sent a note to Seventh Army headquarters along with a fruitcake baked by her companion, Alice B. Toklas. "We have waited for you all so long and here you are," wrote Gertrude Stein. "I cannot tell you enough what it means to see you to hear you to have you here with us." (Of Stein's prose, an American officer wrote: "I understand that she puts together a lot of repetitions which have significance only to those whose minds are in a higher sphere than mine.")

In Grenoble, the fleeing Germans set fire to 37 Rue Maréchal Pétain, said to be the Gestapo headquarters. As victims' bodies turned up here and there, a notice posted at the prefecture advised, "Bring your documents on atrocities to the third floor." A separate room was set aside to record denunciations of collaborators. One drizzly afternoon, several thousand citizens with umbrellas or newspapers folded into rain hats gathered in a factory yard where six French fascists were tied to execution stakes. Eric Sevareid described the "metallic noise of rifle bolts and then the sharp report" of a firing squad; a French officer administered the coup de grâce with a pistol shot in the ear of each slumped figure as a "terrible, savage cry" rose from the howling crowd. "Mothers with babies rushed forward to look on the bodies at close range," Sevareid wrote, "and small boys ran from one to the other spitting upon the bodies."

A 36th Division patrol entered Lyon on Saturday morning, September 2, followed a day later by the French 1st Division hurrying up the west bank of the Rhône. To reach France's third largest city had taken less than three weeks rather than the three months predicted by Churchill. The Americans were accorded the thin satisfaction of knowing, as the historian Trumbull Higgins later wrote, that "the British opposed to the end the only fully successful military operation in the Mediterranean between the fall of Tunis and the final collapse of Germany."

"In the shops one could buy anything," a 45th Division soldier in Lyon told his journal. "Evening gowns, furs, electric fixtures, furniture, antiques, everything except food"—a sad irony in a city celebrated for gastronomy. Lyon during the German occupation had been considered "the capital of repression" in southern France, with 14,000 arrests in the city and surrounding district, as well as 4,300 murders and 300 rapes. The Resistance now cashed its blood chits. "Too much gunfire on the streets here from the FFI," an American colonel wrote. "It seems they are completely out of control. I'm reminded of a revolution."

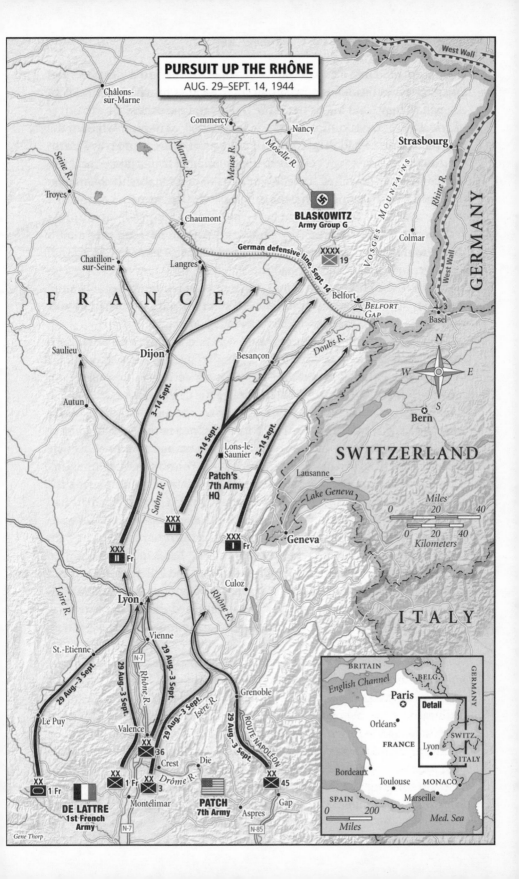

PURSUIT UP THE RHÔNE

AUG. 29–SEPT. 14, 1944

West Wall

Châlons-sur-Marne

Commercy

Nancy

Strasbourg

Seine R.

Marne R.

Meuse R.

Moselle R.

Rhine R.

Troyes

Chaumont

✠ **BLASKOWITZ**
Army Group G

V O S G E S   M O U N T A I N S

Colmar

GERMANY

German defensive line Sept. 14

XXXX 19

Chatillon-sur-Seine

Langres

Belfort

West Wall

F R A N C E

BELFORT GAP

Basel

Saulieu

Dijon

Besançon

Doubs R.

N

Autun

3–14 Sept.

W   E

S

3–14 Sept.

Lons-le-Saunier

SWITZERLAND

Bern

Patch's
7th Army
HQ

Lausanne

3–14 Sept.

3–14 Sept.

Miles
0   20   40

Saône R.

XXX VI

XXX 1 Fr

Lake Geneva

0   20   40
Kilometers

XXX II Fr

Geneva

Loire R.

Lyon

Culoz

Rhône R.

I T A L Y

St.-Etienne

Vienne

Grenoble

29 Aug.–3 Sept.

N-7

Rhône R.

29 Aug.–3 Sept.

29 Aug.–3 Sept.

29 Aug.–3 Sept.

Isère R.

29 Aug.–3 Sept.

ROUTE NAPOLÉON

BRITAIN
BELG.

English Channel

GERMANY

Paris ⊛

Detail

Le Puy

Valence

XX 36

Crest

Die

Orléans

SWITZ.

Lyon

FRANCE

ITALY

XX 1 Fr

XX 3

Drôme R.

PATCH
7th Army

Gap

Bordeaux

MONACO

XX 1 Fr

XX 45

Toulouse

Marseille

DE LATTRE
1st French
Army

Montélimar

Aspres

SPAIN

Med. Sea

N-7

N-85

0   200
Miles

Gene Thorp

Tracers fired into a city hospital that supposedly housed German snipers set the building on fire. Nurses scurried out carrying patients on stretchers, whom they "laid under the plane trees along the parkway by the river near a stack of fresh coffins," Sevareid wrote. Of two dozen bridges in the city, the Germans had demolished all but two. Hundreds of French farmers pushing produce carts aggravated monumental traffic jams, and military convoys often waited three to six hours to cross makeshift spans over the Rhône before swinging northeast toward the Rhine.

Precisely where those convoys should go now confounded the Seventh Army and its commander, Lieutenant General Alexander McCarrell Patch, Jr. DRAGOON's success had put Patch on the cover of *Time* magazine, giving the public another hero to lionize and another battle front to cheer on. "This temporary notoriety will soon die out," the general wrote his wife, Julia. "God protect me from being spoiled by it."

That seemed unlikely. Sandy Patch was tall, gangly, and so taciturn that Truscott believed he had "some difficulty in expressing himself." De Lattre more charitably detected a "mystic turn of mind" in a man with "ascetic features." Possessed of "a temper like the devil before dawn," in one subordinate's phrase, he could also play the accordion and roll a cigarette with one hand from his sack of Bull Durham. Born in the Apache country of southern Arizona to a cavalry lieutenant who had lost a leg chasing horse thieves, Patch had graduated from West Point in 1913 without distinction except as a pole vaulter; he served credibly in France during the last war and began this one in the South Pacific. George Marshall had personally thanked him for a "superb job in New Caledonia and Guadalcanal" as a division and corps commander, then almost cashiered him for indiscreetly discussing the secret American code-breaking that permitted American fighter pilots in April 1943 to ambush and kill Admiral Isoruku Yamamoto, the architect of the Pearl Harbor sneak attack. "I am puzzled as to the course to follow," Marshall had confessed during the investigation. In the end the chief did nothing, preferring to forgive if not forget, and Patch, now fifty-four, had been packed off to Europe.

"It feels as though it was three months ago when we commenced landing on the beaches," Patch wrote Julia in September. "I look now for some very heavy stubborn resistance." Resistance he got, but it was neither especially heavy nor stubborn. After three weeks of running, Blaskowitz halted the Nineteenth Army more than a hundred miles northeast of Lyon at Besançon, a town tucked into an oxbow of the river Doubs and elaborately fortified by the famed seventeenth-century military engineer, Vauban. At Truscott's urging, the 3rd Division pounced before the enemy could dig in, reducing five outer forts in quick order with scaling ladders borrowed from local farmers. Twenty-five tank destroyer shells fired point-blank at the citadel gate unmanned the defenders on September 8, and four thousand men in the garrison surrendered or pelted for the woods on stolen bicycles. "I never saw such confusion in my life," an American officer said. "Germans were flying every which way."

The captured booty included 183,000 gallons of high-octane gasoline, a godsend. Truscott persuaded Patch to exploit the "fleeting opportunity": rather than wait for the French to move forward, as originally planned, three U.S. divisions wheeled east toward the Belfort Gap. That ancient pass, also known as the Gate of Burgundy, had for centuries served as a trade and invasion corridor between the Rhône and the Rhine. Narrowing to just fifteen miles between the Jura Mountains in the south and the Vosges Mountains to the north, the gap in looking east gave onto the Alsatian plain, the Rhine valley, and the Black Forest beyond. Patch's decision to press ahead irked the easily irked De Lattre, who accused the Americans of conspiring to exclude Army B from its fair ration of glory; in response, Patch agreed to permit one French corps to drive toward Belfort between Truscott's right flank and the Swiss border, while another corps, which liberated Dijon on September 11, swung northeast toward Strasbourg. In a September 12 conference, Patch endorsed Truscott's assessment that "the Belfort Gap is the gateway to Germany."

Then the ground shifted. Far from this battlefield, Eisenhower struggled to control an Allied host that stretched from the North Sea to the Côte d'Azur. Prepossessed by the two army groups commanded by Montgomery and Bradley, he devoted little attention and less creative thought to the armies in the south, which now fell under SHAEF. The DRAGOON force he personally had insisted upon now seemed like an awkward appendage, bulling toward what he considered a topographical dead end in the Vosges and the Black Forest. The supreme commander in mid-September told Bradley that he would subordinate Seventh Army to the 12th Army Group but for the political necessity of keeping American suzerainty in the south: De Gaulle surely would demand overall French command of the remaining forces there if Patch was seconded to Bradley. At a minimum, Eisenhower promised, Seventh Army would always support Bradley's larger maneuvers to the north. For that reason, VI Corps and other American forces were to be consolidated, cheek by jowl, with Patton's Third Army, making the U.S. armies contiguous and giving De Lattre the extreme right wing of the Allied line, including the Belfort Gap.

Of these rarefied machinations, Truscott knew nothing. On Thursday, September 14, Patch's Field Order No. 5 arrived at the VI Corps command post. The corps was to pivot northeast, attacking through the Vosges toward Strasbourg. Truscott was "both surprised and disappointed," his headquarters war diary recorded, the "plan being entirely contrary to his conversation with Gen. Patch on [September] 12th." Bedeviled by an abscessed tooth and seething with grievances, Truscott stewed for an evening, nipping from a bottle of "medicinal bourbon." The next morning he composed a letter to Patch that ranged in tone from prickly to impudent.

"The assault on the Belfort Gap should begin at the earliest possible moment," Truscott wrote, before Blaskowitz stiffened his defenses. De Lattre would not be ready until early October, but one French and three American divisions could attack immediately. To fight in the Vosges, as Seventh Army now proposed, would waste "the three most veteran divisions in the American Army. . . . As demonstrated in Italy during last winter in less rugged terrain, the Boche can limit progress to a snail's pace." If Patch did not want VI Corps to force the Belfort Gap, Truscott proposed packing up his divisions for an assault on Genoa to help Fifth Army in Italy. Unaware that the army commander was heeding a SHAEF directive, he closed by asking Patch to refer the matter up the chain of command for adjudication.

Truscott sent the note to the Seventh Army command post, now in a French barracks at Lons-le-Saunier, where Napoléon had persuaded Marshal Ney—"the bravest of the brave"—to rejoin him during the Hundred Days.

Patch phoned at 6:30 P.M. on Saturday, September 16.

Patch: I don't think that letter of yours was advisable. A less sensitive man than I—and I'm not sensitive at all—would see the lack of confidence shown in your leaders.

Truscott: I wrote the letter only because it was something I believe in.

Patch: When I have something on my chest I just have to say it to that person.

Truscott: You have my complete and wholehearted support, once the decision is made. If you think someone else can do the job better, it's all right with me. But I don't think you can find one.

Patch: I know that.

So ended DRAGOON, in bickering frustration.

Truscott's pluck notwithstanding, his ability to force the Belfort Gap and jump the Rhine was dubious at best. With frayed logistical lines stretching three hundred miles, a senior officer observed, VI Corps was "living with just one day's supplies ahead of the game." Blaskowitz on September 19 reported to the German high command that his residual armies were forming a defensive bulwark west of the Vosges, "still able to fight, although much weakened." His greatest fear—a flanking attack southeast toward Belfort by Patton's Third Army—had not come to pass. Of the Army Group G troops who decamped from southern France, more than 130,000 had escaped, although Nineteenth Army salvaged only 165 of 1,600 artillery pieces, and 11th Panzer had barely two dozen tanks left. For his troubles, Blaskowitz was sacked that very day; infuriated by the retreat and by reports of German straggling, Hitler summoned a panzer army commander from Russia to replace him. Blaskowitz soon returned to Dresden. "Hans is now home," his wife wrote her relatives, "planting cabbage."

On the same Tuesday that Blaskowitz was relieved, Truscott received his third star. He, Patch, De Lattre, and their men had reason for pride: in barely a month, they had hastened the German eviction from France, opened new ports and airfields, started the rehabilitation of French industry and commerce from Bordeaux to Burgundy, and demolished two enemy armies by killing, wounding, capturing, or marooning 158,000 Germans.

But ahead lay the granite and gneiss uplands of the Vosges, a primordial badland of cairns, moors, peat bogs, and hogback ridges rising above four thousand feet. Freezing autumn rains had begun here already, Sevareid noted, causing GIs to recall "the Italian winter and to long again for home." The VI Corps war diary recorded, "Looking for skis." In a letter home, Truscott wrote, "I dread the approaching wet and cold and snow and tedious mountain work. The skies weep continuously now." Patrols creeping along the dark flanks of the Vosges could hear the plink of picks and shovels as German sappers burrowed into the hillsides. "There are indications," Truscott told Sarah, "that the beast has every intention of continuing the fight right to the bitter end."

"Harden the Heart and Let Fly"

A WORLD away, although barely two hundred crow-flying miles distant, the Allied cavalcade that had burst from Normandy now spilled across the continental crown, down pilgrim paths and drove roads, through fields of wheat stubble and ripening beets, greeted by pealing church bells and farmers who waved with one hand while tossing buckets of water on their burning crofts with the other.

By the end of August the front stretched from Abbeville on the Somme to Commercy on the Meuse, where a bridge was seized intact on the morning of the thirty-first. A great crescent, extending from Brest nearly to Belgium, was packed with more than two million Allied soldiers and 438,000 vehicles—a two-to-one edge in combat troops over German forces in the west and a twenty-to-one advantage in tanks. The AAF and RAF together massed 7,500 bombers and 4,300 fighters. Montgomery's fifteen divisions in 21st Army Group filled a fast-moving front sixty miles wide across the hedgeless fields between the Seine and the Somme, overrunning or isolating the Rocket Gun Coast. The last of eight thousand V-1s was fired from France on the night of September 1, as launch battalions fled for Holland or Germany; twelve hundred more would be dropped from Luftwaffe aircraft in coming months, but to small effect. "The battle of London is won," Britain's home secretary declared. (Churchill privately proposed that all V-1 equipment and German fortifications along the Channel coast be destroyed to prevent future use by the French, "if they fall out of temper with us.")

In 12th Army Group, Bradley commanded twenty-one divisions, with three more soon to arrive. The First Army zone now spanned sixty-five miles, plated on both flanks by armored divisions, while Patton's Third Army braced the right wing with two corps abreast. The U.S. Ninth Army was created in early September with orders to finish reducing Brest and to contain the enemy garrisons in other Breton ports; the German commander in Brest soon buckled, emerging from the rubble with his Irish setter, a ton of personal luggage, and his fishing tackle. "I deserve a rest," he told his captors. Four Allied airborne divisions also had regrouped in England to await another summons of the trumpet.

Under this onslaught the Wehrmacht stumbled eastward in "a planless flight," as one German general acknowledged. OB West listed eighteen divisions as "completely fit" for combat, while twenty-one others were "totally unfit," sixteen were "partially fit," seven had been "dissolved," and nine were "rebuilding." Flyers signed by Field Marshal Model and passed out along the retreat routes advised, "We have lost a battle, but I tell you we will still win this war!" A proposed defensive line on the Somme never congealed, however, and German soldiers streamed toward the German frontier through Picardy and Belgium, Lorraine and the Ardennes, bellowing, "The Americans will be here in twenty minutes!" Some jumpy demolitionists misplaced their explosives so that trees to be felled as obstructions instead toppled away from the road. In what the OB West war diary called an "ignominious rout," Germans unable to find white flags surrendered by waving chickens.

On came the avenging armies—perhaps not twenty minutes behind German heels, but close enough. "Any Boches today?" an ancient Frenchman was asked near the front at Guise. "Ah, yes, the brutes," he replied, spitting in the road and pointing in all directions. "There, and there, and there, and there." By truck and by foot the pursuers pursued; a battalion from the 1st Division, which covered 272 miles in the last week of August, rode twenty-two miles on August 29 and walked another eight after the trucks circled back for another load of troops. The British 11th Armored Division drove through the entire rainy night of August 30, drivers snoozing during each brief halt. Gun flashes limned the skyline like heat lightning, and shell craters were edged with the gray lace of burned powder until military traffic pounded them smooth. Fleeing German dray horses were cut down by the thousands; they were among a half-million killed in August, always to the regret of Allied cavalrymen. "There was nothing for it," a British trooper said, "but to harden the heart and let fly."

No sentimentality obtained for enemy soldiers. "We blew up everything that didn't look right," a lieutenant in the 60th Infantry told his diary, "especially little haystacks out in the fields, a good place for German snipers." At Braine, near Reims, Patton's vanguard caught two trains with seventy railcars carrying troops and loot from Paris; tank and tank destroyer fire slapped the engines, then automatic weapons stitched the carriages, killing fifty before five hundred others surrendered. A witness with Third Army described "the long ecstatic agony of serving machine guns on living targets," and the pleasure that tank gunners felt in fingering their Sherman triggers, which they called "tits." "The whole west front has collapsed," a German regimental commander wrote on August 31, "and the other side is marching about at will."

Not quite. Fuel shortages, nettlesome since early August, had become grievous as the Allied armies raced eastward. Daily fuel consumption had tripled from six gallons per vehicle in late July to eighteen; a single armored division now burned 100,000 gallons in each day of cross-country fighting. The five-gallon can remained the primary delivery means, and SHAEF logisticians were so desperate that consideration was given to using battleships to haul jerricans of gas to the French beaches. A Canadian corps was immobilized for several days; two of eight divisions in the British Second Army remained on the Seine to allow the other six to move on. A corps in the U.S. First Army stalled for four days, and corps commanders cadged cans of gasoline to keep their staff cars running. Nowhere did the need pinch more than in Third Army. Of seventeen tanks sent to capture a Meuse bridge in Verdun on August 31, all but three ran out of gas en route. Patton's fuel dumps the previous day had received 32,000 gallons, less than one-tenth of Third Army's requirement. His G-4, the army logistician, rated the supply of motor fuel as "extremely critical." "Damn it, Brad," Patton told Bradley, "just give me 400,000 gallons of gasoline and I'll put you inside Germany in two days."

Onward they pushed, on foot when necessary, through villages displaying homemade American flags, crayoned on paper or pillowcases with polka-dot stars. "Vote for Dewey," mischievous GIs yelled, to be answered

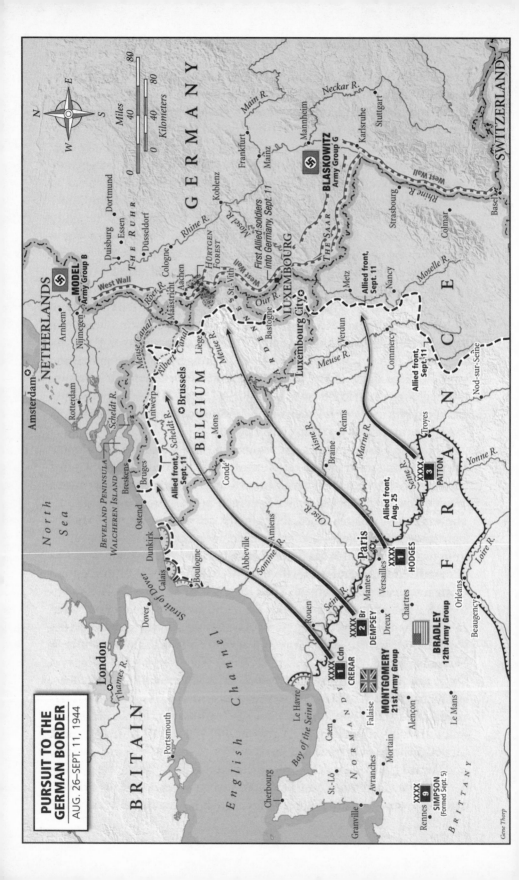

PURSUIT TO THE
GERMAN BORDER
AUG. 26–SEPT. 11, 1944

by cheering, agreeable Frenchmen, "Vote for Dew-ee." An observant soldier told his parents that the locals numbered their building floors beginning above the ground level. "If that was the only mistake the French ever
made," he added, "we wouldn't be here today."

Giddy rumors swirled, including a Swiss claim that Hitler had fled to
Spain. An intercepted German radio report of insurrection in Cologne
stirred great excitement until U.S. analysts realized that the news was dis-
information from an Allied psychological operations team. Still, optimism ran rife. Bradley on September 1 predicted that he would reach the
Rhine by Sunday, September 10, and staff officers selected half a dozen
river crossing sites. Bradley's aide jotted in a diary, "Everything we talk
about now is qualified by the phrase, 'If the war lasts that long.'"

"End the war in '44," soldiers chanted. *Time* reported that officials
from New York to Seattle had begun planning Victory-in-Europe celebrations; a man in Santa Fe had offered $10 "to the first newsboy to reach him
with the *New Mexican* announcing the fall of Germany." With the European war seemingly winding down, Churchill's War Office asked Montgomery whether he could spare an extra army headquarters staff for Burma.
The Pentagon drafted plans to leave one-fifth of all ordnance stocks in
Europe with a postwar occupation force, while one-fifth would be sent to
the Pacific and three-fifths shipped home.

"There is a feeling of elation, expectancy, and almost bewilderment,"
the prime minister's secretary wrote on September 1. Beetle Smith assured
reporters, "Militarily the war is won." Even as Eisenhower tried to tamp
down expectations, he told his diary, "Our military forces can advance
almost at will. . . . The defeat of the German armies is complete, and the
only thing now needed to realize the whole conception is speed."

The Allied juggernaut aimed vaguely for Berlin, intent on ripping out
Germany's political heart. But a nearer, interim target was the enemy's
industrial heart in the Ruhr valley, a sooty ellipse that extended east from
the Rhine for some sixty miles to include the smokestack cities of Essen,
Dortmund, and Duisburg. Two-thirds of German steel and more than
half the country's coal had traditionally come from the Ruhr, and loss of
the region would also devastate the chemical and munitions industries,
with a projected 40 percent drop in artillery ammunition and explosives
production. Hitler would have no choice but to defend this vital region,
and a SHAEF study signed by Eisenhower in May posited that "an attack
aimed at the Ruhr is likely to give us every chance of bringing to battle
and destroying the main German armed forces."

Four paths led to the Ruhr from the west, but most planners considered only two of them suitable for big mechanized armies. One route,

north of the Ardennes—the rugged forested hills that occupied much of southern Belgium and Luxembourg—aimed directly at the Ruhr; it could be supported by Allied seapower and aircraft based in Britain. The second route angled south of the Ardennes, through the so-called Metz Gap. Even before OVERLORD began, Eisenhower had advocated taking both avenues, a strategy of advance on "two mutually supporting axes" that would stretch enemy defenses across a broad front, exploit Allied mobility, and permit shifts in the weight of attack as needed. The southern route also would menace the Saar valley, second only to the Ruhr as an industrial locus in western Germany. SHAEF in late August estimated that the enemy could muster no more than eleven divisions northwest of the Ardennes and five divisions to the south. Eisenhower's planners had proposed that 21st Army Group strike northeast toward the Rhine through Amiens and Liège in the main effort, while 12th Army Group lunged toward Metz and beyond in a subsidiary attack.

Montgomery would have none of it. In a message to Brooke in London on August 18, he had urged channeling both army groups north of the Ardennes "as a solid mass of some forty divisions which would be so strong that it need fear nothing." Concentration of Anglo-American power in the north would utilize the Allied preponderance in armor and bring the war to a quicker close, an issue of particular urgency as Britain ran out of men. Montgomery also argued that a single commander was needed to oversee Allied ground forces driving toward Germany from the Seine—"This is a *whole time* job for one man"—and he claimed that Bradley agreed with this strategic assessment.

Bradley most certainly did *not* agree, nor did most of the other senior Allied generals, including Montgomery's own chief of staff, Major General Francis W. "Freddie" de Guingand. When told that Montgomery proposed to "put everything in one punch," Air Marshal Tedder retorted, "I always thought in a fight it was better to use both hands." Eisenhower on August 23 drove to the 21st Army Group command post in Condé, near Falaise, for a long, tedious conference from which Beetle Smith was excluded at Montgomery's churlish insistence although De Guingand was allowed to remain. When Montgomery proposed halting Patton's Third Army to divert more fuel to the other spearheads, Eisenhower told him, "The American public would never stand for it, and public opinion wins wars." Standing before a map with his hands clasped behind his back, Montgomery replied, "Victories win wars. Give people victory and they won't care who won it."

Montgomery emerged from the caravan at Condé having extracted certain concessions to strengthen his attack, including priority in using the airborne reserve and in drawing supplies. Moreover, the U.S. First Army would swing largely north of the Ardennes rather than south; this would shore up 21st Army Group's right flank, a reinforcement that some SHAEF planners had long considered.

Eisenhower also agreed that a single commander would oversee the assault on Germany, but that generalissimo would not be B. L. Montgomery. Rather, Eisenhower would take the job himself, and before leaving Condé he told Montgomery that at George Marshall's insistence this rearrangement would take effect in another week. In truth, Eisenhower had dictated a secret memo to his staff in mid-May laying out his eventual role as ground commander, while specifying that "nothing must be said . . . to indicate there would ever be any diminution of General M's command or responsibility. . . . The less said the better."

Churchill, "as a solace," promoted Montgomery to the rank of field marshal on September 1, giving him the equivalent of five stars to Eisenhower's four. This, as the prime minister said with no little spite, "will put the changes in command in their proper perspective." Although Eisenhower praised Montgomery to reporters as "not only my very close and warm friend, but . . . one of the great soldiers of this or any other war," the promotion went down badly at SHAEF.

"Damn stupid & I warrant most offensive to Eisenhower & the Americans," Admiral Ramsay told his diary. Patton wrote Bea on September 1 that "the Field Marshal thing made us sick, that is Bradley and me." Even Brooke felt uneasy, telling a colleague that Montgomery "is probably the finest tactical general we have had since Wellington. But on some of his strategy, and especially his relations with the Americans, he is almost a disaster." Militarily the war might be won, as Beetle Smith had averred, but close combat within the Allied high command was just starting.

Late in the morning of Saturday, September 2, Eisenhower flew in his B-25 to Bradley's command post in Chartres. In the middle distance the twin spires of the magnificent cathedral poked the heavens. Patton also arrived, "bumptious and noisy," in a staff officer's description, accoutred with a revolver and his bull terrier, Willie, whom he occasionally introduced as "a sodomy son of a bitch." An aide made drinks with ice from a refrigerator that Eisenhower had given Bradley after complaining, "Goddamn it, I'm tired of drinking warm whiskey every time I come to your headquarters."

On a huge wall map of Europe, a bull's-eye encircled Berlin. Dressed in his combat jacket and jump boots, Bradley argued for crossing the German frontier immediately, thus preventing enemy defenders from shoring up the border fortifications known as the Siegfried Line. He also wanted a bulletproof car and armored jeeps for travel in Germany. "Each town in our path" should be bombed, he believed, to "teach them the lesson of death and destruction they have carried to the rest of the world."

Patton offered to "stake my reputation" on Third Army's ability to fight to the Rhine despite crippling supply shortages. "That reputation of yours hasn't been worth very much," Eisenhower said, smiling broadly. Patton barked with laughter. "Pretty good now," he said.

A message from Beetle Smith warning of approaching storms cut short the conference. No sooner had the B-25 lifted off than flames licked from the right engine. After an emergency landing, Eisenhower folded himself into the rear seat of a tiny L-5 Sentinel for a turbulent 120-mile flight west to the Cotentin Peninsula, where his new headquarters had just opened near Granville, another of those French coastal towns that Englishmen over the centuries had captured, fortified, lost, burned, bombarded, and enjoyed on holiday.

Short of fuel, tossed by gusty winds, and unable to find an airstrip in the pelting rain, the pilot set down on a narrow beach not far from the supreme commander's compound. As he helped push the plane toward the dunes to escape the rising tide, Eisenhower slipped in the sand, badly wrenching his right knee. After hobbling across a salt marsh with an arm around the pilot's neck, anxiously watching for mines, he flagged down a jeep carrying eight astonished GIs, who lifted him into the front seat and drove him to his villa. Two aides carried him to a bedroom.

Eisenhower had hurt his left knee in the 1912 Army football game against Tufts, a serious injury requiring seven hospitalizations over the years. But no mishap was more inopportune than this damage to his "good" knee, now swollen and acutely painful. A doctor slathered the joint in a plaster cast and prescribed indefinite bed rest; Eisenhower refused to allow his blood pressure to be read for fear that the persistent ringing in his ears marked some debilitating condition that would get him sent home.

For more than a fortnight the supreme commander was largely immobilized, leaving Granville briefly only three times in eighteen days. The villa was pleasant enough, with a splendid view of Mont-St.-Michel to the south. Two resident cows provided fresh milk and cream for the mess, and for ninety minutes each day a therapist baked and massaged Eisenhower's aching knee. In scribbled notes to Mamie he apologized for being "always a bit off-key when I try to talk seriously," and he confessed to thinking of their dead son, Doud Dwight, who would have been twenty-seven. To his living son, John, a newly commissioned lieutenant who had proposed they make "an air tour of the United States" after the war, Eisenhower wrote, "Who is going to buy the plane? I am broke and I suspect you are not far from it."

Even for an ambulatory commander, Granville was an ill-chosen headquarters—isolated, remote from the front, and so plagued with signal deficiencies that for three weeks Eisenhower could communicate with his armies only by cable, courier, messages jury-routed through the RAF, or in rare tête-à-tête conferences. His indifference to Seventh Army's exploits in southern France owed something to his sequestration in Granville, but the forced seclusion also allowed him to mull his plan for the push into Germany. Following the hail-fellow session with Bradley and Patton in Chartres, he came to regret his earlier concessions to Montgomery and to reaffirm his commitment to a multipronged advance on a broad front. In a two-hour lunch with Ramsay, Eisenhower complained that Montgomery seemed to covet Bradley's motor transport in order to allow 21st Army Group to "advance alone on Berlin. This would entail a complete standstill order on the U.S. armies." Montgomery's view certainly was more nuanced—he by no means favored halting the U.S. First Army—but Ramsay denounced the ostensible proposal as "Monty-like" and "tripe."

On Monday, September 4, Eisenhower told his lieutenants by cable that "our best opportunity of defeating the enemy in the west lies in striking at the Ruhr and at the Saar." Patton's advance, hamstrung by the fuel priority accorded First Army to support Montgomery, was to be reinvigorated; the two American armies would share equally in the paltry gasoline supply, each receiving 3,500 tons a day. "We must now as never before keep the enemy stretched everywhere," Eisenhower wrote Marshall the same day.

An exasperated Montgomery privately complained that Eisenhower appeared "to have a curious idea that every army command must have an equal and fair share of the battle." Given the logistical limitations, he insisted, "the only policy is to halt the left and strike with the right, or halt the right and strike with the left." The left—his force and First Army—was aimed at the Ruhr and therefore deserved first call on supplies. In a quick, eyes-only rebuttal to Eisenhower on Monday, he wrote:

> We have now reached a stage where one really powerful and full-blooded thrust toward Berlin is likely to get there and thus end the German war. We have *not* enough maintenance resources for two full-blooded thrusts. . . . If we attempt a compromise solution and split our maintenance resources so that neither thrust is full-blooded we will prolong the war. I consider the problem viewed as above as very simple and clear-cut.

Eisenhower replied on Tuesday, affirming his order and further explaining his strategic logic. But so maladroit was the Granville signals operation that the message reached Montgomery in two pieces, backward, and late: the second half arrived on Thursday and the first half on Saturday. A British officer later reported, "Monty walked up and down, waving his arms and saying, 'The war is lost.'"

The misdirected signal was entirely apt for two men talking past each other. Soldiers and historians were to argue the merits of each case for decades. Eisenhower later caricatured Montgomery's scheme as a "preposterous proposal to drive on a single pencil-line thrust straight on to Berlin," and Smith called it "the most fantastic bit of balderdash ever proposed by a competent general." Bradley, who had been victimized in Sicily by what he called Montgomery's "arrogant and egotistical" demand that U.S. forces give way to the British, asserted that "if you try to fight the German on one front only, you're playing right into his hands."

Montgomery's vision had the military virtue of mass—the concentration of combat power—but it ran counter to SHAEF calculations of what was possible for an Allied force still drawing supplies across beaches several hundred miles away. One study estimated that a single-axis thrust to Berlin by three British and two American corps would need nearly 500 truck companies, of which only 347 existed. Even with supplies augmented by airlift and through the docks at Antwerp, a long lunge across Germany would require the "wholesale grounding" of many Allied corps, including twenty-two U.S. divisions relegated to "hibernation." Moreover, the need to protect long open flanks in the enemy heartland meant that a solitary Allied spearhead would be no stronger than six or eight divisions with little air support—"easy prey for the German mobile reserves," as one logistician warned. A British intelligence brigadier at SHAEF concluded that simply encircling and holding the Ruhr would prove impossible without more robust combat forces than now available on the Western Front. "Monty," he added, "was overbidding his hand." Even De Guingand cited fatal shortages of transport and bridging equipment; after the war, he observed that Hitler's eventual defeat required a Soviet offensive of 160 divisions complemented by a massive attack from the west and another eight months of savage air bombardment.

Most strategists would come to similar conclusions. Britain's youngest brigadier in 1944, the future field marshal Lord Carver, wrote:

> In both world wars there were countless examples of single thrusts . . . attracting the enemy's reserves and thus being brought to a halt. . . . The strategy which had been generally successful was one of alternating thrusts, delivering a blow in an unexpected area when the enemy's reserves had been attracted elsewhere.

Two-fisted punching had in fact won through for Montgomery at Ala-mein, Mareth, and Normandy. Likewise, the American historian Russell F. Weigley observed that, for the side playing a strong hand, "the whole history of American strategy since U. S. Grant confirmed that the enemy can be hit with advantage at several places and thus forced to accentuate his weakness through dissipation." As the historian Gerhard L. Weinberg noted, "Whatever Montgomery's talents, mounting rapid thrusts was not one of them."

Nor was the field marshal inclined "to appreciate that in higher strat-egy political factors can sometimes have the same weight as purely military considerations," as Montgomery's biographer Ronald Lewin later acknowl-edged. Eisenhower believed that triumph in Europe must be shared, espe-cially given the expanding American dominance in men and matériel. But this equitable recognition cut no ice with Montgomery: Eisenhow-er's "ignorance as to how to run a war is absolute and complete," he told Brooke, who made this condemnation his own. "Ike knows nothing about strategy and is *quite* unsuited to the post of supreme commander," Brooke confided to his diary. Eisenhower's decision to personally oversee the ground campaign, he wrote, "is likely to add another 3 to 6 months on to the war."

Eisenhower's generalship was without doubt vulnerable to criticism. Montgomery's complaint that "he was extremely susceptible to the per-sonality of the last commander he saw before he made his decision" had a whiff of truth, as did Patton's diary entry on September 2: "Ike is all for caution, since he had never been at the front and has no feel of actual fighting." Beguiled by the pursuit of a battered enemy, he repeatedly gave short shrift to logistical needs and failed to ensure that his directives were heeded. Smith groused that "the trouble with Ike" was that "instead of giving direct and clear orders, [he] dresses them up in polite language." He was a conciliator, Smith added, who rarely issued unequivocal orders and never decreed: *Do as I command and be silent.* If consistent in his views supporting a broad, multipronged assault on Germany, he was "hardly decisive in the way he communicated them to Montgomery," Ste-phen E. Ambrose later wrote. "He allowed Montgomery to carry every argument to its bitter end."

This bitter argument indeed was far from over. "There is never a moment that doesn't have its strain or particular problem," Eisenhower had writ-ten Mamie, and he would confess to her, "God, how wearying and wear-ing it all gets." Yet Allied unity remained the central principle of his command and he would go to great lengths to preserve it, including self-delusion. "The team is working well," he wrote Marshall in September.

"Without exception all concerned have now fully accepted my conception of our problem and are carrying it out intelligently and with energy."

The armies fought on, largely unaware of the generals' quarrels at echelons above reason. All but immobilized for the first five days of September, Third Army at last saw fuel stocks begin to improve. New orders listed Metz and two misspelled German cities, "Maintz" and "Frankfort," as objectives. B-24s were pressed into service as flying gas stations, each carrying two hundred five-gallon cans; Patton encouraged air resupply by awarding bounties of confiscated cognac and champagne to helpful pilots. With almost 300,000 troops, Third Army remained short of everything from grenades and binoculars to radios and wristwatches; army shortages for the week of September 2 included 270,000 pairs of combat boots, 540,000 wool blankets, 6,000 radio tubes, and 48 surgical bullet probes. Patton had given up cigars in a gesture of solidarity with his strapped army—he often smoked twenty a day—but captured German commissaries yielded three million pounds of beef, fifty thousand cases of champagne, and huge stocks of sardines and the Italian silk used for parachutes.

In a breezy session with reporters, Patton first complained that "a goddamn army commander doesn't do anything but sit around and curse," then explained, "I never worried about flanks. That was probably due to my long-felt masculine virility." After lamenting that "when you slow anything down, you waste human lives," he told the scribes, "I hope to go through the Siegfried Line like shit through a goose."

To his northwest, Courtney Hodges's First Army crossed the Belgian border and liberated the Walloon city of Mons early on September 3. "Once again," the 3rd Armored Division reported, "cognac, champagne, and pretty girls." And once again, tens of thousands of retreating Germans faced annihilation. Even with two-thirds of its worn tanks now unfit for combat, the 3rd Armored took 2,500 prisoners, and this on a day when the division was grounded for want of fuel. What one U.S. Army unit described as "a confused, blinded, heterogeneous mass" from twenty or more dismembered Wehrmacht divisions now crawled through southwest Belgium with stolen French cars and Belgian farm wagons, canalized by American roadblocks.

Bounding from the south, the 1st Division fell on the German flank. Shermans churned across the loamy fields trailed by olive-drab clouds of riflemen. Four-barrel .50-caliber antiaircraft guns, depressed as infantry weapons, peppered enemy ranks, and P-47s peeled from the perfect sky to rake the German columns, nose to tail. "Those are magnificent Belgian horses, and I hate to pot them," one pilot radioed. "Well, here goes." Long

Tom 155mm field guns, accustomed to pounding targets a dozen miles away, now served as sniper rifles, shattering half-tracks and haystacks until the air reeked of burning fodder and flesh, both equine and human. "You only want to slaughter us," a captured officer complained.

In addition to some 3,500 enemy dead, another 25,000 would be bagged alive in three days. In batches of fifty they trudged to the cages, booed by passing Belgian Boy Scouts whose mothers were carving steaks from the horse carcasses. Three thousand prisoners temporarily penned in the slag yard of an old redbrick sugar refinery emptied their pockets as ordered, and GIs sifted through the little piles of nail clippers and clasp knives; an American lieutenant held up a discarded condom wrapped in foil and told a chubby *Landser,* "You will not love for a while." With Falaise and the capitulation at Brest, the Mons Pocket was among Germany's worst drubbings in northwestern Europe in 1944.

Thirty miles to the north, the British Second Army also swept into Belgium, after streaking 250 miles in six days. Hitler ordered Boulogne and Dunkirk held as bitter-end fortresses, but the Canadians had taken Rouen and pressed toward Bruges. General Eberbach was caught fleeing in a Volkswagen outside Amiens—"I commanded what used to be the Seventh Army," he told his captors—and the garrison commander at Le Havre would soon surrender in his pajamas, bemedaled nonetheless, along with eleven thousand others.

At eight P.M. on Sunday, September 3, the Welsh Guards rolled into Brussels and ignited a tumultuous celebration. "The joy of Paris was a pallid thing compared to this extravaganza," Moorehead reported. The Guards Armored Division clattered down the Chaussée de Ninove, tank tracks chewing at the cobbles. The great dome of the Palais de Justice, set afire as a parting gesture by the retreating Germans, was likened by a reporter to "a flambeau in the night." Ecstatic Belgians shouted the only English they knew—"Goodbye, Tommy, goodbye!"—and lobbed hydrangeas, apples, and bottles of Lion d'Or beer into the passing vehicles.

Local worthies appeared in sashes and other badges of office to declaim, proclaim, acclaim. The Royal Hampshires found that no sooner did they post a sentry than a happy throng would "bear the man away . . . to regale him." Bistros sent waiters into the streets to fill soldiers' mess tins with champagne and ice cream; the bulging larders caused one Guardsman to grumble that "Belgians felt they had done their bit by eating their way through the war." Undimmed, the celebration would continue for more than a week, fueled by the capture of a German wine dump containing "eighty thousand bottles of a remarkable claret," Moorehead wrote. Countless drunken verses of "Tipperary" could be heard day and night, and effigies of Hitler were paraded through the streets to be beaten, burned, and cursed in Flemish, French, Dutch, and various other liberated tongues.

On Monday at noon British tanks nosed through the outskirts of Antwerp, past houses put to the torch by Belgian resistance fighters for belonging to alleged collaborators. Jubilant crowds reluctantly parted, allowing the 11th Armored Division to race downtown, where nonplussed German soldiers were still sipping beer in sidewalk cafés. By two that afternoon, a tank squadron had reached the docks. Thanks to the Belgian "White Resistance," which had attacked and delayed German demolitionists, the port, sluice gates, and underground oil storage tanks with their capacity of two million barrels remained intact. A sharp firefight around pillboxes in a city park petered out by 9:30 P.M., and surviving defenders surrendered or melted away. After a fruitless search for a cinema to use as a jail, British officers instead converted the local zoo into a prison compound—hungry citizens, it was said, had devoured most of the menagerie. Six thousand captives soon crowded the pens, sorted into separate cages in the lion house for officers, Belgian fascists, and German mistresses. Other ranks filled the bear pits, the tiger pens, the monkey house. "The captives sat on the straw," wrote Martha Gellhorn, "staring through the bars."

With Brittany's ports soon to be forsaken, no liberated city in Europe was more important to the Allied cause than Antwerp. By the mid-sixteenth century it had become the richest town on the Continent, surpassing even Venice and Genoa, with a hundred or more ships at anchor every day, carrying spices from Portugal, grain from the Baltic, silk embroideries from Italy. The Inquisition, a Spanish pillage, and the rise of Holland cost the city its prosperity; not until the nineteenth century did Antwerp ascend again to become a bustling hive of diamond-cutting, cigar-rolling, sugar-refining, and beer-brewing. By the 1930s it ranked with Hamburg, New York, and Rotterdam among the world's finest ports, handling a thousand ships each month, with twenty-nine miles of quays, more than six hundred cranes, nine hundred warehouses, and a vast rail yard. All this was recovered whole on September 4. One early-twentieth-century estimate had calculated that the city's defenses "would require an army of 260,000 men to besiege it effectually, and at least a year to reduce it by starvation." The British had needed but a few hours.

The capture of Antwerp and the exploitation of its port had been stressed since the earliest Allied invasion plans in December 1941. Eisenhower in a message to Montgomery on August 24 reiterated the need "to get a secure base at Antwerp," an order repeated in a formal directive to top commanders on August 29 and September 4. Montgomery echoed the supreme commander, stating his intent "to capture Antwerp," as well as "to destroy all enemy forces in the Pas de Calais and Flanders." But Antwerp had a topographical quirk that required more than simply seizing the docks and the monkey house. Communication with the North Sea from the port required control of the eighty-mile estuary at the mouth of the river Scheldt, including fortified Walcheren Island on the north side of the Scheldt, and the polders around Breskens on the southern bank.

Having sailed these waters in war and in peace for centuries, the Royal Navy was intimately familiar with the estuary. Four thousand British troops had died of fever on Walcheren during a campaign in 1809, with the survivors evacuated ignominiously to England. Churchill himself, as first lord of the Admiralty, had rushed to Antwerp in October 1914 to rally the Belgian government in defense of the port. Admiral Ramsay on September 3 sent a telegram to SHAEF, with a copy to Montgomery, reminding all that "both Antwerp and Rotterdam are highly vulnerable to mining and blocking. If enemy succeeds in these operations, the time it will take to open ports cannot be estimated." The first sea lord, Admiral Andrew Browne Cunningham, told his diary on September 7: "Again impressed on the [Combined Chiefs of Staff] that Antwerp, though completely undamaged, was as much use as Timbuctoo unless the entrance and other forts were silenced and the banks of the Scheldt occupied. I fear this is being overlooked by the generals."

Alas, yes. An Ultra intercept of a Führer order on September 3, stressing the "decisive importance" of holding the Scheldt, was disregarded by Allied commanders; so were subsequent orders from Hitler, including an intercepted message reminding Fifteenth Army that "it must be insured that the Allies cannot use the harbor for a long time." This "incomprehensible" error, the historian Ralph Bennett later concluded, was "a strategic mistake of such magnitude that its repercussions were felt almost until the end of the war." Eisenhower's messages to his top commanders about Antwerp had not specified capturing the Scheldt, and neither Montgomery nor Dempsey, the Second Army commander, attended the issue. Montgomery believed the enemy army's position was hopeless. "The bottle is now corked," he declared, "and they will not be able to get out."

A Royal Marine Commando unit trained for amphibious assault had instead been diverted to besiege Dunkirk from a landward vantage. The 11th Armored Division commander, Major General G. P. B. "Pip" Roberts, had been told little more than to seize the docks and port in Antwerp. His corps commander, Lieutenant General Brian G. Horrocks, later confessed to "suffering from liberation euphoria" that entailed dining with the Belgian queen mother and her lady-in-waiting rather than studying a map. "If I had ordered Roberts not to liberate Antwerp but to bypass the town and advance only fifteen miles northwest . . . we should have blocked the Beveland isthmus" and potentially trapped the Fifteenth Army near the Dutch border, Horrocks wrote in his memoir. "My eyes were fixed on the Rhine."

The British drive soon was stymied. An artillery major directed fire to the north from the top floor of an Antwerp office building while a Belgian secretary brought trays of coffee with cognac and played American blues on the office phonograph. But none of the bridges across the imposing Albert Canal north and east of the city had been captured—fifteen of seventeen still stood as late as September 5—and now they were all blown. An effort to seize a bridgehead across the canal came a cropper when army storm boats were found to have holes in the bottom. "German reaction was swift and most unpleasant," a brigadier reported, and included panzer fire that addled sappers trying to lay a bridge. Enemy battle groups rushed to reinforce the canals, but with other British corps to move forward, Montgomery had already ordered Horrocks to halt for regrouping.

An evacuation of German troops by ferry promptly began across the Scheldt from Breskens, west of Antwerp. In little more than a fortnight, 86,000 men, 600 artillery pieces, 5,000 vehicles, and 4,000 horses, mostly from the Fifteenth Army, escaped to fight another day. The estuary's north-bank fortifications on Walcheren Island and Beveland, already formidable, grew stouter, while a stubborn rear guard of eleven thousand troops showed no sign of abandoning the pocket around Breskens.

Montgomery told London on September 7 that he hoped to be in Berlin in three weeks. But that was unlikely without the fuel, ammunition, food, and other war stuffs that could arrive in bulk only through a big-shoulders port. For now, as the U.S. Army official history later concluded, "Antwerp was a jewel that could not be worn for want of a setting." A British officer in Antwerp offered his own judgment: "Success can be most bewildering."

5. Against the West Wall

"Five Barley Loaves and Three Small Fishes"

VERSAILLES had long proved irresistible to empire builders. A modest seventeenth-century hunting lodge, built above a fenny country village twelve miles southwest of Paris, had quickly grown into the world's most celebrated château, an emblem of both the ancien régime and French regal indulgence. More than twenty thousand nobles, courtiers, merchants, and servants eventually basked in the radiance of the Sun King and his dimmer heirs, crowding together in what one traveler described as "a state of unhygienic squalor." Later, the palace had served as a headquarters for the Prussian army besieging Paris in the starving winter of 1870, when 65,000 Parisians perished despite eating the city's cats, crows, and rats. Here, in January 1871, the German Empire had been proclaimed in the Hall of Mirrors, that exquisite gallery of seventeen reflecting arches facing seventeen arcaded windows. Here too, with a grim and vengeful echo, the treaty to end the First World War was signed in June 1919, as celebratory guns boomed, fountains spurted, and blue-coated Republican Guardsmen held their sabers aloft to salute the Hun's subjugation. Two decades later the Hun was back, for a four-year stay.

It was here that Eisenhower chose to locate his new command post. Even as he recuperated from his bum knee in distant Granville, SHAEF staff officers swarmed into Versailles and made it their own. Headquarters offices filled the plush Trianon Palace Hotel, where a room with a bath that went for 175 francs a night before the war now could not be had at any price except by holders of a SHAEF master pass, a stiff piece of paper the size of a playing card emblazoned with a blue border and a red cross. Waiters in black tie served K-ration lunches on white linen with crystal stemware and plates trimmed in gold. The Clemenceau Ballroom, used by the Allied powers to negotiate the 1919 treaty and more recently by the Germans to decorate Luftwaffe pilots during the Battle of Britain, now served as a map room. Thickets of antennae sprouted in the royal gardens, and latrines lined the stately château trees near the faux farm that had allowed Marie Antoinette to live a Rousseauian fantasy of pastoral simplicity. Staff sections and signal offices filled the great stables built by Louis XIV, each said by one visitor to be "larger than some of our state capitols."

Eisenhower's office occupied a white stone annex behind the hotel; a bronze bust of Hermann Göring found in the foyer was turned to the wall because, as an officer explained, "he has been a bad boy." Eleven paintings, including a Van Dyck, were plucked from the château to appoint the supreme commander's suite, apparently without his knowledge, along with an eighteenth-century desk and other furnishings from the Mobilier National. An incensed lieutenant who in civilian life had been a curator at the Metropolitan Museum of Art managed to have most of the loot put back.

SHAEF by midsummer had already tripled in size from the 1,500 Allied officers and men originally envisioned for the headquarters. Now the roster tripled again, to 16,000; they would fill 750,000 square feet of office space. Eventually 1,800 properties around Versailles were commandeered to house 24,000 Allied garrison troops. A French magazine mocked SHAEF as the Societé des Hôteliers Américains en France, while military wits claimed the acronym stood for Should Have Army Experience First. One officer likened the organization to a sea serpent: "Some had seen its head, some its middle, some its tail. No one had seen all of the sprawling mass."

Another sea serpent had wrapped its tentacles around Paris proper, with even greater speed and adhesion. Created in Britain in May 1942 to succor the logistical needs of the U.S. Army in Europe, the Services of Supply had been renamed the Communications Zone, or COMZ, on June 7 and now comprised half a million troops, or one in every four GIs on the Continent. A vast headquarters near Cherbourg, with five thousand prefabricated buildings and tentage for eleven thousand, was abruptly abandoned when the liberation of Paris triggered a stampede for the capital. COMZ convoys rolled into the City of Light hauling, as an Army major recounted, "tons of files and thousands upon thousands of clerks, typists, guards—its statistical departments, its coding and decoding rooms, its huge telephone exchange, and all the other complicated paraphernalia of big business." COMZ immediately requisitioned 315 hotels and put 48 others on notice of indenture; more than three thousand additional Parisian properties were claimed for the cause, including fourteen million square feet of depot space, 29,000 hospital beds, and "apartments of proper elegance and swank for the brass," in one officer's description. Only after abject pleadings were Parisian children permitted to keep their schools. French officials complained that the Americans' demands exceeded even those of the Germans'.

All this and more was the handiwork of the COMZ commander, Lieutenant General John C. H. Lee, known as John Court House Lee, Jesus Christ Himself Lee, and God A'Mighty Lee. Son of an Iowa insurance agent and given his mother's improbable Christian name, John, Lee had graduated from West Point with Patton in 1909, then made a career as an Army engineer doing river, dam, and harbor duty in places like Detroit, Guam, and Rock Island. *Time* magazine in mid-September called him "a man of exceptionally friendly and attractive personality," an encomium affirmed by almost no one who knew him. A fussy martinet who wore rank stars on both the front and back of his helmet, Lee was said to have a supply sergeant's parsimony in doling out Army kit "as if it were a personal gift," rewarding friends, of whom he had few, and punishing enemies, of whom he had many. He had a knack for risible self-delusion, once standing in a London theater to acknowledge an ovation in fact intended for Eisenhower, sitting in the box above him; he also claimed that Marshall had chosen him for his current job because of "my ability to get along with people." The Army's official history, rarely astringent in describing senior generals, in this case captured the man: "Heavy on ceremony, somewhat forbidding in manner and appearance, and occasionally tactless . . . General Lee often aroused suspicions and created opposition." The Army's chief surgeon in Europe admitted that "he's nobody I'd ever want to go fishing with for a week." Classmate Patton was less circumspect, calling him "a glib liar" and "a pompous little son-of-a-bitch only interested in self-advertisement." Yet field commanders rarely crossed him, fearing reprisal in the supply shed; when Lee visited Third Army, Patton welcomed him with an honor guard, a band, and a banquet.

Booted and bedizened, wearing spurs and clutching a riding crop, Lee kept Bibles in his desk and in his briefcase. He preferred, by his own account, "to start each morning at His altar whereon we lay our problems." He often press-ganged his personal retinue of forty—including a chiropractor, eight correspondence secretaries, and a publicist who had once worked for the movie mogul Samuel Goldwyn—into escorting him to church, which he attended daily and twice if not thrice on Sundays. Then he was off to inspect his vast dominion, either in a black, red-cushioned limousine driven by a Baptist lay preacher, or in a special rail-car, which one minion described as Lee's private "instrument of torture." Regardless of conveyance, he liked to read scripture aloud. Any approaching subordinate was to tender a salute at precisely ten paces, and woe to the soldier whose helmet was cockeyed. A hospital staff's preparations for a Lee visitation included three simple injunctions: "Dress up. Stop all operations. Liquor down the toilet." Even the bedridden, one surgeon recorded, "had to lie at attention, [and] the ambulatory had to get out of their chairs and stand at attention all the time he was on that ward until he called at ease." Excess slop in a mess-hall garbage pail sent him into a pale fury. Whipping out a spoon, he would sample the waste himself, declaring, "You see, I can eat it and you're throwing this away."

In Paris, Lee kept a huge war room in the Hôtel Majestic basement, and three suites upstairs for his own use. (His personal baggage included a piano.) The adjacent Avenue Kléber became known as the "Avenue de Salute," and Lee dispatched officers to patrol the sidewalk and take the names of soldiers who failed to render the proper courtesy. Additional suites were reserved for him in other grand hostels; denizens at one were advised, "The Hôtel George V is considered General Lee's personal residence, and assignments of accommodations carry the understanding that such persons are his guests." The front curb was to be kept clear for his own entourage; other cars "will be required to park around the corner or down on the next block."

"Why didn't somebody tell me some of those things?" Eisenhower later asked after hearing of Lee's idiosyncrasies. The complaint said more about the supreme commander's inattention than about Lee. Not for two weeks did Eisenhower learn of the COMZ land rush in Paris, which he had intended to keep mostly free of Allied soldiers. On September 16, he personally wrote a blistering rebuke to the man he had deemed "a modern Cromwell":

> Due to the heavy shipments of your personnel and supplies to that area before I was aware of it, it is impossible to shift your headquarters at this moment without interfering with your first priority duties. Nevertheless you will immediately stop the entry into Paris of every individual who is not needed at that spot for an essential duty. . . . I regard the influx into Paris of American personnel, including your headquarters, as extremely unwise. . . . I am informed that the dress, discipline and conduct of American personnel in Paris is little short of disgraceful.

Lee was an unrepentant sinner. "I have no regrets," he said. "One should be as far forward as possible."

Lee's "first priority duties" required provisioning a huge fighting force four thousand miles from home with 800,000 separate supply items, eightfold more than even Sears, Roebuck stocked. The task might well have overmatched the most gifted administrator, and certainly it taxed Jesus Christ Himself. Allied invasion architects had assumed that by D+90—September 4—only a dozen U.S. divisions would have reached the Seine, whereupon a pause of one to three months would be imposed to consolidate the lodgment area before resuming the attack across France. No logistician expected to reach the German border until May 1945. In the event, sixteen divisions were 150 miles beyond the Seine on September 4, and barely a week later the Allied line had reached a point not anticipated until D+350.

Battlefield exigencies disrupted and then demolished a supply plan two years in the making. The need for more combat troops to fight through the bocage had been met at the expense of service units—mechanics, fuelers, railroaders, sutlers of all sorts—and the subsequent breakout from Normandy caused Eisenhower in mid-August to pursue the fleeing enemy without pausing to shore up his logistics. The thrill of the chase held sway. Marshall and Eisenhower further accelerated the flow of divisions to the theater, advancing the schedule by two months at a severe cost in cargo shipments. Other afflictions impaired the supply system: the loss of Mulberry A; the demolitions at Cherbourg, Marseille, and Le Havre; the abandonment of ports in Brittany; the Allied bombardment of French rails and roads; the quick advance up the Rhône; and Hitler's stubborn retention of Dunkirk and other coastal enclaves. Liberated Paris pleaded for an air delivery of 2,400 tons in emergency food, medicines, and other goods each day, of which Bradley conceded 1,500—the equivalent of the daily needs of 2.5 combat divisions.

Truck convoys that in July had required just hours for a round-trip to the front now took up to five days to reach the battlefield and return to the beaches. The First Army quartermaster depot moved six times in six weeks while trying to keep pace with the advance, even transforming eighteen artillery battalions into truck units. Moreover, the distance from American factories meant that items ordered in eastern France typically took almost four months to reach the front from home; at any given moment, two thousand tanks were in the pipeline. As Patton told reporters in September, "We cannot make five barley loaves and three small fishes expand like they used to."

Much more than bread and seafood was needed, of course. Purchasing agents roamed across neutral Europe buying Swedish paper, Spanish apricots, Portuguese figs, and bananas from the Canary Islands. Thirty-three woodcutting camps opened in France, Belgium, and Luxembourg to split a million cords of firewood. Nineteen thousand tons of wood pulp shipped from the United States to local factories became fifty million rolls of toilet paper. But efforts to buy military uniforms from French clothiers were undone by language hurdles and the need to convert U.S. measurements into metric equivalents; SHAEF reported that "one-sixteenth of an inch on each of twelve measurements for the seams in a uniform would mean throwing off completely the proper size."

Average daily supply needs totaled 66.8 pounds for every Allied soldier on the Continent: 33.3 pounds of gas, oil, grease, and aircraft fuel; 8 pounds of ammunition, including aerial bombs; 7.3 pounds of engineer construction material; 7.2 pounds of rations; and sundry poundages for medical, signal, and miscellaneous supplies. (Quartermasters found that ravenous troops were eating 30 percent more than the normal ration allocation.) Four advancing armies burned a million gallons of gasoline each day, exclusive of the needs of Patch and De Lattre in southern France, and intensified fighting in the east would mean stupendous ammunition expenditures, including 8 million artillery and mortar shells each month.

Prodigal wastage, always an American trait, made the logistician's life harder. Infantry divisions had been authorized 1,600 M-7 grenade launchers with a replacement rate of 2 per week, but some were losing 500 to 700 a month. Eisenhower described other ordnance losses as "extremely high," and he warned the Pentagon that every month he was forced to replace 36,000 small arms, 700 mortars, 500 tanks, and 2,400 vehicles. Five times more mine detectors were requisitioned than anticipated, and First Army alone used 66,000 miles of field wire each month, stringing almost a hundred miles every hour—double the allotment. Of 22 million jerricans sent to France since D-Day, half had vanished, and SHAEF asked Washington for 7 million more. The need to fly fuel to bone-dry combat units, Eisenhower added, meant that "it is now costing us 1½ gallons of 100-octane [aviation] gasoline to deliver one gallon of 80-octane motor fuel to forward depots."

All this fell largely unforeseen on Lee, who was reduced to sending crates of oranges and other delicacies to Beetle Smith in hopes of retaining SHAEF's confidence. (He regretted not playing bridge as a means of infiltrating Eisenhower's inner circle.) SHAEF certainly shared culpability, not least because it had abandoned plans for a robust network of supply depots across the Continent and relied instead on scattered ad hoc dumps. The SHAEF chief logistician on September 9 warned that "maintenance of the armies [is] stretched to the limit.... The administration situation remains grim." Bradley's top supply officer in 12th Army Group subsequently agreed: "For a period of about one month now the logistical situation has been disorderly and for the past three weeks has been bad."

COMZ improvised, with mixed results. Fuel shortages tended to be a problem of distribution rather than supply, and an elaborate nexus of pipelines was built to reduce reliance on tanker ships, gas trucks, and jerricans. A project called PLUTO—Pipeline Underwater Transport of Oil—laid twenty-one lines across the bottom of the English Channel; pumping stations were dubbed "Bambi" and "Dumbo," in keeping with the Disney motif. The first pipe to Cherbourg was completed in mid-August, but an inconsiderate ship's anchor ruined it within hours. Two days later another line was wrecked after fouling a propeller; still another failed in late August, when ten tons of barnacles grew on the submerged pipeline drum and kept it from rotating. PLUTO proved disappointing—"a scandalous waste of time and effort," in one admiral's view; the Channel lines provided far less than 10 percent of Allied fuel needs on the Continent during the war. Tankers, gas trucks, and jerricans remained indispensable.

A terrestrial innovation was the Red Ball Express, a cargo haulage service begun in late August. Soon seven thousand trucks carried four thousand tons or more each day on one-way highways to First and Third Army dumps, typically a three-day round-trip. MPs posted 25,000 road signs in English and French, and Cub planes monitored the traffic flow. Problems arose immediately. Red Ball burned 300,000 gallons of gasoline a day, as much as three armored divisions in combat. Drivers sometimes loaded six to ten tons of cargo on 2½-ton vehicles; the Red Ball units became known as "truck-destroyer battalions." Despite a twenty-five-mile-per-hour speed limit, seventy trucks on average were wrecked beyond repair every day. On one stretch marked "steep hill and dangerous curve," eight gasoline semi-trailers in a single convoy flipped over, followed by eight more the next day. "The gas splashing inside throws you from side to side," one driver explained. "This affects your steering." Of fifteen thousand U.S. Army vehicles "deadlined" and useless in Europe in the fall of 1944, nine thousand were trucks littering French byways.

Roads deteriorated in the autumn rains, and a dearth of spark plugs, fan belts, and tools hampered mechanics; one company with forty-one trucks possessed a single pair of pliers and one crescent wrench. The daily ruination of five thousand tires—many shredded by discarded ration cans—led to such a desperate shortage that even threadbare spares were stripped from vehicles throughout the United States and shipped to Europe. Pilferage from trucks and dumps grew so virulent that General Lee requested thirteen infantry battalions as guards; over Bradley's bitter protest, Eisenhower gave him five, with shoot-to-kill authority. Red Ball moved over 400,000 tons in three months, and eventually was supplemented by other routes with names like White Ball, Red Lion, and Green Diamond. But as one major general in Paris lamented, "It was the greatest killer of trucks that I could imagine."

A single train could haul the equivalent of four hundred trucks. Eighteen thousand men, including five thousand prisoners of war, labored to rebuild the French rail system, which had been obliterated by years of Allied bombing. Thirty-two trains left Cherbourg over a single, reconditioned track on August 15, creeping across bridges at ten miles per hour, on a two-day trip to Le Mans. A line to Paris opened on September 1, and by the end of the month almost five thousand miles of track had been refurbished. Shortages of skilled train, yard, and rail crews impaired operations; signalmen often were reduced to flagging with lighters and burning cigarettes. Two dozen Army railway battalions eventually arrived from as far away as Persia and Peoria. The Army used 200,000 rail cars in France, of which 31,000 were shipped in pieces from the United States, assembled in Britain, and ferried across the Channel: freight cars, flatcars, tank cars, gondolas, cabooses, and thirteen hundred muscular American engines. By year's end, eleven thousand miles of French and Belgian track had been rebuilt, along with 241 rail bridges.

Without ports, all the roads, rails, and truck-destroyer battalions in Europe had limited utility. A parody by exasperated SHAEF officers held that "the number of divisions required to capture the number of ports required to maintain those divisions is always greater than the number of divisions those ports can maintain." Fifty-four ports had been studied by OVERLORD planners for possible use; Lee narrowed the number under consideration to three dozen, of which half eventually played a role for the Allies. Marseille and other harbors in southern France proved a boon, handling more than one-third of all Allied supplies sent to France in the fall of 1944. Cherbourg tripled its expected cargo capacity, to 22,000 tons a day; it was said that unloaded rations were piled "as high as Napoléon's hand" around the famous statue of *l'empereur* pointing toward England. But SHAEF calculated that combat supply requirements in the coming month would sharply outpace the Allied ability to unload and distribute cargo; the number of ships anchored in Continental waters awaiting berths would exceed two hundred by mid-October.

Clearly the solution was to be found in Antwerp: using rail and road networks, Cherbourg could support a maximum of twenty-one divisions, while Antwerp using rails alone could sustain fifty-four. Cherbourg lay almost four hundred miles from the huge forward depots now under construction at Liège, in eastern Belgium; from Antwerp, the distance was sixty-five miles. Although the Allied port predicament was deemed "grave," the opening of Antwerp would have "the effect of a blood transfusion," Eisenhower promised Marshall. Meanwhile the armies would make do with brute-force logistics, another American specialty. Stevedores man-handling cargo off an old Hog Islander freighter in Rouen were surprised when the Norwegian captain's caged parrot abruptly sang the opening bars of "The Star-Spangled Banner"—voice cracking on the high notes—then squawked, "What a life! Misery! Misery!"

Every Village a Fortress

A STUBBY C-47 transport plane banked east of Brussels on Sunday afternoon, September 10, before leveling off to touch down on the airdrome at Melsbroek, previously used by the Germans but now occupied by the Royal Air Force and code-named B-58. Wearing the rank insignia of a new field marshal, Montgomery strode across the runway as the propellers twirled to a stop, then bounded up the ramp and into the cabin with a pugnacious glint.

There he found Eisenhower, his knee bandaged and throbbing. Only with help had he managed to hobble aboard the plane; Montgomery had insisted on a personal meeting but protested that he was too busy to leave Brussels, so the supreme commander had come to him. After a perfunctory greeting, Montgomery asked that Eisenhower's chief administrative officer, Lieutenant General Sir Humfrey M. Gale, be ejected from the plane, although his own logistician, Major General Sir Miles Graham, would remain. Air Marshal Tedder, the SHAEF deputy commander, could also stay. No sooner had Eisenhower meekly complied than the field marshal pulled a crumpled sheaf of top secret cables from his pocket, including the first half of the bifurcated message of September 5 that had arrived Saturday morning, four days late.

"Did you send me these?"

"Yes, of course," Eisenhower replied. "Why?"

"Well, they're nothing but balls," Montgomery said, "sheer balls, rubbish." In a seething tirade, his reedy voice trilling, he claimed to have been betrayed and insisted that the broad, double-thrust advance on Germany would fail. Was George Patton actually running the war for SHAEF?

A scarlet flush crept up Eisenhower's neck, but his voice was level as he leaned forward, tapped Montgomery's knee, and said, "Monty, you can't speak to me like that. I'm your boss."

The field marshal settled in his seat with a weak smile. "I'm sorry, Ike," he said.

For a long hour they bickered, "a complete dogfight," in Graham's description. Montgomery restated his case for a single thrust; if given transport and fuel from the Canadians and Third Army, plus the four airborne divisions, he was certain he could capture the Ruhr with twenty divisions from the British Second and American First Armies, opening the road to Berlin. Patton's strike toward Metz in the south would weaken the Allied center, he said, leaving none of the armies with sufficient strength to burst ahead.

Eisenhower agreed that the Ruhr remained their main objective, but any lunge toward Berlin—still four hundred miles away—would risk lethal attacks on both flanks. "You can't do that," he told Montgomery. "What the hell?" The broad-front strategy made better strategic sense, he added. It was safer and surer and would keep the enemy off balance.

Eisenhower was intrigued, however, by Montgomery's description of a new plan to drop several parachute divisions into Holland, clearing a corridor for Dempsey's Second Army and other forces to seize a bridgehead over the Rhine. Similar proposals had been advanced before, but this scheme was bigger, stronger, more ambitious, and Eisenhower was willing to try it. The operation would be given a two-word code name: MARKET GARDEN.

At length Montgomery rose, saluted, and trotted down the stairs to the tarmac, a pinched, elfin figure in a beret. "Our fight must be with both hands at present," Tedder wrote shortly after the conference. "Montgomery will of course dislike not getting a blank check."

The aircraft engines coughed and caught. Eisenhower flew off in pain.

For all that had been said, much remained unsaid. The two had barely mentioned Antwerp and MARKET GARDEN got short shrift. Following the meeting, Montgomery sent a carping, thirty-three paragraph note to Brooke. The supreme commander, he complained,

> is completely out of touch with what is going on; he tries to run the war by issuing long telegraphic directives. Eisenhower himself does not really know anything about the business of fighting the Germans. . . . Just when a really firm grip was needed, there was no grip.

Regardless of American requirements, Montgomery had privately concluded that 21st Army Group did not need Antwerp to drive halfway across Germany. Graham, his logistics chief, posited that a fighting division could get by with 350 to 400 tons of daily sustenance, barely half the SHAEF estimate. British units had done so in Africa, albeit under very different combat conditions. If two Allied corps reached Berlin, Montgomery believed, German defenses would be in such "disorder" that the Third Reich would disintegrate. Lesser ports, such as Dieppe and Le Havre, could sustain an advance on the enemy capital; just "one good Pas de Calais port," Montgomery added, would suffice to reach Münster, fifty miles beyond the Rhine, if augmented with daily airlift and more trucks. Unfortunately, the first Pas de Calais port—Boulogne—would not open until mid-October; the same was true of battered Le Havre. Until then only Mulberry B, far from the front, could handle sizable British cargo ships, and autumn weather made that ever riskier. Worse yet, fourteen hundred three-ton

British trucks had just been found to have faulty pistons, and the same defect plagued all the replacement engines. Nevertheless, according to the Canadian official history, Montgomery's staff had assigned the prying open of the Scheldt as a "last priority" for the Canadian First Army.

Another grim battlefield development also had come into play. Montgomery on Saturday had received a secret War Office cable informing him that two explosions in England the previous evening heralded a new German assault against the home island. Without warning, at 6:34 P.M. on September 8, an explosion carved out a crater twenty feet deep in Stavely Road near the Thames, killing three, demolishing eleven houses, and wrecking fifteen more; the blast had been audible in Westminster, seven miles distant. A second explosion rocked Epping sixteen seconds later. Just days earlier, Churchill's government had declared victory against the V-1 in the battle of London; Whitehall now refused to publicly acknowledge a new German threat. Suggestions from the government that natural-gas accidents were responsible inspired caustic jokes about "flying gas mains" and applications by the credulous for damages from local utility companies.

The true culprit, the V-2 rocket, was forty-six feet long, weighed almost thirteen tons, and carried a one-ton warhead. Reaching 3,600 miles per hour and an apogee of sixty miles, it had an impact velocity comparable to fifty big train engines slamming into a neighborhood. The V-2 was the handiwork of a young Prussian Junker named Wernher von Braun, who belonged to the Nazi Party and the SS, and who since 1937 had been working on a liquid-fuel rocket at Peenemünde, a bucolic Baltic fishing village recommended by his mother.

The rocket had long been expected by British intelligence. "Existence of V-2 is established beyond doubt," a secret report on July 11 confirmed. Some analysts feared a warhead of up to six tons, carrying gas or "bacteriological germs" and capable of destroying all buildings within a mile or more of impact. Saturation bombing of Peenemünde killed many German scientists and engineers, delaying the rocket program for two months. But the ruthless use of slave laborers by the thousands and the construction of simple mobile launch equipment had permitted Hitler in early September to authorize the start of Operation PENGUIN. Fourteen V-2s would be fired on average every day in coming months, although they had an annoying tendency to break up in flight. Unlike the V-1, the V-2 could not be defended against—at Mach 5, it was simply too fast. Already 1.5 million Londoners had left the city because of the recent V-1 onslaught, and now the British government also considered evacuating.

The initial volley had been fired from western Holland, and the SS general overseeing PENGUIN had placed his headquarters outside Nijmegen, a Dutch town only ten miles south of Arnhem on the Rhine, a prime objective of Operation MARKET GARDEN. The message from London advising Montgomery of the first rocket attacks also pleaded, "Will you please report most urgently by what approximate date you consider you can rope off the coastal area contained by Antwerp-Utrecht-Rotterdam?" While General Dempsey and others favored a more easterly advance toward the Rhine at Wesel, this new German onslaught further persuaded Montgomery to drive north, deep into Holland. "It must be towards Arnhem," he said.

Tedder was right: Montgomery disliked not getting a blank check. On Monday he cabled Eisenhower that without greater logistical support no offensive toward the Rhine would be possible for almost two weeks, perhaps longer. "This delay," he added in a thinly veiled threat, "will give the enemy time to organize better defensive arrangements and we must expect heavier resistance and slower progress."

Eisenhower had returned from Brussels bruised in spirit and sore of body. "E. is spending a few days in bed on account of his leg," Kay Summersby told her diary on September 11. The supreme commander began dictating notes for a future memoir, "to put down some of the things that might be appropriate for me to say in a personal acc[ount] of the war," as he wrote in his office journal. Regarding the field marshal, he added, "Monty seems unimpressed by necessity for taking Antwerp approaches. . . . Monty's suggestion is simple—give him everything. This is crazy."

Ramsay arrived for a visit on the eleventh to find Eisenhower in pajamas. The admiral noted in his diary:

> He let himself go on subject of Monty, command, his difficulties, future strategy, etc. He is clearly worried & the cause is undoubtedly Monty who is behaving badly. Ike does not trust his loyalty & probably with good reason. He has never let himself go to me like this before.

At a moment when strategic harmony was needed in the Allied high command, dissonance and puerile backbiting obtained. Eisenhower was sympathetic to the British impulse to scourge the V-2 launch sites, and he saw MARKET GARDEN as a bold stroke that could hasten Germany's defeat. Despite the risk of a delay in opening Antwerp, he believed that these disparate objectives could be achieved without crippling the American drive toward the Saar. "There is no reason," he wrote Bradley, "why Patton should not keep acting offensively if the conditions for offensive action are right." As for the field marshal, Eisenhower's private comments had become ever more scathing. "He called him 'a clever son of a bitch,' which was very encouraging," Patton confided to his diary. After the war Eisenhower would be far harsher, telling the author Cornelius Ryan, "He's a psychopath, don't forget that. He is such an egocentric. . . . Essentially he's not an honest man."

That assessment was absurd. Even if solipsistic and at times careless with the truth, Montgomery—who was as responsible as any man for victory in Normandy—was hardly a psychopath. Fortunately for the Allied cause, Eisenhower bit his tongue and soldiered on, game if gimpy. In reply to Montgomery's warning of a fortnight's delay, he sent Beetle Smith to Brussels for more palaver, then agreed to bolster 21st Army Group with an extra thousand daily tons of supplies, by truck and by plane. He also authorized Montgomery to communicate directly with Hodges's First Army on his right flank, rather than routing all messages through Bradley. Montgomery sent thanks, then privately gloated. "Ike has given way," he told a confidant in London. "The Saar thrust is to be stopped. . . . We have gained a great victory."

He was deluded. Eisenhower had offered concessions without conceding. The Saar thrust would continue. And the only victory that concerned three million Allied soldiers in harm's way was the one their commanders were supposed to effect on the battlefield. To Marshall, Eisenhower wrote a petulant note that again distorted Montgomery's argument:

> Montgomery suddenly became obsessed with the idea that his army group could rush right on into Berlin provided we gave him all the maintenance that was in the theater—that is, immobilize all other divisions. . . . Examination of this scheme exposes it as a fantastic idea. . . . I have sacrificed a lot to give Montgomery the strength he needs.

As for the future, Eisenhower proved himself an imperfect seer:

> We will have to fight one more major battle in the West. This will be to break through the German defenses on the border. . . . Thereafter the advance into Germany will not be as rapid as it was in France . . . but I doubt that there will be another full-dress battle involved.

Just after six P.M. on the warm, clear Monday evening of September 11, a jeep carrying a five-man American patrol from Troop B of the 85th Reconnaissance Squadron crept north on the river road from Vianden in northeastern Luxembourg. Thickly timbered hills pitched and yawed in all directions, and blue shadows bled into the dells. The jeep lurched to a halt near the jackstraw wreckage of a blown bridge across the narrow Our River. Staff Sergeant Warner W. Holzinger, a German-speaker from Reedsburg,

Wisconsin, scrambled down the bank, followed by a rifleman and a French interpreter hired by the troop in Paris. Holzinger's orders from the 5th Armored Division urged caution, but added, "Should probing indicate great weakness in some portion of the frontier line, penetration may become possible." The sergeant detected great weakness. With the limpid water barely reaching their boot cuffs, he and his two comrades sloshed twenty yards across the Our to become the first Allied soldiers into Germany.

Up the slope for four hundred yards they trudged to a clutch of houses, where a farmer reported that the German rear guard had scuttled off the previous day. With the man impressed as a guide—"in case he was lying," Holzinger later explained—the GIs hiked to the crest of a knife-blade ridge half a mile above the river for a panoramic view. Raking the hills with his field glasses, Holzinger counted twenty concrete pillboxes tucked among the glades and brakes, including one with a chicken coop attached. Each appeared to be vacant. As dusk thickened, he hurried back across the river to report by radio that his men had found the Siegfried Line.

By midnight, other patrols from the 4th and 28th Infantry Divisions had also crossed the border, to be greeted by hostile stares and white bedsheets draped from upper windows. Three corps abreast, the U.S. First Army approached the German frontier through southern Holland, eastern Belgium, and Luxembourg. Scouts watched for "cuckoos"—local civilians, often ethnic Germans of dubious loyalty, scurrying east—and listened to the *chat-chat-chat* of machine guns said to be "eating away at each other" as outposts traded fire across the lines. Farther south on the same Monday, a patrol from the 6th Armored Division in Patton's army spied French dragoons from Patch's army at Saulieu in Burgundy. A few hours later, a detachment from General Leclerc's French 2nd Armored Division— also part of Third Army—encountered twenty men in three scout cars from De Lattre's 1st Infantry Division outside Nod-sur-Seine, forty miles northeast of Dijon. Straightening his collar as he ran, the local mayor raced toward the rendezvous with the entire village on his heels. There beneath an elm tree on Route Nationale 71, as church bells sang in their belfries, they witnessed officers from the two units shake hands to seal the merger of the Allied liberators who had landed in Normandy with those who had come through Provence.

From the North Sea to the Mediterranean, the Allies now presented an unbroken front. Never had the Third Reich's prospects seemed bleaker. The Wehrmacht in three months had lost fifty divisions in the east, twenty-eight in the west, and territory several times larger than Germany proper. Axis regimes in Romania, Bulgaria, and Finland were suing for

peace. Berlin had begun evacuating southern Greece, dispatching transport planes across the Aegean at night to spirit 37,000 troops from Crete.
The operational life of a U-boat commander now averaged just two
patrols. Advancing Soviet armies had swarmed into the Baltics and halfway across Poland before the Red Army paused to regroup, a delay that
had let the Germans obliterate rebellious Warsaw. After five years of war,
German army casualties exceeded 114,000 officers and 3.6 million enlisted
men, not counting those who returned to duty after recovering from their
wounds.

For all his troubles in the east, Hitler's greatest peril at the moment lay
in the west, where three army groups prepared to pounce on Germany. In
search of a savior, he once again summoned Field Marshal von Rundstedt,
who after his dismissal in July had spent much of his time taking the cure
at Bad Tölz. "I would like to place the Western front in your hands again,"
Hitler told him. Field Marshal Model would remain in harness to command the remains of Army Group B. "My Führer," Rundstedt replied,
"whatever you order, I shall do to my last breath." *Life* declared him not
only "the Wehrmacht's best general," but "Germany's last hope."

From his new headquarters near Koblenz, Rundstedt soon found how
wan hope had become. The German high command, Oberkommando der
Wehrmacht, or OKW, considered its fighting strength in the west to equal
no more than thirteen robust infantry and four motorized divisions; several dozen others were exhausted if not eviscerated. Rundstedt advised
Berlin that "Army Group B has about 100 tanks in working order"; the
oncoming Allies, he added, had "roughly 1,700." General Erich Brandenberger had taken command of Seventh Army after Eberbach's capture
only to be told that "it is unknown where the army headquarters are for the
moment"; when the command post was found, Brandenberger reported,
"everything gave the impression of flight and disorganization." In mid-
September, he calculated the effective strength of his army at three to four
divisions, including such "mongrel units" as one assembled from two hundred postal detachments. Across the front, items from tanks and trucks to
ammunition and uniforms were in short supply. Eighteen new "Volksgrenadier" divisions had been created in late summer from recuperating hospital patients, industrial workers, stragglers, combat veterans, converted
sailors and airmen, and boys. More such divisions would materialize, but
each numbered only ten thousand troops, compared to seventeen thousand in the Wehrmacht's palmy days, and transport was predominately
bipedal or four-hooved.

The Siegfried Line—to Germans, the *Westwall*—stood as a last bastion
before the Rhine. Begun in 1936, its fortifications eventually stretched

from the Dutch border to Switzerland and comprised three thousand pill-boxes and bunkers. Built with walls and ceilings up to eight feet thick, some included fireplaces, tin chimneys, and connecting tunnels. Others were disguised as electrical substations, with dummy power lines, or as barns, with hay bales stacked in the windows. Planned with a shrewd eye for terrain and interlocking fields of fire, the pillboxes were most numerous where approach avenues seemed especially vulnerable; as many as fifteen big bunkers might be found in a single square kilometer. Thousands of dragon's teeth—pyramidal tank barriers of reinforced concrete two to six feet high—also stippled the landscape. By 1939, propaganda films were assuring German audiences that the Fatherland had been made invincible against ground attack from the west.

But years of neglect had ravaged the West Wall. Barbed wire, steel doors, and heavy weapons were plundered for the Atlantic Wall. Saplings and brush soon blocked firing apertures. Farmers laid roadbeds atop the dragon's teeth to reach their fields and transformed pillboxes into tool sheds or storage bins for potatoes and turnips. Bunkers flooded, or were looted, or became hideouts for soldiers straggling back from Normandy. Dank as a troll's lair, the fortifications seemed "more like sewage works than subterranean forts," one visitor reported.

Hitler in mid-August ordered the *Westwall* rehabilitated with a levy of "people's labor." Simply finding keys to locked doors proved exasperating. By September 10, the workforce had grown to 167,000, including girls from the League of German Maidens and boys from the Hitler Youth, as well as others plucked from depots, training schools, police stations, and convalescent homes. Captured weapons from the Eastern Front rearmed some bunkers, although the concussion and large barrel of the MG-42—a notoriously lethal German machine gun developed after the West Wall was designed—proved too much for many pillboxes.

With characteristic agility, Rundstedt manned the fortifications with makeshift units rushed to the front. Even as he complained on September 10 of needing another six weeks to properly rebuild the line, he impro-vised with dismounted panzer crews, border guards, and training battal-ions. The 49th Infantry Division scooped up officers and men from more than a dozen broken battalions and moved into a ten-mile stretch of the wall. The equivalent of two Luftwaffe divisions were deployed along a sixty-mile stretch in Holland. The I SS Panzer Corps officially halted its long retreat on September 14 to help shore up defenses. Within a week, 160,000 stragglers had been redirected to the front, with twenty-one Volksgrenadier divisions and nearly eight panzer divisions stiffening the *Westwall*.

Hitler demanded "a holding of the position until annihilation." He added:

> The fight in the West has spread to the German Reich. The situation no longer permits any maneuvering. Stand your ground or die! . . . Every bunker, every block of houses in a German city, every German village must become a fortress.

The question of how to breach the Siegfried Line now preoccupied Allied generals and privates alike. "It is a monument to stupidity," Patton insisted. "Anything that man makes, man can overcome." But the U.S. Army had little experience in reducing elaborate European fortifications; Corps of Engineer manuals focused more on makeshift fieldworks. A single bunker atop a hill south of Aachen and attacked by the 39th Infantry in mid-September showed how tough the nut could be. Sequentially and without success, GIs fired bazookas and placed pole charges; poured burning gasoline under the door; detonated a beehive explosive charge on the rooftop ventilator, followed by three dozen stacked Teller mines and eleven more beehives; and scorched the embrasures with flamethrowers. Only after three hundred pounds of TNT were tamped into a divot on the roof and detonated with a monumental roar did thirty Germans emerge under a white flag to report that the greatest inconvenience during the ordeal was the occasional snuffing out of their candles.

Ordinary artillery barrages did little against West Wall redoubts except "dust off the camouflage." Napalm and other incendiaries proved disappointing. Experiments showed that twenty-five to fifty pounds of explosives often was needed to break a single dragon's tooth, and large pillboxes required half a ton. Ten to twenty rounds fired from a self-propelled 155mm gun might penetrate six-foot concrete walls, or might not. Engineers learned to use an armored bulldozer hidden within a smoke screen to entomb pillboxes; doors were sealed shut with a jeep-towed arc welder. At a minimum, heavy shelling sometimes made it hard for defenders to breathe by causing the inside concrete walls to powder.

As Rundstedt rushed defenders into the line, two American armies poked and probed, looking for a seam to rip. Patton's brash assurance notwithstanding, his Third Army had yet to even close with the Siegfried Line, which abruptly bent eastward in trace with the border. Reduced to Michelin maps and guesswork—200,000 aerial photos, requiring four acres of paper, would not arrive until mid-September—Patton planned to leap the Moselle and advance to Mainz and Mannheim on the Rhine. He intended to bypass the French city of Metz "if it doesn't fall like a ripe plum," and little resistance was anticipated short of the West Wall.

Hitler had other ideas. German reinforcements swarmed in from Denmark and northern Italy, giving the Metz commander the equivalent of almost five divisions to shore up not only the elaborate constellation of forts around the city but also a defensive line west of the Moselle. Four armored columns from Third Army reached the river north and south of Metz on September 7 to find screaming sheets of enemy artillery and no bridges still standing.

The next morning, a battalion from the 5th Infantry Division slipped across the Moselle from Dornot only to be counterattacked by close-order panzer grenadiers shrieking "Heil, Hitler!" Four American companies dug a last-ditch horseshoe line only three hundred yards wide with the river at their backs; wounded GIs were asked not to cry out in hopes of keeping secret the extent of the casualties. Peppered from the bluffs by German flak guns, the battalion fought off three dozen assaults in sixty hours. "This sure is a hell hole," the unit log noted. Not until nightfall on September 10 were survivors authorized to fall back across the river, evacuating under blistering fire in three bullet-pricked boats that required two men to bail for each man paddling. Others swam with water wings fashioned from inflated condoms, or rode rafts built from empty ammunition cans. In addition to more than 360 battle casualties, the battalion sent another 150 to the hospital with combat exhaustion.

Patton would gain other bridgeheads over the Moselle, and on September 14 the unfortified city of Nancy was captured to become the Third Army headquarters. But his barnyard aspiration—"to go through the Siegfried Line like shit through a goose"—had clearly been checked. He had misjudged enemy grit: a Reuters dispatch reported that captured Germans tended to "thrash about and bite." By attacking on a broad front, Patton had failed to exploit a vulnerable if temporary gap between the German Fifth Panzer and First Armies. For now he was reduced to bluster. "I have studied the German all my life," he told his staff in Nancy. "I know exactly how he will react. . . . He hasn't the slightest idea what I'm going to do. Therefore, when the day comes, I'm going to whip hell out of him."

Farther north, First Army's prospects at first seemed brighter as three corps butted up against the West Wall on a seventy-five-mile front, shoulder to shoulder to shoulder. On the army's right wing, where Sergeant Holzinger had first trespassed across the Our, V Corps soon found itself overmatched by enemy counterblows and scorching fire from stout fortifications in the Ardennes borderlands. The 28th Infantry Division, proud to have tramped through Paris on its postage-stamp march three weeks earlier, now had so little artillery ammunition that guns were restricted to twenty-five rounds a day and only one battalion per regiment could fight at any given time. Three days' brawling in the sinister German uplands known as the Schnee Eifel made little headway, though the Americans took seventeen pillboxes and fifty-eight prisoners in one firefight. Even this modest penetration of the Siegfried Line provoked a counterattack that cost the division fifteen hundred casualties. Once again, as in World War I, the unit's red keystone shoulder flash—honoring its Pennsylvania National Guard heritage—became known as the *Blutiger Eimer*, the Bloody Bucket.

In a sector just to the north, Hemingway on September 12 accompanied the 4th Division into Germany, where he found "ugly women and squatty ill-shaped men." Requisitioning a deserted farmhouse, he shot the heads off several chickens with his pistol, then served a supper of fricassee, peas, onions, and carrots to regimental officers, one of whom wrote, "We all seemed for the moment like minor gods." The moment passed. A counterattack by the 2nd SS Panzer Division sealed a six-mile gap torn in the line and inflicted eight hundred American casualties; one company broke and pelted a mile to the rear. On Friday, September 15, the division command post shuffled back into Belgium, purportedly the 4th Division's first retreat since the Carolina maneuvers of 1941. A promising 5th Armored Division foray also petered out, and the corps bridgehead was soon abandoned, leaving the Ardennes to lapse into an uneasy repose that would last until mid-December.

On First Army's left flank, XIX Corps rolled through the Dutch city of Maastricht on September 14, finding the Germans gone but for three scoundrels burning papers at the Gestapo headquarters. Three days later, the 30th Division crossed into Germany only to encounter pillboxes and fire pits newly manned by Austrians in a Volksgrenadier division. A corps offensive to seize crossings on the Roer River, nine miles distant, was twice postponed for lack of ammunition, heavy weather, and anxiety over an exposed northern flank; this gave the enemy time to entrench and the Americans time "to ponder their apprehensions," as the Army's official history acknowledged.

That left the last, best chance for a quick American breakthrough in the First Army center, where Joe Collins's VII Corps had massed before Aachen with three divisions abreast on a thirty-five-mile front. Collins knew this ground intimately from his three years with the occupation force in Koblenz after World War I. (He prided himself in correctly pronouncing German names.) He also knew that the Aachen Gap had been a major trade gateway since the Roman Empire and, as he put it, "the real route into and out of Germany" since early Christendom. For precisely that reason, Hitler had doubled the strength of the *Westwall* here with twin fortification belts: the Scharnhorst Line almost straddled the Belgian-Dutch border, paralleled a few miles to the east by the thicker Schill Line. Aachen sat in a bowl between the two belts, ancient and vulnerable, the city of Charlemagne and Nazi romanticism, where for seven centuries Holy Roman emperors had been crowned as heirs to the Caesars.

Collins now made a tactical choice he would soon regret. He decided to isolate Aachen rather than capture it. Short of gasoline and ammunition, keen to avoid an urban gunfight like the Cassino bloodletting in Italy, he ordered the 1st Division to seize the hills ringing the city south and east while the 9th Division pushed through the dense woods, seven miles below Aachen, known as the Hürtgenwald—the Hürtgen Forest. Between those two infantry divisions, the 3rd Armored Division would butt northeast toward the village of Stolberg, beyond which lay open ground leading to the Roer and Rhine Rivers. With luck, Collins believed, the Germans would abandon Aachen rather than risk encirclement by fifty thousand American troops chewing through the Scharnhorst and Schill Lines.

The sudden appearance of VII Corps had ignited panic in the city. Antiaircraft crews smashed their gun sights and fled toward Cologne, followed by police, municipal, and Nazi Party officials. Hitler ordered the evacuation of all 160,000 citizens. Terrified of being shot as traitors if they failed to comply, shopkeepers, pensioners, and mothers pushing prams soon clogged the roads leading east.

Into this chaos on the evening of Tuesday, September 12, came General Gerhard Graf von Schwerin, ordered to defend Aachen with the sixteen hundred men and thirty tanks remaining in his 116th Panzer Division, reinforced by two feeble Luftwaffe battalions and some local militiamen he called "Santa Clauses with fowling pieces." A veteran of Africa and Normandy, winner of the Knight's Cross for valor, Schwerin was a Prussian nobleman whom Hitler had described as "a splendid battlefield commander who unfortunately is not a National Socialist." Another officer later added, "He was intelligent, but this often proved a handicap."

Placing his new command post in the opulent Palast Hotel Quellenhof, Schwerin on Wednesday morning did the unthinkable: with the city likely to fall in just hours, he countermanded Hitler's evacuation order. Troops fanned out across Aachen, shooting looters and urging citizens to return to the surer safety of their homes. Then Schwerin sat at his desk and composed an appeal, in English, to be given the American commander whenever he took the city: "I stopped the absurd evacuation of this town; therefore, I am responsible for the fate of its inhabitants and I ask you, in the case of an occupation of your troops, to take care of the unfortunate population in a humane way."

He entrusted the letter to the only official still left in Aachen, a telephone company bureaucrat, then rushed to shore up the crumbling defenses along the city's southeastern perimeter.

A day passed, and then another. By dusk on Friday, the 1st Division had ruptured the Scharnhorst Line to ring Aachen on the west, south, and east. The 9th Division had pushed through the western fringe of the Hürtgen Forest, with its 47th Infantry Regiment on Saturday scooting past the last concrete bastion of the Schill Line to Schevenhütte, ten miles into Germany. The 3rd Armored Division captured a chain of villages—Roetgen, Schmidthof, Rott, Brandt—and edged to the southern lip of Stolberg, where fleeing Germans left half-eaten meals on the tables and half-packed suitcases on the beds.

But the momentum had seeped out of Collins's attack. Of several hundred Sherman tanks authorized for the armored division, only seventy remained fit for combat, hardly more than a battalion; after cantering across France, many now could manage only a low-gear crawl. Trucks, halftracks, and jeeps were equally decrepit. Many GIs lived on captured rations. Resupply required a two-hundred-mile round-trip to Army depots for ammunition, and an even longer journey for fuel. Fifty rounds from a tank destroyer failed to reduce one obdurate pillbox, and in an especially vicious firefight enemy mortars and 88mm guns crippled a dozen Shermans.

The dawning realization that the Americans intended to force the Stolberg corridor rather than assault Aachen revived the German high command. Guns and panzers were shifted, artillery recalibrated, and on Saturday morning the newly rebuilt 12th Infantry Division—nearly fifteen thousand men known as the Wild Buffaloes—poured into the fight aboard buses and trucks. Storm troopers and party officials scuttled back to enforce another demand by Hitler that Aachen be forcibly evacuated of civilians. Schwerin's letter fell into Nazi hands, and he was advised that he would be tried for cowardice by the notorious People's Court, known for administering justice with a noose. He fled to a farmhouse northwest of the city, protected by a cordon of motorcycle troops with machine guns; remarkably, at Rundstedt's urging, Hitler soon forgave him with no more than a reprimand, and a few months later Schwerin would command first a division in Italy and then a corps. "Fate," he explained, "had decided."

A German counterattack on Sunday with fixed bayonets across open ground south of Aachen was smashed by seven hundred rounds from the 32nd Field Artillery Battalion; dead and maimed fusiliers lay in field-gray windrows splashed with crimson. A German reporter in Aachen that Sunday described how "almost in every street a building was burning like a huge torch." GIs poked through a cemetery where fifteen wooden coffins had been abandoned before they could be interred, each with a thumb-tacked card bearing the name of a dead German soldier in Gothic script. A fading spray of red and white dahlias included a farewell message: "To Our Comrades, a Last Greeting."

After five days of fighting, Collins had gashed a twelve-mile hole in the first belt of the West Wall and a five-mile rift in the second. But he lacked the strength to exploit his opening. Stolberg, a meandering stone town folded into a pinched valley, had become a house-to-house battle of precisely the sort he had hoped to avoid. Collins moved his command post into a brick building previously used as a Nazi headquarters in Korneli-münster, barely two miles from the front; here he studied his maps and field reports under nagging artillery fire—staff officers tacked blankets across holes blown in the walls—and pondered what might have been. For him too, fate had decided.

Three German divisions soon sealed off the American salient, with five times as many panzers and assault guns around the city than had been there a week earlier. Hitler demanded fanatical resistance in what he now called "Fortress Aachen." The battle increasingly would move to the cellars, like Stalingrad. "Each and every house will be defended," the Füh-rer added, "to the last man and the last bullet."

A Market and a Garden

SINCE its founding in 1835 as a military garrison on the moors of north-east Belgium, the Flemish town of Bourg-Léopold had seen fortune ebb and flow with each passing army. It was said that here the invading Germans in 1914 had first experimented with chlorinated gas. Between world wars, the cantonment became Europe's largest and most modern, a camp for forty thousand Belgian soldiers and several thousand horses—all for naught against a new generation of German attackers, who bombed Bourg-Léopold in May 1940, then occupied the casern for four years, using the municipal woods to execute more than two hundred men, mostly sus-pected resistance supporters. British bombers in mid-May 1944 had acci-dentally slaughtered seventy-seven townfolk during a raid on the camp, but made amends two weeks later by returning to kill scores of German soldiers in their barracks.

Now the Germans were gone, again, and Allied soldiers swarmed through the cobbled streets. The British XXX Corps had planted its head-quarters outside town, near a honey farm with brightly painted wooden hives, and military policemen in brassards and red caps briskly directed dust-caked convoys to the engineer dumps scattered around Bourg-

Léopold. Nine thousand sappers had assembled two thousand truckloads of road metal, bridge girders, and barge anchors, all sorted into columns with code names for quick deployment.

On the radiant Sunday morning of September 17, dozens of British officers, none below the rank of lieutenant colonel, filed into the dingy cinema on Nicolaylaan, across from the hip-roof train station. They were a vivid lot, sporting chromatic scarves, ascots, and berets affixed with the badges of Scots, Irish, and Welsh Guards, of Grenadier and Coldstream Guards and Household Cavalry. Their costumes, a brigadier recorded, included "sniper's smocks, parachutist's jackets and jeep coats over brightly colored slacks, corduroys, riding breeches or even jodhpurs." After an exchange of barked greetings—some had fought together since before Alamein—they settled into their moviegoer seats to study a huge sketch map of eastern Holland propped against the screen on stage.

At eleven A.M. Lieutenant General Brian Horrocks, in a high-necked wooly beneath his battle-dress blouse and an airborne smock, ambled down the center aisle, provoking another yelping chorus of salutations. Lanky and spare, Horrocks was said by one admirer to possess "an ascetic, almost an ecclesiastical face," and his thick nimbus of white hair added a patriarchal mien to a man barely forty-nine. Mounting the stage, he surveyed the assemblage with a wry smile, then welcomed them with a quip that would be oft-repeated in later years to illustrate his sangfroid: "This is a tale you will tell your grandchildren, and mighty bored they'll be." Much knee-slapping ensued.

Horrocks was made for such moments. He had been born in an Indian hill station, the son of a knighted army surgeon, and as a young officer was severely wounded in the gut and captured at Ypres in 1914; repatriated after four years in a German prison camp, he squandered his accumulated back pay in an epic six-week spree. In 1919 he was captured again, this time by the Reds while fighting with a British contingent aiding the Whites in the Russian civil war. Again he was repatriated, having managed to survive typhus in a Bolshevik jail. After eighteen years as a captain, and a turn in the 1924 Olympics as the British pentathlon champion, he quickly ascended the ranks when war resumed, although he deemed himself "a not very bright philistine who had been lucky." Evacuated from Dunkirk, he later fought with Montgomery at Alamein and across Africa. While preparing to command the British corps at Salerno, he was struck down by a German fighter during a strafing run on Bizerte; one bullet caught him in the leg and another punctured his lungs and intestines before exiting through his spine. Half a dozen brutal surgeries kept him hospitalized for more than a year, and medicos declared he would never have another field command. Instead, Montgomery summoned him in August to take

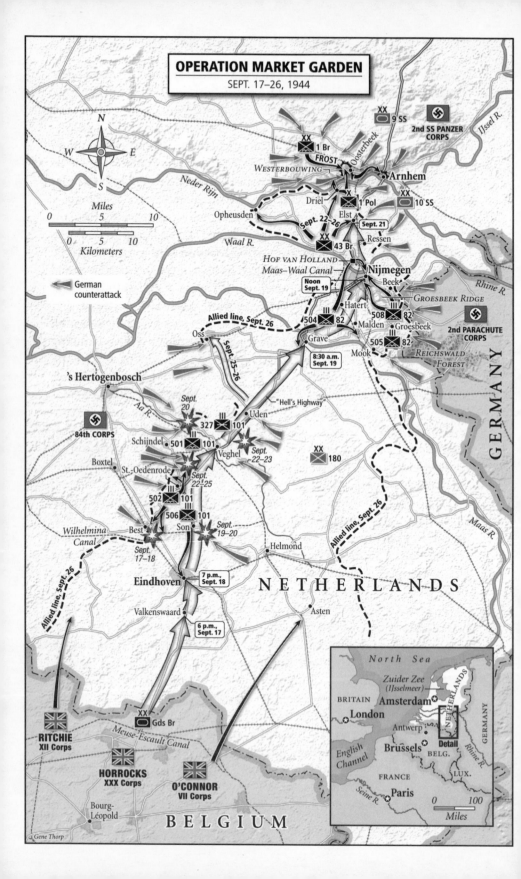

XXX Corps. The botched capture of the Scheldt adjacent to Antwerp was in part Horrocks's fault—as he candidly confessed—and if he now radiated vigorous good humor, some of those hunched in their cinema seats thought he appeared a tad frail.

Eyes alight, graceful hands gliding up and down, he spoke for an hour to review, for a final time, the plan called MARKET GARDEN. The Allied objective was "to dominate the country to the north as far as the Zuider Zee"—a shallow lake off the North Sea, better known as the IJsselmeer— "thereby cutting off communications between Germany and the Low Countries." With luck and élan, a quarter of a million enemy soldiers would be trapped in the western Netherlands, including those from the Fifteenth Army who had escaped across the Scheldt; the attack also would overrun many of the pestiferous V-2 rocket sites. An Allied juggernaut spearheaded by three armored divisions would then pivot east into Germany toward the Ruhr, having outflanked the Siegfried Line. Code names for various Dutch localities had been drawn from Shakespeare, including HAMLET, MACBETH, DUNCAN, BANQUO, OTHELLO, IAGO, YORICK, JULIET, and GUILDENSTERN—even indifferent scholars could not help but notice that things ended badly for this dramatis personae—but the three central characters represented a trio of large towns to be seized: BRUTUS, or Eindhoven, thirteen miles north of the current Allied line; BELCH, or Nijmegen, fifty-three miles north; and MALVOLIO, or Arnhem, sixty-four miles north. The Zuider Zee lay another thirty miles beyond Arnhem.

Linking these towns was a single narrow highway that ran through drained polders in terrain so excruciatingly flat that elevations varied no more than thirty feet over the course of fifty miles. Nine substantial bridges required capture or, if destroyed, replacement—hence the heaps of engineering matériel—and watercourses to be spanned included three wide rivers, two smaller tributaries, three major canals, and countless ditches, kills, and irrigation channels. Most imposing were the Meuse, known as the Maas once it entered Holland, and the Rhine, or Rijn, which, after widening to its greatest girth upon reaching the Dutch frontier, fractured into several "distributaries" before crossing a broad marshy plain to reach the sea. Two-thirds of the river's flux swept down the river Waal through Nijmegen; the Neder Rijn, or Lower Rhine, which kept the original stream's name but not its grandeur, flowed roughly parallel to the Waal and the Maas as it angled through Arnhem. The city had long been a retirement mecca for wealthy Dutch merchants from the East Indies: "Arnhem," a holiday guide from the 1930s proclaimed, "is an attractive residential center amidst delightful scenery, and with an exceedingly healthy atmosphere."

Horrocks paused, glancing at his notes and then at the map behind him before continuing. The deed would be done, he explained, by air and by land. For the largest airborne operation of the Second World War—the MARKET of MARKET GARDEN—the newly created First Allied Airborne Army was even now ascending from fields across England, bound for the Netherlands. Nearly 35,000 soldiers would be plunked down—most by parachute, the rest by glider—in what British planners insisted on calling "a carpet of airborne troops." At the foot of the carpet, in the south, the U.S. 101st Airborne Division would envelop a fifteen-mile corridor that included Eindhoven. In the middle, the 82nd Airborne sector stretched for ten miles, and included both the Nijmegen bridge over the Waal and a nine-span bridge across the Maas at Grave, or rather TYBALT. At the top of the carpet, the British 1st Airborne Division would seize Arnhem and a span across the Neder Rijn.

As this unfolded, the land assault—GARDEN—starting later in the afternoon would gallop north from Belgium with three divisions under XXX Corps in a thrust that was to be, in Field Marshal Montgomery's words, "rapid and violent, and without regard to what is happening on the flanks." Two vehicles abreast at a density of thirty-five trucks, tanks, and personnel carriers per mile would snake up that single highway, twenty thousand vehicles all told. Speed, Horrocks stressed, was "absolutely vital." The first Guards tanks should reach Eindhoven within two to three hours; if the vanguard reached the 1st Airborne paratroopers at Arnhem within forty-eight hours, as he hoped, much of the corps could be across the Rhine by the end of D+3, or Wednesday, September 20.

A SHAEF intelligence summary issued September 16 reported that "the enemy has by now suffered, in the West alone, losses in men and equipment which can never be repaired in this war. . . . No force can, then, be built up in the West sufficient for a counteroffensive or even for a successful defensive." German strength facing the 100,000-man XXX Corps directly across the Dutch border was estimated at six infantry battalions backed by twenty armored vehicles and a dozen field guns; scant enemy activity had been detected in the last two days. Still, no one expected that an assault of such rococo choreography would be easy. The regiment chosen to lead the ground attack, the Irish Guards, concluded that "on the whole it would be much easier for a rich man to get into heaven" than for XXX Corps to reach the Zuider Zee.

The conference ended with few questions. The earlier badinage had subsided, supplanted by knit-browed sobriety as the men filed from the theater. Horrocks thought the Irish Guards officers looked especially pensive.

At an abandoned factory on the south bank of the Meuse–Escaut Canal near Bourg-Léopold, Horrocks climbed an iron ladder to the flat roof. The warm midday sun spangled the dark canal and the irrigation ditches running north into Holland. An occasional German shell swished overhead, and the yap of a machine gun could be heard in the middle distance. Behind him, he spied some of the 350 British guns hidden in woodlots and farmyards. Tanks trundled forward, slowly to avoid raising dust, and sappers reinspected their bridge loads.

Earlier that morning Horrocks had asked an American colonel, "What do you think of the plan?" When told with a shrug, "It's all right," the corps commander laughed gaily, but the Yank saw anxiety in his eyes. Horrocks was in fact fretful. During the mad pursuit across France he had collapsed with a recurrent fever and was confined to his caravan; Montgomery had not only concealed his frailty—"Don't worry," the field marshal said, "I shan't invalid you home"—but invited him to recuperate in his own camp. Whether Horrocks was fit for the rigors ahead remained to be seen. The date also made him uneasy: no attack he had launched on a Sunday had ever fully succeeded.

From a nearby radio came word that the MARKET air armada was well under way. He cocked an ear for the distant drone of planes, a gaunt and lonely figure peering from his rooftop parapet.

Many others invested in MARKET GARDEN also felt perturbations, though for reasons more tangible than superstitions about the Sabbath. Under relentless pressure on Eisenhower from George Marshall and others in Washington to get those airborne divisions into the fight, the plan had been slapped together in less than a week. The First Allied Airborne Army, also created at War Department insistence, and the corps headquarters that preceded it had drafted and discarded eighteen operational plans in the past forty days, including a scheme for seizing airfields in Berlin and other missions with names like WILD OATS, TRANSFIGURE, COMET, and the unfortunate HANDS UP. Even Montgomery seemed exasperated by the frantic cycle of concocting and scuttling plans to sprinkle paratroopers across the Continent. "Are you asking me to drop cowpats all over Europe?" the field marshal had reportedly asked his subordinates.

Some commanders worried about MARKET's dispersal of paratroopers along a fifty-mile corridor. Others opposed GARDEN's tangential line of advance through boggy terrain to the north, *away* from the U.S. First Army axis toward the Ruhr. In contravention of Montgomery's earlier demand for one "full-blooded thrust" into Germany, the two main Allied legions would steadily diverge from each other. "It's a foolhardy thing to do, and you'll take a lot of casualties," Bradley told Eisenhower. "In addition, it's not in accordance with the plan Monty and I made together." "Flabbergasted," as he himself said, at not being consulted before Eisenhower approved MARKET GARDEN, Bradley also resented the diversion of transport planes needed to resupply his armies. The airborne army, he complained, showed "an astonishing faculty for devising missions that were never needed."

Personalities added fat to the fire. Commanding that airborne army was a short, vain, querulous U.S. Army Air Forces lieutenant general named Lewis H. Brereton, a Naval Academy graduate said to be capable of swearing in four languages and whose philandering had drawn a personal rebuke from General Marshall. "Mystify, mislead, and surprise," Brereton liked to tell subordinates, quoting Stonewall Jackson, but some wondered who was being duped. Blamed for ineffective close air support with the ground forces during the Normandy campaign's early weeks, when he commanded the Ninth Air Force, Brereton was "not sincere nor energetic nor cooperative," according to Bradley, who applauded his transfer to the airborne with two words: "Thank goodness." Brereton was disappointed in his new role, but he now oversaw both the U.S. XVIII Airborne Corps and the British I Airborne Corps—four divisions and a Polish brigade in all, as well as a fleet of transport planes.

If Brereton's interactions with his fellow Americans were prickly—the XVIII Airborne chief of staff called him "a stupid ass"—his relations with the British had grown venomous, particularly with his deputy, Lieutenant General Frederick A. M. "Boy" Browning, who would lead the MARKET assault. A handsome, mannered Grenadier Guardsman who had served valiantly in the last war but had yet to see action in this one, Browning was a high-strung mustache-twirler given to designing his own uniforms—false uhlan front, zip opening at the neck, polished Sam Browne belt, gray kid gloves, swagger stick—and occasionally kicking over the furniture. Some British subordinates privately called him "that popinjay," and Americans were wary of what one officer called "too deliberate a smile." Pilot, sailor, bobsledder, and national champion in the high hurdles, Browning nevertheless owed some of his cachet to his wife, the celebrated novelist Daphne du Maurier, whose *Rebecca* had, when translated to film by Alfred Hitchcock, won the Oscar for best picture in 1941. Browning so loathed Brereton that in early September he quit as deputy commander, only to withdraw his resignation a day later. Even now, with planes in the air by the thousands, the two men were seeking a modus vivendi to get them through the battle.

Finally, and most substantively, some officers sensed that the Germans were less supine than presumed. Brigadier E. T. Williams, Montgomery's intelligence chief, cautioned the field marshal that the Allies' "enemy appreciation was very weak" and that no proper study of the ground around Arnhem had been made. (The road bridge over the Neder Rijn had been penciled onto Allied map sheets, which were based largely on Dutch surveys made in the 1920s, before the span existed.) A radio decrypt also revealed that the enemy expected a XXX Corps thrust toward Nijmegen. The Polish commander, General Stanisław Sosabowski, after listening to an excessively chipper review of the battle plan on September 14, burst out, "But the Germans, how about the Germans, what about *them*?" Sosabowski later complained that someone "with a vivid imagination, optimism, and little knowledge was producing parachute battle orders with the same frequency and ease as a conjuror producing rabbits from a top hat." A British brigadier acknowledged a tendency "to make a beautiful airborne plan and then add the fighting-the-Germans bit afterwards."

Guessing which Germans would be fought proved vexing beyond all other vexations. Radio traffic showed that Model's Army Group B headquarters had shifted to Oosterbeek, outside Arnhem. Other intelligence suggested enemy reinforcement of river and canal defenses, but with troops considered "low category"; some improvised Luftwaffe ground units were apparently so rudimentary that they lacked field kitchens. Ultra decrypt XL 9188 in early September revealed that various battered units from Normandy had been ordered to western Holland to refit, and subsequent intercepts indicated that this gaggle included the II SS Panzer Corps. Not until September 15 had the SHAEF high command taken note that the corps' two divisions, the 9th and 10th SS Panzer, seemed to have laagered near Arnhem. Together they had suffered nine thousand casualties at Caen, at Falaise, and in the retreat across France; they had also lost much of their armor, including 120 tanks on August 19 alone. But whether the divisions were still eviscerated, where they were headed, or even precisely where they were now located remained opaque.

Montgomery's senior staff officers almost to a man voiced skepticism about MARKET GARDEN. Beetle Smith grew anxious enough to alert Eisenhower, who hesitated to intervene in tactical dispositions but authorized his chief of staff to raise the issue with the field marshal. Smith flew to Brussels on Friday, forty-eight hours before the assault was to begin, and suggested strengthening the MARKET force to be dropped at Arnhem, perhaps by shifting one of the American airborne divisions farther north. "Montgomery ridiculed the idea and laughed me out of his tent," Smith later reported. "He waved my objections airily aside."

Montgomery's insouciance was understandable, even if his alleged demeanor was not. Five Allied corps were about to descend on a narrow sliver of western Holland where the enemy was "weak, demoralized, and likely to collapse entirely if confronted with a large airborne attack," according to a British Second Army assessment. The German defenses around Arnhem had recently been gauged as no larger than a brigade of three thousand men, with insignificant tank strength. The Dutch underground had noted panzers and SS soldiers near Arnhem, but German infiltration of the resistance had resulted in the capture and execution of several dozen agents and made the Allies distrust information sent from the Netherlands. No conclusive intelligence about the two SS panzer divisions could be teased out, and the partial reports were passed to neither Horrocks nor most airborne commanders. The presence of tanks at Arnhem "was the one awkward fact that would not fit the desired pattern," the intelligence historian Ralph Bennett later wrote, "so the best thing was to sweep it under the carpet."

Boy Browning declared himself ready to sacrifice a third of his MARKET force in simply laying the airborne carpet, but such a gallant immolation would prove unnecessary. At two dozen English airfields on that lovely Sunday morning, the mighty flock had gathered: 1,545 transports and 478 gliders to be escorted by more than 1,000 fighters in two aerial trains across the North Sea for a flight almost three hours long. Hundreds of bombers also flew, bringing the entire winged fleet to 4,676. Tea wagons rattled along the runways with bacon sandwiches and great steaming mugs. "That means business," one crewman said. "They never give you a cup of tea unless you're really going." At Grantham, a British sergeant strutted down the sun-washed flight line in an opera hat, doffing it and bowing to men right and left.

"Emplane!" The order echoed and reechoed. With much grunting and cursing, the thousands heaved themselves aboard—among them many Normandy veterans, who called themselves "the Old Men." Fighters and pathfinders lifted off first, and by noon, just as Horrocks finished his briefing in the Bourg-Léopold theater, more than twenty thousand troops were off the ground, with 330 artillery tubes and 500 vehicles. Men played chess or read the Sunday papers; others dozed or gawked from the tiny windows at "an immense armada of aircraft, some towing gliders, which stretched as far as could be seen," as one lieutenant wrote. "They floated up and down in unison like an outstretched blanket being gently shaken."

The first British pathfinders jumped at 12:40 P.M., followed twenty minutes later by gliders landing every nine seconds—"plowing up dirt like a ship in a heavy sea," in one GI's image. Then, from an altitude of six hundred feet, the parachutists spilled out, so many that astonished witnesses below thought they were snowflakes or flak bursts, and within eighty minutes those twenty thousand Allied cutthroats were deep behind enemy lines. Aircraft losses were modest: sixty-eight planes, including fighters and bombers lost to flak. Gleeful children near Arnhem sang "Jingle Bells" in Dutch to parachutists wriggling from their silks.

That this welcoming chorus congregated several miles west of town underscored one of two tactical complications beclouding the sunny first hours of MARKET. Airborne doctrine held that drop and landing zones should be as close to the mission objective as possible, preferably within five miles; these instead lay seven to eight miles from the Arnhem road bridge. Accusatory fingers subsequently would be pointed either at Major General Roy Urquhart, commander of the 1st Airborne Division, a novice parachutist who was said to lack the requisite experience and credibility to insist on closer drops, or, more plausibly, at air commanders who refused to fly closer because of possible enemy flak and because of congestion in the airspace between Arnhem and Nijmegen.

The second complication was evident just by counting noses: barely half of the 3.5-division force designated for MARKET was on the ground, and no more troops would arrive until the following day or later. General Brereton's troop carrier commanders had insisted that only a single mission fly on Sunday; a second sortie would ostensibly exhaust air and ground crews and leave insufficient time to service and reload the planes (although double missions over the same distance had been flown from Italy in DRAGOON the previous month). Pleas by airborne commanders and by an emissary from Montgomery to Brereton's headquarters failed to reverse the decision, despite an analysis that showed transporting the entire combat force at a deliberate rate could take up to four days. Particularly for the British, the combination of too few men with too far to travel would soon prove fateful, even as paratroopers from the 1st Airborne Division collected their kit and hurried east in search of a bridge to seize.

The day went well enough for the Yanks in the south. Almost seven thousand men from the 101st Airborne spilled across the polders between Veghel and Best, where red flags and billowing orange smoke denoted battalion assembly areas. Dutchmen capered through the fields, shaking hands with their liberators and offering sandwiches, pitchers of milk, and bicycles, for which receipts were issued. Stray Germans here and there were captured or killed in a hundred sharp spasms of violence; under a fruit tree near a captured jam factory, where GIs discovered shelves of preserved apples, pears, and plums, the poet-paratrooper Louis Simpson found a mattress "with a German officer stretched on it. He had been laid there to die in all possible comfort."

Nine road and rail bridges stood in the division sector, but only at Son, four miles north of Eindhoven, did one span cause immediate grief. At a crossing over the Wilhelmina Canal, a bazooka team from the 506th Parachute Infantry knocked out an 88mm gun with a single round, and a sergeant with a tommy gun mowed down six fleeing crewmen. Troopers pressed to within thirty yards of the canal bank, only to see the bridge abruptly levitate from its piers and vanish in a smoky roar. Hardly had the debris stopped raining than GIs swam to the south bank or crossed in rowboats. Using ropes, scavenged doors, and barn wood, engineers threw a narrow catwalk across the stone stubs of the now naked piers, and a thousand men tiptoed to the far bank as an inky evening settled over the battlefield. The 506th was supposed to sprint south and seize Eindhoven and its bridges by eight P.M., welcoming Horrocks's Guardsmen from Bourg-Léopold, but the delay at Son meant that any rendezvous would have to await first light on Monday.

Twenty miles north, 7,300 troops from the 82nd Airborne had also arrived intact in a confetti of green, orange, blue, red, and chartreuse parachutes. All but one of 482 planes and two of 50 gliders reached the target zones below Nijmegen. Among the few jump casualties was the 82nd commander, James Gavin, who fractured two vertebrae in a hard landing between Groesbeek and Mook. Allowing himself little more than a grimace, Gavin shed his parachute, picked up an M-1 rifle, and in less than an hour had set up his command post in a leafy thicket just west of Groesbeek.

With the ascension of Matthew Ridgway to command the XVIII Airborne Corps, Gavin had taken over the 82nd in mid-August. At thirty-seven he would be not only the youngest major general in the U.S. Army during World War II, but also the youngest division commander since the Civil War. That achievement was all the more remarkable given his start in life. Gavin was an orphan (he later concluded that his mother had been an immigrant Irish nun in Brooklyn); adopted as a toddler, he was raised among Pennsylvania's anthracite collieries by a woman who invoked the Holy Family as she beat him with a hairbrush, a broomstick, or a cat-o'-nine-tails specially made in a harness shop. Sometimes she waited until the child was asleep to launch her assault.

After eight years of grammar school, Gavin soaped miners' beards for a barber, delivered boots for a shoemaker, and ran a filling station for an oil company. On his seventeenth birthday he fled to New York and joined the Army. Stationed in Panama, he read and studied diligently enough to win admission to West Point. He lied about his age to avoid disclosing that he had enlisted as a minor. A perpetual student he remained, even now subscribing to *The New Yorker, Time, Reader's Digest,* and the Book-of-the-Month Club. In a loose-leaf notebook titled "Generalship," organized by virtues such as "enterprise" and "intelligence," he copied a phrase he attributed to Voltaire: "That calm courage in the midst of tumult, that serenity of a soul in danger, which is the greatest gift of nature for command." Gavin called it "the courage of two o'clock in the morning." Ridgway had recently praised his young subordinate's "self-possession regardless of the pressure in and out of battle, loyalty, initiative, zeal, sound judgment, and common sense. . . . He adds great charm of manner."

Though Gavin casually referred to war as "the scuffle," he was realistic about human limits. After combat jumps into Sicily, Salerno, and Normandy, he had come to believe that "courage for every man is like a bank account" that must not be overdrawn. MARKET would require another judicious withdrawal. "It looks very rough," he had written in his diary on Thursday about the impending attack. "If I get through this one I will be very lucky."

Eleven bridges could be found in the 82nd sector, and enemy demolitionists blew those at Malden, Mook, and Hatert as paratroopers closed in. But the rivet-skinned, nine-arch span over the Maas at Grave still stood when soldiers from the 504th Parachute Infantry rushed the southern ramp, gutting a concrete flak tower with bazooka rounds through the firing ports, then shooting up two truckloads of absconding Germans and swinging a captured 20mm gun onto the remaining defenders. Shouts, explosions, bullets pinging off the girders—the battle din ebbed at last and a brilliant bouquet of green flares signaled that the hour was won. Engineers snipped detonation wires and ripped out boxes of dynamite painted to resemble bridge steel. In Grave the Dutch sang "Tipperary" as the Germans skulked off, and a message flew up the division chain of command: "Bridge number eleven is ours."

Bridge eleven and all its sisters were worthless if the Germans seized one of the few bits of elevated terrain in Holland, and this beyond all else preoccupied Gavin. Groesbeek Ridge, an unprepossessing eminence three hundred feet high and five miles long southeast of Nijmegen, dominated the Maas, the Waal, and the Maas–Waal Canal; General Browning's orders to the 82nd specified that "the capture and retention of the high ground between Nijmegen and Groesbeek is imperative in order to accomplish the division's task." With eight 75mm howitzers banging away an hour after the jump—each had arrived in seven pieces, by parachute—Gavin spent the afternoon shoring up strongpoints along the ridge and squinting across the nearby German border for signs of an enemy counterattack. Nijmegen and its two grand bridges would have to wait until these approaches were secure.

Near the 82nd command post, a Dutch commando captain stepped into a farmhouse outside Groesbeek to use the telephone. After ringing friends in the north, he emerged to tell Gavin, "Fine. Everything is going as planned, and the British have landed at Arnhem."

So too had the Germans, and with this convergence the heartache began in earnest. Field Marshal Model had been sipping a preluncheon glass of Moselle in his headquarters at the Tafelberg Hotel in Oosterbeek when a staff officer rushed in with news of British glider landings barely two miles away. "Right. Everyone out," Model said. "They're after me and this headquarters." Hurrying down the steps, papers and underwear spilling from his attaché case, he leaped into a staff car and raced to the II SS Panzer Corps headquarters, eighteen miles to the east. By midafternoon he was organizing German counterblows at Arnhem, Nijmegen, and points south. "Imagine!" Model exclaimed. "They almost got me."

They did get the Arnhem commandant, General Friedrich Kussin, who wandered across town in his Citroën to investigate the commotion only to blunder into a fusillade of British rifle and Sten-gun fire that flattened his tires and killed both his driver and batman. Shot in the chest and throat, Kussin flopped from the car to the pavement, quite dead, a revolver in his gloved right hand and an unfinished cigarette in his left, his mouth agape in a rictus of astonishment. Vengeful Dutchmen ripped the rank badges from his collar.

Not much else went right for General Urquhart or his division. Six thousand German troops had bivouacked around greater Arnhem—double the anticipated number; they were mostly grenadiers from the two SS panzer divisions as well as "ear and stomach battalions" composed of soldiers with maladies afflicting those organs. Others hurried into battle aboard farm carts, wood-burning trucks, and even fire engines. Within ninety minutes of the British landings, about four hundred SS soldiers had blocked two of the western approaches to town, forcing the Tommies into a garden-by-garden gunfight on their long tramp toward the bridge.

Ignoring warnings of danger ahead, Urquhart—a strapping, amiable Scot, with combat experience in Africa and Italy—wandered too far forward and found himself first under machine-gun fire and then cut off from the rest of his command in a confused warren of Dutch alleys. Darting through kitchens and across terraces, he and two other officers finally hid in the attic at 14 Zwarteweg, without food, water, or a toilet, as SS troops sniffed through the streets below and positioned an antitank gun near the front door. For forty hours, until the Germans retrenched to the east, the 1st Airborne Division headquarters would be without its commander. Urquhart acknowledged feeling "idiotic, ridiculous, [and] as ineffectual in the battle as a spectator."

A single British parachute battalion won through. Following a southern route through gorse and birch stands near the Neder Rijn, Lieutenant Colonel John D. Frost's 2nd Battalion had woven proffered marigolds
into their helmet nets and captured a few German soldiers said to have
been "snogging with their Dutch girlfriends." Radios proved so erratic
that bugle calls were used instead, and the southern span of Arnhem's rail
bridge blew up in the faces of the platoon sent to secure it. But at eight P.M.
Tommies reached the northern piers of the intact road bridge, and Frost's
men soon burrowed into buildings along the riverbank. Several dozen
paratroopers wrapped their hobnail boots in curtain strips to deaden their
footfalls, then crept onto the span only to be smacked back by cackling
machine guns. British return fire with an antitank gun and a flamethrower
ignited paintwork on the girders. A German attempt to rush 10th SS Panzer troops across the bridge from the south ended with enemy trucks blazing on the ramp and charred bodies smoldering in the roadbed.

A brutal deadlock had begun. Of nearly 6,000 British paratroopers,
only 740 would reach the bridge, enough to revoke German possession of
the span but too few to assert a British claim. Relief battalions pushing
from the west found the streets ever more perilous, not least from German
snipers lashed to tree branches with rope stays. Flames danced all night
from the burning bridge and from wooden houses set ablaze by gunfights
along the embankments. From his makeshift command post a block from
the river, Frost—an Africa veteran who optimistically had shipped his golf
clubs and hunting gun overland to Holland—peered south through the
lurid orange glow, hoping that a new day might reveal Horrocks's tanks
lining the far shore.

That would not happen.

At precisely two P.M. that Sunday, seventeen Allied artillery regiments
had begun a lacerating barrage, as Horrocks and his coterie looked north
and rubbed their hands in gleeful anticipation atop the factory roof near
Bourg-Léopold. Shells gnawed at fields and pine thickets for a thousand
yards on either side of the Eindhoven road, and every five minutes another
eight Typhoons swooped in with rocket fire to savage any lurking ambushers.

At 2:35 P.M., the Irish Guards lieutenant commanding the lead tank
ordered, "Driver, advance!" Like a circus parade the column surged forth,
nose to tail, gears grinding, every chassis groaning beneath ammunition
crates, rations for six days, and enough jerrican fuel to travel another 250
miles after gas tanks ran dry. The artillery barrage now rolled forward,
barely three hundred yards ahead of the armored vanguard; brown dust
and blue exhaust masked the bursting shells. Across the Dutch border

they rumbled at eight miles per hour. "Advance going well," an officer reported by radio. "Leading squadron has got through."

No sooner had the hand-rubbers on the roof congratulated one another than scarlet tongues of German fire licked along the column. Within two minutes, nine Irish Guards tanks had been disemboweled with antitank guns and hand-held Panzerfausts—"a nasty gap of a half a mile littered with burning hulks," as one witness described the scene. Infantrymen hitchhiking on the armored decks dove into roadside ditches, and crews scrambled from their hatches except for a few poor souls who burned down to their tanker boots. An armored bulldozer lurched forward to push the pyres from the concrete roadbed, and Typhoons pirouetted in for another two hundred sorties, rocketing enemy positions real and imaginary.

The German defenders soon were identified as two battalions from the 9th SS Panzer Division—"a complete surprise," British intelligence acknowledged—plus two battalions from the 6th Parachute Regiment. "Our intelligence spent the day in a state of indignant surprise," the Irish Guards war diary recorded. "One German regiment after another appeared which had no right to be there." The consequent "ugly mood" inspired one Irish sergeant to force several prisoners onto his tank at gunpoint to identify hidden enemy emplacements. Even so, another artillery barrage was needed at six P.M. before the Irish Guards staggered into little Valkenswaard to harbor for the night on the central square, now laved in orange light from burning houses. A few dozen scruffy prisoners sat in a cage tucked beneath the municipal bandstand.

For seven miles from the Dutch border to Valkenswaard, double- and triple-banked British vehicles jammed the road, annoyed by occasional enemy mortar rounds. In few spots was this narrow aisle into occupied Holland wider than thirty feet, and the Guards Armored Division now knew vividly what a terrain study had concluded a week earlier: "Cross-country movement in the area varies from impracticable to impossible. . . . All canals and rivers present obstacles, accentuated by the thousands of dikes and shallow drainage ditches." Eindhoven still lay six miles ahead—the 101st Airborne's failure to reach the city by eight P.M. had not mattered—and Arnhem seemed a world away. Despite the quick destruction of those first nine tanks, losses were light: only fifteen dead in the entire Guards Armored Division. Yet the XXX Corps drive stopped cold for twelve hours, and little consideration was given to preserving at least an illusion of momentum, perhaps by letting the fresh Grenadier Guards pass through their battered Irish brethren. Horrocks had urged speed, but there was no speed.

"Things are going very well indeed," Brereton's headquarters told SHAEF. "We have had very few losses." Eisenhower's operations chief phoned with "congratulations on the successful outcome of the operation," the First Allied Airborne Army chief of staff noted in his diary. "Everyone at SHAEF was delighted."

Everyone at SHAEF was deluded: MARKET GARDEN had been lost on the very first day through failure to seize the bridges at Arnhem and Nijmegen, and the failure was compounded by the ponderous overland advance. A titanic, often heroic battle remained to play out, with particular fates by the tens of thousands in the balance. But the margin for victory, always razor thin, now was irretrievably gone.

Eindhoven was home to the Philips electronics company, founded in 1891 by a cousin of Karl Marx's. In addition to making lightbulbs, the firm had expanded to vacuum tubes, radios, X-ray equipment, and, in 1939, the electric razor. Still, with no apologies to Paris, Eindhoven thought of itself as the *Lichtstad*, the city of light. For the past four years, nearly all exports had gone to Germany at Berlin's insistence. But the firm proved deft at sheltering Jews by insisting they were irreplaceable specialists, and several hundred Jewish workers would survive the war.

Now this company town of thatched roofs, clipped lawns, and neat privet hedges was set free. Troopers from the 101st Airborne nudged into Eindhoven from the north early on Monday, September 18, routing a few score Germans and finding all bridges intact. Jubilation burst from every doorway and unshuttered window, a din of tin whistles, toy drums, and singing citizens draped in orange, the Dutch national color. Thousands danced in gyrating circles, offering their liberators apples and gin. "The air seemed to reek with hate for the Germans," an American officer observed.

Not until dusk did XXX Corps arrive from the south, having taken the entire day to crawl six miles. Following a sluggish start from Valkenswaard, the Guards Armored Division encountered more troublesome ambuscades, now stiffened with Panther tanks. Fog at Belgian airfields and other aggravations grounded the Typhoons, and attempts to detour east or west were impeded by frail bridges. "Every time the advance seemed to be progressing," the Grenadier Guards reported, "a canal or stream would intervene with a bridge that invariably broke after a couple tanks had crossed." Pushing at last through orange-bedecked Eindhoven, the Guardsmen halted for the night below Son while engineers finished laying a Bailey bridge over that toppled Wilhelmina Canal highway span. Off again they rolled at dawn on Tuesday, down the tree-lined road known already as Hell's Highway, through St.-Oedenrode and Veghel toward

Grave, an iron thread snaking through one needle's eye after another, now more than thirty-three hours behind schedule.

Reinforcements from England also arrived, though hardly with the ease of the surprise initial drops on Sunday. Almost 150 gliders landed at Son early Monday afternoon, defying gunfire from German marksmen lined up shoulder to shoulder as if on a rifle range. Gavin at the same time found two drop zones east of Groesbeek Ridge infested with enemy troops who had leaked across the German border with more than a dozen 20mm guns. Resupply planes were already on the wing, so an improvised counterattack force fixed bayonets and charged down the ridge to chase off the intruders just in time. A midafternoon lift of nearly four thousand aircraft delivered twelve hundred gliders and seven thousand troops across the battlefield. More than two hundred B-24 bombers, stripped of their ball turrets, bombsights, and waist guns, also spat supplies by parachute, with spotty accuracy. All in all, the 82nd received about 80 percent of its expected replenishment, but the 101st got less than half.

The 101st found more unexpected trouble four miles west of Son at Best, a town of cobblers and boot makers, with a brick factory and a cold-storage plant. Unaware that a thousand Fifteenth Army troops protected the vital German supply road through Best, a solitary company from the 502nd Parachute Infantry arrived to claim both the town and a single-span concrete bridge over the Wilhelmina Canal for an alternative route from Eindhoven. Lieutenant Edward L. Wierzbowski led his platoon to the northern lip of the canal, where five machine guns opened up from the far bank, soon punctuated by mortar rounds. At eleven A.M. on Monday the bridge blew to smithereens, and Wierzbowski and his men spent the day and following night fighting for survival from a shallow trench sixty yards back from the water's edge.

Among seven wounded GIs huddled in an adjacent foxhole was Private First Class Joe E. Mann, a twenty-two-year-old with thin lips, wide-set eyes, and a strong nose, the fifth of nine children from a farm family near Spokane. Mann, the platoon scout, had helped destroy an ammunition dump and an 88mm gun with bazooka rounds before being shot in both arms, which now dangled uselessly in a double sling. On Tuesday morning a swirling fog abruptly lifted along the canal to unveil creeping wraiths in field gray almost atop the American position. GIs managed to scoop away two enemy grenades before they detonated but a third exploded, blinding the platoon machine-gunner, who still managed, groping wildly, to find a fourth and fling it back. The fifth grenade fell behind Mann, who leaned back and absorbed the blast with his torso, saving his comrades in a gesture later commemorated with the Medal of Honor. "My back's gone," he told Wierzbowski. Two minutes later he was dead.

The supreme commander of Allied forces in western Europe, General Dwight D. Eisenhower, crossing the English Channel en route to Normandy from southern England on June 7, 1944. President Roosevelt chose Eisenhower to command Operation OVERLORD as "the best politician among the military men. He is a natural leader who can convince other men to follow him."

An artillery unit bound for Normandy loads equipment into landing vessels in Brixham on the southwest coast of England, June 1, 1944. Seven thousand kinds of combat necessities, from surgical scissors to bazooka rockets, had to reach French beaches in the first four hours of the invasion.

The Allied military high command for Operation OVERLORD, during a meeting in London. Seated, from left to right: Air Chief Marshal Sir Arthur W. Tedder; Eisenhower; General Bernard L. Montgomery. Standing, from left to right: Lieutenant General Omar N. Bradley; Admiral Sir Bertram H. Ramsay; Air Chief Marshal Trafford Leigh-Mallory; Lieutenant General Walter Bedell "Beetle" Smith, Eisenhower's chief of staff.

Eisenhower with paratroopers from the 101st Airborne Division at Greenham Common in the Berkshire Downs, June 5, 1944. "The idea, the perfect idea," Eisenhower advised, "is to keep moving." The tall officer in the dark uniform is Commander Harry C. Butcher, Eisenhower's naval aide.

American soldiers wade from a landing craft toward Omaha Beach and the bluffs beyond on the morning of June 6, 1944.

American and German dead await burial in a makeshift morgue behind Omaha Beach. The 4,700 U.S. casualties at Omaha, including wounded and missing, accounted for more than one-third of the Allied total on D-Day.

Reinforcements and artillery press inland from Omaha Beach two days after the initial invasion. Within a week of D-Day, more than 300,000 Allied troops and 2,000 tanks had arrived in France, but the beachhead remained pinched and crowded.

Montgomery, commander of Allied ground forces in Normandy, confers with war correspondents on June 15. Eisenhower considered him "a good man to serve under, a difficult man to serve with, and an impossible man to serve over."

The remnants of Mulberry A off Omaha Beach after one of the worst June gales in eighty years. A senior American admiral denounced the artificial harbors emplaced off Normandy as "the greatest waste of manpower and steel and equipment . . . for any operation in World War II."

Field Marshal Erwin Rommel, commander of Army Group B in France, seen in a 1940 photo that foreshadows his subsequent wounding four years later during a strafing attack by Allied fighter planes.

Adolf Hitler examines wreckage in an undated German photo captured by the U.S. Army on the Western front. For the first and only time since the Germans overran Paris four years earlier, the Führer in mid-June of 1944 would return to France to confer with his commanders in Margival about the Allied invasion.

A German V-1 flying bomb plummets to earth above a London rooftop. More than ten thousand of the crude weapons were fired at Britain, killing or badly injuring 24,000 people; thousands more V-1s fell on Antwerp.

GIs from the 79th Infantry Division fighting in bocage terrain south of the Cotentin Peninsula in mid-July. Of these bitterly defended hedgerows, a soldier wrote, "Each one of them was a wall of fire, and the open fields between were plains of fire."

Eisenhower and Bradley listen to Major General J. Lawton Collins, right, commander of the U.S. VII Corps, shortly after the capture of Cherbourg. Among the few officers in France with combat experience in the South Pacific, Collins was described by one admirer as "runty, cocky, confident, almost to the point of being a bore."

General Karl-Wilhelm von Schlieben, commander of the German garrison at Cherbourg, shortly after his surrender on June 26. In his pocket was found a menu from a dinner honoring him a few weeks earlier, featuring lobster and champagne.

Brigadier General Theodore Roosevelt, Jr., seen in Ste.-Mère-Église on July 12, hours before he died of a coronary thrombosis. The 4th Infantry Division commander described him as "the most gallant soldier and finest gentleman I have ever known."

Honorary pallbearers at Roosevelt's funeral include Bradley and Lieutenant General George S. Patton at the head of the column on the left, and, on the right, Lieutenant General Courtney H. Hodges and Collins. *(U.S. Army Military History Institute)*

Field Marshal Walter Model took command of the retreating German armies in France in mid-August 1944. "Did you see those eyes?" Hitler once said of Model. "I wouldn't want to serve under him." *(U.S. Army Military History Institute)*

"A warring, roaring comet," as one reporter described George Patton, the U.S. Third Army commander, seen here after his promotion to four-star general in 1945. *(U.S. Army Military History Institute)*

Photographer Robert Capa, left, and Ernest Hemingway, right, accredited as a correspondent for *Collier's* magazine, with their Army driver in France shortly before the liberation of Paris.

Major General Jacques Philippe Leclerc, commander of the French 2nd Armored Division, on the Boulevard du Montparnasse in Paris on the day of liberation, August 25, 1944.

General Dietrich von Choltitz, commander of German forces in Paris, seen shortly after he formally surrendered the city late on the afternoon of August 25.

Sniper fire sends French citizens sprawling or fleeing in the Place de la Concorde on August 26. "It was like a field of wheat suddenly struck by a strong gust of wind," wrote one witness.

General Charles de Gaulle continues singing a hymn in Notre Dame cathedral on August 26 despite gunfire reverberating through the nave during a thanksgiving service. "The most extraordinary example of courage I've ever seen," a BBC reporter declared.

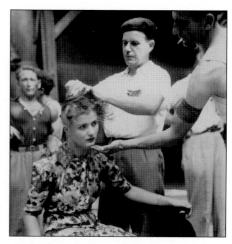

A French woman accused of collaboration with German occupiers is barbered on August 29. Others like her had swastikas painted on their breasts or placards hung around their necks that read, "I whored with the Boches."

Parisians line the Champs-Élysées on August 29 to cheer the U.S. 28th Infantry Division, marching through Paris before taking up pursuit of the German army to the east.

Assault forces from the U.S. VI Corps file ashore near St.-Tropez in southern France during Operation DRAGOON on August 15, 1944.

Major General Lucian K. Truscott, Jr., shown here after his promotion to three-star general in October, commanded the U.S. VI Corps during the invasion of southern France and the subsequent pursuit up the Rhône River. This was Truscott's third amphibious invasion of the war.

Lieutenant General Alexander M. Patch, Jr., commander of the U.S. Seventh Army in southern France, and his son, Captain Alexander M. "Mac" Patch III, shortly before the young officer's death. *(U.S. Military Academy)*

General Jean Joseph Marie Gabriel de Lattre de Tassigny, described by one admirer as "an animal of action," commanded the French First Army as part of the 6th Army Group in southern France. *(©KEYSTONE-FRANCE)*

Lieutenant General John C. H. Lee, the chief American logistician as commander of the Communications Zone. "Heavy on ceremony, somewhat forbidding in manner and appearance, and occasionally tactless," as the Army's official history described him, "General Lee often aroused suspicions and created opposition."

British paratroopers in a C-47 transport plane, bound for Holland in Operation MARKET GARDEN.

More than twenty thousand parachutists and glider troops descended behind German lines on September 17, 1944, in the biggest, boldest airborne operation of the war.

By late September 1944, the once-handsome Dutch town of Nijmegen had been reduced to ruins, although the road bridge leading toward Arnhem, ten miles north, still spanned the Waal River.

GIs from the 1st Infantry Division battle through central Aachen on October 17, 1944, several days before German defenders finally capitulated.

Captain Joseph T. Dawson helped stave off German counterattacks at Aachen. "These bitter tragic months of terrible war leave one morally as well as physically exhausted," he told his family. Here Dawson receives the Distinguished Service Cross from Eisenhower for heroics at Omaha Beach. (*McCormick Research Center, First Division Museum*)

Riflemen from the 110th Infantry Regiment of the 28th Division creep through the Hürtgen Forest near Vossenack in early November. "The days were so terrible that I would pray for darkness," one soldier recalled, "and the nights were so bad that I would pray for daylight."

Eisenhower quizzes Major General Norman D. Cota about the Hürtgen battle at the 28th Division command post in Rott. "Well, Dutch," the supreme commander told him, "it looks like you got a bloody nose."

Sherman tanks push eastward on November 16 as part of Operation QUEEN. After more than three weeks the attack sputtered and stalled, reaching the west bank of the Roer River but not the Rhine, as U.S. commanders had hoped.

The high command contemplates a winter campaign in northern Europe. Conferring in mid-November at the supreme commander's forward headquarters in Reims are, left to right, Field Marshal Sir Alan Brooke, chief of the Imperial General Staff; Eisenhower; Prime Minister Winston S. Churchill.

Nearly out of ammunition and with only three men left unwounded, the lieutenant knotted a filthy handkerchief to his carbine muzzle and surrendered the platoon. The battle at Best, envisioned as a company operation, soon sucked in the entire regiment, and only the arrival of British tanks decided the day by securing the Allied left flank. Fourteen hundred German prisoners would be taken, and more than three hundred enemy corpses counted, including some reportedly shot by their own comrades while trying to give up. Yet the town itself remained just outside Allied lines, and so it would remain for weeks.

An entry in the 82nd Airborne's intelligence log on Monday morning—"Dutch report Germans winning over British at Arnhem"—was more than matched in brevity by a British acknowledgment of "a grossly untidy situation." In a shot-torn town where the bakeries remained open and milkmen still made their rounds, the 1st Airborne Division found itself in great peril. Three battalions had tried and failed to reach Colonel Frost and his men where they still clung to the north ramp of Arnhem's highway bridge. Parachuted supplies had drifted mostly into German hands, and foul weather forced a postponement in the drop of Polish reinforcements. Balky radios, all but worthless in wooded or urban terrain, limited communication between the embattled Arnhem force and the rest of the First Allied Airborne Army to an occasional truncated exchange. General Urquhart would not rejoin his headquarters from the Zwarteweg attic until Tuesday morning, and by that afternoon over half of the British soldiers north of the Neder Rijn were listed as casualties. One brigadier was reduced to describing himself as "a broken-down cavalryman leading little bayonet rushes." Brazen civilians built roadblocks with bodies—German, British, Dutch—laid head to toe like sandbags in a futile effort to keep the SS from roaming freely across town. "Everything," a British account conceded, "had gone awry."

Nothing was right except the courage, and nowhere was courage greater than at the bridge. Living on apples and pears scavenged in the cellars, along with tea, nips of cherry brandy, and Benzedrine, Frost's force by Tuesday had been cudgeled back into a perimeter of ten buildings from an original eighteen. Heavy Dutch furniture barricaded the doors and windows. Buckets, jugs, and vases were filled with water to douse incendiaries. To avoid fratricide the men called to one another from blownout windows with an old African war cry—"Waho, Mohammed!"—using rolled strips of wallpaper for megaphones. A German effort to force the bridge from the south with a dozen armored cars and two Mercedes trucks ended in a fiery welter of wrecked vehicles; another seventy enemy dead paved the ramp. An enemy FW-190 fighter swooped across the river on Tuesday afternoon to drop a bomb—it proved a dud—then clipped the southern tower of the fourteenth-century St. Walburgis church with its left wing before cartwheeling into a small lake. "Great joy all round," wrote a British sapper.

Germans on the south bank of the Neder Rijn unlimbered 40mm flak guns against the British strongholds, then 88mm and even 150mm. Tiger tanks and Nebelwerfer six-barreled rocket launchers—Screaming Meemies—joined the cannonade with high explosives and white phosphorus. "Starting from the rooftops, buildings collapsed like dolls' houses," an SS private recorded. Another German likened the effect of panzer shells on masonry to "the skin peeling off a skeleton." After a shell hit a house near the roofline, "the entire building seemed to shake itself like a dog," a British mortarman reported, and when a second round struck "the walls appeared to breathe out before the whole structure collapsed."

"Arnhem was burning," Frost later recalled. "It was as daylight in the streets, a terrible enameled, metallic daylight. . . . I never saw anything more beautiful than those burning buildings." Despite a BBC report that "everything was going according to plan" in the Netherlands, the 2nd Battalion's predicament had grown hopeless. "It is a pretty desperate thing to see your battalion gradually carved to bits around you," Frost wrote after the war. Before scrambling to another position, paratroopers loosened their helmet straps and sat for a moment with fallen comrades: "Nobody is in such dire need of companionship as a dead man," one major explained. But soon enough, the ripe corpses of British and German alike were tossed from upper windows into the streets below.

By Wednesday the Neder Rijn embankment held by the British was described as "a sea of flame," with enemies pressing from east, north, and west. At 1:30 P.M. mortar shards crippled Frost in both legs; he was carried to a fetid cellar where the floor was so packed with the wounded and dead that orderlies had difficulty squeezing through. "Our building is on fire," wrote a sergeant consigned to the same hole. "We no longer have any means to put it out. In our cellar there is an all-pervading stench of blood, feces, and urine." Germans held prisoner in the basement, including captured crewmen from a V-2 battery, sang *"Deutschland, Deutschland, über alles,"* in hopes the SS would recognize their comrades' voices before flinging in grenades.

Both sides agreed to a two-hour cease-fire late Wednesday to evacuate the wounded and the gibbering shock cases. "Are you British or American?" asked the first SS soldier into Frost's cellar. Doors were ripped from their hinges and used as stretchers to hoist men outside, where "the scene resembled one of those paintings that you see in regimental museums entitled 'The Last Stand,'" a Tommy recalled. Panzer grenadiers offered brandy, chocolate, and congratulations for a fight well fought, "a harder battle than any I had fought in Russia," as one declared. Frost, who would spend six months in a prison hospital, considered his SS captors "kind, chivalrous, and even comforting." But not to all: a Dutch physician who had treated British wounded in the Domestic Science School for Girls was put before a firing squad with four others, and only three hours later did a German officer, hearing moans, administer a coup de grâce with pistol shots to the head. Likewise, a young Dutchman who had fought with the paratroopers, and whose swaddled forearms had been seared by phosphorus, was forced to his knees and executed; a witness described "the heavily bandaged hands sprawled out in front like two grotesque paddles."

The cease-fire expired and the battle resumed, briefly. The last battalion diehards surrendered at five A.M. Thursday, after holding out for more than three days. Eighty-one paratroopers had been killed, and the rest were prisoners. A final message dispatched over one of those feeble radios was heard only by German eavesdroppers: "Out of ammunition. God save the king."

The Arrow That Flieth by Day

A T 4:30 P.M. on Tuesday, September 19, as the Arnhem bridge predicament turned from dreadful to desperate, young General Gavin stood outside a schoolhouse in Malden, three miles west of Groesbeek. Toeing the curb with his jump boot, he awaited the arrival of half a dozen British and American commanders to plot their next move.

Afternoon shadows stretched through the village and thickening clouds drifted overhead. The fine weather had deteriorated: more than a thousand supply planes had taken off from England during the day, only to encounter fog so thick over the Channel that glider pilots could see barely three feet of tow rope. Although many aircraft turned back, forty-five planes and seventy-three gliders had been lost. Only half of an expected sixty-six artillery tubes and 2,300 reinforcement troops reached Holland. The resupply of ammunition and rations was deemed "negligible."

Of five major objectives assigned the 82nd Airborne in GARDEN, four had been taken, but the fifth—a crossing over the Waal in Nijmegen— remained beyond reach. A single battalion from the 508th Parachute Infantry had tried to take the road bridge on Sunday evening, but rather than follow Gavin's instructions to circle along the river bottoms from the Groesbeek Heights, the regimental commander heeded Dutch assurances that cutting through Nijmegen's serpentine streets would be quicker and surer. At ten P.M., enemy troops had spilled from trucks onto a traffic circle near the southern approach to the bridge, and a muddled firefight in the dark foiled the American gambit. Soon 10th SS Panzer soldiers were entrenched among the stone ruins of the Valkhof, the imperial Carolingian redoubt built by Charlemagne in 768 and where his son, Louis the Pious, once housed his hunting falcons.

Nor had the belated arrival of XXX Corps on Tuesday morning carried through to the Waal. Both the 82nd Airborne and flag-waving Dutchmen had welcomed the Guards Armored Division to the nine-arch bridge at Grave at 8:30 A.M., and the first tanks barreled into Nijmegen's suburbs just past noon. Two-thirds of the golden corridor from Bourg-Léopold to Arnhem now belonged to the Allies. But an attempt to rush the river at Nijmegen failed. Three columns made for the road bridge, the rail bridge, and the post office, which Dutch patriots believed housed the detonators to destroy both spans. Only the last of these forays succeeded, and the post office proved empty but for civilians cowering in the cellar and a few dead Germans behind the stamp counter. Enemy commanders were so confident of holding the bridges that the spans remained standing; Model wanted them intact for a counterattack from Arnhem through Nijmegen. As a barrier around the southern ramps, SS engineers had stacked fuel cans in several hundred houses, then bowled thermite grenades through every third door. Another Dutch city was in flames.

Joining Gavin along the Malden curb were the cigar-chewing Colonel Reuben H. Tucker—a thirty-three-year-old Sicily and Anzio veteran from Connecticut who commanded the 504th Parachute Infantry Regiment— and three mud-spattered British colonels, each wearing corduroy trousers, suede chukka boots, and the regimental badges, respectively, of the Irish, Grenadier, and Scots Guards. In addition, each wore what a witness described as "the most amazing air of nonchalance." A trio of British generals also joined the klatch: Major General Allan H. S. Adair, commander of the Guards Armored Division; the tall, angular Horrocks; and Boy Browning, who had arrived in a nearby cabbage patch with his headquarters staff aboard thirty-six gliders. Twirling his mustache more intently than ever, the MARKET commander had exchanged his attaché case and parade-ground battle dress for an airborne smock, with field glasses looped around his neck. But even Browning's renowned poise showed signs of fraying. Earlier in the day he had received another inane congratulatory message from higher headquarters; this one, from Beetle Smith, pronounced SHAEF "extremely pleased with the show," which was unfolding "exactly" as anticipated. Browning in a burst of pique had heaved an ink jar at the photo of a German general tacked up on a wall.

Gavin quickly described the predicament in Nijmegen. On the south bank of the Waal, enemy troops held a kilometer-wide sector, from the rail bridge in the west to the road bridge in the east. This swatch extended three hundred yards from the river into the burning town. As many as five hundred SS men defended each span, with others burrowed around the Belvedere, a seventeenth-century watchtower. Even the riverfront bandstand was now a strongpoint with firing loopholes. German reinforcements could be seen crossing the bridges on foot and by bicycle. Guns firing from the north bank had clobbered several British tanks, and stymied American paratroopers in the city had been reduced to wrapping themselves in drapes and furniture slipcovers to stay warm at night. In frustration, Gavin had urged six hundred Dutch resistance fighters to snipe at enemy troops around the bridges with weapons scavenged from the dead. At this point little was known about the British plight in Arnhem—Browning's radios were hardly better than General Urquhart's—but contrary to earlier intelligence assessments, Gavin was certain that the enemy was not "a broken German army in full retreat." Captured SS men appeared "tough and confident."

Colonel Tucker, whose helmet brim nearly hid his eyes, occasionally removed his cigar to spit. ("Every time he did," a British colonel later wrote, "a faint look of surprise flicked over the faces of the Guards officers.") Gavin believed the only way to eject the enemy from Nijmegen was to outflank him: he proposed that as British tanks and a paratrooper battalion pressed the attack through the town, Tucker's regiment would cross the Waal downstream of the rail bridge to attack the German rear. Given the urgency in reaching Arnhem, rather than wait for nightfall the attack would be launched as soon as possible on Wednesday. But first they needed boats. None could be found along the river.

Browning and Adair said little. Tucker spat. Horrocks was skeptical; a daylight crossing of the Waal—four hundred yards wide, with a current of eight knots—seemed potentially as suicidal as the American assault across the Rapido in central Italy eight months earlier. More than two thousand GIs had been killed or wounded in that fiasco. But Horrocks agreed there was little choice. The XXX Corps engineering train should have several dozen assault boats amid the jumble of bridging equipment. Horrocks would order them found and hurried up Hell's Highway, even though with tens of thousands of soldiers already jamming that narrow ribbon, traffic was nearly at a standstill. Before the conference adjourned, he offered Gavin some advice: "Jim, never try to fight an entire corps off one road."

Two hours later, as dusk sifted over the battlefield and commanders bustled about preparing for the morrow, 120 low-flying Luftwaffe planes pummeled Eindhoven in the only large, long-range air strike by German bombers during the fall of 1944. Philips workers and their celebrating families had been banging those toy drums and chalking their names on British fenders when Dutch rail workers reported rumors of approaching panzers. The orange bunting and Dutch flags abruptly vanished. "All smiles stopped together," Alan Moorehead reported.

> Mothers with their paper caps awry ran along the street to gather up their children. . . . The tin whistles subsided almost on a note and there was no more dancing. . . . Every one of the fat jolly faces was now full of apprehension.

No enemy tanks appeared, but instead "a clear golden cluster of parachute flares burst into light above the town. . . . The streets were like day again." Moments later the bombs began to tumble, igniting half a dozen ammunition trucks in the Stratumsedijk and setting the factory ablaze. Generals Ridgway and Brereton, making their way together toward Nijmegen to ensure that at least six generals would supervise the five-battalion attack on Wednesday, found themselves in an Eindhoven park "flat on our stomachs for almost an hour," as Brereton informed his diary. Ridgway later wrote, "Great fires were burning everywhere, ammo trucks were exploding, gasoline trucks were on fire, and debris from wrecked houses clogged the streets." Women and children sang hymns in a shelter "full of mad cyclonic gusts of air and light," in Moorehead's description. A bomb struck another packed cellar on Biesterweg, incinerating forty-one people. Water pressure failed across the city, and among nine thousand damaged buildings, over two hundred houses were gutted. The city of light burned and burned.

Dawn revealed the full catastrophe. Of more than 1,000 civilian casualties, 227 were dead. Their bodies would be collected at a school in Thijmstraat and placed in narrow coffins with peaked lids and brass handles for burial in a mass grave. Eindhoven had become an obvious military target once GARDEN convoys arrived, but Moorehead raged anyway. "A blind act of malice on the part of the enemy," he fumed. "A hideous, unforgivable thing."

The boats were late arriving on Wednesday, delaying the river assault in Nijmegen until midafternoon. After yet another postponement and more mumbled excuses about the traffic on Hell's Highway, Gavin wheeled on Horrocks. "For God's sake, try!" he snapped. "It is the least you can do." Twenty minutes before the attack was to begin, three British trucks pulled up behind a riverside power plant a kilometer west of town. Rather than the expected thirty-three boats, there were twenty-six—shellfire had wrecked a fourth truck—and frail vessels they were. Nineteen feet long, with plywood bottoms and green canvas sides pegged to the gunwales, the boats were "of a type more suitable for the quieter rivers of England" than for traversing the true Rhine, as a Guardsman conceded. Some carried only two paddles rather than the required eight. "Flimsy, flat-bottomed little things," Captain Henry B. Keep later wrote his mother, "smaller than Daddy's tin ducking boat."

As a Royal Engineer major gave rudimentary instructions behind a dike—"Head them upriver as much as possible," he advised with a shrug— paratroopers from the 3rd Battalion of the 504th Parachute Infantry wolfed down pork chops ladled from a large pot, or dragged on a last ciga- rette. Typhoons clawed the far shore, followed by a fifteen-minute barrage from a hundred artillery tubes. Two dozen British Sherman tanks lurched into view to pop away, first with high-explosive shells and then with white phosphorus to build a milky smoke screen. At 3:02 P.M., a whistle trilled. Four hundred grunting men hoisted the boats onto their shoulders—each vessel weighed six hundred pounds—and staggered across the dike to the steep, muddy lip of the river Waal.

Instantly German fire from three directions diced the river with steel, "like a school of mackerel on the feed," in one soldier's description. Boats bogged in the river mud or capsized in the shallows as men leaped aboard. Others spun in circles or swept downstream with drowning men clinging to the gunwales. From the rail bridge alone, almost three dozen German machine guns cackled, punctuated by a pair of 20mm guns. Hissing bul- lets skipped like hot stones across the water and through the canvas hulls; troopers plugged the leaking holes with caps, gloves, and handkerchiefs. A direct hit from a mortar round flipped a dozen men into the Waal. An engineer shot through the head tumbled overboard with his feet still wedged beneath a seat so that the torso served as a second rudder, swing- ing the boat round and round until comrades smeared with blood and brains could finally heave his corpse into the river. "The man next to me had the middle part of his head blown away, so that his skull dropped on what was left of his lower face," Chaplain Delbert Kuehl recalled. In the same boat, the battalion commander, Major Julian A. Cook, murmured "Hail, Mary, full of grace" over and over as he paddled. "Thy will be done," the chaplain added.

"It was a horrible, horrible sight," a British tank commander later recalled. "Boats were literally being blown out of the water." The three British generals—Browning, Horrocks, and Adair—watched transfixed through field glasses from the top floor of the power plant. A stiff breeze shredded the smoke screen, giving German gunners on the rail bridge and on the opposite embankment a clear view of their targets. Tracers braided and rebraided. The roar of gunfire and ripping canvas carried on the water, and more men pitched over, to be rolled to the center of the boats where steam rose from their leaking wounds. Paddlers without paddles gouged at the boiling Waal with rifle butts, helmets, and entrenching tools in an ecstasy of flailing. "My God," said Horrocks, "look at 'em."

Half made the far shore, tumbling from the cockleshell flotilla to lie gasping and retching in the muddy lee of the north bank. Thirteen surviving boats started back: ballasted with dead men, riddled with holes, and paddled by exhausted U.S. Army engineers. Eleven boats would survive a second passage; four more crossings then ferried over the balance of the 3rd Battalion, followed by 1st Battalion and Colonel Tucker. German prisoners were impressed as galley slaves to paddle on the final circuits in what became known as the "Waal Regatta."

Those vomiting on their knees along the shore soon rose with murder in their eyes. "God help anyone in front of us," one trooper said. With squad rushes they bounded forward in a spree of what one sergeant called "jack-in-the-box shooting," killing fifty Germans near the river before loping six hundred yards to the dike road to kill more with grenades and bayonets. One company slaughtered the enemy garrison at Hof van Holland, a decrepit old Dutch fort, after swimming the moat and scaling the earthworks or storming over a narrow wooden bridge. Other troopers shook themselves out into a skirmish line and stalked toward the bridge, firing from the hip. Captain Keep described his men as "driven to a fever pitch [and] lifted out of themselves—fanatics rendered crazy by rage and lust for killing. . . . I have never witnessed this human metamorphosis so acutely displayed as on this day. The men were beside themselves."

Sensing that the day had turned and pressed by British tanks bulling north through Nijmegen, SS troops sidled onto the rail bridge, only to be raked with Browning Automatic Rifle fire and two captured German machine guns: Tucker's men had seized the northern ramp, waving yellow recognition flags to ward off British fire across the river. German engineers who had been repairing the bridge superstructure were shot dead in their safety harnesses; for days, they would dangle from high in the girders "like a group of gargoyles," Captain Keep told his mother. Other enemy troops dove into the river, pursued by gunfire, or were killed trying to surrender. "Old German men grab our M1s and beg for mercy," a corporal recalled. "They were shot pointblank." A German lieutenant colonel told his diary, "The Americans behaved as they always do, throwing our wounded from the bridge into the Waal, and shooting the few prisoners." Two hundred and sixty-seven enemy bodies would be counted on just the rail bridge.

Paratroopers darting through river grass along the Waal also reached the northern approach to the road bridge at dusk, just as Grenadier Guards tanks in Nijmegen broke past Charlemagne's Valkhof and onto the span, spitting fire. German 88mm rounds tore the air, "ripping and screaming like great Roman candle balls of light," an American commander reported. Shells gouged two British tanks, but one skidded sideways through an enemy roadblock on the far ramp and blew away a pair of roadside anti-tank guns. Fleeing SS troops hied into the gloaming through gooseberry brakes. British engineers combing the girders for explosives found dynamite and detonators lashed to a catwalk eighty feet above the river.

"The most gallant attack ever carried out during the whole of the last war," as Horrocks would call it, was over. The cost included two hundred paratroopers from Tucker's regiment. Model's order to "blow up the road bridge at Nijmegen" came too late. The 10th SS Panzer radioed the bad news: "They're over the Waal."

Montgomery monitored the battle through liaison officers and radio reports. He had neither visited the battlefield during MARKET GARDEN nor seen his field commanders; he was having his portrait painted, again, and seemed entranced by the experience, boasting that the likeness would "create a tremendous sensation at next year's Academy." Yet at 10:50 P.M. on Wednesday he felt confident enough of the view from Brussels to cable Eisenhower:

> Things are going to work out alright. . . . The British airborne division at Arnhem has been having a bad time but their situation should be eased now that we can advance northwards from Nijmegen to their support. There is a sporting chance that we should capture the bridge at Arnhem.

In a subsequent message to Brooke, he added, "I regard general situation on rivers as now very satisfactory." This assessment was nothing less than hallucinatory. Despite the valor at Nijmegen, any "sporting chance" to take the Arnhem bridge had passed. Things in Holland were not going to work out, even if the high command did not yet know it. As a XXX Corps account later acknowledged, "In front, on the flanks, and in the rear, all was not well."

Gavin knew. Even before his first trooper splashed into the Waal, he had been summoned from the power plant in Nijmegen by a frantic call from his chief of staff near Groesbeek: "General, you'd better get the hell back here or you won't have any division left." Racing to his command post, where he was surprised to find a begrimed Ridgway newly arrived after his Eindhoven ordeal, Gavin learned that German paratroopers had overrun Beek in the north and part of Mook in the south, threatening not only Hell's Highway but that priceless Dutch anomaly, the high ground overlooking Nijmegen. Only darkness, Coldstream tanks, and Gavin's pluck saved the day—in one perilous instance he squirmed on his belly across a macadam road beneath enemy grazing fire. Counterattacks at first light on Thursday retook Beek, secured Mook, and slapped the Germans back to the east.

But troubles in the Anglo-American rear had only begun. A panzer attack at Son on Wednesday would have broken through but for ten pugnacious British tanks. Allied intelligence had presumed the enemy incapable of shifting substantial forces to counter MARKET GARDEN; in the event, another 85,000 Germans flooded the battlefield in barely a week. Two additional British corps assigned to safeguard the Allied flanks—XII in the west and VIII in the east—plodded across boggy heathland, averaging just three miles a day against fitful resistance. As of Friday, September 22, the former had yet to reach Best and the latter was stalled southeast of Eindhoven.

That same morning, Hell's Highway was cut for the first time, despite Dutch warnings of enemies massing both east and west between Veghel and Uden. For more than a day—"the blackest moment of my life," Horrocks confessed—panzers blocked the road, severing the supply lifeline to three Allied divisions now north of the Maas. No sooner had British tanks and U.S. paratroopers reopened the route on Saturday afternoon than the Germans struck again six miles north of Son, in fighting so vicious that American gunners fired over open sights at four hundred yards. This time Hell's Highway would be closed for two days, long enough for the enemy to destroy fifty vehicles and seed the roadway with mines.

The new bridgehead over the Waal failed to uncork the advance to Arnhem, as Montgomery had hoped. After a thirty-five-hour delay at Nijmegen to capture the bridges, the XXX Corps vanguard sat for another eighteen hours. Enemy raids and congestion on Hell's Highway played hob: reinforcements from the British 43rd Division took three days to travel sixty miles in reaching the Irish Guards and the 82nd Airborne. Tommies had been delayed while helping GIs at Mook and in clearing Nijmegen, and some supplies promised by SHAEF failed to appear. Gavin also concluded that after five years of war British veterans were excessively cautious, nurturing what he called "Why die now?" sentiments. He found Colonel Tucker in a farmhouse near the rail bridge seething at the delay. "What in the hell are they doing?" Tucker demanded, gnawing his cigar. "Why in the hell don't they get on to Arnhem?"

At 1:30 P.M. on Thursday, September 21, the Irish Guards at last edged forward on a road elevated six feet above the fens, carrying a captured German map that showed enemy guns tucked behind a tree line at Ressen, three miles north of Nijmegen. The map proved accurate: eleven panzers, two 88mm batteries, two infantry battalions, and various other highwaymen waited in ambush. In a reprise of the advance from Bourg-Léopold, the stately British procession abruptly burst into flames, with three Shermans burning and the trailing column "piled up . . . head to tail in silhouette." Misbehaving radios kept Typhoons from attacking, the jammed traffic on Hell's Highway held the artillery too far south, and a British officer eyeing "these sad flat lands" of dikes, ditches, and fruit trees declared, "We're not going to get a yard up this bloody road."

More than a yard they got, yet not much more. In terrain as hostile to armored spearheads as the Norman bocage, the Guards reached Elst—halfway to Arnhem—in three days. "But farther they could not go," a regimental history lamented. Before the week ended, Guards officers with shotguns were roaming the countryside in search of plover and pheasant, determined to make the most of their misery.

The British survivors at Arnhem were now pinched within a three-mile perimeter in leafy Oosterbeek, just west of town above the water meadows of the Neder Rijn. General Urquhart's command post filled the handsome, big-windowed Hartenstein Hotel, handsome no more. Corpses lay stacked like wood in the garden, and even the hotel radiators had been drained to slake the thirst of the wounded. Slit trenches snaked among the laurels and beneath the beech trees. Captured Germans squatted on tennis courts used as prison cages. "In the evening I would go to my trench and smoke a pipe," a paratrooper later wrote. "I used to watch an apple tree which grew nearby, and had red apples on it, and then I watched the stars come up." Not far from here, the poet Philip Sidney had lain mortally wounded after the battle of Zutphen in September 1586. That gentle Sidney had watched the same stars, the same moon climbing the sky with sad steps, brought some comfort.

Between mortar barrages—called "hate" by the British—German loudspeakers played "In the Mood" or broadcast surrender appeals. Tommies answered with maledictory catcalls and Bren-gun fire; snipers notched their rifle butts for every coal-scuttle helmet knocked awry. Each day the weight of metal grew heavier in what the enemy came to call the *Hexenkessel*, the witches' cauldron. German flamethrower teams and fifteen factory-new King Tiger II tanks joined in brawling "from room to room, from the ground floor up, from garden to garden, and from tree to tree," as an SS captain described it. A Dutch woman observed, "You have no idea how much people scream in such circumstances." XXX Corps artillery near Nijmegen ranged the enemy with admirable accuracy and kept the 9th SS Panzer at bay. That too brought some comfort.

Of nearly 9,000 British soldiers inserted north of the Neder Rijn, about 3,600 could still fight, but they had dwindling means. Of 1,500 tons of supplies dropped since September 18, less than 200 tons had been recovered by Urquhart's men, and 66 transport planes—among 629 sorties flown—had been shot down. The cellars and stout-walled houses in Oosterbeek brimmed with wounded men, sick men, dying men, and men newly dead. A gallant Dutch woman, Kate ter Horst, glided among them to read King David's Ninety-first Psalm by flashlight: "Thou shalt not be afraid for the terror by night; nor for the arrow that flieth by day." Urquhart radioed an appeal to Browning on Thursday evening: "Our casualties heavy. Resources stretched to utmost. Relief within twenty-four hours vital."

Relief came, though far too little and much too late. Reinforcement by General Sosabowski's Polish airborne brigade had twice been postponed by bad weather, and the demise of Frost's battalion prompted a new scheme to have the Poles jump on September 21 near Driel, just across the river from Urquhart's bridgehead, rather than parachuting near the now forsaken bridge. More foul weather over the Continent forced many befuddled pilots to turn back—one lost soul ended up in Ireland—and Sosabowski found himself in Driel with only two-thirds of his command, some one thousand men, and no means of crossing two hundred yards of river; a ferry supposedly waiting for him had been cut loose and then sunk to keep it out of German hands. Enemy soldiers further reinforced the north bank, overrunning a single British platoon on the Westerbouwing heights and narrowing Urquhart's river frontage to seven hundred yards.

A night passed, then another. A few Poles slipped into the British camp by dinghy or raft, but a subsequent attempt to storm across provoked sheets of plunging fire—"hell on the river," Sosabowski called it. A battalion from the Dorsetshire Regiment, vanguard of the 43rd Division, also took a try on the night of September 24, after trucks carrying assault boats—many without paddles, again—were late, got lost, or suffered ambush. An hour into the crossing, unbearable machine-gun fire and grenade volleys ended the foray, with more than three hundred of the four hundred waterborne Dorsets soon dead or captured. "Gallant, but quite useless," one British officer concluded. A Polish correspondent waiting at the Hartenstein that Sunday wrote, "Everything would seem to point to our situation having become tragic."

When the end came, it came quickly. In the gloomy XXX Corps command post at Malden on Monday morning, September 25, Browning and Horrocks agreed to cut their losses and extract the 1st Airborne Division from Arnhem that night, under a plan improbably code-named BERLIN. "Never was darkness more eagerly awaited," a clerk in the Hartenstein cellar scribbled in the division diary. Urquhart had studied the surreptitious British withdrawal from Gallipoli in 1915, and on his orders forward trenches thinned out as men slipped toward the river, boots wrapped in rags, faces blackened with ashes and mud, their path marked by white tape. Orderlies trundled the lightly injured in wheelbarrows and on handcarts; medical truces had already remanded twelve hundred wounded into German hands, and many more would be left behind in the care of chaplains and medical officers.

"The night was made for clandestine exits," Urquhart later remarked. Wind and heavy rain tossed the birches in the bottoms and the chestnuts on the Westerbouwing bluffs. XXX Corps artillery pounded the perimeter to further muffle the sounds of flight. Burning houses glowed red and weird. Holding hands in a queue 150 yards long, the men shuffled through the mud flats in groups of fourteen to match the capacity of thirty-seven storm boats crewed by Canadian and British engineers. A sergeant shared out the Benzedrine, and officers put a match to their last secrets. Gunners tossed their sights and breechblocks into the water. Boat by boat they slipped across the obsidian Neder Rijn in the rain, until the bows bumped against a groyne on the far shore where a voice called from the darkness, "All right. Let's be having you." In a barn south of Driel plates of hot stew were ladled out, along with tumblers of Cointreau and mugs of tea laced with rum. Forty trucks and ambulances shuttled the escapees to Nijmegen.

Dawn caught the division not quite all away. The demented whine of enemy machine guns sounded abruptly from the reeds, and mortar rounds stomped along the river. Some men plunged into the water and flailed for the southern bank, or drowned. A final boat was so overloaded that the coxswain could not pull the outboard starter cord. Passengers paddled with hands and rifle butts, but bullets chewed the vessel to flinders; only four of twenty-five aboard lived to reach the safe shore. Three hundred others gathered on the shoreline were captured, but 2,600 had escaped.

Urquhart was among those who got away. Early Tuesday morning, September 26, he appeared red-eyed and muddy at Boy Browning's large, fine house below Nijmegen. Roused from sleep, Browning took twenty minutes to change from pajamas into an immaculate uniform, his Sam Browne belt gleaming like glass.

"I'm sorry we haven't been able to do what we set out to do," Urquhart said.

Browning waved away the apology. "You did all you could," he said crisply. "Now you had better get some rest."

* * *

In the small hours of Friday, September 29, twelve German commandos in wetsuits slipped into the Waal five miles upstream of Nijmegen. Trained in Venice for aquatic skullduggery, all were strong swimmers— one had competed in the Olympics—and together they guided half a dozen tubes, each sixteen feet long, stuffed with nearly a ton of hexanite explosive, and suspended between a pair of air cylinders for buoyancy. Down the dark river they swam, snipping a hole in the new concertina boom before lashing their charges to the bridge piers and setting the detonator timers for a sixty-minute delay. Exhausted and numb with cold, the men staggered from the water a mile downstream, close to where Tucker's regiment had crossed the previous week. Sentries immediately captured ten of the twelve, but at 6:30 A.M. a volcanic sequence of blasts ruptured the Dutch dawn, blowing an eighty-foot gap in the deck of the road bridge and dropping the long central span of the rail bridge into the river. The last casualties of MARKET GARDEN lay on the muddy bed of the Waal.

This rude gesture hardly dampened the Allied high command's insistence that the bold airborne lunge across Holland had been "a decided victory," in Churchill's phrase. Brereton declared the operation a "brilliant success," while Montgomery passed word to the king that he was "well pleased with the gross result of his airborne adventure," which he deemed "90 percent successful" because the ground force had covered nine-tenths of its intended distance. (Air Marshal Tedder tartly observed that "one jumps off a cliff with an even higher success rate, until the last few inches.") Browning claimed that given the chance he would not alter his plan a whit. "Who was to tell at that time," he later said, "that the German Army was going to recover as a fighting force?" Even Urquhart asserted, "We have no regrets."

Brave words from a division commander without a division: two-thirds of those fighting for the 1st Airborne had been killed or captured, and the casualties included eight of nine battalion commanders and twenty-six of thirty rifle company commanders. Allied airborne losses in MARKET approached 12,000, more than half of them British; moreover, in 17,000 air sorties, 261 planes and 658 crewmen were lost. Casualties in Horrocks's XXX Corps totaled 1,500, plus 70 tanks. Cornelius Ryan, whose *A Bridge Too Far* remains the classic narrative of the battle, put total Allied losses at 17,000 in nine days. The II Panzer Corps listed 3,300 killed, wounded, and missing, but other tallies suggested that total German losses were at least double that figure. Dutch road builders and construction crews went on finding skeletons for decades.

Even decided victories and brilliant successes sometimes required scapegoats. Montgomery blamed the weather for his unfulfilled 10 percent. Brereton blamed XXX Corps. Browning blamed Sosabowski; accused of incompetence and insubordination—he was, to be sure, given to prickly impertinence—the Pole was stripped of his command at British insistence, and not for more than sixty years did the Dutch recognize his valor with a posthumous award. Paratroopers quipped that Montgomery was "too busy fighting Eisenhower to fight the Germans," and a Royal Signal Corps private suggested that "a bit more constructive criticism of the plan and less of the 'Ready! Ay, ready!' attitude on the part of the senior commanders wouldn't have been amiss." The operation in fact had lacked what one British general called "a single controlling mind": in that regard it reflected the larger Allied campaign in western Europe. Horrocks at least had the grace to blame himself for various shortcomings, including not dispatching the 43rd Division on a different axis than Hell's Highway and failure to keep a senior Dutch officer at his elbow.

Several hundred fugitive Allied troops eventually slipped back across the lines, often with help from courageous Dutch civilians. But more than six thousand others marched off to captivity for the duration, many singing "Green grow the rushes, O." On a square in downtown Arnhem, a captured British officer put his men through a smart parade drill to "show these bastards what real soldiers look like" before the long column tramped eastward in the custody of what one grizzled sergeant major insisted on calling "the detaining power."

The Dutch too would tramp away. German orders in late September required 95,000 civilians to evacuate Arnhem for northern Holland, and another 50,000 were forced from homes along the Neder Rijn. Soldiers then systematically plundered the city, with one truck collecting sewing machines, another tools, still another household linens, all for distribution in the bombed cities of the Ruhr. Other reprisals included the execution of fifty resistance members accused of helping the British, and jail for others involved in a rail strike that had been called when the first Allied parachutists drifted to earth on that glorious Sunday afternoon so long ago. At a price of five thousand buildings destroyed or damaged in Nijmegen alone, one-fifth of the Netherlands had been liberated. But the rest would endure another nine months of occupation: Allied soldiers did not reenter Arnhem until mid-April 1945. Before then, the "Hunger Winter" reduced the Dutch to eating dogs and tulip bulbs, and sixteen thousand died of starvation anyway. "My country," Prince Bernhard observed, "can never again afford the luxury of another Montgomery success."

Nor could the Allies. MARKET GARDEN had won a sixty-five-mile salient that crossed five major water barriers but led nowhere. Without turning the German flank or gaining a bridgehead over the Neder Rijn, 21st Army Group had nearly doubled the perimeter to be outposted, from

150 to 280 miles. That task would entangle most of Second Army, as well as the two committed U.S. airborne divisions, which, with Eisenhower's tacit approval, would be stuck helping the British hold this soggy landscape until mid-November, eating British oxtail soup and heavy puddings, drinking British rum, and smoking British cigarettes considered so foul that some GIs preferred to inhale torn strips of *Stars and Stripes*. Soldiers stood in empty oil drums to keep their feet dry; when the British sent Gavin a personal caravan with a bed and running water, he hid the thing unused, confessing, "I'd be mortified if my boys knew that I had one." The 82nd and 101st suffered another 3,600 casualties during the restive Dutch autumn, more than the divisions sustained during MARKET. "The fighting has been much more vicious and intense than in Normandy," Gavin wrote. The British remained in the salient so long that those plover-hunting officers eventually turned their shotguns on overwintering ducks, which they stalked on ice skates.

MARKET GARDEN proved "an epic cock-up," as a British major averred, a poor plan with deficient intelligence, haphazard execution, and indifferent generalship. The occasion did inspire heroics and displays of combat leadership as stirring as any in modern warfare; Eisenhower offered Montgomery a fistful of American valor decorations to be awarded in the 1st Airborne Division as the field marshal saw fit: ten Distinguished Service Crosses, ten Silver Stars, ten Bronze Stars. Montgomery shifted his command post to Eindhoven, along with his menagerie of rabbits, canaries, and squirrels, and he sent an aide to Britain to fetch his winter kit, including a heavy dressing gown, thick vests, and wool underwear.

The failure at Arnhem, Montgomery cabled Brooke, "will not affect operations eastward against [the] Ruhr." In this he was mistaken. The battle would be, as the historian Max Hastings wrote, "the last occasion of the war when Eisenhower unequivocally accepted a strategic proposal by Montgomery," and the field marshal's advocacy of a single exploitative thrust into Germany under his command seemed ever less credible. Even Montgomery now acknowledged the primacy of Antwerp. "The opening of the port," he wrote in late September, "is absolutely essential before we can advance deep into Germany." Whether that amounted to more than lip service remained to be seen.

Beyond battlefield consequences, MARKET GARDEN preyed on the mind of every man scarred by this primordial struggle. "There was a change of mood after Arnhem," a British captain wrote. "One just didn't feel the same. We were getting rather tired." Bradley's logistics chief told his diary, "The picture is not very good and it looks like we will have a real struggle from now on." Few could doubt Alan Moorehead's conclusion that "there was only one way—the hard way. All hope of a quick end of the war in 1944 had gone."

Teeming autumn rain fell often, with implications for campaigning on the Continent as portentous as Montgomery's request for woolen drawers. "I am not looking forward to the winter war we have ahead of us," Gavin wrote his daughter. "I wear everything that I can get on, but I feel as though I will never be warm again." In their very bones, they now knew that there was indeed but one way ahead: the hard way.

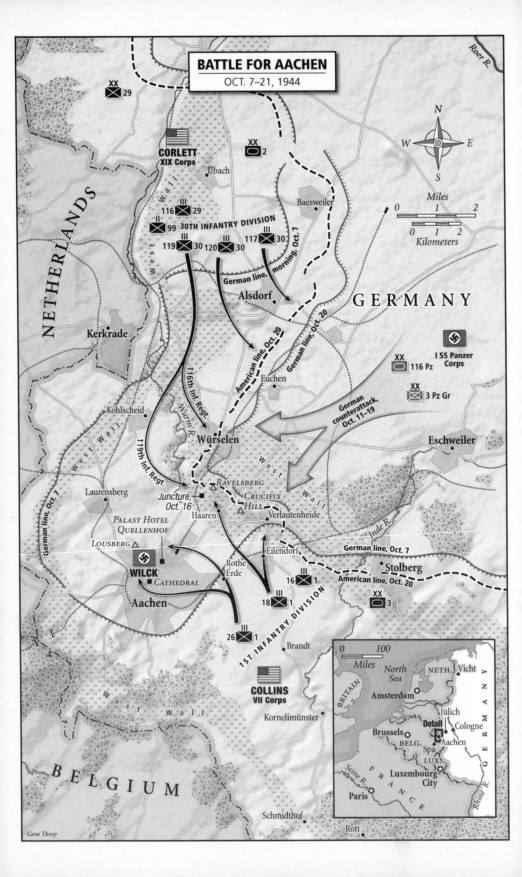

BATTLE FOR AACHEN
OCT. 7–21, 1944

XX 29

CORLETT
XIX Corps

Übach

XX 2

116 III 29

99 II 30TH INFANTRY DIVISION

119 III 30 120 III 30 117 III 30

Baesweiler

German line, morning, Oct. 7

Alsdorf

GERMANY

I SS Panzer Corps

XX 116 Pz

XX 3 Pz Gr

Kerkrade

NETHERLANDS

West Wall

Wall

Köhlscheid

American line Oct. 20

116th Inf. Regt.

German line, Oct. 20

Euchen

Wurm R.

Würselen

West Wall

German counterattack, Oct. 11–19

Eschweiler

119th Inf. Regt.

Laurensberg

Ravelsberg

Juncture, Oct. 16   CRUCIFIX HILL

Haaren

Verlautenheide

Inde R.

PALAST HOTEL
QUELLENHOF

LOUSBERG

German line, Oct. 7

Eilendorf

German line, Oct. 7

WILCK

Rothe Erde

CATHEDRAL

Aachen

18 III 1

16 III 1

American line, Oct. 20

Stolberg

XX 3

1ST INFANTRY DIVISION

26 III 1

Brandt

COLLINS
VII Corps

Kornelimünster

West Wall

BELGIUM

Schmidthof

Rott

Gene Thorp

Roer R.

N
W   E
S

Miles
0   1   2

Kilometers
0   1   2

Inset map:

Miles
0   100

North Sea

BRITAIN

NETH. Vlcht

Amsterdam

Jülich

Detail Cologne

Brussels

BELG. Aachen

GERMANY

Spa

LUX.

Seine R.

FRANCE

Luxembourg City

Paris

Rhine R.

6. THE IMPLICATED WOODS

Charlemagne's Tomb

FOR the most loyal Germans, Aachen had always seemed a city worth dying for. Thermal springs believed to have healing powers had lured first the Romans and then the Carolingians. Here Charlemagne may have been born and here certainly he died, in 814, after creating the First Reich. His holy bones slept in a gold casket in the choir apse of Aachen's great cathedral. From Otto I in the tenth century to Ferdinand I in the sixteenth, thirty kings and twelve queens had been anointed, crowned, and enthroned on the homely marble seat that once held Charlemagne's royal posterior. The cathedral also housed four relics that for the past half millennium had been removed from storage every seven years for veneration by pilgrims: the apparel of the Virgin, the swaddling clothes and loincloth of Christ, and the garment John the Baptist wore at his decapitation.

It was said that the fearless burghers of Aachen had danced rapturously in the streets during the plague of 1374. That native pluck had been put to the test repeatedly during recent bombing attacks. An Allied raid in July 1943 demolished three thousand buildings, and additional strikes in the spring of 1944—with bombs fuzed to explode only after penetrating into the cellars of five-story stone structures—scarred every one of the city's sixty-six churches, including the cathedral. The raids also battered the town hall, originally built on the ruins of Charlemagne's palace and later renovated in the Baroque style to display statues of fifty German rulers along the north façade.

Now smoke rose from Aachen again. General Collins's VII Corps had bored through both bands of the Siegfried Line in mid-September without capturing the city or making further headway toward the Rhine, and he intended to rectify those omissions. By early October, the U.S. First Army had narrowed its front from one hundred miles to sixty, giving Collins greater combat heft; the new Ninth Army had also pushed forward and would soon assume command of the left wing of the American line, abutting the British. Seventy-four American gun batteries began pounding Fortress Aachen, where eighteen thousand German troops had been committed to defend the cradle of Teutonic nationalism unto the last bullet, as Hitler required. Drew Middleton of *The New York Times*, studying the smoke-draped city through field glasses, saw "a gray and brown mass marked here and there by licking tongues of flame and pierced by the steeples of churches and factory chimneys."

To help VII Corps complete Aachen's encirclement before pushing eastward, XIX Corps dispatched the 30th Division—the stalwarts of Mortain—along with a regiment from the 29th Division to punch a hole through the West Wall northwest of the city beginning on October 2. Troops were issued extra rations of chocolate and cigarettes, as well as duckboards to lay across the boggy beet and turnip fields. Napalm fizzled in the wet woodlands, but massed mortar fire chewed through enemy barbed wire, and almost twenty thousand artillery rounds in half a day gutted the German defenses. By October 7, 30th Division troops had surged five miles beyond the West Wall on a six-mile front, bolstered by tanks of the 2nd Armored Division. "We have a hole in this thing big enough to drive two divisions through," reported Major General Leland S. Hobbs, the 30th Division commander. "This line is cracked wide open." A day later, as his men swung south to outflank Aachen, he added, "The job is finished as far as this division is concerned."

Hobbs was dead wrong. Piecemeal enemy counterattacks with reserves pulled from Arnhem in the north and Alsace in the south stalled the division three miles short of Aachen in a dreary slag-and-shaft scape of collieries and mining villages. The job of cinching the noose would require help from the 1st Division, which already held a semicircular twelve-mile front, west, south, and east of the city. At four A.M. on Sunday, October 8, the 18th Infantry attacked northeast of Aachen, bounding from pillbox to pillbox, scorching the firing ports with bazookas, bangalore torpedoes, flamethrowers, and satchel charges. A German redoubt on Crucifix Hill fell by midafternoon, as did the huge white cross on the crest, toppled either by shellfire or vengeful GIs. A day later two companies slipped past enemy pickets without firing a shot and climbed the Ravelsberg, another highground stronghold. Eight more pillboxes surrendered at dawn on Tuesday, October 10, and GIs gobbled down the breakfast lugged uphill that morning by an unwitting German kitchen detail.

Field Marshal Rundstedt warned Berlin that no greater danger now faced the Fatherland in the west than the peril before Aachen. The main German supply route into the city had been crimped, and hardly a mile separated the 1st and 30th Divisions. So confident were the Americans that Major General Clarence R. Huebner, commander of the 1st Division, on Tuesday gave the Aachen garrison twenty-four hours to surrender or face extermination. "There is no middle course," warned the ultimatum, which was delivered by two hundred artillery rounds packed with surrender leaflets, as well as in broadcasts by Radio Luxembourg and booming public-address speakers.

Lest the Germans miss the message, at 10:10 A.M. two lieutenants and a private first class walked up Triererstrasse with a white flag and a copy of Huebner's demand. At a rail underpass in eastern Aachen, a voice called *"Komm!"* Blindfolded and led to a cellar, the envoys upon being unmasked handed the ultimatum to a German officer wearing an Iron Cross and a Russia campaign ribbon; in return they received a signed, stamped receipt. After an exchange of cigarettes and salutes, the trio was guided back to the underpass by sentries nipping from a liquor bottle. Colonel Gerhard Wilck, who in September had replaced the discredited General von Schwerin as Aachen's garrison commander, was not the surrendering sort. The answer was *"Nein."*

Aachen's dismemberment began in earnest on Wednesday morning, when three hundred Allied planes dropped sixty-two tons of bombs on targets stained with red artillery smoke. Five thousand artillery rounds followed over the next two days, then another hundred tons of bombs and five thousand more shells. At precisely 9:30 A.M. on Friday, October 13, troops from the 2nd Battalion of the 26th Infantry simultaneously tossed one thousand grenades over the railroad embankment near Triererstrasse, then scrambled across the tracks and into the inner sanctum of Charlemagne's capital.

They found "a sterile sea of rubble," in one GI's phrase, a ghost town with 20,000 civilians of Aachen's original 165,000 living in dank holes. A garrison of 5,000 troops and policemen defended the inner city, reinforced by constabulary volunteers from Cologne and I SS Panzer Corps grenadiers who had hurried in on Rundstedt's orders. Huebner could muster only two battalions from the 26th Infantry for his assault force, but much had been learned in Italy about urban combat. Aachen would now serve as a test bed for new destructive techniques developed by troops whose battle cry became, "Knock 'em all down!"

Street by street, building by building, room by room, assault squads methodically clawed across the city from east to west, darting between doorways and down alleys smoked with white phosphorus. With Peliserk-erstrasse as a boundary line between the battalions, the 3rd pushed through the foundries and rolling mills on Aachen's northern edge, while the 2nd bulled into the town center at a pace of four hundred yards a day. A tank or tank destroyer perforated each building with crashing fire, floor by floor from street to attic, forcing defenders to the cellars, where grenades finished them off. Bazooka teams knocked down doors, and engineers blew holes in ceilings or walls with beehive charges—"mouseholing" skills learned in Cassino and Ortona—to let riflemen move up, down, and laterally without using defended stairwells. Every closet, every coal bin, every sewer main was searched, and bulldozers piled rubble atop each manhole cover. To further discourage German infiltration, select rooms in cleared houses were booby-trapped, often with a No. 2 green bean can filled with nails, three pounds of dynamite, a No. 8 blasting cap, and a tripwire trigger.

Three captured German streetcars were each packed with a thousand pounds of captured enemy munitions and a delay fuze, then rolled downhill through no-man's-land; the thunderous explosions did little damage but elicited appreciative cheers from the American line. Flamethrowers proved persuasive, even though stone burned poorly: a three-second spurt of fire followed by an ultimatum on Saturday—"Surrender or get fried"— cleared a fetid three-story air raid shelter of more than seventy-five soldiers and a thousand civilians with hands raised. For recalcitrants in bunkers, 1st Division engineers found that mattresses wedged into firing ports amplified the explosive pressures inside so that even small charges would fracture the concrete. An order went out to collect mattresses from every occupied German village.

Another lethal legacy from the Italian campaign was the M-12, an ungainly 155mm gun mounted on a tank chassis that was capable of keeping pace with armored spearheads during the gallop across France. On a single day in Aachen, M-12s fired sixty-four rounds almost point-blank to demolish nine buildings, including a movie theater occupied by a company of enemy riflemen, every one of whom was killed or wounded. As 2nd Battalion edged closer to the rubble that once was the town hall, with its proud façade of German rulers, an M-12 clanked onto Wilhelmstrasse; there a tank destroyer fired sixteen rounds to bore a hole through a house wall. The 155mm gun then used the firing loophole to throw seven rounds down Hindenburgstrasse into the State Theater, five blocks away. German troops in the stronghold pelted west toward the cathedral.

Across the city the Americans crept at a steady, sanguinary fifty feet an hour, shooting, dynamiting, grenading. National Socialist slogans on a broken wall reminded the faithful, *auf Deutsch,* "For this we thank our Führer," and, "You are nothing, the state is all." GIs chalked their own scatological exegesis. Drew Middleton described a soldier firing into the street from a back bedroom, where eiderdown quilts in red silk covered the beds. "The sons of bitching bastards," the GI muttered as he emptied his rifle. "The fucking, fucking bastards."

Knock 'em all down.

* * *

As the house-to-house ruination proceeded, the imminent merger of the 1st and 30th Divisions outside Aachen had hit a snag. Savage German artillery ripped up the ridgelines, searched the dells, and scorched suburban streets—enemy observers could see the Americans plainly—forcing GIs to shelter in captured pillboxes from daybreak until dusk. Not even a radio antenna could protrude without being snipped off by whizzing shell fragments. The 30th Division had suffered two thousand casualties since beginning its assault, and the 1st had lost another eight hundred. Lieutenant General Hodges, the First Army commander, grew impatient and then choleric, proposing to sack Hobbs, the commander of the 30th Division. "He hasn't moved an inch in four days," Hodges complained. "We have to close that gap."

Hodges also castigated the XIX Corps commander, Major General Charles H. Corlett, for shooting two thousand rounds of reserve artillery ammunition. Raised on a ranch in southern Colorado and known as "Cowboy Pete," Corlett had commanded assaults in both the Aleutians and the South Pacific; at Aachen he had already thrown in his last reserves, converted engineers to trigger-pullers, and contemplated shoving cooks and clerks into the line. When Hodges kept pressing the point—"When are you going to close the gap?" he demanded—Corlett jumped into his jeep and drove to First Army headquarters. Unable to find the army commander, he instead roared at the staff, "If you don't think we are fighting, I will take you down and show you."

Worse was yet to come, and much of it would fall on the 1st Division's 16th Infantry. "Every hour seems interminable," Captain Joe Dawson, commander of G Company, had written his family in Waco earlier that week. "Long, long ago I entered this land of horror." In fact just over four months had passed since Dawson landed at Omaha Beach to fight across Easy Red and up the Colleville bluffs; for that passage, he received the Distinguished Service Cross. Since then he had shed twenty-five pounds as well as any illusions he still harbored after the campaigns in North Africa, Sicily, and Normandy. "For over two years," he had recently written his sister, "I've calloused my emotions with countless experiences that will never be recalled to memory if I can find power to erase them forever."

Son of a Baptist preacher and just thirty-one, he looked older. "His face is bony," wrote W. C. Heinz, a reporter for the New York *Sun* who was with Dawson at Aachen, "and he has large ears and very brown eyes." Three miles northeast of Aachen cathedral, G and I Companies occupied a ridge eight hundred feet high and four hundred yards long, with clear vistas not only of the city but also of adjacent Belgium and Holland. Maps and magazines lay scattered on a table in Dawson's pillbox command post, along with a candle, a kerosene lamp, two field phones in leather cases, and a small radio that could pick up Bruno and the Swinging Tigers on Radio Berlin. Soldiers in G Company debated with theological intensity whether the malodorous German corpses along the line deterred enemy frontal attacks. One GI advised, "Just move the ones that are within ten feet."

The past week had brought "periods of quiet and periods of great noise," Heinz wrote; but with five hundred shells hitting the ridge each day—one every three minutes—tranquil moments had grown rare. Great noise returned before dawn on Sunday, October 15, when 3rd Panzer Grenadier Division troops filtered onto the ridge from the east with orders to break the siege of Aachen. "We could hear them singing rousing marching songs as they came through the woods," a sergeant later recalled. Mortars and six artillery battalions blunted the initial assault, but at dawn a dozen panzers stood in a meadow below the pillboxes. By ten A.M. several Tigers had churned uphill through a railroad cut, raking the Americans with main-gun and machine-gun fire. GIs unable to even peer from their foxholes defecated in empty ration cans and flung their scat at the enemy. "G and I Companies are being overrun with tanks and infantry," the regimental log recorded at 12:44 P.M., then added fourteen minutes later, "Situation critical . . . Situation very critical." Dawson called artillery onto his own command post, every concussive thud "like a body being thrown against the door." P-47 fighters roared in at twenty-five feet just before two P.M., guns winking along their wings, and the gray tide ebbed, leaving more dead to stink up the slope. Bing Crosby and Judy Garland sang from the little radio.

At nine P.M. the attackers again advanced, under hissing chandelier flares that stretched the panzer shadows into long, lupine shapes. Two tanks closed to within ten yards of G Company's line before massed artillery again bounced them back. Fires burned in the trees and among the diced bodies. "Much moaning and groaning out in the wooded area," an Army account noted. More German assaults followed, with bayonets fixed. When an officer warned General Huebner of mounting casualties, the division commander drew on his pipe and replied, "If higher authority decides that this is the place and time that the 1st Division is going to cease to exist, I guess this is where we cease to exist."

As the enemy attacks grew feebler, two dozen men from G Company counterattacked with grenades, tommy guns, and their own fixed bayonets, slaughtering all enemies lurking along the line. More than two hundred German corpses were counted across a quarter-mile slope, but it was the sight of a dead GI that made Dawson buckle for a moment. "He doesn't know why, and I don't know why, and you don't know why," the captain told Heinz. "You want to know what I think? I think it stinks." Dawson put his head in his hands and sobbed.

Then the silver voice of Lily Pons, the coloratura soprano, came from the radio. Dawson abruptly straightened. "Shut up. I want to hear this," he said. "It's the 'Bell Song' from *Lakmé.*"

"Puccini," said a lieutenant in the command post.

"No, not Puccini," Dawson said. "Not Puccini, but I can't remember the name of the guy."

At 4:15 P.M. on Monday, October 16, 30th Division scouts edged from the southwest corner of Würselen to meet comrades from the 18th Infantry scrabbling down from the Ravelsberg. Aachen's fate was sealed, though German efforts to crack the encirclement would persist for several days. By one count, the enemy had lost sixty-three of ninety panzers thrown into the battle.

No, not Puccini. Lakmé, an opera in three acts set in British India, was by Léo Delibes.

The tally for G Company totaled forty-eight men, one-third of the unit. Joe Dawson had more memories to erase. Gesturing outside his pillbox to the scorched ridge that would subsequently bear his name in Army nomenclature, Dawson told Heinz, "We died right here." To his family he wrote, "My nerves are somewhat shattered."

In keeping with the Führer's wishes, Aachen's death throes were painful and protracted. From his headquarters a couple miles northeast of the cathedral in the five-story Palast Hotel Quellenhof, once the kaiser's country home, the dutiful Colonel Wilck proclaimed, "We shall fight to the last man, the last shell, the last bullet." The hotel billiard room, beauty parlor, and children's dining room all became strongpoints, and Wilck's men hauled a disassembled 20mm gun to the second floor, piece by piece, then rebuilt it to cover approaches through Farwick Park. Into the park on Wednesday, October 18, swept the 26th Infantry's 3rd Battalion, commanded by Lieutenant Colonel John T. Corley, the Brooklyn-born son of Irish immigrants, whose combat decorations over the war's course would include two Distinguished Service Crosses and eight Silver Stars.

At seven A.M., as mortars pummeled the German line south of the tennis courts, an M-12 rumbled down Roland Street, flanked by tanks and tank destroyers spitting fire into the smart houses fronting the boulevard. Thirty rounds of 155mm fire soon made a shambles of the Palast and the nearby Kurhaus spa; a U.S. platoon rushed across the half-moon driveway into the hotel lobby, killing two dozen defenders in a brisk exchange of grenades that shredded the hunting-scene oils in the reading room. Wilck had retreated hastily to a stout bunker at the north end of Lousbergstrasse, where he held out for three more days, assuring Berlin by radio that "the defenders of Aachen will prepare for their last battle" even as they donated ten thousand marks to charity in a gesture of solidarity with the German *Volk*. "We shall fight on," he vowed.

The colonel instead had packed his bags. On Saturday morning, overzealous GIs shot two German emissaries who emerged from the bunker carrying a white flag. Two more figures soon crept out—nervous American prisoners this time—to inform Corley of Wilck's capitulation. At noon he emerged, a slender man with a pointed chin and hair swept back from his widow's peak, with four hundred bitter-enders behind him. "They marched smartly in column," wrote Don Whitehead, "all well-groomed, with shining black boots." After signing a formal surrender, Wilck told Corley, "Everything belongs to the Americans that was German." Permitted to bid a brief farewell to his men, the colonel scrambled onto a jeep hood. "I am speaking to you at a painful moment," he said. "The American commander has told me that I cannot give you the *Sieg Heil* or *Heil Hitler*. But we can still do it in our hearts." As Wilck climbed down for removal to the cages, he added, "I don't believe in miracles any longer."

Nearly twelve thousand Germans had been captured by the 30th and 1st Divisions, with many hundreds killed. American casualties approached six thousand, among them hundreds treated for combat exhaustion. Joe Dawson, wholly spent, was evacuated to the United States later in the month. "These bitter tragic months of terrible war leave one morally as well as physically exhausted," he wrote his family. Also sent home was General Corlett, the XIX Corps commander, whom Hodges removed ostensibly on grounds of failing health. Corlett, who called his relief "just plain heartbreak," told his staff as he departed, "Anyone who sasses the army commander and disobeys an order ought to be relieved. . . . This is the price one must pay." He was replaced by the capable Major General Raymond S. McLain, who had commanded the 45th Division artillery in Sicily and Italy before taking over the 90th Division in Normandy. A former Oklahoma National Guard soldier with a sixth-grade education, McLain was the only Guardsman to command an Army corps during the war, as well as the only officer without at least a modicum of higher education.

No one would take the waters in Aachen for quite some time. Visitors piled up metaphors to convey the desolation. The city was "as dead as a Roman ruin," an intelligence officer declared, "but unlike a ruin it has none of the grace of gradual decay." The reporter Iris Carpenter wrote that Aachen was "as dead as yesterday." By one calculation, 83 percent of Aachen's houses had been destroyed or damaged. Most streets were impassable except on foot. A horse carcass sprawled in the Palast porte-cochère, and medics laid German dead from the hotel and spa on the beaten grass in Farwick Park. An old woman flagged down passing GIs and asked, "Can you tell me, please, when they will take the dead from my house?" A soldier shook his head and said in a Texas drawl, "These ruins. These people."

A plump, sooty man wandering the streets proved to be the bishop of Aachen. An inspection of his cathedral found the graveyard uprooted and the stained glass shattered. But an Allied bomb that pierced the apse had failed to detonate, and six pious boys had formed a fire brigade to extinguish flames on the roof. Charlemagne's bones lay unmolested though hardly undisturbed. GIs erected a large sign bearing a paraphrase from Hitler, and the English translation: *"Gebt mir fünf Jahre und ihr werdet Deutschland nicht wiedererkennen."* Give me five years and you will not recognize Germany again.

"We can force the Boche to their knees if we go about it the right way," Collins wrote. But what was the right way? Just as Aachen had offered a proving ground for modes of destruction, now this first German city to be captured would serve as a laboratory for military occupation policies. A curfew was imposed from nine P.M. to six A.M., no one could travel more than six kilometers from home without permission, and gatherings of more than five people were prohibited, except for worship services—a fine irony given the battered condition of the churches. The use of cameras, binoculars, and carrier pigeons was banned. Lists of known pigeoneers in western Germany were compiled—it was said that Heinrich Himmler himself, the Reichsführer-SS, was a pigeon fancier—and "clipping details" visited local lofts to snip the birds' flight feathers, leaving them earthbound until their next molt. As an added precaution, a "falconry unit" in England stood ready to deploy to the Continent if enemy agents showed signs of clandestine avian communication.

"We come as conquerors, but not as oppressors," Eisenhower had declared in late September. Even before the broken glass was swept from the cathedral nave, however, complications arose that would perplex the conquerors to the end of the war and beyond. The Combined Chiefs, for example, decreed that "it is not intended to import food supplies into Germany," yet that would consign millions to starvation. The chiefs also ordered the exclusion from office of "active Nazis" and "ardent Nazi sympathizers," but to identify such scoundrels proved difficult, and to run Germany without them sometimes impossible. During the first occupation months, more than fifty key city employees in Aachen were party members, including the only man still alive who understood the region's electrical grid.

An Army study also concluded that two blunders made during the assault had had unintended psychological consequences: an ultimatum had been issued to the commander of a besieged city without affording him an "honorable" way to capitulate, thus prolonging his resistance; and that ultimatum had been made public without recognizing the mortal threat of Nazi reprisals against the families of surrendering soldiers. Indeed, it was in an effort to forestall such retribution that Colonel Wilck had insisted that his capitulation document include a clause attesting to the exhaustion of German food and ammunition stocks.

Still, Aachen was theirs, the "first German city to be taken by an invading army in over a hundred years," Drew Middleton noted. Yet no soldier picking a path through the drifted rubble needed to be told that a hundred more German cities remained untaken—and a thousand towns, and ten thousand villages, each potentially as dead as yesterday.

"Do Not Let Us Pretend We Are All Right"

T HE autumnal struggles at Arnhem and Aachen leached any undue optimism from the Allied high command, except among those too far from the battlefield to know better. The Charlie-Charlies in October ordered SHAEF to immediately establish direct links with Moscow "in anticipation of [the] approach of Allied and Russian forces within the very near future," even though those forces remained more than five hundred miles apart. George Marshall arrived in France for a visit and proclaimed, "We have them licked. All they have is a thin shell and when we break that, they are finished." Beguiled by dubious intelligence to the effect that organized German resistance was unlikely to last beyond December 1, the Army chief subsequently advocated a full-bore offensive to win the war in Europe by year's end. Marshall proposed "playing everything for a conclusion," even as he began earmarking divisions to fight in the Pacific.

Eisenhower took pains to dampen such expectations. "We have facing us now one of our most difficult periods of the entire European war," he warned Marshall in early October. "Deteriorating weather is going to place an increased strain on morale." To his mother in Kansas, he wrote: "Most people that write to me these days want to know when the war in Europe is going to be over. . . . I wish I knew. It is a long, hard, dreary piece of work."

Eisenhower now commanded fifty-eight divisions, including those in southern France, yet a month after crossing the German frontier no Allied soldier stood deeper than twelve miles into Germany. Enemy casualties were accruing at four thousand a day, but Allied losses since June 6 equaled a third of a million. Logistics were "in a bad state," the supreme commander told Marshall, "reminiscent of the early days in Tunisia." Half a dozen U.S. divisions remained in the rear because of insufficient means to support them on the battlefront; moreover, SHAEF logisticians calculated that even if the American armies reached the Rhine near the Ruhr, no more than twenty divisions could be sustained in combat.

To further explain his plight, Eisenhower and his logisticians composed a long essay for the Pentagon on combat realities in Europe. Uniforms wore out "at a rate almost incomprehensible to civilians," twice as fast as U.S. clothing manufacturers could make them. Overcoats, shoes, mess kits, and blankets were also consumed at double the War Department's estimates. Food demands through the winter—even if the war ended, soldiers still had to eat—would require the shipment of 3.5 billion pounds from the United States, equivalent to 340 loaded Liberty ships. "Beef requirements for European theater will call for the slaughtering of . . . approximately 4,000 [cattle] every day," Eisenhower wrote. "Dehydrated egg requirements amount to the equivalent of $2\frac{1}{2}$ billion fresh eggs, or a daily requirement of $6\frac{1}{2}$ million." Tent canvas was short by 100 million square feet. Just the demand for paper was staggering: the U.S. Army since the liberation of Paris had been forced to print ten million maps on the flip side of captured German maps. (Many depicted southern England, having been produced for Operation SEA LION, the aborted 1940 invasion of Britain; sheafs of these had been found in an abandoned enemy depot in Liège.)

The most desperate need was for ammunition, which was expended at a rate exceeding two tons every minute of every hour of every day, despite incessant rationing in the second half of 1944. By late September, fewer than four rounds per day were available for the largest guns, such as the 8-inch howitzer. By early October, ammunition shortfalls were "truly critical" across the front, with many Third Army tubes down to a single shell per day—Patton wanted sixty—and 12th Army Group reported that supplies of artillery ammunition had "reached a state of almost complete collapse." A "silence policy" in V Corps required guns to stand unused for more than a week.

The shortfall partly reflected an inability of U.S. plants to meet demand: a 155mm shell required forty separate manufacturing procedures. The more common 105mm howitzer ammunition was produced and shipped under twelve hundred different lot numbers, each with minor variations in propellant that affected accuracy. (First Army was to spend 25,000 man-hours in the early fall sorting jumbled ammunition to avoid catastrophic short barrages.) Shortages kept American armies largely on the defensive in October—attacking required more firepower than sitting—and Eisenhower blamed a dearth of heavy ammunition for delays in capturing

Aachen. He broadcast an appeal to the home front for greater production, and the War Department dispatched veteran gunners to key plants for pep rallies under a program called "Firepower for Eisenhower."

One senior American general believed that a one-third increase in artillery ammunition "would have saved many lives and shortened the war." Yet General Lee's COMZ insisted there was no shortage on the Continent, and indeed thousands of tons were stacked in Normandy depots and aboard several dozen ammunition ships, most of them waiting to unload. Lee had predicted that 150 ships would be discharged in October, but the actual number was less than 100. On October 20, 246 cargo vessels plied Continental waters; the wait for berths in various anchorages often lasted weeks, sometimes months. Entire fleets now served as floating warehouses for munitions and other matériel.

The War Department, trying to supply a global war with limited shipping, grew exasperated: in October, a cable warned SHAEF that "no further commodity-loaded ships" would be sent to Europe until empty ships began sailing home. Eisenhower was horrified, and more than two dozen Liberty ships were sent back to the United States, some before emptying their holds. To encourage stevedores and boost morale, Bronze Stars were handed out to efficient hatch crews, and band concerts serenaded workers on the docks.

If only Antwerp were free. "We have captured a port which resembles Liverpool in size, but we cannot use it," Montgomery had written in September. "If we could use it, all our maintenance troubles would disappear." Eisenhower stressed freeing the Scheldt and opening the port "as an indispensable prerequisite for the final drive into Germany." Even during MARKET GARDEN, the supreme commander had summoned twenty-three general officers to Versailles to discuss strategy—pleading the press of battle, Montgomery sent his chief of staff as a proxy—and to emphasize Antwerp "as a matter of urgency." Eisenhower told Beetle Smith a week later, "I am terribly anxious about Antwerp." Yet the supreme commander also insisted that both Montgomery and Bradley "must retain as first mission the gaining of the line of the Rhine north of Bonn as quickly as humanly possible."

Montgomery had assigned clearing the Scheldt to the Canadian First Army, which included a British corps and the Polish 1st Armored Division, for a total of six divisions. Allied air attacks intensified against enemy targets on diamond-shaped Walcheren Island and the Beveland peninsula, which formed the Scheldt's north shore. Allied ground troops squeezed the Breskens Pocket on the southern lip of the estuary, held by a formidable force of eleven thousand Germans, including Eastern Front veterans reinforced with both naval guns and seventy field artillery pieces. "The whole energies of the [Canadian] Army will be directed towards . . . Antwerp," Montgomery decreed—yet he ordered the Canadians to simultaneously isolate the enemy garrison at Dunkirk and capture the occupied French ports of Boulogne and Calais. The latter ports eventually fell and the Breskens Pocket slowly shrank, but the MARKET GARDEN stalemate south of Arnhem allowed the German Fifteenth Army to shift reinforcements to the Scheldt defenses. With enemies still entrenched on both banks of the estuary, no Allied ship dared venture upstream.

Thus the days and weeks rolled by, and big-shouldered Antwerp remained dormant. "We need this place more than we need FDR," Major General Everett Hughes wrote his wife. Although Montgomery acknowledged the port's primacy, neither he nor Eisenhower demanded that all other tasks be subordinated to this one. Dempsey's Second Army continued to look beyond the Rhine toward the Ruhr; control of a large port was a less urgent matter for the smaller British force. Even Field Marshal Brooke had doubts about Montgomery's priorities. "Antwerp must be captured with the least possible delay," he told his diary in London. "I feel that Monty's strategy for once is at fault." Montgomery would acknowledge as much after the war, conceding "a bad mistake on my part" in demanding too much of the Canadians. "I reckoned that the Canadian Army could do it *while* we were going for the Ruhr," he added. "I was wrong."

But in October 1944, the field marshal displayed no indulgence for those who questioned his judgment. Admiral Ramsay warned that to clear the Scheldt of mines would take weeks, even after German defenders were finally flicked from the banks of the waterway. "I think the army is not taking this operation seriously enough," he told his diary in early October. After another SHAEF meeting, Ramsay wrote, "Monty made the startling announcement that we could take the Ruhr without Antwerp. This afforded me the cue I needed to lambaste him. . . . I let fly with all my guns at the faulty strategy we had allowed." Montgomery took such criticism badly, and he accused the admiral of undercutting him. "Request you will ask Ramsay from me," the field marshal wrote Eisenhower, "by what authority he makes wild statements to you concerning my operations about which he can know nothing."

No less troublesome than the arcane issues of shipping and logistics were parallel questions of strategy and command. After a brief respite, Montgomery had again hectored Eisenhower over the supreme commander's preference for the broad, multipronged assault on Germany first adopted in May. Even as MARKET GARDEN came unglued, the field marshal had pressed once more for a single axis, preferably that of 21st Army Group, with nine reinforcing divisions from the U.S. First Army also under his command. Montgomery proposed that other Allied forces "stop in place where they are," donating transport and other war stuffs to his expedition. Eisenhower had tried to paper over the dispute by suggesting that his vision and Montgomery's could be reconciled, but in late September the field marshal rebuffed him with a tart cable:

> I can not agree that our concepts are the same. . . . If you want to get to the Ruhr you will have to put every single thing into the left hook and stop everything else. It is my opinion that if this is not done you will not get to the Ruhr.

Unchastened by the destruction of the 1st Airborne Division and the larger misadventure in Holland, Montgomery now overplayed his hand. During a private conference with George Marshall in Montgomery's tidy caravan in Eindhoven on Sunday, October 8, the field marshal complained about a "lack of grip" since Eisenhower had taken field command of the campaign, with battles that were "ragged and disjointed. . . . We [have] now got ourselves into a real mess." The chief of staff's icy blue stare implied demurral. "Marshall listened but said little," Montgomery subsequently wrote. "It was clear that he entirely disagreed." Marshall later confessed to nearly losing his famous temper at what he termed Montgomery's "overwhelming egotism."

Eisenhower's patience, too, finally wore thin. On the same Sunday that Marshall visited Eindhoven, SHAEF planners at Versailles warned that in failing to uncork the Scheldt "fifteen divisions are held impotent for lack of success in this relatively small operation. . . . Our advance into Germany may be delayed into spring." As it happened, high winds that very day ripped up Cherbourg's port and Mulberry B.

"This reemphasizes the supreme importance of Antwerp," Eisenhower cabled Montgomery in an "eyes only" message on Monday:

> Unless we have Antwerp producing by the middle of November our entire operations will come to a standstill. I must emphasize that, of all our operations on the entire front from Switzerland to the Channel, I consider Antwerp of the first importance.

Montgomery would assert that this was the first time Eisenhower had issued clear instructions on the matter, a claim the British official history subsequently judged "hardly justified." More likely, given Eisenhower's reluctance to issue unequivocal orders, it was the first time the field marshal had detected a tone of exasperation or even disapproval. "You can rely on me to do every single thing possible to get Antwerp opened,"

Montgomery replied promptly, and on the same day he instructed the Canadians in his firmest directive yet that "the opening of this port will take priority over all other offensive operations." Yet a week would pass before the Canadian army, clearly overmatched by the task at hand, was substantially reinforced, even though Eisenhower drove home his point with another testy cable on Tuesday:

> Nothing that I may ever say or write with respect to future plans in our advance eastward is meant to indicate any lessening of the need for Antwerp, which I have always held as vital, and which has grown more pressing as we enter the bad weather period.

Instead of replying directly, Montgomery that day sent Beetle Smith a caustic sixteen-paragraph memorandum titled "Notes on Command in Western Europe." Beginning with an assertion that "the present organization for command within the Allied forces in Western Europe is not satisfactory," the paper lambasted Eisenhower's generalship and proposed that he either move his headquarters forward to "take direct command of the operations against the Ruhr" or delegate field command in Europe to either Montgomery or Bradley. "I do not believe we have a good and sound organization for command and control," the field marshal wrote.

> It may be that political and national considerations prevent us having a sound organization. If this is the case I would suggest that we say so. Do not let us pretend we are all right, whereas actually we are very far from being all right.

Eisenhower waited three days to reply with his own thirteen-paragraph letter, carefully vetted by Marshall before the chief flew back to Washington on Friday. "The questions you raise are serious ones," Eisenhower wrote. "However, they do not constitute the real issue now at hand. That issue is Antwerp. . . . The Antwerp operation does not involve the question of command in any slightest degree." After pointing out the "woeful state" of American and French supply, and noting that "by comparison you are rich," Eisenhower again reviewed the reasoning behind his preference for a broad attack arranged by army groups under his command. Then the master bridge player laid down his trump card:

> If you, as the senior commander in this theater of one of the great Allies, feel that my conceptions and directives are such as to endanger the success of operations, it is our duty to refer the matter to higher authority for any action they may choose to take, however drastic.

The threat could hardly be misconstrued: if a general was to be cashiered, it would not be Eisenhower. Montgomery promptly amended his battle plan so that "the whole of the available offensive power of Second Army will now be brought to bear" in scouring the approaches to Antwerp. To subordinates he cabled, "I must impress on army commanders that the early use of Antwerp is absolutely vital. . . . We must accept heavy casualties to get quick success." The field marshal directed Second Army's XII Corps to pivot toward the Scheldt from the western flank of the Nijmegen corridor, permitting the Canadians—whose advance had covered hardly a mile a day—to concentrate on the Breskens Pocket and the eastern avenues to Walcheren Island. Montgomery now had the weight of two armies squeezing the seven German divisions that had neutralized Antwerp.

To Eisenhower the field marshal wrote, "You will hear *no* more on the subject of command from me. I have given you my views and you have given your answer. That ends the matter." He closed this pretty fiction with another: "Your very devoted and loyal subordinate, Monty."

Dwight David Eisenhower turned fifty-four years old on Saturday, October 14. He celebrated with a joyride in his old Cadillac—a newer model from Detroit was somewhere in the hold of yet another ship waiting for a berth. With Kay Summersby behind the wheel, he had traveled from Versailles to Verdun to spend Friday night with Bradley before the two generals pushed on the next morning to the Belgian town of Verviers, twenty miles southwest of the intensifying street battle in Aachen.

The U.S. First Army headquarters encampment rambled through the muddy grounds of a dilapidated three-story château, where an honor guard greeted Eisenhower, Bradley, and his three army commanders—Patton, Hodges, and the new Ninth Army commander, Lieutenant General William H. Simpson—and George VI, who was touring the front. After lunch in a spartan dining hall, Patton sipped his coffee, puffed on a cigar, and entertained the table with war stories from North Africa. "I must have shot a dozen Arabs myself," he told the monarch, provoking derisive hoots of laughter.

Bidding farewell to king and comrades, Eisenhower and Bradley then drove south through the somber Ardennes, past Belgian towns that soon would be all too familiar: Malmédy, St.-Vith, Vielsalm. In bucolic Bastogne, the smell of fresh bread wafted from the cooling racks of a mobile Army bakery. Farmers stacked hay bales for the coming winter and dairymen herded their cows to the barn, hardly glancing at the speeding limousine that carried the most famous general in Europe, if not in all the war-torn world.

This was Eisenhower's third consecutive birthday overseas. A profile in *Time* that month observed that he "has not visibly aged . . . but he gives a subtle impression of having grown bigger as a man and as a commander. For lack of exercise, he is slightly thicker around the middle and there are often tired lines under his snapping blue eyes. . . . Even in times of crisis, he is relaxed, genial and confident on the surface—whatever goes on underneath." True enough: he *was* thicker, confident, tired. Certainly he had grown as a commander since his fifty-second birthday, spent on Grosvenor Square in London on the eve of TORCH, when they were all callow and unblooded; or since his fifty-third, passed at the Hôtel St.-Georges in Algiers while reading dispatches from the swollen Volturno River, where the arduous Allied attack north of Naples suggested what lay ahead for those bent on a winter campaign in Italy.

Yet even *Time*'s omniscience missed nuances in the man and in the general he had become. He seemed transparent and simple but was neither. A reviewer of his published diary fragments long after the war would be struck by a "closed, calculating quality"; the historian Eric Larrabee later described him as "a veiled man" who was "so seemingly forthright, so ready to volunteer his thoughts, yet in the end so secretive, so protective of his purposes and the hidden processes of an iron logic behind them." Every commander wore a mask, and Eisenhower wore his while still conveying sincerity, rectitude, and humanity. "I have a feeling that he was a far more complicated man than he seemed to be," wrote Don Whitehead, "a man who shaped events with such subtlety that he left others thinking that they were the architects of those events. And he was satisfied to leave it that way."

He would never be a Great Captain, and perhaps his war had grown too big for such an archaic figure. Eisenhower was romantic enough to regret this failing: a lifelong admirer of Hannibal, he privately hoped that a double envelopment of the Ruhr would echo the Carthaginian destruction of the Romans at Cannae. He had long recognized that his task was not to be a field marshal, but rather to orchestrate a fractious multinational coalition, to be "chairman of the board"—the phrase was his—of the largest martial enterprise on earth. The master politician Franklin Roosevelt had chosen him as supreme commander from among thirteen hundred U.S. Army generals because he was not only a "natural leader," in the president's judgment, but also a military man with exceptional political instincts. E. J. Kingston McCloughry, a British air vice marshal who worked at SHAEF, wrote that Eisenhower "had a genius of getting along with most people, combining the art of persuasion and of inspiring good will."

He was by temperament a reconciler, an adjudicator, a compromiser; the recent contretemps with Montgomery showed Eisenhower as a man willing, perhaps too willing, to split the difference, to turn the other cheek.

Without doubt his orders could be opaque and imprecise, either because he failed to see the battlefield clearly or because he was reluctant to intrude on subordinate prerogatives—as in the Antwerp debacle, or in the incomplete attempts to annihilate the enemy at Messina and Falaise. In addition to his accolade for the supreme commander, Kingston McCloughry also damned with faint praise, deeming him "shrewd without being subtle, and understanding without being profound.... Perhaps Eisenhower's greatest advantage compared with, say, Montgomery, was that he was all too conscious of his own limitations."

And yet who could gainsay the greatness that had begun to enfold him? Churchill recognized that "no one knew better than he how to stand close to a tremendous event without impairing the authority he had delegated to others." Knowing full well how corrosive forces gnawed at every military confederation, from chauvinism to vanity, Eisenhower insisted that an allied commander must "solve problems through reasoning rather than by merely issuing commands." A collaborative forbearance was key to Allied unity, and Allied unity would win the war. This was his catechism, his "iron logic," and it had become the most profound article of faith in his life.

Except in the crow's-feet crinkling his eyes and the deepening furrows on his forehead, few could see the strain from years of decisions that by now had consigned tens of thousands to their deaths. Only in a handwritten reply to a waspish letter from Mamie did he let the mask slip a bit as he began his fifty-fifth year. "We've now been apart for 2½ years and at a time under conditions that make separations painful and hard to bear," he wrote. "The load of responsibility I carry would be intolerable unless I could have the belief that there is someone who wants me to come home— for good. Don't forget that I take a beating, every day."

The miles slid past, and with them the day. At dusk the Cadillac crossed the Belgian border and soon rolled into Luxembourg City. Here Bradley had just shifted the 12th Army Group command post from damp tents in Verdun to steam-heated stone buildings in the grand duchy. Only twelve miles from the German border—hardly enough distance to safely position a regimental headquarters, much less that of an army group—the capital was still reeling from four years of occupation. Overrun in less than a day in 1940, Luxembourg had been integrated into the Third Reich, and relentlessly germanized: the occupiers renamed the country Gau Moselland, changed the street names, banned the local French dialect, and conscripted ten thousand men into the Wehrmacht. Now Adolf Hitler Strasse had once again become the Avenue de la Liberté, and banners above the boulevard proclaimed, "We wish to remain what we are."

Bradley's office on the Place de Metz occupied a brownstone belonging to the state railway, but the limousine continued across the Pétrusse River, where tanneries, breweries, and shoemaker shops lined the bottoms near the ruined buttresses of Count Siegfried's thousand-year-old castle. On the Avenue de la Gare, the two generals climbed out at the Hôtel Alfa, a seven-story building with a mansard roof and balconies overlooking the train station.

Here in the dining room, to Eisenhower's surprise and evident delight, a party had been organized, with martinis, champagne, and an enormous four-star cake baked by a pastry chef in Paris. An orchestra played into the night, dreamy songs from another time they hardly remembered, and for a few sweet hours the war went away, even with the enemy but a dozen miles to the east and still scheming to reclaim Gau Moselland. Happy birthday, they sang, happy birthday, dear Ike, raising their glasses to a man they trusted and admired, the very man who would lead them to victory and then would lead them home.

The Worst Place of Any

I N late October, the U.S. First Army headquarters moved into winter quarters in the Belgian town of Spa. A flourishing resort since the 1500s—Karl Baedeker had called it "the oldest European watering-place of any importance"—Spa reached its zenith in the eighteenth century with visits by Peter the Great and other potentates keen to promenade beneath the elms or to marinate in the sixteen mineral springs infused with iron and carbonic acid. The town declined after the French Revolution, then revived itself, as such towns do—in Spa's case, by peddling varnished wood-ware and a liqueur known as Elixir de Spa. Here the Imperial German Army had placed its field headquarters during the last weeks of World War I: in the Grand Hôtel Britannique on the Rue de la Sauvenière, Field Marshal Paul von Hindenburg concluded that the cause was lost. The last of the Hohenzollerns to wear the crown, Kaiser Wilhelm II, arrived here from Berlin in October 1918, to fantasize about unleashing the army on his own rebellious *Volk;* instead he chose abdication and exile in the Netherlands.

Now GIs hauled the roulette wheels and chemin-de-fer tables from the casino on the Rue Royale, replacing them with field desks and triple bunks beneath the crystal chandeliers. "We'll take the 'hit' out of Hitler," they sang. Tests by Army engineers confirmed that every one of the city's eleven drinking water sources was polluted, but a decent black market meal could be had at the Hôtel de Portugal—horsemeat with mushroom caps seemed to be a Walloon specialty in these straitened times. As for the thirsty, each general in First Army received a monthly consignment of a case of gin and half-cases of scotch and bourbon; lesser officers combined their allotments in a nightly ritual to make twelve quarts of martinis for the Hôtel Britannique mess, a grand ballroom with mirrors on three walls and exquisite windows filling the fourth. Headquarters generals also requisitioned the hilltop mansion of a Liège steel magnate as their bivouac; Belgian guests occasionally were invited to movie screenings in a nearby school, where soldiers tried to explain in broken French the nuances of *Gaslight* and *A Guy Named Joe*. Drew Middleton reported that fleeing German troops had left behind in an Italian restaurant a recording of "Lili Marlene"; GIs played the disc incessantly while assuring skeptical Belgians that "the song had been taken prisoner . . . and could no longer be considered German." Almost hourly, the clatter of a V-1 bound for Antwerp from one of the launch sites in the Reich could be heard in the heavens above Spa.

Lieutenant General Courtney H. Hodges moved his office into Hindenburg's old Britannique suite and settled in to ponder how to wage a late autumn campaign in northern Europe. Hodges was an old-school soldier: he had flunked out of West Point—undone by plebe geometry—and had risen through the ranks after enlisting as a private in 1905. The son of a newspaper publisher from southern Georgia, he was of average height but so erect that he appeared taller, with a domed forehead and prominent ears. Army records described the color of his close-set eyes as "#10 Blue." "God gave him a face that always looked pessimistic," Eisenhower once observed, and even Hodges complained that a portrait commissioned by *Life* in early September made him appear "a little too sad."

A crack shot and big-game hunter—caribou and moose in Canada, elephants and tigers in Indochina—Hodges had earned two Purple Heart citations after being gassed in World War I but tore them up as excessively "sissy." He smoked Old Golds in a long holder, favored bourbon and Dubonnet on ice with a dash of bitters, and messed formally every night, in jacket, necktie, and combat boots. He had been seen weeping by the road as trucks passed carrying wounded soldiers from the front. "I wish everybody could see them," he said in his soft drawl. One division commander said of him: "Unexcitable. A killer. A gentleman." A reporter wrote that even in battle "he sounds like a Georgia farmer leaning on the fence, discussing his crops." Bradley, who as Hodges's subordinate used to shoot skeet or hunt quail with him on Sunday mornings at Fort Benning, later recalled, "He was very dignified and I can't imagine anyone getting familiar with him." Now his superior, Bradley still called him "sir."

First Army was the largest American fighting force in Europe, and Hodges was the wrong general to command it. Capable enough during the pursuit across France, he now was worn by illness, fatigue, and his own shortcomings—"an old man playing the game by the rules of the book, and a little confused as to what it was all about," a War Department observer wrote. "There was little of the vital fighting spirit." Even the Army's official histories would describe his fall campaign as "lacking in vigor and imagination," and among senior commanders he was "the least disposed to make any attempt to understand logistic problems." He was "pretty slow making the big decisions," a staff officer conceded, and he rarely left Spa to visit the front; for nearly two months the 30th Division's General Hobbs never laid eyes on him. Peremptory and inarticulate, Hodges "refused to discuss orders, let alone argue about them," one military officer later wrote. He sometimes insisted that situation reports show even platoon dispositions—a finicky level of detail far below an army commander's legitimate focus—and he complained in his war diary that "too many of these battalions and regiments of ours have tried to flank and skirt and never meet the enemy straight on." He believed it "safer, sounder, and in the end, quicker to keep smashing ahead." "Straight on" and "smashing ahead" would be Hodges's battlefield signature, with all that such frontal tactics implied.

Peevish and insulated, ever watchful for hints of disloyalty, Hodges showed an intolerance for perceived failure that was harsh even by the exacting standards of the U.S. Army. Of thirteen corps and division commanders relieved in 12th Army Group during the war, ten would fall from grace in First Army, the most recent being General Corlett of XIX Corps after Aachen. When the frayed commander of the 8th Division requested brief leave after his son was killed in action, Hodges sacked him. The Army historian Forrest Pogue described one cashiered officer waiting by the road for a ride to the rear, belongings piled about him "like a mendicant. . . . The sickness of heart was there, and the look of tired, beaten, exhausted helplessness could not be effaced."

Such a command climate bred inordinate caution, suppressing both initiative and élan, and First Army's senior staff made it worse. "Aggressive, touchy, and high-strung," Bradley later wrote of the staff he had created before ascending to 12th Army Group. "Critical, unforgiving, and resentful of all authority but its own." Three rivalrous figures played central roles in this unhappy family: Major General William B. Kean, the able, ruthless chief of staff, who was privately dubbed "Captain Bligh" and to whom Hodges ceded great authority; Brigadier General Truman C. Thorson, the grim, chain-smoking operations officer nicknamed Tubby but also called Iago; and Colonel Benjamin A. Dickson, the brilliant, turbulent intelligence chief long known as Monk, a histrionic man of smoldering grievances.

Not least of First Army's quirks as it prepared to renew the drive toward the Rhine was what one correspondent called a "slightly angry bafflement" at continued German resistance, a resentment that the enemy did not know he was beaten. As this colicky command group settled into Spa and prepared for the coming campaign, they all agreed that they would simply have to take the "hit" out of Hitler.

On October 28, Eisenhower reiterated his plan for winning the war. "The enemy has continued to reinforce his forces in the West," he cabled his lieutenants. "Present indications are that he intends to make the strongest possible stand on the West Wall, in the hope of preventing the war spreading to German soil." Antwerp, he declared, remained "our first and most important immediate objective." Canadian First Army troops had captured Breskens a week earlier, and the dwindling enemy pocket on the Scheldt's southern bank seemed certain to collapse within days if not hours. Canadian troops also were advancing along the north edge of the estuary; German defenders trapped on the Beveland Peninsula and Walcheren Island had been reduced to little more than a "White Bread" division comprising soldiers with digestive ailments. Eisenhower finally felt confident that the entire Scheldt soon would be cleansed of Germans, and Antwerp open to shipping shortly thereafter.

With that accomplished, he added, the final battle for Europe would unfold in "three general phases": an unsparing struggle west of the Rhine; the seizure of bridgeheads over the river; and finally a mortal dagger thrust into the heart of Germany. Seven Allied armies would advance eastward apace, arrayed from north to south: the Canadian First; the British Second; the U.S. Ninth, First, Third, and Seventh; and the French First. The enemy's industrial centers in the Ruhr and the Saar remained paramount objectives in the north and center, respectively, with Berlin as the ultimate target.

First Army's capture of Aachen and breach of the Siegfried Line in the adjacent Stolberg corridor left barely twenty miles to traverse before the Rhine. Here lay the most promising frontage on the entire Allied line. Hodges, with assistance from Simpson's Ninth Army, was to sweep forward another ten miles to the Roer River, overrun Düren on the far bank, then press on toward Cologne and the Rhine. Joe Collins's VII Corps would again lead the attack, but first V Corps on his right was to clear out the Hürtgen Forest and capture the high-ground village of Schmidt, providing First Army with more maneuver room and forestalling any counterattack into VII Corps' right flank by enemies who might be skulking in the forest dark.

Four compact woodland tracts formed the Hürtgen, eleven miles long and five miles wide in all. Forest masters for generations had meticulously pruned undergrowth and regulated logging, leaving perfectly aligned firs as straight and regular as soldiers on parade, in what one visitor called "a picture forest." But some of its acreage grew wild, particularly along creek beds and in the deep ravines where even at midday sunlight penetrated only as a dim rumor. Here was the Grimm forest primeval, a place of shades. "I never saw a wood so thick with trees as the Hürtgen," a GI later wrote. "It turned out to be the worst place of any."

The Hürtgenwald had been fortified as part of the Siegfried Line, beginning in 1938. German engineers more recently had pruned timber for fields of fire, built log bunkers with interlocking kill zones, and sowed mines by the thousands on trails and firebreaks; along one especially vicious trace, a mine could be found every eight paces for three miles. The 9th Division in late September had learned how lethal the Hürtgen could be when trying to cross the forest as part of the initial VII Corps effort to outflank Aachen. One regiment took four days to move a mile; another needed five. By mid-October the division was still far short of Schmidt and had suffered 4,500 casualties to gain three thousand yards—a man down every two feet—and no battalion in the two spearhead regiments could field more than three hundred men. More and more of the perfect groves were gashed yellow with machine-gun bullets or reduced to charred stumps—"no birds, no sighing winds, no carpeted paths," Forrest Pogue reported. A commander who offered his men $5 for every tree found unscarred by shellfire got no takers. Pogue was reminded of the claustrophobic bloodletting of May 1864 in another haunted woodland, one in eastern Virginia: "There was a desolation," he wrote, "such as one associated with the Battle of the Wilderness."

Nearly half of the 6,500 German defenders from the 275th Division had been killed, wounded, or captured in checking the 9th Division; reinforcements included two companies of Düren policemen known as "family-fathers" because most were at least forty-five years old. More bunkers were built, more barbed wire uncoiled, more mines sown, including nonmetallic shoe and box mines, and lethal round devices said to be "no larger than an ointment box." Enemy officers considered it unlikely that the Americans would persist in attacking through what one German commander called "extensive, thick, and nearly trackless forest terrain."

That underestimated American obstinacy. The Hürtgen neutralized U.S. military advantages in armor, artillery, airpower, and mobility, but Hodges was convinced that no First Army drive to the Roer was possible without first securing the forest and capturing Schmidt, from which every approach to the river was visible. He likened the menace on his right flank to that posed by German forces in the Argonne Forest to the American left flank during General John J. Pershing's storied offensive on the Meuse in the autumn of 1918. This specious historical analogy—the Germans could hardly mass enough armor in the cramped Hürtgen to pose a mortal threat—received little critical scrutiny within First Army, not least because of reluctance to challenge Hodges. In truth, "the most likely way to make the Hürtgen a menace to the American Army," the historian Russell F. Weigley later wrote, "was to send American troops attacking into its depths."

No consideration was given to bypassing or screening the forest, or to outflanking Schmidt from the south by sending V Corps up the vulnerable attack corridor through Monschau, fifteen miles below Aachen. Senior officers in First Army would spend the rest of their lives trying to explain the tactical logic behind the Hürtgen battle plan. "All we could do was sit back and pray to God that nothing would happen," General Thorson, the operations officer, later lamented. "It was a horrible business, the forest. . . . We had the bear by the tail, and we just couldn't turn loose." Even Joe Collins, who enjoyed favorite-son status with Hodges, conceded that he "would not question Courtney." After the war Collins said:

> We *had* to go into the forest in order to secure our right flank. . . . Nobody was enthusiastic about fighting there, but what was the alternative? . . . If we would have turned loose of the Hürtgen and let the Germans roam there, they could have hit my flank.

No less regrettable was a misreading of German topography. Seven dams built for flood control, drinking water, and hydroelectric power stood near the headwaters of the Roer, which arose in Belgium and spilled east through the German highlands before flowing north across the Cologne plain and eventually emptying into the Maas southeast of Eindhoven. Five of the seven dams lacked the capacity to substantially affect the river's regime, but the other two—the Schwammenauel and the Urft—impounded sizable lakes that together held up to forty billion gallons. In early October, the 9th Division's intelligence officer had warned that German mischief could generate "great destructive flood waves" as far downstream as Holland. Colonel Dickson, First Army's intelligence chief, disagreed. Opening the floodgates or destroying the dams would cause "at the most local floodings for about five days," Dickson asserted. No terrain analysis was undertaken, nor were the dams mentioned in tactical plans. "We had not studied that particular part of the zone," Collins later acknowledged. "That was an intelligence failure, a real combat intelligence failure."

By late October, as First Army coiled to resume its attack, unnerving details about the Roer and its waterworks had begun to accumulate. A

German prisoner disclosed that arrangements had been made to ring Düren's church bells if the dams upstream were blown. A German engineer interrogated in Spa intimated that a wall of water could barrel down the Roer. Inside an Aachen safe, an American lieutenant found Wehrmacht plans for demolishing several dams; by one calculation, a hundred million metric tons of water could flood the Roer valley for twenty miles, transforming the narrow river to a half-mile-wide torrent. A top secret memo to Hodges from Ninth Army's General Simpson on November 5 cited a Corps of Engineers study titled "Summaries of the Military Use of the Roer River Reservoir System," which concluded that the enemy could "maintain the Roer River at flood stage for approximately ten days . . . or can produce a two-day flood of catastrophic proportions." An American attack over the Roer might be crippled, with tactical bridges swept away and any troops east of the river isolated and annihilated. Obviously neither the First Army nor the Ninth, farther downstream, could safely cross the Roer and make for the Rhine until the dams were neutralized. Simpson proposed to Hodges that he immediately "block these [enemy] capabilities." A flanking attack toward Schmidt from Monschau in the south would also permit capture of Schwammenauel, Urft, and their sisters.

Yet First Army hewed to its plan for a frontal assault, afflicted by what General Thorson later called "a kind of torpor in our operations." Hodges in late October had told Bradley that the Roer reservoirs were half empty—unaware that they were being replenished—and that "present plans of this army do not contemplate immediate capture of these dams." It was assumed that, if necessary, bombers could blow open the reservoirs whenever the Army asked. Bradley would later claim that by mid-October "we were very much aware of the threat they posed" and that the "whole point" of the renewed attack through the Hürtgen was "to gain control of the dams and spillways." That was untrue. Not until November 7 did Hodges order V Corps to even begin drafting plans to seize the dam sites, and not until December 4 would Bradley's war diary note: "Decided must control Roer dam."

By that time another frontal assault through horrid terrain had come to grief, and officers at Spa were reduced to feeble maledictions. "Damn the dams," they would tell one another again and again. "Damn the dams."

Attacking the worst place of any now fell to Major General Dutch Cota and his 28th Division, still recovering from the September skirmishes that had revived the division's World War I nickname, the Bloody Bucket. The 28th had regained full strength but only with many replacements untrained as infantrymen, under officers and sergeants plucked from antiaircraft units and even the Army Air Forces. Hemingway, who for several

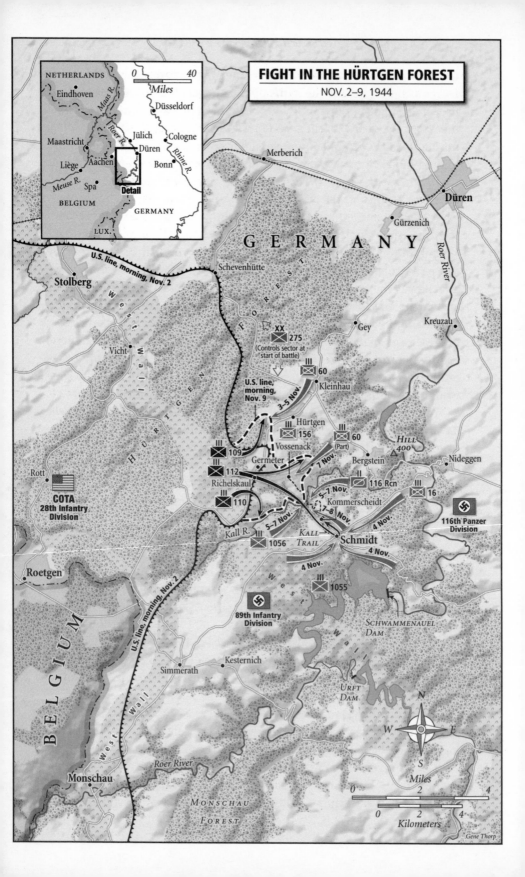

FIGHT IN THE HÜRTGEN FOREST
NOV. 2–9, 1944

NETHERLANDS

Eindhoven

Düsseldorf

0   40
Miles

Maastricht
Jülich
Cologne

Liège
Aachen
Düren

Meuse R.
Spa
Bonn

BELGIUM
Detail
GERMANY

LUX.

Merberich

Düren

Gürzenich

G E R M A N Y

Stolberg

Schevenhütte

Roer River

Kreuzau

Vicht

Gey

XX 275
(Controls sector at
start of battle)

III 60

Kleinhau

U.S. line,
morning,
Nov. 9

3–5 Nov.

Hürtgen

III 156

III 60
(Part)

HILL
400

Vossenack

Germeter

Nideggen

III 109

III 112

7 Nov.

Bergstein

Richelskaul

II 116 Rcn

III 16

Rott

III 110

5–7 Nov.

Kommerscheidt

**COTA
28th Infantry
Division**

7–8 Nov.

4 Nov.

**116th Panzer
Division**

Kall R.

5–7 Nov.

II 1056

*KALL
TRAIL*

Schmidt

4 Nov.

Roetgen

4 Nov.

III 1055

U.S. line, morning, Nov. 2

West Wall

**89th Infantry
Division**

*SCHWAMMENAUEL
DAM*

B E L G I U M

Kesternich

Simmerath

*URFT
DAM*

N

W   E

S

Monschau

Roer River

Miles

0   2   4

MONSCHAU

FOREST

0   2   4
Kilometers

Gene Thorp

weeks would live in a fieldstone house south of Stolberg, suggested that it would "save everybody a lot of trouble if they just shot them as soon as they got out of the trucks."

In late October the Bloody Bucketeers—as they called themselves with sardonic pride—assembled beneath the yellow-gashed firs. GIs heaved logs into the firebreaks in hopes of tripping mines, or probed the ground inch by inch with a bayonet held at a thirty-degree angle or with a No. 8 wire. Dead men from the 9th Division still littered the forest, bullet holes in their field jackets like blood-ringed grommets. After a soldier ran over a Teller mine with his jeep, a lieutenant wrote, "His clothing and tire chains were found seventy-five feet from the ground in the tree tops. It snows every day now." A few men had overshoes; the rest, trying to avoid trench foot by standing on burning Sterno blocks, soon lost any scruples about stripping footwear from the dead.

Foul weather, supply shortages, and the slow arrival of two more divisions caused First Army to postpone VII Corps's main attack toward Düren until mid-November. An offensive in the north by 21st Army Group also was pushed back. But Hodges saw no reason to delay clearing the Hürtgen and seizing Schmidt. On Wednesday, November 1, after lunch in Spa with the V Corps commander, Major General Leonard T. Gerow, Hodges made a rare visit to a division command post. He drove twenty miles to Rott, strode into the two-story *Gasthaus* at 23 Quirinstrasse, where Cota had put his headquarters, and voiced his pleasure that the 28th Division was obviously "in fine fettle, rarin' to go." The battle plan, Hodges informed Cota, was "excellent."

In fact, it was badly flawed. For two weeks across the 170-mile front of the First and Ninth Armies, the 28th Division would be the only U.S. unit launching an attack, attracting the undivided attention of German defenders who already knew precisely where the *Blutiger Eimer* division was assembling. The "excellent" plan, imposed on Cota by V Corps staff officers squinting at a map far from the front, required him to splinter his force by attacking on three divergent axes: one regiment to the north, another to the southeast, and a third to the east, toward Schmidt. Cota's misgivings had been waved away despite his warrant that the attack had no more than "a gambler's chance" of success. A large sign posted in the forest warned, "Front line a hundred yards. Dismount and fight."

At nine A.M. on November 2, a cold, misty Thursday, GIs heaved themselves from their holes like doughboys going over the top. Eleven thousand artillery rounds chewed up German revetments and flayed the forest with steel from shells detonating in the tree canopy. But the brisk *brrrr* of machine-gun fire from pillboxes on the division's right flank mowed down men in the 110th Infantry Regiment—"singly, in groups, and by platoons," the division history recorded. By day's end the 110th had gained not a yard, and by week's end the regiment would be rated "no longer an effective fighting force."

The attack hardly began better for the 109th Regiment on the left flank. German sappers driving charcoal-fueled trucks had hauled enough mines from a Westphalian munitions plant to lay a dense field in a swale across the road from Germeter to Hürtgen village. The 109th had advanced barely three hundred yards when a sharp *pop!* was followed by a shriek and a GI clutching his bloody foot. More pops followed, more shrieks, more maimed boys. After thirty-six hours the regiment would hold only a narrow, mile-deep salient into enemy territory, a salient almost mirrored by Germans infiltrating the U.S. ranks.

Against such odds, and to the surprise of American and German alike, the division's main attack won through in the center. A battalion from the 112th Infantry was pinned wriggling to the ground by enemy fire near Richelskaul, but seven Shermans churned down the wooded slope from Germeter, each trailing clouds of infantrymen holding a rear fender and trotting in the tank tracks to avoid mines. The Shermans fired four rounds apiece to dismember the church steeple in Vossenack and any snipers hidden in the belfry, and two hundred white-phosphorus mortar shells set the village ablaze. One block wide and two thousand yards long, Vossenack straddled a saddleback two miles from Schmidt, visible through the haze to the southeast. Soft ground, mines, and Panzerfaust volleys wrecked five Shermans, but before noon burning Vossenack belonged to Cota's men, who burrowed into the northeast nose of the ridgeline.

At dawn on Friday, November 3, the attack resumed. From Vossenack the ridge plunged into the crepuscular Kall gorge, a deep ravine carved through the landscape by a stream rushing toward the Roer. Two American battalions in column spilled down a twisting cart track, then forded the icy Kall near an ancient sawmill and emerged from the beeches limning the far ridge to pounce on the drab hamlet of Kommerscheidt. The 3rd Battalion scampered southeast for another half mile and at 2:30 P.M. fell on the astonished garrison at Schmidt, capturing or killing Germans eating lunch, riding bicycles, or nipping schnapps on the street. From rooftops in the sixteenth-century town, the entire Hürtgen swam into view, along with the meandering Roer two miles to the east and the sapphire Schwammenauel reservoir a mile south. A believing man with imagination could almost see the end of the war.

Telephoned congratulations from division and corps commanders across the front poured into Cota's *Gasthaus* in Rott, ten miles to the west. General Hodges himself sent word that he was "extremely, satisfied." The plaudits, Cota later said, made him feel like "a little Napoleon."

*   *   *

The bad news from Schmidt reached Field Marshal Model that same afternoon at Schlenderhan castle in the horse country west of Cologne, hardly twenty-five miles from the battlefield. There by chance Model had just started a map exercise with his top commanders, positing a theoretical American attack near the Hürtgenwald. Sketchy reports indicated that in fact a strong assault against the German LXXIV Corps threatened to over-run the Roer dams that generated much of the electricity west of the Rhine.

Model ordered the corps commander back to his post, but other officers—including two army commanders—were instructed to continue the war game, using dispatches from the front to help orchestrate the battle. Low clouds and fog had impaired Allied fighter-bombers for the past two days; with luck, reinforcements could hasten, unimpeded, on the good roads threading the Roer valley. Confrontation with the Americans would first fall to the 116th Panzer Division, which had fought through Yugoslavia and southern Russia as far as the Caspian Sea before surviving more recent battles in the west, at Falaise and Aachen. The reconnaissance battalion already was galloping toward Schmidt, followed in trace by the bulk of the division and by troops from the 89th Division.

Three isolated American rifle companies and a machine-gun platoon from the 112th Infantry defended Schmidt, unaware of the Wehrmacht high command's keen interest in them but unnerved by snipers and hay-stacks on a hillside that seemed to move in the moonlight. Exhausted after Friday's trudge through the Kall gorge in heavy overcoats with full field packs, the 3rd Battalion sent out no patrols and scattered sixty antitank mines—delivered during the night by tracked Weasel cargo carriers—on three approach roads without attempting to implant or camouflage them. No panzer counterattack was considered likely given Allied air superior-ity and the destruction of German armor in the past two months. Oblivi-ous to his men's vulnerability, Cota remained in Rott; not for three more days would he visit the front. Having already committed his only division reserve to help the hard-pressed 110th Infantry in the south, the little Napoléon had lost control of the battle before it really began.

Just before sunrise on Saturday, November 4, German artillery fire crashed and heaved from three directions around Schmidt. A magnesium flare drifted across the pearl-gray dawn, and wide-eyed GIs spied a long column of Panthers and Mk IVs snaking toward them from the northeast, easily swerving around the pointless mines. German machine-gun bullets ripped through foxholes; scarlet tank fire blew the town apart, house by house. Mortar pits were overrun, bazooka rounds bounced off panzer hulls like marbles, and yowling enemy infantrymen raced toward Schmidt from the south, west, and east, some banging on their mess kits in a luna-tic tintinnabulation.

At 8:30 an American platoon on the southern perimeter broke in panic, unhinging the defense. Soon the entire battalion took to its heels, Companies I, K, and L scrabbling through gardens and over fences, "ragged, scattered, disorganized infantrymen," in one lieutenant's account. Barking officers grabbed at their soldiers' herringbone collars in an attempt to turn them, but hundreds leaked down the road toward Kommerscheidt, forsaking their dead and wounded. Two hundred others stampeded in the wrong direction—southwest, into German lines—and of those only three would elude capture or worse. By ten A.M., Schmidt once again belonged to the Reich.

The fight for the Hürtgen had taken a turn, though not for several hours did the command post in Rott get word that an infantry battle had become a tank brawl. Lowering clouds grounded Allied pilots for a third day, and U.S. intelligence was slow to realize that enemy observers with Zeiss optics on Hill 400, just two miles north of Schmidt, could see even a rabbit cross the meadows on either flank of the Kall gorge. Confusion soon turned to chaos, calamity to farce. A tank company trying to negotiate the steep Kall trail managed, with a great deal of winching around the hairpin turns, to get three Shermans across the ravine to help repel an initial German lunge at Kommerscheidt from Schmidt. But five other tanks stood disabled, repeatedly throwing tracks on the treacherous switchbacks and blocking the path, which at nine feet was precisely as wide as a medium tank. After nightfall, in relentless rain and stygian darkness, engineers hacked at the trace with picks and shovels—a bulldozer broke down half an hour after arriving—but even the nimble Weasels seemed clay-footed, and the ammunition trailers they towed had to be unhitched and manhandled around each sharp turn into and out of the gorge.

In Rott, Cota's perplexity only deepened. Radios worked fitfully, and messengers were ambushed or forestalled by descending curtains of artillery. Was the Kall trail open? No, came the reply, then yes, then no. Engineers detonated captured Teller mines in a futile attempt to blow apart a rocky knob blocking a switchback above the pretty stone bridge spanning the creek; three hundred pounds of TNT finally reduced the obstruction. Tank crews showed little sense of urgency—"Everybody appeared to treat the disabled tanks with the same kind of warm-hearted affection an old-time cavalryman might lavish on his horse," the Army's official history acknowledged. Not until 2:30 A.M. on Sunday, November 5, just before moonrise, were the stalled Shermans finally shoved over the brink into the gorge.

A fretful General Gerow, the V Corps commander, drove into Rott a few hours later, clucked at Cota, and soon returned with Hodges and Joe Collins. Pulling on an Old Gold, the army commander also berated Cota and then rounded on Gerow in a crimson tirade—"tougher than I had ever heard him before," Collins later recalled. "He was pushing Gerow awfully hard." Cota was reduced to scribbling another order that might or might not reach the 112th Infantry: "It is imperative that the town of Schmidt be secured at once." He ended the message: "Roll on."

Had the generals seen the battlefield clearly, reclaiming Schmidt would have been the least of their concerns. Enemy forces now crowded the 28th Division on three sides, threatening the Bloody Bucket with annihilation. Nine Shermans and nine tank destroyers had traversed the Kall to reach the remnants of two infantry battalions huddled in what was described as a "covered wagon" defense in Kommerscheidt. Just the rumor of another panzer attack sent spooked riflemen scouring for the gorge, but any illusion of refuge there soon vanished. On Sunday night, reconnaissance troops from the 116th Panzer clattered down the Kall creek bed past an old sawmill, through ferns half as high as a man. Army engineers grooming the trail ran for their lives, as German sappers mined the switchbacks, set up ambushes, and effectively cut off more than a thousand GIs east of the ravine.

Dawn on Monday laid bare the American plight. Panzer drumfire from Schmidt soon reduced nine Shermans to six, and nine tank destroyers to three. GIs unable to leave their flooded rifle pits, described as "artesian wells," were once again reduced to defecating in empty C-ration cans. Those gimlet-eyed German observers on Hill 400 lobbed twenty artillery rounds or more onto each position, shifting guns hole by hole by hole; sobbing men waited in terror as the footfall drew closer.

A relief battalion from the 110th Infantry that had been ordered to huddle together for warmth in Vossenack—"just like cattle do in a storm," as one survivor reported—attracted a thirty-minute artillery barrage. Men were "killed right and left as they were milling around. . . . Everybody was trying to jump over a bleeding body to find shelter." One company lost 41 of 127 men, another 75 of 140. "Lieutenant, are my legs still there?" a wounded soldier asked his platoon leader. "Please tell the truth."

Soldiers in the claustrophobic forest debated whether they could stave off the enemy long enough to finish smoking the carton of cigarettes they carried, or merely an open pack, or perhaps only the Lucky Strike they had just lighted. Examining a badly wounded man for injuries in the dark woods, a 28th Division medic reported, was "like putting your hand in a bucket of wet liver." A surge in head wounds stirred debate in the ranks about whether German snipers were aiming at the keystone insignia—the bloody bucket—painted on their helmets. "So this is combat," a lieutenant new to the Hürtgen reflected. "I've only had one day of it. How does a man stand it, day in and day out?"

How, indeed? The morning wore on, and the existential crisis sharpened. The 2nd Battalion of the 112th Infantry, whose two sister battalions were trapped in Kommerscheidt, finally broke after four nights of murderous shelling on the exposed nose west of the Kall gorge. An abrupt, piercing scream unmanned Company G, which fled for the rear through Vossenack, and the contagion instantly infected the ranks. "Pushing, shoving, throwing away equipment, trying to outrun the artillery and each other," an officer reported, the men scorched up the ridge toward their original positions at the beginning of the Hürtgen battle four days earlier. A lieutenant who considered the pell-mell flight "the saddest sight I have ever seen," added, "Many of the badly wounded men, probably hit by artillery, were lying in the road where they fell, screaming for help."

Officers managed to rally seventy stouthearts near the ruined Vossenack church—no one had yet seen a single German in the village—and four tank platoons rushed down from Germeter. Cota ordered two road-repairing companies from the 146th Engineers into the line as riflemen. Still in their raincoats and hip boots, the engineers battled infiltrators all night around the church; Germans at one point occupied the tower and the basement while GIs held the nave. On Tuesday morning, November 7, the engineers helped beat back a panzer grenadier assault, keeping Vossenack in American hands except for the eastern fringe, dubbed the Rubble Pile, which the Germans would hold for another month. The 112th Infantry's 2nd Battalion was considered "destroyed as a fighting unit," another unit smashed to pieces.

"The 28th Division situation is going from bad to worse," First Army's war diary noted on Tuesday. Cota could only agree. A relief force of four hundred men had fought across a firebreak in the Kall gorge to reach Kommerscheidt on Sunday, but none of the accompanying tanks or tank destroyers could bull through German roadblocks. Artillery and mortar barrages pounded Kommerscheidt through the night, and catcalling enemy infiltrators crept so close in the encroaching draws that Jewish GIs hammered out the telltale "H"—for "Hebrew"—on their dogtags. As the gray skies spat sleet, fifteen panzers and two infantry battalions renewed the attack on Tuesday morning, shooting up farmsteads and garden shacks. By midday the Americans had fallen back to entrenchments along the eastern lip of the gorge, and Kommerscheidt too was lost.

Reeling from lack of sleep and grieving for his gutted command, Cota phoned Gerow to propose that survivors marooned across the ravine retreat to a new line west of the Kall. Shortly before midnight on Tuesday, Gerow called back with permission. Hodges, he added, was "very dissatisfied. . . . All we seem to be doing is losing ground." Not until three P.M. on Wednesday, November 8, did the withdrawal order reach the battered last-stand redoubt. Soldiers at dusk fashioned litters from tree limbs and overcoats. Others smashed radios, mine detectors, and the engine blocks on four surviving jeeps; three antitank guns were spiked and the only functioning Sherman booby-trapped. Soldiers shed their mess kits and other clattering gear—the senior officer among them mistakenly threw away his compass—and engineers abandoned two tons of TNT with which they had planned to demolish pillboxes in Schmidt.

Come nightfall, American artillery smothered Kommerscheidt with high explosives to hide the sounds of withdrawal, and two columns slipped into the gorge. A smaller group of litter-bearers carried the wounded down the trail, past GI corpses crushed to pulp by the earlier armor traffic, while several hundred "effectives" set out cross-country, each grasping the shoulder of the man in front and moving through woods so dark they produced the illusion of walking into a lake at midnight. Charles B. MacDonald, the author of the Army's official account, described the retreat:

> Like blind cattle the men thrashed through the underbrush. Any hope of maintaining formation was dispelled quickly by the blackness of the night and by German shelling. All through the night and into the next day, frightened, fatigued men made their way across the icy Kall in small irregular groups, or alone.

Of more than two thousand American soldiers who had fought east of the Kall, barely three hundred returned. German pickets in the gorge let some wounded pass; others were detained for two days near a log dugout above the rushing creek, whimpering in agony until a brief cease-fire permitted evacuation. The dead accumulated in stiff piles, covered with fir branches until Graves Registration teams could bear them away.

Eisenhower and Bradley had driven to Rott on Wednesday morning, perplexed at reports of an attack gone bad. In the command post at 23 Quirinstrasse, the supreme commander listened to Cota's account and then said with a shrug, "Well, Dutch, it looks like you got a bloody nose." Hodges and Gerow arrived a few minutes later for a hurried conference. With Germans still entrenched on the high ground at Schmidt, any November offensive to the Rhine now stood in jeopardy.

After Eisenhower left, Hodges gave Cota yet another tongue-lashing. Had the regiments been properly deployed and dug in? If they had been, even under heavy German artillery casualties "would not be high nor would ground be lost." During the battle, Hodges complained, the division staff appeared to have "no precise knowledge of the location of their units and were doing nothing to obtain it." The First Army commander wanted Cota to know that he was "extremely disappointed." Before driving back to Spa, Hodges told Gerow that "there may be some personnel changes made."

The gray weather grew colder. Sleet turned to heavy snow, and winter's first storm was on them. Vengeful GIs rampaged through German houses, smashing china and tossing furniture into the streets. "I've condemned a whole regiment of the finest men that ever breathed," a distraught officer told the reporter Iris Carpenter. "I tell you frankly, I can't take much more of it."

Survivors from the Kall were trucked to Rötgen, where pyramidal tents had been erected with straw floors and stacks of wool blankets. Medics distributed liquor rations donated by rear-echelon officers. Red Cross volunteers served pancakes and beer, and the division band played soldierly airs. "Chow all right, son?" a visiting officer asked one soldier, who without looking up replied, "What the fuck do you care? You're getting yours, aincha?"

On Thursday, November 9, the 28th Division began planting a defensive barrier of five thousand mines around the cramped salient held in the Hürtgen. Patrols crept through the lines searching for hundreds of missing GIs in the once perfect ranks of trees, now quite imperfect. The weeklong battle had been among the costliest division attacks of the war for the U.S. Army, with casualties exceeding 6,000. The Bloody Bucket was bloodier than ever: one battalion in the 110th Infantry was reduced to 57 men even after being reinforced, and losses had whittled the 112th Infantry from 2,200 to 300. "The division had accomplished very little," the unit history conceded. In less than six months, Dutch Cota had gone from a man lionized for his valor at Omaha Beach and St.-Lô to a defeated general on the brink of dismissal: such was war's inconstancy. He was permitted to keep his command partly because so many other leaders had been lost in the division that four majors and a captain led infantry battalions. In mid-November, the 8th Division arrived in the Hürtgen to replace the 28th, which was shunted to a placid sector in the Ardennes for rest and recuperation. To his troops, Cota issued a message of encouragement, which closed with the injunction "Salute, March, Shoot, Obey."

German losses for the week had totaled about 3,000. "We squat in an airless cellar," a German medic wrote his parents. "The wounded lie on bloodstained mattresses. . . . One has lost most of his intestines from a grenade fragment." Another soldier, with an arm and a foot nearly severed, pleaded, "Comrades, shoot me." On the American side of the line, U.S. quartermaster troops dragged dead Germans feetfirst from a wrecked barn, while a watching GI strummed his guitar and belted out "South of the Border." But the enemy kept his death grip on the forest. Single American divisions continued to gnaw and be gnawed: attacks in coming days by the 4th and 8th Infantry Divisions, like those by the 9th and the 28th, gained little at enormous cost, with battalions reduced to the size of companies and companies shaved to platoons. "The days were so terrible that I would pray for darkness," one soldier recalled, "and the nights were so bad that I would pray for daylight."

In less than three months, six U.S. Army infantry divisions would be tossed into the Hürtgen, plus an armored brigade, a Ranger battalion, and sundry other units. All told, 120,000 soldiers sustained 33,000 casualties in what the historian Carlo D'Este would call "the most ineptly fought series of battles of the war in the West." A captured German document reported that "in combat in wooded areas the American showed himself completely unfit," a harsh judgment that had a whiff of legitimacy with respect to American generalship.

As the attack continued to sputter in late November, Hodges himself showed the strain. "He went on and on about how we might lose the war," Major General Pete Quesada, the commander of IX Tactical Air Command, said after one unhappy conference. Despite the setback, Hodges and his command group soldiered on: at a November dinner party in the Spa generals' mansion, the table was decorated with the distinctive black "A" of First Army's shoulder flash, originally adopted in 1918. For dessert, each guest received an individual cake with the officer's name stenciled in pink frosting, and with coffee the film *Janie* was shown, a romantic comedy starring Joyce Reynolds.

One soldier-poet composed a verse that ended, "We thought woods were wise but never/Implicated, never involved." Yet in the Hürtgen surely terrain and flora were complicit, the land *always* implicated. An engineer observed that the forest "represented not so much an area as a way of fighting and dying." A coarse brutality took hold in Allied ranks, increasingly common throughout Europe. Fighter-bombers incinerated recalcitrant towns with napalm, and one potato village after another was blasted to dust by artillery. "*C'est la* bloody goddam *guerre*," soldiers told one another. Among those sent to the rear for psychiatric examination were two GI collectors, one with a cache of ears sliced from dead Germans and another with a souvenir bag of teeth. Through the long winter, feral dogs in the forest would feed on corpses seared by white phosphorus. "This was my personal Valley of the Shadow," a medic wrote. "I left with an incredible relief and with a sadness I had never so far known."

From his fieldstone house near Vicht, furnished with a potbelly stove and a brass bed in the living room, Hemingway rambled about in a sheepskin vest that "made him bulk bigger." Sometimes on request he ghostwrote love letters for young GIs, reading his favorite passages to fellow journalists. He would memorably describe the Hürtgen as "Passchendaele with tree bursts," but not even a Hemingway could quite capture the debasement of this awful place. A soldier asked Iris Carpenter as she scribbled in her reporter's note pad, "Do you tell 'em their brave boys are livin' like a lot of fornicatin' beasts, that they're doin' things to each other that beasts would be ashamed to do?" A veteran sergeant who believed the Hürtgen more wretched than anything he had experienced in North Africa, Sicily, or Normandy, quoted *King Lear*, act IV, scene 1: "The worst is not / So long as we can say 'This is the worst.'"

To a soldier named Frank Maddalena, who went missing in the forest in mid-November, his wife, Natalie, mother of his two children, wrote from New York: "I see you everywhere—in the chair, behind me, in the shadows of the room." In another note she added, "Still no mail from you. I really don't know what to think anymore. The kids are fine and so adorable. Right now, I put colored handkerchiefs on their heads and they are dancing and singing. . . . When I walk alone, I seem to feel you sneaking up on me and putting your arms around me."

No, that did not happen, would not, could not. This is the worst.

Part Three

7. The Flutter of Wings

A Town Too Small for the Tragedy

A STATELY procession of nineteen cargo ships glided up the gray Scheldt in a pelting rain on Tuesday morning, November 28. Seamen and anxious war correspondents crowded the rails, squinting for mines. Three small coasters had made the run to Antwerp without mishap on Sunday, the first Allied vessels to sail the estuary since 1940; but not until this initial convoy was safely berthed could the port be considered fully open, almost three months after its capture. Photographers and dignitaries lined the wharves, including Belgian worthies and legates from both SHAEF and 21st Army Group. As tugs bullied the Quebec-built merchantman S.S. *Fort Cataraqui* to her pier, a brass band crashed through "Heart of Oak," a spirited naval march with lyrics by the celebrated eighteenth-century actor and impresario David Garrick:

> Heart of oak are our ships, jolly tars are our men,
> We always are ready; Steady, boys, steady!
> We'll fight and we'll conquer again and again.

Stevedores made fast the freighter, then fell on her and her trailing sisters with cranes and cargo slings. From nineteen holds poured war stuffs of every sort, and not a moment too soon: COMZ three days earlier had warned of more dire shortages on the Continent, with "persistently low" ammunition stocks and "no days of supply whatsoever of items such as Prestone [antifreeze], overshoes, sleeping bags, tires, radios, field wire, replacement engines, axles, general purpose and combat vehicles."

A protocol oversight had excluded Canadian army emissaries from the dockside welcoming committee, a lamentable snub: the Canadian First Army had sustained nearly thirteen thousand casualties in winning the Scheldt. The protracted "struggle in the polders" had ultimately required massed flamethrowers, gunfights from windmill to windmill, and the bombardment of ancient Dutch dikes to flush German defenders from Walcheren Island with North Sea floodwaters. Amphibious assaults across the Scheldt and the North Sea to Walcheren in early November included fire support from the 15-inch guns of the battleship *Warspite* and the monitors *Erebus* and *Roberts*. Pipers piped, landing craft beat toward the island from Ostend, and Royal Marines were greeted by a small boy in an orange sash standing on the ruptured dike, waving a Dutch flag and shouting, "Good morning! Good morning!" But not until the German commander was rousted from his bed in Middelburg to surrender the last two thousand defenders was the battle declared won, at noon on November 8.

With enemy shore guns finally silenced, more than two hundred minesweepers in fifteen flotillas had scoured the eighty-mile estuary seventeen times in three weeks under Operation CALENDAR. Each ship's crew painted a white chevron on the funnel for every mine discovered and destroyed. Sweeps mounted on truck beds probed the Scheldt's marshy banks, while divers cleared every square inch of the thousand acres around Antwerp's docks, feeling their way along the silty bottom through the frigid, turbid basins. No mines were found for three days in mid-November, and the Royal Navy proclaimed the Scheldt safe only to rescind the declaration after nine explosions on November 22 and 23 sent the sweepers back to work. Two hundred and sixty-seven mines had been cleared before the *Fort Cataraqui* could lead her convoy up the channel.

Twenty more ships arrived in the next two days, and by mid-December Antwerp would be unloading 23,000 tons a day—half of all U.S. cargo arriving in northwestern Europe, exclusive of Marseille. Day and night, ships steamed in and out of the great port, past endless rows of squat warehouses, bells ringing, whistles tooting, gulls screaming. Six thousand civilian stevedores and nine thousand quay workers swarmed over the docks, complemented by as many military laborers. Unloading began as the first hawser was tossed to waiting hands on the wharf, and typically thirteen hours later the last cargo net rose from the final hold before the empty vessel cast off to make for the open sea. In addition to more than two hundred berths and six hundred cranes, Antwerp boasted the densest rail network in Europe, with nineteen miles of track per square mile; even so, thanks to shortages of rolling stock and COMZ miscalculations, within a fortnight 85,000 tons of matériel was piled high beneath tarpaulins and in sheds behind the quays, awaiting more railcars and the construction of depots in Lille, Mons, and elsewhere. A dozen ammunition ships had been scheduled among the first convoys, but fears that an accidental explosion or a V-weapon would wreck the port more savagely than any enemy saboteur caused delays until the vessels could be diverted to isolated berths in a far corner of the harbor.

Explosions had already become all too commonplace in Antwerp that fall, beginning with the first V-2 rocket to hit the city on October 7, followed by the first V-1 flying bomb four days later. Both V-1s and V-2s struck on October 13, damaging paintings in the Museum of Fine Arts and killing or wounding more than two dozen butchers in the municipal slaughterhouse. ("Something beastly fell in Antwerp yesterday," British intelligence reported.) An orphanage that also served as a hospital was subsequently demolished, killing thirty-two people, including a surgical team and several orphans crushed beneath a collapsing wall. On November 27, just hours before the first convoy steamed up the Scheldt, a V-2 detonated in Teniersplaats as a military convoy rolled through the intersection, killing 157 and rupturing water mains so that body parts and women's handbags floated in a new downtown lake; the torso of a military policeman was found on a rooftop two hundred feet from the blast.

Barely above sea level, Antwerp lacked subway tunnels and deep cellars for shelter; GIs now called it "the city of sudden death." Sixteen thousand troops assigned to the port had been housed in brick apartment buildings, but the onslaught forced them to tent encampments dispersed outside town. Army engineers took emergency courses on how to extricate buried survivors from collapsed buildings. Window glass became scarce, as it had in London. A V-weapon hit a public toilet, crushing several men beneath heavy porcelain urinals, and streetwalkers could be seen brushing debris from their fur coats after an explosion in the red-light district. The shattering of a fragrance shop perfumed the air for days, "a heavy, incongruous, unwanted smell," the GI magazine *Yank* reported. The revived city opera gamely staged *La Bohème* and then *Carmen*; a naval officer recounted how a V-1 growled overhead during one performance "while the cast continued singing, and not a soul moved from their seats in the packed auditorium."

Hitler had long recognized Antwerp's strategic value, and in mid-October he had ordered all V-2s concentrated exclusively on either the port or London. German launch crews over the course of six months would fling 1,712 V-2s and 4,248 V-1s at Antwerp—usually more than thirty each day, but sometimes fourfold that number. Sixty-seven thousand buildings in greater Antwerp would be damaged or destroyed, including two-thirds of all houses; two cargo ships and fifty-eight smaller vessels would be sunk. Despite the battering of rail lines, roads, quays, and cranes, good fortune and V-weapon imprecision allowed port operations to remain largely unimpaired. Equally important was a stupendous Allied defensive effort involving 22,000 antiaircraft artillerymen who were secretly organized into a unit named Antwerp X. Three parallel defensive belts southeast of the city, each roughly six miles apart, deployed six hundred guns that hammered away around the clock, with new gun barrels and ammunition stocks flown from the United States as needed. Seventy-two searchlights and six thousand miles of new telephone wire strengthened the city's early warning system, and more than three million sandbags helped shield Antwerp against blast.

German V-1 crews in December abruptly opened a new attack azimuth by launching from the northeast, shortening the warning period from eight minutes to less than four. Sometimes as many as eight flying bombs approached Antwerp simultaneously, a U.S. study reported, with "the characteristic roar of the motor in flight, the stream of flame flying to the rear, the cutoff, silent dive, and violent detonation." Yet nimble gun crews proved proficient: by one calculation, 211 V-1s would strike within eight miles of central Antwerp, while 2,200 others were destroyed in midair or crashed in open tracts. Hundreds of others flew far afield, failed to leave the launch rail, or otherwise misfired.

The V-2, of course, was a different beast, and invulnerable against Allied defenses. "The angel of death is abroad in the land," Churchill had said of the missile, "only you can't hear the flutter of his wings."

Nearly twelve hundred seats were filled in the Rex Cinema on bustling Avenue De Keyser for the Friday afternoon matinee on December 15. During the occupation, only German films were screened, and Belgian moviegoers since Antwerp's liberation in early September had been keen to catch up on years of American and British movies unavailable since the war began. Shortages of film stock—cellulose was also an ingredient in gunpowder—had not prevented Hollywood from producing thirteen hundred films in the past three years. More than a quarter of them were war movies, but today the Rex, which occupied a former pub owned by the Belgian Socialist Party, was showing a classic western: *The Plainsman,* a Cecil B. De Mille melodrama starring Gary Cooper as Wild Bill Hickock and Jean Arthur as Calamity Jane. The film had limited merits as a history of the American frontier—in 113 minutes, De Mille also managed to get Abraham Lincoln, Buffalo Bill Cody, General George Armstrong Custer, and a Cheyenne chief named Yellow Hand onto the screen—but the audience seemed rapt.

At 3:20 P.M., just after Gary Cooper learned of Custer's death at the Little Bighorn, a searing white light flashed across the auditorium as a V-2—unheard and unseen, launched from a new site in Holland—blew through the roof. The one-ton warhead detonated in the mezzanine with a roar audible on the Scheldt, "spewing up the inside" of the theater, as a witness reported. In an instant the huge screen pitched forward, and the balcony and ceiling plummeted onto patrons seated on the main floor.

Two hundred rescuers toiled for a week with cranes, bulldozers, and acetylene torches. One crew freed a GI who had been trapped for hours, *Yank* reported:

When he stumbled out, he held two dead children in his arms. A Red Cross worker tried to take them away from him, but he savagely refused. . . . He had been sitting next to their mother whose head had been blown off. . . . The town is too small for the tragedy.

Recovery teams ultimately retrieved 567 bodies, more than half of them Allied soldiers, Navy gun crews, and merchant mariners. Four were German prisoners paroled for the afternoon. Another 200 servicemen were badly injured. Belgian victims included husbands, wives, and children fused together by the blast. Searchers found a dead girl in the balcony, a *Yank* reporter wrote, "half smiling, with the lipstick and makeup on her face untouched. Next to her was a row of soldiers looking straight ahead as if they were still absorbed in the movie." The city zoo became a morgue, but the stench in the Rex grew so awful that chemical decontamination squads had to spray bodies still pinned in the wreckage before work could continue.

Those who perished before the final reel of *The Plainsman* never saw Wild Bill shot in the back while playing cards in Deadwood, nor a heartbroken Calamity Jane cradling his body at the end of the movie. City officials promptly closed all cinemas and other theaters for the duration. Carmen would not sing again in Antwerp until peace returned and the angel of death was no longer abroad in the land.

"Faith in a Friendly Universe"

DESPITE the travails of the Hürtgen Forest, Omar Bradley's optimism rebounded, and he assured his lieutenants that Operation QUEEN—the 12th Army Group assault designed to scourge enemy defenses east and north of Aachen—would be "the last big offensive necessary to bring Germany to her knees." Bradley shuttled between Luxembourg City and Spa, consolidating his divisions, encouraging his commanders, and scrutinizing weather forecasts. A successful lunge through the German lines to Düren could carry across the Roer River another twenty-five miles to the Rhine, he believed, replicating the breakout from St.-Lô to the Seine.

Just past the meridian on November 16, twenty-four hundred heavy bombers dropped ten thousand tons of high explosives and incendiaries on targets near Aachen—so much brimstone that a surrendering German confessed, "I feel very good about being captured." Then gusts of white flame leaped from twelve hundred artillery tubes across the front, and shells by the tens of thousands detonated downrange "like yellow blossoms bursting on a gray wallpaper," wrote the correspondent W. C. Heinz.

Fluorescent orange sheets draped the decks of surging Sherman tanks, identifying them as friendly to the fighter-bombers swarming overhead, and infantry shock battalions again surged eastward toward the Roer, in that hunched scamper of exposed men trying to make themselves small. The sound of musketry became general, and it was said that the soldiers "all had the same expression because they had no expression at all." In some sectors, sixty-inch searchlights, each like a tiny sun with 800 million candlepower, would point the way through the autumnal gloom, illuminating minefields and bedazzling defenders.

The entrenched enemy quickly stiffened. In Collins's VII Corps, which spearheaded First Army on the right with nine attacking infantry regiments and an armored combat command, some companies managed only eight hundred yards before dusk. Tanks made a modest dent in the Stolberg corridor, but at a price: forty-four of the sixty-four Shermans at the point of the spear. In four days, the 1st Division would advance two miles and lose a thousand men; the next two miles cost another three thousand casualties. The 104th Division, commanded by Major General Terry de la Mesa Allen, who had led the adjacent Big Red One in Africa and Sicily, outflanked the town of Eschweiler, where still-hot food and burning candles evidenced an enemy decamping in haste. But even after a week, General Hodges would find the Roer several miles beyond his grasp, and the battle reduced to a "house-by-house killing match." Nor did Ninth Army on the left fare much better in attacking the plashy, mine-infested crescent between the rivers Wurm and Roer, where fifty stone villages had been converted into Wehrmacht citadels. As of November 22, XIX Corps had advanced three or four miles, fighting not only Model's legions, but mud, despair, and a dozen types of mine.

Thirty days hath November, and only on two of them did it neither rain nor snow. Rainfall was triple the monthly average. Rain grayed the soldiers, as it had in Italy, melding them with the mud until they seemed no more than clay with eyes, as ugly as the beet and cabbage fields in which they fought. Radios and mine detectors shorted out, trucks bogged to the bumpers, and frozen mud made wool coats unbearably bulky. "Men were forced to discard their overcoats because they lacked the strength to wear them," a staff officer noted. "Their hands are so numb that they have to help one another on with their equipment." Riflemen tied kerchiefs around the triggers and bolts of their M-1s in a futile effort to keep them clean; condoms or the waxed paper from ration crackers covered the muzzles. Army ordnance shops and French fabricators made a million or more "duck bills," five-inch steel cleats welded onto tank tracks to widen their purchase and give them better traction in the mud. A single Sherman could wear over three hundred of the things and still get stuck.

This was "thee or me" combat, in a First Army phrase, and it made men sardonic, fatalistic, and deeply sad. A soldier in the 5th Division wrote home, "They say cleanliness is next to Godliness. I say it's next to impossible. . . . If I am killed and go to hell it can't be any worse than infantry combat." A nineteen-year-old comrade wrote, "With every heartbeat I seemed to hear a voice, relentlessly, and ever louder, saying, 'It's coming, it's coming, it's coming, nearer, nearer.'" A quartermaster soldier almost hit by a German shell told Robert Capa, "That one sounded like, 'You ain't goin' back to Alabama.'" Most soldiers now "didn't bother to button our flies," a GI in the 78th Division reported. "Convenience for frequent emptying of a nervous bladder was preferable to pissing your pants." An intelligence officer who would serve six terms as governor of Arkansas, Major Orval E. Faubus, found that he could no longer recall when the hollyhocks bloomed in his native Ozarks. "One forgets so much," he mused. When his young son wrote that he had just seen *Snow White*, Faubus buckled. "I wonder," he asked, "why I had to love him so much."

Even the best soldiers frayed. Lieutenant Colonel Creighton Abrams, a storied tank commander who eventually would wear four stars, wrote his wife:

> My heart and soul have been torn and seared by so many things already, by losses, by frustrations, by errors. . . . I haven't been dry, I haven't been warm, except for quick naps I haven't slept for two weeks. There's no time to eat right, there's no time to think—it's attack, attack, attack.

"War happens inside a man," Eric Sevareid concluded. "It happens to one man alone. It can never be communicated. . . . A million martyred lives leave an empty place at only one family table." Among the empty chairs was that of Captain Thomas F. O'Brien, a New Hampshire boy killed on his birthday in the opening hours of Operation QUEEN. "He did not suffer very long," the company war diary recorded, "perhaps ten minutes." Succeeding him in command of the 16th Infantry's Cannon Company was his best friend, Captain Jack E. Golden, who like many 1st Division veterans battled recurrent malaria contracted in the Mediterranean. "I feel about eighty years old now," Golden told his family in Texas. He was twenty-two.

> You get so tired you stop doing small things that are important to your safety and if you get tired enough you don't care whether you live or die. . . . We gamble life and death. Daddy, you will understand this. Just like in cards you may win night after night but you can't be lucky always. . . . I am always scared to death.

As fresh reserves came forward, legions of dead men were removed to the rear. Each field army developed assembly lines to handle five hundred bodies a day; under government regulations, twenty-five sufficed to open a new temporary cemetery. Great pains were taken to identify remains whenever possible. Innovative techniques allowed fingerprints to be lifted from bodies long buried and for hidden laundry marks to be extracted from shredded uniforms. Graves Registration artisans meticulously reconstructed mutilated faces with cosmetic wax so that Signal Corps photographs could be taken to help identify those without dogtags. Reuniting a dead man and his name was the last great service that could be rendered a comrade gone west.

For the living, small pleasures helped pass the time, since, as one soldier told his diary in November, "the process of making history is 90 percent boredom." Blackjack and poker games raged in muddy beet-and-turnip burrows ten feet square, each illuminated by an old canteen filled with kerosene and a sock wick. During mail call, wrote the soldier-poet Karl Shapiro, "war stands aside for an hour. . . . A world is made human." One officer told his wife that he had spent thirty minutes in an abandoned house "pulling the chain of a sit-down latrine and listening to the melodious crashing of water, just like home."

Even for those who would outlive the war and die abed as old men in the next century, these were the most intense moments they would ever know. "I've learned what it means to be alive, to breathe and to feel," a lieutenant in the 82nd Airborne wrote his sister. "I have seen men do such things, both good and bad, that surely the recording angel in heaven must rejoice and despair of them." None could doubt that war would transform them, that at least some corner of the soul would never be what it once was. "I can see now," a soldier in the 84th Division wrote his father on November 26, "how a man changes greatly."

Operation QUEEN sputtered and stalled. After more than three weeks, Ninth Army closed to the west bank of the Roer, but not to the Rhine as Bradley had hoped. VII Corps in First Army would not reach the Roer until mid-December, requiring thirty-one days to move seven miles, or fifty feet an hour. Together the two armies suffered 38,000 battle casualties. In the three months since Staff Sergeant Holzinger became the first GI to set foot on German soil, the Allies had nowhere penetrated the border by more than twenty-two miles. Total American losses for the fall—killed, wounded, died of wounds, died of illness, died in accidents, missing, captured, sick, injured, battle-fatigued, imprisoned, suicides—climbed to 140,000.

The face reconstructors and the grave diggers stayed busy. SHAEF in

October had set quotas for valor awards lest they be disbursed too promiscuously; each infantry division could give out three Distinguished Service Crosses, thirty-five Silver Stars, and seventy-nine Bronze Stars for every week in combat. Now the quotas seemed niggardly, and Eisenhower ordered the policy revised.

The Roer, already in spate from daily rain, remained susceptible to deliberate flooding. After several postponements for bad weather and at least one mission in which the navigators got lost, the Royal Air Force in early December dropped nearly two thousand tons on the Schwammenauel, the Urft, and other dams. Many direct hits did only enough damage to create a bit of sloshing downstream, and the RAF soon went back to smashing cities. SHAEF censors banned all reference to the dams in press dispatches, as if the enemy might not have noticed the Allies' belated interest. Had even one of the four Army corps in QUEEN been able to fight on to the Rhine, the German plan for a surprise winter offensive—already far advanced—would no doubt have been disrupted if not undone. But no crossing of the Roer was yet feasible and the Rhine remained beyond reach.

Certainly the enemy had been badly hurt. The initial bombing had pulverized several Roer towns. Various German units disembarking from trains or otherwise vulnerable in Jülich and Düren were butchered. Of eight infantry battalions in one Volksgrenadier division, none could now muster even a hundred men. Twenty-two thousand gallons of napalm encouraged 8,000 Germans to surrender in the Ninth Army sector, among 100,000 prisoners who passed through 12th Army Group cages that fall. Enemy commanders were reduced to throwing clerks, engineers, and even veterinarians into the line. "Great losses," a German officer added, "were occasioned by numerous frostbites."

Yet there was no sign that Germany was on her knees, as Bradley had anticipated, and even he felt a resurgent gloom. "It is entirely possible," he told a War Department visitor, "for the Germans to fight bitter delaying actions until 1 January 1946."

Winter always seemed to catch the U.S. Army by surprise. The Americans had been unprepared for winter campaigning in the Atlas Mountains of Tunisia in 1942 and in the Apennines of Italy in 1943, and they were just as unready in 1944. Even before OVERLORD, War Department queries about cold-weather preparations had been mostly dismissed with a resentful scowl by Eisenhower's provisioners. Arctic clothing tested at Anzio was offered to SHAEF but rejected as unnecessary. The Army's quartermaster general in mid-August had predicted that "the war would not go into another winter," and Major General Robert M. Littlejohn, the chief quartermaster in Europe, agreed that "the serious fighting cannot long continue." In mid-September, Hodges assured his uneasy medical officers, "Don't you know that this war is going to be over in a few weeks?" A late requisition for winter clothing was submitted to the War Department "as a precautionary measure," but it included only enough to outfit one army of 350,000 soldiers at a time when four American armies were fighting in western Europe.

The alarming German resilience of late October had inspired Littlejohn to urge Bradley to expedite shipments of cold-weather kit to the battlefront. "General, the weather is getting cold. Soon you will need some winter clothing," the quartermaster told him in Luxembourg City. Bradley waved off the warning, saying, in Littlejohn's recollection, "The men are tough and can take it." Supply-line sclerosis and delays in opening Antwerp aggravated matters, as did the severe wear on all uniforms and equipment: even as theater commanders in late September belatedly requested 850,000 heavy overcoats—double the number contemplated just a month earlier—plus five million sets of wool undershirts and drawers, quartermasters faced a need to reclothe a million ragged U.S. soldiers, as well as 100,000 French troops and throngs of German prisoners. "We can't fight a winter war in the same clothes that we use in the summer," Captain Jack Golden wrote his family. "We should have learned a little last winter in Italy."

Instead, as the Army official history conceded, "front-line troops fought through a large part of the winter inadequately clothed." Far less than half of the requested underwear reached the theater, despite Littlejohn's contention that "wool is essential to combat, as much as ammunition." Shortages of wool socks in medium sizes forced Army laundries to try shrinking size 12 pairs, even as unintended shrinkage remained a galling problem, with a "high failure rate in all woolens." Three field launderings were typically enough to ruin a pair of socks, so the Army had to buy seven million new pairs a month.

The Army listed seventy different articles of winter clothing, guaranteeing a thousand permutations of confusion. Six different field jackets reached Europe, for example, and seven types of trousers. The "jacket, field, M-43" came in nineteen sizes, while the "jacket, field, pile" liner came in only thirteen, thus confounding mathematical efforts to match them. Attempts to develop decent sleeping bags were byzantine. The Harvard University Fatigue Laboratory invented a measuring unit of insulation called the "Clo," with one Clo defined as the protection provided by an ordinary business suit when worn in an Alaskan winter. A single bag of quilted down and waterfowl feathers rated seven Clos, while two layers of Army blankets covered with a cotton windbreaker earned four. More than sixty bag variants were tested, including some made of chopped chicken and turkey feathers, milkweed floss, and reindeer hide, but the materials mattered little if the bags failed to reach the field armies, as, in 1944, they commonly did.

The Army was said to believe that every GI was fashioned from four elements—a belly, genitalia, a bundle of conditioned reflexes, and a pair of feet. Insufficient attention was paid to the last of these components, for among body parts it was the foot that most plagued the American war effort in Europe. Four types of GI footgear were available in late fall, "none of which were entirely satisfactory," as a Pentagon investigation found. Combat boots fitted in warm weather were often too tight to accommodate more than a single pair of socks, and in rain and snow the boot was "nothing but a sponge tied around the soldier's foot," as General Littlejohn acknowledged. Far too few overshoes had been requisitioned, and virtually none larger than size 11 arrived before March 1945; half of the several million pairs eventually shipped to Europe proved too delicate to tug over a combat boot. The "shoepac," a rubber-and-leather boot designed to be worn with two pairs of heavy socks, was ill-fitting and leaky. Until December, only enough were requisitioned for a small fraction of the GIs who needed them, and far too few in widths E, EE, and EEE.

And so the soldier suffered. The first case of trench foot—a crippling injury to blood vessels and tissue caused by prolonged exposure to cold, wet conditions—had been reported on September 27. Within weeks, the syndrome was epidemic. "We are making some progress in the prevention of trench foot," Eisenhower wrote Marshall on November 27. That was untrue. In November and December trench foot and other cold weather health problems hospitalized 23,000 men, nearly all of them combat infantrymen—a loss equivalent to the infantry strength of five and a half divisions. By late November, trench foot accounted for one-quarter of all hospital admissions. In Third Army, where trench foot was particularly virulent, physicians reported that almost none of the afflicted soldiers would return to duty before spring; four in ten eventually were evacuated home as disabled. A 30th Division account described "long lines of cots on which lay soldier after soldier, their feet sticking out from under the blankets, with a little ball of cotton wool separating each toe."

Almost nothing had been learned from the Italian campaign, despite ample warnings after the experience of the previous winter. Nor had the Americans learned from the British or the Germans, who enforced prophylactic measures such as dry socks, foot massages, frequent inspections, and soldier education. Many GIs were told to lace their boots tighter, precisely the wrong advice. Bradley, who acknowledged soldiers "not having their wet shoes off for periods of five to ten days," warned in late November that 12th Army Group could lose a thousand men to trench foot every day. In the event, 46,000 troops would be hospitalized by spring, almost 10 percent of admitted casualties in Europe, an avoidable calamity even worse than the malaria epidemic that had decimated Allied armies in Sicily. By Army regulation, trench foot patients, unlike frostbite victims, were ineligible for the Purple Heart, and some commanders likened the disgrace of trench foot to that of a venereal disease.

As every buck private knew, the weather would get worse before it got better. First Army meteorologists in one forecast put the chance of sunshine at "1 in 1,000." Axle-deep mud caused a soldier to write that he had "never realized its omnipresence, persistency, and mucilaginous qualities. I especially dislike wading through it to get food." Soldiers complained that conditions were so awful that they risked "trench body." Men coped as they could by rubbing peppermint extract on their toes, or wedging newspaper in their shoes and around their genitals, or kneeling rather than standing in foxholes, or building sleeping platforms above warm dungheaps, or fashioning homemade footwear from wool blankets and overshoes. An antiaircraft gunner who noticed Eisenhower's fleece-lined boots during a visit to the front offered five hundred francs for the pair. The supreme commander pulled off the boots and offered them in trade for "one dead Kraut."

The soldiers' misery contributed to a spike in combat exhaustion, a medical diagnosis coined in Tunisia to replace the discredited "shell shock" of World War I. The brutal fighting, oppressive conditions, and recognition that the war was far from over took a profound psychic toll, not least among troops said to be "ghosted," haunted by the memory of dead comrades. "Each moment of combat imposes a strain so great that men will break down in direct relation to the intensity and duration of their exposure," the theater surgeon general told Eisenhower. "Thus psychiatric casualties are as inevitable as gunshot and shrapnel wounds in warfare."

Those evacuated from the front with combat exhaustion—some were so badly unhinged they had to be immobilized by tying their boot laces together and lashing gun belts around their arms—were said to be "going back to the kitchen." So many thousands now headed to the kitchen that SHAEF censors banned disclosure of their numbers; the public would not know that the U.S. Army alone hospitalized 929,000 men for "neuropsychiatric" reasons in World War II, including as many as one in four admissions during the bitter fall of 1944. "I can't take much more of this fighting because it is getting the best of me," an infantryman wrote his family. "This nerve business I've been trying to cover up from my own men, but I'm sure they have noticed it because I've noticed it in some of them."

In contrast to the Army's nonchalance about cold-weather injuries, the military had learned much in the Mediterranean about combat exhaustion, and that experience served the ranks well in western Europe. Most patients were treated as temporarily disabled and kept close to the front, to preserve their self-respect and emotional links to their unit. Division clearing stations now usually included a psychiatrist; as in Italy, exhausted patients often were put into a deep sleep, sometimes for days, with "Blue 88s," sodium amytal or nembutal capsules. Of every one hundred exhaustion patients hospitalized in the European theater, ninety returned to duty in some capacity, although many were finished as killer riflemen.

But neither competent treatment nor all the Blue 88s in Europe could efface war's capacity to fracture men's psyches. "Between the physical fear of going forward and the moral fear of turning back, there is a predicament of exceptional awkwardness," an American Civil War veteran had once observed, and that dilemma still obtained. "The only way one could get out of battle," a Canadian psychiatrist wrote, "was death, wounds, self-inflicted wounds, and going 'nuts.'" Lieutenant Paul Fussell, who would narrowly survive the war to become one of its shrewdest expositors, believed that "after five months of combat duty, a frontline officer is used up, neurasthenic beyond saving." Most experts concluded that soldiers wore out for good after 200 to 240 days of battle, although two psychologists monitoring the advance into Germany posited that a GI's combat skills began to decline after a month of fighting, with many "close to a vegetative state" after forty-five days. One soldier who had been wounded for a second time tried to explain in a letter home why he was still hospitalized. "I'm not badly injured," he wrote. "But I guess I'm hurt, Pop. Hurt inside—in my brain."

How to mitigate such psychic battering would remain a quandary, as it had been since Homer's day. "Morale is a darkling plain, littered with dead clichés, swept by pronunciamentos, and only fitfully lit up by the electrical play of insight," an AAF study declared. The Army's surgeon general recommended that frontline infantrymen be relieved for six months after completing two hundred days in combat, but the nation lacked enough replacements to effect such a solution. "Under present policy no man is removed from combat duty until he has become worthless," a report to Eisenhower noted. "The infantryman considers this a bitter injustice." One chaplain was reduced to suggesting that "sound mental health requires a satisfactory life-purpose and faith in a friendly universe." On the battlefields of Europe in 1944, no such cosmology seemed likely.

George Patton had encamped in a villa with a grilled gateway at 10 Rue Auxerre in Nancy, not far from the World War I battlefields where he had first won glory as a tank commander. Owned by a French coal baron, the mansion was said by one visitor to be "filled with the most impossible bric-a-brac, including gilded angels three feet high and cherubs hanging from the ceilings, cheap and showy statuary lining the halls along with dull green, brown, and purple tapestries." Aides drove to Burgundy on wine-buying sprees, and Willie the timid bull terrier often dozed on a chair by the sideboard. Eleven-inch German rail guns twenty-five miles away had found Third Army's range, occasionally lobbing 600-pound shells into Nancy, including three rounds that broke the windows and doorjambs at No. 10 one night, while wrecking the house across the street.

Patton swanned about Lorraine with studied insouciance, loudly singing the obscene verses of "Lilly from Piccadilly" in his open jeep with its bleating klaxon and three-star insignia front and rear. To one reporter he showed off his famous ivory-handled pistol—"I killed my first man with it"—but he turned down a $250,000 offer for his diary from the Hearst newspaper empire. The discretion was well-advised: recent entries suggested that "Ike is the best general the British have" and that Third Army had been "halted to save Monty's face." Patton also speculated that supply allocations in the field were somehow adjusted to affect electoral politics at home, "a most sinister idea." When Eisenhower ordered fifty thousand men in XV Corps transferred from Third Army to Seventh Army for better logistical support through Marseille, Patton confided to his diary that the new 6th Army Group commander in southern France, Lieutenant General Jake Devers, "is a liar and, by his glibness, talked Eisenhower into giving him the corps. . . . May God rot his guts."

Incessant rain made Patton even more peevish. Picking up a spoon in the Rue Auxerre dining room during another downpour, he bent it double and grumbled, "How long, O Lord, how long?" To Bea he wrote, employing his unique orthography, "Send me a couple of bottles of pink medicin. When I am not attacking I get bilious. . . . It is raining like hell—what a country."

Because of the *Westwall*'s eastward bow, which traced the German border, Third Army still had not approached the Siegfried Line. The removal of XV Corps and other large units had shrunk Patton's strength by 100,000 men, to 250,000, although as Bradley's right wing he still mustered six infantry and three armored divisions, along with thirty-eight additional field artillery and fourteen tank destroyer battalions on a seventy-five-mile front. In keeping with Eisenhower's strategy to close on the Rhine along the entire Allied line—the same concept that had spawned Operation QUEEN and the relentless head-butting in the Hürtgen—Third Army's immediate target remained the industrial Saar and the great river beyond. Yet the Rhine remained 130 miles away. Between here and there stood not only scores of manure-stacked Lorraine villages and obdurate German defensive works, but also one of the most rigorously fortified cities in Europe.

Metz had become an obsession for Patton. His earlier plan to blow past the city on his way to Berlin had been frustrated by supply shortages, unexpected enemy resistance, Allied politics, and those relentless rains that robbed the American Army of its mobility. Now he was determined to reduce this ancient citadel with a double envelopment and a direct thrust across the Moselle, which virtually enfolded Metz and provided a natural breastwork to the west.

Patton claimed that Metz had not fallen to assault since being sacked by Huns in 451, but in fact the Germans had taken it from the French in 1870, only to lose it again after World War I. Fortified and refortified over the centuries—Vauban told Louis XIV that the city was designed to defend not just a province but all of France—Metz was now a sprawling constellation of forty-three forts. Some were built to bolster the interwar Maginot Line, but the most modern works faced west. More than a dozen nineteenth-century redoubts arranged in an inner circle currently served as strongpoints, while a casemated outer ring, built by Germans after the Franco-Prussian War and strengthened upon Hitler's annexation of Lorraine in 1940, included fuming guns nested in rotating steel turrets, deep dry moats sixty feet wide, and interlocking fields of fire that swept all avenues. Mines, barbed wire, and murderous machine-gun nests complemented the concrete bastions. Patton's explanation that "we're using Metz to blood the new divisions" vexed Bradley, although not enough to overrule his army commander. "Leave it alone," Bradley urged. "For God's sake, lay off it. . . . You are taking too many casualties for what you are accomplishing." Patton ignored the criticism, telling his diary that "the tent maker"— Omar—was "too conservative. . . . I wish he had a little more daring."

Daring had thus far gained naught. The September fiasco at Dornot was followed by an October debacle at Fort Driant, described by one historian as "probably the most formidable and well-prepared fortification that the American Army attempted to reduce in all of World War II." A three-hundred-acre slab of concrete overlooking the Moselle valley, five miles southwest of Metz, Driant was said by Army intelligence to be "manned by about 100 old men and boys, whose morale is low." Not true: it was stoutly defended by diehards behind walls seven feet thick, with a pentagonal central fort supplied through arterial tunnels. Neither American bombs, nor napalm, nor point-blank artillery salvos by Third Army's biggest guns had any discernible effect; nor did day after day of infantry attacks that included pouring hot oil through Driant's gun embrasures. "We were attempting to assault a medieval fortress in a medieval man-

ner," wrote a reporter with the 5th Infantry Division. Patton ordered his XX Corps to throw every last man at Driant if necessary because, as his chief of staff noted in the command diary, "he could not allow an attack by this army to fail."

It failed anyway. After a week's hard fighting, GIs had reduced only two peripheral barracks outside Driant, while the enemy still held five main casemates. Patton scolded his generals, suggesting that miscreants atone for their failings by personally leading the next attack, "or not come back." But by mid-October the assault had collapsed—Third Army's first substantial reverse. (Efforts were made to keep the bad news out of the papers.) In an October 19 letter to Lieutenant General Jimmy Doolittle, commander of Eighth Air Force, Patton wrote, "Those low bastards, the Germans, gave me my first bloody nose when they compelled us to abandon our attack on Fort Driant in the Metz area." He requested "a revenge bombardment," with "large bombs of the nastiest type, and as many as you can spare, to blow up this damn fort so that it becomes nothing but a hole."

Even the largest, nastiest bombs failed to reduce Driant, and Patton now planned a bigger, broader attack on Metz, the biggest and broadest of his life. After stockpiling ammunition for several weeks, he wrote in his diary on Sunday, November 5:

> Had a bad case of short breath this morning—my usual reaction to an impending fight or match. Went to church. . . . Had Marlene Dietrich and her troupe for lunch. Later they gave us a show. Very low comedy, almost an insult to human intelligence.

A day later he met with the reporters covering Third Army. "I told you we were going to be stopped for a while, and I was correct," he told them. "Now we are going to start again. You do some lying and say this is simply what we called in the last war 'correcting a line.'" To Bea he confessed, "I am having indigestion and the heaves as I always do before a match. I suppose I would be no good if I did not; it is not fear as to the result but simply anxiety to get started."

Rain fell for a third consecutive day, giving Patton what one correspondent described as "a tired, aged appearance." Two senior commanders arrived at the house on Rue Auxerre at seven o'clock on Tuesday evening, dripping amid the bric-a-brac and the cherubim peering down from the ceiling. The officers pleaded for a postponement of the attack until the skies cleared and the swollen rivers subsided. Patton refused.

He woke at three A.M. on Wednesday, November 8, to the thrum of rain on the roof. Patton had deliberately chosen this day to commemorate the TORCH landings in Morocco two years before; now, padding around the bedroom, he reminded himself to forgo the counsel of his fears and thumbed through a copy of Rommel's World War I memoir, *Infantry Attacks*. He was sufficiently consoled by the account of foul weather on the Western Front in September 1914 to once more fall asleep.

Four hundred guns roused him again at 5:15, a sound he likened to "very many doors all slamming at once." Third Army would shoot tens of thousands of shells that day; through the front curtains, this first barrage made the northeastern sky gleam as if kindled by heat lightning. The rain had stopped, and stars sprinkled the heavens above Nancy. "I thanked God for His goodness to me," Patton scribbled in his diary.

Bradley phoned at 7:45 to wish him luck, then put Eisenhower on the line. "I expect great things of you," the supreme commander said. "Carry the ball all the way." At ten A.M., from a XII Corps observation post overlooking the Moselle south of Metz, Patton watched hundreds of fighter-bombers pirouette in the morning sun before blistering enemy command posts and artillery batteries. "I'm almost sorry for those German bastards," he muttered. Smoke screens boiled across the river, at its highest flood stage since 1919, and three infantry divisions from XII Corps lunged forward, to be followed by a fourth in the afternoon. Two armored divisions coiled in the brakes and hollows, ready to exploit any fracture in the German line. The rains returned at five P.M., but Patton sensed momentum in his attack. At supper that night, an aide reported, "for the first time in days he was relaxed and talkative."

Doolittle's air fleets on Thursday brought more of those big, nasty bombs Patton favored—1,300 heavies dumping 2,600 tons on seven Metz forts in Operation MADISON. Dropped through dense overcast by bombardiers relying on murky radar images, more than 98 percent of the payloads missed their targets, often by miles. The infantry soldiered on, resupplied with rations, plasma, ammunition, and toilet paper tossed from the cockpit doors of single-engine spotter planes flying at ten to twenty feet, too low for German antiaircraft crews to depress their 20mm guns. As part of a XX Corps attack north of the city, gutful troops from the 358th Infantry scampered across the roof of Fort Koenigsmacker, blowing open steel doors with satchel charges and dumping gasoline and thermite grenades down ventilation shafts. Though badly flayed by German machine guns, the men rejected an order to fall back, replying by radio, "This fort is ours." Soon it was: almost four hundred Germans emerged with their hands raised, the first Metz bastion to fall.

Almost half a mile wide, the Moselle rose farther until water lapped through villages fronting the river. Floodwaters inundated German minefields, which helped eight battalions from the 90th Division get a purchase on the far bank, but building a bridge to carry tanks took days. Engineers blue with cold and wearing flak jackets struggled to hold bridge pontoons in place against the bully current and crashing artillery. "The air seemed filled with white tracers," a nineteen-year-old soldier in the 5th Division reported. "Men would get up in front of me, head toward the trees and, as a string of tracers would pass through them, [fall] to the ground or into the stream."

"Groans, suffering, and pain. Men shot to pieces," a surgical technician entered in his diary. "All wards were completely filled, also the barber shop, supply tent, pharmacy, and laboratory tents. And finally, the mess tent filled up." A surgeon toiling over the mangled legs of a soldier whose jeep triggered a mine described "bolts, washers, [and] bushings in the muscle, as on a work bench." Another GI was wounded when a shell detonated in a barnyard, "filling his thigh from knee to buttocks with manure, all tightly packed . . . as into a sausage." Wounded men who had narrowly escaped death lay in silence on the ward cots, the surgeon added, "like somebody rescued from the ledge of a skyscraper." Patton spent his fifty-ninth birthday on November 11 "by getting up where the dead were still warm," as he wrote Bea. "However the enemy must be suffering more, so it is a question of mutual crucifiction [*sic*] till he cracks."

On November 14, nearly a week into the offensive, engineers finished a Bailey bridge north of the city. Early the next morning, the 10th Armored Division rumbled over the Moselle in a spitting sleet storm, threatening a wide envelopment in tandem with the 90th Division, twenty miles above Metz, complemented by a shallower swing in the south by the 6th Armored and 80th Infantry Divisions. As other forces pinched the city's near flanks, the 95th Division battered German garrison forces west of the river; many of these were the overage or infirm troops known as *Halb-soldaten*, half soldiers. Eisenhower arrived for a visit on November 15, tromping about in the mud before dining with Patton on the Rue Auxerre. "It was very jolly," an aide noted, "and the two generals sat up and talked until after two A.M."

Battlefield advances made them jolly. The next day, Patton more than doubled the daily artillery allocation for XII Corps to twenty thousand rounds, explaining, "If we win now we will not need shells later; if we do not use the shells now, we will not win the war." Hitler had twice rebuffed Rundstedt's suggestion to abandon Metz, but Nazi functionaries fled in stolen Renaults and Citroëns. The city water system had been smashed, ammunition was short, and reinforcements were so feeble—including constables armed with ancient French rifles and decrepit supernumeraries wearing brassards in lieu of uniforms—that a Wehrmacht general described them as "drops of water on a hot stone." The phones failed on November 17 as the last German civilians were evacuated to the east by a police escort from Darmstadt. A new garrison commander summoned from the Eastern Front, General Heinrich Kittel, was made to swear an oath to defend the city "to the last man and cartridge," the usual immolation blithely demanded of those in harm's way by those far from it.

At 10:30 A.M. on November 19, the two wings of Third Army completed the encirclement of Metz when soldiers from the 5th Division met cavalry troopers from the 90th seven miles east of the city, in Retonfey. Patton's two corps now held a line ten to twenty miles east of where they had begun eleven days earlier. In Metz, the end came quickly, with mercifully few room-to-room brawls. Six thousand prisoners were captured; General Kittel was discovered on November 21 in an underground field hospital, suffused with morphine after being badly wounded while fighting in the line. The city formally surrendered at 2:35 P.M. the next day.

Patton drove into Metz as the conquering hero, sirens wailing to herald his arrival, punctuated by the "steamboat trombone" on his personal jeep. "It was very pleasant to drive into a town which has not been captured for more than 1,300 years," he wrote, still insisting on his fictitious version of history. To Bea he added, "I will be hard to live with. I have been a sort of demi-god too long." He personally interrogated General Anton Dunckern, the bug-eyed security commander for Lorraine, who had been apprehended by a 5th Division patrol while trying to slink out of Metz with an aide. After threatening to turn him over to the French, who "know how to make people talk," Patton told an interpreter, "If he wanted to be a good Nazi, he could have died then and there. It would have been a pleasanter death than what he will get now." When Dunckern protested that he had been captured by Americans and should therefore remain in U.S. custody, Patton snapped, "When I am dealing with vipers, I do not have to be bothered by any foolish ideas. . . . I understand German very well, but I will not demean myself by speaking such a language."

An honor guard played ruffles and flourishes for the victors. Patton sprinkled medals among his legions, acclaiming what he deemed "one of the epic river crossings of history," and Metz formally returned to French custody. GIs in muddy boots and frayed uniforms stood at attention in a central square, as a military band with colors flying preceded French soldiers in black berets, white leggings, and Sam Browne belts, each with two submachine guns slung over his shoulders.

Little mention was made of the outlying forts, several of which remained defiantly unconquered. Sherman tanks blackened those works with thousands of rounds of French white-phosphorus ammunition, using special firing pins improvised by Third Army armorers. Fort St.-Privat surrendered on November 29, yielding more than five hundred prisoners, scores of whom had phosphorus burns. Fort Driant, that hard nut, would hold out until December 8, and Fort Jeanne d'Arc was the last to fold, on December 13.

By that time Third Army's left wing had finally closed on the Saar River and the Siegfried Line, although Patton's right remained short of the German frontier. The sixty-mile advance in the Lorraine campaign had liberated another five thousand square miles of France, but at a cost in three months of nearly a hundred thousand U.S. battle and nonbattle casualties. Third Army had yet to breach the *Westwall*, much less reach the Rhine, and the long autumn amounted to what one historian would call "Patton's bloodiest and least successful campaign," a season of unimaginative and dispersed frontal attacks of the sort he ridiculed when lesser generals launched them. Unable to resist the prestige of bagging Metz, he had forfeited the single greatest advantage the Americans now held over their adversaries—mobility—by permitting much of his army to be drawn into a sanguinary siege.

In a note to Henry L. Stimson, the secretary of war, Patton proposed that as part of any surrender terms the Germans be required to keep Lorraine, "this nasty country where it rains every day and where the whole wealth of the people consists in assorted manure piles." He also summoned the Third Army chaplain, Colonel James H. O'Neill, to his office in an old French barracks in Nancy. "Chaplain, how much praying is being done in the Third Army?" Patton asked.

"I'm afraid to admit it," O'Neill said, "but I do not believe that much praying is going on."

"We must ask God to stop these rains," Patton said, staring through his high windows at the sopping landscape outside. "These rains are the margin that holds defeat or victory." O'Neill typed out an improvised appeal on a three-by-five card, and engineers reproduced a quarter-million copies to be distributed throughout Third Army. "Restrain these immoderate rains with which we have had to contend," the text asked.

> Grant us fair weather for Battle. Graciously hearken to us as soldiers who call upon Thee that, armed with Thy power, we may advance from victory to victory, and crush the oppression and wickedness of our enemies, and establish Thy justice among men and nations. Amen.

To his diary a week later Patton confided, "It has certainly rained less since my prayer."

To the Land of Doom

FAR above the killing fields, the struggle for command of the skies had long tilted in the Allies' favor, allowing some four thousand Anglo-American heavy bombers flying from England and Italy to get on with what an airman called "the murder business": the gutting of the German homeland with well over one million tons of high explosives, incendiaries, and fragmentation bombs.

Allied hopes for strategic bombing early in the war had proved too optimistic, especially the belief that precision strikes would quickly eviscerate the enemy war economy, and so spare ground forces the blood-letting that had characterized World War I. Imprecise targeting, bad weather, and savage German defenses had forced Allied strategists to use the bomber fleet as a blunt instrument, a bludgeon rather than a scalpel. Terrible aircraft losses in the first three months of 1944, including almost 800 U.S. heavies shot down, had been stanched in the spring by the belated arrival of the P-51 Mustang, a fighter with sufficient range to escort bombers to any target on the Continent. An unexpected surge in German aircraft production, with 10,000 single-engine fighters built from May through September, had again challenged Allied hegemony; during the summer, another 900 bombers went down from Eighth Air Force alone. But the Luftwaffe now was in a death spiral, having lost 31,000 planes before D-Day and another 13,000 from June through October. By July, novice German fighter pilots typically received less than thirty flying hours in training before being hurled into combat, less than one-tenth the Anglo-American average; the life expectancy of a Luftwaffe pilot could be measured in weeks if not hours. "Each time I close the canopy before take-off," wrote one airman, "I feel that I am closing the lid of my own coffin."

Of necessity, antiaircraft flak had become the primary German defense. Flak was credited with destroying 6,400 Anglo-American planes in 1944 and damaging 27,000 others. A standard 88mm flak gun fired a 17-pound shrapnel grenade that climbed thirteen thousand feet in six seconds before bursting into fifteen hundred shards that could perforate any plane within two hundred yards. Fortunately for Allied crews, sixteen thousand 88mm shells were required on average to bring down a single heavy bomber. Flak nevertheless "held an evil, hypnotic fascination," an American pilot acknowledged. Heavier German guns were deployed to reach high-flying B-17s, and by war's end 1.2 million Germans would man the Reich's ground-based air defenses.

British bombers, flying mostly at night, tried to avoid what a BBC reporter over Berlin described as "a wall of light." A blue-tinted searchlight beam, guided by radar, would fix on an approaching plane, drawing other searchlights into a brilliant cone so that "the bomber appeared to ride at its moving vertex" while gunfire converged on the target. "The only hope," an RAF crewman said, "was to get clear before the searchlights could form a cone." American bombers, flying by day, sought to counter German search and fire-control radars with an expanding array of electronic jammers; one study estimated that effective jamming meant that 25 percent fewer planes were destroyed and 50 percent fewer were spared serious flak damage compared to those flying without countermeasures. Still, as the poet-airman Randall Jarrell wrote:

> Six miles from earth, loosed from its dream of life,
> I woke to black flak and the nightmare fighters.
> When I died they washed me out of the turret with a hose.

Air supremacy provided an invaluable advantage to Allied ground forces and spared the lives of many Anglo-American fliers, even if that meant little to those washed out with a hose. The Allied strategic air effort in Europe cost some eighty thousand lives and ten thousand aircraft, and the vast tactical air war in direct support of ground forces added more losses. In the first half of 1944, battle casualty rates for every 1,000 bomber crewmen serving six months in combat included 712 killed or missing and 175 wounded: 89 percent. By one calculation, barely one in four U.S. airmen completed twenty-five missions over Germany, a minimum quota that was soon raised to thirty and then thirty-five on the assumption that the liberation of France and Belgium and the attenuation of German airpower made flying less lethal.

Perhaps less lethal, but hardly less stressful: the seven British crewmen aboard a Lancaster bomber sometimes spoke of being joined by "the eighth passenger"—fear. Of 7,374 Lancasters built, 3,349 would be lost in action. A British airman had just a one-in-five chance of surviving the loss of his plane, in part because the Lancaster had only a single emergency exit. For an American crewman, the chance was three in five. (The B-17 Flying Fortress had four exits.) In British Bomber Command, two of every five fliers did not live to complete a tour of duty, a mortality rate far exceeding that of British infantrymen on the Western Front in World War I.

The simplest missions could be fatal: an American B-24 returning to base from a training flight clipped a tree in Lancashire during a violent thunderstorm, then cartwheeled through the village of Freckleton. A wall of flame one hundred feet high burned for two hours, engulfing the infants' wing of Holy Trinity School and the Sad Sack Snack Bar, which catered to airmen. Of the sixty-one dead, more than half were children, including some who had been evacuated from London to escape the V-weapon barrage. Bing Crosby, in England on a goodwill tour, found himself too stricken to sing at the sight of the burned children in a local hospital ward. Instead he stood outside in a corridor, crooning "Don't Fence Me In" and "White Christmas" as elegies to innocence and youth.

High though the war's cost in men and machines, the U.S. industrial and military base by the fall of 1944 was producing far more planes, pilots, gunners, bombardiers, and navigators than needed to replace combat losses; during the winter, the training of new pilots, which had climbed to more than 100,000 annually, would be cut by over 70 percent. Yet General Henry H. "Hap" Arnold, chief of the Army Air Forces, fretted over reports of "incipient weaknesses" among bomber crews in Europe, which he described as "lack of respect (amounting to near hatred) for certain very senior general officers; . . . lack of desire to kill Germans; lack of understanding of political necessity for fighting the war; general personal lassitude." Low morale did plague at least part of the force; a rest-and-recuperation program in Atlantic City, Miami, and Santa Monica was abandoned because the interlude at home seemed to make airmen more resentful of civilians, bellicose toward their officers, and reluctant to return to combat. An officer in the 319th Bombardment Group described a fellow pilot as "so shot that he spills food at the table, jerks all night in his sleep, and is highly irritable. . . . He'll kill a whole crew someday and it will be called 'pilot error.' Oh well, such is war." Lieutenant Joseph T. Hallock, a twenty-two-year-old flying in B-17s, told the reporter Brendan Gill, "Sometimes I feel as if I'd never had a chance to live at all, but most of the time I feel as if I'd lived forever." At precarious moments over Germany, he confessed, he would whisper: "God, you gotta. You gotta get me back. God, listen, you gotta."

In the airman's world, those afflicted with "the clanks"—a paralyzing inability to shake a sense of dread—were known as "dead men flying." Bailing out of a stricken "kite" was called "giving birth," and "chop girls" were English women shunned by superstitious crews because they had befriended airmen who then went missing in action. Temperatures of minus sixty degrees Fahrenheit left brown frostbite patches on foreheads and buttocks, at least until deployment of the F-3 heated suit, with 250 watts flowing through wired jackets, trousers, and felt slippers to give eight Clos of insulation. Plastic surgeons learned to rebuild burned-away faces; after sculpting new lips from skin grafted off an arm, they tattooed them red and then added tiny black dots to simulate mustache whiskers.

In the airman's world, a B-17 pilot sat in the five-foot cube of his cockpit with "an oxygen mask full of drool" amid the roar of four engines. He fiddled with 130 switches, dials, gauges, levers, and pedals long enough to dump his payload of bombs—"big ugly dead things," in one officer's phrase—and then fled for home. In this world, Germany was known as "the Land of Doom." In this world, the pilot John Muirhead took pains not to grow close to his Flying Fortress crewmates, because "if I didn't know them, I would not grieve."

How best to destroy the Land of Doom had perplexed air strategists for years. The Combined Chiefs at the Casablanca conference in January 1943 called for "the progressive destruction and dislocation of the German military, industrial, and economic system" in order to undermine the enemy "capacity for armed resistance." But where was a big modern state most vulnerable? Some analysts studied the U.S. industrial system in search of "instructive hints to what might be German weak points," such as the single plant in Chicago that processed 90 percent of all tantalum, a corrosion-resistant metal critical to radar and radio production. Others scrutinized Germany directly, reviewing thousands of intelligence reports. One conclusion: sustained bombing of enemy steel plants was pointless, because the Reich was using only 20 percent of its steel-making capacity.

But Germany did have an Achilles heel: oil. The Allied powers controlled more than 90 percent of the world's natural oil, compared to just 3 percent for the Axis. German schemes to exploit Soviet oil fields in the Caucasus had been thwarted by battlefield reverses in Africa and Russia. By the spring of 1944, this vulnerability became increasingly evident to Allied intelligence analysts. Shortages impeded the training of some combat divisions, fuel cuts were imposed on the German navy, and fleets of vehicles were converted to wood-burning engines. Nearly all Luftwaffe aviation fuel came from synthetic-oil plants, and German chemists sought energy substitutes in such unlikely European flora as acorns and grapes. An OSS analysis asserted that further reduction of the Reich's oil production would have "rapid and drastic effects upon her military capacity." Ultra intercepts revealed Berlin's alarm at Allied raids on the vast Romanian petroleum facilities around Ploesti and against oil targets in Germany. British intelligence by late May had concluded that sustained air attacks on German oil production would cause disastrous industrial shortages within three to six months. "Oil," warned a decrypted message from Japanese officials in Berlin to Tokyo, "is Germany's problem."

No one believed that more than Lieutenant General Carl A. Spaatz, commander of the U.S. Strategic Air Forces in Europe. Taciturn and unpretentious, with passions for fishing and cribbage, "Tooey" Spaatz was an aviation pioneer who had shot down three German planes in World

War I and helped set a world record for staying aloft in 1929 through innovative midair refueling. *Time* claimed that he now kept "the finest poker table in London. . . . He bets with a heavy hand [and] bluffs outrageously." Uncanny in his ability to draw an inside straight, Spaatz sometimes played with a kitten tucked into his uniform blouse for luck. The need to destroy the Luftwaffe, and Eisenhower's decision to focus on German transportation targets before Normandy, had delayed a full-force blow at the enemy's oil industry. Yet even before D-Day, the supreme commander had heeded Spaatz's pleas by authorizing several oil raids, among them a mid-May attack by nine hundred bombers that also resulted in the destruction of sixty Luftwaffe fighters desperately struggling to defend the target.

No sooner had OVERLORD forces come ashore than Spaatz declared, on June 8, that the "primary strategic aim of United States Strategic Air Forces is now to deny oil to enemy armed forces," a decree that remained in force until the war ended. An estimated 30 percent of German production came from the Ploesti refineries, with another 36 percent from two dozen synthetic plants that converted brown coal to gasoline and aviation fuel. Sixty crude-oil refineries in Germany, Austria, Hungary, Poland, and Czechoslovakia provided the rest. Fifteenth Air Force in Italy would target refineries in Romania, Vienna, and Budapest, along with synthetic-oil plants in Silesia, Poland, and the Sudetenland. Eighth Air Force in England would focus on seven large synthetic plants in central Germany, as well as some twenty refineries mostly in northern Germany. British intelligence in late July posited that oil shortages could cause a German military collapse by the end of 1944.

That estimate was too rosy, but German production did plummet through the summer. Ploesti had been wrecked by bombers even before the Red Army overran the region in August, and of ninety-one oil facilities remaining in Hitler's hands only three were at full production by early fall.

Not everyone subscribed to the oil strategy. A directive from the Combined Chiefs on September 25 gave first priority to enemy petroleum targets, followed by the German transportation system and tank production facilities. But Bomber Command resisted the edict. Its leadership was determined to finish the job of sowing terror and chaos by destroying German cities, a project that had begun with incendiary attacks on the medieval town centers of Lübeck and Rostock in the spring of 1942. The British Air Ministry had long studied the science of "fire-raising," examining the combustible qualities of German pantries, attics, and furnishings, and collecting insurance maps to study firewall patterns in German buildings. Allied bombers would ultimately drop eighty million incendiary sticks, twenty-two-inch hexagonal rods with a magnesium-zinc case that burned for eight minutes at two thousand degrees Fahrenheit. The firestorm that incinerated Hamburg in the summer of 1943, killing 41,000 and "de-housing" nearly a million, "simulated the atmosphere of another planet," a German writer recorded, "one incompatible with life."

Air Chief Marshal Arthur T. Harris, the Bomber Command leader, in late 1943 had sent Churchill a list of forty-seven German cities, of which nineteen were deemed "virtually destroyed" and another nineteen "seriously damaged." Harris argued that Germany would surrender after the destruction of "between 40 percent and 50 percent of the principal German towns," which he believed could happen by April 1, 1944. "We shall take out one German city after another," Harris said, "like pulling teeth." Rumors circulated through Germany that lime pits already had been dug for future bomb victims in Berlin.

Yet April passed without a surrender, and British bomber losses were dreadful. Allied intelligence found "no grounds for supposing that the effects of area bombing on civilian morale would contribute to Germany's collapse." The Japanese ambassador in Berlin shared that view: he advised Tokyo that "internal collapse will certainly not be brought about by means of air raids."

Harris believed otherwise. Known to subordinates as both "Bomber" and "Butcher," imbued with what Churchill called "a certain coarseness," he was described by one admiring journalist as "a tiger with no mercy in his heart." With a bowling-pin shape that no uniform could flatter, Harris was given to wearing a mulberry-colored velvet smoking jacket and chain-smoking Camels or partaking of ceremonial snuff. Though sometimes saturnine—he bathed his stomach ulcers with Dr. J. Collis Browne's Mixture, which contained peppermint oil and anhydrous morphine—he never tired of showing dinner guests his private "Blue Book," bulging with aerial photos of skeletonized German cities. Often he drove his black Bentley at lunatic speeds, remanding the ostensible chauffeur to the backseat, and he was not above taking a pony trap from his headquarters at High Wycombe to Chequers, the prime minister's nearby country house west of London. When Churchill grumbled, "I'm sick of these raids on Cologne," Harris replied, "So are the people of Cologne."

In the British official history's portrait:

> He had a tendency to confuse advice with interference, criticism with sabotage, and evidence with propaganda. He resisted innovations and was seldom open to persuasion. . . . Seeing all issues in terms of black or white, he was impatient of any other possibility.

Harris believed that bombers should be clubs to bash the German *Volk*. To a colleague he wrote, "If the Germans were asked today, 'Oil plants or

cities?' they would reply, 'Bomb anything you fancy except the cities.'"
Accordingly, more than half of Bomber Command's payloads during the
war would fall on urban centers. Each morning, in a command center
known as the Hole, Harris would decide which German city would suffer
that night, each with an ichthyic code name: CATFISH, for Munich; WHITE-
BAIT, for Berlin. His animating principle, as the official history explained,
was "that in order to destroy anything it is necessary to destroy everything." By the late fall of 1944, Harris claimed that forty-five of sixty listed
German cities had been "virtually destroyed," at a rate of more than two
each month, with a dwindling number awaiting evisceration. These were
mostly in the east: Halle, Magdeburg, Leipzig, Dresden. Air Chief Marshal Charles F. A. Portal argued in early November that "the air offensive
against oil gives us by far the best hope of complete victory in the next
few months." Harris disagreed, and instead urged completion of what he
called "the city programme." Portal replied on November 12, "If I knew
you to be as wholehearted in the attack on oil as in the past you have been
in the matter of attacking cities, I would have little to worry about."

Harris's resolve to crack the enemy's will and effect a surrender with
terror raids would be found wanting both militarily and morally. "The idea
that the main object of bombing German industrial cities was to break the
enemy's morale proved to be totally unsound," he acknowledged in 1947.
Yet the postwar U.S. Strategic Bombing Survey concluded that "bombing
seriously depressed the morale of German citizens. Its psychological effects
were defeatism, fear, hopelessness, fatalism, and apathy." At any given time
two thousand Allied aircraft might be above Germany, and as Randall
Jarrell wrote:

> In bombers named for girls, we burned
> The cities we had learned about in school—
> Till our lives wore out.

While British Bomber Command believed in leveling entire cities, the
Americans considered themselves "precision bombers," a term that
implied attacks exclusively against military targets out of revulsion at
indiscriminately killing civilians. But because the skies of central Europe
were chronically overcast, half of Eighth Air Force's bomb tonnage was
dropped using "blind bombing" radar techniques; often, as few as one out
of ten bombs fell within half a mile of an obscured target. Even when conditions were ideal for bombardiers—this was the case in roughly one sortie of seven—less than a third of all bombs detonated within a thousand
feet of the aiming point. The term "precision bombing," Spaatz conceded,

was intended "in a relative, not a literal sense." Bad weather also caused frequent diversions to secondary targets such as rail yards, a practice that amounted to emptying bomb bays over city centers. Such attacks on transportation targets gradually restricted the movement of German war commodities, notably coal, while razing urban precincts. "The way to stop the killing of civilians," Hap Arnold asserted in a memo that could have been dictated by Bomber Harris, "is to cause so much damage and destruction and death that the civilians will demand that their government cease fighting." Eighth Air Force would devote more than 20 percent of its payloads to city bombing, the historian Richard G. Davis subsequently calculated, while making efforts to conceal the extent of such attacks. And press censors blocked any hint that precision bombing was often terribly imprecise.

The Americans were no less intent than the British on refining the techniques of havoc. In the Utah desert, Hollywood set designers and engineers from Standard Oil built two facsimile working-class neighborhoods, one German and the other Japanese, with replicas of furniture, bed coverings, and other household inflammables; repeated fire-bomb experiments led to the development of incendiaries that could punch through stout German roofs. The M-76 Block Burner, another American innovation first used in March 1944, spattered incendiary gel in big, burning gobs. "Aerial incendiaries," a U.S. Army study concluded, "probably caused as much death and destruction as any other weapon used in World War II."

Air Chief Marshal Harris never believed in the oil plan, which he described to Portal as "a faith to which I am not only not a convert, but against which I have waged . . . unrelenting opposition." Harris would be condemned both during and after the war for a mulish recalcitrance that impeded a unified assault on the Reich's weakest link, but in his grudging, tardy fashion he did comply with the directives of the Allied high command. Bomber Command's first daylight strategic assaults of the war fell on oil targets in August and September 1944; by November, British and American bombers were flying a comparable number of sorties against oil. Thereafter Bomber Command flew more than twice as many missions as Eighth Air Force, and in the final year of the strategic air war in Europe, Harris's planes would drop nearly 100,000 tons, compared with 73,000 tons for Eighth Air Force. Arguably the British attacked to greater effect since their bombers carried larger payloads and bigger bombs, and frequently dropped those bombs with greater accuracy. Analysts concluded that the Americans attacked petroleum targets with too many small bombs incapable of cracking blast walls, too few incendiaries, and too many bombs—about 14 percent—that proved defective, often because of faulty fuzes.

The inclement fall weather gave Germany a bit of breathing room, as did crash programs dedicated to smoke generation, camouflage, the dispersal of targets, and repair. By late autumn, 350,000 workers—mostly foreign slaves—toiled to repair and hide oil facilities. Defenses became more ferocious: the vast Leuna synthetic-oil plant west of Leipzig, which was attacked twenty-one times at a cost of eighty-two Allied bombers, became the single most heavily defended industrial plant in Germany, bristling with more than five hundred heavy flak guns.

But the die had been cast. For a time in late fall, Rundstedt limited divisions in the west to 1,200 gallons of gasoline a day rather than the standard 7,200. Aviation-fuel production by the end of November had dropped to a quarter of the May level; the Luftwaffe was even forced to minimize aircraft taxiing, and some planes were pulled to the runway by oxen. Attacks on oil-hydrogenation plants also led to dwindling nitrogen stocks, which in turn severely constricted German ammunition production. Likewise, the destruction of synthetic-oil facilities brought the added benefit of impairing production of synthetic rubber, as well as of other chemicals used in explosives.

No industrial disparity during the war had greater importance than the gap between German and American fuel production. From 1942 through 1944, Berlin's refineries and plants generated 23 million tons of fuel; during the same period, the United States produced more than 600 million tons. By the spring of 1945, after more than 500 Allied attacks against some 130 oil targets, German petroleum output would decline to 12 percent of what it had been a year earlier. For want of the commodity most vital in a modern society, the Reich was dying.

The German people were dying, too. From the Air Ministry rooftop in King Charles Street, while watching London burn after a Luftwaffe raid in 1940, Harris had mused, "They are sowing the wind." Now came the whirlwind: some 131 German cities and towns would be attacked from the air during the war, leaving 400,000 dead and seven million homeless.

For those on the ground, the ordeal always began with the shriek of warning sirens, signaling that it was time to turn off the gas, turn on the radio, fill the bathtub, get out the flashlight. In cinemas the words *"Flieger Alarme"* appeared on the screen. Hurrying to the shelters during daylight raids, citizens craned their necks to look for the bright beads of approaching bombers dragging their white contrails. "People alongside us started counting the tiny silver dots," one German recalled. "They had already got to four hundred, but there was still no end to be seen." At night, civilians wore fluorescent badges to avoid colliding in the dark as they made their way by following the phosphorescent paint slathered on street curbs.

Three thousand municipal air-raid shelters had been built by the regime, far too few even when supplemented by mine shafts and subway tunnels. "I had the feeling of having ended up in an underworld, in filth and disorder," a diarist in Krefeld wrote. "It went well with a sign saying in bright letters, 'The People are grateful to their Führer.'" Shelter dwellers wrapped themselves in wet sheets and covered their eyes with gauze, opening their mouths to protect eardrums against concussion and drawing shallow breaths when the ventilators were closed because of fires raging above. A German medic in Hamm reported, "Children with scarlet fever and diphtheria . . . keep being found in bunker rooms. Hopefully we will be spared typhus this time."

"In Cologne life is no longer possible," a diarist wrote in an entry that no doubt would have pleased Harris. "No water, gas, or electricity, and no food." Stuttgart's inner city "ceased to exist" after raids in mid-September: "We had to climb over the dead to get away from the sea of fire," one woman recalled. "I couldn't help thinking, 'We've been living through the day of judgment.'" Bombs battered Essen in 39 of the air war's 60 months; 272 raids left only 5,000 of 65,000 buildings undamaged. From the air, an Allied crewman wrote in his logbook, the burning city resembled "an immense pot, boiling over."

The iron and steel center of Duisburg was bombed nearly three hundred times; during one twenty-four-hour period in November, Bomber Command dropped as much tonnage on the city as had fallen on London during the entire war. In Hanover, a man who rode through the charred ruins on his bicycle after one raid wrote, "The night had done its work. . . . All you could say, over and over, was, 'That too, oh, and that too!'" In Osnabrück, where the ruins were sardonically dubbed "Hermann Göring Square," a single fourteen-minute raid on September 13 dropped 181,000 incendiaries and 2,171 high-explosive bombs; more followed a month later. Five thousand died in Braunschweig in "one great maelstrom of fire" on October 15. Seven thousand died in Heilbronn—one-tenth of the population—during raids in early December. Delay-fuzed bombs kept rescue crews at bay while flames loped through the half-timbered town; among the dead were hundreds in cellars where ventilation pumps had sucked in carbon monoxide. Goebbels told his diary, "A large industrial town ablaze from end to end is a hideous sight." He proclaimed "Politeness Week," urging civic amiability.

Even from the Dutch coast, pilots could see Cologne burning, wrote the novelist and poet W. G. Sebald, like "a fiery speck in the darkness, like the tail of a motionless comet." Names of former residents were chalked on charred apartment walls, with crosses next to those killed; survivors received 210 Reichmarks toward the cost of burying their dead, according to the historian Jörg Friedrich. Helmut Kohl, a future German chancellor who was fourteen in 1944, described shoveling debris from a destroyed house near Mannheim where residents had suffocated in the basement: "They lay there with blue faces." Police assigned to work in morgues and cemeteries were fortified with alcohol. "Do you still remember when we were in school we read Schiller's 'The Bell'?" a girl in Hanover wrote an SS corporal at the front. " 'Many must go into the hostile world.' Then we did not think much about it. . . . Monotonously and cheerlessly we spend our best years, we bury our youth."

On and on it went, high explosives and incendiaries falling nearly every night and every day by the thousands of tons, week after week, month upon month. Deranged mothers, unwilling to abandon their dead children when evacuating Hamburg, carried away the roasted or asphyxiated corpses in cardboard suitcases. A firefighter in Krefeld reported, "The heat was so great that we could not touch the metal on our helmets." A one-hour RAF attack on Darmstadt ignited a firestorm that drew 3,000 firefighters with 220 engines from across the region. "Burning people raced past like live torches," a witness reported, "and I listened to their unforgettable final screams." Among the dead were knots of human beings so thoroughly fused together by the heat that tools were needed to pry the bodies apart for burial. Nurses soaked the sheets of burn victims in salad oil as a palliative. One survivor wrote, "I saw a man dragging a sack with five or six bulges in it as if he were carrying heads of cabbages. It was the heads of his family, a whole family, that he had found in the cellar."

Here then, the annihilative whirlwind—this vortex, this gyre of flame, this destroyer of worlds. "The destruction will go on," wrote one man in Berlin, "until the world has bled to death."

"Providence Decrees and We Must Obey"

A FTER advancing nearly four hundred miles in the month following the invasion of southern France, the DRAGOON juggernaut had gained hardly fifteen miles in the subsequent six weeks. In mid-November, it remained pinned along the western slope of the Vosges Mountains: as Lucian Truscott had feared, the failure to force the Belfort Gap near the

Swiss border had enabled the German Nineteenth Army, spavined though it was, to make a stand. Nine weak enemy divisions straddled the high ground along an eighty-mile front from Switzerland to the Rhine–Marne Canal. Opposing them was the 6th Army Group, formally created in September from two armies: Patch's Seventh on the left, in the north, and De Lattre's French First on the right, in the south. Eisenhower's transfer of XV Corps from Third Army to Seventh—much to Patton's annoyance—gave the Franco-American host four corps, nearly half a million men. They now steeled themselves for what was described as "the first crossing of the Vosges in history under winter battle conditions."

Few could feel optimistic. The Vosges massif loomed like a granite glacis thirty miles deep and seventy miles wide; cleft by few passes, the range was so thickly wooded that a Guadalcanal veteran like Patch was reminded of jungle fighting. "Mountains, woods, and rain are things I do not like anymore, at least in a war," John Dahlquist, the 36th Division commander, wrote his wife in November. "But I will probably see a lot more of them before I am through, so I had better get philosophical about them." Italy veterans in the 36th, 45th, and 3rd Divisions had little stomach for another winter campaign in the uplands, and "alarming mental and physical lethargy" was reported in at least one regiment.

The season had been marked by straggling and desertion; replacements were described as "inept and poorly trained," and the mud was so deep that even airstrips for spotter planes had to be corduroyed with logs painted olive drab. Trench foot, frostbite, mines, and steel-jawed bear traps planted by the Germans added to the misery. The first snow had fallen on October 27, and GIs smeared Vaseline on their tent seams in a vain effort to stay dry. Winter clothing arrived late, despite emergency shipments flown into Dijon aboard B-24s. Six hundred thousand men and almost a million tons of matériel had come through Marseille and Toulon and across the Côte d'Azur beaches by early November. But a long trek to the front, various miscalculations, and a thriving black market in the French ports—20 percent of the cargo unloaded in Marseille was stolen, often by Army freebooters—made for shortages of food, ammunition, and fuel.

"Dear Family," wrote Lieutenant June Wandrey, a nurse in Seventh Army,

> If it wasn't against the family tradition to commit suicide, I'd do it, as wherever I'd go it would be warmer than it is here. . . . I'm tired of the noises of war, the trauma of war, the sleeplessness of war, the hunger of war. . . . Our cook was a mortician in civilian life. He embalms all our food.

The season also had been marked by the usual heartbreak, a reminder that even as millions perished in the global conflagration, they died one by one. Among those killed in late October was Dahlquist's aide, Lieutenant Wells Lewis, son of the Nobel Prize–winning novelist Sinclair Lewis. A Harvard graduate named for H. G. Wells, young Lewis died in Dahlquist's arms after being shot in the head by a sniper. "It is over two years since I last saw my son," his mother wrote Dahlquist. "For a soldier to die in his General's arms is in the great tradition, a literary symbol which I know Wells himself would appreciate."

Killed the same week, by antitank fire, was Patch's only son, Captain Alexander M. "Mac" Patch III, a company commander in the 79th Division who had returned to combat four days earlier after recuperating from a bullet wound to the shoulder suffered in Normandy. General Patch ordered Mac's body brought to his headquarters at Épinal. "So long, son," he said at the open grave, then muttered, "Well, he is not cold and wet and hungry."

Two weeks later Patch wrote to his wife, Julia: "I've been dreading my first letter from you after you had heard from me. It came today." He continued:

> You, and only you, know how deeply hurt I am. . . . It is our private, strictly private grief. No one else's. My hardest period is over. It was during the period after Mac's death, when I kept getting letters from you— such happy letters. . . . You would tell me in those letters to please not let him get back to his outfit too soon. And I could hardly stand it, knowing I *had* done just that. I shall never be able to forgive myself.

"I cannot and must not allow myself to dwell upon our irreparable loss," he told her. "As I write, the tears are falling from my eyes. . . . Providence decrees and we must obey."

The good soldier soldiered on, but Omar Bradley later wrote that "the psychological effect on Patch has been so devastating as to impair his effectiveness as an army commander." Reflecting on Patch's loss, General Dahlquist told his wife, "It is almost beyond comprehension that the human being can stand so much."

The town of Baccarat had been liberated in late October and its famous crystal works captured intact, including an elegant service ordered by Hermann Göring but instead confiscated by Allied officers from which to sip champagne. Dahlquist also bought 100,000 gallons of beer from a French brewery, and engineers rigged pumps to siphon it to the troops. Many toasts were drunk—to the dead, to the living, to fickle life itself. "Rain has started again," Dahlquist wrote home, "and how I hate it. It makes the job ten times harder."

Perpetual friction with the French made the job harder still. General de Lattre de Tassigny, that animal of action, struggled to whip his quarter of a million men into an army rather than a mob. "Our African soldiers felt lost in the dark forests," De Lattre later wrote. Colonial troops still wearing summer uniforms were "unsuited to the winter climate," he added, and cruelly susceptible to trench foot; some French troops wore wooden shoes. On De Gaulle's orders, many colonials were sent to the rear to make room for untrained FFI irregulars. This *blanchiment,* or whitening, was intended to nurture French national unity; De Gaulle also wished both to relieve the African troops, who had carried a disproportionate burden of France's fight in the Mediterranean, and to bring some 400,000 Resistance fighters—many of them communists—under military control. The colonials had once made up more than half the manpower of the French army; now that share would decline to about one-third. Senegalese and Cameroonians shambled from the Vosges front, handing their rifles, helmets, and greatcoats to white Frenchmen trotting into the line. This "crusade" for French self-respect, as De Lattre called it, would add to the French First Army some 137,000 maquis, a "vibrant and tumultuous force" with thin combat skills and paltry logistical support. De Lattre found himself waging what he called "a battle against shortage, anarchy, and complaisance."

Base 901, the French supply organization, in late fall consisted of twelve hundred men with two hundred vehicles. American logisticians calculated that an eight-division army should have more than 100,000 support troops, but De Lattre would never have even a third of that number. Consequently he relied on the Americans—with all of the pathologies that dependency engendered—for everything from the one-third liter of wine included in French rations to the ten pounds of crushed oats, fourteen pounds of hay, and two ounces of salt needed each day for a mountain mule. For every French soldier in Europe, the U.S. Army billed De Gaulle $6.67 per day in support costs.

Franco-American frictions intensified as winter approached. When only 25,000 uniforms could be found for French troops, in a Canadian warehouse in Algiers, De Lattre announced that unless his men received wool clothing he would be "forced to withdraw them from combat." To the 6th Army Group headquarters, he wrote: "This army has been discriminated against . . . in a way seriously prejudicial to its life and to its capabilities for action." The French First Army, he charged, received less than a third of the ammunition, fuel, and rations provided Seventh Army, causing an "asphyxiation of the front line." U.S. quartermasters bitterly denied the allegation and countered that reckless French troops had ruined three thousand pyramidal tents at a time when canvas was "extremely critical." An American general wrote of De Lattre, "He goes into these tirades at least twice a week, at which time he seems to lose his balance." One ill-advised tantrum, launched in the presence of a visiting George Marshall, included allegations that Truscott's VI Corps had pilfered gasoline allocated to the French. The chief of staff walked out. Later, he rounded on De Lattre with pale fury. "You celebrated all the way up the road. You were late on every damn thing. And you were critical of Truscott, who is a fighter and not a talker," Marshall said. The chief finished with the worst epithet he could conjure: "*You* are a politico."

"It was our duty," De Lattre subsequently explained, "to be dissatisfied."

Now Truscott was gone, initially summoned by Eisenhower to organize the new Fifteenth Army as an occupation force—"You won't like it," the supreme commander warned—but then just as abruptly dispatched instead to command Fifth Army in Italy, after General Mark W. Clark took over all Allied forces there. At a farewell ceremony in the Vosges, a band crashed through "The Dogface Soldier" as tears streamed down Truscott's rough cheeks. His successor as commander of VI Corps was Major General Edward H. Brooks, a New Englander who had commanded both the 11th and 2nd Armored Divisions.

With Truscott's departure, the dominant figure on the southern front was the officer who would orchestrate the offensive to breach the Vosges: Lieutenant General Jacob Loucks Devers, the 6th Army Group commander. Now fifty-seven, Devers was the grandson of a blacksmith and son of a jeweler in York, Pennsylvania. There young Jake had climbed a ladder every Sunday with his father to make sure the courthouse clock on East Market Street was correct to the second. A classmate of Patton's at West Point, he played baseball, basketball, and lacrosse, later returning to teach mathematics; the academy yearbook described him as "clever"—always suspect in the Army—and as "an exceedingly earnest youth with rather Puritanical views." A gifted artilleryman and administrator, Devers, like De Lattre, was among the youngest officers in his army to become a general, jumping over nearly five hundred more senior colonels to win his first star in 1940. As chief of the armored force for two years, he helped modernize a tank arm rife with traditionalists nostalgic for the horse. ("I made a lot of mistakes today," he would tell subordinates during maneuvers. "So did you.") With Marshall and McNair as patrons, in May 1943 he became commander of U.S. forces in Europe until Eisenhower's return to London for OVERLORD, whereupon Devers was bundled off to the Mediterranean as the eventual commander of the forces that now formed the right wing of the Allied armies in northwestern Europe.

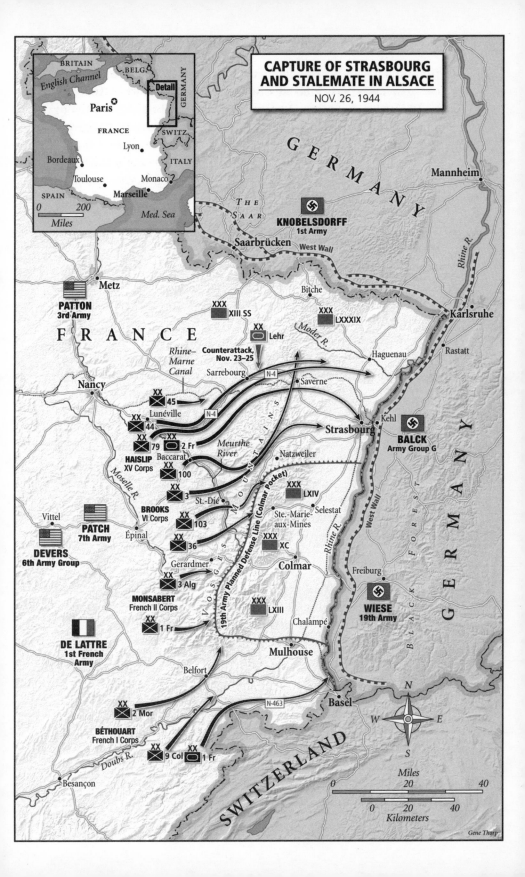

CAPTURE OF STRASBOURG AND STALEMATE IN ALSACE

NOV. 26, 1944

BRITAIN
BELG.
English Channel
GERMANY
Detail
Paris
FRANCE
SWITZ.
Lyon
Bordeaux
ITALY
Toulouse
Monaco
SPAIN
Marseille
Med. Sea
0   200
Miles

GERMANY

Mannheim

THE SAAR

KNOBELSDORFF
1st Army

Saarbrücken   West Wall

Bitche

Karlsruhe

Rastatt

Metz

PATTON
3rd Army

F R A N C E

XXX XIII SS

XXX LXXXIX

XX Lehr

Moder R.

Haguenau

Rhine–
Marne
Canal

Counterattack,
Nov. 23–25

Sarrebourg   N-4

Saverne

Nancy

Kehl

XX 45

Lunéville   N-4

Strasbourg

BALCK
Army Group G

XX 44

XX 79   XX 2 Fr

Baccarat

Meurthe
River

Natzweiler

HAISLIP
XV Corps

XX 100

(Colmar Pocket)

XXX LXIV

XX 3

St.-Dié

Ste.-Marie-
aux-Mines

Selestat

BROOKS
VI Corps

XX 103

XXX XC

Vittel

PATCH
7th Army

XX 36

Colmar

Freiburg

DEVERS
6th Army Group

Épinal

Gerardmer

XX 3 Alg

XXX LXIII

WIESE
19th Army

MONSABERT
French II Corps

XX 1 Fr

Chalampé

DE LATTRE
1st French
Army

Mulhouse

Belfort

N-463

Basel

N

XX 2 Mor

W   E

BÉTHOUART
French I Corps

S

XX 9 Col   XX 1 Fr

Miles
0   20   40

Doubs R.

0   20   40
Kilometers

Besançon

SWITZERLAND

Gene Thorp

Capable and decisive, he had a knack for provoking the enmity of his peers. Perhaps it was his brazen ambition—it was said that when Marshall appointed him to a committee to recommend general officers worthy of further promotion, Devers listed himself first. Perhaps it was his overeager smile, the mien "of a boy who hasn't grown up," as one British general said. He and Mark Clark detested each other to the point of not speaking, and Devers's classmate Patton considered him "a very small caliber man." In Beetle Smith's assessment, "Devers talks too much and doesn't care what he says." Bradley condemned him, with both barrels, as "overly garrulous . . . egotistical, shallow, intolerant, not very smart, and much too inclined to rush off half-cocked."

Worse yet, according to a recent entry in Patton's diary after a conference in Paris, "Ike hates him." The supreme commander evidently nursed old resentments: Devers's reluctance in 1943 to shift bomber squadrons from England to North Africa had displeased Eisenhower, as did his refusal a year later to release Truscott from the Mediterranean for OVER-LORD. "E. says that [Devers] talks a lot but never gets down to facts," Kay Summersby told her diary. Devers brought out the conniver in E., who told Marshall, "I have nothing in the world against General Devers," but allowed that he had previously harbored an "uneasy feeling" about him. When Marshall asked Eisenhower to assess thirty-eight senior American generals in Europe, Devers ranked twenty-fourth on the supreme commander's list and elicited the only pejorative comments of the lot:

> Enthusiastic but often inaccurate in statements and evaluations; loyal and energetic. . . . He has not, so far, produced among the seniors of the American organization here that feeling of trust and confidence that is so necessary to continued success.

Eisenhower sold Devers short. The top U.S. airman in the Mediterranean, Lieutenant General Ira C. Eaker, considered him "the ablest commander I saw in the war." Among other skills, Devers was second only to Eisenhower in his ability to reconcile national differences and forge an effective Allied military coalition. While acknowledging in his diary that De Lattre "is a very difficult man to handle, hears only the things he wants to hear [and is] a temperamental personality who causes more trouble within his own staff and troops than he does with us," Devers showed a sure touch in dealing with a warrior he recognized as "a great inspirational leader"—even if "I never did learn to pronounce that name." De Lattre spoke no English, and French had been Devers's worst subject at West Point, but they shared what Devers called "that common language— the gesture and the smile." More practically, Henry Cabot Lodge, Jr., a former U.S. senator who had been schooled in France and now wore a lieutenant colonel's uniform, served as an able liaison between the two.

As for his compatriots, Devers displayed more than a little naiveté. To his diary in November he described Bradley as "the same fine character as always"; in fact, Devers had modeled his headquarters after that of 12th Army Group, which he admired. Though he brooded, in a letter to his wife, about possible "enemies" at SHAEF and "the undercutting that goes on," he believed Eisenhower and Smith to be friendly, "in their way." But even the bouncy sangfroid and the too-ready smile sometimes slipped a bit as his troops prepared to fling themselves into the Vosges. "Nobody but an utter fool would do what I'm about to do," he told subordinates. "That's the reason why we'll take them by surprise—they won't be expecting us." A staff officer close to Devers concluded, "He's lonely as the devil."

SHAEF's orders called for 6th Army Group to shield Bradley's southern flank, destroy the enemy in Alsace west of the Rhine, breach the Siegfried Line, and secure river crossings near Karlsruhe and Mannheim, respectively forty and seventy miles northeast of Strasbourg—all in service of Eisenhower's plan to cleanse the Rhine's left bank from Switzerland to Nijmegen before pushing across Germany in 1945. Privately the planners in Versailles expected little from the southern front, given the difficulties of the past six weeks. New, unblooded units now weighted the American force, including the 100th and 103rd Infantry Divisions and the 14th Armored Division, not to mention those callow amateurs flocking to De Lattre's flag.

Devers had grander ambitions. German forces along the Vosges were believed to have a strength equivalent to no more than four infantry and two panzer divisions. The general calculated that an offensive launched in mid-November ought to break onto the Alsatian plain and reach the Rhine in two weeks, before swinging north to isolate the Saar. A vengeful urgency now gripped the French: the Germans had begun scorched-earth reprisals, dragging many able-bodied Alsatians between sixteen and sixty across the Rhine as forced laborers, while SS brigands burned farms, villages, and towns rather than cede winter shelter to the Allies. "Don't get stuck in those mountains," Devers warned his subordinates. "You'll never get out."

De Lattre made the first move, attacking on Tuesday, November 14, after heavy snow created what he described as "a Scandinavian landscape." Various deceptions—including phony command posts and an announcement that French troops would begin holiday leave in mid-November—suggested that the army either had designs on the High Vosges to the north or was moving into winter quarters. Instead, De Lattre sent blacked-out convoys bearing his I Corps along the Doubs River near the Swiss frontier. A two-hour artillery barrage caught the Germans unawares, and French infantrymen surged forward at noon. Two divisions straddling the Doubs hooked north into the Belfort Gap, which sundered the Vosges from the Jura Mountains and Swiss Alps to the south. Moroccan riflemen killed a German division commander who had been trapped along the river by the artillery barrage; his effects included a map and notes detailing defensive positions on the German left flank.

By Thursday, French tanks were "decisive everywhere," De Lattre reported. German gunners firing captured Russian howitzers had little ammunition, and thirty new 88mm antitank weapons arrived without sights and other vital components. Among the few reserves slapped into the crumbling line were riflemen pedaling through the snow on bicycles and an *Ohren-Bataillon* of deaf soldiers. French shock troops swarmed into Belfort town, surprising Wehrmacht bakers at their dough trays. Three French tank columns with lights burning clattered east along Highway N-463, and at 6:30 P.M. on Sunday, November 19, a patrol from the 1st Armored Division reached the slate-blue Rhine, thirty miles east of Belfort and four miles above the Swiss border. Gleeful batteries lobbed a few shells across the river, the first French artillery to fall on German soil since 1940.

Having forsaken a substantial wedge of southern Alsace despite Hitler's order not to yield a centimeter, the Nineteenth Army belatedly stiffened. Confusion in the French ranks helped. While a weak detachment wheeled north up the Rhine toward the bridge at Chalampé, other forces keen to liberate their Alsatian *frères* instead swung toward Mulhouse, seven miles west of the river. Twenty German *Feldpost* workers were captured at pistol-point while sorting the military mail on Monday morning, and sixty other deep sleepers surrendered on their cots. But Waffen-SS troops and a brigade of new Panthers sent straight from the factory in Nuremberg rebuilt the enemy line. Savage brawling in Mulhouse persisted for four days; south of Chalampé, a counterattack on Thursday, November 23, clubbed the French away, just three miles short of the bridge. De Lattre's forces would come no closer for the next two and a half months: having captured fifteen thousand Germans at a cost of nine thousand casualties, the French First Army for the moment was a spent force.

Hopes for a decisive breakthrough now rested on Seventh Army's eight divisions packed along Devers's left wing. Here, where the High Vosges descended to the Low Vosges, the Saverne Gap provided a topographic counterpoint in the north to the Belfort Gap in the south. Barely a hundred yards wide in spots, the defile carried the main rail line to Strasbourg, as well as the Rhine–Marne Canal and an ancient roadbed, described by an eighteenth-century travel writer as "one of the masterpieces of man." Twelve thousand infantrymen from a pair of Major General Wade Haislip's XV Corps divisions had been gnawing at the western approaches to the gap since November 13, past moldering World War I trenches and conifers bent beneath wet snow. Four German defensive lines lay athwart the gap, manned by a few thousand Volksgrenadiers held in check by the threat of SS reprisals, producing what Seventh Army intelligence called "ersatz morale."

By November 19, American firepower began to tell. Shelling "left little more of the woods than an old man's scraggly beard," and retreating Germans could be seen silhouetted against flaming houses they had put to the torch. On that Sunday, even as De Lattre's men were spitting into the Rhine, the 44th Division rambled for nine miles along Highway N-4, and the 79th Division just to the south broke through to Sarrebourg. Tricolors appeared. French policemen pulled on uniforms hidden away four years earlier. Cries of *"Kamerad!"* could be heard from more surrendering Germans, including artillerymen overrun before they could limber their guns. Rain turned to snow, then back to rain—"as hard as I have ever seen it rain anywhere," Devers told his diary on Monday. But not even the harshest weather would save a German line now cracked beyond repair.

Into the breach pried open by the infantry rode a familiar swashbuckler sporting a kepi and wielding a malacca cane. In August, General Philippe Leclerc's French 2nd Armored Division had captured Paris; now, seconded to XV Corps, Leclerc eyed another enslaved *ville* in need of liberation. During his anabasis in Africa almost three years earlier, he and his warriors had taken a dramatic vow after capturing the Italian garrison at Koufra: "We swear not to lay down our arms until our colors, our beautiful colors, again fly from the Strasbourg cathedral." For the past several days, between catnaps on the drawing-room floor of a forest château, Leclerc had studied maps of the logging tracks and farm paths spilling onto the Alsatian plain, his eyes narrowed and his lips pursed. "Beat the devil," Haislip told him at last. "Leclerc, this is your country. Strasbourg is yours."

En avant then, again. Pursued by French outriders in Sherman tanks, horse-drawn German caissons and gun carriages lurched around one hairpin turn after another, eastward through the Saverne Gap. "The brave horses were galloping as fast as they could," a witness recounted.

They reached one more bend and then, under the staccato fire of the machine guns, saw themselves abandoned in a second by the German gun crews and drivers. The teams, running wild, were caught up by the armor, which were careful not to immobilize them across the road.

French tankers pulled abreast of the runaways and shouldered fifteen guns and fifty or more draft teams into the ditch in a whinnying moil of equine legs and spinning wagon wheels. As enemy soldiers emerged from the thickets with their hands high, the French detachment commander radioed Leclerc, "Now I am exploiting." Among eight hundred prisoners captured in Saverne town on November 22 was a German general, described as "upright and gloved, in his long leather coat." Frog-marched before Leclerc, he punctuated his sentences with a slight inclination of the torso while insisting, "All is not lost."

Tout au contraire. "Advance without losing a second," Leclerc commanded, and at 7:15 A.M. on Thursday, November 23—Thanksgiving—five columns of Shermans and armored cars swept toward Strasbourg in teeming rain. "We went roaring across the plains," an American liaison officer reported. Sixteen strongholds named for martial demigods like Foch and Ney guarded the city's western approaches, but they were toothless without heavy guns or German reserves. At 10:30 French tanks spilled into downtown Strasbourg, machine-gunning astonished Wehrmacht officers caught packing their sedans or window-shopping with their wives on the boulevards. Booming 75mm fire shattered seven antitank guns near the Parc de la Citadelle before German crews could fire a shot, and trailing French howitzers cut loose from a city park, drawing return fire from enemy batteries across the river that "sent windowpanes tinkling into the streets," according to *The New York Times.* A coded radio message advised Leclerc, *"Tissu est dans iode"*—the cloth is in the iodine. The French vanguard was advancing through Strasbourg toward the Rhine bridges.

As rain drummed off his kepi, Leclerc now made for the city in an open jeep with an escort of light tanks, half-tracks, and seventy men. Through the downpour he soon spied the pink sandstone spire of Strasbourg cathedral, Goethe's "sublimely towering, wide-spreading tree of God," which at nearly five hundred feet had been the world's tallest building for more than two centuries. A tricolor flew from the pinnacle. "Now we can die," Leclerc muttered.

But not yet. A captured German engineer was persuaded to phone his headquarters at noon on Thursday with a French surrender ultimatum; he managed to reach General Hermann Balck, the Army Group G commander, only to be told, "If you don't immediately stop your activities in Strasbourg, your family will land in the concentration camp." Most of the city already was lost to the Reich, and a furious Hitler threatened to demote every officer in Nineteenth Army by one grade. But the Rhine bridge leading to Kehl on the German shore remained in enemy hands. Blockhouses and an effective straggler line, reinforced by mortar and artillery fire, halted the French less than six hundred yards from the river. A stalemated struggle for the western bridgehead settled into what a French officer described as "a solid artillery argument," with the Germans unwilling to retreat the final half-mile into Germany, and Leclerc unable to cudgel them across the Rhine.

"Lots of dead civilians in Strasbourg," an American engineer informed his diary. "Children still playing in the street as though nothing had happened." French and American forces finished mopping up isolated enemy outposts, using city parks and a brewery as detention centers for six thousand Wehrmacht soldiers and fifteen thousand interned German civilians. "One by one," a French account noted, "we captured the human contents of the other forts, barracks, offices, and hospitals."

Strasbourg's emancipation brought two significant discoveries. Thirty miles southwest of the city, at Natzweiler, GIs overran their first concentration camp. Most of the seven thousand inmates still alive had been evacuated to the east, but ample evidence of atrocity remained. Built in 1941, Natzweiler had housed French *résistants,* Jews, homosexuals, and others deemed socially unfit; many had toiled in nearby granite quarries or munitions factories. A chamber built in an adjacent hotel had been used for poison-gas experiments, mostly against Gypsies imported from Auschwitz, and it was said that victims chosen for extermination were plied with sweets and cakes. Other human experiments involved typhus, yellow fever, and mustard gas. The corpses of gassed Jews were trucked by the score to a Strasbourg anatomy laboratory for dissection or preservation in alcohol as part of an SS study on "racial inferiority." Other bodies were cremated, with families reportedly charged seventy-five Reichmarks to retrieve a clay urn of ashes. Seventeen thousand had died at Natzweiler and its satellite camps.

The second discovery was no less portentous. Close on the heels of Leclerc's armored spearhead was an American intelligence unit codenamed ALSOS, carrying secret instructions from the physicists J. Robert Oppenheimer and Luis W. Alvarez on clues to look for in investigating "the Y program"—the German atomic bomb effort. Evidence discovered in Paris and at the Philips factory in Eindhoven pointed to the University of Strasbourg as a key atomic research center. ALSOS agents darted through laboratories, offices, and homes, arresting German physicists and chemists; they retrieved unburned scraps of scientific papers stuck in the chimney of a potbelly stove. Their chief target, the physicist Carl Friedrich von Weizsäcker, a close collaborator of the Nobel Prize–winner Werner

Heisenberg, was away in Germany, but his papers, computations, and correspondence remained in Strasbourg to be confiscated by the agents.

As Lieutenant General Leslie R. Groves, Jr., the director of the Manhattan Project, later wrote SHAEF, the Strasbourg seizures provided "the most complete, dependable and factual information we have obtained bearing upon the nature and extent of the German effort in our field. Fortunately it tends to confirm our conclusion that the Germans are now behind us." Far behind: top secret assessments found that "the enemy had made practically no progress" in building a bomb, that "the effort is not large," and that "no evidence was uncovered of any uranium work on a production scale." Despite the Y program's supposedly high priority, captured documents showed that German scientists had been forced to file a "certificate of urgency" for permission to buy "two slide rules for carrying out a project of military importance." Colonel Boris T. Pash, the ALSOS commander, reported that interrogations and other evidence confirmed that "the Nazis had not progressed in atomic development as far as our own project had early in 1941."

Leclerc and his lieutenants bivouacked in the ballroom of the nineteenth-century Kaiserpalast, used for four years as the Wehrmacht headquarters and said by a 2nd Armored Division officer to be the only building in Strasbourg to which, "because of its pretentious design, it was pleasant to give a German name." Shopkeepers switched their storefront signage back to French, reversing the changes of 1940, but the process of "dis-annexation" would be protracted and painful. More than half a million residents of Alsace and Lorraine had been deported to Germany as laborers, with another 140,000 forcibly drafted into the German army. Leclerc posted placards warning that "for every French soldier shot down in the city, five German hostages will be shot," a threat promptly disavowed by Devers as a violation of the Geneva Conventions. "There is no question that the French hate with the greatest bitterness," wrote the intelligence officer J. Glenn Gray. "They feed themselves on hatred. It is all strange and horrible."

A ceremony near the cathedral commemorated Strasbourg's return to French sovereignty with ringing bells and the usual bellowing of "La Marseillaise," although the din from antiaircraft guns peppering eight Luftwaffe intruders distracted the celebrants. In a message to De Gaulle, Leclerc proclaimed the vow of Koufra fulfilled.

Hitler in a 1940 visit to Strasbourg had also made a pledge: "We will never give it back." The Führer had kept his promise as well. He had not returned the city. The French had taken it.

For nearly three months Seventh Army had made ready to vault the Rhine. Two river-crossing schools, on the Rhône and on the Doubs, taught

GIs the intricacies of bridge construction, raft and ferry tactics, and the swift-water operation of storm boats. Eight hundred outboard-motor operators were now trained, and engineers had scrutinized the German capacity to generate floods on the river, extracting private assurances from the Swiss that upstream weirs would be safeguarded. SHAEF rejected a proposal to capture a bridgehead with two airborne divisions—MARKET GARDEN had cast a pall over such initiatives—and now eight infantry battalions were charged with seizing the far bank.

Even if the bridge from Strasbourg to Kehl remained standing, that avenue led only to the labyrinthine Schwarzwald, the Black Forest, so Seventh Army planners had long eyed a crossing site at Rastatt, a Baroque German town twenty-five miles farther north. Patrols found few defenders along the river there; Devers, who alarmed his headquarters by vanishing for more than a day while personally questioning scouts in the bottoms above Strasbourg, envisioned an advance from Rastatt to Karlsruhe, then a pivot west *behind* the Siegfried Line bunkers, thus trapping the German First Army between Patch and Patton. Even as Leclerc's tanks cavorted through Strasbourg, convoys thirty-five miles long had begun rolling toward riverfront assembly areas with DUKWs, bridging equipment, and boats stacked on trucks. On Thanksgiving night, Patch's engineers told him they could cross the Rhine on forty-eight hours' notice.

Eisenhower knew almost nothing of Devers's plans. On Friday morning, November 24, he and Bradley drove into the Vosges, following a brief conference with Patton in Nancy. They found Devers and Patch waiting for them in Lunéville at 11:30 A.M.; the small convoy then wheeled down Highway N-4 through spattering rain for thirty miles to the XV Corps command post at Sarrebourg. Devers looked "happy and boyish as usual," wrote Bradley's aide, Major Chester Hansen, although "Patch appeared grave, much older." After lunch with Haislip, at two P.M. they continued south another thirty miles through Baccarat to the VI Corps command post at St.-Dié, where the *Cosmographiae Introductio*—the book that had first used the name "America" for the New World—had been published in 1507. Now St.-Dié's textile mills, lumber yards, and eleventh-century church lay in ashes, pillaged by German demolitionists with incendiary grenades and dynamite. Residents with "square, impassive Alsatian faces" huddled in the rain along the charred walls that had once been their homes, wrote Hansen. Eisenhower called it "one of the most appalling sights of wanton destruction I've ever seen."

A final forty-mile drive to the west brought the convoy to the 6th Army Group headquarters in Vittel at six P.M. Revived by a boisterous cocktail party with ample scotch, the travelers enjoyed a late dinner at the elegant Heritage Hotel. After coffee, Devers led Eisenhower and Bradley to his penthouse suite, where the three men sat at a table.

The supreme commander wasted no time. Patton that same morning had pleaded for the return of XV Corps from Seventh Army, and Bradley agreed that the transfer of at least two divisions was warranted to reinforce Third Army's seventy-mile front. Despite the capture of Metz, Patton remained roadbound and not yet on the Saar.

"He's in the mud, and he's up against a concrete bastion," Devers said sympathetically.

Eisenhower frowned. New reports of a German counterattack from the north against Haislip's troops were unsettling: seventy tanks from the Panzer Lehr Division had routed cavalrymen eating their Thanksgiving turkey, and only massed artillery and timely help from Patton's 4th Armored Division would blunt the enemy advance. Eisenhower was even more nonplussed to learn that much of Seventh Army was heading for the Rhine at Rastatt. A crossing there, he complained, was "a helluva way to get to Berlin."

"Ike, I'm on the Haguenau river, moving north," Devers said, his voice rising. "I've got everything in the woods there to cross the Rhine. On the other side there are a lot of pillboxes, but they're not occupied."

"Those pillboxes are like hedgerows," Bradley said.

"Brad, we haven't got any hedgerows. We've got pillboxes, and the pillboxes aren't occupied," Devers said. "We can do this with a minimal force—as a raid, really—and this will cause the Germans no end of trouble."

The conversation dragged into the small hours of Saturday morning, the tone ever sharper. Devers noted that SHAEF had encouraged opportunism in seizing Rhine bridgeheads. Why flinch now? Shouldn't Seventh Army be strengthened rather than Third? Was it unreasonable to think that Patton's army should be shifted to the 6th Army Group so that together they could envelop the Saar?

Devers grew shrill. Eisenhower's plan to clear the entire west bank of the Rhine before advancing into central Germany seemed pointless. Was SHAEF intent on destroying the enemy or simply on occupying territory? Yet Devers undercut his own argument by describing the lunge across the Rhine at Rastatt not as a great wheeling movement by an army group, but as a sally that would take only "a matter of hours." Further, he likened it to Patton's effort in August 1943 to loop behind the enemy with an amphibious landing by a single battalion on the north coast of Sicily at Brolo—a misbegotten analogy, since that operation had ended in calamity.

Eisenhower remained immovable, and in truth he had made up his mind days earlier. The advances through Alsace, though welcome and applauded, were "far from the Ruhr," he observed, and a Rhine crossing here led to no "definitely decisive area." Weary of arguing, he gave Devers explicit orders: Seventh Army would immediately pivot northward, west of the Rhine, while the French finished expelling the enemy from Alsace below Strasbourg. Although reportedly "mad as hell" at Devers's obstinacy, Eisenhower offered a compromise, telling him that XV Corps would remain under 6th Army Group and even be strengthened with another armored division.

The trio of generals retired for a few hours' sleep, not a happy man among them. Orders went forth the next morning. Seventh Army Staff Memorandum X-376 on Saturday advised commanders that the plan "has recently been changed. At the present, no crossing of the Rhine River is contemplated and the direction of the advance will turn north astride the Vosges Mountains and generally parallel to the Rhine." Letter of Instruction No. 3 from 6th Army Group ordered the French First Army to extirpate the remaining Germans west of the river, with Leclerc's 2nd Armored Division driving south from Strasbourg under De Lattre's command. SHAEF planners began concocting a collaborative attack by Patton and Patch, while noting that "although the joint Third Army–Seventh Army offensive is not the most important sector of the front, it offers the best chance of quick returns and of getting the main offensive underway once more."

To his diary Devers confided, "The decision not to cross the Rhine was a blow to both Patch and myself, for we were really poised."

Even the Army official history, published half a century after the event and disinclined to second-guess the high command, found Eisenhower's decision "difficult to understand." The supreme commander "had opted for an operational 'strategy' of firepower and attrition—the direct approach—as opposed to a war of opportunistic maneuver." After encouraging a bloody attack through the Vosges, SHAEF possessed neither a coherent strategic goal for its southern wing nor the agility to exploit unexpected success. Even Patton believed Devers should have jumped the Rhine, yet little thought seems to have been given either in Versailles or in Luxembourg City to using Third Army's tank legions to exploit a bridgehead at Rastatt. In "misusing 6th Army Group," as one Army historian later charged, Eisenhower unwittingly gave the Germans a respite, allowing Hitler to continue assembling a secret counteroffensive aimed at the Ardennes in mid-December. Crossing the Rhine after Thanksgiving might well have complicated German planning for what soon would be known as the Battle of the Bulge.

Surely the supreme commander's personal distaste for Devers informed these events. Some also believed he played favorites with Bradley, his classmate and confidant. Devers emerged from the midnight session in Vittel wondering whether he was "a member of the same team." In a letter to his wife a day later he scornfully referred to unnamed "great strategists" and lamented not receiving "a little encouragement . . . to bring the war to a quicker end." In his diary he added, "The tragedy to my mind has been that the higher command has not seen fit to reinforce success on the flank."

Yet Devers made errors of his own—not least, he failed to recognize how feeble the French were. Six of eight German infantry divisions in the Nineteenth Army had been destroyed, leaving a fifty-thousand-man remnant in a rectangular Alsatian pocket that extended for forty-five miles along the Rhine and twenty-five miles west toward the High Vosges. Although Hitler on November 26 decreed that "to give up Alsace is out of the question," Rundstedt estimated that the pocket, which centered on the town of Colmar, could hold out for only three weeks. Devers told his diary, "It is hoped that the French Army will be able to destroy the Germans in their sector by 15 December."

This was not to be. De Lattre would claim that thirty German battalions reinforced the pocket "with the help of darkness and fog," but in fact only a few thousand more troops arrived west of the Rhine in the fortnight after Hitler's decree. French exhaustion, losses among junior officers, and "confusion I have never seen anywhere," as an American general put it, allowed the Germans to cauterize their lines.

Still more disheartening was the internecine bickering among Frenchmen who loathed one another at least as much as they loathed the enemy. Leclerc flatly refused Devers's order to march south from Strasbourg to join De Lattre's command, declaring, "I will not serve with any commanders who previously obeyed Vichy and whom I consider to be turncoats." For their part, De Lattre's men disdainfully refused to use Leclerc's nom de guerre, calling him instead by his antebellum name, Hauteclocque. Paris seemed unable to resolve the bickering, and Devers confessed to his diary, "Having a great deal of trouble keeping the French at their job of closing the pocket." He later added, "This was the only failure in command I ever had in war." Even when reinforced with the U.S. 36th Infantry Division, De Lattre failed to crack the Colmar Pocket; it was to remain an open wound in the Allied flank for months and the source, as an American colonel wrote, of "a great deal of consternation and ill-feeling between Jakey Devers and Eisenhower."

Seventh Army engineers trucked their storm boats back to supply dumps near Lunéville to await a brighter day. German dynamite on December 2 dropped the Kehl bridge into the Rhine with a thunderous splash, and the Strasbourg bridgehead escaped by boat to the Fatherland. Two railroad spans and three pontoon bridges closer to Colmar would keep the pocket victualed through the winter. Vicious sniper and artillery fire regularly swept back and forth across the river. Loudspeaker broadcasts from Kehl warned Alsatians that the Reich would soon return to reclaim Strasbourg.

"SHAEF treats us as bastard children," a Seventh Army officer later wrote his family, "slightly ashamed of our progress." Once again, an apparent battlefield victory was etched with vexation. Perhaps the taste of ashes was the flavor of war itself.

THE SIEGFRIED LINE
CAMPAIGN
SEPT. 11–DEC. 15, 1944

8. A Winter Shadow

"We Are All So Human That It Is Pitiful"

N INE million Allied propaganda leaflets fluttered over Germany every day, one thousand tons of paper each month, six billion sheets by war's end, all urging insurrection or surrender. In the early days of this "nickeling," airmen shoveled sheaves of leaflets into the slipstream from B-17 bomb bays thirty thousand feet over Brussels in hopes of littering occupied Paris; many instead drifted as far afield as Italy. Mass production of the T-1 Monroe Leaflet Bomb, beginning in April 1944, greatly improved accuracy: a barometric nose fuze blew open the five-foot-long cylinder two thousand feet above the target, scattering eighty thousand leaflets over one square mile. A single B-24 could sprinkle a million pages over five enemy towns during a single sortie.

Psychological-warfare teams studied previous surrender appeals, such as those used by the Japanese at Corregidor, searching for a key to unlock German intransigence. Many leaflets included a *Passierschein,* a safe-conduct pass, signed by Eisenhower and stressing the humane treatment accorded prisoners—for example, they would get the same food served "the best fed Army in the world." Bradley's army group alone also fired fifteen thousand artillery propaganda shells every month, each packed with five hundred leaflets, and loudspeaker appeals encouraged defection along the front, a practice known as "hog calling." Radio Luxembourg had begun German-language broadcasts in late September, with airtime devoted to composers banned by the Nazis, information programs such as *The Voice of SHAEF,* and dire war news, including street-by-street damage reports of recent bombing raids.

Millions of time-fuze incendiaries were dropped with instructions printed in nine languages to encourage sabotage, particularly by non-German slave laborers. OSS "Field Manual No. 3" offered advice to sabo-teurs on how to insinuate sawdust, hair, sugar, or molasses into German fuel tanks, preferably one hundred grams for each ten gallons of gasoline. A half-pint of urine or salt water would also do the trick. "Try to commit acts for which large numbers of people could be responsible," the manual advised. "For instance, if you blow out the wiring in a factory at a central fire box, almost anyone could have done it."

Still Germany fought on. Some Allied strategists believed that the insistence on unconditional surrender, announced by Roosevelt at the Casablanca conference in January 1943, was prolonging the war. Joseph Goebbels and other Nazi propagandists claimed that the demand "means slavery, castration, the end of Germany as a nation." A U.S. government analysis warned that most Germans felt they had "nothing to lose by continuing the war." Others argued that the Reich kept fighting out of fear of the Russians and the Gestapo "rather than any phrase coined at a conference," as John J. McCloy, the assistant secretary of war, put it. Proposals for "conditional unconditional surrender," similar to the modified terms under which Italy had capitulated, found no favor with Roosevelt. "I want at all costs to prevent it from being said that the unconditional surrender principle has been abandoned," the president had declared even before OVER-LORD. Germans must recognize, he later added, "that the whole nation has been engaged in a lawless conspiracy against the decencies of modern civilization."

Eventual Allied victory had long been an article of faith, of course. Even before the Normandy landings, SHAEF commissioned seventy-two studies on how to govern postwar Germany, under a plan now code-named ECLIPSE. Yet no consensus existed on the construct of postwar Europe, or the political architecture of a future Germany, or, as the experience in Aachen had revealed, the nuances of occupation. Roosevelt inclined toward a hard peace following the hard war—he proposed feeding the eighty million Germans three bowls of soup a day from U.S. Army vats, a gesture of largesse given that he had at first suggested just one bowl daily. In this the president reflected his people: polls showed that more than four in five Americans supported unconditional surrender and the reduction of Germany to a third-rate power. SHAEF in the summer of 1944 drafted a "Handbook for Military Government in Germany," recommending enlightened benevolence in rebuilding the postwar economy and administrative apparatus. "This so-called Handbook is pretty bad," Roosevelt wrote Secretary of War Stimson. "All copies should be withdrawn." So they were, notwithstanding a SHAEF officer's lament that "nobody ever reads handbooks anyhow"; no revision was issued until December. Even Eisenhower's decree that "we come as conquerors, but not as oppressors" proved problematic when translated into German, because *Eroberer*—conqueror—implied plunder and annexation *auf Deutsch*. The issue eventually reached the War Department's top linguist, who substituted *ein siegreiches Heer*—a victorious army—as less inflammatory.

The victorious Red Army in the east helped focus the Anglo-Americans on postwar matters when Washington and London realized that Soviet troops could soon occupy Germany as far west as the Rhine. A War Department analysis prophesied:

> The defeat of Germany will leave Russia in a position of assured military dominance in eastern Europe and in the Middle East, [bringing] a world profoundly changed in respect to relative national military strengths, a change more comparable indeed with that occasioned by the fall of Rome than with any other change occurring during the succeeding fifteen hundred years. . . . The British Empire will emerge from the war having lost ground both economically and militarily.

Winston Churchill also perceived that his nation's empire was imperiled and he sought to stave off decline in his own fashion. In mid-October, during a private meeting in Moscow with Stalin, the prime minister had jotted a few notations on a sheet of paper in proposing an allocation of postwar influence between Moscow and London in southeastern Europe. He suggested 90 percent for the Soviets in Romania, a similar British preponderance in Greece, 75 percent for Moscow in Bulgaria, and an even split in Yugoslavia and Hungary. Stalin penciled a blue tick mark on the paper and told Churchill to keep what the prime minister called his "naughty document." Although the "percentages agreement" had no legal force and proved a poor forecast of subsequent events, the Americans were incensed upon eventually learning of this nefarious sidebar arrangement, which contravened Roosevelt's antipathy toward spheres of influence in postwar Europe.

That fall, a separate controversy had come to dominate the discussion of Germany's future. The disavowal by the White House of SHAEF's handbook emboldened the U.S. treasury secretary, Henry Morgenthau, Jr., to propose that Germany be dismembered and that the constituent pieces be reduced to neutered agricultural states incapable of armed aggression. Roosevelt waxed enthusiastic at this scheme. As the historian Warren F. Kimball later wrote, the president and Morgenthau, "like the two Jeffersonian gentlemen farmers they pretended to be," proposed scrubbing stains from the German character by "starting them out again as farmers." Morgenthau's explanation of his plan at an Anglo-American strategy conference convened in Quebec in mid-September had drawn baleful stares from Churchill, who called it "unnatural, unchristian, and unnecessary." But when Morgenthau predicted that to eradicate German competition for coal and steel markets would guarantee British prosperity for twenty years, the prime minister changed his tune virtually overnight, endorsing "the re-creation of an agricultural state as had existed in the last quarter of the nineteenth century" by shuttering the Ruhr and the Saar. As for the Germans, Churchill added, "They brought it on themselves."

Others in the Anglo-American brain trust were appalled. Anthony Eden, the British foreign secretary, "flew into a rage," while his American counterpart, Cordell Hull, called Morgenthau's proposal "a plan of blind vengeance." Stimson warned of "enormous general evils" from such a "Carthaginian peace," not least because the raw materials for Europe's antebellum livelihood had derived largely from the Ruhr and the Saar. Plans were also afoot to deed a vast swatch of farmland in eastern Germany to Poland, which left unanswered the question of how the Germans could live as farmers if the land became Polish. Even George Marshall bridled at Morgenthau's vision, particularly his proposal to summarily shoot Nazi leaders upon capture.

Predictably, the scheme soon leaked. "The papers have taken it up violently," Stimson noted with satisfaction. An editorial in London called Morgenthau's Germany "a ruined no-man's land in which no wheels turn," and the British cabinet denounced the treasury secretary's "unwisdom," adding, "A policy which condones or favors chaos is not hard; it is simply inefficient." Roosevelt deftly disavowed the plan, telling Stimson with a grin, "Henry Morgenthau pulled a boner." The German newspapers also took it up violently, warning of "a life and death struggle" against Anglo-American "cannibals," whose "satanic plan of annihilation" was, needless to say, "inspired by the Jews." Even six billion leaflets could go only so far to persuade Germans that a tolerable peace would follow from surrender.

This contretemps cooled Roosevelt's enthusiasm for postwar strategizing. "I dislike making detailed plans for a country which we do not yet occupy," he told Hull in late October, while publicly assuring the Germans that they would not be enslaved. Precisely how the occupation would be configured was put off until another season, along with ancillary questions of military governance. An early proposal had considered carving the Reich into as many as seven disparate states; a more practical agreement drafted by the British Foreign Office in early 1944 posited three occupation zones, with the Soviet Union given the eastern 40 percent of the country except for Berlin, which would be administered jointly by the Allied victors. Roosevelt for months had resisted a proposed American occupation sector contiguous to France; his distrust of De Gaulle ran very deep. But at Quebec the president at last conceded that the concentration of U.S. forces on the right of Eisenhower's line argued for an American zone in Bavaria and the German southwest, with guarantees of access to North Sea ports in the British sector.

No formal ratification of this plan, or any other, was forthcoming. Eisenhower initially believed postwar Germany should be administered under a single Allied commander, but more recently he had conceded that "the Russians will . . . take exclusive responsibility for administering the eastern portion of Germany." Some U.S. strategists continued to advocate occupation zones converging on Berlin like pie slices, rather than placing the German capital deep within the Soviet sector; the U.S. ambassador to Britain, John G. Winant, denounced such a proposal as "not having any faith in Soviet intentions."

With postwar politics unresolved, military planners could only continue to sketch big arrows across their maps, aimed at Berlin. Roosevelt had shied away from Morgenthau's draconian solution, but he remained ardently committed to unconditional surrender. As for the rest, the president had told Churchill: "Something 'big' will come out of this war: a new heaven and a new earth."

Montgomery's promise to Eisenhower that "you will hear *no* more on the subject of command from me" had hardly been made before it was broken. Those big arrows on war room maps may have pointed toward the Ruhr and beyond, but his sharpest darts were aimed at the supreme commander. In private rants to his British colleagues, the field marshal continued to disparage Eisenhower, his plan, and his generalship. "He has never commanded anything before in his whole career," Montgomery wrote Brooke in mid-November. "Now, for the first time, he has elected to take command of very large-scale operations and he does not know how to do it." In another note, on November 21, he added, "There is a feeling of optimism at SHAEF. There are no grounds for such optimism." Brooke, who should have known better, fed these disloyal tantrums, replying to Montgomery on November 24, "You have always told me, and I have agreed with you, that Ike was no commander, that he had no strategic vision, was incapable of making a plan or of running operations when started." On a visit to London two days later, Montgomery added, "Eisenhower is quite useless. . . . He is completely and utterly useless."

On Tuesday afternoon, November 28, the blind, callow, useless Eisenhower arrived for an overnight visit at the 21st Army Group headquarters in the Belgian town of Zonhoven, east of Antwerp. Here he heard more of the same from Montgomery directly, albeit in more diplomatic language. Strutting and frowning amid the wall maps in his office trailer, pinching his cheek between thumb and forefinger, the field marshal for several hours railed about lack of progress on the Western Front and urged that a single commander oversee the Allied main effort against the Ruhr. As Eisenhower, exhausted, prepared for bed, Montgomery's aide Lieutenant Colonel Christopher C. "Kit" Dawnay brought the supreme commander a whiskey and soda, then repaired to Montgomery's office, where the field marshal dictated a note to Brooke. "We talked for three hours," Montgomery reported. "He admitted a grave mistake has been made" and agreed that "I should be in full operational command north of the Ardennes with Bradley under me."

An astonished Dawnay interjected, "Ike does *not* agree, sir."

"Send that message," Montgomery snapped. The next morning, following more tedious palaver before Eisenhower pressed on to inspect British, Canadian, and Polish troops, Montgomery told Brooke in a postscript, "He thinks Bradley has failed him as an architect of land operations. There is no doubt he is now very anxious to go back to the old set-up we had in Normandy . . . and to put Bradley under my operational command."

Montgomery evidently had second thoughts about his interpretation of Eisenhower's comments, because on Thursday, November 30, he sent him a "personal and confidential" cable "to confirm the main points that were agreed on during the conversations." Earlier in the fall, he wrote, Eisenhower had consented to place the main Allied weight in the north, to eradicate the enemy west of the Rhine, and to seize bridgeheads across the river.

> We have achieved none of this; and we have no hope of doing so. We have therefore failed; and we have suffered a strategic reverse. . . . We must get away from the doctrine of attacking in so many places that nowhere are we strong enough to get decisive results.

The Belgian Ardennes naturally divided the Western Front, he added; the two sectors, north and south, should each have separate commanding generals.

> Bradley and I together are a good team. We worked together in Normandy, under you, and we won a great victory. Things have not been so good since you separated us. I believe [that] to be certain of success you want to bring us together again; and one of us should have the full operational control north of the Ardennes; and if you decide that I should do that work—that is O.K. by me.

On Friday, December 1, Eisenhower's Cadillac circled south across the Pétrusse River in Luxembourg City, where he found Bradley bedridden with the flu in the Hôtel Alfa, his face badly swollen with hives. Clutching Montgomery's message in his fist, a scarlet flush creeping up his neck, "Ike was as angry as I had ever seen him," Bradley later recorded. This missive from the field marshal could only be interpreted as a condemnation of his

leadership; Montgomery even had the temerity to propose another strategy session from which all others would be excluded except the two chiefs
of staff, Smith and De Guingand, "who must not speak."

After a splenetic diatribe to which the disfigured Bradley could do little more than sniffle, Eisenhower calmed himself long enough to dictate
a fifteen-paragraph reply, again demonstrating his remarkable ability to
turn the other cheek with composure and equanimity. "There are certain
things in your letter [with] which I do not concur," he began.

> I am not quite sure I know exactly what you mean by strategic
> reverse. . . . I do not agree that things have gone badly since Normandy,
> merely because we have not gained all we had hoped to gain. In fact, the
> situation is somewhat analogous to that which existed in Normandy for
> so long.

He reminded Montgomery that British logistics in the north had been
so stretched that merely providing five hundred extra tons of supplies
each day "cost Bradley three divisions," by stripping them of motor transport in order to feed and arm 21st Army Group. "Had we not advanced on
a relatively broad front we would now have the spectacle of a long narrow
line of communication, constantly threatened on the right flank."

> I have no intention of stopping Devers and Patton's operations as
> long as they are cleaning up our right flank and giving us capability of
> concentration. . . . It is going to be important to us later on to have two
> strings to our bow.

Only in reply to the suggestion of muzzling the chiefs of staff did
Eisenhower offer the back of his hand. "It makes no difference to me
whether your chief of staff attends or whether Bradley's does. Mine will be
there unless some unforeseen circumstance prevents. . . . I will not by any
means insult him by telling him that he should remain mute."

He finished by subtly suggesting that only one of them could see the
horizon.

> I most definitely appreciate the frankness of your statements, and
> [the] usual friendly way in which they are stated, but I beg of you not to
> continue to look upon the past performances of this great fighting force
> as a failure merely because we have not achieved all that we could have
> hoped. . . . We must look at this whole great affair stretching from Mar-
> seille to the lower Rhine as one great theater.

As was now amply evident, Montgomery simply could not play the loyal, stalwart lieutenant. Subordination held little appeal for a solipsist. Even the king's equerry had noted in his diary that "such canalized egotism, though maybe necessary to a successful general . . . makes a man an exacting companion. . . . Sometimes I wonder whether Monty's undoubted genius does not occasionally bring him to the verge of mental unstability." If that was overdrawn—self-involvement need not imply imbalance— nevertheless Eisenhower's biographer Stephen E. Ambrose later wrote of Montgomery: "He had no competence in the fine art of persuasion. He was accustomed to working on a problem alone, then handing down a solution. . . . He could not get his ideas across without appearing either patronizing or offensive, or both."

A British official who watched Montgomery in a meeting described how he "sat up like a little bird with his head on one side, sharp as a needle, and with very bright eyes. . . . A most striking man with his bright eyes and long beaky nose [but] a bit *naif* in political matters." Brooke confided to his diary that Montgomery "goes on harping over the system of command in France. He has got this on the brain. . . . He cannot put up with not being the sole controller of land operations."

But others in the highest British circles took up his twin themes of abject failure in the west and Eisenhower's manifest deficiencies. "We have of course sustained a strategic reverse on the Western Front," Churchill told the South African soldier and statesman Jan Smuts on December 3. To Roosevelt, the prime minister cabled three days later, "We have definitely failed to achieve the strategic object which we gave to our armies five weeks ago. We have not yet reached the Rhine in the northern part." The president replied with sanguine assurances—"a decisive break in our favor is bound to come"—but even Admiral Ramsay, who was among Eisenhower's staunchest allies, told De Guingand that he saw "no prospect of Ike getting any wiser."

Some of Montgomery's partisans were more savage. Brooke noted that during a luncheon at SHAEF's new forward headquarters in Reims, Kay Summersby had been "promoted to hostess, and sat at the head of the table. . . . Ike produced a lot of undesirable gossip that did him no good." In subsequent diary entries, Brooke added, Eisenhower "is detached and by himself with his lady chauffeur on the golf links at Reims. . . . I think he is incapable of running the war even if he tries."

The fairways at Reims were in fact carpeted with SHAEF tents, rendering them unfit for sport, and Eisenhower's British military assistant, Lieutenant Colonel James F. Gault, later attested that during their long wartime association the supreme commander never swung a golf club. Yet the calumny continued. "Eisenhower completely fails as supreme commander. . . .

The war is drifting in a rudderless condition," Brooke wrote. "We must take the control out of Eisenhower's hands."

At Montgomery's request, another high-command conclave was scheduled for Thursday morning, December 7, in Maastricht, the first Dutch city to be liberated in September and, it was asserted, the oldest town in the Netherlands, a claim bitterly disputed by Nijmegen. Here the Romans had quarried limestone and bridged the Maas, and here blessed Saint Servatius had placed his bishopric in the fourth century. Here too a four-month siege by Spanish brigands in 1579 ended in plunder and eight thousand locals put to the sword; another siege a century later, under Louis XIV, ended when that ubiquitous French military engineer, Vauban, reduced the Maastricht citadel by digging parallel trenches ever closer to the fortifications, a technique embraced by besiegers for the next two centuries. The Dutch could take solace only in having killed the celebrated French captain of musketeers Charles d'Artagnan, who was felled by a musket ball to the throat and subsequently immortalized in the novels of Alexandre Dumas.

Eisenhower and Tedder spent Wednesday night at the Hôtel Alfa in Luxembourg City with a still-ailing Bradley before the trio drove together to Maastricht. In a conference room at U.S. Ninth Army headquarters, Eisenhower—smartly tailored in the waist-length uniform jacket that came to be named for him—opened the session by applauding the Allied butchery of enemies during the fall, which had inflicted attrition "very much greater than our own." SHAEF intelligence had estimated that current operations were chewing through twenty German divisions a month, while only a dozen could be newly formed each month, and five eviscerated divisions refitted. Yet with the Rhine in spate from autumn rains, Eisenhower added, "it might not be possible to effect a major crossing until May." Since the beginning of November, the British Second Army had advanced less than ten miles.

At Eisenhower's request, Montgomery then took the floor to tender his views. "The master plan," as the field marshal called it, must cut off the Ruhr and force the enemy into mobile warfare to further strain German supplies of fuel and other matériel. The only suitable region for mobile combat, he believed, lay north of the Ruhr. "We must, therefore, concentrate the whole of our available effort on the drive across the Rhine north of the Ruhr, operations on the rest of the front being purely containing ones."

Eisenhower agreed, then disagreed. True, it was vital to isolate the Ruhr and force the enemy to move; the crux of his strategy was to provoke the Germans to give battle so they could be decisively defeated. But converging

Allied attacks from disparate points would require Rundstedt to shift his forces across a wider front: an invasion avenue from Frankfurt toward Kassel, now in Patton's sights, appeared "quite practicable."

Montgomery begged to differ. He could "not agree that a thrust from Frankfurt offered any prospect of success." This, he added, was a fundamental disagreement between his vision and Eisenhower's.

Round and round they went, "another long and tedious affair," in Bradley's phrase. Montgomery again argued for separate commands north and south of the Ardennes. Eisenhower countered that he intended to make command arrangements based on operations yet to come, "not by geographical factors" already behind the Allied line. The Ruhr, he pointed out, offered an obvious demarcation, with 21st Army Group to the north and 12th Army Group to the south. Again Montgomery disagreed. This, he said, was "a second fundamental difference of view."

The session ended with the supreme commander attempting to reconcile the irreconcilable. In what Bradley called "a classic Eisenhower compromise," Montgomery's drive in the north was affirmed as the main Allied attack; the field marshal would be reinforced, with up to ten divisions from the U.S. Ninth Army placed under his command. Bradley would retain command of Hodges's First Army and Patton's Third, respectively north and south of the Ardennes, protected on the right flank by Devers's army group. The broad-front strategy was upheld once more, with all seven Allied armies in action. The Ruhr would be devoured by a double envelopment from north and south, much as Hannibal had devoured the Romans in 216 B.C. at Cannae, a legendary battle of annihilation that had long kept an excessively powerful grip on Eisenhower's imagination.

"The meeting was affable on the surface but quite unproductive," Tedder subsequently wrote Air Marshal Portal. "Monty's almost contemptuous way of refusing to discuss or hear of anything except only his particular ideas makes real discussion quite impossible. . . . Ike depressed about it last night and wondered what was the use of having such meetings."

Others also were disheartened. "Another balls up," Montgomery told Tedder. "Everything has been a balls up since September 1." To Brooke on Thursday night he wrote:

> I personally regard the whole thing as quite dreadful. We shall split our resources and our strength, and we shall fail. . . . You have to get Eisenhower's hand taken off the land battle. I regret to say that in my opinion he just doesn't know what he is doing. And you will have to see that Bradley's influence is curbed.

Bradley a few days later wrote of Montgomery, "He refused to admit that there was any merit in anybody else's views except his own . . . largely colored by his desire to command the whole show." Should 12th Army Group ever fall under Montgomery's command, Bradley told Eisenhower, he would interpret the arrangement as "an indication that I had failed" and would ask to be relieved. Eisenhower's confidant General Everett Hughes wrote his wife from Paris, "We are all so human that it is pitiful. We never grow up."

A churlish, dolorous mood had taken hold, belying their station as the winning generals of winning armies in a winning, righteous cause. As so often happens in battle, exhaustion and strain had got the best of them, and a thousand fraught decisions from which dangled lives by the tens of thousands gnawed at every commander with a beating heart. War, that merciless revealer of character, uncloaked these men as precisely as a prism flays open a beam of light to reveal the inner spectrum. Here they were, disclosed, exposed, made known, and if rectitude was to obtain, they would have to fight their way to that high ground just as surely as they would have to fight their way across the Rhine.

Staking Everything on One Card

AN iron sky roofed the gray-green Taunus Hills on Monday morning, December 11, as a motorcade carrying Adolf Hitler and a fifty-man entourage of staff officers and SS bodyguards rolled across the Hessian landscape toward another of those remote boltholes the regime had built for itself in better days. The convoy sped south from the Giessen train station toward Frankfurt for fifteen miles before climbing west, past the heel-clicking sentries outside the neo-Gothic Schloss Ziegenberg; the cars traveled a final mile beneath a camouflage canopy suspended from trees above the narrow roadbed. With a crunch of tires on gravel, the convoy pulled to a stop and the Führer climbed from the rear seat of his limousine, his face puffy and spectrally pale.

To the unschooled eye, the seven half-timbered buildings of the Adlerhorst—the Eagle's Eyrie—resembled a farm hamlet, or perhaps a rustic hunting camp. Several houses had wooden porches with flower baskets. Interior furnishings included oak floor lamps and tasseled shades; deer-antler trophies hung on the knotty-pine paneling. But a closer look revealed the cottages to be bunkers with thick concrete walls and reinforced roofs; the architect Albert Speer had designed them in 1939 as a field headquarters for campaigns in the west, including the drive on Dunkirk so long ago. Outbuildings were disguised as haystacks or barns, and a maze of subterranean passages with heavy metal doors and peepholes linked one sector to another. Artificial trees supplemented the native conifers to thwart aerial snooping. Hidden antiaircraft batteries ringed the compound. A concrete bunker half a mile long and masked as a brick retaining wall led across a shallow glen to Schloss Ziegenberg, with its single stone tower dating to the twelfth century. After centuries of neglect the castle had been refurbished in the 1800s, and in recent years it had served as a rehabilitation hospital for wounded officers.

Hitler shuffled into his private chalet, known as Haus 1. Since his meeting with Rundstedt and Rommel at Margival in June, the Führer, like his empire, was even more diminished. His limp was pronounced. Doctors had recently removed an abscess from his vocal cords, and the long overnight trip from Berlin to Giessen aboard the Führer train, *Brandenburg,* had further worn him. "He seemed near collapse," one officer later wrote. "His shoulders drooped. His left arm shook as he walked." In a few hours he would unveil to his field commanders his planned masterstroke for snatching victory from his enemies, much as Frederick the Great had when Prussia faced certain defeat by her European adversaries in the winter of 1761–62. "Genius is a will-o'-the-wisp if it lacks a solid foundation of perseverance and fanatical tenacity," Hitler had recently told an aide. "This is the most important thing in all human life." Destiny had brought him to this moment, to this dark wood, and he was ready, as General Alfred Jodl, his operations chief, put it, "to stake everything on one card." But first he needed rest.

Even a delusional megalomaniac could sense that the Third Reich faced obliteration. Soviet armies now coiling in Poland and the Balkans stood within a bound of the German homeland. Romania, Bulgaria, and Finland had departed the Axis, with German possessions in Hungary, Yugoslavia, Albania, and Greece imperiled. Gone were Belgium, Luxembourg, half of Holland, and all of France but for the Alsatian enclave and a few besieged ports. In Italy, Field Marshal Kesselring struggled to hold the Gothic Line, the last defensive position across the peninsula short of the Po valley.

German war production was likewise attenuated. The Wehrmacht in September fired seventy thousand tons of explosives, but factories produced only half that amount. From January through October, 118,000 military trucks had been lost and just 46,000 new ones built, although dwindling gasoline stocks often immobilized vehicle fleets anyway. Allied bombardment of the Ruhr nearly halved steel production from October to November, and by December electrical power generated in Germany had plunged by one-third. Mountains of coal accumulated in the Ruhr, even as profound shortages afflicted other regions because those mountains could not be moved. The regime had imposed a sixty-hour industrial workweek with holidays abolished, except in tank and aircraft factories: there, workers toiled seventy-two hours a week. "Heroes of National Socialist Labor" received extra food, vitamins, and vacations in the Tyrol as incentives; defeatism and sabotage were rewarded with firing squads. Seven million prisoners-of-war and foreign workers, many of them slaves, provided a quarter of the country's labor force for farms, mines, and factories.

To shore up a military now losing almost fifty thousand killed in action each month, Hitler had mustered another three-quarters of a million men by lowering the draft age to sixteen, raising it to fifty, and ordering what he deemed "rear-area swine" combed from the home front. (A nurse's aide described hospitalized soldiers tearing open their wounds at night to delay healing, "out of sheer terror of being sent back to the front.") A reserve of more than thirty divisions, including Volksgrenadier and panzer units, had been built to preserve an offensive strike force, even as German armies retreated on all fronts. In October, a home guard dubbed the Volkssturm— People's Storm—also was created under Himmler's SS; the joke went around that retirement homes now bore the sign "Closed because of the call-up." The levy robbed German industry of skilled workers, but by December Hitler's armies comprised 243 divisions with 3.6 million soldiers, of whom 2 million were older than thirty. If imposing in number and ideological fervor, the force was a pale shadow of the earlier Wehrmacht. Fewer and fewer companies had more than one officer, and some units were so poorly kitted out for combat that they were known as "bow and arrow infantry."

Secret weapons always beguiled the Führer, and never more so than now. Some were as simple as a rifle that could shoot around corners—tests reportedly showed fair accuracy at four hundred meters. Others required the mobilization of a nation hard-pressed to make even gasoline and electricity. The first jet aircraft had taken to the skies in the fall, flying, as one pilot put it, "as if an angel were pushing." The Luftwaffe by year's end would receive more than five hundred Me-262s and Ar-234s, but they remained mostly ineffective in combat—a warplane is only as good as its pilot—and susceptible to accidents, fuel shortages, Allied air raids, and production snafus, including blade fractures in the engine turbines.

No less innovative were new "electro" U-boats with streamlined hulls and increased battery capacity intended to allow longer submersion and far greater underwater speeds than conventional submarines. German yards by November were turning out a new boat every couple days, but these too were bedeviled by defects—mostly discovered after the submarines were delivered to the navy—as well as by Allied sea mines and bomb damage to boats and bases. Well into 1945, German submarines continued to attack Allied ships in waters as distant as the Gulf of St. Lawrence and the U.S. Eastern Seaboard. But scarcely any vessels would be sunk by the new U-boats, and the entire German submarine fleet sent fewer than one hundred Allied and neutral ships to the bottom in the final nine months of the war.

The miracles of the German jet, the electro-boat, and the gun that shot around corners proved to be no miracles at all. If German arms were to forestall the nation's imminent defeat, the enemy must be crushed by soldiers conventionally outfitted with rifles, howitzers, and tanks. That killing blow, Hitler had concluded, must be struck in one great, bold, and unexpected attack.

Dusk enfolded the Taunus Hills at five P.M., when two buses arrived at Schloss Ziegenberg. Heavy rain dripped from the pine boughs as a clutch of senior officers queued up to board. Many believed they had been summoned to the castle to toast Rundstedt's sixty-ninth birthday on Tuesday, but a terse request that each man surrender his sidearm and briefcase in the Ziegenberg cloakroom suggested a less festive occasion. For half an hour the buses lurched this way and that through the forest, as corps and division commanders chatted quietly or stared out the rain-streaked windows. The circuitous route, intended to obscure that they were traveling barely a kilometer across the glen, ended at Haus 2, the Adlerhorst officers' club, which a covered walkway connected to the Führer's Haus 1.

A double row of armed SS guards formed a cordon from each bus to the club's main door; a steep flight of steps, now ringing beneath the heavy footfall of black boots, led to a subterranean situation room. As directed, each officer took his seat around a long rectangular table, with an SS man at port arms behind each chair in an attitude of such scowling intimidation that one general later admitted fearing "even to reach for a handkerchief." Rundstedt and Model, the two senior German commanders in the west, sat impassively elbow to elbow.

Ten minutes later Hitler hobbled in and sat with a grimace behind a small separate table at the head of the room, flanked by Jodl and the tall, monocled Wehrmacht chief, Field Marshal Wilhelm Keitel. Field generals privately referred to the pair as *Nick-Esel*, the nodding donkeys, part of the larger circle of *Jaleute*, yes-people. The Führer's hands trembled as he pulled on his spectacles and picked up a manuscript. Those who had not seen him since the July 20 assassination attempt were stunned by his appearance; one general wrote that he looked like "a broken man, with an unhealthy color, a caved-in appearance . . . sitting as if the burden of responsibility seemed to oppress him." Manipulating his dangling left arm with his right hand, "he often stared vacantly, his back was bent, and his shoulders sunken," another officer reported.

Then he spoke, and color flushed into the pallid cheeks. The dull eyes once again seemed to kindle from within. For the first fifty minutes he delivered a soaring harangue on history, fate, and how he had battled against "the policy of encirclement of Germany," devised by Churchill with "international world Jewry behind it."

> Never in history was there a coalition like that of our enemies, composed of such heterogeneous elements with such divergent aims. Ultra-capitalist states on the one hand; ultra-Marxist states on the other. . . . Even now these states are at loggerheads. . . . These antagonisms grow stronger and stronger from hour to hour. If now we can deliver a few more heavy blows, then at any moment this artificially bolstered common front may suddenly collapse with a gigantic clap of thunder.

As the Allies approached each other from east and west, the strain on this unholy alliance would grow insuperable. Canada, he predicted, would be the first to yank its troops from the theater. "World historical events have their ups and downs," the Führer declared.

> Rome would not be thinkable without a Second Punic War. . . . There would be no Prussia without the Seven Years' War. . . . The palm of victory will in the end be given to the one who was not only ablest, but—and I want to emphasize this—was the most daring.

Toward that end he had a plan, originally code-named WACHT AM RHEIN, Watch on the Rhine, but recently renamed HERBSTNEBEL, Autumn Mist. This he would now disclose on pain of death to any man who betrayed the grand secret.

It had come to him as in a fever dream, when he was bedridden and yellow with jaundice in September. Brooding over what Jodl called "the evil fate hanging over us," the Führer had again been hunched at his maps when his eye fixed on the same unlikely seam through the Ardennes that German invaders had already ripped twice in this century. A monstrous blow by two panzer armies could swiftly reach the Meuse bridges between Liège and Namur, carving away Montgomery's 21st Army Group in the north from the Americans in the south, and eradicating the enemy threat to the Ruhr. Destroying thirty divisions in the west would wipe out a third of the Anglo-American force, requiring Churchill and Roosevelt to sue for peace; conversely, exterminating thirty Bolshevik divisions in the east, among more than five hundred, could hardly deal a decisive blow. Therefore Germany's destiny must, he proclaimed, be "sealed in the West." As for the offensive's ultimate objective, Hitler in a conference with his senior generals had abruptly blurted out a single word: "Antwerp."

The naysayers promptly said nay. Rundstedt, who would command this great offensive, had learned of the plan only after it coagulated in Hitler's imagination; the Führer's order came as a "great surprise." The field marshal favored strategic defense—"no offensive under any conditions," as one lieutenant put it. Yes, he had led the vanquishing German armies through the Ardennes in 1940, but then he had commanded seventy-one divisions altogether, more than double the force allotted to HERBSTNEBEL, and those units were far stronger than the current Wehrmacht divisions. The invasion of the Soviet Union in 1941 had included 123 divisions and 2,500 attack planes, five times the strength of the force available for this offensive. Given the strained supplies of fuel, ammunition, and manpower, and with little Luftwaffe support, Rundstedt concluded that the force was "much, much, *much* too weak" to sustain a winter attack across 125 miles to Antwerp.

Although uncertain why the Allied drive across Europe had stalled, Rundstedt within the sanctity of his sitting room had told trusted aides, "The soldier can do nothing but buy time for the political leader to negotiate." His chief of staff, General Siegfried Westphal, wrote that "the distant objective of Antwerp cannot be reached with the forces available, for then impossibly long flanks would be exposed on both sides of the attacking wedge. . . . The entire planning of this offensive strikes me as failing to meet the demands of reality." Hitler brushed aside the objections, telling Rundstedt, "I think I am a better judge of this than you are, Field Marshal. I have come here to help you."

Even Model, who claimed to love those who craved the impossible, also demurred, calling the Führer's scheme "damned moldy." The Army Group B commander would provide most of the forces for HERBSTNEBEL, and like Rundstedt he considered Antwerp far too ambitious. Both men favored a truncated plan—dubbed "the small solution," in contrast to Hitler's grandiose "large solution"—with a wheeling movement north around Aachen that would cut off the U.S. First and Ninth Armies and destroy ten to fifteen divisions. The two army commanders anointed by the Führer to lead the attack, Generals Hasso von Manteuffel and Sepp Dietrich, had also endorsed the small solution in a six-hour conference with Hitler at the Reich Chancellery in Berlin on December 2. Not only was the small solution better suited to the force available, they argued, but Wehrmacht soldiers would fight desperately to reclaim the swatch of Germany now held by the Americans.

The Führer was unmoved. Only a brutal drubbing would achieve the political objective of forcing the Anglo-Americans to the bargaining table. Only a victory as dramatic as the Reich's recapture of Antwerp could convince the enemy that the campaign was bootless, endless, hopeless. He promised thirty-eight divisions for the attack, supported by two thousand planes—an enduring fantasy that had taken on a life of its own even as autumn fighting further whittled away German strength. The final attack blueprint approved by Hitler on December 9 was virtually unchanged from the vision he had revealed earlier in the fall. A copy sent to Rundstedt was annotated by the Führer: "Not to Be Altered."

And thus was the plan fixed: three armies under Model's Army Group B would attack across a hundred-mile front. The first echelon alone included two hundred thousand men in twenty divisions with two thousand artillery pieces and nearly a thousand tanks and assault guns. A second wave carried five more divisions and hundreds of additional panzers. A fourth field army, the Fifteenth, was positioned north of the assault area with six infantry divisions to tie up American forces near Aachen. In all, Model had thirty or more divisions for HERBSTNEBEL.

With the possible exception of the Vosges, no more rugged terrain existed between the North Sea and the Alps than the coniferous Ardennes, a shaggy, corrugated tableland less than 2,500 feet high but fissured with deep stream beds across the sixty miles between the German border and the Meuse. The French belief that it was an "almost impenetrable massif" had been disproved in August 1914, when four German armies with more than a million men eventually poured through the Ardennes. Between wars, the governments of Belgium and Luxembourg, keen to exploit automobile *tourisme,* built ten all-weather roads that led westward from the German frontier across many stout stone bridges. Still, the delusion of impermeability prevailed until May 1940, when the Germans shoved a mechanized host through the region in three days, nearly twice as fast as predicted even in Wehrmacht march tables, with young Rommel's panzer division grabbing the first bridgehead across the Meuse at Dinant.

Hitler had been consumed for weeks by the minutest details of HERBSTNEBEL, from the provision to each shock trooper of at least three blankets to the banishment of Alsatian troops from frontline units as security risks. Of all the German armored vehicles built in November, 1,345 were shipped to the west, only 288 to the east. Divisions in Norway had been required to divert many of their motor vehicles to the Western Front.

Campaign planners intended to replicate 1940, one officer said: "to hold the reins loose, and let the armies race." Jodl wanted German forces on the Meuse within forty-eight hours; field commanders believed four to six days was a more realistic timetable. No significant interference was expected from Montgomery's 21st Army Group until the panzer vanguard had reached Brussels. Vague plans called for summoning Wehrmacht reinforcements from Italy, Denmark, and Norway after Antwerp fell.

Two tank armies would form the point of the spear: on the right wing, in the north, the main blow would be delivered by Sixth Panzer Army under Dietrich, a squat former butcher's apprentice with an underslung jaw, a harpoon nose, and a taste for schnapps. A tank sergeant in World War I and a favorite of Hitler's since the early 1920s, Dietrich had once led the Führer's Mercedes-mounted personal guard, which he armed with revolvers and hippopotamus whips. More recently he had commanded SS troops in France, Yugoslavia, Greece, and Russia, reportedly boasting in 1943 that of his original 23,000 men, only 30 remained alive and uncaptured. He was accused in one hideous episode of ordering more than four thousand Russians shot in retaliation for six German deaths. Rundstedt deemed Dietrich "decent but stupid," yet accepted him as the paramount tactical commander for HERBSTNEBEL. Dietrich would lead nine divisions with more than 1,000 guns and 120,000 soldiers, a third of them in Waffen-SS units. His lead echelons included five hundred tanks and assault guns, many of which were to funnel into Belgium through the five-mile-wide Losheim Gap—an upland passage exploited by German horse cavalry in 1914 and by Rommel in 1940—then hurry down five roads to reach the Meuse near Liège before wheeling northwest toward Antwerp.

On the left, Fifth Panzer Army with seven divisions was to sweep to the Meuse through southern Belgium and Luxembourg, shielding Dietrich's flank against counterattack from the southwest. Manteuffel, the Fifth Panzer commander, an elfin five-foot-two and 120 pounds, was a veteran of both Russia and Africa, tormented by migraines but described in one efficiency report as "a daredevil, a bold and dashing leader." His army had received a thousand artillery tubes and ample ammunition, but Manteuffel fretted more about fuel: hilly terrain and icy roads, he warned, required two to five times the standard petrol allocation. Model's logisticians had calculated that four and a half million gallons would suffice to reach the Meuse, plus another four million to seize Antwerp; only three million gallons had been delivered to the armies so far, much of it stockpiled far to the rear, in the Rhine valley. "If you need anything," Model advised, "take it from the Americans." Even more strapped was the German Seventh Army, positioned with seven divisions on the far left wing as another shield against counterattack from the southern flank; Hitler ordered Himmler to round up two thousand horses to enhance its mobility.

A thousand trains beginning in early December had hauled the HERBST-NEBEL legions across the Rhine, where they disembarked at night between Trier and München-Gladbach before marching in darkness toward the front. Security remained paramount. No open fires were allowed; to minimize smoke, only charcoal could be used for cooking. Any officer initiated into the plan took multiple secrecy oaths and then was forbidden to travel by airplane lest he be shot down and captured. Gestapo agents sniffed for leaks. Manteuffel personally started a rumor—by means of loud, theatrical dinner conversation at a restaurant—that his army intended to attack through the Saar in January.

Maps remained sealed until the eleventh hour. No motor vehicles could approach within eight kilometers of the front line, a restriction that hampered reconnaissance and artillery coordination. To forestall deserters, only on the final night would shock troops move into their assault trenches. Storch planes buzzing low overhead provided "noise curtains" to conceal engine sounds. The attack, originally scheduled for late November and then postponed until December 10, had been delayed again for nearly a week to stockpile more fuel and permit further positioning. *Null Tag*—Zero Day—now was fixed for Saturday, December 16, the date celebrated as the birthday of that most exquisite German, Ludwig van Beethoven.

In the club's cellar Hitler brought his two-hour oration to a close, eyes still bright, voice still strong. He would repeat the performance again the following night to a second tranche of senior generals.

"The army must gain a victory. . . . The German people can no longer endure the heavy bombing attacks," he told them. "We have many exhausted troops. The enemy also has exhausted troops, and he has lost a lot of blood." Reich intelligence estimated that the Americans alone "have lost about 240,000 men within a period of hardly three weeks." (This figure bore no relation to reality.) "Technically," he said, "both sides are equal."

The central weather office in Berlin predicted poor flying weather over the Ardennes for a week; that would negate Allied air superiority. "Troops must act with brutality and show no human inhibitions," Hitler said. "A wave of fright and terror must precede the troops."

> War is of course a test of endurance for those involved. . . . Wars are finally decided when one side or the other realizes that the war as such can no longer be won. Our most important task is to force the enemy to realize this. He can never reckon upon us surrendering. Never! Never!

Finally spent, Hitler ended his monologue. Rundstedt rose slowly from his chair, the field-gray apotheosis of Prussian dignity. On behalf of his generals, he pledged loyalty to the Führer and vowed that they would not disappoint him. Hardly a month earlier, the field marshal had voiced "grave doubts" about this desperate scheme. Now he proved that he too was one of the *Jaleute*, the yes-men. He too was a nodding donkey.

The Light Line

FOR three months after her glorious liberation, Paris suffered. "She was largely without light or gas or heat," wrote Alan Moorehead. "There were still no buses in the streets, no taxis. Every boulevard was a river of bicycles." Shortages of soap and warm water resulted in an epidemic of ugly leg sores. "You could more easily take a bath in champagne than in hot water," Martha Gellhorn added. "Since there was no leather for shoes, women clattered about the streets on platform soles made of wood, sounding like horses' hooves." Restaurant patrons dined in their overcoats on carrot-and-turnip soup.

The small fuel ration was restricted to adults over seventy-five, children under three, and the certifiably sick. A cord of black-market firewood sold for $120, or 6,000 francs at official exchange rates. The rich sometimes bought sawdust by the ton to burn in their stoves; they also purchased black-market gasoline for the trucks that delivered it. An American officer wrote home that his flat was "cold as charity," and another soldier, assigned a dank, sepulchral room, reported that "on many nights we opened the windows and slept in sleeping bags." A SHAEF officer who attended the opera described heavily muffled musicians, and patrons in formal dress swaddled in lap robes. "Like opening a refrigerator door," he wrote, "a cold wave rolled out on us from backstage as the curtain was lifted." Isaiah Berlin wrote a friend that the city seemed "empty and hollow and dead, like an exquisite corpse." As for actual corpses, the Paris crematorium received only enough gas to operate for two hours a day, so bodies were burned quickly or not at all.

By late November conditions began to brighten and the city "was again alive," according to Forrest Pogue. Tacticians defined the "light line" as the boundary between Allied field armies and the far rear; west of the line, nighttime blackouts no longer were mandatory. Paris again became *la ville lumière*, not least because the great coal fields around Valenciennes had been liberated intact and were soon disgorging the seven thousand tons a day needed to keep city utilities operating and the subway running. By mid-December, SHAEF reported that "electricity consumption in

Paris is 94% of the peacetime figure," with "an unnecessary amount of lighting used."

For liberators behind the light line, life was good, and for the brass in Paris, life was splendid. A PX open only to general officers stocked perfume, bracelets, fountain pens, and new Zippos. General Everett Hughes described hunting partridge near Versailles, with "all the farm hands for miles around acting as beaters." General Lee, the COMZ commander, ensured that fresh milk, butter, and fruit filled Eisenhower's larder, and the White House even sent the supreme commander a bushel of Chesapeake oysters. Frontline troops groused about "all those goddamned chair-borne infantry at the Hôtel Majestic," where Court House Lee kept his headquarters. "The COMZ set-up is shocking," wrote Pogue. "Working on a schedule of 8:30–5:30 (more nearly 4:30); off one afternoon a week." Denizens of the Majestic messed in a swank three-story café on the corner of the Champs-Élysées and Rue de Berri, where French waitresses served meals on starched tablecloths and a GI orchestra played from a mezzanine balcony.

The Majestic was hardly unique. Fifty-one generals lived in the George V, by Lee's careful count, and more filled the Hôtel Palais Quai d'Orsay, where desk clerks and porters wore frock coats. SHAEF's offices in the city occupied the J. P. Morgan bank on the elegant Place Vendôme, near the house where Frédéric Chopin died and opposite Napoléon's column, made from melted-down enemy cannons captured at Austerlitz. SHAEF officers dined in the Hôtel Meurice, that last-ditch redoubt of General Choltitz, where the cupboards still smelled of Wehrmacht boot leather. A ditty percolating through the ranks advised:

> Don't go forward of army group,
> Your proper place is SHAEF.
> Don't mind a bit
> If you're called a shit,
> Just say, "Thank God I'm safe."

The British occupied twelve hotels in Paris, the Canadians two; Americans filled well over three hundred. Champagne cost 300 to 600 francs a bottle—$6 to $12 at official exchange rates, $1.20 to $2.40 at black market rates—although imbibers were required to turn in two empty bottles to get a full one, and stoppers were at a premium because of Spanish cork shortages. A December 2 memo from COMZ, titled "Whiskey and Gin for General Officers," allocated a total of six cases for each army commander through January, with four cases permitted corps commanders, three cases for division commanders, and two cases for every brigadier general. Aides could retrieve the tipple from a warehouse at the Belgium Exposition Grounds in Brussels.

For GIs without stars on their shoulders, Paris seemed a fantastic sanctuary, the ne plus ultra of life outside the combat zone. The Army's first leave center opened in Paris in late October. That was followed by the first of fifty-one GI clubs on the Continent. Located in the Grand Hotel on Boulevard des Capucines, the initial club in Paris charged 30 cents a night for a bed; Major Glenn Miller's orchestra played each evening, even after the band leader disappeared in mid-December during a foul-weather flight over the English Channel. Soon ten thousand soldiers a day poured into the city on forty-eight-hour passes. "Just returned from a trip to Paris," a Seventh Army soldier wrote his wife. "It was wonderful, but I slept on the floor because the bed was just too much like sleeping in butter." A woman working for the OSS described fleets of *vélos*, odd contraptions like "canvas-covered bathtubs and drawn or propelled by motorcycles or bicycles," carting around GIs "who little count the cost in their exuberance at being alive." The writer Simone de Beauvoir concluded that "the easygoing manner of the young Americans incarnated liberty itself."

Troops packed movie theaters along the Champs-Élysées, and two music halls featured vaudeville shows. Post Number One of the American Legion served hamburgers and bourbon, and bars opened with names intended to entice the homesick, like The Sunny Side of the Street and New York. Army special services organized activities ranging from piano recitals to jitterbug lessons, while distributing thousands of hobby kits for sketching, clay modeling, and leather craft. The Bayeux Tapestry, long tucked away for safekeeping, reemerged in an exhibit at the Louvre, with the segment depicting the Norman defeat of the Anglo-Saxons in 1066 tactfully folded from sight.

In early December, Gertrude Stein and Alice B. Toklas returned to Paris from exile in southern France with their dog, Basket, and the Red Cross arranged GI tours of their apartment. Soldiers organized in groups of fifty, often bearing gifts of cigarettes and soap, also visited Picasso in his studio on Rue des Grand Augustins, where Hemingway had left behind a box of grenades. Callers to the atelier were "stratified," wrote one observer: "on the ground floor there were GIs and American journalists; then came communist deputies and prominent party members who showed signs of impatience; then came old acquaintances; and finally one came to Picasso." When the artist—who sometimes received guests in his underwear—was shown photos of war damage in London, he exclaimed, "*C'est épouvantable!* And that is happening all over the world?"

For many soldiers, of course, culture was the least of their interests.

From deuce-and-a-half truck beds rumbling toward the Tuileries came shouts of "We're all going to get laid, French-style!" COMZ counted at least 230 brothels in the city, plus six thousand licensed prostitutes working the streets. Another seven thousand were unregistered, according to Paris police estimates, and of the unregistered more than a third carried venereal disease. A typical transaction cost three packs of Chesterfields, and a survey found that among soldiers who spent two days or more in Paris, two-thirds had intercourse at least once, often in what were called "Where am I?" rooms. In Pigalle, solicitations from aggressive streetwalkers—known as "body snatchers"—could be heard from every corner. "Come along, ba-bee," they cooed, "come along." Soldiers replied, *"Coushay avec?"* or simply, "Zig zig?" One quartermaster private disclosed on his required "VD contact form" that he picked up nine different women around the same Parisian intersection, took them to six different hotels, and essayed seven "sexual exposures," all within eight hours. "Our soldiers," an American officer wrote, "were devastated by aphrodisiac dreams."

They were devastated by more than dreams. The venereal-disease rate in the European theater quickly doubled, and more than two-thirds of all infections acquired in France originated in Paris. The U.S. Army, which had tracked VD in the ranks since 1830, considered a rate below 30 cases per 1,000 troops annually to be "acceptable"; by mid-October the rate in Europe was twice that. It doubled again among the Army Air Forces, and—at 222 per 1,000—was sevenfold the "acceptable" figure in COMZ's Loire encampments. Confronted by another threat to Allied strength, Eisenhower counterattacked by declaring "all brothels, bordellos and similar establishments" off-limits.

Twenty-nine prophylactic dispensaries sprouted across Paris, with huge signs declaring, "Pro Station Here." Mandatory "short-arm" inspections by medical "pecker checkers" increased sharply. Naval commanders at a hotel on the Avenue Marceau barred entry to any woman unless she produced "proof of chastity." A December issue of *Army Talks* warned, "Don't forget the Krauts were fooling around France a long time before we got here. . . . So any dame you get now is plenty second-hand."

Still the VD rate climbed. Soldiers excused from duty while being treated for syphilis or gonorrhea were said to be "whores de combat," and the Good Conduct ribbon became known as the "No-Clap Medal." Women who swapped sex for rations or chocolate were called "Hershey bars," while a brothel was a "house of horizontal refreshment." The French Foreign Ministry asked SHAEF to consider "assigning a certain number of houses of prostitution for the Allied nationals' use" because of "a noteworthy recrudescence of clandestine prostitution" and increasing VD among

French civilians. Eisenhower declined. When Patton proposed providing bordellos with penicillin because "it is futile to attempt to go against human nature," the supreme commander replied tartly, "I most emphatically do *not* agree. . . . To run the risk of being short in this important drug merely in order that brothels in France may be supplied with it is absolutely unacceptable to me." Patton for once held his tongue.

Paris soldiered on, or perhaps sashayed. Vendors near the Eiffel Tower sold pinwheels and balloons, and among pitched stalls at the stamp market, collectors by the hundreds examined specimens with magnifying lenses. French communists tossed clenched-fist salutes to British officers in red-banded uniform caps, mistaking them for Soviets, and young women bicycled down the boulevards with billowing skirts and big hats, a vivid apparition that brightened everyone's morale. In November, De Gaulle's government had closed public dance halls as unseemly, since some two million French citizens remained incarcerated in German labor camps or prisons. But surreptitious dancing continued across Montmartre, and cabarets and nightclubs remained open. Among them was the Sphinx, which Bill Mauldin described as "jammed with French civilians, all smoking [black market] Camels" and served by waitresses who "wore lace caps and high-heeled shoes, with absolutely nothing between."

A lively tableau could also be found in the Hôtel Scribe, abode of many of the nearly one thousand journalists accredited to SHAEF, including the likes of William Shirer, George Orwell, and Robert Capa. "It was an American enclave in the heart of Paris," De Beauvoir wrote. "White bread, fresh eggs, jam, sugar and Spam." (The bar, always crowded, featured a medley of intoxicants called the Suffering Bastard.) Collectively the correspondents filed more than 100,000 words from Paris each day, plus hundreds of photographs and thousands of feet of movie film. Two dozen SHAEF censors sat in a suite on the second floor of the hotel, scrutinizing the copy while occasionally glancing at a long list of "hot stops"—details not to be publicly disclosed, such as troop movements and unit strengths—scrawled in colored chalk on a blackboard. The triple bleating of buzzers in the Scribe lobby announced a new press release, according to the Australian reporter Osmar White, and wire services hired "nimble French youths to race from the briefing room to the dispatching office on the first floor with 'flashes.'"

Sporadic privation would beset Paris for the duration, including shortages of milk, bread, and even government stationery. Reams embossed with the Vichy letterhead were reused, with *"État Français"* struck out and *"République Française"* typed in. Particularly alarming to GIs was a theaterwide cigarette shortage: U.S. Army soldiers alone smoked more than a million packs a day in Europe, and COMZ put the total need for December at 84 million packs. A two-month supply—along with more than one million blankets and sleeping bags—was discovered aboard offshore cargo ships, unable to berth for weeks because priority was given to ammunition and fuel. Until the crisis eased, cigarettes were diverted from rear-echelon troops behind the light line to the front, and Eisenhower began rolling his own as a gesture of solidarity with his men.

Not least among the problems for Court House Lee and others attempting to victual the Allied host was a virulent and ingenious black market. Coffee, gasoline, tires, blankets, boots, soap, and morphine were bought and sold in staggering volume at enormous profit. A pack of Lucky Strikes that cost a nickel at the post exchange on the Champs-Élysées could be peddled on the sidewalk outside for $2. A twenty-pound can of coffee or fifty D-ration chocolate bars brought $300, and the standard soldier musette sack became known as a "black market bag." British Commandos financed their stay at the Ritz by peddling a two-hundred-pound keg of Danish butter for one hundred pounds sterling. An entire train with three engines and forty boxcars full of cigarettes and other PX supplies vanished without a trace during a journey from Normandy to Paris, despite a prolonged search by agents in Cub spotter planes. The distribution of five thousand captured German horses to French farmers was halted in the fall to prevent their diversion to black-market butchers, which did not stop Osmar White from enjoying a "superbly camouflaged horse steak with vintage Château Latour" at an illicit restaurant off Rue du Faubourg St.-Honoré.

Eisenhower's provost marshal estimated that in December eighteen thousand American deserters roamed the European theater, plus another ten thousand British absconders. The equivalent of a division of military fugitives was believed to be hiding in the Parisian demimonde, often joining forces with local black marketeers to peddle K rations for 75 cents from the tailgates of stolen Army trucks—hundreds of such vehicles vanished every day—or simply selling the entire deuce-and-a-half for $5,000. Eventually four thousand military policemen and detectives worked the streets of Paris. From September through December they arrested more than ten thousand people, including French civilians caught selling marijuana to soldiers. A five-story French army barracks on the Boulevard Mortier became a detention block capable of holding more than two thousand miscreants, while the merely AWOL were rounded up and trucked back to the front in lots of sixteen under MP guard. Many soldiers in an Army railway battalion in Paris were arrested and court-martialed en masse for pilferage; nearly two hundred of them drew prison sentences, some as long as fifty years—later commuted for those who agreed to combat duty.

Still, the malfeasance and misconduct would thrive through the end of the war, to the point that Paris, the city of light, the city of learning, the city of love, earned yet another nickname: "Chicago-sur-Seine."

Shortly before six P.M. on Tuesday, December 12, at roughly the hour that Hitler was meeting his second group of HERBSTNEBEL generals at the Adlerhorst, Eisenhower rode in a limousine through the dim streets of London toward 10 Downing Street for a meeting with Churchill and *his* military brain trust. After flying from Versailles the previous day, the supreme commander had kept busy with appointments in his high-windowed corner office overlooking Grosvenor Square, followed this afternoon by a courtesy call on Ambassador Winant at the U.S. embassy down the street.

As his car sped southeast across Piccadilly toward Whitehall, Eisenhower could see that London, unlike Paris, showed little evidence of revival. Blackout restrictions remained in force, and the few cars on the road were described by one visitor as "little points of blue light dragging darkness after them but leaving blackness behind." At Claridge's, a doorman flashed his torch to guide patrons across the sidewalk. Toy and cake shops stood empty a fortnight before Christmas, and even potatoes were in short supply. The city's most popular diversions included a new film adaptation of *Henry V* starring Laurence Olivier and a waxwork exhibit depicting German atrocities. "Horrors of the Nazi Concentration Camps. Come inside and see real Nazi tortures," the marquee beckoned. "Children's amusement section no extra charge."

A national ban on making ice cream had been lifted in November, and, with the threat of German invasion now gone, the antique Home Guard stood down with a fine parade. But what would be the coldest winter in fifty years had set in, its miseries exacerbated by millions of broken windows and missing roof tiles. The homeless and unnerved still retreated to shelters and subways at dusk with their deck chairs and rugs—"cave dwellers getting their cave ready for the night," an American airman recorded—sometimes sleeping five deep on steel shelves erected across the platforms. Much of the Tate Gallery collection had been stored in unused Underground stations on the Piccadilly and Central Lines; the Elgin Marbles now resided in an empty tunnel under Aldwych. An all too familiar sight on London's streets was a telegram delivery boy carrying bad news past twitching parlor curtains as he sought the proper address. "This is a priority," the messengers were told as they set out. "It's death."

As in Antwerp, death could also arrive directly, as a consequence of Hitler's decision to concentrate his V-2 rockets almost exclusively on the

Belgian port and the British capital. Churchill in mid-November had finally confirmed that those mysterious detonations since early September were *not* exploding gas mains. More than one thousand of the rockets would fall on British soil, about half in greater London. Like the V-1, the V-2, dubbed Big Ben, would have little military impact; according to official German calculations the effort invested by Berlin in the V-weapons was roughly equivalent to that of producing 24,000 fighter planes. Further, the V-2 rocket—a hundred times more expensive to build than the V-1—proved less effective than the flying bomb as a terror weapon. Not least among the reasons was the very futility of defending against a missile streaking across the heavens at Mach 5. Since they afforded no protection anyway, neither Allied antiaircraft batteries nor fighter squadrons were tied down, as they had been during the V-1 onslaught.

Radar usually detected V-2 launches from the Netherlands, but warning sirens were deemed pointless; only transport authorities got a minute or two of notification to close subway floodgates beneath the Thames. "You just strolled along, daydreaming, till you were hit," one witness said. Because the odds against shooting down a V-2 with ground fire were considered as high as a thousand to one, dupery had to suffice as a countermeasure. False intelligence about where the Big Bens hit, fed that fall to the Germans through agents controlled by British counterintelligence, persuaded enemy rocketeers that they were overshooting central London. Soon the mean point of impact migrated eastward, a shift that by war's end was credited with sparing an estimated 1,300 British lives, 10,000 other casualties, and 23,000 houses.

That was cold comfort for the nearly three thousand Britons killed by V-2s, or the tens of thousands whose homes were obliterated. "Never have I seen buildings so cleanly swept away, and these are 3- or 4-story tenement houses," a survivor reported. One of the worst attacks occurred shortly after noon on November 25 in the working-class borough of Deptford, where a Saturday sale on saucepans had drawn a long queue at the local Woolworth's. A young mother outside the store described "a sudden airless quiet, which seemed to stop one's breath, then an almighty sound so tremendous that it seemed to blot out my mind completely." A survivor recalled that as the smoke cleared:

> A horse's head was lying in the gutter. There was a pram hood all twisted and bent and there was a little baby's hand still in its wooly sleeve. Outside the pub there was a crumpled bus, still with rows of people sitting inside, all covered in dust and dead. Where Woolworth's had been, there was nothing.

The blast killed 168 and injured even more. "The slogan of 'London can take it' will prevail," a British government official wrote Harry Hopkins, Roosevelt's close aide. "But there may be quite a lot to take."

No V-weapons fell on Whitehall during Eisenhower's Tuesday night visit, but the specter was never farther away than the nearby gutted shops and blown-out windows patched with beaverboard. At six P.M., Churchill welcomed the supreme commander to his map room, where they were joined by Tedder, Brooke, and several other senior British officers. Brooke, as part of his conspiracy with Montgomery to "take the control out of Eisenhower's hands," had tried to arrange a direct meeting with George Marshall; the Army chief declined the invitation and instead told Eisenhower to make his own case in London.

Eisenhower now commanded sixty-nine divisions on the Western Front, a force he expected to expand to eighty-one divisions by February. Using the prime minister's huge wall maps, upon which various battlefronts were delineated with pushpins and colored yarn, the supreme commander once again reviewed his campaign scheme: how Montgomery's 21st Army Group, bolstered by the U.S. Ninth Army, would angle north of the Ruhr, while Bradley's 12th Army Group swung farther south, shielded on the right flank by Devers's 6th Army Group. The twin envelopment would exploit Allied mobility and force the enemy to burn his dwindling fuel stocks by defending a wide, perilous front.

Brooke—his narrow raptor face as intent as the visage of a peregrine watching a pigeon—told his diary later that night:

> Ike explained his plan, which contemplates a double advance into Germany, north of Rhine and by Frankfurt. I disagreed flatly with it, accused Ike of violating principles of concentration of force, which had resulted in his previous failures. I criticized his future plans and . . . I stressed the importance of concentrating on one thrust. . . . Ike does not hope to cross the Rhine before May!!!

Two years earlier, under similar circumstances in Casablanca, Brooke had assailed Eisenhower over a proposed offensive across Tunisia. Unprepared and intimidated, Eisenhower had mounted a halfhearted defense before retreating in disarray from the room. This time he held his ground, parrying Brooke's objections and explaining his rationale with patience and coherence. Closing to the Rhine from Holland to Alsace would give Allied forces the "capability of concentration" for an eventual double thrust. Winter flooding along much of the river now precluded attacks farther east anyway. The fighting in October and November had been grim indeed—Allied troops still occupied only five hundred square miles of Germany—but Wehrmacht divisions were bleeding to death, and with them, the Reich.

"Ike was good," wrote Admiral Andrew Browne Cunningham, the first sea lord. "Kept an even keel. He was obviously impressed by [Brooke's] arguments but refused to commit himself." The debate continued over cocktails and dinner, quickly becoming the same tautological gyre that characterized so many Anglo-American strategic conversations.

The evening ended in stilted silences and muzzy talk about postwar Allied unity, to which the supreme commander pledged to devote "the afternoon and evening of my life." Brooke grew so frustrated that he contemplated resigning, particularly after Churchill chimed in to endorse Eisenhower's broad-front concept. In his diary Brooke conceded that he had "utterly failed . . . in getting either Winston or Ike to see that their strategy is fundamentally wrong." A day later, the prime minister asserted that he had simply been acting the gracious host in refusing to gang up on the only American at table.

Eisenhower flew back to Versailles on Wednesday morning, weary and hardly less dispirited than Brooke. "Field Marshal Brooke seemed disturbed by what he calls our 'dispersion' of the past weeks of this campaign," he cabled Marshall. To Mamie he admitted craving a three-month vacation on a remote beach. "And oh, Lordy, Lordy," he added, "let it be sunny."

Eisenhower knew that more was at stake in this tedious contretemps than the march routes of armies. Every additional day of war left Britain weaker and less capable of preserving the empire or shaping the postwar world.

"I greatly fear the dwindling of the British Army is a factor in France as it will affect our right to express our opinion upon strategic and other matters," Churchill had cabled Montgomery. German intelligence believed that fourteen British divisions still awaited deployment to the Continent, but the prime minister and Brooke knew otherwise. Indeed, Britain was so hard-pressed that even after cannibalizing two existing divisions to fill the diminished ranks in other units, commanders faced "an acute problem in the next six months to keep the army up to strength," as one staff officer in London warned. Wastage in infantry riflemen especially was running at a rate higher than the War Office could make good: a British rifle-company officer who landed in France on June 6 had nearly a 70 percent probability of being wounded by the end of the war, and a 20 percent chance of being killed.

Nor was Britain's plight unique. "All of us are now faced with an unanticipated shortage of manpower," Roosevelt had written Churchill in

October. The American dearth was even more problematic, if only because U.S. troops provided the preponderance of Eisenhower's strength. In December, the American armed forces comprised twelve million, compared with five million for the British, but insatiable and competing global demands pressed even that multitude. A million Army troops were now in the Pacific, while the Army Air Forces had requested 130,000 men to fly and maintain the new B-29 bomber—beyond the 300,000 workers already building the Superfortress. Almost five million American men had been granted occupational deferments, and many soldiers were being furloughed to work in hard-pressed critical industries. In December, 2,500 were sent home to make artillery ammunition and another 2,000 to make tires; thousands more went to foundries, toolmakers, and other plants. Even now Marshall felt pressure from Congress to trim Army manpower so that the production of consumer goods, from toasters to Buicks, could resume.

To swell the ranks, Selective Service exemptions for fathers were belatedly abolished: one million would be drafted in 1944–45. The average age of draftees had climbed from twenty-two in 1940 to twenty-six in 1944, and many new privates were over thirty-five. A ban on shipping eighteen-year-olds overseas was rescinded in August. Induction standards for "physically imperfect men," already loosened, were further relaxed in October. Draft examiners were advised that "such terms as 'imbecile' and 'moron' will not be used," but 330,000 inductees, some of whom could fairly be classified as at least dull-witted, were subsequently discharged for sundry mental defects. A three-page primer advised examiners how to detect malingering, including feigned epilepsy, bed-wetting, and tachycardia "induced by ingestion of drugs such as thyroid extracts." Would-be draft dodgers "may shoot or cut off their fingers or toes, usually on the right side. . . . Some may put their hands under cars for this purpose."

The need for more soldiers—fit or unfit, willing or unwilling, whole or maimed—grew ever more acute as the fall months passed. U.S. battle casualties in Europe had doubled from October to November, to two thousand a day; on December 7, the figure hit three thousand. The trench foot epidemic caused nonbattle casualties to also double in November, to 56,000. Consequently, even as the last of the U.S. Army's eighty-nine divisions prepared for deployment to Europe, and even though more than three hundred thousand individual replacement troops had arrived since D-Day, Bradley's 12th Army Group reported in December that every division already in the theater was below its authorized strength. "The life expectancy of a junior officer in combat was twelve days before he was hit and evacuated," Bradley asserted. Patton advised his diary on December 3,

"Our situation is bad; 11,000 short in an army of three armored divisions and six infantry divisions."

All combat arms felt pinched—the "handling and delivery of armored replacements has been a colossal failure," an Army investigator wrote—but none more than the infantry, that breed apart, described by one private as "a black line on a war map." Using obsolete data from World War I and from other World War II theaters irrelevant to Europe, the War Department had predicted that infantry losses would amount to 64 percent of all casualties. The forecast was a botch: by December, the actual figure was 83 percent, and even higher for divisions that saw especially intense fighting. In January 1944, the Army had estimated a need for 300,000 replacement infantrymen worldwide that year. The eventual number was nearly double, 535,000.

Of more than eight million soldiers in the Army as the year ended, barely two million were serving in ground units. That was simply not enough, particularly since the Navy, Marines, and Air Forces tended to get a disproportionate share of the smartest and most physically able young men. The severest shortage was of that priceless creature known as a "745," the rifleman, so called for his military occupational specialty number. An infantry division might have more than 14,000 soldiers, with another 24,000 troops sustaining the division in ancillary support units, but the point of the spear comprised just 5,200 riflemen in twenty-seven rifle companies. (Others manned mortars and machine guns, cookstoves and radios, stethoscopes and bulldozers and clerical desks.) "We find ourselves totally out of infantry rifle replacements because of the War Department's inability to ship the numbers that are necessary," Bradley's personnel chief warned. As casualties mounted, the shortages grew more desperate and the combat soldier's fatalism deepened. As one veteran wrote, "Nobody gets out of a rifle company. It's a door that only opens one way, in. You leave when they carry you out." Lieutenant Paul Fussell believed that "no infantryman can survive psychologically very long unless he's mastered the principle that the dead don't *know* what they look like."

Frantic efforts were made to muster more riflemen into battle. The Army already had culled privates and noncommissioned officers from forty divisions while they were still training in the United States. Seventeen of those divisions had lost at least two-thirds of their infantry privates and countless junior officers, who then were sent overseas as individual replacements while new recruits filled the ranks behind them. Not only were the original divisions devastated by this turnover—the 65th Division reported that some platoons had churned through as many as sixteen platoon leaders even before leaving the United States—but also many GIs found themselves in battle without sufficient training. "We had to take them over behind a hill right in the middle of the action and show them how to load their rifles," one warrant officer complained.

Crash programs to convert quartermaster soldiers and other support troops into riflemen also began in late November. These so-called "miracle men," or "retreads," often proved wanting, and at least one regiment trying to rebuild after the Hürtgen bloodletting refused to accept hundreds of infantry novices. "State of mind of men being converted into riflemen is, on the whole, not good," an inspection report advised. A survey of infantry divisions found that nearly three-fourths of respondents agreed that "the infantry gets more than its share of the men who aren't good for anything else." Lieutenant Fussell wrote that the implicit message to an infantryman was: "*You* are expendable. Don't imagine that your family's good opinion of you will cut any ice here."

Even the deployment of intact divisions was beset with snafus. Under a plan known as the "Red List," twenty-nine divisions that were ostensibly "fully equipped and ready for combat within fifteen days after landing" arrived overseas beginning in September. In the event, tanks and other heavy equipment meant for these divisions were routed to embarkation ports through a warehouse complex in Elmira, New York, which was already inundated with thousands of military railcars each month. Congestion and confusion led to chaos—thirty workers in Elmira toiled full-time just to strip off erroneous shipping labels—and the Army conceded that an "inability to keep up with paperwork eventually bogged down the entire operation." As a result, many units arrived in Europe without critical combat gear, including three divisions that docked in Marseille so bereft of communications equipment that SHAEF spent months making up the shortages.

The Red List was a paragon of efficiency compared to the Army's individual replacement system. Tens of thousands of soldiers were disgorged onto the Continent woefully unprepared for combat; as Eisenhower conceded, each arrived with the "feeling of being a lost soul . . . shunted around without knowing where he is going or what will happen to him." Many lacked mess kits, bayonets, or even rank insignia; replacement lieutenants and captains used adhesive tape to simulate the bars on their shoulders. So many also lacked weapons that the War Department shipped fifty thousand World War I–vintage rifles to Europe. "We left Fort Meade with no rifles, we arrived in Scotland with no rifles, we arrived in France with no rifles, [and] we arrived in Belgium with no rifles," a soldier recalled.

Replacements traveled for days in unheated French "forty-and-eight" boxcars, considered suitable for forty men or eight horses, although as Eisenhower wrote Marshall, "We have reduced the figure to thirty-five enlisted men per car in order that by tight squeezing men can at least lie down." They then spent weeks or months in replacement centers known as "stockage depots," often sleeping on straw in flimsy tents, waiting to join a unit even as their physical fitness and combat skills deteriorated. A *Stars and Stripes* exposé reported that "many replacements had not bathed in thirty days."

"We want to feel that we are a part of something," one GI in a stockage depot explained. "As a replacement we are apart from everything. . . . You feel totally useless and unimportant." Inactivity, *Stars and Stripes* added, became "a form of mental cruelty." The Army attempted to mitigate the fears of novice troops headed for combat by segregating "salt waters"— new replacements arriving from the United States—from wounded or sick soldiers just out of the hospital. "The battle veterans," a battalion commander explained, "scared the pants off the green boys."

Court House Lee proposed on December 1 that the word "replacement" be supplanted by "reinforcement." " 'Replacement,' " he told Bradley, "carries a cannon fodder implication that we could overcome by using another term." The change would take effect shortly after Christmas, but no euphemism could obscure the fact that "the morale of our officers and enlisted men coming though the replacement system is completely shot," an inspector general's report warned. Even so, U.S. ground forces in Europe since June 6 had received almost half a million replacements, most of them "salt waters," and for all its flaws and indignities the system had kept the field armies reasonably strong for seven months.

Now the Army's ability to replenish its ranks was in jeopardy. SHAEF on December 8 predicted a shortage of 23,000 riflemen by year's end, enough to preclude any attack into Germany. After returning from London, Eisenhower on December 15 ordered rear-echelon units to comb out more combat troops, and an eight-week course to convert mortar crews and other infantrymen into 745s was truncated to two weeks. At least a few officers wondered whether the time had come to allow black GIs to serve in white rifle companies, but for now that radical notion found few champions in the high command.

No one was more fretful than Omar Bradley, whose army group numbered 850,000 men and almost four thousand tanks, yet mustered less than 80 percent of its authorized strength in riflemen. He contemplated breaking up newly arriving divisions to cannibalize infantry as the British had, despite what he conceded would be "tremendous wastage." So irked was Bradley at the Pentagon's failure to provide enough trigger-pullers— "Don't they realize that we can still lose this war in Europe?" he had asked

Eisenhower—that he told SHAEF he planned to fly to Versailles from Luxembourg City to explain his troubles in detail. The conference was scheduled for Saturday morning, December 16—Beethoven's birthday.

"Go Easy, Boys. There's Danger Ahead"

To be sure, there were clues, omens, auguries. Just as surely, they were missed, ignored, explained away. For decades after the death struggle called the Battle of the Bulge, generals, scholars, and foot soldiers alike would ponder the worst U.S. intelligence failure since Pearl Harbor and the deadliest of the war. Only from the high ground of history could perfect clarity obtain, and even then the simplest, truest answer remained the least satisfying: mistakes were made and many men died. What might have been known was not known. What could have been done was not done. Valor and her handmaidens—tenacity, composure, luck—would be needed to make it right. The trial ahead would also require stupendous firepower and great gouts of blood in what became the largest battle in American military history, and among the most decisive.

Allied intelligence first recognized in September that the Germans had created Sixth Panzer Army under a swashbuckling commander, Sepp Dietrich. Also that month, an intercepted message to Tokyo from the Japanese ambassador in Berlin described Hitler as intent on amassing a million new troops for combat in the west, "probably from November onwards." Ultra decrypts in late October revealed that the Luftwaffe was stockpiling fuel and ammunition at eleven airfields north of Aachen; subsequent intelligence showed German aircraft strength in the west quadrupling, to perhaps 850 planes, reversing a policy of concentrating squadrons defensively in the Fatherland. Prisoner reports and a captured German order indicated that the celebrated enemy commando leader Otto Skorzeny—the man who had freed Benito Mussolini from a mountaintop jail—was collecting soldiers who could "speak the American dialect," perhaps for an infiltration mission. The U.S. First Army had flown 361 reconnaissance sorties over western Germany since mid-November, spotting unusual processions of hooded lights on both banks of the Rhine, as well as hospital trains west of the river and canvas-covered flatcars apparently carrying tanks or trucks. In early December, Allied intelligence reported nearly two hundred troop trains moving forward.

None of this suggested an enemy offensive, at least not to the minds of those scrutinizing the evidence. The Sixth Panzer Army and the added Luftwaffe planes were seen as a counterattack force designed to shield the Ruhr but unable to mount "a true counter-offensive"—in SHAEF's judgment—because of fuel shortages and the German military's general decrepitude. An intercepted Luftwaffe order for aerial reconnaissance of the Meuse bridges, a site curiously far afield for those only protecting the Ruhr, was deemed a ruse. A rumor of German intentions to recapture Antwerp was dismissed in a 21st Army Group intelligence review on December 3: "The bruited drive on Antwerp . . . is just not within his potentiality." After all, hundreds of confirmed reports portrayed a battered, reeling foe.

Those nearest the front—the tactical units splayed along the Siegfried Line—proved no more prescient. U.S. V Corps officers interviewing German prisoners in early December discounted reports of intensified training in infiltration techniques and assault tactics. Tanks maneuvering west of the Rhine were assumed to be green units undergoing seasoning, much as novice American units were seasoned in the Ardennes. A woman interrogated on December 14 described the forest near Bitburg as jammed with German equipment, and four Wehrmacht soldiers captured on December 15 reported more combat units arriving at the front; but these and various other clues provoked little alarm. None of the seven First Army divisions around the Ardennes foresaw an enemy offensive; the 99th Division instead averred that "the entire German army [is] disintegrating."

Several factors fed this disregard, including a failure to recognize that Hitler rather than the prudent Rundstedt was directing German field armies in the west. "The war from the military side would now seem to be in the hands of soldiers," a 21st Army Group analysis stated, "a change making the enemy easier to understand but harder to defeat." No sensible field marshal was likely to risk losing the Sixth Panzer Army—the Reich's last mobile reserve in the west—in a winter offensive. In imagining their German counterparts, Forrest Pogue observed, American commanders believed that because "*we* would not attack under these conditions, therefore *they* would not attack under these conditions." To assume otherwise required the ability "to forecast the intentions of a maniac," Bradley's intelligence chief later wrote.

Top Allied officers also had become overly enchanted with Ultra, as they had before Kasserine Pass in 1943. By late 1944, the cryptologists at Bletchley Park were daily providing about fifty intercepted German messages detailing troop movements and unit strengths. "They had become so dependent on Ultra that if it wasn't there," a SHAEF officer said, "then there wasn't anything there." Montgomery's intelligence chief, Brigadier E. T. Williams, agreed. "Instead of being the best, it tended to become the *only* source," he wrote soon after the war ended. "We had begun to lean: that was the danger of Ultra." Intercepts had provided provocative clues—about those Luftwaffe planes on western airfields, for instance—and also raised troubling questions for those inclined to be troubled. Why was the

Italian front required to ship one thousand trucks to Rundstedt? Why was Hitler's personal guard moving toward the Western Front? Why were Sixth Panzer Army troop trains so far forward, if Dietrich's mission was to protect the Ruhr? But ruthless German security about HERBSTNEBEL and strict radio silence by the units committed kept the inner secret from reaching Allied ears.

Some would later claim clairvoyance. Colonel Monk Dickson, the tempestuous First Army intelligence chief, wrote in Estimate No. 37, issued on December 10, that "the continual buildup of forces west of the Rhine points consistently to his staking all on the counteroffensive." But Dickson placed the expected German blow in the wrong place—north of the Ardennes, "between the Roer and the Erft"—and at the wrong time, "when our major ground forces have crossed the Roer River." Further, his fractious relations with SHAEF and 12th Army Group intelligence officers, who considered him a windy alarmist, undermined Dickson's vague warning, as did his subsequent departure from Spa for a four-day holiday in Paris.

A suggestion in early December by Eisenhower's intelligence chief, Major General Kenneth W. D. Strong, that the Sixth Panzer Army could possibly attack through the Ardennes sufficiently aroused Beetle Smith that he bundled off Strong to see Bradley. In a forty-five-minute meeting in Luxembourg City, either Strong failed to convey a sense of alarm or Bradley refused to take counsel of his fears. The U.S. Army's VIII Corps was spread thin along the border highlands, Bradley acknowledged, but ample reinforcements had been positioned behind the front if needed. Bradley had apparently persuaded himself that the enemy here lacked fangs: during a recent drive through the Ardennes he had mused, "I don't think they will come through here. At least they can't do much here. Don't believe they will try." Back in Versailles, Strong recounted the conversation to Smith, who chose not to trouble Eisenhower with the matter.

Perhaps the only genuine prescience could be found farther south, where Patton and his Third Army intelligence officer, Brigadier General Oscar W. Koch, sensed what others did not: that a dangerous, desperate enemy remained capable of wreaking havoc. Koch insisted that the German reversal in recent months "has *not* been a rout or a mass collapse." Hitler, he believed, was "playing for time." On December 7, he noted a "large panzer concentration west of the Rhine in the northern portion of Twelfth Army Group's zone of advance"; two days later, he pointed out the vulnerability of VIII Corps in the Ardennes. On December 14, Koch cited the persistent mystery over the location of at least fourteen German divisions, most of them armored, which together could spearhead a counteroffensive. An attack near Aachen might be more likely than one through the Ardennes, he added; but Patton's intuition suggested otherwise. "The

First Army is making a terrible mistake in leaving the VIII Corps static," he had told his diary, "as it is highly probable that the Germans are building up east of them."

Yet in other Allied high councils a confident swagger prevailed, a conviction that no German reserves would be committed west of the Siegfried Line. A "sudden attack in the West may with some certainty be said to have lapsed," British air intelligence concluded on December 6. Chagrined that so few officers seemed to be reading his turgid reports, Brigadier General Edwin L. Sibert, Bradley's intelligence chief, dragooned the *New Yorker's* former managing editor, now in uniform, to punch up the prose in his December 12 assessment. Full voice was given 12th Army Group's optimism. "Attrition is steadily sapping the strength of German forces on the Western Front," the analysis declared, "and the crust of [German] defense is thinner, more brittle and more vulnerable." An abrupt enemy collapse seemed quite possible, and "given time and fair weather we can make progress against him anywhere."

Montgomery needed no ghostwriter to affirm his views. On December 15, he wrote that Hitler's plight was so dire "that he cannot stage major offensive operations." That same day, the field marshal scribbled Eisenhower a note requesting leave to return to Britain for Christmas. Montgomery included an invoice for a five-pound bet wagered in October 1943, when he had challenged Eisenhower's prediction that the war would end by Christmas 1944.

"I still have nine days," the supreme commander replied, "and while it seems almost certain that you will have an extra five pounds for Christmas, you will not get it until that day."

Marlene Dietrich cut a wide swath through the Ardennes in mid-December. Dressed in a tailored wool uniform with drop-seat long underwear, blond tresses peeking out beneath her helmet brim, she bounced in a truck from encampment to encampment with her USO troupe, changing three or four times a day into the nylons and sequined gown suitable for crooning "Falling in Love with Love" and "See What the Boys in the Back Room Will Have." Sipping calvados to ward off the cold, she handed out postcard photos of herself affixed with lipstick autographs and collected weapons given her by smitten soldiers; her baggage eventually included eleven pistols. Sometimes she told jokes about Hitler, whom she called "an embittered vegetarian." She blamed the war on "his thwarted love life," explaining that "unfortunately for the world, the first girl laughed." It was said that at the Ritz in Paris earlier that fall she had paraded down a corridor wearing a chic chapeau and nothing else, asking, "Don't I look cute?" It was also said, by her, that she had slept with Patton, who gave her the code name LEGS. When the film director Billy Wilder asked about rumors of an affair with Eisenhower, she replied, "But, darling, how could it have been Eisenhower? He wasn't even at the front!"

On a rainy Thursday evening, December 14, Dietrich performed in the tidy Belgian town of Bastogne, headquarters of VIII Corps. She tried not to scratch at the lice as she sang "Lili Marlene." A night later she was in northern Luxembourg, at Diekirch, hardly six miles from her native Germany, singing in a smoky, crowded hall for hundreds of GIs in General Dutch Cota's 28th Division, still recuperating after their trial in the Hürtgen Forest. The troops stamped and whistled and could have listened all night, but reveille would come early, and on Saturday she was booked to entertain the 99th Division back in Belgium. *Underneath the lantern by the barrack gate,* the soldiers sang to themselves as they crawled into their bedrolls. *Darling, I remember the way you used to wait.*

The U.S. Army's *Guide to the Cities of Belgium* assured soldiers that the Ardennes was a fine place to "practice your favorite winter sport"; the region was said to have become a "quiet paradise for weary troops." "Dear Mom and Dad," a GI had recently written. "It is a wonderfully crisp and sunny day—much like you'd see this time of year in the Adirondacks. Plenty of snow." A soldier who dined on fried chicken and French fries in a warm bivouac wrote his mother, "I'll be getting fat if this deal lasts." In Honsfeld, a few miles from the Losheim Gap, soldiers waiting for La Marlene's appearance on Saturday watched a movie with a defective sound track, shouting their own invented dialogue. Farther west, GIs in Vielsalm received another USO troupe, including a comedian who sang while eating crackers. For $10, a soldier at the front could wire home Christmas flowers, but the bouquets and accompanying telegrams terrified more than a few mothers who mistook the gifts for death notifications.

Among visitors to the First Army headquarters in Spa on Friday, December 15, was a delegation of professional baseball players, including Mel Ott and Bucky Walters. They found few senior officers in the command post: most were on leave either in Paris, like Colonel Dickson, the G-2, or in London, like the G-3 operations officer, the G-4 logistician, and the top artillery, ordnance, and antiaircraft officers. General Hodges, the army commander, politely chatted up the guests for half an hour, then excused himself and returned to his billet, worn down by fatigue and a bad cold. Visiting the 106th Division at the same hour was a soldier named Theodore Geisel, known professionally as Dr. Seuss. Geisel, who was making a propaganda film with director Frank Capra, later composed a bit of doggerel to commemorate his experience of the next couple days: "The retreat we beat was accomplished with a speed that will never be beaten."

Ten thousand Belgian civilians had been evacuated from the border areas north of the Losheim Gap, not least because many were ethnic Germans of whom Hitler claimed, "Inwardly they have always remained connected with Germany." A few farmers were permitted to harvest late potatoes and tend the dairy herds, but the unmilked cows made such a racket with their lowing that butchers set up ten slaughter pens; Army trucks then hauled the beef to quartermaster depots in Brussels and Antwerp. Another roundup was scheduled for Saturday morning in Bütgenbach, command post for the 99th Division. Along the front, where conifers grew in such precise rows that they were described as a "cornfield forest," company radios tuned into Axis Sally, the propagandist whose signature line GIs loved to mimic: "Go easy, boys. There's danger ahead."

Of the 341,000 soldiers in the U.S. First Army, 68,822 were in VIII Corps, anchoring the army's right flank with three divisions in the line. They held an eighty-five-mile front—three times the length advised for a force of such strength under Army tactical doctrine—that snaked down the Belgian border through Luxembourg to Third Army's sector. At two spots, the corps line extended across the border into Germany's Schnee Eifel, a snowy hogback that was a topographical extension of the Belgian Ardennes. Intelligence officers calculated that 24,000 enemy soldiers currently faced VIII Corps, so few that First Army in recent days had ordered a deception program to feign an American buildup in the Ardennes; the intent was to lure more Germans, weakening Rundstedt's lines to the north and south. Some VIII Corps troops wore phony shoulder flashes, drove trucks with bogus unit markings, broadcast counterfeit radio traffic, and played recordings of congregating tanks—all to suggest a preponderance that did not exist. In reality, some infantry regiments that typically should have held a 3,500-yard front in such broken country—two miles—now were required to hold frontages of six miles or more.

For much of the fall, four veteran U.S. divisions had occupied this region, mastering the terrain and rehearsing both withdrawal and counterattack plans. But in recent weeks they had been supplanted by two bloodied divisions from the Hürtgen—those weary troops seeking a quiet paradise—and the newly arrived 106th Infantry Division, which was not only the greenest Army unit in Europe but also the youngest. The first division into combat with substantial numbers of eighteen-year-old draftees, the 106th was plunked onto the Schnee Eifel and across the Losheim Gap, echeloned a mile or so west of the Siegfried Line like an ill-fitting stopper in a bottle.

As with so many newer divisions, the 106th had trained diligently for months at home only to be ripped apart by levies from other units shipping overseas first. By August 1944, more than seven thousand men had been transferred out of the division, including many aggressive infantrymen who were replaced by rear-echelon converts with suspect combat skills. After arriving at Le Havre on December 6, the 106th had been trucked across France to reach the Ardennes front at seven P.M. on December 11, "numb, soaked, and frozen," as the military historian R. Ernest Dupuy later wrote. Man for man, foxhole for foxhole, across a twenty-eight-mile sector, they replaced troops of the 2nd Infantry Division, who bolted for showers and hot food in the rear.

Few soldiers of the 106th had ever heard a shot fired in anger, and some failed to zero their rifles to ensure accurate marksmanship. Radio silence precluded the testing and calibration of new sets. Battalions reported shortages of winter clothing, maps, machine-gun tripods, and mortar, antitank, and bazooka ammunition. Trench foot soon spiked when green troops neglected to dry their socks properly. Despite orders to mount an "aggressive defense," few patrols ventured forward, and German war dogs terrorized those that did.

Go easy, boys. There's danger ahead.

"The woods are of tall pines, dark and gloomy inside. After a snow it is all in black and white," an artilleryman wrote his wife from an outpost near Losheim. "This was the Forest of Arden from Shakespeare's *As You Like It*." In the bard's comedy, the forest is a pastoral refuge for characters who choose to devote themselves to love. Few soldiers trying to stay warm in an Ardennes copse in mid-December found such lyricism in the landscape. V-1 flying bombs launched from western Germany rattled overhead day and night, angling toward Antwerp. Forward strongpoints—a few dozen men consigned to the low ground of crossroads villages—were sardonically dubbed "sugar bowls" because of their topographic vulnerability.

A departing 2nd Division colonel told his 106th replacement, "It has been very quiet up here and your men will learn the easy way."

Straw and rags muffled gun wheels and horses' hooves as twenty German divisions lumbered into their final assembly areas on Friday night, December 15. Breakdown crews with tow trucks stood ready along roads that now carried only one-way traffic, and military policemen were authorized to shoot out the tires of any vehicle violating march discipline. For the last kilometer leading to the line of departure, soldiers portaged ammunition by hand or on their backs. Quartermasters issued ration packets of "special vitalizing and strengthening foods," including fifty grams of genuine coffee, grape-sugar tablets, chocolate, fruit bars, and milk powder. "Some believe in living but life is not everything!" a soldier from the 12th SS Panzer Division wrote his sister. "It is enough to know that we attack and will throw the enemy from our homeland. It is a holy task."

Two hundred thousand assault troops packed into an assembly area three miles deep. The initial blow by seven panzer divisions and thirteen of infantry, bolstered by almost two thousand artillery tubes and a thousand tanks and assault guns, would fall on a front sixty-one miles wide. Five more divisions and two heavy brigades waited in the second wave, giving the Germans roughly a five-to-one advantage over the opposing U.S. forces in artillery and a three-to-one edge in armor. The best of Rundstedt's divisions had 80 percent of their full complement of equipment, others but half. Panzer columns carried enough fuel to travel one hundred miles under normal cruising conditions, which existed nowhere in the steep, icy Ardennes. Few spare parts or antitank guns were to be had, but for a holy task perhaps none were needed.

Hitler had indeed staked the future of his Reich on one card. The final OB West war diary entry on Friday night declared, "Tomorrow brings the beginning of a new chapter in the campaign in the West."

In the red-roofed Belgian army barracks that served as the VIII Corps command post in Bastogne, champagne corks popped on Friday night to commemorate the anniversary of the corps's arrival in Britain a year earlier. The commander, Major General Troy H. Middleton, had reason to be proud of his men's combat record in Normandy and in the reduction of Brest. A Mississippian who had enlisted as a private in 1910, Middleton by November 1918 was the youngest American colonel in World War I and, in George Marshall's judgment, "the outstanding infantry regimental commander on the battlefield in France." Leaving the Army in 1937 to become dean and then vice president of Louisiana State University, Middleton returned to uniform in 1942, commanding the 45th Division through the Sicily and Salerno campaigns before taking corps command as an Eisenhower favorite. Now he drank a final toast to battles past and future before retiring to his sleeping van.

A few miles to the east, the faint clop of horses and a growl of engines in low gear drifted to American pickets along the Our River, demarcating Luxembourg from Germany. Their report of disturbing noises in the night ascended the chain of command from one headquarters to the next, with no more heed paid than had been paid to earlier portents. Middleton's command post in Bastogne issued a weather forecast for Saturday—"Cloudy, snow beginning around 1300. Visibility 2 miles"—and a three-word battle summary for the Ardennes: "Nothing to report."

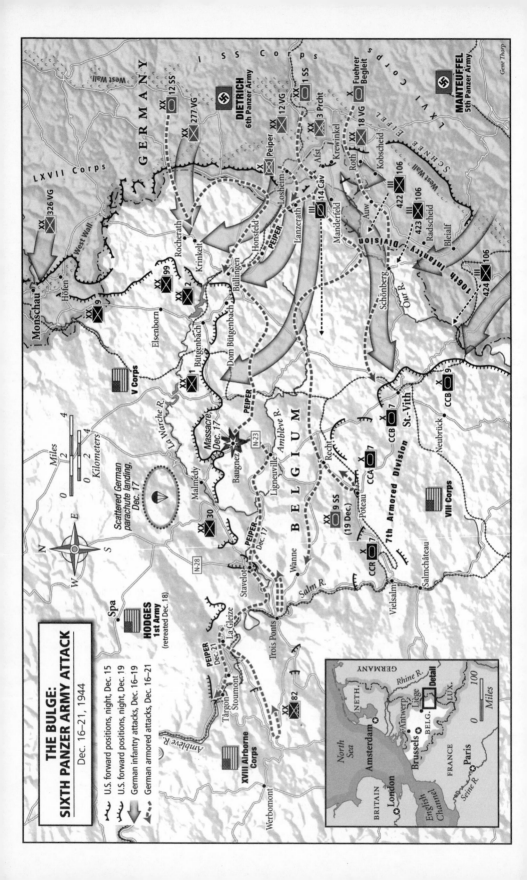

THE BULGE:
SIXTH PANZER ARMY ATTACK
Dec. 16–21, 1944

U.S. forward positions, night, Dec. 15
U.S. forward positions, night, Dec. 19
German infantry attacks, Dec. 16–19
German armored attacks, Dec. 16–21

9. THE BULGE

A Rendezvous in Some Flaming Town

S HEETS of flame leaped from the German gun pits at precisely 5:30 A.M. on December 16. Drumfire fell in crimson splashes across the front with a stink of turned earth and burnt powder, and the green fireballs of 88mm shells bored through the darkness at half a mile per second as if hugging the nap of the Ardennes hillcrests. The Screaming Meemie shriek of Nebelwerfer rockets echoed in the hollows where wide-eyed GIs crouched in their sugar bowls. Then enemy machine guns added their saw-mill racket to the din, and rounds with the heft of railroad spikes splintered fir boughs and soldiers' bones alike. The thrum of panzer engines now carried from the east, along with a creak of bogey wheels, and as the artillery crashed and heaved, a rifleman in the 99th Division reflected, "You'd think the end of the world is coming."

For some, yes, soon enough. A pearly dawn leaked down the slopes, hurried by hissing German flares that glazed the snow with metallic tints of red and silver. Through the trees the infantry emerged as bent shadows, some in snow suits or white capes, others in greatcoats of *Feldgrau* with flanged helmets or duck-bill caps, shouting and singing above the whip-crack of rifle fire. One GI, hiding in a barn among cows now excused from the Saturday-morning slaughter, whispered, "The whole German army's here." Along the thin American line, men dug in deeper, scratching furrows with helmets and mess tins. Others scuttled to the rear, past the first dead men, who wore the usual deadpan expressions. Only the living were surprised.

The battle was joined, this last great grapple of the Western Front, although hours would elapse before American commanders realized that the opening barrage was more than a feint, and days would pass before some generals acknowledged the truth of what Rundstedt had told his legions in an order captured early Saturday: *Es geht um das Ganze.* Everything is at stake. The struggle would last for a month, embroiling more than a million men drawn from across half a continent to this haunted upland. The first act of the drama, perhaps the most decisive, played out simultaneously across three sanguinary fields scattered over sixty miles—on the American left, on the American right, and in the calamitous center. "Your great hour has struck," Rundstedt had also declared. "You bear in yourselves a divine duty to give everything and to achieve the superhuman for our Fatherland and our Führer."

No man embraced the field marshal's sentiments with greater fervor than the slender young SS lieutenant colonel barking at the jammed traffic northwest of Losheim on Saturday morning. Joachim Peiper's great hour had indeed struck, yet he was already late. A highway bridge across a rail cut had been demolished in September by retreating German troops, but engineers assigned to repair the span could not get past the mule wagons, horse-drawn artillery carriages, and Tiger tanks clogging the narrow approach road. A stalled column of tanks and personnel carriers snaked for miles back into Germany.

As commander of the 1st SS Panzer Regiment, proudly wearing the death's-head insignia above the visor of his peaked cap, Peiper had been given the specific divine duty of streaking across Belgium with a task force of almost six thousand men and seventy-two tanks to seize the Meuse crossings at Huy, between Liège and Namur. Although only twenty-nine, he was an obvious choice as the *Spitze*—the point—of Sixth Panzer Army's attack and indeed all of HERBSTNEBEL. A Berliner born into a military family, fluent in English and French, and handsome in the approved Aryan mode, Peiper in 1938 had served as Heinrich Himmler's personal adjutant, even marrying one of his secretaries shortly before the invasion of Poland. Much of his war had been spent in the east, burning villages and slaughtering civilians with such abandon that his unit was nicknamed the Blow Torch Battalion. Two brothers, also SS men, were now dead, but Peiper's devotion to the Reich was undimmed. With Allied bombers terrorizing German cities, he did not question Hitler's orders to wield fear and terror as weapons.

In early December, after a test run in a Panther near Bonn, Peiper reported that a tank regiment could cover eighty kilometers in a single night, "if I had a free road to myself." But when assigned his route to the Meuse in December he had complained that "these roads were not for tanks but for bicycles." The Saturday chaos proved his point, and although he urged his young troopers to "run down anything in the road ruthlessly," most of *Null Tag* had slipped past before the column finally found a detour through Losheim at 7:30 P.M.

More troubles awaited. Both German and American mines cost Peiper five tanks before the task force reached Lanzerath at midnight; an hour later, he ordered two Panthers to take the point, guided through the tenebrous woods by troops waving white handkerchiefs. Shortly before 6 A.M. on Sunday the *Spitze* clattered into Honsfeld to find American vehicles parked in doorways and exhausted GIs slumbering inside. Here the atrocities commenced. Eight soldiers rousted outside in their underwear and bare feet, shouting *"Kamerad"*—comrade, I surrender—were lined up in the street and murdered with a machine gun. Five others emerged from a house with a white flag; four were shot, and the fifth, pleading for mercy, was crushed beneath a tank. Four more Americans, also carrying a large white banner, were shot, too. Peiper's men stripped boots from the dead and pressed on to Büllingen, two miles northwest.

German intelligence had correctly identified Büllingen as a likely fuel dump, and SS crews, after raking a dozen parked spotter planes with gunfire on an airstrip outside town, seized fifty thousand gallons of gasoline by ten A.M. Several American soldiers hiding in a cellar strangled their pet dog to keep her from barking, but two hundred other men were rounded up. Before being marched to prison cages in the rear, GIs were forced to fuel the panzers with jerricans in the treeless square that in happier days had served as the town cattle market. Already many hours behind schedule and still sixty miles from Huy, with orders to ignore his exposed flanks and all diversions, Peiper now pivoted southwest—unwittingly giving the Americans a priceless tactical reprieve. Had he swung northwest a few miles to Bütgenbach and then Elsenborn, where the 12th SS Panzer Division was attacking from the east, he likely would have encircled as many as thirty thousand GIs in the beset 2nd and 99th Divisions, who were struggling to fall back to defensible ground.

This serendipity proved catastrophic for Battery B of the 285th Field Artillery Observation Battalion, which early that morning had hurriedly decamped from Germany with orders to move to Luxembourg. At 11:45 A.M., 140 men in thirty-three vehicles stopped for a Sunday lunch of hash, peas, and pineapple outside the Walloon town of Malmédy, ten miles west of Büllingen. An hour later the march south resumed, past Army engineers taping TNT to ash trees to be blown down as roadblocks if necessary. As the convoy sped through Malmédy on Highway N-23, Belgian civilians gestured ahead, yelling, *"Boches! Boches!"*

Boches there were, and in a particularly foul mood after clumping down a muddy farm trace barely passable even by tracked vehicles. Three miles below Malmédy, at the crossroads hamlet of Baugnez, Peiper's SS column collided with Battery B shortly before one P.M. For two minutes German machine-gun and tank fire peppered the American convoy until Peiper, furious at the destruction of fifteen fine Detroit trucks, managed to call a cease-fire. A few GIs had been killed, a few others escaped through the woods or hid in a ditch, but more than one hundred surrendered, some with white rags tied to their rifle barrels. As Panthers shoved the burning chassis off the road, prisoners were herded with hands high into eight rows on a snowy field, where their captors stripped them of rings, cigarettes, watches, and gloves. Peiper watched for a few minutes from his personnel carrier, then pushed on down the N-23 toward Ligneuville behind his vanguard.

No one would ever be certain which German soldier fired the first shot, but at 2:15 P.M. an abrupt fusillade from two panzer machine guns chewed into the ranks of prisoners still standing with their hands raised. "At the first outburst of fire everyone fell to the ground, including myself," recalled Private First Class Homer D. Ford, an MP who had been captured while directing traffic at the crossroads. For two minutes gunfire tore into the writhing, bleating ranks. Then SS men stalked through the bloody pile, kicking groins and—with the fatal verdict *"Da kriegt noch einer Luft,"* This one's still breathing—firing pistol shots into the skulls or hearts of those yet alive. Ford lived to bear witness:

> I was wounded in the left arm while the group was being sprayed on the ground. . . . I was laying in the snow . . . and I was afraid they would see me shivering but they didn't. . . . I could hear them pull the trigger back and then the click.

For twenty minutes executioners prowled the field, bellowing in English, "You sons of bitches!" An American medic permitted to attend a wounded soldier was then shot along with his patient. A dozen GIs who had fled into a scruffy café at the crossroads were flushed when the building was set ablaze, and shot down as they scattered. For the next two hours, passing SS convoys fired into the mounded bodies until even the SS tired of the sport. The faces of the dead quickly assumed a deep claret color as the blood in their capillaries froze.

Unaware for the moment that his minions had just committed one of the most infamous battlefield crimes of the war, Peiper arrived at Ligneuville in midafternoon. He was disappointed to find that American officers had just fled, but he spent thirty minutes wolfing down the lunch they left behind in the dining room of the Hôtel du Moulin, a three-story hostel with a wrought-iron balcony. Here a German sergeant led eight U.S. prisoners out back to dig graves for three dead Germans; he then shot the Americans in the head, killing seven. The eighth fled bleeding through the forest only to be later captured again and sent to a camp.

The *Spitze* pushed westward that Sunday as winter's blue shadows grew long. In empty Belgian schoolhouses, Christmas decorations covered walls now perforated with bullet holes; a French lesson chalked on a blackboard read, "God made me to know Him, to love Him, and to serve Him in this world, and to be happy with Him in the next." Twilight had fallen when Peiper reached the wooded bluff above Stavelot on the Amblève River. A single squad of American combat engineers held the town, but when three panzers rushed the only bridge, a mine crippled the lead tank, giving Peiper pause. Perhaps the defenders were stronger than he realized. His march column, strung out for fifteen miles across Belgium, would have to close ranks for an assault into Stavelot, and after three nights of little sleep his men desperately needed rest. He gave the order: they would halt until dawn, still forty-two miles from the Meuse.

Behind him, near Malmédy, more than eighty corpses lay in the snow with their ruddy death masks. But at least a dozen GIs had feigned death for more than two hours and now they rose as if resurrected to pelt through the woods. Soon word of the massacre passed from foxhole to foxhole and up the chain of command, reaching First Army headquarters in Spa even before Peiper decided to stop for the night. Vows to give no quarter spread through the ranks; there were formal decrees in at least two regiments. "American troops are now refusing to take any more SS prisoners," the Ninth Army war diary would note, "and it may well spread to include all German soldiers." *Es geht um das Ganze.* Everything is at stake.

Peiper had bored a small, vicious hole through the American left flank, but that aperture would have to be widened considerably if the bulk of Sixth Panzer Army was to ram through. Much of the weight of General Dietrich's attack fell on the 99th Division, another neophyte unit that had been wedged by V Corps into a twenty-mile swatch of the Ardennes front, between Monschau in the north and Lanzerath in the south. By Sunday morning, various battalions had been chopped to pieces in what Captain Charles P. Roland called "a red nightmare," and much of the division reeled west in confusion. Soldiers siphoned gasoline from wrecked jeeps to ignite flame pits across forest trails, but the enemy came on, bayoneting GIs in their holes and firing point-blank through cellar windows.

"One of our young lieutenants danced a rubber-legged jig as he twisted slowly, making the blue bullet hole between his eyes visible," Roland later wrote. Artillerymen spiked their guns with thermite grenades, and drivers opened radiator petcocks before abandoning their trucks to flee on foot through the woods. Signalmen smashed switchboards, adjutants burned secrets, and skittish soldiers shot one another by mistake, including one clutch of GIs who accidentally killed their own major, then wounded a captain trying to calm them down. In the Bütgenbach villa where he kept his command post, the division commander, Major General Walter E. Lauer, played a piano in the living room with studied insouciance even as one frightful dispatch arrived after another; his casualties would climb to two thousand and keep climbing. Lieutenant Richard H. Byers, a lanky gunner from Cleveland, watched tracers flicker overhead in neon sheets and recalled lines written by the poet Alan Seeger before he was killed in France in 1916: "I've a rendezvous with death / At midnight in some flaming town."

Two towns, actually: three miles from the German border, the twin Belgian villages of Krinkelt and Rocherath stood in the path of the 12th SS Panzer Division. The Murder Division, responsible for liquidating so many Canadian prisoners in Normandy, had been rebuilt with more Hitler Youth teenagers and 130 tanks and assault guns. Two panzer grenadier battalions probed the villages on Sunday only to butt against veterans from the U.S. 2nd Infantry Division who had been hustled into the line so quickly that some had Christmas packages from home dangling on their belts and rifle barrels; one witness thought they looked "more like postmen than soldiers."

A full-throated German assault at first light on Monday failed to win through, and fighting swept from house to house, room to room, alley to muddy alley, with grenades, knives, tank destroyers, and artillery salvos called by American officers onto their own heads. Smoke spiraled in thick braids above the mêlée as men from both sides were captured, freed, and recaptured. Antitank guns and skulking bazooka teams, along with almost thirty thousand artillery rounds, knocked out so many Panthers and other tracks that a German officer called the villages "a perfect panzer graveyard." An enemy gambit to outflank the American line by attacking through Höfen, ten miles north, ended with a battalion of Volksgrenadiers littering the snow like gray stepping-stones. Burial details counted 554 German bodies, for only a dozen U.S. casualties.

At dusk on Tuesday, with the last remnants of the 99th Division bundled to the rear except for stouthearts fighting with the 2nd Division, the Americans slipped from Krinkelt and Rocherath in thick fog, abandoning those flaming towns for better ground a thousand yards west—a boomerang crest two thousand feet high, running from southwest to northeast and unmarked on Belgian military maps. American commanders named this high ground after a nearby village: Elsenborn Ridge. Here Major General Gerow, the V Corps commander, believed the German attack could impale itself.

Corps gunners muscled hundreds of tubes into the lee of the ridge, along with 90mm antiaircraft guns to be used as artillery. Troops shoveled dirt into empty wooden ammunition boxes for field fortifications and burrowed down in the shale slope, roofing the hollows with pine logs and doors ripped from their hinges in a nearby Belgian barracks. Riflemen from the 2nd Division filled the ridgeline on the right and those from the 99th held the left, braced by the veteran 9th Infantry Division taking positions below Monschau in the north. An officer described a command post near Elsenborn as "a Gilbert and Sullivan opera . . . a big crowd of officers, all with map cases, binoculars, gas masks, etc., milling about. Nobody knew anything useful, even where the enemy was." Loony rumors flitted about, including reports of Tiger tanks being dropped by parachute. "I want to throw back my head and give voice to that empty feeling with a long animal howl," Lieutenant Byers wrote his wife. Then a colonel walked in and proclaimed, "You need worry no longer. The 1st Division is here."

Just so. At a moment when artillery prowess was most in demand, no better gunner was to be found in the U.S. Army than the owlish, bespectacled pipe-smoker known as Mr. Chips: Major General Clift Andrus, who a week earlier had taken command of the 1st Division when General Clarence Huebner became Gerow's deputy at V Corps. Andrus soon would orchestrate time-on-target fire missions from as many as thirty-five battalions— more than four hundred guns shooting at a single target simultaneously. Also welcome was the arrival of the division's 26th Infantry Regiment to straddle the trunk road from Büllingen to Malmédy.

Here for three days and nights German paratroopers and the 12th SS Panzer smashed against the defensive bulkhead again and again. One message to Andrus's headquarters advised, "Attack repulsed. Send litters." Then: "Much happening out there. We are killing lots of Germans."

The heaviest blows fell on the 26th Infantry's 2nd Battalion, commanded since the battle of El Guettar in Tunisia by Lieutenant Colonel Derrill M. Daniel, a Ph.D. entomologist wise in the ways of insect pests. A night attack from Büllingen by twenty truckloads of whooping, dismounted German infantry supported by panzers churning through deck-deep mud was repulsed with white phosphorus and antitank guns firing high-velocity British sabot ammunition at exhaust flames and engine noises. Hours later eight Panthers punched through the battalion line in a rampage of machine-gun and 75mm fire until bazooka teams and scorching antitank volleys threw them back. Thursday brought worse yet, with a three-hour cannonade before dawn by German howitzers and Nebelwerfers; then two battalions of paratroopers and SS panzer grenadiers spilled from a piney wood in the west, trailed by thirty panzers. The 2nd Battalion's right flank crumbled, and SS tanks wheeled up and down the line, crushing GIs in their foxholes.

"Get me all the damned artillery you can get," Daniel radioed. Ten thousand rounds in eight hours—among the fiercest concentrations in the European war—kept enemy infantry at bay, but panzers closed to within a hundred yards of the battalion command post in a farm compound called

Dom Bütgenbach. For much of the day Daniel and his staff crouched in a cellar with the wounded, burning classified papers and massing fires as tank and machine-gun rounds blistered the four-foot stone walls. Sleeting counterfire from Shermans and new 90mm tank destroyers finally winkled out the last attackers from behind a barn by shooting right through it; only one panzer escaped. An eerie silence descended with the night.

Army patrols reported enemy dead "as common as grass," and grave diggers would count nearly 800 bodies, along with the wrecked hulks of forty-seven panzers and self-propelled guns. Daniel took 250 casualties—this just three weeks after ruinous losses in the Hürtgen—and during the protracted fight at Elsenborn Ridge 5,000 others were killed or wounded or went missing in the 2nd and 99th Divisions alone.

But the American line held. Here Sixth Panzer Army reached its high-water mark, on what would become known as the north shoulder of the Bulge. Dietrich needed an eight- to twelve-mile cushion on his right flank to keep German assault columns unmolested by American artillery as they lumbered toward the Meuse. Instead, the juggernaut was forced to shear away from the main road through Bütgenbach to seek secondary avenues farther south; three routes allocated to the I SS Panzer Corps remained blocked, with others under fire. An attack farther north near Monschau failed abjectly when one German division arrived late to the battle and the other was knocked back. Only Peiper's foray showed clear promise in this sector. The 12th SS Panzer Division had been mauled, again, and other SS units seemed muscle-bound and clumsy.

The Americans by contrast demonstrated agility and a knack for concentrating firepower. Sixty thousand fresh troops had been shuttled into the Ardennes on Sunday, December 17, among the quarter-million reinforcements who would arrive within a week. Four U.S. infantry divisions clotted the north shoulder so effectively that OB West's war diary acknowledged "the Elsenborn attack is gaining only quite insignificant ground," while Army Group B lamented "slower progress than anticipated." The tactical fortunes of Dietrich and his lieutenants seemed increasingly doubtful, to the point that Rundstedt and Model, watching the offensive come unstitched, agreed to abruptly shift the German main effort from Sixth Panzer Army to Manteuffel's Fifth Panzer Army in the south. With northern routes denied or constricted, a new urgency obtained on the German left, and the roads leading through Luxembourg toward Bastogne and thence to the Meuse were now more vital than ever.

Two armored corps abreast had come down like wolves on the fold in Manteuffel's Saturday-morning attack, each corps falling on little more than an American regiment at an unnerving ratio of ten wolves for each sheep. Cota's 28th Division, still recuperating from six thousand Hürtgen casualties, held an impossibly wide twenty-five-mile front along the Our River, with all three infantry regiments on line. Instead of facing two German divisions across the river, as Army intelligence had surmised, Cota's men found themselves fighting five, plus heavy enemy reinforcements.

As artillery and mortar barrages shredded field-phone wires and truck tires, German infiltrators forded the Our in swirling fog to creep up stream beds behind the American pickets. Forward outposts fell back, or perished, or surrendered. "While I was being searched they came across my teeth wrapped in a handkerchief in my pocket," a captured engineer recorded. "These they kept." German shock troops soon rushed American gun lines illuminated by flares and by searchlights ricocheting off the low clouds; howitzer crews fired over open sights before spiking their tubes. An American armored column rushing down a ridgetop road known as Skyline Drive blundered into a German ambush: eleven light tanks were destroyed in as many minutes, "like clay pipes in a shooting gallery." From his command post in Wiltz, a brewing and tanning town ten miles west of the Our, Cota repeated orders from General Middleton at the VIII Corps headquarters in Bastogne, another ten miles farther west: "Hold at all costs." A soldier scribbled in his diary, "This place is not healthy anymore."

Yet as in the north, frictions and vexations soon bedeviled the German attack. A bridge for the 2nd Panzer Division collapsed into the Our after only ten tanks had crossed. Engineers eventually built two spans stout enough to hold a Panther, at Gemünd and Dasburg, but steep, hairpin approach roads, pocked by American artillery, reduced traffic to a crawl. Although Cota's flank regiments yielded ground in the face of flame-throwers and panzer fire, they imposed a severe penalty on the German timetable.

Along the American right, where four infantry divisions from the enemy's Seventh Army formed HERBSTNEBEL's southern lip, the 109th Infantry over three days would fall back slowly for four miles to Diekirch before joining forces with part of the 9th Armored Division. Another Hürtgen convalescent, the 4th Infantry Division, helped parry an enemy sweep into the American rear. On Cota's left, two battalion kitchens in the 112th Infantry were quickly overrun, but cooks fought with rifles and Manteuffel's LVIII Panzer Corps bled badly in getting a foothold across the Our. By Sunday night, the weight of metal and numbers won through for the Germans, but the 112th withdrew in good order to the northwest, largely intact although now splintered away from the rest of the 28th Division. With Cota's permission, the regiment continued sidling north to help defend the Belgian town of St.-Vith.

That left Cota a single regiment, the 110th Infantry, holding an eleven-

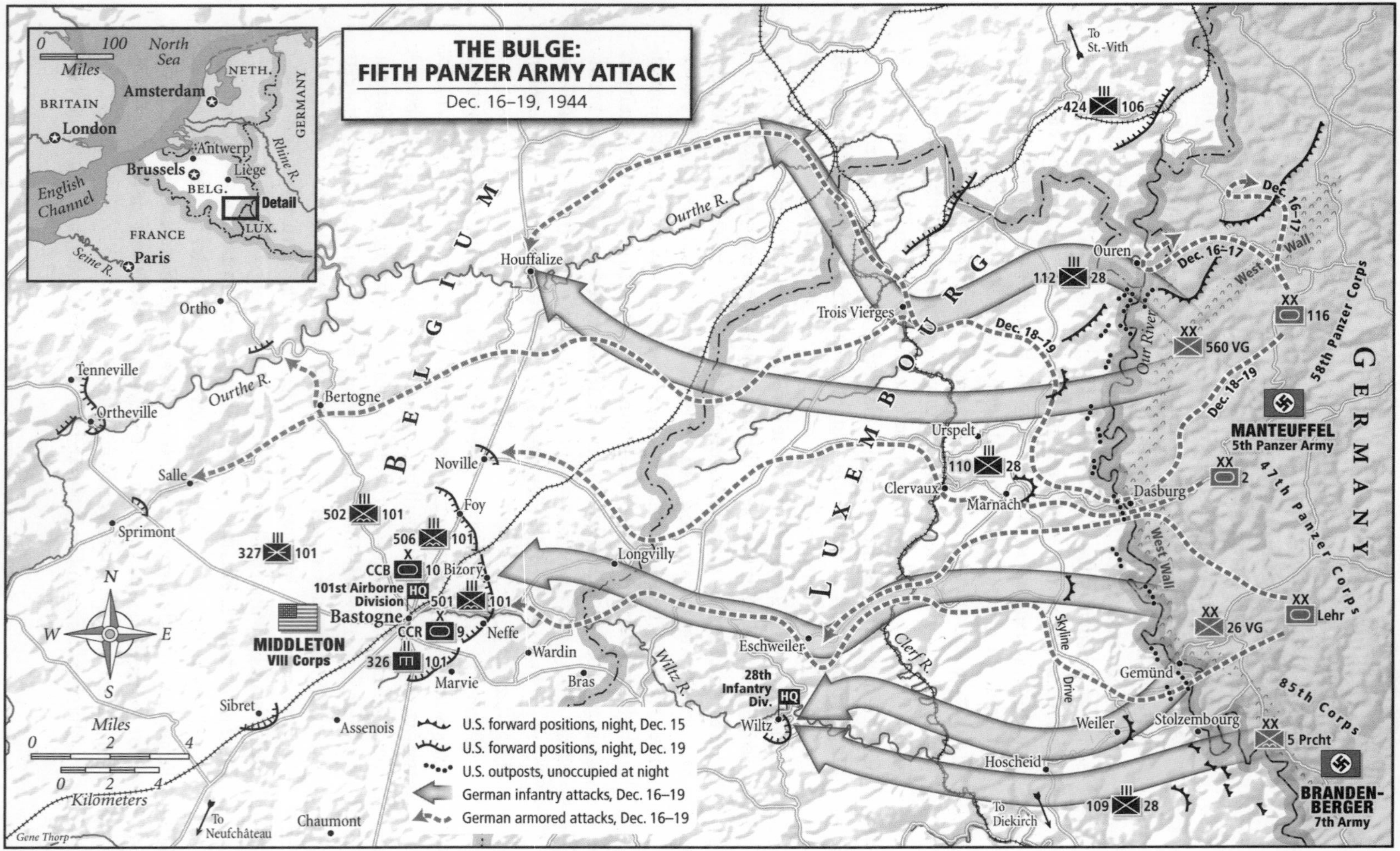

THE BULGE:
FIFTH PANZER ARMY ATTACK
Dec. 16–19, 1944
0 100 Miles
North Sea
NETH.
GERMANY
BRITAIN
Amsterdam
London
Antwerp
Rhine R.
Brussels
Liège
BELG.
English Channel
Detail
FRANCE
LUX.
Seine R.
Paris
To St.-Vith
424 106
Houffalize
Ourthe R.
Ouren
Dec. 16–17
West Wall
112 28
Trois Vierges
Dec. 18–19
116
58th Panzer Corps
560 VG
Our River
GERMANY
BELGIUM
LUXEMBOURG
Ortho
Tenneville
Ortheville
Bertogne
MANTEUFFEL
5th Panzer Army
Urspelt
110 28
Noville
Clervaux
Marnach
Dasburg
2
47th Panzer Corps
Salle
Foy
502 101
506 101
Sprimont
327 101
Longvilly
CCB 10 Bizory
101st Airborne Division
HQ
501 101
Bastogne
CCR 9
Neffe
MIDDLETON
VIII Corps
N
W
E
S
Eschweiler
Wardin
326 101
Marvie
Bras
Wiltz R.
Clerf R.
Skyline Drive
Lehr
26 VG
Gemünd
85th Corps
28th Infantry Div.
Wiltz
Sibret
Assenois
Weiler
Stolzembourg
5 Prcht
Miles
0 2 4
0 2 4
Kilometers
U.S. forward positions, night, Dec. 15
U.S. forward positions, night, Dec. 19
U.S. outposts, unoccupied at night
German infantry attacks, Dec. 16–19
German armored attacks, Dec. 16–19
Hoscheid
To Diekirch
109 28
BRANDENBERGER
7th Army
To Neufchâteau
Chaumont
Gene Thorp

mile front in the division center. Here Manteuffel swung his heaviest blow, with three divisions in XLVII Panzer Corps instructed to rip through to Bastogne, specifically targeted for quick capture under a Führer order. By midday Sunday the 110th was disintegrating, though not without a scrap. In the medieval town of Clervaux, various nobles for nine centuries—notably, John the Blind and the House of Burgundy—had occupied a feudal castle on a rocky spur overlooking the road to Bastogne. Now one hundred GIs, including clerks and bakers, barricaded themselves inside, firing from arrow slits in the Tower of the Witches at Germans in long leather coats scampering below. Wailing pleas for salvation rose from the dungeon, where dozens of women and children had taken refuge.

A mile up the road, in the three-story Hotel Claravallis, the flinty regimental commander, Colonel Hurley E. Fuller, advised Cota by radio of his peril: at least a dozen panzers on the high ground firing into Clervaux; the castle besieged; ammunition short; artillery overrun or retreating. "Hold at all costs," Cota repeated. "No retreat. Nobody comes back."

At 7:30 on Sunday evening, Fuller was again on the radio to division headquarters, likening his predicament to the Alamo, when a staff officer rushed in to report enemy tanks on the street outside. "No more time to talk," Fuller told one of Cota's lieutenants, and then slammed down the handset just before three shells demolished the hotel façade. He bounded to the third floor to grab his carbine and coat, only to find ten terrified soldiers crouched in Room 10. As the sound of German voices carried up the stairway, an explosion blew in the window. Glass, plaster, and steel sprayed the room, killing a lieutenant and wounding five other men. Hurriedly bandaging the eyes of a blinded soldier, Fuller led him by the hand to Room 12, where an iron ladder extended from the window across a fifteen-foot gap to crude steps cut into a shale cliff behind the hotel. Out and up they climbed, one by one, the blind man clutching Fuller's belt from behind. Reaching the bluff above the ruby glow of burning Clervaux, Fuller set a course west for Bastogne, but to no avail: chaos and gunfire soon scattered the absconders. Within hours Fuller had been captured in a thicket near Wiltz, to be bundled off by boxcar to a prison camp near Leipzig.

The castle too was burning. Flames danced from the tower roof and black smoke stained the whitewashed inner walls. A final radio call went out Monday morning, December 18, before a panzer battered down the heavy wooden gates. At one P.M. the little garrison hoisted a white flag in surrender. Silence settled over Clervaux but for crackling fires and the shatter of glass from German looting. In a small inn that once housed the

Red Cross club, a sign in the front window still proclaimed, "Of course we're open."

Not far from Clervaux, frightened civilians in another Luxembourg town wielded hammers and axes to demolish a huge sign erected in the fall to welcome the Americans. On the heels of the retreating 109th Infantry, three thousand men, women, and children fled Diekirch in bitter cold at midnight on Tuesday, abandoning four hundred others too old, infirm, or stubborn to leave. On Cota's order, undelivered Christmas packages and letters were piled in a Wiltz courtyard, doused with gasoline, and burned; the division command post pulled out Tuesday, first to Bastogne, then to Sibret, and eventually to Neufchâteau. A gaggle of Army bandsmen, engineers, paymasters, and sawmill operators fought as a rear guard until overrun by whistle-blowing German paratroopers, who reduced Wiltz with machine pistols and forty panzers.

"This was the end," the official Army history recorded. "Shots, blazing vehicles, and screaming wounded." Some GIs escaped by night in groups of ten with map scraps and radium-dial compasses. Several hundred others were captured, including one young officer who described being propped on a German staff car as a hood ornament, legs dangling over the grille, and driven east through march columns of Wehrmacht reinforcements who were "laughing at me as the trophy."

The 110th Infantry had been annihilated, with 2,500 battle casualties. Sixty American tanks were reduced to smoking wreckage. Yet once again space had been traded for time, a few miles for forty-eight hours, and once again that bargain favored the defenders. The southern shoulder was jammed almost as effectively as the northern. Fifth Panzer Army now marched on Bastogne, true enough, but the stumbling, tardy advance by three bloodied divisions hardly resembled the blitzkrieg of Hitler's fever dream.

Only in the center of the German onslaught did HERBSTNEBEL find unalloyed success. Here many of the fourteen thousand green soldiers in the 106th Division sheltered in captured Siegfried Line pillboxes, as enemy spearheads to the left and right tried on Saturday to envelop them in a pincer movement around the Schnee Eifel hogback. General Manteuffel hoped to capture St.-Vith within a day; the five main roads and three rail lines converging on that Belgian market hub, sixteen miles to the west, were vital given the hazards of moving cross-country through the Ardennes. On no segment of the Western Front were GIs more outnumbered, yet sharp firefights that morning imperiled the German timetable here as elsewhere. After one enemy column was slapped around, a German soldier shouted, in English, "Take a ten-minute break. We'll be back." A GI answered, "Fuck you, we'll still be here."

Not for long, at least on the left flank. Here about half of the sixteen hundred troopers in the 14th Cavalry Group plugged the Losheim Gap with flimsy armored cars and a few tank destroyers in eight sugar-bowl strongpoints under the group commander, Colonel Mark A. Devine, Jr., a beetle-browed disciplinarian with a penchant for telling Belgian mayors, "Your damn town is dirty. Clean it up." Facing paratroopers from the southern edge of Sixth Panzer Army and Volksgrenadiers from the northern edge of Fifth Panzer Army, the cavalry buckled. "Front lines still intact. Things well in hand," Devine reported from Manderfeld, but German shock troops gobbled up the sugar bowls one by one: Krewinkel, Afst, Kobscheid. A final radio message from Roth—"Tanks seventy-five yards from command post. Firing direct fire. Out"—was followed by silence. At four o'clock on Saturday afternoon, after an enemy shell wounded a staff officer and knocked Devine to the floor of his command post, he received permission from the 106th Division headquarters in St.-Vith to pull back two miles. Troopers put Manderfeld to the torch and retreated to the next ridgeline, blowing up eight of a dozen tank destroyers to forestall capture.

Devine's behavior now grew odd; perhaps he was suffering effects from the concussive blast. As his troopers dug in, he drove to St.-Vith, where for hours he loitered around the hectic 106th Division offices, eating bread, cheese, and then a breakfast of hot cakes and coffee. One officer thought his demeanor unremarkable, but the assistant division commander found him "almost incoherent. . . . He was nervous, could barely control his actions." The chief of staff described him as "excited and anxious." The division commander, Major General Alan W. Jones, anxious himself, offered scant advice other than to hold tight.

Instead, at daybreak on Sunday Devine returned to his men and, though there was little enemy pressure, ordered them to fall back farther, this time without authorization. He again drove to St.-Vith early in the afternoon, bursting into Jones's office. "The Germans are right behind us!" he warned, his face flushed. "They've broken through in the north. My group is practically destroyed." Sent back to his cavalrymen, the colonel ordered yet another retreat contrary to orders, now to Poteau, *west* of St.-Vith and seventeen miles from the original front.

At dusk on Sunday, Devine set out once more for St.-Vith, this time driving southeast with his executive officer and entire senior staff in a convoy of three jeeps and an armored car, each burning blackout lights. Thwarted by torrents of traffic crawling west, the little procession turned around in the dark only to hear a sharp command of *"Halt!"* a mile east of Recht. As an approaching German picket did a double take at the white star insignia on the armored car, an officer in the lead jeep pulled a pistol and shot the enemy soldier in the face. A sergeant then unleashed a cackling burst from a .50-caliber machine gun, and in the ensuing gunfight the Americans scattered through the woods. At midnight a disheveled, incoherent Devine appeared in the Poteau tavern serving as his command post, where he told a subordinate, "I want you to take over"; at four A.M. Monday, he was evacuated to Vielsalm by the unit dentist. A battalion surgeon later found Devine in La Roche with "a wild gleam in his eye," directing traffic and urging passersby to counterattack immediately. Six grams of sodium amytal put him into a deep sleep and removed him from the front.

The damage had been done, but even a stalwart stand by the 14th Cavalry likely would not have long postponed the catastrophe that followed. With the American left flank abruptly unhinged, German paratroopers on Sunday had cantered through Manderfeld to Lanzerath, brushing sleeves with Colonel Peiper's SS column and further pressuring the 99th Division to the north as well as imperiling the 106th Division in the south.

In St.-Vith, General Jones, a stocky native of Washington State with brilliantine hair and a Clark Gable mustache, sought counsel from the VIII Corps commander, General Middleton. Except for an engineer battalion, virtually all division reserves had been hustled into the fight. Should the 106th's infantry regiments, entrenched along a twenty-eight-mile front, pull back?

"You know how things are up there better than I do," Middleton said in a phone call from Bastogne. "But I agree it would be wise to withdraw them." In one of those mischances so common in war, a brief disruption on the line apparently kept Jones from hearing the second sentence. He hung up, telling his staff in St.-Vith, "Middleton says we should leave them in," even as Middleton told subordinates in Bastogne, "I just talked to Jones. I told him to pull his regiments off the Schnee Eifel." The 106th would stand pat, despite howling barbarians on both flanks. "He felt that he could hold," Middleton later observed. "He made a mistake. . . . He had a fighting heart."

Jones also believed that help was on the way. VIII Corps promised that combat commands from both the 7th and 9th Armored Divisions would soon arrive, perhaps within hours. That optimism failed to account for the "indescribable confusion" of double- and triple-banked traffic "hurtling to the rear," in one major's description. "It was a case of every dog for himself . . . the most perfect traffic jam I have ever seen." Another officer conceded, "It wasn't orderly, it wasn't military, it wasn't a pretty sight." A tanker plowing against the exodus at one mile per hour reported that "the fear-crazed occupants of the vehicles fleeing to the rear had lost all reason."

By midday on Sunday, only the advance guard from Combat Command B of the 7th Armored Division had arrived in St. Vith. The commander, a newly promoted brigadier general named Bruce C. Clarke, had been preparing to leave for Paris to undergo gallstone surgery when word came that "Alan Jones is having some trouble at St. Vith." Clarke, a craggy engineer from upstate New York, found that General Jones's trouble included Germans on three sides, a disintegrating cavalry group, and fretful anxiety over his son, a lieutenant somewhere on the Schnee Eifel. Division staff officers stomped about, burning maps and flinging equipment into truck beds for evacuation. At one P.M., Jones phoned Middleton again, telling the corps commander, "Things are looking up. . . . We are going to be all right." After ringing off he told an astonished Clarke that Middleton had "enough troubles already" without worrying about the 106th Division.

The crackle of small-arms fire sent both generals hurrying to the third floor of the division command post in steep-roofed St. Josef's Kloster, where the devout had long cared for the sick, schooled the young, and bathed the bodies of the dead. Muzzle flashes twinkled along a bluff just east of town. "I've thrown in my last chips," Jones said, turning to Clarke. "I've got nothing left. You take it now." And with that General Jones soon joined the frantic exodus to the west.

Jones's stand-fast decision had left two infantry regiments, the 422nd and 423rd, and five artillery battalions exposed to entrapment on the Schnee Eifel. On Sunday the trap snapped shut when German columns from north and south converged in Schönberg, just across the Belgian border east of St.-Vith. South of town a third regiment, the 424th Infantry, had earlier that day managed to beat back the enemy envelopment and thus escape entrapment, but by dusk nine thousand other GIs were surrounded on a bleak, snowy German moor. An icy west wind soughed through the fir stands, carrying the fateful whine of panzer engines from the American rear. GIs huddling for warmth in foxholes along the West Wall listened impassively, displaying, one officer recorded, "absolutely no expression."

At 2:15 on Monday morning, a radio message from General Jones at last ordered the two regiments to retreat toward Schönberg, where an armored spearhead from St.-Vith would help them break out. Ammunition, food, and water were to be dropped by parachute. Colonel George L. Descheneaux, commander of the 422nd Infantry, bowed his head. "My poor men," he said. "They'll be cut to pieces."

Cooks made towering stacks of pancakes, then destroyed their kitchens. In dense fog at dawn the anabasis began, a serpentine column of battalions trudging through the snow, vaguely following a compass azimuth of 270 degrees, while a parallel procession of trucks, jeeps, and towed artillery bumped along cow paths and game trails. Men listened for V-weapons overhead and sought to follow the sound westward. Even Descheneaux muttered, "Where the hell are we?" Huge orange panels were readied to mark a drop zone, but no drop came. Bad weather and "command incoordination," as the AAF later termed the confusion, kept some planes grounded in England, while two dozen others shuttled emergency supplies between airfields in Belgium and France, futilely seeking information about the besieged regiments.

By midday the Germans had found them though Allied pilots could not. Artillery and mortar salvos fractured the columns, killing or wounding hundreds and scattering regiments, battalions, and companies across the tableland. Unsure where to shoot, given enemy fire falling from at least three directions, gunners began to spike their guns. With mortar ammunition gone and many riflemen reduced to just a few rounds, wet, cold, hungry troops crawled down ravines or sheltered among the firs and waited for dark. Another radio message from General Jones, now in Vielsalm, advised that no armored relief column was likely to appear. He added:

> Attack Schönberg. Do maximum damage to enemy there. Then attack toward St. Vith. This mission is of greatest importance to the nation. Good luck.

At daybreak on Tuesday, three battalions from the 422nd Infantry, quite lost but still game, moved out abreast only to be lacerated by German tank and machine-gun fire. Mortars walked through the ranks with a heavy footfall. GIs again went to ground, although not before unleashing a five-minute fusillade against shadowy figures in a nearby stream bed who proved to be comrades from the 423rd Infantry. Their commander, Colonel Charles C. Cavender, leaned against a tree, a study in dejection. "Well, Colonel," the regimental chaplain said, "this isn't exactly as we planned, is it?" Cavender shook his head. "No, Chaplain, it isn't."

By one P.M., at least one battalion had been pared to just fifty men. Relentless cannonading flayed the pastures between Radscheid and Auw. An icy breeze stirred the hair of helmetless boys sprawled on their backs, pupils fixed and sightless, "their skin that yellow-white of the newly dead," one lieutenant noted. Benny Goodman and Artie Shaw records blared from German loudspeakers, interspersed with promises of "showers, warm beds, and hotcakes." A GI sobbing in a ditch shouted, "Go blow it out your ass, you German son of a bitch!" Spirits soared for a moment when a clanking Sherman appeared on the Schönberg road; then enemy crewmen inside the captured tank opened fire, and all hope perished.

At 2:30 P.M., with two thousand of his men now packed into a last-stand perimeter four hundred yards across, Colonel Descheneaux summoned his subordinates. "We're still sitting like fish in a pond," he told them. "I'm going to save as many men as I can, and I don't give a damn if I'm court-martialed." The order filtered through the ranks: "Destroy all weapons and equipment. We are about to surrender." As soldiers smashed their rifles against tree trunks and tossed the last ammunition clips into a creek, a major knotted together two white handkerchiefs and set off in search of parley. Descheneaux sat on the lip of a slit trench, weeping. Half a mile away, Colonel Cavender had reached the same conclusion, giving his regiment thirty minutes to destroy all weapons and fling away any German souvenirs. An artillery officer stood on an ambulance waving a snow cape, bellowing, "We surrender."

A few diehards lay low or scampered into the forest, but rank upon rank marched forward with hands raised. More than seven thousand would surrender, in the worst reverse for American arms in the European theater and the greatest U.S. mass capitulation of the war excepting Bataan. "I've lost a division quicker than any division commander in the U.S. Army," General Jones lamented. Two days later, having been relieved of command, he collapsed from a heart attack and was assigned to the "Detachment of Patients" near Paris; "evacuation order no. 13" authorized his return to Washington with a government per diem of $7.

Long columns of prisoners plodded toward Germany, Jones's son among them, past wounded men wailing for help from the snow meadows. Wehrmacht reinforcements tramped by, trundling machine guns in wheelbarrows and catcalling about how panzers had already crossed the Meuse. In that gray tide making for St.-Vith, a captured gunner observed "tanks towing other tanks; tanks towing buses without engines; buses and trucks with red crosses all over them loaded down with ammo and troops."

"Do not flee," the German guards called out. "If you flee, you will be machine weaponed." Many GIs had lost their overcoats and blankets, and at night they lay back to belly for warmth. Some chewed wax candles to ward off hunger, or wolfed down potato skins found in hog troughs. Through Rhineland towns they marched, pelted with stones and maledictions. "The Germans made us take off our overshoes and give them to the civilians," a squad leader from the 423rd Infantry told his diary; in Koblenz, he added, a man in a business suit "hit me in the head with his briefcase. Guard said he was upset over recent bombing."

Among those transported by train into captivity was a twenty-two-year-old private first class named Kurt Vonnegut, Jr., bound for a Dresden work camp. "Bayonets aren't much good against tanks," the future novelist wrote his family in Indiana.

> The supermen marched us, without food, water or sleep to Limburg . . . where we were loaded and locked up, sixty men to each small, unventilated, unheated box car. . . . The floors were covered with fresh cow dung. . . . Half slept while the other half stood.

More than a hundred miles east of the battle, at the Adlerhorst compound in the Taunus Hills, adjutants and headquarters clerks sorted through the latest reports on the Ardennes fighting. Given the disappointments on both flanks of his offensive, Herr Hitler took heart at field dispatches from the Schnee Eifel. The Meuse, Antwerp, victory—all remained in play. To his generals the Führer proclaimed, "Success—complete success—is now in our grasp."

"Why Are You Not Packing?"

A LEADEN overcast in Luxembourg City had prevented Omar Bradley from flying to Versailles on Saturday morning to press his case for more infantry reinforcements. A driver instead stocked the commanding general's Cadillac hamper with Coca-Cola, and at eight A.M. he headed west on roads glazed with ice, skipping the morning war-room briefing that would have alerted him to the German attack. A flattering portrait of Bradley had just appeared in *Time*, his second cover story in six months, but wrapped in a fur-trimmed arctic coat and nursing a bottle of soda in the limousine's rear seat, he looked worn and tired. Five hours later he stopped for lunch at the Ritz in rainy Paris, noting the "lifeless chimneys" around the Place Vendôme. The first rumor of troubles to the east circulated through the hotel dining room; before long, Hemingway, feverish from the flu in his book- and bottle-strewn suite upstairs, would appear in the lobby to proclaim, "There's been a complete breakthrough. This thing could cost us the works. . . . Load those clips. Wipe every cartridge clean."

Shortly before three P.M., a SHAEF colonel tiptoed into Eisenhower's office in the Trianon Palace Hotel in Versailles, where Bradley and four others had just settled around a conference table with the supreme commander. The officer carried a sketchy dispatch from the front suggesting "strong and extensive attacks" in the Ardennes; an alarming number of German divisions already had been identified. Scrutinizing a map that showed blows against the U.S. V and VIII Corps, Major General Strong, the SHAEF intelligence chief, wondered aloud if the enemy had designs on the Meuse and then Brussels. Beetle Smith indelicately recalled recent warnings to 12th Army Group of resurgent strength in Sixth Panzer Army, but Bradley remained skeptical. This was likely nothing more than a spoiling attack, he said, intended to disrupt the Allied assault toward the Rhine; the rumpus would soon peter out. As the meeting broke up, Strong cautioned that "it would be wrong to underrate the Germans."

Eisenhower and Bradley dined that night at the supreme commander's handsome stone villa in St.-Germain-en-Laye, previously occupied by Rundstedt. Despite sour tidings from the Ardennes, they were in a celebratory mood: word had just arrived from Washington of the president's decision to nominate Eisenhower for a fifth star. After spending sixteen years as a major, Eisenhower had ascended from lieutenant colonel to general of the Army in forty-five months. The two friends shared a bottle of champagne, and then nipped from a fifth of Highland Piper Scotch while playing five rubbers of bridge.

Eisenhower in a subsequent cable to Marshall would confess that "all of us, without exception, were astonished" at the strength of HERBSTNEBEL, and nearly a week would elapse until SHAEF intelligence confirmed German ambitions of cleaving the Allied armies in half. Yet the supreme commander sensed on the battle's first day that the trouble in the Ardennes went beyond a spoiling attack. Before repairing to St.-Germain for the evening, he had insisted that Bradley phone his headquarters to shift the 7th Armored Division to St.-Vith from the north, and the 10th Armored Division from the south toward Bastogne. When Bradley replied that Patton would resent the latter order, Eisenhower snapped, "Tell him that Ike is running this damn war."

Other moves quickly followed. SHAEF's only experienced combat reserve consisted of the 101st and 82nd Airborne Divisions; both had hoped for another month to recuperate from MARKET GARDEN and the harsh subsequent weeks near Nijmegen, but neither would get another day. Army tactical doctrine, learned in World War I, called for containing an enemy salient by first crimping the shoulders of any incursion. Paratroopers from both divisions were ordered to the Ardennes posthaste to help crimp. The deployments of one armored division and three infantry divisions from Britain to the Continent would be accelerated, as would troopship sailings to France from the United States. Commanders at the front were told that Meuse bridges were to be held at all costs, or blown into the river if necessary. Patton also was instructed to prepare to swing north, and to take Middleton's beleaguered VIII Corps under his wing. "By rushing out from his fixed defenses," Eisenhower added in an order to subordinates, "the enemy may give us the chance to turn his great gamble into his worst defeat." Supply dumps would be defended, evacuated, or burned as required, and defenses around Paris strengthened. Even so, a French officer visiting Versailles on Monday asked General Strong, "Why are you not packing? Aren't you making any preparation to leave?"

In a message to Marshall, Eisenhower assured the chief that "in no quarter is there any tendency to place any blame upon Bradley"; he had "kept his head magnificently." Yet only grudgingly did Bradley acknowledge his peril. While returning to his headquarters—this time in an armored limousine escorted by MPs—he turned his practiced bird hunter's eye to the passing landscape and cheerfully pointed out pheasants in roadside fields. Upon learning in Luxembourg City that at least fourteen German divisions were attacking, he muttered, "Where in hell has this son of a bitch gotten all his strength?" With the fighting front barely a dozen miles away, his room in the Hôtel Alfa was moved to the rear of the building as a precaution against stray artillery, and he now avoided the front door, entering through the kitchen. Aides removed the three-star insignia from his jeep and covered those on his helmet. Frequent air-raid sirens and booming antiaircraft guns woke him repeatedly despite the sleeping sedatives he took. During a brief moment of panic, staff officers buried secret documents in the headquarters courtyard, disguising the cache as a grave and marking it with a wooden cross and dog tags.

Still Bradley affected nonchalance. Logisticians and engineers were told to continue working on the army group's "Rhine crossing plan." After supper on Monday, December 18, upon studying a map that showed at least four U.S. divisions retreating westward and others threatened with encirclement, he told an aide, "I don't take too serious a view of it, although the others will not agree with me."

Among those who no longer agreed was Courtney Hodges. At his headquarters in Spa, the First Army commander had shared Bradley's defiant attitude of denial for more than a day after the German attack began. An engineer company was sent to work as usual on a rail bridge in Bütgenbach on Sunday, and Hodges initially refused to suspend an attack toward the Roer. At a Christmas party a staff officer who was said to have once sung professionally belted out "Oh, what a beautiful mornin' / Oh, what a beautiful day," from *Oklahoma!* Reporters threw their own party in Room 6 of the Hôtel Portugal in Spa on Sunday, marching with glasses raised, as one correspondent wrote, "briskly up, over, and across the bed, and around the room, with everybody bellowing a quite unprintable ditty, beginning with 'Monday I kissed her on the ankle.'"

Fourteen First Army divisions held a 165-mile front from Aachen to

Luxembourg, and with most of Hodges's senior staff still on leave in London or Paris, deep unease began roiling the Hôtel Britannique command post as Sunday wore on. Church bells pealed to signal a civilian curfew from six P.M. to seven A.M. Mortar crews outside Spa scattered tin pans and crockery around their pits as a makeshift alarm against infiltrators. Cooks, press censors, and Belgian fusiliers rallied to perimeter strong-points. Birds were mistaken for German paratroopers, and improvised patrols of Army lawyers and accountants scrambled off in pursuit. Soldiers in muddy boots tromped through the Britannique cocktail lounge, hauling out dental chairs and sick-bay instruments from behind the mahogany bar. Fearful of German reprisals, Belgian gendarmes freed twenty-one jailed collaborators; MPs rounded them up again. "Thermite grenades were issued with which we could destroy our papers," Forrest Pogue informed his diary, and among those building bonfires in Spa on Sunday night was Major General Pete Quesada, the tactical air commander. Tunisia veterans reminisced about the surprise German offensive in February 1943, when the Army had retreated eighty miles through Kasserine Pass.

Perhaps the prospect of a similar debacle discomfited General Hodges, for at midday on Sunday he closed his office door in the Britannique, sat at his desk, and laid his head on his arms. He took no calls, and for the better part of two days showed symptoms of incapacitation. The precise combination of fatigue, illness, and despair would never be clarified; Major General Ernest N. Harmon, among the Army's toughest combat commanders, later claimed that Hodges was "probably the most shaken man I have ever seen anywhere who pretends to have the carriage necessary for high command." Rumors reached Luxembourg City that the First Army commander "almost went to pieces"; Eisenhower and Bradley apparently considered relieving Hodges, by one account, but chose to wait while General Ridgway's XVIII Airborne Corps rushed to reinforce the front. First Army's capable if autocratic chief of staff, Major General Bill Kean, effectively took command until late Monday, December 18, when Hodges recovered his balance enough to order Spa evacuated.

Officers fussed over how to pack newly pressed pinks-and-greens and whether to take their liquor cabinets until reports put German panzers first at six miles, then just two miles from Spa. Both sightings proved false, but they accelerated the evacuation. "I imagine that the Germans felt like [this] when they had to leave Paris," Pogue wrote. Belgian schoolchildren assembled on a playground to sing "The Star-Spangled Banner" while their parents ripped down American flags and photos of President Roosevelt. Sobbing, a Jewish woman begged the headquarters to "take my child where the Germans can't hurt him." Twelve hundred patients and medicos emptied the 4th Convalescent Hospital within ninety minutes, bolting for Huy. By ill fate, V-1s hit two fleeing convoys, killing two dozen GIs and leaving charred truck chassis scattered across the road.

When Hodges tarried at the Britannique on Monday, one officer whispered to him, "Save yourself, General. It's bad enough if we get overrun without your getting captured." At ten P.M. the command group pulled out for Chaudfontaine, near Liège, where a new headquarters opened at midnight in the Hôtel des Bains. Left behind in Spa were secret maps, and food simmering on the stove. An officer entering the Britannique on Tuesday morning found tables set for breakfast, trees decorated for Christmas, and papers strewn everywhere.

A British liaison officer reported to Montgomery that Hodges was "completely out of touch"—First Army officers flagged down passing truck drivers in Chaudfontaine to ask what they knew about the fighting. Though no longer paralyzed, Hodges remained isolated and ill-informed: not until a week into the German offensive would he visit any unit in the field, and many subordinates were uncertain where the First Army command post had gone. "We can't lose three months' gains in three days very often," a captain wrote his family, "or we'll be beating out a reverse invasion."

Evacuation of the vast supply dumps in eastern Belgium seemed far more ambitious than the abandonment of a headquarters hotel, but the task was capably done. Some stockpiles were beyond either removal or destruction—for instance, the eight million rations around Liège. Quartermasters in Paris also calculated that even if the biggest depots along the Meuse were captured, enough stocks could be found in the rear to last ten days or more, until emergency shipments arrived from the United States. But smaller supply depots, hospitals, and repair shops were ordered to move west of the river. With help from 1,700 First Army trucks and 2,400 railcars, some 45,000 tons of matériel and 50,000 vehicles would be shifted out of harm's way, along with a quarter-million rear-echelon soldiers, patients, and supernumeraries.

Three miles of primacord was used to blow up grenades, mines, and bangalore torpedoes—as well as twenty tons of sugar, rice, and flour—in an exposed dump near Malmédy. Most critical was the 3.5 million gallons of gasoline within ten miles of Lieutenant Colonel Peiper's SS spearhead, largely in five-gallon cans grouped in thousand-can stacks. Near Stavelot, where the fuel dump covered several square miles of woodland, 800,000 gallons of gas and 300,000 gallons of grease and oil were spirited away beginning Sunday night, as Peiper approached the town; another 134,000 gallons was ignited in a roadblock conflagration on Highway N-28. More than two million additional gallons were quickly evacuated from Spa using ten-ton tractor-trailers and railcars rushed to a nearby siding. Except for several minor caches captured by the Germans, Rundstedt's tanks and trucks would be forced to rely on their own dwindling fuel stocks.

Crows or starlings might have been mistaken for German parachutists near Spa, but more than a thousand actual airborne troops were due to be dropped north of Malmédy on *Null Tag* to further disrupt American defenses.

Nothing went right for the enemy. Airdromes designated for training proved not to exist, half the Ju-52 pilots had never flown in combat, and many paratroopers were either novices or had not jumped since the attack on Holland in 1940. "Don't be afraid. Be assured that I will meet you personally by 1700 on the first day," General Dietrich had told the mission commander, Colonel Friedrich von der Heydte. "Behind their lines are only Jewish hoodlums and bank managers." After confusion and blunders delayed the jump for a day, a howling crosswind on Sunday morning scattered paratroopers up to fifty kilometers from the drop zone. Two hundred jumpers were mistakenly dropped near Bonn, and American gunners shot down several planes. With a single mortar, little ammunition, and no functioning radios, von der Heydte rounded up three hundred men, who stumbled into a losing firefight before fleeing in small groups for the Fatherland; the colonel surrendered after briefly hiding outside Monschau. Two-thirds of the original thousand were killed or captured. That was the end of what proved the last German airborne operation of the war.

Operation GREIF, or "condor," proved no more competent. Under the flamboyant Viennese commando officer Otto Skorzeny, 2,000 men had been recruited into the 150th Armored Brigade for behind-the-lines sabotage, reconnaissance, and havoc. Their motor fleet included a dozen Panthers modified to resemble Shermans, German Fords painted olive drab, and a small fleet of captured U.S. Army trucks, jeeps, and scout cars. Some 150 men who spoke English—only 10, mostly former sailors, were truly fluent in the vernacular—would lead raiding parties X, Y, and Z to seize three Meuse bridges. They were issued captured or counterfeit identification documents, as well as GI uniforms, many of which had been purloined from American prisoners under the pretext of disinfection. To mimic American cigarette-smoking techniques and other mannerisms, the men studied Humphrey Bogart in *Casablanca*.

All for naught. Sixth Panzer Army's troubles on the north shoulder disrupted Skorzeny's timetable, and a set of GREIF orders discovered on a dead German officer alerted the Americans to skullduggery. First Army

MPs on Monday, December 18, stopped three men in a jeep near Aywaille who were unable to give the day's password; a search revealed German pay books and grenades. Four others on a Meuse bridge in Liège included a GI imposter who carried both the identification card of a Captain Cecil Dryer and the dogtags of a Private Richard Bumgardner. He and his comrades were found to be wearing swastika brassards beneath their Army field jackets. In all, sixteen infiltrators were swiftly captured in American uniforms and another thirty-five were killed without effecting a single act of sabotage on the Meuse. Most of Skorzeny's brigade eventually was dragooned into battle as orthodox infantry near Malmédy, where inexperience and a lack of artillery led to heavy casualties. Skorzeny himself suffered a nasty head wound.

The sole accomplishment of GREIF was to sow hysteria across the Western Front. A voluble, imaginative German lieutenant captured in Liège claimed to be part of a team sent to kill Eisenhower. Colonel Skorzeny, he said, had already infiltrated American lines with 60 assassins. The ostensible figure quickly grew to 150, and rumors flew that they could be posing as GIs escorting several captured German generals to SHAEF headquarters. Soon hundreds of jeeps carrying suspected killers and blackguards had been reported crisscrossing France; more than forty roadblocks sprang up around the Café de la Paix in Paris, where Skorzeny and his henchmen were expected to rendezvous. Police bulletins described Skorzeny as six feet, eight inches tall—a considerable exaggeration—with "dueling scars on both cheeks," supposedly incurred while brawling over a ballerina in Vienna. It was said that some infiltrators carried vials of sulfuric acid to fling in the faces of suspicious sentries; that many spoke English better than any GI; that they recognized one another by rapping their helmets twice, or by wearing blue scarves, or by leaving unfastened the top button of a uniform blouse. It was said that some might be costumed as priests, or nuns, or barkeeps. The Army official history dryly recorded that "Belgian or French café keepers who for weeks had been selling *vin ordinaire,* watered cognac, and sour champagne to the GIs were suddenly elevated by rumor, suspicion, and hysteria to captaincies in the Waffen SS."

MPs at checkpoints sought to distinguish native English speakers from frauds with various shibboleths, including "wreath," "writhe," "wealth," "rather," and "with nothing." Some asked the identity of the Windy City, since an intelligence report advised that "few Germans can pronounce Chicago correctly." Other interrogatories included: What is the price of an airmail stamp? What is Sinatra's first name? Who is Mickey Mouse's girlfriend? Where is Little Rock? Robert Capa, burdened with a Hungarian accent and an ineradicable smirk, was arrested for failing to know the capital of Nebraska. Forrest Pogue, when asked the statehouse location in his native Kentucky, carefully replied, "The capital is Frankfort, but you may think it is Louisville." When the actor David Niven, serving as an officer in 21st Army Group, was asked, "Who won the World Series in 1940?" he answered, "I haven't the faintest idea. But I do know that I made a picture with Ginger Rogers in 1938."

Cooks, bakers, and clerks were tutored in the mysteries of bazookas, mortars, and mines. Trigger-happy GIs gunned down four French civilians at a roadblock, and an Army doctor was shot in the stomach after answering a sentry's challenge with, "You son of a bitch, get out of my way." Promiscuous gunfire could be heard in Versailles near the Trianon Palace, now entombed in concertina wire, and a fusillade behind Beetle Smith's house one night brought the chief of staff out in his pajamas, cradling a carbine. "We deployed into the garden and began shooting right and left," Robert Murphy, a visiting diplomat, later recounted. "The next morning a stray cat was found in the garden riddled with bullets."

With Skorzeny and his cutthroats presumed to be still at large, Eisenhower reluctantly agreed to move from the St.-Germain villa to smaller quarters near his office. Each day his black limousine continued to follow the usual route to and from SHAEF headquarters, but with the rear seat occupied by a lieutenant colonel named Baldwin B. Smith, whose broad shoulders, prominent pate, and impatient mien made him a perfect body double for the supreme commander.

The real Eisenhower, traveling with Tedder in a bulletproof Cadillac first used in Africa, arrived in Verdun for a war council on Tuesday morning, December 19. At an ancient French army barracks within a muddy quadrangle, he soon was joined by Bradley, Jake Devers, and Patton, who drove up smoking a cigar in a jeep with plexiglass doors and a .30-caliber machine gun mounted on a swivel. At 11:30 A.M. they climbed upstairs to a dank stone squad room with a single potbellied stove, a large table, and a map unfurled across a wall. Bradley, already in a testy mood, pointed to a red arrow labeled "20 German tanks" approaching Namur on the Meuse, farther west than previously reported. "What the hell is this?" he demanded. An intelligence officer hurried to the map, snatched off the errant marker, and apologized for the error.

"The present situation is to be regarded as one of opportunity for us and not of disaster," Eisenhower said, settling into his chair. "There will be only cheerful faces at this conference table." From the other end, Patton chimed in, "Let's have the guts to let the bastards go all the way to Paris. Then we'll cut 'em off and chew 'em up."

Two staff officers reviewed the battlefront in detail. At least seventeen German divisions had joined the attack already; the identities of most were known. The heaviest pressure could be felt at St.-Vith and Bastogne, two vital road centers. Atrocities had been documented. Daily Luftwaffe sorties over St.-Vith had declined sharply from six hundred on Sunday, although a persistent overcast also had grounded Allied planes. Seven French infantry battalions would help defend the Meuse, along with half a dozen COMZ engineer regiments. American strength in the Ardennes had doubled since Saturday, to about 180,000 troops in ten infantry and three armored divisions. More would soon follow.

Eisenhower then spoke. Devers's 6th Army Group would assume the defensive in Alsace, he said, and contribute reserves for the Ardennes. Scattered forces must be pulled together for "positive concerted action." Holding the high ground south of Liège would keep supply depots outside enemy artillery range. By squeezing the shoulders of the German salient, shoring up the Meuse, blunting the enemy advance, and creating "a supply desert," they could smash Rundstedt's bulge—as it was now called— with an American counterblow again aimed at the Rhine. Third Army, which currently held an eighty-mile front with three corps facing the Saar, would pivot north to knife into the exposed German left flank.

Peering down the long table at Patton, Eisenhower asked in his booming voice, "George, how soon can you get an attack off?"

"On December 22," Patton replied, "with three divisions—the 4th Armored, the 26th, and the 80th."

Leaning forward, Eisenhower quickly calculated space, time, and divisions on his fingers. The maneuver required making a sharp left turn with a full corps, then moving nearly a hundred miles over winter roads. "Don't be fatuous, George. If you try to go that early, you won't have all three divisions ready and you'll go piecemeal," he said. "I'd even settle for the 23rd if it takes that long to get three full divisions."

"I'll make a meeting engagement in three days," Patton said, "and I'll give you a six-division coordinated attack in six days." Someone chuckled. The uneasy shuffle of boots could be heard on the bare floor. Glancing at a staff officer for confirmation, Patton added, "We can do that."

Before leaving the barracks, Patton phoned his headquarters to issue various movement orders: XII Corps was to wheel toward Luxembourg in tandem with the III Corps drive into Belgium. "Everyone is a son-of-a-bitch to someone," he told his staff by way of encouragement. "Be better sons-of-bitches than they are."

Eisenhower declined Bradley's invitation to stay for lunch; he would eat a sandwich in the Cadillac on the way back to Versailles. Turning to Patton before getting into the car, Eisenhower said, "George, every time I get promoted I get attacked."

Patton chuckled. "Yes, and every time you get attacked I bail you out."

They shook hands, Eisenhower smiling broadly. He seemed not only sanguine, but brimming with a "great expansive exuberance," as Major Chester Hansen, Bradley's aide, noted in his diary.

"There's something about the guy, the way he brushes along, the way he breaks out in a big grin, the way his voice, harsh and loud, cracks out, that disarms all within his vicinity," Hansen had concluded. "That's the way he is, gay, loud, democratic, dynamic, thinking fast, acting fast, spreading confidence."

Eisenhower had urged his lieutenants in Verdun "to avoid any discouragement or feeling of disappointment in the changed situation." However, a new development left Bradley not only discouraged and disappointed but also furious.

British intelligence on Tuesday evening concluded that the road to Namur was in fact vulnerable, and that if German shock troops crossed the Meuse there they could reach Brussels within hours. Montgomery confided to Brooke that he had told SHAEF's deputy operations officer, Major General J. F. M. Whiteley, "that Ike ought to place me in operational command of all troops on the northern half of the front. I consider he should be given a direct order by someone to do so." In Versailles, Whiteley and Major General Strong, also British, agreed that the Ardennes battlefield would best be managed by two commanders—Montgomery in the north and Bradley in the south—rather than by 12th Army Group alone.

Bradley's subordinate generals to the north were frustrated by their commander's isolation, which allowed only fitful telephone and radio contact; they also complained that not a single staff officer from the army group had visited First Army, Ninth Army, or their affiliated air forces since the offensive began on Saturday. When Eisenhower had proposed that 12th Army Group shift its headquarters to a more central locale, Bradley absurdly replied, "That would startle the people of Luxembourg too much. They would think we were defeated and *had* to get out."

Rousted from his bed by Whiteley and Strong on Tuesday night, Beetle Smith listened to their proposal to expand Montgomery's role and their warnings of "further deterioration" at the front. Then he rounded in anger on the staff officers. Clearly these two Britishers did not consider the Yanks capable of handling the crisis, Smith charged. Where did their loyalties lie? Such faithless impertinence was intolerable. Both men should consider themselves relieved of their duties, and return to England immediately.

As Whiteley and Strong slunk away in the face of this tirade, Smith phoned Eisenhower, finding the supreme commander still in his office at eleven P.M. Fuming, Smith described the bifurcation proposal while grudgingly conceding that it had merit: among other benefits, Montgomery would more likely commit British reserves to the battle if he commanded them. Eisenhower, staring at a huge wall map, promptly agreed. With a grease pencil he drew a line on the map from Givet on the Meuse east through the Ardennes to Prüm in Germany. St.-Vith fell north of the line, Bastogne south.

While the supreme commander pondered this demarcation, Smith phoned Bradley in Luxembourg City:

> Ike thinks it may be a good idea to turn over to Monty your two armies in the north and let him run that side of the Bulge from 21st Group. . . . It seems the logical thing to do. Monty can take care of everything north of the Bulge and you'll have everything south.

Bradley answered cautiously. He noted that no hint of this scheme had arisen in Verdun that morning. Although three enemy armies were now interposed between his command post and the bulk of his army group to the north, he considered his communication difficulties insignificant. "I'd question whether such a changeover is necessary," he added.

By Wednesday morning, when Eisenhower called personally to confirm the reconfiguration, Bradley had worked himself into a seething distemper. "By God, Ike, I cannot be responsible to the American people if you do this. I resign." General Strong, who had been grudgingly pardoned by Smith and was listening to the phone conversation in Eisenhower's office, watched a deep flush creep up the supreme commander's neck. "Brad, I—not you—am responsible to the American people. Your resignation therefore means absolutely nothing." Bradley continued to protest, if in a lower key, until Eisenhower ended the conversation with a peremptory, "Well, Brad, those are my orders." He then phoned Montgomery at his command post in Zonhoven. "We've now got two battles, two separate battles," Eisenhower said, bellowing into the receiver. "I think you'd better take charge of the northern one, and leave Bradley to deal with the southern one."

At 12:52 P.M., a SHAEF log entry confirmed that "Field Marshal Montgomery has been placed in charge of the northern flank." He would command the U.S. First and Ninth Armies, as well as his own army group; Twelfth Army Group was left with only Patton's Third Army. An officer in Bradley's headquarters reported that he was "absolutely livid. Walked up and down and cursed Monty."

Schadenfreude, as Montgomery now demonstrated, was by no means an exclusively German trait. Amid the dogs, goldfish, and singing canaries in his Zonhoven encampment, he had written Brooke just before midnight on Tuesday that "it looks as if we may now have to pay the price for the policy of drift and lack of proper control."

> There is great confusion and all signs of a full scale withdrawal. There is a definite lack of grip and control, and no one has a clear picture.... Everyone knows something has gone wrong and no one knows what or why.... The general situation is ugly as the American forces have been cut clean in half and the Germans can reach the Meuse at Namur without any opposition.

Little of this was true. The Americans had *not* been cut in half, no full-scale withdrawal had begun, and no German was near Namur, except perhaps a few lost paratroopers. But First Army surely needed help, and once given the opportunity the field marshal threw himself into battle with, as one writer later observed, "the energy and verve that were as characteristic as his peacockery." Having been alerted to the impending command change at 2:30 Wednesday morning, he had dispatched a major to Chaudfontaine for a "bedside conference" with Hodges, who was roused from sleep to learn that four British divisions were moving toward the Meuse to secure the riverbanks and bridges. Roadblocks also had been built on the Brussels highway with vehicles and piled carts.

The field marshal himself arrived in Chaudfontaine at 1:30 P.M. on Wednesday in a green Rolls-Royce flying a Union Jack and five-star pennant from the front fenders, accompanied by outrider jeeps with red-capped MPs. As usual he was dressed without orthodoxy in fur-lined boots, baggy corduroy trousers, and as many as eight pullovers. "Unwrapping the bearskin in which he was enveloped," Iris Carpenter reported, "he picked up his box of sandwiches, his thermos jug of tea, and his situation map all chalked over with his grease pencil, and marched inside." An American officer described him as "a monkey on a stick jumping up and down . . . a pompous conquering hero," but as he stalked into the Hôtel des Bains he seemed to a British officer "like Christ come to cleanse the temple." Neither image did Montgomery justice. Politely declining Hodges's offer of lunch—"Oh, no, I've got my own"—he propped his map on a chair and said calmly, "Now let's review this situation. . . . The first thing we must do is tidy up the battlefield."

Three hours later they had both a plan and an understanding. Hodges and his staff appeared tired and dispirited, British officers later reported, but determined to hold fast. Although Hodges feared that two First Army divisions had been surrounded—in fact, only two-thirds of the star-crossed 106th was lost—he stoutly resisted Montgomery's proposal to withdraw the north shoulder, perhaps as far as the Meuse. The field marshal for now relented: First Army would dig in where it could and, with help from General Simpson's Ninth Army, assemble a strike force to counterattack the Germans from the north, complementing Patton's blow from the south. Dempsey's Second Army would continue to feed forces down from Holland, and British stocks would help make good American losses, including 100 25-pounder guns with 300,000 rounds of ammunition; 20,000 snow suits; 2,000 trip flares; and 350 Sherman tanks with duck-bill cleats affixed for better traction. By nine o'clock that evening, all Meuse bridges would be rigged for demolition, and, as the British XXX Corps soon reported, "the enemy's hopes of bouncing the Meuse crossings have almost vanished."

As he returned to Zonhoven, Montgomery considered relieving Hodges; but whatever ailed the First Army commander appeared to have passed. "Hodges is not the man I would pick," Montgomery reported, "but he is much better." Eisenhower concurred in a private cable to the field marshal: "Hodges is the quiet reticent type and does not appear as aggressive as he really is. Unless he becomes exhausted he will always wage a good fight."

SHAEF ordered the new command arrangement to remain secret. Censorship, already tightened to prevent full disclosure of the HERBST-NEBEL reverses, also ensured that Americans at home would be spared knowing that much of the U.S. Army in Europe now was led by a wee Brit in a black beret. "They seemed delighted to have someone to give them orders," Montgomery told Brooke, with some justification. Brooke warned him not to gloat, but the field marshal could not help himself. "The Americans have taken a 1st Class bloody nose," he wrote a friend in London. "I am busy sorting out the mess."

As for Bradley, Eisenhower proposed awarding him a Bronze Star as a sop for losing two-thirds of his command. He also asked Marshall to consider giving him a fourth star. "I retain all my former confidence in him," Eisenhower wrote the chief. "It would have a fine effect generally."

War in the Raw

CIVILIAN refugees with woeful tales of burning villages and Germans in close pursuit tumbled into Bastogne, "an ancient town in the dreariest part of the Ardennes," as a tourist guidebook had once described it. Dray carts piled high with furniture and scuffed baggage clogged the main square despite Army placards warning that "unattended vehicles will be impounded by military police." Shops along the Grand-Rue pulled tight their shutters after the power failed on Sunday, and by midday Monday, December 18, the grumble of artillery could be heard even in the cellar corridors of the Sisters of Notre Dame, a boarding school where hundreds took refuge.

The first paratroopers from the 101st Airborne arrived at dusk on Monday after a sleet-spattered hundred-mile drive from Reims. XVIII Airborne Corps under General Ridgway had been directed to help seal the twenty-mile gap between V Corps and VIII Corps, with Gavin's 82nd Airborne making for Werbomont, southwest of Spa, and the 101st bound for Bastogne. Sergeants had trotted through the troop barracks the previous night, bawling, "Get out of the sack. You ain't reserve no more," and officers interrupted a ballet performance in mid-jeté to order paratroopers in the audience to assemble for battle.

Since leaving Holland in November the 101st had been plagued with several dozen AWOL incidents each week, as well as the usual drunken brawls; troopers held contests to see who could punch out the most windows in Reims. Worse yet, many of the division's senior leaders were absent. They included the commander, Major General Maxwell D. Taylor, who had flown to Washington; his assistant commander, who was in England with seventeen officers to lecture on MARKET GARDEN; and the chief of staff, who had killed himself with a pistol a week earlier. That left command to the division artillery chief, a short, genial brigadier general from Washington, D.C., named Anthony Clement McAuliffe. Having graduated from West Point at the end of World War I, McAuliffe had risen slowly through the ranks of the interwar Army as a gunner with an interest in both technological and sociological innovation: before joining the 101st, he had worked on development of the jeep and the bazooka, and on a study of race relations in the service. He had parachuted into Normandy and landed by glider in Holland; now he drove to Bastogne at the head of a division he led by default.

Several thousand replacement troopers who had received barely a week of field training jammed into open cattle trucks behind him—"like olives in a jar," as one account noted. Some, without helmets or rifles, pleaded for both from the retreating GIs who clogged every road west of Bastogne. COMZ dispatched an emergency convoy hauling five thousand entrenching shovels, two thousand sets of wool drawers, and five thousands pairs of arctic overshoes, sizes six to fourteen. Through Monday night and early the next morning, twelve thousand cold, sodden paratroopers and glidermen poured into Bastogne, where the American predicament was described as "fluid and obscure." By ten A.M. on Tuesday, all four regiments had arrived, accompanied by a few disoriented artillery and armor units press-ganged along the way. General McAuliffe put his command post in the Hôtel de Commerce, facing the train station, and his first wounded into a local seminary. Early Wednesday morning, after a

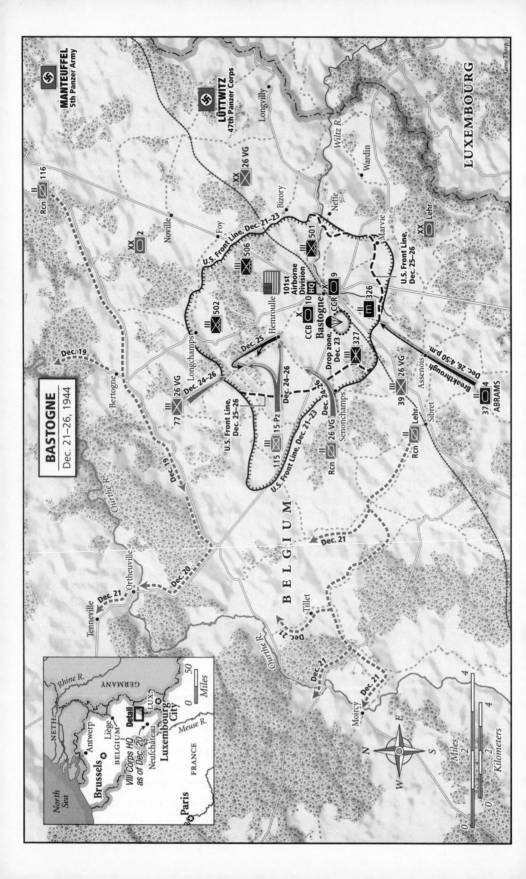

BASTOGNE
Dec. 21–26, 1944

MANTEUFFEL
5th Panzer Army

LÜTTWITZ
47th Panzer Corps

LUXEMBOURG

BELGIUM

Gene Thorp

116 Rcn

2

26 VG

Noville

Foy

Longvilly

Wiltz R.

Wardin

Bizory

Neffe

Marvie

U.S. Front Line,
Dec. 25–26

Lehr

U.S. Front Line, Dec. 21–23

506

501

Lehr

101st
Airborne
Division
HQ

9

502

Hemroulle

CCB

10

Bastogne

CCR

326

327

Drop zone,
Dec. 23

Dec. 25

Dec. 24–26

15 Pz

Dec. 19

Bertogne

Dec. 19

Longchamps

26 VG
77

Dec. 24–26

U.S. Front Line,
Dec. 25–26

115

U.S. Front Line, Dec. 21–23

26 VG

Senonchamps

Dec. 24–26

39

26 VG

Assenois

Rcn

Lehr

Sibret

Breakthrough,
Dec. 26, 4:50 p.m.

37   4
ABRAMS

Dec. 19

Dec. 20

Ourthe R.

Ortheuville

Dec. 21

Tenneville

Dec. 21

Ourthe R.

Tillet

Dec. 21

Dec. 21

Dec. 21

Moircy

N
E
S
W

Miles
0   2   4

Kilometers
0   2   4

Inset map:

North Sea

NETH.

Brussels

Antwerp

Liège

Rhine R.

GERMANY

BELGIUM

Detail

VIII Corps HQ
as of Dec. 20

Neufchâteau

LUX.

Luxembourg
City

Meuse R.

FRANCE

Paris

Miles
0   50

few parting words of encouragement, General Middleton decamped in his Packard for a new VIII Corps headquarters in Neufchâteau, eighteen miles southwest.

Bearing down on Bastogne were three divisions from Fifth Panzer Army, well aware of U.S. reinforcements thanks to careless American radio chatter. Little in the battle had unfolded according to the German master plan, starting with that nettlesome resistance by Cota's 28th Division in Luxembourg. Fuel shortages pinched harder with each passing hour. Panzer tracks chewed up byroads so severely that wheeled vehicles by the score were abandoned in mud sloughs; with few engineers to clear mines, tank crews took up the task with harrows and rollers found in farm sheds. Foot soldiers slouching westward almost outpaced Manteuffel's motorized columns, and Field Marshal Model now privately doubted that HERBSTNEBEL could achieve even the modest goals of the so-called small solution, much less the seizure of Antwerp.

Bastogne and its seven radial roads assumed ever greater importance— "an abscess on our line of communication," in a German commander's phrase—and field-gray spearheads smashed into the feeble roadblocks east of town, setting Army half-tracks ablaze with tracer rounds, then picking off GIs silhouetted against the flames. Two straggling artillery battalions at Longvilly fired over open sights at two hundred yards before the survivors stumbled back into Bastogne, half their howitzers lost. Forty Sherman tanks were demolished in a single night, and defenders in Neffe retreated under showers of incendiary grenades. "We're not driven out," one officer radioed, "but burned out." Under the onslaught of those three divisions— 2nd Panzer, 26th Volksgrenadier, and Panzer Lehr—the American defenses buckled and bent.

But did not break. The Longvilly gunfight cost the Volksgrenadiers four precious hours of daylight on Tuesday. Farther north on the same day, U.S. combat engineers dynamited culverts and bridges, felled trees, and laid abatis with such obstructive skill that the frustrated LVIII Corps countermarched up various blind alleys in search of easier routes west.

No less vital in delaying the enemy was a combat command from the 10th Armored Division, which Middleton on Monday night had ordered to defend a trio of strongpoints outside Bastogne. An especially vicious brawl unfolded in Noville, a foggy sinkhole four miles north of town, where fifteen Sherman tanks and other armor arrived in time to confront much of the 2nd Panzer Division. A murky dawn on Tuesday brought the telltale rattle of German tank suspensions, followed by vague gray shapes drifting from the east. The Americans answered with artillery—aimed "by guess and by God" because of map shortages—and even pistol fire. Soon the fog lifted like a raised curtain to reveal German armor and grenadiers spread thickly across a slope half a mile distant. American tank destroyers ripped into nine panzers, leaving three in flames. German infantrymen turned and fled, pursued by bullets.

All morning and through the afternoon the battle raged. A battalion of 101st paratroopers from Bastogne attacked on a dead run at two P.M., colliding in a brutish mêlée with another German assault just beginning to boil across a smoky ridgeline. Enemy barrages pounded Noville to rubble, killing the paratrooper commander and badly wounding his 10th Armored counterpart; only artillery counterfire kept grenadiers on three sides from overrunning the American redoubt.

At midday on Wednesday, December 20, a radio message to the Hôtel de Commerce advised, "All reserves committed. Situation critical." McAuliffe authorized survivors to fall back into Bastogne at five P.M., cloaked in smoke and darkness; for want of a tank crew, paratroopers drove one of the four remaining Shermans. American casualties exceeded four hundred men, but the 2nd Panzer had lost over six hundred, plus thirty-one panzers and at least two days in the division's drive toward the Meuse. A few hours after Noville fell, Gestapo agents murdered seven Belgians who had survived the siege, including a schoolmaster and the village priest.

Strongpoints east of Bastogne, now reinforced by the 501st Parachute Infantry, proved just as formidable for Panzer Lehr and the 26th Volksgrenadier. Barbed wire and musketry near Neffe snared German skirmishers in what paratroopers called a "giant mantrap." "We took no prisoners," a captain reported. "We mowed them down as if they were weeds." Renewed enemy attacks on Wednesday ran into "a dam of fire" laid by scores of guns firing from Bastogne.

Little profit had been found in frontal assaults, and belatedly the Germans revised their tactics. Manteuffel urged 2nd Panzer to press westward past the Ourthe River despite gasoline shortages so severe that the division wasted a day waiting for fuel trucks. Panzer Lehr would leave a regiment to besiege Bastogne with the 26th Volksgrenadier, but most of the division now sidled to the left to bypass the town on the south.

Among the few heartening reports to reach Fifth Panzer Army on Wednesday was the annihilation of a 101st Airborne medical detachment, which had failed to post sentries at a crossroads encampment west of Bastogne. Shortly before midnight a German patrol of six panzers and halftracks raked the medical tents and trucks with gunfire—"the bullets were so close that I thought I would have to brush them off," one private reported. Within minutes the division surgeon had been captured, along with ten other medical officers, more than a hundred enlisted men, and litters, wounded patients, surgical instruments, and penicillin.

* * *

"Above all," Middleton had instructed McAuliffe, "don't get yourself surrounded." Precisely how eighteen thousand Americans, under orders to hold Bastogne at all costs against forty-five thousand Germans, should avoid encirclement was not clear, particularly in weather so dismal that Allied aircraft on Wednesday flew a total of twenty-nine sorties in Europe, only nine of them over the Ardennes. A day later, on Thursday morning, December 21, an enemy column severed the last open road south, and Bastogne was indeed cut off. Resurgent optimism flared through the German chain of command.

At 11:30 on Friday morning, a delegation of four Germans carrying a white flag appeared in a spruce copse dusted with new snow southwest of Bastogne. "We are *parliamentaires*," an English-speaking captain told an American officer, then presented a note composed on a captured American typewriter, with each umlaut inserted by hand, and addressed *"an den amerikanischen Kommandeur der eingeschlossen Stadt Bastogne."* An appended translation to the American commander of the surrounded city of Bastogne explained:

> The fortune of war is changing.... There is only one possibility to save the encircled U.S.A. troops from total annihilation: In order to think it over, a term of two hours will be granted beginning with the presentation of this note. If this proposal should be rejected, one German artillery corps and six heavy AA battalions are ready to annihilate.... All the serious civilian losses caused by this artillery fire would not correspond with the well-known American humanity.

The note had been authorized by Lieutenant General Heinrich von Lüttwitz, commander of XLVII Panzer Corps.

At 12:25 P.M. the ultimatum reached McAuliffe in his smoke-stained command post, which reeked of cordite from a bombing raid the previous night. Encircled or not, the 101st remained almost at full strength; only five battalions among the four regiments had so far seen intense combat. Six hundred stragglers, mostly from the 28th Division, had been fed a hot meal and mustered into Team Snafu, a quick-reaction battalion. The Bastogne arsenal included forty Shermans; armor officers mimeographed useful tips on tank tactics for their infantry brethren. Six artillery battalions were arrayed in circular gun pits to allow each battery to shoot at every compass point, although McAuliffe, a field artilleryman for a quarter-century, had advised his cannoneers not to fire "until you see the whites of their eyes." Vehicles were slathered with whitewash for camouflage, and Belgian linen closets provided sheets for snow capes. The men now received only two meals a day, but cooks had whipped up excellent flapjacks from doughnut flour discovered in a Red Cross pantry.

Perhaps inspired by the legendary epithet uttered by a French general when asked to surrender at Waterloo—*"Merde!"*—McAuliffe offered a one-word answer to the ultimatum: "Nuts." A paratrooper officer then handed it to the *"parliamentaires,"* whereupon a baffled German officer asked, "Is the reply negative or affirmative?"

"The reply is decidedly *not* affirmative," the American said. "If you don't understand what 'nuts' means, in plain English it is the same as 'go to hell.' . . . We will kill every goddamn German that tries to break into this city."

"We will kill many Americans. This is war."

Only after the event did an irate Manteuffel learn of Lüttwitz's gambit. "This is crazy," he told the corps commander. "Now we must find the artillery and bomber force to make good your threat and level the town."

As Bastogne was a poisonous thorn in General Manteuffel's left flank, St.-Vith had become an irksome nettle on his right. The town had been named for Saint Vitus, a Sicilian boy martyred during the reign of Emperor Diocletian, and the holy patron of dancers, dogs, and chronic oversleepers. Various unpleasantries had befallen St.-Vith since its founding in the twelfth century, including pillages in 1543, 1602, and 1689, but none was uglier than the battle that engulfed the town in December 1944. Despite swift destruction of the 106th Division on the Schnee Eifel, the German plan to occupy St.-Vith by six P.M. on December 17 fell short, and Manteuffel's frustration grew longer day by day.

Gunfights had erupted around the town on December 18 and 19, but German lunges were thrown back, first by two engineer battalions, then by General Clarke's Combat Command B from the 7th Armored, bolstered on his right by remnants from the 106th and a combat command from the 9th Armored Division. Now the easternmost U.S. redoubt of any size in the Ardennes, St.-Vith in three days had become a breakwater, with a "German tide rushing past on the north and south and rising against its eastern face," in the description of the Army official history.

With supply lines cut, howitzers were limited to seven rounds per gun each day. Gunners rummaged for ammunition in abandoned dumps; some batteries reported firing "old propaganda shells just to keep projectiles whistling around German ears." Riflemen on December 20 were told that "for every round fired, a corpse must hit the ground." In St.-Vith's pinched streets, broken glass crunched beneath the hooves of cattle fleeing a burning slaughterhouse. Exhausted officers gobbled amphetamines, and greasy smoke blackened the faces and uniforms of soldiers trying to stay warm over sand-filled tins soaked in gasoline. One soldier later described mounting a local counterattack with a "cold, plodding, unwilling, ragged double line plunging up to their knees in snow." A survivor from the 106th wrote, "Here I was to grow into an old man and die over and over again."

Manteuffel on December 20 ordered two Volksgrenadier divisions to finish off the town, supported by SS tanks. On Thursday, December 21, German artillery tree-bursts lacerated American trenches, as gray waves of infantry swept through the dense woods and Panthers fired flat-trajectory flares to blind Sherman crews. "Goddamn it," a company commander radioed at 7:35 P.M. "They're blasting my men out of their holes one at a time." Half an hour later, Clarke's line had been punctured in three places. At ten P.M. he ordered his troops to fall back onto high ground a kilometer west of town, but nearly a thousand GIs had been killed or captured, and twenty thousand others remained vulnerable in a shrinking salient east of the Salm River.

General Hodges had given XVIII Airborne Corps responsibility for all First Army forces south of Stavelot, and Matt Ridgway now struggled to control a corps front that abruptly tripled in width from twenty-five miles to eighty-five. If the 101st Airborne could continue to fight effectively while surrounded, Ridgway wondered why a comparable combat force in the Salm salient could not do the same. But by early Friday, December 22, that force showed signs of disintegration: patrols simply vanished; an entire battalion staff at Neubrück, three miles south of St.-Vith, had been killed or captured; Clarke reported that his combat command had lost half its strength and would soon be supine.

"This terrain is not worth a nickel an acre," Clarke added, and urged withdrawal. The 7th Armored Division commander, Brigadier General Robert W. Hasbrouck, now encamped at Vielsalm, twelve miles west of St.-Vith, warned that fuel and ammunition shortages had become dire. Just after eleven A.M., Hasbrouck told Ridgway in a message, "If we don't get out of here . . . before night, we will not have a 7th Armored Division left." To an old friend, Brigadier General William M. Hoge, whose combat command in the 9th Armored also faced dismemberment, Ridgway said, "We're not going to leave you in here to be chopped to pieces. . . . We're going to get you out of here." Hoge replied plaintively, "How can you?"

Reluctantly, Ridgway in midafternoon on Friday ordered Hasbrouck to withdraw all U.S. forces across the Salm. Montgomery, who had watched the St.-Vith drama with mounting anxiety, rejoiced. "They can come back with all honor," he said. "They put up a wonderful show."

Fourteen hours of December darkness and a cold snap that froze the mud on Friday night allowed most to escape, narrowly averting a catastrophe even worse than the Schnee Eifel surrender. A radio dispatch to a field commander instructed, "Your orders are: Go west. Go west. Go west." GIs urinated on frozen M-1 rifle bolts to free them, then tramped single file on forest trails and farm tracks, each man gripping the belt or pack straps of the comrade ahead. Others flattened themselves onto tank hulls beneath a scorching fretwork of enemy tracers. German artillery searched roads and junctions, and only the late arrival of a ninety-truck convoy lugging five thousand shells permitted prodigal counterfire by gunners west of the Salm. "Wrapped in scarves and mufflers, only their eyes showing," as one lieutenant wrote, retreating troops made for the bridges at Salmchâteau and Vielsalm; Hasbrouck stood on a road shoulder to welcome his men to safety. An 82nd Airborne trooper south of Werbomont called to a passing column, "What the hell you guys running from? We been here two days and ain't seen a German yet." A weary voice replied, "Stay right were you are, buddy. In a little while you won't even have to look for 'em."

Ridgway estimated that fifteen thousand troops and one hundred tanks escaped. As many tanks were lost, and casualties east of the Salm approached five thousand, atop losses incurred on the Schnee Eifel. Clarke and Hasbrouck would long resent Ridgway for delaying the withdrawal, but the fighting retreat meant that nearly a week went by before Fifth Panzer Army controlled St.-Vith and the radiant roads that Manteuffel had hoped to take in two days. "Nobody is worried down here," Ridgway told First Army by phone at nine P.M. Friday night. "We're in fine shape."

German troops ransacked St.-Vith yet again "in a kind of scavenger hunt," snarling traffic so profoundly that both Model and Manteuffel dismounted and hiked into town from Schönberg. The field marshal even stood at a crossroads with arms flailing to wave tanks and trucks westward. "Endless columns of prisoners," a Volksgrenadier officer wrote. "Model himself directs traffic. He's a little, undistinguished-looking man with a monocle. Now the thing is going. . . . All the advancing units are picking up American vehicles to become motorized."

Looting was best done quickly: beginning on Christmas Day, Allied bombers would drop seventeen hundred tons of high explosives and incendiaries on St.-Vith, obliterating the train station, St. Josef's Kloster, and the fourteenth-century Büchelturm stone tower. The raids reduced most houses to stone dust and ash, entombing hundreds of Belgian civilians. With roads smashed by the bombs, German engineers routed traffic through the rail yards and along a circuitous dirt track to let the conquerors of St.-Vith continue their pursuit. "We shall throw these arrogant big-mouthed apes from the New World into the sea," a German lieutenant wrote his wife. "They will not get into our Germany."

A GI shivering in an Ardennes foxhole asked, after his first glimpse of a German Me-262 jet streaking overhead, "How come *we* don't ever have any secret weapons?" Yet thousands of enemy troops now sensed what many American soldiers still did not know: that a secret weapon no bigger than a radio tube was being used in ground combat for the first time across the Bulge, enhancing the killing power of U.S. artillery with what one enthusiast would call "the most remarkable scientific achievement of the war" except for the atomic bomb.

The new weapon's origin dated to 1940, with a recognition that on average 2,500 antiaircraft artillery shells would be needed to bring down a single enemy plane. Both field artillery and antiaircraft rounds exploded either on contact or when a fuze detonated the shell after a preset flight time; neither technique offered killing precision. Scientists and engineers instead sought a fuze that could sense proximity to the target, causing a shell to blow up not when it randomly reached an altitude of ten or fifteen thousand feet, but rather when it detected an airplane within the kill radius of exploding fragments. Such a fuze would have to withstand the stupendous strain of cannonading, including a g-force of twenty thousand upon leaving a gun muzzle and the centrifugal forces of a shell spinning at five hundred rotations per second. It would also have to be simple enough to build by the millions on an assembly line, and sufficiently miniaturized to squeeze into a shell nose roughly the size of an ice cream cone.

The resulting device, eventually known by the code designations "VT" or "T-98," and by the code name "pozit," contained a tiny radio transmitter, which broadcast a signal in flight. When the beam bounced off a solid object, a receiver in the fuze detected the reflected signal and tripped a firing circuit that detonated the shell. A 5-inch pozit shell, fired by U.S.S. *Helena* in the South Pacific, had for the first time brought down a Japanese plane in January 1943. But for eighteen months the fuze could be used only over open water or friendly territory, for fear that if the enemy retrieved a dud, Axis engineers could copy the design. Pozit shells were secretly used against V-1s aimed at London—British officials considered them up to five times more effective than time-fuzed rounds—and to defend Cherbourg harbor and the Mulberries off Normandy. More recently, British Lancaster bombers had flown an emergency consignment of pozit fuzes from a Cincinnati plant to Antwerp for use against German flying bombs.

Pozit variants had been developed for the field artillery, using radio signals bounced off the approaching ground to detonate shells fifty or seventy-five feet up. Experiments in North Carolina showed that regardless of terrain, weather, or darkness, even entrenched targets were highly vulnerable to a lethal spray of steel shards from such airbursts. One senior Army general called it "the most important new development in the ammunition field since the introduction of high explosive projectiles."

With approval from the Charlie-Charlies, SHAEF in late fall fixed Christmas as the day gunners in Europe could open fire with pozit shells. More than a thousand commanders and staff officers were briefed on the secret, with firing demonstrations in six Allied armies. Hitler hastened the day: when HERBSTNEBEL began, Eisenhower moved up the release by a week. A gunner in the 99th Division described "piles of shells with many men using wrenches and hammers to bang off the one [fuze] and install the other." Within days of the first use by field artillerymen, reports described "the slaughter of enemy concentrations east of Bastogne and interdictions of the principal enemy supply routes west of St. Vith." Twelfth Army Group cheerfully reported that the pozit fuze "is a terror weapon." SHAEF concluded that "the enemy has been severely upset."

Three hundred American companies would soon mass-produce nearly two million fuzes a month at $20 each. "The new shell with the funny fuze is devastating," Patton wrote the Army's ordnance chief in late December. "The other night we caught a German battalion, which was trying to cross the Sauer River, with a battalion concentration and killed by actual count 702." Such exaggerations—and Patton's tallies often proved inflated— were common, and many unsubstantiated claims of pozit lethality would emerge from the Bulge. In the event, fewer than 200,000 pozit rounds were fired by 12th Army Group in the Battle of the Bulge: a modest fraction of the total, although it did include one-quarter of the Army's heaviest shells. Nor was the new technology flawless. Tall trees, chimneys, steeples, and straying spotter planes could cause premature detonations.

Yet the pozit would prove as demoralizing to German troops as it was heartening to GIs. Some enemy officers called it the "electro shell" or "magnetic igniter," believing that terrestrial magnetism triggered the fuze. "It hangs in the air until it finds just the right place to explode," one captured soldier insisted. Shell fragments were said to slice through thick logs atop enemy bunkers, and a single 155mm airburst reportedly could shred every square foot within a seventy-five-yard diameter. Such mayhem was "pure manslaughter," another German prisoner complained. "The devil himself could not escape."

But what of the devil's henchmen? No better target could be found for pozit fire than Lieutenant Colonel Peiper's homicidal *Spitze* at the head of the 1st SS Panzer Division, and for several days American gunners had been shooting the new shells at the column as it tacked across Belgium.

Peiper's drive toward the Meuse seemed ever more quixotic. After halting for the night outside Stavelot following the killing spree near Malmédy, the SS spearhead had turned southwest toward Trois-Ponts, unaware of the huge Allied fuel dumps just to the north. U.S. engineers blew all three bridges in Trois-Ponts, including one with German soldiers atop the span. Thwarted and desperate for gasoline, Peiper swung north through broken terrain along the Amblève, harried by both P-47 fighter-bombers—at least two panzers and five half-tracks were demolished from the air—and artillery. Gunners from the 30th Division fired 3,000 rounds at one bridge approach, cooling their red-hot tubes with cans of water.

More spans were demolished by American defenders or were too frail for sixty-ton Tiger tanks. Probes toward Werbomont and Târgnon proved bootless, as did a German scheme to drop fuel cans into the Amblève in hopes that Peiper would recover a few of them downstream. A two-day fight engulfed the St. Edouard Sanatorium, perched on a hill in Stoumont, while 260 convalescent Belgians cowered in the cellar. Panzers fired point-blank through the windows, counterattacking Shermans did the same, and grenades clattered back and forth down the corridors. A priest gave general absolution to his terrified flock when part of the roof collapsed, but the Germans finally withdrew without a single civilian badly hurt.

Peiper had traveled some sixty miles, but sixteen more still separated him from the Meuse. With the risk of encirclement growing, at dusk on Thursday, December 21, he ordered his men to fall back four miles from Stoumont to La Gleize, a hamlet of thirty houses hemmed in by hills. Here his fifteen hundred survivors and two dozen remaining tanks dug in with more than a hundred American prisoners in tow. That night in a farmhouse cellar, Peiper took time to explain himself to a captured battalion commander, Major Hal D. McCown. "We're eliminating the communist menace," the young lieutenant colonel said in his excellent English. "We will keep what is best in Europe and eliminate the bad." The "bad" evidently included Belgian civilians murdered in recent days, along with more defenseless GIs.

By late Friday, American machine guns, tanks, tank destroyers, and artillery had so battered La Gleize that SS troops called it *der Kessel,* the cauldron. Self-propelled guns fired point-blank over open sights from a nearby château. Gripping a machine pistol, Peiper dashed between rubble piles, shouting encouragement while his adjutant burned secrets in the cellar. Luftwaffe transport planes at eight P.M. dropped gasoline and ammunition to the besieged men, but GIs recovered most of the supplies except for a few bundles containing cigarettes, schnapps, and a crate of Luger pistols. Army Air Forces bombers targeting La Gleize hit Malmédy instead, an error that would be repeated twice, killing more than three dozen GIs and many Belgians.

"Position considerably worsened. Meager supplies of infantry ammunition left," Peiper radioed early Saturday morning. "This is the last chance of breaking out." Not until two P.M., as the Americans pressed nearer, did permission to retreat arrive in a coded message from I SS Panzer Corps. White-phosphorus and pozit shells carved away the La Gleize church, where German troops sheltered under choir stalls. A soldier caught removing the SS runes from his uniform was placed against a broken wall and shot for desertion. Peiper used the bombardment to mask the sound of explosives scuttling his last twenty-eight panzers, seventy half-tracks, and two dozen guns.

At two A.M. on Sunday, December 24, the SS men crept south from the village in single file, led by two Belgian guides. Major McCown was prodded along at gunpoint, although more than 300 wounded Germans and 130 other American prisoners remained behind in the La Gleize cellars. Crossing the Amblève on a small bridge, the column snaked down a ridgeline near Trois-Ponts into the Salm river valley. At daybreak, when spotter planes appeared overhead, Peiper hid his men beneath tree boughs and parceled out provisions: four biscuits and two swigs of cognac each. During a brief firefight with an American patrol, McCown slipped away, whistling "Yankee Doodle" as he wandered through the woods until challenged by pickets in an 82nd Airborne outpost.

At a ford in the frigid Salm, the tallest SS troops formed a human chain to help the column cross the forty-foot water gap. Early Christmas morning, Peiper would reach the German line at Wanne, a few miles southeast of La Gleize. Of his original 5,800 men, 770 remained. Hurried along by more gusts of American artillery, their uniforms stiff with ice, they left a blood spoor across the snow. Peiper and some of his henchmen were later accused of murdering 350 unarmed Americans and 100 or more Belgian civilians in their weeklong spree. But for now justice would be deferred, and a day of reckoning delayed until after the war.

Across the Ardennes, heavy snow had been followed on Saturday, December 23, by killing cold in the continental weather phenomenon known as a Russian High. Alan Moorehead described a "radiant world where everything was reduced to primary whites and blues: a strident, sparkling white among the frosted trees, the deep blue shadows in the valley, and then the flawless ice blue of the sky." Radiators and even gas tanks froze. Airborne troopers refused to allow grave diggers to collect frozen German corpses, which were stacked like sandbags around infantry redoubts. GIs donned every scrap of clothing they could scavenge, including women's dresses worn as shawls. "Everyone seems about the same age," wrote Martha Gellhorn, "as if weariness and strain and the unceasing cold leveled all life."

Troops fashioned sleds from sheet metal, and olive-drab vehicles were daubed with camouflage paint improvised from lime wash and salt. Belgian lace served for helmet nets, and mattress covers, often used as shrouds for the dead, made fine snow suits. Inflated surgical gloves dipped in paint decorated hospital Christmas trees, but "in this cold the life of the wounded is likely to go out like a match," wrote the paratrooper Louis Simpson. GIs suffering from head and chest wounds filled one ward, in a nurse's description, "with breathing giving a rattle that sounds like an untuned radio going through the tent."

Clumsy skirmishes and pitched battles flared along the front, without deference to the holiday season. Peiper's repulse and Sixth Panzer Army's shortcomings had extinguished hopes for a breakthrough on the German right; 237,000 American mines, 370 roadblocks, and 70 blown bridges further impeded the north shoulder. In the far south, faltering progress by Seventh Army had exposed Manteuffel's left flank even as Fifth Panzer Army tried to lance the Bastogne abscess. So desperate were shortages of spare parts and gasoline that new panzers in the Rhine valley were being cannibalized to avoid burning fuel by sending them intact into battle.

But west of St.-Vith, in the German center, grenadiers vaulted the Salm and Ourthe Rivers, and by December 23 panzer spearheads approached Marche, more than twenty miles beyond Vielsalm and a short bound from Dinant, on the Meuse. Model had shoehorned a dozen divisions along a twenty-five-mile battlefront. Although plagued with fuel and ammunition shortages, they remained a potent killing force on the march.

New anxiety beset First Army headquarters, which had again fallen back, to Tongres, near Maastricht, only hours before German bombs demolished the Hôtel des Bains in Chaudfontaine. Ridgway evinced his usual grit, telling his division commanders by phone at six A.M. on December 24:

> The situation is normal and entirely satisfactory. The enemy has thrown in all of his mobile reserves, and this is his last major offensive effort in the West in this war. This corps will halt that effort, then attack and smash him.

Others were far less sanguine, yet the Russian High brought clear skies for the first time since the German attack began, and Allied aircraft took wing in great flocks. In a campaign known as "processing the terrain," twelve thousand offensive sorties were flown in the two days before Christmas, battering highways, airfields, and bridges, as well as rail centers in Koblenz, Trier, and Cologne. Whooping GIs craned their necks as wave upon wave of Marauders and Fortresses, Liberators and Lancasters appeared from the west in the heaviest attacks of the war. "The bombers have fine, feathery white streams of vapor streaked across the sky," a 99th

Division soldier wrote his wife, "and the fighters scrawl wavy designs as they try to murder each other." Ice and deep snow entombed German convoys west of the Rhine; horse-drawn plows could hardly clear enough routes for three attacking armies. Model's resupply and reinforcement echelons offered fat targets for Allied fighter-bombers, known as "Jabos" to enemy soldiers. "We prefer to walk instead of using a car on the main highway," a German lieutenant near St.-Vith told his diary. "The American Jabos keep on attacking everything that moves on the roads. . . . [They] hang in the air like a swarm of wasps."

Clear skies also permitted resupply of Bastogne, besieged but unbowed after the rejected surrender ultimatum. Shortly before noon on Saturday, the first C-47s dropped parachute bundles originally intended for the doomed 106th Division on the Schnee Eifel. By four P.M., more than 240 planes had delivered 5,000 artillery shells, almost as many mortar rounds, 2,300 grenades, a dozen boxes of morphine, 300 units of plasma, and 1,500 bandages. Jeeps tore around the drop zone on the western edge of Bastogne, where paratroopers scooped up the bundles and hauled ammunition directly to gun batteries and rifle pits. More sorties the next day would bring rations, a quarter-million machine-gun rounds, and almost one thousand radio batteries. General McAuliffe also had the invaluable services of Captain James E. Parker, a fighter pilot who had arrived several days earlier as an air support officer with enough radio crystals in his pocket to talk directly to the P-47 squadrons now bound for Bastogne. Swarming wasps by the hundreds attacked fast and low with napalm and high explosives, vectored by Parker to Manteuffel's panzers, trucks, and assault guns. Tracks in the snow made them easy to find.

Bastogne was reprieved but hardly delivered. German attacks from the west and southwest grew so intense on Saturday night that despondent American officers shook hands goodbye. Despite aerial replenishment, the garrison was reduced to five hundred gallons of gasoline and a day's rations; 101st Airborne gunners who had been rationed to ten rounds daily heeded McAuliffe's advice to look for the whites of enemy eyes. With a defensive perimeter only sixteen miles in circumference, every corner of Bastogne came under fire. The town, one major wrote, "seemed to have been sandblasted with steel filings."

More than three thousand civilians remained trapped with the Americans, and carbolic acid sprinkled in cellars did little to relieve the stench of excrement. Several hundred wounded GIs lay in sawdust on a church floor; others languished in a Belgian army garage ripe with the odor of gas gangrene. Dust grayed their hair, a witness observed, and "their faces were old with suffering and fatigue." Two surgeons toiled by flashlight in a tool-room operatory, lopping off limbs. The moribund lay along a wall reserved for the hopeless; other buildings served as a morgue and a ward for trench-foot victims. The walking wounded filled a roofless structure formerly used as an indoor rifle range. Scavengers found coffee and Ovaltine in an VIII Corps warehouse, as well as a cache of sugar hidden behind a wall. This booty went to the wounded, along with cognac and crème de menthe served as analgesics. Two thousand burlap bags discovered in a storeroom were used by troopers in foxholes to wrap their boots.

Napalm fires ringed the town, and the chatter of machine guns carried on the wind as the short day faded. A chaplain in vestments held Christmas Eve services with a portable field organ and candles guttering on an improvised altar. "Do not plan, for God's plan will prevail," he advised. "Those who are attacking you are the enemies of Christ." In a vaulted seminary chapel, where tattered canvas covered holes in the stained glass, soldiers sang "O Little Town of Bethlehem." In the whitewashed Belgian barracks that served as the 101st headquarters, a GI clerk sat at a switchboard humming, off-key, "Santa Claus Is Coming to Town." A coded message from Patton that afternoon had promised, "Xmas eve present coming up. Hold on." Yet no sign of a relief column from the south had been reported. McAuliffe hid his disappointment from the men, but told General Middleton in a phone call, "We have been let down."

At 5:10 P.M., an intrepid pilot in an L-4 Grasshopper, guided by flashlights, landed on a snowy field with a crate of penicillin. That was the last good thing to happen in Bastogne on Christmas Eve. Barely two hours later, beneath a brilliant moon that silvered the streets, German bombers struck the town in the first of two raids. One bomb landed on an aid station near the Neufchâteau road, caving in the roof, burying twenty soldiers, and killing a civilian nurse. Flames crackled around the Hôtel de Ville. Several patients burned to death on their litters, and the smell of charred flesh added to the other stinks that wafted through Bastogne on this holiest of holy nights.

Patton attended a candlelight communion service on Christmas Eve in the crowded, frigid Episcopal church in Luxembourg City, ensconced with Bradley in a pew once reserved for the German kaiser. A Red Cross volunteer described Patton's "brick-red face, with its round, receding forehead sparsely framed by silvery-white hair.... I saw a tired, aging man, a sorrowful, solitary man, a lonely man, with veiled eyes behind which there was going on a torment of brooding and introspection." She may have misread her man: even if the Ardennes had worn him down, battle lightened his heart as nothing in this world.

Scanning the starry sky outside, Patton muttered, "Noel, noel, what a night to give the Nazis hell." Careering about in an open jeep, one pistol holstered outside his parka and another tucked into his waistband, blue eyes watering from the cold, he barked at MPs to keep the convoys moving, and he personally challenged sentries to ensure that they knew the day's password. This was a moment to "root-hog or die," he told his staff. "If those Hun bastards want war in the raw, then that's the way we'll give it to them." He had asked God for fair weather, just as Achilles petitioned Zeus to lift the fog before the walls of Troy. The Almighty had heeded his supplication, he informed his diary—"a clear cold Christmas, lovely weather for killing Germans."

Patton had made good on his brash promise at Verdun to attack north with three divisions by December 22. The feat was prodigious, requiring most of Third Army to swing sharply left while keeping the Saar front secure. The maneuver also required distributing fifty-seven tons of new maps, uprooting and reinstalling an extensive signal-wire network, and stockpiling fuel and ammunition, including shells for twelve hundred guns in the army's 108 artillery battalions. No SS prisoners were to be taken alive, Patton told his staff. At his urging, an extra skin of armor plate was welded to the front of some Sherman hulls, for a total thickness of four inches, and these "Jumbo" tanks were to lead the columns churning north. "Drive like hell," Patton urged. "We have an opportunity of winning the war."

Both commander and commanded had also made missteps. Poor MP radio security allowed German eavesdroppers to track Third Army troop movements by route, unit, and destination; a surprise dagger thrust would soon become a plodding frontal assault on a thirty-mile front. Tank crews that failed to sweep the snow off their fluorescent recognition panels were strafed by P-47s. The hard freeze permitted cross-country mobility for the first time since October, but ice caused many a skidding wreck. When the 4th Armored Division was seven miles south of Bastogne, Patton ordered a perilous night attack that gained only four hundred yards and left one tank battalion with just fourteen Shermans. A German ambush in Chaumont—an "ugly, manure-strewn hell of a village"—smacked a combat command back more than a mile at a cost of eleven more Shermans and thirty-six hours. "The troops built little fires of anything that would burn," an armored officer wrote. "The dead lay frozen and stiff and when the men came to load them in trucks, they picked them up and put them in like big logs of wood."

"This was probably my fault, because I had been insisting on day and night attacks," Patton confessed to his diary. Even now, after almost four decades as a soldier, he reflected on how "it takes a long time to learn war . . . to really learn how to fight." He had predicted that Third Army would reach Bastogne on December 24, but with 4th Armored making little progress—German paratroopers kept infiltrating back into cleared villages—Patton twice phoned an irate Eisenhower to apologize for delays. "This snow is God-awful," he said. "I'm sorry." To a subordinate Patton added, "I am unhappy about it."

In search of a seam through enemy defenses, Combat Command R early Christmas morning looped thirty miles from 4th Armored's right flank to the division's far left, near Neufchâteau. Reduced to twenty Shermans, the 37th Tank Battalion led the attack north under Lieutenant Colonel Creighton W. Abrams, Jr., the thirty-year-old son of a New England railroad mechanic and among sixty men in the West Point class of 1936 who would eventually earn generals' stars. When a blown bridge halted the battalion, Abrams, chewing a cigar and eating aspirin by the handful, ordered a bulldozer to demolish a stone wall and push the debris into the creek as a causeway.

On Monday afternoon, December 26, the battalion crested a ridge three miles southwest of the Bastogne perimeter. Thirteen artillery batteries fired more than five hundred rounds into the farm village of Assenois. With friendly shells falling close enough to wound several GIs, Shermans and half-tracks charged through streets darkened by smoke and dust, as Volksgrenadiers poured from the cellars in what the official history would call a "shooting, clubbing, stabbing melee." Before surrendering with five hundred other defenders, a German officer reported by telephone, "They are through Assenois and going to Bastogne."

Five Shermans and a half-track raced north under Lieutenant Charles Boggess. Gunfire ripped through the fir trees, shooting down surprised Germans standing in a mess line, and three tank shells killed a dozen more in a concrete blockhouse. Boggess spotted colored parachutes scattered in a field and foxholes flanking the road ahead. "Come here!" he yelled, standing in his turret. "This is the 4th Armored." Several helmeted figures in olive drab emerged from their holes, and at 4:50 P.M. the siege of Bastogne was over. Twenty minutes later, McAuliffe greeted Abrams with a polite "It's good to see you, Colonel."

"Kilroy Was Stuck Here," someone had chalked on the charred wall of a ruined barn. Now that ubiquitous, sardonic liberator had himself been liberated. Seventy ambulances and supply trucks soon rolled into the smoldering town, and seven hundred enemy prisoners marched out; a 101st Airborne sergeant scrutinized their footwear, smashing his rifle butt onto the toes of any German wearing GI boots. The eight-day defense of a drab market town in Belgium had cost more than two thousand American casualties. Losses in the 4th Armored added another thousand to the tally, and the division's tank strength hardly equaled that of a battalion. But

Rundstedt's chief of staff would later list the "failure to conquer Bastogne" first among seven factors that caused HERBSTNEBEL to fail.

Patton had his own assessment. Never averse to historical grandiosity, he told reporters a few days later that the battle at Bastogne would be considered "just as important as the battle of Gettysburg was to the Civil War."

"Glory Has Its Price"

TIME in the last week of December chose Eisenhower as its "Man of the Year." A flattering cover portrait depicted the supreme commander flanked by American and British flags, with legions of soldiers and tanks stretching behind him into the middle distance. The honor rang a bit tinny given the current German salient in Allied territory, which now measured forty miles wide by sixty miles deep. U.S. losses in the last fortnight of December included almost 600 tanks, 1,400 jeeps, 700 trucks, 2,400 machine guns, 1,700 bazookas, 5,000 rifles, and 65,000 overcoats. The enemy had accumulated such a large American motor pool that pilots were ordered to bomb any column that included both Allied and German vehicles.

Of greater concern was a German armored spearhead ripping a seam between the U.S. VIII Corps in the south and XVIII Airborne Corps in the north. Fatigue, dispersion, empty fuel tanks, and ammunition shortages impaired the enemy drive. In some instances, half a German brigade towed the other half, and ordnance trucks often had to make a four-night round-trip drive to Bonn for artillery shells. But on Christmas Day the 2nd Panzer Division was only five miles from Dinant, soon drawing near enough to the Meuse to draw fire from British tanks. Four divisions in Joe Collins's VII Corps, now nearly 100,000 strong, were ordered to counterpunch on a fifty-mile front, with Major General Ernie Harmon's 2nd Armored Division smashing into the enemy vanguard after a seventy-mile road march from the Roer River that took less than a day.

Savage fighting raged from the Salm to the Meuse for three days. As Typhoons and Lightnings screamed over the treetops at Foy–Notre Dame, just east of Dinant, Harmon's tanks rumbled through a wood in nearby Celles, destroying or capturing 142 vehicles and taking nearly five hundred prisoners. On December 26, Manteuffel authorized survivors from 2nd Panzer to flee on foot, abandoning equipment from six battalions. Farther east, a British flame-throwing tank persuaded two hundred Germans to emerge with raised hands from a last-stand château in Humain, while thirteen artillery battalions drove the 2nd SS Panzer out of Manhay. In confused fighting at Sadzot—known to GIs as Sad Sack—enemy crews mortared their own platoons; the engagement turned out to be Sixth Panzer Army's last sally before Model ordered Dietrich onto the defensive.

Eisenhower for the past week had been looking for counteroffensive opportunities that would trap the overextended Germans and fulfill his ambition of annihilating enemy forces west of the Rhine. An Ultra intercept decoded just after Christmas revealed that Model's army group was fast running short of serviceable tanks and assault guns; despite recent losses, the U.S. First, Third, and Ninth Armies alone had almost four thousand tanks. But disagreement over when and where to strike back divided Allied commanders.

Patton favored driving from the south through the base of the German salient, toward Bitburg and then east, in hopes of bagging the entire enemy pocket. Collins, in a memorandum on Wednesday, December 27, laid out three options and endorsed "Plan No. 2," a strong attack from the north toward St.-Vith, complemented by Third Army's lunge from the south. Montgomery hesitated, suspecting that Rundstedt had enough combat strength for another attack that could punch through the Americans to Liège. Collins thought not. "Nobody is going to break through these troops," he told Montgomery. "This isn't going to happen." If the Allies failed to attack closer to the base of the salient, they risked leaving a corridor through which retreating Germans could escape, he told the field marshal. "You're going to push the Germans out of the bag," Collins added, "just like you did at Falaise."

Falaise could hardly be blamed solely on Montgomery, who through much of the European campaign had evinced a bold streak—in MARKET GARDEN, for instance, and in encouraging the Americans to blow past the Brittany cul-de-sac. But now he turned cautious, perhaps discouraged by First Army's early drubbing. He had doubted Patton's ability to reach Bastogne or impede Manteuffel, and he doubted that the poor roads leading south toward St.-Vith would support Collins's scheme. Rather than gamble on an attempt by First and Third Armies to sever the forty-mile base of the salient, he thought a more prudent counterstrike would aim the two armies' main blows across the waist of the bulge at Houffalize, north of Bastogne, shooing away the enemy rather than trapping him, and only after the German offensive had, as he put it, "definitely expended itself."

Eisenhower chafed at Montgomery's caution. When he learned on Wednesday that the field marshal was at last ready to consider counterattacking, the supreme commander exclaimed sarcastically, "Praise God from whom all blessings flow!"

"Monty is a tired little fart," Patton informed his diary the same day.

"War requires the taking of risks and he won't take them." Yet others were just as circumspect as Montgomery. Beetle Smith in a staff meeting on Wednesday suggested telling "our masters in Washington that if they want us to win the war over here they must find us another ten divisions." Bradley also favored pinching the enemy at Houffalize, not least because Eisenhower had promised to return First Army to his command when the town fell. First Army planners agreed that poor roads precluded hitting the base of the Ardennes salient, and Monk Dickson, the intelligence chief, endorsed Montgomery's view that Rundstedt could strike again; he counted seventeen uncommitted German divisions. Deteriorating weather further encouraged prudence: a five-day spell of clear skies ended on Thursday, December 28, and with it the comfort provided by Allied air fleets.

Montgomery later asserted that he had left selection of the northern attack azimuth to Hodges, who after the high anxiety of HERBSTNEBEL much preferred the more conservative route toward Houffalize. Perhaps the last straw for Hodges came when another V-1 detonated three hundred yards from the First Army headquarters in Tongres, breaking most of the windows; sixty-five men were wounded by flying glass. In the First Army command diary, an aide wrote, "Hodges has had enough of exposed flanks for the last two weeks."

Delayed by fog, snowbanks, and further reports of assassins afoot, Eisenhower's command train on early Thursday afternoon pulled into a rail siding in the Belgian town of Hasselt, five miles south of Zonhoven. Bodyguards bounded through the station, searching for potential malefactors, and machine-gun crews crouched on the platform to lay down a suppressive cross fire, as needed. Montgomery hopped aboard at 2:30 P.M. to find Eisenhower in his study, eager to discuss a counteroffensive that would turn the tables in the Ardennes once and for all. While Smith and De Guingand, the two chiefs of staff, waited in an unheated corridor, Montgomery sketched the plan: four corps would squeeze the enemy salient from the north and northwest, complementing the three already attacking from the south under Patton. The two wings would plan to meet in Houffalize, halfway down the length of the bulge.

Yet the field marshal was vague about precisely when this cataclysmic counterblow would fall. Building a combat reserve was vital, Montgomery said. His own direct observation and the reports of his "gallopers"—young British liaison officers who reported to him personally from far corners of the battlefield—led him to conclude that First Army still lacked the strength to confront an enemy force that included at least seven panzer divisions, with enough residual power to launch "at least one more full-blooded attack." Better to let the enemy first impale himself with a final futile lunge toward the Meuse. Then, deflecting Eisenhower's impatient request for a date certain, Montgomery urged development of a "master plan for the future conduct of war," one in which "all available offensive power must be allotted to the northern front," preferably with a single commander who "must have powers of operational control."

With this ancient theme again resurrected, Eisenhower brought the meeting to a close and showed Montgomery to the platform. Machine-gunners folded their tripods, bodyguards reboarded, and the train chuffed back to Versailles via Brussels. Despite Montgomery's insistence that the necessary conditions fall in place before an Allied counterblow was launched, the supreme commander believed that he had extracted a commitment for an attack from the north to begin in four days, on Monday, January 1.

That was incorrect. Montgomery returned to his Zonhoven field camp and cabled Brooke that Eisenhower was "definitely in a somewhat humble frame of mind and clearly realizes that the present trouble would not have occurred if he had accepted British advice and not that of American generals." He further believed, after a recent conference with Bradley, that the later also finally recognized the limitations of his generalship. "Poor chap," Montgomery had written Brooke, "he is such a decent fellow and the whole thing is a bitter pill for him." But 21st Army Group had put the cousins back on track. "We have tidied up the mess," he told the British chief, "and got two American armies properly organized." Montgomery also wanted the War Office to know that although he cabled London about his operations each night, no such report went to SHAEF. "You are far better informed, and in the picture, than is Ike," he confided.

And then, with the chronic nescience of a political naïf, he overplayed his hand, again. In a note to Eisenhower on Friday, December 29, Montgomery wrote:

> We have had one very definite failure. . . . One commander must have powers to direct and control the operation; you cannot possibly do it yourself, and so you would have to nominate someone else.

He enclosed a proposed order for Eisenhower to issue to both 12th and 21st Army Groups, decreeing that "from now onwards full operational direction, control, and coordination of these operations is vested in the [commander-in-chief of] 21 Army Group." In summation, he told the supreme commander, "I put this matter up to you again only because I am so anxious not to have another failure." However, he added, without "one man directing and controlling . . . we will fail again."

By chance, Montgomery's note arrived just before a personal message to Eisenhower from George Marshall, who noted that "certain London papers" were calling for the field marshal to command "all your ground forces." The chief added:

> Under no circumstances make any concessions of any kind whatsoever. You not only have our complete confidence but there would be a terrific resentment in this country following such action. . . . Give them hell.

Precisely who should get hell was ambiguous, but Eisenhower settled on Montgomery. "They are all mad at Monty," Kay Summersby told her diary on Friday, subsequently adding, "Bedell [Smith] and E. agree that Monty has changed considerably since the day in Italy over a year ago when he said he wanted to join the team."

The supreme commander's patience finally snapped when the agreeable De Guingand arrived in Versailles on Saturday, December 30, with the disagreeable news that no offensive would be launched from the north until at least January 3, leaving Patton to fight alone in the south against a ferociously reinforced enemy. Convinced that he had been deceived, Eisenhower stormed about his office, ordering staff officers to find the message confirming Montgomery's commitment to a January 1 attack—a futile search, De Guingand assured him, because "knowing Monty, the last thing he would do is commit himself on paper."

"All right, Beetle," Eisenhower said, turning to his chief of staff as the familiar scarlet flush crept up his neck. "I'm going to send a telegram . . . to the Joint Chiefs of Staff that I've had trouble with this man and it's either they can relieve me if they'd like to—that would be perfectly all right—but one of the two of us has to go."

Now fully alive to Montgomery's peril, and aware both of Marshall's stern note and the thinly concealed American yen to have Harold Alexander command 21st Army Group, De Guingand proposed driving immediately to Zonhoven. "Won't you please hold up that telegram 'til I get back?" he asked Eisenhower.

"All right, Freddie, I'll hold this up until tomorrow morning. But I don't think you ought to try and get up there, not tonight, because the weather is so bad."

After De Guingand hurried out to begin the treacherous two-hundred-mile drive to Montgomery's camp, Eisenhower dictated a frosty cable to the field marshal:

> I do not agree that one army group commander should fight his own battle and give orders to another army group commander. . . . You disturb me by predictions of "failure" unless your exact opinions in the matter of giving you command over Bradley are met in detail. I assure you

that in this matter I can go no further. . . . We would have to present our differences to the CC/S [Combined Chiefs of Staff].

Already in fragile health, De Guingand arrived in Zonhoven at midnight, as Alan Moorehead later told Forrest Pogue, "nearly exhausted, a little hysterical, full of whisky. . . . He said to Monty, 'I must see you at once.'" As the chief of staff described the surly mood in Versailles, Montgomery paced around his caravan.

"If you keep on, one of you will have to go," De Guingand said, "and it won't be Ike."

Montgomery scoffed. "Who would replace me?"

"That's already been worked out," De Guingand said. "They want Alex."

Montgomery's bluster abruptly dissolved, precisely as it had when the battle of Mareth turned against him in March 1943. "What shall I do, Freddie?" he asked. "What shall I do?"

De Guingand had already drafted an apology to Eisenhower, which he now pulled from his battle dress. "Sign this," he said. Montgomery scratched his signature and summoned an orderly to have the message delivered, eyes only:

> Dear Ike . . . Whatever your decision may be you can rely on me one hundred percent to make it work and I know Brad will do the same. Very distressed that my letter may have upset you and I would ask you to tear it up. Your very devoted subordinate, Monty.

The crisis passed but the scars would linger. Soon after sending his apologetic note to Eisenhower, Montgomery privately cabled Brooke, "The general tendency at SHAEF and among the American command is one of considerable optimism. . . . I cannot share this optimism." Eisenhower thanked Montgomery for "your very fine telegram," but the incessant friction with the field marshal kept him awake at night. "He's just a little man," he would say after the war. "He's just as little inside as he is outside."

No sooner had Eisenhower suppressed this insurrection on his northern flank than his southern flank erupted, first with insubordination by 6th Army Group, then in a German attack hardly less cheeky than HERBST-NEBEL.

Although he commanded ten French and eight American divisions, General Devers had accomplished little in Alsace since Eisenhower's refusal in late November to permit the Rhine crossing near Strasbourg. The U.S. Seventh Army's combat power had been dissipated by the requirement to move in two opposite directions: north, to shore up Bradley's flank, and south, to help General de Lattre eradicate the enemy salient around Colmar. Neither gambit yielded conspicuous success. After punching half a dozen holes through the German border to the north, GIs found the Siegfried Line impenetrable; they were reduced to tacking up latrine placards along the West Wall that read, "Shit on Hitler's Home."

The Colmar Pocket, as wide as the Bulge in Belgium and about half as deep, also proved unyielding. General Dahlquist's 36th Division, attached to De Lattre's First Army, reported that their French brothers-in-arms showed little interest in completing the liberation of Alsace, even as German forces aggressively shored up the salient. "The enemy attacked on three fronts today," Dahlquist told his diary in mid-December, later adding, "The French left our division holding the bag for almost two weeks." Squabbling between rival French factions persisted, aggravated by General Leclerc's declaration that neither he nor his 2nd Armored Division cared to serve under a Vichy traitor like De Lattre. "I have now two problem children, Leclerc and De Lattre," Devers wrote George Marshall.

At Verdun on December 19, Eisenhower had ordered 6th Army Group to help Bradley in the Bulge by contributing troops and shifting to the defensive. Three days later, Devers halted further attacks against the Colmar Pocket, leaving Hitler still master of 850 square miles of France. But Eisenhower was willing to cede much more: a SHAEF staff officer on December 26 brought Devers a map drawn by the supreme commander personally, which made plain that the Franco-American armies were to fall back nearly forty miles to an ostensibly more defensible line along the Vosges, abandoning Strasbourg and the Alsatian plain. Devers on December 27 flew to Versailles to argue that a retreat from the Rhine would anger the French, embolden the Germans, and bring the hard-won Saverne Gap within range of enemy artillery. Eisenhower stood fast, spooked by intelligence reports of German legions massing across from the U.S. Seventh Army. The 6th Army Group, he told Devers, must move "back to the Vosges line and hang on" until the Ardennes struggle subsided. Supply dumps were to be shifted into the mountains, and Devers was to sequester two U.S. divisions, one armored and one infantry, as a SHAEF reserve west of the Vosges. Devers told his diary:

> The Germans undoubtedly will attack me now. . . . The position I give up is much stronger than the one to which I go. . . . Giving up the town of Strasbourg is a political disaster to France.

De Gaulle thought so too: on December 28, he sent General Alphonse Juin, now the French military chief of staff, to Versailles to make inquiries about a rumored retreat in Alsace. A gallant Algerian, distinguished by

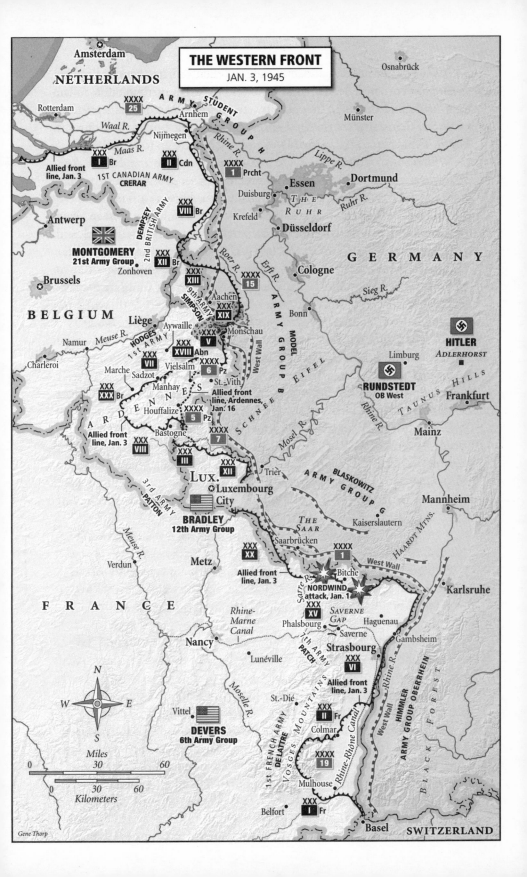

THE WESTERN FRONT
JAN. 3, 1945

Gene Thorp

his Basque beret and left-handed salute—his right arm had been maimed in 1915—Juin cornered Beetle Smith, who told him that no firm decision had been made and that SHAEF's action was "simply the study of a plan." In truth, Smith had drafted the final order that morning. Juin motored back to Rue St.-Dominique and warned De Gaulle, "They are up to something."

While Smith prevaricated, Devers temporized. He moved his command post seventy miles west, to Vittel, but ordered his staff to prepare plans for three intermediate fallback positions leading to a final line along the eastern face of the Vosges. When General Patch was told to ready his Seventh Army for withdrawal, he winked at a staff officer and said, "Ain't going to do it. We aren't that bad off." De Lattre was even more recalcitrant, decrying "a psychosis of retreat" that would force the Allies to capture the same ground twice. He took two days to translate Devers's withdrawal directive into his own General Order No. 201, which on December 30 instructed French subordinates "to maintain the integrity of the present front" by yielding not a single square centimeter of Alsatian soil. Devers cabled Eisenhower that falling back to the Vosges could take two weeks.

Once again the supreme commander's neck flushed deep red. "Call up Devers and tell him he is not doing what he was told," he barked at Smith. "Tell him to obey his orders and shorten his line." In a phone call from Vittel, Devers feebly claimed that Eisenhower's earlier instruction had been discretionary. "I won't go to him with that story," Smith snapped. "He thinks you've been disloyal." Another written order from Eisenhower left no wiggle room:

> The political pressure to retain French soil, which you are undoubtedly experiencing, must be resisted if it leads to any risk of your losing divisions. . . . You must not endanger the integrity of your units east of your main position, the Vosges. You must be prepared to accept the loss of territory east of the Vosges and all its political consequences.

Devers capitulated, telling subordinates that all forces would have to retreat to the Vosges no later than January 5. "Eisenhower," he advised his diary, "has given me no alternative." As for the supreme commander, he was now so vexed at a man whom he had long disliked that he considered sacking Devers and giving command of his army group to Patch.

"You can kill a willing horse by overdoing what you require of him," Devers wrote in his diary. "SHAEF has given me too much front, and taken away too many of my troops. This is unsound." A message from De Gaulle through Juin urged the Allies not to surrender Strasbourg "but to make it a Stalingrad."

The final day of the year ticked by with fresh snow and more omens. A reconnaissance flight at last light detected German artillery lumbering forward into new gun pits. Seventh Army placed all troops on high alert and canceled holiday celebrations. A reporter who insisted on toasting the departure of 1944 declared, "Never was the world plagued by such a year less worth remembering." Devers's diary entry for December 31 was just as cheerless: "Patch called me. . . . He was sure he was going to be attacked during the night."

The attack indeed fell that night, the last substantial German offensive of the war in western Europe. Hitler had given another Adlerhorst pep talk to commanders in Army Group G, conceding failure in the Ardennes, but offering another chance to thrash the Americans in Operation NORD-WIND, North Wind. A lunge by eight divisions southwest down the Vosges axis would recapture the Saverne Gap and link up with Nineteenth Army troops occupying the Colmar Pocket; in addition, the attack would force Patton to withdraw from Bastogne to parry this new threat. French troops in Alsace were weak and disorganized, the Führer promised, and the U.S. Seventh Army was overextended along a 126-mile perimeter.

The Americans were also alert and entrenched. Ultra intercepts provided no specific enemy attack order, but ample intelligence revealed the German order of battle and unit boundaries below Saarbrücken. Patch had little doubt that the main attack would come against the Seventh Army left, west of the Haardt Mountains, with a complementary attack to the east between the mountains and the Rhine.

"German offensive began on Seventh Army front about 0030 hours," Patch's chief of staff wrote in a diary entry on Monday, January 1. "Krauts were howling drunk. Murdered them." Shrieking Waffen-SS troops, silhouetted by moonlight that glistened off snowfields near the Sarre River, hardly dented the American left wing. A single .30-caliber water-cooled machine gun, slewing left and right with long, chattering bursts, was credited with slaying more than one hundred attackers. Volksgrenadier corpses piled up in a kill sack soon dubbed "Morgue Valley." "Gained only insignificant ground," the Army Group G war diary recorded; then, by nightfall on Tuesday: "The attack has lost its momentum."

The most flamboyant German sally occurred on New Year's Day, an attack by nine hundred Luftwaffe planes flying at treetop altitude across the Western Front. Operation BODENPLATTE, Baseplate, also known as the "Hangover Raid," included pilots said to be wearing dress uniforms with patent-leather shoes and white gloves after celebrating the arrival of 1945. The raiders caught seventeen Allied airfields by surprise, destroying 150 parked planes and damaging more than 100 others.

Montgomery's personal aircraft was among those wrecked. But German losses approached 300 planes, some shot down by their own antiaircraft gunners who, for reasons of secrecy, had not been informed of BODENPLATTE. Worse still was the loss of 237 German pilots, including veteran airmen, instructors, and commanders. "We sacrificed our last substance," one Luftwaffe officer said.

Even as NORDWIND collapsed on the German right, an ancillary New Year's attack ten miles to the east spilled from old Maginot Line bunkers to gain traction through corrugated terrain below Bitche. Bypassing American strongpoints in the Low Vosges, the 6th SS Mountain Division bent the Seventh Army line sufficiently to alarm SHAEF and terrify Strasbourg, thirty miles southeast. Propaganda broadcasts from Radio Stuttgart reported German shock troops assembling to seize the city, with reprisals certain to fall on Alsatians who had helped the Allies. Rumors of Seventh Army detachments packing to leave along the Rhine "spread like a powder fuze and caused a general panic," according to a French lieutenant.

Lowered tricolors and the sight of official sedans being gassed up added to the dread. Journalists reported that roads west were clogged with "women pushing baby carriages [and] wagons piled high with furniture," as Strasbourg steeled itself for yet another reversal of fortune. One soldier spied inverted dinner plates laid across a road in the thin hope that they sufficiently resembled antitank mines to delay, at least briefly, the Hun's return.

Charles de Gaulle, once again referring to himself in the third person, declared that the abandonment of Strasbourg would not only be "a terrible wound inflicted on the honor of the country," but also "a profound blow to the nation's confidence in de Gaulle." On Tuesday, January 2, he told De Lattre in a handwritten note, "Naturally the French Army cannot consent to the abandonment of Strasbourg. . . . I order you to take matters into your own hands." At nearly the same moment, Devers cabled De Lattre to pull his left wing back toward the Vosges no later than Friday morning, necessarily exposing the city. The American order had "a bomb-like effect" in the French army headquarters, one staff officer observed, and it provoked an anguished "*Ça, non!*" from De Lattre, now confronted by conflicting orders from two masters in what he called "a grave problem of conscience."

De Gaulle saw no dilemma. When De Lattre proposed waiting "until the Allied high command has given its consent" to defend Strasbourg, De Gaulle replied, "I cannot accept your last communication." De Lattre's sole duty, De Gaulle added, was to France; it was said that at an afternoon reception in Paris, Madame de Gaulle snubbed Madame de Lattre. Strasbourg's mayor sent the army commander a photograph of the spectacular cathedral with an inscription, "To General de Lattre, our last hope." Confined to his cot by residual lung inflammation from a World War I gassing, the long-suffering De Lattre now suffered more.

At nine P.M. on Tuesday, General Juin appeared at Beetle Smith's office in Versailles, tossed his left-handed salute, and then spent five hours warning of "extremely grave consequences" that would cause "the supreme commander to be severely judged" should Strasbourg be abandoned. After repeating himself incessantly, Juin at two A.M. pulled from his pocket a letter in which De Gaulle threatened to withdraw French forces from SHAEF command. "We are dependent on them," De Gaulle had told Juin, "but inversely they are dependent on us."

"Juin said things to me last night, which, if he had been an American, I would have socked him on the jaw," a bleary-eyed Smith told Eisenhower during a staff meeting Wednesday morning, January 3. For more than an hour in the supreme commander's office, joined by Strong and Spaatz, they debated their course. Smith still believed that withdrawal to the Vosges was imperative; 6th Army Group reported pressure across the entire front from NORDWIND. Devers had now accepted Eisenhower's order "to forget Strasbourg," but to forsake the city would threaten Allied unity. Strasbourg's military governor had warned Patch, "You will cover the American flag with ineradicable shame," and dispatches from the city at five that morning predicted "terrible reprisals" and "mass massacres." Evacuation plans had already been drafted, beginning with a thousand civil servants that afternoon although only two hundred railcars were available to transport at least a hundred thousand civilians. Buffeted by contradictory demands, De Lattre appeared to have fallen in step with De Gaulle by ordering the 3rd Algerian Division to prepare for deployment to Strasbourg.

"Next to the weather," Eisenhower would tell George Marshall, the French "have caused me more trouble in this war than any other single factor. They even rank above landing craft." The art of command at times requires tactical retreat for strategic advantage, in a headquarters no less than on a battlefield, and by midday on Wednesday the supreme commander sensibly recognized that in the interest of Allied comity he would have to yield. De Gaulle had requested a meeting at three P.M., but before formally acceding to French demands Eisenhower intended to land a punch or two.

Smith phoned Devers to ask how close German forces were to the Alsatian capital.

"About thirty miles," Devers replied.

"Well, keep them as far away as you can," Smith said. "It looks now as if you will have to hold Strasbourg."

*   *   *

The crowded stage in this melodrama grew more congested at 2:15 P.M. with the arrival of Churchill and Brooke after a turbulent flight from England in filthy weather. Eisenhower whisked them from the airfield to his house for a quick lunch, and then to a conference room in the Trianon Palace. De Gaulle soon appeared, stiff and unsmiling, with Juin on his heels. The men settled into armchairs arranged in a circle around a situation map spread across the floor, and De Gaulle handed Eisenhower a copy of his letter ordering De Lattre to defend Strasbourg.

Eisenhower gestured to the map of Alsace, which showed three German corps bearing down from the north, as well as half a dozen enemy divisions threatening attack from the Colmar salient. "In Alsace, where the enemy has extended his attack for two days, the Colmar pocket makes our position a precarious one," he said. The long front exposed French and American soldiers alike. Moreover, Devers not only had no reserves, he had been told to forfeit two divisions to reinforce the Ardennes, where fighting remained savage.

"Alsace is sacred ground," De Gaulle replied. Allowing the Germans to regain Strasbourg could bring down the French government, leading to "a state bordering on anarchy in the entire country."

"All my life," Churchill said pleasantly, "I have remarked what significance Alsace has for the French."

Even so, Eisenhower said, he resented being pressured to amend military plans for political reasons. The threat to pull French forces from SHAEF command seemed spiteful, given all that the Allies had done for France; the Combined Chiefs already had agreed to equip sixteen French divisions, and De Gaulle had recently asked for a total of fifty. Should *le général* choose to fight independently, SHAEF would have no choice but to suspend supplies of fuel and munitions to the French army. This crisis could have been averted, Eisenhower added, had De Lattre's troops fought well and eradicated the Colmar Pocket, as ordered.

By now the supreme commander's face had grown beet red. De Gaulle stared down his great beak. General Eisenhower, he said, was at "risk of seeing the outraged French people forbid the use of its railroads and communications. . . . If you carry out the withdrawal, I will give the order to a French division to barricade itself inside Strasbourg and before the scandalized world you will be obliged to go in and free it."

The prime minister chose this moment to gently lower himself from his chair to the floor with feline grace. Laying an index finger on the map, he murmured, "Strasbourg, this point."

Having lost his composure, Eisenhower now regained it. Very well, he conceded, Strasbourg would be defended. Sacred Alsace would remain French, the withdrawal order to Devers canceled. Ringing for tea, he confided to De Gaulle in a low voice, "I am having a lot of trouble with Montgomery."

The conference ended. "I think you've done the wise and proper thing," Churchill told Eisenhower. Buttonholing De Gaulle in a corridor outside, the prime minister said, in his sibilant, fractured French, that Eisenhower was "not always aware of the political consequences of his decisions," but was nonetheless "an excellent supreme commander." De Gaulle said nothing, but before Eisenhower bade him adieu at the front door of the Trianon Palace, Deux Mètres told him, "Glory has its price. Now you are going to be a conqueror." To a dinner companion the next night, De Gaulle said, "Imagine, asking us to withdraw our troops from Strasbourg. Could you believe it?" The contretemps, he said, revealed that "these Americans . . . equate politics with sentiment, the military art with logic."

As the happy news of salvation spread through Strasbourg late Wednesday afternoon, jubilant crowds belted out "La Marseillaise." A tricolor rose again before the Caserne de Gendarmerie, and a Seventh Army loudspeaker truck rolled through the city, urging calm. Eisenhower authorized Devers to keep the new SHAEF reserve for his own use; Strasbourg was to be defended "as strongly as possible"—primarily by French troops—but without risking "the integrity of your forces, which will not be jeopardized."

NORDWIND would drag on, with three more attacks against the Americans of at least corps size, and another against the French up the Rhine–Rhône Canal from Colmar. Seventh Army's right wing bent back ten miles and more, particularly along the Rhine near Haguenau, and enemy troops ferried across the river at Gambsheim closed to within a few miles of Strasbourg before being cuffed back. But these paltry territorial gains, which cost 23,000 irreplaceable German casualties, carried little strategic heft; Patch held the Saverne Gap and the Rhine–Marne Canal, and Patton was not diverted from the Ardennes. Hitler denounced as "pessimistic" reports from Alsace that NORDWIND had failed for want of sufficient infantry. Yet he was reduced to using Volksgrenadiers who had trained together for barely a month, among them recruits from eastern Europe who spoke no German, and a convalescent unit known as the "Whipped Cream Division" because of its special dietary needs.

"We must believe in the ultimate purposes of a merciful God," Eisenhower had written Mamie after his confrontation with De Gaulle. "These are trying days." Rarely had the burden of command weighed more heavily on him. Bodyguards still shadowed his every move, he found no time for exercise, and despite his regular letters home his wife chided him for not writing often enough.

He had new worries, too: recent intelligence suggested the Germans might soon use poison gas, and it was also said that enemy scientists were developing a ray capable of stopping Allied aircraft engines in flight. Further, he suffered yet another significant loss: on January 2, ice on the wings combined with pilot error during takeoff had caused the crash of a twin-engine Hudson at airfield A-46, five miles south of Versailles. The fiery accident killed Admiral Ramsay—among Eisenhower's staunchest and most valued advisers—who was flying to Brussels for a conference with Montgomery about the defenses at Antwerp. On Sunday, January 7, a French naval band played Chopin's funeral march as a gun carriage bore Ramsay's coffin to a hillside grave above the Seine. The supreme commander joined mourners in the shuffling cortège.

Later that afternoon, Eisenhower's office calendar recorded: "E. leaves office early, 4:30 & goes home. He is very depressed these days."

The Agony Grapevine

SHAEF on January 5 confirmed an American press report that the U.S. First and Ninth Armies now fought under British command. The statement from Versailles claimed that the arrangement had been made "by instant agreement of all concerned," but failed to explain that the reconfiguration was only temporary. Smug accounts in London newspapers began describing GIs as "Monty's troops"; privately encouraged by the field marshal, the press clamored for a "proper" chain of command in northwestern Europe, under a single battle captain.

"We have nothing to apologize for," Bradley told his staff. "We have nothing to explain." Major Hansen wrote in his diary, "Many of us who were avowed Anglophiles in Great Britain have now been irritated, hurt, and infuriated by the British radio and press. All this good feeling has vanished."

On Saturday, January 6, Montgomery cabled Churchill that he planned to summon reporters to explain "how [the] Germans were first 'headed off,' then 'seen off,' and now are being 'written off.'" He also intended to rebut any suggestion of American failure in the Ardennes. "I shall show how the whole Allied team rallied to the call and how national considerations were thrown overboard. . . . I shall stress the great friendship between myself and Ike."

On the same day, he wrote a confidant in London, "The real trouble with the Yanks is that they are completely ignorant as to the rules of the game we are playing with the Germans." When Brigadier Williams, the intelligence chief, asked why he intended to hold a press conference, Montgomery explained that Eisenhower's generalship had been impugned, and "I want to put it right." Williams offered two words of counsel: "Please don't." Others in his headquarters, smelling condescension, also sought to dissuade him. Alan Moorehead pleaded with De Guingand to muzzle Montgomery, lest he "make some bloody awful mistake."

"That's a funny position for a newsman to take," De Guingand said.

"I want to win the war," Moorehead replied.

In a double-badged maroon beret and a parachute harness—"dressed like a clown," in Moorehead's description—the field marshal appeared before a gaggle of correspondents in Zonhoven on January 7. No doubt he meant well. Praising the American GI as "a brave fighting man, steady under fire, and with that tenacity in battle which stamps the first-class soldier," he also saluted Eisenhower as "the captain of our team," declaring, "I am absolutely devoted to Ike. We are the greatest of friends." No mention was made of Bradley, and an assertion that British troops were "fighting hard" exaggerated their role as reserves very much on the fringe of the battlefield.

Much of the recitation, however, was devoted to describing the field marshal's own brilliance upon taking command almost three weeks earlier. "The first thing I did," Montgomery said, "was busy myself in getting the battle area tidy—getting it sorted out":

> As soon as I saw what was happening I took certain steps myself to ensure that if the Germans got to the Meuse they would certainly not get over that river. And I carried out certain movements so as to provide balanced dispositions. . . . I was thinking ahead. . . . The battle has been most interesting. I think possibly one of the most interesting and tricky battles I have ever handled.

Montgomery likened "seeing off" the enemy to his repulse of Rommel in Egypt in 1942. He closed by declaring, without a scintilla of irony, "Let us have done with the destructive criticism that aims a blow at Allied solidarity."

"Oh, God, why didn't you stop him?" Moorehead asked Williams as reporters scattered to file their stories. "It was so awful." Many British officers agreed. The field marshal had been "indecently exultant," as one put it, displaying "what a good boy am I" self-regard, in De Guingand's phrase, and conveying what another general called his "cock on a dunghill mood." A headline in the *Daily Mail*—"Montgomery Foresaw Attack, Acted 'On Own' to Save Day"—captured the prevailing Fleet Street sentiment, although Churchill's private secretary told his diary, "Monty's triumphant, jingoistic, and exceedingly self-satisfied talk to the press on Sunday has given wide offense." A mischievous German radio broadcast mimicked the BBC with a phony news flash that quoted Montgomery as describing the Americans as "'somewhat bewildered.'...The battle of the Ardennes can now be written off, thanks to Field Marshal Montgomery."

"He sees fit to assume all the glory and scarcely permits the mention of an army commander's name," the Ninth Army war diary complained. "Bitterness and real resentment is [sic] creeping in." No one was more bitter or resentful than Bradley, whose "contempt had grown into active hatred" for Montgomery, reported one British general at SHAEF. Air Marshal Tedder informed his diary that cooperation between Bradley and the field marshal was now "out of the question."

Bradley twice called Versailles on Tuesday, January 9, "very much upset over the big play up Monty is getting in the British press," Kay Summersby noted. He, too, summoned reporters, using a map and a pointer to render his own version of events, which included the dubious assertion that American commanders had consciously taken "a calculated risk" in thinning out defenses in the Ardennes. Privately he denounced Montgomery's "attempt to discredit me so he could get control of the whole operation." The field marshal, he asserted, wanted to "be in on the kill, and no one else."

In another call to Eisenhower, Bradley warned, "I cannot serve under Montgomery. If he is to be put in command of all ground forces, you must send me home."

Eisenhower assured him that he had no plans to expand the field marshal's authority, then added, "I thought you were the one person I could count on for doing anything I asked you to do."

"This is one thing I cannot take," Bradley replied.

Once again Eisenhower sought to mollify, to mediate, and to keep his temperamental subordinates concentrated on the task at hand: evicting Rundstedt from the Bulge and resuming the march on Germany. But in a note to Brooke he admitted, "No single incident that I have encountered throughout my experience as an Allied commander has been so difficult."

Heading off, seeing off, and writing off the Germans proved more problematic than Montgomery's facile catchphrases implied. Rundstedt in late December had reported that both panzer armies in HERBSTNEBEL "are forced completely into the defensive." Some German strategists urged Hitler to shift his armor to the Eastern Front—the Soviets had encircled Budapest in late December—but the Führer replied that the east "must take care of itself." Twenty infantry and eight panzer divisions remained committed to the Bulge in early January. Such a host would not be easily expelled, even though German infantry regiments were half the size of their American counterparts and U.S. armored divisions on average mustered more than twice as many tanks as their German equivalents. The "German soldier is fighting with great determination and bravery," a SHAEF assessment concluded. "Desertions few."

Yet many enemy commanders had been killed or wounded, and some Volksgrenadier companies near Bastogne had fewer than thirty men. Mortars and antitank guns were muscled to the rear for want of ammunition. German rations would be cut twice in January, to eleven ounces of bread and an ounce of fat per day. Potatoes and vegetables ran short. Motorcycle scouts combed the countryside for gasoline, which OB West allocated virtually drop by drop. One division traveled by bicycle for more than a week. In a schoolhouse hospital, a German doctor asked a shrieking, wounded *Landser,* "Are you a soldier or a pants-crapper?"

"Ten shells for their one," a U.S. Third Army soldier told the journalist Osmar White. "That's the secret of it." Work details of German prisoners were forced to break stone for road repairs, with a GI guard yelling, "Get along there, you cocksucking sonofabitch." They were the fortunate ones: to his diary, Patton disclosed "some unfortunate incidents in the shooting of prisoners. (I hope we can conceal this.)" Others were executed legally, among them eighteen of Skorzeny's saboteurs, convicted by military commissions within days of their apprehension and sentenced to be "shot to death with musketry." Three of the condemned requested that captured German nurses in an adjacent cell serenade them with Christmas carols. "We had to stop them after a while," an Army captain reported. "They were disturbing our troops." The reporter W. C. Heinz witnessed the firing-squad execution of the trio. "I looked at the ground, frost-white, the grass tufts frozen, the soil hard and uneven," Heinz wrote. "This view I see now, I told myself, will be the last thing their eyes will ever see." Trussed and then blindfolded, with paper circles pinned over their hearts, "the three stood rigid against the posts like woodcuts of men facing execution" until the fatal volley left them limp and leaking blood.

A final German lunge at Bastogne lingered into the second week of January, with fighting as fierce as any seen in the Ardennes. The number of German divisions battling Third Army increased from three to nine. Dreadful weather again grounded much of the Allied air force and forced American gunners to use blowtorches and pinch bars to free frozen gun carriages. Patton had hoped to seize Houffalize in a one-day bound of seventeen miles; instead, his drive north with III and VIII Corps averaged barely a mile a day. First Army's attack from the north, finally launched by Montgomery on January 3, moved no faster. Fog, snow, mines, rugged terrain, blown bridges, and a stubborn enemy reduced Collins's VII Corps to a crawl and cost five thousand casualties in the plodding advance on Houffalize. On January 8, Hitler authorized Model to at last abandon the western half of the Bulge, but not for three days did GIs see signs of a general withdrawal, yard by grudging yard. The Führer on January 14 rejected a plea from Rundstedt and Model to pull back to the Rhine; the retreat instead must halt at the West Wall, whence the offensive had begun.

At 11:40 A.M. on Tuesday, January 16, a cavalry patrol from the north met an armored infantry patrol from the south outside Houffalize to link the First and Third Armies. One thousand tons of Allied bombs and countless pozit shells had "completely removed" the Walloon market town, Patton wrote. "I have never seen anything like it in this war." Waiting for bulldozers to plow a path through the rubble, he composed a snatch of doggerel:

> Little town of Houffalize,
> Here you sit on bended knees.
> God bless your people and keep them safe,
> Especially from the RAF.

A day later, Eisenhower returned First Army to Bradley. Hodges sent Montgomery five pounds of coffee as thanks for his ministrations, and on January 18 moved the army headquarters back to the Hôtel Britannique in Spa. The place was largely intact except that the furniture had been upended and a Christmas tree, denuded of ornaments, was "tilting drunkenly in one corner." Ninth Army for now would remain under British command, despite carping from Bradley, who finally took SHAEF's hint by shifting his command post from isolated Luxembourg City to Namur, a riverine city once famed for fine knives. There in ducal splendor he and his staff occupied a baroque château with marble floors, velvet drapes, and full-length oils of Belgian nobility. A crystal chandelier dangled above his desk, and smirking cherubs looked down on the twenty-foot map board, propped against the wall frescoes. Bradley was billeted in the posh Hôtel d'Harscamp—"Whore's Camp" to GIs—from which a magnificent vista gave onto Namur's cathedral and the Meuse valley beyond. Once again was he sovereign of all he surveyed.

Village by village, croft by croft, American soldiers reclaimed what they had lost. Middleton deployed his VIII Corps headquarters back to Bastogne, where 101st Airborne paratroopers gave him a receipt certifying that the town was "used but serviceable" and "Kraut disinfected." The 7th Armored Division reentered ruined St.-Vith on January 23, capturing a German artillery officer whose latest diary entry read, "The battle noises come closer to the town. . . . I'm sending back all my personal belongings. One never knows."

Hitler had already decamped, leaving the Adlerhorst at six P.M. on January 15 and returning to Berlin the next morning aboard the *Brandenburg*. There would be no jackboots in Antwerp or even across the Meuse, no sundering of Allied armies, no petitions for peace from Washington and London. "I know the war is lost," he said, according to his Luftwaffe adjutant. "The superior power is too great. I've been betrayed." Still, he had extracted his armies from the Ardennes at a deliberate pace and in good order. Manteuffel abandoned fifty-three tanks along the roadside on a single day for want of fuel or spare parts, but many others escaped. In the south alone, thirteen divisions from Fifth Panzer Army and Seventh Army crossed five bridges thrown over the Our. The enemy, Eisenhower admitted to the Charlie-Charlies, "will probably manage to withdraw the bulk of his formations." Nearly two weeks would pass after the capture of Houffalize before the retreating Germans slammed the last steel door in the West Wall.

The east, meanwhile, could no longer "take care of itself." The Red Army had massed more than 180 divisions and nine thousand aircraft north of the Carpathians for a winter offensive; launched on January 12, the attack threatened the Reich from Hungary to the Baltic as never before. On January 22, Hitler ordered Sixth Panzer Army to Hungary to protect approaches to the few oil fields still in German possession. For weeks, Dietrich's weary divisions trudged across the Fatherland at a clopping pace to save gasoline. Tractors towed vehicles by the hundreds. The Eastern Front, a German historian later wrote, "showed itself again to be a suction pump which weakened other fronts."

In the west the war receded, this time for good. Once again Belgium and Luxembourg had been liberated. Children shrieked with joy while sledding near a stone quarry in Luxembourg, oblivious to the heckle of Thunderbolt cannons above the skulking enemy just to the east. The milky contrails of bombers bound for Cologne or Duisburg or Berlin etched the sky from horizon to horizon. Across the Ardennes women stood in their doorways, eyeing the olive-drab ranks tramping by. "Are you sure?" they asked. "Are you sure they have really gone for good?"

The dead "lay thick," wrote Martha Gellhorn as the guns fell silent, "like some dark shapeless vegetable." For weeks the iron ground precluded burials except with earth-moving equipment and air compressors; many of the three thousand civilians killed in the Ardennes were wrapped in blankets and stored in church crypts to await a thaw. At the American cemetery in Henri-Chapelle, fifteen miles east of Liège, grave diggers with backhoes worked around the clock to bury as many as five hundred GIs a day. Each was interred in a hole five feet deep, two feet wide, and six and a half feet long, but only after their overshoes had been removed for reuse. One dog tag was placed in the dead man's mouth, the other tacked to a cross or a Star of David atop the grave. Those whose tags had been lost first went to a morgue tent for photographs and dental charting. Fingertips were cleaned and injected with fluid to enhance prints, while technicians searched for laundry marks, tattoos, and other identifying clues, all to avoid conceding that here was yet another mother's son known but to God.

Among the dead gathered by Graves Registration teams combing the Bulge were a few score murdered by Peiper's men near Malmédy, recovered in two feet of snow when the Baugnez crossroad was recaptured in mid-January. Investigators carried the frozen corpses, stiff as statuary, to a heated shed. There field jackets and trouser pockets were sliced open with razor blades to inventory the effects, like those of Technician Fifth Grade Luke S. Swartz—"one fountain pen, two pencils, one New Testament, one comb, one good-luck charm"—and Private First Class Robert Cohen, who left this world carrying thirteen coins, two cigarette lighters, and a Hebrew prayer book.

An Army tally long after the war put U.S. battle losses in the Ardennes and Alsace from December 16 to January 25 at 105,000, including 19,246 dead. Thousands more suffered from trench foot, frostbite, and diseases. Even as American losses in the Pacific spiraled, roughly one in ten U.S. combat casualties during World War II occurred in the Bulge, where 600,000 GIs had fought, fourfold the number of combatants in blue and gray at Gettysburg. More than 23,000 were taken prisoner; most spent the duration in German camps, living on seven hundred calories a day and drinking ersatz coffee "so foul we used to bathe in it," as one captured officer later recalled. Families of soldiers from the obliterated 106th Division organized the "Agony Grapevine," conceived by a Pittsburgh lumberman whose son had gone missing on the Schnee Eifel. Volunteers with shortwave radios kept nightly vigils, listening to German propaganda broadcasts that sometimes named captured prisoners.

Of more than sixty thousand wounded and injured, those who had come closest to death often lay wide-eyed on their hospital cots, as one surgeon wrote, "like somebody rescued from the ledge of a skyscraper." Many would need months if not years to recover; a wounded officer described a jammed hospital courtyard in March filled with broken men on stretchers, "like the scene of the aftermath of the Battle of Atlanta in *Gone With the Wind*." A soldier wrote his parents in Nevada of narrowly surviving a gunfight on January 13, when a German shell scorched past him. "I looked down and my rt. hand was gone. . . . Dad, you'll have to be patient with me until I learn to bowl left-handed."

German losses would be difficult to count with precision, not least because the Americans tended to inflate them. (Patton at times concocted figures from whole cloth, or assumed that enemy casualties were tenfold the number of prisoners taken.) A U.S. Army estimate of 120,000 enemy losses in the month following the launch of HERBSTNEBEL was surely too high, and Bradley's claim of more than a quarter-million was preposterous. One postwar analysis put the figure at 82,000, another at 98,000. The official German history would cite 11,000 dead and 34,000 wounded, with an indeterminate number captured, missing, sick, and injured.

Model's success in extricating much of his force structure—in late January, Germany still listed 289 divisions, the same number counted by SHAEF on December 10—belied the Reich's true plight. "He bent the bow until it broke," Manteuffel said of the Army Group B commander. German forces in the west had virtually no fuel reserves and only about a third of the ammunition they needed. The Luftwaffe was so feeble that Hitler likened air warfare to "a rabbit hunt." More than seven hundred armored vehicles had been lost in the Ardennes, German manpower reserves were exhausted, and the Reichsbahn was so badly battered that as of January 19 all rail freight shipments were banned except for coal and Wehrmacht matériel. After more than five years of war, four million German soldiers had been killed, wounded, or captured. Hitler professed to find solace in a letter Frederick the Great had written during the Seven Years' War: "I started this war with the most wonderful army in Europe. Today I've got a muck heap."

Patton sensed the kill. "When you catch a carp and put him in the boat," he told reporters, "he flips his tail just before he dies. I think this is the German's last flip." Manteuffel came to the same conclusion. The Bulge had left the Wehrmacht so enfeebled, he warned, that Germany henceforth would be capable of fighting only "a corporal's war."

Few U.S. generals had enhanced their reputations in the Ardennes, except for battle stalwarts like McAuliffe. An American Army that considered itself the offensive spirit incarnate had paradoxically fought best on the defensive, as it had at Salerno, Anzio, and Mortain. The cautious January counterattack designed by Bradley and Montgomery, with Eisenhower's consent, extruded Germans from the Bulge rather than maneuvering or cudgeling them out; intended to "trap the maximum troops in the salient," the riposte trapped almost no one. Among top commanders, Patton proved the most distinguished. His remarkable agility in fighting the German Seventh Army, half the Fifth Panzer Army, and portions of the Sixth Panzer Army was best summarized in Bradley's six-word encomium: "One of our great combat leaders."

Churchill sought to repair Anglo-American discord with a gracious speech in the Commons. "United States troops have done almost all the fighting and have suffered almost all the losses," he said. "They have lost sixty to eighty men for every one of ours." The Bulge "is undoubtedly the greatest American battle of the war and will, I believe, be regarded as an ever-famous American victory." To his secretary, the prime minister later remarked that there was "no greater exhibition of power in history than that of the American Army fighting the battle of the Ardennes with its left hand and advancing from island to island toward Japan with its right." Montgomery also showed unwonted courtesy in notes to Eisenhower and "my dear Brad," telling the latter, "What a great honour it has been for me to command such fine troops." But honeyed words hardly mollified those determined to resent the continued British control of an American field army under Eisenhower's reconfiguration. "Why isn't Ike a man?" Patton wrote in his diary on January 24. "We will attack and win, in spite of Ike and Monty."

Eisenhower claimed that the German offensive "had in no sense achieved anything decisive." In fact, HERBSTNEBEL had hastened the Third Reich's demise. Hitler's preoccupation with the west in late 1944—and the diversion of supplies, armor, and reserves from the east—proved a "godsend for the Red Army," in the estimate of one German historian. Half of the Reich's fuel production in November and December had supported the Ardennes offensive, and now hundreds of German tanks and assault guns fighting the Russians were immobilized on the Eastern Front for lack of gasoline. By January 20, the Soviet juggernaut of two million men had torn a hole nearly 350 miles wide from East Prussia to the Carpathian foothills, bypassing or annihilating German defenses. Bound for the Oder River, Stalin's armies would be within fifty miles of Berlin at a time when the Anglo-Americans had yet to reach the Rhine. Here, a thousand kilometers from the Ardennes, was the greatest consequence of the Battle of the Bulge.

With the German tide receding, Eisenhower resumed sketching big arrows on the map. His timetable had been disrupted by six weeks or so, but his basic scheme for ending the war remained unaltered: Allied forces would continue destroying enemy forces west of the Rhine; they would seize bridgeheads over the river "when the ice menace is over" in March; and then they would advance into the German heartland. In a long message to the Combined Chiefs on January 20, he reiterated that Montgomery's attack north of the Ruhr was "our principal purpose," but believed "this area will be most strongly held by the enemy." SHAEF victualers also reckoned that no more than thirty-five Allied divisions could be supported above the Ruhr until new rail bridges spanned the Rhine. All the more reason then, in Eisenhower's calculation, for a second axis: he envisioned the bulk of Bradley's army group attacking from Mainz and Karlsruhe toward Frankfurt and Kassel—a corridor whose use Patton had long touted.

At present the Western Allies mustered 3.7 million soldiers in 73 divisions along a 729-mile front, with U.S. forces providing more than two-thirds of that strength. Eisenhower also had almost 18,000 combat aircraft—complemented by air fleets in Italy—and overwhelming dominance in artillery, armor, intelligence, supply, transportation, and the other sinews of modern combat. The Pentagon accelerated the sailing dates of seven U.S. divisions, diverted two others not previously earmarked for Europe, and combed out units in Alaska, Panama, and other quiescent theaters, where Marshall believed "plenty of fat meat" could be found. So desperate was the need for rifle-platoon leaders that an emergency school for new lieutenants opened in the Louis XV wing of the Château de Fontainebleau, with classes in map-reading, patrolling, and camouflage. Many of these students were among the almost 30,000 U.S. enlisted men who received battlefield commissions during the war. Army draft levies, which had just increased from 60,000 to 90,000 men a month, would jump again in March to 100,000. SHAEF expected the western armies to grow to 85 divisions by May.

That would have to suffice. Britain had nearly run out of men and the American replacement pool was described as "almost depleted," with much hard fighting still to come against Germany and Japan. Eisenhower asked for a hundred thousand Marines; he would get none. Patton calculated that victory in western Europe required "twenty more divisions of infantry"; that was a pipe dream. Eisenhower would have to win with the forces now committed to his theater, and no more.

The Battle of the Bulge had affirmed once again that war is never linear, but rather a chaotic, desultory enterprise of reversal and advance, blunder and élan, despair and elation. Valor, cowardice, courage—each had been displayed in this spectacle of a marching world. For magnitude and unalloyed violence, the battle in the Ardennes was unlike any seen before in American history, nor like any to be seen again. Yet as always, even as armies and army groups collided, it was the fates of individual soldiers that drew the eye.

"Everybody shares the same universals—hope, love, humor, faith," Private First Class Richard E. Cowan of the 2nd Infantry Division had written his family in Kansas on December 5, his twenty-second birthday. Two weeks later he was dead, killed near Krinkelt after holding off German attackers with a machine gun long enough to cover his comrades' escape. "It is such a bitter dose to have to take," his mother confessed after hearing the news, "and I am not a bit brave about it." Cowan would be awarded the Medal of Honor, one of thirty-two recognizing heroics in the Bulge. Like so many thousands of others, he would be interred in one of those two-by-five-by-six-and-a-half-foot graves, along with his last full measure of hope, love, humor, and faith. The marching world marched on.

Affixed to a wall in Montgomery's caravan, amid the photos of Rommel and Rundstedt and the field marshal himself, was a copy of Sir Francis Drake's meditation before his attack on Cádiz in 1587. "There must be a beginning of any great matter," Drake had written, "but the continuing unto the end until it is thoroughly finished yields the true glory." So too in this great matter, this struggle for civilization itself. The moment had come to seize the true glory.

Part Four

10. ARGONAUTS

Citizens of the World

MORNING sun and a tranquil breeze carried hints of an early Mediterranean spring across Grand Harbour, where strains of "The Star-Spangled Banner" could be heard from a Royal Navy band practicing aboard H.M.S. *Sirius* on Friday, February 2. Not since Eisenhower's arrival with his headquarters in July 1943, just before the invasion of Sicily, had the little island of Malta seethed with such excitement. Hundreds of Allied officers now swarmed through the capital, Valletta, where an Anglo-American strategy conference code-named CRICKET had convened to consider the weightiest matters of war and peace.

Sixteen thousand tons of Axis bombs had pulverized Malta from 1940 to 1943, clogging every street with drifted rubble and giving Valletta the gaunt, haunted mien of the Maltese themselves. Difficulties in finding enough intact buildings to house the CRICKET legations had exasperated conference planners, who warned that "a certain amount of inconvenience must be expected." (They also cautioned that "spreading of rumors and gossip in Malta is a national pastime, so please discuss nothing in public.") The Americans alone occupied sixteen barracks, palazzi, and improvised hostels, including the local YWCA and the Lascaris Bastion, a dank warren excavated eons ago by the Knights of St. John, a monastic order founded during the First Crusade. The honey-hued sandstone long favored by Maltese builders was so porous that even buildings unbruised by enemy bombs were said by one airman to resemble "ventilated cold-storage vaults." Allied officers took their meals in winter garb, and an admiral described trying to sleep while wrapped in a dressing gown, raincoat, overcoat, and several blankets. To provide more billets, nine U.S. Navy ships had berthed in Grand Harbour, lauded by a visitor as "perhaps the most astonishing natural anchorage in the world." An LST from Naples served as a floating garage for staff cars.

To compensate for any discomfort, every officer was permitted seventy pounds of luggage, and CRICKET's British hosts assigned each a batman to fetch the daily newspaper. "The shine he put on my shoes lasted for weeks," an American delegate marveled. An efficient valet service pressed uniforms overnight, and bars opened punctually at six P.M. A twenty-piece orchestra played until midnight in Admiralty House, once home to the Captain of the Galleys; marble scrolls on the wide staircase listed the name of every British sea dog to command the Mediterranean fleet for the past century and a half, Lord Nelson among them. A local librarian gave walking tours to explain Malta's exotic history, beginning with the Phoenicians and the Carthaginians: how shipwrecked Saint Paul converted the Maltese to Christianity with proselytizing fervor and perhaps a miracle or two; how the knights in the sixteenth century paid the Holy Roman emperor Charles V an annual rent of one falcon, due on All Souls' Day, a curiosity used by Dashiell Hammett in his novel *The Maltese Falcon;* how Turkish brigands captured Fort St. Elmo in 1565, nailing defenders to wooden crosses that were floated across Grand Harbour; how the Maltese retaliated by decapitating Turkish prisoners and ramming the severed heads into cannon breeches, then firing them at the enemy redoubt. Malta clearly was a place of no quarter.

At 9:30 A.M. on Friday, the pugnacious gray prow of the cruiser U.S.S. *Quincy* glided past that same Fort St. Elmo, escorted by U.S.S. *Savannah*, revived and refitted after nearly being sunk by a German glide bomb off Salerno seventeen months earlier. A half-dozen Spitfires wheeled overhead like osprey, and whooping crowds lined the rooftops and the beetling seawalls around the quays. "The entrance to the harbor is so small that it seemed impossible for our big ship to get through," a passenger on *Quincy* wrote.

As the cruiser crept at four knots along the stone embankment, a solitary figure could be seen sitting on the wing bridge, wrapped in a boat cloak with a tweed tam-o'-shanter atop his leonine head and a cigarette holder clenched between his teeth. For this journey he had been assigned a sequence of code names—BRONZE, GARNET, STEEL, and, from the British, ADMIRAL Q—but now there was no hiding his identity. Tars and swabs came to attention on weather decks across the anchorage. A field piece at the fort boomed a slow salute of twenty-one rounds, and that band aboard *Sirius* tootled through the much-rehearsed American anthem to herald the arrival of Franklin D. Roosevelt, president of the United States. The diplomat Charles E. Bohlen described the moment:

> The sun was glistening on the waves and a light breeze was snapping the flags flying from the British warships and walls of the city. . . . Roosevelt sat on deck, his black cape around his shoulders, acknowledging salutes

from the British man-of-war and the rolling cheers of spectators crowding the quays. He was very much a historical figure.

Across the harbor, on the quarterdeck of H.M.S. *Orion*, another historical figure stood in a naval uniform, puffing a cigar and waving his yachtsman's cap until the American president spotted Winston Churchill and waved back. An abrupt hush fell across the harbor. "It was one of those moments," another witness wrote, "when all seems to stand still and one is conscious of a mark in history." *Quincy* eased her starboard flank against Berth 9. Thick hawsers lassoed the bollards, and the harbor pilot signaled belowdecks: "Through with engines."

Since leaving Washington eleven days earlier, Roosevelt had traveled just under five thousand miles. Sea voyages always enchanted him and this trip had been no different, despite an annoying cold that confined him to his cabin for part of the passage. He devoted little time to the briefing books and studies prepared by the State Department, preferring to sleep or watch movies—*Laura, Our Hearts Were Young and Gay, To Have and Have Not*—or thumb through pulp mysteries packed for the trip, with portentous titles like *Death Defies the Doctor* and *Blood upon the Snow*. A special elevator hoisted him to the flag bridge, where he liked to sit in an admiral's swivel chair, staring at the pewter sea and the destroyers darting fore and aft. A strong-swimming Secret Service agent stood near, prepared to leap overboard with the president in his arms should *Quincy* be torpedoed or mined. But two suspected submarine contacts proved to be fish, and the only peril encountered was a nasty swell two days out of Newport News that caused the destroyer *Satterlee* to roll sixty-one degrees. After supper, Roosevelt often played poker or gin rummy for half a penny a point, ruminating on the recent election—he had just won a fourth term, by 432 electoral votes to 99—and on the subsequent inauguration, held not at the Capitol but on the White House portico, with thirteen of his grandchildren capering about.

To celebrate the president's sixty-third birthday on January 30, his traveling companions had wheeled four cakes into his cabin—one for each term—followed by a fifth that displayed a big question mark etched in frosting. *Quincy*'s crew gave him a brass ashtray fashioned from a shell casing fired at Normandy on D-Day.

With *Quincy* made fast, the tweet of a bosun's whistle shortly after ten A.M. announced the first visitors, and George Marshall trooped up the gangplank accompanied by Admiral Ernest J. King, the U.S. Navy chief. They found the president basking topside in a wicker chair near a port gun mount. The officers exchanged silent looks of dismay at Roosevelt's appearance: he was haggard and ashen, with violet circles beneath his eyes. Bohlen, who also boarded the cruiser, later wrote:

> I was shocked by Roosevelt's physical appearance.... He was not only frail and desperately tired, he looked ill. I never saw Roosevelt look as bad as he did then, despite a week's leisurely voyage at sea.

Time magazine had catalogued the many rumors about the president's health: that he had been secretly rushed to the Mayo Clinic, that three psychiatrists attended him when he traveled, that he was anemic. The truth was worse. Not for decades would it be revealed that his blood pressure had climbed from 128 over 82, in 1930, to 260 over 150, in December 1944. In the past year he had shed nearly thirty pounds. ("Can't eat," he had complained in December. "Cannot taste food.") An examination by a cardiologist disclosed "a bluish discoloration of his skin, lips, and nail beds," with labored breathing, "bouts of abdominal distress," and symptoms of an enlarged heart and fluid in the lungs—all leading to a diagnosis of congestive heart failure. He had indeed been anemic, from chronic bleeding hemorrhoids exacerbated by his inability to stand or walk, and he had suffered symptoms of a mild heart attack in August while giving a speech in Washington State. For various ailments he was periodically treated with phenobarbital and injections of codeine. His personal physician ordered that as little as possible be revealed to Roosevelt, who took the prescribed green digitalis pills without asking what they were and made fitful efforts to halve his daily smoking and drinking to ten cigarettes and one and a half cocktails, as recommended. "Lots of sleep & still need more," he would write his secretary from Valletta later on Friday. Each day the White House press office leafed through official photographs in search of images to show the public that did not suggest a decrepit, dying man. That task had become almost impossible.

Yet if the body was frail, the inner man remained steadfast. To the end of his days Roosevelt would be, as the scholar James MacGregor Burns later wrote, an "improviser, a practical man, a dreamer and a sermonizer, a soldier of the faith, a prince of the state." Today he was eager to hear of Allied progress on the Western Front, and since Eisenhower had chosen not to attend CRICKET—he pled the demands of battle—Marshall and King spent more than half an hour describing to Roosevelt the SHAEF plan for reaching the Rhine, seizing bridgeheads, and advancing by two complementary avenues toward the Ruhr. They also outlined Montgomery's alternative single-prong thrust in the north. Calling for a map, the president reminisced about bicycling through the Rhineland as a young man, green and carefree. He knew that terrain, knew it well, he said, and

Eisenhower's scheme made perfect sense. As commander-in-chief, he approved.

Another trill of the bosun's pipe announced Churchill's arrival on the quarterdeck, beaming and natty in his tailored blue uniform with a handkerchief peeking from the breast pocket. He too was traveling under various noms de guerre—Colonel Warden, Colonel Kent, TUNGSTEN, CHROME—and, at age seventy, he too had been ill, arriving by plane in Valletta three days earlier febrile and out of sorts. "His work has deteriorated a lot in the last few months," his physician, Charles Moran, noted in his diary on Wednesday. "He has become very wordy." Sunshine, whiskey, and a few winning hands of bezique seemed to restore him, and for an hour over lunch he prattled to Roosevelt about his "complete devotion to the principles enunciated in America's Declaration of Independence." The president smiled indulgently; he often complained of "pushing Winston uphill in a wheelbarrow" when it came to applying those principles to Britain's imperial possessions. The war in Europe would likely end this year, Roosevelt said, although the defeat of Japan might not come until 1947. Peace would bring a chance to remake a principled world.

Churchill retrieved an eight-inch cigar, firing it with a small candle on a tobacco tray at his elbow. Citizens in too many countries feared their own governments, he said, and they must be freed from such fear. "As long as blood flows from my veins," he added with a theatrical flourish, "I will stand for this." Roosevelt could only agree; together they would spread the Four Freedoms around the globe, including freedom from fear. But for now the president intended to see a bit of Malta before they reconvened for dinner. As Churchill turned to go, Roosevelt confided that he had slept ten hours every night since leaving Washington, but had yet to feel "slept out."

Off he went for thirty miles in a touring car on this sparkling day, escorted by the island's governor-general, through battered Valletta and Ghajn Tuffieha and walled Mdina. Maltese peasants and tradesmen snatched the caps from their heads as the convoy sped by, saluting with a knuckle touched to the brow. By 4:30 that afternoon Roosevelt was back aboard *Quincy*, where Churchill eventually joined him for cocktails in the wardroom. The prime minister, having insisted on a leisurely bath, was half an hour late. The Charlie-Charlies also arrived, except for Hap Arnold, the Army Air Forces commander, recuperating at home from his fourth heart attack.

To president and prime minister the chiefs reported "complete agreement" on Eisenhower's plan for concluding the war in Europe. Churchill, who was uncommonly chatty even by his voluble standard, tendered advice about reserve divisions along the Rhine. He also proposed occupying as much of Austria as possible to keep the Russians at bay; the prime minister had long recognized that the maneuvering of armies would shape postwar politics, but this was the first time he had suggested positioning Anglo-American troops to impede Soviet expansion.

Roosevelt nodded now and again but said little. At eight o'clock, dinner was served.

This amiable gathering concealed the most rancorous confrontation of the war between the British and American high commands. The donnybrook had begun innocently enough three days earlier, when the Combined Chiefs met at noon on Tuesday for the 182nd time since first making common cause in January 1942. Above Grand Harbour, in a former market building known as Montgomery House and made so noisome by kerosene heaters that the officers preferred to sit bundled in their overcoats, a SHAEF delegation led by Beetle Smith once more presented Eisenhower's plan: destroy the enemy west of the Rhine, jump the river, then advance "into the heart of Germany" on two axes. Straightening the line along the Rhine, from Alsace to Holland, would forestall further German counterattacks by using the river as a defensive barrier while the Allies coiled for their final offensive. The entire U.S. Ninth Army would reinforce Montgomery in the north, Smith said; the second lunge toward Frankfurt and Kassel, by Bradley's 12th Army Group, would help envelop the Ruhr from the south and deliver a right-hand roundhouse punch should the left hook of 21st Army Group be stymied.

Again Field Marshal Brooke took on the role of naysayer. Thin, sallow, and round-shouldered, privately known as Colonel Shrapnel, Brooke was both formidable and easily parodied. "Men admired, feared, and liked him: in that order, perhaps," the *Economist* magazine observed. His civil passions were homely and endearing: lake fishing, Cox's Orange Pippin apples, mimicry, a bit of opera, wildlife photography (in which he was a pioneer), and, most especially, birds—he could go on and on about Knipe's *Monograph of the Pigeons*. Raised in France, the youngest of nine children born to a baronet from Northern Ireland, he had hoped to become a physician. Instead, as a young soldier Brooke proved to be "a gunner of genius in the great barrage-duels of the First World War," a biographer wrote. Exploiting both mathematics and psychology, he was particularly adept at the creeping barrage and a practice known as "searching back," intended to catch unwary enemies as they emerged from cover.

The tactic befitted the man. Never convivial, Brooke after another five years of world war was often dyspeptic and dispirited. "I don't feel that I can stand another day working with Winston," he had confided to his diary a few days earlier. "He is finished and gone, incapable of grasping any military situation and unable to get a decision." But it was the cousins who most irked him, particularly as British clout dwindled and American influence grew. Now, as if again "searching back" at the Somme, he targeted Smith.

The British chiefs, Brooke said in his clipped staccato, believed the Allies had "not sufficient strength available for two major operations." One attack avenue must be chosen, and only one. Montgomery's route in the north appeared "the most promising," given its proximity to both Antwerp and the Ruhr. Bradley's southern assault would dilute Allied strength by diverting bridging kit and other matériel. The Bulge had revealed the folly of Eisenhower's broad-front strategy in spreading an attack too thin. "Closing up the Rhine on its whole length," as SHAEF proposed, could retard the advance. Would Montgomery have to wait on the riverbank until the Colmar Pocket was eradicated? Until Bradley's forces crossed the Roer and cleared the Saar?

This argument had dragged on for five months, but Smith kept his poise to rally in defense of the SHAEF plan. Eisenhower intended to support "every single division which could be maintained logistically" in the north, he said, but topography required Montgomery to attack the Rhine on a narrow, four-division front that "might bog down" if confronted by Rundstedt's residual host. Montgomery himself had acknowledged that barely two dozen divisions could be supported east of the Rhine in his sector until rail bridges spanned the river; Eisenhower was committed to supplying three dozen there, plus another ten divisions to exploit any breakthrough. But why should nearly forty other American and French divisions remain dormant when Germany clearly lacked sufficient strength to defend the entire Western Front? Putting all eggs in a single basket, Smith added, would be risky.

Marshall concurred, warning that it was "not safe to rely on one line of advance only." The session adjourned without agreement, and Smith hurriedly cabled Eisenhower in Versailles. The British "will insist on something in writing to clinch the fact that the main effort on the north is to be pushed," he wrote; they also wanted assurances that an attack on the Ruhr would not be delayed "until you have eliminated every German west of the Rhine." The supreme commander replied promptly:

> You may assure the Combined Chiefs of Staff in my name that I will seize the Rhine crossings in the north just as soon as this is a feasible operation and without waiting to close the Rhine throughout its length. Further, I will advance across the Rhine in the north with maximum strength and complete determination.

This pleased Brooke not at all, given Eisenhower's continued insistence on bifurcating his force. To his diary on Wednesday, Colonel Shrapnel confided, "When we met at 2:30 P.M. the situation was more confused than ever, as Bedell Smith had sent another wire to Ike which was also impossible and Ike had wired back. So we were again stuck. . . . I am feeling very tired, and old!"

Worse was to come. As Brooke prepared to climb into bed at midnight in the San Anton Palace, Smith appeared at his door for further discussion. The conversation grew warm. Brooke wondered whether Eisenhower had "his hands too full," and whether his headquarters was too far from the front. Was he in fact "strong enough" for the job, or too readily swayed by whichever commander had seen him last? "Goddamn it," Smith barked. "Let's have it out here and now." For an hour they traded jabs, until spent by exhaustion and the late hour. "I think the talk did both of us good," Brooke wrote before falling asleep, "and may help in easing the work tomorrow."

That was unlikely. Alerted by Smith to the late-night altercation, George Marshall had had enough. Not only did the British carping imply lack of faith in Eisenhower, but Brooke and his ilk appeared to champion Montgomery against his superior officer. "Please leave this to me," Marshall told Admiral King.

As the chiefs convened again on Thursday afternoon, February 1, Marshall asked that the room be cleared of all subordinate officers and note-takers. No sooner had Brooke taken his chair than Marshall bored in. Why were the British so worried about the influence that Bradley and Patton had on Eisenhower? What about Roosevelt's influence? Did the British consider that pernicious, too? "The president practically never sees General Eisenhower, and never writes to him. That is at my advice because he is an Allied commander," Marshall said, eyebrows knit and voice rising to a wrathful timbre. In fact the British chiefs could not be "nearly as much worried as the American chiefs of staff are about the immediate pressures of Mr. Churchill on General Eisenhower." The prime minister never hesitated to hector the supreme commander directly, day or night, circumventing the Combined Chiefs. "I think your worries," Marshall declared, "are on the wrong foot."

He had not finished. Should the British succeed in interposing a ground commander between the supreme commander and his three army group commanders, Marshall intended to resign—or so he had told Eisenhower. Montgomery was behind much of this pother, Marshall charged; despite being given "practically everything he asked for," including the U.S. Ninth Army, he plainly craved "complete command." If truth be told, Montgomery was an "over-cautious commander who wants everything," an "impudent and disloyal subordinate" who treated all American officers with "open contempt."

A stunned silence followed this tirade. After the war Brooke would write: "Marshall clearly understood nothing of strategy and could not even argue out the relative merits of various alternatives. Being unable to judge for himself he trusted and backed Ike, and felt it his duty to guard him from interference." But Admiral Cunningham, the first sea lord, later observed that "Marshall's complaint was not unjustified."

For now, American indignation carried the day. Brooke fell silent, the chiefs promptly agreed to endorse SHAEF's master plan, and the last great internecine tempest of the war subsided. For another month, the British conspired to replace Tedder as deputy supreme commander with Harold Alexander, whom they considered more pliant despite Brooke's dismissal of him as "a very, very small man [who] cannot see big." Eisenhower, braced by Marshall, advised London that if Alexander should arrive at SHAEF from Italy, he would find few military duties to occupy him. Spaatz would succeed Tedder as senior airman in the west, and there would be "no question whatsoever of placing between me and my army group commanders any intermediary headquarters."

Few could doubt that the Americans now had the whip hand. "The P.M. was sore," Kay Summersby jotted in her diary, "but E said he would get over it."

Light rain spattered Luqa airdrome southwest of Valletta in the smallest hours of Saturday, February 3. A fleet of twenty-five transport aircraft, collectively known as Mission No. 17, stood beneath arc lights on the bustling flight line. Trucks and staff cars crept along the runway in search of this plane or that. Baggage handlers hoisted suitcases and crates into the bays—sealed boxes with secret documents bore black bands and yellow tags—while flight chiefs with clipboards carefully scrutinized the blue-and-white passes of the passengers clambering into the cabins. CRICKET was over; now would come ARGONAUT, a conference with Joseph Stalin at the Crimean resort of Yalta, on the Black Sea.

Roosevelt in recent months had proposed venues from Scotland to Jerusalem. Stalin, pleading ill health and the demands of his great offensive against Germany's Eastern Front, countered with Yalta, a proposal that sent Anglo-American officials paging through their Baedeker guides. "I emphasized the difficulties that this decision made for you, but that in consideration of Marshal Stalin's health you were prepared to meet them," W. Averell Harriman, the U.S. ambassador to Moscow, had written Roosevelt in late December. Among the difficulties cited, aside from the seven-hour, fourteen-hundred-mile flight from Malta to a remote locale and

Roosevelt's own precarious health: "toilet facilities will be meager [and] there are no bars"; travelers were advised to bring sleeping bags and ample "bug powder"; electric current at Yalta was an odd 330 volts; and the Turkish government had given overflight permission for Mission No. 17, but "cannot guarantee that the planes will not be fired upon." To a man the president's advisers had opposed his making such an arduous journey, but Roosevelt insisted. As his aide Harry Hopkins later remarked, "his adventurous spirit was forever leading him to go to unusual places."

Roosevelt and Churchill had agreed to limit their respective entourages to 35 people; instead, a total of 700 were flying from Malta, with more descending on the Crimea by train from Moscow and others arriving by ship. The Americans numbered 330, among them 14 generals, 15 full colonels, 18 bodyguards, and 8 cooks and stewards. The British travel roster ran on for eleven pages, including 62 signalers, 58 Royal Marines, a catering captain, a pair of cinema operators, 5 map-room officers, and 17 members of Churchill's personal staff. Each traveler had been told to "invent a suitable and plausible cover story to account for departure and absence" from home, and the British Board of Trade discreetly issued 2,400 ration coupons for purchases of clothing suitable for "a place abroad where the climate is cold." Churchill alone requested an extra 72 coupons to buy new uniforms and underwear.

In view of the rustic conditions anticipated at Yalta, the commissary list prepared by British provisioners for transport aboard Mission No. 17 included 144 bottles of whiskey, 144 bottles of sherry, 144 bottles of gin, 200 pounds of bacon, 200 pounds of coffee, 50 pounds of tea, 100 rolls of toilet paper, 2,500 paper napkins, 650 dinner plates, 350 tea cups and saucers, 500 tumblers, 100 wineglasses, 20 salt and pepper shakers, 400 sets of cutlery, 36 tablecloths, and 13 sugar bowls. Moreover, R.M.S. *Franconia,* bound for Yalta through the Dardanelles, carried a supplemental 864 bottles of whiskey and gin, 180 bottles of sherry, 20,000 American cigarettes, 500 cigars, and 1,000 boxes of matches. A separate shipment designated "Yalta Voyage 208" included several hundred bottles of Rhine wine, vermouth, Gordon's gin, Johnnie Walker Red Label and King George IV whiskies, and 1928 Veuve Clicquot champagne, as well as 20,000 Chesterfield and Philip Morris cigarettes, 500 Robert Burns cigars, and a carton of toilet paper. For good measure, a consignment for Yalta entrusted to the British ambassador in Moscow included a dozen bottles of 1928 Château Margaux, cognac, beer, 10,000 Players cigarettes, and 48 bottles of White Horse, Black & White, and Vat 69 whiskies. No one would go thirsty. Churchill advised the White House that whiskey "is good for typhus and deadly on lice."

"We left Malta in darkness," an Army colonel wrote, "like migrating swans." The first plane lifted into the low ceiling at 1:50 A.M., blue flame spurting from the exhaust manifolds as the pilot pushed the throttle to full power on Luqa's short runway. Other aircraft followed at ten-minute intervals. The flight plan would take these swans across the Mediterranean almost to German-occupied Crete, followed by a ninety-degree left turn over the Aegean, past Athens and Samothrace, before the planes crossed European Turkey and the Black Sea. With radio silence imposed, pilots extinguished their lights at takeoff. Passengers set their watches ahead two hours and tried to sleep.

Churchill boarded a four-engine C-54 Skymaster provided him by the Army Air Forces; he claimed that British artisans had used five thousand animal hides to upholster the plush cabin. Huddled in his greatcoat, the prime minister resembled "a poor hot pink baby about to cry," in the description of his daughter Sarah, who was in his traveling party.

Down the flight line stood C-54 No. 252, named *Sacred Cow,* which would be making her maiden flight with a passenger identified on the manifest only as "The Admiral." Soon a caged elevator hoisted Roosevelt in his wheelchair into the plane's aft cabin. Churchill would later recall that the president's face "had a transparency, an air of purification." There was "a faraway look in his eyes."

Spitfire and P-38 fighter escorts already droned overhead. Aircrews in recent weeks had experimented to determine the lowest possible altitude that balanced safety and comfort: the flight would be made at 6,000 feet. The engines coughed and caught. Silver propellers whirred beneath a wet moon. At 3:30 A.M. *Sacred Cow* nosed into the night and banked to the east.

A Fateful Conference

WEDGED into a natural amphitheater between the Black Sea and the Crimean Mountains, Yalta seemed to have been built for drama. The towering peaks, bearing the gray scars of ancient avalanches, loomed above the town like "a vision of the Sierras," as Mark Twain had written in *The Innocents Abroad.* Anton Chekhov, who wrote *The Cherry Orchard* and *Three Sisters* at his villa in Yalta, observed in "The Lady with the Pet Dog":

> The stories told of the immorality in such places as Yalta are to a great extent untrue . . . tales of easy conquests, of trips to the mountains, and the tempting thought of a swift, fleeting love affair. . . . The town with its cypresses had quite a deathlike air, but the sea still broke noisily

on the shore; a single barge was rocking on the waves, and a lantern was blinking sleepily on it.

That sea—to the ancients, Pontus Euxinus, Sea Friendly to Strangers— had broken noisily on a shore occupied by Cimmerians and Scythians, Greeks and Genoese, Tartars and Russian princes. Two thousand annual hours of sunshine—comparable to Nice—suggested salutary conditions on the Crimean coast, and the first of three dozen sanatoriums for tuberculars and other invalids had been financed by progressive intellectuals, including Chekhov and Maxim Gorky. In 1920, by Lenin's decree, Yalta became a workers' spa, a proletarian paradise of fig, mulberry, and beech groves overlooking an inky sea of imponderable depth.

Then came the Germans. Three years of warfare, including the epic siege at nearby Sevastopol, utterly despoiled the Crimea, and Stalin's invitation to the Anglo-Americans had triggered weeks of frenzied efforts to make Yalta presentable. Thousands of Red Army soldiers filled bomb craters, refurbished gutted houses, and shoveled manure from nineteenth-century palaces that the Germans had used to stable their horses. Fifteen hundred rail coaches ran from Moscow, a four-day journey, bringing carpets, window glass, and even brass doorknobs, which the absconding enemy had sawed off and carried away. Chefs, waiters, chambermaids, maîtres d's, linens, beds, curtains, dishes, and silverware were gathered from the Hotels Metropol, National, Splendide, and Moscow for duty at Yalta. Each night a Russian convoy swept across the Crimea, rooting through farmhouses, boarding rooms, and schools for shaving mirrors, washbowls, coat hangers, clocks, and paintings. Swarms of plasterers, plumbers, painters, electricians, and glazers worked around the clock. Five hundred Romanian prisoners-of-war planted shrubs and semitropical flowers in riotous profusion.

British and American support ships were diverted to Sevastopol when it was found that Yalta's coastal waters remained clogged with German mines. ("They didn't leave a map," a Russian officer explained with a shrug.) From the ships' holds, office furniture, two hundred tons of radio equipment, and all that tipple aboard *Franconia* was trucked for fifty miles— and nine hundred hairpin turns—across the mountains. A "sanitary survey," conducted in Yalta on January 28 by U.S. Navy physicians, found a "marked infestation with bed bugs"; hundreds of mattresses and pillows were sprayed with a 10 percent solution of DDT dissolved in kerosene. Linens were dusted with DDT powder and, for good measure, Russian kitchen staffs received instruction in "hygienic practices."

Four Soviet regiments arrived to safeguard Yalta, in addition to 160 fighter planes, several antiaircraft batteries, and Stalin's security cordon of

620 men, reinforced by a personal bodyguard of a dozen Georgians carrying tommy guns. Seventy-four thousand security checks were made within a twenty-kilometer diameter of the town, and 835 suspected "anti-Soviet elements" arrested. Three concentric circles of sentries ringed the Soviet, British, and American compounds, and the woods grew stiff with shadowy agents. Eavesdroppers with listening bugs and directional microphones also arrived from Moscow, intent on overhearing as many private conversations as possible.

Despite the efforts of all those Soviet maids and maîtres d's, ARGO-NAUT would be more rough-hewn than earlier conclaves in venues like Casablanca, Quebec, and Washington. "Regret necessity for nineteen full colonels sleeping one room," a terse message to the British delegation warned. Lieutenant General Hastings Ismay, the prime minister's military assistant, later wrote, "It would have been difficult to find a more unget-at-able, inconvenient, or unsuitable meeting place."

Yet apprehension ran far deeper than concerns over crowded quarters and bed bugs. "This may well be a fateful conference," Churchill had told Roosevelt. "The end of this war may well prove to be more disappointing than was the last." ARGONAUT would help shape the postwar world. Now all that remained was for the Argonauts themselves to arrive.

Sacred Cow touched down at 12:10 P.M. on Saturday at Saki airfield on the Crimean west coast, followed twenty minutes later by the prime minister's upholstered Skymaster. Wearing his cape and a gray fedora with the brim turned up, Roosevelt descended in the caged elevator to the icy runway, where a Secret Service agent lifted him into a Russian jeep. He was greeted by Vyacheslav Molotov, the Soviet foreign minister, known privately to the Americans as "Stone Ass." With Churchill standing at his elbow smoking a cigar, the president took the salute of a high-stepping, white-gloved honor guard from whose rifles live ammunition had been confiscated. All twenty-five planes from Mission No. 17 stood in perfect alignment as the captain of the guard marched past holding a sword "straight in front of him like a great icicle," wrote Charles Moran. A band crashed through three national anthems and then the "Internationale."

> We will destroy this world of violence,
> Down to the foundations, and then
> We will build our new world.
> He who was nothing will become everything.

"The president looked old and thin and drawn," Moran added. "He sat looking straight ahead with his mouth open, as if he were not taking things in." Three large tents stood near the crude control tower. Tables inside were heaped with platters of salmon, sturgeon, whitefish, caviar, and black bread. Beside steaming glasses of tea stood pitchers of vodka, as well as bottles of cognac and champagne. Marshall, muffled in a fur-lined khaki overcoat, glanced disapprovingly at this repast and muttered, "Let's get going."

Soon a weaving convoy of sedans and buses followed the unpaved road to Yalta, eighty miles and five hours away. No photograph or Movietone footage could have more vividly conveyed to the Western Allies the intensity of the war being waged by their eastern comrades: mile upon mile of gutted buildings, barns, crofts, trains, tanks, trucks. Peasant women in shawls and knee boots waved from barren fields and from orchards reduced to flinders. Except for a few sheep, no livestock could be seen, or farm machinery, or men for that matter, apart from the sentries in great-coats and astrakhan hats, one every hundred yards, saluting each passing vehicle with an abrupt extension of their rifles at a thirty-degree angle. Churchill passed the time by reciting Lord Byron's epic poem *Don Juan*. Beyond bleak Simferopol, the terrain lifted from snowy moor to mountain. The Route Romanoff followed a high, winding trace around the limestone flank of Roman-Kosh, the highest peak in the Crimea, before descending to the serpentine coastal road above the sea, each mile warmer than the mile before, until shortly before six P.M. they came to Yalta. Female traffic wardens waved them through with a waggle of red and yellow flags.

Churchill and the British contingent peeled away for their assigned billets in the Villa Vorontsov, described by Ismay as "a fantastic mixture of bogus Scottish castle and Moorish palace"; its furnishings, another guest said, radiated "an almost terrifying hideosity." Built for a Russian governor in the early nineteenth century, with a handsome view of the Black Sea, the estate had served as a headquarters for Field Marshal Erich von Manstein during the Germans' Crimean offensive. Great logs now burned in the hearths, and Russian housekeepers in black livery scurried about in an effort to accommodate the visitors. When Sarah Churchill mentioned that caviar was improved by lemon juice, a tub holding a lemon tree heavy with fruit appeared in the foyer. When Air Marshal Portal noted that a large glass tank lacked fish, goldfish swam on the instant.

Alas, Moran complained, "nothing is left out but cleanliness." Bedbugs soon brought American fumigators with their DDT sprayers—too late for Churchill's badly gnawed feet, although a bigger, bug-free bed was shipped by special train from Moscow. Generals and admirals now shared cells built for serfs—"We sleep in droves like prep school boys in dormitories," one officer wrote his wife—and just two bathrooms with cold taps served the entire villa. Sarah wrote her mother of seeing "3 field marshals queuing for a bucket" to relieve themselves. Yalta, the prime minister would harrumph, was surely "the Riviera of Hades." Perhaps only Brooke was happy: "I picked up a great northern diver, scoters, cormorants, many gulls and other diving ducks," he told his diary. "Also dolphins feeding on shoals of fish."

Ten miles away the Americans settled into the fifty-room Villa Livadia, a two-story, flat-roofed palace of limestone and marble set on a sea bluff. Suitcases and musette bags were piled in the grand foyer, as the travelers arrived to be greeted by servants who bowed at the waist and addressed Roosevelt as "Your Excellency." ("The president did not seem displeased," one general noted.) Here too the guests found an odd mixture of elegance and inconvenience. Waiters in swallowtail coats carried silver trays with little cakes and scalding tea in tall glasses, and caviar hillocks seemed to rise from every oak table. In a makeshift salon, a Russian barber and manicurist stood ready to groom the Americans, and the lush grounds around Livadia offered fifteen kilometers of walking paths lined with cedars, yews, and black cypresses shaped like exclamation points. Yet only four bathtubs and nine lavatories served more than one hundred Americans living on two floors in the villa; cards thumbtacked to the doors listed bathroom assignments by age, rank, and sex. (The president's daughter, Anna, was one of two women in the traveling party.) For the impatient, auxiliary latrines were dug in a nearby deer park. A notice to all delegates asked, "Please do not pilfer rooms and dining services for souvenirs."

An air of tragedy hung over Livadia, which had been built in 1911 as a summer palace for the last czar, Nicholas II, and his czarina, Alexandra, at a cost of two million rubles, paid in gold. Orthodox priests had spattered holy water and swung smoldering censers to bless each room. Little imagination was required to see the royal couple with their four daughters and ailing son arriving by imperial train from St. Petersburg, snacking on reindeer tongue and smoked herring as they cavorted through the villa or aboard the three-masted, twin-funneled royal yacht anchored below the bluff. It was said that lion-head embellishments on the marble benches outside the front entrance caricatured the czar; that he slept in a different room every night to foil assassins; that a private outside staircase had been used by the mystical Rasputin to visit the czarina. After abdicating in 1917, Nicholas futilely petitioned to retire at Livadia; instead, he and his family were murdered, and the villa became first a tuberculosis asylum and then a German division headquarters in 1941. Hitler had promised the estate to Rundstedt after the war for services rendered, and thus it escaped the torch.

Now Roosevelt slept in the czar's first-floor suite, whose décor was described as "early Pullman car," with brass lamps shaded in fringed orange silk and bottle-green harem cushions scattered across the floor. Marshall was assigned another royal bedroom upstairs, and Admiral King, to the great mirth of his comrades, occupied the czarina's boudoir.

At four o'clock on Sunday afternoon, the heavy wooden doors flew open and a Secret Service squad marched into the Livadia foyer, followed by a Soviet security phalanx at port arms. From a black Packard in the semicircular driveway emerged a short ursine figure in a round military cap and a greatcoat adorned with epaulets and six brass buttons. His trousers were tucked into boots of soft Caucasus leather with elevated heels, and on the khaki tunic of his marshal's uniform he wore the red ribbon and five-pointed star of a Hero of the Soviet Union. The impenetrable dark eyes and gray pushbroom mustache were softened by a slight smile that revealed irregular teeth, more black than bone in tint, and even the fading light showed that beneath a heavy coating of talcum powder his cheeks were dimpled with the smallpox scars he had incurred at age six. All conversation stopped—Russian servants were careful not to rattle the teacups—and junior officers pressed forward, necks craned, as if to catch a fleeting glimpse of Grendel.

Joseph Stalin intrigued even Franklin Roosevelt, who now greeted the marshal with a broad grin and an extended hand from behind the desk of his makeshift study in the palace. They shared native shrewdness, political acumen, and a conviction that their respective nations were about to become superpowers—a recent coinage that they would help define. In other respects the wealthy patrician had little in common with this son of a drunk cobbler and a mother born into serfdom. Roosevelt a few weeks later would tell his cabinet, preposterously, that during Stalin's youthful study for the priesthood "something entered into his nature of the way in which a Christian gentleman should behave"; in fact, he had left the seminary to specialize in bank robbery, extortion, and—as the first editor of the Bolshevik newspaper *Pravda*—manipulation of the masses. Calm, laconic, and often courteous, with, in Brooke's estimation, "a military brain of the highest caliber," he was also vindictive, enigmatic, and a murderer to rival Hitler. Still, Roosevelt repeatedly told his lieutenants, "I can handle Stalin." As for the marshal's perspective: he had observed a few months earlier that "Churchill is the kind of man who will pick your pocket of a *kopeck*. . . . Roosevelt is not like that. He dips his hand only for bigger coins."

Beneath a painting of a farmer plowing his field and a chandelier with bulbs of varying size and brilliance, they made small talk. The president was pleased they could have a private conversation before Churchill joined them. Stalin spoke a few snatches of English, perhaps learned from Hollywood movies, notably, "You said it!," "So what?," and "What the hell goes on around here?" With Bohlen translating and taking notes, Roosevelt assured the marshal that he was "living in comfort" at Livadia, where all plenary sessions would convene for the president's convenience. He observed that Allied military fortunes had "considerably improved" since their last meeting, in Teheran fourteen months earlier. With armies from east and west now edging closer, he hoped that General Eisenhower would be able to communicate directly with Soviet field commanders rather than routing all messages through the Combined Chiefs. The shocking pillage of Crimea made him "more bloodthirsty than a year ago," the president added, and he urged Stalin to consider offering a dinner toast "to the execution of fifty thousand officers of the German army."

The marshal replied that the carnage was much worse farther north in Ukraine; there the enemy's *Lebensraum* plan to settle ten million German colonists in the east had resulted in genocide. *Everyone* had become more bloody-minded, he said, for the Germans were "savages and seemed to hate with a sadistic hatred the creative work of human beings."

Roosevelt offered Stalin a cigarette and lighted another for himself. The British, he said, were "a peculiar people and wished to have their cake and eat it too." As for the French, he wholeheartedly agreed with Churchill's tart rationale for excluding De Gaulle from ARGONAUT. ("I cannot think of anything more unpleasant and impossible," Churchill had recently written Anthony Eden, his foreign secretary, "than having this menacing and hostile man in our midst.") Yet the president believed it might make sense for France to have a postwar occupation zone in Germany, along with the Big Three.

Why, Stalin asked, given how little France had contributed to winning the war?

"Only out of kindness," Roosevelt replied.

Stalin nodded. "That," he said in his thick Georgian accent, "would be the only reason to give France a zone."

They parted with another handshake. Later, tamping tobacco into his pipe, the marshal gestured toward the ailing man in the wheelchair and mused aloud, "Why did nature have to punish him so?"

Upon Churchill's arrival at 5:10 P.M., the first plenary session began with twenty-eight men convening in what had once been the Livadia state dining room. Half sat around a circular table covered in white damask and the rest perched on chairs along the walls. Measuring fifty by thirty feet, the chamber had double walnut doors at one end and a huge conical fireplace, now blazing merrily, at the other; half a dozen arched windows gave onto the garden. In this high-ceilinged room Nicholas and Alexandra in 1911 had celebrated the sixteenth birthday of their eldest daughter, the Grand Duchess Olga Nikolaevna, with a dress ball and a cotillion supper; as an autumn moon sailed above the Black Sea, the czar gave Olga a necklace of thirty-two diamonds and pearls. It was said that even in November the scent of roses had perfumed the night.

Much of ARGONAUT's initial meeting was given over to reports from the front. Speaking without notes, General Marshall offered a concise summary of circumstances in the west. The German salient in the Ardennes had been eliminated, he said, and Eisenhower hoped to cross the Rhine in March. Montgomery was readying an offensive southeast toward the Rhine above Düsseldorf, supported by the U.S. Ninth Army, which would drive northeast toward the same objective. The Ruhr would then be enveloped rather than assaulted frontally. A supporting attack by Bradley's army group would angle toward Frankfurt and beyond, with Devers's army group shielding the right wing. Tens of thousands of tons of cargo now arrived every day in European ports—this even though more than sixty V-1s and V-2s had pummeled Antwerp just two days earlier. Allied bombing continued to batter the Reich, Marshall added: in less than a year German oil production had dwindled to 20 percent of its peak.

The Soviet account, read by General of the Army Aleksei I. Antonov, was electrifying. The winter offensive launched east of Warsaw in mid-January had advanced three hundred miles in three weeks; the Germans evidently had expected Stalin to await better weather and so were caught out. Red Army troops outstripped even the ten to twelve miles a day their commanders had hoped for, and Soviet soldiers now stood on the Oder River, less than fifty miles from Berlin. Enemy forces in East Prussia had been cut off, with Soviet legions sweeping toward Stettin, Danzig, and Königsberg on the Baltic. Industrial Silesia had been overrun. Red Army political officers were nailing up signs with messages scrawled in diesel oil: "You are now in goddamn Germany." Antonov estimated that forty-five German divisions already had been destroyed in the offensive.

The Soviets currently possessed a seven-to-one superiority over the Germans in tanks, eleven-to-one in infantry, twenty-to-one in artillery. Hitler had shifted reserves from the west, but many were diverted to Budapest, or to screen Vienna and the Hungarian oil fields. Stalin chimed in to say that on the central front in western Poland, Soviet divisions outnumbered German by 180 to 80. Neither he nor Antonov noted the liberation near Kraków a week earlier of Auschwitz, among the most heinous of Nazi concentration camps. Only a few thousand inmates had been found alive, but subsequent investigation would reveal the extermination of more than a million people, mostly Jews, and unspeakable medical experiments. The Germans had not had time to cart away seven tons of women's hair shorn from victims, or 348,820 men's suits and 836,515 dresses, neatly baled, or the pyramids of dentures and spectacles whose owners had been reduced to ash and smoke.

"Our wishes," Antonov said, "are to speed up the advance of the Allied troops on the Western front." German defenses had congealed east of Berlin; although Eisenhower in Versailles was offering three-to-one odds that the Russians would enter the enemy capital by March 31, that proved optimistic. Many Soviet divisions had been pared to fewer than four thousand men, with shortages of air support and artillery ammunition. Bridgeheads on the Oder remained pinched. Rain, snow, and mud slowed the armies' momentum, as did the need to shift supply lines from Russian rail gauges to narrower western European tracks. Enemy counterattacks threatened the flanks in East Pomerania. Antonov put Red Army casualties in the past three weeks at 400,000, almost quadruple U.S. losses in the Bulge. When Admiral King complimented Soviet valor, Stalin replied, "It takes a very brave man not to be a hero in the Russian army."

Valor, yes, but also iniquity. Soviet atrocities were now rampant in the east; they included the burning of villages, wanton murder, and mass rape in East Prussia, Silesia, and elsewhere. By late 1945, an estimated two million German women would be sexually assaulted by Red Army assailants, and that figure excluded Poles and liberated Soviet women who had been kidnapped by the Wehrmacht to Germany as slave laborers. In Königsberg, nurses would be dragged from operating tables to be gang raped. "Our men shoot the ones who try to save their children," a Soviet officer said. German fathers executed their daughters to spare them further defilement, and raped women were nailed by their hands to the farm carts carrying away their families as part of the migration of 7.5 million Germans to the west over the next few months. "They are going to remember this march by our army over German territory for a long, long time," a Russian soldier wrote his father. Of these things, nothing was said—not in the Livadia salon that day, nor at any point during ARGONAUT.

At 8:30 P.M., Roosevelt, Churchill, Stalin, and eleven others adjourned to dinner "in very good humor," according to Bohlen's notes. Great care had been taken not to have thirteen at table lest the number discomfit the superstitious Roosevelt. Filipino mess boys served caviar, sturgeon, beef and macaroni, fried chicken, fruit, and layer cake, washed down with vodka and five types of wine. "The world will have its eyes on this conference," Churchill declared. "If it is successful, we will have peace for a hundred years." The prime minister was described by one diplomat as "drinking buckets of Caucasian champagne"; Stalin sipped only half his vodka during the innumerable toasts before discreetly recharging his glass with water.

Not until the final half hour did political issues arise, when table talk turned to the postwar epoch soon to come. "We three have to decide how to keep the peace of the world," Stalin said, "and it will not be kept unless we three decide to do it." Surely it was "ridiculous to believe that Albania would have an equal voice with the three great powers who had won the war," he continued, adding that the Soviet Union would "never agree to have any action of the great powers submitted to the judgment of the small powers."

Roosevelt agreed that "the great powers bore the greater responsibility," and should dictate the peace. But smaller nations could hardly be ignored. "We have, for instance," he said, "lots of Poles in America who are vitally interested in the future of Poland."

"But of your seven million Poles, only seven thousand vote," Stalin interjected, apparently concocting his statistics from thin air.

Great nations, Churchill declared, "should discharge their moral responsibility . . . with moderation and great respect for the rights of the small nations." Rising to his feet, he proposed a toast to "the proletariat masses of the world," then added, "The eagle should permit the small birds to sing and care not wherefore they sing."

Shortly after eleven P.M. the gathering dissolved. Much work lay ahead, but president, prime minister, and marshal agreed they had made a good start. Not everyone agreed. "A terrible party I thought," Anthony Eden noted in his diary. "President vague and loose and ineffective." Churchill had "made desperate efforts and too long speeches to get things going again. Stalin's attitude to small countries struck me as grim, not to say sinister."

Stalin's attitude toward Germany was far grimmer. He made this clear when the conference reconvened late Monday afternoon, February 5. "I should also like to discuss . . . the dismemberment of Germany," he told Roosevelt and Churchill, reminding them that at Teheran the president had proposed carving the Fatherland into five lesser states. "Hasn't the time come for decision? If you think so, let us make one."

"We are all agreed on dismemberment," Churchill said, "but the actual method, the tracing of lines, is much too complicated a matter to settle here in five or six days. It requires very searching examination of geography, history, and economic facts. . . . We reserve all rights over their land, their liberty, and their lives. . . . It is not necessary to discuss it with the Germans."

"No," Stalin agreed, "simply to demand from them."

Roosevelt asserted that he still favored "the division of Germany into five or seven states," but in fact the Anglo-Americans had backed away from such draconian solutions since their brief flirtation the previous fall with Henry Morgenthau's agrarian scheme.

"We are dealing with the fate of eighty million people and that requires more than eighty minutes to consider," Churchill said. Whatever the Allies decided must not leak to the enemy, he added. "Eisenhower doesn't want that. That would make the Germans all the harder. We should not make this public."

"No," Stalin said, a cigarette jutting from his mustache, "these questions for the moment are only for us. They should *not* be public until the time of surrender."

Glancing at a note slipped to him by Harry Hopkins, Roosevelt proposed deferring the matter until the three foreign ministers could devise a method for secretly studying dismemberment options. On the related issue of how postwar Germany should be occupied, the president observed that zones had been agreed upon by the European Advisory Commission in London but not yet approved by the Big Three governments. With a shuffle of paper he passed around a crude, hand-drawn map showing the tripartite division of Germany, including a jointly administered Berlin.

Churchill now raised the question of giving France an occupation zone, perhaps carved from the British and U.S. sectors, since the "French might be able to be of real assistance" in a protracted postwar period.

How long would U.S. forces likely remain in Europe? Stalin asked Roosevelt. "I can get the people and Congress to cooperate fully for peace but not to keep an army in Europe for a long time," the president replied. "Two years would be the limit."

"Germany should be run by those who have stood firmly against Germany and have made the greatest sacrifices," Stalin said. "We cannot forget that in this war France opened the gates to the enemy."

Churchill could hardly let the marshal's shabby amnesia pass unchallenged. ("He loves France like a woman," Moran told his diary later that evening.) But rather than remind Stalin of his 1939 nonaggression pact with Hitler, and of Moscow's congratulatory telegrams to Berlin following every subsequent Wehrmacht victory, the prime minister slyly mused that every nation had "difficulties in the beginning of the war and made mistakes." In postwar Europe, he insisted, "France must take her place."

But who should pay for the catastrophe? Much of the Soviet Union lay in ruins—Roosevelt and Churchill had seen that for themselves in the Crimea—and rebuilding would require many years. Since shortly after the German invasion in 1941, Stalin had pressed for reparations. Now, he said, the Soviets had a specific plan: German heavy industry would be reduced by 80 percent through confiscation of aviation plants, synthetic-oil facilities, and the like, and the Soviet Union would require payment from Berlin of $1 billion in German goods annually for a decade, with a like sum to the Anglo-Americans.

On this issue, too, Washington and London had second thoughts. Roosevelt said the United States now coveted nothing from postwar Germany. (U.S. officials privately estimated that whatever German assets survived the war would be worth at most $200 million.) Yet he also did not want Germans to have a higher living standard than the Soviet people. Churchill's opposition was stouter; privately he considered Stalin's reparations plan "madness." Germany, like France, would be an important counterweight to Soviet power in Europe, and he was also reluctant to bankrupt a future trading partner.

Recalling the oppressive conditions imposed by the Treaty of Versailles in 1919, the prime minister told Stalin that he was "haunted by the specter of a starving Germany." If the victors wanted a German dray horse to pull their wagon, he added, they "would at least have to give it fodder." Stalin scoffed. "Care should be taken," he said, "to see that the horse did not turn around and kick you." This matter was likewise deferred: a commission would be appointed to examine reparation issues.

On it went for six more days of hammer-and-tongs work, the three leaders and their lieutenants like smiths attempting to forge a new world. Roosevelt privately complained of Churchill's protracted monologues—"now we are in for ½ hour of it," the president scribbled on a notepad when the prime minister launched into another allocution. As Churchill's rhetoric soared, swooped, and pirouetted, Air Marshal Portal reported, "he ran away from the interpreter & was untranslatable." Other delegates sought brief respites from the conference hall. One evening the U.S. chiefs watched *National Velvet*, a new film starring Mickey Rooney and a twelve-year-old actress named Elizabeth Taylor. Moran visited the villa once owned by his fellow physician Chekhov, admiring a wooden stethoscope and a bronze bust of Tolstoy. A clutch of British generals toured Crimean War battlefields, where Brooke attempted to make sense of the Light Brigade's charge at Balaclava by thumbing through old maps and a guide to the campaign.

Back at the Villa Livadia, no issue occupied the Argonauts more than Poland's fate, which was discussed in seven of the eight plenary sessions. The United States and Britain currently recognized a Polish government-in-exile in London—"a decent but feeble lot of fools," in Churchill's opinion—while Moscow supported a provisional, pro-Soviet regime in Warsaw. "If we separate still recognizing different Polish governments, the whole world will see that fundamental differences between us still exist," Churchill asserted. "The consequences will be most lamentable." Some 150,000 Polish soldiers fought alongside the Western Allies, but with ten million Red Army troops in eastern Europe and all of Poland now occupied, Stalin held trump.

Rising from his chair, Stalin called Poland "the corridor through which the enemy passed into Russia. Twice in the past thirty years our enemies, the Germans, have passed through the corridor." Unpersuaded, Churchill reminded the marshal that Britain had gone to war in 1939 to restore Polish sovereignty. "We could never be content with any solution that did not leave Poland a free and independent state," he said. Roosevelt, seeking to mediate, asked the Soviets, "How long will it take you to hold free elections?" Molotov replied: "Within a month's time."

In the event, elections would not be held in Poland for two years, and they were hardly free. But no confrontation short of armed conflict was likely to reverse Stalin's conviction that stupendous Soviet losses in the Great Patriotic War had purchased the right to determine eastern Europe's political contours, as the historian Warren F. Kimball would later observe. "All the Balkans except Greece are going to be Bolshevized, and there is nothing I can do to prevent it," Churchill had lamented even before Yalta. "There is nothing I can do for poor Poland either." Poland's eastern and western borders eventually would be shifted west. By annexing eastern Poland—an area roughly the size of Missouri—the Soviet Union gained a wider buffer; in turn, much of Pomerania, East Prussia, and Silesia would be peeled away from Germany and appended to western and northern Poland. Following the war, Soviet puppets would rule in Warsaw, and the Red Army troops who had reentered Poland in 1944 subsequently remained for almost half a century. "Terrible and humbling submissions must at times be made to the general aim," Churchill later wrote.

For Roosevelt, two paramount concerns shaped his views on Poland and other matters. The first reflected a January memorandum from the Joint Chiefs, declaring that prompt Soviet entry into the war against Japan "is necessary to provide maximum assistance to our Pacific operations." In the Philippines, MacArthur had yet to capture Manila. In the central Pacific, the next American assault—against the flyspeck island of Iwo Jima—was not scheduled until mid-February. In Burma, the British remained months away from capturing Rangoon. And in New Mexico, there was no guarantee that the atomic bomb, a secret not shared with Moscow, would work. If the Pacific war were to last eighteen months after the victory in Europe—with huge American casualties, as feared by the Pentagon—Soviet help in tying down the Japanese in Manchuria and providing air bases in eastern Siberia would be vital to the Joint Chiefs. By entangling Moscow in Asia, the United States might also curb Soviet ambitions in Europe.

Stalin at the Teheran conference had tentatively committed the Soviet Union to war against Japan; now he firmly agreed to shift twenty-five divisions to the Far East and provide additional military aid within three months after Germany's surrender. In exchange, Moscow would receive territories lost by imperial Russia in 1905 after the Russo-Japanese War, plus the Kuril Islands and guarantees regarding ports and railroads in the Far East. These penalties and others to be imposed by the Western Allies would ensure that Japan forfeited its entire empire. To preserve the illusion of Soviet neutrality in the Pacific and to forestall a preemptive Japanese attack, the agreement, formally signed on February 10, would for now remain secret, locked in a White House safe. Chagrined U.S. negotiators complained that in "trading with the Russians you had to buy the same horse twice."

The second issue preoccupying Roosevelt, and the matter nearest his heart, was creation of a world organization capable of keeping the peace by balancing the security requirements of the great powers against the rights of small nations. He entertained what one adviser termed "pet ideas" of building strategic military bases around the globe controlled by what he called the "United Nations"; the U.N. would keep the United States committed to the wider world after the war, and offer a forum for Soviet engagement with the West. An elite security council within the organization would give smaller nations a voice while providing the great powers with a veto. Earlier discussions on the United Nations had stumbled over the precise configuration of that council, and over Moscow's insistence on individual memberships for all sixteen Soviet republics. Molotov at Yalta agreed to pare the number to two or three extra votes. "This is not so good," Roosevelt wrote, likening the demand to giving individual membership to all forty-eight U.S. states. But in the end he relented, ceding Moscow two extra votes in a future general assembly, for Ukraine and Belorussia, in addition to a seat on the security council for the Soviet Union. This deal also would remain secret.

ARGONAUT staggered to an end. They were "tired all through," in Churchill's phrase, not least from two more grand banquets that closed out the conference. Stalin hosted the first, at nine P.M. on February 8, in the Yusupov Palace, a Moorish Revival villa once owned by the prince who had helped orchestrate Rasputin's murder. Bohlen counted forty-five toasts, while mosquitoes stung exposed ankles under the table and one inebriant repeatedly barked, "Drink it down!" Stalin hailed Churchill as "the bravest governmental figure in the world . . . a man who is born once in a hundred years." Churchill in return called Stalin "the mighty leader of a mighty country. . . . We regard Marshal Stalin's life as most precious to the hopes and hearts of all of us." The prime minister invoked a beguiling image of "standing on the crest of a hill with the glories of the future possibilities stretching before us."

Roosevelt, who had tossed down two cocktails before dinner, toasted Stalin as the "chief forger of the instruments which had led to the mobilization of the world against Hitler"; "the atmosphere of this dinner," he added, "[is] that of a family." Guests hopped around the table clinking glasses; only the foolish had failed to heed Russian advice to coat their stomachs with butter and oily salmon before the first sip of vodka. A huge man in a black alpaca jacket stood behind Stalin's chair, advising the marshal on what to eat and drink. When Roosevelt asked the identity of a pudgy Soviet guest sporting pince-nez, Stalin replied, "Ah, that one. That's our Himmler." It was Lavrenty P. Beria, the sadistic murderer and rapist who served as chief of the secret police.

Churchill hosted the final dinner at the Villa Vorontsov on Saturday, February 10, the last night of ARGONAUT. Soviet agents arrived early to peer behind the walls and under the table, flipping chairs and chests. A British honor guard in regimental finery lined the front steps to welcome the nine guests; for half an hour the three leaders loitered in Churchill's map room, studying battle lines east and west. Churchill broke into song, a rousing version of "When We've Wound Up the Watch on the Rhine," and Roosevelt joked, "This singing by the prime minister is Britain's secret weapon." During the lavish meal—the menu included sturgeon in aspic, suckling pig, white fish in champagne, mutton shashlik, wild goat of the steppes, quail, and partridge—Churchill stood and lifted his glass to Stalin. "The fire of war has burnt up the misunderstandings of the past," he said. "We feel we have a friend whom we can trust." The president added, "We are here at Yalta to build up a new world, which will know neither injustice nor violence, a world of justice and equity." Stalin daubed his eyes with a handkerchief. As he departed the villa behind his booted bodyguards, the British staff gathered in the foyer to be led by their prime minister in three rousing cheers for the marshal. *Hip, hip, hooray!*

They were done. A communiqué approved by the three leaders on Sunday morning affirmed their "sacred obligation" to maintain in peace the same Allied unity that had prevailed in war. A "declaration on liberated Europe" within the statement also endorsed "a world order under law" and "the right of all peoples to choose the form of government under which they will live." "We will meet again soon, in Berlin," Roosevelt told Stalin in a farewell from the Villa Livadia at 3:45 P.M. He gave the marshal a book titled *Target: Germany*, published by the Army Air Forces, with vivid photographs of bomb damage. Two Russian servants arrived bearing Georgian wine, caviar, butter, oranges, and tangerines for the Americans. Stalin also promised to ship to Washington the desk Roosevelt used at Livadia because he had "worked so hard there."

Churchill had begun the day in a querulous mood, sourly singing snatches of "The Soldiers of the Queen" after breakfast. He lamented both his failure to safeguard Poland—he decried the communiqué as "this bloody thing"—and the unmistakable decline of British influence in shaping the postwar world. But the prospect of sailing home from Sevastopol aboard *Franconia* cheered him. A former chef from the *Queen Mary* had been press-ganged to cook on the return voyage, and Stalin's couriers delivered bulging hampers of gifts: seven kilos of caviar, seventy-two bottles of champagne, eighteen bottles of vodka, a case of chocolate, seven cases of fruit, and various wines, liqueurs, and cigarettes.

"Papa, genial and sprightly like a boy out of school, his homework done, walked from room to room saying, 'Come, come on,'" wrote Sarah Churchill. Stalin, she added, "like some genie, just disappeared."

"I am a bit exhausted but really all right," Roosevelt wrote Eleanor as he headed back to Washington. His spirits were high enough to mimic both Stalin, in a faux Slavic accent—"I had not thought of it. It is a good idea. I will sign"—and Churchill, whom he imitated putting up his hands defensively, like a boxer on the ropes. "Churchill is acting now as if he is always afraid of getting hit," the president said. But there would be no rest for the weary, not yet. After a night aboard a Navy ship in Sevastopol, Roosevelt boarded the *Sacred Cow* at Saki airfield on Monday morning, February 12, and flew to Egypt. He had proposed a rendezvous with De Gaulle in Algiers, but the Frenchman—said by the U.S. embassy in Paris to be "in a sulky mood" at being excluded from ARGONAUT—brusquely declined.

Instead the president again boarded *Quincy,* moored adjacent to the Suez Canal, and welcomed a succession of potentates whose influence, he suspected, would expand in a postwar, postcolonial world. First came young King Farouk I of Egypt, wearing a fez and sunglasses, followed by the diminutive Emperor Haile Selassie of Ethiopia, the Conquering Lion of the Tribe of Judah, Elect of God, and descendant of Solomon and Sheba. Finally the destroyer U.S.S. *Murphy* pulled along *Quincy's* starboard flank to deliver the imposing, black-robed King Ibn Saud of Saudi Arabia, with an entourage that included a fortune-teller, a food taster, bodyguards carrying scimitars, a royal coffee server and his deputy, nine slaves, and a herd of sheep whose numbers diminished with each bloody butchering on *Murphy's* fantail. A Navy navigator provided bearings to Mecca for the proper positioning of prayer rugs. The king presented Roosevelt with a gold knife, perfume, and Arab robes, including "harem attire" for Eleanor; the president reciprocated with a wheelchair—the monarch was barely ambulatory—and a supply of penicillin. "2 Kings & 1 Emperor in 2 days," Roosevelt wrote his secretary. "All goes well but again I need sleep."

Escorted by a cruiser and seven destroyers, *Quincy* steamed for home. The president spent much of the voyage basking in a sun with little power to brighten his eye or bronze his cheek. "He had," as Churchill would write in his memoir, "a slender contact with life." At nine A.M. on February 28, he would arrive back at the White House, completing a journey of 13,842 miles. "It's been a global war," he told Eleanor, "and we've already started making it a global peace."

"We really believed in our hearts that this was the dawn of the new day we had all been praying for," said Harry Hopkins, who suffered from liver disease and had less than a year to live. "We were absolutely certain that we had won the first great victory of the peace." Other delegates shared his exuberance. "For what we have gained here," Marshall said, "I would have gladly stayed a whole month." Even Brooke was chipper, telling his diary, "Conference is finished and has on the whole been as satisfactory as could be hoped for, and certainly a most friendly one."

Roosevelt and Churchill warranted Marshal Stalin's good faith. "Stalin doesn't want anything other than security for his country," the president said. "He won't try to annex anything and will work for a world of democracy and peace." The prime minister would tell his war cabinet, "Stalin I'm sure means well to the world and Poland. . . . He will not embark on bad adventures." He added, "I don't think I'm wrong about Stalin," whom he had called "that great and good man."

Public reaction was overwhelmingly favorable once the joint communiqué revealed the first details of ARGONAUT. *The New York Times* claimed the agreements "justify and surpass most of the hopes placed on this fateful meeting." Polling results given the White House in mid-March would show that only 11 percent of Americans surveyed deemed the conference "unsuccessful"; although 38 percent knew too little to have an opinion, a solid majority agreed that the Polish arrangement was "about the best that could be worked out." In a spasm of optimism, *Time* averred that "all doubts about the Big Three's ability to cooperate in peace as well as in war seem now to have been swept away."

Within weeks the bloom had left the rose. Churchill sat listening to *The Mikado* on a gramophone, lamenting "the shadows of victory" and fretting that he had trusted Stalin as Neville Chamberlain had once trusted Hitler. "We had the world at our feet," he mused. "Twenty-five million men marching at our orders by land and sea. We seemed to be friends." Provisional agreements made at Yalta soon came unstitched. The Western Allies effectively scuttled the deal to dismember Germany and to extract reparations collectively. Moscow in turn consolidated its grip on eastern Europe, installing a Communist regime in Bucharest and deporting tens of thousands of ethnic Germans to the Ural Mountains as slave laborers. Polish leaders deemed anti-Soviet were arrested in utter disregard of the "declaration on liberated Europe"; exiled Poles in London decried the "partition of Poland, now accomplished by her allies." The sentimentality of ARGONAUT quickly faded, along with delusions that Russian xenophobia and Leninist dogma could be sweet-talked away. Marshall alerted the Joint Chiefs to reports of "increasing Russian non-cooperation with U.S. military authorities," and Roosevelt would complain in mid-March, "We can't do business with Stalin. He has broken every one of the promises he made at Yalta." To a friend in Washington he added, "I didn't say the result was good. I said it was the best I could do."

Recriminations followed, inflamed by the eventual revelation of secret concessions regarding United Nations membership and the enticements that had induced Moscow to make war on Japan. A stigma soon stained Yalta, "a connotation of shameful failure, if not outright treason," as one British historian wrote, "matching that attached to the Munich Conference of September 1938." For decades the Western delegates would be blamed for everything from the Soviet domination of Eastern Europe to the rise of Communist regimes in China, northern Korea, and Indochina.

Roosevelt's frailty came to be seen as both the proximate cause of craven negotiating and a metaphor for the West's weak answer to Stalin's belligerence. "The shrewdness has gone, and there is nothing left," Moran wrote of Roosevelt during the conference. "The president's opinions flutter in the wind." Yet those working in closest proximity found, as Churchill later told the Commons, "an extraordinary effort of the spirit over the flesh, of willpower over physical infirmity." The president evinced both a reasonable command of complex issues and, the historian S. M. Plokhy would write, "his trademark ability to make alliances, strike deals, and maneuver in order to achieve his main goals." Eden wrote that although Roosevelt "gives the impression of failing powers . . . I do not believe that the president's declining health altered his judgment." Photos from Yalta would show a wasting man, gray and thin; U.S. Navy color movie footage shows a man indeed gray and thin, but also animated and plainly alert. Reporters ferried to the *Quincy* for the 992nd press conference of Roosevelt's presidency found him articulate, droll, and quick; asked whether the conference had laid a foundation for an enduring peace, Roosevelt replied, "I can answer that question if you can tell me who your descendants will be in the year 2057. . . . We can look as far ahead as humanity believes in this sort of thing."

Two generations later, Yalta can be seen as neither the portal to Roosevelt's "world of justice and equity" nor a disgraceful capitulation to red fascism but, rather, an intricate nexus of compromises by East and West. Roosevelt "largely followed through on earlier plans, and gained most of what he wished," the historian Robert Dallek concluded, including Soviet support for the United Nations and participation in the defeat of Japan, an obligation punctually fulfilled by Moscow's declaration of war three months after the German surrender. That declaration may not have "saved two million Americans," as Admiral King had envisioned at Yalta, but along with two atomic bombs it encouraged Tokyo's decision to surrender. With the Soviet Union killing far more Germans in combat than all other Allied forces combined, at a fell price of 26 million Soviet lives, Stalin was not to be denied what the diplomat George F. Kennan called "a wide military and political *glacis* on his Western frontier." If Roosevelt sounded plaintive and exasperated, his explanation also captured the political reality of Europe in February 1945: *It was the best I could do.*

War had held the Big Three together—the common cause of crushing Germany proved stronger than the centrifugal forces that beset any alliance. Now the entropy of peace threatened to unknot those ties, as postwar interests and imperatives emerged. Even Roosevelt and Churchill, who had met on nine occasions to spend 120 days together during the war, felt the bonds of blood and history fraying week by week. When the reporters aboard *Quincy* asked Roosevelt whether Churchill hoped to reassemble the antebellum imperial empire, the president replied, "Yes, he is mid-Victorian on all things like that. . . . Dear old Winston will never learn on that point. . . . This is, of course, off the record." But Churchill knew. Roosevelt "cannot leave the empire alone," he told Moran. "It seems to upset him." Eden shrewdly suspected that the president "hoped that former colonial territories, once free of their masters, would become politically and economically dependent upon the United States."

Moran in February observed, "We have moved a long way since Winston, speaking of Roosevelt, said to me in the garden at Marrakesh [in January 1943], 'I love that man.'" Perhaps it was too much to expect such attachments to survive when so much had perished. Speaking to the Commons a few days after his return from Yalta, the prime minister warned: "We are now entering a world of imponderables. . . . It is a mistake to look too far ahead. Only one link in the chain of destiny can be handled at a time."

Yet for those who felt destiny as a following wind, the morrow beckoned and the imponderable held more promise than peril. "The Americans pitch their song on a higher note," Moran wrote. "They feel they are on top of the world."

"Only Our Eyes Are Alive"

F ROM the Swiss border to the North Sea, across the fronts of almost eighty Allied divisions in seven armies, none of this mattered at the moment, not a whit. What preoccupied several million soldiers was the effort to find a bit of warmth in the frozen night, and perhaps a lukewarm meal rather than congealed hash in a cold can, and to live to see the next dawn, and then the next, and the next after that. The autumn rallying cry of "Win the War in '44" had been supplanted by the sour "Stay Alive in '45." A soldier in the 70th Division spoke for many GIs in a letter to his parents in Minnesota: "My mind is absolutely stripped of any traces of reason for war. . . . Maybe the overall picture justifies what goes on up here, but from an infantryman's point of view, it's hard to see."

The harshest winter in decades compounded the misery, even after the German retreat from the Bulge. "My hands shivered like tuning forks," wrote one private in Lorraine. "But worst of all, the cold had settled in my spine. . . . I was a bundle of icy vibrations." A soldier in the 84th Division described awakening in a slushy foxhole to find his feet "encased in a block of ice up to my ankles"; comrades chipped him free with bayonets. Impassioned debates raged over "whether sleeping with hands in the crotch or the armpits was the best way to avoid frostbite." Troops jerked awake by gunfire left patches of hair stuck to the icy ground. Soldiers fashioned crude igloos or huddled over tiny fires fueled with cardboard scraps from K-ration boxes. GIs became adept at chopping a small divot from the frozen ground with a pickax, then detonating a quarter-pound TNT block to finish excavating a foxhole. Graffiti scribbled on a concrete fortification in Lorraine read: "Austin White, Chicago, Ill., 1918. Austin White, Chicago, Ill., 1945. This is the last time I want to write my name here."

A SHAEF plan to cut one million cords of firewood by February 1 fell short by 964,000 for want of tools and lumberjacks. Coal production in Europe fell 40 percent in January, partly because Belgian miners went on strike; frozen canals impeded deliveries of what stock there was. GI work details spent a month slicing peat from Norman bogs for fuel before abandoning the task as pointless. Sled dogs shipped from Alaska and Labrador to evacuate the wounded in snowy terrain arrived after the spring thaw, and so gave the field armies only useless, barking mouths to feed.

A lieutenant in the 99th Division wrote his wife in January:

To date, I've slept on a mattress, a steel deck, a wet concrete floor with a little straw on top, dirt floors, a bed, a stretcher, on an LST, in a truck, in a foxhole, across the front seats of a jeep, in a rope hammock, in cellars, first, second, and third floors, in a pillbox, on the back window shelf of a command car, in haylofts, on snow, and in shacks.

There were horrors to see, hear, and smell, horrors to relive and remember because they could never be forgotten. A soldier from the 75th Division described an hour in a foxhole with a mortally wounded comrade and no morphine: "I tried to knock him out. I took off his helmet, held his jaw up, and just whacked as hard as I could. . . . That didn't work. Nothing worked. He slowly bled to death." Another GI assigned to police corpses from the battlefield wrote:

Everywhere we searched we found bodies, floating in the rivers, trampled on the roads, bloated in the ditches, rotting in the bunkers, pretzeled into foxholes, burned in the tanks, buried in the snow, sprawled in doorways, splattered in gutters, dismembered in minefields, and even literally blown up into trees.

When a reporter asked a private in the 23rd Infantry what he wanted Americans at home to know, he said, "Tell 'em it's rough as hell. Tell 'em it's rough. Tell 'em it's rough, serious business. That's all. That's all." A nurse in Seventh Army wrote her family in January: "Admitted a 19-year-old from Texas last night who had both legs blown off by a shell. He was unhappy because now he could never wear his nice cowboy boots. He died before he could be taken to surgery." Another nurse, in a Third Army shock ward dubbed the Chamber of Horrors, said, "Maybe it's a good thing their mothers can't see them when they die."

Prison-camp guards opened the locked boxcars on a freight train carrying captured Germans across France to find that 104 had suffocated. Their pleas and shouts had been ignored, and investigators found "evidence of teeth marks and clawing on inner walls." Eisenhower wrote Marshall, "I certainly loathe having to apologize to the Germans. It looks as if this time I have no other recourse." His message to Berlin, sent through the Swiss, read: "The supreme commander profoundly regrets this incident and has taken steps to prevent its recurrence."

War made the warriors sardonic, cynical, old before their time. "Will you tell me what the hell I'm being saved for?" a captain in the 30th Division mused after surviving a bloody attack on the West Wall. Another soldier replied, "For the Pacific." To a GI in the 100th Division, "it wasn't so much fear of death as the uncertainty of life." One squad leader found his battle-weary men "impassive, lethargic, uncommunicative." Some deliberately extended an arm or leg from their foxholes in hopes of the proverbial million-dollar wound, but for most "each succeeding town came and each succeeding town went, and we continued dying a thousand deaths." After the Germans ambushed his patrol, a soldier in the 275th Infantry wrote, "Things didn't go exactly as planned. They usually don't." To Lieutenant Paul Fussell, the bitterest lessons of combat were indeed "about the eternal presence in human affairs of accident and contingency, as well as the fatuity of optimism at any time or place."

> All planning was not just likely to recoil ironically; it was almost certain to do so. Human beings were clearly not machines. They were mysterious congeries of twisted will and error, misapprehension and misrepresentation, and the expected could not be expected of them.

There was nothing for it but obduracy, to soldier on even for those who were not soldiers. "How hard I have become," an American Red Cross volunteer told her diary in February. "Emotions which formerly would have wracked my soul leave me almost untouched. It's a hardness of survival." A soldier in the 84th Division described seeing GIs using a severed German head as a soccer ball in an icy pasture; when a mortar round blew apart a U.S. trooper in a nearby street, he added, "I sat and ate my food. I had not known him." J. Glenn Gray, a counterintelligence officer, wrote in his journal, "Yesterday we caught two spies. . . . One had to be severely beaten before he confessed. It was pretty horrible. . . . I thought of the *Hamlet* line as most appropriate, ''Tis bitter cold and I am sick at heart.'"

Not all would learn to hate. Nor would all find satisfaction, even exhilaration, in killing the Huns, Heinies, Hermanns, Lugerheads, Jerries, Fritzes, Boches, Krauts, Katzenjammers, Squareheads. A survey of four thousand GIs found that although four-fifths expressed strong hatred toward German leaders, less than half voiced hatred toward German soldiers. But by late winter enough haters and killers filled the ranks to constitute a ferocious killing engine. After Malmédy, an officer in the 35th Division wrote: "A hatred such as I have never seen has sprung up among us against Hitler's armies and all of Germany." A British soldier added, "The question of killing does not present itself as a moral problem any more—or as a problem at all."

"Slowly it is beginning to dawn on them that the only good German is a dead German," the XII Corps chief of staff wrote his parents. "The result is that we're killing more and taking fewer prisoners." While smashing up a German house, a 2nd Division soldier bellowed, "Screw the bastards and all their works. Shit on them. Piss on them." A Canadian soldier wrote, "When the Jerries come in with their hands up, shouting '*Kamerad*,' we just bowl them over with bursts of Sten fire." A lieutenant in the 15th Infantry told his diary, "Sergeant Burton, somewhat inebriated, shoots two Krauts who are trying to surrender. . . . Some of our best men are the most murderous."

Fussell described how GIs in his 103rd Division found some fifteen Germans cowering in a deep crater in the forest.

> Their visible wish to surrender—most were in tears of terror and despair—was ignored by our men lining the rim. . . . Laughing and howling, hoo-ha-ing and cowboy and good-old-boy yelling, our men exultantly shot into the crater until every single man down there was dead. . . . The result was deep satisfaction.

"Killing is an obsession," a private in the 86th Division wrote his parents. "What code could withstand it?"

At 7:30 A.M. on Wednesday, January 31, a U.S. Army weapons carrier clanked up to a gray farmhouse with orange shutters outside Ste.-Marie-aux-Mines, an Alsatian town long celebrated for mineralogy, fifteen miles northwest of Colmar. A scrawny, handcuffed twenty-four-year-old private from Michigan named Eddie D. Slovik stepped from the rear bay, escorted by four MPs. A Vosges snowstorm had delayed their journey from Paris through the Saverne Gap, and Private Slovik was late for his own execution. No task gripped Eisenhower with more urgency than clearing the Colmar Pocket to expel the enemy from Alsace and shore up the Allied right wing. But first, a dozen riflemen were to discharge a single, vengeful volley in the high-walled garden of 86 Rue du Général Bourgeois.

As a miscreant, Private Slovik was more bumbling than iniquitous. First arrested at age twelve, he quit school at fifteen, and served jail time for burglary, assault, and embezzlement. Originally declared 4-F by a draft board and exempted from conscription for what the British would call "LMF"—lack of moral fiber—he was reclassified 1-A, an indication of the desperate need for infantrymen. Inducted in late 1943, Slovik arrived in France in August 1944, was assigned to the 28th Infantry Division, and promptly deserted. Perhaps his only endearing trait was a uxorious devotion to his wife, Antoinette, to whom he wrote 376 letters, in pencil, during his 372 days in the Army. "I fought to make you love me," he told her, adding, "I think I'm going to have a lot of trouble. Army life don't agree with me."

In this he was not unique. Indiscipline had become a nagging worry for Eisenhower: nearly 11,000 general courts-martial would be convened for serious crimes committed in Europe by U.S. soldiers, in addition to 126,000 special and summary courts-martial for lesser infractions. "Disciplinary conditions are becoming bad," Eisenhower had told his diary in November. A month later he advised subordinates, "The large incidence of crimes such as rape, murder, assault, robbery, housebreaking, etc., continues to cause grave concerns." A French prefect lamented that "the liberators have turned into looters, rapists, and killers," and a newspaper in Cherbourg declared, "Never has one witnessed such debauchery." ("Unfortunately," a U.S. Army provost marshal conceded, "the editorial is justified.") General Juin wrote Eisenhower that civilian women dared "not to go about their daily chores even when accompanied by a man for fear of being accosted by American soldiers." Although less than one-half of one percent of Allied troops in Europe were implicated in serious offenses, a SHAEF memo in late January noted that "a considerable percentage of the French civil population" believed that GIs behaved badly, if not criminally.

Severe punishment had a fitful deterrent effect. A study of military offenders found that many had "mental ages of seven or eight"; some were psychopaths or chronic alcoholics. Of fourteen hundred convictions for violating Article of War No. 64—striking an officer, drawing a weapon on an officer, or "willful disobedience"—the average sentence for infractions in combat was fifteen years' imprisonment. Thirty-year sentences for felonious behavior were not uncommon, and any jail term over six months also drew a dishonorable discharge. Four hundred and forty-three death penalties were imposed on GIs, most for murder or rape, and a severely disproportionate number fell on black soldiers, often after dubious due process. Seventy executions took place in Europe, including several public hangings; War Department Pamphlet 27-4 specified that the hangman's rope was to be "manila hemp, 1¼ inches in diameter . . . stretched to eliminate any spring," and coated "with wax, soap, or grease to ensure a smooth sliding action through the knot."

Desertion, defined by the U.S. military as an unauthorized absence of two months or more, was as old as warfare, and historically it was a capital crime punished by a firing squad. The British had handed down more than 3,000 death sentences from 1914 to 1920, and had executed about 10 percent of those condemned—before abolishing the death penalty for cowardice and desertion in 1930. The German military issued 50,000 military death sentences in World War II, with half or more carried out. Twenty-one thousand soldiers would desert from the U.S. Army during the war; less than half had been caught by the late 1940s. Of nearly 2,000

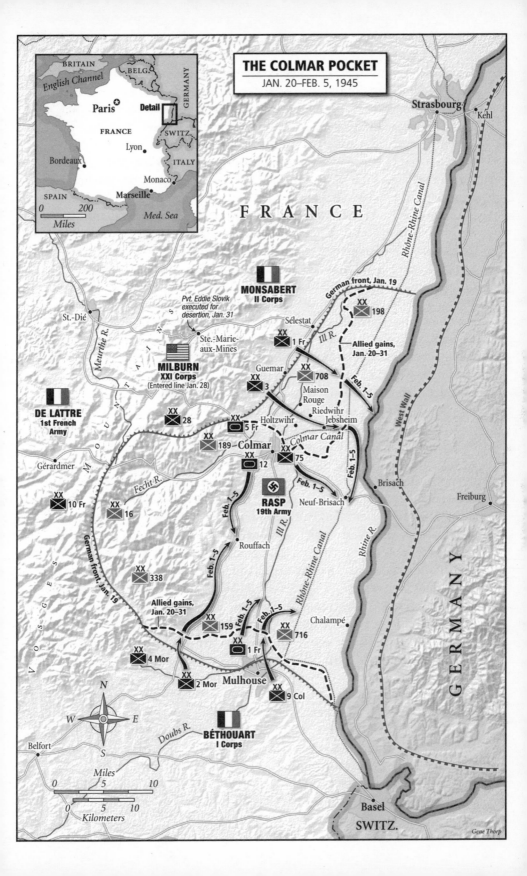

THE COLMAR POCKET
JAN. 20–FEB. 5, 1945

BRITAIN
English Channel
BELG.
GERMANY
Paris
Detail
FRANCE
SWITZ.
Lyon
ITALY
Bordeaux
Monaco
Marseille
SPAIN
Med. Sea
0   200
Miles

FRANCE

Strasbourg
Kehl

Rhône-Rhine Canal

German front, Jan. 19

MONSABERT
II Corps

XX 198

St.-Dié

Pvt. Eddie Slovik
executed for
desertion, Jan. 31

Sélestat

XX 1 Fr

Ill R.

Allied gains,
Jan. 20–31

Ste.-Marie-
aux-Mines

Feb. 1–5

MILBURN
XXI Corps
(Entered line Jan. 28)

Guemar

XX 3

XX 708

Maison
Rouge
Riedwihr

West Wall

DE LATTRE
1st French
Army

XX 28

XX 5 Fr

Holtzwihr

Jebsheim

Feb. 1–5

XX 189 Colmar

Colmar Canal

Feb. 1–5

XX 75

Gérardmer

XX 16

Fecht R.

XX 12

RASP
19th Army

Neuf-Brisach

Brisach

Freiburg

XX 10 Fr

Feb. 1–5

Ill R.

XX 338

Rouffach

Feb. 1–5

Allied gains,
Jan. 20–31

Rhône-Rhine Canal

Rhine R.

GERMANY

XX 159

Feb. 1–5

Feb. 1–5

XX 716

Chalampé

XX 4 Mor

XX 1 Fr

German front, Jan. 19

XX 2 Mor Mulhouse

XX 9 Col

N
W   E
S

BÉTHOUART
I Corps

Belfort

Doubs R.

Miles
0   5   10

Kilometers
0   5   10

Basel
SWITZ.

Gene Thorp

deserters convicted in Europe, 139 received death sentences. But the United States had not actually executed a deserter since 1864.

Slovik was arrested in October after living for weeks with a Canadian unit. Offered amnesty if he went to the front, he refused, vowing, "I'll run away again if I have to." He was convicted following a two-hour court-martial in the Hürtgen Forest on November 11. From a jail cell in Paris he appealed his death sentence to Eisenhower in a six-paragraph clemency plea. "How can I tell you how humbley sorry I am for the sins I've comitted. . . . I beg of you deeply and sincerely for the sake of my dear wife and mother back home to have mercy on me," he wrote, according to the author William Bradford Huie. "I Remain Yours for Victory, Pvt. Eddie D. Slovik." Unfortunately for the condemned, the supreme commander reviewed the petition at the nadir of the Bulge, on December 23, during a session in his Versailles office known as "the Hanging Hour." Eisenhower not only affirmed the sentence, but decreed that as a lesson to shirkers it be carried out by Slovik's putative unit, the 109th Infantry Regiment, in General Dutch Cota's 28th Division. "Darling," Slovik wrote Antoinette, "I'm in a little trouble."

The MP guards had lost the handcuff key during the trip through the Vosges, and a hacksaw was used to free the prisoner's wrists so that he could be properly bound with nylon parachute cord. A priest heard his confession and handed him twenty-eight letters from the wife who would soon be a widow. Cota convened the firing squad of twelve specially chosen sharpshooters to remind them that they were "the finest marksmen in the Army"; a physician gave a tutorial on the location of the heart, but, considering the point-blank range of twenty yards, chose not to pin a target on Slovik's chest. He was hooded with a black sack, sewn by a local seamstress in accord with the Army regulation "to cover the head and neck of the prisoner and to obscure all light." A blanket was draped over his shoulders against the cold. Slovik declined to make a final statement other than to ask, "Please shoot straight so I won't have to suffer."

Gray overcast roofed the garden at ten A.M. as Cota, clutching a brass-handled swagger stick, stood in the snow with forty-two other witnesses. Murmuring a prayer, the condemned man shuffled through an archway and was lashed to a six-foot stake. The firing squad appeared in quick step, halted, faced right, shouldered rifles, and on command cut loose a smoking volley. Eleven bullets struck Slovik, including two in the left arm; not one hit his heart. Even the Army's finest marksmen trembled at such an awful moment. Three physicians with stethoscopes listened to the wounded man's shallow breathing and irregular heartbeat as the squad prepared to reload. "The second volley won't be necessary," a doctor pronounced at 10:08 A.M. "Private Slovik is dead." Cota, who in the past eight months had endured Omaha Beach, St.-Lô, the Hürtgen Forest, and the Bulge, later described this episode as "the toughest fifteen minutes of my life."

A priest anointed the body with oil. Slovik would be buried outside a World War I cemetery at Oise-Aisne, near Soissons, in row three of Plot E—a hidden, unsanctified tract reserved for the dishonorable dead. *'Tis bitter cold, and I am sick at heart.*

Eisenhower acknowledged a gnawing obsession with the Colmar Pocket. He called it "the one sore on the whole front," and insisted that "we must get cleaned up in the south, even if it is going to hold up the offensives in the north."

In this he would be further frustrated, for Hitler showed no inclination to forswear his 850-square-mile swatch of Alsace, stubbornly held by 23,000 Wehrmacht troops. Deep trenches zigged and zagged across snowy terrain now seeded with minefields, and more than a dozen Alsatian villages had been converted into fortresses around the pocket's 130-mile perimeter. Perpetual smoke screens hid rail and road bridges across the Rhine, as well as ten ferry sites, frustrating AAF bombers trying to sever German supply routes. Allied engineers upstream had released more than two hundred floating contact mines, to no avail. The Führer even awarded an Iron Cross for valor to one particularly durable span near Brisach.

General Devers's initial effort to reduce the pocket through Operation CHEERFUL, an ill-named double envelopment, had foundered in late January on French inadequacy. In the south, General de Lattre's I Corps fired off the entire French artillery ammunition consignment in a fruitless barrage, then lost half its tanks to mines and antitank guns. By early February, after eleven days of flopping around on "polished ice terrain," not a single objective had been captured. The French II Corps, attacking from the north on a seven-mile front, did a bit better, but enemy graffiti scribbled on walls throughout the pocket—*"Elsass bleibt deutsch,"* Alsace remains German—still obtained.

Franco-American fraternity, always delicate, grew brittle. "Having gained surprise in both north and south, we have been unable to exploit," Devers told his diary. "Continual trouble with Gen. de Lattre. . . . Situation on the front does not look good." The French, he lamented, lacked "the punch or the willingness to go all out." General Leclerc's refusal to take orders from De Lattre, again, led Devers to observe that if he "were in the Russian army he would be shot." When Devers repeatedly pressed De Lattre to close up his straggling line, the Frenchman snarled, "Goddamn it! Am I commander here or not? If I am, let me command. If not, relieve me."

Eisenhower privately complained, "We have certainly been let down by the French."

American units had their own difficulties. Cota's 28th Division, consigned to De Lattre's French First Army in mid-January, was described as "exhausted and depleted" after the Bulge. When the veteran 3rd Division joined the French II Corps in attacking north of Colmar, soldiers donned mattress covers or improvised nightshirts for camouflage and carried wooden planks to cross the countless streams braiding the marsh flats. But no plank would support a Sherman M-4, and the first tank in an armored column crashed through a frail bridge over the Ill River at Maison Rouge; the mishap left three infantry battalions exposed to a panzer counterattack on the far bank. Terrified GIs scoured across the plain "in flight and panic," splashing through the icy, steep-banked Ill while enemy grazing fire lashed their backs with white tracers. "It was like a goddamned scene from Civil War days," a captain reported. One regiment lost 80 percent of its combat kit and 350 men, many of them taken prisoner while hiding in boggy burrows. "Our clothes were so frozen after we were captured," wrote one private, "that we rattled like paper." As a taunt, enemy gunners fired leaflet canisters stuffed with the names of GIs now in German custody.

Audie Murphy helped redeem the day with valor uncommon even by his standards. Since advancing up the Rhône and across the Vosges with the 3rd Division, Murphy—who was still not yet old enough to vote or to shave more than once a week—had collected two Silver Stars, a battlefield commission, and a severe wound that turned gangrenous and cost him several pounds of flesh whittled from his right hip and buttock. Rejoining the 15th Infantry in mid-January after two months' recuperation, he soon took command of the same company he had joined as a private in North Africa two years earlier; it was now reduced to eighteen men and a single officer, himself. On January 26, two hundred German infantrymen with half a dozen panzers attacked from the woods near Riedwihr. Clutching a map and a field phone, Second Lieutenant Murphy leaped onto a burning tank destroyer and for an hour repulsed the enemy with a .50-caliber machine gun while calling in artillery salvos. He "killed them in the draws, in the meadows, in the woods," a sergeant reported; the dead included a dozen Germans "huddled like partridges" in a nearby ditch. "Things seemed to slow down for me," Murphy later said. "Things became very clarified." De Lattre described the action as "the bravest thing man had ever done in battle," but Murphy reflected that "there is no exhilaration at being alive." He would receive the Medal of Honor.

At last an Allied preponderance began to crush the pocket. An exasperated Eisenhower committed a U.S. corps, the XXI, for a total of four

American divisions to bolster De Lattre's eight; the reinforcements gave Devers better than a five-to-one advantage in men, tanks, and artillery ammunition. "God be praised!" the French commander exclaimed. By Friday, February 2, the 28th Division had cleared Colmar's outskirts, then stood aside to let French tanks liberate the town. "Your city," De Lattre said, "has found the motherland and the tricolor once more."

By February 5, columns from north and south had joined at Rouffach, cleaving the Geman pocket in half. From the north the 3rd Division enveloped Neuf-Brisach, another of Vauban's seventeenth-century strongholds, known as the City of Ramparts. Brutal fighting with tanks, mortars, bazookas, and grenades swept across the Jewish cemetery. GIs bellowed "Hindy ho, you bastards!"—an approximation of *"Hände hoch,"* Hands up—although one regiment reported that "the men did not take any prisoners because they would have gotten in the way." Hundreds of Germans pelting south from Neuf-Brisach were butchered by artillery, like "clay pigeons in green uniforms." A French patriot showed GIs a narrow tunnel leading from a dry moat beneath the citadel's northeast wall, but only seventy-six German soldiers were found alive within.

At eight A.M. on Friday, February 9, enemy demolitionists dropped the last bridge into the Rhine at Chalampé with a spectacular splash. "My dear French comrades," De Lattre said, "you have been artisans of a great national event. . . . Germany passed its last night in France." (Actually a corner of northeastern Alsace was to remain in Hitler's custody for a few more weeks, as well as several French ports.) The pocket was finally eradicated, even if the job had taken three times longer than the week De Lattre had anticipated. Trucks hauled German bodies to yet another mass grave—"entangled among each other like so many frozen, dead chickens in packing cases," in a GI's description. Colmar had cost 20,000 Franco-American casualties, by De Lattre's tally; the Germans reported more than 22,000 killed or missing. Fewer than 500 men had escaped from each of the eight German divisions defending Hitler's purchase on Elsass.

As the U.S. Army concluded with justification, Germany's Nineteenth Army "had been sacrificed for no appreciable gain." The German host that had begun retreating within hours of the Allied landings in southern France six months earlier was now a silent, spectral memory, a legion of shades.

Pulverizing the Reich from above now intensified with a fury no nation had ever endured. Thousand-bomber Allied raids had become common, even quotidian. The first 22,000-pound British "earthquake bomb" was dropped on Bielefeld in early spring, gouging a crater thirty feet deep and wrecking a hundred yards of rail viaduct. Forty more would fall, each with a power exceeded among air munitions only by the atomic bomb. The M-47 100-pound phosphorus bomb fell for the first time in late January; deemed an "excellent antipersonnel incendiary weapon" by AAF tacticians, each canister carried six times the hellfire of a 155mm artillery phosphorus round. Innovative applications of napalm also flourished because, as Robert A. Lovett, the U.S. assistant secretary of war, explained, "If we are going to have a total war we might as well make it as horrible as possible." SHAEF issued a forty-three-page list of German monuments, historic sites, and objets d'art to be spared, "symbolizing to the world," in Eisenhower's words, "all that we are fighting to preserve." In a letter to his family, an American corporal put such rarefied sentiments in perspective. "Thanks to the Allied air forces," he wrote, "most of Europe resembles Stonehenge more than anything else." One enemy city after another had been reduced to what the German writer W. G. Sebald would call "lifeless life."

British air strategists considered taking the war to small German municipalities, but concluded that bombers could obliterate only "thirty towns a month at the maximum"; destroying one hundred such *Dörfer* would "account for only 3 percent of the population." A more lucrative target was Berlin, known to pilots as "Big B," which housed not only the regime but 5 percent of Germany's *Volk*. Two months had passed since Berlin was last clobbered, and George Marshall at Malta advocated bombing Big B again to impede German reinforcement of the Eastern Front and to curry Soviet goodwill. In this the British eagerly concurred: Bomber Harris had long urged bludgeoning Berlin until "the heart of Nazi Germany ceases to beat." By one calculation, a no-holds-barred bombardment could kill or injure 275,000 Germans; it would also "create great confusion" and "might well ruin an already shaky morale."

Skeptics objected only to be shouted down. General Doolittle, the Eighth Air Force chief, believed that "the chances of terrorizing into submission" people who had already been bombed repeatedly since 1942 were "extremely remote." Flight crews dreaded the most viciously defended city in Europe. "Big B is no good as a target," one airman said. "I don't believe in spite bombing." But in a note scribbled to Beetle Smith, Eisenhower had written, "I agree the project would be a good one."

THUNDERCLAP, as the "project" was code-named, dumped 2,279 tons of bombs on Berlin on February 3, at a cost of almost two dozen B-17s lost to flak. The single heaviest raid to hit Big B in the war proved a disappointment: only one ton in three detonated within a mile of the aim point, and some groups managed to miss the world's sixth largest city altogether. The German regime claimed 20,000 dead, and the AAF official history later put the figure at 25,000; subsequent analyses lowered the THUNDERCLAP death toll to 2,893, plus another 2,000 injured. No one surrendered.

Even so, bombs smashed rail stations, marshaling yards, and neighborhoods—also electronics, leather, and printing plants; hotels; newspaper offices; and various government buildings, including the Air Ministry, the Foreign Office, Gestapo headquarters, and the Reich Chancellery. "It was a sunny, beautiful morning," a German woman wrote. "Blooming blue hyacinth, purple crocuses, and soon-to-bloom Easter lily. . . . One should never enjoy such things." Terror swept a subway station, according to a Wehrmacht account, and "the people literally ripped clothes from each other's bodies. They totally forgot themselves in their panic and were hitting each other." Others were said to herd together "like deer in a storm." A survivor recounted how phosphorus bombs "emptied themselves down the walls and along the streets in flaming rivers of unquenchable flame." The raid rendered 120,000 Germans homeless. A diarist described Berliners as "marching backwards in time" to become cave-dwellers and added, "Only our eyes are alive."

Other elaborate air missions followed throughout February, among them Operation CLARION, an assault by 3,500 bombers and almost 5,000 fighters meant to further eviscerate German transportation and remind small-town Germans in "relatively virgin areas" of their mortality. Trains, rail stations, barges, docks, and bridges were bombed and strafed, but neither a general collapse of the Reichsbahn nor weakened civilian will could be detected. "Perhaps it was a case," the AAF posited, "of trying to injure the morale of a people who had no morale."

Most infamous of the winter raids was the attack on Dresden by more than eight hundred Bomber Command aircraft during the night of February 13, followed over the next two days by almost as many Eighth Air Force bombers. Discrete blazes confederated into a firestorm with superheated winds capable of uprooting trees and peeling shingles from rooftops. "Chimney stacks fell down just from the echo of my voice," a schoolgirl later reported. "I saw a pile of ashes in the shape of a person. . . . It was my mother." Asked to assess the raid, Bomber Harris replied, "Dresden? There is no such place as Dresden." Nazi officials claimed 200,000 dead in a city jammed with refugees from the east, but an exhaustive inquiry more than half a century later lowered the figure to 25,000. Among those hauling bodies to cremation pits were SS squads experienced in such matters from duty at Treblinka; also pressed into service was Private First Class Vonnegut, captured on the Schnee Eifel two months earlier. "Dear people," he wrote his family in Indiana:

> We were put to work carrying corpses from air raid shelters; women, children, old men; dead from concussion, fire or suffocation. Civilians

cursed us and threw rocks as we carried bodies to huge funeral pyres in the city.

Each night and each day, bombing snuffed out another corner of the Reich. More than one German dwelling in every five was destroyed from the air, leaving 7.5 million homeless during the war and more than 400,000 Germans dead. Devastation scorched seventy cities, and carbonized bodies lay stacked in countless black windrows. Of the vast Krupp factory in Essen, a witness would report that "the biggest armament works in the world is incapable of producing a hairpin." *Time* described how Duisburg, Düsseldorf, Dortmund, Wuppertal, Bochum, and other industrial hubs "burned like torches for a night, smoldered for a day, then lay blackened and dead."

Yet still the lifeless life lived on. Even General Spaatz decried "the chimera" of bringing Germany to her knees from twenty thousand feet. Only subjugation and occupation would persuade the Reich that the Reich was finished. Only conquest would end the war.

Field Marshal Montgomery had a conqueror's glint in his eye as he set in motion the battle he hoped would lead to Berlin. Montgomery's plan was to begin on Thursday, February 8, with 340,000 troops in the Canadian First Army plowing southeast up the left bank of the Rhine from Nijmegen in Operation VERITABLE. Two days later, in Operation GRENADE, the U.S. Ninth Army with another 300,000 men would lunge northeast across the Roer on a forty-mile front, reinforced on the right flank by 75,000 First Army men from Joe Collins's VII Corps. This American horde, bristling with two thousand guns and fourteen hundred tanks, was to join the Canadians shoulder to shoulder on the Rhine before enveloping the industrial Ruhr.

But no crossing could be made on the Roer—a modest stream that paralleled the Rhine—until the Schwammenauel and Urft dams upstream were seized to prevent the Germans from uncorking floodwaters at an indelicate moment. Efforts in the late fall to capture or bomb the waterworks had failed, and "damn the dams" remained a tiresome malediction in American headquarters. Not until those bugaboos were eliminated could the Roer be vaulted, the Rhine attained, and the Ruhr captured.

The Urft fell easily in early February, but only because German defenders had rallied round the Schwammenauel and the twenty billion gallons it impounded. For nearly a week the green 78th Division, reinforced by a regiment from the 82nd Airborne and eventually the veteran 9th Division, had retaken ground won and then lost in the Hürtgen battles of late fall: the Kall gorge—where dozens of decaying, booby-trapped corpses of

28th Division troops still lined the trail—and then Kommerscheidt, and finally ruined Schmidt, captured in a cellar-to-cellar gunfight on February 8 after forty battalions of U.S. artillery made the rubble bounce. The Schwammenauel stood two miles away.

At eight P.M. on Friday, February 9, a battalion of the 309th Infantry crept from a tangled wood to find the dam intact and imposing: 170 feet high, 1,200 feet across, and almost 1,000 feet thick at its base. German mortar and artillery rounds rained down, and muzzle flashes winked from the far shoreline, answered by an eventual forty thousand U.S. shells. Silvered by flare light, five engineers and an escort of riflemen trotted across the dam as an ominous rumble rose from the Schwammenauel valve house below. Finding that a bridge across the sluiceway had been destroyed, the men hopped over a guardrail and slid down the dam's northern face to enter a doorway far below. Stifling heat and pressure made breathing difficult— "it was like going in a tunnel under the sea," one lieutenant recalled—but no explosives were found within. Engineers had calculated that German demolitionists would need a half million pounds of TNT to blow a hole in the massive structure.

But mortal wounds had already been inflicted. Other patrols found the gatehouse, power room, and discharge valves thoroughly wrecked: an unstoppable cascade of water fifteen feet wide was pouring from floodgates ninety feet below the dam's lip. German dynamite also had jammed open the valve on a penstock carrying water from Urft reservoir to the Schwammenauel basin, guaranteeing that the Roer valley would be flooded for days by 100 million tons of water.

Snowmelt and rain had already made the Roer unruly, as readings taken at gage stations every two hours made evident. Now the river rampaged. The ominous code word "Johnstown" alerted Ninth Army of inundations to come, although with a rising tide rather than a wall of water. Overnight the Roer rose eight inches, and kept rising.

With Montgomery's concurrence, Lieutenant General Bill Simpson, the Ninth Army commander, postponed his attack at the Roer for twenty-four hours, then delayed it again indefinitely. Engineers reported that currents upstream were racing at nearly ten miles an hour, too swift for bridging, and aerial scouts above Linnich downstream found that a river usually one hundred feet wide from bank to bank now stretched a thousand yards, and in some spots more than a mile.

For nearly a fortnight, fifteen American divisions would wait on the west bank for the reservoirs to drain and the torrent to abate. Fortunately, patience and common sense were among the military virtues accorded Simpson, the son of a Confederate Army veteran who became a Pecos River rancher. Lean, angular, and six foot four, with a helmet that fitted his shaved head like a skullcap, Simpson credited his wife as "the balance wheel that settled me down." Combat experience in the Philippines, Mexico, and the Meuse-Argonne taught him as a young officer to "never send an infantryman where you can send an artillery shell." "He is excellent in every respect," Eisenhower told Marshall, and Bradley called Ninth Army "uncommonly normal." An admiring AAF officer wrote that Simpson "had the perfect calm, poise, and surety of an experienced professor. He displayed no anxiety, no uncertainty, and his whole headquarters reflected his character."

While Simpson bided his time, the Canadian First Army, composed of both British and Canadian corps, of necessity carried the weight of the Allied attack. The ponderous, muddy trudge from Nijmegen—"a bitter slugging match," in Eisenhower's phrase—averaged a bit more than a mile a day through the sloughs and thickets between the Rhine and the Maas, bagging eleven thousand enemy prisoners and reducing a score of German villages to half-timbered ash. "Machine guns are crackling now like fire rushing wildly through dry bracken," wrote R. W. Thompson, a reporter for London's *Sunday Times.* The sight of evening barrages, he added, "reminds me of the Jabberwock: 'with eyes of flame came wiffling through the tulgy wood, and burbled as he came.'" Rundstedt on February 12 reported that Army Group B had fewer than three hundred tanks and an infantry strength of under seven divisions; each German battalion was said to face the equivalent of an Allied division. As in Sicily and Normandy, Montgomery's forces would pin down substantial enemy reserves, permitting an American breakthrough.

At length Ninth Army was ready to take up the cudgels. Hoping to catch the enemy by surprise several days before the Roer spate had fully subsided, Simpson on Thursday, February 22, ordered Operation GRE-NADE launched the next morning; he then watched Bing Crosby in *Going My Way,* tossed down a nightcap, and went to bed. Hardly had the crooning ended than, at 2:45 A.M. Friday, two thousand massed guns cut loose. "The light from the flash of the cannon and explosion of the rounds was so brilliant," a lieutenant colonel in XIX Corps reported, "that you could read a document in the dark of night without any impression that there was flickering light."

Forty-five minutes later three corps plunged forward on a seventeen-mile front. Enemy fire and an unruly current still flowing at seven miles per hour would cost the assault six hundred storm boats. A footbridge installed at 4:24 A.M. promptly collapsed when rammed by a careering river craft. A falling tree and German gunners sank more foot spans, as mortar rounds walked across the water and plunging machine-gun fire

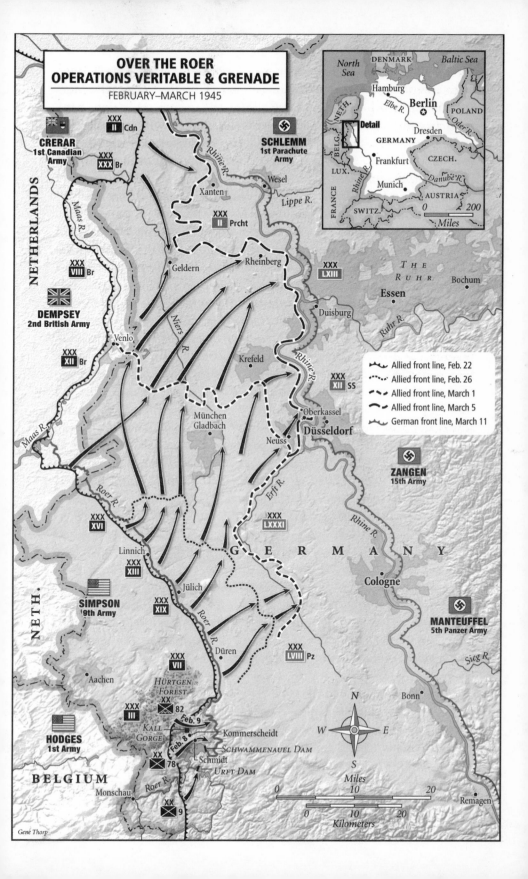

OVER THE ROER
OPERATIONS VERITABLE & GRENADE
FEBRUARY–MARCH 1945

Legend:
- Allied front line, Feb. 22
- Allied front line, Feb. 26
- Allied front line, March 1
- Allied front line, March 5
- German front line, March 11

Inset map:
North Sea · DENMARK · Baltic Sea · Hamburg · **Berlin** · POLAND · Elbe R. · Oder R. · NETH. · Detail · Dresden · BELG. · GERMANY · LUX. · CZECH. · Frankfurt · FRANCE · Rhine R. · Munich · Danube R. · AUSTRIA · SWITZ.
0 200 Miles

Main map labels:

CRERAR 1st Canadian Army — XXX II Cdn — XXX XXX Br

SCHLEMM 1st Parachute Army — XXX II Prcht

Rhine R. · Xanten · Wesel · Lippe R. · Geldern · Rheinberg · XXX LXIII · THE RUHR · Essen · Bochum

NETHERLANDS · Maas R. · XXX VIII Br

DEMPSEY 2nd British Army · Niers R. · Duisburg · Ruhr R.

Venlo · XXX XII Br · Krefeld · Rhine R. · XXX XII SS · Oberkassel · Düsseldorf

Maas R. · München Gladbach · Neuss · ZANGEN 15th Army

Roer R. · Erft R. · XXX XVI · XXX LXXXI · GERMANY

Linnich · XXX XIII · Cologne

SIMPSON 9th Army · Jülich · XXX XIX · Roer R. · MANTEUFFEL 5th Panzer Army

NETH. · Düren · XXX LVIII Pz · Rhine R. · Sieg R.

Aachen · XXX VII · HÜRTGEN FOREST · XXX III · XX 82 Feb. 9 · Bonn

HODGES 1st Army · KALL GORGE · Feb. 8 · Kommerscheidt · Schwammenauel Dam · XX 78 · Schmidt · Urft Dam

BELGIUM · Roer R. · Monschau · XX 9 · Remagen

Compass: N W E S

Miles 0 10 20
Kilometers 0 10 20

Gene Thorp

chewed through GIs flailing for shore. One bridge built by 30th Division engineers was knocked out eight times before being abandoned. The damp cold prevented a battalion in Joe Collins's VII Corps on the right flank from starting even a single outboard motor, and other boats swamped, sank, or were shot to driftwood by either enemy artillery or white-phosphorus rounds fired short from U.S. guns. A battalion commander reported "indescribable confusion."

But within hours brute force won through. Anchor cables held fast and by seven A.M. three footbridges crossed the flood; a sturdier span opened at four P.M. Friday, bearing the first vehicles. By nightfall, the bridgehead was four miles deep, and three feeble German counterattacks had been slapped aside. Of fourteen hundred U.S. casualties, most were engineers. Simpson's headquarters kept a one-page chart listing each battalion in thirteen infantry regiments with the notation "crossing" or "over" as appropriate. By dawn on Saturday, twenty-eight battalions from six divisions had reached the far shore, with ten more to follow by nightfall. A separate list of "cities captured"—mostly German villages, really—grew to sixteen. On Saturday evening, nineteen bridges spanned the Roer, seven of them fit for tanks. Scouts found beer on tap in a *Gasthaus*; other GIs captured a Nebelwerfer battery before it could fire a shot. "It looks like things are beginning to break a bit," the 30th Division commander reported.

By Monday, February 26, as three corps fanned across a bridgehead twenty-five miles wide, Ninth Army was advancing three or four miles a day with VII Corps shielding the right flank. On Tuesday, Simpson committed his armor under orders to exploit, and columns of Shermans clattered across the Cologne plain toward Düsseldorf. Swarming fighter-bombers heckled the fleeing foe; villages with streetlights burning and trolleys running fell without a shot fired. Abruptly the war seemed to have returned, as one Army historian later wrote, "to the halcyon days of August and September." By Thursday, March 1, Simpson's spearhead had reached Neuss, within rifle shot of the Rhine. From the rooftop of a seven-story grain elevator, American officers with telescopes reported seeing "the dead, lifeless giant of Düsseldorf. . . . Of the sea of factory chimneys, one smoked; of the miles of railroad yards in the foreground, not one car moved."

Eight bridges spanned the great river on Ninth Army's front, and one by one German engineers blew them into the water. A ruse to seize the crossing at Oberkassel almost succeeded: the strike force moved at night, with Shermans tricked up as panzers and with German-speaking GIs perched on the fenders. The deception was unmasked only at dawn by a gimlet-eyed enemy soldier on a bicycle who bellowed in alarm. Gunfire raked the street, sirens wailed, and a pell-mell rush for the ramp ended abruptly when bridge girders, towers, and roadbed plunged into the river with a roar and another of those mighty, disheartening splashes.

Simpson now proposed a quick amphibious assault over the Rhine north of Düsseldorf. A thrust by XIX Corps could shorten the war by weeks, he believed; patrols reported that "the enemy is completely disorganized and has neither defensive forces on this side nor the far side of the Rhine capable of stopping a fast crossing." Montgomery declined with a curt "Don't go across," adding that any attempt by Ninth Army to invade the "industrial wilderness" of the Ruhr without extensive, deliberate preparation was "unwise" and would risk precious bridging matériel. The field marshal's rationale was quite plausible, but an incensed Simpson believed Montgomery coveted for himself and the British the glory of the first Rhine crossing—"a selfish idea," in the army commander's estimation. American officers increasingly derided the British as the "time out for tea army."

GRENADE was over. Ninth Army in less than two weeks had driven more than fifty miles from the Roer to the Rhine. The Canadian First Army had covered forty miles, against stiffer opposition. The two forces met on March 3 at Geldern, west of Duisburg. Together they had suffered 23,000 casualties while capturing 51,000 Germans and killing or wounding 38,000 more.

Despite the staggering losses, enemy survivors escaped in good order across the Rhine before blowing six final bridges in Duisburg and Wesel. Allied armies had begun to mass along the great river, if piecemeal and without a clear sense of how or where to cross. Still, Rundstedt told Hitler that the German plight on the Western Front was "bad everywhere," and even the Führer was forced to acknowledge "a heavy heart."

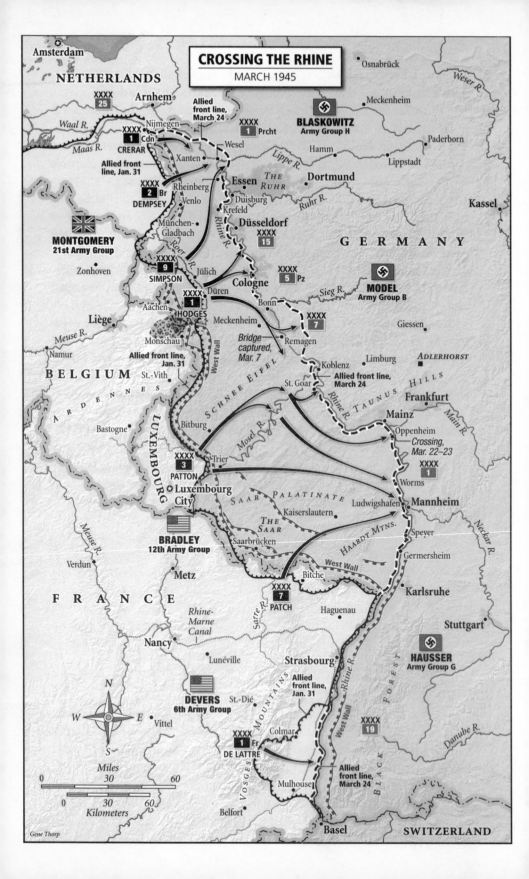

CROSSING THE RHINE
MARCH 1945

Amsterdam

NETHERLANDS

• Osnabrück

Weser R.

XXXX 25

Arnhem

• Meckenheim

Allied front line, March 24

Waal R.

Nijmegen

XXXX 1 Cdn **CRERAR**

XXXX 1 Prcht

BLASKOWITZ
Army Group H

• Paderborn

• Hamm

• Lippstadt

Wesel

Maas R.

Allied front line, Jan. 31

Xanten

Lippe R.

THE RUHR

Dortmund

Kassel

Rheinberg

Venlo

Essen

Duisburg

Ruhr R.

XXXX 2 Br **DEMPSEY**

München-Gladbach

Krefeld

Düsseldorf

Rhine R.

XXXX 15

MONTGOMERY
21st Army Group

G E R M A N Y

• Zonhoven

Roer R.

Jülich

XXXX 9 **SIMPSON**

Düren

Cologne

XXXX 5 Pz

MODEL
Army Group B

XXXX 1 **HODGES**

Bonn

Sieg R.

• Giessen

Aachen

Liège

Meckenheim

XXXX 7

Monschau

Bridge captured, Mar. 7

Remagen

ADLERHORST

Namur

Meuse R.

West Wall

Allied front line, Jan. 31

Koblenz

• Limburg

B E L G I U M

St.-Vith

Schnee Eifel

St. Goar

Allied front line, March 24

TAUNUS HILLS

Frankfurt

Bitburg

Mosel R.

Rhine R.

Mainz

• Bastogne

L U X E M B O U R G

Trier

Oppenheim

Main R.

XXXX 3 **PATTON**

Luxembourg City

SAAR PALATINATE

Crossing, Mar. 22–23

XXXX 1

Worms

Kaiserslautern

Ludwigshafen

Mannheim

BRADLEY
12th Army Group

THE SAAR

Saarbrücken

Speyer

HAARDT MTNS.

Neckar R.

Verdun

Metz

West Wall

Germersheim

F R A N C E

Bitche

Karlsruhe

XXXX 7 **PATCH**

Haguenau

Stuttgart

Rhine-Marne Canal

Sarre R.

Nancy

Lunéville

Strasbourg

Allied front line, Jan. 31

HAUSSER
Army Group G

N

W   E

S

St.-Dié

V O S G E S

M O U N T A I N S

Rhine R.

West Wall

DEVERS
6th Army Group

• Vittel

Colmar

XXXX 1 Fr **DE LATTRE**

B L A C K   F O R E S T

XXXX 19

Danube R.

Miles
0   30   60

Mulhouse

Allied front line, March 24

Kilometers
0   30   60

Belfort

Basel

SWITZERLAND

Gene Thorp

11. CROSSINGS

The Inner Door to Germany

INTO the Rhineland they pounded, and across the Saar and down the Mosel, where violets and myrtle had begun to bloom and the first early buds stippled the fruit trees. Engineers corduroyed cart tracks through smitten glades, and filled roadside ditches with bricks and stone from granulated villages to fashion an extra lane for the endless convoys rolling east. "This is better than the other sort of war," a British lieutenant reflected. "You feel you're getting somewhere."

German refugees trudged away from the beaten zone, lugging suitcases and favorite lamps and tablecloth peddler packs. Martial slogans could still be seen on the broken walls—*"Führer befehl, wir folgen!"* Führer, command us and we'll follow!—but so could slatherings of despair, including *"Hitler weg! Krieg weg!"* Down with Hitler! Down with war! Churches posted "In Memoriam" notices for dead soldiers by the hundreds, the thousands, the tens of thousands. U.S. Army trucks trundled to the rear with coal-scuttle helmets as hood ornaments, each open bed packed with prisoners. "They stood facing the rear, their gray-green uniforms dirty," wrote W. C. Heinz, "all of them rocking together with the motion of the trucks." German women held up babies or tossed bread from their doorways as they studied the passing blur of faces in hopes of a recognition. "I am in the fodderland," Audie Murphy would write to his family. "It is much different than the other countrys ive been in. The Houses are nicer and more modern but still arnt as good as ours."

As two dozen British, Canadian, and American divisions in 21st Army Group closed on the Rhine in the north, Hodges's First Army also made for the river between Cologne and Koblenz, with thirteen divisions in three corps abreast. "It is impossible not to be elated," the headquarters diary noted on March 3. Farther south, twelve divisions in Patton's Third Army overran the rubble that once was Bitburg, then pivoted through the Saar-Palatinate in tandem with fourteen divisions from Patch's Seventh Army. Together, they would attack on a seventy-mile front along the flanks of the Haardt Mountains. Any town that spurned surrender demands from a "bullshit wagon"—a Sherman fitted with loudspeakers audible two miles away—was scourged with tank and howitzer shells until eventually a white flag or two popped up; the obstinate died. "On the road yesterday I could look ahead and see at least a dozen towns burning and fires sprouting out from various and sundry places all over the horizon," Major General Alvan C. Gillem, Jr., commander of XIII Corps, wrote his wife in Georgia. Of 1,700 buildings in Jülich, 300 remained intact; of 9,322 in Düren, described by an engineer as "the most totally destroyed city I have ever seen," 13 stood undamaged. Doors torn from their hinges were used to cover German bodies awaiting burial, and big paper sacks served as coffins for want of lumber.

"Everything smelled of death," Iris Carpenter wrote after viewing another place reduced to slag. "Bulldozers scraped a road through the heart of the town which was little more than a smoldering rockery." Allied fighter-bombers harried the fleeing enemy in what one pilot called a "rat hunt: You beat the ground. You flushed the vermin." Artillery barrages ignited open-pit coal seams, Alan Moorehead noted, giving "a lovely play of light and gold flowing heat." To his family in Virginia, a logistics officer wrote in early March, "The earth is certainly scorched."

Nearer the Rhine, however, the swift bound of Allied armies captured intact a *gemütlich* land of bucolic farmsteads and bulging larders. "The cattle, so numerous, so well fed. Chickens and pigs and horses were running everywhere," Moorehead wrote. "Every house seemed to have a good linen cupboard." The reporter R. W. Thompson catalogued "fine stocks of ironmongery, metal goods, oil stoves, furniture, and mattresses. The paper in the deserted offices was of fine quality." In a former candy factory, Martha Gellhorn found "vast stocks of sugar, chocolate, cocoa, butter, almonds," as well as rooms chock-full of Dutch and French cheese, Portuguese sardines, Norwegian canned fish, and syrup by the barrel.

Here was a world of Dresden plates, pewter steins, and trophy antlers arranged *just so* on parlor walls, of Goethe and Schiller bound in calfskin, of boiled eggs in brine vats and the smell of roasting goose. Here was a world of damask tablecloths and silverware in handsome hutches, of Third Reich motherhood medals for stalwart childbearing, and French cosmetics looted from Paris or Lyon. Every house seemed to display a crucifix or Christian texts over the bedsteads; some flew Allied flags, or posted signs claiming that the occupants were Dutch or Belgian, and never mind that discolored patch of wallpaper where the Führer's portrait had hung until the day before. "No one is a Nazi. No one ever was," Gellhorn wrote. "It would sound better if it were set to music. Then the Germans could sing this refrain."

Here too was a world to be looted. "We're advancing as fast as the looting will permit," a 29th Division unit in München-Gladbach reported. German towns were "processed," houses "liberated" from attic to cellar, with everything from Leica cameras to accordions pilfered. A corps provost marshal complained of "gangsterism" by GIs who were "looting and bullying civilians"; some were caught exhuming a medieval grave in a hunt for jewels, while others ripped up floorboards or searched gardens with mine detectors. W. C. Heinz watched a soldier on a stolen bicycle with half a dozen women's dresses draped over his arm carefully stow both bike and garments in a jeep trailer. Plundering MPs were known as the "Lootwaffe": according to a soldier in the 45th Division, a "typical infantry squad involved two shooting and ten looting." Moorehead described how "German cars by the hundred were dragged out of garages ... painted khaki and driven away." French troops hauled German motorcycles, typewriters, and Friesian cows back to Lorraine. British soldiers pillaged a hardware shop, carrying away screws, nails, and hinges simply from "a desire to do some unhindered shoplifting," a *Daily Telegraph* reporter concluded.

That which escaped plunder often was vandalized in what one private called "the chaotic air of a drunken, end-of-the-world carnival." A Canadian soldier recounted his own rampage through a Westphalian house:

> First I took a hammer and smashed over 100 plates, and the cups along with them. Then I took an axe to the china cabinets and buffets. Next I smashed all the furniture. .... I put a grenade in the big piano, and after I poured a jar of molasses into it. I broke all the French doors and all the doors with mirrors in them and threw the lamps into the street. I was so mad.

"I did not feel sorry for the Germans," said Major Peter Carrington, a British officer. "After all they had proved enormously inconvenient."

Allied commanders also found themselves struggling to enforce SHAEF's "non-fraternization" edict, which forbid "mingling with Germans upon terms of friendliness, familiarity, or intimacy," and specifically proscribed "the ogling of women and girls." Violations incurred a $65 fine, so the pursuit of pretty German girls—dubbed "fraternazis" and "furleins"—was soon known as "the $65 question." "Don't play Samson to her Delilah," an Armed Forces Network broadcast warned. "She'd like to cut your hair off—at the neck." But "goin' fratin'" became epidemic, often with cigarettes or chocolate as "frau bait." "To frat" was a synonym for intercourse; non-fraternization was referred to as "non-fertilization." GIs argued that "copulation without conversation is not fraternization," and Patton advised, "Tell the men of Third Army that so long as they keep their helmets on they are not fraternizing." Many a troop truck rolled through a Rhenish village with some leather-lunged soldier bellowing pathetically at young women on the sidewalk, *"Bitte, schlafen mit."* Please sleep with me.

General Hodges ordered champagne served in his mess on Monday, March 5, to celebrate First Army's imminent arrival on the Rhine. Toasts were raised "to an early crossing." A day later VII Corps punched into Cologne, Germany's fourth largest metropolis, that city of mystics and heretics, of Saint Ursula and eleven thousand virgins said to have been massacred by barbarians for their faith, the city where Karl Marx had edited the *Rheinische Zeitung* and where priests had once celebrated a thousand masses a day. Now, of 770,000 residents only 10,000 remained. Two dozen Bomber Command raids in the past three years left Cologne resembling "the open mouth of a charred corpse," in the image of the poet Stephen Spender. Like other dead cities it had the same odd shapelessness that afflicted dead men, a loss of structure and contour as well as life.

Volkssturm pensioners fought from behind overturned trams, and enemy snipers darted through the rubble. Building by broken building, block by broken block, Sherman gunners systematically burned out upper floors with white phosphorus while GI infantrymen grenaded the cellars. A cavalry charge across Cologne's airfield by 3rd Armored Division tanks smashed sixteen 88mm antiaircraft guns trying to form a skirmish line. The twin-spired thirteenth-century cathedral still stood, though wounded by bombs, shells, and incendiaries that had left the ceiling and stained glass in shards across the nave floor. Nazi flags could be found "dumped like scarlet garbage into the corners of alleys," wrote the journalist Janet Flanner. "The destroyer of others is herself destroyed."

Hodges on Wednesday, March 7, reported that Cologne had fallen. Yet so had the city's link to the east bank of the Rhine: a twelve-hundred-foot segment of the Hohenzollern bridge had been blown into the river at noon the previous day. First Army's hopes for an early crossing seemed ever more faint.

"The Rhine. I don't know what I expected. Another Mississippi, I suppose," an engineer sergeant told his diary. "The damn thing flows north." Indeed it did. From Switzerland, where the river was fed by 150 glaciers, to the North Sea, the European father of waters formed an extraordinary moat against invasion from the west. Although it was only the world's fifteenth-largest river in volume, ranking between the Euphrates and the Rhône, the Rhine was broad, deep, and fast enough that engineers compared any crossing to "a short sea voyage." "At no place is the river fordable, even at low water," the U.S. Army Corps of Engineers reported, and winter floods had been the highest in a quarter century, with currents in some stretches approaching eleven miles an hour. Most of the thirty-one Rhine bridges within Germany had been demolished by men with a rare aptitude for destruction. Thanks to the aerial bombardment of German factories, the river flowed relatively unpolluted for the first time in a generation, but so much wreckage clogged its bed that the Allies could not simply sail upstream from Nijmegen. A "top secret and private" note from Churchill's office to Beetle Smith likened the difficulties faced by seven Allied armies in catapulting eighty divisions across the river to "another D-Day."

Plans to jump the Rhine had been drafted even before the Normandy landings. Exhaustive studies examined bank, current, weather, and ice conditions, as well as Roman accounts of erecting a trestle bridge before the birth of Christ, and French records of nineteenth-century pile-driving near Strasbourg. Army engineers in Vicksburg, Mississippi, scrutinized historical hydrology data, aided by intelligence agents in Switzerland and daily gage readings intercepted in German radio broadcasts to river pilots. More than 170 models of the Rhine were built, and a hydraulics laboratory in Grenoble conducted elaborate experiments. A Rhine River Flood Prediction Service opened in January; mindful of the Roer debacle, diplomats pressed the Swiss to protect seven headwater dams with soldiers and artillery.

River-crossing schools on the Loire trained hundreds of outboard-motor operators, pile-driving specialists, and DUKW drivers. A steel mill in Luxembourg extruded 54,000 tons of massive I-beams for bridge building. Boatyards in Florida, Minnesota, and Michigan built hundreds of seventeen-foot plywood craft designed to carry a dozen riflemen and three engineers each; nested and crated in clusters of six, the vessels were whisked to Europe by cargo plane or fast ship. French boatwrights, shown a photograph of a storm boat in January, set to work using blueprints drawn by a naval architect. Trees were felled, plywood milled, and screws and nails fashioned from surplus wire; five weeks after placing the order, the U.S. Army picked up seven hundred boats. Seagoing landing craft, capable of carrying a Sherman tank or sixty men, sailed from England to Antwerp and up the Albert Canal before being hauled overland to the Rhineland on trailers so enormous that bulldozers led the convoys to knock down any building crimping the roadway. Other big craft for this "inland navy" were trucked three hundred miles from Le Havre; they arrived, a witness reported, "festooned with treetops, telephone wires, and bits of buildings from French villages."

By early March, forward depots contained 1,100 assault boats, 124 landing craft, 2,500 outboard motors, 5 million board feet of lumber, 6,000 bridge floats, and enough steel and pilings to build more than 60 bridges. Everyone agreed, however, that it would be far simpler to capture one already built.

Just such a bridge still stood fifteen miles south of Bonn at Remagen, an ancient Roman town straddling a road built by Marcus Aurelius. Here the Rhine scoured a curving basalt gorge: to the north, Siegfried had slain his dragon at Drachenfels, bathing in the creature's blood to become invulnerable; to the south, Julius Caesar built two spans over the river, in 55 and 53 B.C., during his Gallic campaigns. The current bridge had been completed in 1918 and named for General Erich Ludendorff, the progenitor of the final, fatal German offensives on the Western Front in the Great War. More than a thousand feet long and wide enough for two trains to pass abeam, the span featured symmetrical arches resting on four stone piers, with embrasured stone towers at either end. Wooden planks could be laid on the rail tracks to permit motor traffic. On the east bank, the tracks vanished into the Dwarf's Hole, a tunnel bored through the steep six-hundred-foot hill called the Erpeler Ley. Local aesthetes complained that the bridge marred the dramatic riverscape; they complained more when it drew repeated Allied air attacks, including a January raid that killed three dozen civilians.

Retreating German soldiers had tramped across the Ludendorff in late 1918, and now retreating German soldiers were tramping over it once again, mingling with refugees, livestock, and an occasional hospital train carrying broken boys. A teenage antiaircraft gunner described a snaking procession making for the bridge through Remagen's jammed streets on Wednesday morning, March 7, "with cannons being pulled by horses, by motor vehicles, and yes, even by soldiers." Fewer than a thousand defenders remained in the area; most were Volkssturm militia of doubtful martial value, and all fell under a confused, fractured command architecture. Field Marshal Model had promised reinforcements, but none had arrived.

Sixty zinc-lined boxes for explosives had been fitted to the bridge in 1938, linked by cables through heavy conduits to an electrical firing switch inside the rail tunnel. The premature blowing of a bridge near Cologne— apparently triggered by an American bomb—had led to a Führer order that explosive charges would be emplaced only when the enemy was within five miles of a bridge, and igniters were to be withheld until "demolition seems to be unavoidable." On Wednesday morning, sketchy reports put U.S. Army outriders near the western bluffs above Remagen. Explosives were laid, but Army Group B described the Americans as a thin screening force to mask an Allied thrust toward Bonn and Cologne. Little urgency obtained.

Their enemy was nearer than they knew. On the previous night, March 6, the U.S. III Corps commander, Major General John Millikin, had phoned Major General John W. Leonard, commander of the 9th Armored Division. "Do you see that little black strip of a bridge at Remagen?" Millikin asked as both men squinted at their maps. "If you happen to get that, your name will go down in glory."

At 8:20 A.M. on this gray, misty Wednesday, a tank-and-infantry task force left Meckenheim, ten miles from the river. Leading the column in the advance guard was Lieutenant Karl H. Timmermann, who had commanded Company A of the 27th Armored Infantry Battalion for less than twenty-four hours. Timmermann had been born not far to the southeast, in Frankfurt; his doughboy father had taken a German war bride in 1919 before moving back to Nebraska. In a note scribbled in a Meckenheim cellar, the weary young officer told his wife:

> There is no glory in war. Maybe those who have never been in battle find [a] certain glory and glamour that doesn't exist. . . . Tell mom that we'll be on the Rhine tomorrow.

Now Lieutenant Timmermann would prove himself wrong: for a brief, vivid moment glory would be his. Summoned by two waving scouts shortly before one P.M., he hurried forward in his jeep to find a hazy, panoramic view of the Rhine gorge below. "Jesus, look at that," a sergeant muttered. "Do you know what the hell river that is?" Through field glasses Timmermann watched cows, horses, soldiers, trucks, and civilians cross beneath the bridge arches in a lumbering parade. Just below, white flags and bedsheets flapped from Remagen windowsills. Two locomotives with steam up stood on the far bank.

As three platoons descended through the town, leapfrogging from doorway to doorway, Timmermann bounded past the handsome St. Apollinaris Church and a sign that read, "Citizens and Friends: Preserve Our Parks." A spatter of German musketry provoked booming return fire from a platoon of new M-26 Pershing tanks, each brandishing a 90mm gun. Tearful Germans pointed to cellars where Volkssturm stragglers crouched in terror. A captured enemy general in an elaborately braided uniform proved upon interrogation to be a railroad station agent.

Shortly before two P.M. a dark geyser of earth and paving stones abruptly blossomed above the western ramp; the blast left a smoking hole thirty feet wide, intended to keep American tanks from gaining the bridge. Heckling gunfire erupted from the Ludendorff towers. Bullets pinged and sparked among the girders. GIs fixed bayonets before darting past the last houses above the river. "I'll see you on the other side," the 27th Armored Infantry commander told Timmermann, "and we'll all have a chicken dinner. . . . Move on." Timmermann raked the far bank with his glasses.

Tiny figures loped along the shoreline and into the tunnel. "They look like they want to get us on the bridge before they blow it up," he said.

Barely half a mile away, pandemonium swept the eastern shore. Civilians and shrieking children cowered in the Dwarf's Hole as billowing smoke from white-phosphorus shells drifted down the tunnel. German soldiers ran this way and that along the bridge ramp, including several engulfed in orange flame from American tank shells chewing up the riverbank and smacking the Erpeler Ley. Three junior officers argued over whether the demolition order should be put in writing. Shouts of "Blow the bridge!" carried across the water, and at length a captain shouted, "Everybody lie down! Open your mouths to protect your eardrums." He turned the key on the firing switch.

Nothing happened. He turned it again, and again, without effect. A German sergeant sprinted ninety yards onto the bridge, lighted the primer cord by hand, and pelted back to the tunnel, chased by bullets.

With a doleful boom the timber planks rose from the railbed like jackstraws. Dust and black smoke boiled from the piers. The Ludendorff seemed to levitate momentarily as if expending a great sigh, then settled back onto its stone foundations, insulted but intact.

No one would ever be certain why fourteen hundred pounds of explosives failed to detonate properly: faulty charges, faulty blasting caps, perhaps a tank shell that severed the main demolition cable, perhaps, as some averred, a miracle.

Reprieved, Lieutenant Timmermann and his men raced onto the bridge, slashing wires and pitching charges into the water. Four Pershing tanks and a dozen Shermans arrayed on the west bank hammered the eastern tower until riflemen could clear out a German machine-gun nest. Sergeant Alex Drabik of Toledo reached the far bank first, in a zigzagging, stumbling sprint that cost him his helmet. Eight others followed on his heels, including Timmermann.

By late afternoon, Company A had 120 men across. A platoon began to scale the Erpeler Ley, dodging stones rolled down the slope by a flak battery holding the crest. After a single warning shot, five German engineers surrendered in the Dwarf's Hole; GIs blew apart the master demolition switch with a carbine. A 90mm tank round from across the river smashed through a German locomotive tugging a long string of boxcars, and the train halted with a sharp lurch, a white plume of steam sighing from the firebox. GIs crouched in a ditch as a passenger train from the north pulled into the tiny Erpel station; middle-aged soldiers with rifles spilled onto the platform only to be greeted with mispronounced shouts of *"Hände hoch."* A single German guard at the eastern exit of the rail tunnel also was seized, and twenty minutes later two hundred others emerged under a white flag to march in their long leather coats, hands high, across the bridge they had neither saved nor destroyed. Before surrendering, Captain Willi Bratge, the Remagen commandant, told a subordinate to deliver a message to the German high command. "Inform them that the demolition of the bridge was unsuccessful," Bratge said, "and that the Americans have crossed."

Night fell, a sodden, moonless night, "dark as a pocket," as one officer recorded, so dark that engineers felt for the street curbs in Remagen with their feet. Bulldozers slowly filled the crater on the western ramp and three artillery battalions unlimbered. Soldiers ripped lumber from German houses to patch the rail planks. Exhausted drivers napped at their wheels as great knots of convoy traffic converged at the bridge, awaiting orders to cross. By ten P.M. three depleted rifle companies occupied the far shore, thwarting a counterattack by a hundred German engineers and antiaircraft crewmen who were repulsed near the Erpeler Ley while carrying half a ton of explosives.

At last nine Shermans—narrower than the Pershings—crept across at midnight, guided by foot soldiers wearing luminous buttons on their belts. German tracer fire searched the span, usually a few feet too high. "Ominous and nerve-wracking creaking" rose from the bridge, a captain reported, all the more ominous when the tenth vehicle to cross, a tank destroyer, skidded to the right near one of the eastern piers and plunged partway through a hole in the deck. For several hours—"the most harrowing minutes of my life," one officer acknowledged—the vehicle remained stuck, blocking all traffic. Engineers debated pushing it over the side, or jacking it up, or winching it out, or blowing it to pieces. Just as dawn peeked above the Erpeler Ley, the damnable thing was muscled out and towed away. The desperate effort to deepen the bridgehead resumed apace, through what a Wehrmacht general now called "the inner door to Germany."

Ancient, stately Reims, known by the undignified Allied code name BASSINET, had been home to SHAEF's forward headquarters since mid-February. The city was renowned both for enthroning more than two dozen French kings, beginning with the fifth-century conversion to Christianity of Clovis the Frank, and for champagne, fermented in chalky warrens that ran for miles underground. Allied staff officers often held blind tastings at day's end, sipping from one bottle after another to debate the merits of Krug and Taittinger and Moët & Chandon.

Eisenhower messed in the borrowed house of a Heidsieck Monopole champagne baron, not far from the Cathédrale Notre-Dame, and on March 7 he had invited several airborne commanders to supper, among them Ridgway, Gavin, and Maxwell Taylor. He had just complained about the soup when a whispering aide summoned him to the telephone for a call

from Bradley. Harry Butcher could hear the supreme commander's booming voice:

> Brad, that's wonderful. Sure, get right on across with everything you've
> got. It's the best break we've had. . . . To hell with the planners. Sure, go
> on, Brad. . . . We'll make good use of it even if the terrain isn't too good.

Returning to the dining room with a jubilant grin on his face, Eisenhower ordered champagne for the table. "That was Brad," he said. "He's
got a bridge across the Rhine. And he apologized for it, said it was badly
located at Remagen."

They drank to the bridge, and to the valiant lads who had seized it. Yet
before long the supreme commander would realize that this remote site
created almost as many problems as it solved. "Nobody ever would have
selected *that* bridge," General Millikin conceded. Poor roads and rugged
terrain; a sclerotic bottleneck at Remagen; the shift of Allied legions to
bolster Montgomery's planned crossing ninety miles north—such exigencies made exploitation harder than simply flinging First Army over the
Ludendorff, or the Ludy, as it was soon called.

For the moment, Eisenhower would commit five divisions across the
Rhine, with orders to gain the autobahn seven miles beyond the river. By
Thursday evening, March 8, eight thousand GIs occupied a bridgehead
two miles wide and a mile deep. Mindful of the German frogmen who
had destroyed the Nijmegen rail bridge, engineers strung three protective
booms upstream, including one with a steel net dangling ten feet below
the river surface. Searchlights swept the water from dusk until dawn, cavalrymen fired at suspicious flotsam, and boat crews dropped depth charges
every five minutes, detonating seven tons of explosives each night.

As engineers toiled to strengthen the fragile Ludy, the first ferry
crossed the Rhine at dawn on Friday, soon joined by two more hauling
gasoline and ammunition. Construction crews also began work on a floating treadway bridge a few hundred yards downstream. Power boats bullied each new segment through the river, to be appended to the growing
span with four-foot spikes hammered home by "suicide squads" braving
German mortar and artillery barrages. A particularly vicious shelling
demolished nineteen floats in ten minutes, killing or wounding seventeen
engineers. Among them was Private First Class Marion Priester, age
twenty, who tried to close a wicked chest wound with his hands before
announcing, "Boys, I've had it." As a comrade reported, "He died before
he hit the ground." Yet by five o'clock on Sunday afternoon, thirty-two
hours after work had begun, the first jeep crossed the thousand-foot
bridge. A second span was finished a few hours later. By Monday, three

infantry divisions and part of an armored combat command held a bridge-head fourteen miles wide and four miles deep.

Loss of the Ludendorff was an unalloyed disaster for the German high command. In an order decrypted by Ultra, Rundstedt demanded that both bridge and bridgehead "be immediately destroyed with lasting effect." Model directed the 11th Panzer Division to lead a counterattack from Düsseldorf, a fantasy given the profound shortages of fuel and munitions. Still, more than a hundred guns soon battered the bridgehead, a round every two minutes, among them three shells that hit the Ludy on March 9, punching another fifteen-foot hole in the deck and setting an ammunition truck on fire. Joining the cannonade was the "Karl" mortar, a 600mm behemoth that weighed 137 tons and fired a 2-ton projectile with little accuracy and less effect, although one enemy shell was said to have hit a Remagen bank, filling the street with fluttering Reichsmark notes.

Hermann Göring sought volunteers to fly suicide missions into the bridge, a proposal also intercepted by Allied eavesdroppers even before it was rejected as impractical by German commanders. Nearly four hundred Luftwaffe sorties were flown over Remagen, including missions by jet planes and antiquated Stuka dive-bombers; all could just as well have been deliberately suicidal. The marauders soon encountered twenty-five barrage balloons and nearly seven hundred antiaircraft guns—the Army's densest concentration of World War II—under orders to shoot anything with wings. Each approaching enemy plane was said by one officer to "cost the American taxpayer a million dollars in antiaircraft ammunition," and gunners would claim more than a hundred aircraft shot down. The intense fire inflicted two hundred friendly casualties on the ground, mostly welts and bruises from the spent .50-caliber slugs that fell like hard rain. On Hitler's command, V-2 launch sites in Holland also fired eleven rockets at the bridge, the only tactical use of the weapon during the war. None struck home; the single near miss killed three GIs and a barnyard full of livestock several hundred yards from the river.

The debacle at Remagen clearly called for recrimination and reprisal, and the Führer wasted no time. Rundstedt, who had already infuriated Hitler by ridiculing the *Westwall* as a "mousetrap," was relieved of command for the second time in nine months. Given another bauble to pin to his uniform and a curt "I thank you for your loyalty" from the Führer, Rundstedt once again repaired to Bad Tölz to take the cure for his rheumatism. "No one," his chief of staff wrote, "can jump over his own shadow." He was succeeded on March 10 as the OB West commander by Field Marshal Albert Kesselring, who for the past two and a half years had been the Allies' archnemesis in North Africa, Sicily, and Italy.

Harsher fates befell four junior officers deemed to have bungled the Ludendorff demolition. A drumhead court-martial tried, convicted, and condemned them within thirty minutes. Denied clergy and stripped of rank insignia, each was shot in the back of the neck and buried in a shallow grave. The letters they had been permitted to write their families were then burned.

Such rough justice was said to create a "bridge psychosis" throughout the German ranks: officers devoted colossal tonnages of TNT to blowing bridges and culverts across the shrinking Reich. But neither Kesselring nor a kangaroo court could stem the American flood tide at Remagen.

Among those crossing the Rhine on March 12 was the 5th Platoon of Company K of the 394th Infantry Regiment. Singular only because they were black, these GI riflemen were among fifty-three platoons of "colored" infantry mustered from volunteers to help remedy manpower shortages after the Bulge. Many had surrendered sergeant's stripes earned as cooks, drivers, and laborers in black service battalions for the privilege of fighting as privates. "Hitler was the one that got us out of the white folks' kitchen," one black observer later said.

"Get it moving," yelled a first sergeant in the 394th. "You ain't in the quartermaster no more. You're in the Army now." They of course had already been in the Army, among 900,000 African-Americans to serve in olive drab, but now they were partially integrated as black platoons under white officers within white companies, scattered through eleven divisions. Despite the creditable records of two black divisions in Italy and the Pacific, and of black artillery and tank battalions before and during the Bulge, resistance to integrating combat regiments ran deep. "A colored soldier cannot think fast enough to fight in armor," Patton told his diary, and some argued that teaching black riflemen to shoot white Germans would lead to the shooting of white Americans at home. "We were going to make liars out of the whites," a black soldier later said. Another wrote, "I am an American negro, doing my part for the American government to make the world safe for a democracy I have never known." For many white combat soldiers in Germany, the simple truth was voiced by an artillery forward observer in the 394th Infantry: "We were short-handed and they were welcome."

Repairs on the Ludendorff continued for nine days even as tactical bridges carried most of the traffic across the Rhine. Between air raids and enemy shellings, two hundred welders, riggers, ironworkers, and carpenters swarmed over the structure, patching chords, stringers, and holes in the deck. Measurements showed the Ludy settling a bit on the upstream side, to the south, but engineers believed the structure had been stabilized.

It had not. Just before three P.M. on Saturday, March 17, a rivet sheared away with a sharp *pop!* Others followed, as if musketry swept the girders.

A vertical hanger snapped. Dust billowed from the quaking deck. Timbers splintered and the squeal of steel on steel echoed against the Erpeler Ley. "Men on the deck dropped their tools and started to run," an engineer colonel later testified. Many found themselves sprinting uphill as the center span twisted counterclockwise and buckled. Then the entire bridge seemed to fold in on itself, "gracefully, like an old slow-motion movie," before pitching into the Rhine with a white splash.

Of those who rode the Ludy down, twenty-eight died and another sixty-three were injured. A major's body found atop the east pier was recognizable only by his oak-leaf rank insignia; others vanished into the Rhine forever. Scaffolding and deck timbers threatened to ram through the treadways downstream until engineers with axes and poles pushed the debris away while boatmen fished survivors from the river. Precisely why the bridge collapsed would remain uncertain. Weakened by earlier Allied bombing and the botched demolition, the span had since been assaulted by hard winds, heavy traffic, welding, incessant hammering, V-2s, artillery, and the vibration of a thousand shells fired from an Army 8-inch howitzer battery less than a mile away. "Most of us," an engineer told his diary, "are glad the damned thing is gone."

Late Saturday night, seven German frogmen who had trained in a Vienna swimming pool slipped into the Rhine with orders to destroy the tactical bridges using plastic explosives. None got close before being captured, killed, or forced to shore by exhaustion, gunfire, and blinding searchlights. Within a week, eight Army bridges would span the Rhine near Remagen, feeding a bridgehead now twenty-five miles wide and eight miles deep. The Frankfurt autobahn, finally severed on March 16, would serve as a trunk road into the Fatherland's central precincts.

On Monday, March 19, Eisenhower approved shoving nine First Army divisions across the Rhine in anticipation of forming a common front with Third Army once Patton jumped the river below Koblenz. "The war is over, I tell you," Hodges repeatedly proclaimed in Spa. "The war is over." The war was not over, nor would giddy repetition make it so. But the inner door to Germany had swung wide, never to be shut again.

Two If by Sea

FIELD Marshal Kesselring's buoyant optimism and Bavarian bonhomie had served him well through five years of war. A toothy, ruthless sophisticate whom the Americans derisively called Smiling Albert, he was descended from brewers, vintners, and an occasional soldier of fortune; his father had been a schoolmaster in Bayreuth, home of Richard Wagner.

Kesselring's Allied adversaries in the Mediterranean knew all too well that he was an exceptional field commander, responsible for the long, fighting withdrawal from El Alamein to northern Italy. Energetic and confident, he also possessed that priceless attribute of successful generalship—luck—and was celebrated for his narrow escapes. Having learned to fly at age forty-eight before transferring from the artillery to the Luftwaffe, he had survived being shot down five times. "I don't believe you can be a military commander unless you're an optimist," Hitler said of Kesselring. The new OB West commander's marching orders from the Führer were concise, explicit, and impossible to fulfill: "Hang on."

Now Kesselring's luck showed signs of deserting him. In October, his staff car had collided with a German gun, an accident from which he was still recuperating. He found travel difficult, and his ability to personally inspect the battlefront was impaired. Exactly how many troops he commanded was uncertain; since the beginning of the Rhineland battles in February, a quarter-million Germans had vanished, mostly into Allied prison camps. Wehrmacht maps showed divisions where not even regiments remained, and staff officers estimated that German strength in the west had been pared to "at the very best one hundred combatants to every kilometer of front." Directives and queries from Berlin inclined toward the hallucinatory: for instance, could the Channel Islands garrison hold out for another year? Rumors circulated in the ranks that the Americans intended to shoot all German corporals to forestall the rise of another Hitler.

Field commanders in mid-March urged Kesselring to complete the Wehrmacht's evacuation across the Rhine; clinging to enclaves west of the river was deemed hopeless if not disastrous. The field marshal disagreed, fearful that retreat would degenerate into rout. In line with Hitler's "hang on" policy, on March 17 he ordered "the retention of present positions," while telling subordinates that "annihilation . . . is to be avoided."

Yet only three days later even the Reich's last optimist had to acknowledge that the Americans had "torn our front wide open." The enemy might be delayed, but not stopped. "The best general," Kesselring mused, "cannot make bricks without straw."

George Patton had taken brief leave in Paris, where Beetle Smith took him hunting in an old royal preserve outside the city. Patton shot three ducks, three hares, and a pheasant. Later he sat in a box at the Folies Bergère, sipping champagne and acknowledging an adulatory ovation from the audience. The revue girls, he noted, were "perfectly naked, so much so that no one is interested." Hurrying back to the front, he resolved to remain within sound of the guns for the duration.

Battlefield carnage always inflamed Patton's imagination, and the

Saar-Palatinate proved particularly vivifying. In Trier, for instance, twenty air raids and Third Army onslaughts had reduced the city to 730,000 cubic yards of rubble. "The desolation is frozen, as if the moment of combustion was suddenly arrested, and the air had lost its power to hold atoms together," wrote Private First Class Lincoln Kirstein, who would soon found the New York City Ballet. "Hardly a whole thing is left." The entrance to the old Roman amphitheater still stood and that, coupled with his nightly read-ings from Caesar's *Gallic Wars,* sufficed for Patton to inform his diary in mid-March that he "could smell the sweat of the legions." It was all there for him: gladiators grappling with wild beasts; legionnaires and centurions "marching down that same road" now carrying his own legions; Caesar himself mulling how best to bound across the Rhine.

Rarely, perhaps never, had his generalship been nimbler, surer, more relentless. With Patch's Seventh Army also sweeping like a scythe from the south, the Americans would count ninety thousand prisoners cap-tured in the Saar, three thousand square miles overrun, and irreplaceable German steel, chemical, and synthetic-oil plants flattened or seized. Ameri-can mobility unhinged the enemy, and firepower flayed him. "Scarcely a man-made thing exists in our wake," one division commander reported. The butcher's bill increased each day, of course. "Lots of young men dying miserably, or fighting to keep from dying," a nurse wrote in her diary, "hanging onto my hand until it hurts, as if I could keep them from slip-ping into that dark chasm." Patton urged on those still standing. "Roads don't matter," he declared. "Terrain doesn't matter. Exposed flanks don't matter." When a self-propelled gun got wedged under a rail overpass, Pat-ton told the hapless artillery commander, "Colonel, you can blow up the goddamn gun. You can blow up the goddamn bridge. Or you can blow out your goddamn brains, I don't care which."

By Wednesday, March 21, three corps from Third Army had reached the Rhine. General Middleton's VIII Corps vaulted the Mosel to envelop Koblenz and reported "not a shot, not a round of shellfire, indeed not a sign of the enemy." Fewer than two thousand disheartened German defend-ers soon paddled across the Rhine in heavy fog. Forty miles upstream at Mainz, and beyond to Worms in Seventh Army's sector, enemy rear guards fled on any conveyance that could float. More bridges were blown, at Lud-wigshafen and Germersheim. "We're going to cross the Rhine," Patton declared on Thursday, "and we're going to do it before I'm a day older."

He made good his boast. At Oppenheim, a wine town and barge har-bor midway between Mainz and Worms, two battalions from the 5th Division crossed by stealth in assault boats at 10:30 P.M., surprising enemy soldiers in their bedrolls. By daybreak on Friday, March 23, six infantry battalions had reached the far shore with just twenty casualties before pressing eastward behind the marching fire known as "walking death." Tanks followed by ferry, and then across a floating bridge; GIs ripped down roadside fences to accommodate three columns of traffic on the far bank. Patton recorded how he "drove to the river and went across the pontoon bridge, stopping in the middle to take a piss in the Rhine, and then pick up some dirt on the far side . . . in emulation of William the Conqueror."

"Brad, we're across!" he bellowed in a phone call to Namur. "And you can tell the world Third Army made it before Monty." Bradley obliged him: the American crossing, he informed reporters, had been accomplished without aerial bombardment, without airborne assault, even without artillery fire. Within a day the 5th Division bridgehead was five miles deep. To "produce a proper feeling of rivalry," Patton ordered all three Third Army corps to race for Giessen and a juncture with First Army.

"I love war and responsibility and excitement," he wrote Bea. "Peace is going to be hell on me. I will probably be a great nuisance."

Churchill had proposed riding into battle in a British tank during Operation VARSITY PLUNDER, the 21st Army Group attack over the Rhine. "I'm an old man and I work hard," he later explained. "Why shouldn't I have a little fun?" Dissuaded, he instead donned the uniform of a colonel in the 4th Queen's Own Hussars—the regiment in which he had been commissioned half a century earlier—and on the afternoon of March 23, he boarded a C-47 Dakota with Brooke to fly to Venlo, on the Dutch-German border. An Anglo-American smoke screen fifty miles long already hugged the river, "a thick black haze," one witness reported, "for all the world like Manchester or Birmingham as seen from the air."

They found Montgomery's command post in a pine forest, occupying a clearing once used by an equestrian school. Photos of Rommel and Rundstedt still adorned the caravan walls, like the vanquished ghosts from battles past. After supper, the prime minister repaired to Montgomery's map wagon, where caged canaries sang their arias. A few hours earlier, the field marshal explained, he had put his master plan in motion with a code phrase to his lieutenants: "Two if by sea." The British were coming.

Under Montgomery's command, more than 1.2 million Allied soldiers now leaned forward, in an operation that rivaled OVERLORD for complexity and grandeur. Three armies crowded the west bank of the Rhine, with the British Second squeezed between the Canadian First to the north and the U.S. Ninth to the south, all imperfectly concealed by that smoky miasma. On the east bank, arrayed around Wesel, their foe was reduced to what a German general called the "shadow of an army" that could "only pretend to resist." The British Army might be melting away—the bloody slog from Nijmegen had cost the equivalent of thirty-five infantry battalions, for which there were few replacements—but Montgomery intended to stage one last, glorious military pageant, worthy of an empire.

The plan for PLUNDER called for three corps, two British and one American, to assault the river that night. Less than twelve hours later, in VARSITY, they would be followed by an Anglo-American airborne corps that would descend onto the reeling enemy—a reversal of previous battle sequences. Sixty thousand engineers had gathered on this stretch of the Rhine. Fifty-five hundred artillery tubes stood elevated and poised to fire: a single 105mm howitzer could spray almost two tons of lethal fragments over nine acres in an hour. Fifteen thousand tons of bombs had been dropped in the past three days to soften up the battlefield. The British alone had amassed 120,000 tons of matériel, half of it ammunition; American stocks were larger still. Churchill already had chalked a message on one huge shell: "Hitler Personally."

With a final pinch of his cheek and clipped assurances that all would be well, Montgomery retired to his sleeping trailer. The distant grumble of guns signaled that PLUNDER had commenced. Churchill and Brooke strolled among the pines in the balmy evening, reflecting on how far they had come in the past thirty months, from Alam Halfa and Alamein in Egypt to Hitler's inner keep. Just before ten P.M. Churchill took a final draw on his cigar and then he, too, turned to bed, an aging hussar in need of sleep.

Twenty miles east, the Rhine attack had grown febrile with "the unbearable whip and lash of the guns," in Alan Moorehead's phrase. Flame and steel seared the far shore with as much hellfire as several thousand tubes could deliver. Concussion ghosts drifted back across the river, rippling the battle dress of Tommies assembled in water meadows, where they drained their rum mugs and blackened their cheeks with teakettle soot. Commandos "appeared in long files, coming out of the woods," wrote Eric Sevareid. "There was the sound of creaking boots and straps. . . . They were slightly bent under their packs. Some were singing." Into storm boats and amphibious Buffaloes they clambered, and soon the flotillas beat for the far shore, following an azimuth of Oerlikon tracers that stretched to the east like bright strands of rubies. Chandelier flares hissed overhead, dripping silver light into the river. "If you happen to hear a few stray bullets, you needn't think they're intended for you," a British officer had told his troops. "That, gentlemen, is a form of egotism."

From the second floor of a holiday villa overlooking the Rhine, Moorehead watched a Pathfinder aircraft orbit above Wesel's church spires to mark the target for British bombers. He thought the plane resembled "a single hurrying black moth in the air."

> He shot his clusters of red flares into the center of the town, which meant—and how acutely one felt it—that Wesel had just about ten min-

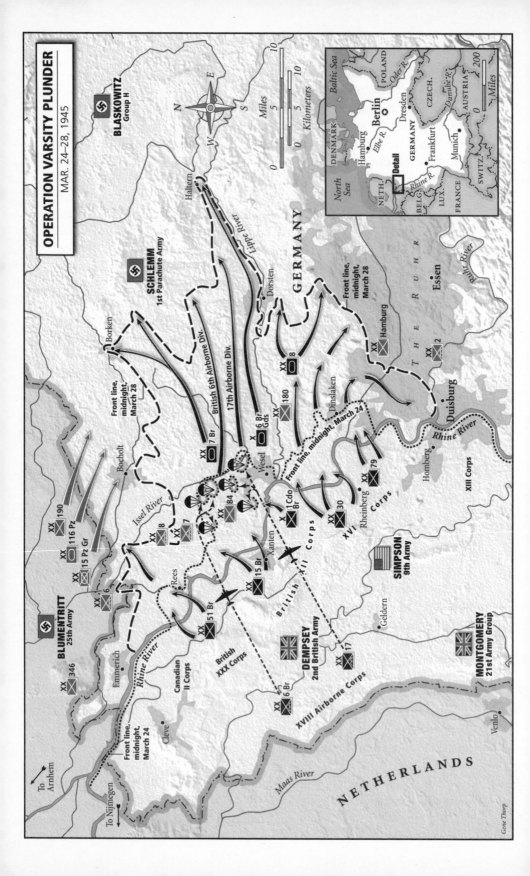

OPERATION VARSITY PLUNDER
MAR. 24–28, 1945

utes to live. Then the Lancasters fill[ed] the air with roaring and at last the cataclysmic, unbelievable shock of the strike. . . . Buildings and trees and wide acres of city parkland simply detached themselves from the earth. . . . A violent wind came tearing across the river.

"A great crimson stain of smoke and flame poured up like a huge open wound," wrote R. W. Thompson, "and the river seemed the color of blood." A British major wondered in his diary "if more than mortal powers had been unleashed." The bombers flew off, a thousand tons lighter, and a violet pall draped Wesel as the Commandos, who had gone to ground on the east bank, now rose to claim their prize. "Burglar-like and in single file, the leaders paying out a white tape, the whole brigade crept into the town," Moorehead wrote. Wesel, or rather its charred carcass, soon was theirs. Two British corps, the XII and XXX, surged over the river in force.

A few miles upstream, 40,000 Ninth Army gunners cut loose at one A.M. with a barrage exceeding a thousand shells a minute. An hour later Simpson's XVI Corps, swollen to 120,000 men, hoisted the first of seven hundred assault boats up over a dike and into the river. Medical heating pads had been used to warm the outboard motors, and now the frenzied yank of starter cords sent, in one writer's description, "shoals of small boats scudding across the water" under a three-quarter moon. Machine-gun tracers guided the initial waves until colored airfield landing lights could be emplaced on the far shore. German resistance evinced "no real fight in it," a lieutenant reported, and the two assault divisions tallied only thirty-one casualties. On the near shore, beachmasters in white helmets hectored stragglers, and twenty-ton cranes hoisted the larger landing craft into the Rhine.

By Saturday morning, March 24, thirteen U.S. infantry battalions held the east bank on an eight-mile front. Engineers in five equipment dumps west of the river whipped off camouflage covers—garnished fishing nets, chicken wire, tar paper, and fabric darkened with coal dust—to reveal endless acres of pontoons, stringers, trusses, and anchor cables. The bridge-builders set to work on the river with a will, and a way.

Rested and exultant, Churchill shortly before ten A.M. on Saturday settled into an armchair placed for his benefit on a hillside in Xanten, five miles west of Wesel. A clement sun climbed through a cloudless sky, marred only by the milky contrail of a V-2 streaking southwest toward Antwerp, or perhaps London. Booming British guns battered targets far beyond the Rhine, and the orange starbursts of exploding shells twinkled through the morning haze. Gazing at the pageant of boats and rafts plying the river below him, the prime minister mused, "I should have liked to have deployed my men in red coats on the plain down there and ordered them to charge. But now my armies are too vast."

A deep droning from the rear grew insistent. Churchill sprang to his feet with unwonted agility. Flocks of Allied fighters abruptly thundered overhead, trailed by tidy formations of transport planes, low enough for those on the ground to discern paratroopers standing in each open jump door. Following behind, as far as eye could see or imagination conjure, came aerial tugs, each towing a glider or two. The prime minister capered downhill for several steps, shouting, "They're coming! They're coming!" Just north of Wesel the first red and yellow parachutes blossomed, in Moorehead's description, "like enormous poppies."

Here then was VARSITY. The British 6th Airborne Division, flying in column from eleven airdromes in East Anglia, had merged south of Brussels with the U.S. 17th Airborne Division, flying from a dozen fields near Paris. Protected by three thousand Allied fighters, their combined amplitude darkened the sky: seventeen hundred transports and thirteen hundred gliders, bringing to battle seventeen thousand paratroopers and glidermen. Their orders were to seize the high ground and woodland above Wesel in reinforcement of the PLUNDER bridgeheads—"to loosen up the scrum," as a British airborne commander put it, "and set the armies behind us swanning."

In this they would be modestly effectual, seizing ten landing zones and drop zones with alacrity. But the stupendous bomb tonnage, the tens of thousands of artillery shells, and the hundreds of attack sorties against suspected antiaircraft positions had failed to winkle out all the enemy batteries, or to discourage mobile 20mm flak guns rushed to the field. "About the time we crossed the Rhine, holes started appearing in the wings and fuselage," an officer in the 513th Parachute Infantry Regiment later wrote. "Flak hitting on the plane body reminded me of the noise made by hail on a corrugated iron roof." Paratroopers groggy from Dramamine narrowed their shoulders and squeezed tight their buttocks as bullets punched through steel floor matting. A battalion commander in the same regiment reported that as his parachute opened, "I looked back and saw the left wing of our aircraft burst into flame. Almost immediately the entire aircraft was afire and falling." Sevareid watched as another plane "parted with a wing."

> The body of the plane plummeted earthward while the wing followed, fluttering and scudding like a big leaf. Another plane was streaming fire from both engines. The flames were beautiful golden ribbons.

Enemy tracers ignited wooden glider frames and fabric skins. A flight lieutenant reported seeing a British Hamilcar disintegrate in midair, the occupants "falling like puppets." A parachutist corporal watched another glider bank above a landing zone when ground fire "cracked it open like an egg and the jeep, gun, blokes all fell out." Of four hundred 6th Airborne gliders, only eighty-eight landed unscathed, and another thirty-two were destroyed on the ground by German artillery and incendiaries. One-quarter of the British glider pilots were casualties. More than fifty American gliders were destroyed by gunfire or in collisions with trees, poles, and other gliders in what one officer called "a flaming hellhole."

"Controls hit by flak in air," a glider account noted. "Wings and nose gone. Pilot and co-pilot hit. 12 EM WIA [enlisted men wounded-in-action]." On Landing Zone N, many glider men reportedly were "slain in their seats, and many loads burned or destroyed by mortars." Robert Capa, who jumped with an American battalion, watched as German marksmen riddled paratroopers helplessly snagged on a tall tree; hearing Capa swear furiously in his native Hungarian, a GI told him, "Stop those Jewish prayers. They won't help you now." A low-flying B-17 Flying Fortress carrying other combat cameramen and reporters fled in flames back across the Rhine. A survivor who bailed out of the stricken bomber watched as "all around us . . . burning and disabled C-47s crashed into the fields."

The morning proved even more hazardous for the new C-46 Curtiss Commando, flying in combat for the first time. Much larger than the C-47, with twin jump doors and a bay that carried twice as many paratroopers, the C-46 also was more vulnerable "due to the position and size of the fuel tanks and maze of hydraulic lines," a Pentagon study later concluded. Bullets striking aluminum often generated sparks up to five inches wide, while leaking gasoline from punctured C-46 tanks tended to dribble through the hot exhaust stacks toward the fuselage. The AAF also had chosen not to install self-sealing fuel bladders in the three thousand C-46s eventually bought. The self-sealing technology had been developed since the 1920s and further refined after the dissection of German Messerschmitt fighters shot down in England during the Battle of Britain in 1940. Two layers of rubber lined the fuel tank, one vulcanized and impermeable, the other more absorbent; the latter, when saturated with gasoline from a bullet puncture, expanded to plug the hole, like blood clotting in a wound. Self-sealing tanks had been installed in fighters and recently in some C-47s. But production priorities, and concern about adding weight and reducing fuel capacity, caused the Pentagon to exclude the C-46, despite earlier airborne calamities in Sicily and noisy charges by one disaffected lieutenant colonel that the decision was "criminal negligence" and "little short of murder."

"I saw pieces of the plane's skin tearing off when shells whizzed through," a sergeant who survived VARSITY later recalled. "There was another C-46 alongside us with the jumpers already in the door. Suddenly it was hit and flames shot from its wing roots." That spectacle recurred again and again above Wesel. "The C-46 seemed to catch on fire every time it was hit in a vital spot," crewmen reported. Of the seventy-three C-46s flown by the 313th Troop Carrier Group, nineteen were destroyed and thirty-eight damaged. Investigators found that fourteen of those lost were "flamers," planes "destroyed by fire originating [in the] gas tanks." The 52nd Troop Carrier Wing, which had flown in Sicily, Normandy, and Holland, concluded that "the C-46D is not a suitable troop carrier aircraft for combat operations."

One final calamity remained to unspool in VARSITY. Just after one P.M., as the airborne divisions finished the three-hour assault, waves of Eighth Air Force B-24 Liberators flew over the battlefield dropping six hundred tons of ammunition, gasoline, and other supplies from as low as one hundred feet. At that altitude, the lumbering, four-engine bombers became shooting-gallery targets, and 15 of 240 Liberators were lost, with another 104 damaged.

Among those shot down just north of Wesel was B-24 J 42-50735, nick-named *Queen of Angels* and flying from Suffolk with the 704th Bombardment Squadron. The eight dead crewmen included First Lieutenant Earle C. Cheek of Missouri, the navigator, "a genial friend, a good companion, and a lovable comrade," according to the unit chaplain. Cheek had survived many harrowing sorties in bombing runs from Italy and then from England: crewmen wounded on his thirteenth mission; an emergency landing in France on his fifteenth; two engines knocked out on his seventeenth; and flak damage to the wings, tail, and bomb bay over Magdeburg on his twenty-first. This was his thirtieth, the one that would fulfill his quota and send him home. "It shouldn't take much longer," he had written his girlfriend in Texas on March 18. "There are so many things we could do together."

The sole survivor from *Queen of Angels,* a waist gunner who bailed out almost at the treetops, subsequently wrote Cheek's mother in Missouri, "The ship crashed about 500 yards from where I landed and killed the rest of the boys, leaving me as the only survivor. . . . This is about the hardest letter I ever wrote to anyone." Another officer in the bomb group confirmed the disaster: "They were last seen with one engine on fire and going toward a crash landing in enemy territory. . . . Fate is definite and there is no altering—the suit always fits."

Churchill at day's end returned to Montgomery's encampment in the pine clearing. With His Majesty's forces now firmly entrenched east of the Rhine, the prime minister was in high feather. "The German is whipped," he declared. "We've got him. He is all through." During dinner, Churchill entertained the mess with dramatic recitations from *The Life of the Bee,* an ode by the Belgian Maurice Maeterlinck to the most orderly society on earth, with chapters entitled "The Swarm" and "The Massacre of the Males."

The prime minister and his field marshals then pushed back from the table and strolled to the map caravan to hear British officers describe VARSITY PLUNDER's progress.

All in all, the reports ratified Churchill's buoyancy. From the 51st Highland Division on the left to the American 79th Division on the right, the Allied bridgehead extended for twenty-five miles along the east bank and reached as deep as seven miles beyond the water's edge. Engineers were at work on various spans: the first tank-bearing bridge would open in the Ninth Army sector within a day. Three thousand enemy prisoners had been bagged on this Saturday, and PLUNDER ground units had made contact with airborne troops. The uncommonly fine weather would continue for at least another day.

The utility of VARSITY's vertical envelopment would long be debated, much as Montgomery's operatic staging of PLUNDER would be ridiculed as unnecessary by the likes of Patton and Bradley. Enthusiasts believed the airheads had disrupted enemy artillery, kept counterattacking Germans away from the river crossings, and opened an alley toward the Ruhr. General Brereton, commander of the First Allied Airborne Army, deemed the day a "tremendous success."

Yet VARSITY bore a taint, a reminder that rarely in war did success and sorrow exclude each other from the battlefield. Given the supine state of enemy defenses, no objective seized by paratroopers would have long eluded a three-corps ground assault. No great depth had been added to the Allied purchase over the Rhine, nor had bridge building been expedited. The two airborne divisions incurred nearly 3,000 casualties, including more than 460 dead. In addition to C-46 and B-24 losses, some 300 C-47s had been damaged and another 30 destroyed. Troop carrier crews suffered another 357 casualties, more than half of them dead or missing. Relatively few gliders could be salvaged. Once again, airborne forces appeared to be coins burning a hole in the pockets of Allied commanders, coins that simply had to be spent. Soldiers soon mocked the operation as VARSITY BLUNDER, and burial squads with pruning saws and ladders took two days to cut down all the dead. *Fate is definite. The suit always fits.*

The next morning, March 25, Churchill, Brooke, and Montgomery attended Palm Sunday services celebrated by a Presbyterian chaplain in a captured German church near the river. The prime minister offered his troops a brief homily on "an influence, supreme and watchful, which guides our affairs." Then with a V-for-victory waggle he was off with his entourage to the river town of Rheinberg for a rendezvous with Eisenhower, Bradley, and Simpson.

Together in the brilliant sunshine the six men picnicked on fried chicken served upon a white tablecloth in the garden of a colliery manager's house.

"Our men muttered about camouflage," a British lieutenant reported, "and helped themselves to a few cakes left behind." Strolling close to the river, where soldiers swarmed with a purposeful buzz worthy of Maeterlinck, Brooke congratulated Eisenhower on Allied successes in recent days. The supreme commander would later quote him as saying, "Thank God, Ike, you stuck by your plan. You were completely right," a statement repudiated by Brooke. "It will be clear that I was misquoted," the field marshal subsequently wrote, "as I am still convinced that he was completely wrong."

For the moment such disputes seemed picayune. After Eisenhower and Bradley took their leave, Churchill's mischievous eye lighted on a nearby landing craft. "I am in command now that Eisenhower is gone," he declared. "Why don't we go across and have a look?" Across the Rhine they went, prowling about for half an hour, ears cocked to the to-and-fro shriek of artillery. The prime minister "seemed more perturbed about lighting his cigar in the wind than about shellfire," a British officer noted, but at length an anxious Simpson told Montgomery, "Get him out of here before he gets killed."

Back on the west bank, Churchill scrambled onto the iron trusses of a demolished rail span as German shells in search of American bridge-builders began to plump the river three hundred yards upstream and even nearer downstream. "Prime Minister," Simpson pleaded, "there are snipers in front of you, they are shelling both sides of the bridge, and now they have started shelling the road behind you." By Brooke's account, Churchill "put both his arms round one of the twisted girders of the bridge and looked over his shoulder at Simpson with pouting mouth and angry eyes." At length he climbed back to shore and shambled off to safety.

After presenting Montgomery with a fine set of *Marlborough: His Life and Times*—Churchill's four-volume paean to his illustrious warrior ancestor—the prime minister reboarded his plane and flew home to London, a dozen Spitfires his attending courtiers. "He never fought a battle that he did not win, nor besieged a fortress that he did not take," Churchill had written in volume one. "He quitted war invincible."

In short order, seven Allied armies finished jumping the river. On the far left wing, Canadian First Army troops funneled through the Wesel bridgehead. Simpson bridled at the pinched frontage allocated his Ninth Army and at what he considered the languid British pace. But by March 27, 21st Army Group had advanced twenty miles beyond the Rhine to begin enveloping the north rim of the Ruhr.

On the right flank, in the south, Patch's Seventh Army had crossed in a two-division assault at Worms early on March 25, supported by three dozen amphibious tanks. XV Corps captured twenty-five hundred Germans at a cost of only two hundred American casualties, and within seventy-two hours Patch built enough momentum to burst from the bridgehead against an enervated enemy pared to fewer than six thousand combat effectives.

The French, who had been first on the Rhine in November, were last to leap it, whipped on by De Gaulle, who cabled General de Lattre, "My dear General, you must cross the Rhine, even if the Americans do not help you and you are obliged to use rowboats.... Karlsruhe and Stuttgart await you, even if they do not want you." General Devers readily assented, but the retreating Germans had sunk all watercraft at Speyer, forcing the French to make do with a single rubber boat; ten riflemen at a time paddled across until a bigger flotilla could be assembled. A solitary company would hold the east bank at dawn on March 31, enough to plant a tricolor and satisfy Deux Mètres, at least for the moment.

"This is the collapse," a British Second Army intelligence assessment concluded on March 26. "The enemy no longer has a coherent system of defense between the Rhine and the Elbe. It is difficult to see what there is to stop us now." Hodges's First Army agreed, in intelligence estimate No. 77: "The enemy is capable of collapse or surrender in successive groups."

Alas, the enemy was capable of more than that, and gouts of blood would yet be spilled. But the Allied conquest intensified and accelerated. Eleven thousand daily air sorties contributed to what SHAEF called "a systematic annihilation of the German armed forces." March proved the heaviest bombing month of the war: 130,000 tons. Upon returning from his Rhineland expedition, Churchill suggested in a March 28 memo that "the moment has come when the question of bombing German cities simply for the sake of increasing the terror, through other pretexts, should be revised. Otherwise we shall come into control of an utterly ruined land." An outraged Bomber Harris counterattacked so vigorously, accusing Churchill of "stigmatizing a policy for which he had been personally responsible," that the prime minister withdrew his minute. Yet the strategic bomber fleets soon found their war "petering out in diminuendo," as one officer wrote, simply for lack of targets to pulverize.

Not so for the ground forces, surging across a 250-mile front. The war had again become mobile and mechanized, precisely the war for soldiers with "machinery in their souls," as John Steinbeck described his fellow Americans. A war of movement, distance, and horsepower was suited, as *Time* rhapsodized, to "a people accustomed to great spaces, to transcontinental railways, to nationwide trucking chains, to endless roads and millions of automobiles, to mail-order houses, department stores and supermarkets."

The United States in the past year had outproduced all Axis nations combined by a factor of two. Not least in that preponderance, American factories during the war turned out seven times more trucks than Germany; now, with more than 700,000 vehicles on the Continent, the

U.S. Army drove hell-for-leather across the Reich "like a vast armed workshop." Eisenhower's armies burned four million gallons of gasoline a day, delivered by eighty-six ocean tankers, through thirty-five hundred miles of pipeline, and in thirty million jerricans. Having erected ten bridges a day on average since June 6, including fourteen major road spans over the Meuse, the U.S. Army would throw fifty-seven more across the Rhine. The traffic those bridges carried included more than six thousand tanks.

The terrible swift sword was fully drawn. Many now dared indulge in the hope, as a British captain wrote, that "with luck, one might be able to see the end." In a message to Marshall that was as close to gloating as he would permit himself, Eisenhower wrote:

> Naturally I am immensely pleased. . . . I hope this does not sound boastful, but I must admit to a great satisfaction that the things that Bradley and I have believed in from the beginning and have carried out in the face of some opposition from within and without, have matured so splendidly.

"The Enemy Has Reason to Fear Him"

No sword was swifter or more terrible than Patton's. When a sniper took a potshot at a Third Army staff officer, Patton ordered German houses burned in retaliation. "In hundreds of villages there is not a living thing, not even a chicken," he told his diary. "Most of the houses are heaps of stone. They brought it on themselves. . . . I did most of it." As his vengeful divisions approached Frankfurt, another "brick and stone wilderness," he wrote Bea that Eisenhower had recommended his promotion to full general, but "at the moment I am having so much fun that I don't care what the rank is. . . . I hope things keep smooth. It seems too good to be true." *Time* featured him on a cover with the caption: "Third Army's Patton. The enemy has reason to fear him."

In a personal note to his fearsome general, Eisenhower wrote:

> I am very proud of the fact that you, as one of the fighting commanders who has been with me from the beginning of the African campaign, have performed so brilliantly throughout. We are now fairly started on that phase of the campaign which I hope will be the final one. I know that Third Army will be at the finish.

Curiously, it was unfinished business from Africa that now distracted Patton, ensuring that things would not "keep smooth" and marring the start of his drive into the German heartland. His beloved son-in-law, Lieutenant Colonel John Knight Waters, a West Point cavalryman, had been captured in Tunisia on Valentine's Day, 1943, during the early hours of the German offensive that culminated at Kasserine Pass. Waters eventually found himself interned as POW No. 4161 with fifteen hundred other American officers in Oflag 64, a prison camp in northern Poland, where listening to the BBC on an illicit radio was known as "reading the canary"; where a hissed warning of "Goon up!" signaled an approaching guard; and where "kriegies" (from *Kriegsgefangenen,* or war prisoners) organized a dance band, a theatrical troupe, a glee club, a camp newspaper, and a five-thousand-volume library.

Waters kept a pocket notebook, titled "Remembrances," which began with a laconic scribble on February 14, 1943: "Captured. Night in cactus." For the next two years his spare entries recorded events small and large, including Red Cross and Swedish YMCA inspections, and, on June 6, 1944, the one-word annunciation: "Invasion." Each calendar day was crossed off in red pencil as it ended. Rarely did Waters give voice to the drear monotony of Oflag 64, as in his October 1, 1944, entry: "And so another month begins. When will this end?"

He also maintained a "Wartime Log," wrapped in brown burlap with a liberty bell drawn on the front cover and an epigraph from the British novelist Henry Seton Merriman: "War is a purifier; it clears the social atmosphere and puts womanly men and manly women into their right places. It is also a simplifier." Here Waters kept a meticulous chart of "P.O.W. Rations," showing daily allotments that typically included 35.7 grams of meat per man—a bit more than an ounce—plus 318 grams of barley bread, 200 grams of cabbage, 100 grams of carrots, 143 grams of cow turnips, and so forth. He carefully peeled food labels from relief-package cans and pasted them into the volume—Top-O peanut butter, Kroger's Country Club Quality Fruitcake, Richardson & Robbins plum pudding—as if to extract a few final calories of nourishment from the memories. Each letter to POW No. 4161 was carefully listed by date, travel time, and censor number. Every parcel from home or the Red Cross was logged, with notations such as "badly damaged" or "good shape," and a catalogue of the contents, which ranged from pencils, shoelaces, and vitamin pills to a cribbage board, MacDonald cigarettes, and, oddly, ice skates.

The great Russian winter offensive had abruptly put the kriegies of Oflag 64 on the road, under guard, with millions of other refugees, war prisoners, and concentration-camp inmates trudging west ahead of the Red Army. On January 21, Waters and his comrades marched out of the camp, carrying stolen cutlery stamped with swastikas and with the secret radio hidden inside an officer's bagpipes. For five weeks they tacked across northern Germany in a horrid three-hundred-mile anabasis. "Zero weather

& blizzard," Waters scrawled in his journal on January 28. Men died, or were shot, or vanished. "Toughest day yet," he wrote on February 22. Survivors studied their own stool like sheep entrails, for portents of illness; some chose not to wash rather than sponge away body oils that might provide a thin film against the cold. Starving men described the lavish meals they intended to devour when they got home, or concocted elaborate menus and lists of memorable restaurants where someday they hoped to dine again.

On February 26, the column was herded into boxcars to travel by rail at a glacial pace for another ten days to an eighth-century Bavarian town fifty miles east of Frankfurt. "Reached Hammelburg at 6 P.M.," Waters wrote on March 8. "Deloused, etc." Marched from the rail yard down Hermann-Göring-Strasse, the men found themselves entering a constellation of prisons that included a vast compound with thirty thousand enlisted men, mostly Soviets. Also here was Oflag XIII-B, a cantonment of five thousand Allied officers, including Serbs held since 1941 and fifteen hundred Americans captured during the Bulge from the 28th, 99th, and 106th Infantry Divisions, as well as the star-crossed 14th Cavalry Group. The camp's senior officer was Colonel Charles C. Cavender, who had surrendered his 423rd Infantry Regiment on the Schnee Eifel nearly three months earlier.

Conditions at Hammelburg were wretched: a diet of beet or cabbage soup, black bread, and turnip marmalade; a single, cold, four-minute shower each week; eighty men wedged into each shabby hut; and the risk of accidental slaughter by marauding Allied aircraft. "Air alerts all day. Worse than ever," Waters wrote on March 19. "Distant rumbling."

Patton had hoped to hear of Colonel Waters's liberation in mid-January. But SHAEF on February 9 advised him that Soviet intelligence listed Waters among a number of American prisoners apparently spirited westward. Fragmentary Allied intelligence and Red Cross reports more than a month later suggested that he might be among new arrivals at Hammelburg. On March 23, the day Third Army crossed the Rhine in force, Patton wrote Bea, "We are headed right for John's place and may get there before he is moved." Two days later he added, "Hope to send an expedition tomorrow to get John."

The dubious honor of rescuing the commanding general's kinsman sixty miles behind enemy lines fell to a tall, tough, redheaded captain from the Bronx named Abraham J. Baum. The twenty-four-year-old son of an immigrant Russian Jew, Abe Baum had studied costume design and worked as a pattern cutter in Manhattan's Garment District; he enlisted after Pearl Harbor and rose through the ranks as a decorated officer in the 4th Armored Division. Without disclosing his blood interest, Patton ordered XII Corps to dispatch an armored column to Hammelburg and

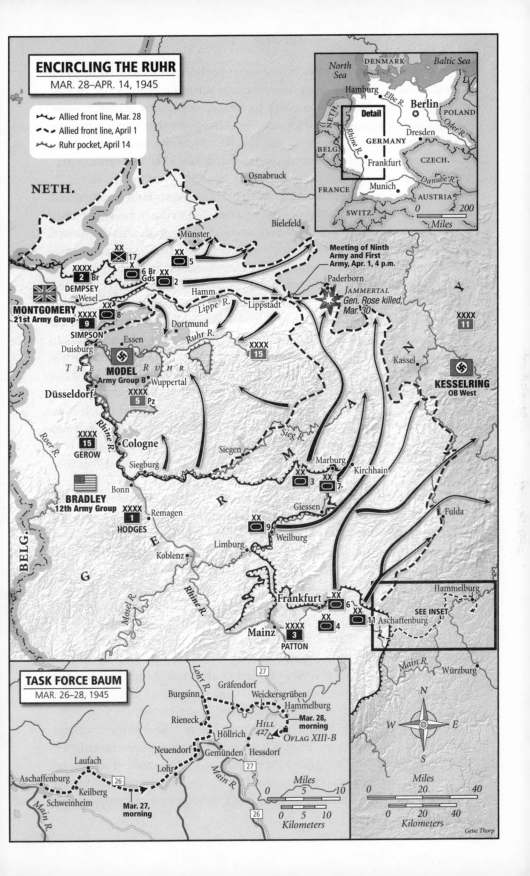

ENCIRCLING THE RUHR
MAR. 28–APR. 14, 1945

⌇⌇⌇ Allied front line, Mar. 28
- - - Allied front line, April 1
⌇⌇⌇ Ruhr pocket, April 14

Detail

North Sea · DENMARK · Baltic Sea
Hamburg · Elbe R. · POLAND
NETH. · Berlin · Oder R.
Rhine R. · GERMANY · Dresden
BELG. · CZECH.
FRANCE · Frankfurt · Danube R.
Munich · AUSTRIA
SWITZ. · Miles · 0 · 200

NETH.

Osnabruck

Bielefeld

Münster

XX 17
X 6 Br Gds
XX 5
XX 2

XXXX 2 Br
DEMPSEY
Wesel
MONTGOMERY
21st Army Group
XXXX 9
SIMPSON
XX 8

Hamm
Lippe R.
Lippstadt

Meeting of Ninth
Army and First
Army, Apr. 1, 4 p.m.

Paderborn
JAMMERTAL
Gen. Rose killed,
Mar. 30

XXXX 11

Dortmund
Ruhr R.

XXXX 15

Kassel

Essen
MODEL
Army Group B
Wuppertal

Duisburg
THE RUHR

Düsseldorf

XXXX 5 Pz

KESSELRING
OB West

Rhine R.
Roer R.
XXXX 15
GEROW
Cologne
Siegburg
Sieg R.
Siegen

Marburg
Kirchhain

XX 3
XX 7

BELG.
Bonn
BRADLEY
12th Army Group
XXXX 1
HODGES
Remagen

Giessen

Fulda

XX 9
Weilburg
Limburg
Koblenz

G E R M A N Y

Mosel R.
Rhine R.

Frankfurt
XX 6
XX 11 Aschaffenburg

SEE INSET

Hammelburg

Mainz
XXXX 3
PATTON
XX 4

Main R.
Würzburg

N
W   E
S

TASK FORCE BAUM
MAR. 26–28, 1945

Lohr R.
27
Gräfendorf
Burgsinn
Weickersgrüben
Hammelburg
Rieneck
Höllrich
HILL 427
Oflag XIII-B
Mar. 28, morning
Neuendorf
Gemünden
Hessdorf
Laufach
26
Lohr
Aschaffenburg
Keilberg
Schweinheim
Main R.
27
Mar. 27, morning
26

Miles
0   5   10
Kilometers
0   5   10

Miles
0   20   40
Kilometers
0   20   40

Gene Thorp

stage a raid that he privately hoped would eclipse Douglas MacArthur's recent rescues of imprisoned Americans at several camps in the Philippines. To ensure that Waters could be recognized, he pressured his aide, Major Alexander C. Stiller, a former Texas Ranger, to accompany the column, ostensibly "for the thrills and laughs." Only en route would Stiller confess to Baum that one of the prisoners they hoped to free was the husband of Patton's only daughter.

Patton had proposed sending an entire four-thousand-man armored combat command eastward but was persuaded that a smaller, nimbler task force would have better odds of success. Baum's column comprised just over three hundred soldiers in sixteen tanks, twenty-seven half-tracks, three motorized assault guns, and seven jeeps. Exhausted from the Rhine crossings, with little sleep in the past four days, the men carried but fifteen maps among them. Some of Patton's subordinates harbored serious doubts about the foray, not least because Hammelburg lay east of a corps driving north. Lieutenant Colonel Creighton Abrams, whose unit was to provide much of the armored firepower, smacked his fist against a field table during a planning meeting late Monday afternoon, March 26. "What the hell is this all about?" he demanded. "It just doesn't make sense." As Baum's force galloped away a few hours later, Patton wrote Bea, "I have been as nervous as a cat all day as everyone but me thought it was too great a risk. I hope it works. . . . If I lose the column it will possibly be a new incident." To his diary he added, "I do not believe there is anything in that part of Germany heavy enough to hurt them."

He was quite wrong. After skirmishes near Aschaffenburg, the column reached Highway 26 at 2:15 A.M. on Tuesday, March 27, making fair time while cutting phone wires and, at first light, gunning down German troops doing calisthenics on a parade ground. American tank and machine-gun fire ripped through barges, tugboats, and German trains along the Main River, east of Lohr; Major Stiller described how enemy soldiers "jumped off and scattered like quail" from an armored antiaircraft *Zug*. In Gemünden, defenders rallied to blow a bridge "in a spume of stone and concrete," and Panzerfaust fire demolished three tanks while wounding Baum in the knee and hand. Detouring north onto a gravel road, the task force freed seven hundred Russian prisoners from a work detail shortly before noon on Tuesday—"Mazel tov," Baum told a German civilian—then again pivoted east before clattering into Hammelburg around 3 P.M.

Here trouble awaited them. An American map found in the wreckage at Gemünden, and reports from a Storch observation plane tracking the olive-drab procession, suggested Hammelburg as the column's likely destination. A German assault-gun battalion lumbered into town from the east while Baum and his men approached from the west. A running gunfight broke out when the Americans nosed up a twisting road toward the prison compound, which sat on a high plateau south of town. Enemy shells scorched through the column from below, and by the time American return fire beat back the attack, more vehicles had been demolished, including three half-tracks. Baum's fuel reserve and ammunition track were ablaze, and camp guards armed with old Belgian rifles had tumbled into a skirmish line outside the fence. The Oflag air-raid siren shrieked maniacally.

Drumfire and coiling black smoke had roused the prisoners, and the sight of five-pointed white stars in the distance provoked jubilant pandemonium. A kriegie priest captured in the Ardennes offered absolution to those who wanted it, but most stood braying at the windows until tank rounds began to slam through the cantonment. The Shermans riddled guard towers and a water tank, and also ignited several buildings in an adjacent compound: Baum's gunners had mistaken Serb uniforms for German. Prisoners dropped to the floor, and word circulated through the barracks: "No smoking, no lights."

With consent from a German commandant eager to surrender, five volunteers led by Colonel Waters marched out the main gate amid the battle din and flitting tracers, waving an American flag and a bedsheet tied to a pole. Several hundred yards from the camp, making for Baum's left flank, they passed a barnyard enclosed by a plank fence. Waters turned just as a German soldier thrust his rifle between the slats and, without aiming, pulled the trigger. The bullet hit POW No. 4161 just below the right hip, chipping his coccyx and exiting through his left buttock. He fell like a stone. Carried in a blanket sling to a nearby German hospital, where he was refused treatment, Waters was then hauled back to the camp and entrusted to Serb surgeons equipped with little more than paper bandages and a table knife for a scalpel.

Baum's tanks meanwhile had crashed through the perimeter fence to be greeted by whooping, back-slapping prisoners. Many appeared ready to bolt, with bedrolls under their arms and pockets stuffed with Red Cross food cans rifled from the mess pantry. Baum had anticipated finding 300 American officers. Instead he confronted 1,291, according to the latest head count; the milling throng reminded him of Times Square.

It was now 6:30 P.M., with daylight fading and the enemy undoubtedly convening another attack. Clambering onto the hood of a jeep, Baum quieted the men and told them, "There are far more of you than we expected. We don't have enough vehicles to take all of you." He pointed west. "When I left, the lines were about sixty miles back in that direction, at the River Main." He could squeeze a hundred or so onto his tanks and half-tracks. The rest would have to walk, or wait in Hammelburg for eventual liberation. A dismayed murmur ran through the throng.

Evening's first stars glittered overhead as hundreds of officers, on foot and outfitted by Baum with a few compasses and maps, tramped into the gloaming, vaguely heading west. Separately, with tanks in the vanguard and every hull upholstered with kriegies, Baum's motorized procession eventually rolled west by southwest, hoping to collide with Patch's Seventh Army.

Instead they promptly found more trouble. Gunfire and Panzerfausts launched from the shadows harassed them. Vehicles burned, casualties mounted. Scouts reported ambushes and roadblocks with panzers ahead at Höllrich and at Hessdorf, where Baum had hoped to pick up Highway 27. Sometime after three A.M. on Wednesday, he ordered the column to shelter atop a dark knob identified on the map as Hill 427, only four miles southwest of Oflag XIII-B. The wounded were carried into a stone barn as the last gasoline was drained from eight half-tracks to fill six surviving tanks. All but a dozen of the hitchhiking kriegies formed into a column of twos and tramped back toward Hammelburg under a white flag, surely the better part of valor. They would reach the camp at 9:30 A.M. to find that German patrols had already rounded up many of the officers who had set out on foot the previous night.

Just after eight A.M., Baum and his depleted band started to edge down Hill 427. "A sheet of hell," as he subsequently put it, abruptly engulfed the ridgeline with tank, artillery, mortar, and machine-gun fire. "At daylight," Major Stiller later wrote, "they destroyed us." As one olive-drab vehicle after another burst into flame, a final Morse message was tapped over the radio— "Task Force Baum surrounded. Under heavy fire. Request air support."

"Every man for himself," Baum hollered. Into the trees he ran, with Stiller on his heels. The baying of dogs echoed across the slope. One by one the GIs were captured or shot down. A German soldier found Baum and Spiller burrowed beneath a den of leaves; when Baum fumbled for his .45 automatic, the German raised his own pistol and shot him in the left thigh, his third wound of the expedition. They, too, would return to Hammelburg, Baum sprawled in a horse cart. "Get a good sleep, boys," a guard told the Americans. "You had a hard night."

After his wounding, John Waters managed to scratch a few spare entries into his "Remembrances" journal:

March 27: "Shot while under white flag by German."
March 28: "Operation & hospital. Suffering."
March 29: "Hosp. Morphine."
March 30: "Hosp. Suffering."

Not for some days would Patton learn details of the failed raid, although German propaganda broadcasts celebrated the repulse at Hammelburg as a signal victory for the Reich. A few officers from Oflag XIII-B escaped their pursuers and eventually stumbled into American lines with fragmentary accounts of salvation, flight, and gunfire. Most prisoners and their erstwhile rescuers, including Stiller, were force-marched to another camp near Munich, where they would await Seventh Army's arrival a month later. Task Force Baum had been obliterated, every vehicle lost and nearly every man captured in addition to the fifty-seven killed, wounded, or missing. An uncertain number of prisoners had died in the escapade.

Patton both evaded responsibility—blaming Major General Manton S. Eddy, the XII Corps commander, for dispatching an undersized force—and prevaricated. To reporters on March 30 he claimed that Task Force Baum was intended largely as a feint. "I felt by hazarding a small force I would confuse the enemy completely as to where we were going," he said. "It did work, for they thought I was going to Nuremberg." Later he would insist that he had first learned of Waters's internment at the camp long after the raid. To Bea on March 31, he wrote:

> I had known of the camp there for a week but did not know definitely he was in it. I sent a force to capture it but fear that the force was destroyed. However it was the proper thing to do.

As details of the fiasco emerged and criticism intensified, Patton unsuccessfully tried to suppress the story. "They are trying to make an incident out of my attempt to rescue John," he told Bea. "How I hate the press." Ten days after the raid, when troops from the 14th Armored Division overran Hammelburg, they found that those too ill or too damaged to travel to Munich had been left in the Serb dispensary, including Colonel Waters and Captain Baum. Patton sent an Army surgeon and two small planes to evacuate his son-in-law to a Frankfurt hospital; the young officer would recover from his injuries and later attain four-star rank. Baum and other wounded Americans were left behind at the camp for several more days. Eventually the former pattern cutter was promoted to major and awarded the Distinguished Service Cross for "loyal, courageous devotion to duty," a decoration pinned on his hospital pajamas by Patton.

Patton had abused his authority, issuing reckless, impulsive orders to indulge his personal interests. As in the slapping incidents in Sicily, his deportment, compounded this time by mendacity, was unworthy of the soldiers he was privileged to lead. Yet with victory so near, his superiors had no heart for public rebukes. Bradley considered the raid "foolhardy," but kept silent. "Failure itself was George's own worst reprimand," he concluded. In cables to Marshall, Eisenhower referred to the raid as "a wild goose chase" and "Patton's latest crackpot actions." The Third Army commander had "lost a full company of medium tanks and a platoon of light tanks. Foolishly he then imposed censorship on the movement."

"Patton is a problem child," Eisenhower added, "but he is a great fighting leader in pursuit and exploitation."

Lovers' Quarrels Are a Part of Love

E ISENHOWER's office in Reims occupied the second floor of the Collège Moderne et Technique de Garçons, three stories of red brick on Rue Henri Joliauer. His windows overlooked a rail marshaling yard and the city's seedy train station; beyond the tracks, German prisoners with push brooms swept the cathedral close. Military convoys crawled through the narrow streets at all hours in a clangor of grinding truck gears and straining engines. SHAEF's forward headquarters now accommodated more than five thousand Allied officers and enlisted men, double the intended number, and they filled not only the *collège* but a music conservatory, various offices on Rue Talleyrand, French military casernes, and the Hôtel du Lion d'Or, where at night jitterbugging soldiers danced in a cabaret with rifles slung over their shoulders.

"France smells wonderful these days," a SHAEF lieutenant wrote home after exploring Reims.

> We get the variegated odors of roast beef, onion and oil dressing, and naturally French pastry. The air is scented with the blossoming chestnut trees. . . . The lilacs were in full bloom, the wisteria dripped from their vines, and all those fruit trees! I nearly was overcome.

Such vernal delights were largely wasted on the supreme commander, who despite recent battlefield successes showed alarming signs of dispirited exhaustion. Eisenhower "looked terrible," Bradley conceded, beset with an aching knee, respiratory miseries, and a painful cyst on his back that required surgical excision. Kay Summersby described his waspish mood as "truly vile"; his "physical and mental condition was worse than we had ever known it," she later wrote. "Beetle was positive that he was on the verge of a nervous breakdown." Smith was hardly in the pink himself, tormented by a bleeding ulcer and an infection that had confined him to bed for several days, further burdening Eisenhower. In his diary, Everett Hughes had written, "Ike shouts and rants. Says 'I have too many things to do.' . . . He acted like a crazy man. . . . On defensive, guard up, worried, self-isolated."

The supreme commander needed rest. With Smith he flew to Cannes in late March and spent five days at a borrowed villa doing little but sleep, sunbathe, and play an occasional rubber of bridge. For the first forty-eight hours, he woke only long enough to lunch on the terrace before shuffling back to bed. "I just can't concentrate," he complained. But the break proved salutary, and he returned to Reims restored and ready to finish the war. Still, as he confessed to Mamie, "Those of us that are bearing real responsibility in this war will find it difficult to ever be restful [or] serene again."

He also returned from the Riviera with a revised battle plan. "Ike has learnt his lesson and he consults me before taking any action," Montgomery had told Brooke earlier in March. But on Wednesday, March 28, only a day after Montgomery had informed Eisenhower that he was beginning his drive from the Rhine toward the river Elbe with the U.S. Ninth Army and British Second Army, the supreme commander delivered a thunderbolt message:

> As soon as you have joined hands with Bradley in the Kassel-Paderborn area, Ninth United States Army will revert to Bradley's command. Bradley . . . will deliver his main thrust on the axis Erfurt–Leipzig–Dresden to join hands with the Russians. The mission of your army group will be to protect Bradley's northern flank. . . . Devers will protect Bradley's right flank.

This plan, Eisenhower assured him, "is simplicity itself." In a clear tweak at the field marshal's presumption, he added, "As you say, the situation looks good."

The supreme commander had his reasons for shifting the main attack avenue from the Allied north to the center, none of which he had discussed with Montgomery or Churchill during their Palm Sunday picnic on the Rhine. Not least, as Eisenhower had written Marshall, "I get tired of trying to arrange the blankets smoothly over several prima donnas in the same bed." Now they would have separate beds. Moreover, Montgomery's armies in the north would have to cross the fenny Westphalian plain, a lowland of watercourses that could easily impede armored columns; the corridor farther south presented few obstructions and offered fine highways for the mobile Americans. With ten thousand German soldiers now surrendering every day, the Wehrmacht tottered toward annihilation, although some Allied intelligence officers worried that diehards might escape to the Alps or organize guerrilla brigades. Speed was paramount, and SHAEF had concluded, in General Whiteley's words, that "if anything was to be done quickly, don't give it to Monty."

Montgomery was gobsmacked by what he called "the blow from Ike. . . . A very dirty work, I fear." Without General Simpson's heft, 21st Army Group was unlikely to reach the Elbe soon, much less Berlin. "The violent pro-American element at SHAEF is pressing for a set-up which will clip the wings of the British group of armies," he wrote London. "The Americans then finish off the business alone." To Brooke, he went further. "This new plan of Ike's," he warned, "will prolong the war." Montgomery elicited less sympathy than he might have hoped. "Monty has only himself to blame for the suspicion with which the Americans treat him," said Admiral Cunningham, the first sea lord.

There was more. Since OVERLORD, Allied planners had presumed that Berlin was their ultimate objective. "Berlin is the main prize," Eisenhower had affirmed in September. "There is no doubt whatsoever in my mind that we should concentrate all our energies and resources on rapid thrusts to Berlin." Now he changed his mind. In a "personal message to Marshal Stalin" cabled that same fateful Wednesday, with a copy to the Charlie-Charlies, the supreme commander disclosed that "the best axis" would carry his legions to Leipzig and Dresden in southeast Germany, a hundred miles from the capital. To Montgomery he added in a subsequent note, "In none of this do I mention Berlin. That place has become, so far as I am concerned, nothing but a geographical location. . . . My purpose is to destroy the enemy's forces and his powers to resist."

Again he had cause. The Red Army was thirty miles from Berlin, on favorable terrain with more than a million men who had been massing for this assault since January; the Anglo-Americans remained well over two hundred miles from the capital. Bradley and other commanders estimated that taking Berlin might cost between ten thousand and one hundred thousand American casualties alone. Marshall had cautioned Eisenhower against "unfortunate incidents," including fratricide between forces approaching from east and west. (On a single day in early April, U.S. and Soviet planes would inadvertently tangle five times, with exchanges of gunfire.) Postwar occupation zones already had been established, and the partition of Berlin would take effect regardless of who captured the city. A race to Berlin, or Vienna, or Prague would bleed U.S. forces needed in the Pacific, and perhaps corrode Moscow's commitment to make war on Japan. By angling southeast, Bradley's spearhead would cut the Reich in half, severing Bavaria and Austria from Berlin, and help forestall the scorched-earth decree Hitler had issued on March 19, "Destructive Measures on Reich Territory." Finally, Eisenhower well understood that Roosevelt's vision of an enduring peace was predicated on cooperation with the Soviets, a comity unlikely to be enhanced by a rivalrous dash to the Reichstag. As he later asked an interviewer, "What would you have done with Berlin if we had captured it?"

None of this went down easily in London. Not only did Eisenhower's new plan steal Montgomery's thunder—this, when the British had suffered twenty thousand casualties in the past two months—but in directly corresponding with Stalin the supreme commander appeared, in British eyes, to exceed his authority. When it was suggested that Eisenhower had impinged on the prerogatives of his superiors, Marshall and the other U.S. chiefs demurred. "The commander in the field," they wrote Brooke and his confederates on March 30, "is the best judge of the measures which offer the earliest prospect of destroying the German armies or their power to resist."

A day later Churchill lowered his beaver and entered the lists. "We might be condemned to an almost static role in the north," he warned the British chiefs, and on Sunday he wrote Roosevelt:

> Berlin remains of high strategic importance. . . . The Russian armies will no doubt overrun all Austria and enter Vienna. If they also take Berlin, will not their impression that they have been the overwhelming contributor to our common victory be unduly imprinted in their minds?

"Laying aside every impediment and shunning every diversion," the prime minister advised, "the allied armies of the north and center should now march at the highest speed towards the Elbe." Yet the Americans were not to be headed. In a deft rebuff from his vacation cottage in Warm Springs, Georgia, Roosevelt told Churchill that "the British Army is given what seems to me very logical objectives on the northern flank."

Eisenhower would further assure Marshall, "I shall not attempt any move I deem militarily unwise merely to gain a political prize unless I receive specific orders from the Combined Chiefs of Staff." No such directive was forthcoming, nor had Eisenhower's marching orders changed significantly from the charge given him the previous spring—to "enter the continent of Europe" and destroy Germany's armed forces.

He had accomplished the former; now he would fulfill the latter. The Allied juggernaut in the west had grown to almost four and a half million, including ninety divisions. They faced a tatterdemalion enemy: sixty-five divisions so depleted that their combined combat strength barely equaled two dozen. Gasoline had grown precious enough that a sour joke in German ranks described a new "fifty-man panzer crew"—one man to steer, one to shoot, and forty-eight to push.

Montgomery had not quite yielded. But when he asked SHAEF for ten American divisions to reinforce a British thrust toward Lübeck and then Berlin—"I consider that Berlin has definite value as an objective," he said—Eisenhower brought him up short. "You must not lose sight of the fact that during the advance to Leipzig you have the role of protecting Bradley's northern flank," the supreme commander replied. "It is not his role to protect your southern flank. My directive is quite clear." Montgomery answered meekly, "It is quite clear to me what you want."

Churchill saw that further bickering was pointless. In a graceful capitulation, he first pronounced the Anglo-Americans "the truest friends and comrades that ever fought side by side," and then sent Roosevelt a scrap of wisdom from the Roman playwright Terence: "I will use one of my very few Latin quotations, '*Amantium irae amoris integratio est.*'" Lovers' quarrels are a part of love.

With Armed Forces Radio playing "The Last Round-Up," the U.S. First, Third, and Ninth Armies trundled onto the German *Autobahnen* and stepped on the gas. The wide double highways were described as "real dream roads . . . as smooth as a highly polished floor," although the cloverleaf ramps baffled those who had never encountered them before. Truck drivers kept themselves awake by singing "Onward, Christian Soldiers." T Force intelligence units would fall on each captured city in search of not only Nazi villains but also industrial secrets; thirty-five mobile microfilm teams rooted through factories and universities. From Wehrmacht depots, they also collected fine German maps of the Soviet Union, just in case.

Towns fell quickly: Limburg, Weilburg, Giessen—Hodges won a box of cigars from Patton by getting there first—Marburg, Kirchhain. "This mad, Alice in Wonderland rush forward through Germany," in one major's description, was both exhilarating and ruthless. Enemy soldiers who resisted were shot down on the instant. Enemy villages that failed to surrender were razed. When SS troops in search of gasoline and vehicles captured an American field hospital in late March, false rumors that doctors had been murdered and nurses raped led to a feverish, malignant manhunt, which left five hundred enemy troops dead before eight hundred others were allowed to capitulate. "How I want the war to end," wrote one soldier. "The danger now begins to frighten me. To die at this stage—with the door at the end of the passage, the door into the rose garden, already in sight, ajar—would be awful."

The hour had come to cinch the noose around the Ruhr. With Ninth Army spanking east and soon to rejoin his command, Bradley on Wednesday, March 28, ordered First Army to hurry north for a rendezvous with Simpson's vanguard, the 2nd Armored Division, while Patton's Third Army angled northeast toward Kassel, shielding Hodges's right flank. The First and Ninth Armies were to meet in Paderborn, an eighth-century bishopric founded by Charlemagne—or rather, they were to meet in what remained of the town: in a thirty-minute raid on Tuesday, RAF Lancasters had dropped 75,000 incendiaries, igniting three thousand individual fires that merged into a single blaze fed by half-timbered houses. It was said that the very air had first turned yellow, then peat brown, then pitch black. Here the enemy intended to stand, with a defensive line of sixty Panthers and Tigers below the town, crewed mostly by SS fledglings and reinforced with a motley brigade of Luftwaffe, Volkssturm, Hitler Youth, and Waffen-SS zealots.

General Collins's VII Corps led the First Army cavalcade, and on a cool, drear Good Friday, March 30, four columns from the 3rd Armored Division converged on Paderborn after a forty-five-mile gallop from Marburg the previous day. In a southern precinct known as Jammertal—Wailing Valley—an ambush brought the American sally to a halt, with tank and Panzerfaust fire skewering one Sherman in the flank and blowing a track from a second. Stabbing volleys from King Tigers caught others in the open at short range, and tracers bounced off the asphalt roads like flaming marbles. Seventeen Shermans, seventeen half-tracks, and a small fleet of Army trucks, jeeps, and ambulances soon brightened the dull day with their pyres; the only saving grace was the inability of panzer gunners to depress their machine guns low enough to rake GIs cowering in a roadside ditch. Napalm dumped along a ridgeline by P-47s did little more than further illuminate the calamity.

Flame, smoke, and percussive gunfire brought the division commander hastening to the front, and no soldier seemed more likely to redeem the day than Major General Maurice Rose. Tall and taciturn, with an addiction to Camel cigarettes and a fondness for musical comedy, Rose was considered the best armored commander in the U.S. Army by Collins and other admirers. Having earned battle honors at St.-Mihiel during the last war, and in North Africa, Sicily, and Normandy during this one, he now led a unit of nearly four hundred tanks, many carrying infantrymen clustered on the hull like barnacles. The son and grandson of rabbis from White Russia, Rose had grown up speaking Yiddish at home in Denver before joining the Colorado National Guard at age sixteen; beginning in 1918, on various Army forms he repeatedly declared himself to be either Methodist, Episcopalian, or generically Protestant, a conversion perhaps inspired by residual anti-Semitism in the officer corps. Near Marburg two days earlier, when a reporter had asked Rose about his plans after the war, he replied, "I have a son. He's four years old now, and I don't know him. We're going to get acquainted."

No, they would not. Moving up the spearhead's eastern edge at dusk in a convoy of three jeeps, two motorcycles, and an armored car, Rose and his command group abruptly took fire from both flanks. "We're in a hell of a fix now," he murmured. Chased by machine-gun bullets, the convoy bolted forward; but at last light, four panzers emerged from the darkness, each emitting the twin exhaust-flame signature of a Tiger. A quick swerve by one tank pinned Rose's jeep against a plum tree. "It looks like they have us," he said. The Tiger commander popped from his turret hatch with a submachine gun, yelling and gesticulating as the general, his aide, and the jeep driver stood in the road with hands high, laved by the faint light of

Shermans afire in a nearby field. As Rose reached for his pistol to drop it in the road, the German fired. Two slugs hit him in the right hand, another ripped into his right cheek. Four stitched his chest, four more struck him in the head, and a final three hit him in the groin, thigh, and lower back. His two comrades tumbled into a ditch, then fled through the dark wood, leaving behind their commander's riddled corpse.

That night as the enemy retreated into Paderborn, a platoon recovered Rose's body and laid him in a grain bin, wrapped in a blanket with an MP honor guard. "It can't be him. I'm sure it ain't him," a young lieutenant said. Told that the dead man had been irrefutably identified, the lieutenant persisted, "I sure hope it ain't him." Rose would be interred in a temporary grave under a wooden cross, then reburied in the majestic Margraten cemetery beneath a Star of David at the insistence of Jewish chaplains who recited Kaddish over his grave. In 1949 a Latin cross was reinstated after a hearing board affirmed his conversion. Under any insignia, a gallant soldier was gone, and his hard death foretold a Reich that would also die hard.

A war-crimes investigation by Lieutenant Colonel Leon Jaworski, who three decades later won fame as a special prosecutor in the Watergate scandal, ruled Rose's shooting accidental. By then, reprisal had run its red course. Feral American troops smashed the villages south of Paderborn, burning houses and executing wounded enemy soldiers. Twenty-seven Germans, said to have been shot after surrendering, were later discovered behind the Etteln cemetery, and eighteen more were counted in Dörenhagen. Some GIs reportedly prevented the Germans from burying their dead, and bodies lay corrupting in the sun and rain for days as a reminder to the living of what war had wrought. Carrion crows hopped about, stiff-legged and unsentimental. It had come to this.

Fanatical resistance in Paderborn caused General Collins to revise his attack. Early Saturday morning, March 31, he ordered the 3rd Armored Division to pivot twenty miles west, where the Ninth Army's 2nd Armored Division was nearing Lippstadt. Here opposition promised to be lighter: the town now was defended mostly by Volkssturm militia with armbands for uniforms and ancient Czech rifles for weaponry. Beaten Wehrmacht columns from the Rhine trudged eastward through the streets, pushing their kit in barrows and stolen prams. A Nazi boss had combed a military hospital for engineers to sabotage bridges over the river Lippe using explosives found in a V-1 storage shed and bombs from an airfield magazine, but the job was botched and the spans in Lippstadt still stood. It was said that a German surgeon had begun removing the telltale blood group tattoos from the inner left arms of Waffen-SS soldiers, leaving a scar that resembled a bullet wound.

Easter Sunday dawned bright and warm. Army chaplains in village churches near the American gun lines hastily celebrated the holy morning as howitzers popped away. "Every time a battery would fire the candles on the altar would flicker and the loosened window panes would rattle," a paratrooper wrote his parents. "The church was crowded with GIs in their filthy combat clothes." Pealing bells in Lippstadt also summoned the faithful, and pious Germans hurried to Mass even as exploding shells walked down Barbarossastrasse. The last garrison troops wobbled away on bicycles, and home guardsmen plundered their barracks for underwear and mattresses.

At noon, observation planes reported vanguards of the 2nd and 3rd Armored Divisions approaching each other from west and east, respectively, the former led by a sergeant named Werner Osthelmer, who had emigrated from Lippstadt eight years earlier to open a butcher shop in Detroit. Shortly after four P.M. the columns met with back-slapping chortles to complete the Ruhr's encirclement. Refugees and liberated slave laborers looted stores in downtown Lippstadt, smashing bank windows and lighting their cigarettes with hundred-mark notes.

The "largest double envelopment in history," in Eisenhower's cock-a-hoop phrase, had thrown a cordon seventy-five miles wide by fifty miles deep around the Reich's industrial core. Precisely who had been trapped within those four thousand square miles remained uncertain, although Allied intelligence believed the pocket contained shards of the Fifteenth and Fifth Panzer Armies, and two corps from the First Parachute Army. Among those snared was Field Marshal Model, whose Army Group B now faced extermination. Model had no appetite for last-ditch fighting among the Ruhr's bombed factories, gutted cities, and slag pits, but Hitler forbade withdrawal on pain of death. Instead the field marshal was reduced to waiting for reinforcement by a new, largely imaginary Twelfth Army, while every uniformed *Landser* in his command was bundled into the Ruhr perimeter, including schoolboy fanatics in short pants, known as "Ascension Day Commandos" for their willingness to die. "All fear comes from the Devil," Model wrote his wife in an Easter letter. "Courage and joy come from the Lord. . . . We all must die at some time or other."

To bring that day closer for his foe, Bradley ordered four corps to reduce the Ruhr Pocket. Ninth Army, now restored to 12th Army Group, would squeeze from the north, clearing one grimy, skeletonized city after another. Some were too enfeebled to resist, like Duisburg and Essen. Others fought on, like Hamm, which would take four days to smite senseless. First Army pressed from the south, in terrain less urban but more rugged, gnawing away four to six miles each day and freeing slave workers by the tens of thousands. Marching fire and thermite grenades usually proved irresistible to enemy holdouts; against one recalcitrant nest, at a Siegburg factory where German paratroopers used machine lathes to burrow into a deep subbasement, fifty flamethrowers encouraged surrender. After his 7th Armored Division captured the LXXXI Corps commander and twenty thousand soldiers, General Hasbrouck began a letter to his wife, then wrote, "There are so many interruptions from excited staff officers at higher headquarters that I will have to stop."

"What is there left to a commander in defeat?" Model asked his staff. "In ancient times, they took poison." The *Ruhrfestung*, Fortress Ruhr, was shrinking by the hour. Ammunition and food stocks dwindled with the American capture of grain and flour reserves near Hamm. Contact with the high command grew spotty, and fatuous orders from Berlin were "scarcely read, much less passed on," as Model's chief of staff conceded. Probes of the U.S. perimeter revealed no weak points for a possible breakout. General Ridgway of XVIII Airborne Corps sent a letter through the lines, urging Model to emulate Robert E. Lee at Appomattox:

> Eighty years ago this month, his loyal command reduced in numbers, stripped of its means of effective fighting and completely surrounded by overwhelming forces, he chose an honorable capitulation. This same choice is now yours.

The plea fell on deaf ears. Moscow had accused Model of complicity in a half-million deaths in Latvia early in the war, and he had no intention of facing Soviet justice. "A field marshal does not become a prisoner," he declared. "Such a thing is just not possible." Instead, he dispatched an aide to slip through the cordon to help the Model family flee westward from Dresden and to burn his personal papers. Then the field marshal ordered Army Group B disbanded, sparing himself the stigma of surrendering a unit that now no longer existed. "Have we done everything to justify our actions in the light of history?" he asked his chief of staff.

With the pocket disintegrating, Model and three fugitive officers drove to the Düsseldorf racetrack before picking their way on a logging road through a thicket northeast of the ruined city. Swatting mosquitoes in the dark, they listened to a radio broadcast from Berlin in an Opel-Blitz signals truck and heard Goebbels condemn the *"verrätische Ruhrarmee,"* the treacherous army of the Ruhr.

"I sincerely believe that I have served a criminal," Model mused. "I led my solders in good conscience . . . but for a criminal government." Sealing his wedding ring and a letter to his wife inside an envelope, he walked to a gnarled oak tree. "You will bury me here," he told a subordinate, then blew his brains out with a Walther service revolver.

* * *

A B-26 crewman flying low over the Ruhr in April spied what he thought was "a dark plowed field." On closer scrutiny, he reported, "it proved to be acres of massed humanity . . . packed together closer than a herd of cows."

Allied intelligence originally estimated that 80,000 Germans had been trapped in the Ruhr Pocket. On April 5, the figure jumped to 125,000. A day later Eisenhower told Marshall that he believed 150,000 were in the pocket, of whom "we will capture at least 100,000." Those figures proved far too modest: in the event, 323,000 enemy prisoners would be taken from seven corps and nineteen divisions. This multitude, larger than those bagged at Stalingrad or Tunis, included twenty-four generals and a dry-shod admiral. "I had some nice days during my military career, yes, it was lots of fun," a German commander told his interrogators. "But now I wish I were dead."

American planners had assumed a need for cages to hold 900,000 German prisoners by the end of June; instead, by mid-April the number exceeded 1.3 million, and the final Ruhr bonanza would sharply increase that tally. "We have prisoners like some people have mice," Gavin complained to his daughter. A guard from the 78th Division who set out on foot with sixty-nine Germans in his custody reached a regimental stockade near Wuppertal with twelve hundred. Enemy troops throughout the pocket could be seen waving "handkerchiefs, bed sheets, table linen, shirts"—on this battlefield, a division history observed, "the predominant color was white." One unit rode bicycles into captivity, maintaining a precise military alignment to the end. Another arrived aboard horse-drawn wagons, clip-clopping in parade formation. The men unhitched and groomed their teams, then turned them free into the fields as they themselves repaired to captivity.

The official Army history described the surrendering rabble:

> Young men, old men, arrogant SS troops, dejected infantrymen, paunchy reservists, female nurses and technicians, teenage members of the Hitler Youth, stiffly correct, monocled Prussians, enough to gladden the heart of a Hollywood casting director. . . . Some [came] carrying black bread and wine; others with musical instruments—accordions, guitars; a few bringing along wives or girlfriends in a mistaken hope that they might share their captivity.

A single strand of barbed wire often sufficed for an enclosure. GI sentries cradled their carbines and stifled yawns. Within the cordon sat supermen by the acre. Singing sad soldier songs and reminiscing about better days, they scavenged the ground for cigarette butts and plucked the lice from their field-gray tunics.

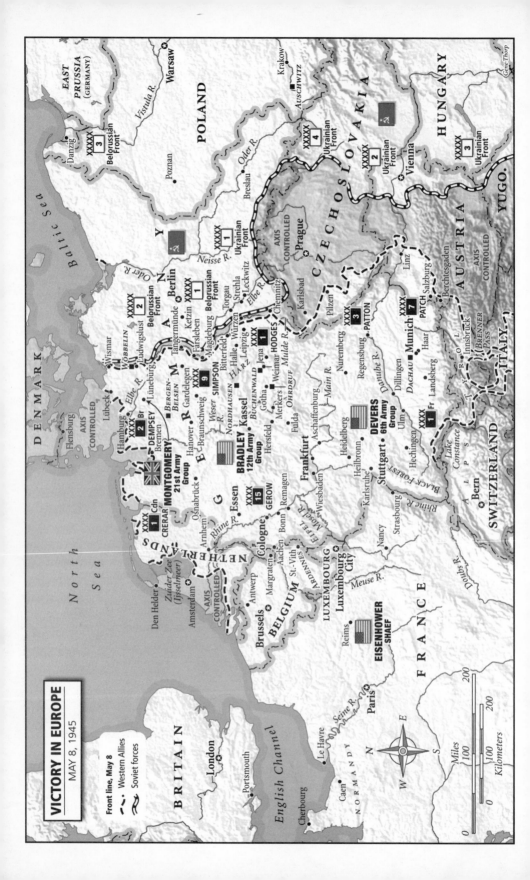

12. VICTORY

Mark of the Beast

For the final destruction of the Third Reich, General Bradley—newly awarded a fourth star, and now dubbed "Omar the Warmaker" by the *Stars and Stripes* newspaper—shifted his command post to Wiesbaden, just west of Frankfurt. Eisenhower joined him there on Wednesday evening, April 11, after a flight from Reims in a B-25 bomber. Early the next morning they squeezed into a Piper Cub and flew eighty miles northeast, following the autobahn trace to the market town of Hersfeld. Here Patton, who also had been promoted to four-star general, awaited them with an armored cavalry escort and a convoy of jeeps, including one adorned with the supreme commander's five-star rank insignia. East they sped for twenty miles, through a lowland corridor known as the Fulda Gap, arriving at 10:30 A.M. in the Thuringian village of Merkers. A tank battalion guarded the entrance to a nineteenth-century potassium mine, where GIs had made a discovery that Patton believed Eisenhower should see.

A photograph of the Führer still graced the timekeeper's office wall in the mine mouth, and an exhortatory sign proclaimed, *auf Deutsch*, "Thy Strength Is Nothing: The People's Strength Is All!" The XII Corps commander, General Eddy, led them onto a rickety freight elevator, and as they slowly descended the pitch-black shaft Patton quipped, "If that clothesline should part, promotions in the United States Army would be considerably stimulated." Sixteen hundred feet down, the lift doors opened. A sentry snapped a salute, and upon recognizing his visitors exclaimed, "Jesus Christ!" In a wide gallery Patton pointed to currency-engraving plates used by the Reichsbank, and stacked bales of money designated for the Wehrmacht. Eyeing the bills, Bradley said, "I doubt the German army will be meeting payrolls much longer."

Treasures already had been discovered in other mines: in a damp Siegen iron pit on April 2, soldiers found six enormous crates labeled "Aachen Cathedral," which included a silver bust of Charlemagne imbedded with a fragment of the emperor's skull. Other boxes in the Siegen lode held paintings by Rembrandt, Van Dyck, and Van Gogh, and the original manuscript of Beethoven's Sixth Symphony. Yet no trove would surpass that found in the Merkers workings, as Eisenhower realized upon stepping through a hole blown in a bank-vault door by Army engineers using half a stick of dynamite.

Here in "Room No. 8," a chamber 150 feet long and 75 feet wide, more than 7,000 bags of gold and other loot recently transferred from Berlin—in some cases by double-decker bus—lay in neat rows under lights dangling beneath the twelve-foot ceiling. In addition to 8,307 gold bars and 55 crates of bullion, the repository included 3,682 sacks of German currency, 80 more of foreign currency, 3,326 bags of gold coins—among them 711 filled with U.S. $20 gold pieces, each sack worth $25,000—8 bags of gold rings, and a pouch of platinum bars. At the back of the room, in more than 200 satchels, suitcases, and trunks, each tagged "Melmer" after a kleptomaniacal SS captain named Bruno Melmer, were valuables stolen from concentration-camp victims: pearls, watch cases, gold tooth crowns, Passover cups, cigarette cases, spoons. Much of the metal had been hammered flat to save space. Other galleries and shafts nearby yielded two million volumes from Berlin libraries, 400 tons of patent records, 33 wooden cases of Goethe memorabilia from Weimar, paintings by Rubens and Goya, and costumes from the Berlin state theaters. "If these were the old free-booting days when a soldier kept his loot," Bradley told Patton, "you'd be the richest man in the world."

Patton facetiously proposed converting the 250 tons of gold—most of the Reich's reserve—into medallions "for every son of a bitch in the Third Army." Eventually valued by SHAEF in excess of half a billion dollars, the treasure in the Merkers shaft lay within what soon would become the Soviet occupation zone. There was not a moment to lose, and plans already had been made to spirit the booty to Frankfurt—in the American zone—using thirty ten-ton trucks guarded by two MP battalions, seven infantry platoons, and air cover from P-51 Mustangs. The artworks were to be wrapped in German army sheepskin coats, thousands of which were also found in the mine.

Similar removals were under way throughout the designated Soviet sector on grounds of "military necessity," provoking shrill, ineffectual protests from Moscow that not only treasure but also equipment and skilled personnel were disappearing westward. Among those brought into the American fold were a thousand German chemists, engineers, physicists, physicians, and mathematicians, as well as various intellectual fruits, whisked away under a program code-named AIRMAIL. The haul included: 241 scientists from the Institute of Physics and Chemistry in Halle, along with new aircraft designs; 45 technical experts from an IG Farben plant in Bitterfeld, with 500 tons of potassium bichromate and 200 tons of potassium permanganate; and, from a Zeiss plant in Jena, 213 experts in radar and other disciplines, plus a new German bombsight. Other swag included ground-to-air missile designs, material supporting 340,000 German patents, and enough V-2 components to build seventy-five rockets.

Patton had one more discovery to show Eisenhower. After a quick lunch at the XII Corps command post, the traveling party flew by small plane to Gotha to join another convoy for a ten-mile excursion to the south. A German deserter's tale of an elaborate headquarters in remote Ohrdruf had intrigued Eisenhower the previous week, and he had authorized Patton to dispatch a flying column from the 4th Armored Division in hopes of capturing the enemy high command. By ill fortune, the raiders had just missed Field Marshal Kesselring, bagging only a few German soldiers masquerading as patients in a local hospital. The mysterious headquarters also proved disappointing: built inside huge underground tunnels in 1938, with telephone exchanges, carpeted offices, flush toilets, and a movie theater, the compound had never been used. Himmler had planned to refurbish the complex as a retreat for Hitler and present it to the Führer on April 20 for his fifty-sixth birthday.

Yet the expedition had hardly been fruitless, because here the Americans liberated a concentration camp in Germany for the first time. Known as S-3 and opened the previous fall, Ohrdruf was among more than eighty satellite camps of a penal facility that soon would become even more notorious: Buchenwald. Bradley described the traveling party's visit to S-3:

> We passed through the stockade. More than 3,200 naked, emaciated bodies had been flung into shallow graves. Others lay in the streets where they had fallen. . . . A guard showed us how the blood had congealed in the coarse black scabs where the starving prisoners had torn out the entrails of the dead for food.

An inmate pointed out a gallows where condemned men were strangled with piano wire. Others had been murdered with a pistol shot to the nape of the neck. As Allied forces had approached from the west, Patton informed his diary, SS guards "had some of the slaves exhume the bodies and place them on a mammoth griddle composed of 60-centimeter railway tracks laid on brick foundations. They poured pitch on the bodies and then built a fire of pinewood and coal under them," leaving "bones, skulls, charred torsos." Most guards then fled, disguised in mufti, although a few were beaten or stabbed to death by vengeful inmates as the first Americans arrived. "You search the face to find what it is that is lacking, to find the mark of the beast," a reporter wrote after scrutinizing SS visages. The camp still reeked of feces and burned hair. Another burial trench dusted with lime "was almost filled with ash and human debris from which, here and there, emaciated limbs projected," wrote Osmar White, the Australian correspondent assigned to Third Army. "Patton," Bradley noted, "walked over to a corner and sickened."

When a young GI giggled nervously, Eisenhower fixed him with a baleful eye. "Still having trouble hating them?" he asked. To other troops gathered round him in the compound, the supreme commander said, "We are told that the American soldier does not know what he is fighting for. Now at least he will know what he is fighting against."

Eisenhower and Bradley agreed to spend Thursday night at the Third Army bivouac in Hersfeld. After supper they retired to Patton's caravan with a sheaf of maps for a long discussion about where best to fling their armies. The destruction of Model's Army Group B left a hole 125 miles wide in the center of the German front for exploitation by 12th Army Group, which now boasted 1.3 million soldiers in twelve corps and forty-eight divisions. Two obvious invasion routes veered north and south of the Harz Mountains, once the Ruhr was cleared: under 12th Army Group's plan, Ninth Army would take the upper route, toward Magdeburg, and First Army the lower, across the Thüringen plain toward Leipzig. Third Army, already farther east on Bradley's right wing, would allow her two sister armies to come abreast and then swing southeast, while Patch's Seventh Army pivoted through lower Bavaria and Austria to shield Patton's flank. The new Fifteenth Army, under General Gerow, would trail the combat legions to take up occupation duties.

Despite great bounds now being made by all forces—Simpson's Ninth Army had traveled 226 miles since jumping the Rhine—Eisenhower wanted the American line to advance no farther east than Chemnitz, near the Czech border. As for Berlin, he reiterated his determination to leave the city to the Soviets, who were about to launch their final assault on the capital.

"Ike, I don't know how you figure that one," Patton said. "We had better take Berlin and quick, and go on to the Oder."

Eisenhower shook his head. "It has no tactical or strategic value," he said, with a hint of exasperation. Not only did an advance on Berlin risk colliding with the Red Army, but it would also hamper U.S. forces with even greater hordes of refugees and prisoners than those already burdening every field commander.

Another anxiety weighed on Eisenhower: he shared fears that the Nazi regime intended to retreat to a so-called National Redoubt in the Alps from which to wage a protracted guerrilla war or stage a sanguinary last stand. Either would allow Germans to claim that the Third Reich had never surrendered. How did a police state perish—with a supine whimper or a bloody bang? No one at SHAEF was sure, but Allied intelligence had convinced itself—and the supreme commander—that Hitler's regime would seek to fight on in the mountains with Götterdämmerung theatricality.

As early as the fall of 1943, Allied planners had envisioned a final shootout in heavily fortified Alpine eyries. Eisenhower warned Marshall, in September 1944, that German fanatics "may attempt to carry on a long and bitter guerrilla warfare." To Bradley in February he proposed training shock battalions to attack "nests of guerrillas which will have to be forcibly eradicated." An impregnable mountain fortress at altitudes up to twelve thousand feet could extend from Salzburg in the east to Lake Constance in the west, and even into Italy through the Brenner Pass. British intelligence voiced doubts: a quarter-million Ultra intercepts during the war had given no hint of such plans except for a vague message to Tokyo in mid-March from the Japanese embassy in Bern alluding to possible "last battlegrounds or redoubts." British agents in Austria found "no sign of preparations for organized resistance." A War Department study in early April reported "no indications that any fortifications are being constructed in Bavaria or Austria to prevent an Allied ingress into the 'redoubt area' from the north."

Far more credulous was Eisenhower's intelligence chief, Major General Strong, who later explained that "after the Ardennes, I was taking no more chances with the Germans." Convinced that it would be "true to German form to die together," Strong in March issued a dire warning: Allied air reconnaissance of twenty Alpine locales showed extensive construction work, perhaps fortifications for a German resistance network he likened to the French maquis. "Some of the most important ministries and personalities of the Nazi regime," he added, "are already established in the Redoubt area." An excitable press also conjured Nazi diehards darting among the Alpine crags and cols. *Collier's* magazine in late January told readers of a vast guerrilla training camp near the Führer's vacation home in Berchtesgaden, and *The New York Times* suggested that the National Redoubt, with countless gun emplacements, would prove more obdurate than Cassino.

An OSS psychological portrait of Hitler, titled "His Life and Legend," examined eight possible fates for the Führer, from natural death—"a remote possibility"—and escape to a neutral country—"extremely unlikely"—to capture, "the most unlikely possibility of all." Suicide was deemed "the most plausible outcome," but the study concluded that "in the end he might lock himself into this symbolic womb and defy the world to get him." Other OSS assessments, fed by a gullible station in Switzerland, reported that food, arms, and ammunition had been stockpiled in Berchtesgaden for at least eighteen months; that 150 trucks brought more war matériel to the redoubt each day; that farmers in the Alpine region could feed 750,000 men 2,500 calories a day, although the diet would be "somewhat unbalanced, with an almost complete absence of sugar"; and that Redoubt factories were capable of making small arms and antitank guns, despite shortages of coke, lead, zinc, and explosives. General William J. Donovan, the director of the Office of Strategic Services, sent Roosevelt a personal memorandum in late March asserting that the Nazis had "made careful plans to go underground."

The correspondent William L. Shirer wondered whether SHAEF intelligence had been "infiltrated by British and American mystery writers," but no imaginations were more feverish than those in Seventh Army. "Vast stores of meat and canned goods are reported being cached in caves and subterranean warehouses in the Salzburg area," Patch's intelligence chief claimed on March 25. It was said that three to five long freight trains had added to the stockpiles each week since February 1, and that secret hydro-powered assembly plants could even produce Messerschmitt fighter planes. All this, a Seventh Army analysis warned in late March, could "create an elite force, predominately SS and mountain troops, of between 200,000 and 300,000 men . . . thoroughly imbued with the Nazi spirit."

The truth was less flamboyant. The previous fall a Nazi gauleiter in the Tyrol, upon learning of OSS anxiety about a possible Alpine stronghold, resolved to encourage the American "redoubt psychosis" in hopes that Allied demands for unconditional surrender would soften if confronted by German intransigence. Thus did the tail wag the dog. Hitler in fact had evinced little interest in defensive warfare; not until spring were tank obstacles constructed in the northern Alps, along with a few field positions hastily cobbled together against a Soviet advance from Hungary. Kesselring dismissed any heroic stand in the mountains as "merest make-believe," and captured German generals expressed genuine puzzlement about a redoubt, even when American interrogators in Wiesbaden dramatically unveiled a wall map depicting a secret "Valhalla."

Hardly more credible was the so-called Werewolf movement. Conceived by Himmler as a paramilitary insurgency and named for a lycanthropic, flesh-eating character from a German novel about the Thirty Years' War, the Werewolf commandos accomplished little more than to scribble a bit of graffiti—"Traitor, take care, the Werewolf is watching"— and assassinate the mayor of Aachen for collaboration. General Donovan briefly considered hiring Basque assassins to hunt down all Werewolves, but nothing came of it.

Yet at SHAEF the myth of the National Redoubt persisted almost to the end of the war. "We may be fighting one month from now and it may even be a year," Bradley would caution visiting congressmen in late April;

A boy's body burns after
a V-2 rocket explosion in
central Antwerp in late
November 1944. German
launch crews would fire
more than 1,700 V-2s at
Antwerp during a six-month
period, in addition to some
4,200 V-1 flying bombs.

A French woman welcomes
an American soldier on
November 25, two days
after French and U.S. troops
liberated Strasbourg, the
capital of Alsace.

Two GIs from the
9th Infantry Division
shelter beneath a
Sherman tank on
December 11 in the
smashed German town
of Geich, near Düren.

At a Belgian crossroads in the early hours of the Battle of the Bulge, German soldiers strip boots and other equipment from three dead GIs. After U.S. troops captured this film, an Army censor redacted the road sign to Büllingen and other landmarks.

German soldiers smoke captured American cigarettes in front of a U.S. Army armored car on December 17, the second day of Operation HERBSTNEBEL, the attack through Belgium and Luxembourg.

General Hasso von Manteuffel commanded the Fifth Panzer Army in the Battle of the Bulge. An elfin veteran of campaigns in both Russia and Africa, Manteuffel was described by one superior as "a daredevil, a bold and dashing leader."

General Sepp Dietrich, the one-time butcher's apprentice and beer-hall brawler, commanded the Sixth Panzer Army. He is seen here in a Nuremberg jail cell, awaiting trial for war crimes in late 1945.

Lieutenant Colonel Joachim Peiper led a vanguard of six thousand SS troops across Belgium in a vain effort to seize crossings on the Meuse river. Convicted of mass murder, he would be condemned to death, though his sentence was later commuted.

Command of the 101st Airborne Division at Bastogne fell to Brigadier General Anthony C. McAuliffe, a short, genial artilleryman.

Major General Matthew B. Ridgway, left, commander of the XVIII Airborne Corps, confers during the Battle of the Bulge with Major General James M. Gavin, commander of the 82nd Airborne Division. (*U.S. Army Military History Institute*)

Montgomery, center, was given command early in the Bulge of all Allied forces in the northern Ardennes. His army commanders as of late December 1944 included, left to right: Lieutenant General Sir Miles Dempsey, British Second Army; Lieutenant General Courtney H. Hodges, U.S. First Army; Lieutenant General William H. Simpson, U.S. Ninth Army; General Harry D. G. Crerar, Canadian First Army. (©*Illustrated London News Ltd / Mary Evans Picture Library*)

GIs from the 347th Infantry Regiment in a mess line north of Bastogne on January 13, 1945, shortly before the convergence of the U.S. First and Third Armies in the Ardennes.

A young SS soldier captured by the U.S. 3rd Armored Division in Belgium on January 15.

A German saboteur, captured while wearing a U.S. Army uniform during the Battle of the Bulge, is lashed to a stake moments before his execution by a firing squad in Belgium. *(U.S. Army Military History Institute)*

President Franklin D. Roosevelt and Prime Minister Churchill aboard the U.S.S. *Quincy* in Grand Harbour, Malta, on February 2. Anna Roosevelt Boettiger, left, and Sarah Churchill Oliver accompanied their fathers on the long journey to the Crimea.

The Big Three at Yalta: Churchill, Roosevelt, and Joseph Stalin on the terrace of the Villa Livadia. The president had but two months to live.

A self-propelled 155mm "Long Tom" pounds enemy targets to the east. After overcoming ammunition shortages early in the summer and fall of 1944, American gunners by early 1945 often fired ten shells or more for every one fired by the enemy.

German mortar fire causes GIs to shelter among concrete dragon's teeth along the Siegfried Line. Known to Germans as the *Westwall* and begun in 1936, the fortifications, which included three thousand bunkers and pillboxes, stretched from the Dutch border to Switzerland.

Lieutenant General Jacob L. Devers, left, commander of the 6th Army Group, with Patch, his Seventh Army commander. Capable and decisive, with a talent for handling his prickly French subordinates, Devers also had a knack for provoking his American peers.

Lieutenant Audie Murphy, right, is congratulated by Major General John W. "Iron Mike" O'Daniel, commander of the 3rd Infantry Division. Murphy, a fifth-grade dropout from Texas, earned both a battlefield commission and the Medal of Honor for his valor in France. (*U.S. Army Military History Institute*)

U.S. Seventh Army 155mm howitzers hammer a German observation post across the Rhine in Brisach in mid-February, shortly after the last enemy troops were expelled from the Colmar Pocket in Alsace.

The Ludendorff railroad bridge, seen from the east on the morning of March 17, with the German town of Remagen visible across the Rhine. Four hours after this photo was taken, the "Ludy" abruptly collapsed into the river, killing twenty-eight U.S. soldiers who were making repairs on the captured span.

Soldiers of the 89th Division, part of Patton's Third Army, crossing the Rhine at St. Goar on March 26. One battalion came under fire even before launching its assault boats, and German defenses included a gasoline-soaked barge set ablaze in midstream. The division suffered almost three hundred casualties in reaching the east bank.

"In Cologne life is no longer possible," wrote a German diarist, and the poet Stephen Spender compared the shattered city to "the open mouth of a charred corpse." Although the Rhine bridges and thousands of buildings were destroyed, the great cathedral survived.

The wreckage of a B-24 Liberator in a German field. Of 240 low-flying Liberators that dropped supplies to Allied troops in the Rhine crossing operation called VARSITY PLUNDER, fifteen were lost and 104 damaged.

Churchill stands on a demolished Rhine rail bridge on March 25 during VAR-SITY PLUNDER. When U.S. officers demanded that he return to a safer position, the prime minister "put both his arms round one of the twisted girders of the bridge and looked over his shoulder...with pouting mouth and angry eyes." *(William Simpson Collection, U.S. Army Military History Institute)*

Major General Maurice Rose, commander of the 3rd Armored Division, receives the Croix de Guerre and an embrace from a French general in mid-March. Less than three weeks later, Rose, considered among the U.S. Army's finest armored commanders, would be shot dead. *(U.S. Army Military History Institute)*

Lieutenant Colonel John K. Waters, captured in Tunisia in 1943, survived two years of German captivity and a failed raid on the Hammelburg prison camp, a scheme concocted by his father-in-law, George Patton. Seen here in a hospital bed after his eventual liberation, Waters went on to attain four-star rank. *(Courtesy of George Patton "Pat" Waters)*

The booty discovered by Third Army troops in an old potassium mine below the German town of Merkers included gold bars, gold coins, art works, and valuables stolen from concentration camp victims. "If these were the old free-booting days when a soldier kept his loot," Omar Bradley told Patton, "you'd be the richest man in the world."

Canadian infantrymen march through a Dutch town on April 9. The starving Dutch had been reduced to eating nettle soup, laundry starch, the occasional cat or dog, and 140 million tulip bulbs.

The Pegnitz river in Nuremberg on April 20, Hitler's fifty-sixth birthday and the day this shattered city—reduced to "alluvial fans of rubble"—fell to the U.S. XV Corps.

Dead inmates discovered in the concentration camp at Buchenwald after its liberation on April 11 by the U.S. 6th Armored Division. An estimated 56,000 victims had been murdered at Buchenwald and its subcamps.

Soldiers from the U.S. 45th and 42nd Divisions arrived at Dachau camp, near Munich, on April 29. Investigators later concluded that vengeful GIs gunned down at least twenty-eight SS guards after they had surrendered.

Prisoners by the acre: an aerial photograph taken on April 25 shows some of the 160,000 Germans herded into a temporary encampment near Remagen. American stockades alone held more than 1.3 million enemy soldiers by mid-April, even before the haul from the Ruhr was complete.

Perched above Hitler's vacation home in the remote Bavarian village of Berchtesgaden, a lavish mountaintop chalet known as the Eagle's Nest had been built by the Nazi regime as a fiftieth birthday present for the Führer. American troops seized the area in early May, shortly after Hitler's suicide in Berlin.

Field Marshal Gerd von Rundstedt following his capture by American troops south of Munich on May 2. The former OB West commander is accompanied by a medic wearing a brassard, and his son, a German lieutenant.

The victorious American commanders, on May 11, 1945. Seated from left to right: Simpson; Patton; General Carl A. Spaatz, U.S. Strategic Air Forces Europe; Eisenhower; Bradley; Hodges; Lieutenant General Leonard T. Gerow, Fifteenth Army. Standing from left to right: Brigadier General Ralph F. Stearley, IX Tactical Air Command; Lieutenant General Hoyt S. Vandenburg, Ninth Air Force; Beetle Smith; Major General Otto P. Weyland, XIX Tactical Air Command; Brigadier General Richard E. Nugent, XXIX Tactical Air Command.

On the night of May 7, hours before the official end of the war in Europe, jubilant Americans celebrate with the British at Piccadilly in central London.

A bugler blows "Taps" at the close of Memorial Day ceremonies in May 1945 at the U.S. military cemetery at Margraten, Holland.

Smith told reporters that "possibly 100 to 125" German divisions could move into the Alps. SHAEF compiled a list of more than two hundred caves in southern Germany and Austria, and called for relentless air reconnaissance. Eisenhower had already ordered Devers's army group to drive toward the mountains to prevent reinforcement of a redoubt, with assistance from the First Allied Airborne Army if necessary, and forces would be dispatched to Salzburg for the same purpose. Nearly three dozen U.S. and French divisions now flooded southern Germany and Austria.

Another intelligence summary from General Strong on April 22 cited "no less than 70 examples of underground construction" and other signs of Nazi resistance in the Alps, where fragments of one hundred divisions, including SS and panzer units, were believed to have congregated. Even if a well-organized defense appeared "increasingly dubious," Strong wrote, "it seems that Hitler or one of his satellites will try to fight on in the south." In the event, not until the last week of April would the Führer sign a directive calling for a mountainous *Kernfestung*—an inner fortress—as a "last bulwark of fanatical resistance." That too was an illusion. "In the end," a German general told his interrogators after the war, "the catastrophe was allowed to run its course."

Shortly after midnight on Friday, April 13, Eisenhower and Bradley retired to their guest quarters in the Third Army encampment. Patton was skeptical of any redoubt, which he would call "so much hot air" and "a figment of the imagination," but he now kept a carbine by his cot because of rumors that glider-borne German assassins might descend behind American lines. The approach of peace made him melancholy. "Sometimes I feel that I may be nearing the end of this life," he would write Bea that week. "What else is there to do? Well, if I do get it, remember that I love you." He continued to scribble battlefield poetry, as if to perpetuate the war in his imagination; *Collier's* had just rejected an especially awful verse, "The Song of the Bayonet," which began: "From the hot furnace, throbbing with passion / First was I stamped in the form to destroy." To a friend he wrote:

> War for me has not been difficult, but has been a pleasant adventure.... The best thing that could happen to me would be to get a clean hit in the last minute of the last fight and then flit around on a cloud and watch you tear my reputation to pieces.

Glancing at his wristwatch before going to bed, Patton found that it had stopped. He turned on the radio to learn the time, only to hear a flash bulletin released moments earlier. Forgoing all thought of sleep, he hurried from his caravan to tell Eisenhower and Bradley the fatal news.

* * *

Franklin D. Roosevelt, a man who had never fired a shot in anger and yet became the greatest soldier in the most devastating war in history, was dead. He had crossed over at the fag end of an existential struggle that would be won in part because of his ability to persuade other men to die for a transcendent cause. Churchill, who would sob like a child at the president's passing, subsequently wrote that "he altered decisively and permanently the social axis, the moral axis, of mankind by involving the New World inexorably and irrevocably in the fortunes of the Old. His life must therefore be regarded as one of the most commanding events in human destiny." Roosevelt's chief of staff said simply, "How could a man die better?"

His passing came at the Little White House in Georgia; desperate for rest, he had traveled to Warm Springs with his stamp collection, aboard the presidential railcar *Ferdinand Magellan*. In his final hours on Thursday, Roosevelt posed for a portrait—the painter, after starting with his eyes, at one point reportedly stepped away from her easel to measure his nose—and signed into law a bill to expand the Commodity Credit Corporation. While preparing for lunch, he abruptly lifted his right hand to his forehead, then pitched forward from a cerebral hemorrhage. He was carried to a bedroom and dressed in pajamas. His blood pressure spiked to 300 over 190 and, two hours after being stricken, he stopped breathing. An injection of adrenaline to the heart had no effect. At 3:35 P.M. he was pronounced dead. "Nothing worked," his physician said. "And that was it." The Secret Service tested his breakfast for poison and found none.

J. Austin Dillon, an Atlanta funeral-home director, arrived seven hours later at the clapboard house with gorgeous roses around the white-pillar porch. He waited until Eleanor Roosevelt emerged dry-eyed from the bedroom, where the first lady had bade her husband farewell. Dillon found the president beneath a sheet with a gauze sling tied beneath his chin to keep his mouth clamped shut. After placing the rigid body on an embalming table under several bright floor lamps, Dillon bathed Roosevelt's face, shaved him, and then injected embalming fluid in the right carotid artery and jugular vein, slowly, to avoid swelling. More injections followed, down the femoral and radial arteries, six bottles in all, before the thoracic and abdominal cavities were aspirated and then each incision carefully sutured. "It was," Dillon later confessed, "one of the most difficult cases in every respect." After toiling for five hours, Dillon cleaned the president's nails, daubed a touch of rouge on his cheeks, and dressed him in a double-breasted blue suit with a white shirt and a dark blue necktie. He summoned Roosevelt's valet, Arthur Prettyman, who gently combed the president's hair.

On Friday, the daily casualty list with next of kin published in the nation's newspapers included this entry: "Army-Navy Dead: ROOSEVELT, Franklin D., commander-in-chief; wife, Mrs. Anna Eleanor Roosevelt, the White House." In Europe, Eisenhower decreed that "wearing of mourning badges, firing of salutes, dropping national and regimental colors and standards will be dispensed with in view of war conditions." A lieutenant in the 15th Infantry told his diary, "This is a shock. He has been president since I was fourteen years old."

Roosevelt had at last found the abiding rest he needed. How could a man die better?

Dragon Country

To an American pilot in his cockpit, the spectacle of Allied armies surging eastward seemed as if "the very crust of the earth itself had shaken loose and was rushing like hell for the Elbe." From a tank turret or a jeep seat, the war was hardly less vivid for those racing at forty miles per hour into Austria like "an irresistible molten mass," or for those watching captured Germans "running to the rear without guard, their hands clasped behind their heads, and gulping for breath," as a GI in the 86th Division described them in a letter home.

This was Dragon Country, in the phrase of the correspondent R. W. Thompson, even if at times the dragons seemed toothless, extinguished, pathetic. Flimsy barricades were called "Sixty-one Roadblocks" by German civilians, supposedly because they provoked sixty minutes of laughter from American soldiers, who then needed one minute to demolish them. A Seventh Army patrol overran an infantry school where two hundred conscripts drilled with wooden sticks and simulated the racket of machine guns by drumming on water cans. (The commandant insisted on surrendering his sword.) Troops from the 84th Division captured a German soldier with a map showing that Hanover's defenses were concentrated in the south and southwest; attacking from the north and northwest, GIs seized the city in a few hours. The university town of Heidelberg surrendered without a fight, red geraniums blooming in the window boxes beneath hundreds of white flags. Seventy thousand enemy soldiers infested the Harz Mountains, but the German Eleventh Army to which they belonged soon proved to be, in one assessment, "less an army than a conglomeration." Day after day the army commander, General Walter Lucht, dodged his American pursuers—first in a village, then in a limestone quarry, a forester's cottage, a cave, and a monastery—before finally repairing to the leafy copse where he was captured.

GIs in one town found a father, mother, and daughter who had hanged themselves as well as the family dog. "The shame of German defeat," their suicide note read, "is too much to bear." Perhaps the war was too far gone even for pathos. After seeing an elderly couple weeping before their burning farmhouse, a company commander in the 2nd Infantry Division wrote, "What right had they to stand there sobbing and blaming us for this terror? What right did they and their kind have to any emotions at all?" Alfried Krupp, an industrialist whose slave factories had armed the Reich, also was said to have wept upon his arrest for war crimes; one of his 125 servants ran after him with a packed weekend bag as he was led away near Essen, as if the misunderstanding could be resolved in a day or two. In Krupp's 260-room Villa Hügel, described by one critic as "the most hideous building in Germany," soldiers found twenty walnut wardrobes lining a dressing room two stories high, with white wolf-skin rugs, gold gooseneck water taps spilling into a bathtub scooped from a huge block of marble, a table that could seat sixty-five diners, and a ceiling mural of a goddess astride a crescent moon, her hair pinned up with a star.

"Brilliant spring sunshine. The song of the lark, the flash of the kingfisher, the white flare of a deer running through the forest shade," wrote R. W. Thompson, advancing on Bremen with British troops. "From behind the window curtains, faces watch us fearfully." Osmar White described "old men leaning on sticks, snatching at their hats" in obeisance to their conquerors, and frantically denying the accusatory query, *"Liebst Du den Führer?"* No! they cried. No, I don't love the Führer! White recorded the roadside interrogation by GIs of a passerby:

> *Kommen Sie hier.* Where are you going?
> To my father's house.
> Why are you going?
> My mother has been killed. I am going to keep house for my father. . . .
>   Is it permitted? Is it not forbidden?
> No. It is not forbidden as far as I know.

And yet dragons lurked. For every enemy platoon that surrendered, another fought savagely, often unto death: in April, 10,677 U.S. soldiers would be killed in action in Europe, almost as many as in June 1944. Goebbels in a radio broadcast in mid-April warned that houses displaying white flags would be considered "plague bacteria." Other decrees urged that shirkers and capitulators be hanged with placards around their necks identifying them as cowards; placarded miscreants soon dangled from streetlamps and telephone poles across the Reich. "If we lose the war," a Nazi official warned, "it means slavery for every German, and certain death for every party member." A party leader in the Harz told German women in April that they would be "abducted and taken to Negro brothels."

Some Luftwaffe pilots received training in how to ram their aircraft into Allied bombers, as well as political indoctrination on the nexus between Jews, Bolshevists, and the Western democracies. "By consciously staking your lives," Göring told his kamikazes, "save the nation from extinction." Few such "total commitment missions" succeeded in the air, but suicidal SS and Hitler Youth gangs were reported across the front. A Seventh Army patrol on April 14 killed several young boys carrying potato-masher grenades. "It's a heartbreaking sight," a reporter wrote of such juvenile soldiers. "These children's faces have nothing childlike about them."

Although the National Redoubt in the Alps was a brown pipe-dream, makeshift bastions here and there stoked SHAEF's fear of a Germany bent on self-immolation. In Aschaffenburg, Bradley reported that "women and children lined the rooftops to pelt our troops with hand grenades," while wounded veterans hobbled from their hospital beds into the firing line. In Heilbronn, on the Neckar River, already smashed by years of bombing, German officers shot down Hitler Youth detachments when they broke and ran under American mortar fire. Heilbronn held out for nine days, until April 13, and the detritus that once had been a pretty medieval town was said by an Army historian to retain "a noticeable stench all during the summer of 1945."

"Why don't the silly bastards give up?" asked a Coldstream Guards corporal. That enigma perplexed every Allied soldier at one moment or another. Imminent, ineluctable disaster had enhanced a perverse sense of German national cohesion, inflamed by terror, misery, and unhappy memories of the last, lost world war. Lurid propaganda—regarding Soviet atrocities in the east, the Allied demand for unconditional surrender, and those "Negro brothels"—fueled the resistance.

"Mother, you asked me when I was coming home. I don't know," Captain Jack Golden had written his family in Seymour, Texas, a few weeks earlier. "I don't see any end to the war. I can't see what the Germans hope to gain but they aren't giving up." Now twenty-three, a graduate of Texas A&M University, Golden had been overseas for more than two years; he had seen enough combat in North Africa and in landings at Gela and Omaha Beach to earn two Silver Stars and a Purple Heart. "I am getting a little tired and I am so nervous that I bite people's head off at the least mishap," he confessed in his looping cursive. The cannon company he commanded in the 16th Infantry Regiment, part of the 1st Division, had fired more than 75,000 rounds since June 6, he added. "We don't count what went on in Africa and Sicily. That is too long ago. Seems like another war."

In an April 3 letter from Germany, Golden expressed relief that his brother, a lieutenant in the Army Air Forces, was headed home on leave. "It will take a little worry off my mind. Every time I saw a bomber go down, I prayed it wasn't Bill." He continued:

> There are too many German towns that we haven't had time to fire our artillery into. I think we should fire about a thousand rounds into every town. Do them all good. . . . Enough. Enough.

That would be his last letter home. On Sunday, April 15, in the Harz foothills, two ambushers with machine pistols stepped from behind a house in Amelunxen onto the same road that a 16th Infantry rifle company had just cleared. They shot Captain Golden dead in his jeep. Jack's passing would be, his family acknowledged, "the greatest trial of our lives." In a condolence note to his parents, Secretary of War Stimson wrote, "The loss of a loved one is beyond man's repairing." *Enough. Enough.*

"Half the nationalities of Europe were on the march," wrote Alan Moorehead, "bundles on their shoulders, trudging along the ditches in order to avoid the passing military traffic." In fact, nearly *all* the nationalities of Europe were on the march, in what one witness called "that monstrous, moving frieze of refugees." Allied officers estimated that 4.2 million "displaced persons" from forty-seven nations trudged through 12th Army Group's sector of Germany alone. They were among some 11 million unmoored souls wandering across central Europe in the spring of 1945.

Some were on forced marches, including Allied prisoners-of-war evacuated by their captors to camps deeper within the shrinking Reich. Darrell W. Coates, a turret gunner shot down and captured in 1942, kept a journal as he and four thousand others from Stalag 17B were prodded across Austria just ahead of Soviet forces approaching from the east.

> *April 9*: Most of us refused to move until they fed us. Bayonets and rifle fire quickly changed our minds.
>
> *April 11*: We were very hungry this nite and we boiled grass in the rain so that we would have something inside us.
>
> *April 14*: Rain again as usual. . . . Miserable as hell. Marched till after 6 P.M.
>
> *April 15*: Hurry up Patton for Christ sake.
>
> *April 19*: Get soup tonight. They must have just run a horse harness through hot water. Tastes like hell.

Others were liberated before the Germans could move them. "Everyone is yelling and jumping around," Lieutenant Bernard Epstein, who had been captured in the Bulge, told his diary on April 12 after Ninth Army troops drove through the gates of Oflag 79, near Braunschweig. "An American officer beside me with one leg amputated is so overcome he can't talk. He's blowing his nose and tears are streaming down his cheeks." Given the dearth of food and medical supplies, many were in wretched condition. "Smaller wounds were covered with toilet paper," wrote Lieutenant June Wandrey, a Seventh Army nurse from Wisconsin. "Their brutal amputations were covered with rags.... Their bodies were covered with scratches, inflicted when they clawed at their body lice." Some British prisoners captured at Dunkirk or in the Western Desert had been incarcerated for four years or more. "So," one Tommy said, eyeing his liberators, "that's what a jeep looks like." Trucked westward to the Allied rear, the men cheered wildly at the sight of every ruined German town.

Of the shambling millions, many hundreds of thousands were slave laborers freed when factories were bombed or encampments overrun. SHAEF broadcasts in various languages by Radio Luxembourg offered instructions both to those not yet freed—"Take shelter and await the Allied armies. Form small groups of your own nationality and choose a leader"—and to those already at liberty: "Do *not* move out of your district. Wait for orders. Keep discipline.... Let your behavior be a credit to your national honor."

Instead, starvation, revenge, indiscipline, and chaos often created what Allied officers called a "liberation complex." SHAEF had presumed that refugees "would be tractable, grateful, and powerless after their domination for from two to five years as the objects of German slave policies." As an Army assessment concluded, "They were none of these things.... Newly liberated persons looted, robbed, murdered, and in some cases destroyed their own shelter." Freed laborers plundered houses in the Ruhr, burning furniture for cook fires and discarding slave rags to dress in business suits, pajamas, and evening clothes ransacked from German wardrobes. Ravenous ex-prisoners licked flour off the floor of a Farsleben bakery. In Osnabrück, "rampageous" Russian slaves died after swilling V-2 rocket fuel discovered in a storage yard. Others smashed wine barrels and liquor bottles in a Hanover cellar, drinking so heavily from a sloshing, six-inch-deep pool of alcohol on the floor that several collapsed in a stupor and drowned before U.S. MPs could close the entrance.

Thousands of refugees carried tuberculosis, diphtheria, and other contagions. As medical officers charted typhus outbreaks in the Rhine valley, roadblocks were thrown up to keep migrating eastern European hordes from advancing farther west. Pilgrims were dusted with DDT and herded into new camps, where a SHAEF sermon blared from public address loudspeakers: "Alleluia! The Lord is victorious, and the spirit of unrighteousness has been reduced to dust and ashes!"

Still the moving frieze moved on. "Some went barefoot even in the frost, others wrapped their feet in blanket strips and sacking," wrote Osmar White.

> There were farm carts, milk floats, bakers' wagons, buggies, sometimes drawn by skinny horses but more often by teams of men and women. Once I saw an ancient steamroller, belching smoke and sparks, towing a long line of drays and carts on the Berlin–Frankfurt autobahn. These processions were amazing and ludicrous . . . heavily salted with suffering.

Shallow graves were "marked by a truss of straw tied on as a crosspiece." Those were the fortunate dead; many found no grave at all. On a road in upper Bavaria, the 90th Division medical battalion described discovering bodies in sad attitudes of liberation: "One man died in the position of massaging his feet. One died taking a drink from a tire rut. He remained on his hands and knees with his face in the rut for two days."

For the liberators, this great floodtide of misery was unnerving. "It's too big," an 82nd Airborne paratrooper wrote in a letter home. "Personally I don't give a damn. . . . It makes you hard." After passing four hundred Italian slave laborers swaddled in rags, Eric Sevareid took inventory of his own sentiments: "a kind of dull satisfaction, a weary incapacity for further stimulation, a desire to go home and not have to think about it anymore—and a vague wondering whether I could ever cease thinking about it as long as I lived."

There was worse to see and to think about—much worse. Ohrdruf had been but the first concentration camp liberated by Western armies in the Fatherland, and it was hardly the most heinous. Others followed in short order, and new discoveries revealed the Reich's full depravity. "If the heavens were paper and all the water in the world were ink and all the trees turned into pens," a rabbi told a war correspondent, "you could not even then record the sufferings and horrors."

Nordhausen was overrun by the 3rd Armored and 104th Infantry Divisions, which found what one witness described as "a charnel house" of several thousand corpses. "Men lay as they had starved, discolored and lying in indescribable human filth," a medic reported. "One hunched-down French boy was huddled up against a dead comrade, as if to keep warm."

In nearby tunnels used to assemble V-weapons, GIs beat up a captured German scientist, then beat him up again for the benefit of a Signal Corps photographer. General Collins ordered two thousand German civilians to carry Nordhausen's dead half a mile for burial in two dozen mass graves. "There is no greater shame for any German," Collins told them, "than to be a citizen of this town."

Soldiers who in years of combat had seen things no man should ever see now gawked in disbelief at the iniquities confronting them. "There was no fat on them to decompose," Major Ralph Ingersoll wrote after viewing corpses at Landsberg. "You are repelled by the sight of your own leg, because in its shape it reminds you of one of those legs. It is a degenerating experience." At the Wöbbelin camp near Ludwigslust, General Gavin ordered local civilians to open the mass graves of camp victims and lift the dead into wagon beds lined with evergreen boughs; they were to be reinterred in graves dug on the town square. "Each body was pulled out, handed up and wrapped in a white sheet or tablecloth," an 82nd Airborne lieutenant wrote his sister. "We were united in a bond of shame that we had ever seen such things." Gavin arranged for a film crew to record the proceedings, and years later he wept while watching the footage. "It was a defining moment in our lives," a paratrooper said. "Who we were, what we believed in, and what we stood for."

Such a moment arrived for the British Army, and the civilized world, on April 15 when the 11th Armored Division stumbled upon the Bergen-Belsen camp, fifty miles south of Hamburg. "We came into a smell of ordure—like the smell of a monkey camp," a British intelligence officer reported, and a "strange simian throng" greeted them at the gates. Over forty thousand men, women, and children jammed a compound designed for eight thousand; since January they had survived on watery soup, fourteen ounces of rye bread a day, and a kind of beet called mangel-wurzel, normally used as livestock feed. But for the past four days they had received neither food nor water and were reduced to eating the hearts, livers, and kidneys of the dead. Plundered bodies lay in such numbers that it was "like trying to count the stars," a medic reported. Ten thousand corpses littered the camp: two thousand lined a pit on the southern perimeter and others were stacked four deep around the crude hospital. "Both inside and outside the huts," the British Army reported, "was an almost continuous carpet of dead bodies, human excreta, rags, and filth." One soldier recounted seeing "a woman squatting gnawing at a human thigh bone. . . . In war you see humanity at the end of its tether." A wire-service reporter admitted to "peeping through fingers like a frightened child."

The living looked like "polished skeletons," in the phrase of a BBC correspondent, with faces resembling "a yellow parchment sheet with two holes in it for eyes." Among the survivors—"these clowns in their terrible motley," as an intelligence officer described them—medics tallied ten thousand cases of tuberculosis, ten thousand of typhus, and twenty thousand of enteritis. Still others had typhoid. A *Life* magazine reporter described an inmate who hobbled up and muttered something in German. "I couldn't understand what he said and I shall never know for he fell dead at my feet in the middle of his sentence." Of those still alive in what British doctors called "the horror camp," thirteen thousand died of their insults after liberation, passing at a rate of a thousand a day. The dead were bulldozed into pits, or carried to mass graves by barefoot German guards, who were hectored by Tommies and clubbed with rifle butts. A month later, after the last survivors had been evacuated, Bergen-Belsen would be burned to the ground.

An estimated quarter-million concentration camp inmates had died since the beginning of the year in death marches from one confinement to another, murdered outright by their guards or succumbing to malnutrition, exposure, and disease. Allied soldiers found the spoor of these perambulations across Germany, but few discoveries were more appalling than that made by a battalion from the U.S. 102nd Infantry Division on April 15 outside Gardelegen, twenty-five miles north of Magdeburg. In and around a smoldering brick barn lay more than a thousand charred bodies of political prisoners, Jews, and other inmates who had been evacuated mostly from camps around Nordhausen. By the time the columns of prisoners reached Gardelegen, hundreds had already been executed. The remnant was locked into the barn, which had been strewn with gasoline-soaked straw and potato sacks. A fusillade of rifle, machine-gun, and Panzerfaust fire, supplemented by fifty grenades, turned the structure into a flaming abattoir, as dying men screamed for mercy in Russian, Polish, French, Hungarian, and Dutch. Others sang "La Marseillaise," the "Internationale," or the Polish national anthem while roasting alive. By the time American soldiers arrived, the flames had subsided, although wisps of smoke rose from the bodies for days. Few of the 1,016 victims from the burning barn were ever identified by name.

For the U.S. Army, the camp at Buchenwald offered a uniquely searing epiphany of liberation because of its size and the clear evidence of systemic evil. Built in 1937 outside Weimar, a city that had once been home to Goethe, Schiller, and Franz Liszt, Buchenwald and its satellites had grown to more than 100,000 inmates by March 1945, with offenders categorized by triangle insignia on their uniforms: red for political prisoners, pink for homosexuals, green for criminals, yellow for Jews. Just after noon on April 11, a warning over the public address system advised, "All S.S. men leave the camp immediately." Sentries "ran with long strides into the forest," a witness reported, and at 3:15 P.M. a white flag rose above the camp. An hour later, outriders of the Third Army's 6th Armored Division burst through the main gate, which stood beneath a large sign proclaiming *Recht oder Unrecht, mein Vaterland.* Right or wrong, my Fatherland. They found twenty-one thousand survivors from thirty-one nations—engineers, lawyers, professors, editors, and a thousand boys under age fourteen—living on six hundred calories a day. As one liberator said of the liberated, "They were so thin and so dried out that they might have been monkeys or plaster of Paris and you had to keep saying to yourself, these are human beings."

An intricate, awful world soon was revealed: the cement cellar "strangling room," where the condemned were garroted and hung on forty-five wall hooks, those still struggling to be bashed with a wooden mallet; Block 46, where gruesome medical experiments were conducted; the dissecting room, where inmate tattoos were excised, tanned, and fashioned into lampshades, wall hangings, and a pair of gloves for the commandant's wife. "Inmates were beaten with fists, sticks, clubs, dog whips, riding crops, rubber hoses, ox-tail whips, leather belts, rifle butts, shovels, spade handles, and rocks," an Army report noted. "Also they were bitten by dogs." Others were strung up by their hands for hours from tree boughs in a grove known to SS guards as the "singing forest" because of the victims' cries. Music blared from the loudspeakers to mask gunfire at the camp stables or rifle range by the execution squad, "Detail 99."

The SS had murdered at least 56,000 inmates in Buchenwald and its subcamps. Many then were consigned to six brick ovens that could reduce a "charge" of eighteen bodies to bone ash in twenty minutes. A verse in gold and black lettering above the crematorium door caught Osmar White's eye:

> *Worms shall not devour but flames*
> *Consume this body. While I lived*
> *I always loved the heat and light.*

Patton marched the burghers of Weimar through Buchenwald, and sent photos to George Marshall. As if to nurture some living thing in this cantonment of death, Patton personally watered the parched plants in a greenhouse. The journalist Edward R. Murrow, rarely at a loss for imagery, found that Buchenwald beggared the imagination. "The stink was beyond all description," he told his radio audience. "For most of it I have no words. . . . If I've offended you by this rather mild account of Buchenwald, I'm not in the least sorry."

Shocking evidence of German torture and murder had been emerging for many months as Allied armies overran crime scenes at Breedonck prison in Belgium, or in camps like Natzweiler in France and Majdanek in Poland. Yet not until the revelations of April 1945 did the vast criminality of the Nazi regime spark enduring outrage in the West. Hyperbolic propaganda about World War I atrocities "had left an enduring legacy of skepticism," the U.S. Army acknowledged; a survey in early December found that barely one-third of British citizens believed atrocity stories about the Germans. Graphic film footage from Europe had been suppressed because Hollywood worried about nauseating moviegoers or creating ill-will toward newsreel companies. But photography and eyewitness accounts from Bergen-Belsen, Buchenwald, and other hellholes now filled newspapers and cinema screens. Warner Bros. and other studios collaborated with the Pentagon in releasing atrocity documentaries. By mid-April, another survey showed that more than four in five Britons were convinced that the Reich had done evil on a monumental scale.

Even war-weary soldiers felt a new sense of purpose. "What kind of people are these that we are fighting?" an anguished GI in the 8th Infantry Division asked after viewing Wöbbelin. If the answer to that question remained elusive, the corollaries—What kind of people are *we*? What kind of people should we be?—seemed ever clearer. Complete victory would require not only vanquishing the enemy on the battlefield, but also bearing witness to all that the war had revealed about the human heart. "Hardly any boy infantryman started his career as a moralist," wrote Lieutenant Paul Fussell, "but after the camps, a moral attitude was dominant and there was no disagreement on the main point." A rifleman in the 157th Infantry agreed. "I've been in the Army for thirty-nine months," he said. "I've been overseas in combat for twenty-three. I'd gladly go through it all again if I knew that things like this would be stopped."

Berliners received an extra allocation of "crisis rations" to commemorate Hitler's birthday on Friday, April 20: a pound of bacon or sausage, half a pound of rice, and an ounce of coffee. Allied planes pummeled the city for much of the day, and citizens risked their lives to queue for the special groceries. "With these rations we shall now ascend into heaven," one woman told her husband. A commemorative postage stamp also was issued, with a cancellation imprint that read, "We are defending Europe against Bolshevism." Both stamp and slogan seemed uncommonly ironic for a regime not known for its wry humor: the Red Army now squeezed the city from north, south, and east. Soviet artillery, delivering a long-range birthday salute, hit downtown Berlin for the first time this day. Soon enough, firing became general, massacring shoppers outside the Karstadt department store and shredding the Reichstag cupola. "No express trains are moving in or out," a Berlin diarist wrote. "All transportation is at a standstill. Postal and telegraph services have ceased. We are cut off from the world, for better or worse at the mercy of the oncoming catastrophe."

In April, almost four thousand suicides would be reported in Berlin; an SS report noted that "the demand for poison, a pistol, or other means of ending life is great everywhere." "The pastor shot himself and his wife and daughter," wrote a sixteen-year-old girl in the Friedrichshagen district. "Mrs. H shot her two sons and herself and slit her daughter's throat. . . . Our teacher, Mrs. K., hanged herself; she was a Nazi." A shortage of coffins meant that the dead were sometimes wrapped in newspapers.

Still, a birthday parade meandered through the Olympic Stadium, where German girls sang, "Lift our banners, in the fresh morning breeze." Some of the party faithful celebrated so exuberantly with schnapps that vomit stained their uniform tunics. Slogans on broken walls around the capital declared "We Will Never Surrender!" and, more ambiguously, "For All This, We Thank the Führer."

The man himself took the passing of another year in stride, accepting murmured birthday greetings from his staff in the thirty-room bunker complex beneath the Reich Chancellery. Much of Hitler's life since leaving the Adlerhorst had been spent in this labyrinth, with its storerooms of canned beef, incessant ventilator hum, and pathetic tongue of red carpet in the foyer. Here he had been joined by his mistress, Eva Braun, a Bavarian *Mädchen* who supposedly danced the Charleston well. Ashen and stooped, wrapped in a gray field coat that cloaked his trembling left arm and leg, the Führer on his birthday climbed up thirty-seven steps to the bomb-pitted Chancellery garden to present a few Hitler Youth skirmishers with Iron Crosses and pats on the cheek. It was his last ascent to the surface world.

Back behind three steel doors in his bunker late that afternoon, he convened his paladins for what would be their final conference together: Göring; Goebbels; Himmler; the architect Albert Speer; the foreign minister, Joachim von Ribbentrop; the Wehrmacht chiefs. Hitler waved away suggestions that he flee the city, as so many privileged "golden pheasants" had fled. "Jodl," he told his operations chief, "I shall fight as long as the faithful fight next to me, and then I shall shoot myself." That evening, a few adjutants and secretaries toasted him in his study. "Führer's birthday," his secretary, Martin Bormann, noted in a diary. "Unfortunately not really a birthday atmosphere." When Hitler retired for the night, the party moved upstairs to the ghostly Chancellery for champagne and dancing to the only gramophone record available, *"Blutrote Rosen Erzählen Dir vom Gluck."* Red roses bring you happiness.

The U.S. Seventh Army marked the day by conquering Nuremberg, a city of astronomers, printers, and toymakers, now designated on American maps as "Nazi Circus Town." Here the party had held its crepuscular rallies, and here the Germans had concocted the laws stripping Jews of their citizenship. For three days General Haislip's XV Corps had bored into the city. The 3rd and 45th Divisions, together since the invasion of Sicily, attacked from the north and southeast, respectively. Battalions abreast, the assault cracked the German gun ring. GIs then battled room by room and cellar by cellar, before breaching the medieval walls of the old city to overwhelm two thousand last-ditch soldiers, 150 armed firemen, and squads of civilian snipers. By Friday at four P.M., all resistance had ended but for two hundred subterranean fanatics whose extermination would take another six hours.

Little remained of the city other than "alluvial fans of rubble," an officer scribbled in his diary. At 6:30 that evening, 3rd Division soldiers gathered in Adolf-Hitler-Platz to raise the national colors on an improvised flagpole and sing the division anthem, "The Dogface Soldier." Their commander, Major General O'Daniel, whose son had been killed in Holland during MARKET GARDEN, rocked on the soles of his boots and bawled to his men: "Casablanca. Palermo. Anzio. Rome. The Vosges. Nuremberg."

A quieter commemoration unfolded a day later. On the southeast edge of the city, Zeppelin Field had been designed by Speer to accommodate a hundred thousand true believers, who in the 1930s were delivered here over a special rail spur for Nazi rallies. Modeled on the Pergamon Altar, the grandstand was crowned with an immense swastika encircled with a copper-clad wreath. Here the XV Corps rabbi, David Max Eichhorn, arrived in a jeep emblazoned with a Star of David and bearing a Torah from the shattered Jewish community in the Alsatian town of Haguenau. A second jeep carried five Jewish GIs from the 45th Division. Halting before the Zeppelin podium, they carried the holy ark up the steps, removed the Torah, and offered God prayers of thanksgiving and deliverance.

Army demolitionists subsequently blew the swastika to atoms, and a band played "The Stars and Stripes Forever." "One believes but can never fully comprehend," Eichhorn told his diary. "I have never beheld a more satisfying heap of ruins."

"God, Where Are You?"

WAR correspondents had begun offering odds on which American unit would be first to encounter the Russians as the Allied armies drew ever closer in eastern Germany. Men in the 84th Division painted welcome signs with Cyrillic lettering, and the appearance in a 69th Division command post of two brigands in Cossack attire caused great excitement until their accents unmasked them as British reporters playing a practical joke. An American order suspended artillery fire beyond the Elbe for fear of hitting the Russians; it was rescinded after cheeky Wehrmacht troops exploited the lull to sunbathe along the east bank. SHAEF and Moscow adopted recognition signals to prevent fratricide: red flares and a single white stripe around tank turrets for Soviet forces, green flares and a double stripe for the Yanks. GI scouts with field glasses scanned the fens along the Mulde River in search of the counterparts they now called "GIvans." A giddy report on April 23 identified a Russian tank, which closer scrutiny revealed as a grassy hummock with a clothesline strung across it.

East of Leipzig on the foggy morning of Wednesday, April 25, three patrols from First Army's 69th Division ventured into the uplands beyond the Mulde, ignoring orders from the U.S. high command to remain within five miles of the river. At 11:30 A.M., in the farm hamlet of Leckwitz, one group of three dozen GIs encountered a solitary Soviet horseman with Asian features mounted on a small pony; the rider swiftly galloped away. Continuing two miles to the Elbe, near Strehla—some twenty-five miles beyond the Mulde—the men spied soldiers milling along the east bank, medals glinting on their chests. After commandeering a sailboat and using hands and rifle butts to paddle across, the Americans shook hands with their Russian comrades from the 175th Rifle Regiment, exchanging smiles and extravagant gestures. But a message radioed to the regimental command post confused Strehla with Groba, four miles south; when an Army reconnaissance plane took ground fire without spotting any Soviets, the report was discounted as erroneous.

Twenty miles north and two hours later, Second Lieutenant William D. Robertson, a slender young intelligence officer, drove into the tenth-century river town of Torgau with three enlisted men in his jeep. Black smoke curled from a burning glass factory. The streets, lined with chestnuts and hawthorns, stood empty except for a few freed slave laborers and two sedans of German soldiers blind drunk on champagne. Gunfire could be heard from the Elbe, just east.

Lacking either green flares or a radio, Robertson smashed the glass door of an apothecary shop on Mackensenplatz, where his men scavenged enough tempera paint to convert a bedsheet into a crude flag with five horizontal red stripes, and blue stars daubed onto a white field. Climbing to the battlements of the hulking Hartenfels Castle above the river, they unfurled their colors, bellowing, "Cease fire! American. Amerikanski. Russia. America. . . . We have no flares!"

After a brief, unnerving riposte of Soviet machine-gun fire that chewed at the castle walls, two Red Army soldiers could be seen creeping across the twisted girders of the demolished Elbe bridge. Robertson and his men pounded down the stairs to meet them halfway before crossing to the far bank for a shared meal of sardines and canteen cups filled with cognac. When afternoon shadows grew long, Robertson drove back to his battalion encampment in Wurzen, carrying four soldiers from the 173rd Rifle Regiment wedged into his jeep as proof of the rendezvous.

Thursday morning brought the full, overwrought merger of east and west. A flying column of fifteen jeeps packed with photographers and correspondents arrived in Torgau to find a scene "like an Iowa picnic," in one lieutenant colonel's description, albeit with promiscuous celebratory gunfire. Soviet soldiers had looted a nearby accordion factory and "Song of the Steppes" carried down the river. Half a dozen varnished shells from the Torgau Racing Club—the only river craft to be found—shuttled GIs and reporters to the east bank for black bread and apples washed down with vodka.

"The Russians all looked as if they hadn't had time for a bath since Stalingrad," Martha Gellhorn would later write, but their tunics were upholstered with "handsome enamel decorations for killing Germans." Red Army teamsters "handled the horses . . . rather like the chariot races in *Ben-Hur*. The pack trains had everything on them: bedding [and] pots and pans and ammunition, and also women." Above it all rose a "splendid Slavic roar and the clang of wheels on cobbles." GIs traded cigarette lighters and nail clippers for the lacquered red stars on Soviet caps. Hundreds of freed Russian slave laborers, mostly women in colorful kerchiefs, waited along the west bank for a seat on a makeshift ferry to begin their long journey home.

At three P.M. the 69th Division commander, Major General Emil F. Reinhardt, stepped uneasily into a wobbly shell. A stout Russian mother sat in the bow with her baby in a carriage balanced across the gunwales. "Get that woman off the boat," an Army officer shouted. "The general needs that boat." Unwilling to budge, the woman sat as rigid as a ship's figurehead until the coxswain swung out into the river with mother, child, and the squatting general as passengers. "Reinhardt's still lucky," a reporter quipped. "Washington had to stand." On the far shore a Soviet general advanced to greet him with an outstretched hand.

An unbroken Allied line now stretched from the North Sea to the Urals, cutting Germany in half and reducing the Reich to shards of a state. So little was left to wreck that Eighth Air Force flew its last bombing raid on April 25, almost at the same hour as the Torgau junction. Fifteenth Air Force, flying from Italy, quit a day later. In the north, a German rump still hugged the North Sea and the Baltic, through Schleswig-Holstein and portions of Mecklenburg and Brandenburg. But this territory was no longer contiguous with Berlin: Soviet armies encircling the city from north and south had met at Ketzin, twenty miles west of the capital. This too occurred on April 25.

Nothing now could thwart the Soviet juggernaut of two and a half million troops and six thousand tanks, although in destroying some ninety German divisions a trio of Soviet army groups in just the three weeks after April 16 would suffer more than three hundred thousand casualties, a bloodletting that made Eisenhower's aversion to Berlin seem prudent. The city's final agony had begun, and with it the rape of at least ninety thousand German women. Many smeared themselves with mud or dotted their skin with red spots to simulate typhus. Russian soldiers defiled them anyway, then ripped out water faucets and unscrewed lightbulbs to carry home as plunder. German strangers shook hands in the dying capital and urged one another, *"Bleib übrig"*: Survive. A diarist described the city as "a hilly landscape of bricks, human beings buried beneath it, the stars above; the last moving things are the rats."

In the south, the Reich had been reduced to swatches of Czechoslovakia and Yugoslavia, plus a narrowing belt that stretched from the Black Forest through lower Bavaria to the Austrian Tirol and Salzburg. Patton crossed the Czech border and each day ticked off fifteen or twenty miles toward Linz; on April 23, the entire Third Army reported fewer than fifty casualties while capturing nine thousand German soldiers. Patch's Seventh Army raced south from Nuremberg to seize intact a bridge over the Danube at Dillingen. Fleets of Sherman tanks led the breakneck pursuit, past grazing cows and farmers agape at their plows. The 10th Armored Division alone captured twenty-eight towns in a single day. Few signs of a National Redoubt could be detected.

"We are constantly suffering from misunderstandings with the French," a recent SHAEF memo had lamented, and perhaps inevitably these final battles would be marred by another snarling brouhaha of the sort that had characterized the Franco-American confederation since the North African campaign. In southwest Germany, General Devers had meticulously choreographed the capture of Stuttgart with three goals in mind: to prevent the escape of the enemy's Nineteenth Army; to expedite the U.S. attack into western Austria; and, secretly, to capture German atomic scientists at the Kaiser Wilhelm Institute for Physics in remote Hechingen. On Devers's order, French troops were to seize Stuttgart, but not until the U.S. VI Corps had outflanked the city to block escape routes south. Other American forces would then barrel through, sweeping into Austria before Nazi bitter-enders could cohere for a last stand.

General de Gaulle had other ideas. Washington and London had yet to specify a postwar French zone of occupation in Germany, and General de Lattre's French First Army seemed relegated to a minor role in the coup de grâce about to befall the Third Reich. Stuttgart offered a wide door to the Danube, Bavaria, and Austria, which, in De Gaulle's calculation, would "support our intentions as to the French zone of occupation." Holding a large tract of Roman Catholic southern Germany could enhance French prestige and perhaps provide a French client state abutting Alsace.

With Deux Mètres urging him on, De Lattre deftly used one French corps to surround the southern half of the Black Forest and another to envelop Stuttgart from the south and east. French tanks rumbled into the city on April 21—"like a merry-go-round," De Lattre reported—and two days later the occupation was complete. When Devers on April 24 ordered his French subordinate to stand clear, De Gaulle stepped in. "I order you to keep a French garrison in Stuttgart . . . until the French zone of occupation has been settled," he told De Lattre. Moreover, French field commanders were to ignore both Devers and Eisenhower. "French forces," De Gaulle said, "should be employed in accordance with the national interest of France, which is the only interest that they should serve." De Lattre apologized to Devers, but declared that he could "answer only to the French government." Seventh Army's chief of staff complained in his diary, "Penny politics by penny people."

"The good and upright Devers was angrier than I have ever seen him," De Lattre's chief of staff reported, particularly after much of the German Nineteenth Army—though reduced to just seventeen thousand men—scampered off. Insult soon followed injury. The U.S. VI Corps approached the Danube city of Ulm to find that De Lattre's tanks had arrived ten hours earlier, forty-four miles outside the designated French sector. When Devers again protested—"This is an absurdity which cannot exist and must not exist"—De Lattre pleaded that the city held special significance for France as the battlefield where Napoléon had routed the Austrian army in 1805. Again ignoring orders to decamp, the French general pressed his attack until a tricolor flew above Ulm. "De Lattre," Devers later concluded, "was trying to be Napoleon."

This opéra bouffe now grew sinister. German civilians fled Stuttgart to seek American protection from predatory French colonial troops. An English woman married to a German claimed that "every female between twelve and eighty" in her village had been assaulted. "Hens and women," she added, "were the main thing they were after." The U.S. 100th Division warned General Patch, "Situation in Stuttgart worst imaginable. . . . Rape, pillage and plunder have been rampant." A reporter asserted that thousands of women were herded into a tunnel and raped; a French commander was said to have responded, with a shrug: "What can you do with the Moroccans?"

After advising De Lattre that "Stuttgart is chaotic," Devers drove into the city at nine A.M. on Friday, April 27, to see for himself. He found the dire reports to be "greatly exaggerated"—rather than fifty thousand women raped, the figure was "fewer than two thousand," some of whom had been violated by rampaging foreign workers or renegade Germans. Seventh Army noted dryly, "French procedure in occupying a German city is traditionally different from that of American forces."

Eisenhower now intervened. In a tart cable to De Gaulle on April 28, he promised to inform London and Washington that "I can no longer count with certainty upon the operational use of any French forces they may contemplate equipping in the future." The new U.S. president, Harry S. Truman, added his own rebuke in a note to De Gaulle.

But with a war to finish, neither Devers nor the supreme commander wanted to prolong this Gallic distraction. French troops for the moment would remain in Stuttgart, where the execution of a few rapists apparently persuaded Devers that "conditions were very much better." Patch's legions meanwhile pressed south. American intelligence agents outflanked the French to arrest some of the German scientists they sought in Hechingen, although the top prize, the Nobel physicist Werner Heisenberg, had pedaled off to Bavaria on his bicycle the previous day and would not be snared for another week.

Bickering over the French occupation zone would continue until a formal settlement was signed in late June. In addition to a sector in Berlin, Paris received a stretch of the Rhineland as far north as Remagen, but not Karlsruhe, Wiesbaden, or Stuttgart, as De Gaulle desired. France and the United States, whose blood camaraderie dated to the American Revolution, would emerge from the war as wary allies, their mutual mistrust destined to shape postwar geopolitics for decades.

Devers coined the perfect epigraph. "For many months we have fought together," he wrote De Lattre, "often on the same side."

A final monstrosity awaited discovery by American soldiers, further confirming not only the Reich's turpitude but the inexorable moral corrosion of war, which put even the righteous at risk.

Ten miles northwest of Munich, a former gunpowder factory of the Royal Bavarian Army had, in March 1933, received the first of 200,000 prisoners. In the next twelve years, nearly a quarter of them would be murdered there and at the 170 subcamps to which Dachau metastasized. By the evening of April 28, when swastika flags were lowered and white flags raised at the main compound, 31,000 inmates from forty-one nations remained behind the electrified fence. Another 13,000 had died in the previous four months, mostly from typhus and starvation.

On a chilly, sunless Sunday morning, April 29, the 45th Infantry Division, bound for Munich and badly frayed after vicious gunfights in Aschaffenburg and Nuremberg, arrived in Dachau town. "There are flower beds and trees, small shops, bicycles on the ground, churches with steeples, a mirror-like river," an Army physician wrote. There was more, as I Company of the 157th Infantry discovered upon following a rail spur toward the prison compound. Thirty-nine train cars—gondolas, passenger carriages, and boxcars—sat on the siding. Either in the cars or scattered along the tracks lay 2,310 decomposing corpses, some naked, others in tattered blue-and-white camp livery; most were Poles who had starved to death after being forcibly evacuated from Buchenwald. While GIs wept at the sight, four Waffen-SS soldiers emerged from hiding with hands high. A lieutenant herded the men into a boxcar and then emptied his pistol into them. Another GI pumped rifle rounds into those still moaning. "You sons of bitches," the lieutenant shrieked. "You sons of bitches."

As the Americans made for a side gate of the camp, thousands of inmates stood baying at the fence in a great keening babel. A decrepit old man offered a GI a stained cigarette. "Take it," another inmate said in English. "That's the only thing the guy owns in this world. That's his everything." Other prisoners cornered kapos and suspected informers, clubbing them with shovels. Howling inmates pursued remaining Waffen-SS troops, some of whom were masquerading in prison garb. "They tore the Germans apart by hand," a soldier reported. Rabbi Eichhorn, who arrived at Dachau that afternoon, wrote, "We stood aside and watched while these guards were beaten to death, beaten so badly that their bodies were ripped open. . . . We watched with less feeling than if a dog were being beaten." Inmates desecrated dead and dying Germans with sticks and rocks, crushing skulls and severing fingers. One guard's "body was strewn all over the place," a witness reported, "arms out of sockets." After entering the compound, soldiers from I Company herded several dozen Germans against the eight-foot stucco wall of a coal yard where, without warning, a gunner manning a light machine gun on a tripod opened fire. Others joined in with carbines and a Browning Automatic Rifle. By the time an officer halted the fusillade, seventeen victims lay dead. A battalion surgeon refused to treat the SS wounded.

At the same hour, the vanguard of the 42nd Infantry Division arrived at the main gate to be welcomed by the infamous *Arbeit Macht Frei* signage and, a brigadier general recounted, "a yelling, seething mass of prisoners who broke through the steel wire fence at several places. . . . In this process several were electrocuted." Sixteen Germans were rousted from a guard tower near the Würm River canal. Witnesses subsequently disagreed on whether any resisted, but upon being disarmed and assembled in two ranks the men were gunned down by soldiers from both the 42nd and 45th Divisions. Seven bodies lay like bloody bundles on the canal bank, with others heaved into the water "amidst a roar unlike anything ever heard from human throats," an Associated Press reporter wrote.

The rampage spent itself. Medics arrived, and grave diggers. "I haven't the words to tell you how horrible it really is," an Army nurse wrote her husband. Doctors and soldiers assumed a spectral appearance upon being dusted with DDT powder each time they emerged from the compound. The 45th Division commander, Major General Robert T. Frederick, among the Army's most valiant combat soldiers and the recipient of eight Purple Hearts, found Dachau too unnerving to discuss. To subordinates who had not been inside the fence, Frederick advised, "I wouldn't bother. It's just a mess."

The Seventh Army inspector general soon arrived to investigate the "alleged mistreatment of German guards." Word of bloodletting also reached Eisenhower, who subsequently spoke with high-ground eloquence in demanding that every division, corps, and army in Europe investigate extrajudicial killings by U.S. forces. "America's moral position will be undermined and her reputation for fair dealing debased," Eisenhower said, "if criminal conduct . . . by her armed forces is condoned and unpunished by those of us responsible for defending her honor."

At least twenty-eight SS men had been gunned down after surrendering at Dachau, the inspector general concluded; he recommended that four U.S. soldiers be court-martialed for murder. Others believed that the death toll was higher and the culpability wider. A judge advocate officer confirmed "a violation of the letter of international law, in that SS guards seem to have been shot without trial." But not a single prosecution followed, just as little would come of Eisenhower's call for a comprehensive legal accounting from his subordinates across Europe. General Patch rejected much of the inspector general's report, citing "an apparent lack of comprehension" of battle stresses. General Haislip, who soon succeeded Patch as Seventh Army commander, noted "the unbalancing effects of the horrors and shock of Dachau on combat troops already fatigued by more than thirty days' continuous action."

No doubt. Yet here surely was victor's justice, tinged with the sour smell of sanctimony, a reminder that honor and dishonor often traveled in trace across a battlefield, and that even a liberator could come home stained if not befouled.

In a letter to her family about treating Dachau survivors, Lieutenant Wandrey, the Seventh Army nurse, invoked a wrenching conundrum:

> I'm on night duty with a hundred corpse-like patients, wrecks of humanity. . . . Many have tuberculosis, typhus, enterocolitis (constant diarrhea) and huge bed sores. . . . Patients wear just pajama shirts as they can't get the bottoms down fast enough to use commodes.
>
> God, where are you?

*   *   *

As a specially designated "Führer City," Munich was known to Hitler's regime as both the "Capital of the Movement" and the "Capital of German Art." To the U.S. Army it was, in Eisenhower's phrase, the "cradle of the Nazi beast." But for three days German insurgents hoping to spare the city further destruction had battled SS troops with sufficient ardor to help prevent the demolition of bridges across the river Isar. Resupplied with 400,000 gallons of gasoline delivered by air on April 29, four American divisions fell on the Führer City the next day, lunging across ten Isar spans before noon to reach the ruined city center. "Window by window" shelling with 240mm howitzers further ruined the ruins, and by nightfall on Monday, April 30, Munich had fallen. Across the Feldherrnhalle, site of annual festivities commemorating the 1923 putsch, GIs found a confession painted in huge white letters: "I am ashamed to be German."

Three hundred miles north on that same Monday, Soviet souvenir-hunters prowled through a morgue full of dead German soldiers near Berlin's Tiergarten, plucking Iron Crosses and swastikas from field-gray tunics. Other Red Army troops prepared to celebrate May Day by roasting an ox in Pariserplatz. Terrified Berliners by the thousands crowded a shelter beneath the Anhalter train station, where excrement and urine had risen ankle-deep. A number of SS troops convened behind the Schultheiss brewery to shoot themselves, but resistance persisted here and there across the capital in what a Soviet writer called "post-mortal convulsions."

Far below the Reich Chancellery, listed on Soviet maps as Objective 106, Hitler ate a late lunch with his two secretaries and his dietician. Dressed in a uniform jacket and black trousers, he then shook hands with his staff, murmuring a few words of farewell before retreating to his study. Eva Braun, wearing a blue dress trimmed in white, joined him at 3:30 P.M. Only a rattle of ventilator fans and the distant grumble of artillery broke the silence. Ten minutes later, aides opened the study door to find Braun slumped on a sofa, dead from cyanide. Next to her sat the lifeless Führer, a bullet hole from a Walther PPK 7.65mm pistol in his right temple.

Twelve years and four months after it began, the Thousand-Year Reich had ended. Humanity would require decades, perhaps centuries, to parse the regime's inhumanity, and to comprehend how a narcissistic beerhall demagogue had wrecked a nation, a continent, and nearly a world. "Never in history has such ruination—physical and moral—been associated with the name of one man, the chief instigator of the most profound collapse of civilization in modern times," wrote Hitler's biographer Ian Kershaw. Stalin, upon hearing the news, would need but a moment to compose the Führer's epitaph: "So—that's the end of the bastard."

Henchmen wrapped the two bodies in blankets, carried them up four flights to the shell-pocked garden, doused them in gasoline, and let them burn for three hours, a small, pleasing blaze within the larger conflagration. "The chief's on fire," a drunk SS bodyguard called down into the bunker. "Do you want to come and have a look?" A chauffeur later complained that the ventilation fans wafted a stench of seared flesh through the labyrinth. "We could not get away from it," he said. "It smelled like burning bacon."

Hitler's death, like his life, would prove predicate to a lie. Rather than disclosing that he had died by his own hand in a squalid rat trap, German radio on Tuesday, May 1, announced that he had "fallen for Germany" while "fighting to the last breath against Bolshevism." The Wehrmacht high command decreed that the Führer's "faithful unto death" example was to be "binding for all soldiers."

But collapse now came with gravitational certainty: the jig was up. The last Soviet shells fell on Berlin at three P.M. on Wednesday, May 2, followed by a silence more ominous for Germans than the din of battle. Defenseless and disemboweled, the city gave itself over to an occupation that was to last half a century.

Fifty miles due west along the Elbe, where Simpson's Ninth Army held the American left wing, tens of thousands of "hysterical, screaming Germans" fled the pursuing Red Army. "I saw German soldiers pushing old women out of boats in which they were trying to cross the river," wrote James Wellard, a Chicago newspaper reporter at Tangermünde. Some shinnied across a catwalk laid over a blown rail bridge, or built plank rafts for baggage and bicycles; others paddled skiffs or fashioned water wings from empty fuel cans even as Soviet artillery searched the shoreline and German rear guards with submachine guns fought within earshot. Refugees "kept leaping into the fast-moving river and kept being washed back on shore," Wellard added. "Dead, dying, and living were scrambled."

Simpson agreed to accept surrendering Wehrmacht troops only if they brought their own food, kitchens, and medical supplies. More than seventy thousand eventually reached the west bank, where they tossed their battle kit onto piles of rifles, pistols, and field glasses before making for the cages in long, singing columns. A German colonel reported that "quite a few people who were not able to cross the Elbe killed themselves."

On every fighting front, similar dramas reached their operatic crescendos.

In Italy, an offensive by a million and a half Allied soldiers from twenty-six countries had broken through the Po river valley on April 23. Five days later Mussolini and his mistress, gunned down by partisans, were strung up by their heels from a rusty beam outside a Milan gas station. "You had the feeling," wrote Philip Hamburger in *The New Yorker*, "as you have at the final curtain of a good play, that events could not have been otherwise." Allied troops soon swept into Verona, Genoa, and Venice. On April 29, at Field Marshal Alexander's palatial headquarters in Caserta, German emissaries capitulated unconditionally. The surrender of nearly one million men from Army Group C, effective at noon on May 2, brought to an end the Mediterranean struggle that had begun five years earlier.

Along the Continent's northern lip, Canadian troops pressed into the Netherlands with the prodigal use of flamethrowers and a sense of urgency: the starving Dutch had been reduced to eating nettle soup, laundry starch, the occasional cat or dog, and 140 million tulip bulbs. It was said that night watchmen in an Amsterdam mortuary rattled their keys to keep rats off the corpses, and that the Dutch were using the same hinged-bottom coffins over and over.

Allied engineers also feared that German demolitionists would flood western Holland by blowing the sea dikes. Secret negotiations led to a truce and safe passage for relief supplies by air beginning April 29 and by road on May 2. The subsequent surrender by General Blaskowitz of Army Group H and "Fortress Holland" triggered national jubilation: bonfires, singing, and dancing by a vast orange throng, even though more than 200,000 civilians were suffering from malnutrition. "The people here are obviously making up for five years of repression," wrote a British brigadier. Gray columns of captured Germans snaked toward Den Helder for embarkation on trawlers and sweeps, thence across the IJsselmeer for the long trudge to prison.

"They left like tramps and criminals," wrote Marsland Gander, a scribe for the *Daily Telegraph*.

> They were allowed ten horses and five carts for every 180 men. . . . Two bicycles among every 500 men could be retained for the purposes of delivering messages. . . . Every man was searched and stripped of loot before he stepped on board the evacuation craft, being allowed only one fountain pen and one wristwatch. The piles of discarded property on the

quayside and in warehouses included bicycles, sewing machines, furniture, radio sets, cases of gin, clothing, scent.

"It was," Gander added, "a time of fairy-tale gladness."

Farther east, where four British divisions outflanked Bremen, the port had fallen on April 27 following a five-day gunfight. A Tommy found Germans "looting, drinking, [and] fighting among each other" in a city he deemed "among the most debauched places on the face of God's earth." Montgomery crossed the lower Elbe with his usual deliberation even as Eisenhower repeatedly hectored him to hurry—the Soviets were making for Denmark. It was a near-run thing: British tanks seized Lübeck on May 2, and paratroopers sprinted another forty miles to capture Wismar on the Baltic, sealing the Jutland Peninsula and blocking entry to Denmark just two hours before the Red Army arrived. Hamburg surrendered without a fight on May 3, as Ridgway's XVIII Airborne Corps—screening Montgomery's right flank—racked up a quarter of a million prisoners in two days.

Among Anglo-American armies, Patton's Third was now the farthest east. Czech villages hoisted pretty archways over approach roads, with flower garlands and signs proclaiming, "Welcome Americans"; identical arches on the far side of town proclaimed, "Welcome Russians." The British had urged that Third Army capture Prague, because, as Churchill cabled Truman, such a prize "might make the whole difference to the postwar situation in Czechoslovakia." Eisenhower was tempted, despite Marshall's warning that "I would be loath to hazard American lives for purely political purposes." But Stalin had heeded American requests to halt on the Elbe, and thus the supreme commander affirmed his earlier commitment to stop along a line between Pilzen and Karlsbad in Bohemia. Patton's legions beat for Linz and Pilzen, ceding Salzburg to Seventh Army and Prague to the Soviets.

Austrian partisans seized Innsbruck on May 2, and two days later VI Corps clattered into the city during a snowstorm, camping in a golf resort hotel with tennis courts and a Viennese orchestra. Just before eleven A.M. on Friday, May 4, a patrol from the 411th Infantry crossed the Brenner Pass to clasp hands with comrades from Fifth Army, a juncture of the European and Italian theaters two terrible years in the making. At Innsbruck's city hall, General Erich Brandenberger surrendered the dregs of his Nineteenth Army in an elaborate ceremony with a written American script that specified the positioning of flags, orderlies, bandsmen, and even pencils. U.S. officers tendered neither salutes nor handshakes, but permitted Brandenberger's men to keep their pistols along with one rifle and ten rounds of ammunition for every ten soldiers to preserve "internal security."

At almost the same hour, Devers arrived by staff car with Generals Patch, Haislip, and O'Daniel at a sculptor's studio in a sylvan glade outside Haar, southeast of Munich. Plaster cast models and statuary ranging from the miniature to the monumental filled the studio, where Lieutenant General Hermann Foertsch stood at rigid attention, ready to surrender both his First Army and Army Group G. As Devers and his lieutenants took their seats at a table, Foertsch bowed slowly from the hips. After a brief discussion of surrender provisions, including how to notify far-flung German units in the Alps that their war was over, Devers reiterated that all Army Group G soldiers between Switzerland and Czechoslovakia would now become prisoners.

"This is *unconditional* surrender," Devers said. "Do you understand that?"

For a full minute Foertsch remained as stiff as the statues around him, a witness recorded, "the muscles of his face working like those of a man about to have convulsions." Then with a slight cant of his head he replied in precise English, "I can assure you, sir, there is no power left at my disposal to prevent it."

Few locales were more freighted with Teutonic sentiment than Berchtesgaden, a remote Bavarian village eighty miles southeast of Munich. Hitler had retreated here after the failed 1923 putsch, and here, in a log hut, he had written the second volume of *Mein Kampf*. Brisk book sales had financed his beloved vacation home—later known as the Berghof—on the Obersalzberg slopes above the town, with views of the mountain where Charlemagne and his mystic army were said to slumber. Other Nazi cronies also bought houses here to create a bucolic enclave conducive to pastoral husbandry—Bormann kept one hundred beehives on his tract—or the plotting of world domination.

As a gift for the Führer's fiftieth birthday, and also as a venue for diplomatic receptions, the regime had hired almost four thousand workers to build a lavish mountaintop château nearby, dubbed the Eagle's Nest. It came with the requisite spectacular vistas, as well as a grand Carrara marble fireplace donated by Mussolini; a Gobelin tapestry covered the wall above the hearth, like a pelt. Visitors drove up a serpentine road through five tunnels bored through the granite mountain, then ascended another four hundred feet to the summit in an Otis elevator appointed with Venetian glass, green leather benches, and brass fittings.

RAF bombers on April 25 had roiled this little brown world with a punitive raid that badly battered the Bormann and Göring houses, as well as Hitler's Berghof and an adjacent SS barracks. Emboldened German looters then rifled the Obersalzberg, stealing Himmler's furniture and

Bormann's collection of a thousand watercolors and drawings. News of the Führer's death inspired SS bodyguards to burn his personal effects on May 1, and then set fire to the house as Allied armies drew near.

Flames still licked from various ruins when two battalions of the 3rd Infantry Division tramped into Berchtesgaden through meadows spangled with wildflowers at four P.M. on May 4. Under orders from General O'Daniel, officers posted a heavy guard on bridges across the Saalach River, barring both the approaching French 2nd Armored and the 101st Airborne Divisions from entering the village. "You've had Paris and you've had Strasbourg," the XV Corps commander, General Haislip, told a fuming General Leclerc. "You can't expect Berchtesgaden as well." GIs lowered a Nazi flag and tore it into two-inch shreds for souvenirs.

Despite bombing, arson, and plunder, soldiers still found much to pillage on the Obersalzberg. Table linen, teacups, and spoons monogrammed "A.H." could be found in the Berghof cellars, as well as phonograph records, magazines dating to 1930, and the toilet seat from a green-tiled water closet. GIs pilfered light fixtures, bedsprings, and high-command situation maps for various theaters. An officer poking through Eva Braun's closet remarked, "What impressed me most was the number of coat hangers in her wardrobes. There must have been more than two hundred of them." A nearby guesthouse yielded an espresso machine, a beer tap, and deep-freeze ice cream tubs.

RAF bombs had spared the Eagle's Nest, but suspected booby traps in the elevator shaft meant a long, steep climb to the summit. Scouts found a dining room with blackout curtains and twenty-six chairs, furniture and paneling of cembra pine, and a pristine kitchen with a butcher's block that appeared never to have felt a cleaver's bite. Mussolini's fireplace was so enormous, a visitor wrote, that "an ox could turn on the spit." Soon three thousand Allied soldiers a day would tramp up to the Eagle's Nest as tourists, ten thousand on Sundays. Bored, gum-chewing paratroopers were pressed into duty as guides.

Göring's booty proved especially vast and varied, much of it crammed into a warehouse with a large bank vault inside: eighteen thousand bottles of wine and liquor; five thousand Minox cameras the size of cigarette lighters; two dozen suitcases stuffed with women's underwear; an impressive cache of pornographic movies; and a bulletproof, fourteen-passenger Mercedes sedan. In nearby rail tunnels and other repositories, paratroopers found much of his notorious art collection, said to be worth more than $500 million: hundreds of paintings by the likes of Rembrandt, Rubens, and Van Dyck, as well as a Vermeer forgery, *Christ with the Woman Taken in Adultery;* terra-cotta saints, satyrs, and warriors; tapestries, antique furniture, gold chalices, porcelain figurines. An inn was converted into a temporary gallery with a placard outside that read: "Hermann Goering Art Collection—Through Courtesy of the 101st Airborne Division." "Ah, war!" sighed Göring's personal curator, who was seized along with the swag. "Goodbye, goodbye."

The *Reichsmarschall* himself soon materialized, having offered his services to Eisenhower "in reorganizing the German Reich." Arrested by the 36th Division thirty-five miles southeast of Salzburg, with an entourage of seventy-five vassals that included a chef, a butler, and a valet, Göring was fed fried chicken and photographed in front of a Texas Lone Star flag, his many chins cascading to the Iron Cross at his throat. To ward off SS assassins, he was permitted to keep four machine pistols overnight. "He is a fat slob, very anxious to talk about how the mistakes were Hitler's and Ribbentrop's," General Dahlquist told his diary. Wearing sky-blue gloves, he claimed in a breezy session with correspondents that accounts of unpleasantries at Bergen-Belsen and Buchenwald were "merely propaganda reports." "I am no prophet," he added. "It is hard to say what will happen in the future." His marshal's baton, sixteen inches long and encrusted with 640 diamonds, twenty gold eagles, and twenty platinum crosses, became a prop to sell war bonds in the United States.

And then there was one. The last German headquarters still at large in the Alps was that of Field Marshal Kesselring, the Anglo-Americans' longtime nemesis. Two reporters tracked down the OB West commander as he awaited the end of the war aboard a five-car train along the Austrian border. Assuming they were Eisenhower emissaries come to negotiate his personal surrender, Kesselring invited them to a lunch of ham, cabbage, potatoes, and beer. Upon discovering his error, Smiling Albert chuckled and muttered, "Well, bugger me."

An American major subsequently invited Kesselring to move to the Berchtesgadener Hof, where he was given the finest room and permitted to keep his pistol, medals, and marshal's baton—"Six of these I have left behind in the ruins of command posts," he lamented—before being remanded to a more austere cell in Luxembourg where war-crimes interrogators awaited him. Asked before his departure to assess Hitler, the field marshal took a deep breath and replied, "Hitler was the most remarkable historical character I ever knew."

A Great Silence

FIELD Marshal Montgomery's final wartime encampment crowned a hilltop on the Lüneburg Heath, thirty miles southeast of Hamburg in a landscape of beech, birch, and half-timbered farmhouses with blue- or pink-tinted plaster. "The lovely colors of the countryside spread away for miles, pools of dark green in the clumps of pine, purple in the heather," wrote Alan Moorehead, who nonetheless considered this an "abode of witches and warlocks and sprites." Tommies fished unconventionally in a nearby trout hatchery, with revolvers and grenades. The spires of two Lüneburg churches soared above the treetops to the north, and pathetic groans could be heard from local hospitals jammed with damaged German soldiers. A sign in an abandoned Luftwaffe barracks still insisted "*Der Führer Hat Immer Recht*"—The Führer Is Always Right—and a storage room there had yielded fine maps of England, Scotland, and the Soviet Union, reminders of the Reich's foiled ambitions.

At 11:30 A.M. on Thursday, May 3, a German sedan escorted by two British armored cars crawled past the village of Wendisch Evern. The small convoy halted beneath a Union Jack that had been hoisted over a trio of camouflaged caravans. Four officers stepped from the sedan, two in gray army greatcoats and two in the long leather watch coats of German naval officers. The door of the middle caravan swung open and an elfin figure in battle dress and khaki trousers emerged, hands clasped behind his back in a pose of severest rectitude. Drawing themselves to attention, the four Germans snapped salutes, which Montgomery returned with the casual brush of a finger against his black beret.

"Who are you?" he bellowed. "What do you want?" A slight, sallow officer in a high-peaked cap stepped forward to introduce himself as Admiral Hans-Georg von Friedeburg. Under the Führer's last political testament, Grand Admiral Karl Dönitz had succeeded Hitler as head of state, or what remained of a state, in a provisional capital in Flensburg, near the Danish border. Admiral von Friedeburg had in turn succeeded Dönitz as commander-in-chief of the German navy, or what remained of a navy.

"I have never heard of you," Montgomery shouted. One British staff officer whispered to another, "He's been rehearsing this all his life."

Undaunted, Friedeburg on Dönitz's authority proposed surrendering the three German armies fleeing the Soviets between the Baltic and Berlin. "Certainly not," Montgomery replied. "Those armies are fighting the Russians, so they must surrender to the Russians. The subject is closed." He would accept only individual soldiers giving up with raised hands, "in the usual way."

After mulling the matter for a moment, the field marshal added, "Will you surrender to me all the German forces between Lübeck and the Dutch coast, and all supporting troops such as those in Denmark?" That would be a tactical battlefield surrender by enemies opposing 21st Army Group, not a strategic capitulation to undermine Moscow. When Friedeburg protested that he had no authority for such an arrangement, Montgomery cut him off. "I wonder," he said, "if you really know what your position is?"

Calling for a map, he quickly pointed out the catastrophe befallen German forces on every front, while delivering a tongue-lashing about concentration camps and the suffering caused by the Reich. "You had better go to lunch and think it over," the field marshal said. He personally would "be delighted to continue fighting." Escorted to a tent, the four Germans dined alone on a table laid with a white sheet. As his comrades nipped from bottles of red wine and cognac, Friedeburg wept—"an embarrassing scene," Moorehead wrote—then agreed to take Montgomery's counterproposal to the high command. He drove off at midafternoon, promising to return the following day.

At five P.M. on a rainy Friday, May 4, the field marshal bounded into the Lüneburg press tent, "jaunty, hands stuffed deep into the pockets of his light naval duffle-coat," R. W. Thompson recorded. "Had a good tea?" Montgomery asked the reporters. "Forces to be surrendered total over a million chaps. No so bad, a million chaps. Good egg!" A colonel soon appeared to announce that Friedeburg and his delegation had returned. "Ha! He is back. He was to come back with the doings," the field marshal said. "Tell them to wait." For half an hour he rambled on, then popped to his feet. "And now we will attend the last act. These German officers have arrived back. We will go and see what their answer is."

The answer was yes. Friedeburg trudged into Montgomery's caravan for a brief tête-à-tête, where he reported that Grand Admiral Dönitz—invariably called Donuts by Allied soldiers—had agreed to the British terms. Dönitz had also instructed Friedeburg to open negotiations with Eisenhower directly; the grand admiral clearly hoped that every hour of delay would allow thousands more Wehrmacht troops and German refugees to escape to the west. Eyes bright, Montgomery gestured to a photo on the wall. "Tell me," he said, "is this a good likeness of Field Marshal Rundstedt? I always like to study my opponents." Yes, Friedeburg said, the resemblance was excellent.

At 6:20 P.M., the admiral emerged from the trailer and, bracketed by two British officers, walked fifty yards to a tent with the side flaps raised. Two BBC microphones sat on a square table covered with an army blanket. "It was a grey evening," Moorehead wrote, "grey heather, grey heavy clouds, grey coats on the Germans and grey in their faces." Montgomery arrived directly. "This," he murmured to reporters, "is a great moment."

Friedeburg and his comrades rose from their chairs to salute stiffly. Montgomery took his chair, his biographer would write, "the simple, tortoiseshell-rimmed reading spectacles set upon the sharp foxish nose, with five rows of decorations below his lapel, the small gold chain linking the breast pockets of his battle dress, the bony, sinewy hands resting upon the table." Holding a document titled "Instrument of Surrender," he read aloud the seven paragraphs in his reedy voice, ending with "The decision of the Allied Powers will be final if any doubt or dispute arises as to the meaning or interpretation of the surrender terms." Picking up a pen, he dipped it into an inkpot and told Friedeburg, "You will now sign the document."

Once all German signatures had been affixed, Montgomery added his own, then began to write "April," crossed out the "A," and dated the document "4 May 1945, 1830 hrs." The capitulation would take effect the next morning at eight A.M. and remain valid until superseded by a general surrender to be signed under SHAEF auspices. He sat back with a sigh, removing his glasses. "That," he said, "concludes the formal surrender."

"The tent flaps were let down," R. W. Thompson reported, "and we walked away." To commemorate what he now called "Victory Hill," Montgomery ordered that an oak plaque be erected on the moor the next day. The marker was stolen within hours, but no one would forget what had transpired on Lüneburg Heath. Recounting the day's events in a letter to Brooke before going to bed, the field marshal wrote, "It looks as if the British Empire part of the German war in Western Europe is over. I was persuaded to drink some champagne at dinner tonight."

Foul weather on Saturday, May 5, spoiled plans to whisk Friedeburg to Reims for a quick end to the war. Instead, he flew to Brussels aboard a British plane before being driven south for 135 miles, arriving shortly after five P.M. at SHAEF's headquarters in the redbrick Collège Moderne et Technique de Garçons, hard by the sooty rail yards. Humming to himself while putting on a fresh collar in the washroom, Friedeburg then walked into Beetle Smith's second-floor office. Within twenty minutes, negotiations had collapsed.

Smith and Major General Strong, who together had handled the Italian capitulation for Eisenhower two years earlier, flatly rejected the admiral's proposed surrender of only those German forces making for the west. The supreme commander, they told Friedeburg, would "not in any circumstances" accept terms other than unconditional surrender to SHAEF and to the Soviet high command simultaneously. Germany's predicament was hopeless, Smith added; he pointed to several theater maps strewn across his desk, including a phony plan, drawn for Friedeburg's benefit, that showed attack arrows from east and west aimed at the Wehrmacht remnants in Bohemia and Yugoslavia. The admiral's eyes again welled with tears, but he was adamant: authority for such a surrender could only come from Dönitz.

Smith walked down the hall to find Eisenhower pacing his office and smoking one cigarette after another. Friedeburg would cable Dönitz, Smith told him, but no surrender was likely for hours, perhaps longer. The admiral had been placed under guard in a house on Rue Godinot and fortified with pork chops, mashed potatoes, and whiskey. "The let-down was horrible," wrote Kay Summersby. "Everyone left in a gray mood."

Eisenhower stalked from the headquarters with Telek, his pet Scottie. Fuming, he returned to his château and tried to lose himself in William Colt MacDonald's *Cartridge Carnival*, a pulp western ablaze with gunplay, cattle rustling, and crooked gambling. "I really expected some definite developments and went to bed early in anticipation of being waked up at 1, 2, 3 or 4 A.M.," he wrote Mamie the next morning. "Nothing happened and as a result I was wide awake, very early—with nothing decent to read. The Wild Wests I have just now are terrible—I could write better ones, left-handed."

A new negotiator arrived in Reims at six o'clock on Sunday evening— General Alfred Jodl, the OKW operations chief—with instructions from Dönitz to "find salvation in the west" by explaining "why we wish to make this separate surrender to the Americans." Joining Friedeburg in Smith's office, Jodl smugly assured the Anglo-Americans, "Eventually, you'll have to fight the Russians."

After ninety minutes of haggling, Smith informed Eisenhower that Jodl and Friedeburg were plainly stalling. "You tell them," the supreme commander snapped, "that forty-eight hours from midnight tonight, I will close my lines on the Western Front so no more Germans can get through. Whether they sign or not—no matter how much time they take." In a radio message to Flensburg, Jodl told Dönitz, "Eisenhower insists that we sign today. . . . I see no alternative—chaos or signature." The grand admiral complained of "sheer extortion" but gave his consent: "Full power to sign."

SHAEF typists for days had been hammering out surrender drafts in English, French, Russian, and German. A version intended to be final had been prepared in Reims on Saturday, but some considered it the wrong document. An earlier, authorized "instrument of surrender," written by the European Advisory Commission the previous summer, had been approved subsequently by Washington, London, Moscow, and Paris. A slightly modified instrument, drafted after the Yalta conference, added a proviso empowering the victors to dismember Germany. But France had only recently been informed of this second, secret version, and now even Moscow seemed ambivalent.

In the absence of firm instructions from the Combined Chiefs, Smith chose to ignore both variants. He opted instead for a third, abridged document, cribbed from a copy of the German surrender in Italy, which *Stars and Stripes* had just published. Revisions requested by Smith and others in Reims were adapted by a British officer who had been an actor and theater manager in civil life. At the frantic urging of the U.S. embassy in London, a "general enabling clause" was inserted, authorizing the Allies to impose additional military and political conditions as needed. A SHAEF captain painstakingly translated various amendments into German, pecking at a typewriter with a single finger.

This hasty pudding would have to serve. Pared to 234 words in five paragraphs, the document was rushed to the typing pool, which in short order produced eight copies of the "Act of Military Surrender," each bound in a plain gray cover.

At two A.M. on Monday, May 7, seventeen reporters and photographers were herded up a stone stairway and through a narrow corridor to the second-floor SHAEF war room. Thirty feet square and used in antebellum days for table tennis and chess by students attending the *collège,* the warm, fusty room contained fifteen unpadded chairs and a heavy oak table. Huge maps hung like tapestries on the faded blue walls, displaying the disposition of Allied armies and airfields from the Arctic Circle to the Aegean Sea. Charts showed weather conditions, SHAEF casualties, and the number of German prisoners, now in seven figures.

"Get ready, gentleman, they're coming."

A hissing bank of klieg lights flickered to life. Jodl and Friedeburg walked to the table, erect and glassy-eyed. "The effect of make-believe was, if anything, heightened by the arrival in the room of the German uniforms," one witness reported. Photographers scuttled about, bent double. The eleven-man Allied delegation followed, including Generals Spaatz and Strong, a Soviet major general, and Beetle Smith. Each took his seat behind a name plate printed on a cardboard strip. Smith looked "ghastly, ill, and exhausted," wrote Osmar White from a perch in the press gallery. In his office down the hall, Eisenhower feigned Olympian detachment, pacing and smoking.

Strong laid a copy of the surrender document before Jodl. Only the click of camera shutters and a scratching of pen nibs broke the silence. When Smith and others had finished countersigning each sheet, Jodl stood, leaning forward slightly with his fingertips pressed against the tabletop. "I want to say a word," he told Smith in English, then added, in German with Strong translating, "The German people and the German armed forces are, for better or worse, delivered into the victors' hands. . . . In this hour I can only express the hope that the victor will treat them with generosity."

The surrender ceremony had lasted ten minutes. Smith and Strong led Jodl, his cheeks streaked with tears, to Eisenhower's office. They found the supreme commander seated behind a desk upon which miniature flags of the Allied nations were displayed. Purple circles rimmed his eyes and his jowls sagged. Jodl bowed.

"Do you understand the terms of the document of surrender you have just signed?" Eisenhower asked.

"*Ja. Ja.*"

"You will officially and personally be held responsible if the terms of the surrender are violated. That is all."

Jodl saluted, then executed a smart about-face and withdrew under the supreme commander's cold gaze for an eventual appointment with the hangman.

Thus was peace made in Europe. "I suppose this calls for a bottle of champagne," Eisenhower said, managing a grin. A cork popped to feeble cheers. Photographers appeared, and a newsreel crew. At Smith's suggestion, various staff officers attempted to compose a suitable cable telling the Charlie-Charlies that the war was over.

As each draft grew more grandiloquent, the supreme commander thanked his lieutenants and then dictated the message himself: "The mission of this Allied force was fulfilled at 0241, local time, May 7, 1945. Eisenhower."

The sharp odors of soap and antiseptic still lingered in the Hotel Fürstenhof near Kassel, where until recently a military hospital had occupied the inn. A week earlier the 12th Army Group headquarters had moved here from Wiesbaden; Omar Bradley occupied a second-floor corner room, sleeping with the window open and a bone-handled .38-caliber pistol by his pillow. At 4:45 A.M. on Monday, a jangling telephone roused him from a deep slumber. "Brad?" Eisenhower's voice bawled from the receiver. "Brad, it's all over." A cease-fire would be imposed immediately, although not until 11:01 P.M. on Wednesday would the surrender officially take hold, allowing time to notify German garrisons in Norway and crews aboard U-boats across the Atlantic.

Bradley climbed from the bed, his hair deranged in gray wisps. Slipping into his frayed West Point bathrobe, he telephoned his army commanders: Hodges in Weimar, Patton in Regensburg, Simpson in Braunschweig, Gerow in Bonn. "Stop them in place," Bradley said. "No sense in taking casualties." He dressed and ambled downstairs to breakfast, a canvas map case under his arm. "Now our troubles really begin," he told a staff officer. "Everyone will want to start for home immediately." Opening his map board, he smoothed the tiny flags symbolizing each of the forty-three American divisions under his command, arrayed across a 640-mile front. Clutching a grease pencil, Bradley wrote his final entry on the map— "D+335"—then threw open the black-out curtains to gaze on the sun-splashed world outside.

"For the first time in eleven months, there is no contact with the enemy," the First Army intelligence log noted in Weimar. At 8:15 Monday morning, seventy miles west of Prague, an order to "cease all forward movement" reached the 1st Division, which, since landing in Algeria thirty months earlier, had dispensed 21,000 Purple Hearts. "It's about goddamn time," one GI remarked. At his command post in a former German barracks in Regensburg, Patton listened to staff officers describe the disposition of the half-million men under his command. Peace still held little appeal for him. To an aide he mused, "Wonder what the rivers in Japan are like? See if you can get some terrain maps of Japan." Rising to his feet, with Willie the white bull terrier on his heels, he strode from the command post and down the barracks steps, snapping his fingers.

As word spread of the German surrender, some rambunctious soldiers celebrated with honking horns or what one officer called "mad, dangerous" gunfire; ".30- and .45-calibers coming back down like a hailstorm," a GI near Salzburg reported. General Gavin advised his diary, "This is it. After two years. One doesn't know whether to cry or cheer or just simply get drunk." The 3rd Armored Division—which had hoarded champagne since crossing the Rhine for precisely this moment—drank a toast to Eisenhower, their victorious commander.

Yet many felt subdued—"curiously flat," in Moorehead's phrase. Elation seemed misplaced. So many were gone, so many broken. "I should be completely joyous on this occasion. As it is, it comes more as an anticlimax," a soldier wrote his family. "I remember the many who marched with me, and who also loved life but lost it and cannot celebrate with us today." An eerie, profound silence fell across much of the battlefield, and even those astonished to have survived felt too weary, or numb, or haunted for hosannas. "I am in a let-down mood," Devers confessed. In Thuringia, the correspondent W. C. Heinz watched soldiers wander aimlessly among the lilacs and blossoming apple trees, as if baffled to find themselves in a land so benign and beautiful. "We did not know how to kill time," Heinz wrote.

For the first time in nearly six years, the sun set on a Europe without front lines, a Europe at peace. "Lights scintillated—truck lights, jeep lights, tent lights, flashlights, building lights, farmhouse lights," wrote a major in the 29th Division. "Everything lit up." Night stole over the Continent, creeping west from the Vistula to the Oder, and then to the Elbe and the Rhine and the Seine. Darkness enfolded a thousand battlefields, at Remagen and St.-Vith, Arnhem and St.-Lô, Caen and Omaha Beach. Darkness fell, and the lights came on again.

Epilogue

T HE *Daily Mail* in London reported that a dozen elderly men stood for hours on Monday, May 7, "with ropes in their hands and hope in their hearts, waiting to send the bells of St. Paul's clanging in the paean of triumph." In vain they stood: no paean clanged, nary a bell pealed. Moscow had objected to proclaiming the war's end until a proper capitulation of German forces on the Eastern Front was signed in Berlin, validating the surrender improvised by SHAEF. The war in Europe was over, yet not quite finished.

No matter that word of the Reims ceremony had leaked. A German radio broadcast from Flensburg on Monday announced the end, and an Associated Press reporter who had witnessed the signing disobeyed Eisenhower's news embargo by sending word to New York, where ticker tape soon fluttered. "It will seem that it is only the governments who do not know," Churchill cabled Stalin at 4:30 P.M. Monday.

But Stalin remained adamant. For years the Nazis had claimed that the German army in World War I was never defeated, in part because the armistice had been signed on French soil; no such canard would be tolerated this time. Churchill and Truman reluctantly agreed to withhold confirmation of the surrender. V-E Day—victory in Europe—would not become official until Tuesday, May 8. Eisenhower dispatched a SHAEF delegation to meet the Soviets at a former German military engineering school in Karlshorst, ten miles southeast of central Berlin. Here the Germans would surrender, again, after nine hours of noisy haggling and more opéra bouffe. General de Lattre, representing France, bitterly decried the absence of a French flag from among the victorious national colors arrayed in the conference hall. He objected further when a tricolor hurriedly sewn by a Russian tailor—using cloth from a Nazi banner, a bedsheet, and denim overalls—turned out Dutch, with the red, white, and blue stripes stacked horizontally rather than aligned vertically. A bemused Harry Butcher wrote from Karlshorst, "It is much easier to start a war than to stop one."

Notwithstanding a BBC announcement at six P.M. on Monday that V-E Day must await the morrow, a boisterous, expectant throng jammed

Piccadilly and Trafalgar Square. "V-E Day may be tomorrow," the *Daily Mail* declared, "but the war is over tonight." Bonfires glazed the clouds with an orange tint that reminded some of the 1940 Blitz. Yet as word of the postponement spread, the festive spirit fizzled. "Move along," a policeman ordered. "It's all off."

In Paris, a celebration that began Monday night would run riot until midday Thursday. Jeeps packed with GIs and comely French women rushed about as crowds shouted, "*Salut! Vive les États Unis!* American Army, heep heep, whoo-ray!" Snaking throngs danced down the Champs-Élysées as sirens sounded a final all clear and church bells rang across the city. A witness in Avenue Kléber reported mobs of "people going from anywhere to anywhere." So many filled the Place de la Concorde that American MPs struggled to open a corridor into the U.S. embassy; thousands joined the Yanks in singing, or at least humming, "The Battle Hymn of the Republic." For the first time since the war began, lights illuminated the Arc de Triomphe, the Opéra, and other grand landmarks. The Garde Républicaine trotted on horseback from the Madeleine in their plumed dragoon helmets, and at least one laughing girl seemed to share every saddle. French gunners unlimbered a howitzer before the palace in Versailles to fire salutes down the Avenue de Paris.

The rest of the world soon caught the celebratory spirit. A crowd estimated at five thousand gathered before the U.S. embassy near Red Square in Moscow to huzzah the American ally; Yanks spotted in the street were playfully tossed into the air. Half a million celebrants filled Times Square, and enormous headlines splashed across page one of *The New York Times* proclaimed, "The War in Europe Is Ended! Surrender Is Unconditional; V-E Will Be Proclaimed Today." In Washington, lights bathed the Capitol dome for the first time since December 1941, although streets remained quiet, perhaps because the battle for Okinawa had become a cave-by-cave bloodbath. Federal bureaucrats were ordered to report to work as usual on Tuesday, lest peacetime lollygagging take root. "This is a solemn but glorious hour," Truman told the nation. "We must work to finish the war. Our victory is only half won. The West is free, but the East is still in bondage to the treacherous Japanese."

V-E Day dawned in London with what one resident called "intense Wagnerian rain" and thunder so violent that many woke fearing a return of German bombers. By midmorning the storm had rolled off, the sun broke through, and those St. Paul's bell-ringers leaned into their work. British lasses with cornflowers and poppies in their hair swarmed about, wrote Mollie Panter-Downes in *The New Yorker,* "like flocks of twittering, gaily plumaged cockney birds." Tugs on the Thames tooted a Morse "V," and vendors peddled tin brooches of Montgomery's bereted head in silhouette. Buglers blew "cease fire" while students in Green Park clapped ash can lids like cymbals. Crates of whiskey and gin, labeled "Not to Be Sold Until Victory Night," were manhandled into hundreds of pubs, where many an elbow was bent prematurely. The Savoy added *La Tasse de Consommé Niçoise de la Victoire* to the menu, along with *Le Médaillon du Soldat*. Crowds outside Buckingham Palace chanted, "We want the king!" and the king they got, along with the queen and two princesses, who appeared waving from a balcony six times during the day. To the strains of "Rule, Britannia!," former Home Guardsmen set fire to a Hitler effigy.

Early in the afternoon Churchill left 10 Downing Street by the garden gate. Crowds cheered him to the echo as he rode in an open car from Horse Guards Parade to the House of Commons. There the prime minister read the surrender announcement to a standing ovation before leading a procession of House members on foot to the twelfth-century St. Margaret's church, on the grounds of Westminster Abbey, for a service of thanksgiving. Thence he was driven by car to Buckingham Palace for tea, through adulatory throngs that bayed, "Winnie! Winnie!" "We all roared ourselves hoarse," the playwright Noël Coward told his diary after standing outside the palace. "I suppose this is the greatest day in our history." Churchill sent an aide to fetch a cigar, which he fired with a flourish before the ecstatic crowd. "I must put one on for them," he confided. "They expect it."

Searchlights at dusk picked out St. Paul's dome and cross, likened by one witness to "a marvelous piece of jewelry invented by a magician." Big Ben's round face glowed with lunar brilliance. More bonfires jumped up in Green Park, fueled with tree branches and the odd bench. As the day faded in the west, Churchill appeared on the Ministry of Health balcony to peer down at the seething crowd spilling across Whitehall. "This is your hour," he told them, flashing his stubby fingers in the trademark V. "We were the first, in this ancient land, to draw the sword against tyranny." Chandelier flares floated overhead, dripping light, and the throng linked arms in deliverance to sing Elgar's "Land of Hope and Glory," weeping together in sorrow and in joy, for all that was lost and all that had been won.

By the time Japan surrendered on September 2, 1945, the Second World War had lasted six years and a day, ensnaring almost sixty nations, plus sundry colonial and imperial territories. Sixty million had died in those six years, including nearly 10 million in Germany and Japan, and more than twice that number in the Soviet Union—roughly 26 million, one-third of them soldiers. To describe this "great and terrible epoch," as George Marshall called it, new words would be required, like "genocide"; and old words would assume new usages: "Holocaust." The war "was a savage, insensate affair, barely conceivable to the well-conducted imagination," wrote Lieutenant Paul Fussell. "The real war was tragic and ironic, beyond the power of any literary or philosophic analysis to suggest." To one victim, Ernie Pyle, this global conflagration had been simply "an unmitigated misfortune."

For the Allies, some solace could be derived from complete victory over a foe of unexampled iniquity. An existential struggle had been settled so decisively that Field Marshal Brooke, among many, would conclude "that there is a God all-powerful looking after the destiny of the world." In Europe, the Western Allies in 338 days had advanced more than seven hundred miles, liberated oppressed peoples by the tens of millions, seized a hundred thousand square miles of Germany and Austria, captured more than four million prisoners, and killed or badly wounded an estimated one million enemy soldiers. While bleeding far less than the Soviets, the West at war's end had retained the most productive and economically vital quadrants of the Continent.

A British military maxim held that "he who has not fought the Germans does not know war." Now the Americans, Soviets, and others also knew war all too well. The cohesion and internal coherence of the Allied coalition had assured victory: the better alliance had won. Certainly it was possible to look at Allied war-making on any given day and feel heartsick at the missed opportunities and purblind personalities and wretched wastage, to wonder why the ranks could not be braver or at least cleverer, smarter or at least shrewder, prescient or at least intuitive. Yet despite its foibles, the Allied way of war won through, with systems that were, as the historian Richard Overy would write, "centralized, unified, and coordinated," quite unlike Axis systems.

In contrast to the Axis autocracy, Allied leadership included checks and balances to temper arbitrary willfulness and personal misjudgment. The battlefield had offered a proving ground upon which demonstrated competence and equanimity could flourish; as usual, modern war also rewarded ingenuity, collaboration, organizational acumen, and luck, that trait most cherished by Napoléon in his generals. The Anglo-American confederation in particular, for all the high-strung melodrama, could be seen in retrospect to effect a strategic symbiosis: British prudence in 1942 and 1943, eventually yielding to American audacity in 1944 and 1945, had brought victories in the Mediterranean that proved a necessary prelude to the decisive campaign that began at Normandy. The war here had indeed formed a triptych, with the campaigns in North Africa, Italy, and western Europe each providing a panel to fashion the whole. Churchill composed his own aphorism, much quoted: "There is only one thing worse than fighting with allies, and that is fighting without them."

"Our resolution to preserve civilization must become more implacable," an American observer had written in 1939. "Our courage must mount." Resolution and courage both proved equal to the cause, as did more material contributions. The Americans had provided more than two-thirds of Eisenhower's 91 divisions, and half of the Allies' 28,000 combat aircraft. Thirteen U.S. divisions in Europe suffered at least 100 percent casualties— 5 more exceeded 200 percent—yet American combat power remained largely undimmed to the end. The entire war had cost U.S. taxpayers $296 billion—roughly $4 trillion in 2012 dollars. To help underwrite a military budget that increased 8,000 percent, Roosevelt had expanded the number of those taxpayers from 4 million to 42 million. The armed forces had grown 3,500 percent while building 3,000 overseas bases and depots, and shipping 4.5 tons of matériel abroad for each soldier deployed, plus another ton each month to sustain him. "I felt," one Frenchman wrote in watching the Yanks make war, "as if the Americans were digging the Panama Canal right through the German army."

What Churchill called the American "prodigy of organization" had shipped 18 million tons of war stuff to Europe, equivalent to the cargo in 3,600 Liberty ships or 181,000 rail cars: the kit ranged from 800,000 military vehicles to footwear in sizes 2A to 22EEE. U.S. munitions plants had turned out 40 billion rounds of small arms ammunition and 56 million grenades. From D-Day to V-E Day, GIs fired 500 million machine-gun bullets and 23 million artillery rounds. "I'm letting the American taxpayer take this hill," one prodigal gunner declared, and no one disagreed. By 1945, the United States had built two-thirds of all ships afloat and was making half of all manufactured goods in the world, including nearly half of all armaments. The enemy was crushed by logistical brilliance, firepower, mobility, mechanical aptitude, and an economic juggernaut that produced much, much more of nearly everything than Germany could— bombers, bombs, fighters, transport planes, mortars, machine guns, trucks—yet the war absorbed barely one-third of the American gross domestic product, a smaller proportion than that of any major belligerent. A German prisoner complained, "Warfare like yours is easy."

There was nothing easy about it, of course. But the United States emerged from World War II with extraordinary advantages that would ensure prosperity for decades: an intact, thriving industrial base; a population relatively unscarred by war; cheap energy; two-thirds of the world's gold supply; and great optimism. As the major power in western Europe, the Mediterranean, and the Pacific, possessing both atomic weapons and a Navy and Air Force of unequaled might, the United States was ready to exploit what the historian H. P. Willmott described as "the end of the period of European supremacy in the world that had existed for four centuries." If the war had dispelled American isolationism, it also encouraged American exceptionalism, as well as a penchant for military solutions and a self-regard that led some to label their epoch "the American century." "Power," as John Adams had written, "always thinks it has a great soul."

The war was a potent catalyst for social change across the republic. New technologies—jets, computers, ballistic missiles, penicillin—soon spurred vibrant new industries, which in turn encouraged the migration of black workers from south to north, and of all peoples to the emerging west. The GI Bill put millions of soldiers into college classrooms, spurring unprecedented social mobility. Nineteen million American women had entered the workplace by war's end; although they quickly reverted to traditional antebellum roles—the percentage working in 1947 was hardly higher than it had been in 1940—that genie would not remain back in the bottle forever. The modest experiment in racially integrating infantry battalions ended when the war did, despite nearly universal agreement that black riflemen had performed ably and in harmony with their white comrades. A presidential order in 1948 would be required to desegregate the military, and much more than that would be needed to reverse three centuries of racial oppression in America.

But tectonic plates had begun to shift. "Glad to be home," a black soldier from Chicago observed as his troopship sailed into New York harbor. "Proud of my country, as irregular as it is. Determined it could be better."

In battered Europe, enormous tasks remained. Those who had outlived the war must "learn how to reassemble our broken world," as Pyle had put it. The last debris of the Third Reich had to be swept up, including 400,000 German troops adrift in Norway. Grand Admiral Dönitz and his bureaucrats stayed busy in Flensburg for two weeks after the surrender—writing reports, exchanging memos, even posing for an official regime photo—until SHAEF authorities finally arrived to hustle them off to jail. ("Any word from me would be superfluous," Dönitz said.) An Allied Control Council would assume power over Germany in early June on behalf of the victors, and Anglo-American troops vacated the Soviet zone a month later. SHAEF moved from Reims to Frankfurt and became USFET, U.S. Forces in the European Theater, even as those forces—more than three million strong—began heading home. Not least among the jobs at hand was the disposal of 211,000 tons of German poisonous gas munitions found in the U.S. and British zones alone, including 90,000 tons of mustard bombs and 3.7 million gas artillery shells—a reminder of how much worse the war could have been. Military authorities considered shipping some of the stuff to the Pacific for use against the Japanese, then concluded that the 160,000 tons of U.S. gas munitions stockpiled in Europe and the Mediterranean offered an ample reserve, if needed.

"On the continent of Europe we have yet to make sure that . . . the words 'freedom,' 'democracy,' and 'liberation' are not distorted from their true meaning as we have understood them," Churchill told Britons in mid-May. "Forward, unflinching, unswerving, indomitable, till the whole task is done and the whole world safe and clean." Part of that cleansing required the investigation and prosecution of those culpable for murdering six million Jews, half a million Gypsies, and others, many others. Three thousand tons of documents relating to the camps would be captured and parsed. In Room 600 of the Nuremberg courthouse, the most celebrated of all war-crimes tribunals would hear testimony from 360 witnesses and review 200,000 affidavits. Of two dozen major Nazi defendants, ten would be hanged in October 1946, from gallows built in a jail gymnasium.

Individual Allied governments also conducted hundreds of additional trials. The Western powers alone arrested 200,000 suspected culprits, charging more than 5,000 with major war crimes. Of 48 defendants tried by a British military court in Lüneburg for crimes relating to Bergen-Belsen, 11 would be executed by an experienced hangman specially flown to the Continent. From 1945 to 1948, American military tribunals tried 1,672 Germans—military officers, politicians, diplomats, industrialists, physicians, jurists—in 489 trials.

The path to justice often proved circuitous. Seventy-four defendants were tried in a Dachau courtroom for murdering GIs and Belgian civilians at or near the Malmédy crossroads during the Bulge, and forty-three of them received death sentences, including their commander, Colonel Joachim Peiper. But confessions had been coerced, by threats to defendants' relatives, physical force, and other wrongful inducements; all capital sentences were commuted. Released from Landsberg prison in 1956, Peiper found a job managing American sales for Porsche. Later he worked for Volkswagen and as a translator, remaining active in Waffen-SS veterans associations. In 1976, Peiper burned to death when his house in Alsace was fire-bombed by a killer who also had slashed the hoses of the local fire department. The crime remained unsolved.

Eisenhower's avowed "number 1 plan" after the war was "to sit on the bank of a quiet stream and fish." That would not happen: the victorious commander was destined for grander things. Among the many accolades he received was a graceful note from Montgomery. "I owe much to your wise guidance and kindly forbearance," the field marshal wrote. "I know my own faults very well and I do not suppose I am an easy subordinate; I like to go my own way. But you have kept me on the rails in difficult and stormy times."

No laurel meant more to Eisenhower than Marshall's encomium:

> You have completed your mission with the greatest victory in the history of warfare. . . . You have made history, great history for the good of all mankind, and you have stood for all we hope for and admire in an officer of the United States Army.

Ahead lay fifteen more years of service, as Army chief of staff, president of Columbia University, commander of the new NATO military alliance, and president of his country. But first Eisenhower would return to London, where three years earlier he had arrived as a new and quite anonymous major general responsible for planning the liberation of Europe. Now a mob instantly congregated when he tried to take a quiet stroll through Hyde Park—"Ike! Good old Ike!" they cried—and two bobbies had to escort him back to the Dorchester Hotel. "It's nice to be back in a country where I can almost speak the language," he had quipped.

On Tuesday, June 12, in an open landau pulled by a pair of high-stepping bays, he rode to the Guildhall, London's eight-hundred-year-old city hall, still scarred from the Blitz. Here he would receive a sword of honor and Britain's formal thanks. A band played Handel's "See the Conquering Hero Comes" as policemen mounted on five white chargers led the carriage into Gresham Street, where thousands of spectators let loose a roar that sent pigeons flapping from the church belfries. Inside, a string orchestra had just finished "My Old Kentucky Home" when a bailiff bellowed from the door, "The supreme commander of the Allied Expeditionary Force!" Eisenhower climbed to the dais to be welcomed with applause by the great men of England, Churchill foremost among them. For twenty minutes, pale and a bit nervous, he spoke without notes of their common cause, their shared sacrifice, and their joint victory. "I had never realized that Ike was as big a man until I heard his performance today," Brooke told his diary. One line from Eisenhower's address would be engraved over his tomb in Kansas a quarter-century later: "Humility must always be the portion of any man who receives acclaim earned in the blood of his followers and the sacrifices of his friends."

Blood there had surely been, and sacrifices beyond comprehension. Battle casualties among armies of the Western Allies since D-Day exceeded three-quarters of a million, of whom at least 165,000 were dead. Added to that were 10,000 naval losses, half of them dead, and 62,000 air casualties—half of them dead, too, in the 12,000 Allied planes lost over Europe.

British, Canadian, Polish, and ancillary forces in 21st Army Group tallied combat losses of 194,000 in eleven months, including 42,000 killed. French battle casualties in northwestern Europe reached 69,000, of whom 12,600 had died. Ghastly as such losses were, they paled beside those suffered by other combatants. Of all German boys born between 1915 and 1924, one-third were dead or missing. Some 14 percent of the Soviet population of 190 million perished during the war; the Red Army suffered more combat deaths at Stalingrad alone than the U.S. armed forces did in the entire war. Soviet forces also had killed roughly nine times more Germans than the United States and Britain combined.

American soldiers bore the brunt for the Western armies in the climactic final year: the 587,000 U.S. casualties in western Europe included 135,576 dead, almost half of the U.S. total worldwide. Of 361,000 wounded GIs, the quick and the lucky escaped with superficial scars, like the veteran who years later wrote that "my left index finger still carries the mark where a tiny shell fragment entered it once, back there one raving afternoon." Others were less fortunate, among them the 1,700 left blind from all theaters, and the 11,000 with at least partial paralysis of one or more limbs. The Army also tallied 18,000 amputations, most of which occurred after June 1944. A single hospital in Michigan treated more amputees than the total number of amputations incurred by the entire U.S. Army in World War I. "You didn't always remember their name," one surgeon later said, "but you did remember their stump."

Seventy-five thousand Americans had been listed as missing or captured during the European campaign; thousands still were not accounted for at war's end, leaving their loved ones with the particular anguish of uncertainty. "Darling, come to me in a dream tonight and tell me that you're alive and safe," Myra A. Strachner had written from the Bronx on April 18, after Private First Class Bernie Staller went missing. "Please! I know you want to tell me." Private Staller's secret eventually would out: he had been killed by German artillery a month earlier, at age nineteen. For others, the mystery endured. An estimated 25,000 GIs lay in isolated graves around the Continent, many of them hidden or lost.

No sooner had the ink dried on the surrender documents than mobile teams fanned across Europe to seek the dead and missing, including 14,000 Americans believed killed in air crashes behind enemy lines and others who had died in German prison hospitals. Similar searches began from the Arctic Circle to Cape Town, from the Azores to Iran. Graves

Registration units labored to confirm the identities of more than 250,000 American dead in 450 cemeteries scattered across 86 countries, two-thirds of them in Europe or the Mediterranean. For an estimated 44,000 lost at sea, nothing could be done.

Within weeks, 700 bodies were disinterred in Czechoslovakia. Hundreds more emerged from scattered graves in eastern Germany, where the Soviets grudgingly permitted three American recovery squads to roam the countryside. Thirteen hundred sets of American remains were unearthed in the Low Countries, many from MARKET GARDEN polders. Millions of land mines made tromping around the Hürtgen Forest and the Siegfried Line perilous, but a nine-month hunt through western Germany would find 6,220 Americans on battlefields large and small. In three years, European fields, forests, orchards, and cellars would yield 16,548 isolated GI dead; over the subsequent decades they would continue to give up a skull here or a femur there.

Even as this search began, all twelve U.S. military cemeteries on German soil were emptied; no dead GI would knowingly be left in the former Reich. By the thousands, and then by the tens of thousands, the dead were reinterred at thirty-eight temporary sites, mostly in France, of which ten eventually became permanent American cemeteries. The solicitude accorded them could be seen at the Ninth Army cemetery in Margraten, where on May 30, 1945, Memorial Day, Dutch citizens gathered flowers from sixty villages and spread them like a brilliant quilt across seventeen thousand graves.

The power of a well-wrought grave was beyond measure. Patricia O'Malley, who was a year old when her father, Major Richard James O'Malley, a battalion commander in the 12th Infantry, was killed by a sniper in Normandy, later wrote of seeing his headstone for the first time in the cemetery at Colleville, above Omaha Beach.

> I cried for the joy of being there and the sadness of my father's death. I cried for all the times I needed a father and never had one. I cried for all the words I had wanted to say and wanted to hear but had not. I cried and cried.

In 1947, the next of kin of 270,000 identifiable American dead buried overseas would submit Quartermaster General Form 345 to choose whether they wanted their soldier brought back to the United States or left interred with comrades abroad. More than 60 percent of the dead worldwide would return home, at an average cost to the government of $564.50 per body, an unprecedented repatriation that only an affluent, victorious nation could afford. In Europe the exhumations began that July: every grave was opened by hand, and the remains sprinkled with an embalming compound of formaldehyde, aluminum chloride, plaster of Paris, wood powder, and clay. Wrapped in a blanket, each body was then laid on a pillow in a metal casket lined with rayon satin.

Labor strikes in the United States caused a shortage of casket steel, and repatriation was further delayed by a dearth of licensed embalmers, although government representatives made recruiting visits to mortician schools around the country. In warehouses at Cherbourg, Cardiff, and elsewhere the dead accumulated. Finally the *Joseph V. Connolly,* the first of twenty-one ghost ships to sail from Europe, steamed down the Scheldt with 5,060 dead soldiers in her hold. Thirty thousand Belgians bade them adieu from the Antwerp docks, while pledging to look after the 61,000 Americans who would remain in those ten European cemeteries, "as if," one man vowed, "their tombs were our children's."

On Saturday, October 27, the *Connolly* berthed in New York. Stevedores winched the caskets from the ship two at a time in specially designed slings. Most then traveled by rail in a great diaspora across the republic for burial in their hometowns. Among those waiting was Henry A. Wright, a widower who lived on a farm in southwestern Missouri, near Springfield. One by one his dead sons arrived at the local train station: Sergeant Frank H. Wright, killed on Christmas Eve 1944 in the Bulge; then Private Harold B. Wright, who had died of his wounds in a German prison camp on February 3, 1945; and finally Private Elton E. Wright, killed in Germany on April 25, two weeks before the war ended. Gray and stooped, the elder Wright watched as the caskets were carried into the rustic bedroom where each boy had been born. Neighbors kept vigil overnight, carpeting the floor with roses, and in the morning they bore the brothers to Hilltop Cemetery for burial side by side beneath an iron sky.

Thus did the fallen return from Europe, 82,357 strong. As the dead came home, so too the things they carried. Two hundred miles north of the Wright farm, the Army Effects Bureau of the Kansas City Quartermaster Depot filled a large warehouse at 601 Hardesty Avenue, just below a majestic bend in the Missouri River. From a modest enterprise that had begun with half a dozen employees in February 1942, the Effects Bureau had expanded to more than a thousand workers, and by August 1945 they were handling sixty thousand shipments a month, each laden with the belongings of American dead from six continents.

Hour after hour, day after day, shipping containers were unloaded from rail freight cars onto a receiving dock and then hoisted by elevator to the depot's tenth floor. Here with assembly-line efficiency the containers traveled by conveyor belt from station to station down to the seventh floor as inspectors pawed through the crates to extract classified documents, pornography, ammunition, and perhaps amorous letters from a girlfriend that would further grieve a grieving widow. The prevailing rule on Hardesty Avenue was said to be "Remove anything you would not want returned to your family if *you* were the soldier." Workers used grinding stones and dentist drills to remove corrosion and blood from helmets and web gear; laundresses took pains to scrub bloodstains out of field jackets and uniform blouses. A detailed inventory was pinned to each repacked container before it was stacked in a storage bin. And all the while banks of typists in an adjacent room hammered out correspondence to the next of kin, up to seventy thousand letters a month, asking where the soldier's last possessions should be sent.

Over the years, Effects Bureau inspectors had found tapestries, enemy swords, a German machine gun, an Italian accordion, a tobacco sack full of diamonds, walrus tusks, a shrunken head, a Japanese life raft. Among thousands of diaries also received in Kansas City was a small notebook that had belonged to Lieutenant Hershel G. Horton, a twenty-nine-year-old Army officer from Aurora, Illinois. Shot in the right leg and hip during a firefight with the Japanese in New Guinea, Horton had dragged himself into a grass shanty and, over the several days that it took for him to die, he had scribbled a final letter in the notebook. "My dear, sweet father, mother, and sister," he wrote. "I lay here in this terrible place, wondering not why God has forsaken me, but rather why He is making me suffer."

This, the profoundest of all mysteries, would be left for the living to ponder. Soldiers who survived also would struggle to reconcile the greatest catastrophe in human history with what the philosopher and Army officer J. Glenn Gray called "the one great lyric passage in their lives." The war's intensity, camaraderie, and sense of high purpose left many with "a deplorable nostalgia," in the phrase of A. J. Liebling. "The times were full of certainty," Liebling later wrote. "I have seldom been sure I was right since." An AAF crewman who completed fifty bomber missions observed, "Never did I feel so much alive. Never did the earth and all of the surroundings look so bright and sharp." And a combat engineer mused, "What we had together was something awfully damned good, something I don't think we'll ever have again as long as we live."

They had been annealed, touched with fire. "We are certainly no smaller men than our forefathers," Gavin wrote his daughter. Alan Moorehead, who watched the scarlet calamity from beginning to end, believed that "here and there a man found greatness in himself."

The anti-aircraft gunner in a raid and the boy in a landing barge really did feel at moments that the thing they were doing was a clear and definite good, the best they could do. And at those moments there was a surpassing satisfaction, a sense of exactly and entirely fulfilling one's life.... This thing, the brief ennoblement, kept recurring again and again up to the end, and it refreshed and lighted the whole heroic and sordid story.

In Moorehead's view, the soldier to whom this grace was granted became, "for a moment, a complete man, and he had his sublimity in him." For those destined to outlive the war and die abed as old men half a century hence, the din of battle grew fainter without ever fading entirely. They knew, as Osmar White knew, that "the living have the cause of the dead in trust." This too was part of the sublimity.

"No war is really over until the last veteran is dead," a rifleman in the 26th Division would conclude. Of the 16,112,566 Americans in uniform during the Second World War, the number still living was expected to decline to one million by late 2014, and, a decade later, in 2024, to dip below a hundred thousand. By the year 2036, U.S. government demographers estimated, fewer than four hundred veterans would remain alive, less than half the strength of an infantry battalion.

Yet the war and all that the war contained—nobility, villainy, immeasurable sorrow—is certain to live on even after the last old soldier has gone to his grave. May the earth lie lightly on his bones.

Notes

The following abbreviations appear in the endnotes and bibliography. Some stack locations and box numbers change as archivists reconfigure their collections. A list of additional manuscripts, monographs, and unpublished documents used in this book appears online at **www.liberationtrilogy.com**.

a.p. author's possession
AAAD Rick Atkinson, *An Army at Dawn*
AAF Army Air Forces
AAFinWWII W. F. Craven and J. L. Cate, eds., *The Army Air Forces in World War II*, vol. 3
AAR after action report
AB After the Battle
AB Div airborne division
AD armored division
admin administration
AF air force
AFHQ micro Allied Forces Headquarters microfilm, NARA RG 331
AFHRA Air Force Historical Research Agency
AFIA American Forces in Action publications and background papers
AG Army Group
ag adjutant general
AGF Army Ground Forces
ALH Howard L. Gleck et al., "The Administrative and Logistical History of the ETO," part 5, WD, May 1946, a.p.
ALM Audie Leon Murphy papers, USMA Special Collections, West Point, N.Y.
ANSCOL Army-Navy Staff College Collection, NWC Lib, U.S. National Archives
AR action report
Ardennes Hugh M. Cole, *The Ardennes: Battle of the Bulge, USAWWII*
AS Armored School
ASEQ Army Service Experiences Questionnaire, MHI
ASF Army Service Forces
AU Air University
bde brigade
Beck Alfred M. Beck et al., *The Corps of Engineers: The War Against Germany, USAWWII*
BLM Bernard Law Montgomery
bn battalion
BP Martin Blumenson, *Breakout and Pursuit, USAWWII*
CARL Combined Arms Research Library, Fort Leavenworth, Kans.
CBH Chester B. Hansen, including papers, diary, MHI
CBM Charles B. MacDonald, including papers, MHI
CCA Gordon A. Harrison, *Cross-Channel Attack, USAWWII*

CCS Combined Chiefs of Staff

CE U.S. Army Corps of Engineers

CEOH U.S. Army Corps of Engineers, Office of History

Chandler Alfred Chandler, ed., *The Papers of Dwight David Eisenhower: The War Years*

CI Combat Interview, ETO

CINCLANT Commander-in-Chief, Atlantic Fleet

CJB Clay and Joan Blair collection, MHI

CJR Cornelius J. Ryan, including papers, Ohio University, Athens, Ohio

CMH U.S. Army Center of Military History, Fort McNair, Washington, D.C.

CNO Chief of Naval Operations

co company

Coakley Robert W. Coakley and Richard M. Leighton, *Global Logistics and Strategy 1943–1945, USAWWII*

COHQ Combined Operations Headquarters, U.K.

Col U OHRO Columbia University Oral History Research Office, N.Y.

corr correspondence

COS chief of staff

CSI U.S. Army Combat Studies Institute, Fort Leavenworth, Kans.

DA Department of the Army

Danchev Alex Danchev and Daniel Todman, eds., *War Diaries, 1939–1945: Field Marshal Lord Alanbrooke*

DDE Dwight David Eisenhower

DDE Lib Dwight D. Eisenhower Presidential Library, Abilene, Kans.

diss dissertation

div division

DOB Rick Atkinson, *The Day of Battle*

DTL Donovan Technical Library, Fort Benning, Ga.

E entry

ET Exercise Tiger collection, MHI

ETO European Theater of Operations

FA field artillery

FAJ *Field Artillery Journal*

FCP Forrest C. Pogue, including background material for *The Supreme Command*, MHI

FDR Lib Franklin D. Roosevelt Presidential Library, Hyde Park, N.Y.

FMS Foreign Military Studies

FOIA Freedom of Information Act

FRUS *Foreign Relations of the United States: The Conferences at Malta and Yalta*

Ft. K Ft. Knox, Ky.

Ft. L Ft. Leavenworth, Kans.

FUSA First U.S. Army

GCM Lib George C. Marshall Research Library, Lexington, Va.

Germany VII Horst Boog et al., *Germany and the Second World War*, vol. 7, *The Strategic Air War in Europe and the War in the West and East Asia, 1943–1944/45*

Germany IX Ralf Blank et al., *Germany and the Second World War*, vol. 9, part 1, *German Wartime Society, 1939–1945*

GS V John Ehrman, *Grand Strategy*, vol. 5

GS VI John Ehrman, *Grand Strategy*, vol. 6

GSP George S. Patton, Jr., including papers, Library of Congress

HCB Harry C. Butcher, including papers

HD Historical Division

HI "Hospital Interviews," NARA RG 407 E 427, ML #2233

HIA Hoover Institution Archives, Stanford University, Palo Alto, Calif.

Hinsley F. H. Hinsley, *British Intelligence in the Second World War*, abridged

HKH Henry Kent Hewitt papers

Hq headquarters
ID infantry division
IFG Samuel Eliot Morison, *The Invasion of France and Germany, 1944–1945*
IG inspector general
IJ Infantry Journal
inf infantry
intel intelligence
IS Infantry School, Ft. Benning, Ga.
IWM Imperial War Museum, London
JAG U.S. Army judge advocate general
JB Joseph Balkoski
JCS Joint Chiefs of Staff
JLC J. Lawton Collins
JLD Jacob L. Devers, including papers
JMG James M. Gavin, including papers
JMH Journal of Military History
JT John Toland, including papers
LC Hugh M. Cole, *The Lorraine Campaign, USAWWII*
LHC Liddell Hart Centre for Military Archives, King's College, London
LHD John Toland, *The Last Hundred Days*
lib library
LKT Jr. Lucian K. Truscott, Jr., including papers
LO Charles B. MacDonald, *The Last Offensive, USAWWII*
LOC MS Div Library of Congress Manuscript Division
LSA Roland G. Ruppenthal, *Logistical Support of the Armies*, vols. 1 and 2, *USAWWII*
MB Martin Blumenson
MBR Matthew B. Ridgway
MEB Magna E. Bauer
MHI U.S. Army Military History Institute, Carlisle, Pa.
MHUC Medical Historical Unit Collection, MHI
micro microfilm
ML miscellaneous AG records, ETO
MMB Mark M. Boatner III, *The Biographical Dictionary of World War II*
MMD 29th Infantry Division Archives, Maryland Military Department, Fifth Regiment
    Armory, Baltimore
MP military police
MRC FDM McCormick Research Center, First Division Museum, Cantigny, Ill.
msg message
mss manuscript
MTOUSA Mediterranean Theater of Operations, United States Army
n.d. no date
NARA National Archives and Records Administration, College Park, Md.
NATOUSA North African Theater of Operations, United States Army
Naval Guns Morton L. Deyo, "Naval Guns at Normandy," ts, n.d., SEM, NHHC, box 87
NHHC Naval History and Heritage Command, Washington, D.C.
NSA National Security Agency
NWC Lib National War College Library
NWWIIM National World War II Museum archives, New Orleans
NYT New York Times
obit obituary
OCMH Office of the Chief of Military History
OCNO Office of the Chief of Naval Operations
OCS Office of the Chief of Staff
OH oral history

ONB Omar N. Bradley, including papers
OPD Operations Division, War Department
OR observer report
OSS Office of Strategic Services
PIR Robert M. Littlejohn, ed., "Passing in Review," MHI
Para parachute
PP Martin Blumenson, *The Patton Papers, 1940–1945*
PP-pres Papers, Pre-presidential
Proceedings *U.S. Naval Institute Proceedings*
qm quartermaster
regt regiment
RG record group
RN Royal Navy
ROHA Rutgers University Oral History Archives of World War II, New Brunswick, N.J.
Ross William F. Ross and Charles F. Romanus, *The Quartermaster Corps: Operations in the War Against Germany, USAWWII*
RR Jeffrey J. Clarke and Robert Ross Smith, *Riviera to the Rhine, USAWWII*
s.p. self-published
SC Signal Corps
SEM Samuel Eliot Morison Office Files
SGS Secretary General Staff
SLAM S.L.A. Marshall, including papers, MHI
SLC Charles B. MacDonald, *The Siegfried Line Campaign, USAWWII*
SMH Society for Military History
SOOHP Senior Officer Oral History Program
SOS Services of Supply
STM Sidney T. Mathews
Sylvan William C. Sylan and Francis G. Smith, Jr., *Normandy to Victory*
td tank destroyer
Texas MFM Texas Military Forces Museum, Austin
Three Years Harry C. Butcher, *My Three Years with Eisenhower*
TR Theodore Roosevelt, Jr., including papers, LOC MS Div
ts typescript
TSC Forrest C. Pogue, *The Supreme Command, USAWWII*
TT Charles B. MacDonald, *A Time for Trumpets*
UK NA National Archive, Kew, U.K. (formerly Public Record Office)
USAF HRC U.S. Air Force Historical Research Center
USAF U.S. Air Force
USAREUR U.S. Army, Europe
USAWWII *United States Army in World War II*
USFET U.S. Forces, European Theater
USHMM U.S. Holocaust Memorial Museum
USMA Arch U.S. Military Academy Special Collections and Archives, West Point, N.Y.
USMC U.S. Marine Corps
USN U.S. Navy
USNAd "U.S. Naval Administration in World War II"
USNI OHD U.S. Naval Institute, Oral History Department, Annapolis, Md.
USSAFE U.S. Strategic Air Forces Europe
UTEP University of Texas at El Paso
UT-K University of Tennessee, Knoxville, Center for the Study of War and Society
VC C. P. Stacey, *The Victory Campaign*, vol. 3, *Official History of the Canadian Army in the Second World War*
VHP Veterans' History Project, National Folklife Center, Library of Congress
VW L. F. Ellis, *Victory in the West*

WaS S. W. Roskill, *The War at Sea, 1939–1945*, vol. 3, part 2
WD War Department
WP *Washington Post*
WSC Winston S. Churchill
WWII World War II
XO executive officer
YCHT York County Heritage Trust, York, Pa.
YU Yale University Library, Manuscripts and Archives

Prologue

1 *A killing frost*: *The New Yorker Book of War Pieces*, 308–9; Peckham and Snyder, eds., *Letters from Fighting Hoosiers*, vol. 2, 95 (*"Three inches"*).

1 *Nearly five years*: Settle, *All the Brave Promises*, 13, 84; Ziegler, *London at War, 1939–1945*, 243–45 (*zinc phosphate*).

1 *Privation lay on the land*: Fussell, *Wartime*, 200, 203; "A Yank in Britain," ts, n.d., Thor M. Smith Papers, HIA, box 2, 31 (*"Squander Bug"*); *Times* (London), May 15, 1944, 1 (*"artificial teeth"*); Stafford, *Ten Days to D-Day*, 203–4 (*"bombed upholstery"*).

1 *Other government placards*: Fussell, *Wartime*, 201; Calder, *The People's War*, 380–81 (*two ounces* and *roast cormorant*); Essame, *Patton: A Study in Command*, 128 (*"Woolton pie"*).

2 *More than fifty thousand*: *VW*, vol. 1, 29; Joseph R. Darnall, "Powdered Eggs and Purple Hearts," ts, 1946, MHUC, MHI, box 24, 72–74 (*parachute flares*); Moynihan, ed., *People at War, 1939–45*, 169 (*"searchlights"*); Ackroyd, *London Under*, e-book, chapter 12 (*"slave ship"*); Ziegler, *London at War, 1939–1945*, 277, 270–71 (*own beds*).

2 *Even during these short summer nights*: *Times* (London), May 15, 1944, 5; Simpson, *Selected Prose*, 117 (*"profoundly dark"*); Reynolds, *Rich Relations*, 414 (*"battlefield of sex"*); Longmate, *The G.I.'s*, 276 (*"Marble Arch style"*); Eustis, *War Letters of Morton Eustis to His Mother*, 191 (*"madhouse after dark"*).

2 *Proud Britain soldiered on*: Joseph R. Darnall, "Powdered Eggs and Purple Hearts," ts, 1946, MHUC, MHI, box 24, 92; *Daily Mail* (London), May 15, 1944, 3 (*pedaled their bicycles*); *Times* (London), May 15, 1944, 2 (*"colt of the first class"*), 5, 8; Stafford, *Ten Days to D-Day*, 17; Brown, *Many a Watchful Night*, 78.

3 *"French sailors with their red pompoms"*: Calder, *The People's War*, 307.

3 *Savile Row tailors*: Taylor, *Swords and Plowshares*, 86; Capa, *Slightly Out of Focus*, 132 (*pocket flask*); Bradley, *A Soldier's Story*, 181 (*pumpkin hue*).

3 *Nowhere were the uniforms*: Forrest Pogue refers to American MPs as Snowballs. Pogue, *Pogue's War*, 15. More common was the British term, Snowdrop. Mollo, *The Armed Forces of World War II*, 235; "History of SHAEF, Feb. 13–June 6, 1944," July 1944, NARA RG 319, 2-3.7 CB 8, appendix 3 (*146 engraved invitations*); Middleton, *Our Share of Night*, 308 (*"big men"*); Naval Guns, 19 (*hard, narrow benches*); http://www.oldpauline lodge.org.uk/School.htm; http://www.stpaulsschool.org.uk/page.aspx?id=8362; http://www.archive.org/stream/historyofstpaul00uoft.

4 *Top secret charts and maps*: Kennedy, *The Business of War*, 328 (*blankets*); D'Este, *Decision in Normandy*, 82–83 (*frock coat*); "Presentation of OVERLORD Plans," May 15 1944, PP-pres, DDE Lib, series VI, box 1 (*King George VI*); D'Este, *Eisenhower: A Soldier's Life*, 500 (*Churchill bowed*).

4 *these big men*: IFG, 223 (*"Mediterraneanites"*); Chandler, 1901 (*"in my blood"*).

4 *The Anglo-Americans pounced*: see *AAAD* and *DOB*.

5 *Elsewhere in this global conflagration*: Weinberg, *A World at Arms*, 651, 656–57; Liddell Hart, *History of the Second World War*, 513, 520; Gilbert, *The Second World War*, 519, 615–17; Mansoor, *The GI Offensive in Europe*, 11 (*six Marine Corps divisions*).

5 *The collapse of Berlin's vast empire*: Charles V. P. von Lüttichau, "Germany's Strategic Situation," n.d., NARA RG 319, OCMH, R-93, box 15 (*German casualties*); Kimball, *Forged in War*, 257; *GS* V, 279 (*193 divisions*); *Germany VII*, 522 (*almost two thousand tanks*);

Webster and Frankland, *The Strategic Air Offensive Against Germany*, vol. 4, appendix 44, 456 (*seventy thousand tons*). No two estimates of German troop dispositions precisely agree.

5 *In 1941, when Britain*: Wilson, ed., *D-Day 1944*, 280; Maurice Matloff, "Wilmot Revisited," in *D-Day: The Normandy Invasion in Retrospect*, 114–15 ("*iron-mongering*").

6 *Cometh the hour*: D'Este, *Decision in Normandy*, 83; Bradley and Blair, *A General's Life*, 240–41; Eisenhower, *Eisenhower at War, 1943–1945*, 231–32; Powers, "The Battle of Normandy," *JMH* (July 1992): 455+ (*skid-proof socks*).

6 "*at peace with his soul*": Naval Guns, 19; *CCA*, 269 (*June 5*); Hamilton, *Master of the Battlefield*, 581 ("*I consider it*"); Miller, *Ike the Soldier*, 599–600 ("*I have no sympathy*").

6 *A wiry, elfin figure*: Eisenhower, *Eisenhower at War, 1943–1945*, 231–32 (*padded shoes*); Chalmers, *Full Cycle*, 187; D'Este, *Patton: A Genius for War*, 595 (*sharp rap*); Liebling, *Mollie & Other War Pieces*, 128 (*ruddy, truculent*); *PP*, 411–12 (*bespoke overcoat*); CBH, June 1 and 2, 1944, box 4; Allen, *Lucky Forward*, 23 ("*son-of-bitchery*"); GSP to Beatrice, Feb. 3, 1944, GSP, LOC MS Div, box 11, folder 15 ("*bad for the soul*").

7 *With a curt swish*: Hamilton, *Master of the Battlefield*, 577–78 (*salmon*); Moorehead, *Montgomery*, 36 ("*pointed flint*"); http://www.stpaulsschool.org.uk/page.aspx?id=8362; http://www.archive.org/stream/historyofstpaul00uoft; *The Pauline*, March 1946, 50–52; Montgomery, *A Field-Marshal in the Family*, 306–8 (*prayers in Latin*).

7 *Glancing at his notes*: "Address on 15 May 1944: Brief Presentation of Plans Before the King," IWM, PP/MCR, C46, Lt. Col. Christopher "Kit" Dawnay Collection, micro R-1.

7 *The Bay of the Seine*: "Strategy of the Campaign in Western Europe, 1944–1945," USFET General Board study no. 1, n.d., 6–8, 14; "The Planning and Tactical Background of the Invasion of the Continent of Europe," n.d., Numa A Watson Collection, MHI; *CCA*, 72–73 ("*strategically unsound*"); ALH, I-183; *WaS*, 15 ("*impudent reconnaissance*"); George E. Creasy, OH, Feb. 4, 1947, FCP, MHI; Mason, ed., *The Atlantic War Remembered*, 345; www.msubmus.co.uk.

8 *Upon returning from Italy*: GS V, 283; *CCA*, 165; *LSA*, vol. 1, 185 (*230 additional support ships*); *WaS*, 8.

8 *As he unfolded his plan*: Moorehead, *Montgomery*, 192–93; James, *The Counterfeit General Montgomery*, 53; Howarth, ed., *Monty at Close Quarters*, 62, 66 ("*essentially didactic*"); Hamilton, *Master of the Battlefield*, 591 (*two thousand clerks*).

8 *Montgomery pressed ahead*: Hinsley, 439–40, 459–60; "Address on 15 May 1944: Brief Presentation of Plans Before the King," IWM, PP/MCR, C46, Lt. Col. Christopher "Kit" Dawnay Collection, micro R-1 ("*Last February*"). The German high command in the west at the time of the invasion had forty-eight infantry and ten panzer divisions. Ludewig, *Rückzug*, 31–42.

9 *Some officers in SHAEF*: ALH, I-201; *WaS*, 13 (*one and one-third divisions*).

9 *Montgomery envisioned*: Cirillo, "The Allied High Command," lecture to British Army Doctrine and Development Directorate, n.d., a.p.; Crosswell, *Beetle*, 607, 633; *CCA*, 188; GS V, 284 (*Paris*).

9 *Precisely how that titanic*: ALH, II-73–87.

11 *But that lay*: "History of COSSAC," May 1944, file #95, NARA RG 498, ETO HD, 7; *CCA*, 10 ("*ugly piece of water*"); Smith, *The English Channel*, 12; Room, *Placenames of the World*, 6; www.jpmaps.co.uk/map/id.22553; http://en.wikipedia.org/wiki/English_Channel; Benjamin A. Dickson, "G-2 Journal: Algiers to the Elbe," MHI, 104 ("*already assaulted*"); memo, Aug. 21, 1942, NARA RG 165, E 421, JPS studies, box 603 (*tunneling*).

11 "*Nothing must stop them*": "Address on 15 May 1944: Brief Presentation of Plans Before the King," IWM, PP/MCR, C46, Lt. Col. Christopher "Kit" Dawnay Collection, micro R-1; Ismay, *The Memoirs of General Lord Ismay*, 351.

11 *None departed*: "Instructions for Visitors," SHAEF, May 4, 1944, NARA RG 331; *PP*, 456 (*tumbler of whiskey*); memo, W. H. S. Wright to Henry Stimson, July 25, 1944, NARA

RG 337, E 54, AGF top secret general corr, folder 319.1 ("*biding his time*"); GSP to Bea, Apr. 9, 1944, GSP, LOC MS Div, box 11, folder 16.

11 *At 2:30:* D'Este, *Warlord,* 665 ("*Risks must be taken*"); D'Este, *Decision in Normandy,* 87–88 ("*I am hardening*"); Thompson, *The Imperial War Museum Book of Victory in Europe,* 2 (*most prodigious undertaking*).

12 *Shortly after six P.M.:* Thomas W. Mattingly and Olive F. G. Marsh, "A Compilation of the General Health Status of Dwight D. Eisenhower," Mattingly Collection, DDE Lib, n.d., box 1, 53; *Three Years,* 550 (*ringing*), 538–39 ("*The strain is telling*").

12 *As the drear suburbs:* Eisenhower in 1946 described Churchill's statement as "shocking." OH, DDE, June 3, 1946, SLAM, A. S. Nevins Papers, MHI. Churchill had used the phrase to George Marshall three months earlier. Reynolds, *In Command of History,* 395.

12 *"You will enter":* "History of SHAEF, Feb. 13–June 6, 1944," July 1944, NARA RG 319, 2-3.7 CB 8, 14–17. Technically, the naval portion of the invasion was code-named NEPTUNE; for simplicity, OVERLORD—code for the overall invasion plan—has been used for all facets of the operation. Ambrose, *The Supreme Commander,* 338 ("*feet in the stirrups*").

12 *For years he had pondered:* Wilson, ed., *D-Day 1944,* 314–15, 324–25.

13 *Planners had even coined:* Gilbert, *D-Day,* 28–29 (*PINWE*); Chandler, 1869 ("*Film Planning Commission*"); memos, SHAEF, Apr. 4 and 23, 1944, NARA RG 331, E 6, box 9, "leave and furlough," 210.7-12 (*CIRCON*); *Three Years,* 526 ("*fog dispeller*"); Blair, *Ridgway's Paratroopers,* 200 (*gliders*).

13 *For every PINWE item:* Richard Collins, SOOHP, 1976, Donald Bowman, MHI, II, 14–15 ("*what parts would burn*"); memos, Apr. 27, May 12, 26, 27, 1944, NARA RG 331, E 1, "Liquidation of German Personalities," box 1.

13 *As the invasion drew nearer:* John W. Castles, Jr., memoir, ts, n.d., USMA Arch (*biological warfare* and *Geiger counters*); Chandler, 1860 ("*radioactive poisons*"); Groves, *Now It Can Be Told,* 199–202 ("*unknown etiology*").

14 *Perhaps less far-fetched:* memo, "Gas Intelligence," Maj. Gen. P. G. Whitefoord [sic], Jan. 20, 1944, NARA RG 331, E 27, SHAEF, box 83; *DOB,* 272; Kleber and Birdsell, *The Chemical Warfare Service,* 5, 655 (*two dozen kinds of gas*).

14 *Fifteen hundred British civilians:* "Historical Report of G-1 Section," June 19, 1944, XIX District, NARA RG 407, E 427, pre-invasion planning file 100, box 19231; Brig. Gen. Alden H. Waitt, "Summary Report of Situation in ETO," July 5, 1945, NARA RG 337, AGF OR, box 2 (*160,000 tons*); "Chemical Warfare Plan," June 2, 1944, NARA RG 334, E 315, ANSCOL, box 89 (*secret SHAEF plan*).

14 *"Everybody gets more":* Miller, *Ike the Soldier,* 588.

14 *Thirty minutes after leaving:* Williams, "Supreme Headquarters for D-Day," *AB,* no. 84 (1994): 1+; "Chief Engineer's Report on Camouflage Activities in the ETO," Nov. 15, 1945, Howard V. Canan Papers, HIA, box 3 (*garnished nets*).

14 *Here hundreds of staff officers: Three Years,* 531 ("*oldish*"); Eisenhower, *Eisenhower at War, 1943–1945,* 157 (*double socks*); Raymond H. Croll, ts, 1974, MHI, 240–55 (*language classes*).

15 *Eisenhower's office:* Summersby, *Eisenhower Was My Boss,* 129–32; Davis, *Soldier of Democracy,* 466; D'Este, *Eisenhower: A Soldier's Life,* 490 (*golf ball*).

15 *Vernal twilight lingered:* Eisenhower, *Eisenhower at War, 1943–1945,* 197; Eisenhower, *Strictly Personal,* 57 (*bomb shelter*); Chandler, 1852; Summersby, *Eisenhower Was My Boss,* 138, 162 ("*Bad Woman*"); Larrabee, *Commander in Chief,* 448 ("*don't have to think*").

15 *"A man must develop":* Miller, *Ike the Soldier,* 598; Eisenhower, *Eisenhower at War, 1943–1945,* 213 (*last troop reserves*); "Notes on the Planning of Operation Overlord," 21st AG, n.d., UK NA, WO 216/139, 29–30 (*Double Intense*); "Casualties and Effects of Fire Support on the British Beaches in Normandy," Army Operational Research Group, Report No. 261, n.d., UK NA, CAB 106/967 (*above 40 percent*).

15 *Love's Tables:* "A Moving Army," SOS, ts, n.d., NARA RG 498, UD 602, ETO HD; Cosmas and Cowdrey, *Medical Service in the European Theater of Operations,* 202 (*12 percent*);

"The United States Navy Medical Department at War, 1941–1945," vol. 1, part 3, Bureau of Medicine and Surgery, 1946, 719; Field Order No. 35, 1st ID, Apr. 16, 1944, NARA RG 407, E 427, 301-3.9 (*gas warfare*); Naval Guns, 21 ("*one-third to one-half*"); "Report of Operations," 12th AG, vol. 2, G-1 section, n.d., CARL (*combat drownings*); Casualty Division History, n.d., NARA RG 498, ETO HD, admin file #4 (*punch cards*).

16 *Recent exercises and rehearsals*: Thompson, *The Imperial War Museum Book of Victory in Europe*, 9 ("*hopping about*"); Waugh, *Men at Arms*, 140; "Comments on Exercise TIGER," NARA RG 407, E 427, FUSA, n.d., file 455 (*DUCK, OTTER*); Yung, *Gators of Neptune*, 160 ("*got confused*"); "Rough Draft of Gen. Maxwell Taylor's Report," with jumpmaster reports, 101st AB Div, July 1, 1944, GCM Lib.

16 *The imaginary biffing turned*: Lewis, *Exercise Tiger*, 20; Bradbeer, *The Land Changed Its Face*, 37–47; "A History of the United States Naval Bases in the United Kingdom," 1944, NARA RG 498, HD, admin file #217; Fergusson, *The Watery Maze*, 324. All in ET: "Report of Enemy Navy Action," Apr. 30, 1944, HQ, Sub Area V; "Exercise Tiger News Letter," Jan. 1996; Arthur D. Clamp, "The American Assault Exercises at Slapton Sands, Devon, in 1944," n.d., AR, Twelfth Fleet, May 3, 1944, including reports from *LST-511, LST-496, LST-58, LST-499, LST-289, LST-531, LST-507*, Task Force 125, *H.M.S. Saladin*; German E-boat logs; also, corr and transcripts. Also, "Notes on Utah Beach and the 1st Engineer Special Brigade," n.d., NARA RG 498, ETO HD, admin file #359a.

16 *Survivors on rafts*: Lewis, *Exercise Tiger*, 104; L. R. Talbot, "Graves Registration in the European Theater of Operations," 1955, chap. 26, PIR, MHI, II, 2–3 (*embalmers*); Joseph R. Darnall, "Powdered Eggs and Purple Hearts," ts, 1946, MHUC, MHI, box 24, 90–91.

17 *Drowned men continued to wash ashore*: The precise death toll remains uncertain. CCA, 270; John Connell, "Over Age in Grade," ts, n.d., MHI; Ingersoll, *Top Secret*, 103–5; Hoyt, *The Invasion Before Normandy*, 155–61; MacDonald, "Slapton Sands: The 'Cover-Up' That Never Was," *Army* 38, no. 6 (June 1988): 64+ (*remained secret*).

17 *Eisenhower grieved*: CCA, 270 (*LSTs*); DDE to GCM, Apr. 29, 1944, GCM Lib, corr, box 67, folder 5.

17 "*the man who can do the average thing*": Eisenhower, *General Ike*, 219; *AAAD*, 286 (*expected to be relieved*); Chandler, 1898 (*Hollywood*); D'Este, *Eisenhower: A Soldier's Life*, 511 ("*generous and lovable*"); Chalmers, *Full Cycle*, 261 ("*a very great man*"); *DOB*, 310 ("*best politician*").

17 "*When it comes to war*": D'Este, *Decision in Normandy*, 50n; Danchev, 546 ("*No real director*"); Ferrell, ed., *The Eisenhower Diaries*, 111 ("*They dislike to believe*").

18 *He needed sleep*: Chandler, 1865, 1891, and vol. 5, chronology, 153; Williams, "Supreme Headquarters for D-Day," *AB*, no. 84 (1994): 1+; "The U.S. Army Special Train *Alive*," n.d., NARA RG 498, ETO HD, admin file #16 (*Monsters*); Ambrose, *Eisenhower: Soldier, General of the Army, President-Elect, 1890–1952*, vol. 1, 294 ("*the human soul*").

18 *By the tens of thousands*: LSA, vol. 2, 231; Ross, 289 (*four thousand in early 1942*); Coakley, 370 (*twenty now could be found*); "An Army in Transit," n.d., NARA RG 498, ETO HD, admin file #241, 7–37 (*more than 100,000*).

18 *Down the gangplanks*: Robert W. Coakley, "The Administrative and Logistical History of the ETO," 1946, CMH, 8-3.1 AA2, vol. 3, 102–8; "Blankets," n.d., NARA RG 498, ETO HD, admin file #500; Amy, lecture, Apr. 8, 1944, NY Port of Embarkation, HIA, Henry J. Amy papers, box 2 (*pillowcases*).

19 "*You are something*": Randall Jarrell, "The Sick Nought," 1914; Karl Cocke, "U.S. Army Replacement Policies, WWII, Korea, and Vietnam," DA, 1990, MHI, chart (*eleven thousand*); Kennedy, *Freedom from Fear*, 710 (*average GI was twenty-six*); Crosswell, *Beetle*, 789 (*teenagers*); "Activities and Organization of COMZ," May 28, 1945, NARA RG 498, ETO HD, admin file #89, 57 (*grade school education*); "Army Life," WD pamphlet 21-13, Aug. 10, 1944, NARA RG 407, AGO Cent File 1940–45, box 3638 (*$50 a month*).

19 *The typical soldier*: Wiltse, ed., *Physical Standards in World War II*, 19–29, 37–42, 163, 193–94.

20 *But what of their souls?*: Cawthon, "Pursuit: Normandy, 1944," *American Heritage* (Feb. 1978): 80+ (*"amateurs"*); "Memorandum," May 1944, NARA RG 330, E 94, Surveys of Attitudes of Soldiers, ETO, B-46 (*April survey*); corr, Charles L. Easter to Marion Page, Aug. 14, 1944, USMA Arch (*"civilian at heart"*).

20 *Skepticism and irony*: Reynolds, *Rich Relations*, 324 (*"Sums up my attitude"*); Rottman, *FUBAR: American Soldier Slang of World War II*, 98, 152; Dickson, *War Slang*, 208; Richler, ed., *Writers on World War II*, 487 (*"ambiguous farce"*); Cawthon, *Other Clay*, 147 (*"If it's not ironic"*); Yardley, "The Fight of Their Lives, and Not Just on the Battle-field," *WP*, Mar. 6, 2009, C1 (*"corrupt, inefficient"*); Scannell, *Argument of Kings*, 122 (*"madness"*).

20 *"War is all foreground"*: *Reporting World War II*, vol. 1, xxi; Simpson, *Selected Prose*, 120–21; Reynolds, *Rich Relations*, 400 (*"quarrelsome continent"*); Schrijvers, *The Crash of Ruin*, 258 (*recent Army survey*).

21 *Certainly they believed*: Scannell, *Argument of Kings*, 112, 121 (*"drab khaki world"*); Steidl, *Lost Battalions*, 31 (*"unseen powers of God"*).

21 *And so four by four*: "The Role Played by Communications Zone in the War Against Germany," n.d., NARA RG 498, ETO HD, admin file #479 (*1,200 camps*); *VW*, vol. 1, 34 (*133 airfields*); Eustis, *War Letters of Morton Eustis to His Mother*, 190 (*"Thomas Hardy"*); Sevareid, *Not So Wild a Dream*, 482 (*"old steady manner"*); Bernard Paget, OH, FCP, Feb. 18, 1947, MHI (*Home Guard*); "A Yank in Britain," ts, n.d., Thor M. Smith Papers, MHI, 75 (*road signs*).

21 *Nearly 400,000 prefabricated huts*: Botting, *The Second Front*, 66; "Construction in the United Kingdom," Oct. 1944, NARA RG 498, ETO HD, admin file #506 (*20 million square feet*); *LSA*, vol. 1, 255 (*"Spamland"*); "Marshalling [*sic*] for OVERLORD," Dec. 1945, NARA RG 498, ETO HD, admin file #547, 14 (*School of Hygiene*); Amy, lecture, Apr. 8, 1944, NY Port of Embarkation, HIA, Henry J. Amy papers, box 2; Robert W. Coakley, "The Administrative and Logistical History of the ETO," 1946, CMH, 8-3.1 AA2, vol. 2, 189 (*GLUE*); H. H. Dunham, "U.S. Army Transportation in the ETO," 1946, CMH 4-13.1 AA 29, 160–61 (*"exposure to weather"*); "A Yank in Britain," ts, n.d., Thor M. Smith papers, MHI, 32 (*red tape*).

22 *No alliance in the war*: "Britain," n.d., NARA RG 498, ETO HD, admin file #23 (*"Red-coats"*); Hastings, *OVERLORD*, 49; Wieviorka, *Normandy*, 111 (*twice a month*); Reynolds, *Rich Relations*, 298 (*Goatland*); Ross, 313 (*shoe sizes*); *A Short Guide to Great Britain*, 29; "Quartermaster Procurement in the United Kingdom, 1942–1944," n.d., NARA RG 498, ETO HD, admin file #154 (*tent pegs*); Thomas V. Barber, "Quartermaster Procurement," n.d., chap 41, PIR, MHI, 4–5 (*beer*).

22 *The British displayed forbearance*: Mass Observation Archive, University of Sussex Library, MO, FR 2454, provided author by Prof. Donald L. Miller (*"irritate me"*); *Meet the Americans*, 1; Margaret Mead, "Army Talks: The Yank in Britain," Mar. 15, 1944, NARA RG 498, ETO HD, admin file #23; Reynolds, *Rich Relations*, ix (*Orwell*).

22 *Occasional bad beheavior*: Schrijvers, *The Crash of Ruin*, 159 (*royal swans*); Francis L. Sampson, *Look Out Below!*, 1958, in CJR, box 97, folder 21 (*grenades*); Kennedy, *Free-dom from Fear*, 709 (*haystacks*); "Army Life," WD, pamphlet 21-13, Aug. 10, 1944, NARA RG 407, AGO Cent File 1940–45, box 3638 (*"men who refrain"*); "Legal Ques-tions Arising in the Theater of Operations," NARA RG 407, E 427, AG WWII Opera-tions Reports, no. 87, 31–32 (*"bastardy proceedings"*); Longmate, *The G.I.'s*, 285 (*"drive carefully"*).

23 *Both on the battlefield and in the rear*: Lewis, *Exercise Tiger*, 48 (*"delicate hothouse"*); Hastings, *OVERLORD*, 293 (*"the chaps that mattered"*).

23 *The loading of invasion vessels*: Bykofsky and Larson, *The Transportation Corps: Opera-tions Overseas*, 259; ONB, OH, 1975, Charles Hanson, MHI, IV-19 (*Seven thousand kinds of combat necessities*). This oral history with Bradley, conducted in fourteen ses-sions over ten months, had been closed to the public until made available to the author in January 2010.

23 *evocative of the Marx Brothers*: Van Creveld, *Supplying War*, 210; William E. Depuy, SOOHP, 1979; Romie L. Brownlee and William J. Mullen III, MHI, 18 (*Selfridges*); Marshall, ed., *Proud Americans*, 138.

23 *In twenty-two British ports*: Gilbert, *D-Day*, 108; H. H. Dunham, "U.S. Army Transportation in the ETO," 1946, CMH, 4-13.1 AA 29, 120–23 (*301,000 vehicles*); "Ordnance Diary," Dec. 1, 1945, NARA RG 498, ETOUSA HD, UD 602, box 1 (*2,700 artillery pieces*); "Historical Report, Office of the Chief Signal Officers," vol. 1, Jan. 1945, NARA RG 498, ETOUSA HD, UD 602, box 1 (*telephone poles*); Waddell, *United States Army Logistics*, 41 (*7 million tons*); Frank A. Osmanski, "Critical Analysis of the Planning and Execution of the Logistic Support of the Normandy Invasion," Dec. 1949, Armed Forces Staff College, MHI, 99 (*41.298 pounds*); *LSA*, vol. 1, 441 (*500-ton bales*); "Ports: How an Army Is Supplied," Oct. 1944, NARA RG 498, ETO HD, admin file #521, 1-3 (*war flats*); "The Reminiscences of Alan Goodrich Kirk," 1962, John Mason, Col U OHRO, 302 (*ferries*); Capa, *Slightly Out of Focus*, 136.

23 *Armed guards from ten cartography depots*: "Supply and Maintenance on the European Continent," NARA RG 407, E 427, AG WWII Operations Reports, 97-USF5-0.3, #130, 26; Beck, 565 (*210 million maps*); IFG, 68 (*charts*); Wieviorka, *Normandy*, 178 (*aerial photos*); "Reconnaissance in a Tactical Air Command," 10th Photo Group, Ninth AF, 1945, CARL, N-9395, 3–4; Allen, "Untold Stories of D-Day," *National Geographic* (June 2002): 2+ (*watercolors*); Coles and Weinberg, *Civil Affairs*, 864–65 ("*restraint and discipline*"); Bradley, *A Soldier's Story*, 224 (*Gone with the Wind*); Field Order No. 35, 1st ID, Apr. 16, 1944, NARA RG 407, E 427, 301-3.9 (*Field Order No. 35*); memo, XXX Corps, May 18, 1944, NARA RG 407, ML #753, box 19123 (*Pink List*).

24 *Day after night after day*: Leppert, "Communication Plans and Lessons, Europe and Africa," lecture, Oct. 30, 1944, NARA RG 334, E 315, ANSCOL, box 199, L-7-44, 14 (*radio crystals*); Field Order No. 35, 1st ID, Apr. 16, 1944, NARA RG 407, E 427, 301-3.9; Perret, *There's a War to Be Won*, 475 ("*marksmanship medal*"); Beck, 308 ("*Hagensen packs*"); "The Administrative History of the Operations of the 21 Army Group," Nov. 1945, NARA RG 334, E 315, ANSCOL, box 458, GB 21-AG AH, 29 (*metal crosses*); Ross, 683 (*mattress covers*).

24 *Four hospital ships made ready*: Martha Gellhorn, "The First Hospital Ship," in *Reporting World War II*, vol. 2, 151; Dowling, lecture, Feb. 28, 1945, NARA RG 334, E 315, ANSCOL, box 207; Cosmas and Cowdrey, *Medical Service in the European Theater of Operations*, 167, 245 ("*dirty trap*"); Frank Davis, OH, Nov. 24, 1944, 68th General Hospital, NARA RG 112, E 302, interview #109 (*steam tables*); Ambrose, *The Supreme Commander*, 413; MacKensie, *Men Without Guns*, 97; Nalty, *Strength for the Fight*, 181 (*black and white donors*); Robert R. Kelley, OH, Jan. 27, 1945, Office of the Chief Surgeon, NARA RG 112, E 302, interview #130; Paul R. Hawley, OH, John Boyd Coates, Jr., et al., 1962, MHUC, 56 (*pallets*).

24 *A new Manual of Therapy*: memo, Office of the Chief Surgeon, Mar. 28, 1944, James B. Mason papers, HIA, folder 1 (*morphine poisoning* and *whole blood*); Cosmas and Cowdrey, *Medical Service in the European Theater of Operations*, 182; Paul R. Hawley, OH, John Boyd Coates, Jr., et al., 1962, MHUC, 54 (*carbon dioxide tanks*).

25 *But whole blood would keep*: Cowdrey, *Fighting for Life*, 245; "The Evolution of the Use of Whole Blood in Combat Casualties," U.S. Army Medical Department, Office of Medical History, http://143.84.107.69/booksdocs/wwii/blood/chapter3.htm; Cosmas and Cowdrey, *Medical Service in the European Theater of Operations*, 175–76, 193; Gellhorn, "The First Hospital Ship," in *Reporting World War II*, vol. 2, 151.

25 *On Tuesday, May 23*: "Stories of Transportation," vol. 1, Frank S. Ross Papers, HIA, box 20, 203; memo, W. H. S. Wright to Henry Stimson, July 25, 1944, NARA RG 337, E 54, AGF top secret general corr, folder 319.1 ("*One Way*"); A. C. Doyle's *Sir Nigel*, chapter 13, in Wilson, ed., *D-Day 1944*, 197 ("*We sat on a hilltop*").

25 *Mothers held their children*: Watney, *The Enemy Within*, 20, 49 ("*boomerang*" and "*girl-saint*"); Ziegler, *London at War, 1939–1945*, 278–79 ("*half empty*"); Fussell, *Wartime*, 109 (*Whore's Lament*).

25 *By late in the week*: Moorehead, *Eclipse*, 100 (*"Civilians must not talk"*); Burgett, *Curra-hee!*, 69–70 (*German uniforms*); Watney, *The Enemy Within*, 63 (*Cherbourg*); Scannell, *Argument of Kings*, 121 (*diversionary attack*); Ziegler, *London at War, 1939–1945*, 282 (*death beam*); *AAFinWWII*, 92 (*icebergs*); Wilson, ed., *D-Day 1944*, 198 (*"shock kept the wounded"*); Longmate, *The G.I.'s*, 316 (*"Don't be surprised"*).

26 *Security remained paramount*: Hinsley and Simkins, *British Intelligence in the Second World* War, vol. 4, 250–54 (*"certain defeat"* and *600,000 monthly visitors*); Stafford, *Ten Days to D-Day*, 15 (*"handsome"*); "History of SHAEF, Feb. 13–June 6, 1944," July 1944, NARA RG 319, 2-3.7 CB 8, 14–19; Gilbert, *D-Day*, 67; CCA, 270 (*counterintelligence agents*).

26 *Camouflage inspectors roamed*: "Chief Engineer's Report on Camouflage Activities in the ETO," Nov. 15, 1945, Howard V. Canan papers, HIA, box 3; "Concealment and Display of Camps," Plan FORTITUDE, section II, "Implementation," n.d., Thaddeus Holt papers, MHI, box 8 (*Garnished nets*); "Camouflage," historical report #18, Aug. 1945, CEOX, box X-32, folder 18, 38 (*"tone-down paint"*); "The Concealment Aspect of Beach Group Work," Camouflage Development and Training Center, Farnham, U.K., Sept. 22, 1944, CARL, N-5122, 4–5 (*Standard Camouflage Color 1A*); "Marshalling [sic] for OVERLORD," CE, Dec. 1945, NARA RG 498, ETO HD, admin file #547, 28 (*"contours"*).

26 *Deception complemented the camouflage*: "History of SHAEF, Feb. 13–June 6, 1944," July 1944, NARA RG 319, 2-3.7 CB 8, chapter 3 (*"strategic dispositions"*); Howard, *Strategic Deception in the Second World War*, 110–11 (*Pas de Calais*); http://webarchive .nationalarchives.gov.uk/+/http://www.mod.uk/aboutus/dday60/fortitude.htm (*"Big-bobs"*).

26 *The British genius for cozenage*: Hinsley and Simkins, *British Intelligence in the Second World* War, vol. 4, 239; Penrose, ed., *The D-Day Companion*, 58–59; Hesketh, *Fortitude*, xi–xiii, 46–52; Howard, *Strategic Deception in the Second World War*, 114, 131 (*German hallucination*); Hinsley, 118–19, 450; Holt, *The Deceivers*, 561–62; James, *The Counterfeit General Montgomery*, 53–66 (*strutted about*).

27 *As May slid toward June*: LSA, vol. 1, 369 (*waterproofing*); Beck, 317 (*fifty-four inches*); Thompson, *The Imperial War Museum Book of Victory in Europe*, 10 (*"wren's tail"*); *VW*, vol. 1, 137 (*Sherman tank*); Gilbert, *D-Day*, 104 (*white stripes*); Howarth, *Dawn of D-Day*, 126; Drez, ed., *Voices of D-Day*, 64 (*push brooms*).

27 *Soldiers drew seasickness pills*: Royce L. Thompson, "D-Day Personal Loads," OCMH, Dec. 4, 1951, CMH 2-3.7 AE P-11; Cawthon, *Other Clay*, 42 (*"braying"*); memo, Cleave A. Jones to G. S. Eyster, SHAEF, July 17, 1944, NARA RG 498, UD 603, ETO HD, SLAM 201 file, box 1 (*"skunk suits"*).

27 *"We're ready now"*: TR to Eleanor, May 30, 1944, TR, box 10; Ross, 695 (*quartermaster box*).

28 *"I am a free man"*: John M. Thorpe, "A Soldier's Tale, to Normandy and Beyond," Nov. 1982, IWM, 84/50/1, 80; Airborne Museum, Ste-Mère-Église, V-mail shown to author by curator Phil Jutras, May 1994 (*"If I don't come out"*); corr, May 30, 1944, Joseph T. Dawson collection, MRC FDM, 1991.65, box 3 (*"destiny of life"*).

28 *Eisenhower left Bushy Park*: Chandler, vol. 5, 155; corr, T. Smith to family, June 17, 1944, Thor M. Smith Papers, HIA; Williams, "Supreme Headquarters for D-Day," *AB*, no. 84 (1994): 1+; Stafford, *Ten Days to D-Day*, 178 (*three telephones*); "Normandy, 1944–1973," *AB*, no. 1 (1973): 2 (*Georgian mansion*); Kingston McCloughry, *Direction of War*, 138 (*nautical almanacs*).

28 *"The intensity of the burdens"*: Overy, *Why the Allies Won*, 158; *Three Years*, 558 (*"jitters"*); Richard Collins, SOOHP, 1976, Donald Bowman, MHI, II, 16; R. H. Winecke, CI, NARA RG 407, E 427-A, folder 170; E. T. Williams, "Reports Received by U.S. War Department on Use of Ultra in the European Theater," SRH-037, Oct. 1945, NARA RG 457, E 9002, NSA, box 18, 2; memo, H. R. Bull to W. B. Smith, May 26, 1944, NARA RG 331, E 1, SHAEF SGS, box 76.

28 *Such a robust force*: diary, Oct. 14, 1944, N. T. Tangye, IWM, P 180 (*"nincompoop"*);

Blumenson, *The Battle of the Generals*, 141 (*"peculiar knack"*); CCA, 186 (*"speculative operation"*); Ambrose, *Eisenhower: Soldier, General of the Army, President-Elect, 1890–1952*, vol. 1, 303 (*"futile slaughter"*); VW, vol. 1, 139 (*"two airborne divisions"*).

29 *"soul-racking problem"*: Eisenhower, *Crusade in Europe*, 263; CCA, 279.

29 *Emerging from his canvas hideaway*: Ambrose, *Eisenhower: Soldier, General of the Army, President-Elect, 1890–1952*, vol. 1, 303; Chandler, 1894 (*"It must go on"*).

29 *A leafy hilltop*: VW, vol. 1, 67–69; IFG, 77; CBH, June 3, 1944, box 4, MHI (*Late spring warmth*); memo, W. H. S. Wright to Henry Stimson, July 25, 1944, NARA RG 337, E 54, AGF top secret general corr, folder 319.1 (*barrage balloons*).

30 *Soldiers still braying and bleating*: Cawthon, *Other Clay*, 48; Pogue, *Pogue's War*, 55 (*"If any of you fellows"*); E. Jones, ts, n.d., IWM, 94/41/1, 4 (*"real white bread"*); Balkoski, *Utah Beach*, 66–67; memoir, Ralph Eastridge, 1995, NWWIIM (*"a man could have jumped"*); D. K. Reimers, "My War," June 4, 1944, MHI, 67 (*"which was Clara"*).

30 *As always where land met sea*: Pogue, *Pogue's War*, 47; ETOUSA pamphlet 370.5, Jan. 1944, Charles E. Rousek papers, MHI (*"Preparation for Overseas Movement"*); "War Diary of Force 'U,'" June 2, 1944, SEM, NHHC, box 82, folder 46 (*Eighteen LCTs*); Lewis, "Landing Craft," lecture, Sept. 18, 1944, NARA RG 334, E 315, ANSCOL, box 199, 9 (*immersion rate*); AR, Don P. Moon, Force U, June 26, 1944, NARA RG 498, ETO HD, admin file #217 (*ships were overloaded anyway*).

30 *The deadweight included*: "History of SHAEF, Feb. 13–June 6, 1944," July 1944, NARA RG 319, 2-3.7 CB 8, chapter 3; Wilson, ed., *D-Day 1944*, 204 (*"annoying and mysterious"*); Pogue, *Pogue's War*, 92 (*"sparse and gray of hair"*); Tobin, *Ernie Pyle's War*, 205 (*"scarecrow"*), 164–67 (*"All I do is drink"*).

31 *"I'm no longer content"*: Miller, *The Story of Ernie Pyle*, 321–30; Tobin, *Ernie Pyle's War*, 221 (*"fucking throat"*), 168 (*"too late"*).

31 *In claustrophobic holds*: Harold S. Frum, "The Soldier Must Write," 1984, June 1, 1944 entry, GCM Lib (*"I love my fellow man"*); Liebling, *Mollie & Other War Pieces*, 177; Brown, *Many a Watchful Night*, 10 (*On* Augusta); Marshall, ed., *Proud Americans*, 138 (*"old uneasiness"*).

31 *More than five hundred weather stations*: R. J. Ogden, "Meteorological Services Leading to D-Day," Royal Meteorological Society, Occasional Papers on Meteorological History, July 2001, 2, a.p.; Stagg, *Forecast for Overlord*, 51 (*reconnaissance planes*); Charles C. Bates, "Sea, Swell and Surf Forecasting for D-Day and Beyond: The Anglo-American Effort, 1943–1945," 2010, a.p., 6 (*British beach watchers*); Charles C. Bates, e-mail to author, Nov. 11 and 23, 2007; Hogben, "The Most Important Weather Forecast in the World," *London Review of Books* 16, no. 10 (May 26, 1994): 21+.

31 *Each Allied invasion constituent*: J. M. Stagg, "Report on the Meteorological Implications," SHAEF, June 22, 1944, CARL, N-11359.

32 *Eisenhower had never been fortunate*: Chandler, 1761; Eisenhower, *Eisenhower at War, 1943–1945*, 248; Charles C. Bates, "Sea, Swell and Surf Forecasting for D-Day and Beyond: The Anglo-American Effort, 1943–1945," 2010, a.p., 13–15 (*Cyclonic disturbances*); diary, Kay Summersby, DDE Lib, PP-pres, box 140 (*"very depressed"*).

32 *At 4:30 A.M. on Sunday*: Ryan, *The Longest Day*, 48; Botting, *The Second Front*, 62; "Memorandum of Record," June 4, 1944, Arthur S. Nevins papers, MHI.

32 *"A series of depressions"*: "Report on the Meteorological Implications," June 22, 1944, UK NA, CAB 106/976, 9–11; Stagg, *Forecast for Overlord*, 124 (*depression L5*); Bates and Fuller, *America's Weather Warriors, 1814–1985*, 92–94 (*"quite impossible"*).

32 *Eisenhower polled his lieutenants*: Kingston McCloughry, *Direction of War*, 138–39 (*"No part"*); Stagg, *Forecast for Overlord*, 102 (*"we must postpone"*).

32 *At that moment the lights failed*: Kingston McCloughry, *Direction of War*, 138–39 (*"Jesus!"*); *Three Years*, 560 (*Sunday papers*).

33 *Banks of gray cloud*: J. H. Patterson, ts, n.d., IWM, 05/491, 1/7, 3 (*"spindrift was flying"*); IFG, 80–81 (*"pyramidical waters"*); Bradley, *A Soldier's Story*, 257 (HORNPIPE BOWSPRIT);

memo, W. H. S. Wright to Henry Stimson, July 25, 1944, NARA RG 337, E 54, AGF top secret general corr, folder 319.1 (*frantic blinkering*).

33 *But bombardment squadrons from Belfast*: Naval Guns, 26; S. C. Donnison, diary, June 3, 1944, IWM, 94/50/1 (*"three-quarter gale"*); History of the Second World War (periodical), part 65, 1974, 1796; "The Invasion of Normandy," USNAd, vol. 5, 395–96; Yung, *Gators of Neptune*, 176; "Memorandum of Record," June 4, 1944, Arthur S. Nevins papers, MHI (*"somewhat out of hand"*).

33 *As anchors dropped and engines died*: Rick Atkinson, foreword, *Instructions for American Servicemen in France During World War II*, Chicago: University of Chicago Press, 2008, v–xiii; Collier, *Fighting Words*, 159 ("Encore une verre"); *Medicine Under Canvas*, 77th Evacuation Hospital, 1949, 120 ("mama-oiselle"); Collins, *Lightning Joe*, 196–97 (*"Holy God"*); Liebling, *Mollie & Other War Pieces*, 175 (*"If God be for us"*); Linderman, *The World Within War*, 238 (*"twenty dollars a card"*); A. J. Liebling, "Cross-Channel Trip," in *Reporting World War II*, vol. 2, 136 (*"Voltaire used the same gag"*); Ambrose, *Pegasus Bridge*, 67 (Stormy Weather).

34 *the "D" in D-Day*: AAR, 146th Engineer Combat Bn, CEOH, box X-37A. There are various explanations for the term; some authorities assert it was first used in an Army order in 1918, with the "D" used as a code letter rather than an abbreviation.

34 *The strange, tempestuous Sunday*: Kersaudy, *Churchill and De Gaulle*, 338–47.

34 *The sad story was this*: Eden, *The Reckoning*, 525–26 (*greeted De Gaulle on the tracks*); "History of SHAEF, Feb. 13–June 6, 1944," July 1944, NARA RG 319, 2-3.7 CB 8, 55–57; "The War of Will, Words and Images," n.d., Wallace Carroll papers, LOC MS Div, box 1, 18–19; Kersaudy, *Churchill and De Gaulle*, 346–47 (*"in chains if necessary"*); Fenby, *The General*, 638–39; Beevor, *D-Day*, 21 (*"gangster"*).

34 *No sooner had Churchill stormed*: Eisenhower, *General Ike*, 147 (*Deux Mètres*); Dallek, *Franklin D. Roosevelt and American Foreign Policy, 1932–1945*, 462 (*"balancing a chip"*); "Memorandum of Record," June 4, 1944, Arthur S. Nevins papers, MHI (*he revealed to De Gaulle*); Aron, *France Reborn*, 27 (*"your forged notes"*); Fenby, *The General*, 638–39; Coles and Weinberg, *Civil Affairs*, 699 (*"violation of national sovereignty"*); "History of SHAEF, Feb. 13–June 6, 1944," July 1944, NARA RG 319, 2-3.7 CB 8, 55–57 (*French liaison officers*); "Preparations for D-Day," n.d., C. D. Jackson papers, DDE Lib, box 3; De Gaulle, *The Complete War Memoirs of Charles de Gaulle*, 559; Chandler, 1907; Davis, *Soldier of Democracy*, 494 (*"I cannot follow Eisenhower"*).

35 *"there is no room in war for pique"*: Foot, *SOE in France*, 386; Beevor, *D-Day*, 21 (*"treason"*); Fenby, *The General*, 641–42; memo, John J. McCoy to GCM, Apr. 26, 1944, GCM Lib, box 76, folder 3 (*"Frog File"*); Roberts, *The Storm of War*, 488 (*the hand that fed him*); Reynolds, *In Command of History*, 456 (*"not a scrap of generosity"*); Ferrell, ed., *The Eisenhower Diaries*, 118 (*"sorry mess"*); memo, W. B. Smith to Hastings L. Ismay, Jan. 23, 1944, NARA RG 331, SHAEF SGS, Geog Corr, box 108 (*"Joan of Arc complex"*); Ambrose, *The Supreme Commander*, 386 (*"To hell with him"*).

35 *At 9:30 P.M. the supreme commander again*: Wilmot, *The Struggle for Europe*, 224–25 (*"unexpected developments"*); Charles C. Bates, "Sea, Swell and Surf Forecasting for D-Day and Beyond: The Anglo-American Effort, 1943–1945," 2010, a.p., 15–16 (*H.M.S. Hoste*); "Report on the Meteorological Implications," June 22, 1944, UK NA, CAB 106/976, 9–11.

35 *Eisenhower polled his subordinates*: Bates and Fuller, *America's Weather Warriors*, 94; "Memorandum of Record," June 4, 1944, Arthur S. Nevins papers, MHI.

35 *For a long minute*: CCA, 272–74; Crosswell, *Beetle*, 622; George E. Creasy, OH, Feb. 4, 1947, FCP, MHI; Kingston McCloughry, *Direction of War*, 138–39 (*"We'll go"*); Stagg, *Forecast for Overlord*, 112–15 (*"Don't bring any more"*).

36 *Across the fleet*: "So appears this fleet majestical / Holding due course to Harfleur," *Henry V*, act III, prologue, 16–17.

36 *"Up anchor!"*: Naval Guns, 23–28; Wilson, ed., *D-Day 1944*, 110; Moorehead, *Eclipse*, 105 (*"Ships were heaving"*); Roskill, *White Ensign*, 371; "War Diary of Force 'U,'" June 5,

1944, SEM, NHHC, box 82, folder 46; John A. Moreno, "The Death of Admiral Moon," n.d., a.p. 225+ (*"England expects"*).

36 *By midmorning the heavy skies*: Brown, *Many a Watchful Night*, 12 (*"tropical in its colors"*); Stafford, *Ten Days to D-Day*, 264 (*chalk cliffs*); John F. Latimer, n.d., NARA RG 38, E 11, U.S. Navy WWII Oral Histories (*"one's eye for beauty"*); Liddle, *D-Day by Those Who Were There*, 91 (*"Road to the Isles"*); Sylvan, 8 (*Rome had fallen*).

36 *Leading the fleet*: VW, vol. 1, 67–69; "Report by the Allied Naval Commander-in-Chief, Expeditionary Force," Oct. 1944, NARA RG 407, ML #624, box 19117, 144; Wilson, ed., *D-Day 1944*, 109; "The Invasion of Normandy," USNAd, vol. 5, 437–39; "Navigational Aspects of the Passage and Assault in Operation OVERLORD," Nov. 1944, bulletin Y/39, COHQ, CARL, N-6530.18, 1–3; Howarth, *Dawn of D-Day*, 202–3 (*"street lamps"*).

37 *As the invasion convoys swung*: Belfield and Essame, *The Battle for Normandy*, 83 (*"all ways at once"*); Balkoski, *Omaha Beach*, 176 (*Lousy Civilian Idea*); Lewis, "Landing Craft," lecture, Sept. 18, 1944, NARA RG 334, E 315, ANSCOL, box 199, 12–13; *IFG*, 84; Howarth, *Dawn of D-Day*, 145 (*"an ominous impression"*); Settle, *All the Brave Promises*, 6 (*"swallow a pork chop"*).

37 *For those who could eat*: AAR, "Report on Operation Neptune," HQ Co, CT 16, June 16, 1944, NARA RG 407, 2-3.7 BG, AFIA; Cawthon, *Other Clay*, 48 (*"edge of eternity"*); Thompson, *The Imperial War Museum Book of Victory in Europe*, 27–29 (*"in case you stop one"*); Gaskill, "Bloody Beach," *American Magazine* (Sept. 1944): 26+ (*"Happy D-Day"*); McKee, *Caen: Anvil of Victory*, 141, 360 (*"Bring me my bow of burning gold"*); Sommers, "The Longest Hour in History," *Saturday Evening Post* (July 8, 1944): 22+ (*stripped each bridge*); Heinz, *When We Were One*, 10–11 (*"dress blues"*); diary, Cyrus C. Aydlett, June 6, 1944, NWWIIM (*"Mr. Whozits"*); Lankford, ed., *OSS Against the Reich*, 56–57 (*punching bag*).

38 *"The first six hours"*: Wilson, ed., *D-Day 1944*, 207; diary, Jack Shea [Cota aide], Nov. 1, 1944, NARA RG 407, CI 81, 29th ID, box 19138, 4–5 (*"You're going to find confusion"*).

38 *"The government paid $5 billion"*: Robert K. Skagg, 741st Tank Bn, OH, June 18, 1944, NARA RG 407, 2-3.7 BG, AFIA; corr, Philip Cole to Ralph Ingersoll, Apr. 21, 1946, Thaddeus Holt papers, MHI, box 1 (*"alone and conspicuous"*).

38 *"We are starting"*: TR to Eleanor, June 3, 1944, TR, box 10; Renehan, *The Lion's Pride*, 236–37; Balkoski, *Utah Beach*, 180 (*"I'll see you tomorrow morning"*).

38 *Far inland, at more than a dozen airfields*: Saunders, *The Red Beret*, 148; Thompson, *The Imperial War Museum Book of Victory in Europe*, 33 (*"a good stamp"*).

39 *American paratroopers smeared*: Davis, *Soldier of Democracy*, 481; Rapport and Northwood, *Rendezvous with Destiny*, 82 (*minstrel act*); corr, Charles L. Easter to Marion Page, July 7, 1944, USMA Arch (*"$10,000 jump"*); Albert Hassenzahl, VHP, AFC/2001/001/5222 (*"I'm not going to die"*); Burgett, *Currahee!*, 77–78; Otis L. Sampson, "Destination," n.d., JMG, MHI, box 12 (*brass-knuckle grip*); Carl Cartledge, 501st PIR, ts, n.d., NWWIIM (*"one for pain"*); Alosi, *War Birds*, 57 (*Carrier pigeons*); Astor, *June 6, 1944*, 128 (*trimmed the margins*).

39 *"We look all pockets"*: Simpson, *Selected Prose*, 119; Fauntleroy, *The General and His Daughter*, 107 (*"I have tried"*); diary, May 25 and June 5, 1944, JMG, MHI, box 10.

39 *"Our landings in the Cherbourg-Havre area"*: Chandler, 1908.

40 *Just after six P.M.*: Eisenhower, *Eisenhower at War, 1943–1945*, 252–53; Holt and Holt, *Major & Mrs. Holt's Battlefield Guide to the Normandy Landing Beaches*, 45 (*"It's very hard really"*); Beevor, *D-Day*, 27 (*"The idea, the perfect idea"*).

40 *At aircraft number 2716*: manifest, aircraft 2716, in "D-Day Experience of Eugene D. Brierre," ts, March 1998, NWWIIM; Taylor, *General Maxwell Taylor*, 77; Taylor, *Swords and Plowshares*, 75–76; Crosswell, *Beetle: The Life of General Walter Bedell Smith*, 623 (*"light of battle"*); Holt and Holt, *Major & Mrs. Holt's Battlefield Guide to the Normandy Landing Beaches*, 45 (*"I hope to God"*).

40 *Red and green navigation lights*: Drez, ed., *Voices of D-Day*, 72–73; corr, Charles L. Easter to Marion Page, July 7, 1944, USMA Arch; Tapert, ed., *Lines of Battle*, 157–58 (*"Give

me guts"); McNally, *As Ever, John*, 42 (*crew chiefs*); Burgett, *Currahee!*, 80 ("*Flap your wings*"); Rapport and Northwood, *Rendezvous with Destiny*, 79–80 ("*Stay, light*").

40 "*Our flag bridge is dead quiet*": Naval Guns, 31; John F. Latimer, ts, n.d., NARA RG 38, E 11, U.S. Navy WWII Oral Histories, 12 ("*trying to slip into a room*").

40 *Small craft struggled*: notes, Force O, n.d., NARA RG 407, 2-3.7 BG, AFIA ("*Men sick*"); Keegan, *Six Armies in Normandy*, 135; Chalmers, *Full Cycle*, 223 (*thirty degrees*); "The Invasion of Normandy," USNAd, vol. 5, 405–8; McKernon, *Corry*, 32 ("*Seasick*").

CHAPTER 1: INVASION

The Far Shore

45 *The singing stopped*: Robert H. George, "Ninth Air Force," 1945, AFHRA, study no. 36, 62–63; Baedeker, *Northern France*, 161 (*famed for cattle*); Rapport and Northwood, *Rendezvous with Destiny*, 85 ("*Say hello*"); Wright and Greenwood, *Airborne Forces at War*, 50–58.

45 *Then France vanished*: Taylor, *Swords and Plowshares*, 77; Drez, ed., *Voices of D-Day*, 64–69 ("*lighted tennis balls*"), 136 ("*keg of nails*"); 101st AB Div, CI #223, July 11–29, 1944, NARA RG 407, E-427-A (*jinking*); Carl Cartledge, 501st PIR, ts, n.d., NWWIIM ("*thick enough*"); John C. Warren, "Airborne Operations in World War II, European Theater," 1956, AFHRA, historical study no. 97, 45.

45 *Even as the cloud bank thinned*: corr, Michael C. Chester to JMG, Mar. 30, 1959, JMG papers, MHI, 1–5; 101st AB Div, CI #223, July 11–29, 1944, and "Operation of 507th PIR," n.d., CI #170, NARA RG 407, E 427-A; Gerald J. Higgins, 101st AB Div COS, OH, Feb. 5, 1946, SLAM, MHI, box 2 (*bundles got stuck*); "Report of Investigation of Operation NEPTUNE," Aug. 9, 1944, Air Inspector, HQ, USSAFE, NARA RG 498, ETO, SGS, 333.5 (*failed to descend to the specified jump height of 500 feet*); Astor, *June 6, 1944*, 144–45 ("*anything in my jump pants*"); corr, Charles L. Easter to Marion Page, July 7, 1944, USMA Arch ("*wall of flame*"); Tapert, ed., *Lines of Battle*, 157–58 ("*a thousand years*"); Guy Remington, "Second Man Out," in *The New Yorker Book of War Pieces*, 340 (*burning shreds*); Beevor, *D-Day*, 63 ("*watermelons falling*").

46 "*I pulled up my knees*": Astor, *June 6, 1944*, 142; Balkoski, *Utah Beach*, 112, 134.

46 *Operation ALBANY*: "Notes on Utah Beach and the 1st Engineer Special Brigade," n.d., NARA RG 498, ETO HD, admin file #359A, 53–54; "Interview with Dr. Simon, Carentan," Sept. 1, 1945, SLAM, MHI, box 2; Ruppenthal, *Utah Beach to Cherbourg*, 3; Balkoski, *Utah Beach*, 53–54; memo, "Glider Operation NEPTUNE," 82nd AB Div IG, Aug. 4, 1944, MBR papers, MHI, box 21.

47 *At four A.M., as thousands*: Beevor, *D-Day*, 71 ("*ravens*"); OH, J. Milnor Roberts, Jr., SOOHP, 1982, HIA, box 1, 72–74 ("*shoot an arrow*"); "Operation MARKET: Air Invasion of Holland," n.d., Hq, IX Troop Carrier Command, NARA RG 334, E 315, ANSCOL, Act R, A-66, box 48, 56; Paul M. Davis and Amy C. Fenwick, "Development and Procurement of Gliders," Mar. 1946, AFHRA, study no. 47, 164–67; John C. Warren, "Airborne Operations in World War II, European Theater," 1956, AFHRA, historical study no. 97, 61 (*rarely if ever flown at night*); Lewis E. Johnston, ed., "The Troop Carrier D-Day Flights," 2003, a.p., 64 ("*typewriter keys*"); Blair, *Ridgway's Paratroopers*, 222, 235 (*Rommel's asparagus*); Albert J. Randall, First Airborne Surgical Team, ts, June 8, 1945, "Medical Department Activities in ETO," Office of the Surgeon General, NARA; Astor, *June 6, 1944*, 160; Ryan, *The Longest Day*, 128–39; Otis L. Sampson, "Destination," ts, n.d., JMG papers, MHI, box 12, 12 ("*bees out of a hive*").

47 *Of more than six thousand jumpers*: "Rough draft of Gen. Maxwell Taylor's report," with jumpmaster reports, 101st AB Div, July 1, 1944, GCM Lib; Capt. R. H. Brown, HQ, 506th PIR, NARA HI (*telephone books*); "Employment of 75mm Pack Howitzers," WD Observer Bd, Aug 1, 1944, CARL, N-7344; McNally, *As Ever, John*, 44 ("*men lying in the straw*").

47 "L'invasion est arrivé": Two versions of this anecdote can be found in Baldwin, *Battles Lost and Won*, 268, and Drez, ed., *Voices of D-Day*, 92; Taylor, *Swords and Plowshares*, 79–81 ("Allez me tuer"); author visit, May 2009; John C. Warren, "Airborne Operations in World War II, European Theater," 1956, AFHRA, historical study no. 97, 42; corr, Maxwell D. Taylor to SLAM, Feb. 25, 1946, SLAM, MHI, box 2; Gerald J. Higgins, 101st AB Div COS, OH, Feb. 5, 1946, SLAM, MHI, box 2; Ruppenthal, *Utah Beach to Cherbourg*, 22.

48 *Five hours after leaping*: Balkoski, *Utah Beach*, 123–25.

48 "Wir fahren gegen England": Howarth, *Dawn of D-Day*, 90–92; author visits, May 1996 and May 2009, including Musée Airborne exhibits; Jutras, *Sainte-Mère-Église*, 11; Holt and Holt, *Major & Mrs. Holt's Battlefield Guide to the Normandy Landing Beaches*, 49–50 (*listening to the BBC*).

48 *"almost no chance to sustain"*: "Capture of Ste. Mère Église," Regimental Study No. 6, n.d., CMH, 2–8.

48 *Alas, the drops in Operation* BOSTON: Gilmore, ed., *U.S. Army Atlas of the European Theater in World War II*, 18–20; memo, "Glider Operation NEPTUNE," 82nd AB Div IG, Aug. 4, 1944, MBR papers, MHI, box 21 (*Less than half of the following gliders*); JMG, "Account of D-Day," ts, n.d., JMG papers, MHI, box 12; AAR, JMG, Aug. 16, 1944, "Debriefing Conference—Operation NEPTUNE," CARL, N-12198; Booth and Spencer, *Paratrooper*, 179–81; AAR, "508 Regiment After the Drop," n.d., MMD, 26–29 ("*he could not take any prisoners*").

49 *Of the division's three parachute infantry regiments*: Howarth, *Dawn of D-Day*, 93.

49 *"with eyes open"*: Ryan, *The Longest Day*, 114–17.

49 *Lieutenant Colonel Edward C. Krause*: Wills, *Put on Your Boots and Parachutes!*, 82; AAR, 3rd Bn, 505th PIR, NARA RG 407, E 427-A, CI #170; "Capture of Ste. Mère Église," Regimental Study No. 6, n.d., CMH, 2–8; Balkoski, *Utah Beach*, 152.

50 *"I am in Ste. Mère"*: Marshall, *Night Drop*, 18; CCA, 289; Balkoski, *Utah Beach*, 113 (*first town in France*).

50 *By dawn, 816 planes*: Balkoski, *Utah Beach*, 113; Blair, *Ridgway's Paratroopers*, 236–37 (*only one of six regiments*); John C. Warren, "Airborne Operations in World War II, European Theater," 1956, AFHRA, historical study no. 97, 36, 59 (*advance weather plane*); Ruppenthal, *Utah Beach to Cherbourg*, 15 ("*not an unmixed evil*"); McNally, *As Ever, John*, 44 (*wires snipped*); Wills, *Put on Your Boots and Parachutes!*, 88 (*lie on their backs*).

50 *an American light bomber flew*: AAR, "Reconnaissance in a Tactical Air Command," 10th Photo Group, XIX Tactical Command, Ninth AF, 1945, CARL, N-9395.

50 *Fifty miles to the east*: Arthur, *Forgotten Voices of World War II*, 301–2 (*stuffed moose head*); VW, vol. 1, 156.

50 *Two parachute brigades*: VW, vol. 1, 149–50; Wilmot, *The Struggle for Europe*, 234–35; Shannon and Wright, *One Night in June*, 52; Saunders, *Royal Air Force, 1939–1945*, vol. 3, 108 (*only seventeen dropped*); Saunders, *The Red Beret*, 159 (*wrapped around his legs*).

51 *Less fortunate were the men*: Thompson, *The Imperial War Museum Book of Victory in Europe*, 41; Liddle, *D-Day by Those Who Were There*, 76 (*tea bags*), 81 ("*silken circles*"); Shannon and Wright, *One Night in June*, 83 (*Dives muck*).

51 *Amid calamity came a celebrated success*: Urquhart, *A Life in Peace and War*, 49 (*Saxon king*); Holt and Holt, *Major & Mrs. Holt's Battlefield Guide to the Normandy Landing Beaches*, 217–19 ("*Flying Morgue*"); Liddle, *D-Day by Those Who Were There*, 66 (*spiked with rum*); Ambrose, *Pegasus Bridge*, 5–13 ("*Cow Cow Boogie*"); Chatterton, *The Wings of Pegasus*, 138; Thompson, *The Imperial War Museum Book of Victory in Europe*, 36 ("*a giant sheet*"); Howarth, *Dawn of D-Day*, 46–47.

51 *"Anything that moved"*: Ambrose, *Pegasus Bridge*, 76–83.

52 *One platoon commander fell dead*: Holt and Holt, *Major & Mrs. Holt's Battlefield Guide to the Normandy Landing Beaches*, 217–21 (*asked in vain to be shot*).

52 *Across the Orne and Dives*: Chatterton, *The Wings of Pegasus*, 140–41; Howarth, *Dawn of D-Day*, 64 (*double bed*); Ryan, *The Longest Day*, 108–9 ("*They got my mate*"); VW, vol. 1, 155.

52 *Perhaps the most perilous mission*: VW, vol. 1, 154–55; *By Air to Battle*, 85 (*banded pigeon*); Shannon and Wright, *One Night in June*, 83 (*sixty lengths of bangalore*).

52 *"I went in with 150"*: Liddle, *D-Day by Those Who Were There*, 75.

First Tide

53 *Ship by ship*: "War Diary of Force 'U,' " June 5–6, 1944, SEM, NHHC, box 82, folder 46; *IFG*, 87; Buffetaut, *D-Day Ships*, 75; Robb, *The Discovery of France*, 312 (*Norman pirates*); Colville, *Footprints in Time*, 161 (*"War in these conditions"*); Colville, *The Fringes of Power*, 492.

53 *On the pitching decks below*: John C. Raaen, Jr., "Sir, the 5th Rangers Have Landed Intact," ts, 2000, MMD, 1 (*watched for mines*); Liebling, *Mollie & Other War Pieces*, 188 (*"a passion"*); Alter and Crouch, eds., *"My Dear Moon,"* no pagination (*"extra systoles"*); Reynolds, *How I Survived the Three First Wave Invasions*, 89 (*"The mind can wander"*); Balkoski, *Omaha Beach*, 111 (*"when a bullet hits you"*), 163 (*Horace's* Satires).

53 *At two A.M. the ship's loudspeaker*: Capa, *Slightly Out of Focus*, 139 (*white jackets*); Liebling, *Mollie & Other War Pieces*, 204 (*tinned beef*); Arthur, *Forgotten Voices of World War II*, 305 (*"superb 1812 brandy"*); K. G. Oakley, "Normandy 'D' Day 1944," ts, n.d., IWM, 96/22/1, 1–2 (*"Do not worry"*).

54 *Precisely what the enemy knew*: ALH, vol. 2, 35–36; Hinsley, 466–67 (*5 percent*); Leppert, "Communication Plans and Lessons, Europe and Africa," lecture, Oct. 30, 1944, NARA RG 334, E 315, ANSCOL, box 199, L-7-44, 22–24; "The Invasion of Normandy," USNAd, vol. 5, 479–82; Arthur, *Forgotten Voices of World War II*, 290 (*electronic signature*); Dear, ed., *The Oxford Companion to World War II*, 333 (*simulate two large naval fleets*).

54 *The actual OVERLORD fleets*: Allen, "Electronics Warfare," lecture, Sept. 21, 1944, NARA RG 334, E 315, ANSCOL, L-7-44, 4; Leppert, "Communication Plans and Lessons, Europe and Africa," lecture, Oct. 30, 1944, NARA RG 334, E 315, ANSCOL, box 199, L-7-44, 22–24; "The Invasion of Normandy," USNAd, vol. 5, 479–82 (*Jamming had begun*).

54 *Of particular concern were glide bombs*: DOB, 217–19; Sunset 592, June 6, 1944, NARA RG 457, E 9026, SRS–1869 (*145 radio-control bombers*); Martin J. Bollinger, "Warriors and Wizards: The Development and Defeat of Radio-Controlled Bombs of the Third Reich," ts, 2010, a.p., 326, 345–46; Orus Kinney, "Nazi Smart Bombs," VHP, Jan. 2010, www.kilroywashere.org/003-Pages/03-OrusKinney.html (*"like a man's erect penis"*).

55 *"Each time they woke us"*: Stiles, *Serenade to the Big Bird*, 127; WaS, 42–43; Arthur, *Forgotten Voices of World War II*, 336 (*"a late tea"*); Philip Cole, "Air Planning for Overlord," lecture, Oct. 28, 1944, NARA RG 334, E 315, ANSCOL, box 199, 14–16; Mason, ed., *The Atlantic War Remembered*, 403 (*crash amid the waves*).

55 *Behind the British came*: Balkoski, *Utah Beach*, 87–91.

55 *Less precise was the main American force*: ibid., 92; Juliette Hennessy, "Tactical Operations of the Eighth Air Force," 1952, AFHRA, historical study no. 70, 15–17 (*forty-five coastal fortifications*).

55 *Conditions were far from perfect*: memo, "Statement of Result of D-Day Bombing by 4-Engine Aircraft," Eighth AF, Aug. 8, 1944, NARA RG 407, AFIA, 2-3.7 BG; *AAFinWWII*, 190–93.

56 *For an hour and a half*: Robert W. Ackerman, "The Employment of Strategic Bombers in a Tactical Role," 1954, AFHRA, study no. 88, 78; Crane, *Bombs, Cities & Civilians*, 70–71; memo, "Statement of Result of D-Day Bombing by 4-Engine Aircraft," Eighth AF, Aug. 8, 1944, NARA RG 407, AFIA, 2-3.7 BG (*"many seconds"*); Davis, *Bombing the European Axis Powers*, 357.

56 *Heavy chains rattled*: Naval Guns, 35–36; Breuer, *Hitler's Fortress Cherbourg*, 83 (*"For Chrissake"*); *IFG*, 93 (*"Anchor holding"*).

56 *Aboard* Princess Astrid: J. H. Patterson, ts, n.d., IWM, 05/491, 1/7, 6 (*"Troops to parade"*); Ewing, *29 Let's Go!*, 37–39 (*blackout curtains*); Smith, *The Big Red One at D-Day*, 32 (*"metal shoeboxes"*); diary, Cyrus C. Aydlett, June 6, 1944, NWWIIM (*"a great abyss"*).

56 *Nautical twilight arrived:* "War Diary of Force 'U,'" June 6, 1944, SEM, NHHC, box 82, folder 46; Beevor, *D-Day*, 92 (*"gigantic town"*); Raitberger, "French Remember D-Day Landings," Reuters, May 18, 1994 (*"more ships than sea"*).

56 *Minesweepers nosed close:* Yung, "Action This Day," *Naval History* (June 2009): 20+; Yung, *Gators of Neptune*, 178; *IFG*, 96 (*Two destroyers also took fire*); Naval Guns, 36–37 (*"Commence counterbattery"*).

57 *Soon enough eight hundred naval guns:* "Notes on the Assault," vol. 1, ts, n.d., Sidney Negretto Papers, MHI, box 4; *VW*, vol. 1, 161; Wilson, ed., *D-Day 1944*, 204 (*"air vibrated"*); Naval Guns, 37; Liebling, *Mollie & Other Pieces*, 180 (*"yellow cordite"*); Baker, *Ernest Hemingway*, 501 (*"railway trains"*); Reynolds, *Hemingway: The Final Years*, 96–98, 102; Heinz, *When We Were One*, 10–11; McManus, *The Americans at D-Day*, 261 (*blue steel*); Lankford, ed., *OSS Against the Reich*, 60–61 (*"There is cannonading"*).

57 *"The arc at its zenith":* John F. Latimer, n.d., NARA RG 38, E 11, U.S. Navy WWII Oral Histories, 12; Dailey, *Joining the War at Sea, 1939–1945*, 314 (*height of the splash*); Ryan, *The Longest Day*, 162 (*"monstrous thing"*); Raitberger, "French Remember D-Day Landings," Reuters, May 18, 1994 (*"It is raining iron"*).

58 *Allied planes swaddled:* The smoke plane in *Corry*'s sector was shot down, weakening the screen. Buffetaut, *D-Day Ships*, 83; AR, U.S.S. *Corry*, June 19, 1944, MMD; McKernon, *Corry*, 38–52.

58 *"We seemed to jump":* Karig, *Battle Report: The Atlantic War*, 334;

58 *Most sailors on the destroyer:* W. H. Greear, lecture, n.d., NARA RG 334, E 315, ANSCOL, box 199, 7; Hinsley, 478 (*"overlooked it"*); "The Invasion of Normandy," USNAd, vol. 5, 504; http://www.uss-corry-dd463.com/d-day_u-boat_photos/d-day_photos.htm. The cause of *Corry*'s sinking remained controversial long after the war.

58 *Eight minutes after the first explosion:* AR, U.S.S. *Corry*, June 19, 1944, NARA RG 38, CNO, 370/45/31/1, box 932, 5; Robert Beeman, "The Sinking of the U.S.S. *Corry*, June 6, 1944," ts, n.d., MMD (*necktie*); memo, R. M. Allan, "U.S.S. *Corry*—Sinking of," n.d., SEM, NHHC, box 81; OH, George D. Hoffman, CO, U.S.S. *Corry*, July 11, 1944, NARA RG 38, E 11, U.S. Navy WWII Oral Histories; Balkoski, *Utah Beach*, 214–15; Hinsley, 478; "The Invasion of Normandy," USNAd, vol. 5, 504.

58 *Experience from the Pacific:* Yung, "The Planners' Daunting Task," *Naval History* (June 2009): 12+; *WaS*, 31–33; "Notes on the Assault," vol. 1, ts, n.d., Sidney Negretto Papers, MHI, box 4 (*140,000 shells*); "Enemy Defenses and Beach Obstacles Above Highwater Mark," bulletin Y/23, Nov. 1944, COHQ, CARL, N-6530-12, 7 (*few enemy casemates*); Yung, *Gators of Neptune*, 209 (*Houlgate battery*); AR, Don P. Moon, Force U, June 26, 1944, NARA RG 498, ETO HD, admin file #217 (*none were completely knocked out*); Yung, "Action This Day," *Naval History* (June 2009): 20+ (*pesky St.-Marcouf battery*).

59 *The Channel's idiosyncratic tidal flow:* Wilmot, *The Struggle for Europe*, 220; Babcock, *War Stories*, 97 (*"I can jump"*); Jeffers, *In the Rough Rider's Shadow*, 236 (*"there are shadows"*).

59 *"Away all boats":* Vining, ed., *American Diaries of World War II*, 101.

59 *He was an unlikely vanguard:* Liebling, *Mollie & Other War Pieces*, 221; Howarth, *Dawn of D-Day*, 112–13 (*"frazzle-assed"*); Jeffers, *In the Rough Rider's Shadow*, 4, 243; Morris, *Colonel Roosevelt*, 548.

60 *"achieve the same heights as his father":* Morris, *Edith Kermit Roosevelt*, 173 (*steel-rimmed spectacles*), 307, 330, 461–63, 474, 487; *AAAD*, 85–86; *DOB*, 94–95; Hamilton, "Junior in Name Only," *Retired Officer* (June 1981): 28+; http://www.loc.gov/rr/mss/text/roosvlt.html, TR, LOC MS Div; http://www.nps.gov/archive/elro/glossary/smith-al.htm.

60 *"What man of spirit":* Morris, *Colonel Roosevelt*, 509; Renehan, *The Lion's Pride*, 239 (*"first, best destiny"*); *DOB*, 160; Michael David Pearlman, "To Make Democracy Safe for the World," Ph.D. diss, University of Illinois, 1978, 606 (*"manhood"*); Roosevelt, *Day Before Yesterday*, 450–51 (*"all right to pull strings"*); Eleanor Roosevelt to GCM, Feb. 7, 1944, GCM Lib, box 83, folder 31 (*"matter considered so serious"*).

61 *The Army's chief capitulated:* TR to R. O. Barton, May 26, 1944, TR, LOC MS Div, box 39 (*"the behavior pattern"*); Jeffers, *In the Rough Rider's Shadow*, 5 (*"can't be that rough"*); TR to Eleanor, July 11, 1944, TR, LOC MS Div, box 10; *IFG*, 100.

61 *He was on the wrong beach:* Balkoski, *Utah Beach*, 182; *IFG*, 98; Drez, ed., *Voices of D-Day*, 172–73; Wilson, ed., *D-Day 1944*, 231 (*two thousand yards south*); Naval Guns, 44 (*"Higher than her length"*); Maynard D. Pederson et al., "Armor in Operation Neptune," May 1949, AS, Ft. K, 21 (*the remaining Shermans*).

61 *"We're not where we're supposed to be":* James A. Van Fleet, SOOHP, H. Williams, 1973, MHI, 55–56.

61 *The accidental beach:* "Combat Engineering," CE, Dec. 1945, NARA RG 498, ETO HD, admin file #547, 19–21; Baker, *Ernest Hemingway*, 501 (*"pikemen"*); Ryan, *The Longest Day*, 179 (*"real estate"*); Rollyson, *Nothing Ever Happens to the Brave*, 197 (*"heavy, dry glove"*).

62 *"How do you boys":* Astor, *June 6, 1944*, 229; Balkoski, *Utah Beach*, 236 (*"great day for hunting"*); "Notes on Utah Beach and the 1st Engineer Special Brigade," n.d., NARA RG 498, ETO HD, admin file #359A, 67; Fane and Moore, *The Naked Warriors*, 68 (*"Fire in the hole"*); OH, Herbert A. Peterson, Naval Combat Demolition, Oct. 1, 1944, NARA RG 38, E 11, U.S. Navy WWII Oral Histories, 2–3 (*"no fear of impaling"*).

62 *Through the dunes and across the beach:* Royce L. Thompson, "American Strength in D-Day Landings," n.d., CMH, 2-3.7 AE.P-5; Ingersoll, *Top Secret*, 126 (*"ironed flat"*); Fowle, ed., *Builders and Fighters*, 448–49 (*Four causeways*); Balkoski, *Utah Beach*, 236 (*"arm signal"*).

62 *The mutter of gunfire:* Maynard D. Pederson et al., "Armor in Operation Neptune," May 1949, AS, Ft. K, 28–29; Drez, ed., *Voices of D-Day*, 181 (*shaving cream*); Balkoski, *Utah Beach*, 254 (*horse-drawn 88mm guns*); diary, Cyrus C. Aydlett, June 10, 1944, NWWIIM (*"It sure takes a lot"*); "D-Day Experience of Eugene D. Brierre," ts, March 15, 1998, NWWIIM, 2001.160, 5–6 (*snipped the unit flashes*).

62 *East of Pouppeville:* CCA, 283; Wilson, ed., *D-Day 1944*, 233–34 (*"Where's the war"*); Babcock, *War Stories*, 52 (*"Hey, boy"*).

63 *Eleven miles offshore:* "War Diary of Force 'U,'" June 5–6, 1944, SEM, NHHC, box 82, folder 46; Chandler and Collins, eds., *The D-Day Encyclopedia*, 373 (*delay seven assault waves*).

63 *At age fifty, Admiral Moon:* Alter and Crouch, eds., *"My Dear Moon,"* no pagination; John A. Moreno, "The Death of Admiral Moon," n.d., a.p., 225+.

63 *In his spare office aboard* Bayfield: "Conference on the Operations of the VII Corps," May 16, 1946, SLAM, MHI, box 2; Collins, *Lightning Joe*, 200–201 (*"I had to put my foot down"*); CCA, 329. Historian Joseph Balkoski believes 4th ID casualties for June 6 were "certainly over 300." Balkoski, *Utah Beach*, 322.

63 *"It is our good fortune":* "War Diary of Force 'U,'" June 5–6, 1944, SEM, NHHC, box 82, folder 46.

Hell's Beach

64 *Fifteen miles southeast of Utah:* IFG, 110–11 (*Spanish galleon*); ALH, 21; "Beach 46—Omaha, Tidal Curves," n.d., CARL, N-7374E; "Operation Report Neptune," Provisional Engineer Special Brigade Group, Sept. 1944, NARA RG 407, ML #951, box 24198, 57; CCA, 18; 1st ID, HI; "Operation Report Neptune," Provisional Engineer Special Brigade Group, Sept. 1944, NARA RG 407, ML #951, box 24198, 60 (*two knots to three*).

64 *That Norman tide:* IFG, 138; "The Invasion of Normandy," USNAd, vol. 5, 566; Balkoski, *Omaha Beach*, 41 (*twenty feet deep*), 22; Royce L. Thompson, "American Strength in D-Day Landings," n.d., CMH, 2-3.7 AE.P-5; "Strategy of the Campaign in Western Europe, 1944–1945," n.d., USFET, General Board study no. 1, 25 (*without stranding the boats*); Drez, ed., *Voices of D-Day*, 53 (*only half an hour*).

64 OVERLORD'*s plan called for nine infantry companies:* Omaha Beachhead, AFIA, 42; Buffetaut, *D-Day Ships*, 101. The nine included a Ranger company.

64 *To minimize the risk of German shore fire*: Yung, *Gators of Neptune*, 216; Wilmot, *The Struggle for Europe*, 264; *IFG*, 124. Fourteen hundred tons of naval shells fell at Omaha, one-third the bombardment weight at much weaker Kwajalein Island. "Amphibious Operations: Invasion of Northern France," CINC, U.S. Fleet, Oct. 1944, NARA RG 407, ML #252, 2–27.

65 *The German defenses were fearsome*: "Comparison of British and American Areas in Normandy in Terms of Fire Support and Its Effects," Army Operational Group Report no. 292, Aug. 14, 1945, UK NA, WO 291/270; McManus, *The Americans at D-Day*, 305 (*"murder holes"*); OH, J. D. Small, June 23, 1944, NARA RG 38, E 11, U.S. Navy WWII Oral Histories, 9 (*"like huckleberries"*); Drez, ed. *Voices of D-Day*, 283 (*"New England town hall"*); "The Invasion of Normandy," USNAd, vol. 5, 512; *IFG*, 114–15 (*aerial photos*).

65 *Also undetected and unexpected*: Hinsley et al., *British Intelligence in the Second World War*, vol. 3, part 2, 842–43; Benjamin A. Dickson, "G-2 Journal: Algiers to the Elbe," MHI, 119 (*radio blackout*); Fritz Ziegelmann, "The 352nd Infantry Division," FMS, #B-432, in Isby, ed., *Fighting the Invasion*, 122–24 (*requisitioned milk*), 194–95, 202; Bennett, *Ultra in the West*, 45; Balkoski, *Omaha Beach*, 48–49; Beevor, *D-Day*, 93; Zetterling, *Normandy 1944*, 277–79; Holt, *The Deceivers*, 578; Foot, *SOE in France*, 386–87 (*British tricksters*).

65 *If the Omaha defenses had been thinned*: Murray, "Needless D-Day Slaughter," *MHQ* (spring 2003): 26+; Hinsley et al., *British Intelligence in the Second World War*, vol. 3, part 2, 842–43; Balkoski, *Beyond the Beachhead*, 67, 78; Clay, *Blood and Sacrifice*, 201 (*odds of three to five*).

66 *For those who outlived the day*: "Greek lyric," epigram, Ridgway, *Soldier* (*this high thing*).

66 *"utterly inhuman noises"*: memo, Cleave A. Jones, July 4, 1944, NARA RG 498, UD 603, ETO HD, box 1, SLAM 201 file; Baumgartner et al., *The 16th Infantry, 1798–1946*, 84 (*gas capes*); OH, J. D. Small, June 23, 1944, NARA RG 38, E 11, U.S. Navy WWII Oral Histories, 9 (*"It's yours"*).

66 *They remembered the red splash*: Cawthon, *Other Clay*, 51–53; Lebda, *Million Miles to Go*, 81–82 (*"wind-driven hail"*); Alan Anderson, ts, n.d., 467th AA Bn, NWWIIM (*"corn cobs"*); diary, Jack Shea, ts, Nov. 1, 1944, NARA RG 407, CI, 29th ID, box 24034, 17 (*size of shovel blades*); Howarth, *Dawn of D-Day*, 134 (*"wicked living things"*); Scannell, *Argument of Kings*, 152 (*"insectile whine"*); Gaskill, "Bloody Beach," *American Magazine* (Sept. 1944): 26+ (*frightened animals*); AAR, 146th Engineer Combat Bn, June 30, 1944, CEOH, X-37A (*spoons*); Whitehead, *"Beachhead Don,"* xxii (*barked knuckles*); W. Garwood Bacon, ts, n.d., 7th Naval Beach Bn, NWWIIM (*eardrums*).

66 *"walking in the face"*: Pogue, *Pogue's War*, 67; Gaskill, "Bloody Beach," *American Magazine* (Sept. 1944): 26+; Howarth, *Dawn of D-Day*, 155 (*"dying scream"*).

66 *Army and Navy engineers*: OH, John T. O'Neill, 299th Engineer Combat Bn, June 9, 1944, NARA 407, E 427, ML #2210; Beck, 308, 320; "Combat Engineering," CE, ETOUSA, Dec. 1945, report no. 10, NARA RG 498, ETO HD, admin file #547, 10–16 (*all drifted left*); *Omaha Beachhead*, 42–43; AAR, 299th Engineer Combat Bn, July 1944, NARA 407, E 427, ML #2210 (*Team 14's landing craft*); McManus, *The Americans at D-Day*, 340 (*"V for victory"*); Fowle, ed., *Builders and Fighters*, 438 (*Seven died in Team 11*); AAR, 146th Engineer Combat Bn, June 30, 1944, CEOH, X-37A (*"like fence posts"*).

68 *Demolitionists shinnied up pilings*: Field Order No. 35, 1st ID, Apr. 16, 1944, NARA RG 407, E 427, 301-3.9; Fowle, ed., *Builders and Fighters*, 438 (*the fuse man's fingers*); Howarth, *Dawn of D-Day*, 134 (*"cluster of bees"*); Fane and Moore, *The Naked Warriors*, 56–58 (*engineers screamed*); Yung, *Gators of Neptune*, 187; Balkoski, *Omaha Beach*, 143 (*only six of sixteen gaps*); OH, W. M. Hoge, CO, Provisional Brigade Group, July 3, 1944, NARA RG 498, ETO HD, admin file #493C; *CCA*, 317; *IFG*, 138n.

68 *The fiascos multiplied*: Keegan, *Six Armies in Normandy*, 135 (*"like toads"*); Lewis, "Landing Craft," lecture, Sept. 18, 1944, NARA RG 334, E 315, ANSCOL, box 199, 18; Drez, ed., *Voices of D-Day*, 234 (*nine inches of freeboard*); OH, Robert K. Skagg, 741st

Tank Bn, June 18, 1944, NARA RG 407, AFIA, 2-3.7 BG (*of thirty-two Shermans*); Howarth, *Dawn of D-Day*, 147 ("*a certain gallantry*").

68 *Artillerymen also struggled*: Marshall, "The Mobility of One Man," *IJ* (Oct. 1949): 6+ (*eighteen sandbags*); "111th FA Bn on D Day," n.d., NARA RG 407, AFIA, 2-3.7 BG ("*unseaworthy*"); Balkoski, *Omaha Beach*, 239 ("*I can still hear*").

69 *Two infantry regiments washed*: Balkoski, *Omaha Beach*, 28–29, 161 ("*lose heart*"); OH, 116th Inf, Co A, n.d., NARA RG 407, AFIA, 2-3.7 BG; Marshall, *Battle at Best*, 54–55 ("*inert and leaderless*"); Kershaw, *The Bedford Boys*, 144–51 ("*didn't get to kill*"); Drez, ed., *Voices of D-Day*, 213 ("*like hay*").

69 "*a venetian blind being lifted*": Baumgarten, *Eyewitness on Omaha Beach*, 17; Balkoski, *Beyond the Beachhead*, 125 (LCA-1015); S. L. A. Marshall, "First Wave at Omaha Beach," *Atlantic*, Nov. 1960, www.theatlantic.com/magazine/archive/1960/11/fir; Drez, ed., *Voices of D-Day*, 209 ("*he sat down*"); Ryan, *The Longest Day*, 176 (*safety pins*); Richler, ed., *Writers on World War II*, 508 ("*I run on*"); Cawthon, *Other Clay*, 57 ("*a debacle*").

69 "*the greater portion of the dead*": Baumgartner et al., *The 16th Infantry, 1798–1946*, 107; Pogue, *Pogue's War*, 87 (*rank insignia*); William Haynes, Co. E, 16th Inf, HI, box 24242 ("*big and little stuff*"); Lebda, *Million Miles to Go*, 81–82 ("*twenty thousand bullets*"); Capa, *Slightly Out of Focus*, 139–40 ("Es una cosa").

70 *The four-hundred-ton* LCI 85: AR, *LCI (L) 85*, June 24, 1944, NARA RG 38, CNO, 370/45/3/1, box 1102; AAR, Company A, 1st Medical Bn, n.d., NARA 407, AFIA, 2-3.7 BG; Clay, *Blood and Sacrifice*, 195–96 (*White bandages*); Kenneth C. Davey, "Navy Medicine on Bloody Omaha," in "Sixth Naval Battalion 1998 Reunion," MRC FDM ("*we could hear*").

70 *By 8:30 A.M. the Omaha assault*: McManus, *The Americans at D-Day*, 327; Cowdrey, *Fighting for Life*, 248 ("*Face downwards*").

70 *Two large boats burned furiously*: AR, *LCI 91*, June 10, 1944, MMD; Robert E. Walker, "With the Stonewallers," n.d., MMD (*soles of his boots*); AR, *LCI(L) 92*, Sept. 2, 1944, NARA RG 38, CNO, 370/45/3/1, box 549 (*champagne corks*); "Actions Group, CT 116," n.d., John P. McKnight papers, HIA, box 1; Seth Shepard, "The Story of the LCI(L) 92," June 25, 1944, MMD, 9–12; Drez, ed., *Voices of D-Day*, 223 ("*Terror seized me*" and "*shipwreck*").

70 *Only where escarpment*: 2nd Ranger Bn, AAR, July 22, 1944, and "A Narrative History of the Second Ranger Infantry Battalion," n.d., both in Robert W. Black collection, MHI, box 3; CI, 2nd and 5th Ranger Bn, n.d., NARA RG 407, E 427-A, folder 337; *IFG*, 126–29; Ryan, *The Longest Day*, 182–84.

70 "*ripped-open dirt*": Heinz, "I Took My Son to Omaha Beach," *Collier's* (June 11, 1954): 21+; "Amphibious Operations: Invasion of Northern France," CINC, U.S. Fleet, Oct. 1944, NARA RG 407, ML #252, 2–11 (*Texas's 14-inch barrels*).

71 *Rangers hauled themselves over the lip*: Interview, Leonard G. Lommell with author, May 2008; OH, Leonard G. Lommell, 2nd Ranger Bn, Mar. 16, 1993, NWWIIM; Kingseed, *Old Glory Stories*, 198–99; author visit, May 2009.

71 *Back on Hell's Beach*: Knickerbocker et al., *Danger Forward*, 212–13 ("*They'll come swarming*"); FCP, "The 25th Anniversary of D-Day," *Congressional Record*, June 25, 1969, E5246+ ("*couldn't look back*"); Kingseed, *From Omaha Beach to Dawson's Ridge*, 145–49, 163 ("*The limitations of life*").

71 *From the gray deck of the command ship*: Pyle, *Brave Men*, 246; CBH, June 3 and 6, 1944 (*First Army war room*); Bradley, *A Soldier's Story*, 252–53; Hastings, *OVERLORD*, 92; memoir, William Puntenney, 29th ID, n.d., MMD, 40–41 ("*bunch of hogs*").

71 *At a plotting table in the center*: Hanson W. Baldwin, "Getting the D-Day News Out," in Mason, ed., *The Atlantic War Remembered*, 394; ONB, OH, 1975, Charles Hanson, MHI, VII, 22 ("*get ground quickly*"); Astor, *June 6, 1944*, 212–13 (*expected the two assault regiments*); Bradley and Blair, *A General's Life*, 243–44 (*Photographers were forbidden*).

72 "*Lincolnesque*": "Doughboy's General," *Time* (May 1, 1944): 23+; Pyle, *Brave Men*, 210–11 ("*he spoke so gently*"); Liebling, "Five-Star Schoolmaster," *New Yorker* (March 10, 1951): 40+.

72 *Few could resist the biography*: OH, ONB, Oct. 14, 1946, FCP (*sodbuster twang*); Liebling, "Five-Star Schoolmaster," *New Yorker* (March 10, 1951): 40+; "Doughboy's General," *Time* (May 1, 1944): 23+; CBH, June 3, 1944 (*two flasks of brandy*); Wertenbaker, *Invasion!*, 77 ("*If there's a bird*"), 85–93; ONB, OH, 1975, Charles Hanson, MHI, II, 11, 24–26, 52–53 ("*guidance from God*"); DOB, 96, 114–15; AAAD, 485–86.

72 *Perhaps. But a few wondered*: C. B. Hansen, "General Bradley As Seen Close Up," *NYT Magazine*, Nov. 30, 1947, 14+ ("*superior*"); Blumenson, *The Battle of the Generals*, 37 ("*mediocrity*"); Blumenson, *Patton: The Man Behind the Legend, 1885–1945*, 216 ("*Has a strong jaw*"); Murray, "Needless D-Day Slaughter," *MHQ* (spring 2003): 26+ (*Bradley's design*); "Doughboy's General," *Time* (May 1, 1944): 23 ("*tommyrot*"). I'm grateful for the insights of Prof. Allan R. Millett on this topic.

73 *Now he was not so sure*: Bradley, *A Soldier's Story*, 271–77; Astor, *June 6, 1944*, 212–13 ("*this is carnage*").

73 *Not for some hours would Bradley learn*: Miller, *Division Commander*, 5–14; diary, Jack Shea [Cota aide], ts, Nov. 1, 1944, NARA RG 407, CI, 29th ID, box 24034, 14–17 (*hugging wooden groins*).

73 *Pistol in hand, he sang tuneless*: Kershaw, *The Bedford Boys*, 155; John C. Raaen, Jr., "Sir, the 5th Rangers Have Landed Intact," ts, 2000, MMD, 28–29; McManus, *The Americans at D-Day*, 333; OH, 116th Inf, March 25, 1945, NARA RG 407, AFIA, 2-3.7 BG; diary, Jack Shea, ts, Nov. 1, 1944, NARA RG 407, CI, 29th ID, box 24034, 18–22 ("*Medico, I'm hit*").

74 *Up the bluff they climbed*: diary, Jack Shea, ts, Nov. 1, 1944, NARA RG 407, CI, 29th ID, box 24034, 19–22, 29; OH, 116th Inf, March 25, 1945, NARA RG 407, AFIA, 2-3.7 BG.

74 *"Where the hell have you been"*: OH, 116th Inf, Mar. 25, 1945, NARA RG 407, AFIA, 2-3.7 BG.

74 *"a final stubborn reserve"*: Howarth, *Dawn of D-Day*, 161; Balkoski, *Omaha Beach*, 346 ("*unwilling soul*"), 262 ("*Watch it*"); "16-G on D-Day," n.d., NARA RG 407, AFIA, 2-3.7 BG (*stepping stones*); diary, Stanley Bach, First Army, NARA RG 407, AFIA, 2-3.7 BG ("*Fire everywhere*"); OH, Joseph Dorchak, Co B, 2nd Ranger Bn, HI ("*shot the corpse*").

74 *A dozen destroyers—some so close*: IFG, 143; OH, Maurice F. McGrath, 116th Inf, Sept. 20, 1944, a.p. ("*pick them out*"); Buffetaut, *D-Day Ships*, 108 (*knocked the tower into the nave*); Karig, *Battle Report: The Atlantic War*, 327 ("*simply champion*").

75 *"coagulating haphazardly"*: CCA, 324; "Operation Neptune Report," Provisional Engineer Special Brigade Group, Sept. 30, 1944, CEOH, box X-24, 91–93, 93n ("*Men believed ours*"); Wheeler, *The Big Red One*, 277–82; *Omaha Beachhead*, 82–83, 87 ("*Troops formerly pinned*").

75 *Cota continued his charmed day*: *Omaha Beachhead*, 95; diary, Jack Shea, ts, Nov. 1, 1944, NARA RG 407, CI, 29th ID, box 24034, 23; Balkoski, *Omaha Beach*, 278 ("*Come on down here*").

75 *That left the British and Canadians*: WaS, 46–48; IFG, 183 (*four times longer*); Howarth, *Dawn of D-Day*, 170–71 (*half a dozen gadgets*).

75 *In other respects, "the bitches"*: Drez, ed., *Voices of D-Day*, 293; "Force G and 50 Division," bulletin Y/36, Nov. 1944, COHQ, CARL, N-6530.16, 19–23 (*engine rooms flooded*); Hastings, *OVERLORD*, 105–6 (*Centaur tanks*); Vian, *Action This Day*, 138 (*two battleships and a monitor*); Thompson, *The Imperial War Museum Book of Victory in Europe*, 56 ("*large packs of grouse*"); VW, vol. 1, 197 (*ninety shore guns*); author visit, Crépon, May 25–29, 2009; "Casualties and Effects of Fire Support on the British Beaches in Normandy," Army Operational Research Group (U.K.), report no. 261, n.d., NARA RG 334, E 315, ANSCOL, box 451, 5 ("*not just disorganized*").

75 *During the run to shore*: Hastings, *Winston's War*, 393; diary, S. C. Donnison, June 6, 1944, IWM, 94/50/1 ("*thick as syrup*"); Thompson, *The Imperial War Museum Book of Victory in Europe*, 48, 60; "An Account of the Assault by an Infantry Battalion," bulletin Y/44, Feb. 1945, COHQ, CARL, N-6350.22, 5–6; J. H. Patterson, ts, n.d., No. 4 Com-

mando, n.d., IWM, 05/491, 1/7 (*"Jerusalem"*); Hills, *Phantom Was There*, 178 (*"The Beer Barrel Polka"*).

76 *Closest to Omaha lay Gold*: Roskill, *White Ensign*, 377; "Report on the Battle of Normandy," Royal Engineers, n.d., CARL, N-5785 (*only two boat lanes*); "An Account of the Assault by an Infantry Battalion," bulleting Y/44, Feb. 1945, COHQ, CARL, N-6350.22, 9; Wilmot, *The Struggle for Europe*, 270–72; Ryan, *The Longest Day*, 188 (*"Perhaps we're intruding"*); WaS, 46–48 (*Port-en-Bessin*); VW, vol. 1, 178, 193 (*all four brigades*).

76 *On the eastern lip of the Allied beachhead*: VW, vol. 1, 185.

76 *"Ramp down"*: Hastings, *OVERLORD*, 103; Ryan, *The Longest Day*, 186 (*"Bash on"*); "Report on the Battle of Normandy," Royal Engineers, n.d., CARL, N-5785 (*cleared no beach obstacles*); Collier, *Fighting Words*, 161 (*"shoulders hunched like boxers"*); Arthur, *Forgotten Voices of World War II*, 313 (*"drowning in their own blood"*); Liddle, *D-Day by Those Who Were There*, 12–13 (*"Beach a shambles"*); D'Este, *Decision in Normandy*, 129 (*within thirty feet*); VW, vol. 1, 186, 194–95; Wilmot, *The Struggle for Europe*, 278.

77 *Even so a kilted piper with a dirk*: Millership, "Scots Piper Dodged Bullets," Reuters, June 1, 1994; Burns, "Bill Millin, Scottish D-Day Piper, Dies at 88," *NYT*, Aug. 19, 2010, B9 (*"Highland Laddie"*); Holt and Holt, *Major & Mrs. Holt's Battlefield Guide to the Normandy Landing Beaches*, 202 (*"Get down"*); Arthur, *Forgotten Voices of World War II*, 316–18 (*"parade-ground style"*); Liddle, *D-Day by Those Who Were There*, 189–90.

77 *The wind-whipped tide and a bullying current*: VW, vol. 1, 179–83; VC, 100–106; Collier, *Fighting Words*, 164 (*"Traitors!"*).

77 *Despite such setbacks*: Keegan, *Six Armies in Normandy*, 141 (*half the number expected*); Wilmot, *The Struggle for Europe*, 275 (*two miles inland*); Saunders, *The Red Beret*, 153; Ambrose, *Pegasus Bridge*, 125; author visit, Crépon, May 25–29, 2009; Isby, ed., *Fighting the Invasion*, 199.

77 *Reporters were told to expect*: Ryan, *The Longest Day*, 196–97; Drez, ed., *Voices of D-Day*, 297–301 (*"cycle like mad"*).

77 *Yet the day seemed undimmed*: author visit, Crépon, May 25–29, 2009; Ryan, *The Longest Day*, 206 (*holding up trousers*); Ambrose, *Pegasus Bridge*, 109 (*French women who emerged*); Howarth, *Dawn of D-Day*, 228 (*Norman dialect*); Thompson, *The Price of Victory*, 253 (*antique gramophone*).

A Conqueror's Paradise

78 *As if in pursuit*: AAFinWWII, 159 (*twenty-six bridges*); Irving, *The Trail of the Fox*, Horch photo; Douglas-Home, *Rommel*, 205; Barnett, ed., *Hitler's Generals*, 198 (*youngest but most celebrated*); Fraser, *Knight's Cross*, 457 ("C'est Rommel!").

78 *He had driven home to Herrlingen*: Liddell Hart, ed., *The Rommel Papers*, 470–71; Ryan, *The Longest Day*, 237–38 (*"If I was commander"*).

78 *At 9:30 P.M., with little left*: Ryan, *The Longest Day*, 15; author visit, La Roche–Guyon, May 30, 2009, and "A Visit to La Roche–Guyon Castle," brochure.

79 *"How peaceful the world"*: Fraser, *Knight's Cross*, 471–73; Beevor, *D-Day*, 40 (*"conqueror's paradise"*); Camille Pissarro, "A Square in La Roche–Guyon," Alte Nationalgaleri, Berlin; www.musee-imaginaire.de/lesesaal/renoir/biografi.html; www.artchive.com/artchive /B/braque/castle.jpg.html.

79 *On the chalk cliffs*: Irving, *The Trail of the Fox*, 334, 345–54, 392.

79 *Clacking typewriters*: Speidel, *We Defended Normandy*, 53 (*Edict of Nantes*); Irving, *The Trail of the Fox*, 372–74 ("He's very calm").

80 *There was much to be grim about*: CCA, 275; Germany VII, 586 (*"There are no signs"*); Lewin, *Rommel as Military Commander*, 223 (*away from their posts*); war diary, Seventh Army, June 6, 1944, NARA RG 407, E 427, ML #2201 (*"not a major action"*).

80 *Not until that fantastic armada*: Horst Boog, "Invasion to Surrender: The Defense of Germany," in Brower, ed., *World War II in Europe: The Final Year*, 120 (*German aircraft*

losses); *Germany VII*, 328–30 (*319 serviceable planes* and *dropped their bombs prematurely*); Keegan, *Six Armies in Normandy*, 143; Davis, *Carl A. Spaatz and the Air War in Europe*, 414; Wieviorka, *Normandy*, 207 (*American planes were gray*).

80 "*The enemy, penetrating our positions*": war diary, Seventh Army, June 6, 1944, NARA RG 407, E 427, ML #2201.

80 "*the fighting animal*": Carver, ed., *The War Lords*, 274; Barnett, ed., *Hitler's Generals*, 299; MMB, 462–63; Isby, ed., *Fighting the Invasion*, 48 ("*re-win great fame*").

81 *Hitler's decision in November 1943*: Keegan, *Six Armies in Normandy*, 60–61, 65 ("*Once defeated*"); *Germany VII*, 512; Liddell Hart, ed., *The Rommel Papers*, 458 ("*zone of death*"), 464 ("*The enemy will have a rough time*").

81 *If confident enough to travel*: Keegan, *Six Armies in Normandy*, 60–61 (*200 million*); Cooper, *The German Army, 1933–1945*, 496 (*eight different languages*); Overy, *Why the Allies Won*, 225–27 (*Army Group B relied*); Friederich Freiherr von der Heydte, "A German Parachute Regiment in Normandy," 1954, FMS, #B-839, MHI, 8 ("*Emplacements without guns*").

81 "*Our friends from the East*": Liddell Hart, ed., *The Rommel Papers*, 467–68; F. Ruge, "Coast Defense and Invasion," June 9, 1947, NARA RG 334, E 315, ANSCOL, ONI IR 243, box 642, 9, 14 ("*nailed to the ground*"); "Railway Sabotage in France and Belgium," SHAEF, G-3, n.d., CARL, N-16313 (*armed railwaymen*); Mark, *Aerial Interdiction in Three Wars*, 233–41; *CCA*, 225–30; *AAFinWWII*, 160; *GS* V, 287; memo, Erwin Rommel, Apr. 22, 1944, captured document, NARA RG 498, ETO HD, "Combat Engineering," admin file #547, 8–9 ("*The enemy will most likely*").

82 "*a cock-fight controversy*": Bodo Zimmerman, 1946, FMS, #B-308, MHI, 42–43.

82 "*main battle line must be the beach*": Fraser, *Knight's Cross*, 455; OH, Hans von Luck to author, Hamburg, Mar. 3 and Apr. 7, 1994 ("*If we can't throw*"); *CCA*, 247.

82 *This impertinence found little favor*: Stafford, *Ten Days to D-Day*, 43 ("*unlicked cub*"); Isby, ed., *Fighting the Invasion*, 48 ("*Marshal Laddie*"); Leo Geyr von Schweppenburg, ETHINT 13, Dec. 11, 1947, MHI, 2 (S'engager).

82 *Hitler dithered, then ordered a compromise*: *Germany VII*, 508–20 ("*In the East*"); Wood, ed., *Army of the West*, 4; *CCA*, 243–49; Ose, "Rommel and Rundstedt: The 1944 Panzer Controversy," *Military Affairs* (Jan. 1986): 7+; *CCA*, 333–34 (*eight hours passed*); Beevor, *D-Day*, 150 ("*arrive too late*").

83 "*Der Führer vertraut mir*": Fraser, *Knight's Cross*, 476–78; Isby, ed., *Fighting the Invasion*, 48 ("*the Führer's marshal*"); Young, *Rommel, the Desert Fox*, 151 (*stamp collector*); Margry, "The Death of Rommel," *AB*, no. 80 (1993): 38+ (*confiscated from Jews*); Liddell Hart, ed., *The Rommel Papers*, 485 ("*come round to the idea*"), 468, ("*fate of the German people*").

83 *The struggle in Normandy would depend*: *VW*, vol. 1, 201–4: Lefèvre, *Panzers in Normandy Then and Now*, 65 (*oddments*), 106–8 (*pulverized by naval gunfire*); OH, Hans von Luck to author, Hamburg, Mar. 3 and Apr. 7, 1994; Luck, *Panzer Commander*, 139–44; Reynolds, *Steel Inferno*, 57–58; Daglish, *Operation Goodwood*, 67 (*Parisian fleshpot*); Isby, ed., *Fighting the Invasion*, 241; *VW*, vol. 1, 204–5; Saunders, *Royal Air Force, 1939–1945*, vol. 3, 113 (*almost 250 more British gliders*).

84 *At 10:40 P.M., General Friedrich Dollmann*: war diary, Seventh Army, June 6, 1944, NARA RG 407, E 427, ML #2201. The 21st Panzer commander put his tank losses for June 6 at 25 percent, while official British sources calculate the loss at 40 to 44 percent. The official German history states that 80 of 125 deployed panzers were destroyed. *Germany VII*, 593; Hinsley, 474; *VW*, vol. 1, 204; Reynolds, *Steel Inferno*, 57–58.

84 *Swarming enemy aircraft impeded movement*: Luther, *Blood and Honor*, 70–73; Hastings, *OVERLORD*, 117 (*Grenadiers skulked back*).

84 "*We cannot hold everything*": Speidel, *We Defended Normandy*, 98–99; Ryan, *The Longest Day*, 237–38 ("*I've nearly always succeeded*").

84 *A monstrous full moon*: *VW*, vol. 1, 222; *AAFinWWII*, 562–63 (*first of 241 airdromes*);

Omaha Beachhead, 108 (*only a hundred tons*); Balkoski, *Utah Beach*, 317 (*nineteen airborne battalions*); Astor, *June 6, 1944*, 239 ("*to kill each other*").

84 "*I must have Caen*": notes, Miles Dempsey, May 15, 1944, UK NA, WO 285/1; Hinsley et al., *British Intelligence in the Second World War*, vol. 3, part 2, 841–42; Beevor, *D-Day*, 142; Hastings, *OVERLORD*, 115 ("*not unpleased*").

85 "*My wife, my children!*": Beevor, *D-Day*, 146; Harris G. Warren, "Special Operations: AAF Aid to European Resistance Movements," 1947, AFHRA, study no. 121, 149 (*seventeen Norman towns*); "Historical Record, A.E.A.F.," n.d., UK NA, AIR 37/1057 (*bomber fleets would follow*); Keegan, *Six Armies in Normandy*, 183 (*eleven days*), 185 (*Westminster Abbey*); Hitchcock, *The Bitter Road to Freedom*, 29–33; Gilbert, *D-Day*, 158–59 (*five hundred coffins*); Arthur Layton Funk, "Caught in the Middle: The French Population in Normandy," in Wilson, ed., *D-Day 1944*, 252.

85 *three thousand Normans would be killed*: Hitchcock, *The Bitter Road to Freedom*, 27; Beevor, *D-Day*, 49 (*fifteen thousand French civilians*), 123 (*calvados*); Moorehead, *Eclipse*, 120 ("*excessive hardship*").

85 *As for the liberators*: casualty estimates vary substantially. *VW*, vol. 1, 222–23; Buffetaut, *D-Day Ships*, 122.

85 *The 8,230 U.S. casualties*: historian Joseph Balkoski tabulates 4,720 casualties at Omaha, plus 3,510 at Utah and on the Cotentin Peninsula. *Omaha Beach* and *Utah Beach*, each appendix 1; Reister, ed., *Medical Statistics in World War II*, 13–20 (*first of almost 400,000 men*).

85 *Many were felled by 9.6-gram bullets*: Andrus et al., eds., *Advances in Military Medicine*, vol. 1, 192–201; Capa, *Slightly Out of Focus*, 149 (*corpses into burial sacks*); J. H. Patterson, No. 4 Commando, ts, n.d., IWM, 05/491, 1/7, 13 ("*nothing was being done*"); George E. McIntyre, "As Mac Saw It," ts, n.d., MHI, 159 (*handkerchiefs draped the faces*); OH, Richard Oliphant, NARA RG 38, E 11, U.S. Navy WWII Oral Histories, 2–3 ("*They do not seem to matter*").

85 *Omaha was the worst*: "Operation Report Neptune," Provisional Engineer Special Brigade Group, Sept. 1944, NARA RG 407, ML #951, box 24198, 328–29; "Activities of Medical Detachment," 16th Inf, D-Day, n.d., NARA RG 407, AFIA, 2-3.7 BG; diary, Jack Shea, ts, Nov. 1, 1944, NARA RG 407, CI, 29th ID, box 24034, 37 (*cat's-eye headlights*); Fisher, *Legacy of Heroes*, 33, 38, 64 (*gas gangrene*); Kenneth C. Davey, "Navy Medicine on Bloody Omaha," in "Sixth Naval Beach Battalion 1998 Reunion," 1998, MRC FDM (*bullet in the brain*); "Vierville-sur-Mer," ts, n.d., MMD ("*There were men crying*").

86 "*swollen grayish sacks*": Moorehead, *Gellhorn*, 219.

86 "*I walked along slowly*": Gaskill, "Bloody Beach," *American Magazine* (Sept. 1944): 26+; Andrew T. McNamara, "QM Activities," 1955, PIR, MHI, 128 (*More than double that number*); Pyle, *Brave Men*, 246 (*toes sticking up*); Richard H. Oliphant, "Eleventh Amphibious Force," n.d., NARA RG 498, ETO HD, admin file #217 ("*staring was rude*").

86 *Graves Registration teams*: Perret, *There's a War to Be Won*, 485 (*safety pins*); "Operation Report Neptune," Provisional Engineer Special Brigade Group, Sept. 1944, NARA RG 407, ML #951, box 24198, 341 (*Two inland sites*); Kenneth C. Davey, "Navy Medicine on Bloody Omaha," in "Sixth Naval Beach Battalion 1998 Reunion," 1998, MRC FDM (*fortified with brandy*).

86 "*since Alexander set out from Macedon*": Saunders, *Royal Air Force, 1939–1945*, vol. 3, 114; Gellhorn, *The Face of War*, 134–36 ("*small shabby men*"); *Reporting World War II*, vol. 2, 155 ("*I'd kill him*").

86 "*We will never again have to land*": Balkoski, *Omaha Beach*, 261.

87 "*We have come to the hour*": Stephen E. Ambrose, "Battle Scars Remain But Little Has Changed in Normandy," *International Herald Tribune*, Apr. 22, 1994, 12; Wacker, "The Voices of D-Day," *Retired Officer* (June 1994): 26+ (*scribbling "deceased"*); Crosswell, *Beetle*, 795 ("*dead stock*"); Tapert, ed., *Lines of Battle*, 162–64 ("*I wonder about him*").

CHAPTER 2: LODGEMENT

"This Long Thin Line of Personal Anguish"

89 *Light rain fell in Portsmouth*: www.britishlistedbuildings.co.uk/en-474304-18-gun-battery -and-flanking-battery-king; *Three Years*, 571 (*four white stars*).

89 *"A scene of great confusion"*: Love and Major, eds., *The Year of D-Day*, 84–85.

89 *Mines continued to bedevil*: AR, *Tide*, July 6, 1944, NARA RG 38, CNO, 370/45/3/1, 2–3; OH, George Crane, XO, *Tide*, Sept. 30, 1944, NARA RG 38, E 11, U.S. Navy WWII Oral Histories; AR, *Susan B. Anthony*, June 7, 1944, NARA RG 498, ETO HD, admin file #217; "The United States Medical Department at War, 1941–1945," vol. 1, part 3, Bureau of Medicine and Surgery, 1946, NHHC, 732–33 (*"ship lifted and hogged"*); OH, Byron S. Huie, salvage officer, Aug. 18, 1944, NARA RG 38, E 11, U.S. Navy WWII Oral Histories (*frightened men off the prow*); Liebling, *Mollie & Other War Pieces*, 191 (*"put her nose in the air"*).

90 *"Why in the devil didn't you"*: Bradley, *A Soldier's Story*, 280–81.

90 *"firmly rooted in France"*: Bradley and Blair, *A General's Life*, 256–57; Bradley Commentaries, CBH, MHI, box 41 (*truck's running board*); "The Administrative History of the Operations of 21 Army Group," n.d., NARA RG 334, E 315, ANSCOL, GB 21-AG AH, box 458, 25 (*build their own cages*); memo, F-48 to "Secret Mail Room," Aug. 12, 1944, U.S. Fleet, OPD Information Bulletin, amphibious supplement no. 8, June 9, 1945, GCM Lib, box 1, file 34 (*More than one-third of all shore obstacles*); Bertram H. Ramsay, dispatch, *London Gazette*, Oct. 30, 1947, CMH, 5109+ (*Straits of Dover*); memo, B. B. Talley, Feb. 1948, RG 407, AFIA, 2-3.7 BG (*pinpointed not only enemy gun batteries*); corr, John H. Lauten, 16th Inf, to WD, July 22, 1947, "1st U.S. Infantry Division, G-2 report intelligence activities, MMD (*now being pummeled*).

90 *Yet First Army still had not reached*: CCA, 341, 351 (*Only a quarter*); "A Narrative History of the Second Ranger Infantry Battalion," ts, n.d., Robert W. Black papers, MHI, box 3; OH, Charles M. Bulap, Co E, 2nd Ranger Bn, HI (*Pointe du Hoc*).

90 *Beyond Utah Beach, confusion remained*: "Continuation of Command Narrative," n.d., JMG, MHI, box 12; Blair, *Ridgway's Paratroopers*, 257 (*Benzedrine*), 259–60 (*"where's the picnic?"*).

91 *The 82nd now occupied*: Gavin, *On to Berlin*, 111; CCA, 291 (*no real bridgehead existed west*); Ruppenthal, *Utah Beach to Cherbourg*, 74–75.

91 *"Bridgehead still very shallow"*: Love and Major, eds., *The Year of D-Day*, 84–85; Bradley and Blair, *A General's Life*, 257 (*"pointless interruption"*).

91 *"With the mast swaying"*: *Three Years*, 572–73; Love and Major, eds., *The Year of D-Day*, xvi (*"aura of vinegar"*).

91 *"We've started"*: Eisenhower, *Letters to Mamie*, 190.

91 *Even war could not dim the radiance*: VW, vol. 1, 265; CCA, 339; Aron, *France Reborn*, 30 (*cadging cigarettes*), 24 (*forty thousand*); OH, Lt. Richard Oliphant, NARA RG 38, E 11, U.S. Navy WWII Oral Histories (*White blossoms rioted*); Liddle, *D-Day by Those Who Were There*, 145 (*cows lowed*); Watney, *The Enemy Within*, 108 (*blue smocks*); CBH, July 2, 1944, MHI, box 4 (*fascist salutes*); Lankford, ed., *OSS Against the Reich*, 88 (*shops offered goods*); author visit, Bayeux, May 26–27, 2009; Osmont, *The Normandy Diary of Marie-Louise Osmont*, 45, 49 (*"without overcoats"*).

92 *"belted with gigantic floats"*: Aron, *France Reborn*, 30 and foreword (*Thirty-six thousand French communes*); Drez, ed., *Voices of D-Day*, 293; Donnison, *Civil Affairs and Military Government in North-West Europe*, 74–77 (*"impossible to differentiate"* and *"Looting by troops"*); Middleton, *Our Share of Night*, 315 (*set up a press camp*); Moorehead, *Eclipse*, 113 (*"a dry Sauterne"*).

92 *"only shells with their insides blown out"*: Moorehead, *Eclipse*, 109; Thompson, *The Imperial War Museum Book of Victory in Europe*, 90–91 (*"please stop the shells"*); Scannell, *Argument of Kings*, 157, 165–66 (*"What I can never understand"*); Osmont, *The Normandy Diary of Marie-Louise Osmont*, 41, 46–47 (*"Overhead the hisses"*).

93 *"looking helpless and insignificant"*: CBH, June 8, 1944, MHI, box 4; Pyle, *Brave Men*, 251–52; Tobin, *Ernie Pyle's War*, 173–79.

A Gunman's World

93 *Enemy soldiers by the tens of thousands*: Keegan, *Six Armies in Normandy*, 157; Wilmot, *The Struggle for Europe*, 305 (*French buses upholstered*).

93 *Traveling by five dusty routes*: Lefèvre, *Panzers in Normandy Then and Now*, 81; *VW*, vol. 1, 23; Carell, *Invasion—They're Coming!*, 107–8 (*"bombers hovering"*); Mark, *Aerial Interdiction in Three Wars*, 246 (*six miles per hour*); Wilmot, *The Struggle for Europe*, 300; Cooper, *The German Army, 1933–1945*, 503 (*Not until June 9*). Historian Niklas Zetterling asserts that Panzer Lehr march losses were exaggerated, although delays were significant. *Normandy 1944*, 47, 384–89.

94 *Half a dozen flak battalions*: Carell, *Invasion—They're Coming!*, 114–15; Zetterling, *Normandy 1944*, 48 (*sixty trains*); Keegan, *Six Armies in Normandy*, 156 (Das Reich *matériel and troops*).

94 *"My friends, you are going to appear"*: Hastings, *Das Reich*, 116–26, 170–82; Foot, *SOE in France*, 399 (*"book of iniquity"*).

94 *Evil also shadowed*: Cooper, *The German Army, 1933–1945*, 503; Milner, "Stopping the Panzers," *JMH* (Apr. 2010): 491+; Isby, ed., *Fighting the Invasion*, 241; Zetterling, *Normandy 1944*, 46 (*too low on fuel*); Chandler and Collins, eds., *The D-Day Encyclopedia*, 361 (*former miner and policeman*); Luther, *Blood and Honor*, 72–73 (*broken nineteen bones*); Murray and Millett, *A War to Be Won*, 423 (*tossing live hand grenades*).

94 *Like hornets the grenadiers swarmed*: Milner, "Stopping the Panzers," *JMH* (Apr. 2010): 491+; Luther, *Blood and Honor*, 147 (*chocolate, peanuts*).

95 *Belated salvos from the warships*: *VC*, 132–33; C. P. Stacey, "Operation Overlord and Its Sequel," Canadian Military HQ, report no. 131, n.d., NARA RG 407, E 427, ETO ML, #640, 13–14 (*more than two miles*); OH, Dixon M. Raymond, 1981, Craig W. H. Luther papers, HIA, box 1, 4–5 (*"couple days"*).

95 *Yet Panzermeyer lacked the strength*: Margolian, *Conduct Unbecoming*, 58–64.

95 *"Why do you bring prisoners"*: Luther, *Blood and Honor*, 181–82; C. P. Stacey, "Canadian Participation in the Operations of North-West Europe," Canadian Military HQ, report no. 147, Oct. 1945, NARA RG 407, E 427, ETO ML (*Murder Division*); "Report on the Court of Inquiry," SHAEF, July 1944, NARA RG 331, 290/715/2, E-56, box 2; Margolian, *Conduct Unbecoming*, 102; Hart, *Clash of Arms*, 383–85 (*cycle of atrocity*); McKee, *Caen: Anvil of Victory*, 201 (*"We just shoot them"*); Beevor, *The Second World War*, 594 (*"NPT below rank major"*). War crimes courts later found the 12th SS Panzer Division culpable for sixty-two cold-blooded murders; many scholars and soldiers believe the number of victims was at least double that. Reynolds, *Steel Inferno*, 94.

96 *Canadian battle casualties approached three thousand*: *VC*, 140; Granatstein, *The Generals*, 132 (*"fuck and frontal"*); English, *The Canadian Army and the Normandy Campaign*, 310 (*expanded to more than fiftyfold*).

96 *"They went at it like hockey players"*: Hastings, *OVERLORD*, 125; *CCA*, 373–74 (*Authie impossible to replicate*); Luther, *Blood and Honor*, 175 (*"screamed from rage"*); Milner, "Stopping the Panzers," *JMH* (Apr. 2010): 491+ (*"stupid things"*).

96 *Among the bastards watching*: Bodo Zimmermann, 1946, FMS, #B-308, MHI, 42–43; MMB, 181; Luther, *Blood and Honor*, 170 (*"My dear Meyer"*); *CCA*, 373–74.

96 *Trailers, tents, and four large radio trucks*: Wilmot, *The Struggle for Europe*, 303; Bennett, *Ultra in the West*, 58–59 (*rely increasingly on the radio*), 68–69; George F. Howe, "American Signal Intelligence in Northwest Africa and Western Europe," n.d., SRH 391, NSA, NARA RG 457, E 9002, 134 (*seventeen thousand messages a day*); Hinsley, 486–90.

97 *Geyr now cocked an ear*: Luther, *Blood and Honor*, 179–80.

97 *Geyr escaped with minor wounds*: Wilmot, *The Struggle for Europe*, 303; Bennett, *Ultra in the West*, 68–69 (*fled to Paris*).

97 *Similar decapitations further impaired*: Geyr, "Reflections on the Invasion," *Military*

Review (Jan. 1961): 2+; Luther, *Blood and Honor*, 195; Günther Keil, "919th Grenadier Regiment," n.d., FMS, #C-018, MHI, 36–38 (*"little piece of life"*); Hastings, *OVERLORD*, 173–74 (*wooden leg*); McLean, *Quiet Flows the Rhine*, 2, 130 (*675 World War II German generals*).

97 *"The Seventh Army is everywhere"*: *VW*, vol. 1, 258; "Special Messages," June 11, 1944, UK NA, HW 1/2927 (*intercepted by Ultra*); Leo Geyr von Schweppenburg, ETHINT 13, Dec. 11, 1947, MHI, 6 (*antiaircraft gun carriers*); BP, 33 (*borrow fifteen machine guns*).

98 *Rommel too was unnerved*: Liddell Hart, ed., *The Rommel Papers*, 477–78; Ruge, *Rommel in Normandy*, 183 (*"territory for bargaining"*); Cooper, *The German Army, 1933–1945*, 504–5 (*"every man shall fight"*).

98 *"The battle is not going"*: Liddell Hart, ed., *The Rommel Papers*, 491–93.

98 *Rommel's lament would have delighted*: "Monty's Wartime Caravans," *AB*, no. 20 (1978): 32+; Wilmot, *The Struggle for Europe*, 336. John Colville, who was Churchill's private secretary, reported that Montgomery had even signed some of his own photographs. Colville, *Footprints in Time*, 184–87 (*"three of Rommel"*).

98 *On D+2 he had come home to Normandy*: Montgomery, *A Field-Marshal in the Family*, 7–8; author visit, Creullet, May 29, 2009; Eisenhower, *General Ike*, 115 (*"keep left"*); Kennedy, *The Business of War*, 343 (*"betting book"*); Hamilton, *Master of the Battlefield*, 718 (*"beaten when necessary"*); Hamilton, *Monty: Final Years of the Field-Marshal, 1944–1976*, 419 (*menagerie*); Kingston McCloughry, *Direction of War*, 158 (*"slender, hard, hawk-like"*); J. S. W. Stone, memoir, n.d., LHC, folder 5, 22 (*reading scripture*).

98 *"The way to fame"*: D'Este, *Decision in Normandy*, 504; Moorehead, *Montgomery*, 188–89 (*275 guineas*); Howarth, ed., *Monty at Close Quarters*, 22 (*"Master"*), 79 (*"interesting personage"*); Lewin, *Montgomery as Military Commander*, 349 (*"Cromwellian figure"*); Granatstein, *The Generals*, 113 (*"God Almonty"*); PP, 472 (*"little monkey"*); Hastings, *Armageddon*, 26 (*"little shit"*); Moran, *Churchill: Taken from the Diaries of Lord Moran*, 174 (*"Monty wants to be a king"*); OH, Charles Miles Dempsey, March 12–13, 1947, FCP, MHI (*"Monty is a good man"*).

99 *He had arrived for the second time*: Carver, ed., *The War Lords*, 501; Raymond Callahan, "Two Armies in Normandy," in Wilson, ed., *D-Day 1944*, 261 (*"last great field army"*); Belfield and Essame, *The Battle for Normandy*, 47 (*British Liberation Army*).

99 *"the power of commanding affection"*: Carver, ed., *The War Lords*, 503; Bradley, *A Soldier's Story*, 319–20 (*"tolerant and judicious"*); Moorehead, *Montgomery*, 36 (*"mousetrap"*); Howarth, ed., *Monty at Close Quarters*, 11 (*"a burning glass"*).

99 *"I keep clear of all details"*: Richardson, *Send for Freddie*, 146; Leasor, *The Clock with Four Hands*, 7 (*"Do you agree"*); Howarth, ed., *Monty at Close Quarters*, 28 (*"One was impressed"*); OH, Field Marshal Montgomery of Alamein, Oct. 1, 1966, John S. D. Eisenhower, CBM, MHI, box 6, 9 (*usual bedtime*).

100 *"too many of his best qualities"*: Lewin, *Montgomery as Military Commander*, 342; Carver, ed., *The War Lords*, 501–3 (*"Like Bottom"*); Howarth, ed., *Monty at Close Quarters*, 37 (*"only rude intentionally"*).

100 *"very small-boyish"*: Hamilton, *Master of the Battlefield*, 537, 546 (*"As long as 51 percent"*); Miller, *Ike the Soldier*, 660 (*refuse to attend her funeral*); Irving, *The War Between the Generals*, 170; Moorehead, *Montgomery*, 36; Howarth, ed., *Monty at Close Quarters*, 23 (*"Alone I done it"*).

100 *"Enjoying life greatly"*: Hamilton, *Master of the Battlefield*, 652.

100 *The OVERLORD plan was largely his*: Ellis, *Brute Force*, 374; OH, David Belchem, 21st AG, Feb. 20, 1947, FCP, MHI (*American right to capture Cherbourg*); Wilmot, *The Struggle for Europe*, 311–12 (*"My general policy"*); memo, B. L. Montgomery, Apr. 14, 1944, IWM, Christopher "Kit" Dawnay collection, PP/MCR, C46, Ancillary Collections, micro R-1 (*"armored force thrusts"*).

100 *Thirty-four Allied armored battalions*: Zetterling, *Normandy 1944*, 107; Davis, *Carl A. Spaatz and the Air War in Europe*, 457 (*"gutless bugger"*).

101 *A flanking attack from west of Caen*: D'Este, *Decision in Normandy*, 176–89; *VW*, vol. 1, 254–56.

101 *"The whole show on land"*: Trafford Leigh-Mallory, "Daily Reflections on the Course of the Battle," UK NA, AIR 37/784; Moorehead, *Montgomery*, 217 (*"a gunman's world"*); Hastings, *Inferno*, 524 (*"Bloody murder"*); Lewis, ed., *The Mammoth Book of Eyewitness World War II*, 405–6 (*"Day of Hell"*).

101 *For the Americans in the west*: Friedrich Freiherr von der Heydte, "A German Parachute Regiment in Normandy," 1954, FMS, #B-839, MHI, 16–19; *CCA*, 366–67; Schrijvers, *The Crash of Ruin*, 93 (*"Lousy & undersized"*), 125 (*"I thought of Carthage"*); "FUSA Weekly Report, 6–14 June 1944," in "Memorandum to Harrison," May 27, 1948, CMH.

102 *Bradley late on June 13*: corr, Clarence R. Huebner to G. A. Harrison, Oct. 17, 1947, NARA RG 319, *CCA* historical files, box 164.

102 *"I'm sitting in a little gray stone"*: TR to Eleanor, June 11, 1944, LOC MS, box 10.

102 *No one took a greater proprietary interest*: "General de Gaulle Visit to Normandy, 14 June 1944," UK NA, ADM 1/16018; Aron, *France Reborn*, 45–47 (*"not altogether in accordance"*).

102 *"I wrote to Mr. Churchill"*: Kersaudy, *Churchill and De Gaulle*, 357; Beevor and Cooper, *Paris After the Liberation, 1944–1949*, 29 (*"Has it occurred to you"*); Fenby, *The General*, 142-44.

103 *"We have not come to France"*: Beevor and Cooper, *Paris After the Liberation, 1944–1949*, 109; "General de Gaulle Visit to Normandy, 14 June 1944," UK NA, ADM 1/16018 (*"dislike of smoking"*); Aron, *France Reborn*, 45–47 (*"I missed him in Africa"*).

103 *"a stiff, lugubrious figure"*: Moorehead, *Eclipse*, 122; Beevor and Cooper, *Paris After the Liberation, 1944–1949*, 30 (*saluting gendarmes*); Whitehead, *"Beachhead Don,"* 130–31 ("Vive De Gaulle"); Donnison, *Civil Affairs and Military Government in North-West Europe*, 78–79 (*Several thousand people awaited*); De Gaulle, *The Complete War Memoirs of Charles de Gaulle*, 563–64 (*"women smiled and sobbed"*); author visit, Bayeux, May 27, 2009, historical signage, Place de Gaulle (*"glorious and mutilated"*); Aron, *France Reborn*, 45–47 (*"The path of war"*).

103 *After belting out "La Marseillaise"*: "General de Gaulle Visit to Normandy, 14 June 1944," UK NA, ADM 1/16018 (*fourteen hotel rooms*); Hamilton, *Master of the Battlefield*, 666; De Gaulle, *The Complete War Memoirs of Charles de Gaulle*, 638 ("France would live"); Robb, *The Discovery of France*, 29 (*"cheese"*).

103 *Montgomery wrote Churchill*: BLM to WSC, June 15, 1944, UK NA, CAB 120/867; Guérard, *France: A Short History*, 239 ("Blessed be he").

Terror Is Broken by Terror

104 *In happier days, when the Reich*: Germany IX, 415 (*a force of 28,000 workers*); *World War II Diary of Jean Gordon Peltier*, MRC FDM, 181–82 (*new maple furniture*); Mark Watson, "As I Saw It," in Knickerbocker et al., *Danger Forward*, 269–70 (*bootjack*); Stenbuck, ed., *Typewriter Battalion*, 222–24 (*Potemkin farmhouses*); Speidel, *We Defended Normandy*, 105 (*Soissons Cathedral*).

104 *"the most forbidden place in France"*: Stenbuck, ed., *Typewriter Battalion*, 222–24; Beevor, *D-Day*, 172 (*"meat flies"*); http://www.hitlerpages.com/pagina33.html.

104 *This was Hitler's first return to France*: *CCA*, 140; Fest, *Hitler*, 695–98 ("tipping to the right"); Bodo Zimmermann, 1946, FMS, #B-308, MHI, 111 (*personal command*).

105 *Hitler sat hunched on a wooden stool*: Speidel, *We Defended Normandy*, 106–7; Bertram H. Ramsay, dispatch, *London Gazette*, Oct. 30, 1947, CMH, 5109+. Twenty Allied divisions had landed by D+9, but Rommel put the number at twenty-six. James Hodgson, "The German Defense of Normandy," Sept. 1953, R-24, NARA RG 319, 270/19/30/4-7, box 6, 8–9.

105 *The German Seventh Army opposed them*: Cooper, *The German Army, 1933–1945*, 503; Edward J. Drea, "Unit Reconstitution: A Historical Perspective," Dec. 1983, CSI, 16

(*averaged under eleven thousand*); *VW*, vol. 1, 262 (*casualties had reached 26,000*); *WaS*, 62; James Hodgson, "The German Defense of Normandy," Sept. 1953, R-24, NARA RG 319, 270/19/30/4-7, box 6, 8–9 (*superiority in matériel*).

105 *Anglo-American warplanes harried*: G. Rundstedt, "Experiences from the Invasion Battles of Normandy," June 20, 1944, in *Naval Intelligence Weekly*, Nov. 15, 1944, Sidney Negretto Papers, MHI, box 4; Biddle, *Rhetoric and Reality in Air Warfare*, 280 (*three hundred trains*); *Germany VII*, 328–30 (*German aircraft reinforcements*); F. Ruge, "Coast Defense and Invasion," June 9, 1947, ONI IR 243, NARA RG 334, E 315, ANSCOL, box 642; Buffetaut, *D-Day Ships*, 147 (*Le Havre*).

105 *American tanks had crossed the Cherbourg–Coutances road*: Isby, ed., *Fighting the Invasion*, 30.

105 *"Don't call it a beachhead"*: Keegan, *Six Armies in Normandy*, 165; Blumentritt, *Von Rundstedt*, 235; Speidel, *We Defended Normandy*, 106–7 (*"Cherbourg is to be held"*).

105 *Rundstedt said little*: Barnett, ed., *Hitler's Generals*, 175–76, 191–98; Roberts, *The Storm of War*, 501 (Der alte Herr); Holt, *The Deceivers*, 570–71 (Der schwarze Ritter); Blumentritt, *Von Rundstedt*, 13–15 (*Junker gentry*); MMB, 477–78.

106 *Beset by rheumatism*: Liddell Hart, *The Other Side of the Hill*, 390 (*"psychic resignation"*); Holt, *The Deceivers*, 570–71 (*slept late*); Isby, ed., *Fighting the Invasion*, 47 (*disdained both the telephone*), 50 (*"just as before 1866"*); Liddell Hart, *The German Generals Talk*, 71–72 (*"brown dirt"*); Speidel, *We Defended Normandy*, 89–90 (*"Bohemian corporal"*); "Battle of the Bulge," PIR, MHI, 12 (*"Quatsch!"*); G. Rundstedt, British interrogation, July 9, 1945, NARA RG 407, E 427, ETO ML #2126, box 24231 (*"cheap bluff"*); Barnett, ed., *Hitler's Generals*, 185; Günther Blumentritt, ETHINT 73, Jan. 1946, MHI, 2–4 (*deepened his gloom*).

106 *Now Rundstedt stepped forward*: James Hodgson, "The German Defense of Normandy," Sept. 1953, R-24, NARA RG 319, 270/19/30/4-7, box 6, 8–9; Irving, *The Trail of the Fox*, 387 (*"The fortress is to hold out"*); Wilmot, *The Struggle for Europe*, 326 (*"They must hold here"*).

106 *Rundstedt thought another invasion was likely*: G. Rundstedt, British interrogation, July 9, 1945, NARA RG 407, E 427, ETO ML #2126, box 24231; Holt, *The Deceivers*, 580–81 (*diverted but a single division*); Howard, *British Intelligence in the Second World War*, vol. 5, *Strategic Deception*, 189 (*twenty-one others*); Bodo Zimmermann, 1946, FMS, #B-308, MHI, 86 (*Rundstedt agreed with Marshal Rommel*); Liddell Hart, *The Other Side of the Hill*, 401; Speidel, *We Defended Normandy*, 98–99; CCA, 412–13.

106 *"You must stay where you are"*: Liddell Hart, *The Other Side of the Hill*, 410.

106 *Great things were afoot*: IFG, 46–47; Hinsley, 483–84; *WaS*, 69.

107 *"imagination run wild"*: *Germany VII*, 420; Hinsley, 424 (*Volkswagen factory*); AAFin-WWII, 105 (*thirty-six thousand tons*); "The V-Weapons," AB, no. 6 (1974): 2+ (*simple mobile equipment*); M. C. Helfers, "The Employment of V-Weapons by the Germans During World War II," 1954, OCMH, NARA RG 319, 2-3.7 AW, 85 (*weapon was a flying torpedo*); Irving, *The Mare's Nest*, 299 (*"cherry stones"*).

107 *The first salvo, launched from western France*: Hinsley, 428–29; *Germany VII*, 375 (*"Terror is broken by terror"*).

107 *Rundstedt suggested that the V-1*: Liddell Hart, ed. *The Rommel Papers*, 454n; Goerlitz, *History of the German General Staff, 1657–1945*, 460–61; *Germany VII*, 426–29 (*margin of error*); Speidel, *We Defended Normandy*, 109 (*"easier for peace"*).

107 *They broke for lunch*: Blumentritt, *Von Rundstedt*, 235; Speidel, *We Defended Normandy*, 110; Irving, *The Trail of the Fox*, 386–88 (*three liqueur glasses*).

107 *"What do you really think of our chances"*: Wilmot, *The Struggle for Europe*, 333; Goerlitz, *History of the German General Staff, 1657–1945*, 460–61 (*"Attend to your invasion front"*).

108 *"The discussion had no success"*: *VW*, vol. 1, 269; Bodo Zimmermann, 1946, FMS, #B-308, MHI, 112 (*V-1 flew east rather than west*); *Germany VII*, 432 (*court-martial investigators*); Kershaw, *Hitler, 1936–45: Nemesis*, 643 (*"Only optimists"*).

108 *"cannot escape the Führer's influence"*: Irving, *The Trail of the Fox*, 387; Ruge, *Rommel in Normandy*, 190–97, 234 (*"endless parallels"*).

108 *Rommel retired to his chambers*: author visit, La Roche–Guyon, May 30, 2009; Liddell Hart, ed., *The Rommel Papers*, 492 (*"The long-range action"*).

108 *Even on the Sabbath morn*: http://myweb.tiscali.co.uk/homefront/arp/arp4a.html (*crowed in jubilaton*).

108 *In the Guards Chapel at Wellington Barracks*: "Services Tomorrow," *Times* (London), June 17, 1944, 8; Ziegler, *London at War, 1939–1945*, 290 (*"Te Deum"*); Baker, *Ernest Hemingway*, 501–3 (*"white-hot bunghole"*); Churchill, *Triumph and Tragedy*, 39–40.

109 *Then they heard nothing*: King and Kutta, *Impact*, 198–99; www.flyingbombsandrockets .com/V1; War Damage Report No. 1861, Royal Military Guards Chapel, Aug. 3, 1944, UK NA, IR 37/59 (*blew out walls*); author visit, Guards Chapel and Museum, Apr. 5, 2010; McKee, *Caen: Anvil of Victory*, 133–34 (*"Be thou faithful"*).

109 *Clementine Churchill hastened home*: Churchill, *Triumph and Tragedy*, 39–40; reminiscence, George Laity, Aug. 15, 2005, www.bbc.co.uk/print/ww2peopleswar/stories/66 (*wax tableau*); McKee, *Caen: Anvil of Victory*, 133–34 (*Churchill wept*).

109 *That afternoon he motored to Bushy Park*: Chandler, 1933; *AAFinWWII*, 526–32; CCA, 215–17 (*thirty thousand attack sorties*); www.discoverfrance.net/France/Paris/Monuments -Paris/Eiffel.shtml (*four Eiffel Towers*); M. C. Helfers, "The Employment of V-Weapons by the Germans During World War II," 1954, OCMH, NARA RG 319, 2-3.7 AW, 33–34 (*forty or more times*); Lyall, ed., *The War in the Air*, 374 (*harpoons*).

109 CROSSBOW *countermeasures in the coming weeks*: Hillson, "Barrage Balloons for Low-Level Air Defense," *Airpower Journal* (summer 1989): 37+; *Germany VII*, 430; Lyall, ed., *The War in the Air*, 378 (*learned to use their wings*); Baldwin, *The Deadly Fuze*, 257–58 (*eight times more difficult*); Collier, *The Defence of the United Kingdom*, 383–84 (*guns were shifted from greater London*); Churchill, *Triumph and Tragedy*, 40 (*Bomb Alley*).

110 *Eisenhower's "first priority" edict*: *AAFinWWII*, 532, 528 (*one hundred V-1s were still fired at Target 42 each day*); M. C. Helfers, "The Employment of V-Weapons by the Germans During World War II," 1954, OCMH, NARA RG 319, 2-3.7 AW, 100 (*one-quarter of all combat sorties*); Collier, *The Defence of the United Kingdom*, 387 (*73,000 tons*); Davis, *Carl A. Spaatz and the Air War in Europe*, 432 (*bombers had little impact*); diary, July 4, 1944, Frederick L. Anderson papers, HIA, box 2 (*"give the enemy full credit"*).

110 *A British study calculated*: "CROSSBOW Probable Scale and Effect of Attack on London by Pilotless Aircraft," Jan. 10, 1944, British COS, NARA RG 331, E 3, SHAEF SGS, 290/7/4/4-5, box 132; corr, Bernard Lipford, 115th Inf, NARA RG 407, E 427, HI (*"pushed through the walls"*).

110 *Soon not a pane of glass remained*: King and Kutta, *Impact*, 202, 211; Fussell, *Wartime*, 215 (*"little devilish laughs"*); Eisenhower, *Letters to Mamie*, 197 (*nineteen times*); Ziegler, *London at War, 1939–1945*, 306 (*"How squalid"*).

110 *Fewer and fewer were willing*: King and Kutta, *Impact*, 211; Collier, *The Defence of the United Kingdom*, 395 (*"an ordeal perhaps as trying"*).

How Easy It Is to Make a Ghost

111 *West of Bayeux, the Norman uplands*: Keegan, *Six Armies in Normandy*, 152–53; Davies, "Geographical Factors in the Invasion and Battle of Normandy," *Geographical Review* (Oct. 1946): 613+ (*pre-Cambrian schist*); memo, Cleave A. Jones, July 17, 1944, SHAEF, NARA RG 498, ETO HD, UD 603, SLAM 201 file, box 1 (*sunken lanes*); *Nouveau Petit Larousse*, 1934, http://en.wikipedia.org/wiki/Bocage (*"agreeable shady"*); Wellard, *The Man in a Helmet*, 126 (*"Gethsemane"*); Doubler, *Busting the Bocage*, 21 (*Guadalcanal*).

111 *"I couldn't imagine the bocage"*: OH, ONB, 1974–75, Charles Hanson, MHI, IX-4; "Neptune Monograph," TF 122, Apr. 21, 1944, NARA RG 331, E 23, SHAEF G-3 Plans, 290/7/10/6, box 43 (*amply forewarned*); *The 35th Infantry Division in World War II* (*"fortification like a wall"*); terrain study, Charles H. Bonesteel III, FUSA, Apr. 18, 1944, Arthur S. Nevins papers, MHI (*"Norman bocage"*); OH, Charles H. Bonesteel III, 1973,

Robert St. Louis, SOOHP, MHI, 164; "Appreciation of Possible Development of Operations to Secure a Lodgment Area," May 7, 1944, 21st AG, UK NA, WO 205/118, 2; *St.-Lô*, 4 (*four thousand hedged enclosures*); Cawthon, *Other Clay*, 76 ("*We were rehearsed endlessly*").

111 "*I feel we'll be getting to St. Lô*": CCA, 383.

112 *Tank companies now reported*: Doubler, *Closing with the Enemy*, 43–44; Mack Morriss, "My Old Outfit," in *Reporting World War II*, vol. 2, 539 ("*a wall of fire*"); "Terrain—Cotentin Peninsula," July 8, 1944, VIII Corps, NARA RG 498, G-3 OR, box 10 ("*spitting range*"); Charles H. Coates, "German Defense in Hedgerow Terrain," WD Observer Board, July 27, 1944, NARA RG 334, E 315, ANSCOL, AGF ETO C-117 (*intimacy neutralized Allied air and artillery*); Pyle, *Brave Men*, 255 ("*snipers everywhere*"); msg, 15th Army Group to SHAEF, Feb. 11, 1945, NARA RG 331, SHAEF SGS, 383.6/4 (*sliding scale of rewards*).

112 *Enemy panzers, artillery, and savage small-arms fire*: Simpson, *Selected Prose*, 139, 122 ("*purr of the bullets*"), 125 ("*Some ideas stink*"); Linderman, *The World Within War*, 85 ("*I lie in the grass*"); Shephard, *A War of Nerves*, 252 ("*a soft siffle*"); Whitaker et al., *Victory at Falaise*, 309–10 (*Mortar fragments*).

112 *French civilians waving white strips*: Pyle, *Brave Men*, 284–85 (*eight cents*); Belfield and Essame, *The Battle for Normandy*, 132 ("*plastered to the walls*"); Wilson, ed., *D-Day 1944*, 254 (*stiff-legged as wooden toys*); Rosse and Hill, *The Story of the Guards Armoured Division*, 33 ("*gigantic rake*"); Daglish, *Operation Goodwood*, 96 (*smoke tinted red*); Whitehead, "Beachhead Don," 133 ("*not a building standing whole*"); Peckham and Snyder, eds., *Letters from Fighting Hoosiers*, vol. 2, 120 ("*deserted and silent*").

113 *Each contested town, like each hedgerow*: memo, Royce L. Thompson, "ETO Invasion Casualties," May 27, 1948, OCMH, GCM Lib, Royce L. Thompson collection, box 1; Osmont, *The Normandy Diary of Marie-Louise Osmont*, 88 ("*white as sheets*" and "*like hunted animals*"); Shephard, *A War of Nerves*, 252; memo, July 15, 1944, NARA RG 498, ETO, SGS, 333.5, 290/50/10/11/7-1, box 35; memo, First Army IG, Aug. 7, 1944, NARA RG 338, First Army AG Gen'l Corr, OIG, box 218 (*five hundred cases of suspected* "*S.I.W.*"); memo, Cleave A. Jones, July 17, 1944, SHAEF, NARA RG 498, ETO HD, UD 603, SLAM 201 file, box 1 ("*Have we 100 divisions*").

113 "*Things are always confusing*": Pyle, *Brave Men*, 269, 305; Hadley, *Heads or Tails*, 90 ("*make a ghost*"); Holt and Holt, *Major & Mrs. Holt's Battlefield Guide to the Normandy Landing Beaches*, 133 (*slain by a mortar splinter*); L. F. Skinner, "The Man Who Worked on Sundays," n.d., IWM, 01/13/1, 18 ("*I buried him close*").

113 *Only the sharpest weather eye*: WaS, 64; Stagg, *Forecast for Overlord*, 126; Bates and Fuller, *America's Weather Warriors*, 96; Woodward, *Ramsay at War*, 164–65 (*SHAEF forecasters predicted*); Karig, *Battle Report: The Atlantic War*, 352–56 (*chance of a June gale*); "Operation OVERLORD: Report on the Effect of Bad Weather, 19–23 June 1944," SHAEF, n.d., NARA RG 498, ETO HD, admin file #220 (*three hundred to one*).

113 *More than two hundred ships now plied*: "Report by the Allied Naval Commander-in-Chief," Oct. 1944, NARA RG 407, ML, #624, 94–95; CCA, 423 (*218,000 tons*); Bynell, "Logistical Planning and Operations—Europe," lecture, March 16, 1945, NARA RG 334, E 315, ANSCOL, box 207, 5 (*30 percent less than planned*); LSA, vol. 2, 392–93 (*anchored off the wrong strand*); "Amphibious Operations: Invasion of Northern France," CINC, U.S. Fleet, Oct. 1944, NARA RG 407, ML #252, box 24148, 5–13 (*officers in small boats*); Waddell, *United States Army Logistics*, 65, 134 ("*Please, oh, please*").

114 *But shortages were more common*: Waddell, *United States Army Logistics*, 75–76, 83 (*strict firing limits*); Bynell, "Logistical Planning and Operations—Europe," lecture, Mar. 16, 1945, NARA RG 334, E 315, ANSCOL, box 207, 5; Charles F. MacDermut and Adolph P. Gratiot, "History of G-4 Com Z ETO," 1946, CMH, 8-3.4 AA, 73 (*bundles of maps*); "Supply and Maintenance on the European Continent," NARA RG 407, E 427, AG WWII operations report no. 130, 97-USF5-0.3.0, 41; "G-4 History," n.d., NARA RG 498, ETO HD, admin file #553A-C, 22 (*145,000 tons*); Howard, lecture, Aug.

8, 1944, NARA RG 334, E 315, ANSCOL, L-6-44, H-83, box 191, 9 (*expected to shoot 125 rounds*).

114 *Salvation appeared to be rising*: Churchill, *Triumph and Tragedy*, 8 ("*synthetic harbors*"); H. D. Bynell, lecture, Oct. 31, 1944, NARA RG 334, E 315, ANSCOL, L-7-44, box 199, 6 (*$100 million*); "Invasion Harbors Towed to France," British Information Services, Oct. 17, 1944, Hanson Baldwin papers, YU, box 109, folder 862 (*another ten thousand now bullied*); Keegan, *Six Armies in Normandy*, 161; *IFG*, 25–26; "Prefabricated Ports," Oct. 1944, British Information Services, Hanson Baldwin papers, YU, box 109, folder 862; *WaS*, 28 (*160 tugs*); *VW*, vol. 1, 88–90; *IFG*, 25–26; *WaS*, 26–27 ("*journey of self-immolation*"); Karig, *Battle Report: The Atlantic War*, 347 (*antique side-wheelers*); "Mulberry B," SHAEF G-4, Nov. 1944, NARA RG 498, ETO HD, admin file #44 (*enormous tricolor*).

114 *To this suicide fleet were added*: "Prefabricated Ports," Oct. 1944, British Information Services, Hanson Baldwin papers, YU, box 109, folder 862; "Mulberry B," SHAEF G-4, Nov. 1944, NARA RG 498, ETO HD, admin file #44 (*ten miles of floating piers*); *VW*, vol. 1, 88–90 (*two million tons*); www.nycgovparks.org/sub_your_park/historical_signs/hs_historical_sign.php?id=8771 (*seventeen times more concrete*); Mason, ed., *The Atlantic War Remembered*, 377 ("*One storm will wash*"); "Task Force 128: Report on Installation of Mulberry A," n.d., DDE Lib, A. Dayton Clark papers, box 2 (*unloading had begun at Mulberry A*); Karig, *Battle Report: The Atlantic War*, 352–56 (*LSTs could be emptied*).

115 *one of the worst June gales in eighty years*: Woodward, *Ramsay at War*, 164–65; log, H.M.S. *Despatch*, June 19, 1944, UK NA, WO 32/12211; "Construction Battalions in the Invasion of Normandy," Nov. 30, 1944, SEM, NHHC, box 81, folder 28, 39–40 (*Anchors dragged and fouled*); Thompson, *The Imperial War Museum Book of Victory in Europe*, 96 ("*Storm continues*").

115 *Swept away they were, pier by pier*: "Task Force 128: Report on Installation of Mulberry A," n.d., DDE Lib, A. Dayton Clark papers, box 2; *IFG*, 177 (*gunshots from sailors*); Buffetaut, *D-Day Ships*, 140–42; *CCA*, 423–26; Karig, *Battle Report: The Atlantic War*, 352–56 (*Distress calls jammed*); Love and Major, eds., *The Year of D-Day*, 93 ("*a damnable spell*").

115 *After eighty hours, the spell broke*: *WaS*, 64 ("*a rent in the sky*"); log, H.M.S. *Despatch*, June 19, 1944, UK NA, WO 32/12211 (*Force seven gusts*); OH, Byron S. Huie, Jr., Aug. 18, 1944, NARA RG 38, E 11, U.S. Navy WWII Oral Histories, 5–6 ("*Not even a thousand-bomber raid*"); Belfield and Essame, *The Battle for Normandy*, 102–3; Fergusson, *The Watery Maze*, 346–47 (*small tanker deep in the dunes*); AAR, 21st Weather Squadron, AAF, 1944, NARA RG 498, ETO HD, admin file #493-A (*sea wrack*); *VW*, vol. 1, 272–73 (*two miles of articulated steel pier*).

115 *Mulberry A was a total loss*: R. W. Crawford, "Guns, Gas and Rations," June 1945, SHAEF G-4, NARA RG 498, ETO HD, admin file #145; Chalmers, *Full Cycle*, 238–39 (*Gooseberries were positioned*); Mason, ed., *The Atlantic War Remembered*, 377 ("*formidable abortion*").

116 *Mulberry B ultimately did prove*: Buffetaut, *D-Day Ships*, 136 (*completed in mid-July*); Hickling and Mackillop, "The OVERLORD Artificial Harbors," lecture, Nov. 6, 1944, CARL, N-12217; Charles C. Bates, "Sea, Swell and Surf Forecasting for D-Day and Beyond: The Anglo-American Effort, 1943–1945," 2010, a.p., 20 (*Port Winston*); H. D. Crerar, "Notes on Conference Given by C-in-C 21 Army Group," June 22, 1944, National Archives of Canada, RG 24, vol. 1054 2, file 215A21.016 (9) ("*at least six days behind*"); *WaS*, 65–66 (*until late July*); *VW*, vol. 1, 274 (*Rommel had exploited the bad weather*); "Supply and Evacuation by Air," n.d., NARA RG 407, E 427, AG WWII Operations Reports, 97-USF5-0.3.0, no. 26 (*hand grenades were flown*); *LSA*, vol. 1, 407 (*eight coasters deliberately beached*).

116 *With the beaches again in disarray*: memo, R. C. Partridge and C. H. Bonesteel III, Dec. 31, 1943, NARA RG 407, ETO ML, #205, box 24143 ("*overwhelm us*"); "Official Study of Port of Cherbourg," 1945, NARA RG 498, ETO HD, admin file #492 (*supplying up to thirty divisions*); Coles and Weinberg, *Civil Affairs*, 721 ("*most important port*").

116 *Great misfortune had befallen Cherbourg*: "Official Study of Port of Cherbourg," 1945, RG 498, ETO HD, admin file #492 (*pillage by the heriditary enemy*); Baedeker, *Northern France*, 158–61; "Cherbourg, Gateway to France: Rehabilitation and Operation of the First Major Port," 1945, NARA RG 319, ETO HD, 8-3.1 AE (*financed with German reparations*).

116 *Now Cherbourg was again besieged*: CCA, 420–22; Whitehead, "*Beachhead Don*," 146–47 (*French farmers tossed roses*); Pyle, *Brave Men*, 273–75 ("*terribly pathetic*"); Bradley, *A Soldier's Story*, 308 (*Strauss waltzes*); *Three Years*, 596–97 (*hog calling*); Fussell, *Wartime*, 255 ("*bumf*"); Lasky, "Military History Stood on Its Head," *Berlin Journal* 14 (spring 2007), American Academy of Berlin: 20+ ("Ei sörrender").

117 *An American ultimatum*: Ruppenthal, *Utah Beach to Cherbourg*, 172–77, 189; Whitehead, *World War II: An Ex-Sergeant Remembers*, 79 ("*All you sons-a-bitches*").

117 *In radio messages decrypted by Ultra*: CCA, 431–34 ("*bunker paralysis*"); Sunset 604, June 25, 1944, NARA RG 457, E 9026, SRS-1869 ("*greatly worn out*"); Reardon, ed., *Defending Fortress Europe*, mss, 165 (*five thousand cows*); Saunders, *Royal Air Force, 1939–1945*, vol. 3, 123 (*four U-boats*); CCA, 434 ("*You will continue to fight*").

117 *Schlieben's miseries multiplied*: "The Reminiscences of Alan Goodrich Kirk," 1962, John Mason, Col U OHRO, NHHC, 349–50 (*bombardment force split*); Karig, *Battle Report: The Atlantic War*, 362–65.

117 *Great salvos soon arced*: OH, John F. Latimer, n.d., NARA RG 38, E 11, U.S. Navy WWII Oral Histories, 19–20 ("*more concentrated firing*"); Morton L. Deyo, "Cherbourg," Feb. 1956, SEM, NHHC, box 81, file 33; *IFG*, 198–205 (*most pugnacious German battery*).

118 *Six miles east of Cherbourg*: Buffetaut, *D-Day Ships*, 151–52; AR, U.S.S. *Texas*, July 12, 1944, NARA RG 38, CNO, 370/45/3/1, box 1470, 3–5; *IFG*, 205–12 (*eight hundred rounds dumped on Battery Hamburg*).

118 *In this General Collins was ready to oblige*: memo, Cleave A. Jones, June 22, 1944, SHAEF, NARA RG 498, ETO HD, UD 603, SLAM 201 file, box 1; Johnson, *History of the Twelfth Infantry Regiment in World War II*, 111 (*four hundred feet above*); Collins, *Lightning Joe*, 221 ("*The view of Cherbourg*").

119 "*you can make the other fellow conform*": OH, JLC, Jan. 21, 1954, CBM, NARA RG 319, OCMH, 2-3.7 CB 3; CBH, July 15, 1944, MHI, box 4 (*gift for persuasion*); Keegan, *Six Armies in Normandy*, 159 (*nonchalance about casualties*); Berlin, *U.S. Army World War II Corps Commanders*, 3–5 (*youngest of the thirty-four*), 16 ("*concentration and decision*"); diary, JMG, May 16, 1944, MHI, box 10 ("*runty, cocky*"); Collins, *Lightning Joe*, 2–3 (*New Orleans emporium*); OH, JLC, 1972, Charles C. Sperow, SOOHP, MHI, 6 (*malarial shakes*); Arlington National Cemetery website, http://www.arlingtoncemetery .net/josephla.htm; corr, JLC to Brentano's, Oct. 24, 1944, JLC papers, DDE Lib, box 3, 201 file (Moby Dick); Carafano, *After D-Day*, 186 ("*An order is but an aspiration*").

119 *Now Cherbourg was nearly his*: Ruppenthal, *Utah Beach to Cherbourg*, 193; Wertenbaker, *Invasion!*, 150–52 (*GIs fought to the docks*); Johnson, *History of the Twelfth Infantry Regiment in World War II*, 112.

119 *General von Schlieben had by now retreated*: Carell, *Invasion—They're Coming!*, 177 ("*swing a cat*"); CCA, 438 ("*Documents burned*"); memo, Cleave A. Jones, June 26, 1944, SHAEF, NARA RG 498, ETO HD, UD 603, SLAM 201 file, box 1 ("*It was good*").

119 *Within minutes a German soldier*: Wertenbaker, *Invasion!*, 158–59; Breuer, *Hitler's Fortress Cherbourg*, 232; Bradley, *A Soldier's Story*, 313 (*a printed menu*); Mittelman, ed., *Hold Fast!*, 17 ("*I too am tired*").

120 *a "looter's heaven"*: corr, Thor M. Smith to family, July 5, 1944, Smith papers, HIA; Whitehead, "*Beachhead Don*," 159–60 ("*shaving cream*"); OH, Albert Mumma, July 22, 1944, NARA RG 38, E 11, U.S. Navy WWII Oral Histories, 11 (*Hôtel Atlantique*); memo, Cleave A. Jones, June 26, 1944, SHAEF, NARA RG 498, ETO HD, UD 603, SLAM 201 file, box 1 (*canned octopus*); "Cherbourg, Gateway to France: Rehabilitation and Operation of the First Major Port," 1945, NARA RG 319, ETO HD, 8-3.1 AE; Andrew T. McNamara, "QM Activities of II Corps," 1955, PIR, MHI, 136 (*two bottles of wine and*

three of liquor); Mason, ed., *The Atlantic War Remembered*, 411–15 (*"one big drunk"*); Wertenbaker, *Invasion!*, 162–63. Capture of the oil tanks "ranked with the seizure of the Remagen bridge" across the Rhine nine months later, in one logistian's analysis. *LSA*, vol. 1, 500.

120 *Those who had inspected the port*: Frank A. Osmanski, "Critical Analysis of the Planning and Execution of the Logistic Support of the Normandy Invasion," Dec. 1949, Armed Forces Staff College, Osmanski papers, MHI; *CCA*, 441–42 (*"a masterful job"*); "Official Study of Port of Cherbourg," 1945, NARA RG 498, ETO HD, admin file #492 (*"completely wrecked"*); "Port Plans, Pre-Invasion," n.d., NARA RG 319, *LSA* background files, 2-3.7 CB 6 (*Trainloads of explosives*); F. K. Newcomer, Jr., "Analytical Study of the Rehabilitation of the Port of Cherbourg," n.d., NARA RG 334, E 315, NWC, ANSCOL, box 234, 14–18; Beck, 352.

121 *Countless booby traps seeded the ruins*: "Cherbourg Port Reconstruction," Office of the Chief Engineer, ETO, March 1945, NARA RG 334, E 315, NWC, ANSCOL, USA ETO Z-2, box 1128, 30–32; Mason, ed., *The Atlantic War Remembered*, 410 (*four hundred mines*); *IFG*, 217 (*eight magnetic and eight acoustical sweeps*); Harlan D. Bynell, "Logistical Planning and Operations—Europe," lecture, Oct. 31, 1944, NARA RG 334, E 315, NWC, ANSCOL, L-7-44, box 199, 9 (*tedious, dangerous reconstruction*); *LSA*, vol. 2, 71–75; "Official Study of Port of Cherbourg," 1945, NARA RG 498, ETO HD, admin file #492 (*not until mid-July*); Beck, 355 (*deepwater basins*); "Port Plans, Pre-Invasion," n.d., NARA RG 319, *LSA* background files, 2-3.7 CB 6 (*"One cannot avoid noticing"*).

121 *"this most pregnant victory"*: WSC to J. Stalin, June 29, 1944, "Strategy and Operations, vol. 2," UK NA, CAB 120/421.

121 *22,000 VII Corps casualties*: Ruppenthal, *Utah Beach to Cherbourg*, 199; Coles and Weinberg, *Civil Affairs*, 731 (*sewn from American parachutes*), 735 (*firearms and pigeons*); Wertenbaker, *Invasion!*, 162–63 (*"the fucking generals"*).

121 *Prisoners by the acre*: Wertenbaker, *Invasion!*, 153; Moorehead, *Eclipse*, 138 (*"lines of invective"*); OH, Albert Mumma, July 22, 1944, NARA RG 38, E 11, U.S. Navy WWII Oral Histories, 7 (*floatable conveyance*); memo, W. H. S. Wright, July 25, 1944, NARA RG 337, E 54, AGF Top Secret Gen'l Corr, box 2, folder 319.1 (*ballads from the Seven Years' War*); Blumentritt, *Von Rundstedt*, 238–39; MMB, 138; Keegan, *Six Armies in Normandy*, 160–61.

122 *"To Alton C. Bright"*: Babcock, *War Stories*, 213–16.

122 *In a nearby nineteenth-century French naval hospital*: Cosmas and Cowdrey, *Medical Service in the European Theater of Operations*, 261–63; Joseph R. Darnall, "Powdered Eggs and Purple Hearts," 1946, MHUC, Professional Papers, Group 1, box 24, 133 (*"stinking in their blood-soaked dressings"*); Sforza, *A Nurse Remembers*, no pagination (*"dirty instruments everywhere"*); Wertenbaker, *Invasion!*, 164 (*"Perhaps more men should know"*), 159.

122 *Two bordellos promptly opened*: "Official Study of Port of Cherbourg," 1945, NARA RG 498, ETO HD, admin file #492; Hitchcock, *The Bitter Road to Freedom*, 49 (*"Collaborators' Wagon"*), 382n; Beevor, *D-Day*, 449 (*smelled for miles*), 516.

122 *"cosmoline gun-metal preservative"*: Babcock, *Taught to Kill*, 84.

CHAPTER 3: LIBERATION

A Monstrous Blood-Mill

123 *One million Allied soldiers*: The millionth soldier landed on July 5. Dispatch, Bertram H. Ramsay, *London Gazette*, Oct. 30, 1947, CMH, 5109+.

123 *the invasion increasingly resembled the deadlock at Anzio*: OH, ONB, June 7, 1956, CBM, NARA RG 319, OCMH, 2-3.7, 270/19/5/4, box 184; Sylvan, 31 (*labyrinthine burrows*); Faubus, *In This Faraway Land*, 157 (*"They keep lobbing mortars"*); Thompson, *The Imperial War Museum Book of Victory in Europe*, 137 (*daily casualties in Normandy*); msg, Dietrich von Choltitz, July 15, 1944, in James Hodgson, "The Battle of the Hedgerows,"

Aug. 1954, NARA RG 319, OCMH, R-54, box 8, IV-27 (*"a monstrous blood-mill"*); Zuckerman, *From Apes to Warlords*, 280 (*"I can't afford to stay here"*).

123 *"concentrate all available air"*: ALH, vol. 2, 104.

123 *The supreme commander's jitters*: Crosswell, *Beetle*, 657 (*Chesterfields*); Miller, *Ike the Soldier*, 662 (*"slow-up medicine"*); *Three Years*, 584, 602 (*sucking panes*); diary, June 30 and July 8, 1944, Barbara Wyden papers, DDE Lib, box 1 (*"How I suffer!"*); Eisenhower, *Eisenhower at War, 1943–1945*, 348 (*back of a P-51 Mustang*); Davis, *Soldier of Democracy*, 501 (*"Marshall would raise hell"*); diary, CBH, July 2, 1944, MHI, box 4 (*"Shoot the bastard"*).

124 *"the Dogfight"*: Jackson, *Overlord*, 174.

124 *"I am familiar with your plan"*: DDE to BLM, July 7, 1944, NARA RG 331, E 1, SHAEF SGS, 381.

124 *Montgomery's reply a day later*: Copp and McAndrew, *Battle Exhaustion*, 116–17 (*Canadian 3rd Division*); BLM to DDE, July 8, 1944, DDE Lib, PP-pres, box 83 (*"I am, myself, quite happy"*); BLM to DDE, July 8, 1944, NARA RG 331, E 1, SHAEF SGS, 381 (*"the battle is going very well"*).

124 *"I like him very much"*: D'Este, *Eisenhower: A Soldier's Life*, 564; Hamilton, *Monty: Final Years of the Field-Marshal, 1944–1976*, 273 (*"making sure I'm not sacked"*).

124 *"Chief Big Wind"*: Crosswell, *Beetle*, 659; Kingston McCloughry, *Direction of War*, 144 (*"something of a dictator"*); Tedder, *With Prejudice*, 556 (*told Churchill in late June*); "Excerpts from Diary, D/SAC," kept by Wing Commander Leslie Scarman, July 8, 1944, NARA RG 319, *Supreme Command* background files, 2-3.7 CB 8 (*"The problem is Monty"*); Trafford Leigh-Mallory, "Daily Reflections on the Course of the Battle," June 15, 19, 27, July 17, 1944, UK NA, AIR 37/784 (*"egg-bound"*).

125 *Churchill too grew waspish*: WSC to A. Brooke, June 18, 1944, and WSC to H. Ismay, July 16, 1944, "Strategy and Operations, vol. II," UK NA, CAB 120/421; Parkinson, *A Day's March Nearer Home*, 334–41 (*anthrax looked promising*); Addison, *Churchill, the Unexpected Hero*, 194–95 (*"one by one by bombing attack"*).

125 *"a cold-blooded calculation"*: Addison, *Churchill, the Unexpected Hero*, 194–95.

125 *whether Allied poison gas would shorten*: Eisenhower had reiterated SHAEF's no-first-use policy in late June 1944. ALH, vol. 2, 116.

125 *"It would be absurd"*: Addison, *Churchill, the Unexpected Hero*, 194–95; Parkinson, *A Day's March Nearer Home*, 334–41 (*"harassing effect"*); margin note, SHAEF chief of staff meeting minutes, July 5, 1944, NARA RG 331, E 3, SGS, 290/7/4/4-5, box 128 (*"I will not be party"*).

125 *Montgomery's battle plan required*: Hogan, *A Command Post at War*, 91–95 (*little imagination*); Blumenson, *The Battle of the Generals*, 113 (*three corps abreast*); BP, 125–27 (*"more or less confused"*).

126 *Beyond Omaha Beach, on the left flank*: BP, 109–14 (*congestion, fratricide*), 82–84 (*"That is exactly what I don't want"*); Baker, *Ernest Hemingway*, 511 (*"the deads"*); Hogan, *A Command Post at War*, 100 (*nine generals*); Belfield and Essame, *The Battle for Normandy*, 187 (*"the sadness of it"*).

126 *"too softhearted to take a division"*: Bradley, *A Soldier's Story*, 333.

126 *Roosevelt had been frantically busy*: Jeffers, *In the Rough Rider's Shadow*, 261; BP, 86, 131; corr, TR to Eleanor, June 17, 24, July 3, 7, 1944, TR, LOC MS Div, box 10; Renehan, *The Lion's Pride*, 239 (*"a desperate weariness"*); Michael David Pearlman, "To Make Democracy Safe for the World," Ph.D. diss, University of Illinois, 1978, 603 (*"Maybe my feet hurt"*).

126 *After a conference with Collins*: "Official Statement of the Military Service and Death of Theodore Roosevelt, Jr.," Aug. 29, 1958, TR, LOC MS Div, box 39; corr, R. O. Barton to Eleanor Roosevelt, July 13, 1944, TR, LOC MS Div, box 32 (*"The show goes on"*).

127 *An Army half-track bore Roosevelt*: Liebling, *Mollie & Other War Pieces*, 220 ("Libérateurs").

127 *Roosevelt never knew*: Medal of Honor recommendation, R. O. Barton, June 27, 1944, TR, LOC MS Div, box 39; Wheeler, *The Big Red One*, 300–301 (*Marshall made certain*);

corr, Elizabeth Beston Henry to Eleanor Roosevelt, July 25, 1944, TR, LOC MS Div, box 26 (*"Elizabethan quality"*).

127 *"a very ancient place"*: Baedeker, *Northern France*, 162–63.

127 *Although sacked by Vikings*: Balkoski, *Beyond the Beachhead*, 268; Weigley, *Eisenhower's Lieutenants*, 138 (*Calvinist apostates*); BP, 146 (*bombers returned every day*); Aron, *France Reborn*, 104 (*ten living inhabitants*).

127 *Eight roads and a rail line*: Mansoor, *The GI Offensive in Europe*, 153; Doubler, *Busting the Bocage*, 15; Whitehead, *"Beachhead Don,"* 190 (*fifty-mile front*); *Reporting World War II*, vol. 2, 541 (*"big-stuff bombs"*); BP, 150–51 (*"moth-eaten"*), 140 (*"on their last legs"*); Mayo, *The Ordnance Department*, 250 (*Civil War battlefields*); Daglish, *Operation Goodwood*, 27 (*five hundred yards a day*); *St.-Lô*, 51 (*29th Infantry Division*).

128 *"Everything about him was explosive"*: Cawthon, *Other Clay*, 27–28, 34 (*"Twenty-nine, let's go!"*); Cawthon, "Pursuit: Normandy, 1944," *American Heritage* (Feb. 1978): 80+ (*"eradicator of lethargy"*); "Memoirs of Charles Hunter Gerhardt," July 1964, MHI; Gerhardt biographical material, MMD; Miller, *Division Commander*, 71 (*"Loose Reins"*); e-mail, Roy Livengood to author, Nov. 8, 2008 (*"General Chickenshit"*); OH, Charles L. Bolte, Maclyn Burg, Jan. 29, 1975, MHI, 172–77 (*"describe the resuscitation"* and *"dashing Indian fighter"*); Ewing, *29 Let's Go!*, 283 (*"hard, exacting, aggressive"*); Balkoski, *Beyond the Beachhead*, 253–54 (*a corps of three divisions*).

128 *By late afternoon on July 15*: BP, 154; OH, 2nd ID, July 13–18, 1944, NARA RG 407, E 427-A, CI, folder 12 (*slabs of TNT*); Cawthon, "July, 1944: St. Lô," *American Heritage* (June 1974): 4+ (*"jerked with a rope"*); Linderman, *The World Within War*, 346 (*"the end of everything"*).

128 *Before dawn on Monday, July 17*: Balkoski, *Beyond the Beachhead*, 262; memoir, William Puntenney, ts, n.d., MMD, 59–63 (*killing the new commander*); *St.-Lô*, 110–11 (*undershirts*); BP, 167 (*plasma bags*); Robert E. Walker, "With the Stonewallers," ts, n.d., MMD, 65 (*"unbearably sorry scene"*).

129 *But German defenses were melting*: BP, 170–71; Johns, *The Clay Pigeons of St. Lo*, 198, 233–34 (*stone sarcophagus*); Whitehead, *"Beachhead Don,"* 195 (*"Here among the dead"*); Miller, *Division Commander*, 90 (*slashed his arm*); *St.-Lô*, 117–19 (*seventeen strongpoints*); Balkoski, *Beyond the Beachhead*, 278 (*Howie's body arrived by jeep*).

129 *"You couldn't identify anything"*: "Between Collaboration and Resistance: French Literary Life Under Nazi Occupation," New York Public Library, exhibition, June 2009; Carpenter, *No Woman's World*, 59 (*"On this lake"*); Blumenson, *Liberation*, 28 (*"liberated the hell"*); Bair, *Samuel Beckett: A Biography*, 242–44; Perloff, "In Love with Hiding," *Iowa Review* (2005): 82 (*"capital of ruins"*); Linderman, *The World Within War*, 117 (*"fence posts, teacups, doorbells"*); AAR, George V. Bleier, Jr., graves registration, 11th Inf, n.d., NARA RG 407, ETO G-3 OR, 290/56/5/1-3, box 11 (*booby-trapped German bodies*); "Graves Registration Service," NARA RG 407, E 427, AG WWII operations reports, 97-USF5-0.3.0, no. 107, 10 (*"jerked by a rope"*).

129 *"If there was a world beyond"*: Cawthon, "Pursuit: Normandy, 1944," *American Heritage* (Feb. 1978): 80+.

129 *"eaten the guts out"*: OH, 2nd ID, July 13–18, 1944, NARA RG 407, E 427-A, CI, folder 12.

130 *"Here!"*: Whitehead, *"Beachhead Don,"* 198; Balkoski, *Beyond the Beachhead*, 278. Many bodies of the division dead had yet to be recovered.

130 *Rommel rose with the sun*: Irving, *The Trail of the Fox*, 372–74; Liddell Hart, *The Rommel Papers*, 463–64 (*"can take your mind off"*).

130 *Troubles he had*: Ruge, *Rommel in Normandy*, 228; VW, vol. 1, 307; memoir, J. S. W. Stone, n.d., LHC, folder 5, 54 (*"funk holes"*).

130 *"Militarily things aren't at all good"*: Liddell Hart, *The Rommel Papers*, 491–93; Davis, *Carl A. Spaatz and the Air War in Europe*, 460 (*six thousand half-ton bombs*); BP, 120 (*forty minutes*); Moorehead, *Eclipse*, 145 (*"nothing more to see"*); Aron, *France Reborn*, 106 (*Eight thousand French refugees*); VW, vol. 1, 316 (*a single battalion*).

130 *On any given day now:* Liddell Hart, *The Rommel Papers,* 496, 486–87 (*Only 10,000 replacements*); *BP,* 181 (*80,000 artillery rounds*); Ruge, *Rommel in Normandy,* 213–19 ("*bleeding white*"); James Hodgson, "The Battle of the Hedgerows," Aug. 1954, NARA RG 319, OCMH, R-54, box 8, IV-5 (*1.6 million German casualties*).

131 *That bloodletting had intensified:* Gilbert, *The Second World War,* 544; Megargee, *Inside Hitler's High Command,* 210; Erickson, *The Road to Berlin,* 228 (*shuffle through Moscow*).

131 *Rommel's disaffection grew:* Lewin, *Rommel as Military Commander,* 230; Young, *Rommel, the Desert Fox,* 165 ("*without the least regard*"); Speidel, *We Defended Normandy,* 84–85 (*dangerous talk*); Beevor, *D-Day,* 326–30 (*would consider taking command*); Barnett, ed., *Hitler's Generals,* 200 (*Rundstedt had been removed*); Günther Blumentritt, ETHINT 73, Jan. 8–11, 1946, MHI, 2–4 ("*make an end to the whole war*"); Carver, ed., *The War Lords,* 197 (*250,000-mark gratuity*); *CCA,* 447 ("*I will be next*").

131 *Rundstedt's successor:* MMB, 282–83 (*Cunning Hans*); Barnett, ed., *Hitler's Generals,* 404–5; Speidel, *We Defended Normandy,* 120–22 ("*obstinate self-will*"); Keegan, *Six Armies in Normandy,* 240 ("*couldn't be grimmer*"); Liddell Hart, ed., *The Rommel Papers,* 486–87 ("*growing worse every day*"); *VC,* 179 (*Kluge had endorsed*).

131 *Fried eggs and brandy:* Ruge, *Rommel in Normandy,* 233; "Rommel's Accident," *AB,* no. 8 (1975): 42+; Luther, *Blood and Honor,* 229 ("*Who do you think*").

131 *During a conference at St.-Pierre:* Belfield and Essame, *The Battle for Normandy,* 149; McKee, *Caen: Anvil of Victory,* 256 (*efforts to conceal the noise*); *Germany VII,* 596–97 (*still expected in the Pas de Calais*).

132 *Dietrich agreed that an attack seemed imminent:* Daglish, *Operation Goodwood,* 83–86; Liddell Hart, *The Tanks,* vol. 2, 362 (*ear pressed to the ground*); Irving, *The Trail of the Fox,* 417–18 ("*I obey only you*").

132 *The car raced east on Route D-4:* Fraser, *Knight's Cross,* 510. Conflicting claims were advanced for this action. The British official RAF history credits Spitfires of Squadron No. 602, flying from airfield B11. Saunders, *Royal Air Force, 1939–1945,* vol. 3, 121.

132 *Slugs stitched the left side of the Horch:* "Rommel's Accident," *AB,* no. 8 (1975): 42+; Young, *Rommel, the Desert Fox,* 170–71 (*Rommel lay in the roadbed*).

132 *He was grievously hurt:* Brown, *Bodyguard of Lies,* 743–44; "Rommel's Death Reported," (Melbourne, Australia) *Argus,* Aug. 23, 1944, 16.

132 *Not for weeks would Reich propagandists:* Bodo Zimmermann, 1946, FMS, #B-308, MHI, 121–22.

133 *Rommel was right about the Allied attack:* Trafford Leigh-Mallory, "Daily Reflections on the Course of the Battle," July 18, 1944, UK NA, AIR 37/784 ("*Aircraft were spread out*"); McKee, *Caen: Anvil of Victory,* 258–59 ("*little dots detach themselves*").

133 *The first bombing wave alone:* D'Este, *Decision in Normandy,* 371; "Operation Goodwood," Oct. 1946, (U.K.) Military Operational Research Unit, report #23, CARL, R-14999, 15, 22 (*twenty-five pounds of high explosives*); Watney, *The Enemy Within,* 217 ("*canopy of noise*"); Copp, ed., *Montgomery's Scientists,* 85; *VW,* vol. 1, 338–39 ("*unalterable dignity*"); Liddell Hart, *The Tanks,* vol. 2, 366–67 ("*Move now!*"); Daglish, *Operation Goodwood,* 11 (*biggest tank battle fought by Britain*).

133 *Operation GOODWOOD massed three British and Canadian corps:* "Operation Goodwood," Oct. 1946, (U.K.) Military Operational Research Unit, report #23, CARL, R-14999, 7, 18–22; *VW,* vol. 1, 329–30, 336; *TSC,* 186–87 ("*draw the main enemy forces*").

133 *That modest, credible battle plan:* Callahan, *Churchill & His Generals,* 214–15; B. L. Montgomery, "Notes on Second Army Operations," July 15, 1944, National Archives of Canada, RG 24, vol. 1054 2, file 215A21.016(9) ("*engage the German armor*"); BLM to A. Brooke, July 14, 1944, Alanbrooke papers, LHC, 6/2/27; Beevor, *D-Day,* 321 ("*Russian style*" breakthrough).

134 *Montgomery had overegged the pudding:* AAR, "Operation Goodwood," 1945, UK NA, CAB 106/959, 4–8; "Lessons from Operation Goodwood," July 1944, UK NA, AIR 37/858; Liddell Hart, *The Tanks,* vol. 2, 360–61; Daglish, *Operation Goodwood,* 31–32 (*titanic battle*); Chandler, 2003–04 ("*burst into flames*").

134 *"to paint his canvas in rather glowing colors"*: OH, M. Dempsey, March 8, 1951, G. S. Jackson, UK NA, CAB 106/1061; OH, M. Dempsey, Mar. 28, 1952, B. H. Liddell Hart, UK NA, CAB 106/1061 (*"did not take Eisenhower into his confidence"*); Hamilton, *Master of the Battlefield*, 760 (*"had to be overconfident"*).

134 *"like a fleet raising anchor"*: Daglish, *Operation Goodwood*, 101–03; AAR, "Operation Goodwood," 1945, UK NA, CAB 106/959, 4–8 (*one vehicle every twenty seconds*); "Operation Goodwood," Oct. 1946, (U.K.) Military Operational Research Unit, report #23, CARL, R-14999, 5 (*long fields of fire*), 15, 22; Watney, *The Enemy Within*, 217 (*"angry women swishing"*); Liddell Hart, *The Tanks*, vol. 2, 363–64 (*three hundred yards every two minutes*); William Steel Brownlie, "And Came Safe Home," ts, n.d., IWM, 92/371, 18 (*"grey wall of shellbursts"*); *VW*, vol. 1, 340–41 (*rail embankment*).

134 *Torrid orange sheaves*: Daglish, *Operation Goodwood*, 131; OH, Hans von Luck, with author, Mar. 3, Apr. 7, 1994, Hamburg; Luck, *Panzer Commander*, 157 (*"like torpedoes"*); AAR, "Operation Goodwood," 1945, UK NA, CAB 106/959, 4–8 (*"great difficulty in locating"*); Baynes, *The Forgotten Victor*, 203–4 (*sixteen Shermans stood burning*); Rosse and Hill, *The Story of the Guards Armoured Division*, 42.

136 *Many more tanks soon burned*: Belfield and Essame, *The Battle for Normandy*, 155; Liddell Hart, *The Tanks*, vol. 2, 362–63; "Operation Goodwood," Oct. 1946, (U.K.) Military Operational Research Unit, report #23, CARL, R-14999, 18; "Lessons from Operation Goodwood," July 1944, UK NA, AIR 37/858 (*smokeless powder*); Howard and Sparrow, *The Coldstream Guards, 1920–1946*, 268 (*"Violent, impassable fire"*).

136 *"Some tank crews are on fire"*: John M. Thorpe, "A Soldier's Tale, to Normandy and Beyond," ts, Nov. 1982, IWM, 84/50/1, 96–98; William Steel Brownlie, "And Came Safe Home," ts, n.d., IWM, 92/371, 19 (*"burnt and injured men"*); Arthur, *Forgotten Voices of World War II*, 337 (*"horrible graveyard"*).

136 *"Operations this morning a complete success"*: *VW*, vol. 1, 344–46, 355–57; BLM to DDE, July 18, 1944, DDE Lib, PP-pres, box 83 (*"Am very well satisfied"*); Fraser, *And We Shall Shock Them*, 335 (*pure fantasy*); McKee, *Caen: Anvil of Victory*, 278 ("Second Army attacked and broke through"); "Caen: The Big Break-Through," (U.K.) *Daily Mail*, July 19, 1944, 1.

137 *"E worried"*: desk calendar, July 19, 1944, Barbara Wyden papers, DDE Lib, box 1; *VW*, vol. 1, 347–50 (*"groaning with enemy"*); Copp and McAndrew, *Battle Exhaustion*, 124–25 (*"men who were still alive"*); Rosse and Hill, *The Story of the Guards Armoured Division*, 46 (*"tropical violence"*); Howard and Sparrow, *The Coldstream Guards, 1920–1946*, 270 (*rum rations*).

137 *The offensive had liberated another thirty-four square miles*: "Operation Goodwood," Oct. 1946, (U.K.) Military Operational Research Unit, report #23, CARL, R-14999, 15, 22; AAR, "Operation Goodwood," 1945, UK NA, CAB 106/959, 4–8 (*Canadian First Army vanguard*); Daglish, *Operation Goodwood*, 170, 183 (*panzer forces were lured*); Reynolds, *Steel Inferno*, 186–87; Liddell Hart, *The Tanks*, vol. 2, 369. Most of the lost British tanks were soon repaired or replaced. "Operation Goodwood," Oct. 1946, (U.K.) Military Operational Research Unit, report #23, CARL, R-14999, 15, 22.

137 *After nearly seven weeks*: TSC, 189–93; Everett S. Hughes to wife, July 22, 1944, Hughes papers, LOC, box 2; *VW*, vol. 1, 353 (*"Allies in France Bogged Down"*); Daglish, *Operation Goodwood*, 11 (*"limited meaning"*); Trafford Leigh-Mallory, "Daily Reflections on the Course of the Battle," July 28, 1944, UK NA, AIR 37/784 (*"The fault with us"*).

138 *"Then we must change our leaders"*: "Excerpts from Diary, D/SAC," July 21, 1944, NARA RG 319, TSC background files, 2-3.7 CB 8; Orange, *Tedder: Quietly in Command*, 271 (*"I do not believe"*); Tedder, *With Prejudice*, 566; Kershaw, *Hitler, 1936–45: Nemesis*, 693 (*at least two hundred others*); Warlimont, *Inside Hitler's Headquarters*, 477; Evans, *The Third Reich at War*, 642–43; Megargee, *Inside Hitler's High Command*, 222 (*stiff-armed Nazi Heil*). Martin Gilbert put the number of executed at more than five thousand (*The Second World War*, 558). Andrew Roberts reports that fifty-eight hundred linked to the plot were arrested in 1944, and a similar number in 1945 (*The Storm of War*, 482).

138 *"What do your people think"*: D'Este, *Decision in Normandy*, 398; Chandler, 2020(n) (*"get on his bicycle"*), 2018–19 (*"Time is vital"*), 2026 (*"I could lie down"*).

The Bright Day Grew Dark

139 *Wearing the West Point bathrobe*: corr, Chester B. Hansen to wife, n.d., CBH, MHI; diary, CBH, July 28 & 12, 1944, MHI, box 4 (*sedatives at bedtime* and *"biggest thing"*); Pyle, *Brave Men*, 213 (*"frightful country ahead"*); Bradley, *A Soldier's Story*, 330; OH, ONB, June 7, 1956, CBM, NARA RG 319, OCMH, 2-3.7, box 184; Whitehead, *"Beachhead Don,"* 136 (*long beech twig*).

139 *"Take all the time you need, Brad"*: OH, M. Dempsey, March 28, 1952, B. H. Liddell Hart, UK NA, CAB 106/1061; OH, J. Lawton Collins, 1972, Charles C. Sperow, SOOHP, MHI, 195 (*bocage copse*); Weigley, *Eisenhower's Lieutenants*, 162–63; memo, B. L. Montgomery to ONB, July 21, 1944, NARA RG 407, ML, box 24143; DDE to ONB, July 24, 1944, in *BP*, 331 (*"Pursue every advantage"*). The attack sector chosen by Bradley also avoided the area's larger rivers. Prados, *Normandy Crucible*, 86.

139 *That advantage lay mainly in airpower*: Davis, *Bombing the European Axis Powers*, 386; Carafano, *After D-Day*, 102 (*more than one hundred howitzers*); Bradley, *A Soldier's Story*, 341 (*fifteen hundred heavies*); *AAFinWWII*, 231 (*swatch five miles wide*); diary, CBH, July 19, 1944, MHI, box 4 (*bomb every sixteen feet*).

140 *Very little in Bradley's vision appealed*: Report of Investigation, Aug. 14, 1944, HQ, USSAFE, Frederick L. Anderson Papers, HIA, box 84, folder 10, 1–2, 5–6; "Handbook for Bombardiers," TM 1-251, March 31, 1941, Frederick L. Anderson Papers, HIA, box 93; "Use of Heavy Bombers in a Tactical Role," Oct. 1944, SHAEF, NARA RG 334, E 315, ANSCOL, box 94 (*Only if the planes attacked perpendicular*); report, signature illegible, July 27, 1944, UK NA, AIR 37/762 (*"between the Army's legs"*).

140 *Bradley agreed to pull his assault battalions*: *BP*, 220–21. An AAF colonel reported warning Bradley that 3 percent of the bombs would fall short, but he mistakenly believed that Bradley had acceded to a perpendicular flight path, whereas Bradley still believed the bombers would attack parallel to the road, which would make "short" drops less risky. OH, John R. De Russey, Eighth AF liaison officer, Sept. 9–12, 1947, NARA RG 319, *CCA* background files.

140 *"nothing more than tools to be used"*: Bradley, *A Soldier's Story*, 154; Pyle, *Brave Men*, 214 (*"I've spent thirty years"*).

140 *Pyle spent Monday night, July 24*: Pyle, *Brave Men*, 296; Tobin, *Ernie Pyle's War*, 199 (*"your own small quota"*); Cawthon, "July, 1944: St. Lô," *American Heritage* (June 1974): 4+ (*"they area"*).

140 *Now he had returned to the front*: Field Order 44, 305th Bomb Group, July 25, 1944, NARA RG 18, AAF WWII, 190/58/17/1, box 925; "Investigation of Bombing of Ground Troops," Aug. 16, 1944, FUSA IG, NARA RG 338, FUSA AG gen'l corr., box 216; *BP*, 222–23 (*Allied white-star insignia*); corr, J. H. Phillips to Ray E. Porter, WD, May 6, 1944, James H. Phillips papers, HIA (*geometric design*).

142 *"like kids at a football game"*: Carafano, *After D-Day*, 119; Nichols, ed., *Ernie's War*, 333; Tobin, *Ernie Pyle's War*, 195 (*"heavy rip"*).

142 *Not much had gone right with* COBRA: "World Battlefronts, Western Front," *Time* (Dec. 4, 1944) (*three barometers*).

142 *Flying from Stanmore*: Sullivan, "The Botched Air Support of Operation COBRA," *Parameters* (March 1988): 97+; Davis, *Carl A. Spaatz and the Air War in Europe*, 470–72; AAR, 305th Bomb Group, July 24, 1944, NARA RG 18, AAF WWII, 190/58/17/1, box 925 (*"not to bomb short"*); memo, "Bombing Errors Committed on the Normandy Battle Front, 24 July 1944," HQ, Eighth AF, July 30, 1944, Frederick L. Anderson papers, HIA, box 84, folder 10 (*chaff bundle smacked the nose*); "The Effectiveness of Third Phase Tactical Air Operations," AAF Evaluation Board, Aug. 1945, NARA RG 334, E 315, ANSCOL, box 15; "Investigation of Bombing of Ground Troops," Aug. 16, 1944, FUSA IG, NARA RG 338, FUSA AG gen'l corr, box 216 (*"As a fiasco"*).

142 *Bradley's fury knew no bounds*: Bradley, *A Soldier's Story*, 347; Bradley and Blair, *A General's Life*, 278–79; memo, ONB, July 25, 1944, in diary, CBH, MHI, box 4 (*At 10:30 P.M. he phoned Bradley*); T. Leigh-Mallory to ONB, July 19, 1944, UK NA, AIR 37/762 (*had left that meeting early*); BP, 229–37.

143 *From his farmyard redoubt*: Tobin, *Ernie Pyle's War*, 198; Pyle, *Brave Men*, 298–301 (*"Goddammit"*).

143 *The star-crossed 30th Division took more casualties*: Hewitt, *Workhorse of the Western Front*, 36–37.

143 *"that awful rush of wind"*: Sullivan, "The Botched Air Support of Operation COBRA," *Parameters* (March 1988): 97+; *History of the 120th Infantry Regiment*, 35–36 (*Bombs entombed men*); Alosi, *War Birds*, 64 (*cows into trees*); Regan, *Blue on Blue*, 166–67 (*"beating you with a club"*); "Investigation of Bombing of Ground Troops," Aug. 16, 1944, FUSA IG, NARA RG 338, FUSA AG gen'l corr, box 216 (*body part*); "Operations of 30th Infantry Division, 24 Jul–1 Aug 1944," n.d., CMH, 8-3.1, part 5, 6–7 (*"American Luftwaffe"*).

143 *Just over fifteen hundred heavies dropped*: Sullivan, "The Botched Air Support of Operation COBRA," *Parameters* (March 1988): 97+; BP, 236–37 (*three dozen bombed American troops*); AAFinWWII, 233–34 (*forty-two medium bombers*); Juliette Hennessy, "Tactical Operations of the Eighth Air Force," 1952, AFHRA, historical study no. 70, 53–56 (*Red marking smoke*); diary, July 25, 1944, Hoyt S. Vandenberg papers, LOC MS Div, box 1 (*five-knot southerly breeze*); Sylvan, 68–71; diary, CBH, July 25, 1944, MHI, box 4 (*corpse was spotted sixty-five feet away*); DDE to GCM, July 26, 1944, GCM Lib, box 67, folder 10 (*"I warned him time and again"*); Individual Deceased Personnel File, Lesley J. McNair, a.p. under FOIA, U.S. Army Human Resources Command, Dec. 2008 (*"6 Lt. Gen. stars"*).

144 *By the time the last medium bomber flew off*: BP, 222–23; Pyle, *Brave Men*, 301 (*"Anybody makes mistakes"*).

144 *"That's a job for artillery"*: Bradley, *A Soldier's Story*, 349.

144 *"I fired three rounds and they all bounced off"*: Hewitt, *Workhorse of the Western Front*, 37; *History of the 120th Infantry Regiment*, 37 (*"Just his legs"*); BP, 246 (*no more than a mile*); Kenneth W. Hechler, "VII Corps in Operation COBRA," n.d., CMH, 8-3.1 AK, part 2 (*"enemy artillery was not touched"*).

144 *Africa veterans like Eisenhower and Bradley*: Reardon, ed., *Defending Fortress Europe*, mss, 179 (*"worn out"*); BP, 240 (*flipping tanks*); James Hodgson, "Thrust-Counterthrust: The Battle of France (21 Jul–25 Aug 44)," March 1955, NARA RG 319, R-58, 20–21 (*"half-crazed soldiers"*); Spayd, *Bayerlein*, 167 (*"Everything was burned"* and *"Only the dead can still hold"*); "Air Power in the ETO," USFET General Board study no. 56, n.d., NARA RG 407, E 427, 97-USF5-0.30, 16–17 (*70 percent of his men*). An Eighth Air Force study put German physical casualties at less than 10 percent. Kenneth W. Hechler, "VII Corps in Operation COBRA," n.d., CMH, 8-3.1 AK, part 2 (*"conveyor-belt bombing"* and *"feeling of helplessness"*).

145 *Unaware of the size of the American host*: Kenneth W. Hechler, "VII Corps in Operation COBRA," n.d., CMH, 8-3.1 AK, part 2; Bennett, *Ultra in the West*, 43; Hinsley, 500 (*thirty Allied divisions*).

145 *"The front has, so to speak, burst"*: James Hodgson, "Thrust-Counterthrust: The Battle of France (21 Jul–25 Aug 44)," March 1955, NARA RG 319, R-58, appendix, 30.

145 *Collins had massed 120,000 troops*: Kenneth W. Hechler, "VII Corps in Operation COBRA," n.d., CMH, 8-3.1 AK, part 2; "List of Weapons Available to VII Corps for the Attack of July 25," Aug. 4, 1944, NARA RG 407, AFIA, 2-3.7 BG (*six hundred artillery tubes*); "Artillery in Operation Cobra," n.d., NARA RG 407, E 427, ML #2229 (*140,000 rounds*); Cooper, *Death Traps*, 51–52 (*rugged tusks*); Mark J. Reardon, "Conquering the Hedgerows," ts, 2009, a.p.; Mayo, *The Ordnance Department*, 254–55 (*oxygen acetylene cylinders*); AAFinWWII, 239–41 (*"hazing the Hun"*).

145 *Collins had not planned to launch*: Persons, "St. Lô Breakthrough," *Military Review*

(Dec. 1948): 13+; OH, J. Lawton Collins, 1972, Charles C. Sperow, SOOHP, MHI, 196–99; Collins, *Lightning Joe*, 242–43; *BP*, 246; Hewitt, *Workhorse of the Western Front*, 41 (*feeling for booby traps*).

146 With the new day, the American onslaught: Doubler, *Busting the Bocage*, 58 ("*Russian style*"); Weigley, *Eisenhower's Lieutenants*, 155 (*under three minutes*); "Operations of 30th Infantry Division, 24 Jul–1 Aug 1944," n.d., CMH, 8-3.1, part 5, 18 (*sunken road to St.-Gilles*); *BP*, 253–54, 275 (*killed the Das Reich commander*); Seventh Army documents, July 26, 1944, NARA RG 407, ML #488, box 24154 (*seven punctures*); Hart, *Clash of Arms*, 390 (*abandonment of two Panther companies*); Kenneth W. Hechler, "VII Corps in Operation COBRA," n.d., CMH, 8-3.1 AK, part 2 (*no further reinforcements*).

146 "Rem"—remnants: Benjamin A. Dickson, "G-2 Journal: Algiers to the Elbe," MHI, 130; *BP*, 250–51 ("*busted wide open*").

146 French farmers flitted: Schrijvers, *The Crash of Ruin*, 194; George E. McIntyre, "As Mac Saw It," ts, n.d., MHI, 273–74 (*copies of* Life); Hastings, *OVERLORD*, 261–62 ("*holes in his head*").

146 On Friday enemy forces leaked to the rear: *BP*, 278–79, 287 ("*Things on our front really look good*").

147 Ahead lay Avranches: Abram et al., *The Rough Guide to France*, 389; *BP*, 308 ("*We face a defeated enemy*"), 323 ("*It's a madhouse here*"), 333 (*ten thousand tactical air sorties*).

Ministers of Thy Chastisement

148 Down metalled roads and farm lanes: Liebling, *Mollie & Other War Pieces*, 232; Pogue, *Pogue's War*, 193 (*scolding dawdlers*); Belfield and Essame, *The Battle for Normandy*, 228 (*grayed their hair*); Lee Miller, "The Siege of St. Malo," in *Reporting World War II*, vol. 2, 233 ("*Cartier clips*").

148 On they marched, south, east, and west: diary, CBH, July 17, 1944, MHI (*copper urns*); Lankford, ed., *OSS Against the Reich*, 152 (*perfume*); AAR, "Battle of Mortain," n.d., NARA RG 165, 330 (Inf), 120-0.3, 42 (*crude swastikas*); Pogue, *Pogue's War*, 199, 209, 134 ("*My wife doesn't understand me*"); "Combat Diary of Edward McCosh Elliott, 1944," n.d., 2nd Bn, Glasgow Highlanders, IWM, 99/61/1, VI-18 (*tricolor nosegays*); Joseph R. Darnall, "Powdered Eggs and Purple Hearts," ts, 1946, MHUC, Group 1, MHI, box 24, 190 ("*I speeg Engless*"); Neal Beaver, 3rd Bn, 508th PIR, ts, n.d., MMD (*jugs of calvados*); Rottman, *FUBAR: American Soldier Slang of World War II*, 55.

148 German tourist posters still hung: Lee Miller, "The Siege of St. Malo," in *Reporting World War II*, vol. 2, 233; Cawthon, "Pursuit: Normandy, 1944," *American Heritage* (Feb. 1978): 80+ (*Milwaukee German*); Watney, *The Enemy Within*, 186 ("*A German*"); Keegan, *Six Armies in Normandy*, 259 ("*No matter how many orders are issued*").

148 In hasty bivouacs the surging columns: Perry Wolff, "Why We Fight," panel, International Conference on WWII, NWWIIM, Apr. 10, 2008; McManus, *The Deadly Brotherhood*, 254 ("*a little piece of metal*"); Beevor, *D-Day*, 390 ("*We buried him darkly*").

149 SHAEF planners in late July estimated: ALH, vol. 2, 114–17; *PP*, 524 ("*roaring comet*"); Allen, *Lucky Forward*, 26 ("*gamecock with brains*").

149 The first glimpse of Lieutenant General George S. Patton, Jr.: Codman, *Drive*, 159 ("*Could anything be more magnificent?*"); D'Este, *Patton: A Genius for War*, 630, 636–37 ("*goddamned bastards*").

149 At noon on Tuesday, August 1: Allen, *Lucky Forward*, 71–72 ("*win or die*"); *PP*, 491 ("*very happy*").

149 "There are apparently two types": *PP*, 464.

150 "Patton has broken out again": msgs, GCM to DDE, W. B. Smith to GCM, DDE to GCM, etc., Apr. 26–May 3, 1944, NARA RG 165, E 422, WD, OPD, history unit, box 4; affidavits, GSP, LOC MS Div, box 12, folder 1.

150 Narrowly pardoned, Patton spent the spring: corr, Everett S. Hughes to wife, May 12, 1944, LOC MS Div, Hughes papers, box II:3, folder 1 (*guns and saddles*); diary, CBH,

July 2, 1944, MHI, box 4 (*offered Eisenhower $1,000*); White, *Conquerors' Road*, 34 (*"neurotic and bloodthirsty"*); Patton, *The Pattons*, 109 (*tattoo parlor*); GSP to Beatrice, July 3, 1944, GSP, LOC MS Div, box 12 (*"Can't stand the times between wars"*).

150 He also reflected deeply on generalship: Essame, *Patton: A Study in Command*, 122–24; Collins, *Lightning Joe*, 248–49 (*"I'm in the doghouse"*); Blumenson, "Bradley-Patton: World War II's 'Odd Couple,'" *Army* (Dec. 1985): 56+ (*"I didn't ask for you"*); Bradley, *A Soldier's Story*, 356 (*"judicious, reasonable"*); speech, GSP, n.d., George Smith Patton Papers, HIA, folder 1 (*"raise up on their hind legs"*).

150 "*I had to keep repeating to myself*": PP, 499; Koch and Hays, *G-2: Intelligence for Patton*, 61 (*"I'm going to Berlin"*).

150 First he was going to Brest: Waddell, *United States Army Logistics*, 46; IFG, 297; LSA, vol. 2, 467–74 (*failed to dampen the ardor*).

151 But the collapse of the German left wing: Ganz, "Questionable Objective: The Brittany Ports, 1944," *JMH* (Jan. 1995): 77+; BP, 370 (*£5 and "Take Brest"*); GSP to Robert Howe Fletcher, Apr. 25, 1945, LOC MS Div, box 13 (*"sixth sense"*); Price, *Troy H. Middleton: A Biography*, 189 (*ten thousand Krauts*).

151 Third Army's other spearhead, the 4th Armored Division: BP, 357–59; Ganz, "Patton's Relief of General Wood," *JMH* (July 1989): 257+ (*because he had tutored his classmates*); Carr, "The American Rommel," *MHQ* (summer 1992): 77+ (*rose gardener*); Raines, *Eyes of Artillery*, 213 (*Piper Cub*).

151 "*We're winning this war*": Price, *Troy H. Middleton: A Biography*, 188; BP, 361–65 (*"Dear George"*); D'Este, *Patton: A Genius for War*, 631 (*Proposing to reach Chartres*); Hirshson, *General Patton: A Soldier's Life*, 508–9 (*bloody siege at Lorient*).

151 "*the main business lies to the east*": BP, 431–32; Ganz, "Questionable Objective: The Brittany Ports, 1944," *JMH* (Jan. 1995): 77+.

152 The Brittany campaign soon proved bootless: BP, 340 (*"last cartridge"*); Blumenson, *The Battle of the Generals*, 164 (*siege of St.-Malo*); Mitcham, *Retreat to the Reich*, 214 (*seventy-five strongpoints*); "Combat Engineering," CE, report No. 10, Dec. 1945, NARA RG 498, ETO HD, admin file #547, 47–53 (*walls up to twenty-five feet thick*); OH, ONB, June 7, 1956, CBM, NARA RG 319, OCMH, 2-3.7 (*garrison was too dangerous*); diary, GSP, Sept. 9, 1944, LOC MS Div, box 3, folder 5 (*"We must take Brest"*).

152 The war ended with not a single cargo or troopship: Balkoski, *From Beachhead to Brittany*, 331; memo, "Fighting in Cities," Ninth Army, Oct. 26, 1944, NARA RG 498, G-3 Observers' Rpt, box 9 (*half a million American shells*); Ganz, "Patton's Relief of General Wood," *JMH* (July 1989): 257+ (*"colossally stupid"*); M-516, Aug. 4, 1944, and M-517, Aug. 6, 1944, National Archives of Canada, RG 24, vol. 1054 2, file 215A21.016(9) (*"We have unloosed the shackles"*).

152 Montgomery's plan was a simple, handsome thing: BLM, "Task of First Canadian Army," Aug. 4, 1944, National Archives of Canada, RG 24, vol. 1054 2, file 215A21.016(9); BP, 435, 449–52 (*struggling ten miles toward Vire*); VW, vol. 1, 386, 408.

153 "*a queer script of its own*": Catton, *A Stillness at Appomattox*, 149.

153 Such a place was Mortain: *The Green Guide to Normandy*, 309; Beevor, *D-Day*, 401 (*children wearing tags*).

153 The last German occupier in Mortain: BP, 466n; Hewitt, *Workhorse of the Western Front*, 51 (*civilians tossed flowers*); SLC, 102.

153 Of keen interest was stony, steep Montjoie: author visit, signage, May 29, 2009; Weiss, *Fire Mission*, 5, 25, 35, 75–76.

154 "*a unique opportunity, which will never return*": James Hodgson, "Thrust-Counterthrust: The Battle of France," March 1955, NARA RG 319, R-series, R-58, 80; TSC, 203 (*"he should keep his eyes riveted"*).

154 "*such an attack if not immediately successful*": Rosengarten, "With Ultra from Omaha Beach to Weimar, Germany," *Military Affairs* (Oct. 1978): 127+; Hans Eberbach, "Panzer Group Eberbach and the Falaise Encirclement," Feb. 1946, FMS, #A-922, MHI, 9–10; BP, 442; order of battle, Gilmore, ed., *U.S. Army Atlas of the European Theater in World War*

II, 52 (*a dozen divisions in four corps*); Mitcham, *Retreat to the Reich*, 120–21 ("*recklessly to the sea*").

155 *Swirling fog lifted and descended*: AAR, "Battle of Mortain," n.d., NARA RG 165, 330 (Inf), 120-0.3, 4–5; Baily and Karamales, "The 823rd at Mortain," *Armor* (Jan.–Feb. 1992): 12+ (*26,000 Germans*); BP, 461 (*120 tanks*); Lefèvre, *Panzers in Normandy Then and Now*, 62 (*imperial cavalry*); Hewitt, *Workhorse of the Western Front*, 57 (*firing by earshot*); "Armored Reconnaissance in the ETO," n.d., NARA RG 337, AGF OR #157 ("*all-gone feeling*"); Robert J. Kenney, "Somewhere in France," ts, 1978, 1st Bn, 117th Inf, a.p. (*Wounded men mewed*).

155 *But almost nothing went right in the German attack*: Isby, ed., *Fighting the Breakout*, 128–29 (*not one reached the front*); BP, 464–65 (*three of six enemy spearheads*); war diary, Seventh Army, Aug. 6, 1944, NARA RG 407, E 427, ML, #2201 ("*uninspired and negative*").

155 *The German weight fell heaviest on St.-Barthélemy*: Baily and Karamales, "The 823rd at Mortain," *Armor* (Jan.–Feb. 1992): 12+; Reynolds, *Steel Inferno*, 216–17 (*let the panzers roll through*); McManus, *The Americans at Normandy*, 381–82 (*delayed six hours*); Baedeker, *Northern France*, 180 (*Abbaye Blanche*); author visit, signage, May 29, 2009 (*sixty-six men with bazookas*); OH, 120th Inf, Aug. 1944, NARA RG 407, E 427-A, CI, folder 96; AAR, "Battle of Mortain," n.d., NARA RG 165, 330 (Inf), 120-0.3, 13–14 (*More than sixty enemy vehicles*).

156 "*First really large concentration*": VC, 233; Featherston, *Saving the Breakout*, 133–35; Saunders, *Royal Air Force, 1939–1945*, vol. 3, 132; BP, 464–65.

156 "*Hundreds of German troops began spilling*": Featherston, *Saving the Breakout*, 133–35. Pilots claimed four times more vehicle kills than could be confirmed by later ground investigation. Copp, ed., *Montgomery's Scientists*, 175.

156 *sorties mistakenly hit American revetments*: OH, 120th Inf, Aug. 1944, NARA RG 407, E 427-A, CI, folder 96; OH, Brig. Gen. James M. Lewis, 30th ID, Aug. 25, 1944, NARA RG 407, E 427-A, CI, folder 96 (*raked the two roads leading west*); VW, vol. 1, 414 ("*well-nigh unendurable*").

156 "*exceptionally poor start*": war diary, Seventh Army, Aug. 6, 1944, NARA RG 407, E 427, ML, #2201.

156 *two traitorous French guides*: Reardon, *Victory at Mortain*, 99; OH, 120th Inf, Aug. 1944, NARA RG 407, E 427-A, CI, folder 96 (*hospital larder*); BP, 487 ("*Looks like hell*").

156 *Lieutenant Weiss, with his field glasses*: Weiss, *Fire Mission*, 53, 68–69, 82, 105; Hewitt, *Workhorse of the Western Front*, 69–74; Alosi, *War Birds*, 68 ("*No birds were singing*").

157 *Nor were the Germans advancing*: Reardon, *Victory at Mortain*, 117, 143; Baily and Karamales, "The 823rd at Mortain," *Armor* (Jan.–Feb. 1992): 12+ (*fewer than six thousand infantrymen*); VW, vol. 1, 416 ("*If only the Germans will go on attacking*").

157 "*Bruised them badly*": McManus, *The Americans at Normandy*, 399–400.

157 "*We have to risk everything*": Hewitt, *Workhorse of the Western Front*, 66.

157 "*thorn in the flesh*": BP, 488–90.

157 *Hitler on August 9 again demanded*: Hans Eberbach, "Panzer Group Eberbach and the Falaise Encirclement," Feb. 1946, FMS, #A-922, MHI, 9–12 ("*very unpleasant*"); Rudolph Freiherr von Gersdorff, "Avranches Counterattack, Seventh Army," n.d., FMS, #A-921, 27-31; OH, 120th Inf, Aug. 1944, NARA RG 407, E 427-A, CI, folder 96 ("*don't surrender*"); Ralph A. Kerley, "Operations of the 2nd Battalion, 120th Infantry at Mortain," 1949, IS, 14.

157 *Each night more slain soldiers on Hill 314*: Ralph A. Kerley, "Operations of the 2nd Battalion, 120th Infantry at Mortain," 1949, IS, 19 (*bolster morale*); OH, 120th Inf, Aug. 1944, NARA RG 407, E 427-A, CI, folder 96; AAR, "Battle of Mortain," n.d., NARA RG 165, 330 (Inf), 120-0.3, 24 (*turnips, cabbages*); Weiss, *Fire Mission*, 124 (*surgical tape*); Hewitt, *Workhorse of the Western Front*, 67 (*half the bundles drifted*); Reardon, *Victory at Mortain*, 267 ("*I want Mortain demolished*").

158 "*The attack failed*": Warlimont, *Inside Hitler's Headquarters*, 449; Liddell Hart, *The Other Side of the Hill*, 416–17 ("*where I lose my reputation*").

158 *French civilians returning to wrecked Mortain*: Schrijvers, *The Crash of Ruin*, 200 ("*crying and rocking*"); corr, Thor M. Smith to family, Aug. 28, 1944, HIA, box 1 ("*obliberated*"); Weiss, "Normandy: Recollections of the 'Lost Battalion' at the Battle of Mortain," *Prologue* (spring 1996): 44+ ("*Not much to write home about*").

158 *Ultra's big ears had given the Allied high command*: Lewin, *Ultra Goes to War*, 405–9; Sunset 647-649, Aug. 7-9, 1944, NARA RG 457, E 9026, SRS-1869; Hinsley et al., *British Intelligence in the Second World War*, vol. 3, part 2, 246; Prados, *Normandy Crucible*, 181; Bennett, *Ultra in the West*, 118–19; Sunset 650, Aug. 10, 1944, NARA RG 457, E 9026, SRS-1869 ("*decisive thrust* must *lead*").

159 *Encouraged by Eisenhower, Bradley kept*: Chandler, 2060; Reardon, *Victory at Mortain*, 152; memoir, John W. Castles, Jr., n.d., USMA Arch ("*I am General Patton's commanding officer*").

159 *Certainly they were thinking of it*: Keegan, *Six Armies in Normandy*, 251 (one-tenth of *France's landmass*); *Three Years*, 789 ("*obstinated*"); Greenfield, ed., *Command Decisions*, 308; VC, 216–24; Liddell Hart, *The Tanks*, vol. 2, 383–86 ("*blind leading the blind*"); Copp and Vogel, *Maple Leaf Route: Falaise*, 94–99 (*stalling in confusion*); BP, 479; "Battlefield Tour: Operation Totalize," Sept. 1947, HQ, British Army of the Rhine and Canadian Army Historical Section, CMH, 65 ("*Push on, you dogs!*").

159 *As this unspooled, Bradley was once again poring*: Featherston, *Saving the Breakout*, 144–45; Bradley and Blair, *A General's Life*, 294–95 (*roadside K-ration lunch*); diary, Aug. 8, 1944, Hobart Gay papers, MHI, box 2, 446 (*sharp turn at Le Mans*).

159 *An exuberant Eisenhower followed Bradley*: Blumenson, *The Battle of the Generals*, 190–91; PP, 505 ("*If I were on my own*").

160 "*This is a first priority*": VC, 236; Hills, *Phantom Was There*, 211 ("*ministers of Thy chastisement*").

160 "*greatest tactical blunder*": McManus, *The Americans at Normandy*, 391; Bradley, *A Soldier's Story*, 375 ("*This is an opportunity*").

160 *Leclerc instead fanned out on all available roads*: Blumenson, *The Battle of the Generals*, 204–5; Essame, *Patton: A Study in Command*, 166–67 (*giving the Germans six hours*).

160 *Patton was peeved but undeterred*: Essame, *Patton: A Study in Command*, 166–67; D'Este, *Decision in Normandy*, 429 ("*push on slowly*"); diary, CBH, Aug. 12, 1944, MHI, 1944, box 4 ("*Shall we continue*").

160 "*Nothing doing*": Blumenson, *The Battle of the Generals*, 206–7; Blumenson, *Patton: The Man Behind the Legend, 1885–1945*, 223 (*Bradley wrongly believed*); Greenfield, ed., *Command Decisions*, 313 (*nineteen German divisions*); Bradley, *A Soldier's Story*, 376–77 ("*I did not consult*"); PP, 509 ("*a great mistake*"); Codman, *Drive*, 163 ("*beside himself*").

161 *Canadian difficulties further unstitched*: Granatstein, *The Generals*, 114; English, *Patton's Peers*, 32–33; BLM to Brooke, July 26, 1944, Alanbrooke papers, LHC, 6/2/27 ("*I fear he thinks*").

161 *Worse yet, the Germans on August 13*: "Operations of the First Canadian Army in North-west Europe," Oct. 1945, Historical Section, Canadian Military HQ, report no. 146, NARA RG 407, E 427, ML; Stacey, *The Canadian Army, 1939-1945*, 202; Copp and Vogel, *Maple Leaf Route: Falaise*, 117 ("*molten fire bath*"); VW, vol. 1, 430–31 ("*troops burnt yellow flares*"); VC, 240–44 ("*dust like I've never seen*").

161 *Bradley now made another momentous decision*: BP, 523–27; ONB, Aug. 15, 1944, "Twelfth U.S. Army Group Directives," CMH ("*Due to the delay*").

163 "*For the first and only time*": Bradley, *A Soldier's Story*, 379; OH, ONB, June 7, 1956, CBM, NARA RG 319, OCMH, 2-3.7, 270/19/5/4, box 184; Prados, *Normandy Crucible*, 216–21, 251.

163 *The two most senior Allied field commanders*: Weigley, "From the Normandy Beaches to the Falaise-Argentan Pocket," *Military Review* (Sept. 1990): 45+; Belchem, *All in the Day's March*, 208; Hastings, *OVERLORD*, 301; Beevor, *D-Day*, 455; Blumenson, *The Battle of the Generals*, 217–18 (*little effort to confirm*); Kennedy, *The Business of War*, 344 ("*squeaking and scuffling*"); D'Este, *Decision in Normandy*, 449 ("*These are great days*").

163 *Bradley was quick to fault Montgomery*: Bradley, *A Soldier's Story*, 376–79; Wertenbaker, *Invasion!*, 91 (*"quality all the great generals had"*); Weigley, "From the Normandy Beaches to the Falaise-Argentan Pocket," *Military Review* (Sept. 1990): 45+ (*"operational forethought"*).

163 *Nor was Eisenhower much help*: Weigley, *Eisenhower's Lieutenants*, 216; diary, CBH, Aug 12, 1944, MHI, 1944, box 4 (*"garbed in suntans"*); Essame, *Patton: A Study in Command*, 171 (*"never really got the feel"*).

164 *Whatever shortcomings vexed the Allied high command*: memos, Seventh Army, Aug. 12, 15, 19, 1944, NARA RG 407, M.L. #483, box 24154; Hans Eberbach, "Panzer Group Eberbach and the Falaise Encirclement," Feb. 1946, FMS, #A-922, MHI, 20 (*"strength of a company"*); Lucas and Barker, *The Killing Ground*, 122 (*"Such tiredness"*); BP, 516–19 (*"five minutes before midnight"*).

164 *Then Kluge vanished*: Mitcham, *Retreat to the Reich*, 138–39; Hans Eberbach, "Panzer Group Eberbach and the Falaise Encirclement," Feb. 1946, FMS, #A-922, MHI, 24 (*"Ascertain whereabouts"*); Speidel, *We Defended Normandy*, 142 (*might have defected*).

164 *Shortly before midnight he appeared*: Reardon, ed., *Defending Fortress Europe*, mss, 378–79; Hans Eberbach, "Panzer Group Eberbach and the Falaise Encirclement," Feb. 1946, FMS, #A-922, MHI, 24 (*"live in another world"*); VC, 254; Reardon, *Victory at Mortain*, 277 (*in a borrowed car*); Blumenson, *The Battle of the Generals*, 227–28 (*Hitler affirmed the decision*).

164 *The order would be Kluge's last*: Reardon, ed., *Defending Fortress Europe*, mss, 382–83; MMB, 369 (*Prussian music director*); Wilmot, *The Struggle for Europe*, 436 (*"Hitler's fireman"*); Kershaw, *"It Never Snows in September,"* 76 (*stabilize the field after defeats*); Charles V. von Lüttichau, "Diary of Thuisko von Metzch," May 1952, NARA RG 319, R-10, 32 (*firing squads*); Barnett, ed., *Hitler's Generals*, 320–26 (*"a good sergeant"*); Kessler, *The Battle of the Ruhr Pocket*, 4 (*"Did you see those eyes?"*).

165 *"Den lieb' ich"*: Lewin, *Montgomery as Military Commander*, 312; Hans Eberbach, "Panzer Group Eberbach and the Falaise Encirclement," Feb. 1946, FMS, #A-922, MHI, 26 (*"My intention is to withdraw"*).

165 *Legend had it*: author visit, Falaise, May 29, 2009; Abram et al., *The Rough Guide to France*, 398; *The Green Guide to Normandy*, 74, 237; Baedeker, *Northern France*, 185–86.

165 *Bullet holes dinged the hoary castle keep*: VC, 250–51; Lucas and Barker, *The Killing Ground*, 124 (*last Tigers had rumbled*); Carell, *Invasion—They're Coming!*, 260–61 (*two teenagers*).

165 *Ultra had decrypted Kluge's withdrawal order*: Sunset 657, Aug. 16, 1944, NARA RG 457, E 9026, SRS-1869; Hinsley, 508.

165 *Bradley now confessed*: Bradley, *A Soldier's Story*, 379; Weigley, *Eisenhower's Lieutenants*, 211 (*three jeeps, nine officers*); BP, 515, 529–30; diary, Aug. 16–17, 1944, Hobart Gay papers, MHI, box 2, 446 (*poised to attack in an hour*).

166 *Napoleonic it was not*: Blumenson, *The Battle of the Generals*, 239–42; VC, 257–59; "The Battle of the Falaise Pocket," *AB*, no. 8 (1975): 1+ (*"comparatively easy business"*); VW, vol. 1, 442–43 (*"damage was immense"*).

166 *"inferno of incandescent ruins"*: author visit, Trun, May 29, 2009, signage; Kennedy, *The Business of War*, 344 (*"Shoot everything"*); Saunders, *Royal Air Force, 1939–1945*, vol. 3, 135 (*Shambles*); "Closing of the Chambois Gap," n.d., CMH, 8-3.1 AK, part 1, 22–23 (*"streams in the gutters"*); Colby, *War from the Ground Up*, 230–41 (*"vertebrae"*); Keegan, *Six Armies in Normandy*, 275 (*"lifted me in the air"*); Maczek, *Od Podwody do Czolga, Wspomnienia Wojenne 1918–1945*, 167–68 (*toasts drunk*).

166 *With eastbound roads now cut*: Zuckerman, *From Apes to Warlords*, 282; VW, vol. 1, 446–47 (*by compass course*); Horrocks, *Corps Commander*, 46–50 (*Three thousand Allied guns*); diary, D. K. Reimers, "My War," Aug. 19, 1944, MHI, 151 (*"The pocket surrounding the Germans"*).

167 *"We always hit something"*: Raines, *Eyes of Artillery*, 220; Saunders, *Royal Air Force, 1939–1945*, vol. 3, 133 (*"Many go barefoot"*), 136–37 (*telltale glint*); Copp, ed., *Montgom-*

ery's Scientists, 189 (*"Heavy firing into the sunken road"*); McKee, *Caen: Anvil of Victory*, 350 (*"I saw a truck crew"*); Keegan, *Six Armies in Normandy*, 271–73 (*"surrounded by fire"*).

167 *Two death struggles*: Copp and Vogel, *Maple Leaf Route: Falaise*, 121 (*"grey-clad men"*); Freiherr von Lüttwitz, Oct. 1945, FMS, #A-904, MHI, 21–22 (*"awful heap"*); OH, Dixon M. Raymond, n.d., Craig W. H. Luther papers, HIA, box 1, 7–8 (*"gun boiled away"*); Reynolds, *Steel Inferno*, 264 (*"like burrs"*); Stacey, *The Canadian Army, 1939–1945*, 205–6.

167 *Three miles northeast, eighteen hundred men*: Maczek, *Od Podwody do Czolga, Wspomnienia Wojenne 1918–1945*, 167; Mieczkowski, ed., *The Soldiers of General Maczek in World War II*, 50–52 (*Poles caught the brunt*); "The Battle of the Falaise Pocket," *AB*, no. 8 (1975): 1+ (*escaping Germans streamed past*); Whitaker et al., *Victory at Falaise*, 277–87 (*SS bodies roasted*).

168 *"Merde pour la guerre"*: Saunders, *Royal Air Force, 1939–1945*, vol. 3, 136–37; Hastings, *OVERLORD*, 305 (*"more of an execution"*); OH, Dixon M. Raymond, n.d., Craig W. H. Luther papers, HIA, box 1, 7–8 (*"shot them down in droves"*); Carpenter, *No Woman's World*, 75 (*urinated on the body*).

168 *"one of those paintings of Waterloo"*: "The Battle of the Falaise Pocket," *AB*, no. 8 (1975): 1+; Collier, *Fighting Words*, 170 (*"the end of Germany"*); DOB, 168 (*escaped seemingly sure destruction at Messina*).

168 *"All German formations"*: Blumenson, *The Battle of the Generals*, 241–42, 254–57.

168 *After liberating Orléans and Chartres*: "Memoranda for Record," Aug. 19, 1944, XII AG, NARA RG 407, ML #205; BP, 566–70, 574–75; AAR, "Bridging the Seine," XV Corps, Nov. 1944, NARA RG 498, G-3 OR, box 10; Gerhard Graf von Schwerin, ETHINT 18, Oct. 1945, MHI, 1.

169 *"inextricable confusion"*: Gerhard Graf von Schwerin, ETHINT 18, Oct. 1945, MHI, 6–7; AAFinWWII, 272 (*sixty Seine crossing sites*); Keegan, *Six Armies in Normandy*, 285 (*improvised ferries*); BP, 557, 581 (*25,000 vehicles*); Wilmot, *The Struggle for Europe*, 433 (*cider barrels*), 424 (*twelve of fifteen division commanders*); Luck, *Panzer Commander*, 165 (*empty fuel cans*); Hastings, *OVERLORD*, 309 (*dead cow*); Zuckerman, *From Apes to Warlords*, 282 (*95 percent of German troops*); TSC, 215. Historian John Prados estimates that 115,000 got away (*Normandy Crucible*, 249, 262).

169 *Yet by any measure the defeat at Falaise*: Weigley, *Eisenhower's Lieutenants*, 214; diary, D. K. Reimers, "My War," Aug. 24, 1944, MHI, 157 (*"Life in the cages"*); Beevor, *D-Day*, 460–61; BP, 535–36 (*"When you receive these lines"*); Warlimont, *Inside Hitler's Headquarters*, 454 (*"western thriller"*).

169 *Allied investigators counted*: Ellis, *Brute Force*, 391. Various tallies have been offered. 21st Army Group reported finding 571 German guns, 358 tanks and self-propelled guns, and 4,700 trucks, cars, and armored tracks in the pocket. "The Operations of 21 Army Group," 1946, CARL, N-133331, 15. Ludewig puts panzer losses at Falaise at more than 400, over half the total fleet. Ludewig, *Rückzug*, 99–100.

169 *No Seine ferry could carry a Tiger*: Lefèvre, *Panzers in Normandy Then and Now*, photo (*charred on the docks*); Westermann, *Flak*, 260; Ellis, *Brute Force*, 391; VW, vol. 1, 448 (*twenty-five hundred trucks and cars*); Wilmot, *The Struggle for Europe*, 434 (*"five to ten tanks each"*); Ludewig, *Rückzug*, 164 (*Fifth Panzer Army*); Keegan, *Six Armies in Normandy*, 283–84 (*Army Group Center*); Callahan quoted in Blumenson, *The Battle of the Generals*, 272 (*"remarkable resurgence"*).

170 *Eisenhower took a quick tour*: corr, Thor M. Smith to family, Aug. 28, 1944, HIA, box 1 (*"bloated dead"*); Thompson, *The Imperial War Museum Book of Victory in Europe*, 139 (*paybooks*); "The Battle of the Falaise Pocket," *AB*, no. 8 (1975): 1+ (*bulldozed mass grave*); Skibinski, *Pierwsza Pancerna*, 311 (*"coal monuments"*); Hastings, *OVERLORD*, 312 (*evacuate gases*); Saunders, *Royal Air Force, 1939–1945*, vol. 3, 136–37 (*rear seat of a limousine*); BP, 558 (*"avenging angel"*).

170 *Troops cleansing the pocket wore gas masks*: Lyall, ed., *The War in the Air*, 428; *Reporting World War II*, vol. 2, 217 (*"Everything is dead"*); Moorehead, *Eclipse*, 158 (*"waiting to die*

in the water"); Stacey, *The Canadian Army, 1939–1945,* 205–6 (*eight thousand slaughtered horses*); Lucas and Barker, *The Killing Ground,* 158–59 (*Not until 1961*).

170 "*Thank you for liberating us*": Copp, *Cinderella Army,* 27; Ambrose, *Eisenhower: Soldier, General of the Army, President-Elect, 1890–1952,* vol. 1, 331 (*Many recalled November 1918*); memo, BLM, Aug. 20, 1944, NARA RG 407, ML, box 24143 ("*beginning of the end*").

The Loveliest Story of Our Time

171 *Warm summer rain:* Marshall, *Battle at Best,* 226 ("*booming like bitterns*").

171 *Tricolor pennants flew:* Keegan, *Six Armies in Normandy,* 306; Hills, *Phantom Was There,* 217–18 (*white silhouette*); Beevor and Cooper, *Paris After the Liberation, 1944– 1949,* 31; Yeide and Stout, *First to the Rhine,* 201.

171 *Scores of frisky "warcos":* Moorehead, *Eclipse,* 160; Lankford, ed., *OSS Against the Reich,* 168–69 (*any procession into Paris*), 160–62 ("*Paris/Orléans*"); Baker, *Ernest Hemingway,* 521; Reynolds, *Hemingway: The Final Years,* 105–6; Voss, *Reporting the War,* 185–90 ("le grand capitaine"); Capa, *Slightly Out of Focus,* 179 ("*spitting short sentences*"); Babcock, *War Stories,* 178 ("*just in case*").

171 *Astride the road outside Limours:* Beevor, *D-Day,* 387; Baker, *Ernest Hemingway,* 525 ("*Like the Scarlet Pimpernel*"); Clayton, *Three Marshals of France,* 39–42 (*child's toy printing set*); MMB, 310; Porch, *The Path to Victory,* 583–84; OH, SLAM, 1973, George J. Stapleton, MHI, V, 19–24 ("*Have no fear*"); Marshall, *Battle at Best,* 226.

172 "*a weird assortment of private cars*": Whitehead, "*Beachhead Don,*" 211–12; Marshall, *Battle at Best,* 226 (*Veterans of the Franco-Prussian War*); Lankford, ed., *OSS Against the Reich,* 171 ("*wreck one's constitution*").

172 *By Thursday evening the spearhead remained five miles:* BP, 611–14.

172 "*advancing on a one-tank front*": Keegan, *Six Armies in Normandy,* 308; Blumenson, "Politics and the Military in the Liberation of Paris," *Parameters* (summer 1998): 4+ ("*slam on in*"); Zaloga, *Liberation of Paris 1944,* 67–68 ("Tenez bon").

173 *Eisenhower had long planned:* "Crossing of the Seine and Capture of Paris," Aug. 17, 1944, SHAEF, planning staff, Post-Neptune, NARA RG 331, E 23 ("*eight divisions*"); Wieviorka, *Normandy,* 350–1; Keegan, *Six Armies in Normandy,* 291–92; Beevor and Cooper, *Paris After the Liberation, 1944–1949,* 39 (*convoys were hijacked*); Riding, *And the Show Went On,* 308 (*Jewish deportees*).

173 "*Paris is worth 200,000 dead*": Zaloga, *Liberation of Paris 1944,* 34, 24; Keegan, *Six Armies in Normandy,* 296 ("*holier-than-thouery*").

173 *The moment grew riper:* Beevor and Cooper, *Paris After the Liberation, 1944–1949,* 37 (*foretelling catastrophe*), 40 (*opened their windows*); "Paris," AB, No. 14, 1976, 11+; Collins and Lapierre, *Is Paris Burning?,* 149–50 (*four hundred such redoubts*), 133 ("*things are going to get bad*"), 219; Jacques Kim, ed., *La Libération de Paris,* 1944, no pagination, in HIA, Boris T. Pash papers, box 4, folder 4 (*portraits of Hitler*); Thornton, *The Liberation of Paris,* 165 ("*pictures of Delacroix*"); Aron, *France Reborn,* 262 (*Hèrmes scarves*); Riding, *And the Show Went On,* 309 ("*For every Parisian*"); Collier, *The Freedom Road, 1944–45,* 165 (*Swedish ball-bearing factory manager*).

175 "*If the enemy tries to hold Paris*": Chandler, 2088–89.

175 "*Gestapo small fry*": Thornton, *The Liberation of Paris,* 127, 121 (*Ash from burning documents*); Joseph R. Darnall, "Hospitalization in European Theater of Operations, " n.d., MHUC, Group 1, box 24, 25 (*clogged the plumbing*); Collins and Lapierre, *Is Paris Burning?,* 72–73 ("*back for Christmas*"); Blumenson, *Liberation,* 13 ("la ville sans regard"); Beevor, *D-Day,* 485 (*toilet brushes*).

175 *With his main thrust delayed by skirmishers:* "Paris," AB, No. 14, 1976, 11+ ("Les Américains!"); BP, 615; Maule, *Out of the Sand,* 214 ("*Rejoice!*").

175 *From a balcony of the Hôtel Meurice:* MWB, 89–90; Neiburg, *The Blood of Free Men,* 85. Choltitz had been linked to the murder of Jews in the Crimea. Roberts, *The Storm of War,* 495–96.

176 "*field of ruins*": BP, 598.

176 "*It has been my fate*": Collins and Lapierre, *Is Paris Burning?*, 24, 158 ("*Our task is hard*"); Ludewig, *Rückzug*, 138 (*Saxon*), 143 (*eight centuries*).

176 *With only twenty thousand men:* Germany VII, 615; Ludewig, *Rückzug*, 144–47; Blumenson, "Politics and the Military in the Liberation of Paris," *Parameters* (summer 1998): 4+ ("*Ever since our enemies*"); BP, 609 (*told superiors of placing explosives*); Aron, *France Reborn*, 279–80 ("*prudent and intelligent attitude*"), 284–85; Maule, *Out of the Sand*, 214 ("*the Allies are here*"). Choltitz's role in saving Paris would be vigorously debated for more than sixty years after the war. http://www.ina.fr/recherche/recherche/search/la+liberation+de+paris

176 *Leclerc managed to slide his entire division:* "Paris," AB, No. 14, 1976, 11+; BP, 615 (*12th Infantry reached Notre Dame*); Keegan, *Six Armies in Normandy*, 309; Beevor and Cooper, *Paris After the Liberation, 1944–1949*, 45 (*women curled their hair*); Aron, *France Reborn*, 286 (*colors flew from the Eiffel Tower*); Thornton, *The Liberation of Paris*, 173 (*Animals set loose*), 187 (*scent of mothballs*).

176 "*The rip tide of courage*": *Reporting World War II*, vol. 2, 251, 260 (*Yiddish*); Marshall, *Battle at Best*, 246–47 ("*not less than five thousand bullets*"); Moorehead, *Eclipse*, 168–69 (*from the rumble seats*); chronology, Aug. 25, 1944, 1556 hours, GSP, LOC MS Div, box 53, folder 1 ("*massacred or made prisoners*"); "Paris," AB, no. 14, 1976, 11+ (*surrendered to a Signal Corps photographer*); Collins and Lapierre, *Is Paris Burning?*, 313, 325 (*weapons in the cloakroom*); Aron, *France Reborn*, 286–87 (*lunch at the usual hour*).

177 "*Germany's lost the war*": Collier, *The Freedom Road, 1944–45*, 170; Collins and Lapierre, *Is Paris Burning?*, 312 (*packed a valise*), 307 ("*our last combat*"); Beevor, *D-Day*, 508 ("*silent from the effort*"); Aron, *France Reborn*, 287–89 ("*particularly not today*").

177 *Just down the street, fighting swept:* Tillier et al., *Paris*, 131; Choltitz, *Soldat Unter Soldaten*, 268–69 ("*Sprechen deutsch?*").

177 *A furious mob punched and spat:* Beevor, *D-Day*, 510; Aron, *France Reborn*, 291–92 ("*Oh, no*"). Choltitz would be court-martialed in absentia after his capture. Ludewig, *Rückzug*, 148–49.

178 *Teams of French and German officers:* Collins and Lapierre, *Is Paris Burning?*, 338–39; Germany VII, 615; Riding, *And the Show Went On*, 313 (*Louvre*).

178 "*German spoken*" signs: "Inside Paris," *Newsweek*, Aug. 28, 1944, 25+; Pogue, *Pogue's War*, 199 ("*Supplier of the Boche*"); Marshall, *Battle at Best*, 212 ("*Leave her alone*"); Edsel, *The Monuments Men*, 121 ("*Arrests and Purges*"); Aron, *France Reborn*, 423 ("*a psychosis*"); Riding, *And the Show Went On*, 318 (indignité nationale). Biographer Jonathan Fenby notes that the Aron figure was disputed, and that an Interior Ministry study found that the Resistance carried out 9,673 summary executions during the war. In Paris, 126,000 people were arrested for collaboration. *The General*, 659–60, 722.

178 *At ten P.M., the first of an eventual eighteen hundred:* AAR, "T Force and T Branch," n.d., 12th AG, NARA RG 331, E 180, SHAEF, box 44; "T Force—The CIC in Paris," Military Intelligence Service, No. 25, Jan. 1945, NARA RG 498, ETO HD, admin file #494L, 66+; AAR, T Force, n.d., 6th AG, G-2, Boris T. Pash papers, HIA, box 4, file 6; Gellhorn, *The Face of War*, 180–82 ("*Revenge me*"); Moorehead, *Eclipse*, 178 ("*a knock on my door*").

178 "*a great city where everybody is happy*": Liebling, *Mollie & Other War Pieces*, 235; Prinsburg (Minn.) *Record News*, Sept. 1944, 2 ("*never in my life been kissed*"); George E. McIntyre, "As Mac Saw It," n.d., MHI; Collier, *Fighting Words*, 172 ("*Had we ever been away?*"); Nicholas, *The Rape of Europa*, 292 (*treasures from the Jeu de Paume*); Thornton, *The Liberation of Paris*, 154 (*Bank of France cellars*).

179 "*You've got just thirty seconds*": OH, SLAM, 1973, George J. Stapleton, MHI, V, 19–28; Collier, *Fighting Words*, 173 ("*seventy-three dry martinis*"); Carpenter, *No Woman's World*, 113 (*raspberries in liquer*); Marshall, *Battle at Best*, 212 ("*It's the law*"); Blumenson, *Liberation*, 156 ("*the day the war should have ended*").

179 "*Paris seems to have*": Nichols, ed., *Ernie's War*, 354; Pyle, *Brave Men*, 314 ("*the loveliest, brightest story*").

179 *De Gaulle entered the city*: De Gaulle, *The Complete War Memoirs of Charles de Gaulle*, 648 ("*Nothing was missing*"); Aron, *France Reborn*, 293 (*whence he had fled*); Foote, *SOE in France*, 416 (*blotting paper*); Beevor and Cooper, *Paris After the Liberation, 1944–1949*, x (*He uttered hardly a word*); D'Este, *Decision in Normandy*, 517; *VW*, vol. 1, 488, 493; Collins and Lapierre, *Is Paris Burning?*, 349 (*Coleman lanterns*). Jonathan Fenby writes that de Gaulle made a perfunctory reference to "our dear and admirable Allies." *The General*, 679–80. Michael Neiberg calls it "the best speech of his life." *The Blood of Free Men*, 237.

180 "*City is scarcely damaged*": memo, N. H. Vissering, SHAEF G-4, Aug. 30, 1944, NARA RG 331, SHAEF SGS, Geog Corr, box 108; "The Coal Situation on the Continent," n.d., "G-4 History," NARA RG 498, ETO HD, admin file #553A-C; Harold S. Frum, "The Soldier Must Write," 1984, GCM Lib (*charcoal burners*); "Paris Is Free!," *Time* (Sept. 4, 1944): 34+ (*cafés in Montparnasse*); Wieviorka, *Normandy*, 354 (*two thousand Resistance fighters and twenty-five hundred civilians*); Zaloga, *Liberation of Paris, 1944*, 83– 90 (*twelve hundred casualties in the eastern suburbs*); Lankford, ed., *OSS Against the Reich*, 175–77 ("*After a noisy hour*"); Chandler, 2108 ("*We should not blame the French*"). Some question whether Hitler personally asked, "Is Paris burning?" Neiberg, *The Blood of Free Men*, 214.

180 *At three P.M. on Saturday, August 26, De Gaulle appeared*: Aron, *France Reborn*, 297–300 ("*confides his safety*"); Foote, *SOE in France*, 416 ("*nunnery*").

180 *A million people or more lined the boulevard*: Beevor and Cooper, *Paris After the Liberation, 1944–1949*, 53; Thornton, *The Liberation of Paris*, 204–5 (*shots rang out*); Moorehead, *Eclipse*, 170–73 ("*like a field of wheat*"); Lankford, ed., *OSS Against the Reich*, 175–77 ("*firing wildly with machine guns*"); corr, P. B. Rogers to family, Sept. 23, 1944, Pleas B. Rogers papers, MHI (*fired "to beat hell"*).

181 "*The huge congregation, who had all been standing*": Beevor and Cooper, *Paris After the Liberation, 1944–1949*, 56; Voss, *Reporting the War*, 90–91 (*FFI fighters fired at the organ pipes*); Blumenson, *Liberation*, 166 ("*extraordinary example of courage*"); Maule, *Out of the Sand*, 226 ("*Have you no pride?*").

181 "*The first wild shots*": Aron, *France Reborn*, 300.

181 *So ended the great struggle*: Keegan, *Six Armies in Europe*, 317; Fritz Bayerlein, ETHINT 67, Aug. 15, 1945, MHI, 7.

181 *German casualties in the west*: memo, DDE to CCS, Aug 30, 1944, NARA RG 331, E 1, SHAEF SGS, 381; D'Este, *Decision in Normandy*, 517; Zetterling, *Normandy 1944*, 82; Ellis, *Brute Force*, 355–56; Zaloga, *Armored Thunderbolt*, 169; memo, DDE to CCS, Aug 30, 1944, NARA RG 331, E 1, SHAEF SGS, 381 ("*very badly cut up*"); Keegan, *Six Armies in Normandy*, 316 (*early warning network*); "The Process of Collapse of the German Armies," Aug. 29, 1944, OSS, research and analysis, no. 2458, NARA RG 334, E 315, ANSCOL, box 922 (*monthly casualties of a quarter million*); "Age-Distribution of Dead in the German Ground Forces," Apr. 3, 1945, OSS, research and analysis, no. 1087.6, NARA RG 334, E 315, ANSCOL, box 888.

182 *Americans killed, wounded, missing, or captured*: The figures include air crews. D'Este, *Decision in Normandy*, 517.

182 *In half a million sorties flown*: *VW*, vol. 1, 488.

182 *The 82nd Airborne had given battle*: Gavin, *On to Berlin*, 12.

182 *Normandy paid a fell price*: Blumenson, *Liberation*, 73 (*of 3,400 Norman villages and towns*); Vigneras, *Rearming the French*, 306 (*24,000 FFI fighters*); Wieviorka, *Normandy*, 131; Neiberg, *The Blood of Free Men*, 13; Kedward, *France and the French*, 298; http://www.discoverfrance.net/France/Paris/Monuments-Paris/Eiffel.shtml.

182 *Most prominent among the German dead*: Ruge, *Rommel in Normandy*, 246; Marshall, *A Ramble Through My War*, 232 (*merely lifting the eyelid*); Margry, "The Death of Rommel," *AB*, no. 80 (1993): 38+ ("*Just one thought*").

182 *The killers would come to Herrlingen*: Liddell Hart, ed., *The Rommel Papers*, 501–5; Margry, "The Death of Rommel," *AB*, no. 80 (1993): 38+ ("*another of the old ones*"); Douglas-Home, *Rommel*, 210 ("*His heart belonged*").

183 *"If I ever was brave"*: Miller, *The Story of Ernie Pyle*, 345.

183 *"a flat, black depression"*: Pyle, *Brave Men*, 319; Miller, *The Story of Ernie Pyle*, 364 (*"I have had all I can take"*); CBH, Sept. 2, 1944, box 4 (*"worn out, thin"*).

183 *For many rank-and-file troops*: corr, T. M. Smith to family, Aug. 8, 1944 (*"spreading like a disease"*), and Aug. 15, 1944 (*"just a damn fool"*), HIA, Thor M. Smith papers, box 1; Pogue, *George C. Marshall of Victory*, 430 (*holiday gifts*); corr, P. B. Rogers, Aug. 17, 1944, Pleas B. Rogers papers, MHI (*"space for a long time"*).

183 *"fundamental inability to make sound strategic judgments"*: Megargee, *Inside Hitler's High Command*, 232–36; Overy, *Why the Allies Won*, 227 (*tactical edge*); "The Effectiveness of Third Phase Tactical Air Operations," AAF Evaluation Board, Aug. 1945, NARA RG 334, E 315, ANSCOL, box 15 (*thirty-one airfields*); Murray and Millett, *A War to Be Won*, 416–17; Thompson, *The Imperial War Museum Book of Victory in Europe*, 135 (*"much more amusing"*).

183 *"a vivid moral structure"*: Fussell, *The Boys' Crusade*, ix.

183 *Soviet troops in Poland*: Some historians put the toll at Majdanek at three hundred thousand or more. Weinberg, *A World at Arms*, 708.

184 *"I have just seen the most terrible place"*: Robert H. Abzug, "The Liberation of the Concentration Camps," in *Liberation 1945*, 35–36; "Murder, Inc.," *Time* (Sept. 11, 1944): 36 (*"Children's shoes"*); William J. vanden Heuvel, "Comments on Michael Beschloss' *The Conquerors*," *SHAFR Newsletter*, March 2003, 27+ (*"systematic murder"*).

184 *"The saviors come not home"*: Harold S. Frum, "The Soldier Must Write," 1984, GCM Lib; Whitehead, *"Beachhead Don,"* 365 (*"like a lamb"*).

184 *It will be my cross*: Carroll, *Behind the Lines*, 69–73.

184 *"It is summer"*: Stiles, *Serenade to the Big Bird*, 215.

184 *A final gesture of American arms*: Eisenhower, *Crusade in Europe*, 316 (*"show of force"*); Huie, *The Execution of Private Slovik*, 106–7 (*Benjamin Franklin*).

185 *Hurriedly trucked to Versailles*: Miller, *Division Commander*, 100; Bradley, *A Soldier's Story*, 396 (*"Khaki Bill"*); Ent, ed., *The First Century*, 165 (*three-cent postage stamp*).

Chapter 4: Pursuit

"The Huntsman Is Hungry"

189 *Naples in August 1944 still carried scars*: Taylor and Taylor, eds., *The War Diaries*, 128 (*carved from the bones of saints*); Kennett, *G.I.: The American Soldier in World War II*, 204–5 (*one-third of all arriving cargo*); Lewis, *Naples '44*, 134–35 (*civilian suits*); Richler, ed., *Writers on World War II*, 477 (*"kingdom come"*).

189 *The city was "colorful"*: Fairbanks, *A Hell of a War*, 224; Taylor and Taylor, eds., *The War Diaries*, 448 (*touch their testicles*); Lewis, *Naples '44*, 93 (*"romantic frustration"*); Vining, ed., *American Diaries of World War II*, 114 (*prices had jumped thirtyfold*); diary, Cyrus C. Aydlett, July 15, 1944, NWWIIM (*"Piece ass!"*).

189 *More than ever Naples was a military town*: Fisher, *Cassino to the Alps*, 292–99.

190 *under Plan 4-44*: Hewitt, "Planning Operation Anvil-Dragoon," *U.S. Naval Institute Proceedings* (July–Aug. 1954): 731+; "Southern France," n.d., NARA RG 319, OCMH background files, chapter 10 (*nine hundred vessels*); IFG, 238–39.

190 *By August 13, the 36th and 45th Infantry Divisions*: "Southern France," n.d., NARA RG 319, OCMH background files, chapter 10; Mauldin, *Up Front*, 198–99 (*moldering corpses*); Even, *The Tenth Engineers*, 38 (*makeshift aircraft carrier*); Wyant, *Sandy Patch*, 114–15 (*"Many a New Day"*); Taggart, ed., *History of the Third Infantry Division*, 202 (*never glanced up*).

190 *Pacing the bridge of the flagship*: OH, "The Reminiscences of Admiral H. Kent Hewitt," Col U OHRO, 1962, 6: 1–3; *AAAD*, 21–23; *DOB*, 30–32.

191 DRAGOON *had begun dreadfully*: Hewitt, "Planning Operation Anvil-Dragoon," *U.S. Naval Institute Proceedings* (July–Aug. 1954): 731ff.; John A. Moreno, "The Death of Admiral Moon," n.d., a.p., 225+; Alter and Crouch, eds., *"My Dear Moon,"* no pagination;

OH, "The Reminiscences of Admiral H. Kent Hewitt," Col U OHRO, 1962, 24: 33–35 (*"I don't think it's as bad"*).

191 *At seven the next morning*: Alter and Crouch, eds., *"My Dear Moon,"* no pagination (*"I am sick"*); Individual Deceased Personnel File, Don P. Moon, a.p., obtained under FOIA, 2008 (*"Cause: suicide"*); corr, JLC to Mrs. Don P. Moon, Aug. 17, 1944, JLC papers, DDE Lib, box 3, 201 file (*"a casualty of this war"*).

191 *At two P.M. on August 13, under clear skies*: Hewitt, "Planning Operation Anvil-Dragoon," *U.S. Naval Institute Proceedings* (July–Aug. 1954): 731+; Moran, *Churchill: Taken from the Diaries of Lord Moran*, 179 (*"All that they felt"*).

192 *Vesuvius had begun to recede*: Hewitt, "Planning Operation Anvil-Dragoon," *U.S. Naval Institute Proceedings* (July–Aug. 1954): 731+; Pawle, *The War and Colonel Warden*, 315–16 (*light tropical suit*); Taggart, ed., *History of the Third Infantry Division*, 202 (*"It's Churchill!"*); Reitan, *Riflemen*, 41.

192 *Colonel Kent*: Jackson, *The Mediterranean and the Middle East*, vol. 6, part 2, 174.

192 *on a fortnight's bathing holiday*: Jenkins, *Churchill: A Biography*, 752–53; Reynolds, *In Command of History*, 3 (*"benevolent hippo"*); Macmillan, *War Diaries*, 502 (*portable map room*).

192 DRAGOON, *originally called* ANVIL: A recent history on the German retreat from France states that the two Wehrmacht armies in Army Group G together numbered sixteen divisions on June 6, 1944. Ludewig, *Rückzug*, 48.

192 *Shipping shortages and delays in capturing Rome*: Charles V. von Lüttichau, "Army Group G Prepares to Meet the Invasion," 1957, OCMH, NARA RG 319, R-series #103, box 16; H. Maitland Wilson, "Dispatch, Invasion of Southern France," 1944, NARA RG 498, ETO HD, admin file #108, 4–31; *CCA*, 76n, 100; "The Invasion of Southern France, Operation Dragoon," ETOUSA, 1944, NARA RG 498, ETO HD, admin file #314; *TSC*, 220–21 (*"decisive theater"*); Howard, *The Mediterranean Strategy in World War II*, 61; Ambrose, *The Supreme Commander*, 338; OH, Charles de Gaulle, Jan. 14, 1947, FCP, MHI; De Gaulle, *The Complete Memoirs of Charles de Gaulle*, 613–14.

192 *The British disagreed, politely at first*: *TSC*, 221–22 (*"bleak and sterile"*); *IFG*, 229–30 (*"great hazards"*); Eisenhower, *Crusade in Europe*, 301 (*would take three months*); memo, British chiefs, June 26, 1944, NARA RG 165, E 422, OPD, history unit, box 12 (*"unacceptable to us"*); H. Maitland Wilson, "Dispatch, Invasion of Southern France," 1944, NARA RG 498, ETO HD, admin file #108, 31; Macmillan, *War Diaries*, 470 (*"eliminate the German forces"*); Kennedy, *The Business of War*, 333 (*"dagger under the armpit"*).

193 *"We need big ports"*: Chandler, 1938; Howard, *The Mediterranean Strategy in World War II*, 67 (*threading the gap*); Pogue, *George C. Marshall: Organizer of Victory*, 408 (*"Austrians held off the Italians"*); OH, John E. Hull, 1974, James W. Wurman, SOOHP, MHI, III-54, V-26 (*"not more than seven divisions"*); Barker, "The Ljubljana Gap Strategy," *JMH* (Jan. 1992): 57+ (*dash to Vienna*); Moran, *Churchill: Taken from the Diaries of Lord Moran*, 233 (*"Winston is a gambler"*); Danchev, 561–65 (*"damned fools"*).

193 *The prime minister would have none of it*: Kimball, ed., *Churchill & Roosevelt: The Complete Correspondence*, vol. 3, 523 (*forestall Soviet domination*), 214–23 (*"complete ruin"*).

193 *Still Churchill persisted*: diary, CBH, Aug. 7, 1944, MHI, box 4 (*"beautifully colored speech"*); dispatch, Henry Maitland Wilson to CCS, n.d., CMH, UH 0-1, 23 (*"greatest secrecy"*); msg, U.S. JCS, Aug. 5, 1944, NARA RG 331, AFHQ micro, R-323-A (*"extremely unwise"*); Jackson, *The Mediterranean and the Middle East*, vol. 6, part 2, 174 (*"utmost confusion"*); *IFG*, 231 (*insufficiently seaworthy*); Chandler, 2057 (*no major Breton port would open*), 2066–67; *Three Years*, 635 (*"Ike said no"*), 639 (*"lay down the mantle"*), 644; Strong, *Intelligence at the Top*, 197 (*wept copiously*); Churchill, *Triumph and Tragedy*, 68–71 (*"no more to be done"*).

194 *Denouncing the "sheer folly"*: Moran, *Churchill: Taken from the Diaries of Lord Moran*, 173.

194 *"strong and dominating partner"*: *TSC*, 226.

194 *"We have been ill-treated"*: Pogue, *George C. Marshall: Organizer of Victory*, 412–13; Roberts, *Masters and Commanders*, 501 (*"lying down"*), 500 (*"Winston is very bitter"*); Hastings, *Armageddon*, 232 (*"one of the stupidest strategic teams"*); Wilson, ed., *D-Day 1944*, 38 (*"The only times I ever quarrel"*).

194 *"an Englishman's idea of cooperation"*: Brower, ed., *World War II in Europe: The Final Year*, 59; Pogue, *George C. Marshall: Organizer of Victory*, 491 (*"always a disperser"*); Howard, *The Mediterranean Strategy in World War II*, 67 (*incoherent*); Brower, ed., *World War II in Europe*, 42 (*"slogan not a strategy"*); *VW*, vol. 2, 19; *TSC*, 246–47 (*"tearing the guts out"*).

195 *Certainly the fraught imperatives*: Powers, "The Battle of Normandy," *JMH* (July 1992): 455+; Roberts, *Masters and Commanders*, 505 (*"full-blown professionals"*); pamphlet, "Beachheads and Mountains," MTO, U.S. Army, June 1945, Theodore J. Conway papers, MHI, box 2 (*one in every ten*).

195 *"He must always be right"*: Roberts, *Masters and Commanders*, 500.

195 *"He was literally frothing"*: Danchev, 571; Colville, *The Fringes of Power*, 564 (*"corrective sneering"*), 522 (*black bristles of the hair brushes*); Hastings, *Winston's War*, 411 (*"his own vivid world"*); Buhite, *Decisions at Yalta*, 15 (*"Of course I am an egotist"*).

195 *"that unresting genius"*: Fraser, *Alanbrooke*, 22.

195 *"The P.M. is very tired"*: Moran, *Churchill: Taken from the Diaries of Lord Moran*, 194; Macmillan, *War Diaries*, 474 (*"old and weary"*); Foreman, "Winston Churchill, Distilled," *Wall Street Journal*, Dec. 10, 2009, D6 (*"economy of effort"*).

195 *Already this Mediterranean sojourn had revived him*: Addison, *Churchill, the Unexpected Hero*, 184 (*Champagne lunches*); Kimball, *Forged in War*, 22 (*Churchill was no alcoholic*); msg, U.S. JCS, Aug. 5, 1944, NARA RG 331, AFHQ micro, R-323-A (*"DRAGOON will be successful"*).

196 *In the smallest hours of Tuesday, August 15*: "Invasion of Southern France," n.d., Office of the Theater Historian, NARA RG 498, ETO HD, admin file #607, 11–12; *IFG*, 255–57 (*one hundred fathoms*); Robichon, *The Second D-Day*, 163 (*"deluge of metal"*).

196 *"Nancy has a stiff neck"*: De Lattre de Tassigny, *The History of the French First Army*, 64. In southern France, the OSS had twenty-eight agent networks radioing reports on German defenses and troop movements. Waller, *Wild Bill Donovan*, 264.

196 *Each soldier aboard the combat loaders*: Stephen J. Weiss, "Operation ANVIL-DRAGOON: The Allied Invasion of Southern France," n.d., a.p.; Garland, *Unknown Soldiers*, 277 (*"Swilled coffee"*), 309 (*"sunstorms"*); Langan W. Swent, "Personal Diary," Aug. 14, 1944, HIA, box 1 (*"things are so quiet"*).

196 *Catoctin's malfunctioning ventilation system*: Will Lang, draft cable to *Life*, Aug. 1, 1944, LKT Jr. papers, GCM Lib, box 21 (*"predatory" face*); corr, Don E. Carleton to Sarah Truscott, July 1944, LKT Jr. papers, GCM Lib, box 1 (*silver nitrate*); Mauldin, *The Brass Ring*, 241 (*"one of the really tough generals"*).

196 *Truscott's was an unorthodox path*: biographical material, LKT Jr. papers, GCM Lib, box 21, folder 7; Jeffers, *Command of Honor*, 215 (*unlucky dabbler*); Heefner, *Dogface Soldier*, 9–13 (*renounced strong drink*).

197 *"willpower, decision, and drive"*: description by Ernest Harmon in Layne Van Arsdale, ed., "Allied Biographies," USAREUR staff ride, Alsace, May 2009; Ambrose, *Eisenhower: Soldier, General of the Army, President-Elect, 1890–1952*, vol. 1, 296 (*lamented his inability to get Truscott released*); Will Lang, draft cable to *Life*, Aug. 1, 1944, LKT Jr. papers, GCM Lib, box 21 (*"Bullshit"*); Jeffers, *Command of Honor*, 215 (*"hunters by instinct"*).

197 *" far removed from the softening touch"*: LKT Jr. to Sarah, July 19 and Aug. 14, 1944, LKT Jr. papers, GCM Lib, box 1; *DOB*, 586.

197 *The enemy never had a chance*: *IFG*, 251; OH, Paul D. Adams, 1975, Irving Monclova and Marlin Lang, SOOHP, MHI (*Quaker guns*); signals report, appendix H, "Airborne Diversion in Support of Operation Dragoon," NARA RG 331, AFHQ micro, R-69 Spec, box 294; John C. Warren, "Airborne Missions in the Mediterranean, 1942–1945," 1955, AFHRA, study no. 74, 92–93; Holt, *The Deceivers*, 619–20 (*attack at Genoa*).

198 *The usual anarchy and intrepidity*: "Report on Airborne Operations in Dragoon," Oct. 30, 1944, Allied Force HQ, HIA, 10; *RR*, 104; John C. Warren, "Airborne Missions in the Mediterranean, 1942–1945," 1955, AFHRA, study no. 74, 99–102; "The Night Landing in Provence, Aug. 1944," n.d., SEM, NHHC, box 87, file 97, 2–3.

198 *At eight A.M., eleven American assault battalions*: "Invasion of Southern France," n.d., WD HD, CMH, 8-3 SF, 50; "Operation Dragoon," Dec. 1944, COHQ, bulletin Y/42, CARL, N-6530.20.

198 *Among those at the point of the spear*: certificate of service, ALM; Simpson, *Audie Murphy, American Soldier*, 1 (*"greatest folk hero"*); Graham, *No Name on the Bullet*, 16–17 (*"can't remember"*); Audie L. Murphy Memorial Website, http://www.audiemurphy.com /biography.htm (*eighteen*); Arlington National Cemetery website, http://www.arlington cemetery.mil/History/Military/HF_AudieMurphy.aspx; Hubler, "He Doesn't Want to Be a Star," *Saturday Evening Post* (Apr. 18, 1953): 34+ (*fainted*).

198 *Sharpshooting now served him well*: Simpson, *Audie Murphy, American Soldier*, 121–22; Murphy, *To Hell and Back*, 176–77 (*"My whole being"*).

199 *Only on the invasion right flank*: WaS, 97; *IFG*, 267–68; *RR*, 115–18; Swent, "Personal Diary," Aug. 9, 1944, HIA, box 1 (*radio-controlled landing craft*); Greear, "Operation Neptune and Landing on Coast of Southern France," lecture, Nov. 1944, NARA RG 334, E 315, ANSCOL, box 199, 12–13 (*same frequencies*); LKT Jr., "Comments on 'Dragoon Secondary Attack Against Fortress Europe,'" n.d., NARA RG 319, OCMH, 2-3.7 CC2, 2–3 (*"milled around at high speed"*); OH, Herbert A. Peterson, Oct. 1, 1944, NARA RG 38, E 11, U.S. Navy WWII Oral Histories, 5 (*"As a general proposition"*).

199 *"All ships and craft reached their final assault"*: msg, HKH, Aug. 15, 1944, NARA RG 331, AFHQ micro, R-323-A.

199 *"quietest beachhead I have ever seen"*: Langan W. Swent, "Personal Diary," Aug. 15, 1944, HIA, box 1.

199 *By the close of this D-Day*: "Invasion of Southern France," n.d., WD HD, CMH, 8-3 SF, 56; *RR*, 123–24, 63, 70 (*less than 300,000*); "Operation Dragoon," Dec. 1944, COHQ, bulletin Y/42, ANSCOL, NARA 334, E 315, box 465 (*preferred to surrender*); Warlimont, *Inside Hitler's Headquarters*, 451 (*"worst day of my life"*); MMB, 45; Bonn, *When the Odds Were Even*, 68 (*SS atrocities in Poland*); Pallud, "The Riviera Landings, *AB*, no. 110 (2000): 2+ (*one-quarter of his infantry divisions*); Charles V. von Lüttichau, "The Invasion," 1957, NARA RG 319, OCMH, R-series # 104, box 16, 12–13; Jackson, *The Mediterranean and the Middle East*, vol. 6, part 2, 189; Ludewig, *Rückzug*, 57–61 (*"Russians in France"*). Demands from the Normandy front had reduced the 11th Panzer Division to barely one hundred tanks and assault guns.

200 *By twilight on Tuesday*: Le Victorieux, n.d., translation, Robert T. Frederick papers, HIA, box 4; Seventh Army war diary, Aug. 16, 1944, MHI (*"weak at most points"*); Sevareid, *Not So Wild a Dream*, 432 (*"faintly sourish smell"*); "The Night Landing in Provence, Aug. 1944," n.d., SEM, NHHC, box 87, file 97, 1 (*"What happiness"*); OH, Theodore J. Conway, 1978, Robert F. Ensslin, SOOHP, MHI, III-21 (*VI Corps crystal*); Conway, "Operation Anvil," lecture, n.d., Norfolk, Theodore J. Conway papers, MHI, box 2, 16 (*"best invasion I ever attended"*).

200 *"frog blackmoors"*: Orange, *Tedder: Quietly in Command*, 273.

200 *the Kimberly ventured no closer*: Churchill, *Triumph and Tragedy*, 94–95; Moran, *Churchill: Taken from the Diaries of Lord Moran*, 180 (*"a querulous mood"*); Pawle, *The War and Colonel Warden*, 315–16 (*"a lot more exciting"*).

The Avenue of Stenches

201 *The immediate objective of DRAGOON*: memo, Joint Security Council, July 4, 1944, NARA RG 165, E 422, WD OPD, history unit, box 39; *RR*, 137; *IFG*, 282; *The Seventh United States Army in France and Germany*, vol. 1, 151 (*three more divisions*).

201 *Known for now as Army B*: Yeide and Stout, *First to the Rhine*, 23; De Lattre de Tassigny, *The History of the French First Army*, 67 (*New Caledonians, Tahitians*); Porch, *The Path*

to *Victory*, 596 (*boots tied around their necks*); Vigneras, *Rearming the French*, 229, 245, 248, 258, 264–66; memo, Charles L. Kades, "Allied Civil Affairs Administration in Southeastern France," Oct. 30, 1944, CARL, N-3972, 14–17 (*cherished wine transports*).

201 *The gimlet-eyed commander of this force*: Salisbury-Jones, *So Full a Glory*, 16; Aron, *France Reborn*, 317–18 ("*animal of action*"); Clayton, *Three Marshals of France*, 26–27 ("jupiterien"), 22–23 ("*greatest soldier to serve France*"); OH, "The Reminiscences of Admiral H. Kent Hewitt," Col U OHRO, 1962 copy at NHHC, 24:28 ("*very volatile*"); Truscott, *Command Missions*, 403 ("*thin hair graying*"); Yeide and Stout, *First to the Rhine*, 25 ("*What have you done*").

201 *De Lattre sprang from minor gentry*: Clayton, *Three Marshals of France*, 22–33.

202 *Loyal to Vichy for more than two years*: Codman, *Drive*, 220–21 (*outside his office door*), 222 ("*a nocturnal*"); Porch, *The Path to Victory*, 594–95 ("*lived on stage*"); Clayton, *Three Marshalls of France*, 117–18 (*might sit for days*).

202 *The* DRAGOON *landing plan for Army B*: Aron, *France Reborn*, 314 ("*the price we must pay*"); OH, JLD, 1968, Thomas E. Griess, YCHT, box 110 (*torrent of French*); Porch, *The Path to Victory*, 594–96 ("*ardent to the point of effervescence*").

203 *The Germans waited, too*: RR, 138–40; Charles V. von Lüttichau, "Army Group G Prepares to Meet the Invasion," 1957, NARA RG 319, OCMH, R-series #103, 24 (*fortifications at Toulon*); Wilt, *The French Riviera Campaign of August 1944*, 121 (*both garrisons reinforced*); Jackson, *The Mediterranean and the Middle East*, vol. 6, part 2, 191

203 *Toulon was the greatest naval base*: *The Seventh United States Army in France and Germany*, vol. 1, 155–59; de Belot, *The Struggle for the Mediterranean, 1939–1945*, 260 (*range of twenty-two miles*); Hewitt, "Planning Operation Anvil-Dragoon," *U.S. Naval Institute Proceedings* (July–Aug. 1954): 731+; *IFG*, 290–91; AR, U.S.S. *Quincy*, Sept. 6, 1944, NARA RG 38, CNO, 57 (*chasing the interlopers back into their smoke*); OH, John F. Latimer, n.d., NARA RG 38, E 11, U.S. Navy WWII Oral Histories, 23; OH, Glynn Markham, n.d., WWII Oral History Collection, Samuel F. Proctor Archive, Department of History, University of Florida ("*spitting against the wall*").

203 *De Lattre had assumed as much*: Yeide and Stout, *First to the Rhine*, 111; "Invasion of Southern France," Office of the Theater Historian, n.d., NARA RG 498, ETO HD, admin file #607, 145–50; *The Seventh United States Army in France and Germany*, vol. 1, 154.

203 *By last light on Monday, August 21*: Salisbury-Jones, *So Full a Glory*, 144 (*Monks from a local monastery*); De Lattre de Tassigny, *The History of the French First Army*, 77–78 (*borrowed policeman's uniform*), 92–94 ("*Three hours later*"); *The Seventh United States Army in France and Germany*, vol. 1, 158–59; "Invasion of Southern France," Office of the Theater Historian, n.d., NARA RG 498, ETO HD, admin file #607, 160–62 (*blew up their remaining ammunition*); Hewitt, "Planning Operation Anvil-Dragoon," *U.S. Naval Institute Proceedings* (July–Aug. 1954): 731+ (*more than a thousand shells*).

204 *Marseille fell at almost the same moment*: LSA, vol. 1, 163–64; De Lattre de Tassigny, *The History of the French First Army*, 99–102; Robichon, *The Second D-Day*, 292–93 ("*figures from another world*"), 289–90 (*civilians in nightclothes*); Salisbury-Jones, *So Full a Glory*, 147 (*city soon grew indefensible*); Aron, *France Reborn*, 335 (*spread his maps*).

204 "*It would be purposeless*": Aron, *France Reborn*, 342; RR, 80.

204 *Thirty-seven thousand prisoners*: Wilt, *The French Riviera Campaign of August 1944*, 130–31; "Supply and Maintenance on the European Continent," n.d., USFET General Board, NARA RG 407, E 427, 97-USF5-0.3.0, no. 130, 50. Toulon received its first Liberty ship on Sept. 20. LSA, vol. 2, 122.

205 *Marseille was devastated even beyond Allied fears*: H. H. Dunham, "U.S. Army Transportation in the ETO," 1946, CMH, 4-13.1 AA 29, 283–84 ("*German masterpiece*" and *five thousand mines*); Aron, *France Reborn*, 343 ("*chaos of steel*"); OH, HKH, June 26, 1945, NARA RG 38, E 11, U.S. Navy WWII Oral Histories, 21 (*blimps*).

205 *Yet the Allies had their port*: LSA, vol. 2, 122; *The Seventh United States Army in France and Germany*, vol. 2, 331 (*12,500 tons of cargo*); De Lattre de Tassigny, *The History of the French First Army*, 115 ("*no German not dead or captive*").

205 *Following his abdication and removal to Elba*: Young, *Napoleon in Exile: Elba*, 136, 229, 283, 292–93, 304–18; Norwich, *The Middle Sea*, 456.

205 *The Route Napoléon led, indirectly, to Waterloo*: Conway, "Operation Anvil," lecture, n.d., Norfolk, Theodore J. Conway papers, MHI, box 2, 18–24; memo, LKT Jr. to A. Patch, July 21, 1944, NARA RG 319, OCMH 2-3.7 CC2, Hamilton mss.

206 *To command this scratch assemblage*: OH, Frederic B. Bates, Oct. 6, 1967, Raymond Henle, HIA, http://millercenter.org/scripps/archive/oralhistories/detail/2000,1; Layne Van Arsdale, ed., "Allied Biographies," USAREUR staff ride, Alsace, May 2009.

206 *An order radioed from the German high command*: Hinsley, 509 (*deciphered by British cryptologists*); Jackson, *The Mediterranean and the Middle East*, vol. 6, part 2, 193–93. Historian Joachim Ludewig writes that Blaskowitz did not receive the withdrawal order until the morning of August 18, and that Nineteenth Army got it that afternoon (*Rückzug*, 82). David T. Zabecki points out that "Army Group B and Army Group G were not quite the same," in that the former was designated an *Armeegruppe*, tantamount to an oversized army in Allied terms, and the latter a *Heeresgruppe*, the equivalent of an Allied army group (Corr. to author, May 9, 2012).

206 *Now the U.S. Seventh Army could speed north*: Donald S. Bussey, "Ultra and the U.S. Seventh Army," May 12, 1945, NARA RG 457, E 9002, NSA, SRH-022; Arthur L. Funk, "General Patch, Ultra, and the Alpine Passes, 1944," n.d., University of Florida, a.p., 3–8 (*NOVOCAINE*); Beavan, *Operation Jedburgh*, 258–59.

206 *Truscott put the spurs to Butler*: Butler, "Task Force Butler," *Armored Cavalry Journal*, part 1 (Jan.–Feb.): 12+ ("*dignified weep*"), and part 2 (March–Apr. 1948): 30+; memo, F. B. Butler, March 3, 1947, NARA RG 319, OCMH background files, Hamilton mss, box 7.

206 *Task Force Butler covered forty-five miles*: John A. Hixson, "Analysis of Deep Attack Operations: U.S. VI Corps, Task Force Butler, Aug. 1944," March 1987, CSI, 27–33; Yeide and Stout, *First to the Rhine*, 69; Butler, "Task Force Butler," *Armored Cavalry Journal*, part 1 (Jan.–Feb. 1948): ff. (*formed a fire brigade*); OH, 2nd Bn, 143rd Inf and 117th Cavalry Recon Squadron, n.d., NARA RG 407, E 427-A, CI, folder 117; Jackson, *The Mediterranean and the Middle East*, vol. 6, part 2, 197.

207 *Across folded limestone hills*: "Invasion of Southern France," n.d., WD HD, CMH, 8-3 SF, 109; Sevareid, *Not So Wild a Dream*, 440–42 ("*through civilized, settled Provence*").

207 *In Gap, nearly a hundred miles from the sea*: Arthur L. Funk, "Allies and Maquis," n.d., NARA RG 319, RR background files, FRC 5; Butler, "Task Force Butler," *Armored Cavalry Journal*, part 2 (Mar.–Apr. 1948): 30. (*sixty B-17s*); OH, 117th Cavalry Recon Squadron, n.d., NARA RG 407, E 427-A, CI, folder 117 (*wearing full packs*).

207 *"You will move at first light"*: "Invasion of Southern France," n.d., WD HD, CMH, 8-3 SF, 199–200; John A. Hixson, "Analysis of Deep Attack Operations: U.S. VI Corps, Task Force Butler, Aug. 1944," March 1987, CSI, 27–33; Truscott, *Command Missions*, 437; Jackson, *The Mediterranean and the Middle East*, vol. 6, part 2, 197; RR, 147 (*dash toward the river*).

207 *By now supply shortages threatened to undermine*: "Supply and Maintenance on the European Continent," n.d., USFET General Board, NARA RG 407, E 427, 97-USF5-0.3.0, no. 130, 50; *The Seventh United States Army in France and Germany*, vol. 1, 218–20 (*three hundred-mile round-trip*); Leo J. Meyer, "Moving Men and Supplies in Southern France," n.d., NARA RG 319, E 99, OCMH background files, 314.7, box 1, 14-17a (*only eleven thousand gallons*); "History of Ordnance Service in the MTO," n.d., vol. 2, CMH, 8-4 JA, 188–89 (*tire patches*).

208 *Even so, by late Monday afternoon the vanguard*: Yeide and Stout, *First to the Rhine*, 74–75; RR, 149 (*Fifty Wehrmacht vehicles*).

208 *VI Corps had severed the enemy escape route*: Yeide and Stout, *First to the Rhine*, 75–78; RR, 149 (*full-throated attack*).

208 *"Everything has gone better"*: LKT Jr. to Sarah, Aug. 17, 21, 29, Sept. 1, 3, 13, 1944, GCM Lib, box 1.

208 *His opponent felt dreadful*: Yeide and Stout, *First to the Rhine*, 80 ("*pre-technical days*");

Charles V. von Lüttichau, "Breakout and Withdrawal to the Dijon Salient," Sept. 1958, OCMH, NARA RG 319, R-series #106, 5 (*save itself by fleeing*); Ganz, "The 11th Panzers in the Defense, 1944," *Armor* (Mar.–Apr. 1944): 26+ ; Giziowski, *The Enigma of General Blaskowitz*, 323–24 (*dangled ropes*).

209 *Truscott took the German feint*: De Lattre de Tassigny, *The History of the French First Army*, 356–57 ("*carved out with an axe*"); OH, "The Invasion of Southern France," Seventh Army, NARA RG 407, E 427-A, CI, folder #368, 160–62 ("*Tell General O'Daniel*"); RR, 164.

209 *At Montélimar, Task Force Butler struggled*: RR, 144–50; "Operation Dragoon," Dec. 1944, COHQ, bulletin Y/42, CARL, N-6530.20 (*Army's swift advance had outrun P-47s*).

209 *This pleased Truscott not at all*: Truscott, *Command Missions*, 426–27; msg, LKT Jr. to J. Dahlquist, Aug. 22, 1944, LKT Jr. papers, GCM Lib, box 12, folder 6 ("*Don't you understand*").

210 *In truth, Dahlquist was overmatched*: photos, biographical notes, John E. Dahlquist papers, MHI; Steidl, *Lost Battalions*, 24, 57, 142–46 (*given to brooding*); corr, John E. Dahlquist to Ruth, Oct. 29, 1944, Dahlquist papers, MHI ("*I get winded*"); corr, John E. Dahlquist to Homer Case, June 5, 1945, Dahlquist papers, MHI (*Half his transport had yet to be unloaded*); Yeide and Stout, *First to the Rhine*, 76 (*Spanish consul's car*); LKT Jr., "Comments on 'Dragoon Secondary Attack Against Fortress Europe,'" n.d., NARA RG 319, OCMH, 2-3.7 CC2, Hamilton mss, 3 (*carrying three dozen men*); "Invasion of Southern France," n.d., WD HD, CMH, 8-3 SF, 237 ("*Your primary mission*").

210 *The battalion withdrew "at night from a hill"*: Yeide and Stout, *First to the Rhine*, 85.

210 *The German capture of a 36th Division battle plan*: "Invasion of Southern France," n.d., WD HD, CMH, 8-3 SF, appendix B, v–xii; Yeide and Stout, *First to the Rhine*, 92 ("*Come on, you bastards*").

210 "*John, I have come here*": Truscott, *Command Missions*, 430–31.

211 *More than eight battalions—some one hundred guns*: "Invasion of Southern France," n.d., WD HD, CMH, 8-3 SF, 243; Holt, *The Deceivers*, 621 (*asphalt caught fire*); OH, 3rd Bn, 143rd Inf, n.d., NARA RG 407, E 427-A, CI, folder 117 (*2,500 mortar rounds*); Lucian Heichler, "German Defense of the Gateway to Antwerp," Dec. 1953, NARA RG 319, R-series #23, 21–27; Turner and Jackson, *Destination Berchtesgaden*, 62; Giziowski, *The Enigma of General Blaskowitz*, 330–31 (*splashed across the Drôme*).

211 *In a confused mêlée*: RR, 166.

211 *Task Force Butler, reduced to hardly more than a battalion*: OH, 3rd Bn, 36th ID, n.d., NARA RG 407, E 427-A, CI, folder 117.

212 "*That's the first time I ever saw a Texan*": Murphy, *To Hell and Back*, 188–89.

212 *The battle of Montélimar was over*: Conway, "Operation Anvil," lecture, n.d., Norfolk, Theodore J. Conway papers, MHI, box 2, 22–24 ("*concept was daring*"); "Invasion of Southern France," n.d., WD HD, CMH, 8-3 SF, 245 (*sixty thousand U.S. artillery shells*); Wilt, *The French Riviera Campaign of August 1944*, 141 ("*I fumbled it badly*"); RR, 167–68 (*Blaskowitz's losses exceeded ten thousand*); Lucian Heichler, "German Defense of the Gateway to Antwerp," Dec. 1953, NARA RG 319, R-series #23, 31–32; Charles V. von Lüttichau, "Breakout and Withdrawal to the Dijon Salient," Sept. 1958, OCMH, NARA RG 319, R-series #106, 16–17 (*338th Division mustered barely one thousand*); Ludewig, *Rückzug*, 178–79 ("*almost a miracle*").

212 "*carnage compounded*": Truscott, *Command Missions*, 432–33; Taggart, ed., *History of the Third Infantry Division*, 222 (*Avenue of Stenches*); Simpson, *Audie Murphy, American Soldier*, 125 (*gas masks*).

212 "*some degree of satisfaction*": Truscott, *Command Missions*, 432–33; OH, "The Invasion of Southern France," Seventh Army, NARA RG 407, E 427-A, CI, folder #368, 176–77 (*ten thousand square miles*); RR, 167 (*captured 23,000 Germans*).

212 *Two field-gray torrents streamed*: Dean H. Krasomil, "German Operations in Southern France: The Withdrawal of the LXIV Corps," March 1954, NARA RG 319, R-series #47, 4–18; *Germany VII*, 650–61 ("*improper remarks*"); Ludewig, *Rückzug*, 80 (*kidnapped whenever possible*).

213 *Allied air strikes and FFI marauders*: Steidl, *Lost Battalions*, 20 (*8 million francs*); "German Surrenders," *AB*, no. 48 (1985): 1+ (*making bonfires*).

213 *The other retreating gaggle*: Wilhelm Heinrich Scheidt, "German Operations in the West," Sept. 1945, OKW Historical Section, NARA RG 407, ML #874, VI, 13–15 ("*trekking Wehrmacht*"); *Germany VII*, 657–61 (*138,000 men*); Marshall, *A Ramble Through My War*, 131 ("*moving bushes*"); *The Seventh United States Army in France and Germany*, vol. 1, 220–21 (*Field Order No. 4*); OH, Viscount Portal, Feb. 7, 1947, FCP ("*swine*"); Wilt, *The French Riviera Campaign of August 1944*, 157 (*shot up a train*). Stalin renewed his suggestion in October 1944. *TSC*, 406.

213 *By early September, almost 200,000 Allied soldiers*: IFG, 276; Garland, *Unknown Soldiers*, 282 ("*liberation, libation*"); Collier, *Fighting Words*, 177 ("*festooned with humanity*"); Marshall, *A Ramble Through My War*, 151 ("*hand out British flags*"); Pallud, "The Riviera Landings," *AB*, no. 110 (2000): 2+ (*cakes of butter*).

213 "*Sometimes the sheets on the hotel beds*": Gray, *The Warriors*, 155; Sevareid, *Not So Wild a Dream*, 457–59 (*painted by Picasso*); corr, Gertrude Stein to A. M. Patch, Jr., n.d. and Nov. 15, 1944, Alexander M. Patch, Jr., papers, USMA Arch, box 1; Wyant, *Sandy Patch*, 141 ("*a lot of repetitions*").

214 *In Grenoble the fleeing Germans*: Sevareid, *Not So Wild a Dream*, 454; Mauldin, *The Brass Ring*, 227–28 (*pistol shot in the ear*).

214 *A 36th Division patrol entered Lyon*: Truscott, *Command Missions*, 434; Higgins, *Soft Underbelly*, 220 ("*British opposed to the end*").

214 "*In the shops one could buy*": Garland, *Unknown Soldiers*, 312; Aron, *France Reborn*, 354 ("*capital of repression*"); diary, Sept. 19, 1944, Kingsley Andersson papers, HIA, box 1 ("*Too much gunfire*").

216 *Tracers fired into a city hospital*: Sevareid, *Not So Wild a Dream*, 462; Coles and Weinberg, *Civil Affairs*, 768–69 (*spans over the Rhône*). One recent German account asserts that all thirty-three bridges around Lyon were blown (Ludewig, *Rückzug*, 192).

216 *Precisely where those convoys should go*: A. M. Patch, Jr., to Julia, Sept. 14, 1944, Patch papers, USMA Arch, box 1 ("*temporary notoriety*").

216 *Sandy Patch was tall, gangly*: Truscott, *Command Missions*, 383 ("*expressing himself*"); Colley, *Decision at Strasbourg*, 27 ("*mystic turn of mind*"); "Patch of Provence," *Time* (Aug. 28, 1944), 22+ ("*devil before dawn*"); Strobridge and Nalty, "From the South Pacific to the Brenner Pass: General Alexander M. Patch," *Military Review* (June 1981): 41+ (*Apache country*); memo, J. N. Wenger, June 17, 1943; memo, E. J. King "for Gen. Marshall only," June 21, 1943; memo, A. M. Patch, Jr., June 29, 1943; "eyes only," GCM to A. M. Patch, Jr., June 29, 1943; memo, GCM to E. J. King, July 28, 1943, GCM Lib, box 78, folder 49 ("*I am puzzled*").

216 "*It feels as though it was three months ago*": A. M. Patch, Jr., to Julia, Sept. 14, 1944, Patch papers, USMA Arch, box 1; Giziowski, *The Enigma of General Blaskowitz*, 355 (*Blaskowitz halted the Nineteenth Army*); Yeide and Stout, *First to the Rhine*, 168–70 (*scaling ladders*); RR, 189; Sevareid, *Not So Wild a Dream*, 466 (*stolen bicycles*); Wilt, *The French Riviera Campaign of August 1944*, 154 ("*never saw such confusion*").

217 *The captured booty included*: Wilt, *The French Riviera Campaign of August 1944*, 150–51 ("*fleeting opportunity*"); *The Seventh United States Army in France and Germany*, vol. 2, 399; Salisbury-Jones, *So Full a Glory*, 161 (*irked De Lattre*); RR, 182–83, 223 (*Patch agreed to permit*); Truscott, *Command Missions*, 443 ("*gateway to Germany*").

217 *Then the ground shifted*: RR, 228–29; Chandler, 2146–47 (*supreme commander in mid-September*); Mansoor, *The GI Offensive in Europe*, 207 (*making the U.S. armies contiguous*).

217 "*surprised and disappointed*": diary, VI Corps, Sept. 14–15, 1944, Don E. Carleton papers, HIA, box 1.

218 "*The assault on the Belfort Gap*": LKT Jr. to A. M. Patch, Jr., Sept. 15, 1955, LKT Jr. papers, GCM Lib, box 12, folder 6; Truscott, *Command Missions*, 443–44; Wyant, *Sandy Patch*, 138 (*Lons-le-Saunier*).

218 *Patch phoned at 6:30 P.M.*: "Telephone Conversation Between Gen. Patch and Gen. Trus-cott," 1830 hrs, Sept 16, 1944, NARA RG 319, OCMH 2-3.7 CC2, Hamilton mss.

218 *So ended DRAGOON*: *RR*, 563 (*"just one day's supplies"*), 237 (*barely two dozen tanks left*); John W. Mosenthal, "The Establishment of a Continuous Defensive Front by Army Group G," Nov. 1955, NARA RG 319, OCMH, R-series, #68, 3–11 (*"still able to fight"*), 13–15 (*Blaskowitz was sacked*); Ludewig, *Rückzug*, 180 (*His greatest* fear); Charles V. von Lüttichau, "Army Group G Operations in Southern France," Aug. 1956, NARA RG 319, OCMH, R-series #87, 36 (*130,000 had escaped*); Charles V. von Lüttichau, "Breakout and Withdrawal to the Dijon Salient," Sept 1958, NARA RG 319, OCMH, R-series #112, 28 (*only 165 of 1,600 artillery pieces*); Giziowski, *The Enigma of General Blaskowitz*, 361 (*"planting cabbage"*). Ludewig estimates that at least 160,000 Germans from southern and southwestern France reached Dijon (*Rückzug*, 267–68).

219 *On the same Tuesday that Blaskowitz was relieved*: Pogue, *George C. Marshall*, 415. The official Army history acknowledges that "it is impossible to ascertain with any degree of accuracy" the casualties in Army Group G for late summer 1944. *RR*, 197.

219 *But ahead lay the granite and gneiss uplands*: author visit, May 24–28, 2009; Taggart, ed., *History of the Third Infantry Division*, 237–38; Sevareid, *Not So Wild a Dream*, 473 (*"long again for home"*); diary, VI Corps, Sept. 28, 1944, Don E. Carleton papers, HIA, box 1 (*"Looking for skis"*); LKT Jr. to Sarah, Sept. 16, Oct. 18, 1944, LKT Jr. papers, GCM Lib, box 1.

"Harden the Heart and Let Fly"

219 *A world away*: Robb, *The Discovery of France*, 42; Roach, *The 8.15 to War*, 170 (*waved with one hand*).

219 *By the end of August the front stretched*: BP, 667; Gilmore, ed., *U.S. Army Atlas of the European Theater in World War II*, 65; LC, 2–3 (*more than two million Allied soldiers*); *AAFinWWII*, 596 (*7,500 bombers and 4,300 fighters*); "Strategy of the Campaign in Western Europe, 1944–1945," n.d., USFET General Board study no. 1, 50 (*Montgomery's fifteen divisions*); King and Kutta, *Impact*, 221–23; Hinsley, 570 (*Luftwaffe aircraft*); Howard, *British Intelligence in the Second World War*, vol. 5, *Strategic Deception*, 177; *Germany VII*, 434; Churchill, *Triumph and Tragedy*, 48 (*"battle of London is won"*); corr, WSC to A. Eden, Sept. 2, 1944, "Strategy and Operations, vol. II," UK NA, CAB 120/421 (*"fall out of temper"*).

220 *In 12th Army Group, Bradley commanded*: LC, 4–5; Balkoski, *From Beachhead to Brit-tany*, 316–17; Mitcham, *Retreat to the Reich*, 214 (*fishing tackle*).

220 *Under this onslaught the Wehrmacht*: Alfred Jodl, ETHINT 52, Aug. 2, 1945, MHI, 6 (*"planless flight"*); Mitcham, *Retreat to the Reich*, 222 (*OB West listed eighteen divisions*); Ludewig, *Rückzug*, 191 (*"We have lost a battle"*); "Penetration of Siegfried Line," 4th ID, n.d., CARL, N-12159.1 (*"Americans will be here"*); *Germany VII*, 624 (*"ignominious rout"*); Boesch, *Road to Huertgen*, 110 (*waving chickens*).

220 *"Any Boches today?"*: Knickerbocker et al., *Danger Forward*, 272.

220 *By truck and by foot the pursuers pursued*: *Blue Spaders*, 69; Horrocks, *Corps Com-mander*, 71–72 (*"harden the heart"*); Pyle, *Brave Men*, 310 (*gray lace of burned powder*); SLC, 15 (*among a half-million killed*).

221 *"We blew up everything"*: Will Thornton, "World War II 'M' Co. History as Told by the Survivors," n.d., a.p.

221 *At Braine, near Reims*: Wellard, *The Man in a Helmet*, 158 (*Patton's vanguard*); White, *Conqueror's Road*, 10 (*"ecstatic agony"*), 25 (*"tits"*); Kershaw, *"It Never Snows in Septem-ber,"* 19 (*"west front has collapsed"*).

221 *Fuel shortages, nettlesome since early August*: Waddell, *United States Army Logistics*, 63 (*tripled from six gallons*); LC, 24–25 (*100,000 gallons* and *Patton's fuel dumps*), 117–18 (*tanks sent to capture a Meuse bridge*); OH, Lt. Gen. Sir Humphrey Gale, Jan. 27, 1947, FCP; VW, vol. 2, 72 (*battleships*); Greenfield, ed., *Command Decisions*, 332 (*stalled for four days*); diary, Sept. 6, 1944, CBH, MHI, box 4 (*corps commanders cadged cans*); "G-4

Periodic Report," Third Army, Sept. 5, 1944, Walter J. Muller papers, HIA, box 6 (*"extremely critical"*); Bradley, *A Soldier's Story*, 402 (*"Damn it, Brad"*).

221 *Onward they pushed, on foot*: Heinz, *When We Were One*, 220 (*polka-dot stars*); Kennett, *G.I.: The American Soldier in World War II*, 194 (*"Vote for Dewey"*); Schrijvers, *The Crash of Ruin*, 131 (*"If that was the only mistake"*).

223 *Giddy rumors swirled*: Hastings, *Armageddon*, 14 (*fled to Spain*); Sylvan, 133–34 (*insurrection in Cologne*); OH, A. F. Kibler, 12th AG, May 29, 1946, NARA RG 407, ML #501, box 24155 (*river crossing sites*); diary, CBH, Sept. 1, 1944, MHI, box 4 (*" 'If the war lasts' "*); diary, Raymond G. Moses, Sept. 4, 1944, MHI, box 1.

223 *"End the war in '44"*: Perret, *There's a War to Be Won*, 359; "Ready for V-Day?," *Time* (Sept. 4, 1944): 17 (*"first newsboy"*); Hamilton, *Monty: Final Years of the Field-Marshal, 1944–1976*, 12 (*spare an extra army headquarters*); memo, E. E. MacMorland to H. B. Sayler, July 29, 1944, Henry B. Sayler papers, DDE Lib, box 4 (*Pentagon drafted plans*).

223 *"There is a feeling of elation"*: Colville, *The Fringes of Power*, 507.

223 *"Militarily the war is won"*: *Three Years*, 657; Ferrell, ed., *The Eisenhower Diaries*, 127 (*"advance almost at will"*).

223 *The Allied juggernaut aimed vaguely for Berlin*: OH, W. B. Smith and H. R. Bull, Sept. 14, 1945, OCMH WWII Europe Interviews, MHI; *SLC*, 28; *LO*, 294 (*Two-thirds of German steel*); "Industrial Value of the Ruhr to the German War Effort," Oct. 30, 1944, British Brief and Action Report, JIC, NARA RG 331, E 3, box 132 (*40 percent drop in artillery ammunition*); *VW*, vol. 1, 82 (*"every chance of bringing to battle"*).

223 *Four paths led to the Ruhr*: "Strategy of the Campaign in Western Europe, 1944–1945," n.d., USFET General Board study no. 1, 42–50; *BP*, 658–59 (*Eisenhower's planners had proposed*).

224 *Montgomery would have none of it*: *BP*, 658–59; *VW*, vol. 1, 459–61; OH, David Belchem, Feb. 20, 1947, FCP, MHI (*preponderance in armor*).

224 *Bradley most certainly did* not *agree*: Bradley and Blair, *A General's Life*, 314; De Guingand, *Operation Victory*, 411; OH, Lord Tedder, Feb. 13, 1947, FCP, MHI (*"better to use both hands"*); *VW*, vol. 1, 461 (*Smith was excluded*); Wilmot, *The Struggle for Europe*, 468 (*"Victories win wars"*).

224 *Montgomery emerged from the caravan*: Ambrose, *Eisenhower: Soldier, General of the Army, President-Elect, 1890–1952*, vol. 1, 340–41; *BP*, 659–60 (*First Army would swing largely north*); draft memo, W. B. Smith, "Command and organization after D-day 'Overlord,'" May 23, 1944, Raymond G. Moses papers, MHI, box 1 (*some SHAEF planners had long considered*).

225 *Eisenhower also agreed that a single commander*: Ambrose, *Eisenhower: Soldier, General of the Army, President-Elect, 1890–1952*, vol. 1, 340–41; "General Eisenhower's Comments on Command," May 18, 1944, Arthur S. Nevins papers, MHI (*"nothing must be said"*).

225 *Churchill, "as a solace"*: Moran, *Churchill: Taken from the Diaries of Lord Moran*, 254; Roberts, *Masters and Commanders*, 512 (*"proper perspective"*); Ambrose, *Eisenhower: Soldier, General of the Army, President-Elect, 1890–1952*, vol. 1, 345 (*"close and warm friend"*).

225 *"Damn stupid"*: Love and Major, eds., *The Year of D-Day*, 129; *PP*, 535 (*"made us sick"*); Hamilton, *Master of the Battlefield*, 799 (*"almost a disaster"*).

225 *Late in the morning of Saturday, September 2*: Chandler, vol. 5, chronology, 165; diary, CBH, Sept. 2, 12, 15, 21, 1944, MHI, box 4.

226 *A message from Beetle Smith*: Williams, "Supreme Headquarters for D-Day," *AB*, no. 84 (1994): 1+; Baedeker, *Northern France*, 179.

226 *Eisenhower slipped in the sand*: Thomas W. Mattingly and Olive F. G. Marsh, "A Compilation of the General Health System of Dwight D. Eisenhower," n.d., DDE Lib, Thomas W. Mattingly papers, box 1; Eisenhower, *Crusade in Europe*, 326; Ambrose, *Eisenhower:*

Soldier, General of the Army, President-Elect, 1890–1952, vol. 1, 347–48 (*refused to allow his blood pressure*).

226 *For more than a fortnight:* Chandler, vol. 5, chronology, 165–67; *Three Years,* 661 (*Two resident cows*); Eisenhower, *Letters to Mamie,* 195 ("*off-key*"), 210–11 (*dead son*); Chandler, 2141 ("*Who is going to buy the plane?*").

227 *Even for an ambulatory commander:* D'Este, *Eisenhower: A Soldier's Life,* 593; Crosswell, *Beetle,* 700 (*through the RAF*); *BP,* 686 (*reaffirm his commitment to a multipronged advance*); Love and Major, eds., *The Year of D-Day,* 132 ("*Monty-like*").

227 *On Monday, September 4: LSA,* vol. 1, 492; *TSC,* 253 ("*now as never before*").

227 *An exasperated Montgomery:* Roberts, *Masters and Commanders,* 531 ("*curious idea*"); "Notes on Conversation with Monty, 18.5.46," R. W. W. "Chester" Wilmot papers, LHC, LH 15/15/127 (*first call on supplies*).

227 "*We have now reached a stage*": BLM to DDE, Sept. 4, 1944, DDE Lib, PP-pres, box 83; Chandler, 2120–21.

227 *Eisenhower replied on Tuesday:* Weigley, *Eisenhower's Lieutenants,* 278–79; OH, Arthur Coningham, Feb. 14, 1947, FCP, MHI ("'*The war is lost*'").

228 *The misdirected signal was entirely apt:* corr, DDE to H. L. Ismay, Jan. 14, 1959, LHC, 4/12/131 ("*preposterous proposal*"); Crosswell, *Beetle,* 687 ("*balderdash*"); Bradley Commentaries, CBH, MHI, box 41 ("*arrogant and egotistical*").

228 *Montgomery's vision had the military virtue of mass:* Strong, *Intelligence at the Top,* 199–201 (*counter to SHAEF calculations*); *LSA,* vol. 2, 10–11 (*nearly five hundred truck companies* and "*wholesale grounding*"); *LSA,* vol. 1, 487–88. A three-corps drive to Berlin in late September even under optimal conditions would require grounding five corps, according to SHAEF (*TSC,* 253–54).

228 *Moreover, the need to protect long open flanks: TSC,* 260; Frank A. Osmanski, "Critical Analysis of the Planning and Execution of the Logistic Support of the Normandy Invasion," Dec. 1949, Armed Forces Staff College, Osmanski papers, MHI ("*easy prey for the German mobile reserves*"); OH, E. J. Foord, Dec. 12, 1946, R. W. W. "Chester" Wilmot papers, LHC, LH 15/15/27 ("*overbidding his hand*"); De Guingand, *Operation Victory,* 412 (*Hitler's eventual defeat*).

228 *Most strategists would come to similar conclusions:* : Dan van der Vat, obituary, "Field Marshal Lord Carver," *The Guardian,* Dec. 12, 2001 (*youngest brigadier*); Keegan, ed., *Churchill's Generals,* 162–63 (*In both world wars*).

229 *Two-fisted punching:* Weigley, *The American Way of War,* 352; Wilson, ed., *D-Day 1944,* 334 ("*Whatever Montgomery's talents*").

229 "*political factors can sometimes have the same weight*": Lewin, *Montgomery as Military Commander,* 298.

229 *Eisenhower's "ignorance":* Hamilton, *Master of the Battlefield,* 799; Danchev, 575 ("*quite unsuited*"), 585 ("*3 to 6 months*").

229 "*extremely susceptible to the personality*": "Notes on Conversation with Monty, 18.5.46," R. W. W. "Chester" Wilmot papers, LHC, LH 15/15/127.

229 "*Ike is all for caution*": diary, Sept. 2, 1944, GSP, LOC MS Div, box 3, folder 7.

229 "*the trouble with Ike*": Crosswell, *Beetle,* 696, 702, 708, 722.

229 "*hardly decisive in the way he communicated*": Stephen E. Ambrose, "Eisenhower as Commander: Single Thrust Versus Broad Front," in Chandler, vol. 5, 47.

229 "*There is never a moment*": Eisenhower, *Letters to Mamie,* 195, 217; Chandler, 2158 ("*team is working well*").

230 *The armies fought on, largely unaware: LC,* 52 (*first five days of September*); *LSA,* vol. 1, 513; war diary, Leroy Irwin, Sept. 6, 1944, 5th ID, Hugh Cole papers, MHI ("*Frankfort*"); *AAFinWWII,* 277 (*flying gas stations*); Semmes, *Portrait of Patton,* 205 (*bounties of cognac and confiscated champagne*); "G-4 Periodic Report," Third Army, Sept. 5, 1944, Walter J. Muller papers, HIA, box 6 (*army shortages*); Allen, *Lucky Forward,* 41, 101–2; *PP,* 549 (*fifty thousand cases of champagne*).

230 *"a goddam army commander"*: PP, 542; Blumenson, *Patton: The Man Behind the Legend, 1885–1945*, 240–41 (*"shit through a goose"*).

230 *To his northwest, Courtney Hodges's First Army*: BP, 694–95 (*"pretty girls"*); Blue Spaders, 71–72 (*"heterogeneous mass"*).

230 *Bounding from the south, the 1st Division*: Stanhope B. Mason, "Reminiscences and Anecdotes of World War II," 1988, MRC FDM, 1994.126, 87, 206–10; OH, C. A. Wollmer, 83rd Armored Reconnaissance Bn, n.d., NARA RG 407, E 427, HI; Heinz, *When We Were One*, 197, 213 (*rake the German columns*); Knickerbocker et al., *Danger Forward*, 274 (*"Belgian horses"*); George W. Williams et al., "Exploitation by the 3rd Armored Division—Seine River to Germany," AS, Ft. K, 1949, NARA RG 337, 44–45 (*"You only want to slaughter us"*).

231 *In addition to some 3,500 enemy dead*: Wheeler, *The Big Red One*, 311–12; Pallud, "The Battle of the Mons Pocket," AB, no. 115 (2002): 2+ (*steaks*); AAR, 1st ID, Oct. 31, 1944, a.p., 1–6; Heinz, *When We Were One*, 200–204 (*"You will not love"*).

231 *Thirty miles to the north, the British Second Army*: BP, 686; VW, vol. 2, 15 (*surrender in his pajamas*), 6; Wilmot, *The Struggle for Europe*, 471 (*fleeing in a Volkswagen*); *Taurus Pursuant*, 67 (*"what used to be"*).

231 *At eight P.M. on Sunday, September 3*: VW, vol. 2, 5; "Advance of 30 Corps Across R. Seine to Brussels and Antwerp," War Office, n.d., NARA RG 407, ML #226; Moorehead, *Eclipse*, 191 (*"a pallid thing"*); Collier, *Fighting Words*, 177 (*"a flambeau"*); Fitzgerald, *History of the Irish Guards in the Second World War*, 450–53 (*"Goodbye, Tommy"*).

231 *Local worthies appeared in sashes*: Daniell, *The Royal Hampshire Regiment*, vol. 3, 231; Fitzgerald, *History of the Irish Guards in the Second World War*, 450–53 (*Bistros sent waiters*); Hastings, *Armageddon*, 7 (*"eating their way"*); Moorehead, *Eclipse*, 191 (*"a remarkable claret"*).

232 *On Monday at noon British tanks*: J. B. Churcher, "A Soldier's Story," 159th Inf Bde, LHC, 52–54 (*houses for belonging to alleged collaborators* and *search for a cinema*); Collier, *Fighting Words*, 177–79 (*still sipping beer*); VW, vol. 2, 5, 10–11, 414–15 (*two million barrels*); Freeman W. Burford, "The Inside Story of Oil in the European War," Nov. 25, 1946, NARA RG 319, 2-37 CB 6; "Advance of 30 Corps Across R. Seine to Brussels and Antwerp," War Office, n.d., NARA RG 407, ML #226 (*petered out by 9:30 P.M.*); Moorehead, *Eclipse*, 192–93 (*cages in the lion house*); Moorehead, *Gellhorn*, 227 (*"sat on the straw"*).

232 *With Brittany's ports soon to be forsaken*: Baedeker, *Belgium and Holland*, 150–52 (*"at least a year to reduce it"*); Lucian Heichler, "German Defense of the Gateway to Antwerp," Dec. 1953, OCMH, NARA RG 319, R-series #22, 2; LSA, vol. 2, 104 (*thousand ships each month*).

232 *The capture of Antwerp and exploitation*: Weinberg, *A World at Arms*, 700; Chandler, 2090, 2100, 2116; msg, Montgomery, Aug. 26, 1944, M-520, National Archives of Canada, RG 24, vol. 1054 2, file 215A21.016 (9) (*"destroy all enemy forces"*).

233 *Having sailed these waters*: WaS, 142–43; Fergusson, *The Watery Maze*, 352 (*campaign in 1809*); Jenkins, *Churchill: A Biography*, 248–50 (*rushed to Antwerp*); VW, vol. 2, 10–11; Love and Major, eds., *The Year of D-Day*, 131; Roskill, *Churchill and the Admirals*, 245 (*"Timbuctoo"*).

233 *"decisive importance" of holding the Scheldt*: Bennett, *Ultra in the West*, 147–48; Ralph Bennett, "Ultra and Some Command Decisions," in Laqueur, ed., *The Second World War*, 231 (*strategic mistake*); Crosswell, *Beetle*, 706 (*"bottle is now corked"*).

233 *A Royal Marine Commando unit*: Roskill, *White Ensign*, 397; *Taurus Pursuant*, 56–58 (*seize the docks*); Horrocks, *Corps Commander*, 79–81 (*"My eyes were fixed"*).

234 *The British drive soon was stymied*: Moulton, *Battle for Antwerp*, 30; Ludewig, *Rückzug*, 214 (*Fifteen of seventeen*); J. B. Churcher, "A Soldier's Story," 159th Inf Bde, LHC, 52–54 (*"swift and most unpleasant"*); Copp, *Cinderella Army*, 38–39 (*reinforce the canals*); Moulton, *Battle for Antwerp*, 52; Lamb, *Montgomery in Europe, 1943–1945*, 201–4; Horrocks, *Corps Commander*, 84.

234 *An evacuation of German troops by ferry*: Weigley, *Eisenhower's Lieutenants*, 293; Lucian Heichler, "German Defense of the Gateway to Antwerp," Dec. 1953, OCMH, NARA RG 319, R-series #22, 13–14 (*5,000 vehicles*); Ludewig, *Rückzug*, 272 (*eleven thousand troops*).

234 *Montgomery told London on September 7*: Orange, *Coningham*, 215; *SLC*, 207 ("*a jewel that could not be worn*"); Hills, *Phantom Was There*, 247 ("*most bewildering*").

CHAPTER 5: AGAINST THE WEST WALL

"Five Barley Loaves and Three Small Fishes"

235 *Versailles had long proved irresistible*: Abram et al., *The Rough Guide to France*, 213 ("*unhygienic squalor*"); McCullough, *The Greater Journey*, 296, 303 (*starving winter of 1870*); Tillier et al., *Paris*, 252; http://en.wikipedia.org/wiki/Palace_of_Versailles; Macmillan, *Paris 1919*, 474–78 (*Republican Guardsmen*).

235 *And it was here that Eisenhower*: Baedeker, *Paris and Its Environs*, 376 (*175 francs*); memo, war room procedures, Mar. 19, 1945, Sidney H. Negrotto papers, MHI (*SHAEF master pass*); memoir, 1974, Raymond H. Croll papers, MHI, 277–89 (*K-ration lunches*); http://www.normandybattlefields.com/normandy_today.htm; Pogue, *Pogue's War*, 202–3 (*Thickets of antennae*); Abram et al., *The Rough Guide to France*, 213 (*Marie Antoinette*); *TSC*, 276–78; Hammon, "When the Second Lieutenant Bearded General Eisenhower," *Military Affairs* (Oct. 1983): 129+ ("*state capitols*").

236 "*he has been a bad boy*": diary, CBH, Sept. 22, 1944, MHI, box 4; Bradley, *A Soldier's Story*, 422.

236 *Eleven paintings, including a Van Dyck*: Coles and Weinberg, *Civil Affairs*, 868–69; Hammon, "When the Second Lieutenant Bearded General Eisenhower," *Military Affairs* (Oct. 1983): 129ff.; Nicholas, *The Rape of Europa*, 302.

236 *SHAEF by midsummer had already tripled*: *TSC*, 276–77 (*750,000 square feet*) and appendix B, 529–34. SHAEF's authorized strength on Feb. 1, 1945, was 16,312.

236 *Eventually 1,800 properties*: *LSA*, vol. 2, 497; Larrabee, *Commander in Chief*, 473 (*French magazine*); OH, Adolph Rosengarten, Jr., Dec. 22, 1947, FCP, MHI (*Should Have Army Experience First*); OH, Ford Trimble, Dec. 17, 1946, FCP, MHI (*sea serpent*).

236 *Another sea serpent had wrapped*: "Activities and Organization of COMZ," U.S. Senate hearing, May 28, 1945, NARA RG 498, ETO HD, admin file #89, 1–5; Robert W. Coakley, "The Administrative and Logistical History of the ETO," vol. 2, 1946, CMH, 8-3.1 AA 2, 119–28; "U.S. Army Operations in the ETO from January 1942 to V-E Day," May 1945, NARA RG 498, ETO HD, admin file #353 (*one in every four GIs*); "Engineer Memoirs: General William M. Hoge," 1993, CEOH, 128; Beck, 350 (*tentage*); Ingersoll, *Top Secret*, 207 ("*tons of files*"); memo, Seine Section, COMZ to SHAEF, Sept. 20, 1944, NARA RG 331, SHAEF SGS, Geog Corr, box 108 (*315 hotels*); memoir, n.d., Pleas B. Rogers papers, MHI (*three thousand additional Parisian properties*); corr, "GHH" to Ralph Ingersoll, May 14, 1946, Thaddeus Holt papers, MHI, box 1 ("*elegance and swank*"); Crosswell, *Beetle*, 739 (*permitted to keep their schools*); *TSC*, 322–23 (*Americans' demands exceeded*).

237 *All this and more was the handiwork*: "Miracle of Supply," *Time* (Sept. 25, 1944): 8+ ("*exceptionally friendly*"); "The Tendons of an Army," n.d., NARA RG 498, ETO HD, admin file #531, 5–6; John Kennedy Ohl, "General Brehon B. Somervell and Logistics in the European Theater of Operations in World War II," 1993, Alexandria, Va., Historical Office, U.S. Army Materiel Command, 20–22 ("*personal gift*"); Irving, *The War Between the Generals*, 78 (*standing in a London theater*); John C. H. Lee, "Service Reminiscences," n.d., Lee papers, MHI, box 1 ("*my ability to get along*"); *LSA*, vol. 2, 267 ("*Heavy on ceremony*"); Cowdrey, *Fighting for Life*, 224 ("*fishing with for a week*"); *PP*, 555–57 ("*glib liar*"); diary, GSP, Aug. 7, 1944, LOC MS Div, box 3, folder 7 ("*pompous little son-of-a-bitch*"); D'Este, *Patton: A Genius for War*, 649 (*Patton welcomed him*).

237 *Booted and bedizened*: Pogue, *George C. Marshall: Organizer of Victory*, 391 (*riding crop*); "Miracle of Supply," *Time* (Sept. 25, 1944): 8+ (*Bibles in his desk* and *red-cushioned*

limousine); John C. H. Lee, "Service Reminiscences," n.d., Lee papers, MHI, box 1 (*"at His altar"*); "Engineer Memoirs: Major General William E. Potter," 1983, CEOH, 35 (*personal retinue of forty*); Irving, *The War Between the Generals*, 92 (*eight correspondence secretaries*); "The U.S. Army Special Train *'Alive,'*" n.d., NARA RG 498, ETO HD, admin file #16; John Connell, "Over Age in Grade," n.d., MHI, 49 (*special railcar*); *LSA*, vol. 2, 267 (*"instrument of torture"*); OH, Henry S. Aurand, 1974, William O. Morrison, SOOHP, MHI (*read scripture aloud*); Irving, *The War Between the Generals*, 316 ("*Dress up*"); OH, Leonard D. Heaton, 1978, Robert B. McLean, SOOHP, MHI (*"had to lie at attention"*); "Engineer Memoirs: General William M. Hoge," 1993, CEOH, 125–26 (*"I can eat it"*); Pyle, *Brave Men*, 233.

238 *In Paris, Lee kept a huge war room*: OH, Henry S. Aurand, 1974, William O. Morrison, SOOHP, MHI; Crosswell, *Beetle*, 739 (*three suites upstairs*); Murray and Millett, *A War to Be Won*, 437 (*a piano*); Pogue, *Pogue's War* (*"Avenue de Salute"*); Allen, *Lucky Forward*, 69 (*"General Lee's personal residence"*).

238 *"Why didn't somebody tell me"*: OH, Leonard D. Heaton, 1978, Robert B. McLean, SOOHP, MHI; OH, W. B. Smith, May 13, 1947, FCP, MHI; MMB, 311 (*"modern Cromwell"*).

238 *"Due to the heavy shipments"*: DDE to J. C. H. Lee, Sept. 16, 1944, attached to memo, W. B. Smith to G-1, "Discipline in the Paris Area," Sept. 17, 1944, NARA RG 331, SHAEF SGS, Geog Corr, box 108.

238 *"I have no regrets"*: John C. H. Lee, "Service Reminiscences," n.d., Lee papers, MHI, box 1.

238 *Lee's "first priority duties"*: Crosswell, *Beetle*, 739 (*Sears, Roebuck*); Greenfield, ed., *Command Decisions*, 323 (*assumed that by D+90*); "Strategy of the Campaign in Western Europe, 1944–1945," n.d., USFET, General Board study no. 1, 35; *LSA*, vol. 2, 6–7 (*No logistician expected to reach*).

239 *Battlefield exigencies disrupted*: Frank O. Osmanski, "Critical Analysis of the Planning and Execution of the Logistic Support of the Normandy Invasion," Dec. 1949, Armed Forces Staff College, Osmanski papers, MHI, 43; "Logistics of Overlord," n.d., CARL, N-13587; *LSA*, vol. 1, 479; Crosswell, *Beetle*, 688–89 (*Marshall and Eisenhower further accelerated*); TSC, 258–59; Greenfield, ed., *Command Decisions*, 327 (*2.5 combat divisions*).

239 *Truck convoys that in July*: H. H. Dunham, "U.S. Army Transportation in the ETO," 1946, CMH, 4-13.1 AA 29, 216; Hogan, *A Command Post at War*, 145–46 (*quartermaster depot moved six times*); Weinberg, *A World at Arms*, 761 (*two thousand tanks*); PP, 555–57 (*"five barley loaves"*).

239 *Much more than bread and seafood*: "Quartermaster Procurement," chapter 41, PIR, MHI, 7; "Food Service in the ETO," chapter 47, PIR, MHI, 71; "Quartermaster Procurement on the Continent," n.d., SHAEF QM, NARA RG 498, ETO HD, admin file #154, 1–2 (*"one-sixteenth of an inch"*), 11 (*woodcutting camps*), 14 (*toilet paper*).

240 *Average daily supply needs*: Coakley, 825; "Supply and Maintenance on the European Continent," USFET General Board study no. 130, NARA RG 407, E 427, 97-USF5-0.3.0, 37 (*eating 30 percent more*); TSC, 256–57 (*a million gallons of gasoline*); Charles K. MacDermut and Adolph P. Gratiot, "History of G-4 Com Z ETO," 1946, CMH, 8-3.4 AA, 83 (*ammunition expenditures*); Henry F. Pringle, "Weapons Win Wars," n.d., CMH, 2-3.7 AB.B, 187 (*eight million artillery and mortar shells*).

240 *Prodigal wastage, always an American trait*: memo, "Supply Discipline," ONB, July 23, 1944, Walter J. Muller papers, HIA, box 8; Henry F. Pringle, "Weapons Win Wars," n.d., CMH, 2-3.7 AB.B, 187 (*"extremely high"*); "Supply: Oversea Theaters of Operation," 1945, NARA RG 319, background files, 2-3.7 (*mine detectors*); Waddell, *United States Army Logistics*, 149 (*a hundred miles every hour*); Hastings, *Armageddon*, 23 (*22 million jerricans*); *LSA*, vol. 2, 203 (*7 million more*); Chandler, 2200 (*"it is now costing us"*).

240 *All this fell largely unforeseen*: memo, Raymond G. Moses to ONB, Sept. 26, 1944, and draft memo to W. B. Smith, Nov. 7, 1944, Moses papers, MHI, box 1; Graham and Bidwell,

Coalitions, Politicians & Generals, 259 (*crates of oranges*); OH, J. C. H. Lee, March 21, 1947, FCP, MHI (*regretted not playing bridge*); Frank A. Osmanski, "Critical Analysis of the Planning and Execution of the Logistic Support of the Normandy Invasion," Dec. 1949, Armed Forces Staff College, Osmanski papers, MHI, 29 (*ad hoc dumps*); minutes, Military Shipments Priority Meeting, Sept. 9, 1944, NARA RG 331, E 1, SHAEF SGS, box 54 ("*stretched to the limit*"); memo, Raymond G. Moses to ONB, Sept. 26, 1944, Moses papers, MHI, box 1 ("*For a period of about one month*").

240 *COMZ improvised, with mixed results:* "Pluto: Pipeline Under the Ocean," *AB*, no. 116 (2002): 2+ ("*Bambi*"); Moore, "Operation Pluto," *Proceedings* (June 1954): 647+; Freeman W. Burford, "The Inside Story of Oil in the European War," Nov. 25, 1946, NARA RG 319, CMH background file, 2-.37 CB 6; Mason, ed., *The Atlantic War Remembered*, 417 ("*scandalous waste*").

241 *A terrestrial innovation was the Red Ball Express:* Henry F. Pringle, "Weapons Win Wars," n.d., CMH, 2-3.7 AB.B, 188; Andrew T. McNamara, "QM Activities of II Corps . . . and First Army Through Europe," 1955, chapter 46, PIR, MHI, 142 (*Cub planes*); BP, 691 (*300,000 gallons of gasoline*); "Red Ball," Feb. 3, 1945, NARA RG 498, ETO HD, admin file #281, 1–3, 14, 16–18, 28–29, 40, 55, 56–57, 63–65 ("*steep hill*"); memoir, Robert P. Patterson, ts, 1947 (?), a.p., 273 ("*gas splashing inside*"); "Shipping Situation and Supply Requirements," Nov. 25, 1944, COM Z, G-4, CARL, N-6726 ("*deadlined*"); OH, Henry S. Aurand, 1974, William O. Morrison, SOOHP, MHI (*nine thousand were trucks*). At war's end, the U.S. Army had 464 truck companies in Europe, each typically with 48 trucks (Eudora Ramsay Richardson and Sherman Allan, "Quartermaster Supply in the ETO in WWII," vol. 1, 1947, QM School, Camp Lee, Va.).

241 *Roads deteriorated in the autumn rains:* Waddell, *United States Army Logistics,* 124–31; "Supply: Oversea Theaters of Operations," 1945, NARA RG 319, background files, 2-3.7 (*ruination of five thousand tires*); D'Este, *Patton: A Genius for War,* 649 (*Lee requested thirteen infantry battalions*); "Subsistence in the ETO," 1959, Robert M. Littlejohn papers, HIA (*shoot-to-kill authority*); Gropman, ed., *The Big "L,"* 389 (*400000 tons*); LSA, vol. 2, 140; OH, Henry S. Aurand, 1974, William O. Morrison, SOOHP, MHI ("*greatest killer of trucks*").

241 *A single train could haul:* Gropman, ed., *The Big "L,"* 389–90 (*almost five thousand miles of track*); LSA, vol. 1, 551 (*obliterated by years of Allied bombing*); "Supply and Maintenance on the European Continent," USFET General Board study no. 130, NARA RG 407, E 427, 97-USF5-0.3.0, 30–36; Waddell, *United States Army Logistics,* 118 (*creeping across bridges*); "Military Railway Service," USFET General Board study no. 123, NARA RG 407, E 427, 97-USF5-0.3.0 (*line to Paris* and *as far away as Persia*); H. H. Dunham, "U.S. Army Transportation in the ETO," 1946, CMH, 4-13.1 AA 29, 232 (*flagging with lighters*); "Activities and Organization of COMZ," U.S. Senate hearing, May 28, 1945, NARA RG 498, ETO HD, admin file #89, 21–22 (*thirteen hundred muscular American engines*); memo, COMZ assistant G-5, Feb. 18, 1945, NARA RG 498, ETO HD, admin file #494U (*eleven thousand miles*).

242 "*the number of divisions required to capture the number of ports*": Whipple, "Logistical Bottleneck," *IJ* (March 1948): 6+.

242 *Fifty-four ports had been studied:* R. W. Crawford, "Guns, Gas and Rations," SHAEF G-4, June 1945, NARA RG 498, ETO HD, admin file #145; "American Port Plans, August to November 1944," n.d., NARA RG 319, background files, 2-37 CB 6 (*half eventually played a role*); RR, 575 (*one-third of all Allied supplies*); LSA, vol. 2, 71 (*Cherbourg tripled its expected cargo*); OH, Henry S. Aurand, 1974, William O. Morrison, SOOHP, MHI ("*Napoleon's hand*"); Whipple, "Logistical Bottleneck," *IJ* (March 1948): 6+ (*two hundred by mid-October*).

242 *Clearly the solution was to be found in Antwerp:* LC, 211; LSA, vol. 2, 52 ("*blood transfusion*"); John Connell, "Over Age in Grade," n.d., 11th Port Engineer Special Brigade Group, MHI, 99–100 ("*What a life!*").

Every Village a Fortress

243 *A stubby C-47 transport plane*: Margry, ed., *Operation Market-Garden Then and Now*, vol. 1, 27 *(B-58)*; http://en.wikipedia.org/wiki/Brussels_Airport.

243 *There he found Eisenhower*: Ambrose, *Eisenhower: Soldier, General of the Army, President-Elect, 1890–1952*, vol. 1, 348. Ambrose puts the meeting on Eisenhower's B-25 aircraft.

243 *"Well, they're nothing but balls"*: OH, Miles Graham, Jan. 19, 1949, "Allied Strategy After Fall of Paris," R. W. W. "Chester" Wilmot, LHC, LH 15/15/48; Ambrose, *Eisenhower: Soldier, General of the Army, President-Elect, 1890–1952*, vol. 1, 348–49 *(Patton actually running the war)*.

243 *For a long hour they bickered*: Wilmot, *The Struggle for Europe*, 489 *(capture the Ruhr with twenty divisions)*; TSC, 255.

243 *Eisenhower agreed that the Ruhr*: OH, DDE, n.d., CJR, box 43, file 7 *("What the hell?")*.

244 *"Our fight must be with both hands"*: VW, vol. 2, 22; SLC, 120–22.

244 *"Just when a really firm grip was needed"*: BLM to Brooke, Sept. 10, 1944, AB papers, LHC, 6/2/27.

244 *Regardless of American requirements*: OH, Miles Graham, Jan. 19, 1949, "Allied Strategy After Fall of Paris," R. W. W. "Chester" Wilmot, LHC, LH 15/15/48 *(350 to 400 tons)*; Hinsley, 542 *(Dieppe and Le Havre)*; VC, 310 *("one good Pas de Calais port"* and *"last priority")*; Second Army war diary, "The First 100 Days," Sept. 7, 1944, UK NA, WO 285/9; VW, vol. 2, 131–32 *(would not open until mid-October)*, 15; SLC, 208; Hastings, *Armageddon*, 23 *(fourteen hundred three-ton British trucks)*; Crosswell, *Beetle*, 707.

245 *Another grim battlefield development*: Hamilton, *Monty: Final Years of the Field-Marshal, 1944–1976*, 42 *(War Office cable)*; Longmate, *Hitler's Rockets*, 164–74 *(Stavely Road* and *"flying gas mains")*; Collier, *The Defence of the United Kingdom*, 406; *AAFinWWII*, 542 *(refused to publicly acknowledge)*.

245 *The true culprit, the V-2 rocket*: Collier, *The Defence of the United Kingdom*, 521; *Germany VII*, 438 *(fifty big train engines)*. A 1960 movie based on Von Braun's life, *I Aim at the Stars*, inspired the proposed subtitle, "But Sometimes I Hit London." Mallon, "Rocket Man," review of Michael J. Neufeld, *Von Braun*, *New Yorker* (Oct. 22, 2007): 170+ *(young Prussian Junker)*.

245 *The rocket had long been expected*: minutes, British chiefs of staff meeting, July 11, 1944, NARA RG 331, E 3, box 129; Hinsley, 421–23 *(Saturation bombing of Peenemünde)*; *Germany VII*, 443 *(tendency to break up)*; Howard, *British Intelligence in the Second World War*, vol. 5, *Strategic Deception*, 180–81 *(British government also considered evacuating)*.

245 *The initial volley had been fired*: M. C. Helfers, "The Employment of V-Weapons by the Germans During World War II," 1954, OCMH, NARA RG 319, 2-3.7 AW, 72; Collier, *The Defence of the United Kingdom*, 408 *(outside Nijmegen)*; King and Kutta, *Impact*, 245 *("Will you please report"* and *"It must be towards Arnhem")*; OH, Miles Dempsey, June 4, 1946, R. W. W. "Chester" Wilmot papers, LHC, 15/15/30 *(favored a more easterly advance)*.

246 *"This delay," he added*: VW, vol. 2, 22.

246 *"E. is spending a few days in bed"*: diary, Kay Summersby, Sept. 11, 1944, DDE Lib, PP-pres, box 140.

246 *"Monty seems unimpressed"*: desk calendar, DDE, Sept. 11–13, 1944, Barbara Wyden papers, DDE Lib, PP-pres, box 1.

246 *"He let himself go on subject of Monty"*: Love and Major, eds., *The Year of D-Day*, 137.

246 *At a moment when strategic harmony*: OH, SLAM, 1973, George J. Stapleton, SOOHP, MHI, III, 2–3; VW, vol. 2, 351–52; msg, DDE to ONB, Sept. 15, 1944, ONB papers, MHI *("There is no reason")*; PP, 552 *("'clever son of a bitch'")*; OH, DDE, n.d., CJR, box 43, file 7, 17, 36–37 *("psychopath")*.

247 *He also authorized Montgomery to communicate directly*: Chandler, 2133–34; VW, vol. 2, 24 *("Ike has given way")*.

247 *"Montgomery suddenly became obsessed"*: Chandler, 2144.

247 *Just after six P.M. on the warm, clear Monday*: After various units claimed to have been first into Germany, an Army historical investigation concluded that Holzinger and his patrol had earned the distinction. Emerson F. Hurley, "Study of the First Entry into Germany in World War II," n.d., NARA RG 407, E 427, 605-CAV-0.20; *SLC*, 3.

248 *Up the slope for four hundred yards*: "Unit History, 85th Cavalry Reconnaissance Squadron," 5th AD, n.d., and letter, W. W. Holzinger, Nov. 3, 1947, NARA RG 407, E 429, 95-USF 2-0.3.0; Pogue, *Pogue's War*, 264.

248 *By midnight, other patrols from the 4th and 28th Infantry Divisions*: Pogue, *Pogue's War*, 264; MacDonald, *The Battle of the Huertgen Forest*, 6 (*Three corps abreast*); memo, commanders' conference, First Canadian Army, Oct. 16, 1944, National Archives of Canada, RG 24, vol. 1054 2, file 215A21.016(9) ("*cuckoos*"); Heinz, *When We Were One*, 29, 258 ("*eating away at each other*"); *RR*, 223 (*spied French dragoons*); Robichon, *The Second D-Day*, 295–96; William K. Wyant, "Seventh Army History," n.d., NARA RG 319, background historical file, FRC 4.

248 *From the North Sea to the Mediterranean*: Greenfield, ed., *Command Decisions*, 345; *BP*, 701–2; Roskill, *White Ensign*, 390 (*evacuating southern Greece*); "Germany's War Effort and Its Failure," Oct. 8, 1945, U.K. chiefs of staff committee, Joint Intelligence Subcommittee, ANSCOL, NARA RG 334, E 315, 91 (*operational life of a U-boat commander*); *GS* V, 343–45; *SLC*, 14 (*114,000 officers and 3.6 million enlisted*).

249 *"I would like to place the Western front"*: Rundstedt also had presided over a kangaroo "court of honor" convened to expel from service officers implicated in the July 20 assassination plot. Barnett, ed., *Hitler's Generals*, 201.

249 *From his new headquarters near Koblenz*: Germany VII, 632–35 (*fighting strength in the west*); *VC*, 317–24 ("*roughly 1,700*"); interrogation, Erich Brandenberger, Sept. 1945, Third Army Intelligence Center, NARA RG 407, E 427, ML #978, 1–2, 14 (*two hundred postal detachments*); "Weaknesses in Germany's Capacity to Resist," JIC assessment, UK COS brief and action report, Sept. 27, 1944, NARA RG 331, E 3, SHAEF SGS, box 132 (*tanks and trucks to ammunition and uniforms*); *LC*, 33 (*created in late summer*); *SLC*, 15 (*Begun in 1936*).

249 *The Siegfried Line*: interrogation, Erich Brandenberger, Sept. 1945, Third Army Intelligence Center, NARA RG 407, E 427, ML #978, 11; *SLC*, 34–35 (*Fatherland had been made invincible*); "Combat Engineering," Aug. 1945, CE, historical report no. 10, CEOH, box X-30, 63 (*disguised as electrical substations*), 57; *LC*, 548–51 (*fields of fire*); G-2 analysis, XIX Corps, Sept. 14, 1944, Thomas L. Crystal papers, HIA (*fifteen big bunkers might be found*); "Breaching the Siegfried Line," Dec. 5, 1944, Seventh Army, special intelligence bulletin, NARA RG 200, E 4100 (UD), Garrison H. Davidson personal office file, box 1.

250 *But years of neglect had ravaged the West Wall*: interrogation, Erich Brandenberger, Sept. 1945, Third Army Intelligence Center, NARA RG 407, E 427, ML #978, 17–18; Lucian Heichler, "The Germans Facing V Corps, September 1944," May 1952, NARA RG 319, R-series, #37, 2–5 (*Farmers laid roadbeds*); OH, Gerhard Graf von Schwerin, ETHINT 18, Oct.–Nov. 1945, MHI, 34 (*tool sheds or storage bins*); Rudolf Freiherr von Gersdorff, "The Battle of Schmidt," Nov. 1945, FMS, #A-891, MHI (*hideouts for soldiers*); White, *Conquerors' Road*, 12–13 ("*more like sewage works*").

250 *Hitler in mid-August ordered*: *LC*, 548–51; Wilmot, *The Struggle for Europe*, 478 (*finding keys to locked doors*); Germany VII, 633 (*League of German Maidens*); Cooper, *The German Army, 1933–1945*, 517 (*plucked from depots*); Lucian Heichler, "The Germans Facing V Corps, September 1944," May 1952, NARA RG 319, R-series, #37, 5 (*Captured weapons from the Eastern Front*); Rudolf Christoph Freiherr von Gersdorff, ETHINT 53, Nov. 24, 1945, MHI, 1 (*large barrel of the MG-42*).

250 *With characteristic agility, Rundstedt manned*: *SLC*, 43; Henry P. Halsell, "Hürtgen Forest and Roer River Dams," n.d., CMH, 314.7, I-20 (*improvised with dismounted panzer crews*); Lucian Heichler, "The Germans Opposite XIX Corps," May 1953, OCMH, NARA

RG 319, R-series, #21, 77 (*49th Infantry Division*); Cooper, *The German Army, 1933–1945*, 517 (*two Luftwaffe divisions*); *Germany VII*, 634–35 (*160,000 stragglers had been redirected to the front*).

250 *"holding of the position until annihilation"*: John W. Mosenthal, "The Establishment of a Continuous Defensive Front by Army Group G," Nov. 1955, OCMH, NARA RG 319, R-series, #68, 11; Lucian Heichler, "The Germans Facing V Corps, September 1944," May 1952, NARA RG 319, R-series, #37, 30 (*"Every bunker, every block of houses"*).

251 *"It is a monument to stupidity"*: Semmes, *Portrait of Patton*, 223.

251 *But the U.S. Army had little experience*: Hogg, *The Biography of General George S. Patton*, 116; "Combat Engineering," Aug. 1945, CE, historical report no. 10, CEOH, box X-30, 65–66 (*single bunker atop a hill south of Aachen*).

251 *Ordinary artillery barrages*: SLC, 45 (*"dust off"*); "Breaching the Siegfried Line," XIX Corps, Oct. 2, 1944, CARL, N-7623, 9–15 (*Napalm*), 23–26 (*jeep-towed arc welder*); Kleber and Birdsell, *The Chemical Warfare Service*, 602–3; "Combat Engineering," Dec. 1945, CE, NARA RG 498, ETO HD, admin file #547, 70 (*twenty-five to fifty pounds of explosives*), 66 (*made it hard for defenders to breathe*); memo, Albert H. Peyton to First Army CG, Oct. 20, 1944, NARA RG 407, ETO G-3 OR, box 9 (*large pillboxes required half a ton*).

251 *As Rundstedt rushed defenders into the line*: AAR, "Reconnaissance in a Tactical Air Command," 10th Photo Group, XIX Tactical Air Command, Ninth AF, 1945, CARL, N-9395, 29 (*200,000 aerial photos*); LC, 55; SLC, 37; "Mobility, Unused: Study Based on Lorraine Campaign," Oct. 1952, MHI, OCMH WWII Europe Interviews (*"a ripe plum"*).

251 *Hitler had other ideas*: Doubler, *Closing with the Enemy*, 127 (*elaborate constellation of forts*).

252 *The next morning, a battalion from the 5th Infantry Division*: LC, 139–41, 145–46, 157 (*"hell hole"*); AAR, 2nd Bn, 11th Inf, n.d., NARA RG 407, ETO G-3 OR, box 11; John K. Rieth, "We Seek: Patton's Forward Observers," 2002, a.p., 101.

252 *Patton would gain other bridgeheads*: LC, 93–96; Rickard, *Patton at Bay*, 107, 160, 230–31; Ludewig, *Rückzug*, 22 (*"thrash about and bite"*); Ayer, *Before the Colors Fade*, 166 ("*I have studied the German*").

252 *Farther north, First Army's prospects*: SLC, 46–48, 56.

253 *"We all seemed for the moment"*: Baker, *Ernest Hemingway*, 539–40.

253 *On Friday, September 15, the division command post*: AAR, "Penetration of Siegfried Line," 4th ID, n.d., CARL, N-12159.1; SLC, 52–53, 61–65.

253 *On First Army's left flank, XIX Corps*: SLC, 106, 111–15; MacDonald, *The Battle of the Huertgen Forest*, 58–59.

253 *That left the last, best chance*: SLC, 66, 29; OH, JLC, Jan. 21, 1954, CBM, NARA RG 319, OCMH background file, 2-3.7 CB 3 (*"the real route"*); *Blue Spaders*, 74 (*twin fortification belts*).

254 *Collins now made a tactical choice*: OH, JLC, 1972, Charles C. Sperow, SOOHP, MHI, 219; *Blue Spaders*, 76; Clay, *Blood and Sacrifice*, 213; Collins, *Lightning Joe*, 269, 279; Wheeler, *The Big Red One*, 329 (*Germans would abandon Aachen*).

254 *The sudden appearance of VII Corps*: Lucian Heichler, "The Germans Opposite VII Corps in Sept. 1944," Dec. 1952, CMH, CMH 2-3.7 EB, 12, 18–19.

254 *Into this chaos*: SLC, 71, 81; Gerhard Graf von Schwerin, ETHINT 18, Oct.–Nov. 1945, MHI, 44 (*"Santa Clauses"*); http://www.waffenhq.de/biographien/biographien/schwerin.html; Whiting, *The Home Front: Germany*, 176 (*"splendid battlefield commander"*); Fritz Krämer, ETHINT 24, Nov. 17, 1945, MHI, 1 (*"He was intelligent"*).

254 *"I stopped the absurd evacuation"*: Gerhard Graf von Schwerin, ETHINT 18, Oct.–Nov. 1945, MHI, 37–41.

255 *A day passed, and then another*: MacDonald, *The Battle of the Huertgen Forest*, 37; Reynolds, *How I Survived the Three First Wave Invasions* (*half-eaten meals*).

255 *But the momentum had seeped out of Collins's attack*: SLC, 86; Meyer A. Edwards, Jr., et al., "Armor in the Attack of a Fortified Position," May 1950, AS, Ft. K, NARA RG 337,

62–64 (*two-hundred-mile round-trip*); *Blue Spaders*, 77 (*Fifty rounds from a tank destroyer*). The official Army history contends that the 3rd Armored Division was authorized 232 tanks, but it was one of two "heavy" armored divisions actually authorized more than 300.

255 *The dawning realization that the Americans intended*: Clay, *Blood and Sacrifice*, 214 (*Wild Buffaloes*); Stolberg: *Penetrating the Westwall*, 19; *SLC*, 81–82 (*forcibly evacuated*); Lucian Heichler, "The Germans Opposite VII Corps in Sept. 1944," Dec. 1952, NARA RG 319, R-series, #38, 56; Gerhard Graf von Schwerin, ETHINT 18, Oct.–Nov. 1945, MHI, 48–53 ("*Fate*").

255 *A German counterattack on Sunday*: Wheeler, *The Big Red One*, 332; Lewis, ed., *The Mammoth Book of Eyewitness World War II*, 434 ("*like a huge torch*"); Heinz, *When We Were One*, 23–25 ("*a Last Greeting*").

256 *After five days of fighting, Collins had gashed*: *SLC*, 86; *Blue Spaders*, 84–85 (*meandering stone town*); Collins, *Lightning Joe*, 270; Stanhope B. Mason, "Reminiscences and Anecdotes of World War II," 1988, MRC FDM, 234 (*tacked blankets across holes*); "Aachen: Military Operations in Urban Terrain," 1999, 26th Infantry Regiment Association, 10.

256 *Three German divisions soon sealed*: Lucian Heichler, "The Germans Opposite VII Corps in Sept. 1944," Dec. 1952, CMH, CMH 2-3.7 EB, 83–84, 36 ("*Each and every house*"); *SLC*, 88 ("*the last bullet*").

A Market and a Garden

256 *Since its founding in 1835*: Ivan Sache and Jan Martens, "Presentation of Leopoldsburg," Apr. 14, 2006, http://www.crwflags.com/fotw/flags/be-vlilp.html.

256 *Now the Germans were gone, again*: memoir, J. S. W. Stone, Royal Engineers, LHC, folder 5, 70–71 (*painted wooden hives*); http://home.mweb.co.za/re/redcap/rmp.htm; Horrocks, *A Full Life*, 210; AAR, "Operation Market Garden," 21st AG, n.d., UK NA, AIR 37/1249, appendix D (*two thousand truckloads*).

257 *On the radiant Sunday morning of September 17*: C. D. Renfro, 101st AB, liaison to XXX Corps, "Operation Market," Oct. 10, 1944, NARA RG 407, E 427-A, CI, folder #226; Ryan, *A Bridge Too Far*, 146 ("*sniper's smocks*"); Horrocks, *Corps Commander*, 98–99 (*huge sketch map*).

257 *At eleven A.M. Lieutenant General Brian Horrocks*: Horrocks, *Corps Commander*, 98–99; Moorehead, *Eclipse*, 239 ("*ecclesiastical face*").

257 *Horrocks was made for such moments*: Keegan, ed., *Churchill's Generals*, 225–36; MMB, 238–39; Warner, *Horrocks*, 101–3, 110 (*Montgomery summoned him in August*); Baynes, *Urquhart of Arnhem*, 101 (*a tad frail*).

259 *Eyes alight, graceful hands gliding*: Urquhart, *Arnhem*, 184–85; C. D. Renfro, 101st AB, liaison to XXX Corps, "Operation Market," Oct. 10, 1944, NARA RG 407, E 427-A, CI, folder #226; AAR, Operation Market Garden, 21st AG, n.d., CARL, R-13333, 3 ("*dominate the country*"); Belchem, *All in the Day's March*, 224 (*V-2 rocket sites*); Verney, *The Guards Armoured Division*, 99 (*spearheaded by three armored divisions*); code names, NARA RG 407, E 427-A, CI, folder 226-A (*HAMLET*).

259 *Linking these towns was a single narrow highway*: *SLC*, 131; *GS* V, 527–28 (*Nine substantial bridges*); *SLC*, 131–32; www.rollintl.com/roll/rhine.htm ("*distributaries*"); Baedeker, *Belgium and Holland*, 400 (*retirement mecca*); Middlebrook, *Arnhem 1944*, 49 ("*exceedingly healthy atmosphere*").

259 *Horrocks paused, glancing at his notes*: AAR, "Operations in Holland," First Allied Airborne Army, Dec. 1944, ANSCOL, NARA RG 334, E 315, Act R A-104, box 62, 19; OH, Brian Urquhart, Jan. 24, 1967, CJR, box 108, folder 6 ("*carpet of airborne troops*").

260 *As this unfolded, the land assault*: *SLC*, 133–34; Horrocks, *Corps Commander*, 98–99 ("*absolutely vital*").

260 "*the enemy has by now suffered*": weekly intelligence summary no. 26, SHAEF, Sept. 16, 1944, JMG, MHI, box 15.

260 *German strength facing the 100,000-man XXX Corps*: AAR, Operation Market Garden,

21st AG, n.d., CARL, R-13333, 36; Fitzgerald, *History of the Irish Guards in the Second World War*, 486 (*"easier for a rich man"*).

260 *Irish Guards officers looked especially pensive*: Horrocks, *Corps Commander*, 100.

261 *Tanks trundled forward, slowly*: ibid., 209–10.

261 *"What do you think of the plan?"*: C. D. Renfro, 101st AB, liaison to XXX Corps, "Operation Market," Oct. 10, 1944, NARA RG 407, E 427-A, CI, folder #226.

261 *Horrocks was in fact fretful*: Badsey, *Arnhem 1944*, 11–12; Keegan, ed., *Churchill's Generals*, 236–38 (*"I shan't invalid you"*); Horrocks, *A Full Life*, 210 (*no attack he had launched on a Sunday*).

261 *From a nearby radio came word*: Horrocks, *Corps Commander*, 100–101.

261 *Many others invested in MARKET GARDEN*: Chandler, 1947 (*Under relentless pressure*); office diary, First Allied Airborne Army, Sept. 10–17, 1944, Floyd Lavinius Parks papers, MHI, box 2 (*less than a week*); Greenfield, ed., *Command Decisions*, 334 (*created at War Department insistence*); Brereton, *The Brereton Diaries*, 343 (*eighteen operational plans*); Baynes, *Urquhart of Arnhem*, 76 (*WILD OATS*); Lewin, *Montgomery as Military Commander*, 338 (*"cowpats"*).

261 *Some commanders worried about MARKET's dispersal*: corr, A. C. McAuliffe to A. C. Smith, Feb. 8, 1954, NARA RG 319, OCMH, 2-3.7 CB3; Willmott, *The Great Crusade*, 361–63; Hamilton, *Monty: Final Years of the Field-Marshal, 1944–1976*, 22–24; Weigley, *Eisenhower's Lieutenants*, 295; OH, ONB, 1974–75, Charles Hanson, MHI, V-58-61 (*"foolhardy"*); Bradley Commentaries, CBH, MHI, boxes 41–42 (*"Flabbergasted"*); Bradley, *A Soldier's Story*, 402 (*"astonishing faculty"*).

262 *Personalities added fat to the fire*: Blair, *Ridgway's Paratroopers*, 181; MMB, 61–62; Brereton, *The Brereton Diaries*, 342 (*"Mystify, mislead"*), 308–9; Bradley Commentaries, CBH, MHI, boxes 41–42 (*"not sincere nor energetic"*); Blair, *Ridgway's Paratroopers*, 299 (*"Thank goodness"*); Taylor, *General Maxwell Taylor*, 97.

262 *If Brereton's interactions with his fellow Americans*: Blair, *Ridgway's Paratroopers*, 181 (*"stupid ass"*); Badsey, *Arnhem 1944*, 36 (*false uhlan front*); OH, Eddie Newbury, Browning personal secretary, n.d., CJR, box 108, folder 6 (*kicking over the furniture*); Hastings, *Armageddon*, 36 (*"popinjay"*); diary, July 2, 1944, CBH, MHI, box 4 (*"too deliberate a smile"*); MMB, 66 (*high hurdles*). Hitchcock later directed another movie based on a du Maurier short story, *The Birds* (http://en.wikipedia.org/wiki/Daphne_du_Maurier).

262 *Browning so loathed Brereton*: Brereton, *The Brereton Diaries*, 337–38; Badsey, *Arnhem 1944*, 12.

262 *"enemy appreciation was very weak"*: OH, E. T. Williams, May 1947, FCP, MHI.

263 *The road bridge over the Neder Rijn*: Margry, ed., *Operation Market-Garden Then and Now*, vol. 1, 27; Hinsley, 544 (*radio decrypt*).

263 *"But the Germans, how about the Germans"*: Gavin, *On to Berlin*, 150. Other accounts put this comment a bit earlier, during planning for the stillborn Operation COMET. See http://www.pegasusarchive.org/arnhem/stanislaw_sosabowski.htm.

263 *someone "with a vivid imagination"*: Sosabowski, *Freely I Served*, 140; Middlebrook, *Arnhem 1944*, 8 (*"fighting-the-Germans bit"*). Sosabowski's Polish rank had no direct Anglo-American equivalent, and is variously translated as either brigadier or major general (David T. Zabecki, note to author, May 9, 2012).

263 *Guessing which Germans would be fought*: Hinsley, 544; TSC, 282–83 (*"low category"*), 142; Lucian Heichler, "Holland, Allied Invasion from the Sky," Oct. 1953, NARA RG 319, R-series, #5, 16 (*lacked field kitchens*); Margry, ed., *Operation Market-Garden Then and Now*, vol. 1, 79 (*II SS Panzer Corps*); Zetterling, *Normandy 1944*, 336–39, 344–47 (*nine thousand casualties*); Bennett, *Ultra in the West*, 151–53 (*120 tanks*).

263 *Montgomery's senior staff officers almost to a man*: Crosswell, *Beetle*, 717–18; Powell, *The Devil's Birthday*, 42–43 (*Smith flew to Brussels*); SLC, 122. Biographer Crosswell believes Smith never physically traveled to Montgomery's headquarters (*Beetle*, 717).

263 *"Montgomery ridiculed the idea"*: OH, W. B. Smith and Pink Bull, Sept. 14, 1945, OCMH WWII Europe Interviews, MHI; OH, W. B. Smith, Apr. 18, 1949, SLAM, NARA RG 319, OCMH, 2-3.7 (*"waved my objections"*).

263 *Montgomery's insouciance was understandable*: Ryan, *A Bridge Too Far*, 144 (*"weak, demoralized, and likely to collapse"*); Saunders, *The Red Beret*, 212–13 (*no larger than a brigade*); Hinsley, 543; *SLC*, 121–22; OH, Brian Urquhart, Jan. 24, 1967, CJR, box 108, folder 6; *VW*, vol. 1, 52 (*Dutch underground*); Middlebrook, *Arnhem 1944*, 56; Margry, ed., *Operation Market-Garden Then and Now*, vol. 1, 79; Horrocks, *Corps Commander*, 93; Ralph Bennett, "Ultra and Some Command Decisions," in Laqueur, ed., *The Second World War*, 232. Bennett reports that Browning was included on the Ultra distribution list (*"tanks at Arnhem"*).

264 *Boy Browning declared himself ready*: memo, G-3, 82nd Airborne, Oct. 23, 1945 [*sic*], JMG papers, CJR, box 100, folder 3; *SLC*, 137–39; Hills, *Phantom Was There*, 251 (*"That means business"*); Saunders, *The Red Beret*, 216 (*British sergeant strutted*).

264 *"Emplane!"*: memoir, Dwayne Burns, 508th PIR, n.d., NWWIIM; Ryan, *A Bridge Too Far*, 173 (*more than twenty thousand troops*); Middlebrook, *Arnhem 1944*, 83–85 (*"floated up and down"*).

264 *The first British pathfinders jumped*: McNally, *As Ever, John*, 53 (*"plowing up dirt"*); Kershaw, *"It Never Snows in September,"* 66 (*snowflakes*); *SLC*, 137–39 (*within eighty minutes*); Middlebrook, *Arnhem 1944*, 112 (*"Jingle Bells"*).

265 *That this welcoming chorus congregated*: AAR, "Airborne Division Report on Operation Market," UK 1st Airborne Division, Jan. 10, 1945, CARL, N-5647, 43; *Airborne Forces*, 174; John C. Warren, "Airborne Operations in World War II, European Theater," 1956, AFHRA, historical study no. 97, 149; Murray and Millett, *A War to Be Won*, 441; Urquhart, *Arnhem*, 6–7; Middlebrook, *Arnhem 1944*, 54–55;

265 *The second complication was evident*: MARKET troop carrier commanders argued that the shorter days of mid-September made two missions more difficult to squeeze in (John C. Warren, "Airborne Operations in World War II, European Theater," 1956, AFHRA, historical study no. 97, 150).

265 *Pleas by airborne commanders and by an emissary*: Powell, *The Devil's Birthday*, 33–34; Baynes, *Urquhart of Arnhem*, 92; *SLC*, 131–32 (*up to four days*).

265 *The day went well enough for the Yanks*: "Kinnard's Operation in Holland," 1st Bn, 501st PIR, 1946, Battalion and Small Unit Study No. 1, ETOUSA, history section, CJR, box 100, folder 5; Simpson, *Selected Prose*, 129 (*"laid there to die"*).

265 *Nine road and rail bridges stood*: "Eindhoven," 506th PIR, n.d., NARA RG 407, E 427A, CI, folder #226; OH, Lynn Compton, 506th PIR, n.d., NARA RG 407, E 427, HI; John C. Warren, "Airborne Operations in World War II, European Theater," 1956, AFHRA, historical study no. 97, 105 (*sprint south and seize Eindhoven*).

266 *Twenty miles north, 7,300 troops*: A. D. Bestebreurtje, "The Airborne Operation in Netherlands in Fall 1944," *De Militaire Spectator*, English trans. from Dutch, Jan. 1946, CJR, box 100, folder 4; *SLC*, 159 (*All but one of 482 planes*); Gavin, *On to Berlin*, 161; corr, JMG to CJR, Nov. 16, 1966, and to A. D. Bestebreurtje, July 9, 1973, JMG papers, CJR, box 100, folders 4 and 9.

266 *With the ascension of Matthew Ridgway*: Muir, ed., *The Human Tradition in the World War II Era*, 178; Nordyke, *All American All the Way*, 412 (*youngest major general*); D'Este, "Raw Courage," *World War II* (July–Aug. 2011): 30+.

266 *adopted as a toddler*: memoir, "Beyond the Stars," ts, 1983, James M. Gavin Irrecovable Trust, JMG, MHI, box 2, 3, 10, 21–27 (*invoked the Holy Family*), 410–11; Booth and Spencer, *Paratrooper*, 26–27 (*soaped miners' beards*), 42–43 (*He lied about his age*); West Point application, 1925, JMG, MHI, box 9 (*filling station*); Fauntleroy, *The General and His Daughter*, 124 (*Book-of-the-Month Club*); "Generalship," JMG, MHI, box 10; OH, JMG, 1975, Donald G. Andrews and Charles H. Ferguson, SOOHP, MHI, 23 (*"two o'clock in the morning"*); Nordyke, *All American All the Way*, 412 (*"charm of manner"*).

267 *After combat jumps into Sicily*: Fauntleroy, *The General and His Daughter*, 105 (*"the scuffle"*); Gavin, *On to Berlin*, 152 (*"bank account"*); "Personal Diary," Sept. 14, 1944, JMG, MHI, box 10 (*"looks very rough"*).

267 *Eleven bridges could be found in the 82nd sector*: Field Order No. 11, 82nd AB Div, Sept. 13, 1944, "bridge data" annex, CARL; John S. Thompson, "The Holland Jump," 1944, CJR, box 101, folder 9 (*shooting up two truckloads*); AAR, Reuben H. Tucker, 504th PIR, n.d., and AAR, 2nd Bn, 504th PIR, n.d., NARA RG 407, E 427-A, CI, folder #171 (*ripped out boxes of dynamite*); signage, Grave bridge, author visit, May 2009 (*"Bridge number eleven"*).

267 *Bridge eleven and all its sisters*: memo, JMG to Office of the Theater Historian, July 25, 1945, NARA RG 407, E 427-A, folder 171; memo, G-3, 82nd Airborne, Oct. 23, 1945, CJR, box 100, folder 3 (*"capture and retention"*); SLC, 159 (*eight 75mm howitzers*); Ryan, *A Bridge Too Far*, 221–22 (*seven pieces*).

268 *"Everything is going as planned"*: corr, JMG to A. Bestebreurtje, July 9, 1973, CJR, box 100, folder 9; OH, JMG, Jan. 20, 1967, CJR, box 101, folder 10.

268 *So too had the Germans*: Kershaw, *"It Never Snows in September,"* 68 (*"Everyone out"*); Ryan, *A Bridge Too Far*, 199 (*underwear spilling*); Hastings, *Armageddon*, 41; SLC, 140.

268 *Vengeful Dutchmen ripped the rank badges*: Margry, ed., *Operation Market-Garden Then and Now*, vol. 1, 299; photo, Kershaw, *"It Never Snows in September,"* 95.

268 *Not much else went right*: Urquhart, *Arnhem*, 40–41; Kershaw, *"It Never Snows in September,"* 304–5 (*fire engines*); Middlebrook, *Arnhem 1944*, 117–19.

268 *Ignoring warnings of dangers ahead*: Urquhart, *Arnhem*, 64–66; Baynes, *Urquhart of Arnhem*, 108–11; Ryan, *A Bridge Too Far*, 298 (*"idiotic, ridiculous"*).

269 *A single British parachute battalion*: Sims, *Arnhem Spearhead*, 38 (*"snogging"*); Frost, *A Drop Too Many*, 210–11 (*rail bridge blew up*); Middlebrook, *Arnhem 1944*, 147–48, 152–58; Kershaw, *"It Never Snows in September,"* 99 (*trucks blazing on the ramp*).

269 *A brutal deadlock had begun*: VW, vol. 2, 51; Middlebrook, *Arnhem 1944*, 292–93 (*only 740*); Saunders, *The Red Beret*, 225–26 (*lashed into the tree branches*); Frost, *A Drop Too Many*, 204 (*golf clubs*).

269 *That would not happen. At precisely two P.M.*: Fitzgerald, *History of the Irish Guards in the Second World War*, 489–90; AAR, Operation Market Garden, 21st AG, n.d., CARL, R-13333, 37 (*Typhoons swooped in*).

269 *"Driver, advance!"*: Verney, *The Guards Armoured Division*, 99–101.

269 *The artillery barrage now rolled*: AAR, 2nd Bn, Irish Guards, UK NA, WO 171/1256; Rosse and Hill, *The Story of the Guards Armoured Division*, 127 (*"Advance going well"*).

270 *No sooner had the hand-rubbers on the roof*: Horrocks, *A Full Life*, 211–12; Rosse and Hill, *The Story of the Guards Armoured Division*, 127–28 (*"burning hulks"*); Verney, *The Guards Armoured Division*, 101–3; Hastings, *Armageddon*, 55 (*tanker boots*).

270 *The German defenders soon were identified*: AAR, Operation Market Garden, 21st AG, n.d., CARL, R-13333, 37 (*"complete surprise"*); Rosse and Hill, *The Story of the Guards Armoured Division*, 129 (*6th Parachute Regiment*); Ryan, *A Bridge Too Far*, 230 (*"indignant surprise"*); Fitzgerald, *History of the Irish Guards in the Second World War*, 492–93 (*"ugly mood"*); OH, Giles A. M. Vandeleur, Irish Guards, Aug. 10, 1967, CJR, box 102, folder 17; Margry, ed., *Operation Market-Garden Then and Now*, vol. 1, 216–17, 226; AAR, 2nd Bn, Irish Guards, UK NA, WO 171/1256.

270 *For seven miles from the Dutch border*: Bredin, *Three Assault Landings*, 126; AAR, Operation Market Garden, 21st AG, n.d., CARL, R-13333, 89 (*wider than thirty feet*); "Preliminary Tactical Study of the Terrain," XVIII Airborne Corps, Sept. 11, 1944, CARL (*"impracticable to impossible"*); SLC, 148–49; Verney, *The Guards Armoured Division*, 101–3 (*only fifteen dead*); Margry, ed., *Operation Market-Garden Then and Now*, vol. 1, 227.

271 *"Things are going very well indeed"*: office diary, Sept. 17–18, 1944, First Allied Airborne Army, Floyd Lavinius Parks papers, MHI, box 2.

271 *Eindhoven was home*: Baedeker's Netherlands, 178; www.hansvogels.nl/eindhovenENG

/violet2en.htm; www.frits.philips.com/en/darkcloud.html; Crouch, "Frederik Philips Dies at 100; Businessman Saved Dutch Jews," *NYT*, Dec. 7, 2005; Teulings, "Structure and Logic of Industrial Development: Philips and Electronics Industry," *Social Scientist* 9, no. 4 (Nov. 1979): 3+; http://en.wikipedia.org/wiki/Philips.

271 *Now this company town of thatched roofs*: Moorehead, *Eclipse*, 202–3; "Eindhoven," 506th PIR, n.d., NARA RG 407, E 427A, CI, folder #226 (*all bridges intact*); SLC, 150 ("*reek with hate*").

271 *Not until dusk did XXX Corps arrive*: AAR, 3rd Bn, Irish Guards, Sept. 18, 1944, UK NA, WO 171/1257; AAR, Operation Market Garden, 21st AG, n.d., CARL, R-13333, 39–42 (*stiffened with Panther tanks*); Powell, *The Devil's Birthday*, 113 (*grounded the Typhoons*); Verney, *The Guards Armoured Division*, 103; Forbes, *The Grenadier Guards in the War of 1939–1945*, vol. 1, 122 ("*Every time the advance*"); SLC, 150.

272 *Reinforcements from England also arrived*: "327th RCT at Zon," 327th PIR, n.d., NARA RG 407, E 427A, CI, folder #226-A; H. J. Jablonsky, "Combat Lessons of 82nd Airborne Division," Observers' Board, WD, Dec. 9, 1944, CARL, 5; SLC, 167; Ryan, *A Bridge Too Far*, 311–16 (*four thousand aircraft*); AAR, "Air Resupply and Resupply by B-24 Aircraft," Oct. 29, 1944, 2nd Bombardment Division, CARL, 1–7 (*stripped of their ball turrets*); John C. Warren, "Airborne Operations in World War II, European Theater," 1956, AFHRA, historical study no. 97, 124.

272 *The 101st found more unexpected trouble*: "Combat Diary of Edward McCosh Elliott, 1944," 2nd Bn, Glasgow Highlanders, IWM, 99/61/1, VIII-12; "A Historical Study of Some World War II Airborne Operations," [1951?], WSEG Staff Study No. 3, CARL, N-17309.1; Ryan, *A Bridge Too Far*, 308–09 (*Fifteenth Army troops*).

272 *Among seven wounded GIs*: Nappi, "War Hero Enriches Soul History," (Spokane, Wash.) *Spokesman-Review*, Aug. 14, 2004, www.spokesmanreview.com/tools/story_pf.asp?ID= 20967; Rapport and Northwood, *Rendezvous with Destiny*, 287–99; Marshall, *Battle at Best*, 10–36; Medal of Honor citation, http://www.homeofheroes.com/moh/citations_1940 _wwii/mann.html.

273 *Nearly out of ammunition*: Kershaw, "*It Never Snows in September*," 144; SLC, 152 (*three hundred enemy corpses*); "Battalion and Small Unit Study No. 6," Oct. 1944, NARA 498, ETO HD, UD 602, box 5, 35–36 (*shot by their own comrades*); Marshall, *Battle at Best*, 41.

273 "*Dutch report Germans winning*": SLC, 170.

273 "*grossly untidy situation*": Powell, *The Devil's Birthday*, 110.

273 *In a shot-torn town*: Ryan, *A Bridge Too Far*, 282 (*bakeries*), 218 (*head to toe like sandbags*), 232–33 ("*gone awry*"); Middlebrook, *Arnhem 1944*, 200–202, 209, 281; Saunders, *The Red Beret*, 232–34 ("*little bayonet rushes*"); *Airborne Forces*, 167; SLC, 172–73 (*Balky radios*); Baynes, *Urquhart of Arnhem*, 111 (*would not rejoin his headquarters*); Powell, *The Devil's Birthday*, 130 (*over half of the British soldiers*).

273 *Nothing was right except the courage*: Ryan, *A Bridge Too Far*, 344–45; Sims, *Arnhem Spearhead*, 72 (*cherry brandy*); Mackay, "The Battle of Arnhem Bridge," *Royal Engineer Journal* (Dec. 1954): 305ff. (*Benzedrine* and "*Great joy all round*"); Kershaw, "*It Never Snows in September*," 177 (*perimeter of ten buildings*); Arthur, *Forgotten Voices of World War II*, 359 (*vases were filled with water*); Saunders, *The Red Beret*, 239 (*rolled strips of wallpaper*); Middlebrook, *Arnhem 1944*, 292–95; Margry, ed., *Operation Market-Garden Then and Now*, vol. 2, 465 (*Mercedes trucks*); "Arnhem," *AB*, no. 2 (1973): 1ff.

274 *Germans on the south bank of the Neder Rijn*: Frost, *A Drop Too Many*, 223–25; Kershaw, "*It Never Snows in September*," 177–78 ("*skin peeling*"); Sims, *Arnhem Spearhead*, 74 ("*shake itself like a dog*").

274 "*Arnhem was burning*": Arthur, *Forgotten Voices of World War II*, 359 ("*metallic daylight*"), 354 ("*Nobody is in such dire need*"); Saunders, *The Red Beret*, 236–37 ("*never saw anything more beautiful*"); Mackay, "The Battle of Arnhem Bridge," *Royal Engineer Journal* (Dec. 1954): 305ff. (*Despite a BBC report*); Middlebrook, *Arnhem 1944*, 312 ("*pretty desperate thing*"); Kershaw, "*It Never Snows in September*," 216–17 (*tossed from upper windows*).

274 *"a sea of flame"*: Middlebrook, *Arnhem 1944*, 307.

274 *"Our building is on fire"*: Thompson, *The Imperial War Museum Book of Victory in Europe*, 167–68.

274 "Deutschland, Deutschland": OH, Joseph Enthammer, Arnhem History Museum, John Frost Bridge, author visit, May 2009.

274 *Both sides agreed to a two-hour cease-fire*: Thompson, *The Imperial War Museum Book of Victory in Europe*, 167–68. ("British or American?"), 169 (*offered brandy, chocolate*); Sims, *Arnhem Spearhead*, 85 ("*The Last Stand*"), 88 ("*grotesque paddles*"); Kershaw, "*It Never Snows in September*," 125–26 ("*harder battle than any*"); Frost, *Nearly There*, 80–81; Frost, *A Drop Too Many*, 233 ("*kind, chivalrous*"); exhibit on Dr. Jan Zwolle, Arnhem History Museum, John Frost Bridge, author visit, May 2009 (*put before a firing squad*).

275 *Eighty-one paratroopers had been killed*: Middlebrook, *Arnhem 1944*, 321.

275 *"God save the king"*: Ryan, *A Bridge Too Far*, 430.

The Arrow That Flieth by Day

275 *At 4:30 P.M. on Tuesday, September 19*: OH, JMG, Jan. 20, 1967, CJR, box 101, folder 10, 1–3 (*curb*); Gavin, *On to Berlin*, 170–71.

275 *Afternoon shadows stretched*: Bates and Fuller, *America's Weather Warriors*, 99–100 (*weather had deteriorated*); John C. Warren, "Airborne Operations in World War II, European Theater," 1956, AFHRA, historical study no. 97, 129–33; *SLC*, 154.

275 *Of five major objectives*: "A Historical Study of Some World War II Airborne Operations," [1951?], WSEG Staff Study No. 3, CARL, N-17309.1, 22; AAR, JMG, July 25, 1945, Office of Theater Historian, NARA RG 407, E 427-A, CI, folder #171; Margry, ed., *Operation Market-Garden Then and Now*, vol. 1, 164; *SLC*, 163–66 (*muddled firefight in the dark*); Nordyke, *All American All the Way*, 457 (*10th SS Panzer soldiers*); Baedeker, *Belgium and Holland*, 404; *Baedeker's Netherlands*, 288 (*falcons*).

276 *Nor had the belated arrival of XXX Corps*: VW, vol. 2, 37; Forbes, *The Grenadier Guards in the War of 1939–1945*, vol. 1, 129–33; Margry, ed., *Operation Market-Garden Then and Now*, vol. 2, 349, 360–63; AAR, "The Capture of Nijmegen Bridge," XXX Corps, UK NA, WO 205/1125. No Dutchman explained why the detonators would be placed on the wrong side of the bridges to be destroyed (Fitzgerald, *History of the Irish Guards in the Second World War*, 499–500).

276 *Enemy commanders were so confident of holding the bridges*: Badsey, *Arnhem 1944*, 43; Forbes, *The Grenadier Guards in the War of 1939–1945*, vol. 1, 128 (*bowled thermite grenades*).

276 *Joining Gavin along the Malden curb*: Tucker biographical data, CJR, box 103, folder 23; Chatterton, *The Wings of Pegasus*, 178 ("*air of nonchalance*"); Powell, *The Devil's Birthday*, 118 (*arrived in a nearby cabbage patch*); OH, Eddie Newbury, Browning personal secretary, n.d., CJR, box 108, folder 6 (*Twirling his mustache*); Margry, ed., *Operation Market-Garden Then and Now*, vol. 2, 344 (*airborne smock*); office diary, First Allied Airborne Army, Sept. 19, 1944, Floyd Lavinius Parks papers, MHI, box 2 ("*extremely pleased*"); Badsey, *Arnhem 1944*, 60 (*ink jar*).

276 *Gavin quickly described the predicament*: Kershaw, "*It Never Snows in September*," 193; *SLC*, 175; Gavin, *On to Berlin*, 175, 163 ("*tough and confident*"); Rosse and Hill, *The Story of the Guards Armoured Division*, 134–35 (*riverfront bandstand*); Wills, *Put on Your Boots and Parachutes!*, 141–43 (*on foot and by bicycle*); Otis L. Sampson, "My Last Combat Jump," n.d., Co E, 505th PIR, JMG, MHI, box 15 (*wrapping themselves in drapes*); corr, JMG to CJR, Oct. 2, 1973, and JMG to M. C. Hustinx, March 8, 1947, CJR, box 101, folders 9 & 10 (*six hundred Dutch resistance fighters*); Powell, *The Devil's Birthday*, 118 (*Browning's radios*).

277 *Colonel Tucker, whose helmet brim*: Chatterton, *The Wings of Pegasus*, 178 ("*Every time he did*"); Gavin, *On to Berlin*, 173 (*attack the German rear*).

277 *Browning and Adair said little*: corr, JMG to CJR, Oct. 2, 1973, CJR, box 101, folder 9

(*Horrocks was skeptical*); *DOB,* 347 (*Rapido*); Gavin, *On to Berlin,* 170–71 ("*never try to fight an entire corps*").

277 *Two hours later, as dusk sifted:* Powell, *The Devil's Birthday,* 135; *SLC,* 153 (*only large, long-range air strike*); Bredin, *Three Assault Landings,* 126–28 (*Dutch flags abruptly vanished*); Margry, ed., *Operation Market-Garden Then and Now,* vol. 2, 395–97 ("*All smiles stopped*").

277 *No enemy tanks appeared:* Powell, *The Devil's Birthday,* 135; Brereton, *The Brereton Diaries,* 349–50 ("*flat on our stomachs*"); Booth and Spencer, *Paratrooper,* 228 ("*Great fires were burning*").

278 "*A blind act of malice*": Margry, ed., *Operation Market-Garden Then and Now,* vol. 2, 395–401.

278 *The boats were late arriving:* Horrocks, *Corps Commander,* 112 ("*For God's sake, try!*"); OH, Giles A. M. Vandeleur, Irish Guards, Aug. 10, 1967, CJR, box 102, folder 17 (*there were twenty-six*); Rosse and Hill, *The Story of the Guards Armoured Division,* 137 ("*suitable for the quieter rivers*"); Ryan, *A Bridge Too Far,* 406–8 (*two paddles*); corr, Henry B. Keep to mother, Nov. 20, 1944, JMG, MHI, box 15 ("*Daddy's tin ducking boat*").

279 *As a Royal Engineer major gave rudimentary instructions:* OH, Robert M. Tallon, March 6, 1968, CJR, box 103, folder 20 ("*Head them upriver*"); Nordyke, *More Than Courage,* 225 (*pork chops*); AAR, Reuben H. Tucker, 504th PIR, n.d., and AAR, 2nd Bn, 504th PIR, n.d., NARA RG 407, E 427-A, CI, folder #171; OH, Giles A. M. Vandeleur, Irish Guards, Aug. 10, 1967, CJR, box 102, folder 17 (*milky smoke screen*); AAR, 3rd Bn, 504th PIR, n.d., NARA RG 407, E 427-A, CI, folder #171 (*Four hundred grunting men*).

279 *Instantly German fire from three directions:* AAR, 3rd Bn, 504th PIR, n.d., NARA RG 407, E 427-A, CI, folder #171 ("*mackerel on the feed*"); Ryan, *A Bridge Too Far,* 406–8; *SLC,* 180; OH, Robert M. Tallon, March 6, 1968, CJR, box 103, folder 20 (*direct hit from a mortar round*); Burriss, *Strike and Hold,* 113–15 (*engineer shot through the head*), 116–17 ("*Thy will be done*"); Nordyke, *More Than Courage,* 234 ("*his skull dropped*").

279 "*It was a horrible, horrible sight*": OH, Giles A. M. Vandeleur, Irish Guards, Aug. 10, 1967, CJR, box 102, folder 17.

280 *The roar of gunfire and ripping canvas:* Nordyke, *More Than Courage,* 237, 256; Reuben H. Tucker, ts, n.d., CJR, box 103, folder 23 ("*look at 'em*").

280 *Half made the far shore: SLC,* 181; AAR, 3rd Bn, 504th PIR, n.d., NARA RG 407, E 427-A, CI, folder #171 (*galley slaves*).

280 "*God help anyone in front of us*": Nordyke, *More Than Courage,* 240.

280 "*jack-in-the-box shooting*": OH, Theodore Finkbeiner, Jr., March 4, 1968, CJR, box 102, folder 24; *SLC,* 181.

280 *One company slaughtered the enemy garrison at Hof:* AAR, "The Capture of Nijmegen Bridge," XXX Corps, UK NA, WO 205/1125; Powell, *The Devil's Birthday,* 160; corr, Henry B. Keep to mother, Nov. 20, 1944, JMG, MHI, box 15 ("*driven to a fever pitch*").

280 *Sensing that the day had turned:* AAR, Co. A, 1st Bn, 504th PIR, n.d., NARA RG 407, E 427-A, CI, folder #171 (*yellow recognition flags*); Fitzgerald, *History of the Irish Guards in the Second World War,* 504 (*high in the girders*); corr, Henry B. Keep to mother, Nov. 20, 1944, JMG, MHI, box 15 ("*gargoyles*"); corr, Virgil F. Carmichael, Oct. 13, 1967, CJR, box 102, file 16 (*shot trying to surrender*); Nordyke, *More Than Courage,* 260 ("*Old German men grab*"); Kershaw, "*It Never Snows in September,*" 211–12 ("*throwing our wounded from the bridge*"); *SLC,* 183 (*Two hundred and sixty-seven enemy bodies*).

281 *Paratroopers darting through river grass:* Nordyke, *More Than Courage,* 263 ("*Roman candle balls*"); Forbes, *The Grenadier Guards in the War of 1939–1945,* vol. 1, 137–38 (*skidded sideways*); AAR, "The Capture of Nijmegen Bridge," XXX Corps, UK NA, WO 205/1125 (*detonators lashed to a catwalk*).

281 "*The most gallant attack*": Horrocks, *Corps Commander,* 112; *SLC,* 183; Kershaw, "*It Never Snows in September,*" 211–12 ("*blow up the bridge*"); Nordyke, *More Than Courage,* 264 ("*They're over the Waal*").

281 *Montgomery monitored the battle*: Hamilton, *Monty: The Final Years of the Field-Marshal, 1944–1976*, 73, 76, 87–89.

281 *"Things are going to work out alright"*: msg, BLM to DDE, Sept. 20, 1944, DDE Lib, PP-pres, box 83.

281 *"I regard general situation on rivers"*: Powell, *The Devil's Birthday*, 184.

281 *"all was not well"*: Randal, *A Short History of 30 Corps in the European Campaign*, 35.

281 *"General, you'd better get the hell back here"*: OH, JMG, 1975, Donald G. Andrews and Charles H. Ferguson, SOOHP, MHI, JMG papers, box 1.

281 *Racing to his command post*: corr, JMG to MBR, Jan. 27, 1973, CJR, box 102, folder 6; Gavin, *On to Berlin*, 176–77.

282 *But troubles in the Anglo-American rear*: SLC, 187; "A Historical Study of Some World War II Airborne Operations," [1951?], WSEG Staff Study No. 3, CARL, N-17309.1 (*another 85,000 Germans*); John C. Warren, "Airborne Operations in World War II, European Theater," 1956, AFHRA, historical study no. 97, 150; Margry, ed., *Operation Market-Garden Then and Now*, vol. 2, 569.

282 *That same morning, Hell's Highway*: Ryan, *A Bridge Too Far*, 476–77; Horrocks, *A Full Life*, 228 ("*blackest moment*"); SLC, 189–92; Kershaw, "*It Never Snows in September*," 283–87 (*destroy fifty vehicles*).

282 *The new bridgehead over the Waal*: SLC, 184–86; Crosswell, *Beetle: The Life of General Walter Bedell Smith*, 720 (*supplies promised by SHAEF*); OH, JMG, 1975, Donald G. Andrews and Charles H. Ferguson, SOOHP, MHI, JMG papers, box 1 ("*Why die now?*"); corr, JMG to MBR, Jan. 27, 1973, CJR, box 102, folder 6 (*found Colonel Tucker in a farmhouse*); Powell, *The Devil's Birthday*, 162–63 ("*What in the hell are they doing?*").

282 *At 1:30 P.M. on Thursday*: AAR, 3rd Battalion, Irish Guards, UK NA, WO 171/1257 (*captured German map*); SLC, 185 (*waited in ambush*); Fitzgerald, *History of the Irish Guards in the Second World War*, 508–9 ("*head to tail in silhouette*"); Ellis, *Welsh Guards at War*, 229 ("*these sad flat lands*"); Margry, ed., *Operation Market-Garden Then and Now*, vol. 2, 576–77 ("*not going to get a yard*").

283 *"But farther they could not go"*: Forbes, *The Grenadier Guards in the War of 1939–1945*, vol. 1, 141; T. G. Lindsay, "Operation Overlord Plus," n.d., LHC, 43–44 (*plover and pheasant*).

283 *The British survivors at Arnhem were now pinched*: Urquhart, *Arnhem*, 105–7, 131; Saunders, *The Red Beret*, 242–43 ("*I used to watch an apple tree*").

283 *Between mortar barrages, called "hate" by the British*: Powell, *The Devil's Birthday*, 208 ("*In the Mood*"); *By Air to Battle*, 124–25 (*notched their rifle butts*); Kershaw, "*It Never Snows in September*," 240 ("*room to room*"); Middlebrook, *Arnhem 1944*, 344–46 ("*You have no idea*"); Baynes, *Urquhart of Arnhem*, 147 (*kept the 9th SS Panzer at bay*).

284 *Of nearly 9,000 British soldiers inserted*: Middlebrook, *Arnhem 1944*, 39, 339, 398–400. Urquhart cited eighty-four supply planes lost (AAR, "Airborne Division Report on Operation Market," 1st Airborne Division, Jan. 10, 1945, CARL, N-5647, 34).

284 *"Thou shalt not be afraid"*: *By Air to Battle*, 125; http://www.pegasusarchive.org/arnhem/jimmy_cleminson.htm.

284 *"Our casualties heavy"*: Urquhart, *Arnhem*, 132.

284 *Relief came, though far too little*: Sosabowski, *Freely I Served*, 152, 156, 164; John C. Warren, "Airborne Operations in World War II, European Theater," 1956, AFHRA, historical study no. 97, 138–39 (*forced many befuddled pilots*); Middlebrook, *Arnhem 1944*, 410–11, 341–43 (*narrowing Urquhart's river frontage*); SLC, 186–86; Margry, ed., *Operation Market-Garden Then and Now*, vol. 2, 588–89.

284 *A night passed, then another*: Chmielewska-Szymańska, *Życie i działalność Stanisława Sosabowskiego*, 144–45; Sosabowski, *Najkrótszą Drogą*, 247; Peszke, "The Polish Parachute Brigade in World War II," *Military Affairs* (Oct. 1984): 188ff.

284 *A battalion from the Dorsetshire Regiment*: "Pegasus and the Wyvern," *Royal Engineers Journal* (March 1946): 22ff.; SLC, 196–97; Powell, *The Devil's Birthday*, 215 ("*quite useless*"); Swiecicki, *With the Red Devils at Arnhem*, 82 ("*Everything would seem to point*").

284 *When the end came, it came quickly*: Horrocks, *A Full Life*, 230–32; Urquhart, *Arnhem*, 170–77 (*trundled the lightly injured*); Badsey, *Arnhem 1944*, 76 (*medical truces*).

285 *"The night was made for clandestine exits"*: Powell, *The Devil's Birthday*, 221; author visit, May 24, 2009; Badsey, *Arnhem 1944*, 83 (*shuffled through the mud flats*); Urquhart, *Arnhem*, 170–77 (*"Let's be having you"*); *By Air to Battle*, 130 (*Cointreau and mugs of tea*); Margry, ed., *Operation Market-Garden Then and Now*, vol. 2, 684.

285 *Dawn caught the division*: "Pegasus and the Wyvern," *Royal Engineers Journal* (March 1946): 22+; Tucholski, *Spadochronowa opowieść, czyli o żołnierzach gen. Sosabowskiego i cichociemnych*, 72–73 (*flailed for the southern bank*); Waddy, *A Tour of the Arnhem Battlefields*, 177 (*only four of twenty-five aboard*).

285 *Urquhart was among those*: Urquhart, *Arnhem*, 179–80.

285 *"You did all you could"*: Baynes, *Urquhart of Arnhem*, 151. Historian Max Hastings concluded that Browning "displayed shameful incompetence and merited dismissal with ignominy" (*Inferno*, 561).

286 *In the small hours of Friday, September 29*: "Germans Use Expert Swimmers to Mine Dutch Bridges," *Military Intelligence Service*, no. 25, Jan. 1945, NARA RG 498, ETO HD, admin file #494L, 61+; Margry, ed., *Operation Market-Garden Then and Now*, vol. 2, 706–7 (*air cylinders*); "Forced Crossing of the Rhine, 1945," Aug. 1945, CE, Historical Report No. 20, CEOH, box X-32, folder 20, 14; Randal, *A Short History of 30 Corps in the European Campaign*, 38.

286 *This rude gesture hardly dampened*: Powell, *The Devil's Birthday*, 232 (*"decided victory"*); Brereton, *The Brereton Diaries*, 360–61 (*"brilliant success"*); Hart-Davis, ed., *King's Counsellor*, 258 (*"well pleased with the gross result"*); AAR, Operation Market Garden, 21st AG, n.d., CARL, R-13333, 115 (*"90 percent successful"*); Orange, *Tedder: Quietly in Command*, 279 (*"one jumps off a cliff"*); OH, F.A.M. Browning, Feb. 1955, NARA RG 319, SLC background papers, 2-3.7 CB 3 (*"Who was to tell"*); SLC, 198 (*"We have no regrets"*).

286 *Brave words from a division commander*: Middlebrook, *Arnhem 1944*, 445; SLC, 200 (*losses in* MARKET *approached 12,000*); VW, vol. 2, 54 (*in 17,000 air sorties*); Ryan, *A Bridge Too Far*, 523; Kershaw, *"It Never Snows in September,"* 311 (*total German losses*); De Slag Om Arnhem, 24 (*went on finding skeletons*). A recent German study puts Model's losses around Arnhem alone at 3,300 (Ludewig, *Rückzug*, 278).

286 *Even decided victories and brilliant successes*: AAR, Operation Market Garden, 21st AG, n.d., CARL, R-13333, 115 (*Montgomery blamed the weather*); AAR, "Operations in Holland," First Allied Airborne Army, Dec. 1944, NARA RG 334, E 315, ANSCOL, Act R A-104, box 62; Brereton, *The Brereton Diaries*, 360–61.

286 *Browning blamed Sosabowski*: In 2006, Queen Beatrix awarded the Bronze Lion to Sosabowski, who died in 1967 (Dreel ferry signage, author visit, May 24, 2009. www .ww2awards.com/person/34944).

287 *"too busy fighting Eisenhower"*: Baynes, *Urquhart of Arnhem*, 160, 167 (*"a bit more constructive criticism"*).

287 *"a single controlling mind"*: ibid., 159.

287 *Horrocks at least had the grace*: Horrocks, *A Full Life*, 231; Keegan, ed., *Churchill's Generals*, 236–38 (*had failed to keep a senior Dutch officer*).

287 *Several hundred fugitive Allied troops*: brochure, "Airborne Museum 'Hartenstein,'" Oosterbeek, author visit, May 2009, 12–13; Badsey, *Arnhem 1944*, 83–85; Middlebrook, *Arnhem 1944*, 439 (*more than six thousand others*); Hastings, *Armageddon*, 56 (*"Green grow the rushes"*); Arthur, *Forgotten Voices of World War II*, 364 (*"show these bastards"*).

287 *The Dutch too would tramp away*: "Freedom Trail Arnhem," n.d., city of Arnhem, author visit, May 24, 2009; Powell, *The Devil's Birthday*, 229 (*plundered the city* and *eating dogs and tulip bulbs*); Saunders, *The Red Beret*, 262 (*execution of fifty resistance members*); VW, vol. 2, 416–17 (*rail strike*); Nijmegen signage, author visit, May 22, 2009 (*five thousand buildings*); Hitchcock, *The Bitter Road to Freedom*, 122 (*sixteen thousand died of starvation*); Urquhart, *A Life in Peace and War*, 75 (*"can never again afford"*).

287 *21st Army Group had nearly doubled the perimeter*: SLC, 204–5.

288 *That task would entangle most of Second Army*: Rapport and Northwood, *Rendezvous with Destiny*, 381 (*oxtail soup*); Arthur, *Forgotten Voices of World War II*, 368 (*empty oil drums*); Fauntleroy, *The General and His Daughter*, 134–35 ("*I'd be mortified*"); SLC, 206 (*another 3,600 casualties*); corr, JMG to MBR, Oct. 3, 1944, MBR papers, MHI, box 21 ("*much more vicious*"); T. G. Lindsay, "Operation Overlord Plus," n.d., LHC, 54–55 (*which they stalked on ice skates*).

288 "*an epic cock-up*": Arthur, *Forgotten Voices of World War II*, 346–47.

288 *Eisenhower offered Montgomery a fistful*: corr, DDE to BLM, Oct. 11, 1944, DDE Lib, PP-pres, box 83.

288 *Montgomery shifted his command post*: Biographer Nigel Hamilton considered MARKET GARDEN to be "Monty's worst mistake of the war" (*Monty: Final Years of the Field-Marshal, 1944–1976*, 56, 97, 115).

288 "*will not affect operations eastward*": Fraser, *And We Shall Shock Them*, 348.

288 "*the last occasion of the war*": Hastings, *Armageddon*, 60–61.

288 "*The opening of the port*": BLM, M-527, Sept. 27, 1944, National Archives of Canada, RG 24, vol. 1054 2, file 215A21.016(9).

288 "*There was a change of mood after Arnhem*": Hastings, *Armageddon*, 141.

288 "*The picture is not very good*": diary, Sept. 24, 1944, Raymond G. Moses papers, MHI, box 1.

289 "*I am not looking forward to the winter*": Fauntleroy, *The General and His Daughter*, 57.

CHAPTER 6: THE IMPLICATED WOODS

Charlemagne's Tomb

291 *For the most loyal Germans*: "Concise Guide to Aachen Cathedral," n.d., Europäische Stiftung für den Aachener Dom, www.aachendom.de; "Aachen at a Glance," Aachen Tourist Service, author visit, Sept. 25–27, 2009.

291 *It was said that the fearless burghers*: Friedrich, *The Fire*, 116–17, 246–47.

291 *Now smoke rose from Aachen again*: SLC, 252 (*First Army had narrowed its front*), 281–84 (*eighteen thousand German troops*); "Aachen: Military Operations in Urban Terrain," 26th Infantry Regiment Association, 49 (*Seventy-four American gun batteries*); Middleton, *Our Share of Night*, 345 ("*gray and brown mass*").

292 *To help VII Corps complete Aachen's encirclement*: "Breaching the Siegfried Line," XIX Corps, Oct. 2, 1944, Charles H. Corlett papers, MHI, box 1, 9–15 (*Napalm fizzled*); SLC, 260–61, 279–80 ("*We have a hole*"), 294 ("*job is finished*").

292 *Hobbs was dead wrong*: "German Reaction to XIX Corps Breakthrough Siegfried Line, 2–16 Oct., 1944," n.d., NARA RG 407, ML, box 24130; SLC, 287 (*huge white cross*); "Battle of Aachen, 18th Infantry Regiment," n.d., NARA RG 407, E 427-A, CI (*gobbled down the breakfast*).

292 *Field Marshal Rundstedt warned Berlin*: SLC, 299n; Wheeler, *The Big Red One*, 337 (*hardly a mile separated*); "The Fall of Aachen," n.d., Stanhope Mason papers, MRC FDM, 1994.126 ("*no middle course*").

293 *Lest the Germans miss the message*: "The Fall of Aachen," n.d., Stanhope Mason papers, MRC FDM, 1994.126; "Aachen: Military Operations in Urban Terrain," 26th Infantry Regiment Association, 17–18.

293 *Aachen's dismemberment began in earnest*: "Aachen: Military Operations in Urban Terrain," 26th Infantry Regiment Association, 17–18; Daniel, "The Capture of Aachen," lecture, CO, 2nd Bn, 26th Inf, n.d., Quantico, Va., 8–11 (*tossed one thousand grenades*).

293 *They found a "sterile sea of rubble"*: SLC, 308, 289; Daniel, "The Capture of Aachen," lecture, CO, 2nd Bn, 26th Inf, n.d., Quantico, Va., 5 ("*Knock 'em all down!*").

293 *Street by street, building by building*: "Aachen: Military Operations in Urban Terrain," 26th Infantry Regiment Association, 29–30; "Battle Experiences," Apr. 15, 1945,

NARA RG 407, ML #248, box 24148 (*perforated each building*); Beck, 384 (*beehive charges*); Wheeler, *The Big Red One*, 339 (*bulldozers piled rubble*); "Battle Experiences, Twelfth Army Group," Dec. 5, 1944, NARA RG 337, AGF OR, no. 173 (*No. 2 green bean can*).

294 *Three captured German streetcars*: "1106th Engineer Group South of Aachen," n.d., Stanhope Mason papers, MRC FDM, 1994.126; "Aachen: Military Operations in Urban Terrain," 26th Infantry Regiment Association, 6; Daniel, "The Capture of Aachen," lecture, CO, 2nd Bn, 26th Inf, n.d., Quantico, Va., 15–16 (*"Surrender or get fried"*); "1st Division World War II Combat Achievements Report," chapter XXV, "Aachen," 2nd Bn, 26th Inf, Oct. 14, 1944, MRC FDM; Stanhope B. Mason, "Reminiscences and Anecdotes of World War II," 1988, MRC FDM, 1994.126, 226 (*collect mattresses*).

294 *Another lethal legacy from the Italian campaign*: Mayo, *The Ordnance Department*, 301 (*capable of keeping pace*); author visit, Sept. 25–27, 2009; "Clearing the Area South of the Railroad Tracks," n.d., Stanhope Mason papers, MRC FDM, 1994.126 (*seven rounds down Hindenburgstrasse*).

294 *Across the city the Americans crept*: Middleton, *Our Share of Night*, 349, 354 (*"fucking bastards"*).

295 *As the house-to-house ruination proceeded*: "1st Division World War II Combat Achievements Report," chapter XXV, "Aachen," 2nd Bn, 26th Inf, Oct. 8–9, 1944, MRC FDM; Marshall, ed., *Proud Americans*, 224 (*Not even a radio antenna*); SLC, 302 (*"have to close that gap"*).

295 *Hodges also castigated the XIX Corps commander*: Farrington, ed., *Cowboy Pete*, 9, 13, 21, 103.

295 *"Every hour seems interminable"*: Kingseed, *From Omaha Beach to Dawson's Ridge*, 209–10.

295 *"I've calloused my emotions"*: corr, Joseph T. Dawson to sister, Sept. 19, 1944, MRC FDM, 1991.65.

295 *"His face is bony"*: Heinz, *When We Were One*, 39 (*"large ears"*), 20 (*"Just move the ones"*).

296 *Bruno and the Swinging Tigers*: Alosi, *War Birds*, 91.

296 *"We could hear them singing"*: Wheeler, *The Big Red One*, 340.

296 *By ten A.M. several Tigers had churned uphill*: "Attack on G and I Companies," 16th Infantry, NARA RG 407, E 427-A, CI; Clay, *Blood and Sacrifice*, 216.

296 *"Situation very critical"*: Kingseed, *From Omaha Beach to Dawson's Ridge*, 212–15; Heinz, *When We Were One*, 49 (*"thrown against the door"* and *Judy Garland sang*); Clay, *Blood and Sacrifice*, 216 (*P-47 fighters*).

296 *"Much moaning and groaning"*: "Attack on G and I Companies of the 16th Infantry Regiment," n.d., Stanhope Mason papers, MRC FDM, 1994.126.

296 *"If higher authority decides"*: OH, James K. Woolnough, 1971, W. D. Macmillan and William M. Stevenson, SOOHP, MHI, 18.

296 *As the enemy attacks grew feebler*: "Attack on G and I Companies of the 16th Infantry Regiment," n.d., Stanhope Mason papers, MRC FDM, 1994.126; Heinz, *When We Were One*, 223, 41–42 (*"He doesn't know why"*).

297 *At 4:15 P.M. on Monday, October 16*: SLC, 306; Marshall, ed., *Proud Americans*, 241 (*sixty-three of ninety panzers*).

297 *The tally for G Company*: Kingseed, *From Omaha Beach to Dawson's Ridge*, 219–20 (*"somewhat shattered"*); Heinz, *When We Were One*, 223 (*"We died right here"*).

297 *In keeping with the Führer's wishes*: "Aachen: Military Operations in Urban Terrain," 26th Infantry Regiment Association, 40 (*"We shall fight"*); "Clearing Area South of the Rail Road Tracks," 26th Inf, n.d., and blueprint, map, Palast Hotel, "Aachener Quellenhof," NARA RG 407, E 427-A, CI; *Register of Graduates*, U.S. Military Academy, class of 1938 (*John T. Corley*).

297 *At seven A.M., as mortars pummeled*: "1st Division World War II Combat Achievements Report," chapter XXVI, "Farwick Park, Aachen," 3rd Bn, 26th Inf, Oct. 14, 1944, MRC

FDM; "Clearing Area South of the Rail Road Tracks," 26th Inf, n.d., NARA RG 407, E 427-A, CI (*exchange of grenades*); Robert G. Botsford, "The City of Aachen," in Stanhope B. Mason, "Reminiscences and Anecdotes of World War II," 1988, MRC FDM, 1994.126 (*hunting-scene oils*); *SLC*, 316 (*ten thousand marks*).

298 *The colonel instead had packed his bags*: *SLC*, 316; Whitehead, "*Beachhead Don*," 273–74 ("*They marched smartly*"); "Aachen: Military Operations in Urban Terrain," 26th Infantry Regiment Association, 42 ("*do it in our hearts*"); Knickerbocker et al., *Danger Forward*, 266 ("*I don't believe in miracles*").

298 *Nearly twelve thousand Germans had been captured*: *SLC*, 317–18; Wheeler, *The Big Red One*, 342.

298 "*These bitter tragic months*": Wheeler, *The Big Red One*, 342–43. Promoted to major, Dawson would return to Europe to work with the OSS. An oil industry geologist after the war, he died in 1998.

298 *Also sent home was General Corlett*: corr, ONB to DDE, Oct. 19, 1944, Charles H. Corlett papers, MHI, box 1 (*failing health*); Farrington, ed., *Cowboy Pete*, 104–5 ("*plain heartbreak*"); OH, George I. Forsythe, 1974, Frank L. Henry, SOOHP, MHI, 212 ("*sasses the army commander*"); Berlin, *U.S. Army World War II Corps Commanders*, 6 (*Oklahoma National Guard soldier*); http://digital.library.okstate.edu/encyclopedia/entries/M/MC033 .html.

298 *No one would take the waters in Aachen*: Robert G. Botsford, "The City of Aachen," in Stanhope B. Mason, "Reminiscences and Anecdotes of World War II," 1988, MRC FDM, 1994.126 ("*none of the grace*"); Carpenter, *No Woman's World*, 165 ("*dead as yesterday*" and "*the dead from my house*"); Heinz, *When We Were One*, 226 (*83 percent*); *Reporting World War II*, vol. 2, 546–47 ("*These ruins*").

299 *A plump, sooty man wandering the streets*: Whiting, *The Home Front: Germany*, 178–79 ("Gebt mir fünf Jahre"); Robert G. Botsford, "The City of Aachen," in Stanhope B. Mason, "Reminiscences and Anecdotes of World War II," 1988, MRC FDM, 1994.126 (*graveyard uprooted*); Edsel, *The Monuments Men*, 142–44 (*formed a fire brigade*).

299 "*We can force the Boche to their knees*": corr, JLC to M. S. Eddy, Oct. 24, 1944, JLC papers, DDE Lib, box 3, 201 file; "U.S. Military Government in Germany: Operations During the Rhineland Campaign," 1950, CMH, 8-3.1 DA5, 34–35, 138; Whiting, *The Home Front: Germany*, 178–79 (*curfew was imposed*); Alosi, *War Birds*, 134 ("*clipping details*"); "Pigeon Report," AFHQ G-2 to SHAEF G-2, March 12, 1945, NARA RG 331, SGS, Entry 15, box 112 ("*falconry unit*").

299 "*We come as conquerers*": "U.S. Military Government in Germany: Operations During the Rhineland Campaign," 1950, CMH, 8-3.1 DA5, 34–39, 55a, 57, 105–6; *TSC*, 356–57 ("*not as oppressors*").

299 *An Army study also concluded*: Lerner, *Psychological Warfare Against Nazi Germany*, 276–79.

300 "*first German city to be taken*": Knickerbocker et al., *Danger Forward*, 402.

"*Do Not Let Us Pretend We Are All Right*"

300 *The autumnal struggles at Arnhem and Aachen*: ALH, 142; Cundiff, *45th Infantry CP*, 207 ("*We have them licked*"); Royce L. Thompson, "Proposed CCS Directive to Eisenhower to End ETO War in 1944," Jan. 19, 1950, Historical Section, CMH, 2-3.7 AE.P-9 ("*playing everything for a conclusion*"); OH, W. B. Smith, Sept. 14, 1945, OCMH WWII Europe Interviews, MHI (*fight in the Pacific*).

300 "*We have facing us now*": Chandler, 2208.

300 "*Most people that write to me*": ibid., 2288.

300 *Eisenhower now commanded fifty-eight divisions*: *SLC*, 378, 388, 390; Chandler, 2168 ("*in a bad state*"); *TSC*, 296 (*insufficient means to support them*); *LSA*, vol. 2, 13 (*no more than twenty divisions*).

301 *To further explain his plight*: Chandler, 2281–85; "G-4 History," n.d., NARA RG 498, ETO HD, admin file #553A-C, 82; Cooper, *Death Traps*, 239 (*enemy depot in Liège*).

301 *The most desperate need was for ammunition*: Chandler, 2281 (*two tons every minute*), 2311n; "Ammunition Supply for Field Artillery," n.d., USFET General Board study no. 58, NARA RG 407, E 427, 97-USF-0.3.0, 8–9 (*incessant rationing*), 24–27 ("*complete collapse*"); LSA, vol. 2, 247–48, 255–56 (*Patton wanted sixty*); Waddell, *United States Army Logistics*, 45 ("*silence policy*").

301 *The shortfall partly reflected an inability*: LSA, vol. 2, 269, 274, 255–56 (*largely on the defensive*); "Ammunition Supply and Operations, European Campaign," USFET General Board study no. 100, NARA RG 407, E 427, 97USF-0.3.0 (*25,000 man-hours*); Eiler, *Mobilizing America*, 410 ("*Firepower for Eisenhower*").

302 *One senior American general believed*: "Ammunition Supply for Field Artillery," n.d., USFET General Board study no 58, NARA RG 407, E 427, 97-USF-0.3.0, 28–29 ("*saved many lives*"); corr, Brig. Gen. John H. Hinds to Maj. Gen. Orlando Ward, July 6, 1951, NARA RG 319, E 97, background papers, LSA, vol. 1, box 6 (*thousands of tons were stacked*); Charles K. MacDermut and Adolph P. Gratiot, "History of G-4 Com Z ETO," 1946, CMH, 8-3.4 AA, 86–87 (*actual number was less than 100*); "G-4 History," n.d., NARA RG 498, ETO HD, admin file #553A-C, 56, 87–88 (*246 cargo vessels*); LSA, vol. 2, 128 (*floating warehouses*).

302 *The War Department, trying to supply a global war*: Charles K. MacDermut and Adolph P. Gratiot, "History of G-4 Com Z ETO," 1946, CMH, 8-3.4 AA, 87–89 ("*no further commodity-loaded ships*"); "G-4 History," n.d., NARA RG 498, ETO HD, admin file #553A-C, 92 (*Bronze Stars*).

302 *If only Antwerp were free*: corr, BLM to H. Crerar, Sept. 13, 1944, M-523, National Archives of Canada, RG 24, vol. 1054 2, file 215A21.016(9) ("*We have captured a port*"); minutes, Sept. 22, 1944, conference, SHAEF forward war room, 2:30 P.M., Arthur S. Nevins papers, MHI ("*indispensable prerequisite*" and "*matter of urgency*"); Wilmot, *The Struggle for Europe*, 534 (*sent his chief of staff*); Chandler, 2202 ("*terribly anxious*"), 2212 ("*must retain as first mission*"); Crosswell, *Beetle*, 726.

302 *Montgomery had assigned clearing the Scheldt*: VW, vol. 2, 59–67, 70–71, 104–7, 116; SLC, 220–21.

303 "*We need this place more than we need FDR*": corr, Sept. 23, 1944, Everett S. Hughes papers, LOC MS Div, box II:3, folder 4.

303 *Dempsey's Second Army continued to look beyond the Rhine*: Love and Major, eds., *The Year of D-Day*, 152n; Danchev, 600 ("*Antwerp must be captured*"); Callahan, *Churchill & His Generals*, 220 ("*I was wrong*").

303 *But in October 1944, the field marshal displayed*: ONB to C. Hodges, Sept. 23, 1944, "Memoranda for Record," 12th Army Group, NARA RG 407, ML #205, box 24143 (*Ramsay warned that to clear the Scheldt*); Chalmers, *Full Cycle*, 251 ("*not taking this operation seriously*"); Love and Major, eds., *The Year of D-Day*, 151 ("*I let fly*"); corr, BLM to DDE, Oct. 9, 1944, DDE Lib PP-pres, box 83 ("*he makes wild statements*"). Eisenhower denied getting "wild statements" from Ramsay (Chandler, 2216).

304 "*I can not agree that our concepts*": TSC, 293.

304 *Unchastened by the destruction*: Pogue, *George C. Marshall*, 475 ("*overwhelming egotism*").

304 "*Our advance into Germany may be delayed*": LSA, vol. 2, 107; Chandler, 2215n (*high winds that very day*).

304 "*This reemphasizes the supreme importance*": Chandler, 2215.

304 *Montgomery would assert*: VW, vol. 2, 95 ("*hardly justified*"); corr, BLM to DDE, Oct. 9, 1944, DDE Lib PP-pres, box 83 ("*You can rely on me*"); corr, BLM to Canadian First Army, M-530, Oct. 9, 1944, National Archives of Canada, RG 24, vol. 1054 2, file 215A21.016(9) ("*port will take priority*"); SLC, 220; VW, vol. 2, 85.

305 "*Nothing that I may ever say or write*": Chandler, 2216.

305 "*It may be that political and national considerations*": VW, vol. 2, 85–88.

305 "*The questions you raise are serious ones*": Chandler, 2221–24.

306 *The threat could hardly be misconstrued*: VW, vol. 2, 92, 103, 109.

306 *"You will hear no more"*: corr, BLM to DDE, Oct. 16, 1944, DDE Lib PP-pres, box 83.

306 *a newer model from Detroit was somewhere*: Chandler, 2265.

306 *With Kay Summersby behind the wheel*: Summersby, *Eisenhower Was My Boss*, 191; Chandler, vol. 5, chronology, Oct. 13–14, 1944; Bradley, *A Soldier's Story*, 432–33 (*"I must have shot a dozen"*).

306 *Bidding farewell to king and comrades*: Bradley, *A Soldier's Story*, 433.

307 *"has not visibly aged"*: Eisenhower, *Eisenhower at War, 1943–1945*, 489; Chandler, vol. 5, chronology, Oct. 14, 1942, and Oct. 14, 1943.

307 *Yet even* Time's *omniscience*: John P. Roche, "Eisenhower Redux," *NYT Book Review*, June 28, 1981 (*"calculating quality"*); Larrabee, *Commander in Chief*, 419 (*"veiled man"*); Wilson, ed., *D-Day 1944*, 212 (*"far more complicated"*).

307 *He would never be a Great Captain*: Ambrose, *The Supreme Commander*, 610 (*Cannae*), 338 (*"chairman of the board"*); D'Este, *Eisenhower: A Soldier's Life*, 467 (*exceptional political instincts*); Kingston McCloughry, *Direction of War*, 168 (*"genius of getting along"*).

307 *He was by temperament a reconciler*: Graham and Bidwell, *Coalitions, Politicians & Generals*, 193; *VW*, vol. 2, 92; Kingston McCloughry, *Direction of War*, 168 (*"shrewd without being subtle"*).

308 *"no one knew better than he"*: Churchill, *Triumph and Tragedy*, 31; *DOB*, 50 (*"solve problems through reasoning"*).

308 *"We've now been apart"*: Eisenhower, *Mrs. Ike*, 226.

308 *The miles slid past, and with them the day*: Bradley, *A Soldier's Story*, 432 (*steam-heated stone buildings*); OH, William H. Simpson, 1971, Thomas R. Stone, SOOHP, MHI; OH, James E. Moore, 1984, Larry F. Paul, SOOHP, MHI, 111; "Brief Historical Survey of the War Years in Luxembourg," National Museum of Military History, http://www.luxembourg.co.uk/NMMH/waryears.html (*germanized*); David Lardner, "Letter from Luxembourg," in *The New Yorker Book of War Pieces*, 399–401 (*and conscripted ten thousand*). Lardner was killed in Aachen a week after writing this article.

308 *Bradley's office on the Place de Metz*: MacDonald, *A Time for Trumpets*, 71; author visit, June 4, 2009; *A Walk Through Luxembourg*, tourist booklet, n.d., 2–3, 24, 29.

309 *Here in the dining room*: Summersby, *Eisenhower Was My Boss*, 191; Bradley, *A Soldier's Story*, 433.

The Worst Place of Any

309 *The Belgian town of Spa*: Baedeker, *Belgium and Holland*, 249–53; *PP*, 632–33 (*Hindenburg concluded*); Keegan, *The First World War*, 417–19 (*fantasize about unleashing the army*).

309 *Now GIs hauled the roulette wheels*: Andrew T. McNamara, "QM Activities of II Corps Through Algeria, Tunisia & Sicily and First Army Through Europe," 1955, PIR, MHI, 149; Benjamin A. Dickson, "G-2 Journal: Algiers to the Elbe," MHI, 171 (*triple bunks*); Knickerbocker et al., *Danger Forward*, 333 (*"take the 'hit' out"*); William A. Carter, "Carter's War," 1983, CEOH, box V, 14, XI, 25 (*eleven drinking water sources*), 27 (*grand ballroom with mirrors*); Marshall, ed., *Proud Americans*, 258 (*horsemeat*); OH, Charles G. Patterson, First Army AA officer, 1973, G. Patrick Murray, SOOHP, MHI, 118 (*monthly consignment*); Sylvan, 155 (*hilltop mansion*), 154 (*clatter of a V-1*); *Medicine Under Canvas*, 138 (Gaslight *and* A Guy Named Joe); Middleton, *Our Share of Night*, 344 (*"song had been taken prisoner"*);

310 *Lieutenant General Courtney H. Hodges moved*: Wishnevsky, *Courtney Hicks Hodges*, 10–13 (*"#10 Blue"*); MacDonald, *A Time for Trumpets*, 188 (*"pessimistic"*); Sylvan, 119 (*"a little too sad"*).

310 *A crack shot and big-game hunter*: "Precise Puncher," *Time* (Oct. 16, 1944): cover story; OH, Mildred Lee Hodges (widow), 1973, G. Patrick Murray, SOOHP, MHI, 12 (*"sissy"*), 40 (*dash of bitters*); OH, Charles G. Patterson, First Army antiaircraft officer, 1973, G. Patrick Murray, SOOHP, MHI, 18; Miller, *Ike the Soldier*, 705 (*"I wish every-*

body"); corr, Walter E. Lauer, CG, 99th ID, May 8, 1963, MHI, Maurice Delaval collection, box 13 ("*Unexcitable. A killer*"); Wishnevsky, *Courtney Hicks Hodges*, 187–88 ("*a Georgia farmer*"), 52 ("*sir*"); OH, ONB, [1966?], Kitty Buhler, MHI, 45–47 ("*very dignified*").

310 *First Army was the largest American fighting force*: Beetle Smith called him "the weakest commander we had" (OH, W. B. Smith, May 8, 1947, FCP, MHI).

310 *Capable enough during the pursuit*: Hogan, *A Command Post at War*, 288–90 (*illness, fatigue*); corr, David T. Griggs, advisor to secretary of war, Feb. 22, 1945, to Edward L. Bowles, AFHRA, 519.161-7 ("*a little confused*"); SLC, 619–20 ("*lacking in vigor*" and "*pretty slow*"), 21–22 (*platoon dispositions*); LSA, vol. 2, 349 ("*least disposed to make any attempt*"); Bolger, "Zero Defects: Command Climate in First U.S. Army, 1944–1945," *Military Review* (May 1991): 61+ (*rarely left Spa* and "*refused to discuss orders*"); Sylvan, 144 (*Hobbs never laid eyes on him*), 76 ("*quicker to keep smashing ahead*").

311 *Peevish and insulated*: Hogan, *A Command Post at War*, 184–85, 288–89.

311 *Of thirteen corps and division commanders relieved*: The initial First Army firings were of course under Bradley before he relinquished command to Hodges. Bolger, "Zero Defects: Command Climate in First U.S. Army, 1944–1945," *Military Review* (May 1991): 61+.

311 "*like a mendicant*": Pogue, *Pogue's War*, 111–12.

311 "*Aggressive, touchy, and high-strung*": Bradley, *A Soldier's Story*, 180 ("*Critical, unforgiving*"); Bradley Commentaries, CBH papers, MHI.

311 *Three rivalrous figures*: Hogan, *A Command Post at War*, 28 ("*Captain Bligh*"), 32 (*Tubby*); Bradley Commentaries, CBH papers, MHI; Benjamin A. Dickson, "G-2 Journal: Algiers to the Elbe," MHI, 150, 197 (*Iago*); Baldwin, *Battles Lost and Won*, 497; Dickson obituary, *Assembly*, Sept. 1978.

312 "*slightly angry bafflement*": Baldwin, *Battles Lost and Won*, 318.

312 "*The enemy has continued to reinforce*": Chandler, 2257–59.

312 *Canadian First Army troops had captured Breskens*: The Breskens Pocket dissolved on Nov. 3. The British I Corps under the Canadian army included a British infantry division, the U.S. 104th Infantry Division (as of Oct. 23), and Polish and Canadian armored divisions. *VW*, vol. 2, 107, 111–13; SLC, 215–29.

312 "*three general phases*": Chandler, 2257–59.

312 *First Army's capture of Aachen*: "Approach to and Crossing of the Rhine, 18 Oct. 1944," 12th Army Group, G-3, NARA RG 407, ML, box 24143; OH, "Hürtgen Forest," 28th ID, Nov. 1944, NARA RG 407, E 427-A, CI, folders #74–77 (*the most promising frontage*).

312 *Four compact woodland tracts formed the Hürtgen*: Rush, *Hell in Hürtgen Forest*, 17; Pogue, *Pogue's War*, 272 (*regulated logging*); Heinz, *When We Were One*, 141 ("*picture forest*"); Currey, *Follow Me and Die*, 108 ("*worst place of any*").

313 *The* Hürtgenwald *had been fortified*: Rush, *Hell in Hürtgen Forest*, 19; McManus, *The Deadly Brotherhood*, 62 (*sowed mines*); Weigley, *Eisenhower's Lieutenants*, 366 (*four days to move a mile*); SLC, 337–40 (*4,500 casualties*); Pogue, *Pogue's War*, 272 ("*Battle of the Wilderness*").

313 *Nearly half of the 6,500 German defenders*: Lucian Heichler, "The First Battle of the Hürtgen Forest," March 1954, OCMH, NARA RG 319, R-series #42, 10–17 ("*family-fathers*"); SLC, 335–40, 333–34 ("*extensive, thick, and nearly trackless*"); Mack Morriss, "War in the Huertgen Forest," *Yank*, Jan. 5, 1945, in *Reporting World War II*, vol. 2, 562–63 ("*ointment box*").

313 *That underestimated American obstinacy*: author visit, Sept. 26, 2009; SLC, 323–24 (*Argonne Forest*); Weigley, *Eisenhower's Lieutenants*, 365 ("*to make the Hürtgen a menace*").

314 *No consideration was given to bypassing*: OH, T. C. Thorson, Sept. 12, 1956, and R. F. Akers, June 11, 1956, CBM, NARA RG 319, OCMH, 2-3.7; Hogan, *A Command Post at War*, 182; MacDonald, *The Battle of the Huertgen Forest*, 88; OH, JLC, Jan. 25, 1954, CBM, NARA RG 319, OCMH, 2-3.7 ("*would not question Courtney*").

314 *"We* had *to go into the forest":* OH, JLC, Jan. 25, 1954, CBM, NARA RG 319, OCMH, 2-3.7; OH, "Conversations with General J. Lawton Collins," May 17, 1983, Gary Wade, ed., CSI, report no. 5, CARL (*"they could have hit my flank"*).

314 *Seven dams built for flood control:* Together the two main reservoirs had a capacity of 123,000 acre-feet (*SLC,* 325).

314 *"great destructive flood waters":* Miller, *A Dark and Bloody Ground,* 32; Collins, *Lightning Joe,* 273 (*nor were the dams mentioned in tactical plans*); OH, "Conversations with General J. Lawton Collins," May 17, 1983, Gary Wade, ed., CSI, report no. 5, CARL (*"intelligence failure"*).

314 *By late October, as First Army coiled: SLC,* 327 (*Düren's church bells*), 342; Benjamin A. Dickson, "G-2 Journal: Algiers to the Elbe," MHI, 190; Hogan, *A Command Post at War,* 181; Edgar Holton, former XIX Corps G-2 lieutenant, e-mails to author, June 30, July 23, Aug. 3, 2011 (*Inside an Aachen safe*); XIX Corps history, July 1945, NARA RG 407, E 427, ML #2220, 21–23 (*a hundred million metric tons of water*); memo, W. Simpson to C. Hodges, Nov. 5, 1944, NARA RG 407, E 427, ML #1024 (*"capabilities"*); English, *Patton's Peers,* 119 (*flanking attack toward Schmidt*).

315 *"a kind of torpor":* OH, T. C. Thorson, Sept. 12, 1956, CBM, NARA RG 319, OCMH, 2-3.7.

315 *"present plans of this army":* Hogan, *A Command Post at War,* 181; Weigley, *Eisenhower's Lieutenants,* 434–45 (*replenished*).

315 *Bradley would later claim:* Bradley Commentaries, CBH papers, MHI; Bradley and Blair, *A General's Life,* 341; Bradley, *A Soldier's Story,* 442.

315 *Not until November 7 did Hodges order:* Hogan, *A Command Post at War,* 181; war diary, Dec. 4, 1944, ONB papers, MHI (*"must control Roer dam"*).

315 *"Damn the dams":* OH, T. C. Thorson, Sept. 12, 1956, CBM, NARA RG 319, OCMH, 2-3.7.

315 *Attacking the worst place of any:* OH, "Hürtgen Forest," 28th ID, Nov. 1944, NARA RG 407, E 427-A, CI, folders #74–77; Heinz, *When We Were One,* 239, 244–46 (*"save everybody a lot of trouble"*).

317 *In late October the Bloody Bucketeers:* Currey, *Follow Me and Die,* 28, 87 (*Sterno blocks*); Mack Morriss, "War in the Huertgen Forest," *Yank,* Jan. 5, 1945, in *Reporting World War II,* vol. 2, 562–63 (*No. 8 wire*); Will Thornton, "World War II 'M' Co. History as Told by the Survivors," n.d., a.p. (*"His clothing and tire chains"*); Boesch, *Road to Huertgen,* 162 (*stripping footwear*).

317 *Foul weather, supply shortages, and the slow arrival:* Hogan, *A Command Post at War,* 184–85; Margry, "Battle of the Hürtgen Forest," *AB,* no. 171 (1991): 1+ (*two-story* Gasthaus); author visit, Sept. 26, 2009; Sylvan, 161 (*"fine fettle"*).

317 *In fact, it was badly flawed: SLC,* 346–47; OH, "Hürtgen Forest," 28th ID, Nov. 1944, NARA RG 407, E 427-A, CI, folders #74–77; Carey A. Clark et al., "Armor in the Hürtgen Forest," May 1949, AS, Ft. K, 36; Miller, *Division Commander,* 117 (*"gambler's chance"*); Carpenter, *No Woman's World,* 191 (*"Dismount and fight"*).

317 *At nine A.M. on November 2:* MacDonald and Mathews, *Three Battles,* 259; Ent, ed., *The First Century,* 170–72 (*"singly, in groups"*).

318 *The attack hardly began better for the 109th:* Paul Brückner, "The Battle in the Hürtgen Forest," n.d., a.p. I am grateful to Maj. Gen. (ret.) David Zabecki for his insights about the battle and for various documents, including this one.

318 *The 109th had advanced barely three hundred yards:* MacDonald and Mathews, *Three Battles,* 272; *SLC,* 349–50.

318 *Against such odds, and to the surprise:* MacDonald and Mathews, *Three Battles,* 259–63; *SLC,* 349; Carey A. Clark et al., "Armor in the Hürtgen Forest," May 1949, AS, Ft. K, 36–39 (*wrecked five Shermans*); corr, Edwin M. Burnett to 12th AG, Nov. 6, 1944, NARA RG 498, G-3 OR, box 1 (*burrowed into the northeast nose*).

318 *At dawn on Friday, November 3:* author visit, Hürtgen Forest, Sept. 26, 2009; Currey, *Follow Me and Die,* 113–14 (*astonished garrison at Schmidt*).

318 *"extremely satisfied"*: Sylvan, 163; *SLC*, 352 (*"little Napoleon"*).

319 *The bad news from Schmidt*: General Freiherr von Gersdorff, "The Battle of Schmidt," Nov. 1945, FMS, #A-891 and A-892, MHI.

319 *Model ordered the corps commander*: 116th Panzer Division memorial and cemetery, Vossenack, author visit, Sept. 26, 2009; Henry P. Halsell, "Hürtgen Forest and Roer River Dams," n.d., CMH, 314.7, I-22; General Freiherr von Gersdorff, "The Battle of Schmidt," Nov. 1945, FMS, #A-891 and A-892, MHI.

319 *Three isolated American rifle companies*: Miller, *A Dark and Bloody Ground*, 64–65, 77; MacDonald and Mathews, *Three Battles*, 290–91 (*scattered sixty antitank mines*); AAR, 28th ID, n.d., a.p. from David Zabecki; Bradbeer, "General Cota and the Battle of the Hürtgen Forest," *Army History* (spring 2010): 18+ (*Cota remained in Rott*).

319 *Just before sunrise on Saturday, November 4*: "Combat Experiences," 28th ID hq, March 9, 1945, NARA RG 498, G-3 observers' reports, box 2.

320 *At 8:30 an American platoon*: OH, Jack W. Walker, Co L, 112th Inf, Nov. 1944, NARA RG 407, E 427-A, CI, 28th ID, folders 74–77; Currey, *Follow Me and Die*, 129–34 (*"ragged, scattered, disorganized"*); SLC, 360–61; MacDonald and Mathews, *Three Battles*, 297–300.

320 *stampeded in the wrong direction*: The division history estimates that only 67 of the 200 survived (Ent, ed., *The First Century*, 17).

320 *The fight for the Hürtgen had taken a turn*: author visit, Bergstein, Sept. 26, 2009; e-mail, David T. Zabecki to author, Sept. 22, 2009 (*slow to realize*).

320 *Confusion soon turned to chaos*: SLC, 359–60; MacDonald and Mathews, *Three Battles*, 288, 310 (*nine feet*); Carey A. Clark et al., "Armor in the Hürtgen Forest," May 1949, AS, Ft. K, 61 (*unhitched and manhandled*).

320 *In Rott, Cota's perplexity*: AAR, 893rd TD Bn, Nov. 18, 1944, Nov. 1944, NARA RG 407, E 427-A, CI, 28th ID, folders 74–77; Miller, *A Dark and Bloody Ground*, 73; *SLC*, 359–60 (*"warm-hearted affection"*); MacDonald and Mathews, *Three Battles*, 313.

320 *A fretful General Gerow*: Miller, *Division Commander*, 122–24; OH, JLC, 1973, G. Patrick Murray, SOOHP, MHI (*"tougher than I had ever heard"*); Currey, *Follow Me and Die*, 155 (*"Roll on"*).

321 *Had the generals seen the battlefield clearly*: SLC, 360–63; OH, "Hürtgen Forest," 28th ID, Nov. 1944, NARA RG 407, E 427-A, CI, folders #74–77 (*"artesian wells"*); MacDonald and Mathews, *Three Battles*, 335 (*shifting guns hole by hole by hole*).

321 *A relief battalion from the 110th Infantry*: OH, Anthony R. Seymour, Warren G. Holmes, John Hayducok, 110th Inf, n.d., NARA RG 407, E 427, HI (*"just like cattle"*).

321 *Soldiers in the claustrophobic forest*: Linderman, *The World Within War*, 29 (*cigarettes*), 16 (*"So this is combat"*); Cowdrey, *Fighting for Life*, 260 (*"wet liver"*); memoir, Robert D. Georgen, n.d., 2nd Bn, 110th Inf, NWWIIM (*snipers were aiming*).

322 *"Pushing, shoving, throwing away equipment"*: Miller, *A Dark and Bloody Ground*, 79; Currey, *Follow Me and Die*, 165 (*"saddest sight"*).

322 *Officers managed to rally*: memoir, Thomas E. Wilkins, Co. C, 146th Engineers, n.d., CEOH, box X-37A (*hip boots*); Miller, *A Dark and Bloody Ground*, 79–82 (*Rubble Pile*); Ent, ed., *The First Century*, 172 (*"destroyed as a fighting unit"*).

322 *"The 28th Division situation"*: Sylvan, 167; OH, Richard W. Ripple, CO, 707th Tank Bn, Nov. 14, 1944, NARA RG 407, E 427-A, CI, folders #74–77; Currey, *Follow Me and Die*, 183–86; SLC, 362–65; MacDonald and Mathews, *Three Battles*, 378 (*dogtags*).

322 *Reeling from lack of sleep*: At one point in the ordeal, Cota reportedly fainted (Miller, *Division Commander*, 128–29).

323 *"All we seem to be doing is losing ground"*: Bradbeer, "General Cota and the Battle of the Hürtgen Forest," *Army History* (spring 2010): 18+; OH, Richard W. Ripple, CO, 707th Tank Bn, Nov. 14, 1944, NARA RG 407, E 427-A, CI, folders #74–77 (*battered last-stand redoubt*); OH, George R. Sedberry, Jr., Co C, 112th Inf, n.d., NARA RG 407, E 427, HI (*litters from tree limbs*); OH, G. M. Nelson, CO, 112th Inf, Nov. 13, 1944, NARA RG 407, E 427-A, CI, folders #74–77 (*threw away his compass*); OH, 20th Engineer Combat Bn, Nov. 1944, NARA RG 407, E 427-A, CI, folders #74–77 (*abandoned two tons of TNT*).

323 *Come nightfall, American artillery smothered*: MacDonald and Mathews, *Three Battles*, 380; OH, G. M. Nelson, CO, 112th Inf, Nov. 13, 1944, NARA RG 407, E 427-A, CI, folders #74–77 (*walking into a lake*).

323 *"Like blind cattle the men thrashed"*: SLC, 371.

323 *The dead accumulated in stiff piles*: Babcock, *War Stories*, 275.

323 *Eisenhower and Bradley had driven to Rott*: Sylvan, 167–68; Bradbeer, "General Cota and the Battle of the Hürtgen Forest," *Army History* (spring 2010): 18+ ("*bloody nose*").

324 *"I've condemned a whole regiment"*: Carpenter, *No Woman's World*, 181.

324 *Survivors from the Kall*: AAR, Albert L. Berndt, 112th Inf surgeon, Nov. 10, 1944, NARA RG 407, E 427-A, CI, folders #74–77; Miller, *A Dark and Bloody Ground*, 89 (*soldierly airs*); Carpenter, *No Woman's World*, 232 ("*Chow all right, son?*").

324 *On Thursday, November 9*: Bradbeer, "General Cota and the Battle of the Hürtgen Forest," *Army History* (spring 2010): 18+.

324 *The weeklong battle had been among the costiliest*: Losses included those in units attached to the 28th Division (*SLC*, 374). Division casualties included 750 cases of trench foot (OH, "Hürtgen Forest," 28th ID, Nov. 1944, NARA RG 407, E 427-A, CI, folders #74–77).

324 *The Bloody Bucket was bloodier than ever*: SLC, 372 (*reduced to 57 men*); Bradbeer, "General Cota and the Battle of the Hürtgen Forest," *Army History* (spring 2010): 18+ (*from 2,200 to 300*); Ent, ed., *The First Century*, 172 ("*accomplished very little*"); memo, N. Cota, Nov. 29, 1944, in AAR, 28th ID, n.d., a.p., from David Zabecki ("*Salute, March, Shoot, Obey*").

324 *German losses for the week*: MacDonald, *The Battle of the Huertgen Forest*, 120 (*about three thousand*); corr, Hans-Helmut Jansen to parents, Dec. 5, 1944, trans. David Zabecki, a.p. ("*We squat in an airless cellar*"); Ivan "Cy" H. Peterman, "As I Saw It," in Knickerbocker et al., *Danger Forward*, 304 ("*South of the Border*"); Miller, *A Dark and Bloody Ground*, 60 ("*days were so terrible*").

325 *In less than three months, six U.S. Army infantry divisions*: SLC, 437–38, 492; Charles B. MacDonald, introduction to Boesch, *Road to Huertgen*.

325 *All told, 120,000 soldiers*: MacDonald, *The Battle of the Huertgen Forest*, 195.

325 *"the most ineptly fought series of battles"*: quoted in Hastings, *Armageddon*, 193; 183rd Volksgrenadier Div, n.d., in "Tactical Lessons," First Army, Aug. 1944–Feb. 1945, 5A, USAREUR staff ride, Hürtgen Forest, Dec. 5–8, 2001 (*completely unfit*).

325 *"He went on and on"*: Hogan, *A Command Post at War*, 186; Sylvan, 184 (*individual cake*).

325 *"We thought woods were wise"*: Schrijvers, *The Crash of Ruin*, 6.

325 *"not so much an area"*: Henry P. Halsell, "Hürtgen Forest and the Roer River Dams," n.d., CMH, 314.7, I-32.

325 *Fighter-bombers incinerated recalcitrant towns*: Sylvan, 189; Boesch, *Road to Huertgen*, 142 ("*C'est la bloody goddam guerre*"); Towne, *Doctor Danger Forward*, 150 (*cache of ears*); Baker, *Ernest Hemingway*, 555 (*seared by white phosphorus*); McManus, *The Deadly Brotherhood*, 253 ("*my personal Valley*").

326 *From his fieldstone house near Vicht*: Heinz, *When We Were One*, 243–46 ("*bulk bigger*"); Baker, *Ernest Hemingway*, 556; Reynolds, *Hemingway: The Final Years*, 113–25; Carpenter, *No Woman's World*, 240 ("*fornicatin' beasts*"); William P. Shaw, "Fellowship of Dust: The WWII Journey of Sgt. Frank Shaw," n.d., NWWIIM, 70 (King Lear).

326 *"I see you everywhere"*: Frank Maddalena was declared killed in action a year later (Litoff and Smith, eds., *Since You Went Away*, 247–48).

CHAPTER 7: THE FLUTTER OF WINGS

A Town Too Small for the Tragedy

329 *A stately procession of nineteen cargo ships*: British Pathé newsreel, 1944, http://www.britishpathe.com/record.php?id=23525.

329 *Seamen and anxious war correspondents*: Correspondents sailed with the port headquarters on the U.S.S. *James B. Weaver* (LSA, vol. 2, 110).

329 *Three small coasters had made the run*: *VW*, vol. 2, 127; Rawling, *Cinderella Operation*, 147–48; *VC*, 422–24.

329 *COMZ three days earlier had warned*: "Shipping Situation and Supply Requirements," COM Z, G-4, Nov. 25, 1944, CARL, N-6726.

329 *A protocol oversight had excluded*: *VC*, 422–24 (*snub*). Roughly half of those Canadian First Army casualties were Canadian nationals, with the balance divided among British, Polish, Czech, French, and American units (*SLC*, 229; *VW*, vol. 2, 127–28).

329 *The protracted "struggle in the polders"*: *VC*, vol. 3, 386; *SLC*, 221 (*flamethrowers*); Thompson, *Men Under Fire*, 17 (*windmill to windmill*); Reed, "Assault on Walcheren," *AB*, no. 36 (1982): 1+ (*bombardment of ancient Dutch dikes*); Wilmot, *The Struggle for Europe*, 545–46; Chalmers, *Full Cycle*, 256 ("*Good morning!*"); Woodward, *Ramsay at War*, 192–93 (*rousted from his bed*); Roskill, *White Ensign*, 397; *VW*, vol. 2, 115–23 (*last two thousand*); Rawling, *Cinderella Operation*, 147–48 (*at noon*).

330 *With enemy shore guns finally silenced*: Rawling, *Cinderella Operation*, 147–48; Moulton, *Battle for Antwerp*, 181–82 (*white chevron* and *nine explosions*); Thompson, *Men Under Fire*, 21 (*feeling their way*); Roskill, *White Ensign*, 153 (*Two hundred and sixty-seven mines*).

330 *Twenty more ships arrived*: *LSA*, vol. 2, 110; "G-4 History," ETOUSA, n.d., NARA RG 498, ETO HD, admin file #553A-C, 99. (*23,000 tons*); Edwin T. Bowden, "Quartermaster Operations at the Port of Antwerp," n.d., chapter 22, PIR, MHI, 9; "American Port Plans, August to November 1944," n.d., NARA RG 319, *LSA* background papers, 2-3.7 CB 7, 65–66 (*Six thousand civilian stevedores*); Eudora Ramsay Richardson and Sherman Allan, "Quartermaster Supply in the ETO in WWII," vol. 1, QM School, Ft. Lee, Va., 1947 (*densest rail network*); *LSA*, vol. 2, 111 (*85,000 tons of matériel*); "Clothing and Footwear," chapter 56, PIR, 1959, Robert M. Littlejohn papers, HIA (*depots in Lille, Mons*); "Development of Antwerp," ETOUSA, 1944, NARA RG 498 ETO HD, admin file #244, 15–16 (*ammunition ships*).

330 *Explosions had already become all too commonplace*: King and Kutta, *Impact*, 274. Various accounts give different dates for the initial V-weapon attacks in Antwerp. See *VW*, vol. 2, 149.

331 *Both V-1s and V-2s struck on October 13*: *SLC*, 229 ("*Something beastly*"); Rely, "Antwerp 'City of Sudden Death,'" *AB*, no. 57 (1987) 43+ (*women's handbags*).

331 *Barely above sea level*: King and Kutta, *Impact*, 279–81 ("*city of sudden death*"); "Development of Antwerp," ETOUSA, 1944, NARA RG 498, ETO HD, admin file #244, 17 (*tent encampments*); Antrobus, "V-2 in Antwerp," *Yank*, May 4, 1945, 6+ ("*unwanted smell*"); Thompson, *The Imperial War Museum Book of Victory in Europe*, 195 ("*cast continued singing*").

331 *Hitler had long recognized*: M. C. Helfers, "The Employment of V-Weapons by the Germans During World War II," OCMH, 1954, NARA RG 319, 2-3.7 AW, box 28, 75; Rely, "Antwerp 'City of Sudden Death,'" *AB*, no. 57 (1987): 43+ (*over the course of six months*). The German official history states that of 3,170 V-2s launched, 1,610 were aimed at Antwerp (*Germany VII*, 444).

331 *Sixty-seven thousand buildings in greater Antwerp*: "5th Major Port: A Story of Three Years Overseas," U.S. Army Transportation Corps, 1945, MHI, 68–71; *TSC*, 332 (*two-thirds of all houses*); *VW*, vol. 2, 149–50, 235 (*port operations to remain largely unimpaired*); "The Story of Antwerp," 50th AAA Bde, 1945, NARA RG 498, ETO HD, admin file #244A (*22,000 antiaircraft artillerymen*); film, "Defense of Antwerp Against the V-1," 1947, http://www.archive.org/details/gov.dod.dimoc.20375; Rely, "Antwerp 'City of Sudden Death,'" *AB*, no. 57 (1987): 43+ (*new gun barrels and ammunition*).

332 *German V-1 crews in December*: "The Story of Antwerp," 50th AAA Bde, 1945, NARA RG 498, ETO HD, admin file #244A; "Tactical Employment of Antiaircraft Artillery Units," USFET General Board study no. 38, n.d., NARA RG 407, E 427, AGWWII Operations Reports, 97-USF5-0.30, 40–41 ("*characteristic roar*"); M. C. Helfers, "The Employment of V-Weapons by the Germans During World War II," 1954, OCMH, NARA RG 319, 2-3.7 AW, box 28, 131 (*within eight miles of central Antwerp*).

332 *"The angel of death"*: Roberts, *Masters and Commanders*, 537.

332 *Nearly all twelve hundred seats were filled*: "Ciné Rex: 1935–1993," http://users.telenet.be /rudolf.bosschaerts/rex1e.html (*only German films were screened*); Huntington, "Lights. Camera. War!" *America in World War II* (June 2008): 34+ (*thirteen hundred films*).

332 *At 3:20 P.M., just after Gary Cooper*: Rely, "Antwerp 'City of Sudden Death,'" *AB*, no. 57 (1987): 43+.

333 *Recovery teams ultimately retrieved*: "The Antwerp Story," in "Stories of Transportation," vol. 1, Frank S. Ross papers, HIA, box 20, 407; *SLC*, 230 (*two hundred servicemen*); "Antwerp, 'City of Sudden Death,'" http://www.v2rocket.com/start/chapters/antwerp.html (*city zoo became a morgue*); Antrobus, "V-2 in Antwerp," *Yank*, May 4, 1945, 6+ (*decontamination squads*).

"Faith in a Friendly Universe"

333 *Despite the travails of the Hürtgen Forest*: Sylvan, 175 (*"last big offensive"*); Bradley, *A Soldier's Story*, 438–41; Bradley and Blair, *A General's Life*, 342–43.

333 *Just past the meridian on November 16*: AAR, "Operation Q," IX Tactical Air Command, n.d., Courtney H. Hodges papers, DDE Lib, box 7 (*"I feel very good"*); Heinz, *When We Were One*, 58 (*"yellow blossoms"*), 59 (*"no expression at all"*); Harmon, *Combat Commander*, 219 (*orange sheets*); memo, William L. Blanton, XIII Corps, n.d., NARA RG 407, ETO G-3 OR (*800 million candlepower*).

334 *The entrenched enemy quickly stiffened*: *SLC*, 420–24, 492, 505 (*hot food and burning candles*), 416–18 (*"house-by-house killing match"*); "Further Technical Notes on German Minefields," March 7, 1945, UK War Office, NARA RG 407, ML #225, appendix J (*dozen types of mine*). First Division casualties included those of the attached 47th Infantry.

334 *Thirty days hath November*: *SLC*, 518; "Weather Conditions in the ETO on D-Day and in Nov. 1944," HQ, Air Weather Service, Sept. 1946, NARA RG 319, *CCA* background historical files, box 164 (*triple the monthly average*).

334 *"Men were forced to discard their overcoats"*: *SLC*, 446, 457, 518; Schrijvers, *The Crash of Ruin*, 16 (*condoms*); *LSA*, vol. 2, 492 (*"duck bills"*).

335 *This was "thee or me" combat*: Rosengarten, "With Ultra from Omaha Beach to Weimar, Germany," *Military Affairs* (Oct. 1978): 127+; Nickell, *Red Devil*, 79 (*"They say cleanliness"*), 84–85 (*"With every heartbeat"*); Capa, *Slightly Out of Focus*, 203 (*"'You ain't goin' back'"*); Babcock, *Taught to Kill*, 123 (*"pissing your pants"*); Linderman, *The World Within War*, 306 (*"One forgets so much"*), 311 (Snow White).

335 *"My heart and soul have been torn"*: Sorley, *Thunderbolt*, 62.

335 *"War happens inside a man"*: Sevareid, *Not So Wild a Dream*, 495.

335 *Among the empty chairs*: AAR, Cannon Company, 16th Inf, and "Jack's Letters," Nov. 6, Dec. 8, Dec. 10, 1944, a.p., compiled by Rick Perry.

336 *As fresh reserves came forward*: "Graves Registrations Service," NARA RG 407, E 427, USFET General Board study no. 107; Ross, 219, 688 (*Great pains were taken*).

336 *For the living, small pleasures*: diary, Harold S. Frum, Nov. 11, 1944, "The Soldier Must Write," 1984, GCM Lib (*"90 percent boredom"*); Nickell, *Red Devil*, 80 (*burrows ten feet square*); Tapert, ed., *Lines of Battle*, 214–15 (*"war stands aside"*); corr, T. R. Bruskin to wife, Dec. 5, 1944, a.p. (*"pulling the chain"*).

336 *"I've learned what it means"*: McNally, *As Ever, John*, 52.

336 *"I can see now"*: Blunt, *Foot Soldier*, V-mail photo, 154.

336 *Operation QUEEN sputtered and stalled*: *SLC*, 578, 593, 616–17. *SHAEF in October had set quotas*. The highest awards required authorization from higher headquarters ("Awards and Decorations," USFET General Board study no. 10, n.d., NARA RG 407, E 427, AG WWII operations reports, 97-USF-0.3.0).

337 *The Roer, already in spate from daily rain*: *SLC*, 598 (*nearly two thousand tons*), 581, 594; Weigley, *Eisenhower's Lieutenants*, 434–35; AAR, 12th AG, vol. 14, publicity and psy-

chological warfare, NARA RG 331, E-200A, SHAEF records, box 267, 82–83 (*censors banned all reference*).

337 *Certainly the enemy had been badly hurt*: SLC, 412–14, 583 (*even a hundred men*), 594, 457 (*"numerous frostbites"*).

337 *"It is entirely possible"*: Crosswell, *Beetle*, 798.

337 *Winter always seemed to catch*: Bynell, "Logistical Planning and Operations—Europe," lecture, March 16, 1945, NARA RG 334, E 315, ANSCOL, box 207, 13 (*Arctic clothing tested at Anzio*); *LSA*, vol. 2, 222–24 (*"serious fighting"* and *"precautionary measure"*); "Report of Observers, ETO, 11 March–21 Apr 1945," Apr. 27, 1945, NARA RG 337, AGF OR #371; Cosmas and Cowdrey, *Medical Service in the European Theater of Operations*, 490 (*"Don't you know"*).

338 *"General, the weather is getting cold"*: Robert M. Littlejohn, "Ports and Transportation," n.d., chapter 27, PIR, MHI, 9; Andrew T. McNamara, "QM Activities of II Corps . . . and First Army Through Europe," 1955, chapter 46, PIR, MHI, 147–48 (*delays in opening Antwerp*); *LSA*, vol. 2, 224–26 (*850,000 heavy overcoats*); "Jack's Letters," Feb. 4, 1945, a.p. (*"We can't fight a winter war"*).

338 *"front-line troops fought"*: *LSA*, vol. 2, 227.

338 *Far less than half of the requested underwear*: Ross, 599, 571 (*shrinking size 12 pairs*); Robert M. Littlejohn, "Helpful Hints to Would-Be Quartermaster Generals," 1945, PIR, MHI, 3 (*"wool is essential to combat"*); Erna Risch and Thomas M. Pitkin, "Clothing the Soldier in World War II," 1946, CMH, 4-10.2 AA 16, 244–51 (*seven million new pairs*).

338 *The Army listed seventy different articles*: *LSA*, vol. 2, 233; Morris M. Bryan, "Quartermaster Planning," n.d., chapter 45, PIR, MHI (*"jacket, field, M-43"*); Andrus et al., eds., *Advances in Military Medicine*, vol. 2, 499–500 (*the "Clo"*); "Blankets," NARA RG 498, ETO HD, admin file #500.

339 *The Army was said to believe that every GI*: Sherry, *In the Shadow of War*, 94; "Trench Foot," n.d., NARA RG 407, E 427, AG WWII operations reports, 97-USF5-0.3.0, no. 94, 4–5 (*"none of which"*); "Clothing and Footwear," chapter 56, PIR, 1959, Robert M. Littlejohn papers, HIA (*"nothing but a sponge"*); Ross, 602–3 (*none larger than size 11*); Harold M. Florsheim, "Quartermaster Supply," n.d., chapter 40, PIR, MHI, 27–28; Lawrence B. Sheppard, "Supply of Footwear and Socks in the European Theater," 1945, chapter 31, PIR, MHI; *LSA*, vol. 2, 228–29; Cosmas and Cowdrey, *Medical Service in the European Theater of Operations*, 492–93.

339 *The first case of trench foot*: "Notes Taken at Trench Foot Conference," Jan. 24, 1945, Office of the Chief Surgeon, Paris, Paul R. Hawley papers, MHI, 1–6; Chandler, 2320 (*"We are making some progress"*); Cosmas and Cowdrey, *Medical Service in the European Theater of Operations*, 494; Cowdrey, *Fighting for Life*, 267; corr, D. G. Gilbert to JT, Jan. 28, 1959, JT, LOC, box 38 (*one-quarter of all hospital admissions*); Ellis, *On the Front Lines*, 187 (*"long lines of cots"*).

339 *Almost nothing had been learned*: The official report on trench foot in Italy, completed in Jan. 1944, took a year to reach the ETO (Cosmas and Cowdrey, *Medical Service in the European Theater of Operations*, 489).

339 *Nor had the Americans learned from the British*: "Notes Taken at Trench Foot Conference," Jan. 24, 1945, Office of the Chief Surgeon, Paris, Paul R. Hawley papers, MHI, 6; "German Training on Proper Use of Winter Clothing," July 21, 1945, NARA RG 337, AGF OR #559; monograph, "Cold Weather Injuries," n.d., NWWIIM.

339 *Many GIs were told to lace their boots tighter*: Cosmas and Cowdrey, *Medical Service in the European Theater of Operations*, 490, 496; corr, W. H. Simpson to A. C. Gillem, Jr., Nov. 25, 1944, Alvan Cullom Gillem, Jr., papers, MHI, box 6 (*could lose a thousand men*); *LSA*, vol. 2, 229; "Trench Foot," n.d., NARA RG 407, E 427, 97-USF5-0.30, USFET General Board study no. 94, 1–5 (*Purple Heart*); Cowdrey, *Fighting for Life*, 267; "Trench Foot," XV Corps, Dec. 28, 1944, NARA RG 498, G-3 OR, box 10, 1–2.

340 *As every buck private knew*: Sylvan, 172 ("*1 in 1,000*"); diary, Harold S. Frum, Oct. 21, 1944, "The Soldier Must Write," 1984, GCM Lib ("*never realized its omnipresence*"); Miller, *Ike the Soldier*, 705 ("*trench body*"); monograph, "Cold Weather Injuries," n.d., NWWIIM (*wedging newspaper*); OH, John Cappell, 8th Inf, 4th ID, NWWIIM (*sleeping platforms*); Cosmas and Cowdrey, *Medical Service in the European Theater of Operations*, 492–93 (*making their own footwear*); diary, Manton Eddy, Nov. 15, 1944, FCP, MHI ("*one dead Kraut*").

340 *The soldiers' misery contributed to a spike*: DOB, 508–9; Sherry, *In the Shadow of War*, 96 ("*ghosted*"); "The Execution of Eddie Slovik," *AB*, no. 32 (1981): 28+ ("*Each moment of combat*").

340 *Those evacuated from the front*: Ewing, *29 Let's Go!*, 88 ("*going back to the kitchen*"); "SHAEF Censorship Guidance," No. 11, May 4, 1944, NARA RG 331, E 1, SGS, box 4; Reister, ed., *Medical Statistics in World War II*, 43 (*929,000 men*); Cosmas and Cowdrey, *Medical Service in the European Theater of Operations*, 385–86 (*one in four admissions*); extract, censorship report, Sept. 1944, NARA RG 498, ETO HD, admin file ("*I can't take much more*").

341 *In contrast to the Army's nonchalance*: Copp and McAndrew, *Battle Exhaustion*, 110, 126; "Study of AGF Battle Casualties," AGF G-3, Sept. 25, 1946, NARA RG 337, E 16A, admin div subject file, box 48, 2–3; Cawthon, *Other Clay*, 100 ("*Blue 88s*"); Cosmas and Cowdrey, *Medical Service in the European Theater of Operations*, 385–87 (*ninety returned to duty*); "Combat Fatigue," n.d., NARA RG 407, E 427, 97-USF5-0.30, USFET General Board study no. 91, 1–4; *DOB*, 509.

341 *competent treatment and all the Blue 88s*: Rush, *Hell in Hürtgen Forest*, 309 ("*Between the physical fear*"); Copp and McAndrew, *Battle Exhaustion*, 144 ("*The only way one could get out*"); Fussell, *Doing Battle*, 31 ("*after five months*"); Linderman, *The World Within War*, 356–57 ("*I'm not badly injured*"); "Study of AGF Battle Casualties," AGF G-3, Sept. 25, 1946, NARA RG 337, E 16A, admin div subject file, box 48, 3 (*200 to 240 days*). Ten combat days typically equaled seventeen calendar days.

341 *"Morale is a darkling plain"*: Martin R. R. Goldman, "Morale in the AAF in World War II," 1953, AFHRA, historical study no. 78, 4.

341 *The Army's surgeon general recommended*: Palmer et al., *The Procurement and Training of Ground Combat Troops*, 231–32; "The Execution of Eddie Slovik," *AB*, no. 32 (1981): 28+. ("*Under present policy*"); "Military History of the Second World War: The Corps of Chaplains," 1946, CMH, 4-3 AA, 86 ("*faith in a friendly universe*").

341 *George Patton had encamped in a villa*: Codman, *Drive*, 202–3; Hirshson, *General Patton: A Soldier's Life*, 553 ("*impossible bric-a-brac*"); John K. Rieth, "We Seek: Patton's Forward Observers," 2002, a.p., 101 (*German rail guns*); PP, 566; diary, Oct. 24, 1944, Hobart Gay papers, MHI, box 2, 539 (*broke the windows*).

342 *Patton swanned about Lorraine*: D'Este, *Patton: A Genius for War*, 655, 691, 689; Hirshson, *General Patton: A Soldier's Life*, 521 (*$250,000 offer*); diary, Oct. 28 and 29, 1944, GSP, LOC MS Div, box 3, folder 8; Blumenson, *Patton: The Man Behind the Legend, 1885–1945*, 241; PP, 557–58 ("*May God rot his guts*").

342 *"How long, O Lord"*: Codman, *Drive*, 202–3.

342 *"Send me a couple of bottles"*: PP, 567, 570.

342 *Because of the West Wall's eastward bow*: Allen, *Lucky Forward*, 113 (*removal of XV Corps*); LC, 302–3; Wellard, *The Man in a Helmet*, 169 (*scores of manure-stacked Lorraine villages*).

343 *Patton claimed that Metz had not fallen*: PP, 576 (*Germans had taken it*); Hirshson, *General Patton: A Soldier's Life*, 544 (*Vauban told Louis XIV*); John P. Ludwikosky et al., "735th Tank Battalion in the Reduction of Metz," May 1950, AS, Ft. K, NARA RG 337, 6–7 (*forty-three forts*); Rickard, *Patton at Bay*, 123 (*modern works faced west*); Bradley, *A Soldier's Story*, 427 ("*blood the new divisions*"); Bradley Commentaries, CBH, MHI, box 42 ("*Leave it alone*"); OH, ONB, Dec. 1974–Oct. 1975, Charles Hanson, MHI, VI, 47 ("*too many casualties*"); PP, 566 ("*more daring*").

343 *Daring had thus far gained nought*: Doubler, *Closing with the Enemy*, 130 ("*most formidable*"); Meyer A. Edwards, Jr., et al., "Armor in the Attack of a Fortified Position," May 1950, AS, Ft. K, NARA RG 337, 88–91 ("*100 old men and boys*"); LC, 264–66 (*walls seven feet thick*); Wellard, *The Man in a Helmet*, 173–74 ("*medieval fortress*"); diary, Oct. 4, 1944, Hobart Gay papers, MHI, box 2, 522 ("*could not allow an attack*").

345 *It failed anyway*: Patton, *The Pattons*, 268 ("*or not come back*"); LC, 270–75 (*first substantial reverse*); Wellard, *The Man in a Helmet*, 174 (*bad news out of the papers*); Tapert, ed., *Lines of Battle*, 189–90 ("*Those low bastards*").

345 "*Had a bad case of short breath*": PP, 568–69.

345 "*tired, aged appearance*": Wellard, *The Man in a Helmet*, 185; PP, 568–70 (*pleaded for a postponement*).

345 *He woke at three A.M. on Wednesday, November 8*: PP, 571; LC, 317–19.

346 *Bradley phoned at 7:45*: Codman, *Drive*, 213 ("*almost sorry*" and "*relaxed and talkative*"); PP, 571.

346 *Doolittle's air fleets on Thursday*: Robert W. Ackerman, "The Employment of Strategic Bombers in a Tactical Role," 1954, AFHRA, study no. 88, 86–88; "The Effectiveness of Third Phase Tactical Air Operations in the European Theater," AAF Evaluation Board, Aug. 1945, 4, 162–65; LC, 425.

346 *The infantry soldiered on, resupplied*: AAR, 95th ID, Nov. 1944, AGF OR, CARL, N-6741; Raines, *Eyes of* Artillery, 227; AAR, 1st Bn, 358th Inf, Nov. 1944, http://www.worldhistorycompass.com/peragimus/358journal.html (*scampered across the roof*); Colby, *War from the Ground Up*, 308 ("*This fort is ours*"); Braim, *The Will to Win*, 108–11.

346 *Almost half a mile wide, the Moselle*: Rickard, *Patton at Bay*, 177–79; Nickell, *Red Devil*, 91 ("*The air seemed filled*").

347 "*Groans, suffering, and pain*": Knight, *Would You Remember This?*, 128–29.

347 "*bolts, washers, [and] bushings*": Cowdrey, *Fighting for Life*, 262–63.

347 "*getting up where the dead were still warm*": PP, 573–74.

347 *On November 14, nearly a week*: LC, 408–9, 417 ("Halb-soldaten"); Codman, *Drive*, 213–14 ("*very jolly*").

347 "*If we win now*": PP, 575.

347 *Hitler had twice rebuffed Rundstedt's suggestion*: LC, 418–32.

348 *At 10:30 A.M. on November 19*: Rickard, *Patton at Bay*, 193; LC, 447.

348 *Patton drove into Metz*: Farago, *Patton: Ordeal and Triumph*, 643; PP, 581 ("*I will be hard to live with*"), 577–78 ("*When I am dealing with vipers*"); Wellard, *The Man in a Helmet*, 181–82 (*personally interrogated*).

348 *An honor guard played*: diary, Nov. 23, 1944, Hobart Gay papers, MHI, box 2, 580; Mansoor, *The GI Offensive in Europe*, 206 ("*one of the epic river crossings*"); Nickell, *Red Devil*, 111 (*French soldiers*).

348 *Little mention was made of the outlying forts*: John P. Ludwikosky et al., "735th Tank Battalion in the Reduction of Metz," May 1950, AS, Ft. K, NARA RG 337, 54–55 (*French white phosphorus*); LC, 448–49.

349 "*Patton's bloodiest and least successful campaign*": D'Este, *Patton: A Genius for War*, 666–69; "Mobility, Unused: Study Based on the Lorraine Campaign," Oct. 1952, OCMH WWII Europe Interviews, MHI, 5–7 (*forfeited the single greatest advantage*).

349 "*this nasty country where it rains*": PP, 588–89.

349 "*Chaplain, how much praying*": James H. O'Neill, "The True Story of the Patton Prayer," n.d., chap. 25, PIR, MHI; PP, 591 ("*certainly rained less*").

To the Land of Doom

350 *Far above the killing fields*: AAFinWWII, 280; Miller, *Masters of the Air*, 278 ("*murder business*"); Westermann, *Flak*, 1 (*well over one million tons*); DOB, 495–97.

350 *Terrible aircraft losses in the first three months*: Jean H. Dubuque and Robert F. Gleckner, "The Development of the Heavy Bomber, 1918–1944," 1951, AFHRA, historical study

no. 6, 114–20 (*eight hundred U.S. heavies shot down*); Bernard Boyland, "Development of the Long-Range Escort Fighter," 1955, AFHRA, historical study no. 136, 242–45, 147–61; Kennedy, "History from the Middle: The Case of the Second World War," *JMH* (Jan. 2010): 35+; *AAFinWWII*, 287–88, 303 (*another nine hundred bombers went down*); Hastings, *Armageddon*, 301 (*Luftwaffe now was in a death spiral*), 310 ("*Each time I close the canopy*"); Muller, "Losing Air Superiority: A Case Study from the Second World War," *Air & Space Power Journal* (winter 2003): 55+; Ehlers, *Targeting the Reich*, 319 (*less than thirty flying hours*).

350 *Of necessity, antiaircraft flak*: Westermann, *Flak*, 278, 295 (*1.2 million Germans*); Friedrich, *The Fire*, 40 (*any plane within two hundred meters*); Davis, *Bombing the European Axis Powers*, 594 (*sixteen thousand 88mm shells*); Ferguson, *All's Fair*, 162 ("*evil, hypnotic fascination*"); Davis, *Carl A. Spaatz and the Air War in Europe*, 439 (*Heavier German guns*).

350 *British bombers, flying mostly at night*: Sebald, *On the Natural History of Destruction*, 21 ("*wall of light*"); Friedrich, *The Fire*, 42 ("*moving vertex*"); "An Evaluation of German Capabilities in 1945," USSAFE, Jan. 19, 1945, Frederick L. Anderson papers, HIA, box 80, folder 7 (*electronic jammers*); "Signal Service in ETOUSA," n.d., NARA RG 498, ETO HD, admin file #299, 24 (*effective jamming meant that 25 percent*).

351 "*Six miles from earth*": Randall Jarrell, "The Death of the Ball Turret Gunner," in Stallworthy, ed., *The Oxford Book of War Poetry*, 277.

351 *Air supremacy provided an invaluable advantage*: Millett and Murray, *Military Effectiveness*, vol. 3, *The Second World War*, 64 (*eighty thousand lives*); Crane, *Bombs, Cities & Civilians*, 51 (*battle casualty rates for every 1,000 bomber crewmen*); Linderman, *The World Within War*, 39 (*barely one in four*); "Study of AGF Battle Casualties," HQ, AGF G-3, Sept. 25, 1946, NARA RG 337, E 16A, admin div subject file, box 48, 4; Cowdrey, *Fighting for Life*, 233, 237. Some crews permitted to go home after fulfilling the lower quota were ordered back to Europe when the number increased (Davis, *Carl A. Spaatz and the Air War in Europe*, 439, 446).

351 *Perhaps less lethal, but hardly less stressful*: Tripp, *The Eighth Passenger*, 4–5; Davis, *Bombing the European Axis Powers*, 583–88 (*two of every five fliers did not live*).

351 *The simplest missions could be fatal*: memo, "Bomber Crash at Freckleton," Office of the Chaplain, USSAFE, Aug. 29, 1944, Carl A. Spaatz papers, LOC MS Div, diary, box 18; Russell Brown and Nick Wotherspoon, "The Freckleton Disaster," 2007, http://web.uk online.col.uk/lait/site/B-24%2042-50291.htm; "Freckleton Air Disaster of 1944," BBC News, Aug. 7, 2009, http://news.bbc.co.uk/local/lancashire/hi/people_and_places/history /newsid_8189000/8189386.stm ; "Plane Kills 35 Infants in School," *Daily Telegraph*, Aug. 24, 1944, 3; "Crashing Bomber Wipes Out Nearly All a Village's 4 to 6 Children," *Daily Express*, Aug. 24, 1944, 3.

352 *High though the war's cost in men and machines*: Arnold, *Global Missions*, 530 (*cut by over 70 percent*); corr, H. H. Arnold to C. A. Spaatz, Aug. 14, 1944, Carl A. Spaatz papers, LOC MS Div, personal diaries, box 15 ("*incipient weaknesses*"); *AAFinWWII*, 306 (*rest-and-recuperation program*); corr, 319th Bombardment Group, 438th Bombardment Squadron, n.d., NARA RG 492, MTOUSA, office of the surgeon, 1944, 290/54/33/2 ("*he spills food at the table*"); Brendan Gill, "Young Man Behind Plexiglass," *New Yorker*, Aug. 12, 1944, in *Reporting World War II*, vol. 2, 474–84 ("*God, you gotta*").

352 *In the airman's world, those afflicted*: Crane, *Bombs, Cities & Civilians*, 54 ("*clanks*"); Tripp, *The Eighth Passenger*, 70, 34, 197 ("*dead men flying*"); Stiles, *Serenade to the Big Bird*, 159 ("*giving birth*"); Andrus et al., eds., *Advances in Military Medicine*, vol. 2, 502–3; Jean H. Dubuque and Robert F. Gleckner, "The Development of the Heavy Bomber, 1918–1944," 1951, AFHRA, historical study no. 6, 111–13; Fisher, *Legacy of Heroes*, 16 (*tattooed them red*).

352 *a B-17 pilot sat in the five-foot cube*: Stiles, *Serenade to the Big Bird*, 133 ("*oxygen mask*" and "*dead things*"); Miller, *Masters of the Air*, 316 ("*Land of Doom*"); Crane, *Bombs, Cities & Civilians*, 54 ("*I would not grieve*").

353 *How best to destroy the Land of Doom*: "Target Priorities of the Eighth Air Force," May 15, 1945, Carl A. Spaatz papers, LOC MS Div, box 326, folder VIII A.F., 20 (*"progressive destruction"*); Earle, "Selection of Strategic Bombing Targets," lecture, Apr. 23, 1946, NARA RG 334, E 315, ANSCOL, box 235, 4–12 (*"instructive hints"*).

353 *But Germany did have an Achilles heel*: Overy, *Why the Allies Won*, 228–31 (*whereas the Axis share was 3 percent*); "German Petroleum Situation," OSS, R&A no. 2340, July 13, 1944, NARA RG 334, E 315, ANSCOL, box 919, 3 (*Soviet oil fields* and *"rapid and drastic effects"*); Rostow, *Concept and Controversy*, 45–47 (*wood-burning engines*); Hinsley et al., *British Intelligence in the Second World War*, vol. 3, part 2, 57–58 (*British intelligence by late May*); Hinsley, 580 (*"Germany's problem"*).

353 *No one believed that more*: Carver, ed., *The War Lords*, 568–69 (*Taciturn and unpretentious*); Middleton, "Boss of the Heavyweights," *Saturday Evening Post* (May 20, 1944), 18+ (*fishing and cribbage*); James, *A Time for Giants*, 98–100 (*aviation pioneer*); MMB, 518; "The Man Who Paved the Way," *Time* (June 12, 1944): 23+ (*"finest poker table"*); Davis, *Carl A. Spaatz and the Air War in Europe*, 552 (*inside straight*); *Three Years*, 629 (*played with a kitten*); Miller, *Masters of the Air*, 290 (*mid-May attack by nine hundred bombers*).

354 *No sooner had* OVERLORD *forces come ashore*: "Target Priorities of the Eighth Air Force," May 15, 1945, Carl A. Spaatz papers, LOC MS Div, box 326, folder VIII A.F., 22; Hinsley et al., *British Intelligence in the Second World War*, vol. 3, part 2, 58.

354 *That estimate was too rosy*: TSC, 308; *AAFinWWII* (*only three were at full production*).

354 *Not everyone subscribed to the oil strategy*: VW, vol. 2, 150–51 (*But Bomber Command resisted the edict*); Germany VII, 367 (*Lübeck and Rostock*); Germany IX, 385 (*firestorm that incinerated Hamburg*); Friedrich, *The Fire*, 9 (*"fire-raising"*), 16–17 (*eighty million incendiary sticks*), 167 (*"the atmosphere of another planet"*).

355 *Air Chief Marshal Arthur T. Harris, the Bomber Command chief*: Biddle, *Rhetoric and Reality in Air Warfare*, 229–32 (*"between 40 percent and 50 percent"*); Davies, *No Simple Victory*, 69 (*"like pulling teeth"*); Germany IX, 387 (*lime pits*).

355 *"no grounds for supposing"*: Hinsley, 582–83.

355 *"internal collapse certainly will not be brought about"*: Hinsley et al., *British Intelligence in the Second World War*, vol. 3, part 2, 304.

355 *Harris believed otherwise*: Tripp, *The Eighth Passenger*, 18; Hastings, *Armageddon*, 304–5 (*"a certain coarseness"*); Grayling, *Among the Dead Cities*, 192 (*"tiger with no mercy"*); Zuckerman, *From Apes to Warlords*, 218; Hastings, *Bomber Command*, 278–79 (*ulcers*), 282–83 (*"I'm sick of these raids"*); Probert, *Bomber Harris*, 154–58 (*black Bentley*).

355 *"He had a tendency to confuse advice"*: Webster and Frankland, *The Strategic Air Offensive Against Germany*, vol. 3, part 5, 80.

355 *Harris believed that bombers*: Biddle, *Rhetoric and Reality in Air Warfare*, 249 (*"If the Germans were asked"*); Davis, *Bombing the European Axis Powers*, 566 (*more than half of Bomber Command's payloads*); Hastings, *Bomber Command*, 282–84 (*The Hole*), 386–87 (*"If I knew you"*); Webster and Frankland, *The Strategic Air Offensive Against Germany*, vol. 3, 44 (*"in order to destroy anything"*), 82 (*"virtually destroyed"*); Probert, *Bomber Harris*, 309 (*"city programme"*).

356 *Harris's resolve to crack the enemy's will*: Probert, *Bomber Harris*, 336 (*"proved to be totally unsound"*); Miller, *Masters of the Air*, 473 (*"bombing seriously depressed"*); Germany IX, 458 (*two thousand Allied aircraft*); Randall Jarrell, "Losses," http://www.poemhunter.com/poem/losses/.

356 *While British Bomber Command believed in leveling*: Earle, "Selection of Strategic Bombing Targets," lecture, Apr. 23, 1946, NARA RG 334, E 315, ANSCOL, box 235, 18; Hugh Odishaw, "Radar Bombing in the Eighth Air Force," 1946, Carl A. Spaatz papers, LOC MS Div, box 80, 88, 93, 94–97 (*as few as one out of ten bombs*); Davis, *Carl A. Spaatz and the Air War in Europe*, 504 (*one sortie of seven*); Crane, *Bombs, Cities & Civilians*, 63–67 (*"not a literal sense"*); Biddle, *Rhetoric and Reality in Air Warfare*, 243–45,

258 (*frequent diversions*), 280 (*Such attacks on transportation targets*); Schaffer, "American Military Ethics in World War II: The Bombing of German Civilians," *Journal of American History* (Sept. 1980): 318+ ("*The way to stop the killing*"); Davis, *Bombing the European Axis Powers*, 574 (*20 percent of its payloads*).

357 *The Americans were no less intent*: Miller, *Masters of the Air*, 455; Kleber and Birdsell, *The Chemical Warfare Service*, 622 (*M-76 Block Burner*), 614 ("*as much death and destruction*").

357 *Air Chief Marshal Harris never believed*: Biddle, *Rhetoric and Reality in Air Warfare*, 252 ("*I am not only not a convert*"); Davis, *Bombing the European Axis Powers*, 569 (*oil targets in August and September*), 570 (*flew more than twice as many missions as Eighth Air Force*); Ehlers, *Targeting the Reich*, 287–88 (*British attacked to greater effect*); AAFinW-WII, 795 (*faulty fuzes*).

358 *The inclement fall weather gave Germany*: Hinsley et al., *British Intelligence in the Second World War*, vol. 3, part 2, 58; AAFinWWII, 283–87, 641 (*350,000 workers*); Westermann, *Flak*, 263–64; Doolittle, *I Could Never Be So Lucky Again*, 433 (*most heavily defended*).

358 *But the die had been cast*: Ehlers, *Targeting the Reich*, 266, 279 (*1,200 gallons of gasoline and oxen*); Willmott, *The Great Crusade*, 418–19 (*had dropped to a quarter of the May level*); Westermann, *Flak*, 270; Weigley, *The American Way of War*, 356–57; Miller, *Masters of the Air*, 312–14 (*synthetic rubber*).

358 *No industrial disparity*: Zetterling, *Normandy 1944*, 47; Weigley, *The American Way of War*, 356–57 (*decline to 12 percent*). Air commanders at the end of the war put German motor and aviation production at 2 percent of the earlier peak. "Joint Statement on Strategic Bombing by Air Ministry and U.S. Strategic Air Forces in Europe," Apr. 30, 1945, UK NA, AIR 2/5737, 4.

358 "*They are sowing the wind*": Daglish, *Operation Goodwood*, 96; Sebald, *On the Natural History of Destruction*, 3–4 (*131 German cities and towns*); Germany IX, 475–76 (*400,000 dead*).

358 *For those on the ground, the ordeal*: Hastings, *Armageddon*, 328; Germany IX, 390 ("*People alongside us*"); Friedrich, *The Fire*, 363 (*phosphorescent paint*).

359 *Three thousand municipal air raid shelters*: Foedrowitz, "Air Raid Shelters in Hannover," AB, no. 124 (2004): 2+; Germany IX, 391 ("*filth and disorder*"); Whiting, *The Home Front: Germany*, 144–45 (*opening their mouths*); Friedrich, *The Fire*, 356 ("*Children with scarlet fever*").

359 "*In Cologne life is no longer possible*": Friedrich, *The Fire*, 258, 45.

359 *The iron and steel center of Duisburg*: Webster and Frankland, *The Strategic Air Offensive Against Germany*, vol. 3, *Victory*, part 5, 66; Friedrich, *The Fire*, 201 ("*The night had done its work*"), 176–77, 294–95 (*carbon monoxide*); Germany IX, 461 (*Heilbronn*), 462 ("*a hideous sight*"); Whiting, *The Home Front: Germany*, 140 ("*Politeness Week*").

359 *Even from the Dutch coast*: Sebald, *On the Natural History of Destruction*, 22–23; Friedrich, *The Fire*, 382 (*210 Reichmarks*); Steinhoff et al., *Voices from the Third Reich*, 488 ("*blue faces*"); Wilhelm von Grolmann, "The Collapse of the German Reich as Seen from Leipzig," n.d., FMS, #B-478, MHI, 14–15 (*fortified with alcohol*); corr, "Annemarie," Dec. 29, 1944, Norman D. King papers, HIA, box 1 ("*Do you still remember*"). Friedrich Schiller's "The Song of the Bell" was published in 1798.

360 *On and on it went, high explosives*: Sebald, *On the Natural History of Destruction*, 22–29 (*Deranged mothers*); Friedrich, *The Fire*, 213 ("*The heat was so great*"), 447 ("*a man dragging a sack*"); Hastings, *Bomber Command*, 361–78.

360 "*The destruction will go on*": Lubrich, ed., *Travels in the Third Reich, 1933–1945*, 299.

"Providence Decrees and We Must Obey"

360 *After advancing nearly four hundred miles*: Yeide and Stout, *First to the Rhine*, 227; RR, 335 (*Nine weak enemy divisions*); "A History of the Headquarters Sixth Army Group," vol. 1, NARA RG 331, E 242A, box 157, from James Scott Wheeler (*nearly half a million men*); William K. Wyant, "Seventh Army History," n.d., NARA RG 319, RR background files, FRC 4 ("*first crossing of the Vosges*").

361 *Few could feel optimistic*: RR, 240–42, 245, 291–93 (*"mental and physical lethargy"*); Steidl, *Lost Battalions*, 121–22 (*"Mountains, woods, and rain"*).

361 *The season had been marked by straggling*: RR, 291–93 (*"inept"*); Taggart, ed., *History of the Third Infantry Division*, 257; Pete T. Heffner, Jr., "Lessons Learned in the Vosges Mountains Campaign," Dec. 12, 1944, NARA RG 407, ETO G-3 OR, box 3 (*bear traps*); Aron, *France Reborn*, 445 (*first snow*); *The Seventh United States Army in France and Germany*, vol. 1, 323 (*emergency shipments*); "The Invasion of Southern France, Operation DRAGOON," ETOUSA, G-4, 1944, NARA RG 498, ETO HD, admin file #314 (*Six hundred thousand men*); Gilland, "Logistical Support for the Combat Zone," lecture, 1948, Engineer Officers Advance Course, NARA RG 319, *LSA* background file, 2-3.7 CB 6 (*various miscalculations*); Coles and Weinberg, *Civil Affairs*, 752 (*20 percent of the cargo*); "Supply and Maintenance on the European Continent," NARA RG 407, E 427, USFET General Board study no. 130, 97-USF5-0.30, 50–54 (*shortages of food, ammunition, and fuel*).

361 *"Dear Family"*: Wandrey, *Bedpan Commando*, 141, 144, 190.

362 *The season also had been marked*: diary, Oct. 29, 1944, John E. Dahlquist papers, MHI, box 3; Steidl, *Lost Battalions*, 140–41.

362 *Killed the same week*: corr, Frank McCarthy to Julia Littell Patch, Oct. 22, 1944, GCM Lib, box 78, folder 50; Wyant, *Sandy Patch*, 149–51 (*"So long, son"*); obit, Alexander McC. Patch, Jr., *Assembly*, July 1946, 12 (*"cold and wet and hungry"*).

362 *"I've been dreading my first letter"*: corr, A. M. Patch to Julia, Nov. 6, 10, 14, 1944, Alexander M. Patch, Jr., papers, USMA Arch, box 1.

362 *"I cannot and must not allow"*: Wyant, *Sandy Patch*, 149–50.

362 *"the psychological effect on Patch"*: "Allied Biographies," USAREUR staff ride, May 2009, compiled by Layne Van Arsdale.

362 *"It is almost beyond comprehension"*: Steidl, *Lost Battalions*, 92–95.

362 *The town of Baccarat had been liberated*: Maule, *Out of the Sand*, 242; corr, John E. Dahlquist to Ruth, Nov. 2 and 5, 1944, Dahlquist papers, MHI (*"Rain has started again"*).

363 *Perpetual friction with the French*: De Lattre de Tassigny, *The History of the French First Army*, 167–71 (*"Our African soldiers"*), 179; OH, Albert Kenner, SHAEF chief medical officer, May 27, 1948, FCP, MHI (*susceptible to trench foot*); AAR, "Supply of Petroleum Products in Southern France," June 1945, CARL, N-15081, 3 (*wooden shoes*); Porch, *The Path to Victory*, 565, 591–92, 601–4 (blanchiment); Yeide and Stout, *First to the Rhine*, 179–83 (*137,000 maquis*).

363 *Base 901, the French supply organization*: Vigneras, *Rearming the French*, 187–88, 270 (*$6.67 per day*); "The Service Forces in Southern France," n.d., NARA RG 498, ETO HD, admin file 314, 13-14 (*crushed oats*).

363 *Franco-American frictions intensified*: Vigneras, *Rearming the French*, 325–26; Ross, 122, 205 (*"forced to withdraw"*); Seventh Army war diary, Oct. 1, 1944, MHI, 277–78 (*received less than a third*); De Lattre de Tassigny, *The History of the French First Army*, 162 (*"asphyxiation of the front line"*).

363 *U.S. quartermasters bitterly denied*: The U.S. quartermaster official history contends that the French First Army received twice as much clothing and equipment as Seventh Army (Ross, 205).

364 *countered that reckless French troops had ruined three thousand*: memo, "Housing Tentage Used by French in N. Africa," Nov. 17, 1944, NARA RG 331, E 34, SHAEF, box 60; diary, JLD, Oct. 8, 1944, MHI, original in YCHT (*"He goes into these tirades"*); Pogue, *George C. Marshall*, 476 (*"You celebrated"*).

364 *"It was our duty"*: De Lattre de Tassigny, *The History of the French First Army*, 162.

364 *Now Truscott was gone*: Truscott, *Command Missions*, 446; OH, Theodore J. Conway, 1978, Robert F. Ensslin, SOOHP, MHI, III-26 (*tears streamed*).

364 *With Truscott's departure, the dominant figure*: Markey, *Jake: The General from West York Avenue*, 16 (*grandson of a blacksmith*); Martin Weil, "Gen. Jacob Devers Dies; Leader in World War II," WP, Oct. 1979 (*classmate of Patton's* and *five hundred more*

senior colonels); Colley, *Decision at Strasbourg*, 10 (*"exceedingly earnest youth"*), 155 (*"I made a lot of mistakes today"*); Franklin L. Gurley, "The Relationship Between Jean de Lattre de Tassigny and Jacob L. Devers," March 26, 1994, Sorbonne, NARA RG 319, *RR* background files, FRC 4; MMB, 129–30.

366 *Capable and decisive, he had a knack*: "Battlebook," USAREUR Senior Leader Staff Ride, Alsace, May 2009; OH, Field Marshal Harold Alexander, Jan. 10-15, 1949, SM, CMH, Geographic Files (*"a boy who hasn't grown up"*); *DOB*, 506 (*detested each other*); diary, GSP, Feb. 29, 1944, LOC MS Div, box 3, folder 5 (*"very small caliber"*); notes, Daniel Noce, Dec. 4, 1944, NARA RG 319, *RR* background papers, FRC 5 (*"Devers talks too much"*); Bradley and Blair, *A General's Life*, 210 (*"overly garrulous"*).

366 *"Ike hates him"*: *PP*, 552.

366 *The supreme commander evidently nursed old resentments*: msg, DDE to JLD, Jan. 16, 1944, and JLD to DDE, Jan. 18, 1944, "Eyes Only, General Devers, Incoming," NARA RG 492, MTOUSA, SGS, box 135; Colley, *Decision at Strasbourg*, 86; diary, Kay Summersby, Oct. 20, 1944, DDE Lib, PP-pres, box 140 (*"talks a lot"*); corr, DDE to GCM, July 12, 1944, GCM Lib, box 67, folder 10 (*"I have nothing in the world"*). Eisenhower had advised Marshall that "Devers would be a good bet" to command an army group in southern France. DDE to GCM, July 15, 1944, NARA RG 165, E 422, WD, operations division, history unit, box 55.

366 *"Enthusiastic but often inaccurate"*: Chandler, 2466–69.

366 *Eisenhower sold Devers short*: OH, Ira C. Eaker, Aug. 1, 1975, Thomas E. Griess, JLD, YCHT, box 81 (*"ablest commander I saw"*); diary, JLD, Nov. 7 and 18, 1944, MHI (*"very difficult man to handle"* and *"inspirational leader"*); Franklin L. Gurley, "The Relationship Between Jean de Lattre de Tassigny and Jacob L. Devers," March 26, 1994, Sorbonne, NARA RG 319, *RR* background files, FRC 4 (*"never did learn to pronounce"*); OH, JLD, 1968, Thomas E. Griess, YCHT, box 110, 20 (*"gesture and the smile"*).

367 *"the same fine character as always"*: diary, JLD, Nov. 5, 1944, MHI.

367 *"the undercutting that goes on"*: corr, JLD to wife, Sept. 23, 1944, NARA RG 319, *RR* background papers, FRC 5; OH, Reuben Jenkins, Oct. 14, 1970, JLD, YCHT, box 94, 18–20 (*"lonely as the devil"*).

367 *SHAEF's orders called for 6th Army Group*: *RR*, 351–53.

367 *Devers had grander ambitions*: *The Seventh United States Army in France and Germany*, vol. 2, 402; *RR*, 352–53; OH, JLD, Aug. 1971, Thomas E. Griess, YCHT, 16. (*"Don't get stuck"*).

367 *De Lattre made the first move*: De Lattre de Tassigny, *The History of the French First Army*, 225–30; John W. Price, "Forcing the Belfort Gap," n.d., NARA RG 319, *RR* background files, FRC 5 (*Various deceptions*); *RR*, 414–18; author visit, Belfort, May 2009.

368 *By Thursday, French tanks were "decisive everywhere"*: De Lattre de Tassigny, *The History of the French First Army*, 233–36; *RR*, 410.

368 *Having forsaken a substantial wedge*: Friedrich-Wilhelm von Mellenthin, Army Group G chief of staff, ts, March 1946, FMS #A-999, MHI, 79; Seaman, "Reduction of the Colmar Pocket," *Military Review* (Oct. 1951): 37+ (*Confusion in the French ranks*); De Lattre de Tassigny, *The History of the French First Army*, 253–62 (*German* Feldpost *workers*); *RR*, 431 (*a spent force*).

368 *Hope for a decisive breakthrough*: Seventh Army war diary, Nov. 20, 1944, MHI, 393; Robb, *The Discovery of France*, 227 (*"one of the masterpieces of man"*); Bonn, *When the Odds Were Even*, 111–16 (*"ersatz morale"*).

369 *On November 19, the weight of metal*: OH, 79th ID, Saverne Gap, n.d., NARA RG 407, E 427-A, CI, folder 156; *RR*, 368–71 (*44th Division rambled for nine miles*); *The Seventh United States Army in France and Germany*, vol. 2, 411 (*broke through to Sarrebourg*); Aron, *France Reborn*, 440–41 (*French policemen pulled on uniforms*); diary, JLD, Nov. 20, 1944, MHI (*"as hard as I have ever seen it rain"*).

369 *Into the breach pried open*: Porch, *The Path to Victory*, 538 (*"We swear"*); Maule, *Out of the Sand*, 249 (*"Beat the devil"*).

369 *"The brave horses were galloping"*: "Capture of Strasbourg," French 2nd AD, Jan. 28, 1945, NARA RG 407, E 427-A, CI, folder #247.

370 Tout au contraire: De Gaulle, *The Complete War Memoirs of Charles de Gaulle*, 824 (*five columns*); Colley, *Decision at Strasbourg*, 123–24 (*"We went roaring"* and *"sent window-panes tinkling"*); *The Seventh United States Army in France and Germany*, vol. 2, 413–16 (*Sixteen strongholds*); Yeide and Stout, *First to the Rhine*, 243–44 (*tanks spilled into downtown Strasbourg*).

370 *As rain drummed off his kepi*: Maule, *Out of the Sand*, 252–54; "Capture of Strasbourg," French 2nd AD, Jan. 28, 1945, NARA RG 407, E 427-A, CI, folder #247; Susan Bernstein, "Goethe's Architectonic *Bildung* and Buildings in Classical Weimar," 2000, Johns Hopkins University Press, http://www2.winchester.ac.uk/edstudies/courses/level%20two%20sem%20two/114.5bernstein.html (*"tree of God"*); Porch, *The Path to Victory*, 606 (*"Now we can die"*).

370 *A captured German engineer was persuaded*: Charles V. von Lüttichau, "The Fall of Strasbourg and the Birth of the Colmar Pocket," n.d., NARA RG 319, OCMH, R-series, #129, 2–3, 13–14; *RR*, 380–81; AAR, XV Corps, Jan. 23, 1945, Wade H. Haislip papers, MHI, box 2; "Capture of Strasbourg," French 2nd AD, Jan. 28, 1945, NARA RG 407, E 427-A, CI, folder #247 (*"solid artillery argument"*).

371 *"Lots of dead civilians"*: diary, Nov. 25, 1944, Kingsley Andersson papers, HIA, box 1; "Capture of Strasbourg," French 2nd AD, Jan. 28, 1945, NARA RG 407, E 427-A, CI, folder #247 (*"One by one"*).

371 *Strasbourg's emancipation*: "Natzweiler-Struthof," USHMM, http://www.ushmm.org/wlc/en/article.php?ModuleId=10007260. British troops had overrun the Breendonk internment camp near Antwerp in September (http://www.ushmm.org/wlc/en/article.php?ModuleId=10005423).

371 *Built in 1941, Natzweiler had housed*: Turner and Jackson, *Destination Berchtesgaden*, 97 (*socially unfit*); Yurka N. Galitzine, "Investigation Report on the Life in a German Exter-mination Camp (KZ Natzweiler)," n.d., C. D. Jackson papers, DDE Lib, box 2 (*sweets and cakes* and *urn of ashes*); J. M. Barnes, Royal Army Medical Corps, "Report on a Third Visit to France," Feb. 1945, Boris T. Pash papers, HIA, box 2, folder 1; Evans, *The Third Reich at War*, 607 (*mustard gas*).

371 *The second discovery was no less portentous*: corr, J. R. Oppenheimer and Luis Alvarez to Robert Furman, June 5, 1944, Boris T. Pash papers, HIA, box 3, folder 2; memo, S. A. Goudsmit, "Strassburg [*sic*] Intelligence on German Nuclear Physics," Dec. 17, 1944, and "Progress Report #8—Strasbourg Operation, ALSOS Mission," Dec. 7, 1944, Boris T. Pash papers, HIA, box 2, folders 1 and 3; Pash, *The Alsos Mission*, 155–57; Groves, *Now It Can Be Told*, 212–23.

372 *"most complete, dependable and factual information"*: memo, L. R. Groves to Maj. Gen. Clayton Bissell, March 16, 1945, George Bryan Conrad papers, USMA Archives; memo, S. A. Goudsmit, "Strassburg [*sic*] Intelligence on German Nuclear Physics," Dec. 17, 1944, Boris T. Pash papers, HIA, box 2, folder 1 (*"two slide rules"*); "Alsos Mission History," n.d., and "Report by the Scientific Chief of the ALSOS Mission," n.d., Boris T. Pash papers, HIA, box 2, folder 8; Pash, *The Alsos Mission*, 159 (*"the Nazis had not progressed"*).

372 *Leclerc and his lieutenants bivouacked*: "Capture of Strasbourg," French 2nd AD, Jan. 28, 1945, NARA RG 407, E 427-A, CI, folder #247 (*"its pretentious design"*); Gray, *The Warriors*, 4–5 (*switched their storefront signage*); Aron, *France Reborn*, 437–38 (*deported to Germany*). The French refused to print 6th Army Group guarantees of the Geneva Conventions, forcing Seventh Army to put up its own posters to that effect (Seventh Army war diary, Dec. 6–10, 1944, MHI, 426–35).

372 *"There is no question that the French hate"*: Gray, *The Warriors*, 200.

372 *A ceremony near the cathedral*: "Capture of Strasbourg," French 2nd AD, Jan. 28, 1945, NARA RG 407, E 427-A, CI, folder #247; Franklin Louis Gurley, "Policy Versus Strategy: The Defense of Strasbourg in Dec. 1944," 1992, NARA RG 319, *RR* background files, FRC 5 (*"never give it back"*).

372 *For nearly three months Seventh Army*: Seventh Army war diary, Sept. 26, 1944, MHI, 266.

373 *Eight hundred outboard-motor operators*: "The Crossing of the Rhine," 1945, CEOH, box X-25, folder 2; Seventh Army war diary, Sept. 19, Nov. 7, and Nov. 18, 1944, MHI, 256, 356, 380; corr, Garrison H. Davidson to Hal C. Pattison, CMH, July 23, 1988, NARA RG 319, *RR* background files, FRC 4 (*SHAEF rejected a proposal*).

373 *Even if the bridge from Strasbourg to Kehl*: *The Seventh United States Army in France and Germany*, vol. 2, 419; OH, Reuben Jenkins, Oct. 14, 1970, Thomas E. Griess, JLD, YCHT, box 94, 29–30 (*Patrols found few defenders*); *RR*, 439; Colley, *Decision at Strasbourg*, 150; corr, Garrison H. Davidson, Apr. 21, 1953, CEOH, box X-25 (*On Thanksgiving night, Patch's engineers*).

373 *Eisenhower knew almost nothing*: diary, JLD, Nov. 24, 1944, MHI; Colley, *Decision at Strasbourg*, 135–36 ("*happy and boyish*" and "*impassive Alsatian faces*"); http://www2 .lib.virginia.edu/exhibits/lewis_clark/exploring/ch1-1.html (*the name "America"*); Steidl, *Lost Battalions*, 126 (*St.-Dié's textile mills*); Turner and Jackson, *Destination Berchtesgaden*, 92 (*grenades and dynamite*); Marshall, *A Ramble Through My War*, 168 ("*wanton destruction*").

373 *A final forty-mile drive*: Colley, *Decision at Strasbourg*, 135–36; *RR*, 439–40 (*Heritage Hotel*).

374 *The supreme commander wasted no time*: memo, ONB to G-3, 12th AG, Nov. 26, 1944, NARA RG 319, *RR* background files, FRC 5 (*Bradley agreed that the transfer*); *RR*, 439–40.

374 *"He's in the mud"*: Colley, *Decision at Strasbourg*, 136–38.

374 *New reports of a German counterattack*: *RR*, 382–86; Weigley, *Eisenhower's Lieutenants*, 407 (*only massed artillery*); corr, Robert R. Smith, CMH, to Thomas E. Griess, USMA, Nov. 28, 1978, NARA RG 319, *RR* background files, FRC 4 ("*helluva way to get to Berlin*").

374 *"Ike, I'm on the Haguenau"*: The river at Haguenau is in fact named the Moder, a tributary of the Rhine.

374 *"I've got everything in the woods"*: Colley, *Decision at Strasbourg*, 136–38; *RR*, 439–42; corr, Hal. C. Pattison, CMH, to Garrison H. Davidson, Aug. 1, 1968, NARA RG 319, *RR* background files, FRC 4 (*Patton's army should be shifted*).

374 *Devers grew shrill*: *RR*, 439–42, 575; Colley, *Decision at Strasbourg*, 136–38 (*likened it to Patton's effort in August 1943*); *DOB*, 162–64 (*a misbegotten analogy*).

374 *Eisenhower remained immovable*: corr, Robert R. Smith, CMH, to Thomas E. Griess, USMA, Nov. 28, 1978, NARA RG 319, *RR* background files, FRC 4; *Three Years*, 702–5 (*no "definitely decisive area"*); *RR*, 439–42 ("*mad as hell*").

375 *The trio of generals retired for a few hours' sleep*: Seventh Army war diary, MHI, 400–403; *LC*, 520–21 ("*offers the best chance*").

375 *"The decision not to cross the Rhine"*: diary, JLD, Nov. 24 and 26, 1944, MHI.

375 *Even the Army official history*: *RR*, 563 ("*difficult to understand*"), 445 ("'*strategy' of firepower and attrition*"); Mansoor, *The GI Offensive in Europe*, 207 (*neither a coherent strategic goal*); corr, Robert R. Smith, CMH, to Thomas E. Griess, USMA, Nov. 28, 1978, NARA RG 319, *RR* background files, FRC 4 ("*misusing 6th Army Group*"); Friedrich-Wilhelm von Mellenthin, Army Group G chief of staff, ts, March 1946, FMS #A-999, MHI, 100–112 (*gave the Germans a respite*).

375 *Surely the supreme commander's personal distaste*: corr, Thomas E. Griess, USMA, to Robert R. Smith, CMH, Dec. 19, 1978, NARA RG 319, *RR* background files, FRC 4; OH, Reuben Jenkins, Oct. 14, 1970, Thomas E. Griess, JLD, YCHT, box 94, 35–36 (*played favorites with Bradley*); *RR*, 439–40 ("*member of the same team*"); Colley, *Decision at Strasbourg*, 178, 154 ("*bring the war to a quicker end*"); diary, JLD, Dec. 19, 1944, MHI ("*The tragedy to my mind*").

376 *Yet Devers made errors of his own*: *RR*, 433, 437; Charles V. von Lüttichau, "The Fall of Strasbourg and the Birth of the Colmar Pocket, n.d., NARA RG 319, OCMH, R-series,

#129, 24–26 (*"out of the question"*); diary, JLD, Dec. 2, 1944, MHI (*"It is hoped that the French Army"*).

376 *"with the help of darkness and fog"*: De Lattre de Tassigny, *The History of the French First Army*, 291; memo, Reuben E. Jenkins to JLD, Feb. 24, 1947, Jenkins papers, MHI, box 1, 8 (*only a few thousand more troops*), 6 (*"confusion"*).

376 *Still more disheartening*: Clayton, *Three Marshals of France*, 60–61; Mitchell, *Hitler's Mountain*, 124 (*"I will not serve"*); Porch, *The Path to Victory*, 588 (*his antebellum name*); diary, JLD, Dec. 6, 1944, MHI (*"Having a great deal of trouble"*); Maule, *Out of the Sand*, 260–62 (*"the only failure in command"*); John Hixson and Benjamin Franklin Cooling, "Combined Operations in Peace and War," 1982, MHI, 190–92 (*Even when reinforced*); OH, Russell L. Vittrup, 1989, Henry E. Fitzgerald, 1989, SOOHP, MHI, 124 (*"consternation and ill-feeling"*).

376 *Seventh Army engineers trucked their storm boats*: Colley, *Decision at Strasbourg*, 144; Taggart, ed., *History of the Third Infantry Division*, 278 (*dropped the Kehl bridge*); Yeide and Stout, *First to the Rhine*, 254 (*keep the pocket victualed*); Peter T. Heffner, Jr., VI Corps, Dec. 29, 1944, G-3 OR, NARA RG 498, box 3 (*Loudspeaker broadcasts*).

377 *"SHAEF treats us as bastard children"*: corr, T. R. Bruskin to wife, Apr. 15, 1945, a.p.

CHAPTER 8: A WINTER SHADOW

"We Are All So Human That It Is Pitiful"

379 *Nine million Allied propaganda leaflets*: "The Psychological Warfare Division," 1945, CMH, 8-3.6 BA, 45–48; Robert H. Garey, "Leaflet Operations in the Western European Theater," SHAEF, July 1945, C. D. Jackson papers, DDE Lib, box 9, 1, 19, 25 (*one thousand tons*); Lerner, *Psychological Warfare Against Nazi Germany*, 239–40.

379 *In the early days of this "nickeling"*: "The Psychological Warfare Division," 1945, CMH, 8-3.6 BA, 47; Harris G. Warren, "Special Operations: AAF Aid to European Resistance Movements," 1947, AFHRA, historical study no. 121, 44–45 (*as far afield as Italy*); "Psychological Warfare in the ETO," n.d., USFET General Board study no. 131, NARA RG 407, E 427, 97-USF5-0.30, 32–33 (*T-1 Monroe Leaflet Bomb*); Robert H. Garey, "Leaflet Operations in the Western European Theater," SHAEF, July 1945, C. D. Jackson papers, DDE Lib, box 9, 25 (*A single B-24*). Invented by a bomb squadron armament officer, the munition technically was known as "Bomb, Propaganda, T-1."

379 *Psychological warfare teams studied*: TSC, 344; "Psychological Warfare in the ETO," n.d., USFET General Board study no. 131, NARA RG 407, E 427, 97-USF5-0.30, 8 (*"best fed Army"*), 43 (*"hog calling"*); "The Psychological Warfare Division," 1945, CMH, 8-3.6 BA, 39–42 (Voice of SHAEF). Radio Luxembourg often broadcast damage reports as if they came from a clandestine German station in the Rhineland (AAR, 12th AG, vol. 14, NARA RG 331, E-200A, SHAEF, box 268, 187–91).

379 *Millions of time-fuze incendiaries*: "The Psychological Warfare Division," 1945, CMH, 8-3.6 BA, 53; OSS, "Simple Sabotage Field Manual," Field Manual No. 3, Jan. 1944, 5, 11–14 (*"Try to commit acts"*).

380 *Still Germany fought on*: Murphy, *Diplomat Among Warriors*, 240 (*unconditional surrender*); memo, Wallace Carroll, Office of War Information, Mar. 25, 1944, Wallace Carroll papers, LOC MS Div, box 1, folder: day files Mar. 1944, 1 (*"nothing to lose"*); Matloff, *Strategic Planning for Coalition Warfare, 1943–1944*, 529 (*"phrase coined at a conference"*), 431 (*"I want at all costs"*); TSC, 354–55 (*"a lawless conspiracy"*).

380 *Eventual Allied victory*: McCreedy, "Planning the Peace: Operation Eclipse and the Occupation of Germany," *JMH* (July 2001): 713+ (*seventy-two studies*); Pogue, *George C. Marshall: Organizer of Victory*, 466 (*four in five Americans supported*); Ziemke, *The U.S. Army in the Occupation of Germany, 1944–1946*, 86–90 (*War Department's top linguist*).

380 *The victorious Red Army*: Mosely, "The Occupation of Germany," *Foreign Affairs* (July 1950): 580+.

381 *"The defeat of Germany will leave Russia"*: Matloff, *Strategic Planning for Coalition Warfare, 1943–1944*, 523–24.

381 *Winston Churchill also perceived*: Kimball, *Forged in War*, 286; Reynolds, *In Command of History*, 460–63 (*"naughty document"*). One prominent historian believes Stalin's confirmational tick mark was intended for Romania only, and that in fact he wanted a 90 percent share in Bulgaria rather than Churchill's proposed 75 percent (Plokhy, *Yalta*, 147).

381 *Although the "percentages agreement"*: Hastings, *Winston's War*, 415–19; Jenkins, *Churchill: A Biography*, 759–61.

381 *That fall, a separate controversy*: Kimball, *Forged in War*, 275 (*"two Jeffersonian gentlemen farmers"*), 276 (*"unnatural, unchristian"*); Dallek, *Franklin D. Roosevelt and American Foreign Policy, 1932–1945*, 474 (*"re-creation of an agricultural state"*). Churchill's change of heart may also have been encouraged by a U.S. agreement to continue providing American aid to Britain after the war (Stoler, *Allies in War*, 170).

382 *"They brought it on themselves"*: Moran, *Churchill: Taken from the Diaries of Lord Moran*, 190–91.

382 *Others in the Anglo-American braintrust*: ibid., 193 (*"flew into a rage"*); Grayling, *Among the Dead Cities*, 161 (*"blind vengeance"*); Stimson and Bundy, *On Active Service in Peace and War*, 569–71 (*"general evils"*); Weinberg, *A World at Arms*, 796–97; Pogue, *George C. Marshall: Organizer of Victory*, 467 (*proposal to summarily shoot*).

382 *"The papers have taken it up"*: Stimson and Bundy, *On Active Service in Peace and War*, 580–81; Ziemke, *The U.S. Army in the Occupation of Germany*, 101–05.

382 *"a ruined no-man's land"*: Collier, *The Freedom Road, 1944–45*, 189.

382 *"A policy which condones or favors chaos"*: VW, vol. 2, 147.

382 *"Henry Morgenthau pulled a boner"*: Stimson and Bundy, *On Active Service in Peace and War*, 580–81; TSC, 342 (*"inspired by the Jews"*).

382 *This contretemps cooled Roosevelt's enthusiasm*: Murphy, *Diplomat Among Warriors*, 228 (*"I dislike making detailed plans"*); TSC, 342–43 (*would not be enslaved*), 351; Mosely, "Dismemberment of Germany," *Foreign Affairs* (Apr. 1950): 487+ (*seven disparate states*); Mosely, "The Occupation of Germany," *Foreign Affairs* (July 1950): 580+ (*three occupation zones*); ALH, I-178–79; Weinberg, *A World at Arms*, 792–95.

382 *No formal ratification of this plan*: Ambrose, *Eisenhower: Soldier, General of the Army, President-Elect, 1890–1952*, vol. 1, 280 (*single Allied commander*); Chandler, 1873 (*"eastern portion of Germany"*); Murphy, *Diplomat Among Warriors*, 231–32 (*"not having any faith"*).

383 *"Something 'big' will come out of this war"*: Brower, ed., *World War II in Europe: The Final Year*, 22.

383 *Montgomery's promise to Eisenhower*: Bryant, *Triumph in the West*, 252 (*"He has never commanded anything"*), 254 (*"You have always told me"*); Hastings, *Armageddon*, 153 (*"feeling of optimism"*); Crosswell, *Beetle*, 778 (*"Eisenhower is quite useless"*).

383 *On Tuesday afternoon, November 28*: VW, vol. 2 167–68; Bryant, *Triumph in the West*, 258–59 (*"We talked for three hours"*).

384 *"Ike does not agree"*: Howarth, ed., *Monty at Close Quarters*, 16.

384 *"He thinks Bradley has failed him"*: Bryant, *Triumph in the West*, 258–59.

384 *"We have achieved none of this"*: msg, BLM to DDE, Nov. 30, 1944, DDE Lib, PP-pres, box 83; Chandler, 2325.

384 *On Friday, December 1*: Sylvan, 197 (*hives*); Bradley and Blair, *A General's Life*, 346 (*"as angry as I had ever seen him"*).

385 *"There are certain things in your letter"*: Chandler, 2323–25.

386 *"such canalized egotism"*: Hart-Davis, ed., *King's Counsellor*, 265, 311 (*"mental unstability"*).

386 *"He had no competence in the fine art"*: Ambrose, *The Supreme Commander*, 512.

386 *A British official who watched Montgomery*: Hamilton, *Monty: Final Years of the Field-Marshal, 1944–1976*, 117 (*"like a little bird"*); Danchev, 620 (*"goes on harping"*).

386 *But others in the highest British circles*: Churchill, *Triumph and Tragedy*, 267 ("*We have of course sustained*"); *VW*, vol. 2, 167 ("*We have definitely failed*"); *TSC*, 315 ("*a decisive break*"); Love and Major, eds., *The Year of D-Day*, xliii ("*no prospect of Ike*").

386 *Some of Montgomery's partisans were more savage*: Danchev, 625, 628.

386 *The fairways at Reims*: Sixsmith, *Eisenhower as Military Commander*, 178 (*never swung a golf club*); Danchev, 627–30 ("*Eisenhower completely fails*").

387 *At Montgomery's request, another high-command conclave*: Baedeker, *Belgium and Holland*, 239–40; http://en.wikipedia.org/wiki/Maastricht; www.fortified-places.com/sieges /maastricht1673.html.

387 *Eisenhower and Tedder spent Wednesday*: Bradley and Blair, *A General's Life*, 347; Chandler, vol. 5, chronology, 175; Signal Corps footage, http://www.criticalpast.com/video /65675070150_General-Eisenhower_Omar-Bradley_Bernard-Montgomery_World-War -II (*smartly tailored*); "Extracts from report of Maj. Gen. K. W. D. Strong," Nov. 29, 1944, BLM corr, DDE Lib, PP-pres, box 83 (*twenty German divisions a month*); Hastings, *Armageddon*, 140 (*less than ten miles*), 148.

387 "*The master plan*": "Notes of Meeting at Maastricht on 7.12.1944," Tedder notes, Sidney H. Negrotto papers, MHI, box 4; copy in Harold R. Bull papers, DDE Lib, box 2. *VW*, vol. 2, 167–68.

388 *Round and round they went*: Bradley and Blair, *A General's Life*, 347 ("*tedious affair*"); Ambrose, *The Supreme Commander*, 610.

388 "*The meeting was affable*": corr, D/SAC to CAS, Nov. 7, 1944, NARA RG 319, SC background files, 2-3.7 CB 8 ("*Another balls up*").

388 "*I personally regard the whole thing*": Bryant, *Triumph in the West*, 264–65; Hamilton, *Monty: Final Years of the Field-Marshal, 1944–1976*, 163.

389 *Bradley a few days later wrote*: Hamilton, *Monty: Final Years of the Field-Marshal, 1944–1976*, 163 ("*He refused to admit*"); D'Este, *Eisenhower: A Soldier's Life*, 635 ("*an indication that I had failed*"); corr, Everett S. Hughes to wife, Dec. 1, 1944, Hughes papers, LOC MS Div, box II:3, folder 4 ("*We are all so human*").

Staking Everything on One Card

389 *An iron sky roofed the gray-green Taunus Hills*: Alfred Jodl, ETHINT 51, July 31, 1945, MHI, 24.

389 *To the unschooled eye*: Kappes, "Hitler's Ultra-Secret Adlerhorst," 2003, http://www .militaryhistoryonline.com/wwii/articles/adlerhorst.aspx (*Interior furnishings*); White, *Conquerors' Road*, 54–57 (*heavy metal doors and peepholes*); Raiber, "The Führerhaupt-quartiere," *AB*, no. 19 (1977): 1+ (*Artificial trees*); "Kransberg-die Perle in Taunus," www.kransberg.com (*centuries of neglect*).

390 *Hitler shuffled into his private chalet*: Bullock, *Hitler: A Study in Tyranny*, 762; Percy Ernst Schramm, "The Preparations for the German Offensive in the Ardennes," in Parker, ed., *The Battle of the Bulge: The German View*, 121–22 (*vocal cords*); Günther Blumentritt, "Battle of the Bulge," part 1, n.d., PIR, MHI, 6 ("*He seemed near collapse*"); Overy, *Why the Allies Won*, 274–75 ("*will-o'-the-wisp*"); *Germany VII*, 680 ("*everything on one card*").

390 *Even a delusional megalomaniac*: Greenfield, ed., *Command Decisions*, 345.

390 *German war production*: *Ardennes*, 4–5 (*118,000 military trucks*), 8 (*holidays abolished*); Charles V. P. von Lüttichau, "The Ardennes Offensive: Germany's Situation in the Fall of 1944," OCMH, 1953, part II, NARA RG 319, R-series, #25, box 6, 44, 52, 59, 62, 67, 69 [copy also in CMH, 2-3.7]; Tooze, *The Wages of Destruction*, 595 ("*Heroes of National Socialist Labor*"), 603, 629 (*vitamins*); Hitchcock, *The Bitter Road to Freedom*, 249 (*Seven million prisoners-of-war*).

391 *To shore up a military now losing*: MEB, "Overall View of Germany's Economic, Political, and Military Situation at the Beginning of 1945," May 1950, NARA RG 319, R-series #28, 12; Greenfield, ed., *Command Decisions*, 347; *Ardennes*, 8 ("*rear-area swine*"), 15; Steinhoff et al., *Voices from the Third Reich*, 461 ("*out of sheer terror*"); *TT*, 43; Megargee,

Inside Hitler's High Command, 221 (Volkssturm); Evans, *The Third Reich at War*, 676 ("*Closed because of the call-up*"); Willmott, *The Great Crusade*, 416 (*robbed German industry*); Rush, *Hell in Hürtgen Forest*, 306 ("*bow-and-arrow infantry*").

391 *Secret weapons always beguilded*: Rudolf Lusar, "The German Weapons and Secret Weapons of World War II and Their Subsequent Development," 1956, CMH, 16–17; *Germany VII*, 339 ("*as if an angel*"), 341–48, 353–54; *VW*, vol. 2, 144 (*oddly ineffective*); Muller, "Losing Air Superiority: A Case Study from the Second World War," *Air & Space Power Journal* (winter 2003): 55+.

391 *No less innovative were new "electro" U-boats*: Tooze, *The Wages of Destruction*, 613–16; Spector, *At War at Sea*, 253; Brower, ed., *World War II in Europe: The Final Year*, 128; Hinsley, 600–603; Blair, *Hitler's U-Boat War*, vol. 2, *The Hunted, 1942–1945*, 627, 657–59.

392 *Well into 1945, German submarines continued*: U-boats during the war were credited with sinking three thousand Allied and neutral vessels (Roskill, *White Ensign*, 413–15, 422–23). Clay Blair calculates that in 1944–45, a total of 188 ships were sunk by U-boats (*Hitler's U-Boat War*, vol. 2, *The Hunted, 1943–1945*, 820).

392 *But scarcely any vessels would be sunk by the new U-boats*: Blair, *Hitler's U-Boat War*, vol. 2, *The Hunted, 1942–1945*, 659, 820; Weinberg, *A World at Arms*, 771–72.

392 *Dusk enfolded the Taunus Hills*: Günther Blumentritt, "Battle of the Bulge," part 1, n.d., PIR, MHI, 8–10 (*Many believed they had been summoned*); Spayd, *Bayerlein*, 179–80 (*each man surrender his sidearm*); Kappes, "Hitler's Ultra-Secret Adlerhorst," 2003, http://www.militaryhistoryonline.com/wwii/articles/adlerhorst.aspx.

392 *A double row of armed SS guards*: Spayd, *Bayerlein*, 179–80; *TT*, 47 ("*handkerchief*").

392 *Ten minutes later Hitler hobbled in*: Günther Blumentritt, "Battle of the Bulge," part 1, n.d., PIR, MHI, 1; OH, Hasso von Manteuffel, Oct. 12, 1966, John S. D. Eisenhower, CBM, MHI, box 6, 15–17; Spayd, *Bayerlein*, 180 (*Nick-Esel*); Hasso von Manteuffel, "The 5. Pz Army and the Offensive in the Ardennes," Apr. 1946, FMS, #B-151, MHI, 78–79 ("*a broken man*"); Parker, ed., *The Battle of the Bulge: The German View*, 121–22 ("*stared vacantly*").

393 *Then he spoke*: Parker, ed., *The Battle of the Bulge: The German View*, 4.

393 *"Never in history"*: Wilmot, *The Struggle for Europe*, 578.

393 *As the Allies approached each other*: GS VI, 65; Jacobsen and Rohwer, eds., *Decisive Battles of World War II: The German View*, 401–2 (*Canada*).

393 *"Rome would not be thinkable"*: Parker, ed., *The Battle of the Bulge: The German View*, 4–8 ("*most daring*"); Megargee, *Inside Hitler's High Command*, 218.

393 *Toward that end he had a plan*: The name was changed shortly before the attack for security reasons. HERBSTNEBEL had been the army group code-name (*TT*, 36–38).

393 *It had come to him as in a fever dream*: Alfred Jodl, ETHINT 50, July 26, 1945, K. W. Hechler, CBM, MHI, box 12; Kershaw, *Hitler, 1936–45: Nemesis*, 732; Ardennes, 1–10, 13; Charles V. von Lüttichau, "The Ardennes Offensive: Planning and Preparations," Aug. 1953, OCMH, NARA RG 319, R-series #12, 11–13, 31–33 ("*Antwerp*"); MEB, "The Idea for the German Ardennes Offensive in 1944," May 1952, OCMH, NARA RG 319, R-series #9, 22–23 ("*sealed in the West*").

394 *The naysayers promptly said nay*: MEB, "The Idea for the German Ardennes Offensive in 1944," May 1952, OCMH, NARA RG 319, R-series #9, 109 ("*great surprise*"); Parker, ed., *Hitler's Ardennes Offensive*, 248 ("*no offensive*"); Charles V. von Lüttichau, "The Ardennes Offensive: Germany's Situation in the Fall of 1944," 1953, OCMH, CMH, 2-3.7, 39; *Ardennes*, 72 (*invasion of the Soviet Union*); British interrogation report, Gerd von Rundstedt, July 9, 1945, NARA RG 407, E 427, ML #2126, box 24231 ("*much too weak*"); Jacobsen and Rohwer, eds., *Decisive Battles of World War II: The German View*, 396–97.

394 *"The soldier can do nothing"*: Günther Blumentritt, "Battle of the Bulge," part 1, n.d., PIR, MHI, 6; Blumentritt, *Von Rundstedt*, 268–70 ("*I am a better judge*").

394 *Even Model, who claimed to love*: Lewin, *Montgomery as Military Commander*, 312

("*moldy*"); Westphal, *The German Army in the West*, 180–81 ("*small solution*"); "The Ardennes Offensive," British monograph, Aug. 1, 1945, CMH, Geog Belgium, 370.2, 7–8; OH, Hasso von Manteuffel, Oct. 12, 1966, John S. D. Eisenhower, CBM, MHI, box 6, 15–16; Hasso von Manteuffel, "The 5. Pz Army and the Offensive in the Ardennes," Apr. 1946, FMS, #B-151, MHI, 78-38-45, 71; Fritz Krämer, ETHINT 21, Aug. 14–15, 1945, MHI, 3 (*Wehrmacht soldiers would fight*).

395 *The Führer was unmoved*: Warlimont, *Inside Hitler's Headquarters*, 482–85; *Ardennes*, 34–35 (*promised thirty-eight divisions*), 30–32 (*virtually unchanged*); Hasso von Manteuffel, "The 5. Pz Army and the Offensive in the Ardennes," Apr. 1946, FMS, #B-151, MHI, 73 (*two thousand planes*); *GS* VI, 66–67 ("*Not to Be Altered*").

395 *And thus was the plan fixed*: *Ardennes*, 71–72; *Germany VII*, 681; Cirillo, "Ardennes-Alsace," 3, 10.

395 *With the possible exception of the Vosges*: MacDonald, "The Neglected Ardennes," *Military Review* (Apr. 1963): 74+ ("*impenetrable massif*"); *Ardennes*, 43 (*ten all-weather roads*).

395 *Hitler had been consumed for weeks*: Warlimont, *Inside Hitler's Headquarters*, 482–85 (*Alsatian troops*); "Germany's War Effort and Its Failure," Oct. 8, 1945, UK Chiefs of Staff Committee, NARA RG 334, E 315, ANSCOL, GB JIC (46) 33, 153 (*vehicles built in November*); Merriam, *Dark December*, 105 ("*hold the reins loose*"); Jacobsen and Rohwer, eds., *Decisive Battles of World War II: The German View*, 396–97 (*German forces on the Meuse within forty-eight hours*); Hasso von Manteuffel, ETHINT 46, Oct. 29, 1945, MHI, 9 (*four to six days*). Westphal quoted Jodl as claiming that six days to the Meuse would be "quite permissible for this phase" (*The German Army in the West*, 182).

396 *No significant interference was expected*: *Germany VII*, 682 (*Brussels*); Herbert Büchs, Jodl aide, ETHINT 34, Aug. 31, 1945, MHI, 12–13 (*Vague plans*).

396 *Two tank armies would form the point*: Barnett, ed., *Hitler's Generals*, 411–13, 419; MMB, 133 (*hippopotamus whips*); Belfield and Essame, *The Battle for Normandy*, 166–67 (*of his original 23,000 men*); *TT*, 160–61 ("*decent but stupid*"), 26, 29 (*Losheim Gap*); Jacobsen and Rohwer, eds., *Decisive Battles of World War II: The German View*, 396–97 (*nine divisions*); Cirillo, "Ardennes-Alsace," 11; *Ardennes*, 77 (*wheeling northwest toward Antwerp*).

396 *On the left, the Fifth Panzer Army*: Jacobsen and Rohwer, eds., *Decisive Battles of World War II: The German View*, 396–97; "Battlebook," USAREUR staff ride, Ardennes, Dec. 2001 ("*a daredevil*"); *SLC*, 396 (*a thousand artillery tubes*); Liddell Hart, *The Other Side of the Hill*, 450 (*fretted more about fuel*); "The Ardennes Offensive," British monograph, Aug. 1, 1945, CMH, Geog Belgium, 370.2, 11; Parker, ed., *The Battle of the Bulge: The German View*, 136–37 (*only three million gallons*), 133 (*two thousand horses*); Barnett, ed., *Hitler's Generals*, 327 ("*take it from the Americans*").

397 *A thousand trains beginning in early December*: München-Gladbach's name was changed to Mönchengladbach after the war. "The German Counter-Offensive in the Bulge," Sept. 1945, U.K. War Office, Directorate of Tactical Investigation, CARL, N-13205, 3.

397 *Security remained paramount*: *Ardennes*, 48–51; Hasso von Manteuffel, ETHINT 46, Oct. 29, 1945, MHI, 1–2 (*started a rumor*).

397 *Maps remained sealed*: "The Ardennes Offensive," British monograph, Aug. 1, 1945, CMH, Geog Belgium, 370.2, 12–16, 23; *Ardennes*, 69–70 (*delayed again for nearly a week*).

397 "*The army must gain a victory*": Josef "Sepp" Dietrich, ETHINT 16, July 10, 1945, MHI, 2–3; Parker, ed., *The Battle of the Bulge: The German View*, 9–10 ("*both sides are equal*").

397 *The central weather office in Berlin*: Royce L. Thompson, "Weather of the Ardennes Campaign," Oct. 2, 1953, CMH, 10–12.

397 "*Troops must act with brutality*": Bauserman, *The Malmédy Massacre*, 2–6.

397 "*War is of course a test of endurance*": Warlimont, *Inside Hitler's Headquarters*, 486–87; Bullock, *Hitler: A Study in Tyranny*, 762.

398 *Finally spent, Hitler ended*: Spayd, *Bayerlein*, 180 (*would not disappoint*); *Ardennes*, 28–32 ("*grave doubts*").

The Light Line

398 *For three months after her glorious liberation*: Moorehead, *Eclipse*, 186 ("*without light*"); Pogue, *Pogue's War*, 212 (*leg sores*); Gellhorn, *The Face of War*, 183 ("*bath in champaigne*"); Moorehead, *Gellhorn*, 224 ("*platform soles*").

398 *The small fuel ration*: corr, Pleas B. Rogers to family, Jan. 17, 1945, and Nov. 14, 1944 ("*cold as charity*"), and Oct. 14, 1944 (*crematorium*), Rogers papers, MHI; Richler, ed., *Writers on World War II*, 542–43 (*sawdust by the ton*); memoir, William Henry Baumer, n.d., HIA, box 1, 170 ("*we opened the windows*"); memoir, Raymond H. Croll, 1974, Croll papers, MHI, 300 ("*refrigerator door*").

398 *By late November conditions began to brighten*: Pogue, *Pogue's War*, 212; pamphlet, "Red Ball SOP," Oct. 1, 1944, Ewart G. Plank papers, HIA ("*light line*"); Whipple, "Logistical Bottleneck," *IJ* (March 1948): 6+ (*seven thousand tons a day*); minutes, meeting of chief administrative officers, Dec. 22, 1944, Versailles, NARA RG 331, E 1, SHAEF SGS, box 55 ("*electricity consumption in Paris*").

399 *For liberators behind the light line*: diary, Jan. 22, 1945, Kingsley Andersson, HIA, box 1 (*PX open only to general officers*); corr, E. S. Hughes to wife, Dec. 8, 1944, Everett S. Hughes papers, LOC MS Div, box II:3, folder 4 (*hunting partridge*); diary, CBH, Dec. 27, 1944, MHI, box 4 (*Chesapeake oysters*); Middleton, *Our Share of Night*, 336 ("*chairborne infantry*"); Pogue, *Pogue's War*, 334 ("*COMZ set-up*"), 213 (*French waitresses*).

399 *The Majestic was hardly unique*: OH, J. C. H. Lee, Mar. 21, 1947, FCP, MHI (*Fifty-one generals*); Pogue, *Pogue's War*, 203 (*frock coats*); Beevor and Cooper, *Paris After the Liberation, 1944–1949*, 126 (*Wehrmacht boot leather*).

399 "*Don't go forward of army group*": Rosengarten, "With Ultra from Omaha Beach to Weimar, Germany," *Military Affairs* (Oct. 1978): 127+.

399 *The British occupied twelve hotels*: minutes, SHAEF, Oct. 20, 1944, Versailles, NARA RG 331, SHAEF SGS, Geog Corr, box 108; corr, Thor M. Smith to family, Oct. 25, 1944, HIA, box 1 (*Champagne cost*); ASF, Technical Intelligence Report No. 2426, Apr. 12, 1945, CARL, N-9270 (*black market rates*). SHAEF in December noted that soldiers felt they were "the victims of extreme financial injustice" because the official exchange rate of 50 francs to the dollar was four to five times less than black market transactions (Coles and Weinberg, *Civil Affairs*, 747–48).

399 *stoppers were at a premium*: "The Reminiscences of Alan Goodrich Kirk," Col U OHRO, transcript in NHHC, 374; memo, "Whiskey and Gin for General Officers," Dec. 2, 1944, COMZ, MBR, MHI, box 22.

400 *For GIs without stars*: "Leaves, Furloughs and Passes in the Theater," May 1946, General Board study no. 4, NARA RG 407, AG WWII operations reports, E 427, 97-USF5-0.3.0 (*first leave center*); memo, Nov. 8, 1944, Minutes, NARA RG 331, SHAEF SGS, Geog Corr, box 108; "Special Service Clubs," General Board report no. 121, n.d., NARA RG 407, AG WWII Operations Reports, E 427, 97-USF-0.3.0 (*fifty-one GI clubs*); Pogue, *Pogue's War*, 224 (*Glenn Miller's orchestra*), 230–31 (*ten thousand soldiers a day*); corr, T. R. Bruskin to wife, Sept. 27, 1944, a.p. ("*Just returned from a trip*"); Helen Van Zonneveld, "A Time to Every Purpose," n.d., HIA, 382–83 ("*canvas-covered bathtubs*"); Beevor and Cooper, *Paris After the Liberation, 1944–1949*, 125–26 ("*easygoing manner*").

400 *Troops packed movie theaters*: Pogue, *Pogue's War*, 224 (*hamburgers and bourbon*); Beevor and Cooper, *Paris After the Liberation, 1944–1949*, 130 (*Sunny Side of the Street*); "History of Special Service Operations in the ETO," n.d., NARA RG 498, ETO HD, admin file #573, 46, 51–52 (*activities*); Nicholas, *The Rape of Europa*, 306–7 (*Bayeux Tapestry*).

400 *In early December, Gertrude Stein*: Nicholas, *The Rape of Europa*, 306–7 ("*stratified*"); Pogue, *Pogue's War*, 225 (*cigarettes and soap*); Beevor and Cooper, *Paris After the Liberation, 1944–1949*, 71 (*underwear*); Taylor and Taylor, eds., *The War Diaries*, 525 ("*all over the world?*").

400 *For many soldiers, of course, culture*: Fussell, *The Boys' Crusade*, 41 ("*going to get laid*"); report, Seine Section, COMZ, n.d., NARA RG 498, ETO HD, admin file #599 (*230 brothels*); memo, "Venereal Disease," Feb. 21, 1945, SHAEF G-5, public safety division, NARA RG 331, SHAEF, E-47, box 931 (*more than a third*); Neillands, *The Battle for the Rhine*, 75 (*three packs of Chesterfields*); memo to chief surgeon, COMZ, "Remarks on Attitudes and Behavior of Enlisted Men Related to VD," n.d., NARA RG 330, E 94, attitude surveys, ETO B-24, 1 (*intercourse at least once*); Pogue, *Pogue's War*, 233 ("*Come along*"); Schrijvers, *The Crash of Ruin*, 182 ("*Zig zig?*"); Cosmas and Cowdrey, *Medical Service in the European Theater of Operations*, 541 ("*VD contact form*"); Kennett, *G.I.: The American Soldier in World War II*, 207 ("*aphrodisiac dreams*").

401 *They were devastated by more than dreams*: Cosmas and Cowdrey, *Medical Service in the European Theater of Operations*, 541 (*two-thirds of all infections*); "V.D.," *Army Talks* 46, Dec. 2, 1944, NARA RG 498, ETO HD (*since 1830*); memo, A. W. Kenner, chief medical officer, to R. W. Barker, Nov. 8, 1944, and memo, R. W. Barker to W. B. Smith, Nov. 10, 1944, NARA RG 331, E 1, SHAEF SGS, entry 6, box 45 (*rate in Europe*); G-1 history, n.d., NARA RG 498, ETO HD, admin file #550, 12 (*off-limits*).

401 *Twenty-nine prophylactic dispensaries*: Steckel, "Morale Problems in Combat," *Army History* (summer 1994): 1+; Rottman, *FUBAR: American Soldier Slang of World War II*, 98; "The Reminiscences of Alan Goodrich Kirk," Col U OHRO, transcript in NHHC, 368 ("*proof of chastity*"); "V.D.," *Army Talks* 46, Dec. 2, 1944, NARA RG 498, ETO HD ("*Don't forget the Krauts*").

401 *Still the VD rate climbed*: Nickell, *Red Devil*, 139 ("*whores de combat*"); Rottman, *FUBAR: American Soldier Slang of World War II*, 80 ("*No-Clap Medal*"); Schrijvers, *The Crash of Ruin*, 182 ("*Hershey bars*"); Blunt, *Foot Soldier*, 49 ("*horizontal refreshment*"); corr, French Foreign Ministry to SHAEF, Feb. 24, 1945, NARA RG 331, E 1, SHAEF SGS, entry 6, box 45 ("*noteworthy recrudescence*"); corr, GSP to DDE, Oct. 19, 1944 ("*human nature*"), and DDE to GSP, Oct. 21, 1944 ("*do* not *agree*"), NARA RG 331, E 1, SHAEF SGS, entry 6, box 45.

402 *Paris soldiered on*: corr, Thor M. Smith to family, Oct. 24 and 25, 1944, HIA, box 1 (*stamp market*) and Nov. 17, 1944 (*surreptitious dancing*); Beevor and Cooper, *Paris After Liberation, 1944–1949*, 68 (*clenched-fist salutes*); Mauldin, *The Brass Ring*, 250–51 ("*jammed with French civilians*").

402 *Among the liveliest tableaus*: Beevor and Cooper, *Paris After Liberation, 1944–1949*, 73 ("*American enclave*"); Capa, *Slightly Out of Focus*, 189 (*Suffering Bastard*); TSC, 523–25 (*100,000 words*); "A History of Field Press Censorship in SHAEF," n.d., MHI, 47–52 ("*hot stops*"); White, *Conquerors' Road*, 110 ("*nimble French youths*").

402 *Sporadic privation would beset Paris*: minutes, "Critical Supply Situation in Paris," Jan. 18, 1945, NARA RG 331, SHAEF SGS, Geog Corr, box 108; Beevor and Cooper, *Paris After Liberation, 1944–1949*, 101 (*government stationery*); ETO inspection report, cigarette shortage, Dec. 15, 1944, NARA RG 498, file #44, box 10; Robert M. Littlejohn, "Ports and Transportation," chapter 27, PIR, MHI, 11–12, appendix B (*blankets and sleeping bags*); D'Este, *Eisenhower: A Soldier's Life*, 620 (*rolling his own*).

403 *Not least among the problems for Court House Lee*: Ecker, "G.I. Racketeers in the Paris Black Market," *Yank*, May 4, 1945, 2; Pogue, *Pogue's War*, 231–32 ("*black market bag*"); Durnford-Slater, *Commando*, 205 (*Danish butter*); OH, Henry S. Aurand, 1974, William O. Morrison, SOOHP, MHI (*entire train with three engines*); "The Administrative History of the Operations of 21 Army Group on the Continent of Europe, 6 June [1944]–8 May, 1945," Nov. 1945, NARA RG 334, E 315, ANSCOL, GB 21-AG AH, 53 (*captured German horses*); White, *Conquerors' Road*, 110 ("*camouflaged horse steak*").

403 *Eisenhower's provost marshal estimated*: Hastings, *Armageddon*, 185; Cawthon, *Other Clay*, 165 (*hiding in the Parisian demimonde*); "Subsistence in the ETO," 1959, chapter 55, PIR, Robert M. Littlejohn papers, HIA (*peddle K rations*); report, provost marshal, Seine Section, COMZ, n.d., NARA RG 498, ETO HD, admin file #599-G (*hundreds of such vehicles*); Pogue, *Pogue's War*, 230–31 (*selling the entire deuce-and-a-half and*

"*Chicago-sur-Seine*"); resume, n.d., Pleas B. Rogers papers, MHI (*four thousand military policemen*); "Report of Visit to Paris Detention Barracks," March 9, 1945, NARA RG 498, ETO inspection report, file #37 (*trucked back to the front*); Bykofsky and Larson, *The Transportation Corps: Operations Overseas*, 351; Ecker, "G.I. Racketeers in the Paris Black Market," *Yank*, May 4, 1945, 2 (*fifty years*).

404 *Shortly before six P.M. on Tuesday, December 12*: Chandler, vol. 5, chronology, 175; "The Tendons of an Army," ETOUSA, n.d., RG 490, ETO HD, admin file #531, 2.

404 *As his car sped southeast across Piccadilly*: S. N. Behrman, "The Suspended Drawing Room," in *The New Yorker Book of War Pieces*, 424 (*little points of blue light*); Ziegler, *London at War, 1939–1945*, 309 (*Children's amusement section*).

404 *A national ban on making ice cream*: Ziegler, *London at War, 1939–1945*, 305; Stiles, *Serenade to the Big Bird*, 170 (*cave dwellers*); S. N. Behrman, "The Suspended Drawing Room," in *The New Yorker Book of War Pieces*, 429 (*five deep*); Ackroyd, *London Under*, e-book, chapter 12 (*Elgin Marbles*); Arthur, *Forgotten Voices of World War II*, 372 ("*It's death*").

404 *As in Antwerp, death could also arrive*: M. C. Helfers, "The Employment of V-Weapons by the Germans During World War II," OCMH, 1954, NARA RG 319, 2-3.7 AW, 75; Ziegler, *London at War, 1939–1945*, 298 (*half in greater London*); *Germany VII*, 454–55 (*equivalent to that of producing 24,000 fighter planes*).

405 *Radar usually detected V-2 launches*: "V-2 Countermeasures in the ETO," July 4, 1945, NARA RG 337, AGF OR #506, 18–20, 40–41; Ackroyd, *London Under*, e-book, chapter 12 (*floodgates*); S. N. Behrman, "The Suspended Drawing Room," in *The New Yorker Book of War Pieces*, 421 ("*You just strolled along*"); Collier, *The Defence of the United Kingdom*, 417 (*as high as a thousand to one*); Masterman, *The Double-Cross System*, 181 (*agents controlled by British counterintelligence*); Howard, *British Intelligence in the Second World War*, vol. 5, *Strategic Deception*, 182–83 (*sparing an estimated 1,300 British lives*).

405 *That was cold comfort for the nearly three thousand*: Official British figures listed 9,300 V-2 casualties, including 2,800 fatalities, a bit less than half the corresponding figures for the V-1 attacks (Collier, *The Defence of the United Kingdom*, 527).

405 "*Never have I seen buildings*": Ziegler, *London at War, 1939–1945*, 296–97; Longmate, *Hitler's Rockets*, 209 (*Saturday sale on saucepans*).

405 "*A horse's head was lying in the gutter*": Roberts, *The Storm of War*, 518; http://lewisham warmemorials.wikidot.com/incident:world-war-ii-new-cross-woolworths-v2-rocket; Ziegler, *London at War, 1939–1945*, 298; Sherwood, *Roosevelt and Hopkins*, 836 ("*quite a lot to take*").

406 *No V-weapons fell on Whitehall*: Eisenhower, *Eisenhower at War, 1943–1945*, 551.

406 *Eisenhower now commanded sixty-nine divisions*: GS VI, 18–19; author visit, Churchill Museum and Cabinet War Rooms, London, 2005 (*pushpins and colored yarn*).

406 "*Ike explained his plan*": Danchev, 634–35.

406 *Two years earlier, under similar circumstances*: AAAD, 282–83 (*retreating in disarray*); "U.S. Military Government in Germany: Operations During the Rhineland Campaign," 1950, CMH, 8-3.1 DA5, 28 ("*capability of concentration*"); Eisenhower, *Eisenhower at War, 1943–1945*, 551; Chandler, 2341.

407 "*Ike was good*": Crosswell, *Beetle*, 786.

407 *The evening ended in stilted silences*: Eisenhower, *Eisenhower at War, 1943–1945*, 552 ("*evening of my life*"); Danchev, 634–35 ("*utterly failed*"); Ambrose, *Eisenhower: Soldier, General of the Army, President-Elect, 1890–1952*, vol. 1, 361.

407 *Eisenhower flew back to Versailles*: Carver, ed., *The War Lords*, 533; Chandler, 2341 ("*Brooke seemed disturbed*"); Eisenhower, *Eisenhower at War, 1943–1945*, 550 ("*let it be sunny*").

407 "*I greatly fear the dwindling*": D'Este, *Decision in Normandy*, 265; Howard, *British Intelligence in the Second World War*, vol. 5, *Strategic Deception*, 199 (*fourteen British divisions*); memo, E. I. C. Jacob, Dec. 5, 1944. Also, BLM to A. Brooke, Oct. 26, 1944 ("*acute problem in the next six months*"), and A. Brooke to WSC, Nov. 3, 1944; WSC, "Personal

Minute," Dec. 3, 1944, and "Note on Reduction of 50 Div in 21 Army Group," Dec. 8, 1944, and memo, WSC, Dec. 12, 1944: all in UK NA, WO 215/101; *VW*, vol. 2, 142–43 (*Wastage in infantry riflemen*); Hastings, *Armageddon*, 77 (*20 percent*).

407 *"All of us are now faced with an unanticipated shortage"*: FDR to WSC, Oct. 16, 1944, in NARA RG 165, E 422, WD, OPD, history unit, box 55.

408 *The American dearth was even more problematic*: GS VI, 19; Matloff, *Strategic Planning for Coalition Warfare, 1943–1944*, 409 (*new B-29 bomber*); Eiler, *Mobilizing America*, 400 (*300,000 workers already building*), 397 (*occupational deferments*), 417n (*hard-pressed critical industries*); Bland, ed., *George C. Marshall Interviews and Reminiscences for Forrest C. Pogue*, 390 (*Marshall felt pressure*).

408 *To swell the ranks, Selective Service exemptions*: Kennedy, *Freedom from Fear*, 635; Eiler, *Mobilizing America*, 635 (*many new privates*); Palmer et al., *The Procurement and Training of Ground Combat Troops*, 207, 224 (*ban on shipping eighteen-year-olds*); *LSA*, vol. 2, 506 (*"physically imperfect men"*); Wiltse, ed., *Physical Standards in World War II*, 194 (*"such terms as 'imbecile'"*), 42, 199–200 (*"put their hands under cars"*).

408 *The need for more soldiers*: *LSA*, vol. 2, 316–17 (*two thousand a day* and *trench foot epidemic*); Palmer et al., *The Procurement and Training of Ground Combat Troops*, 217 (*figure hit three thousand*); "Reinforcement System and Reinforcement Procedures in the European Theater," n.d., NARA RG 407, E 427, AG WWII operations reports, 97-USF-0.3.0, study no. 3 (*three hundred thousand individual replacement troops*); Robert J. Greenwald, "Human Logistics: The Supplying of Men, a Study of the Reinforcement System," Jan. 31, 1945, ETOUSA, NARA RG 498, ETO HD, admin file #571-K, 94 (*below its authorized strength*); Bradley Commentaries, Chester B. Hansen collection, MHI, box 42 (*"life expectancy of a junior officer"*); diary, Dec. 3, 1944, GSP, LOC MS Div, box 3, folder 9 (*"Our situation is bad"*).

409 *All combat arms felt pinched*: "Report of Observers, ETO," Apr. 27, 1945, NARA RG 337, AGF OR no. 371 (*"delivery of armored replacements"*); Rush, *Hell in Hürtgen Forest*, 65 (*"black line on a map"*); *LSA*, vol. 2, 506 (*obsolete data*); Greenwald, "Human Logistics: The Supplying of Men, a Study of the Reinforcement System," Jan. 31, 1945, ETOUSA, NARA RG 498, ETO HD, admin file #571-K, 75 (*actual figure was 83 percent*); Palmer et al., *The Procurement and Training of Ground Combat Troops*, 216 (*a need for 300,000*).

409 *Of more than eight million soldiers in the Army*: Weigley, *History of the United States Army*, 440; Palmer, "Procurement of Enlisted Personnel for the AGF: The Problem of Quality," 1946, AGF, historical section S #4, NARA RG 334, E 315, ANSCOL, box 150, 40 (*disproportionate share*); Eric Klinek, "The Army's Orphans: The United States Army Replacement System During World War II and Its Impact on Combat Effectiveness," paper, SMH, Ogden, Utah, Apr. 19, 2008.

409 *The severest shortage was of that priceless creature*: Crosswell, *Beetle*, 797; Weigley, *History of the United States Army*, 464 (*27 rifle companies*); "Reinforcement System and Reinforcement Procedures in the European Theater," n.d., NARA RG 407, E 427, AG WWII operations reports, 97-USF-0.3.0, study no. 3 (*"We find ourselves totally out"*); Fussell, *The Boys' Crusade*, 96 (*"Nobody gets out"*); Fussell, *Doing Battle*, 122 (*"no infantryman can survive"*).

409 *Frantic efforts were made*: Crosswell, *Beetle*, 788 (*Seventeen of those divisions*); Palmer et al., *The Procurement and Training of Ground Combat Troops*, 472–74 (*sixteen platoon leaders*); Report No. ETO-5, n.d., Surveys of Attitudes of Soldiers Fighting in the ETO, NARA RG 330, E 94, 6 (*"show them how to load their rifles"*).

410 *Crash programs to convert quartermaster soldiers*: Robert J. Greenwald, "Human Logistics: The Supplying of Men, a Study of the Reinforcement System," Jan. 31, 1945, ETOUSA, NARA RG 498, ETO HD, admin file #571-K, 84–85; Report No. ETO-5, n.d., Surveys of Attitudes of Soldiers Fighting in the ETO, NARA RG 330, E 94, 13 (*"miracle men"*); Steckel, "Morale Problems in Combat," *Army History* (summer 1994): 1+ (*"retreads"*); Edward J. Drea, "Unit Reconstitution: A Historical Perspective," Dec. 1983, CSI, 19 (*refused to accept hundreds*); inspection report, 16th Reinforcement Depot, Dec. 29–31,

1944, NARA RG 498, 290/57/30/4, box 2, file 3 (*"State of mind of men"*); Crosswell, *Beetle*, 789 (*"aren't good for anything else"*); Fussell, *Doing Battle*, 108 ("You *are expendable"*).

410 *Even the deployment of intact divisions*: "History of the Red List," 1946, CMH, 3-5.1 A BA, 1-4, 55f, 60–66, 75.

410 *The Red List was a paragon of efficiency*: memo, DDE to GCM, Feb. 17, 1945, NARA RG 498, SGS IG, 333.5 (*"feeling of being a lost soul"*); Greenwald, "Human Logistics: The Supplying of Men, a Study of the Reinforcement System," Jan. 31, 1945, ETOUSA, NARA RG 498, ETO HD, admin file #571-K, 34 (*adhesive tape*); "History of the Ground Force Replacement System, ETO," n.d., NARA RG 498, ETO HD file #571A (*World War I–vintage rifles*); OH, Andre Beaumont, n.d., ROHA, http://oralhistory.rutgers.edu (*"We left Fort Meade"*).

410 *Replacements traveled for days*: Robert J. Greenwald, "Human Logistics: The Supplying of Men, a Study of the Reinforcement System," Jan. 31, 1945, ETOUSA, NARA RG 498, ETO HD, admin file #571-K, 16–17, 21; corr, DDE to GCM, Feb. 25, 1945, NARA RG 498, SGS IG, 333.5 (*"We have reduced the figure"*); inspection report, 16th Reinforcement Depot, Dec. 29–31, 1944, NARA RG 498, 290/57/30/4, box 2, file 3 (*"stockage depots"*); Eric Klinek, "The Army's Orphans: The United States Army Replacement System During World War II and Its Impact on Combat Effectiveness," paper, SMH conference, Apr. 19, 2008, Ogden, Utah (*combat skills deteriorated*); "History of the Ground Force Replacement System, ETO," n.d., chapter 4, "Major Problems Encountered by Ground Force Reinforcement Command," NARA RG 498, ETO HD file #571F, 346 (*"had not bathed in thirty days"*).

411 *"We want to feel that we are a part of something"*: Report No. ETO-5, n.d., Surveys of Attitudes of Soldiers Fighting in the ETO, NARA RG 330, E 94, 14; Robert J. Greenwald, "Human Logistics: The Supplying of Men, A Study of the Reinforcement System," Jan. 31, 1945, ETOUSA, NARA RG 498, ETO HD, admin file #571-K, 34–36 (*"scared the pants off"*).

411 *Court House Lee proposed on December 1*: Robert J. Greenwald, "Human Logistics: The Supplying of Men, a Study of the Reinforcement System," Jan. 31, 1945, ETOUSA, NARA RG 498, ETO HD, admin file #571-K, 34–35, 65, 36 (*almost half a million replacements*); Bradley, *A Soldier's Story*, 446–47 (*"cannon fodder implication"*); memo, "Replacement System," July 29, 1944, 9th ID IG, NARA RG 498, box 9, file 34 (*"morale of our officers"*).

411 *Now the Army's ability to replenish its ranks*: Lee, *The Employment of Negro Troops*, 688–89 (*shortage of 23,000*); LSA, vol. 2, 321–28 (*truncated to two weeks*).

411 *No one was more fretful than Omar Bradley*: The tank figure includes those in Ninth Army, temporarily seconded to 21st AG (Royce L. Thompson, "Ardennes Campaign Statistics," Apr. 1952, OCMH, NARA RG 319, E 97, LSA vol. 1, background files, box 7).

411 *mustered less than 80 percent*: "Report of Operations," n.d., 12th AG, vol. 2, G-1 section, CARL, 30; Bradley, *A Soldier's Story*, 446–47 (*"Don't they realize"*).

"Go Easy, Boys. There's Danger Ahead"

412 *Allied intelligence first recognized in September*: Hinsley, 550–55; Bennett, *Ultra in the West*, 189–99; "Estimate No. 37," First Army, G-2, Dec. 10, 1944, USAREUR staff ride, Dec. 2001 (*Skorzeny*); memo, K. W. D. Strong, SHAEF, to army groups, Oct. 19, 1944, NARA RG 331, SHAEF SGS, 383.6/4, box 86.

412 *The U.S. First Army had flown*: Hinsley, 558–59 (*361 reconnaissance sorties*); AAFin-WWII, 679 (*canvas-covered flatcars*); Bennett, *Ultra in the West*, 196 (*two hundred troop trains*).

412 *None of this suggested an enemy offensive*: Royce L. Thompson, "American Intelligence on the German Counteroffensive," vol. 1, Nov. 1949, CMH, 2-3.7 AE P-1 (*counterattack force*); Hinsley, 558–59 (*"true counter-offensive"*); Sibert, G-2, 12th AG, "Military Intelligence Aspects of the Period Prior to the Ardennes Counter Offensive," sent to Hanson

Baldwin, Jan. 2, 1947, CBM, MHI, box 6, 8–9 (*reconnaissance of the Meuse bridges*); *VW*, vol. 2, 175 ("*bruited drive on Antwerp*").

413 *Those nearest the front*: "Estimate of Enemy Capabilities Prior to the Counter-Offensive," n.d., in "History of the Ardennes Campaign," NARA RG 498, ETOUSA HD, UD 584, box 1, 4 (*officers interviewing German prisoners*); *TSC*, 365 (*assumed to be green units*); Royce L. Thompson, "American Intelligence on the German Counteroffensive," vol. 2, "Division Level," March 1949, CARL, N-16829.2 ("*German army [is] disintegrating*"); *Ardennes*, 59–61.

413 *Several factors fed this disregard*: *TSC*, 372 (*Hitler rather than the prudent Rundstedt*); *VW*, vol. 2, 171 ("*in the hands of soldiers*"); 21st AG intelligence review, Dec. 3, 1944, Oscar W. Koch papers, MHI, box 12 (*No sensible field marshal*); Pogue, "The Ardennes Campaign: The Impact of Intelligence," lecture, Dec. 16, 1980, NSA Communications Analysis Association, a.p. ("*we would not attack*"); Sibert, G-2, 12th AG, "Military Intelligence Aspects of the Period Prior to the Ardennes Counter Offensive," sent to Hanson Baldwin, Jan. 2, 1947, CBM, MHI, box 6, 3 ("*intentions of a maniac*").

413 *Top Allied officers also had become overly enchanted*: Bennett, *Ultra in the West*, 191; "Synthesis of Experiences in the Use of Ultra Intelligence by U.S. Army Field Command in the ETO," n.d., NARA RG 457, E 9002, NSA, SRH-006, 12–16.

413 "*They had become so dependent*": OH, Richard Collins, 1976, Donald Bowman, SOOHP, MHI, 8; OH, Ralph Hauenstein, Jan. and Feb. 2102, author, Palm Beach and Naples, Fla. The list of Ultra recipients grew to about six hundred by March 1945 ("List of Recipients," March 25, 1945, Richard Collins papers, MHI, box 1).

413 "*Instead of being the best*": E. T. Williams, "Reports Received by U.S. War Department on Use of Ultra in the European Theater," Oct. 1945, NARA RG 457, E 9002, NSA, SRH-037, 1, 13; Bennett, *Ultra in the West*, 202–3; Lewin, *Ultra Goes to War*, 428–33.

414 *Some would later claim clairvoyance*: "Estimate No. 37," First Army, G-2, Dec. 10, 1944, USAREUR staff ride, Dec. 2001; *TSC*, 366–68 (*a windy alarmist*); OH, E. T. Williams, May 30–31, 1947, FCP, MHI; Strong, *Intelligence at the Top*, 242–43; *TT*, 76–77 (*departure from Spa*); Weigley, *Eisenhower's Lieutenants*, 460.

414 *A suggestion in early December*: OH, W. B. Smith, Apr. 1949, SLAM, OCMH WWII General Miscellany, MHI; *TSC*, 365n (*ample reinforcements had been positioned*); corr, K. W. D. Strong to FCP, Aug. 31, 1951, NARA RG 319, *SC* background files, 2-3.7 CB 8 (*chose not to trouble* Eisenhower); OH, Edwin L. Sibert, May 11, 1951, FCP, NARA RG 319, *SC* background files, 2-3.7 CB 8 ("*I don't think they will come*"). Bradley grew sufficiently concerned that he told Sibert he wanted Eisenhower to reinforce him with the 12th Armored Division.

414 *Perhaps the only true prescience*: *TT*, 52 ("*has* not *been a rout*"); Third Army intel summaries, Dec. 7 and 14, 1944, Oscar W. Koch papers, MHI, box 12 ("*large panzer concentration*" and *persistent mystery*); Blumenson, *Patton: The Man Behind the Legend, 1885–1945*, 245 (*vulnerability of VIII Corps*); *TSC*, 366–67; *PP*, 582 ("*The First Army is making a terrible mistake*").

415 *Yet in other Allied high councils a confident swagger*: "Strategy of the Campaign in Western Europe, 1944–1945," n.d., USFET, General Board study no. 1, 69; Hinsley, 563 ("*sudden attack in the West*"); OH, Edwin L. Sibert, May 11, 1951, FCP, NARA RG 319, *SC* background files, 2-3.7 CB 8 (*punch up the prose*); *TSC*, 369n; intel summary no. 18, 12th AG, Dec. 12, 1944, Oscar W. Koch papers, MHI, box 11 ("*Attrition is steadily sapping*"); Royce L. Thompson, "American Intelligence on the German Counteroffensive," vol. 1, Nov. 1949, CMH, 2-3.7 AE P-1 ("*given time and fair weather*").

415 *Montgomery needed no ghostwriter*: Wilmot, *The Struggle for Europe*, 587n ("*cannot stage major offensive operations*").

415 "*I still have nine days*": *TSC*, 370n.

415 *Marlene Dietrich cut a wide swath*: Weintraub, *11 Days in December*, 28–30; Atkinson, "Ghost of a Chanteuse," *WP*, May 7, 1996; Joseph Edgar Martin, "From Casablanca to Berchtesgaden: A Memoir of World War II," 2003, a.p., 53 (*sequined gown*); Goolrick

and Tanner, *The Battle of the Bulge*, 41 (*lipstick autographs*); Kennett, *G.I.: The American Soldier in World War II*, 202 (*eleven pistols*); Codman, *Drive*, 200–201 ("*the first girl laughed*"); Spoto, *Blue Angel*, 196–200 ("*how could it have been Eisenhower?*").

416 *On a rainy Thursday evening, December 14*: corr, Malcolm Richard Wilkey, March 7, 1983, CBM, MHI, box 1, 3; *TT*, 96–97; McManus, *Alamo in the Ardennes*, 33.

416 *The U.S. Army's* Guide to the Cities of Belgium: Schrijvers, *The Crash of Ruin*, 31, 213; *Ardennes*, 238 ("*quiet paradise*"); Babcock, *Taught to Kill*, 63 ("*crisp and sunny day*"); Richard Henry Byers, "Battle of the Bulge," 1983, a.p., 22–23 ("*I'll be getting fat*"); Toland, *Battle*, 18 (*sang while eating crackers*); Blunt, *Foot Soldier*, 108; OH, Albert Handaly, ROHA, http://oralhistory.rutgers.edu/Interviews/handaly_albert.html (*death notifications*).

416 *Among visitors to the First Army headquarters*: Benjamin A. Dickson, "G-2 Journal: Algiers to the Elbe," MHI, 180–83; Sylvan, 211; Hogan, *A Command Post at War*, 207, 212 (*worn down by fatigue*); Holt, *The Deceivers*, 657 ("*The retreat we beat*").

416 *Ten thousand Belgian civilians*: Schrijvers, *The Unknown Dead*, 12 ("*connected with Germany*"); corr, Ralph G. Hill, Jr., Nov. 10, 1973, Maurice Delaval collection, MHI, box 9 (*Army trucks then hauled the beef*); *TT*, 127–28 (*Another roundup*); corr, John I. Hungerford, June 26, 1957, JT, LOC MS Div, box 36 ("*cornfield forest*"); Marshall, *A Ramble Through My War*, 170 ("*Go easy, boys*").

417 *Of the 341,000 soldiers in the U.S. First Army*: Royce L. Thompson, "Ardennes Campaign Statistics," Apr. 1952, OCMH, NARA RG 319, E 97, *LSA* vol. 1, background files, box 7; *Ardennes*, 56; corr, Troy H. Middleton to theater historians, July 30, 1945, NARA RG 498, ETOUSA HD, UD 584; *TSC*, 371; Price, *Troy H. Middleton: A Biography*, 212–13 (*phony shoulder flashes*); John C. Hollinger, "The Operations of the 422nd Infantry Regiment," 1949, Infantry School, Ft. Benning, Ga. (*frontages*); Lauer, *Battle Babies*, 6–7.

417 *For much of the fall, four veteran U.S. divisions*: SLC, 612–15; Beck, 461 (*eighteen-year-old draftees*); Alan W. Jones, Jr., "The Operations of the 423rd Infantry," 1949, IS, 6 (*across the Losheim Gap*).

417 *As with so many newer divisions*: John C. Hollinger, "The Operations of the 422nd Infantry Regiment," 1949, IS (*seven thousand men had been transferred*); OH, "German Breakthrough in the Ardennes," 106th ID, n.d., NARA RG 407, E 427-A (*arriving at Le Havre*); Dupuy, *St. Vith: Lion in the Way*, 15–16 ("*numb, soaked, and frozen*").

418 *Few soldiers of the 106th had ever heard*: corr, John I. Hungerford, June 26, 1957, JT, LOC MS Div, box 36; Alan W. Jones, Jr., "The Operations of the 423rd Infantry," 1949, IS, 8 (*calibration of new sets*); OH, "German Breakthrough in the Ardennes," 106th ID, n.d., NARA RG 407, E 427-A (*shortages of winter clothing*); Rosser L. Hunter, IG report, "Action of 106th Infantry Division," Jan. 26, 1945, NARA RG 338, FUSA AG, 333.9, 1 ("*aggressive defense*"); report, M. C. Shattuck, VIII Corps, Dec. 13, 1944, NARA RG 498, G-3 OR, box 9 (*German war dogs*).

418 "*The woods are of tall pines*": Richard Henry Byers, "Battle of the Bulge," 1983, a.p., 14; "The Losheim Gap," n.d., ETO HD, NARA RG 498, UD 584, box 4; OH, Mark Devine, 14th Cavalry Group, n.d., NARA RG 407, E 427-A, CI, folder #329 ("*sugar bowls*").

418 "*It has been very quiet*": Dupuy, *St. Vith: Lion in the Way*, 15–16.

418 *Straw and rags muffled gun wheels*: *Ardennes*, 70; OH, Hasso von Manteuffel, Oct. 12, 1966, John S. D. Eisenhower, CBM, MHI, box 6, 21–22 (*authorized to shoot out tires*); Parker, ed., *The Battle of the Bulge: The German View*, 139–40 (*portaged ammunition*); memo, Walter Model, "Maximum Performance Without Sleep," Dec. 17, 1944, NARA RG 498, ETOUSA HD, UD 584 ("*strengthening foods*"); Wilmot, *The Struggle for Europe*, 582 ("*Some believe in living*").

418 *Two hundred thousand assault troops*: *Ardennes*, 72–73, 650.

419 "*Tomorrow brings the beginning*": ibid., 74.

419 *In the red-roofed Belgian army barracks*: *TT*, 189; Price, *Troy H. Middleton: A Biography*, 215–16 (*champagne corks*); Weigley, *Eisenhower's Lieutenants*, 121 ("*outstanding infantry regimental commander*").

419 *A few miles to the east, the faint clop*: Ardennes, 194, 63 ("*Nothing to report*"); Royce L. Thompson, "Weather of the Ardennes Campaign," Oct. 2, 1953, CMH, 22.

Chapter 9: The Bulge

A Rendezvous in Some Flaming Town

421 *Sheets of flame leaped*: Richard Henry Byers, "Battle of the Bulge," 1983, a.p., 26; OH video, I&R platoon, 394th Inf, 99th ID, compiled by NWWIIM, 2008 ("*the end of the world*").

421 *For some, yes*: OH, 14th Cavalry Group, n.d., NARA RG 407, E 427-A, CI, folder 329; Dupuy, *St. Vith: Lion in the Way*, 3; OH video, I&R platoon, 394th Inf, 99th ID, compiled by NWWIIM, 2008 ("*The whole German army*").

421 *The battle was joined, this last great grapple*: As described later in this chapter, Operation NORDWIND, effectively a coda to the Bulge attack, was the last substantial German offensive in the west (OH, 99th ID, Jan. 1945, NARA RG 407, E 427-A, CI, folder 209; *Ardennes*, 82).

421 *Es geht um das Ganze*: "Intelligence Notes on the Breakthrough," 99th ID, G-2, n.d., CBM, MHI, box 4.

422 *No man embraced the field marshal's sentiments*: Royce L. Thompson, "The ETO Ardennes Campaign: Operations of the Combat Group Peiper," July 24, 1952, CMH; *Ardennes*, 260–61; http://www.ss501panzer.com/Trail_KG_Peiper.htm.

422 *As commander of the 1st SS Panzer Regiment*: TT, 198–99, 462–63; "Malmedy Massacre Investigation," U.S. Senate Armed Services Committee, Oct. 1949 (*Blow Torch Battalion*); Bauserman, *The Malmédy Massacre*, 5–6; MMB, 418; Reynolds, *The Devil's Adjutant*, 25 (*Two brothers, also SS men*); memo, European Command judge advocate, March 28, 1949, CMH, LAW 2-7, 2. (*Hitler's orders to wield fear*).

422 *In early December, after a test run*: "An Interview with Obst Joachim Peiper," ETHINT 10, Sept. 7, 1945, MHI, 2–3, 7, 13–14 ("*these roads were not for tanks*").

422 *Both German and American mines cost Peiper*: ibid., 15; Eisenhower, *The Bitter Woods*, 218; Royce L. Thompson, "The ETO Ardennes Campaign: Operations of the Combat Group Peiper," July 24, 1952, CMH (*clattered into Honsfeld*); TT, 203; *Ardennes*, 261; "The Battle of the Bulge," AB, no. 4 (1974): 1+ (*stripped boots*).

423 *German intelligence had correctly identified*: Ardennes, 261, 91; Royce L. Thompson, "The ETO Ardennes Campaign: Operations of the Combat Group Peiper," July 24, 1952, CMH. "An Interview with Obst Joachim Peiper," ETHINT 10, Sept. 7, 1945, MHI, 16 (*fifty thousand gallons*). The official Army history contends that fifty American soldiers were murdered in Büllingen, but Charles B. MacDonald, a particularly capable historian, asserts that a single GI was murdered there (*TT*, 206–9).

423 *This serendipity proved catastrophic for Battery B*: Bauserman, *The Malmédy Massacre*, ix; Schrijvers, *The Unknown Dead*, 37–38 ("*Boches!*"); TT, 213–15.

423 *Boches there were, and in a particularly foul mood*: Royce L. Thompson, "The ETO Ardennes Campaign: Operations of the Combat Group Peiper," July 24, 1952, CMH; Bauserman, *The Malmédy Massacre*, 40–50, 62; Schrijvers, *The Unknown Dead*, 37 (*captors stripped them of rings*).

424 "*Da kriegt noch einer Luft*": Bauserman, *The Malmédy Massacre*, 67.

424 "*I was wounded in the left arm*": affidavit, Homer D. Ford, in memo to ONB, Dec. 29, 1944, NARA RG 498, ETOUSA HD, UD 584; Ed Cunningham, "The Battle of the Bulge," *Yank*, March 2, 1945, in *Reporting World War 2*, 582 ("*then the click*").

424 *For twenty minutes executioners prowled*: TT, 219; author interviews, Bastogne, 50th anniversary, Battle of the Bulge, Dec. 17, 1994 (*claret color*).

424 *Unaware for the moment that his minions*: "An Interview with Obst Joachim Peiper," ETHINT 10, Sept. 7, 1945, MHI, 16–17; "The Battle of the Bulge," AB, no. 4 (1974): 1+ (*wolfing down the lunch*); TT, 229 (*killing seven. The eighth fled*).

425 "*God made me to know him*": McNally, *As Ever, John*, 57–58.

425 *Twilight had fallen when Pieper reached*: Ardennes, 265–66; Royce L. Thompson, "The ETO Ardennes Campaign: Operations of the Combat Group Peiper," July 24, 1952, CMH (*strung out for twenty-five kilometers*).

425 *Behind him, near Malmédy*: Bauserman, *The Malmédy Massacre*, 83 (*word of the massacre passed*); author interviews, Bastogne, 50th anniversary, Battle of the Bulge, Dec. 17, 1994 (*Vows to give no quarter*); Linderman, *The World Within War*, 139; war diary, Ninth Army, Dec. 23, 1944, William H. Simpson papers, MHI, box 11 (*"American troops are now refusing"*).

425 *Peiper had bored a small, vicious hole*: Ardennes, 78, 101–6; Brower, ed., *World War II in Europe: The Final Year*, 225 (*"red nightmare"*); Lauer, *Battle Babies*, 17, 42 (*flame pits*); OH, 99th ID, Jan. 1945, NARA RG 407, E 427-A, CI, folder 209 (*bayoneting GIs*).

425 *"One of our young lieutenants"*: Brower, ed., *World War II in Europe: The Final Year*, 225; OH, 99th ID, Jan. 1945, NARA RG 407, E 427-A, CI, folder 209; Richard Henry Byers, "Battle of the Bulge," 1983, a.p., 33–34 (*killed their own major*), 32 ("I've a rendezvous with death"); TT, 179 (*played a piano*); Ardennes, 123 (*climb to two thousand*).

426 *Two towns, actually*: Royce L. Thompson, "Tank Fight of Rocherath-Krinkelt," Feb. 13, 1952, CMH, 2-37 AE P-12, 2–8; Toland, *Battle*, 80 (*"more like postmen"*).

426 *A full-throated German assault*: Royce L. Thompson, "Tank Fight of Rocherath-Krinkelt," Feb. 13, 1952, CMH, 2-37 AE P-12, 4; Reynolds, *Men of Steel*, 87 (*"perfect panzer graveyard"*).

426 *At dusk on Tuesday, with the last remnants*: USAREUR staff ride, Elsenborn, Dec. 5–8, 2001 (*unmarked on Belgian military maps*).

426 *Corps gunners muscled hundreds of tubes*: Blue Spaders, 99–100 (*Tiger tanks being dropped by parachute*), 99 (*"worry no longer"*); Richard Henry Byers, "Battle of the Bulge," 1983, a.p., 32 (*"throw back my head"*).

427 *Just so. At the moment when artillery prowess*: Albert H. Smith, Jr., ed., "Biographical Sketches," n.d., Stanhope Mason papers, MRC FDM, 1994.126.

427 *Here for three days and nights*: Wheeler, *The Big Red One*, 353–57; Knickerbocker et al., *Danger Forward*, 341 (*"Attack repulsed"*); Blue Spaders, 104 (*"We are killing"*).

427 *The heaviest blows fell*: corr, Derrill M. Daniel to JT, "The Operations of the 2nd Battalion, 26th Infantry, at Dom Bütgenbach," June 9, 1958, CBM, MHI, box 2; TT, 404–5; Blue Spaders, 105; Ardennes, 129–32; Rivette, "The Hot Corner at Dom Bütgenbach," IJ (Oct. 1945): 19+ (*Thursday brought worse yet*).

427 *"Get me all the damned artillery"*: Blue Spaders, 108; Rivette, "The Hot Corner at Dom Bütgenbach," IJ (Oct. 1945): 19+ (*finally winkled out the last defenders*).

428 *Army patrols reported enemy dead*: corr, Derrill M. Daniel to JT, "The Operations of the 2nd Battalion, 26th Infantry, at Dom Bütgenbach," June 9, 1958, CBM, MHI, box 2; TT, 406–7, 410–11 (*five thousand others were killed*).

428 *But the American line held*: Percy E. Schramm, "The Course of Events in the German Offensive in the Ardennes," n.d., FMS, #A-858, MHI, 4, 7; author visit, 1st ID memorial, Dom Bütgenbach, June 2, 2009; Cirillo, "Ardennes-Alsace," 16; TT, 410; Westphal, *The German Army in the West*, 183 (*muscle-bound and clumsy*). Dietrich later claimed that one-quarter of his tanks had been immobilized by various misfortunes simply in moving to the line of departure (USAREUR staff ride, Elsenborn, Dec. 5–8, 2001).

428 *The Americans by contrast demonstrated agility*: MacDonald, "The Neglected Ardennes," *Military Review* (Apr. 1963): 74+; Charles V. von Lüttichau, "Key Dates During the Ardennes Offensive," part 2, April 1952, NARA RG 319, R-series, #11, 104–8 (*"the Elsenborn attack is gaining"*); "Answers to Questions Asked General Westphal," 1954, FMS, #A-896, MHI, 8–9 (*tactical fortunes of Dietrich*). The formal shift of emphasis from north to south occurred on Dec. 20 (*Ardennes*, 134–35).

428 *Two armored corps abreast had come down*: TT, 130–31; David E. Wright, "The Operations of the 1st Battalion, 110th Infantry," 1948, IS, 7 (*Cota's 28th Division*); Royce L. Thompson, "American Intelligence on the German Counteroffensive," vol. 2, "Division Level," March 1949, CARL, N-16829.2, 140–41 (*found themselves fighting five*).

429 *As artillery and mortar barrages shredded:* Ardennes, 181–82; Phillips, *To Save Bastogne,* 52; AAR, 28th ID, Unit Report No. 6, Dec. 1944, JT, LOC MS Div, box 34 (*German infiltrators forded the Our*); corr, Bill Jarrett, May 23, 1945, Norman D. Cota papers, DDE Lib, box 2 ("*While I was being searched*"); Ardennes, 188 ("*clay pipes*"), 198–99 ("*not healthy anymore*").

429 *Yet as in the north, frictions and vexations:* TT, 143–44; Ardennes, 186 (*Engineers eventually built two spans*); "The Breakthrough to Bastogne," vol. 2, n.d., CMH, 8-3.1 AR, 4–6 (*reduced traffic to a crawl*).

429 *On the American right, where four infantry divisions:* Ardennes, 212–13; Ent, ed., *The First Century,* 176 (*would fall back slowly for four miles*). Seventh Army took several days to throw five bridges across the Our. Jacobsen and Rohwer, eds., *Decisive Battles of World War II: The German View,* 405–6.

429 *On Cota's left, two battlion kitchens:* corr, Gustin M. Nelson, CO, 112th Inf, to father, May 1945, CBM, MHI, box 3; Ardennes, 193; Ent, ed., *The First Century,* 174.

429 *That left Cota a single regiment:* The 110th Inf also had only two infantry battalions on line, with the third held to the west in division reserve ("The Breakthrough to Bastogne," vol. 2, n.d., CMH, 8-3.1 AR, 4–6).

431 *Here Manteuffel swung his heaviest blow:* Ardennes, 176–77, 190–91 (*barricaded themselves*); Jacobsen and Rohwer, eds., *Decisive Battles of World War II: The German View,* 394–95 (*under a Führer order*); Clervaux en Ardennes, 12, 26–27 (*John the Blind*); Toland, *Battle,* 99 (*pleas for salvation*).

431 *A mile up the road, in the three-story Hotel:* author visit, Clervaux, June 3, 2009; AAR, 110th Inf, n.d., JT, LOC MS Div, box 35 (*advised Cota by radio*); Toland, *Battle,* 88 ("*Hold at all costs*").

431 *At 7:30 on Sunday evening:* TT, 276–79; AAR, 110th Inf, n.d., JT, LOC MS Div, box 35; corr, Hurley E. Fuller to Norman D. Cota, Feb. 22, 1945, Cota papers, DDE Library, box 2 (*Within hours Fuller had been captured*).

431 *The castle too was burning:* McManus, *Alamo in the Ardennes,* 93–94, 143; Phillips, *To Save Bastogne,* 142–43 (*garrison hoisted a white flag*); Jos. Märtz, "Luxemburg in der Rundstedt-Offensive," JT, LOC MS Div, box 39, 144 (*German looting*); Margaret Henry Fleming, "With the American Red Cross in the Battle of the Bulge," n.d., Columbus WWII Round Table Collection, MHI, box 1 ("*Of course we're open*").

432 *Not far from Clervaux, frightened civilians:* diary, "First Army," Dec. 19, 1944, JT, LOC MS Div, box 36; Ardennes, 226 (*fled Diekirch in bitter cold*); Weintraub, *11 Days in December,* 40 (*Christmas packages and letters*); "The Breakthrough to Bastogne," vol. 2, n.d., CMH, 8-3.1 AR, 31, 37–40 (*A gaggle of Army bandsmen*).

432 "*This was the end*": Ardennes, 210–11; Daniel B. Stickler, XO, 110th Inf, "The Battle of the Bulge," n.d., CBM, MHI, box 3 (*radium-dial compasses*); McManus, *The Deadly Brotherhood,* 160 ("*laughing at me*").

432 *The 110th Infantry had been annhilated:* "The Breakthrough to Bastogne," vol. 2, n.d., CMH, 8-3.1 AR, 31, 40–41; Cirillo "Ardennes-Alsace," 25.

432 *Only in the center of the German onslaught:* Royce L. Thompson, "Intensity of Fighting on a Division Level: The Ordeal of the 106th ID," n.d., CMH, 2-3.7 AE P-5, 135; Dupuy, *St. Vith: Lion in the Way,* 35, 46 (*Siegfried Line pillboxes*); "The Defense of St. Vith, Belgium," n.d., AS, Ft. K, NARA RG 407, E 427, Miscl AG Records, #2280, 2–7 (*hoped to capture St.-Vith within a day*); Ardennes, 145 (*On no segment of the Western Front*), 147 ("*Take a ten-minute break*"); "The Losheim Gap," n.d., NARA RG 498, ETO HD, UD 584, 6–10.

433 *Not for long, at least on the left flank:* "VIII Corps Strength, 16 Dec 1944," n.d., CMH, 2-3.7, AE P-14 (*sixteen hundred troopers*); "The Losheim Gap," n.d., NARA RG 498, ETO HD, UD 584, 3–4, 18 (*put Manderfeld to the torch*); OH, 14th Cavalry Gp, NARA RG 407, E 427-A, CI, folder #329 ("*Your damn town*" and "*Tanks seventy-five yards*"); "The Losheim Gap," n.d., NARA RG 498, ETO HD, UD 584, 2, 14–16; TT, 117 (*the cavalry buckled*); Dupuy, *St. Vith: Lion in the Way,* 28–29 ("*Front lines still intact*"); affidavit,

A. D. "Pat" Dugan, former XO, 14th Cavalry Gp, June 12, 1950, a.p., 2–4 (*knocked Devine to the floor*); "Report of Investigation, Action of 14th Cavalry Group," Jan. 29, 1945, IG, NARA RG 338, First Army AG Gen'l Corr (*eight of a dozen tank destroyers*).

433 *Devine's behavior now grew odd*: corr, M. A. Devine, Jr., to "Gen. Searcy," Feb. 27, 1945, and handwritten notes, n.d., a.p. (*eating bread, cheese*); affidavit, W. M. Hoge, 4th AD, Apr. 20, 1945, a.p. (*thought his demeanor unremarkable*); testimony, Henry B. Perrine, ADC, 106th ID, and William C. Baker, Jr., chief of staff, 106th ID, in IG memo, Feb. 2, 1945, NARA RG 338, First Army AG Gen'l Corr, box 222 (*"almost incoherent"*).

433 *Instead, at daybreak on Sunday Devine*: *Ardennes*, 162–64. On his first two visits to St.-Vith, Devine took a French liaison officer, Aspirant George Guderin (Affidavit, G. Guderin, March 12, 1945, a.p.).

433 *"The Germans are right behind us"*: Toland, *Battle*, 66 (*"They've broken through"*); Morelock, *Generals of the Ardennes*, 338–39; Rosser L. Hunter, "Action of 106th Infantry Division," IG, Jan. 26, 1945, NARA RG 338, FUSA AG, 333.9, 1–6; "Report of Investigation, Action of 14th Cavalry Group," Jan. 29, 1945, IG, NARA RG 338, First Army AG Gen'l Corr; "The Losheim Gap," n.d., NARA RG 498, ETO HD, UD 584, 28, 32.

433 *At dusk on Sunday, Devine set out*: OH, 14th Cavalry Gp, NARA RG 407, E 427-A, CI, folder #329.

433 *Thwarted by torrents of traffic*: corr, Lawrence J. Smith, former 14th Cav S-3, to CBM, Oct. 22, 1983, CBM, MHI, box 5 (*disheveled, incoherent*); testimony, William F. Damon, Jr., in IG memo, Feb. 2, 1945, NARA RG 338, First Army AG Gen'l Corr, box 222 (*"I want you to take over"*); affidavit, Robert N. Pritchard, n.d., a.p. (*evacuated to Vielsalm*).

434 *A battalion surgeon later found Devine*: testimony, Clark P. Searle, surgeon, 820th Tank Bn, in IG memo, Feb. 2, 1945, NARA RG 338, First Army AG Gen'l Corr, box 222. Even before the war ended, and for five years subsequently, Devine sought to explain his actions. Gen. Middleton described him as "better than the average officer" (Corr, Troy H. Middleton, July 20, 1949, a.p.).

434 *The damage had been done*: memo, "Action of 106th Infantry Division," First Army IG to chief of staff, Jan. 26, 1945, NARA RG 338, First Army AG Gen'l Corr; *Ardennes*, 90–91 (*American left flank abruptly unhinged*); "The Losheim Gap," n.d., NARA RG 498, ETO HD, UD 584, 12, 32.

434 *In St.-Vith, General Jones, a stocky native*: Persons, *Relieved of Command*, 159–61; *Ardennes*, 155–57.

434 *"You know how things are up there"*: TT, 128–29; OH, Troy H. Middleton, July 30, 1945, theater historian, NARA RG 498, ETOUSA HD, UD 584 (*"He felt that he could hold"*).

434 *Jones also believed that help was on the way*: Morelock, *Generals of the Ardennes*, 295; Rosser L. Hunter, "Action of 106th Infantry Division," IG, Jan. 26, 1945, NARA RG 338, FUSA AG, 333.9, 1–6 (*VIII Corps promised*); Dupuy, *St. Vith: Lion in the Way*, 113–14 (*"indescribable confusion"*); "The Defense of St. Vith, Belgium," n.d., AS, Ft. K, NARA RG 407, E 427, Miscl AG Records, #2280, 9–10 (*"every dog for himself"*); Baldwin, *Battles Lost and Won*, 329 (*" fear-crazed occupants"*).

435 *By midday on Sunday*: TT, 322–23 (*gallstone*); Clarke, "The Battle for St. Vith," *Armor* (Nov.–Dec. 1974): 1+ (*"some trouble"*); Morelock, *Generals of the Ardennes*, 295–300 (*"enough troubles already"*).

435 *The crackle of small-arms fire*: http://www.cellitinnen-osa.de/en/geschichte-teil3.html; TT, 327 (*"thrown in my last chips"*); Clarke, "The Battle for St. Vith," *Armor* (Nov.–Dec. 1974): 1+ (*"You take it now"*); Rosser L. Hunter, "Action of 106th Infantry Division," IG, Jan. 26, 1945, NARA RG 338, FUSA AG, 333.9, 5 (*joined the frantic exodus*).

435 *Jones's stand-fast decision*: "The Losheim Gap," n.d., NARA RG 498, ETO HD, UD 584, 32; *Ardennes*, 165–67; "Report of Action Against Enemy," 106th ID, Jan. 6, 1945, Alan W. Jones papers, MHI, box 1; John C. Hollinger, "The Operations of the 422nd Infantry Regiment," IS, 1949 (*absolutely no expression*").

435 *"My poor men"*: TT, 340.

436 *Cooks made towering stacks of pancakes*: John P. Kline, "The Service Diary of German

War Prisoner #315136," n.d., CBM, MHI, box 2; OH, 106th ID, "German Breakthrough in the Ardennes," n.d., NARA RG 407, E 427-A, CI, folders 244–245a (*compass azimuth*); Dupuy, *St. Vith: Lion in the Way*, 123 ("*Where the hell are we?*"); "Report on Allied Air Force Operations," May 21, 1945, SHAEF, A-3, CARL, N-9371; Royce L. Thompson, "Air Resupply to Isolated Units, Ardennes Campaign," Feb. 1951, CMH, 2-3.7 AE P, 2–3, 26–29 ("*command incoordination*").

436 *"Attack Schönberg"*: TT, 340.

436 *At daybreak on Tuesday, three battalions*: OH, 106th ID, "German Breakthrough in the Ardennes," n.d., NARA RG 407, E 427-A, CI, folders 244–245a; corr, George A. Curtis, Sept. 7, 1957, CBM, MHI, box 4 ("*this isn't exactly as we planned*").

436 *By one P.M., at least one battalion*: memo, Distinguished Unit Citation nomination, 423rd Inf, CBM, MHI, box 4; "A Glimpse of War," n.d., submitted by Robert Fullam, NWWIIM, 9 ("*their skin that yellow-white*"); OH, 106th ID, "German Breakthrough in the Ardennes," n.d., NARA RG 407, E 427-A, CI, folders 244–245a ("*Go blow it out your ass*"); Alan W. Jones, Jr., "The Operations of the 423rd Infantry," IS, 1949, 26 (*Spirits soared for a moment*).

437 *At 2:30 P.M., with two thousand of his men*: http://www.purplehearts.net/descheneaux/descheneaux.htm ("*like fish in a pond*"); OH, 106th ID, "German Breakthrough in the Ardennes," n.d., NARA RG 407, E 427-A, CI, folders 244–245a ("*Destroy all weapons*"); TT, 343–45 (*Descheneaux sat on the lip*); memo, Distinguished Unit Citation nomination, 423rd Inf, CBM, MHI, box 4; Leo R. Leisse, "Diary of an Ex-P.O.W.," n.d., CBM, MHI, box 5, 2–4 (*Cavender had reached the same conclusion*); Richard A. Hartman, "The Combat History of the 590th Field Artillery Battalion," 1949, CBM, MHI, box 2 ("*We surrender*").

437 *A few diehards lay low*: Ardennes, 170; Morelock, *Generals of the Ardennes*, 275 ("*I've lost a division quicker*"); memos, Jan. 26 and March 8, 1945, 365th Station Hospital, Alan W. Jones papers, MHI, box 1 ("*Detachment of Patients*"); Winton, *Corps Commanders of the Bulge*, 253–56, 412.

437 *Long columns of prisoners plodded*: John P. Kline, "The Service Diary of German War Prisoner #315136," CBM, MHI, box 2 (*wounded men wailing*); OH, Jacques Peterges, Aug. 5, 1981, and Adolf Schür, Aug. 10, 1981, CBM, MHI, box 6 (*catcalling*); William P. Kirkbridge, "Negotiations for the Surrender at Losheimergraben," n.d., Richard H. Byers papers, 99th ID, MHI, box 1 ("*tanks towing other tanks*").

437 *"Do not flee"*: corr, John I. Hungerford to JT, June 26, 1957, CBM, MHI, box 4; Leo R. Leisse, "Diary of an Ex-P.O.W.," n.d., CBM, MHI, box 5, 3–4 (*back to belly*); Roger S. Durham, "The Past Is Present: The World War II Service of George E. Durham," 1996, a.p., 174–75 (*potato skins*); John P. Kline, "The Service Diary of German War Prisoner #315136," n.d., CBM, MHI, box 2 ("*made us take off our overshoes*").

438 *"Bayonets aren't much good"*: Carroll, *Behind the Lines*, 318–20.

438 *"Success—complete success"*: TT, 193.

"Why Are You Not Packing?"

438 *A leaden overcast in Luxembourg City*: Bradley, *A Soldier's Story*, 449 (*Coca-Cola* and "*lifeless chimneys*"); war diaries, Dec. 16, 1944, ONB papers, MHI; "Destroy the Enemy," *Time*, Dec. 4, 1944; Weintraub, *11 Days in December*, 54–55 ("*There's been a complete breakthrough*").

438 *Shortly before three P.M., a SHAEF colonel*: memo, "Conference in War Room," Dec. 16, 1944, Harold R. Bull papers, DDE Lib, box 2; "Excerpts from Diary, D/SAC," Dec. 16, 1944, NARA RG 319, SC background files, 2-3.7 CB 8; Bradley, *A Soldier's Story*, 449; Strong, *Intelligence at the Top*, 212–17 ("*it would be wrong to underrate*").

439 *Eisenhower and Bradley dined that night*: http://www.ibiblio.org/lia/president/Eisenhower Library/_General_Materials/DDE_Biography.html (*ascended from lieutenant colonel to general*); Miller, *Ike the Soldier*, 723 (*Piper Scotch*); diary, Dec. 17, 1944, CBH, MHI, box 4 (*five rubbers of bridge*).

439 *Eisenhower in a subsequent cable to Marshall*: TSC, 375, 376n; *TT*, 186 ("*Tell him that Ike*").

439 *Other moves quickly followed*: DDE, "The Battle of the Ardennes Salient," Dec. 23, 1944, Sidney H. Negrotto papers, MHI; *Ardennes*, 334 (*Army tactical doctrine*); TSC, 380 ("*By rushing out*"); Strong, *Intelligence at the Top*, 219 ("*Why are you not packing?*").

440 *In a message to Marshall*: Chandler, 2368; war diaries, Dec. 17, 1944, ONB papers, MHI (*at least fourteen German divisions*); diary, Dec. 17, 1944, CBH, MHI, box 4 (*sedatives*); memoir, H. Wentworth Eldredge, n.d., Thaddeus Holt papers, MHI (*buried secret documents*).

440 *Still Bradley affected nonchalance*: diary, Dec. 17, 1944, Raymond G. Moses papers, MHI, box 1 ("*Rhine crossing plan*"); diary, Dec. 18, 1944, CBH, MHI, box 4 ("*I don't take too serious*"). Gen. Sibert, the army group G-2, continued to see the offensive as a "diversionary attack" that "cannot be regarded as a major long term threat" (*TT*, 190).

440 *Among those who no longer agreed*: *Ardennes*, 332 (*engineer company*); memoir, H. Wentworth Eldredge, n.d., Thaddeus Holt papers, MHI ("*Oh, what a beautiful mornin'*"); Carpenter, *No Woman's World*, 209 ("*briskly up, over, and across*").

440 *Fourteen First Army divisions*: *Ardennes*, 259; "The Defense of St. Vith, Belgium," n.d., AS, Ft. K, NARA RG 407, E 427, Miscl AG Records, #2280, 5–6 (*165-mile front*); Knickerbocker et al., *Danger Forward*, 338 (*Church bells*); "Defense of Spa," 518th M.P. Bn, n.d., in "History of the Ardennes Campaign," NARA RG 498, ETOUSA HD, UD 584, box 2 (*civilian curfew*); Middleton, *Our Share of Night*, 341 (*tin pans and crockery*); Carpenter, *No Woman's World*, 205–6 (*perimeter strongpoints*); Rosengarten, "With Ultra from Omaha Beach to Weimar, Germany," *Military Affairs* (Oct. 1978): 127+ (*German paratroopers*); Pogue, *Pogue's War*, 296–97 (*lawyers and accountants*).

441 *Soldiers in muddy boots tromped through the Britannique*: "Defense of Spa," 518th M.P. Bn, n.d., in "History of the Ardennes Campaign," NARA RG 498, ETOUSA HD, UD 584, box 2 (*twenty-one jailed collaborators*); Pogue, *Pogue's War*, 294 ("*Thermite grenades*"); Zuckerman, *From Apes to Warlords*, 312 (*among those building bonfires*); OH, Robert A. Hewitt, 1981, Earl D. Bevan, SOOHP, MHI, 175; Benjamin A. Dickson, "G-2 Journal: Algiers to the Elbe," MHI, 183 (*Kasserine Pass*).

441 *Perhaps the prospect of a similar debacle*: The most comprehensive account of this episode is to be found in Hogan, *A Command Post at War*, 212.

441 "*probably the most shaken man I have ever seen*": corr, E. N. Harmon to G. F. Howe, Oct. 21, 1952, OCMH, NARA RG 319, Howe papers, background files to *Northwest Africa: Seizing the Initiative in the West*, USAWWII; Bradley Commentaries, CBH, MHI, boxes 41–42 ("*almost went to pieces*"); Bolger, "Zero Defects: Command Climate in First U.S. Army, 1944–1945," *Military Review* (May 1991): 61+; OH, Adolph Rosengarten, Jr., Dec. 22, 1947, FCP, MHI (*considered relieving Hodges*).

441 *Officers fussed over how to pack*: Pogue, *Pogue's War*, 296–97 ("*I imagine that the Germans*"); Sylvan, 225 (*photos of President Roosevelt*); Carpenter, *No Woman's World*, 212 ("*take my child*"); memo, IG, March 21, 1945, NARA RG 338, First Army AG General Corr, box 223 (*bolting for Huy*); Royce L. Thompson, "Military Impact of the German V-Weapons, 1943–1945," July 31, 1953, CMH, 2-3.7 AE-P-4, 38 (*V-1s hit two fleeing convoys*).

442 *When Hodges tarried at the Britannique*: Carpenter, *No Woman's World*, 213 ("*Save yourself*"); OH, JLC, 1972, Charles C. Sperow, SOOHP, MHI, 229–30; Sylvan, 221 (*opened at midnight*); Morelock, *Generals of the Ardennes*, 150 (*food simmering*).

442 *A British liaison officer*: Hastings, *Armageddon*, 205–7; Hogan, *A Command Post at War*, 217 (*flagged down passing truck drivers*), 223 (*not until a week into the German offensive*); Morelock, *Generals of the Ardennes*, 150 (*uncertain where the First Army command post*); corr, Weldon Hogie to family, Dec. 30, 1944, "Letters Back Home," a.p., 82–83 ("*We can't lose three months' gains*").

442 *Evacuation of the vast supply dumps*: "Operational History of the Advance Section, COMZ," n.d., NARA RG 498, ETO HD, admin file #583F, 109; Robert M. Littlejohn, ed.,

"Battle of the Bulge," 1955, chapter 21, PIR, MHI, 3–4 (*stocks could be found in the rear*); Fest, "The German Ardennes Offensive: A Study in Retrograde Logistics," *Ordnance* (Feb. 1983): 51+; Wendt, "Logistics in Retrograde Movements," *Military Review* (July 1948): 34+.

442 *Three miles of primacord*: "Ardennes, Supply Installations, Withdraw of," FUSA, Apr. 29, 1945, NARA RG 498, ETOUSA HD, UD 584, box 2; Cooper, *Death Traps*, 183 (*fuel dump covered several square miles*); "The Quartermaster in the Bulge," in "History of the Ardennes Campaign," NARA RG 498, ETOUSA HD, UD 584, box 2 (*ignited in a roadblock*); Wendt, "Logistics in Retrograde Movements," *Military Review* (July 1948): 34+.

443 *Crows or starlings might have been mistaken*: "Kampfgruppe von der Heydte," FMS, #B-823, JT, LOC MS Div, box 38; interrogation, F. von der Heydte, Oct. 31, 1945, London, NARA RG 407, E 427, ML #1068; *Ardennes*, 271.

443 *Operation GREIF, or "condor"*: DOB, 244 (*flamboyant Viennese commando*); *Ardennes*, 270 (*150th Armored Brigade*); Skorzeny, *Skorzeny's Special Missions*, 156–58; interrogation, Otto Skorzeny, n.d., ETHINT 12, CBM, box 12; Weingartner, "Otto Skorzeny and the Laws of War," *JMH* (Apr. 1991): 207+ (Casablanca).

444 *found to be wearing swastika brassards*: "The History of the CIC," n.d., Intelligence Center, Ft. Holabird, CBM, box 6, 2–3, 10–12, 19; memo, Richard F. Shappell to Hugh M. Cole, May 14, 1945, FUSA G-2, Operation GREIF, NARA RG 407, E 429, ML #994 (*sixteen infiltrators*); *Ardennes*, 559 (*without effecting a single act*), 360–63; Weingartner, "Otto Skorzeny and the Laws of War," *JMH* (Apr. 1991): 207+.

444 *The sole accomplishment of GREIF*: memo, C. Hodges to SHAEF, Dec. 20, 1944, NARA RG 331, E 1, SGS, "Assassins," box 8; "The History of the CIC," n.d., Intelligence Center, Ft. Holabird, CBM, box 6, 12; memo, FUSA to SHAEF, Dec. 22, 1944, NARA RG 331, E 1, SGS, "Assassins," box 8 (*"dueling scars"*); Toland, *Battle*, 158–59 (*brawling over a ballerina and nuns*); CI News Sheet No. 12, Dec. 26, 1944, 21st AG, in FUSA G-2, Operation GREIF, NARA RG 407, E 429, ML #994 (*sulfuric acid*); Paul E. Kohli, "Stavelot, Belgium, 16–18 December 1944," 1985, Columbus WWII Round Table collection, MHI, box 1, 5 (*spoke English better*); "The History of the CIC," n.d., Intelligence Center, Ft. Holabird, CBM, box 6, 18 (*top button of a uniform*); *Ardennes*, 559 (*"Belgian or French café keepers"*).

444 *MPs at checkpoints sought to distinguish*: FUSA G-2, Operation GREIF, NARA RG 407, E 429, ML #994; "The History of the CIC," n.d., Intelligence Center, Ft. Holabird, CBM, box 6, 18 (*Sinatra's first name?*); Elstob, *Hitler's Last Offensive*, 189 (*Where is Little Rock?*); Capa, *Slightly Out of Focus*, 208 (*capital of Nebraska*); Pogue, *Pogue's War*, 302–3 (*"The capital is Frankfort"*); Weintraub, *11 Days in December*, 59 (*"Who won the World Series"*). Niven was attached to 12th Army Group as a liaison officer.

445 *Cooks, bakers, and clerks were tutored*: Price, *Troy H. Middleton: A Biography*, 223; memo to W. B. Smith, Dec. 21, 1944, NARA RG 331, E 1, SGS, "Assassins," box 8 (*gunned down four French civilians*); war diary, Dec. 22, 1944, Ninth Army, William H. Simpson papers, MHI, box 11 (*"get out of my way"*); Murphy, *Diplomat Among Warriors*, 239 (*"We deployed into the garden"*).

445 *a perfect body double*: "The History of the CIC," n.d., Intelligence Center, Ft. Holabird, CBM, box 6, 14; *TT*, 226.

445 *The real Eisenhower, traveling with Tedder*: diary, Dec. 19–20, 1944, CBH, MHI, box 4; Baldwin, *Battles Lost and Won*, 335 (*"What the hell is this?"*).

445 *"The present situation is to be regarded"*: Eisenhower, *Crusade in Europe*, 371.

445 *Two staff officers reviewed the battlefront*: "Record of Meeting," Dec. 19, 1944, Harold R. Bull papers, DDE Lib, box 2; *TT*, 419–20 (*seventeen German divisions*), 417 (*180,000 troops*); "Allied Air Power and the Ardennes Offensive," n.d., director of intelligence, USSAFE, NARA RG 498, ETOUSA HD, UD 584, box 1 (*Daily Luftwaffe sorties*); "Task Force Thrasher: History of the Defense of the Meuse River," 1945, NARA RG 407, ML #945, box 24198 (*Seven French infantry battalions*).

446 *Eisenhower then spoke*: "Record of Meeting," Dec. 19, 1944, Harold R. Bull papers, DDE

Lib, box 2 ("*positive concerted action*"); "Counter-offensive Measures," SHAEF, Dec. 22, 1944, NARA RG 498, ETOUSA HD, UD 584, box 1 ("*a supply desert*"); *Ardennes*, 487; "The Intervention of the Third Army: III Corps in the Attack," n.d., CMH, 8-3.1 AR, I-1 (*three corps facing the Saar*).

446 "*George, how soon*": Verdun conference participants left varying accounts of this exchange, including one staff officer who recalled Patton saying he could attack in two days (OH, Reuben Jenkins, 6th AG G-3, Oct. 14, 1970, Thomas E. Griess, YCHT, 39–40). Most recalled a claim of three days. "Notes on Bastogne Operation," Third Army, Jan. 15, 1945, NARA RG 407, E 427-A, CI, "The Siege of Bastogne," folder #227.

446 "*On December 22*": *PP*, 599–600. John Nelson Rickard notes that some evidence suggests Patton may have proposed Dec. 21 (*Advance and Destroy*, 106).

446 *Leaning forward, Eisenhower quickly calculated*: OH, Reuben Jenkins, 6th AG G-3, Oct. 14, 1970, Thomas E. Griess, YCHT, 39–40; *TT*, 421 ("*Don't be fatuous*").

446 "*We can do that*": Hirshson, *General Patton: A Soldier's Life*, 577.

446 *Before leaving the barracks, Patton phoned*: "Notes on Bastogne Operation," Jan. 16, 1945, GSP, LOC MS Div, box 49, folder 13; Allen, *Lucky Forward*, 33 ("*Everyone is a son-of-a-bitch*").

446 "*Yes, and every time you get attacked*": Codman, *Drive*, 233–34; diary, Dec. 19, 1944, GSP, LOC MS Div, box 3, folder 9; diary, Dec. 19, 1944, CBH, MHI, box 4 ("*great expansive exuberance*").

447 "*There's something about the guy*": diary, Nov. 8, 1944, CBH, MHI, box 4.

447 *Eisenhower had urged his lieutenants*: "Record of Meeting," Dec. 19, 1944, Harold R. Bull papers, DDE Lib, box 2 ("*avoid any discouragement*").

447 *British intelligence on Tuesday evening*: Belchem, *All in the Day's March*, 247; msg, BLM to Brooke, Dec. 19, 1944, IWM, PP/MCR, C46, Ancillary Collections, micro R-1 ("*Ike ought to place me*"); *Ardennes*, 423–24 (*best be managed by two commanders*).

447 *Bradley's subordinate generals to the north*: *Ardennes*, 423–24; Merriam, *Dark December*, 123; Belchem, *All in the Day's March*, 248–49; notes, phone conversation, A. Coningham and James M. Robb, SHAEF, Dec. 22, 1944, DDE Lib, PP-pres, box 98 (*not a single staff officer*); OH, ONB, Dec. 1974 to Oct. 1975, Charles Hanson, MHI, VI, 34 ("*That would startle the people of Luxembourg*").

447 *Rousted from his bed*: Strong, *Intelligence at the Top*, 224–25.

447 *As Whiteley and Strong slunk away*: Bradley Commentaries, CBH, MHI, boxes 41–42; *Ardennes*, 423–24; *TT*, 422–23 (*drew a line on the map*).

448 "*Ike thinks it may be a good idea*": Bradley, *A Soldier's Story*, 476; Bradley and Blair, *A General's Life*, 363–64 ("*I'd question whether such a changeover*").

448 *By Wednesday morning, when Eisenhower called*: Ambrose, *Eisenhower: Soldier, General of the Army, President-Elect, 1890–1952*, vol. 1, 368; Strong, *Intelligence at the Top*, 226 ("*those are my orders*"), 233; OH, BLM, March 29, 1949, R. W. W. "Chester" Wilmot papers, LHC, LH 15/15/127 ("*I think you'd better take charge*").

448 *At 12:52 P.M., a SHAEF log entry*: corr, H. R. Bull to Hanson Baldwin, Sept. 12, 1946, Harold R. Bull papers, DDE Lib, box 2; OH, Arthur Coningham, Feb. 14, 1947, FCP, MHI ("*absolutely livid*").

448 *Amid the dogs, goldfish, and singing canaries*: Hamilton, *Monty: Final Years of the Field-Marshal, 1944–1976*, 181; Hastings, *Armageddon*, 205–7 ("*now have to pay the price*").

449 "*There is great confusion*": corr, BLM to A. Brooke, Dec. 19, 1944, IWM, PP/MCR, C-46, Ancillary Collections, micro R-1.

449 *Little of this was true*: Weigley, *Eisenhower's Lieutenants*, 505 ("*energy and verve*"); Sylvan, 223 ("*bedside conference*"); "Operations of 30 (Br) Corps During the German Attack in the Ardennes," n.d., NARA RG 498, ETOUSA HD, UD 584, box 2; Belchem, *All in the Day's March*, 247 (*piled carts*).

449 *The field marshal himself arrived*: OH, BLM, Oct. 1, 1966, John S. D. Eisenhower, CBM, MHI, box 6, 6; Hamilton, *Monty: Final Years of the Field-Marshal, 1944–1976*, 246 (*eight pullovers*); Carpenter, *No Woman's World*, 215–16 ("*Unwrapping the bearskin*"); Wishnevsky,

Courtney Hicks Hodges, 161 (*"monkey on a stick"*); Wilmot, *The Struggle for Europe*, 592 (*"Christ come to cleanse"*).

449 *Three hours later they had both a plan*: Hogan, *A Command Post at War*, 219–20; Belchem, *All in the Day's March*, 248–49 (*Hodges feared that two First Army divisions*); Wilmot, *The Struggle for Europe*, 593; *Ardennes*, 426–27; war diary, Ninth Army, Dec. 20, 1944, William H. Simpson papers, MHI, box 11 (*assemble a strike force*); "Operations of 30 (Br) Corps During the German Attack in the Ardennes," and tally of British equipment transfers, n.d., NARA RG 498, ETOUSA HD, UD 584, box 2 (*"enemy's hopes of bouncing"* and *British stocks*); "Combat Engineering," Aug. 1945, Historical Report No. 10, CEOH, box X-30, 89–90 (*all Meuse bridges*).

450 *"Hodges is not the man I would pick"*: OH, W. B. Smith, May 8, 1947, FCP, MHI.

450 *"Hodges is the quiet reticent type"*: Chandler, 2369.

450 *SHAEF ordered the new command arrangement*: "The Old Army Game," *Time* (Jan. 1, 1945): 45; Elstob, *Hitler's Last Offensive*, 462 (*"They seemed delighted"*); Hamilton, *Monty: Final Years of the Field-Marshal, 1944–1976*, 238 (*"a 1st Class bloody nose"*).

450 *As for Bradley*: OH, James M. Robb, n.d., FCP, MHI (*Bronze Star*); Chandler, 2367–68 (*"I retain all my former confidence"*).

War in the Raw

450 *Civilian refugees with woeful tales*: "The Battle of Bastogne, 19–28 Dec. 44," n.d., Battle Studies, CMH, Geog Belgium 370.2, 2; Rapport and Northwood, *Rendezvous with Destiny*, 665 (*"ancient town in the dreariest part"*); "The Battle of the Bulge," *AB*, no. 4 (1974): 1+ (*"unattended vehicles"*); *TT*, 506–7 (*hundreds took refuge*).

451 *The first paratroopers from the 101st Airborne*: *Ardennes*, 305–9; Booth and Spencer, *Paratrooper*, 244 (*"Get out of the sack"*); Toland, *Battle*, 94 (*interrupted a ballet performance*).

451 *Since leaving Holland in November*: memo, MBR to Maxwell D. Taylor, Nov. 12, 1944, MBR papers, MHI, box 21 (*AWOL incidents*); Schrijvers, *The Crash of Ruin*, 171 (*drunken brawls*); Kennett, *G.I.: The American Soldier in World War II*, 209–10 (*troopers held contests*); Marshall, *Bastogne*, 10 (*in England with seventeen officers*); Blair, *Ridgway's Paratroopers*, 362, 513 (*killed himself with a pistol*).

451 *Anthony Clement McAuliffe*: MMB, 351. McAuliffe was born in Washington, D.C., and attended West Virginia University before West Point (http://www.arlingtoncemetery .net/amcauli.htm; http://en.wikipedia.org/wiki/Anthony_McAuliffe#cite_note-2; "Gale Encyclopedia of Biography," http://www.answers.com/topic/anthony-mcauliffe; Blair, *Ridgway's Paratroopers*, 221, 336–37).

451 *Several thousand replacement troopers*: OH, A. C. McAuliffe, Jan. 2, 1945, Paris, in Brereton, *The Brereton Diaries*, 378–82; Bowen, *Fighting with the Screaming Eagles*, 161 (*"olives in a jar"*); "Bastogne," n.d., NARA RG 498, ETOUSA HD, UD 584 (*without helmets or rifles*); "Battle of the Bulge," 101st Airborne miscellany, NARA RG 407, E 427-A, CI, folder #229 (*emergency convoy*); OH, William L. Roberts, CCB, 10th AD, Jan. 12, 1945, NARA RG 407, E 427-A, folder #305 (*"fluid and obscure"*); "The Battle of Bastogne, 19–28 Dec. 44," n.d., Battle Studies, CMH, Geog Belgium 370.2, 2 (*first wounded*); *Ardennes*, 315; Price, *Troy H. Middleton: A Biography*, 248 (*in his Packard*).

453 *Bearing down on Bastogne*: *Ardennes*, 449, 229 (*Foot soldiers slouching westward*); Cirillo, "Ardennes-Alsace," 26; Ritgen, *Die Geschichte der Panzer-Lehr Division im Westen*, no pagination; "The Battle of the Bulge," *AB*, no. 4 (1974): 1+; Charles V. von Lüttichau, "Diary of Thuisko von Metzch," Army Group B, May 1952, and OH with von Metzch, n.d., NARA RG 319, R-series, #10, 25–26 (*Model now privately doubted*).

453 *"an abscess on our line"*: Toland, *Battle*, 119.

453 *Two straggling artillery battalions at Longvilly*: *Ardennes*, 449, 303–4 (*"We're not driven out"*), 319–20.

453 *No less vital in delaying the enemy*: Price, *Troy H. Middleton: A Biography*, 230; OH, William R. Desobry, 1978, Ted S. Chesney, SOOHP, MHI (*"by guess and by God"*); Marshall, *Bastogne*, 57–59 (*ripped into nine panzers*).

454 *All morning and through the afternoon*: OH, William R. Desobry, 1978, Ted S. Chesney, SOOHP, MHI; AAR, 506th PIR, Jan. 8, 1945, in "Battle of the Bulge," NARA RG 407, E 427-A, CI, folder 229 (*pounded Noville to rubble*).

454 *At midday on Wednesday, December 20*: Ardennes, 454–55 ("*Situation critical*"); OH, R. Harwick, 506th PIR, n.d., HI (*four remaining Shermans*); TT, 500; McManus, *Alamo in the Ardennes*, 252; author visit, Noville, Bastogne, June 3, 2009, tourist pamphlet (*Gestapo agents*).

454 *Strongpoints east of Bastogne, now reinforced*: OH, J. Ewell, "Action of 501st Regiment at Bastogne," Jan. 6, 1945, NARA RG 407, E 427-A, CI, folder #230 ("*mantrap*"); OH, Stanfield Stach, 501st PIR, n.d., HI ("*We took no prisoners*"); Marshall, *Bastogne*, 76 ("*dam of fire*"); *Ardennes*, 456–58.

454 *Little profit had been found in frontal assaults*: Ardennes, 321; Jacobsen and Rohwer, eds., *Decisive Battles of World War II: The German View*, 405–6.

454 *Among the few heartening reports*: AAR, Albert J. Crandall, First Airborne Surgical Team, June 8, 1945, "Medical Department Activities in ETO," NARA; Rapport and Northwood, *Rendezvous with Destiny*, 468 ("*bullets were so close*"); "Bastogne," n.d., NARA RG 498, ETOUSA HD, UD 584 (*division surgeon*).

455 "*Above all*," *Middleton had instructed*: "Bastogne," n.d., NARA RG 498, ETOUSA HD, UD 584; "Report on Allied Air Forces Operations," SHAEF, May 21, 1945, CARL, N-9371 (*twenty-nine sorties in Europe*); Jacobsen and Rohwer, eds., *Decisive Battles of World War II: The German View*, 407–9 (*Resurgent optimism*).

455 *At 11:30 on Friday morning*: Rapport and Northwood, *Rendezvous with Destiny*, 510–11.

455 "*The fortune of war is changing*": Devlin, *Paratrooper!*, 529–30.

455 *At 12:25 P.M. the ultimatum reached McAuliffe*: "The Battle of Bastogne, 19–28 Dec. 44," n.d., Battle Studies, CMH, Geog Belgium 370.2, 3; "Bastogne," n.d., NARA RG 498, ETOUSA HD, UD 584; corr, Eugene A. Watts to CBM, Feb. 28, 1985, CBM, MHI, box 1; *Ardennes*, 459 (*only five battalions among the four regiments*); OH, William L. Roberts, CCB, 10th AD, Jan. 12, 1945, NARA RG 407, E 427-A, folder #305 (*mimeographed useful tips* and *two meals a day*); Marshall, *Bastogne*, 133–34 ("*whites of their eyes*"); *Ardennes*, 460–61 (*flapjacks*).

456 *Perhaps inspired by the legendary epithet*: John Glendower Westover, "Selected Memories," vol. 3, MHI, 56, 89–90; OH, Harry W. O. Kinnard, May 2004, author, Arlington, Va.

456 "*We will kill many Americans*": "Bastogne," n.d., NARA RG 498, ETOUSA HD, UD 584.

456 "*This is crazy*": OH, Hasso von Manteuffel, Oct. 12, 1966, John S. D. Eisenhower, CBM, MHI, box 6, 21.

456 *The town had been named for Saint Vitus*: http://saintvitus.com/SaintVitus/Catholic _Encyclopedia.html; http://www.catholic-saints.info/patron-saints/saint-vitus.htm; author visit, St.-Vith, June 2, 2009, signage (*Various unpleasantries*); http://st.vith.be/tourist info/?Geschichtliches; Manteuffel assessment, 1964, in terrain study, Northern Army Group, June 1976, MHI, 11 (*German plan to occupy St.-Vith*).

456 *Gunfights had erupted around the town*: AAR, 106th ID, Jan. 6, 1945, Alan W. Jones papers, MHI, box 1; Morelock, *Generals of the Ardennes*, 306–7 (*easternmost U.S. redoubt*); *Ardennes*, 292–93 ("*German tide*").

456 *With supply lines cut*: Ardennes, 399 (*seven rounds*); AAR, 442nd FA Group, March 18, 1946, Robert W. Hasbrouck papers, MHI, box 1 ("*old propaganda shells*"); Donald P. Boyer, Jr., "Narrative Account of Action of 38th Armored Infantry Battalion," n.d., Robert W. Hasbrouck papers, MHI, box 1 ("*for every round fired*"); Schrijvers, *The Unknown Dead*, 169–70 (*burning slaughterhouse*); "Engineer Memoirs: General William M. Hoge," 1993, CEOH, 134 (*gobbled amphetamines*); Lauer, *Battle Babies*, 83 (*greasy smoke*); Ellis, *On the Front Lines*, 97 ("*cold, plodding, unwilling*"); memoir, Archie Ross, n.d., 424th Inf, NWWIIM ("*grow into an old man*").

457 *Manteuffel on December 20*: "The Defense of St. Vith, Belgium," n.d., AS, Ft. K, NARA RG 407, E 427, Miscl AG Records, #2280, 25; *Ardennes*, 404–6 (*flat-trajectory flares*); Donald P. Boyer, Jr., "Narrative Account of Action of 38th Armored Infantry Battalion,"

n.d., Robert W. Hasbrouck papers, MHI, box 1 (*"They're blasting my men"*); "The Defense of St. Vith, Belgium," n.d., Ft. K, AS, NARA RG 407, E 427, Miscl AG Records, #2280, 29 (*ordered his troops to fall back*); Blair, *Ridgway's Paratroopers*, 385; *TT*, 481 (*twenty thousand others*).

457 *General Hodges had given XVIII Airborne Corps*: war diary, XVIII Airborne Corps, Dec. 19, 1944, MBR papers, MHI, box 59; *Ardennes*, 401 (*twenty-five miles to eighty-five*), 410–13 (*battalion staff at Neubrück*); Morelock, *Generals of the Ardennes*, 308–10, 326 (*lost half its strength*).

457 *"This terrain is not worth a nickel"*: Bruce C. Clarke, "The Battle of St. Vith: A Concept in Defensive Tactics," n.d., CARL, N-8467.297; msg, R. Hasbrouck to MBR, Dec. 22, 1944, Robert W. Hasbrouck papers, MHI, box 1; corr, MBR to JMG, Oct. 6, 1978, Maurice Delaval papers, MHI, box 9; Ridgway, *Soldier*, 120 (*"We're not going to leave you"*).

457 *Reluctantly, Ridgway in midafternoon*: *Ardennes*, 412–13; corr, MBR to JMG, Oct. 6, 1978, Maurice Delaval papers, MHI, box 9; Morelock, *Generals of the Ardennes*, 308–10 (*"They can come back"*).

457 *Fourteen hours of December darkness*: Goolrick and Tanner, *The Battle of the Bulge*, 124 (*"Go west"*); memoir, Roger W. Cresswell, 7th AD, Sept. 23, 1979, Maurice Delaval collection, MHI, box 7 (*each man gripping the belt* and *"only their eyes showing"* and *"Stay right where you are"*); "The Defense of St. Vith, Belgium," n.d., AS, Ft. K, NARA RG 407, E 427, Miscl AG Records, #2280, 36 (*prodigal counterfire*); *TT*, 481, 487 (*Hasbrouck stood on a road*).

458 *Ridgway estimated that fifteen thousand troops*: Blair, *Ridgway's Paratroopers*, 389; *Ardennes*, 422 (*casualties east of the Salm*); *TT*, 487 (*would long resent Ridgway*); Soffer, *General Matthew B. Ridgway*, 71 ("*Nobody is worried*").

458 *German troops ransacked St.-Vith*: *Ardennes*, 412–13.

458 *"Model himself directs traffic"*: Baldwin, *Battles Lost and Won*, 338.

458 *Looting was best done quickly*: "Allied Air Power and the Ardennes Offensive," n.d., director of intelligence, USSAFE, NARA RG 498, ETOUSA HD, UD 584, box 1 (*seventeen hundred tons*); author visit, June 2, 2009, signage, tourist brochure; Schrijvers, *The Unknown Dead*, 183–84; Hastings, *Armageddon*, 211 (*"big-mouthed apes"*).

458 *A GI shivering in an Ardennes foxhole*: Blunt, *Foot Soldier*, 119 (*"How come we don't"*); Baxter, *Scientists Against Time*, 222 (*"most remarkable scientific achievement"*).

459 *The new weapon's origin dated to 1940*: "Employment of VT Fuzes in the Ardennes Campaign," n.d., CMH, 3–6 (*2,500 antiaircraft artillery shells*); Baxter, *Scientists Against Time*, 223–24 (*ice cream cone*).

459 *The resulting device, eventually known*: Baxter, *Scientists Against Time*, 223–24, 235; Green et al., *The Ordnance Department*, 363–66 (*used only over open water*); Appleman et al., *Okinawa: The Last Battle*, 257; "Employment of VT Fuzes in the Ardennes Campaign," n.d., CMH, 3–6, 17; Morton, "The VT Fuze," *Army Ordnance* (Jan.–Feb. 1946): 43+ (*five times more effective*); Baldwin, *The Deadly Fuze*, 275–76 (*Lancaster bombers had flown*).

459 *Pozit variants had been developed*: Cooper, *Death Traps*, 206; corr, Ben Lear to GCM, n.d. (fall 1944), Henry B. Sayler papers, DDE Lib, box 9 (*"most important new development"*); Morton, "The VT Fuze," *Army Ordnance* (Jan.–Feb. 1946): 43+.

460 *With approval from the Charlie-Charlies*: "Employment of VT Fuzes in the Ardennes Campaign," n.d., CMH, 9–11, 21–24 (*"slaughter of enemy concentrations"* and *"terror weapon"*); Richard Henry Byers, "Battle of the Bulge," 1983, a.p., 39 (*"piles of shells"*); "Operational Use of VT Artillery Fuzes," OPD Information Bulletin, Feb. 23, 1945, vol. 4, #2, NARA RG 334, E 315, ANSCOL, box 1164; Green et al., *The Ordnance Department*, 363–66 (*"severely upset"*).

460 *Three hundred American companies*: Baxter, *Scientists Against Time*, 233, 236 (*"The other night we caught"*); *Ardennes*, 655–56; "VT Fuzes," March 29, 1945, NARA RG 337, AGF OR #282 (*exaggerations*); "Employment of VT Fuzes in the Ardennes Campaign," n.d., CMH, 3 (*the Army's heaviest shells*); Green et al., *The Ordnance Department*, 366;

Chester C. Hough, "Effectiveness of VT Fuze," Apr. 18, 1945, NARA RG 337, AGF OR #305.

460 *Yet the pozit would prove as demoralizing*: Baldwin, *The Deadly Fuze*, 284; Carpenter, *No Woman's World*, 232 (*"It hangs in the air"*); memo, "Results of Use of Pozit Fuses," Jan. 10, 1945, V Corps to First Army, NARA RG 498, G-3 OR, box 1 (*single 155mm airburst*); "Effect of Pozit Fuze," Jan. 6, 1945, XV Corps, NARA RG 498, G-3 OR, box 10 (*"The devil himself"*).

460 *But what of the devil's henchmen?*: Guns of the 30th ID first used pozit shells on December 19, and gunners estimated that one-quarter of all rounds fired around La Gleize were so fuzed ("VT Fuzes," March 29, 1945, NARA RG 337, AGF OR #282).

460 *Peiper's drive toward the Meuse*: corr, J. Peiper to John S. D. Eisenhower, Apr. 4, 1967, CBM, MHI, box 6; *TT*, 239–40 (*blew all three bridges*); "An Interview with Obst Joachim Peiper," ETHINT 10, Sept. 7, 1945, MHI, 21 (*Peiper swung north*); Reynolds, *Men of Steel*, 95; *Ardennes*, 337–39 (*cans of water*).

461 *More spans were demolished*: Royce L. Thompson, "The ETO Ardennes Campaign: Operations of the Combat Group Peiper," July 24, 1952, CMH; Toland, *Battle*, 176 (*fuel cans into the Amblève*); Weingartner, *Crossroads of Death*, 58–60; *Ardennes*, 349–50, 364–65; Schrijvers, *The Unknown Dead*, 54–56 (*priest gave general absolution*); *TT*, 445.

461 *Peiper had traveled some sixty miles*: Royce L. Thompson, "The ETO Ardennes Campaign: Operations of the Combat Group Peiper," July 24, 1952, CMH; Reynolds, *Men of Steel*, 125 (*fifteen hundred survivors*); "Kampfgruppe Peiper," n.d., FMS, #C-004, MHI, 12–13 (*a hundred American prisoners*); Hal D. McCown, CO, 2nd Bn, 119th Inf, "Observations of an American Field Officer," n.d., MHI; *TT*, 459 (*"communist menace"*); Schrijvers, *The Unknown Dead*, 42–48; Moriss, "The Defense of Stavelot," *Yank*, Feb. 9, 1945, 8+; Hitchcock, *The Bitter Road to Freedom*, 84–85; "Malmédy Massacre Investigation," Senate Armed Services Committee, Oct. 1949, 2.

461 *By late Friday, American machine guns*: *TT*, 459; Royce L. Thompson, "The ETO Ardennes Campaign: Operations of the Combat Group Peiper," July 24, 1952, CMH (*burned secrets in the cellar*); Reynolds, *Men of Steel*, 126; *Ardennes*, 374–77; *TT*, 457–59 (*Luger pistols*), 465 (*hit Malmédy instead*).

461 *"Position considerably worsened"*: H. Priess, "Commitment of the I SS Panzer Corps During the Ardennes Offensive," March 1946, FMS, #A-877, MHI, 40–43; Reynolds, *Men of Steel*, 133 (*coded message*); Reynolds, *The Devil's Adjutant*, 225–35 (*shot for desertion*); *Ardennes*, 376–77 (*last twenty-eight panzers*).

462 *At two A.M. on Sunday, December 24*: *Ardennes*, 376–77. Other accounts cite fewer German wounded and more American prisoners left behind (Reynolds, *Men of Steel*, 133).

462 *During a brief firefight with an American patrol*: Hal D. McCown, CO, 2nd Bn, 119th Inf, "Observations of an American Field Officer," n.d., MHI; *TT*, 462–63 (*"Yankee Doodle"*).

462 *At a ford in the frigid Salm*: Reynolds, *Men of Steel*, 134–35 (*human chain*); Royce L. Thompson, "The ETO Ardennes Campaign: Operations of the Combat Group Peiper," July 24, 1952, CMH (*German line at Wanne*); *TT*, 462–63; Reynolds, *Men of Steel*, 134–35 (*770 remained*); "Malmédy Massacre Investigation," Senate Armed Services Committee, Oct. 1949, 2; *Ardennes*, 262; Royce L. Thompson, "Bibliography of the Malmédy Massacre Case," Dec. 9, 1954, CMH, Geog Belgium, 370.2.

462 *Across the Ardennes, heavy snow*: Royce L. Thompson, "Weather of the Ardennes Campaign," Oct. 2, 1953, CMH, 29; *Ardennes*, 470; Moorehead, *Eclipse*, 228 (*a "radiant world"*); William A. Carter, "Carter's War," 1983, CEOH, box V-14, XII, 22 (*stacked like sandbags*); Wellard, *The Man in a Helmet*, 209 (*women's dresses*); Lewis, ed., *The Mammoth Book of Eyewitness World War II*, 441 (*"Everyone seems about the same age"*).

462 *Troops fashioned sleds*: "Ardennes, Supply Installations, Withdraw of," FUSA, Apr. 29, 1945, NARA RG 498, ETOUSA HD, UD 584; "Chief Engineers Report on Camouflage Activities in the ETO," Nov. 15, 1945, Howard V. Canan papers, HIA, box 3 (*lime wash and salt*); Schrijvers, *The Crash of Ruin*, 208 (*Belgian lace*); "Third U.S. Army After Action Report," n.d., chapter 21, CMH (*mattress covers*); "Unit History, 93rd Evacuation

Hospital, 1944," Donald E. Currier papers, MHI, box 1, 42–43 (*gloves dipped in paint*); Simpson, *Selected Prose*, 138 (*"out like a match"*); Mary Ferrell, 101st Evacuation Hospital, ts, March 1970, NWWIIM (*"like an untuned radio"*).

463 *Clumsy skirmishes and pitched battles*: Ardennes, 438–39; "Engineer Troops in Ardennes Breakthrough," NARA RG 498, ETOUSA HD, UD 584, box 2, 2 (*impeded the north shoulder*); Liddell Hart, *The Other Side of the Hill*, 463 (*exposed Manteuffel's left flank*); Horst Stumpff, OB West chief armored officer, Aug. 11, 1945, ETHINT 61, MHI, 61 (*new panzers in the Rhine valley*).

463 *But west of St.-Vith in the German center*: Gilmore, ed., *U.S. Army Atlas of the European Theater in World War II*, 142–43; Cirillo, "Ardennes-Alsace," 33 (*twenty-five-mile battlefront*).

463 *New anxiety beset First Army headquarters*: Sylvan, 231; war diary, Dec. 24, 1944, 0615 hrs, MBR papers, MHI, box 59 (*"The situation is normal"*).

463 *Others were far less sanguine*: "Report on Allied Air Force Operations," May 21, 1945, SHAEF, A-3, CARL, N-9371; *AAFinWWII*, 773 (*"processing the terrain"*); Royce L. Thompson, "Weather of the Ardennes Campaign," Oct. 2, 1953, CMH, 29–30 (*GIs craned their necks*); Davis, *Carl A. Spaatz and the Air War in Europe*, 532–33 (*heaviest attacks of the war*); Richard Henry Byers, "Battle of the Bulge," 1983, a.p., 36 (*"The bombers have fine, feathery"*); Ardennes, 649–50 (*horse-drawn plows*); Quesada, "Operations of the Ninth Tactical Air Command," lecture, May 29, 1945, NARA RG 334, E 315, ANSCOL, L-10-45, 13; diary, Martin Opitz, 295th VG Div, Dec. 25, 1944, NARA RG 407, ETO G-3 OR, box 8 (*"The American Jabos"*).

464 *Clear skies also permitted resupply of Bastogne*: "Report on Air Resupply to 101st Airborne Division at Bastogne," Jan. 11, 1945, in "Battle of the Bulge," and OH, Carl W. Kohls, G-4, et al., NARA RG 407, E 427-A, CI, folders #229 and 230. Of 900 sorties to Bastogne, 23 planes would be lost (Royce L. Thompson, "Air Resupply to Isolated Units, Ardennes Campaign," Feb. 1951, CMH, 2-3.7 AE P, 73).

464 *General McAuliffe also had the invaluable services*: OH, James E. Parker, "Air Support Part at Bastogne," Jan. 1, 1945, NARA RG 407, E 427-A, CI, folder #230; Marshall, *Bastogne*, 134–56; "Bastogne," n.d., NARA RG 498, ETOUSA HD, UD 584 (*Tracks in the snow*).

464 *Bastogne was reprieved*: OH, William L. Roberts, CCB, 10th AD, Jan. 12, 1945, NARA RG 407, E 427-A, folder #305; "Bastogne," n.d., NARA RG 498, ETOUSA HD, UD 584 (*rationed to ten rounds*); Ardennes, 474 (*sixteen miles in circumference*); Ingersoll, *Top Secret*, 250 (*"steel filings"*).

464 *More than three thousand civilians remained trapped*: Toland, *Battle*, 255–57; "Medical Evacuation and Supply, Bastogne," n.d., NARA RG 407, E 427-A, CI, folder 230 (*Several hundred wounded*); Cowdrey, *Fighting for Life*, 265–66 (*"their faces were old"*); Rapport and Northwood, *Rendezvous with Destiny*, 469–70 (*toiled by flashlight* and *rifle range*); Cosmas and Cowdrey, *Medical Services in the European Theater of Operations*, 418 (*the moribund lay along a wall* and *cognac*); "Bastogne," n.d., NARA RG 498, ETOUSA HD, UD 584 (*coffee and Ovaltine*); Schrijvers, *The Crash of Ruin*, 166–67.

465 *Napalm fires ringed the town*: Ardennes, 475.

465 *"Do not plan, for God's will"*: Weintraub, *11 Days in December*, 137; Simpson, *Selected Prose*, 140 (*"Those who are attacking you"*); Toland, *Battle*, 255–57 (*"Santa Claus Is Coming"*); Ardennes, 475 (*"Xmas eve present"*); Marshall, *Bastogne*, 169 (*"We have been let down"*).

465 *At 5:10 P.M. an intrepid pilot*: "Medical Evacuation and Supply, Bastogne," n.d., NARA RG 407, E 427-A, CI, folder 230; author visit, Bastogne, June 3, 2009, signage; OH, William L. Roberts, CCB, 10th AD, Jan. 12, 1945, NARA RG 407, E 427-A, folder #305 (*civilian nurse*); Rapport and Northwood, *Rendezvous with Destiny*, 471; "The Battle of Bastogne, 19–28 Dec. 44," n.d., CMH, Geog Belgium 370.2, 4.

465 *Patton attended a candlelight communion*: PP, 606; corr, GSP to Bea, Dec. 25, 1944, GSP, LOC MS Div, box 12; D'Este, *Patton: A Genius for War*, 691 (*enthroned with Bradley*); Codman, *Drive*, 235 (*crowded, frigid*).

465 *"brick-red face"*: PP, 852–53.

465 *Scanning the starry sky outside*: Allen, *Lucky Forward*, 184 (*"Noel, noel"*); Wellard, *The Man in a Helmet*, 210 (*personally challenged sentries*); Allen, *Lucky Forward*, 184 (*"root-hog or die"*); D'Este, *Patton: A Genius for War*, 682–83 (*"war in the raw"*); Blumenson, *Patton: The Man Behind the Legend, 1885–1945*, 251 (*asked God for fair weather*); PP, 606 (*"clear cold Christmas"*).

466 *Patton had made good on his brash promise*: H. P. Hudson, "The Intervention of the Third Army: III Corps in the Attack," n.d., NARA RG 498, ETOUSA HD, UD 584, box 3 (*feat was prodigious* and *"Drive like hell"*); Allen, *Lucky Forward*, 180 (*108 artillery battalions*); Rickard, *Advance and Destroy*, 167 (*No SS prisoners were to be taken alive*); Baily, *Faint Praise*, 120 (*"Jumbo" tanks*).

466 *Both commander and commanded had also made missteps*: Albret Praun, Wehrmacht signal chief, "German Radio Intelligence," n.d., FMS, #P-038, CMH, 84–85; Holt, *The Deceivers*, 647–48, 658–59; Cirillo, "Ardennes-Alsace," 36 (*plodding frontal assault*); Robert R. Summers et al., "Armor at Bastogne," May 1949, AS, CARL, N-2146.71-2, 123 (*first time since October*); *Ardennes*, 526 (*perilous night attack*); Fox, *Patton's Vanguard*, 388 (*just fourteen Shermans*), 382–84 (*"manure-strewn hell of a village"*); "The Intervention of the Third Army: III Corps in the Attack," n.d., CMH, 8-3.1 AR, II, 12–13; Taylor, *General Maxwell Taylor*, 130 (*"The troops built little fires"*).

466 *"This was probably my fault"*: PP, 605.

466 *"it takes a long time to learn war"*: Rickard, *Advance and Destroy*, 172; Fox, *Patton's Vanguard*, 388; Robert R. Summers et al., "Armor at Bastogne," May 1949, AS, CARL, N-2146.71-2, 128–31 (*German paratroopers kept infiltrating*); notes, Dec. 26, 1944, SHAEF main, James M. Robb corr, DDE Lib, PP-pres, box 98 (*Patton twice phoned*); "The Intervention of the Third Army: III Corps in the Attack," n.d., CMH, 8-3.1 AR, II, 12–13 (*"I am unhappy"*).

467 *In search of a seam*: Sorley, *Thunderbolt*, 22, 55 (*eating aspirin*); Fox, *Patton's Vanguard*, 399.

467 *"shooting, clubbing, stabbing melee"*: *Ardennes*, 552–55; "The Intervention of the Third Army: III Corps in the Attack," n.d., CMH, 8-3.1 AR, VIII, 10 (*"They are through Assenois"*).

467 *Five Shermans and a half-track*: Sorley, *Thunderbolt*, 80–81; Toland, *Battle*, 282–83 (*"Come here!"*); Capa, *Slightly Out of Focus*, 212 (*"It's good to see you"*).

467 *"Kilroy Was Stuck Here"*: Capa, *Slightly Out of Focus*, 212; *Ardennes*, 607–9 (*seven hundred enemy prisoners*), 480–81 (*two thousand American casualties*); Hastings, *Armageddon*, 234 (*smashing his rifle butt*); "Bastogne," n.d., NARA RG 498, ETOUSA HD, UD 584 (*division's tank strength*); "Answers to Questions Asked General Westphal," 1954, FMS #A-896, MHI, 11 (*"failure to conquer Bastogne"*).

468 *"as important as the battle of Gettysburg"*: PP, 613.

"Glory Has Its Price"

468 Time *in the last week of December*: "Man of the Year," *Time* (Jan. 1, 1945): cover; TT, 600 (*current German salient*); Royce L. Thompson, "Ardennes Campaign Statistics," Apr. 28, 1952, CMH, 2-3.7 AE P-15; "Ordnance," n.d., "History of the Ardennes Campaign," NARA RG 498, UD 584, box 2; "Tactical Air Operations in Europe," XIX Tactical Air Command, May 1945, Frederick L. Anderson papers, HIA, box 83, folder 1, 56 (*ordered to bomb any column*).

468 *Of greater concern was a German armored spearhead*: Rickard, *Advance and Destroy*, 202–3; *Ardennes*, 430–35, 535 (*four-night round-trip*), 426–27; TT, 577–79 (*five miles from Dinant*); Collins, *Lightning Joe*, 292 (*nearly 100,000 strong*).

468 *Savage fighting raged from the Salm*: William E. Dressler et al., "Armor Under Adverse Conditions," 1949, AS, Ft. K, 41–48; TT, 583; *Ardennes*, 570 (*equipment from six battalions*), 595–603 (*Sixth Panzer Army's last sally*); Harmon, *Combat Commander*, 240 (*British flame-throwing tank*).

469 *Eisenhower for the past week*: Weigley, *Eisenhower's Lieutenants*, 545.

469 *An Ultra intercept decoded just after Christmas*: Sent on December 21, the message took five days to decode (Bennett, *Ultra in the West*, 214); Royce L. Thompson, "Ardennes Campaign Statistics," Apr. 28, 1952, CMH, 2-3.7 AE P-15 (*almost four thousand tanks*).

469 *Patton favored driving from the south*: Ardennes, 610-11; Rickard, *Advance and Destroy*, 191–96.

469 *Collins, in a memorandum on Wednesday*: memo, JLC to C. Hodges, "Plans for Offensive Operations," Dec. 27, 1944, JLC papers, DDE Lib, box 3, 201 file.

469 *Montgomery hesitated*: war diary, Ninth Army, Dec. 28, 1944, William H. Simpson papers, MHI, box 11; corr, JLC to Bruce C. Clarke, Feb. 21, 1975, CARL, N-8467.297; OH, JLC, 1973, G. Patrick Murray, SOOHP, in "Courtney Hodges Story," MHI ("*Nobody is going to break through*"); OH, JLC, 1972, Charles C. Sperow, SOOHP, MHI, 235–38 ("*You're going to push the Germans out*").

469 *Falaise could hardly be blamed solely on Montgomery*: Weigley, *Eisenhower's Lieutenants*, 539; msg, BLM to DDE, Dec. 22, 1944, 2155 hrs, DDE Lib, PP-pres, box 83 (*doubted Patton's ability*); memo, JLC to C. Hodges, Dec. 30, 1944, JLC papers, DDE Lib, box 3 ("*definitely expended itself*").

469 *"Praise God"*: notes, James M. Robb, Dec. 27, 1944, DDE office, DDE Lib, PP-pres, box 98.

469 *"Monty is a tired little fart"*: PP, 608; notes, James M. Robb, Dec. 27, 1944, W. B. Smith office, DDE Lib, PP-pres, box 98 ("*our masters in Washington*"); Rickard, *Advance and Destroy*, 193, 198–99 (*Bradley also favored pinching the enemy at Houffalize*); Hogan, *A Command Post at War*, 225 (*counted seventeen uncommitted German divisions*); *Ardennes*, 614 (*clear skies ended*).

470 *Montgomery later asserted*: OH, BLM, Oct. 1, 1966, John S. D. Eisenhower, CBM, MHI, box 6, 7; Bolger, "Zero Defects: Command Climate in First U.S. Army, 1944–1945," *Military Review* (May 1991): 61+ (*preferred the more conservative route*); Sylvan, 241 ("*Hodges has had enough*").

470 *Delayed by fog, snowbanks, and further reports*: Hamilton, *Monty: Final Years of the Field-Marshal, 1944–1976*, 259–63; Eisenhower, *Crusade in Europe*, 360; *TT*, 609 (*Montgomery sketched the plan*).

470 *Yet the field marshal was vague*: Hamilton, *Monty: Final Years of the Field-Marshal, 1944–1976*, 222 ("*gallopers*"), 259–63 (*a "master plan"*); Wilmot, *The Struggle for Europe*, 605 ("*one more full-blooded attack*"); *TSC*, 385n.

471 *With this ancient theme again resurrected*: *TSC*, 385. Eisenhower glosses over this episode in his memoir (Eisenhower, *Crusade in Europe*, 360–61).

471 *"definitely in a somewhat humble frame of mind"*: Hamilton, *Monty: Final Years of the Field-Marshal, 1944–1976*, 265, 246–48 ("*such a decent fellow*" and "*You are far better informed*"); Hastings, *Armageddon*, 223 ("*We have tidied up the mess*").

471 *"We have had one very definite failure"*: Chandler, 2387.

471 *"I put this matter up to you again"*: corr, BLM to DDE, Dec. 29, 1944, DDE Lib, PP-pres, box 83.

472 *"Under no circumstances make any concessions"*: corr, GCM to DDE, Dec. 30, 1944, Eyes Only Message, Walter B. Smith collection, DDE Lib, WWII documents, box 27; *TSC*, 385–86.

472 *"They are all mad at Monty"*: diary, Kay Summersby, Dec. 29 and 31, 1944, DDE Lib, PP-pres, box 140.

472 *"knowing Monty, the last thing he would do"*: notes, James Robb, SHAEF, Dec. 31, 1944, NARA RG 319, SC background files, 2-3.7 CB 8.

472 *"All right, Beetle"*: OH, DDE, n.d., CJR, box 43, file 7, 33.

472 *Now fully alive to Montgomery's peril*: Chandler, 2387n.

472 *"All right, Freddie"*: OH, DDE, n.d., CJR, box 43, file 7, 34.

472 *"I do not agree that one army group commander"*: corr, DDE to BLM, Dec. 31, 1944, DDE Lib, PP-pres, box 83.

473 *Already in fragile health*: OH, Alan Moorehead, Jan. 21, 1947, FCP, MHI ("*one of you will*

have to go"); *AAAD*, 425 (*Mareth*); Ambrose, *Eisenhower: Soldier, General of the Army, President-Elect, 1890–1952*, vol. 1, 376 (*"What shall I do"*).

473 *"Dear Ike . . . Whatever your decision"*: corr, BLM to DDE, Dec. 31, 1944, DDE Lib, PP-pres, box 83.

473 *"The general tendency at SHAEF"*: Hamilton, *Monty: Final Years of the Field-Marshal, 1944–1976*, 288–89; Chandler, 2389 (*"very fine telegram"*), xxiii (*"He's just a little man"*); OH, John Whiteley, May 15, 1963, CR, box 44, folder 3 (*kept him awake*).

473 *Although he commanded ten French and eight American divisions*: RR, 462–63, 482–83, 492; Garland, *Unknown Soldiers*, 346 (*"Shit on Hitler's Home"*). .

474 *The Colmar Pocket, as wide as the Bulge*: OH, Paul D. Adams, 1975, Irving Monclova and Marlin Lang, SOOHP, MHI; diary, Dec. 12, 1944, John E. Dahlquist papers, MHI, box 3 (*"enemy attacked on three fronts"*); corr, J. E. Dahlquist to Homer Case, June 5, 1945, John E. Dahlquist papers, MHI, box 1 (*"holding the bag"*); corr, JLD to DDE, Dec. 18, 1944, NARA RG 319, *RR* background files, FRC 5; diary, JLD, Dec. 15, 1944, MHI; Franklin L. Gurley, "The Relationship Between Jean de Lattre de Tassigny and Jacob L. Devers," March 26, 1994, Sorbonne, NARA RG 319, *RR* background files, FRC 4 (*"two problem children"*).

474 *At Verdun on December 19*: RR, 486–89, 495–97, 511, 533; notes, Dec. 26, 1944, SHAEF main, James M. Robb corr, DDE Lib, PP-pres, box 98 (*brought Devers a map*); Gurley, "Policy Versus Strategy: The Defense of Strasbourg in Dec. 1944," NARA RG 319, *RR* background files, FRC 5 (*abandoning Strasbourg and the Alsatian plain*); memo, DDE to JLD, Dec. 28, 1944, 1024 hrs, NARA RG 498, ETOUSA HD, UD 584 (*SHAEF reserve west of the Vosges*).

474 *"The Germans undoubtedly will attack me"*: diary, JLD, Dec. 26, 28, 29, 1944, MHI.

474 *De Gaulle thought so too*: DOB, 401 (*left-handed salute*); Gurley, "Policy Versus Strategy," NARA RG 319, *RR* background files, FRC 5 (*"They are up to something"*).

476 *While Smith prevaricated*: John W. Price, "The Strasbourg Incident," 1967, OCMH, NARA RG 319, *RR* background files, FRC 5, 3–5 (*fallback positions*); OH, Russell L. Vittrup, 1989, Henry E. Fitzgerald, SOOHP, MHI, 125–26 (*"Ain't going to do it"*); De Lattre de Tassigny, *The History of the French First Army*, 303–4 (*"psychosis of retreat"*); Gurley, "Policy Versus Strategy," NARA RG 319, *RR* background files, FRC 5 (*"integrity of the present front"*).

476 *"Call up Devers and tell him"*: notes, Jan. 1, 1945, SHAEF main, James M. Robb corr, DDE Lib, PP-pres, box 98.

476 *"I won't go to him with that story"*: Gurley, "Policy Versus Strategy," NARA RG 319, *RR* background files, FRC 5.

476 *"The political pressure to retain French soil"*: corr, DDE to JLD, Jan. 1, 1945, JLD papers, MHI.

476 *Devers capitulated*: diary, JLD, Jan. 1, 1945, MHI (*"no alternative"*); Franklin L. Gurley, "The Relationship Between Jean de Lattre de Tassigny and Jacob L. Devers," March 26, 1994, Sorbonne, NARA RG 319, *RR* background files, FRC 4; Gurley, "Policy Versus Strategy," *JMH* (July 1994): 481+.

476 *"You can kill a willing horse"*: diary, JLD, Dec. 30, 1944, MHI.

476 *"make it a Stalingrad"*: diary, JLD, Jan. 1, 1945, MHI.

476 *The final day of the year ticked by*: war diary, Seventh Army, Dec. 31, 1944, MHI; Cochran, "Protecting the Ultimate Advantage," *Military History* (June 1985): 45+; Bradley, *A Soldier's Story*, 483 (*"Never was the world plagued"*); diary, JLD, Dec. 31, 1944, MHI (*"Patch called me"*).

477 *The attack indeed fell that night*: RR, 493–97, 499–500 (*Seventh Army was overextended*); Bonn, *When the Odds Were Even*, 181–83; Rickard, *Advance and Destroy*, 173, 241 (*force Patton to withdraw*).

477 *The Americans were also alert and entrenched*: Cochran, "Protecting the Ultimate Advantage," *Military History* (June 1985): 45+; Donald S. Bussey, "Ultra and the U.S. Seventh Army," May 12, 1945, SRH-022, and "Reports by U.S. Army Ultra Representatives," 6th Army Group, n.d., SRH-023, NARA RG 457, E 022 (*Patch had little doubt*).

477 *"German offensive began"*: Wyant, *Sandy Patch*, 9–11 (*"Murdered them"*); Bonn, *When the Odds Were Even*, 197, 200, 203–4 (*"Gained only insignificant ground"*); RR, 504–5; Yeide and Stout, *First to the Rhine*, 275 (*"Morgue Valley"*).

477 *The most flamboyant German sally*: TT, 608 (*Hangover Raid*); Miller, *Masters of the Air*, 374 (*white gloves*); VW, vol. 2 190. Richard G. Davis puts the tally of destroyed Allied planes at nearly two hundred, including three dozen American aircraft (*Carl A. Spaatz and the Air War in Europe*, 535).

477 *But German losses approached 300 planes*: Germany VII, 693–94; Miller, *Masters of the Air*, 374 (*"our last substance"*). Miller puts Allied losses at more than 450 planes and German losses at over 400.

478 *Even as* NORDWIND *collapsed*: RR, 505–9; "The Psychological Warfare Division," 1945, CMH, 8-3.6 BA, 78–79 (*Radio Stuttgart*): Gurley, "Policy Versus Strategy," NARA RG 319, RR background files, FRC 5 (*"caused a general panic"*).

478 *Lowered tricolors and the sight of official sedans*: Gurley, "Policy Versus Strategy," NARA RG 319, RR background files, FRC 5; memo, "Misleading Briefing Data," Frank A. Allen, Jr., to JLD, Jan. 16, 1945, and memo, 6th Army Group, Jan. 21, 1945, NARA RG 331, E 240P, SHAEF public relations section, box 38 (*"women pushing baby carriages"*); Fussell, *Doing Battle*, 129 (*inverted dinner plates*).

478 *Charles de Gaulle, once again referring to himself*: De Gaulle, *The Complete War Memoirs of Charles de Gaulle*, 834. De Gaulle's message, written on January 1, took twenty-seven hours to reach De Lattre (OH, Philippe de Camas, asst G-3, French First Army, Oct.–Dec. 1948, Miguel Vigneras, Paris, NARA RG 319, RR background files, FRC 5).

478 *"a bomb-like effect"*: OH, Philippe de Camas, asst G-3, French First Army, Oct.–Dec. 1948, Miguel Vigneras, Paris, NARA RG 319, RR background files, FRC 5; Salisbury-Jones, *So Full a Glory*, 171 (*"Ça, non!"*); Gurley, "Policy Versus Strategy," NARA RG 319, RR background files, FRC 5 (*"problem of conscience"*).

478 *De Gaulle saw no dilemma*: De Gaulle, *The Complete War Memoirs of Charles de Gaulle*, 834–37; Gurley, "Policy Versus Strategy," NARA RG 319, RR background files, FRC 5 (*snubbed Madame De Lattre*); De Lattre de Tassigny, *The History of the French First Army*, 311 (*"our last hope"*).

479 *At nine* P.M. *on Tuesday, General Juin*: Gurley, "Policy Versus Strategy," NARA RG 319, RR background files, FRC 5 (*"extremely grave consequences"* and *"they are dependent on us"*); corr, David G. Barr to JLD, Aug. 15, 1967, NARA RG 319, RR background files, FRC 5 (*pulled from his pocket*).

479 *"Juin said things to me last night"*: notes, Jan. 3, 1945, DDE office and W. B. Smith office, James M. Robb corr, DDE Lib, PP-pres, box 98; "Summary of Directions in Chronological Order Concerning Holding Strasbourg or Not Holding Strasbourg," Jan. 3, 1945, JLD papers, MHI (*"forget Strasbourg"*); John W. Price, "The Strasbourg Incident," 1967, OCMH, NARA RG 319, RR background files, FRC 5, 26 (*"ineradicable shame"*); Seventh Army war diary, Jan. 3, 1945, MHI (*"terrible reprisals"*); Gurley, "Policy Versus Strategy," NARA RG 319, RR background files, FRC 5 (*Evacuation plans*); memo, "Misleading Briefing Data," Frank A. Allen, Jr., to JLD, Jan. 16, 1945, and memo, 6th Army Group, Jan. 21, 1945, NARA RG 331, E 240P, SHAEF public relations section, box 38 (*only two hundred rail cars*).

479 *"Next to the weather"*: Chandler, 2491.

479 *Smith phoned Devers to ask*: "Summary of Directions in Chronological Order Concerning Holding Strasbourg or Not Holding Strasbourg," Jan. 3, 1945, JLD papers, MHI.

480 *The crowded stage in this melodrama*: John W. Price, "The Strasbourg Incident," 1967, OCMH, NARA RG 319, RR background files, FRC 5, 21–22; Danchev, 642 (*Eisenhower whisked them*); Chandler, 2396n (*a copy of his letter*).

480 *Eisenhower gestured to the map*: De Gaulle, *The Complete War Memoirs of Charles de Gaulle*, 834–37 (*"In Alsace, where the enemy"*).

480 *"a state bordering on anarchy"*: memo, DDE to GCM, Jan. 6, 1945, NARA RG 319, RR background files, FRC 5.

480 *"All my life," Churchill said*: De Gaulle, *The Complete War Memoirs of Charles de Gaulle*, 837–39; Porch, *The Path to Victory*, 603 (*asked for a total of fifty*).

480 *By now the supreme commander's face*: Gurley, "Policy Versus Strategy," NARA RG 319, *RR* background files, FRC 5 (*"If you carry out the withdrawal"*); De Gaulle, *The Complete War Memoirs of Charles de Gaulle*, 837–39 (*"I am having a lot of trouble"*).

481 *"I think you've done the wise and proper"*: Eisenhower, *Crusade in Europe*, 384.

481 *"not always aware of the political consequences"*: Kersaudy, *Churchill and De Gaulle*, 300; De Gaulle, *The Complete War Memoirs of Charles de Gaulle*, 838–39 (*"Glory has its price"*); Gurley, "Policy Versus Strategy," NARA RG 319, *RR* background files, FRC 5 (*"Imagine, asking us to withdraw"*); Porch, *The Path to Victory*, 610 (*"equate politics with sentiment"*).

481 *As the happy news of salvation*: Gurley, "Policy Versus Strategy," NARA RG 319, *RR* background files, FRC 5; msg, DDE to JLD, Jan. 7, 1945, and "Summary of Directions in Chronological Order Concerning Holding Strasbourg or Not Holding Strasbourg," Jan. 3, 1945, JLD papers, MHI (*"as strongly as possible"*).

481 NORDWIND *would drag on*: *RR*, 505–9, 513, 527, 564; *VW*, vol. 2, 249 (*enemy troops ferried across the river*); MEB, "Army Group G," Dec. 1956, OCMH, NARA RG 319, R-91, box 14, 18; Giziowski, *The Enigma of General Blaskowitz*, 373 (*Hitler denounced as "pessimistic"*), 371 (*"Whipped Cream Division"*); Bonn, *When the Odds Were Even*, 219 (*recruits from eastern Europe*).

481 *"We must believe in the ultimate purposes"*: Eisenhower, *Letters to Mamie*, 229.

482 *He had new worries, too*: office diary, Jan. 5, 1945, Kay Summersby, DDE Lib, PP-pres, box 140 (*developing a ray*); Gardner, "The Death of Admiral Ramsay," *AB*, no. 87 (1995): 44+; Woodward, *Ramsay at War*, 194; Chalmers, *Full Cycle*, 267.

482 *"E. leaves office early"*: desk calendar, Jan. 7, 1945, Barbara Wyden papers, DDE Lib, box 1.

The Agony Grapevine

482 SHAEF *on January 5 confirmed*: office diary, Jan. 5, 1945, Kay Summersby, DDE Lib, PP-pres, box 140; Weigley, *Eisenhower's Lieutenants*, 565 (*"by instant agreement"*); Eisenhower, *The Bitter Woods*, 465.

482 *"We have nothing to apologize for"*: diary, Jan. 1, 5 and 6, 1945, CBH, MHI, box 5. Even *Stars and Stripes* referred to GIs as "Monty's troops" (Hamilton, *Monty: Final Years of the Field-Marshal, 1944–1976*, 302).

482 *"I shall show how the whole Allied team"*: msg, BLM to WSC, Jan. 6, 1945, UK NA, CAB 120/867.

482 *"The real trouble with the Yanks"*: Hamilton, *Monty: Final Years of the Field-Marshal, 1944–1976*, 411.

482 *When Brigadier Williams, the intelligence chief, asked why*: OH, E. T. Williams, May 30–31, 1947, FCP, MHI; Hamilton, *Monty: Final Years of the Field-Marshal, 1944–1976*, 304 (*"Please don't"*); OH, David Belchem, Feb. 20, 1947, FCP, MHI (*smelling condescension*); OH, Alan Moorehead, Jan. 21, 1947, FCP, MHI (*"some bloody awful mistake"*).

483 *In a double-badged maroon beret*: OH, Alan Moorehead, Jan. 21, 1947, FCP, MHI (*"dressed like a clown"*); *VW*, vol. 2, 425–27 (*"a brave fighting man"*); Wilmot, *The Struggle for Europe*, 610–11 (*No mention was made of Bradley*); *TT*, 611 (*British troops were "fighting hard"*).

483 *"The first thing I did"*: Davis, *Soldier of Democracy*, 530.

483 *"Let us have done with the destructive criticism"*: *VW*, vol. 2, 425–27.

483 *"Oh, God, why didn't you stop him?"*: Hamilton, *Monty: Final Years of the Field-Marshal, 1944–1976*, 303; Colville, *The Fringes of Power*, 551 (*"indecently exultant"* and *"exceedingly self-satisfied"*); Weigley, *Eisenhower's Lieutenants*, 565 (*"what a good boy am I"*); Richardson, *Send for Freddie*, 172 (*"cock on a dunghill"*); Bradley and Blair, *A General's Life*, 382 (*"Montgomery Foresaw Attack"*); *VW*, vol. 2, 428 (*"'somewhat bewildered'"*).

484 *"He sees fit to assume"*: war diary, Ninth Army, Jan. 19, 1945, William H. Simpson papers, "Personal Calendar," MHI, box 11; OH, Frederick E. Morgan, n.d., FCP, MHI

("*active hatred*"); "Excerpt from Diary, D/SAC," Jan. 31, 1945, NARA RG 319, *SC* background papers, 2-3.7 CB 8 ("*out of the question*").

484 *Bradley twice called Versailles*: office diary, Jan. 9, 1945, Kay Summersby, DDE Lib, PP-pres, box 140. The "calculated risk" explanation first emerged from 12th Army Group on Dec. 21 and was widely cited long after the war (Royce L. Thompson, "American Intelligence on the German Counteroffensive," vol. 1, Nov. 1949, CMH, 2-3.7 AE P-1).

484 "*attempt to discredit me*": Bradley Commentaries, CBH collection, MHI, box 41.

484 "*I cannot serve under Montgomery*": Bradley, *A Soldier's Story*, 487–88; diary, Jan. 8, 1945, CBH, MHI, box 5.

484 "*No single incident that I have encountered*": Chandler, 2481.

484 *Heading off, seeing off, and writing off*: Rickard, *Advance and Destroy*, 200–203 ("*must take care of itself*"); *Ardennes*, 650–51 (*twice as many tanks*); Weigley, *Eisenhower's Lieutenants*, 572 ("*Desertions few*").

485 *Yet many enemy commanders had been killed*: *Ardennes*, 615; MEB, "The German Withdrawal from the Ardennes," May 1955, NARA RG 319, OCMH, R-series #59, 20 (*combed the countryside for gasoline*); Rickard, *Advance and Destroy*, 319 (*traveled by bicycle*); Roger S. Durham, "The Past Is Present: The World War II Service of George E. Durham," 1996, a.p., 124 ("*pants-crapper*").

485 "*Ten shells for their one*": White, *Conquerors' Road*, 7, 14 ("*Get along there*"); *PP*, 615 ("*unfortunate incidents*"); *TT*, 226 (*Skorzeny's saboteurs*); FUSA G-2, Operation GREIF, n.d., NARA RG 407, E 429, ML #994 ("*musketry*"); Heinz, "The Morning They Shot the Spies," *True* (Dec. 1949): 28+ ("*We had to stop them*"); "W.C. Heinz, 93, Writing Craftsman, Dies," *NYT*, Feb. 28, 2008.

485 *A final German lunge at Bastogne*: Wilmot, *The Struggle for Europe*, 607–8; Cirillo, "Ardennes-Alsace," 45 (*increased from three to nine*); "Allied Air Power and the Ardennes Offensive," n.d., director of intelligence, USSAFE, NARA RG 498, ETOUSA HD, UD 584, box 1 (*Dreadful weather*); *Ardennes*, 628–29 (*blowtorches and pinch bars*); Rickard, *Advance and Destroy*, 216, 314 (*barely a mile a day*); *LO*, 26–33 (*five thousand casualties*), 39–42 (*must halt at the West Wall*).

486 *At 11:40 A.M. on Tuesday, January 16*: *LO*, 42–43; Weigley, *Eisenhower's Lieutenants*, 561; author visit, Houffalize, June 4, 2009, signage; "Allied Air Power and the Ardennes Offensive," n.d., director of intelligence, USSAFE, NARA RG 498, ETOUSA HD, UD 584, box 1 (*One thousand tons*); *PP*, 632 ("*I have never seen anything like it*"). Of the nearly two hundred civilians killed in Houffalize, almost all died "at the hands of their liberators" (Hitchcock, *The Bitter Road to Freedom*, 87).

486 "*Little town of Houffalize*": D'Este, *Patton: A Genius for War*, 696–97.

486 *A day later, Eisenhower returned First Army*: Sylvan, 262; Benjamin A. Dickson, "G-2 Journal: Algiers to the Elbe," MHI, 203 (*Hôtel Britannique*); Hogan, *A Command Post at War*, 239 ("*tilting drunkenly*"); war diary, Ninth Army, Jan. 30, 1945, William H. Simpson papers, "Personal Calendar," MHI, box 11; Bradley, *A Soldier's Story*, 502 ("*Whore's Camp*").

486 *Village by village, croft by croft*: Fussell, *Wartime*, 122 ("*Kraut disinfected*"); "The Defense of St. Vith, Belgium," n.d., AS, Ft., K, NARA RG 407, E 427, Miscl AG records, #2280, 42 ("*The battle noises*"); *LO*, 51.

487 *Hitler had already decamped*: Raiber, "The Führerhauptquartiere," *AB*, no. 19 (1977): 1+; Kershaw, *Hitler, 1936–45: Nemesis*, 747 ("*I know the war is lost*"); Rickard, *Advance and Destroy*, 290–92 (*five bridges thrown over the Our*); Chandler, 2439 ("*probably manage to withdraw*"). A U.S. Army history estimated that "perhaps one-third" of German armor committed to the Bulge escaped (Cirillo, "Ardennes-Alsace," 52).

487 *The Red Army had massed more than 180 divisions*: *GS*, vol. 4, 80; Warlimont, *Inside Hitler's Headquarters*, 499; *LO*, 51; MEB, "The German Withdrawal from the Ardennes," May 1955, NARA RG 319, OCMH, R-series #59, 1–2, 20; Josef "Sepp" Dietrich, Aug. 8–9, 1945, ETHINT 15, MHI, 22; Percy E. Schramm, "The Course of Events in the German Offensive in the Ardennes," n.d., FMS, #A-858, MHI, 18–21 ("*suction pump*").

487 *In the west the war receded*: Lewis, *The Mammoth Book of Eyewitness World War II*, 444 (*Thunderbolt cannons*); Moorehead, *Eclipse*, 228 (*"Are you sure?"*).

487 *The dead "lay thick"*: Gellhorn, *The Face of War*, 194; Bagnulo, ed., *Nothing But Praise*, 48 (*precluded burials*); Schrijvers, *The Unknown Dead*, 27 (*blankets*), 359. The National Museum of Military History in Diekirch put total civilian dead and wounded in Belgium and Luxembourg at 3,800 (Hitchcock, *The Bitter Road to Freedom*, 385n).

487 *At the American cemetery in Henri-Chapelle*: Joseph T. Layne and Glenn D. Barquest, "Margraten: U.S. Ninth Army Military Cemetery," 1994, NWWIIM, 7–13; Joseph James Shomon, *Crosses in the Wind*, 91–98, 109; "Third U.S. Army After Action Report," chapter 21, CMH (*morgue tent for photographs*).

488 *Among the dead gathered by Graves Registration teams*: Bauserman, *The Malmédy Massacre*, 100–101.

488 *An Army tally long after the war*: The figures included losses from 6th Army Group. TSC, 402. Corr, D. G. Gilbert, chief, Army historical services division, to JT, Jan. 28, 1959, JT, LOC MS Div, box 38. About three-quarters of U.S. casualties were suffered by 12th Army Group; a 1952 monograph put the figure at 71,000 through January 19, 1945 (Royce L. Thompson, "Ardennes Campaign Statistics," Apr. 28, 1952, CMH, 2-3.7 AE P-15).

488 *Thousands more suffered from trench foot, frostbite*: Morelock, *Generals of the Ardennes*, 20.

488 *More than 23,000 were taken prisoner*: OH, William R. Desobry, 1978, Ted S. Chesney, SOOHP , MHI (*"so foul we used to bathe"*).

488 *organized the "Agony Grapevine"*: Frank, "The Glorious Collapse of the 106th," *Saturday Evening Post* (Nov. 9, 1946).

488 *Of more than sixty thousand wounded and injured*: Cowdrey, *Fighting for* Life, 263 (*"ledge of a skyscraper"*); Fussell, *Doing Battle*, 146 (*"Battle of Atlanta"*); Carroll, ed., *War Letters*, 267–68 (*"I looked down"*).

489 *German losses would be difficult to count*: AAAD, 484; Sylvan, 262; Rickard, *Advance and Destroy*, 316 (*120,000 enemy losses*); Bradley, *A Soldier's Story*, 492 (*more than a quarter-million*); Percy E. Schramm, "The Course of Events in the German Offensive in the Ardennes," FMS, #A-851, MHI, 20; *Germany VII*, 694 (*official German history*). Other German historians put total casualties at approximately 68,000, plus the 23,000 in Alsace (Rickard, *Advance and Destroy*, 316; Cirillo, "Ardennes-Alsace," 53).

489 *Model's success*: Rickard, *Advance and Destroy*, 322 (*289 divisions*); OH, Hasso von Manteuffel, Oct. 12, 1966, John S. D. Eisenhower, CBM, MHI, box 6, 7 (*"He bent the bow"*); Greenfield, ed., *Command Decisions*, 356 (*virtually no fuel*); MEB, "Effects of the Ardennes Offensive: Germany's Remaining War Potential," May 1955, OCMH, Foreign Studies Branch, NARA RG 338, R-series, #61, 28 (*"rabbit hunt"*); Zaloga, *Armored Thunderbolt*, 258 (*seven hundred armored vehicles*); Davis, *Carl A. Spaatz and the Air War in Europe*, 537 (*freight shipments were banned*); LO, 8 (*four million German soldiers*). A 1950 study put total German military losses through January 31, 1945, at 8.3 million (MEB, "Overall View of Germany's Economic, Political, and Military Situation at the Beginning of 1945," May 1950, CMH, 2-3.7 EC, 12).

489 *"When you catch a carp"*: transcript, GSP press conference, Jan. 1, 1945, GSP, LOC MS Div, box 12, folder 18.

489 *"a corporal's war"*: Liddell Hart, *The Other Side of the Hill*, 464.

489 *Few U.S. generals had enhanced their reputations*: Millett and Murray, *Military Effectiveness*, vol. 3, *The Second World War*, 80; Rickard, *Advance and Destroy*, 193, 291, 320 (*Patton proved the most distinguished*); ONB, 1945 efficiency report on GSP, DDE Lib, PP pres, box 91.

490 *Churchill sought to repair*: TSC, 389; Bradley, *A Soldier's Story*, 488; Colville, *The Fringes of Power*, 583 (*"no greater exhibition of power"*); TSC, 395 (*"What a great honor"*); diary, Jan. 24, 1945, GSP, LOC MS Div, box 3, folder 9 (*"Why isn't Ike a man?"*).

490 *"had in no sense achieved anything decisive"*: "Biennial Report of the Chief of Staff of the Army," Oct. 1945, NARA RG 498, ETOUSA HD, UD 584, box 2; Franz Kurowski in

Barnett, ed., *Hitler's Generals*, 432 (*"godsend for the Red Army"*); Ehlers, *Targeting the Reich*, 292, 311–14 (*lack of gasoline*); Erickson, *The Road to Berlin*, 447–48, 460–62; Cooper, *The German Army, 1933–1945*, 525–26; Gerhard L. Weinberg, "D-Day: Analysis of Costs and Benefits," in Wilson, ed., *D-Day 1944*, 336 (*within fifty miles of Berlin*).

490 *With the German tide receding*: Rickard, *Advance and Destroy*, 314 (*timetable had been disrupted*).

490 *his basic scheme for ending the war remained unaltered*: Chandler, 2450–54; Weigley, *Eisenhower's Lieutenants*, 547. One SHAEF study, dated December 23, put the number of divisions that could be supported in the north at just twenty-five until rail bridges were built, a figure Montgomery himself considered plausible (ALH, 155–56; TSC, 410).

491 *At present the Western Allies mustered 3.7 million*: LO, 5–7; LSA, vol. 2, 288; MEB, "Effects of the Ardennes Offensive: Germany's Remaining War Potential," May 1955, OCMH, Foreign Studies Branch, NARA RG 338, R-series, #61, 46 (*729-mile front*); TSC, 392–93 (*"plenty of fat meat"*).

491 *So desperate was the need for rifle platoon leaders*: "History, 1945," Ground Forces Training Center, n.d., Harold E. Potter papers, MHI, box 1; corr, Congressional Research Service to Rep. Adam Benjamin, Jan. 1981, a.p. (*thirty thousand U.S. enlisted*); D. M. Giangreco, "Spinning the Casualties: Media Strategies During the Roosevelt Administration," *Passport*, newsletter, Society for Historians of American Foreign Relations, Dec. 2004, 22+ (*ninety thousand men a month*); Chandler, 2453 (*85 divisions*).

491 *That would have to suffice*: "Major Problems Encountered by Ground Force Reinforcement Command," chapter 6, NARA RG 498, ETO HD, admin file #571F, 291–95 (*"almost depleted"*); TSC, 392–93 (*a hundred thousand Marines*); corr, David T. Griggs to Edward L. Bowles, adviser to secretary of war, Feb. 22, 1945, AFHRA, 519.161-7 (*"twenty more divisions"*); Kirkpatrick, *An Unknown Future and a Doubtful Present: Writing the Victory Plan of 1941*, CMH, 1990, 113–14

491 *"Everybody shares the same universals"*: Carroll, ed., *War Letters*, 266; *Ardennes*, 99; Cirillo, "Ardennes-Alsace," 20 (*thirty-two recognizing*).

492 *Affixed to a wall*: "Monty's Wartime Caravans," *AB*, no. 20 (1978): 32+; *VW*, vol. 2, 357.

CHAPTER 10: ARGONAUTS

Citizens of the World

495 *Morning sun and a tranquil breeze*: Dilks, ed., *The Diaries of Sir Alexander Cadogan*, 700–701; Eden, *The Reckoning*, 592 (*"Star-Spangled Banner"*); DOB, 46–51 (*invasion of Sicily*).

495 *Sixteen thousand tons*: "Argonaut," No. AR/2, n.d., UK NA, CAB 120/172 (*"rumors and gossip"*); "Operation Argonaut," n.d., Frederick L. Anderson papers, HIA, box 95, folder 14 (*Lascaris Bastion*); Kuter, *Airman at Yalta*, 69 (*"cold-storage vaults"*); King and Whitehill, *Fleet Admiral King*, 587 (*wrapped in a dressing gown*); Norwich, *The Middle Sea*, 303 (*"astonishing natural anchorage"*); Cherpak, ed., *The Memoirs of Admiral H. Kent Hewitt*, 213–14 (*floating garage*).

495 *To compensate for any discomfort*: Kuter, *Airman at Yalta*, 70–71, 72–73 (*local librarian*); John E. Hull, "Unpublished Autobiography," n.d., MHI, 14-3 (*"shine he put on my shoes"*); Charles H. Donnelly, "Autobiography," May 1979, MHI, 706–10 (*bars opened punctually*); Roberts, *Masters and Commanders*, 540 (*twenty-piece orchestra*); Pawle, *The War and Colonel Warden*, 357 (*marble scrolls*); Norwich, *The Middle Sea*, 302–7; "Argonaut," No. AR/2, n.d., UK NA, CAB 120/172.

496 *At 9:30 A.M. on Friday*: Stettinius, *Roosevelt and the Russians*, 68; notes, Feb. 2, 1945, Anna Roosevelt Halsted papers, FDR Lib, box 84 (*"entrance to the harbor"*).

496 *As the cruiser crept at four knots*: "Trips of the President," FDR Lib, container 21, file 6-1; Churchill, *Closing the Ring*, 642 (ADMIRAL Q); Bishop, *FDR's Last Year*, 292 (*slow salute*).

496 *"The sun was glistening"*: Bohlen, *Witness to History, 1929–1969*, 171.

497 *Across the harbor, on the quarterdeck*: Moran, *Churchill: Taken from the Diaries of Lord Moran*, 234; Bishop, *FDR's Last Year*, 292 (*"Through with engines"*); Eden, *The Reckoning*, 592 (*"one of those moments"*); William M. Rigdon, log, "The President's Trip to the Crimea Conference and Great Bitter Lake, Egypt," Averill Harriman papers, LOC MS Div, 14 (*Berth 9*).

497 *Since leaving Washington*: Guy H. Spaman, "President's Trip," July 5, 1945, Secret Service records, FDR Lib, container 4, file 103-1; Byrnes, *Speaking Frankly*, 22. The physician with Roosevelt aboard *Quincy* reported that he rested well and slept late on the voyage (Bruenn, "Clinical Notes on the Illness and Death of President Franklin D. Roosevelt," *Annals of Internal Medicine* 72, no. 4 (Apr. 1, 1970): 579+).

497 *He devoted little time*: William M. Rigdon, log, "The President's Trip to the Crimea Conference and Great Bitter Lake, Egypt," Averill Harriman papers, LOC MS Div, 1–3 (*Laura and sixty-one degrees*); book list, official files, Yalta trip, FDR Lib, box 3 (Death Defies the Doctor); Bishop, *FDR's Last Year*, 271–72 (*agent stood near*); notes, Jan. 27, 1945, Anna Roosevelt Halsted papers, FDR Lib, box 84 (*half a penny a point*); Dallek, *Franklin D. Roosevelt and American Foreign Policy, 1932–1945*, 481; Brinkley, *Washington Goes to War*, 264 (*thirteen of his grandchildren*).

497 *To celebrate the president's sixty-third birthday*: corr, E. J. Flynn to Helen, Feb. 2, 1945, Edward J. Flynn papers, FDR Lib, box 25; Goodwin, *No Ordinary Time*, 574–75 (*brass ashtray*).

497 *With Quincy made fast*: William M. Rigdon, log, "The President's Trip to the Crimea Conference and Great Bitter Lake, Egypt," Averill Harriman papers, LOC MS Div, 14–18; King and Whitehill, *Fleet Admiral King*, 587 (*violet circles*); Bohlen, *Witness to History, 1929–1969*, 172–73 (*"I was shocked"*).

498 Time *magazine had catalogued*: "The Presidency," *Time* (May 8, 1944): 8; Altman, "For F.D.R. Sleuths, New Focus on an Old Spot," *NYT*, Jan. 5, 2010, D1; Bruenn, "Clinical Notes on the Illness and Death of President Franklin D. Roosevelt," *Annals of Internal Medicine* 72, no. 4 (Apr. 1, 1970): 579+ (*260 over 150* and *"Can't eat"*); Goodwin, *No Ordinary Time*, 494, 496–97 (*digitalis*); Burns, "FDR: The Untold Story of His Last Year," *Saturday Evening Post* (Apr. 11, 1970): 12+; Kimball, *Forged in War*, 341 (*"abdominal distress"*); Tully, *F.D.R. My Boss*, 351–53 (*"Lots of sleep"*); Brinkley, *Washington Goes to War*, 265 (*official photographs*).

498 *Yet if the body was frail*: Burns, "FDR: The Untold Story of His Last Year," *Saturday Evening Post* (Apr. 11, 1970): 12+; King and Whitehill, *Fleet Admiral King*, 587 (*SHAEF plan*).

499 *Another trill of the bosun's pipe*: Argonaut files, UK NA, PREM 4/77/1B; "Trips of the President," FDR Lib, container 21, file 6-1 (*TUNGSTEN*); Moran, *Churchill: Taken from the Diaries of Lord Moran*, 232 (*"very wordy"*); Eden, *The Reckoning*, 590–91 (*bezique*); Leahy, *I Was There*, 294–95 (*Declaration of Independence*); Black, *Franklin Delano Roosevelt*, 1031 (*"pushing Winston uphill"*); Stettinius, *Roosevelt and the Russians*, 70–72 (*defeat of Japan*).

499 *Churchill retrieved an eight-inch cigar*: Stettinius, *Roosevelt and the Russians*, 70–72.

499 *Off he went for thirty miles*: William M. Rigdon, log, "The President's Trip to the Crimea Conference and Great Bitter Lake, Egypt," Averill Harriman papers, LOC MS Div, 16–18; notes, Feb. 2, 1945, Anna Roosevelt Halsted papers, FDR Lib, box 84 (*half an hour late*); Coffey, *Hap*, 349 (*fourth heart attack*).

499 *"complete agreement"*: FRUS, 542–43; Kimball, ed., *Churchill & Roosevelt: The Complete Correspondence*, vol. 3, 523 (*impede Soviet expansion*).

500 *Roosevelt nodded*: FRUS, 542–43, 548 (*eight o'clock*); King and Whitehill, *Fleet Admiral King*, 587.

500 *This amiable gathering concealed*: Wilmot, *The Struggle for Europe*, 666; Charles H. Donnelly, "Autobiography," May 1979, MHI, 711 (*bundled in their overcoats*); FRUS, 464–66, 471 (*"heart of Germany"*); LO, 55–56. SHAEF on January 28 calculated that thirty-three Allied divisions could defend the Rhine line, compared to the forty-two

needed if German forces continued to occupy the Colmar Pocket and other salients west of the river (ALH, 178).

500 *Again Field Marshal Brooke*: DOB, 281–82; Danchev, xv (*"Men admired, feared"*); Kennedy, *The Business of War*, 329 (Monograph of the Pigeons); "Notes About Alan's Childhood and Boyhood," 1943, LHC, Alanbrooke papers, 1/1 (*hoped to become a physician*); Fraser, *Alanbrooke*, 24–29 (*"gunner of genius"*), 215, 448, 514; Keegan, *Six Armies in Normandy*, 47 (*"searching back"*).

500 *The tactic befitted the man*: Danchev, 649.

501 *The British chiefs, Brooke said*: FRUS, 472; Weigley, *Eisenhower's Lieutenants*, 578 (*Bulge had revealed the folly*); minutes, CCS, Jan. 30, 1945, FDR Lib, Map Room conferences, box 29 (*"Closing up the Rhine"*).

501 *This argument had dragged on*: FRUS, 473 (*"every single division"*); minutes, CCS, Jan. 30, 1945, FDR Lib, Map Room conferences, box 29 (*barely two dozen divisions*); GS VI, 91; John E. Hull, "Unpublished Autobiography," n.d., MHI, 14-2.

501 *Marshall concurred*: FRUS, 473; Chandler, 2463–64 (*"You may assure"*).

502 *"I am feeling very tired"*: Danchev, 652.

502 *Worse was to come*: OH, Field Marshal Viscount Alanbrooke, Jan. 28, 1947, FCP, MHI (*"hands too full"*); Ambrose, *The Supreme Commander*, 586–87 (*"Let's have it out"*); Crosswell, *Beetle*, 862–63; Danchev, 652 (*"talk did both of us good"*).

502 *That was unlikely*: SC, 409; GS VI, 90; Crosswell, *Beetle*, 862–63 (*"Please leave this to me"*).

502 *As the chiefs convened again*: Crosswell, *Beetle*, 862–63; Cray, *General of the Army*, 502–3 (*"practically never sees General Eisenhower"*); Pogue, *George C. Marshall*, 516–17 (*"wrong foot"*).

502 *He had not finished*: Chandler, 2461; Cray, *General of the Army*, 500–501; SC, 413; Bland, ed., *George C. Marshall Interviews and Reminiscences for Forrest C. Pogue*, 400–402 (*"everything he asked for"*); Crosswell, *Beetle*, 862–63 (*"over-cautious commander"*).

503 *"Marshall clearly understood nothing"*: Danchev, 653.

503 *"Marshall's complaint was not unjustified"*: Cunningham, *A Sailor's Odyssey*, 626–27; Roberts, *Masters and Commanders*, 577.

503 *For another month, the British conspired*: corr, F. L. Anderson to C. A. Spaatz, Feb. 2, 1945, "Operation Argonaut," HIA, Frederick L. Anderson papers, box 95, folder 14; Orange, *Tedder: Quietly in Command*, 297; Hastings, *Armageddon*, 195 (*"a very, very small man"*); Chandler, 2480–82 (*"no question whatsoever"*).

503 *"The P.M. was sore"*: Orange, *Tedder: Quietly in Command*, 297.

503 *Light rain spattered Luqa airdrome*: Pogue, *George C. Marshall: Organizer of Victory*, 519; Stettinius, *Roosevelt and the Russians*, 28–29 (*Mission No. 17*); "Argonaut," No. AR/2, n.d., UK NA, CAB 120/172 (*black bands and yellow tags*).

503 *Roosevelt in recent months had proposed*: Olsen, "Full House at Yalta," *American Heritage* (Jan. 1972): 1+. Stalin initially proposed Odessa, but that port city remained within range of German bombers (Mason, ed., *The Atlantic War Remembered*, 447–48).

503 *"I emphasized the difficulties"*: memo, A. Harriman to FDR, Dec. 27, 1944, NARA RG 165, E 422, OPD, box 31; cable file, ARGONAUT, NARA RG 165, E 422, OPD, box 31 (*"toilet facilities"*); Sherwood, *Roosevelt and Hopkins*, 844–45 (*"his adventurous spirit"*).

504 *Roosevelt and Churchill had agreed to limit*: memo, William Leahy to GCM, E. King, Dec. 28, 1944, NARA RG 165, E 422, OPD, box 31; Clemens, *Yalta*, 111; Mason, ed., *The Atlantic War Remembered*, 447–48 (*Americans numbered 330*); "Argonaut," No. AR/2, n.d., UK NA, CAB 120/172; admin papers, UK NA, CAB 104/177 (*"plausible cover story"*).

504 *In view of the rustic conditions*: admin papers, UK NA, CAB 104/177; memo, M. Moritz, Malta Command, to E. A. Armstrong, War Cabinet Offices, Feb. 23, 1945; admin papers, UK NA, CAB 104/177 (*"Yalta Voyage 208"*); Harriman and Abel, *Special Envoy to Churchill and Stalin, 1941–1946*, 390 (*"good for typhus"*).

505 *"We left Malta in darkness"*: Charles H. Donnelly, "Autobiography," May 1979, MHI, 719–23; Leahy, *I Was There*, 295–301 (*set their watches ahead*).

505 *Churchill boarded a four-engine C-54*: Kuter, *Airman at Yalta*, 103; Goodwin, *No Ordinary Time*, 575 (*"hot pink baby"*).

505 *Down the flight line stood C-54 No. 252*: http://www.strategic-air-command.com/aircraft /cargo/c54_skymaster.htm; Bishop, *FDR's Last Year*, 300 (*caged elevator*); Gallagher, *FDR's Splendid Deception*, 202 (*"a transparency"*).

505 *Spitfire and P-38 fighter escorts*: memo, Jan. 27, 1945, Naples, "Trips of the President," FDR Lib, container 21, file 6-1; William M. Rigdon, log, "The President's Trip to the Crimea Conference and Great Bitter Lake, Egypt," Averill Harriman papers, LOC MS Div, 17–18.

A Fateful Conference

505 *Wedged into a natural amphitheater*: Twain, *The Innocents Abroad*, 280; Anton Chekhov, "The Lady with the Pet Dog," http://www.enotes.com/lady-pet-text (*"The stories told"*).

506 *That sea—to the ancients Pontus Euxinus*: Thomas Spencer Baynes, ed., *The Encyclopaedia Britannica*, vol. 3, 795, online ed.; "Notes on the Crimea," 1945, "WWII Summit Conferences," Charles H. Donnelly papers, MHI (*Cimmerians and Scythians*); Ponomarenko, *Yalta: A Short Guide*, 11, 19–21 (*Lenin's decree*); Yhagapov and Shekurov, *Greater Yalta*, 19–26; Clemens, *Yalta*, 113 (*three dozen sanatoriums*).

506 *Then came the Germans*: Leasor, *The Clock with Four Hands*, 286–87; corr, E. J. Flynn to wife, Feb. 8, 1945, Edward J. Flynn papers, FDR Lib, box 25 (*brass doorknobs*); John E. Hull, "Unpublished Autobiography," n.d., MHI, 14-4; Mason, ed., *The Atlantic War Remembered*, 449–50; Harriman and Abel, *Special Envoy to Churchill and Stalin, 1941–1946*, 393 (*coat hangers*).

506 *British and American support ships*: Buhite, *Decisions at Yalta*, 4 (*"didn't leave a map"*); Olsen, "Full House at Yalta," *American Heritage* (Jan. 1972): 1+ (*nine hundred hairpin turns*); memo, T. W. Sullivan and L. H. Backus, U.S. Navy physicians, Feb. 18, 1945, Ross T. McIntire papers, FDR Lib, box 4 (*"marked infestation"*).

506 *Four Soviet regiments arrived*: Montefiore, *Stalin: The Court of the Red Tsar*, 480–81; Davies, *No Simple Victory*, 191–92 (*dozen Georgians*); Plokhy, *Yalta*, 58, 233 (*Eavesdroppers*).

507 *"This may well be a fateful conference"*: corr, WSC to FDR, Jan. 8, 1945, GCM Lib, box 62, folder 19; Pawle, *The War and Colonel Warden*, 358 (*"nineteen full colonels"*); Ismay, *The Memoirs of General Lord Ismay*, 384 (*"would have been difficult"*).

507 *Sacred Cow touched down*: William M. Rigdon, log, "The President's Trip to the Crimea Conference and Great Bitter Lake, Egypt," Averill Harriman papers, LOC MS Div, 19; Stettinius, *Roosevelt and the Russians*, 80–81 (*agent lifted him*); Clemens, *Yalta*, 128 (*"Stone Ass"*); Guy H. Spaman, "President's Trip," July 5, 1945, Secret Service records, FDR Lib, container 4, file 103-1 (*ammunition had been confiscated*); Moran, *Churchill: Taken from the Diaries of Lord Moran*, 234 (*"a great icicle"*).

507 *"We will destroy"*: Aron Kots version, http://en.wikipedia.org/wiki/The_Internationale #Russian_lyrics.

508 *Beside steaming glasses of tea*: Charles H. Donnelly, "Autobiography," May 1979, MHI, 719–23; John E. Hull, "Unpublished Autobiography," n.d., MHI, 14-4 (*"Let's get going"*); Houghton, "That Was Yalta," *New Yorker* (May 23, 1953): 86+ (*khaki overcoat*).

508 *Soon a weaving convoy*: Stettinius, *Roosevelt and the Russians*, 81; U.S. Navy color footage, FDR Lib, 71-8: 65–67 (*women in shawls*); Kuter, *Airman at Yalta*, 114–15; Charles H. Donnelly, "Autobiography," May 1979, MHI, 719–23; notes, Feb. 3–4, 1945, Anna Roosevelt Halsted papers, FDR Lib, box 84 (*a few sheep*); William M. Rigdon, log, "The President's Trip to the Crimea Conference and Great Bitter Lake, Egypt," Averill Harriman papers, LOC MS Div, 18–20 (*Route Romanoff*). Author Michael Dobbs notes that at least some of the destruction likely was inflicted by Soviet forces during a 1944 purge of Tatar villages (*Six Months in 1945*, 24–25, 10 [Don Juan]).

508 *Churchill and the British contingent*: Ismay, *The Memoirs of General Lord Ismay*, 386–87;

Dilks, ed., *The Diaries of Sir Alexander Cadogan*, 703 (*"hideosity"*); Churchill, *Triumph and Tragedy*, 347 (*goldfish*).

508 *"nothing is left out but cleanliness"*: Moran, *Churchill: Taken from the Diaries of Lord Moran*, 237–38; Leasor, *The Clock with Four Hands*, 288 (*shipped by special train*); Richardson, *From Churchill's Secret Circle to the BBC*, 198 (*"We sleep in droves"*); Plokhy, *Yalta*, 50 (*"queuing for a bucket"*); Hastings, *Winston's War*, 442 (*"Riviera of Hades"*); Danchev, 656 (*"a great northern diver"*).

509 *Ten miles away the Americans settled*: Kuter, *Airman at Yalta*, 121–22, 138 (*tea in tall glasses*); Olsen, "Full House at Yalta," *American Heritage* (Jan. 1972): 1+; Houghton, "That Was Yalta," *New Yorker* (May 23, 1953): 86+ (*"Please do not pilfer"*).

509 *An air of tragedy*: Clemens, *Yalta*, 113 (*two million rubles*); Massie, *Nicholas and Alexandra*, 156–64 (*reindeer tongue*); Plokhy, *Yalta*, 43–44.

509 *Now Roosevelt slept*: Houghton, "That Was Yalta," *New Yorker* (May 23, 1953): 86+.

510 *At four o'clock on Sunday*: William M. Rigdon, log, "The President's Trip to the Crimea Conference and Great Bitter Lake, Egypt," Averill Harriman papers, LOC MS Div, photo; OH, John E. Hull, 1974, James W. Wurman, SOOHP, MHI, VI-6, 7; Beevor, *Berlin: The Downfall, 1945*, 79 (*Hero of the Soviet Union*); Dobbs, *Six Months in 1945*, 35 (*talcum powder*); Buhite, *Decisions at Yalta*, 17 (*smallpox scars*); Houghton, "That Was Yalta," *New Yorker* (May 23, 1953): 86+ (*rattle the teacups*).

510 *Joseph Stalin intrigued even Franklin Roosevelt*: Bohlen, *Witness to History, 1929–1969*, 180; Fox, "The Super-Powers Then and Now," *International Journal* (summer 1980): 417+; Reynolds, *Rich Relations*, 438. See also William T. R. Fox, *The Super-Powers* (New York: Harcourt Brace, 1944).

510 *In other respects the wealthy patrician*: Montefiore, *Stalin: The Court of the Red Tsar*, 25; Dallek, *Franklin D. Roosevelt and American Foreign Policy, 1932–1945*, 521 (*"a Christian gentleman"*); Plokhy, *Yalta*, 56–57, 77; MMB, 527–28; Overy, *Why the Allies Won*, 259 (*"military brain"*); Murphy, *Diplomat Among Warriors*, 232–33 (*"I can handle Stalin"*); Roberts, *Masters and Commanders*, 486 (*"bigger coins"*).

510 *Beneath a painting of a farmer*: Hastings, *Winston's War*, 444 (*"You said it!"*); Stettinius, *Roosevelt and the Russians*, 99 (*communicate directly*).

511 *The marshal replied that the carnage*: Tooze, *The Wages of Destruction*, 468–69, 477–83; FRUS, 571–73 (*"sadistic hatred"*).

511 *Roosevelt offered Stalin*: Bishop, *FDR's Last Year*, 310–11; Kersaudy, *Churchill and De Gaulle*, 392–93 (*"unpleasant and impossible"*).

511 *"Only out of kindness"*: FRUS, 571–73; Montefiore, *Stalin: The Court of the Red Tsar*, 492 (*"Why did nature"*).

511 *Upon Churchill's arrival*: William M. Rigdon, log, "The President's Trip to the Crimea Conference and Great Bitter Lake, Egypt," Averill Harriman papers, LOC MS Div, photo; Bishop, *FDR's Last Year*, 312–13; Massie, *Nicholas and Alexandra*, 168–69 (*diamonds and pearls*).

512 *Much of* ARGONAUT*'s initial meeting*: Bland, ed., *George C. Marshall Interviews and Reminiscences for Forrest C. Pogue*, 405; FRUS, 575–78. Among other discrepancies, Soviet minutes of the conference quote Marshall as putting German oil production at 40 percent of previous levels (Clemens, *Yalta*, 124). A Soviet account also reported that Churchill seemed bored by the military recitations ("The Crimea and Potsdam Conferences of the Leaders of the Three Great Powers," *International Affairs*, All-Union Society, Moscow [June 1965]: 97).

512 *The Soviet account*: FRUS, 582–83; Erickson, *The Road to Berlin*, 447–48, 461, 471–72; Read and Fisher, *The Fall of Berlin*, 211 (*"You are now in goddam Germany"*).

512 *The Soviets currently possessed a seven-to-one advantage*: Horst Boog, "Invasion to Surrender: The Defense of Germany," in Brower, ed., *World War II in Europe: The Final Year*, 132; FRUS, 582–83 (*180 to 80*); Robert H. Abzug, "The Liberation of the Concentration Camps," in *Liberation 1945*, 35–36; "Auschwitz," USHMM, http://www.ushmm

.org/wlc/en/article.php?ModuleId=10005189; Posner and Ware, *Mengele: The Complete Story*, 3–8 (*medical experiments*); Gill, *The Journey Back from Hell*, 25–27; Weinberg, *A World at Arms*, 798–800 (*seven tons of women's hair*); Read and Fisher, *The Fall of Berlin*, 212 (*pyramids of dentures*).

513 "Our wishes": FRUS, 582–83; Feis, *Churchill, Roosevelt, Stalin*, 498–99; Weinberg, *A World at Arms*, 798–800; Erickson, *The Road to Berlin*, 475–76, 480, 517 (*threatened the flanks in East Pomerania*); Buell, *Master of Seapower*, 487 ("*It takes a very brave man*").

513 By late 1945, an estimated two million German women: Antony Beevor, introduction to Anonymous, *A Woman in Berlin*, xx; Hitchcock, *The Bitter Road to Freedom*, 154–167 (*dragged from operating tables* and *forced migration of 7.5* million Germans); Evans, *The Third Reich at War*, 710 ("*Our men shoot the ones*" and "*They are going to remember*"); Erickson, *The Road to Berlin*, 466–67 (*nailed by their hands*).

513 "in very good humor": FRUS, 589–90.

513 Great care had been taken: notes, Feb. 4, 1945, Anna Roosevelt Halsted papers, FDR Lib, box 84; Sherwood, *Roosevelt and Hopkins*, 852 (*Filipino mess boys*); William M. Rigdon, log, "The President's Trip to the Crimea Conference and Great Bitter Lake, Egypt," Averill Harriman papers, LOC MS Div, 25 (*five types of wine*); Bishop, *FDR's Last Year*, 319 ("*peace for a hundred years*"); Dilks, ed., *The Diaries of Sir Alexander Cadogan*, 707 ("*drinking buckets*"); Stettinius, *Roosevelt and the Russians*, 111 (*recharging his glass*).

514 Not until the final half hour: FRUS, 589–90.

514 "But of your seven million Poles": Stettinius, *Roosevelt and the Russians*, 113.

514 "The eagle should permit": FRUS, 589–90.

514 "A terrible party": Eden, *The Reckoning*, 593.

514 Stalin's attitude toward Germany: FRUS, 611–14, 624–27, 633.

515 Glancing at a note slipped to him: ibid., 612–18, 629, 634.

515 "I can get the people and Congress": Stettinius, *Roosevelt and the Russians*, 127.

515 "Germany should be run by those": FRUS, 612–18.

515 "He loves France like a woman": Moran, *Churchill: Taken from the Diaries of Lord Moran*, 241.

515 rather than remind Stalin: Fenno, ed., *The Yalta Conference*, 48–50; FRUS, 612–18, 629 ("*France must take her place*").

515 But who should pay: Clemens, *Yalta*, 37 (*Stalin had pressed*); Smith, *American Diplomacy During the Second World War*, 132; FRUS, 620–21; Byrnes, *Speaking Frankly*, 26–27.

516 Washington and London had second thoughts: Clemens, *Yalta*, 37–41, 137–39, 172; "The Crimea and Potsdam Conferences of the Leaders of the Three Great Powers," *International Affairs*, All-Union Society, Moscow (June 1965): 101; Byrnes, *Speaking Frankly*, 28 (*$200 million*).

516 Recalling the ruinous conditions: FRUS, 621–23.

516 On it went for six more days: Stettinius, *Roosevelt and the Russians*, 185 ("*in for ½ hour of it*"); Meacham, *Franklin and Winston*, 319 ("*ran away from the interpreter*"); Moran, *Churchill: Taken from the Diaries of Lord Moran*, 243 (*wooden stethoscope*); Danchev, 658–59; Roberts, *Masters and Commanders*, 552–55 (*Crimean War battlefields*).

516 Back at the Villa Livadia: Churchill, *Triumph and Tragedy*, 365; Hastings, *Winston's War*, 417 ("*feeble lot of fools*"); Clemens, *Yalta*, 174–177; Harriman and Abel, *Special Envoy to Churchill and Stalin, 1941–1946*, 411 (*150,000 Polish soldiers*); Montefiore, *Stalin: The Court of the Red Tsar*, 494 (*ten million Red Army troops*).

517 Rising from his chair: Bohlen, *Witness to History, 1929–1969*, 187; Byrnes, *Speaking Frankly*, 30–32 ("*Within a month's time*").

517 elections would not be held in Poland for two years: Kimball, *Forged in War*, 307–8; Dobbs, *Six Months in 1945*, 64, 85 (*Missouri*); Colville, *The Fringes of Power*, 555 ("*All the Balkans except Greece*"); Addison, *Churchill, the Unexpected Hero*, 206–7 ("*Terrible and humbling submissions*").

517 For Roosevelt, two paramount concerns: FRUS, 396; Fenno, ed., *The Yalta Conference*,

96–98; Howarth, ed., *Men of War*, 104; FCP, "Yalta in Retrospect," in Snell, ed., *The Meaning of Yalta*, 201 (*huge American casualties*); Dallek, *Franklin D. Roosevelt and American Foreign Policy, 1932–1945*, 517; Stoler, *George C. Marshall: Soldier-Statesman of the American Century*, 126.

518 *Stalin at the Teheran conference*: Kimball, ed., *Churchill & Roosevelt: The Complete Correspondence*, vol. 3, 527; Harriman and Abel, *Special Envoy to Churchill and Stalin, 1941–1946*, 400, 412 (*"same horse twice"*); Plokhy, *Yalta*, 285–88; Feis, *Churchill, Roosevelt, Stalin*, 535 (*Japan forfeited its entire empire*); Leahy, *I Was There*, 318–21.

518 *The second issue preoccupying Roosevelt*: Leahy, *I Was There*, 315; http://www.un.org/en /aboutun/history/ ("*United Nations*"); Dallek, *Franklin D. Roosevelt and American Foreign Policy, 1932–1945*, 507 (*committed to the wider world*); Clemens, *Yalta*, 216–18 (*all sixteen Soviet republics*); Stettinius, *Roosevelt and the Russians*, 174–75, 187, 281; Plokhy, *Yalta*, 289–92, 366–67; Leahy, *I Was There*, 321 (*would remain secret*). Stalin at one point offered Roosevelt two extra votes for the United States.

518 ARGONAUT *staggered to an end*: Kimball, *Forged in War*, 324 (*"tired all through"*); FRUS, 797–98 (*forty-five toasts*); diary, William D. Leahy, Feb. 8, 1945, LOC MS Div, micro R-4, container 6, 27 (*mosquitoes*); Bishop, *FDR's Last Year*, 384–85 (*"Drink it down!"*); FRUS, 797–98; Churchill, *Triumph and Tragedy*, 361–62 (*"We regard Marshal Stalin's life"*).

519 *Roosevelt, who had tossed down two cocktails*: Bishop, *FDR's Last Year*, 384–85. A staff officer who later rose to four-star rank, John E. Hull, described FDR as drinking heavily at one dinner (OH, 1974, James W. Wurman, SOOHP, MHI, VI-6, 7).

519 *Guests hopped around the table*: diary, William D. Leahy, Feb. 8, 1945, LOC MS Div, micro R-4, container 6, 28; Peckham and Snyder, eds., *Letters from Fighting Hoosiers*, vol. 2, 211 (*butter and oily salmon*); Cunningham, *A Sailor's Odyssey*, 628 (*advising the marshal*); Montefiore, *Stalin: The Court of the Red Tsar*, 493, 516–20 (*"our Himmler"*).

519 *Churchill hosted the final dinner*: Churchill, *Triumph and Tragedy*, 393 (*"The fire of war"*); Bohlen, *Witness to History, 1929–1969*, 178–80; Meacham, *Franklin and Winston*, 320 (*"secret weapon"*); menu, Feb. 10, 1945, Anna Roosevelt Halsted papers, FDR Lib, box 84; Bishop, *FDR's Last Year*, 421–22 (*gathered in the foyer*).

519 *They were done*: Clemens, *Yalta*, 300; FRUS, 972–73 (*"declaration on liberated Europe"*); Black, *Franklin Delano Roosevelt*, 1072 (*"We will meet again"*); William M. Rigdon, log, "The President's Trip to the Crimea Conference and Great Bitter Lake, Egypt," Averill Harriman papers, LOC MS Div, 31 (Target: Germany); Roosevelt, *As He Saw It*, 242–43 (*Two Russian servants*); Bishop, *FDR's Last Year*, 430–31 (*"worked so hard"*).

520 *Churchill had begun the day*: Moran, *Churchill: Taken from the Diaries of Lord Moran*, 248–49, 251 (*chef from the* Queen Mary); Clemens, *Yalta*, 267–68 (*"this bloody thing"*); Argonaut files, UK NA, PREM 4/77/1B (*hampers of gifts*).

520 *"Papa, genial and sprightly"*: Jenkins, *Churchill: A Biography*, 782.

520 *"I am a bit exhausted"*: Goodwin, *No Ordinary Time*, 582; Jonathan Daniels, "The Presidency," in Goodman, ed., *While You Were Gone*, 124 (*"afraid of getting hit"*).

520 *"in a sulky mood"*: Willis, *The French in Germany*, 13.

520 *Instead the president again boarded* Quincy: OH, W. B. McCarthy, U.S.S. *Murphy*, March 8, 1945, NARA RG 38, E 11, U.S. Navy WWII Oral Histories; official file, 200-4-E, ship's logs, FDR Lib, box 67; William M. Rigdon, log, "The President's Trip to the Crimea Conference and Great Bitter Lake, Egypt," Averill Harriman papers, LOC MS Div, 43–49 (*"harem attire"*); Tully, *F.D.R. My Boss*, 352–53 (*"2 Kings & 1 Emperor"*).

521 *"a slender contact with life"*: Churchill, *Triumph and Tragedy*, 397; Roosevelt, *As He Saw It*, 246 (*"It's been a global war"*).

521 *"We really believed in our hearts"*: Sherwood, *Roosevelt and Hopkins*, 870. Hopkins had been treated for stomach cancer as early as 1937 (James A. Halsted, "Severe Malnutrition in a Public Servant of the World War II Era: The Medical History of Harry Hopkins," *Transactions of the American Clinical and Climatological Association*, 86 (1975), http:// www.scribd.com/doc/20368863/Harry-Hopkins-Medical-Bio, 23+).

521 *"For what we have gained here"*: Stoler, *Allies and Adversaries*, 226; Danchev, 661 (*"Conference is finished"*).

521 *"Stalin doesn't want anything"*: Roberts, *Masters and Commanders*, 557–58; Stoler, *Allies in War*, 196 (*"I don't think I'm wrong"*); Reynolds, *In Command of History*, 465 (*"great and good man"*).

521 *"justify and surpass most of the hopes"*: msg, Jonathan Daniels to S. Early, Feb. 13, 1945, official files, FDR Lib, box 3; memo, Hadley Cantril to FDR, "Public Reaction to the Crimea Conference," March 13, 1945, official file 200-4-E, FDR Lib, box 67 (*Polling results*); Byrnes, *Speaking Frankly*, 45 (*"all doubts"*).

521 *"the shadows of victory"*: Colville, *The Fringes of Power*, 562–63; Reynolds, *In Command of History*, 468 (*Neville Chamberlain*); Smith, *American Diplomacy During the Second World War*, 134–35; Clemens, *Yalta*, 269–71, 277, 280–89; Weinberg, *A World at Arms*, 809 (*Moscow in turn consolidated its grip*); Dobbs, *Six Months in 1945*, 114 (*slave laborers*), 110 (*"partition of Poland"*); Kissinger, "The Age of Kennan," review of John Lewis Gaddis, *George F. Kennan: An American Life*, NYT Book Review, Nov. 13, 2011 (*sentimentality of ARGONAUT*); Stoler, *Allies and Adversaries*, 231 (*"Russian non-cooperation"*); Harriman and Abel, *Special Envoy to Churchill and Stalin, 1941-1946*, 444 (*"We can't do business"*); Black, *Franklin Delano Roosevelt*, 1081 (*"the best I could do"*).

522 *Recriminations followed*: I am particularly grateful to Prof. Mark A. Stoler for his insights on Malta and Yalta. His essay "World War II" provides a fine survey of the subsequent historiography after Yalta, in Schulzinger, ed., *A Companion to American Foreign Relations*, 188+ (*"connotation of shameful failure"*).

522 *For decades the Western delegates would be blamed*: Miller, *F.D.R.: An Intimate History*, 506.

522 *Roosevelt's frailty came to be seen*: Moran, *Churchill: Taken from the Diaries of Lord Moran*, 239–41 (*"The shrewdness has gone"*); Feis, *Churchill, Roosevelt, Stalin*, 557; Gallagher, *FDR's Splendid Deception*, 169–70 (*"extraordinary effort"*); Goodwin, *No Ordinary Time*, 585; Plokhy, *Yalta*, 400 (*"trademark ability"*); Eden, *The Reckoning*, 592–93 (*"impression of failing powers"*); U.S. Navy movie footage, FDR Lib, 71-8: 65–67; transcript, 992nd press conference, *Quincy*, Feb. 23, 1945, Anna Roosevelt Halsted papers, FDR Lib, box 84.

523 *Two generations later, Yalta can be seen*: Dallek, *Franklin D. Roosevelt and American Foreign Policy, 1932-1945*, 519, 533 (*"military and political glacis"*); Forrest C. Pogue, "Yalta in Retrospect," in Snell, ed., *The Meaning of Yalta*, 191; Plokhy, *Yalta*, 228, 287, 401 (*"saved two million Americans"*). James MacGregor Burns later wrote that Roosevelt had "reached the limit of his bargaining power" ("FDR: The Untold Story of His Last Year," *Saturday Review* [Apr. 11, 1970]: 12+).

523 *War had held the Big Three together*: Addison, *Churchill, the Unexpected Hero*, 200 (*met on nine occasions*); transcript, 992nd press conference, *Quincy*, Feb. 23, 1945, Anna Roosevelt Halsted papers, FDR Lib, box 84 (*"mid-Victorian"*); Moran, *Churchill: Taken from the Diaries of Lord Moran*, 245 (*"seems to upset him"*); Eden, *The Reckoning*, 593 (*"dependent upon the United States"*).

523 *"We have moved a long way"*: Hastings, *Winston's War*, 459; Churchill, *Triumph and Tragedy*, 401 (*"a world of imponderables"*).

523 *"The Americans pitch their song"*: Moran, *Churchill: Taken from the Diaries of Lord Moran*, 249.

"Only Our Eyes Are Alive"

524 *From the Swiss border*: Bonn, *When the Odds Were Even*, 177–78 (*"Stay Alive"*); L. D. Docken, "My Recollections of the Battle of Phillipsburg in Jan. 1945," 1981, NARA RG 319, RR background files, FRC 5 (*"My mind is absolutely stripped"*).

524 *The harshest winter in decades*: Schrijvers, *The Crash of Ruin*, 21 (*"tuning forks"*); Blunt, *Foot Soldier*, 122 (*"block of ice"*); Fussell, *Doing Battle*, 130 (*"hands in the crotch"*); Murphy, *To Hell and Back*, 233 (*patches of hair*); Blair, *Ridgway's Paratroopers*, 424 (*igloos*);

Blue Spaders, 117 (*quarter-pound TNT block*); Fussell, *The Boys' Crusade*, 41 ("*Austin White, Chicago, Ill.*").

524 *A SHAEF plan to cut one million cords*: LSA, vol. 2, 213; Frank A. Osmanski, "Critical Analysis of the Planning and Execution of the Logistic Support of the Normandy Invasion," Dec. 1949, Armed Forces Staff College, Osmanski papers, MHI; OH, Philip Carlquist, 1978, Emory University, http://sage.library.emory.edu/collection-0608.html; Cowdrey, *Fighting for Life*, 278 (*Sled dogs*).

525 "*To date, I've slept*": Richard Henry Byers, "Battle of the Bulge," 1983, a.p.

525 "*I tried to knock him out*": McManus, *The Deadly Brotherhood*, 141.

525 "*Everywhere we searched*": Blunt, *Foot Soldier*, 156.

525 "*Tell 'em it's rough*": CBM, *Company Commander*, quoted in Ellis, *On the Front Lines*, 332; Wandrey, *Bedpan Commando*, 163 ("*nice cowboy boots*"); Hauser, "Shock Nurse," *Saturday Evening Post* (March 10, 1945): 12+ ("*their mothers can't see them*").

525 *Prison-camp guards opened*: memo, Theater IG to CG, Advance COMZ, Apr. 1, 1945, NARA RG 498, ETO IG, box 19; DDE to GCM, March 18, 1945, memos, NARA RG 498, ETO SGS classified gen'l corr, 383.6, box 51 ("*I certainly loathe*").

525 "*Will you tell me what the hell*": Heinz, *When We Were One*, 231; memoir, Ralph M. Morales, 254th Inf, 1964, NARA RG 319, *RR* background files, FRC 4 ("*a thousand deaths*"); L. D. Docken, "My Recollections of a Raiding Party into Lixing, Feb. 1945," n.d., NARA RG 319, *RR* background files, FRC 5 ("*Things didn't go exactly as planned*"); Fussell, *Doing Battle*, 140 ("*accident and contingency*").

526 "*How hard I have become*": Vining, ed., *American Diaries of World War II*, 106; Blunt, *Foot Soldier*, 138, 86 ("*I sat and ate*"); Gray, *The Warriors*, 233–34 ("*'Tis bitter cold'*").

526 *A survey of four thousand GIs*: "Attitudes of Soldiers in the European Theater," Apr.–May 1945, report no. ETO 85, NARA RG 330, E 94, 6; Schrijvers, *The Crash of Ruin*, 76 ("*A hatred such as I have never seen*"); Ellis, *On the Front Lines*, 286 ("*The question of killing*").

526 "*Slowly it is beginning to dawn*": Peckham and Snyder, eds., *Letters from Fighting Hoosiers*, vol. 2, 165; Christen T. Jonassen, "Living Conditions in the E.T.O.," 1987, Columbus WWII Round Table, MHI, box 1, 4 ("*Screw the bastards*"); Ellis, *On the Front Lines*, 286 ("*When the Jerries come in*"); Toole, *Battle Diary*, 57 ("*Some of our best men*").

527 "*Their visible wish to surrender*": Fussell, *Doing Battle*, 124.

527 "*Killing is an obsession*": corr, Waldo Heinrichs, Jr., to parents, Apr. 30, 1945, MHI, box 1.

527 *At 7:30 A.M. on Wednesday*: Huie, *The Execution of Private Slovik*, 22–25, 34, 60; "The Execution of Eddie Slovik," *AB*, no. 32 (1981): 28+.

527 *Indiscipline had become a nagging worry*: "Military Justice Administration in Theater of Operations," n.d., USFET General Board study no. 83, NARA RG 407, E 427, AG WWII operations reports, 97-USF5-0.30, 1–2 (*11,000 general courts-martial*); desk calendar, Nov. 5, 1944, DDE Lib, Barbara Wyden papers, box 1 ("*Disciplinary conditions*"); memo, DDE, Dec. 13, 1944, NARA RG 331, E 1, SHAEF SGS, box 11 ("*The large incidence of crimes*"); Wieviorka, *Normandy*, 328 ("*liberators have turned into looters*"); "Alleged Lawlessness of American Troops in Normandy Area," Nov. 18, 1944, NARA RG 498, ETO inspection file #40 ("*fear of being accosted*"); Ellis, *On the Front Lines*, 200 (*less than one-half of one percent*); memo, SHAEF G-2 to SHAEF G-1, Jan. 24, 1945, NARA RG 331, E 1, SHAEF SGS, box 11 ("*a considerable percentage*"). Beetle Smith subsequently complained to commanders on March 20, 1945, that "large scale looting is being practiced by both U.S. and British troops in Holland and Germany."

528 *Severe punishment had a fitful deterrent effect*: "The Military Offender in the Theater of Operations," n.d., USFET General Board study no. 84, NARA RG 407, E 427, AG WWII operations reports, 97-USF5-0.30, 1–2 ("*mental ages*" and *dishonorable discharge*); "Military Justice Administration in Theater of Operations," n.d., USFET General Board study no. 83, NARA RG 407, E 427, AG WWII operations reports, 97-USF5-0.30, 7–9.

528 *Four hundred and forty-three death penalties*: "Normandy Executions," *AB*, no. 85 (1994).

At least one author subsequently claimed that fourteen thousand European women were raped by U.S. soldiers. John H. Morrow, Jr., review of J. Robert Lilly, *Taken by Force, JMH* (Oct. 2008): 1324. See also Davies, *No Simple Victory,* 339. SHAEF and Army figures suggest that the numbers, though appalling, were far lower. See AAR, 12th AG, vol. 10, NARA RG 331, E 200A, SHAEF, box 267; Ziemke, *The U.S. Army in the Occupation of Germany, 1944-1946,* 220; and Wieviorka, *Normandy,* 328.

528 *Seventy executions took place in Europe*: corr, Theodore Wyman, Jr., to OCMH, May 5, 1954, NARA RG 319, E 97, *LSA,* vol. 1, background files, box 4,14; Lilly, "U.S. Military Executions," *AB,* no. 90 (1995): 50+; "Normandy Executions," *AB,* no. 85 (1994) ("*manila hemp*").

528 *Desertion, defined by the U.S. military*: "The Execution of Eddie Slovik," *AB,* no. 32 (1981): 28+; Laffin, *Combat Surgeons,* 197–98 (*more than three thousand death sentences*).

528 *The German military issued*: Geoffrey P. Megargee, World War II panel, SMH conference, May 22, 2004, Bethesda, Md.; Rush, *Hell in Hürtgen Forest,* 336; Horst Boog, "Invasion to Surrender: The Defense of Germany," in Brower, ed., *World War II in Europe: The Final Year,* 129. Boog estimates that "somewhat less than half" of the fifty thousand condemned were executed.

528 *Twenty-one thousand soldiers would desert*: DOB, 508; Fussell, *The Boys' Crusade,* 108 (*less than half had been caught*).

528 *Of nearly two thousand deserters convicted in Europe*: "Military Justice Administration in Theater of Operations," n.d., USFET General Board study no. 83, NARA RG 407, E 427, AG WWII operations reports, 97-USF5-0.30, 4. Several dozen others were condemned for mutiny, sedition, or misbehavior before the enemy, i.e., fleeing from battle.

530 *since 1864*: Huie, *The Execution of Private Slovik,* 146.

530 *Slovik was arrested in October*: ibid., 121–22, 150–51 ("*in a little trouble*"), 174, 179–80; Carroll, "A Deserter Begs Eisenhower to Spare His Life," *World War II* (Jan.–Feb. 2012): 21+ ("*How can I tell you*"); Morgan, *Eisenhower Was My Boss,* 134 ("*Hanging Hour*"); "The Execution of Eddie Slovik," *AB,* no. 32 (1981): 28+.

530 *The MP guards had lost the handcuff key*: Huie, *The Execution of Private Slovik,* 203–11, 217–21, 227.

530 *Gray overcast roofed the garden*: "The Execution of Eddie Slovik," *AB,* no. 32 (1981): 28+; Miller, *Division Commander,* 160–62. In a letter to author William Bradford Huie in 1953, General Cota said, "I regret that Private Slovik had to be a product of our replacement system. This was a cruel system . . . and I never liked it." Corr, Dec. 13, 1953, Norman D. Cota papers, DDE Lib, 201 file, box 1.

531 *A priest anointed the body*: L. R. Talbot, "Graves Registration in the European Theater of Operations," 1955, chapter 26 PIR, MHI; Lilly, "U.S. Military Executions," *AB,* no. 90 (1995): 50+.

531 *"the one sore on the whole front"*: diary, JLD, Jan. 27, 1945, MHI; Tedder, *With Prejudice,* 657 ("*we must get cleaned up*").

531 *In this he would be further frustrated*: RR, 533, 538 (*Iron Cross*); OH, 3rd ID, Colmar Pocket, RG 407, E 427-A, CI, 270/65/5/1, folder 26 (*converted into fortresses*); MEB, "The Colmar Pockets, 20 Jan–9 Feb 45," Oct. 1954, NARA RG 319, R-56, 11 (*ten ferry sites*); "Reduction of the Colmar Pocket," Sixth AG, n.d., CARL, N-11980.3, 5 (*floating contact mines*).

531 *General Devers's initial effort*: Seaman, "Reduction of the Colmar Pocket," *Military Review* (Oct. 1951): 37+; *The Seventh United States Army in France and Germany,* vol. 2, 627; "History of Ordnance Service in the Mediterranean Theater," vol. 2, n.d., CMH, 8-4 JA, 196–97; Turner and Jackson, *Destination Berchtesgaden,* 120–21; De Lattre de Tassigny, *The History of the French First Army,* 345–48 ("*polished ice terrain*"); memo, Reuben E. Jenkins to JLD, Feb. 24, 1947, Jenkins papers, MHI, box 1 (*French II Corps*); Yeide and Stout, *First to the Rhine,* 307 ("Elsass bleibt deutsch").

531 *"Having gained surprise"*: diary, JLD, Jan. 24–26, 1945, and Feb. 1, 1945 ("*he would be shot*"), MHI; RR, 537 ("*willingness to go all out*"); OH, Henry Cabot Lodge, Aug. 16,

1973, Thomas E. Griess, JLD, YCHT, box 94, 11–12 (*"Goddamn it!"*); Tedder, *With Prejudice*, 657 (*"let down by the French"*).

532 *American units had their own difficulties*: *The Seventh United States Army in France and Germany*, vol. 2, 629 (*"exhausted and depleted"*); William A. Sutton, "Operation Grandslam, 30th Regiment," 3rd ID, June 2, 1945, Seventh Army Combat Narratives, MHI, 5 (*improvised nightshirts*), 38 (*"Civil War days"*); Taggart, ed., *History of the Third Infantry Division*, 305–9 (*350 men*); Even, *The Tenth Engineers*, 45 (*Maison Rouge*); Melvin J. Lasky, "La Maison Rouge," March 3, 1945, Seventh Army Combat Narratives, MHI, 2–28 (*"flight and panic"*); RR, 544–47; memoir, James T. Cooper, 30th Inf, ts, n.d., Audie Murphy papers, USMA Arch (*"rattled like paper"*).

532 *Audie Murphy helped redeem*: Simpson, *Audie Murphy, American Soldier*, 130–37, 153–60; Taggart, ed., *History of the Third Infantry Division*, 310–11; Murphy, *To Hell and Back*, 240–43 (*"huddled like partridges"*); Graham, *No Name on the Bullet*, 90 (*"Things seemed to slow down"*); De Lattre de Tassigny, *The History of the French First Army*, 361 (*"bravest thing"*).

532 *At last an Allied preponderance*: MEB, "The Colmar Pockets, 20 Jan–9 Feb 45," Oct. 1954, NARA RG 319, R-56, 18–19; De Lattre de Tassigny, *The History of the French First Army*, 375 (*"God be praised!"*); RR, 551.

533 *By February 5, columns from north and south*: Statements collected from GIs by Army historians shortly after the battle included, "We shot the wounded Germans because we only had twenty men and couldn't fool with them." OH, 3rd ID, Colmar Pocket, RG 407, E 427-A, CI, 270/65/5/1, folder 26.

533 *A French patriot showed GIs*: Weigley, *Eisenhower's Lieutenants*, 598–99.

553 *"My dear French comrades"*: Seaman, "Reduction of the Colmar Pocket," *Military Review* (Oct. 1951): 37+ (*"national event"*); De Lattre de Tassigny, *The History of the French First Army*, 397; LO, 238 (*corner of northeastern Alsace*); memo, Reuben E. Jenkins to JLD, Feb. 24, 1947, Jenkins papers, MHI, box 1 (*three times longer*); Graham, *No Name on the Bullet*, 94 (*"frozen, dead chickens"*).

553 *Colmar had cost*: De Lattre de Tassigny, *The History of the French First Army*, 398–99. U.S. casualties were put at eight thousand, although only five hundred killed in action (RR, 556–57).

533 *"sacrificed for no appreciable gain"*: RR, 558. Russell F. Weigley asserts that one Volksgrenadier unit, the first evacuated across the Rhine, escaped reasonably intact (*Eisenhower's Lieutenants*, 598–99).

533 *Pulverizing the Reich from above*: Willmott, *The Great Crusade*, 414; Webster and Frankland, *The Strategic Air Offensive Against Germany*, vol. 3, *Victory*, part 5, 204 (*"earthquake bomb"*); Green et al., *The Ordnance Department*, 470–71 (*only by the atomic bomb*); "Tactical Air Operations in Europe," XIX TAC, May 1945, Frederick L. Anderson papers, HIA, box 83, folder 1, 8–9 (*"antipersonnel incendiary"*); Miller, *Masters of the Air*, 4 (*"horrible as possible"*); "Preservation of Historical Monuments, Art Objects, etc.," Sept. 1944; memo, DDE, June 1, 1944, NARA RG 331, E 1, SHAEF SGS, box 1 (*"symbolizing to the world"*); Schrijvers, *The Crash of Ruin*, 201 (*"Stonehenge"*); Sebald, *On the Natural History of Destruction*, 47 (*"lifeless life"*).

534 *British air strategists considered*: memo, L. S. Kuter to H. H. Arnold, Aug. 9, 1944, Frederick L. Anderson papers, HIA, box 96; corr, F. L. Anderson to C. A. Spaatz, Feb. 2, 1945, in "Operation ARGONAUT," n.d., Frederick L. Anderson papers, HIA, box 95, folder 14; *AAFinWWII*, 724–26; Webster and Noble Frankland, *The Strategic Air Offensive Against Germany*, vol. 3, *Victory*, part 5, 116 (*"ceases to beat"*); Davis, *Bombing the European Axis Powers*, 490–95 (*"already shaky morale"*).

534 *Skeptics objected*: THUNDERCLAP originally was planned in Aug. 1944 only to be postponed six months and revived in truncated form (Transcript, phone conversation, J. Doolittle and F. L. Anderson, Aug. 21, 1944, in "Operation Thunderclap: Attack on German Civilian Morale," Frederick L. Anderson papers, HIA, box 96, folder 2); Ehlers, *Targeting the Reich*, 335 (*"extremely remote"*).

534 *"Big B is no good"*: "Survey of Combat Crews in Heavy Bombardment Groups in ETO," June 1944, Research Branch, Eighth AF, Carl A. Spaatz papers, LOC MS Div, box 18.

534 *"I agree the project"*: DDE, marginalia on "Air Attack on German Civilian Morale," U.K. Chief of Staff Brief and Action Report, Aug. 7, 1944, NARA RG 331, E 3, SGS conferences and briefings, box 129.

534 THUNDERCLAP, *as the "project"*: Davis, *Carl A. Spaatz and the Air War in Europe*, 552–53; Davis, *Bombing the European Axis Powers*, 496–500, 515n; *AAFinWWII*, 724–26; Miller, *Masters of the Air*, 265 (*sixth largest city*).

535 *Even so, bombs smashed*: *AAFinWWII*, 724–26. Among those killed was Roland Freisler, the notorious state secretary in the Reich Justice Ministry and a Wannsee Conference participant (Author visit, Wannsee Conference villa, Berlin, Sept. 30, 2009).

535 *"It was a sunny, beautiful morning"*: "Vor Fünfzig Jahren: Ein Tagebuch," *Frankfurter Allgemeine*, 1994, a.p.; Friedrich, *The Fire*, 352 (*"people literally ripped clothes"*); Miller, *Masters of the Air*, 478 (*"deer in a storm"*); Whiting, *The Home Front: Germany*, 144–45 (*"flaming rivers"*), 422–26 (*120,000 Germans homeless*); Anonymous, *A Woman in Berlin*, 5, 10 (*"Only our eyes"*).

535 *Other elaborate air missions*: Davis, *Carl A. Spaatz and the Air War in Europe*, 571; Schaffer, "American Miltary Ethics in World War II: The Bombing of German Civilians," *Journal of American History* (Sept. 1980): 318+ (*"virgin areas"*); Juliette Hennessy, "Tactical Operations of the Eighth Air Force," 1952, AFHRA, historical study no. 70, 119–21, 126 (*civilian will*); *AAFinWWII*, 735 (*"no morale"*).

535 *Most infamous of the winter raids*: Webster and Frankland, *The Strategic Air Offensive Against Germany*, vol. 3, *Victory*, part 5, 108–9; Biddle, "Dresden 1945: Reality, History, and Memory," *JMH* (Apr. 2008): 413+ (*uprooting trees*); Arthur, *Forgotten Voices of World War II*, 404 (*"Chimney stacks fell"*); Colville, *The Fringes of Power*, 562–63 (*"Dresden?"*); "Death Toll in Second World War Dresden Bombing," *Daily Mail* (U.K.), Oct. 3, 2008, http://www.dailymail.co.uk/news/article-1067489/Death-toll-Second-World-War -Dresden-bombing-25-000-commission-finds.html; *Germany IX*, 390; Sebald, *On the Natural History of Destruction*, 98 (*Treblinka*).

535 *"We were put to work"*: Carroll, *Behind the Lines*, 318–20.

536 *Each night and each day, bombing*: Davis, *Carl A. Spaatz and the Air War in Europe*, 588. The German fatality number of 406,000, calculated in 1990, included Austrians, forced laborers, and prisoners of war (*Germany IX*, 475–76). Max Hastings and W. G. Sebald put the number closer to 600,000. See, respectively, *Armageddon*, 299, and *On the Natural History of Destruction*, 3–4.

536 *Devastation scorched seventy cities*: Hitchcock, *The Bitter Road to Freedom*, 183, 191 (*"burned like torches"*); Collier, *Fighting Words*, 180 (*"a hairpin"*).

536 *Yet still the lifeless life*: Crane, *Bombs, Cities & Civilians*, 105 (*"chimera"*).

536 *Field Marshal Montgomery had a conqueror's glint*: The Canadian First Army offensive also became known as the Battle of the Reichswald (*VW*, vol. 2, 253–57; *LO*, 136–37).

536 *But no crossing could be made on the Roer*: OH, 78th ID, 1945, NARA RG 407, E 427-A, CI, folders 145–149.

536 *The Urft fell easily*: Hogan, *A Command Post at War*, 243; OH, 78th ID, 1945, NARA RG 407, E 427-A, CI, folders 145–149 (*booby-trapped corpses*); Gavin, *On to Berlin*, 262–63; Sylvan, 293 (*forty battalions*); *Lightning: The History of the 78th Infantry Division*, 110.

537 *At eight P.M. on Friday, February 9*: OH, 78th ID, 1945, NARA RG 407, E 427-A, CI, folders 145–149; Sylvan, 296–97 (*forty thousand U.S. shells*); Mittelman, *Eight Stars to Victory*, 309–12; *Lightning: The History of the 78th Infantry Division*, 118–20; Miller, *A Dark and Bloody Ground*, 201 (*ominous rumble*); OH, 303rd Engineer Bn and 78th ID, 1945, NARA RG 407, E 427-A, CI, folders 145–149 (*"tunnel under the sea"*).

537 *But mortal wounds had already*: *LO*, 81–82; *VW*, vol. 2, 264 (*100 million tons*).

537 *Snowmelt and rain*: "Combat Engineering," Aug. 1945, Historical Report No. 10, ETO, CEOH, box X-30, 129; Weigley, *Eisenhower's Lieutenants*, 603.

537 *With Montgomery's concurrence*: Ninth Army war diary, Feb. 8–10, 1945, William H.

Simpson papers, MHI, box 11; *LO*, 143; OH, William H. Simpson, 1971, Thomas R. Stone, SOOHP, MHI.

537 *For nearly a fortnight, fifteen American divisions*: OH, William H. Simpson, 1971, Thomas R. Stone, SOOHP, MHI; *SLC*, 379; Bradley and Blair, *A General's Life*, 340; Stone, "General William Hood Simpson: Unsung Commander of U.S. Ninth Army," *Parameters* 9, no. 2 (June 1981): 44+; Bradley, *Soldier's Story*, 437 (*"uncommonly normal"*); memoir, Richard D. Hughes, n.d., AFHRA, 520.056-234, 60 (*"He displayed no anxiety"*).

538 *While Simpson bided his time*: The Anglo-Canadian operation was known as VERITABLE (*VW*, vol. 2, 264–71; *LO*, 145).

538 *"Machine guns are crackling now"*: Thompson, *Men Under Fire*, 80, 83; *LO*, 141–42.

538 *At length Ninth Army was ready*: Ninth Army war diary, Feb. 22, 1945, William H. Simpson papers, MHI, box 11; OH, George I. Forsythe, 1974, Frank L. Henry, SOOHP, MHI, 180 (*"you could read a document"*).

538 *Forty-five minutes later three corps plunged*: *LO*, 145–55 (*"indescribable confusion"*), 160–62; "Combat Engineering," CE, ETOUSA, report #10, Dec. 1945, RG 498, ETO HD, admin file #547, 129–33 (*six hundred storm boats*); Hubert S. Miller, XIX Corps engineer, "Roer River Crossing," 1947, CARL, N-9924.2, part I, 17 (*knocked out eight times*). VII Corps was still part of First Army (*LO*).

540 *But within hours brute force won*: Hubert S. Miller, XIX Corps engineer, "Roer River Crossing," 1947, CARL, N-9924.2, part I, 12–13; "Combat Engineering," CE, ETOUSA, report #10, Dec. 1945, RG 498, ETO HD, admin file #547, 129–33; Ninth Army war diary, Feb. 23, 1945, William H. Simpson papers, MHI, box 11 (*"cities captured"*); Wilmot, *The Struggle for Europe*, 673 (*nineteen bridges*); *LO*, 167 (*"things are beginning to break"*).

540 *On Tuesday, Simpson committed his armor*: *LO*, 172; Ninth Army war diary, March 12, 1945, William H. Simpson papers, MHI, box 11 (*"dead, lifeless giant"*).

540 *Eight bridges spanned the great river*: *LO*, 174.

541 *"the enemy is completely disorganized"*: Ninth Army war diary, March 4, March 5 (*"unwise"*), and March 27, 1945 (*"time out for tea"*), William H. Simpson papers, MHI, box 11; OH, William H. Simpson, 1971, Thomas R. Stone, SOOHP, MHI (*"Don't go across"* and *"selfish idea"*); *LO*, 178; Wilmot, *The Struggle for Europe*, 677 (*"industrial wilderness"*).

541 GRENADE *was over*: *LO*, 184; *VW*, vol. 2, 277.

541 *Despite the staggering losses*: *LO*, 171 (*"heavy heart"*).

CHAPTER 11: CROSSINGS

The Inner Door to Germany

543 *Into the Rhineland they pounded*: William A. Carter, "Carter's War," 1983, CEOH, box V, XIII-25; Thompson, *Men Under Fire*, 54 (*"other sort of war"*).

543 *German refugees trudged away*: corr, Thor Smith to family, March 13, 1945, Thor M. Smith papers, HIA, box 1; Ed Cunningham, "The Battle of the Bulge," *Yank*, March 2, 1945, in *Reporting World War II*, vol. 2, 585; war diary, Lasky, "Military History Stood on Its Head," *Berlin Journal* 14 (spring 2007), American Academy of Berlin, 20+ (*"wir folgen"*); Botting, *From the Ruins of the Reich*, 3 ("Krieg weg!"); Gander, *After These Many Quests*, 313–14 (*"In Memoriam" notices*); Heinz, *When We Were One*, 156 (*"They stood facing"*), 261 (*tossed bread*); Simpson, *Audie Murphy, American Soldier*, 212 (*"fodderland"*).

543 *As two dozen British, Canadian, and American divisions*: Fraser, *And We Shall Shock Them*, 390; "Report of Rhine River Crossings," May 1945, FUSA, Office of the Engineer, NARA RG 407, Miscl AG records, ML #887, box 19135 (*three corps abreast*); Sylvan, 319 (*"impossible not to be elated"*); *LO*, 114–15, 240, 252; White, *Conquerors' Road*, 33 (*"bullshit wagon"*); 4th AD combat interviews, March–Apr. 1945, NARA RG 407, Miscl

AG records, ML #857, box 19133 (*tank and howitzer shells*); corr, A. C. Gillem to wife, Feb. 25, 1945, Alvan Cullom Gillem, Jr., papers, MHI, box 7 ("*On the road yesterday*"); Friedrich, *The Fire*, 122–24; William A. Carter, "Carter's War," 1983, CEOH, box V, XIII-6 ("*most totally destroyed city*"); Henry L. Barr, "Infantry Living Conditions in Combat Area," n.d., Columbus WWII Round Table Collection, MHI, box 1 (*Doors torn from their hinges*).

544 "*Everything smelled*": Carpenter, *No Woman's World*, 257; White, *Conqueror's Road*, 42–43 ("*rat hunt*"); Moorehead, *Eclipse*, 235 ("*lovely play of light*"); corr, P. B. Rogers to family, March 7, 1945, Pleas B. Rogers papers, MHI ("*certainly scorched*").

544 "*The cattle, so numerous*": Moorehead, *Eclipse*, 230–31.

544 "*Every house seemed to have*": Thompson, *Men Under Fire*, 35.

544 "*vast stocks of sugar*": Martha Gellhorn, "*Das Deutsches Volk*," *Collier's*, May 26, 1945, in *Reporting World War II*, vol. 2, 675.

544 *Here was a world of Dresden plates*: White, *Conquerors' Road*, 20–21; Nickell, *Red Devil*, 154 (*boiled eggs*); Bourke-White, *Portrait of Myself*, 262–63 (*motherhood medals*); Thompson, *Men Under Fire*, 145 (*Christian texts*); Pogue, *Pogue's War*, 356–57 (*Dutch or Belgian*); Martha Gellhorn, "*Das Deutsches Volk*," *Collier's*, May 26, 1945, in *Reporting World War II*, vol. 2, 671 ("*No one is a Nazi*").

544 *Here too was a world to be looted*: Robert E. Walker, "With the Stonewallers," n.d., MMD, 111 ("*We're advancing*"); memo, ONB to GSP, "Misbehavior of Allied Troops," May 7, 1945, GSP, LOC MS Div, box 13 ("*processed*"); memo, FUSA IG, Apr. 23, 1945, NARA RG 338, First Army AG gen'l corr, box 220 (*Leica cameras*); Wellard, *The Man in a Helmet*, 224–25; Marshall, *A Ramble Through My War*, 226 (*medieval grave*); memo, W. B. Smith to ONB, March 20, 1945, NARA RG 331, E 1, SGS, box 11 (*floorboards*); Schrijvers, *The Crash of Ruin*, 205 (*mine detectors*); Heinz, *When We Were One*, 233 (*women's dresses*); Kessler, *The Battle of the Ruhr Pocket*, 45 ("*Lootwaffe*"); Christen T. Jonassen, "Living Conditions in the E.T.O.," 1987, Columbus WWII Round Table collection, MHI, box 1, 2 ("*two shooting*"); Moorehead, *Eclipse*, 253 ("*German cars by the hundred*"); Adams, "Operations of an American Military Government Detachment in the Saar, 1944–45," *Military Affairs* (autumn 1955): 121+ (*motorcycles, typewriters*); Gander, *After These Many Quests*, 312 ("*unhindered shoplifting*").

545 "*drunken, end-of-the-world carnival*": Schrijvers, *The Crash of Ruin*, 171.

545 "*First I took a hammer*": Linderman, *The World Within War*, 244.

545 "*I did not feel sorry*": Thompson, *The Imperial War Museum Book of Victory in Europe*, 260.

545 *Allied commanders also found themselves*: LO, 330 ("Bitte, schlafen mit"); Thompson, *The Imperial War Museum Book of Victory in Europe*, 261 ("*ogling*"); Willoughby, "The Sexual Behavior of American GIs During the Early Years of the Occupation of Germany," *JMH* (Jan. 1998): 155+ ("*$65 question*"); Kennett, *G.I.: The American Soldier in World War II*, 213 ("*Don't play Samson*"); Stafford, *Endgame 1945*, 128–29 ("*To frat*"); Schrijvers, *The Crash of Ruin*, 183 ("*copulation without conversation*"); D'Este, *Patton: A Genius for War*, 653 ("*Tell the men of Third Army*").

546 *General Hodges ordered champagne*: Sylvan, 322; Friedrich, *The Fire*, 221–25 (*only 10,000*); Hitchcock, *The Bitter Road to Freedom*, 182–89 ("*charred corpse*").

546 *Volksstrum pensioners fought*: Cooper, *Death Traps*, 257; Margry, "The Battle for Cologne," *AB*, no. 104 (1999): 2+ (*cavalry charge*); Janet Flanner [Genêt], "Letter from Cologne," March 31, 1945, *New Yorker*, in *Reporting World War II*, vol. 2, 664–68 ("*scarlet garbage*").

546 *Hodges on Wednesday, March 7*: Margry, "The Battle for Cologne," *AB*, no. 104 (1999): 2+; LO, 191.

546 "*The Rhine. I didn't know*": David Pergrin, 291st Engineer Bn, "The Remagen Bridgehead," 1983, CEOH, box X-26, folder 2, 19; "Combat Engineering," historical report no. 10, Aug. 1945, CEOH, box X-30, 148–49 (*150 glaciers*); Michael George Mulhall, *The Dictionary of Statistics*, 515 (*fifteenth-largest*); LSA, vol. 2, 373 ("*short sea voyage*");

"Forced Crossing of the Rhine, 1945," historical report no. 20, Aug. 1945, CEOH, box X-32, folder 20, 1 (*"fordable"* and *eleven miles an hour*); Dziuban, "Rhine River Flood Prediction Service," *Military Engineer* (Sept. 1945): 348+ (*floods had been the highest*); Tooze, *The Wages of Destruction*, 651 (*relatively unpolluted*); ALH, 178 (*wreckage clogged its bed*); corr, H. L. Ismay to W. B. Smith, Dec. 30, 1944, LHC, 4/29/15 (*"another D-Day"*).

547 *Plans to jump the Rhine*: "Forced Crossing of the Rhine," Dec. 1945, CE, NARA RG 498, ETO HD, admin file #547, 4; "Rhine River Crossing," Jan. 26, 1945, ETOUSA, CEOH, box X-24A, folder 2; OH, Franklin F. Snyder, "Water Resources: Hydraulic and Hydrology," 1995, CEOH, 5, 45, 57 (*engineers in Vicksburg*); Dziuban, "Rhine River Flood Prediction Service," *Military Engineer* (Sept. 1945): 348+ (*radio broadcasts* and *Grenoble*); Abrams, *Our Secret Little War*, 62–63 (*170 models*).

547 *River-crossing schools on the Loire*: "Forced Crossing of the Rhine," Dec. 1945, CE, NARA RG 498, ETO HD, admin file #547, 10–12; *The U.S. Army Corps of Engineers: A History*, 145; Henry F. Pringle, "Weapons Win Wars," n.d., CMH, 2-3.7 AB.B, 201–2 (*Boatyards*); "Supply: Oversea Theaters of Operation," 1945, NARA RG 319, *Global Logistics and Strategy, 1943–1945* background files, 2-3.7 (*nested and crated*); We Bought the Eiffel Tower: The Story of the General Purchasing Agent, European Theater, 1949, MHI, 60, 174–75; OH, Alan G. Kirk, Sept. 22, 1945, NARA RG 38, CNO, box 15, 3–4 (*up the Albert Canal*); Davis, *Across the Rhine*, 8 (*bulldozers*); IFG, 318; Karig, *Battle Report: The Atlantic War*, 394–96 (*"festooned with treetops"*).

547 *By early March, forward depots*: Henry F. Pringle, "Weapons Win Wars," n.d., CMH, 2-3.7 AB.B, 201–2 (*2,500 outboard motors*); Davis, *Across the Rhine*, 8 (*1,100 assault boats*).

548 *Just such a bridge still stood*: Hechler, *The Bridge at Remagen*, 3, 49–53; Zaloga, *Remagen 1945*, 35. Some locals referred only to an adjacent subterranean gallery, used as an air raid shelter, as the Dwarf's Hole (http://www.herrlichkeit-erpel.de/EnglischeVersion /Bruecke03_eng.htm).

548 *Local aesthetes complained*: author visit, Friedensmuseum Brücke von Remagen, June 18, 1996.

548 *Retreating German soldiers*: Steinhoff et al., *Voices from the Third Reich*, 410 (*"cannons being pulled"*); Hechler, *The Bridge at Remagen*, 44–45 (*fractured command architecture*); LO, 214 (*Model had promised*).

548 *Sixty zinc-lined boxes*: LO, 213; "The Ludendorff Railway Bridge," *AB*, no. 16 (1977): 2+; Kenneth W. Hechler, "The German Reaction to Remagen," OCMH, July 1957, NARA RG 319, R-series, #101, 6.

549 *"Do you see"*: OH, John W. Leonard, 9th AD, CG, March 16, 1945, NARA RG 407, E 427-A, CI 300, box 19081.

549 *At 8:20 A.M.*: Reavis, "Crossing of Rhine Remembered," *Stars and Stripes*, March 8, 1995, 1; Hechler, *The Bridge at Remagen*, 79 (*"There is no glory"*).

549 *Now Lieutenant Timmermann would prove*: Hechler, *The Bridge at Remagen*, 88; LHD, 201 (*"Do you know what the hell"*); corr, L. E. Engeman, CO, 14th Tank Bn, to JT, Apr. 5, 1964, JT, LOC MS Div, LHD, box 10 (*locomotives with steam up*).

549 *As three platoons descended*: Hechler, *The Bridge at Remagen*, 98; LHD, 202; Hechler, *Hero of the Rhine*, 18–20.

549 *Shortly before two P.M. a dark geyser*: OH, Karl Timmermann, Murray Deevers, William M. Hoge et al., 27th Armored Inf Bn, March–Apr. 1945, NARA RG 407, E 427-A, CI (*"chicken dinner"*); Hechler, *The Bridge at Remagen*, 104–5 (*"before they blow it"*).

550 *Barely half a mile away, pandemonium*: LO, 217; Hechler, *The Bridge at Remagen*, 112–13 (*"Everybody lie down"*).

550 *With a doleful boom*: "Report of Rhine River Crossings," May 1945, FUSA, Office of the Engineer, NARA RG 407, Miscl AG records, ML #887 (*fourteen hundred pounds*); "Engineers at Remagen," n.d., 7, and OH, Sears Y. Coker, 9th Armored Engineer Bn, March 11, 1945, JT, LOC MS Div, LHD, boxes 9 and 10; LO, 230.

550 *Reprieved, Timmermann and his men*: OH, Karl Timmermann, Murray Deevers, William

M. Hoge et al., 27th Armored Inf Bn, March–Apr. 1945, NARA RG 407, E 427-A, CI 300, box 19081.

550 *By late afternoon, Company A*: ibid.; OH, George P. Soumas, 14th Tank Bn, n.d., NARA RG 407, E 427-A, CI 300, box 19081; "Report of Rhine River Crossings," May 1945, FUSA, Office of the Engineer, NARA RG 407, Miscl AG records, ML #887 (*GIs blew apart*); LHD, 210; Hechler, *The Bridge at Remagen*, 128; Kenneth W. Hechler, "The German Reaction to Remagen," OCMH, July 1957, NARA RG 319, R-series, #101, 7 ("*Inform them*"). There is no evidence that this particular message reached a higher headquarters.

551 *Night fell, a sodden, moonless night*: "Engineer Memoirs: General William M. Hoge," 1993, CEOH, 151 ("*dark as a pocket*"); Ben Cothran, "Remagen, 7 March 1945," n.d., JT, LOC MS Div, *LHD*, box 10 (*drivers napped*); OH, Donald J. Russel [sic], 27th Armored Inf Bn, June 12, 1945, NARA RG 407, E 427-A, CI 300, box 19081 (*three depleted rifle companies*); Reichelt, *Phantom Nine*, 210 (*half a ton of explosives*).

551 *At last nine Shermans*: "Engineers at Remagen," n.d., JT, LOC MS Div, *LHD*, box 9, 4 ("*most harrowing*"); OH, George P. Soumas, 14th Tank Bn, n.d., NARA RG 407, E 427-A, CI 300, box 19081 ("*Ominous and nerve-wracking*"); Rudolf Schulz, "The Bridge of Decision," Dec. 1951, JT, LOC MS Div, box 10, *LHD*, 5 ("*inner door*").

551 *Ancient, stately Reims*: "Code Names and Code Words," NARA RG 331, E 1, SGS, 290/7/2-4/1, box 24; Baedeker, *Northern France*, 85, 103; Abram et al., *The Rough Guide to France*, 272–75; memoir, William Henry Baumer, n.d., HIA, box 1, 183 (*blind tastings*).

551 *Eisenhower messed in the borrowed house*: Danchev, 669.

552 "*Brad, that's wonderful*": *Three Years*, 764, 767–78.

552 *Returning to the dining room*: OH, DDE, June 3, 1946, SLAM, A. S. Nevins papers, "Message Log Oral History Interview," MHI; Taylor, *Swords and Plowshares*, 105–6 ("*badly located*").

552 *They drank to the bridge*: Courtney H. Hodges, "Remagen: The Bridge That Changed the War," 1949, Hodges papers, MHI, box 21, 24–25; OH, John Millikin, March 19, 1945, NARA RG 407, E 427-A, CI, folder 339 ("*Nobody ever*"); diary, March 7, 1945, CBH collection, MHI, box 4; Weigley, *Eisenhower's Lieutenants*, 629; David Pergrin, 291st Engineer Bn, "The Remagen Bridgehead," 1983, CEOH, box X-26, folder 2, 17 (*the Ludy*).

552 *For the moment, Eisenhower would commit*: memo, "Telephone Conversation—General Bradley–General Bull," March 9, 1945, Harold R. Bull papers, DDE Lib, box 2; Bradley, *A Soldier's Story*, 510–14 (*gain the autobahn*); author visit, Friedensmuseum Brücke von Remagen, June 18, 1996 (*eight thousand GIs*); OH, Ben J. Cothran, 9th AD, March 14, 1945, NARA RG 407, E 427-A, CI 300, box 19081; "Report of Rhine River Crossings," May 1945, FUSA, Office of the Engineer, NARA RG 407, Miscl AG records, ML #887, box 19135 (*protective booms*); B. C. Andrus, III Corps, March 24, 1945, NARA RG 498, ETO G-3 OR (*Searchlights swept the water*); Beck, 510–11 (*depth charges*); OH, F. Russell Lyons et al., III Corps engineers, March 21, 1945, NARA RG 407, E 427-A, CI, folders 339–340 (*seven tons*).

552 *As engineers toiled*: "Report of Rhine River Crossings," May 1945, FUSA, Office of the Engineer, NARA RG 407, Miscl AG records, ML #887, box 19135; "Combat Engineering," historical report no. 10, Aug. 1945, CEOH, box X-30, 151–60 (*nineteen floats in ten minutes*); David Pergrin, 291st Engineer Bn, "The Remagen Bridgehead," 1983, CEOH, box X-26, folder 2, 32–38 ("*Boys, I've had it*"), 70 (*first jeep crossed*); SC, 424; Courtney H. Hodges, "Remagen: The Bridge That Changed the War," 1949, Hodges papers, MHI, box 21, 31 (*four miles deep*).

553 *Loss of the Ludendorff*: "History of U.S. Strategic Air Force Europe vs. German Air Force," Sept. 1945, SRH-013, NARA RG 457, E 9002, NSA, 338 ("*immediately destroyed*"); Rudolf Schulz, "The Bridge of Decision," Dec. 1951, JT, LOC MS Div, box 10, *LHD*, 3, 7 (*11th Panzer Division*); OH, F. Russell Lyons et al., III Corps engineers, March 21, 1945, NARA RG 407, E 427-A, CI, box 19086, folders 339–340; LO, 228; Zaloga, *Remagen 1945*, 59; OH, Rich Porter, with author, Jan. 27, 2009 (*Reichsmark notes*).

553 *Hermann Göring sought volunteers*: Zaloga, *Remagen 1945*, 56, 59 (*Army's densest concentration*); Hinsley, 592 (*Allied eavesdroppers*); B. C. Andrus, III Corps, March 24, 1945, NARA RG 498, ETO G-3 OR (*barrage balloons*); Paul Semmens, "The Hammer of Hell," n.d., CMH, 156–67 (*nearly seven hundred*); Wishnevsky, *Courtney Hicks Hodges*, 183 ("*a million dollars*"); LO, 228 (*aircraft shot down*); Royce L. Thompson, "Military Impact of the German V-Weapons, 1943–1945," July 31, 1953, CMH, 2-3.7 AE-P-4, 39; M. C. Helfers, "The Employment of V-Weapons by the Germans During World War II," 1954, OCMH, NARA RG 319, 2-3.7 AW, 81; Hechler, *The Bridge at Remagen*, 162; Beck, 510–11.

553 *The debacle at Remagen clearly called*: Blumentritt, *Von Rundstedt*, 279; Carver, ed., *The War Lords*, 199 (*repaired to Bad Tölz*); Westphal, *The German Army in the West*, 192–93 ("*his own shadow*"); LO, 222; AAAD, 166–67; DOB, 93.

553 *Harsher fates befell*: Günther Kraft, "The Shooting of My Father in Consequence of the Remagen Incidents," Apr. 10, 1946, trans. Duscha Ziegel, OCMH, JT, LOC MS Div, LHD, box 10; Zumbro, *Battle for the Ruhr*, 102–5; Hechler, *The Bridge at Remagen*, 178–79 (*letters*). A fifth officer, Captain Willi Bratge, was tried in absentia, having been captured.

554 *Such rough justice*: Spayd, *Bayerlein*, 198 ("*bridge psychosis*"); Colley, *Blood for Dignity*, 93.

554 "*Hitler was the one*": Sherry, *In the Shadow of War*, 101.

554 "*You ain't in the quartermaster*": Charles Roland, "G.I. Joe: The Citizen Soldier in World War II," 1979, MHI, ASEQ, 3rd Bn, 394th Inf, 99th ID, 24.

554 *They of course had already been in the Army*: memo, "Report of Board of Officers on Utilization of Negro Manpower," to GCM, Nov. 17, 1945, and "Negro Platoons in Composite Rifle Companies—World War II Style," "Army Talk," no. 170, Apr. 12, 1947, Alvan C. Gillem, Jr., papers, DDE Lib, box 14; MacGregor, *Integration of the Armed Forces*, 51–53. A proposal by John C. H. Lee to fully integrate them was rejected by Eisenhower after Smith noted that such radical integration contradicted War Department policy (Colley, *Blood for Dignity*, 49; Lee, *The Employment of Negro Troops*, 688–97).

554 *Despite the creditable fighting records*: DOB, 381–83; Lee, *The Employment of Negro Troops*, 648–52, 661–64, 679; Patton, *War as I Knew It*, 160 ("*cannot think fast enough*"); Colley, *Blood for Dignity*, 53–55 ("*make liars out of the whites*"); Reynolds, *Rich Relations*, 315 ("*I am an American negro*"); e-mail, Harry Dewey to author, Dec. 15, 2008 ("*We were short-handed*").

554 *Repairs on the Ludendorff continued*: corr, Justin Dwight Hillyer to Ken Hechler, Oct. 25, 1959, CEOH, box X-26, folder 1.

554 *Just before three P.M. on Saturday, March 17*: Beck, 510–11; David Pergrin, 291st Engineer Bn, "The Remagen Bridgehead," 1983, CEOH, box X-26, folder 2, 100–105 ("*slow-motion movie*").

555 *Of those who rode the Ludy down*: Hechler, *The Bridge at Remagen*, 163–64; OH, F. Russell Lyons et al., III Corps engineers, March 21, 1945, NARA RG 407, E 427-A, CI, box 19086, folders 339–340 (*engineers with axes*); "Report of Rhine River Crossings," May 1945, FUSA, Office of the Engineer, NARA RG 407, Miscl AG records, ML #887, box 19135 (*8-inch howitzer battery*); "Combat Engineering," historical report no. 10, Aug. 1945, CEOH, box X-30, 151–60; David Pergrin, 291st Engineer Bn, "The Remagen Bridgehead," 1983, CEOH, box X-26, folder 2, 107 ("*glad the damned thing*"). Hodges sacked General Millikin the day the bridge fell for failure to properly organize the bridgehead (Sylvan, 335–37).

555 *Late Saturday night, seven German frogmen*: B. C. Andrus, III Corps, Mar. 24, 1945, NARA RG 498, ETO G-3 OR; LO, 228–30; VW, vol. 2, 283.

555 *Eisenhower approved shoving*: LO, 234; Sylvan, 338 ("*The war is over*").

Two If by Sea

555 *Field Marshal Kesselring's buoyant optimism*: Macksey, *Kesselring: The Making of the Luftwaffe*, 6–8; Kesselring, *The Memoirs of Field-Marshal Kesselring*, 9, 13–14, 243 ("*Hang on*"); Warlimont, *Inside Hitler's Headquarters*, 451 ("*I don't believe*"), 506.

556 *Now Kesselring's luck*: Kesselring, *The Memoirs of Field-Marshal Kesselring*, 218–19, 241; MacDonald, *The Mighty Endeavor*, 457 (*quarter-million Germans had vanished*), 239 ("*one hundred combatants*"); Warlimont, *Inside Hitler's Headquarters*, 506 (*Channel Islands garrison*); Steinhoff et al., *Voices from the Third Reich*, 413 (*shoot all German corporals*).

556 *Field commanders in mid-March urged Kesselring*: LO, 244, 257–58; Kesselring, *The Memoirs of Field-Marshal Kesselring*, 249–50 ("*bricks without straw*").

556 *George Patton had taken brief leave*: PP, 643; Codman, *Drive*, 254–57.

556 *In Trier, for instance*: Friedrich, *The Fire*, 248–49.

557 "*The desolation is frozen*": Edsel, *The Monuments Men*, 260–62.

557 "*smell the sweat of the legions*": PP, 655.

557 *Rarely, perhaps never, had his generalship*: Weigley, *Eisenhower's Lieutenants*, 639; LO, 262 ("*Scarcely a man-made thing*"); Wandrey, *Bedpan Commando*, 179 ("*hanging onto my hand*"); Allen, *Lucky Forward*, 254 ("*Roads don't matter*"); Ayer, *Before the Colors Fade*, 193 ("*blow up the goddamn gun*").

557 *By Wednesday, March 21*: LO, 250–51, 259; Allen, *Lucky Forward*, 260 ("*We're going to cross the Rhine*").

557 *He made good his boast*: memo, William Sackville, XII Corps, March 26, 1945, NARA RG 498, ETO G-3 OR, box 9; Allen, *Lucky Forward*, 263; LO, 267–71 ("*walking death*"); diary, GSP, March 24, 1945, LOC MS Div, box 3, folder 11 ("*drove to the river*").

558 "*Brad, we're across*": Codman, *Drive*, 269; LO, 273 ("*feeling of rivalry*").

558 "*I love war*": Semmes, *Portrait of Patton*, 264.

558 *Churchill had proposed riding*: Roberts, *Masters and Commanders*, 561; Hastings, *Winston's War*, 456 ("*I'm an old man*"); Colville, *Footprints in Time*, 184–87; AAR, "Operation Varsity," First Allied Airborne Army, May 19, 1945 (*smoke screen*); Saunders, *The Red Beret*, 287 ("*thick black haze*").

558 *They found Montgomery's command post*: Colville, *The Fringes of Power*, 575; Churchill, *Triumph and Tragedy*, 411; LO, 303 ("*Two if by sea*").

558 *Under Montgomery's command*: SC, 421; LO, 301 ("*pretend to resist*"); Callahan, *Churchill & His Generals*, 222 (*thirty-five infantry battalions*).

559 *The plan for* PLUNDER: VW, vol. 2, 286–87; AAR, "Activities, Final Phase, European War," IX Troop Carrier Command, June 1945, MBR papers, MHI, box 62, 56–76; Harris, "The Bigger They Are the Harder They Fall," *FAJ* (May–June 1938): 229+ (*single 105mm howitzer*); Thompson, *I Was Churchill's Shadow*, 151 ("*Hitler Personally*"). Ninth Army had accumulated 138,000 tons of supplies (LO, 297).

559 *Churchill and Brooke strolled*: Danchev, 674.

559 "*They were slightly bent under their packs*": Sevareid, *Not So Wild a Dream*, 499–502.

559 "*If you happen to hear*": Arthur, *Forgotten Voices of World War II*, 405–6.

559 "*a single hurrying black moth*": Moorehead, *Eclipse*, 240.

561 "*A great crimson stain*": Thompson, *Men Under Fire*, 106–7.

561 "*more than mortal powers*": Allen, *One More River*, 241.

561 "*Burglar-like and in single file*": Moorehead, *Eclipse*, 240; VW, vol. 2, 288–89.

561 *A few miles upstream*: Allen, *One More River*, 247 ("*shoals of small boats*"); "The Rhine Crossing," Aug. 1945, NARA RG 337, E 15A, AGF OR #608 (*a thousand shells a minute*); LO, 305–7 (*seven hundred assault boats* and *thirty-one casualties*); Albert H. Peyton, XVI Corps, March 31, 1945, NARA RG 498, ETO G-3 OR, box 8 (*twenty-ton cranes*).

561 *fishing nets, chicken wire, tar paper*: "Chief Engineers Report on Camouflage Activities in the ETO," Nov. 15, 1945, Howard V. Canan papers, HIA, box 3.

561 *Rested and exultant*: Colville, *The Fringes of Power*, 576; Colville, *Footprints in Time*, 184–87; Moorehead, *Eclipse*, 240–42 ("*my armies are too vast*").

562 "*They're coming!*": Moorehead, *Eclipse*, 244.

562 *Here then was* VARSITY: "Narrative of Operation Varsity," March 31, 1945, First Allied Airborne Army, Floyd Lavinius Parks papers, MHI, box 3; LO, 309; John C. Warren, "Airborne Operations in World War II, European Theater," 1956, AFHRA, historical

study no. 97, 192. Various official histories of VARSITY PLUNDER differ markedly on details of the operation. The fighter and fighter-bomber cover included escort, cover, and patrol missions (*AAFinWWII*, 774).

562 *Their orders were to seize the high ground*: "Visit to ETO," May 5, 1945, NARA RG 337, E 15A, AGF OR #320; Gander, *After These Many Quests*, 286 ("*loosen up the scrum*").

562 *In this they would be modestly effectual*: "Visit to ETO," May 5, 1945, NARA RG 337, E 15A, AGF OR #320; "Narrative of Operation Varsity," March 31, 1945, First Allied Airborne Army, Floyd Lavinius Parks papers, MHI, box 3 (*failed to winkle out*); corr, Paul M. McGuire, 3rd Bn, 513th PIR, to JT, Sept. 6, 1963, JT, LOC MS Div, *LHD*, box 3 ("*holes started appearing*"); A. C. Miller, 2nd Bn, 513th PIR, "Operation VARSITY," Sept. 1963, JT, LOC MS Div, box 3, *LHD* ("*I looked back*").

562 *The body of the plane plummeted*: Sevareid, *Not So Wild a Dream*, 503.

563 "*falling like puppets*": Clark, *Crossing the Rhine*, 319.

563 "*cracked it open like an egg*": Arthur, *Forgotten Voices of World War II*, 412.

563 *Of four hundred 6th Airborne gliders*: Ernest M. Layman, Jr., "The Operations of XVIII Airborne Corps in the Crossing of the Rhine River at Wesel," n.d., JT, LOC MS Div, *LHD*, box 3, 9; *VW*, vol. 2, 291; John C. Warren, "Airborne Operations in World War II, European Theater," 1956, AFHRA, historical study no. 97, 176–77; *LO*, 313.

563 "*Controls hit by flak*": John C. Warren, "Airborne Operations in World War II, European Theater," 1956, AFHRA, historical study no. 97, 184–87.

563 "*Stop those Jewish prayers*": Capa, *Slightly Out of Focus*, 219; Richard C. Hottelet, "Big Jump into Germany," *Collier's*, May 5, 1945, in *Reporting World War II*, vol. 2, 658 ("*burning and disabled C-47s*").

563 *The morning proved even more hazardous*: "A Historical Study of Some World War II Airborne Operations," [1951?], WSEG staff study no. 3, CARL N-17309.1, 136; Eckelmeyer, "The Story of the Self-Sealing Tank," *U.S. Naval Institute Proceedings* (Feb. 1946): 205+ (*sparks up to five inches*); AAR, "Operation Varsity," 52nd Troop Carrier Wing, n.d., MBR papers, MHI, box 62; memo, Maj. Donald W. Nyrop, "Fuel Tanks C-46 Aircraft," Sept. 9, 1944, and H. H. Arnold, "Operational and Tactical Suitability of the C-46A Airplane for Troop Carrier Operations," Aug. 8, 1944, Report of the Army Air Forces Board, both in NARA RG 18, AAF fuel systems, AAF Central Files, 1942–44, file 452.22; Holley, *Buying Aircraft*, 550–51 (*three thousand C-46s*); S. D. Heron, "Development of Aviation Fuels," in Schlaifer, ed., *Development of Aircraft Engines and Fuels*, 640

563 *Two layers of rubber lined the fuel tank*: corr, Lt. Col. David N. Laux to Henry L. Stimson, June 1, 1944; memo, Robert Lovett to Henry L. Stimson, July 18, 1944; memo, Brig. Gen. Mervine E. Gross, "Additional Built-in Fuel Capacity for C-46 Airplanes," Oct. 12, 1944; memo, Lewis H. Brereton, First Allied Airborne Army, Nov. 30, 1944; memo, Col. H. A. Shepard to H. H. Arnold, "Self-Sealing Fuel Cells for C-47 Airplanes," Dec. 13, 1944; memo, Col. S. F. Giffin, "Self-Sealing Tanks and Armor Plate for Troop Carrier C-46 and C-54 Aircraft," Feb. 3, 1945; memo, Col. H. G. Bunker, Apr. 16, 1945; Pearson, "Washington Merry-Go-Round," Apr. 29, 1944, *WP*, all in NARA RG 18, AAF fuel systems, AAF Central Files, 1942–44, file 452.22; John C. Warren, "Airborne Operations in World War II, European Theater," 1956, AFHRA, historical study no. 97, 194 (*some C-47s*).

563 "*I saw pieces*": Allen, *One More River*, 267.

564 "*The C-46 seemed to catch on fire*": John C. Warren, "Airborne Operations in World War II, European Theater," 1956, AFHRA, historical study no. 97, 180; AAR, "Activities, Final Phase, European War," IX Troop Carrier Command, June 1945, MBR papers, MHI, box 62, 80–81 (*seventy-three C-46s*); AAR, "Operation Varsity," 52nd Troop Carrier Wing, n.d., MBR papers, MHI, box 62 ("*not a suitable troop carrier*").

564 *One final calamity remained*: John C. Warren, "Airborne Operations in World War II, European Theater," 1956, AFHRA, historical study no. 97, 189.

564 *Among those shot down*: corr, John E. Cannon to Emma Cheek, Apr. 3, 1945, Earle C. Cheek collection, USMA Arch; e-mail, http://www.Accident-Report.com to author, Dec. 11, 2009.

564 *Cheek had survived many harrowing sorties*: corr, Earle C. Cheek to Doris, family, Nov. 1944–March 1945, Cheek collection, USMA Arch; "Missing Air Crew Report," HQ, AAF, March 27, 1945, a.p., www.Accident-Report.com. Other crewmen on the plane had completed eighteen to twenty-eight missions.

564 *The sole survivor*: corr, A. W. Keenen to Emma Cheek, June 25, 1945; Capt. T. G. Brown to Doris, June 12, 1945; Maj. Gen. Edward F. Witsell to Emma Cheek, Apr. 14, 1945, all in Cheek collection, USMA Arch.

564 *"The German is whipped"*: Eisenhower, *Crusade in Europe*, 390.

564 *Churchill entertained the mess*: Pawle, *The War and Colonel Warden*, 373–74.

565 *Engineers were at work on various spans*: "Visit to ETO," May 5, 1945, NARA RG 337, E 15A, AGF OR #320.

565 *The utility of* VARSITY'*s vertical envelopment*: *VW*, vol. 2, 292; *AAFinWWII*, 774; John C. Warren, "Airborne Operations in World War II, European Theater," 1956, AFHRA, historical study no. 97, 191–93 (*"tremendous success"*). The U.S. Army official history is unusually caustic in evaluating VARSITY (*LO*, 314).

565 *The two airborne divisions incurred*: "Narrative of Operation Varsity," Mar. 31, 1945, First Allied Airborne Army, Floyd Lavinius Parks papers, MHI, box 3; "Visit to ETO," May 5, 1945, NARA RG 337, E 15A, AGF OR #320; AAR, "Operation Varsity: First Allied Airborne Army," May 1945, NARA RG 334, E 315, ANSCOL, ACT R A-105, box 62 (*more than three hundred C-47s*); AAR, "Activities, Final Phrase, European War," IX Troop Carrier Command, June 1945, MBR papers, MHI, box 62, 80–81 (*another 357 casualties*); Thompson, *The Imperial War Museum Book of Victory in Europe*, 234 (*VARSITY BLUNDER*); Clark, *Crossing the Rhine*, 323 (*saws and ladders*).

565 *"an influence, supreme and watchful"*: Kessler, *The Battle of the Ruhr Pocket*, 31.

566 *Together in the brilliant sunshine*: OH, William H. Simpson, 1971, Thomas R. Stone, SOOHP, MHI; Thompson, *The Imperial War Museum Book of Victory in Europe*, 242 (*"Our men muttered"*); Eisenhower, *Crusade in Europe*, 372 (*"Thank God, Ike"*); Danchev, 676–77 (*"I was misquoted"*).

566 *"I am in command now"*: OH, William H. Simpson, 1971, Thomas R. Stone, SOOHP, MHI (*"Get him out of here"*); Churchill, *Triumph and Tragedy*, 416 (*"Why don't we go across"*); "Winston Churchill Visits the Rhine," *AB*, no. 16 (1977): 28+ (*ears cocked*); Davis, *Across the Rhine*, 85 (*"lighting his cigar"*).

566 *"pouting mouth and angry eyes"*: Danchev, 677.

566 *After presenting Montgomery*: Colville, *The Fringes of Power*, 579; Winston S. Churchill, *Marlborough: His Life and Times*, vol. 1 (Chicago: University of Chicago Press, 2002), 15.

566 *In short order, seven Allied armies*: *LO*, 320; OH, William H. Simpson, n.d., CJR, box 44, folder 14, 10–12 (*Simpson bridled*); war diary, Ninth Army, March 27–31, 1945, William H. Simpson papers, "personal calendar," MHI, box 11 (*languid British pace*); *VW*, vol. 2, 294 (*twenty miles beyond the Rhine*).

566 *On the right flank, in the south*: *LO*, 285–89; Wyant, *Sandy Patch*, 189 (*fewer than six thousand combat effectives*).

567 *"My dear General, you must cross"*: *LO*, 321–22; De Gaulle, *The Complete War Memoirs of Charles de Gaulle, 1940–1946*, 845–46; De Lattre de Tassigny, *The History of the French First Army*, 421 (*"even if they do not want you"*), 425 (*A solitary company*).

567 *"This is the collapse"*: Moorehead, *Eclipse*, 244; Benjamin A. Dickson, "G-2 Journal: Algiers to the Elbe," MHI, 203–12 (*"The enemy is capable of collapse"*).

567 *"a systematic annihilation"*: *SC*, 429; Biddle, *Rhetoric and Reality in Air Warfare*, 287 (*heaviest bombing month*); Addison, *Churchill, the Unexpected Hero*, 196–97 (*"stigmatizing a policy"*); memoir, Richard D. Hughes, n.d., AFHRA, 520.056-234, 64 (*"petering out"*).

567 *"machinery in their souls"*: John Steinbeck, *Bombs Away: The Story of a Bomber Team*, (New York: Penguin, 2009), e-book edition.

567 *"people accustomed to great spaces"*: "Miracle of Supply," *Time* (Sept. 25, 1944): 8+.

567 *The United States in the past year*: Wieviorka, *Normandy*, 43.

568 *American factories during the war*: Gropman, *Mobilizing U.S. Industry in World War II*, 133. The Allies collectively outproduced Germany in military trucks by a factor of 12 to 1 (Ellis, *Brute Force*, 348–49).

568 *with more than 700,000 vehicles on the Continent*: "Ordnance Diary," Dec. 1, 1945, NARA RG 498, ETOUSA HD, UD 602, box 1; Nevins, "How We Felt About the War," in Goodman, ed., *While You Were Gone*, 21 (*"armed workshop"*); Freeman W. Burford, "The Inside Story of Oil in the European War," Nov. 25, 1946, NARA RG 319, E 97, *LSA*, vol. 1, background files, box 6 (*four million gallons*); "Combat Engineering," CE, ETOUSA report no. 10, Dec. 1945, NARA RG 498, ETO HD, admin file #547, 7 (*ten bridges a day*); *LSA*, vol. 2, 422–23 (*fifty-seven more across the Rhine*), 454 (*six thousand tanks*).

568 *"one might be able to see the end"*: Hastings, *Armageddon*, 380.

568 *"Naturally I am immensely pleased"*: Chandler, 2544.

"The Enemy Has Reason to Fear Him"

568 *No sword was swifter*: *Three Years*, 797 (*German houses burned*); *PP*, 660 (*"Most of the houses are heaps"*), 656–57 (*"having so much fun"*); Ziemke, *The U.S. Army in the Occupation of Germany, 1944–1946*, 227 (*"brick and stone wilderness"*); D'Este, *Patton: A Genius for War*, 725 (*"reason to fear him"*). The German high command generally was less attentive to Patton individually than Americans liked to believe (Yeide, "The German View of Patton," *World War II* [March–Apr. 2012]: 27+).

568 *"I am very proud of the fact"*: *PP*, 662–63.

569 *His beloved son-in-law*: *AAAD*, 339–44; OH, John K. Waters, 1980, William C. Parnell, III, SOOHP, MHI, 240–58; OH, Brooks Kleber, June 27, 1989, William A. Young, III, Kleber papers, MHI, 8–9; http://www.oflag64.us/Oflag64/Oflag_64_Association_homepage.html.

569 *Waters kept a pocket notebook*: John K. Waters, "Remembrances," a.p., courtesy George Patton "Pat" Waters.

569 *He also maintained a "Wartime Log"*: John K. Waters, "A Wartime Log," a.p., courtesy George Patton "Pat" Waters.

569 *The great Russian winter offensive*: Blatman, *The Death Marches*, 407; "Sketches from the Lives of the Kriegies of Oflag 64," 1997, a.p., 34; OH, Brooks Kleber, June 27, 1989, William A. Young, III, Kleber papers, MHI, 8–18 (*secret radio*).

570 *On February 26, the column was herded*: Margry, "The Hammelburg Raid," *AB*, no. 91 (1996): 1+; Baron et al., *Raid!*, 46–48.

570 *Conditions at Hammelburg were wretched*: Deborah A. Smith, "American Prisoners of War in Germany, 1944–45: Hammelburg," May 10, 1976, and OH, Brooks Kleber, June 27, 1989, William A. Young, III, both in Kleber papers, MHI, 19.

570 *Patton had hoped to hear*: diary, Jan. 18, 1945, GSP, LOC, MS Div, box 3, folder 9; diary, Third Army chief of staff, Feb. 9, 1945, Hobart Gay papers, MHI, box 2, 722 (*Soviet intelligence*); Blumenson, *Patton: The Man Behind the Legend, 1885–1945*, 260–61 (*new arrivals at Hammelburg*); *PP*, 667 (*"We are headed"*); corr, GSP to Beatrice, March 25, 1945, GSP, LOC MS Div, box 13 (*"Hope to send an expedition"*).

570 *The dubious honor of rescuing*: Baron et al., *Raid!*, 21–25; "Interview of Major Abraham J. Baum," Sept. 14, 1945, JT, LOC MS Div, *LHD*, box 1; Margry, "The Hammelburg Raid," *AB*, no. 91 (1996): 1+; Whitaker, "Task Force Baum and the Hammelburg Raid," *Armor* (Sept.–Oct. 1996): 20+; diary, Manton Eddy, XII Corp CG, March 26, 1945, FCP, MHI (*Patton ordered XII Corps*); Alexander C. Stiller, ts, n.d., GSP, LOC MS Div, box 49, folder 13; Blumenson, "The Hammelburg Affair," *Army* (Oct. 1965): 16+ (*"thrills and laughs"*).

572 *Patton had proposed sending*: OH, Abraham Baum, "Interview by Mr. Lake, War Correspondent," n.d., NARA RG 407, E 427; OH, Abraham J. Baum, Apr. 10, 1945, D. G. Dayton and S. J. Tobin, JT, LOC MS Div, *LHD*, box 1 (*fifteen maps*); *PP*, 668–70;

Blumenson, *Patton: The Man Behind the Legend, 1885-1945*, 260–61 (*east of a corps driving north*); Sorley, *Thunderbolt*, 92–93 ("*What the hell*"); corr, GSP to Beatrice, March 27, 1945, GSP, LOC MS Div, box 13 ("*nervous as a cat*"); *PP*, 666 ("*I do not believe*").

572 *After skirmishes near Aschaffenburg*: Baron et al., *Raid!*, 99–109. A meticulous contemporary effort by Peter Domes to reconstruct the raid can be found under "US Schedule," http://taskforcebaum.de/schedule/schedule%20us.html.

572 *American tank and machine-gun fire*: Margry, "The Hammelburg Raid," *AB*, no. 91 (1996): 1+; Alexander C. Stiller, ts, n.d., GSP, MS Div, box 49, folder 13 ("*scattered like quail*"); Baron et al., *Raid!*, 118–19, 133 ("*Mazel tov*"); "Notes on Task Force Baum, Narrative of Capt. Baum," n.d., NWWIIM.

572 *Here trouble awaited them*: Alexander C. Stiller, ts, n.d., GSP, MS Div, box 49, folder 13; Margry, "The Hammelburg Raid," *AB*, no. 91 (1996): 1+.

573 *Drumfire and coiling black smoke*: Herndon Inge, Jr., untitled memoir, n.d., MHI, 711–17; *LHD*, 292 (*offered absolution*), 294 ("*No smoking*").

573 *With consent from a German commandant*: corr, John K. Waters to Harry H. Semmes, Sept. 15, 1953, JT, LOC MS Div, *LHD*, box 1; OH, John K. Waters, 1980, William C. Parnell, III, 277–79; Baron et al., *Raid!*, 156–57 (*coccyx*); Margry, "The Hammelburg Raid," *AB*, no. 91 (1996): 1+ (*paper bandages*).

573 *Baum's tanks meanwhile*: Alexander C. Stiller, ts, n.d., GSP, MS Div, box 49, folder 13; Herndon Inge, Jr., untitled memoir, n.d., MHI, 711–17; OH, Col. Paul R. Goode, May 17, 1945, JT, LOC MS Div, *LHD*, box 2 (*he confronted 1,291*).

573 *It was now 6:30 P.M.*: Baron et al., *Raid!*, 162–64.

574 *Evening's first stars glittered*: OH, Col. Paul R. Goode, May 17, 1945, JT, LOC MS Div, *LHD*, box 2; OH, R. S. Garner, 707th Tank Bn, 28th ID, May 4, 1945, NARA RG 407, Miscl AG records, ML 857, box 19133 (*a few compasses*).

574 *Scouts reported ambushes and roadblocks*: "Notes on Task Force Baum," 4th AD, Apr. 10, 1945, NARA RG 407, E 427, file 604-0.3.0, box 12337; OH, R. S. Gardner, 28th ID, May 4, 1945, 707th Tank Bn, 28th ID, May 4, 1945, NARA RG 407, Miscl AG records, ML 857, box 19133.

574 "*A sheet of hell*": Baron et al., *Raid!*, 202–3; Alexander C. Stiller, ts, n.d., GSP, MS Div, box 49, folder 13 ("*they destroyed us*").

574 "*Every man for himself*": Baron et al., *Raid!*, 202–3; Margry, "The Hammelburg Raid," *AB*, no. 91 (1996): 1+; OH, Brooks Kleber, June 27, 1989, William A. Young, III, Kleber papers, MHI, 21–22 ("*Get a good sleep*").

574 "*March 27: 'Shot'*": John K. Waters, "Remembrances," a.p., courtesy George Patton "Pat" Waters.

575 *Not for some days*: Baron et al., *Raid!*, 250.

575 *Patton both evaded responsibility*: Phillips, *The Making of a Professional*, 184 (*undersized force*); *PP*, 667 ("*I felt by hazarding*"); D'Este, *Patton: A Genius for War*, 717 (*long after the raid*).

575 "*I had known of the camp*": corr, GSP to Beatrice, March 31, 1945, GSP, LOC MS Div, box 13.

575 "*They are trying to make an incident*": corr, GSP to Beatrice, Apr. 13, 1945, GSP, LOC MS Div, box 13.

575 *Ten days after the raid*: Margry, "The Hammelburg Raid," *AB*, no. 91 (1996): 1+; Baron et al., *Raid!*, 244–49 ("*courageous devotion*").

575 *Patton had abused his authority*: Hirshson, *General Patton: A Soldier's Life*, 623; Bradley, *A Soldier's Story*, 542–43 ("*Failure itself*"); Chandler, 2616–17 ("*crackpot actions*").

Lovers' Quarrels Are a Part of Love

576 *Eisenhower's office in Reims*: Williams, "Supreme Headquarters for D-Day," *AB*, no. 84 (1994): 1+; Kessler, *The Battle of the Ruhr Pocket*, 49 (*Military convoys crawled*); SC, 420

(*more than five thousand*); Joseph R. Darnall, "Powdered Eggs and Purple Hearts," 1946, MHUC, group 1, box 24, 180 (*jitterbugging soldiers*).

576 *"France smells wonderful"*: corr, Howard J. Silbar to family, Apr. 15, 1945, Silbar papers, MHI, box 1.

576 *Eisenhower "looked terrible"*: Bradley and Blair, *A General's Life*, 410; Morgan, *Past Forgetting*, 216–17 (*"physical and mental condition"*); Crosswell, *Beetle*, 878–89 (*"Ike shouts and rants"*).

576 *The supreme commander needed rest*: Morgan, *Past Forgetting*, 217–18; Thomas W. Mattingly and Olive F. G. Marsh, "A Compilation of the General Health System of Dwight D. Eisenhower," Mattingly papers, DDE Lib, box 1; D'Este, *Eisenhower: A Soldier's Life*, 679–81 (*"Those of us"*).

577 *"Ike has learnt his lesson"*: Roberts, *Masters and Commanders*, 560.

577 *"As soon as you have joined hands"*: Chandler, 2552, 2593 (*"simplicity itself"*).

577 *"I get tired of trying to arrange"*: ibid., 2521; "Strategy of the Campaign in Western Europe, 1944–1945," n.d., USFET, General Board study no. 1, 97 (*ten thousand German soldiers*); OH, John Whiteley, May 15, 1963, CJR, box 44, folder 3 (*"if anything was to be done"*).

577 *Montgomery was gobsmacked*: *VW*, vol. 2, 299–301; Crosswell, *Beetle*, 887 (*"blow from Ike"*); Hamilton, *Monty: Final Years of the Field-Marshal, 1944–1976*, 446 (*"violent, pro-American"*), 458 (*"prolong the war"*); Roberts, *Masters and Commanders*, 564 (*"only himself to blame"*).

578 *Allied planners had presumed that Berlin*: Chandler, 2561, 2568 (*"In none of this do I mention Berlin"*).

578 *The Red Army was thirty miles from Berlin*: LO, 340–41; GS VI, 132–33; Murphy, *Diplomat Among Warriors*, 229; OH, Arthur Nevins, Aug. 15, 1972, Maclyn P. Burg and John E. Wickman, Nevins papers, DDE Lib, 60; SC, 445; Chandler, 2553n (*"unfortunate incidents"*).

578 *On a single day in early April*: That aircraft incident occurred on April 2 (Chandler, 2602).

578 *Postwar occupation zones already*: Greenfield, ed., *Command Decisions*, 387; Kershaw, *Hitler, 1936–45: Nemesis*, 786 (*"Destructive Measures"*); Ambrose, *Eisenhower and Berlin, 1945*, 29–30, 42; OH, John Whiteley, May 15, 1963, CJR, box 44, folder 3; OH, DDE, n.d., CJR, box 43, file 7, 26 (*"What would you have done"*).

578 *None of this went down easily*: Kimball, ed., *Churchill & Roosevelt: The Complete Correspondence*, vol. 3, 604; SC, 442 (*"The commander in the field"*).

579 *"We might be condemned"*: Greenfield, ed., *Command Decisions*, 380.

579 *"Berlin remains"*: Kimball, ed., *Churchill & Roosevelt: The Complete Correspondence*, vol. 3, 604–5.

579 *"very logical objectives"*: ibid., 608.

579 *"I shall not attempt any move"*: SC, 468.

579 *The Allied juggernaut in the west had grown*: More than two-thirds of the divisions were American (LO, 322).

579 *They faced a tatterdemalion enemy*: 12th AG, G-2 summary no. 43, March 25, 1945, NARA RG 498, ETO HD, UD 603, box 3.

579 *Gasoline had grown precious*: German gasoline production was less than one-tenth what it had been a year earlier ("Target Priorities of the Eighth Air Force," May 15, 1945, Carl A. Spaatz papers, LOC MS Div, box 326, folder VIII A.F., 23); Robert J. C. Osborne et al., "The 9th Armored Division in the Exploitation of Remagen Bridgehead," March 1950, AS, Ft. K, 9 (*"fifty-man panzer crew"*).

579 *Montgomery had not quite yielded*: Chandler, 2594; SC, 446 (*"It is quite clear"*).

580 *Lovers' quarrels*: War Department translation. Kimball, ed., *Churchill & Roosevelt: The Complete Correspondence*, vol. 3, 604, 612.

580 *With Armed Forces Radio playing*: Knickerbocker et al., *Danger Forward*, 380 (*"Last*

Round-up"); Robert J. C. Osborne et al., "The 9th Armored Division in the Exploitation of Remagen Bridgehead," March 1950, AS, Ft. K, 30; Schrijvers, *The Crash of Ruin*, 141 ("*dream roads*"); Triplet, *A Colonel in the Armored Regiments*, 232–33 (*cloverleaf ramps*); Jack A. Marshall, "Once Upon a War," 2009, a.p., 131–32 ("*Onward, Christian Soldiers*"); OH, Andrew J. Boyle, 1971, Frank Walton, SOOHP, MHI, 11–14 (*mobile microfilm teams*).

580 *Towns fell quickly*: Sylvan, 351 (*box of cigars*); corr, Gerald Ritchie, 6th Airborne Div, to Elspeth, Apr. 10, 1945, IWM, P. 182 ("*Alice in Wonderland*"); Patton, *War as I Knew It*, 282; *LO*, 350 (*false rumors*); Graham, *No Name on the Bullet*, 95 ("*How I want*").

580 *The hour had come to cinch*: *LO*, 351–52; Friedrich, *The Fire*, 139 (*the very air had first turned yellow*); Zumbro, *Battle for the Ruhr*, 225–26 (*motley brigade*).

581 *General Collins's VII Corps*: Ossad and Marsh, *Major General Maurice Rose*, 22–23, 33–34; Cooper, *Death Traps*, 277–79 (*roadside ditch*).

581 *Flame, smoke, and percussive gunfire*: OH, JLC, Jan. 25, 1954, CBM, NARA RG 319, OCMH, 2-3.7, *SLC* background files, box 184; OH, JLC, 1972, Charles C. Sperow, SOOHP, MHI, 202; Cooper, *Death Traps*, 191 (*nearly four hundred tanks*); Ossad and Marsh, *Major General Maurice Rose*, 38, 46, 49; memo, Col. E. V. Freeman, memorial division, Office of the Quartermaster General, Nov. 16, 1949, M. Rose individual deceased personnel file, obtained under FOIA, U.S. Army Human Resources Command, July 2008 (*repeatedly declared himself*); Heinz, *When We Were One*, 154 ("*I have a son*").

581 "*We're in a hell of a fix*": corr, George G. Garton, CO, 391st Armored FA Bn, to JT, Apr. 13, 1963, JT, LOC MS Div, box 2 ("*they have us*"); Ossad and Marsh, *Major General Maurice Rose*, 28–35, 312–24, 343.

582 "*It can't be him*": Heinz, *When We Were One*, 154.

582 *Rose would be interred*: memo to Brig. Gen. J. R. Ranck, QM, COMZ, Orleans, France, Dec. 4, 1959, M. Rose individual deceased personnel file, obtained under FOIA, U.S. Army Human Resources Command, July 2008; Palmer and Zaid, eds., *The GI's Rabbi*, 162 (*Kaddish*).

582 *A war-crimes investigation*: Ossad and Marsh, *Major General Maurice Rose*, 339; Zumbro, *Battle for the Ruhr*, 227 (*Feral American troops*).

582 *Fanatical resistance in Paderborn*: Albert R. Cupello et al., "Armored Encirclement of the Ruhr," May 1949, AS, Ft. K, NARA RG 337, 78–79; Kessler, *The Battle of the Ruhr Pocket*, 107–8, 117–18; Zumbro, *Battle for the Ruhr*, 249–58 (*blood group tattoos*).

583 *Easter Sunday dawned*: corr, Paul M. McGuire to JT, Sept. 6, 1963, JT, LOC MS Div, LHD, box 3 ("*Every time a battery*"); Kessler, *The Battle of the Ruhr Pocket*, 107; Zumbro, *Battle for the Ruhr*, 251–54 (*bicycles*).

583 *At noon, observation planes*: *LO*, 359; Kessler, *The Battle of the Ruhr Pocket*, 118 (*Werner Osthelmer*).

583 *Shortly after four P.M. the columns met*: The official Army history put the rendezvous at one P.M., but that appears to be several hours too early (Albert R. Cupello et al., "Armored Encirclement of the Ruhr," May 1949, AS, Ft. K, NARA RG 337, 78–79); Zumbro, *Battle for the Ruhr*, 260; Kessler, *The Battle of the Ruhr Pocket*, 119 (*hundred-mark notes*).

583 "*largest double envelopment*": SC, 438; Zumbro, *Battle for the Ruhr*, 260; *LO*, 353 (*Hitler forbade withdrawal*); Francis Daugherty et al., "7th Armored Division's Part in the Reduction of the Ruhr Pocket," May 1950, AS, Ft. K, NARA RG 337, 63–66 (*imaginary Twelfth Army*); Kessler, *The Battle of the Ruhr Pocket*, 114–15 ("*All fear comes*").

583 *To bring that day closer*: *LO*, 363–66; AAR, "Operations in the Ruhr Valley," 75th ID, n.d., CARL, N-13095 (*thermite grenades*); OH, "Crushing the Rose Pocket," 97th ID, Apr. 7–19, 1945, NARA RG 407, E 427-A, CI, box 19066, folder 208 (*fifty flamethrowers*); corr, Robert W. Hasbrouck to wife, Apr. 16, 1945, Maurice Delaval papers, MHI, box 9 ("*so many interruptions*"); Francis Daugherty et al., "7th Armored Division's Part in the Reduction of the Ruhr Pocket," May 1950, AS, Ft. K, NARA RG 337, 85.

584 "*What is there left?*": Carl Wagener, "Army Group B," n.d., FMS, #B-593, MHI, 34–47.

584 *"Eighty years ago this month"*: Ridgway, *Soldier*, 139–40.

584 *Moscow had accused Model*: Barnett, ed., *Hitler's Generals*, 329; *LO*, 369–72 (*"Have we done everything"*).

584 *"I sincerely believe"*: A decade later, Model's son exhumed his remains in a moldering field marshal's uniform; he was reburied in the German cemetery at Vossenack (Zumbro, *Battle for the Ruhr*, 375–79, 412; Kessler, *The Battle of the Ruhr Pocket*, 3, 206–10); Barnett, ed., *Hitler's Generals*, 329 (*Walther service revolver*).

585 *"a dark plowed field"*: Hastings, *Armageddon*, 419.

585 *Allied intelligence originally estimated*: Frank A. Osmanski, "Critical Analysis of the Planning and Execution of the Logistic Support of the Normandy Invasion," Dec. 1949, Armed Forces Staff College, Osmanski papers, MHI, 45; Benjamin A. Dickson, "G-2 Journal: Algiers to the Elbe," MHI, 203–12 (*125,000*); Chandler, 2587 (*"at least 100,000"*).

585 *Those figures proved far too modest*: "Consumption Rates U.S. Forces from the Rhine to the Elbe," May 11, 1945, NARA RG 498, ETO HD, admin history #27; *LO*, 359 (*seven corps and nineteen divisions*), 372 (*Stalingrad or Tunis*); *SC*, 440 (*dry-shod admiral*); Spayd, *Bayerlein*, 222–23 (*"I had some nice days"*).

585 *"We have prisoners like some people"*: Fauntleroy, *The General and His Daughter*, 181; *LO*, 370; Spayd, *Bayerlein*, 218 (*groomed their teams*).

585 *"Young men, old men"*: *LO*, 370–71.

585 *GI sentries cradled their carbines*: OH, "Crushing the Rose Pocket," 97th ID, Apr. 7–19, 1945, NARA RG 407, E 427-A, CI, box 19066, folder 208.

Chapter 12: Victory

Mark of the Beast

587 *For the final destruction*: Stars and Stripes, March 27, 1945, CBH letters, MHI (*"Omar the Warmaker"*); Bradley, *A Soldier's Story*, 539 (*Eisenhower joined him*); diary, Third Army chief of staff, Feb. 9, 1945, Hobart Gay papers, MHI, box 2, 866–69; Hirshson, *General Patton: A Soldier's Life*, 627–28 (*five-star rank insignia*); Ziemke, *The U.S. Army in the Occupation of Germany, 1944–1946*, 228–29 (*GIs had made a discovery*). Patton's official date of rank as a four-star was April 14.

587 *A photograph of the Führer*: Stafford, *Endgame 1945*, 74; White, *Conquerors' Road*, 68 (*"Thy Strength"*); Codman, *Drive*, 281 (*"If that clothesline"*); Ziemke, *The U.S. Army in the Occupation of Germany, 1944–1946*, 229–31 (*"Jesus Christ!"*); Bradsher, "Nazi Gold: The Merkers Mine Treasure," *Prologue* 31, no. 1 (spring 1999): 7+ (*"meeting payrolls"*).

587 *Treasures already had been discovered*: "Civil Affairs and Military Government Activities in Connection with Monuments, Fine Arts and Archives," NARA RG 407, E 427, USFET General Board study no. 36, 97-USF5-0.3.0, 27–29; Edsel, *The Monuments Men*, 281–83.

588 *Here in "Room No. 8"*: Bradsher, "Nazi Gold: The Merkers Mine Treasure," *Prologue* 31, no. 1 (spring 1999): 7+ (*concentration-camp victims* and *"richest man in the world"*); Tooze, *The Wages of Destruction*, 654 (*double-decker buses*); Nicholas, *The Rape of Europa*, 312, 333–36; Holland and Rothbart, "The Merkers and Buchenwald Treasure Troves," *AB*, no. 93 (1996): 1+; Ziemke, *The U.S. Army in the Occupation of Germany, 1944–1946*, 231 (*each sack worth $25,000*); Slany, *U.S. and Allied Efforts to Recover and Restore Gold and Other Assets Stolen or Hidden by Germany During World War II*, 159–61; memo, Col. B. Bernstein to Brig. Gen. F. J. McSherry, "Contents of Mines in Merkers Area," Apr. 18, 1945, Frank J. McSherry papers, MHI, box 53 (*galleries and shafts nearby*).

588 *Patton facetiously proposed*: memo, Brig. Gen. Frank J. McSherry to DDE, "Gold and Art Treasure Found at Meikers [sic]," Apr. 10, 1945, McSherry papers, MHI, box 53 (*250 tons*); Crosswell, *Beetle*, 899 (*"every son of a bitch"*).

588 *Eventually valued by SHAEF*: Bradsher, "Nazi Gold: The Merkers Mine Treasure," *Prologue* 37, no. 1 (spring 1999): 7+; Ziemke, *The U.S. Army in the Occupation of Germany, 1944–1946*, 229–31 (*ten-ton trucks*).

588 *Similar removals were under way*: William F. Heimlich, "The Eagle and the Bear: Berlin, 1945–1950," n.d., HIA, 46–52 (*AIRMAIL*); OH, Andrew J. Boyle, 1971, Frank Walton, SOOHP, MHI, 13–17; corr, DDE to Harry S. Truman, Aug. 8 and Sept. 24, 1945, NARA RG 498, ETO, secretary general staff, 333.5, box 35. In response to a Soviet protest, Eisenhower told Truman in a top-secret note, "I believe it may be granted that the Russian report is correct. Actually, equipment, documents and personnel exceeding the claims made were evacuated."

589 *Other swag included ground-to-air missile*: William F. Heimlich, "The Eagle and the Bear: Berlin, 1945–1950," n.d., HIA, 46–52; Rudolf Lusar, "The German Weapons and Secret Weapons of World War II and Their Subsequent Development," 1956, CMH (*patents*); Longmate, *Hitler's Rockets*, 375–76 (*seventy-five rockets*). For details of Soviet removals see Dobbs, *Six Months in 1945*, 242–47.

589 *Patton had one more discovery*: diary, Third Army chief of staff, Feb. 9, 1945, Hobart Gay papers, MHI, box 2, 866–69; *LO*, 375–78; Allen, *Lucky Forward*, 279 (*flush toilets*).

589 *the Americans liberated a concentration camp*: Robert H. Abzug, "The Liberation of the Concentration Camps," in *Liberation 1945*, 33; case file, Buchenwald KZ, n.d., Donald McClure papers, HIA, box 1 (*eighty satellite camps*).

589 *"We passed through the stockade"*: Bradley, *A Soldier's Story*, 539.

589 *An inmate pointed out a gallows*: Ziemke, *The U.S. Army in the Occupation of Germany, 1944–1946*, 231; *PP*, 684 (*"mammoth griddle"*); James J. Weingartner, "Early War Crimes Trials," in *Liberation 1945*, 82–83 (*vengeful inmates*); Thompson, *Men Under Fire*, 138 (*"mark of the beast"*); White, *Conquerors' Road*, 91–92 (*"ash and human debris"*); Schudel, "General Witnessed History at Nazi camp, Panama Canal," *WP*, Aug. 7, 2012, B6.

590 *"Still having trouble"*: Codman, *Drive*, 282–83.

590 *Eisenhower and Bradley agreed to spend*: Ziemke, *The U.S. Army in the Occupation of Germany, 1944–1946*, 232–33 (*125 miles*); MacDonald, *The Mighty Endeavor*, 476–77; *LO*, 380.

590 *Despite great bounds*: Ryan, *The Last Battle*, 314 (*226 miles*); *LO*, 384.

590 *"Ike, I don't know"*: diary, Third Army chief of staff, Feb. 9, 1945, Hobart Gay papers, MHI, box 2, 866–69; Weintraub, *15 Stars*, 331 (*hordes of refugees*).

590 *Another anxiety weighed*: *LO*, 407.

590 *How did a police state perish?*: Timothy Naftali, "Creating the Myth of the *Alpenfestung*," in Bischof and Pelinka, eds., *Austrian Memory & National Identity*, 203–46.

591 *As early as the fall of 1943*: Jenkins, "The Battle of the National Redoubt," *Military Review* (Dec. 1946): 3+; Crosswell, *Beetle*, 883 (*"bitter guerrilla warfare"*); memo, DDE to ONB, "Security of Troops," Feb. 20, 1945, NARA RG 331, E 1, SHAEF SGS, file 371.2, box 65 (*"nests of guerrillas"*); Hinsley, 613; Timothy Naftali, "Creating the Myth of the *Alpenfestung*," in Bischof and Pelinka, eds., *Austrian Memory & National Identity*, 213, 236n (*quarter-million Ultra intercepts*); Pogue, *George C. Marshall*, 557 (*"no indications"*).

591 *Far more credulous*: Strong, *Intelligence at the Top*, 255 (*"no more chances"*); OH, Kenneth Strong, May 15, 1963, CJR, box 95, folder 5, 1–2 (*"die together"*); *VW*, vol. 2, 302–4 (*"most important ministries"*); Minott, *The Fortress That Never Was*, 29, 88–94 (*more obdurate than Cassino*).

591 *An OSS psychological portrait*: Walter C. Langer, "A Psychological Analysis of Adolf Hitler—His Life and Legend," n.d., OSS, NARA RG 226, 190/3/6/01, box 1, 244–49; OSS, "Report from Switzerland," March 1, 1945, NARA RG 226, M 1642, R-83, frame 333 (*150 trucks*); memo, R&A London to Chandler Morse, Harold Barger, "Subject: Pickaninny—Economic Capabilities of the Alpine Area," March 29, 1945, OSS, NARA RG 226, E 73, box 3 (*"absence of sugar"*); OSS Berne to OSS director, "Official Dispatch," March 16, 1945, NARA RG 226, M 142, R-30, frames 99–100 (*antitank guns*); memo, William J. Donovan to FDR, March 26, 1945, NARA RG 226, M-1642, R-25, frames 441–42 (*"go underground"*).

592 *The correspondent William L. Shirer*: Miller, *Ike the Soldier*, 761 (*"mystery writers"*);

memo, "Study of the German National Redoubt," March 25, 1945, HQ, Seventh Army, G-2, NARA RG 226, M 1642, R-52, frames 253–59 (*"Vast stores"* and *"Messerschmitt"* and *"imbued with the Nazi spirit"*); Ryan, *The Last Battle*, 213 (*long freight trains*); AAR, *The Seventh United States Army in France and Germany*, vol. 3, 808–10; Minott, *The Fortress That Never Was*, 54 (*hydro-powered*).

592 *The truth was less flamboyant*: Hinsley, 613; Hans [sic] Hofer, Lower Alps gauleiter, n.d., FMS #B-458, ETHINT, vol. 24, MHI, 9–11, 23 (*wall map*); Georg Ritter von Hengl, Apr. 25, 1946, FMS #B-459, 3–11, and #B-461, n.d., 1–3, ETHINT, vol. 24, MHI (*not until spring*); Kesselring, *The Memoirs of Field-Marshal Kesselring*, 277 (*"make-believe"*).

592 *Werewolf movement*: Timothy Naftali, "Creating the Myth of the *Alpenfestung*," in Bischof and Pelinka, eds., *Austrian Memory & National Identity*, 203–46; Beevor, *Berlin: The Downfall, 1945*, 175 (*"Werewolf is watching"*); Whiting, *The Home Front: Germany*, 179–80 (*mayor of Aachen*); Brown, *The Last Hero*, 738–40 (*Basque assassins*).

592 *Yet at SHAEF the myth*: press conference, W. B. Smith, Apr. 21, 1945, in "Operations of the Approach to the Rhine and Across the Rhine," n.d., Sidney H. Negrotto papers, MHI; D'Este, *Eisenhower: A Soldier's Life*, 696–98; Bradley, *A Soldier's Story*, 536 (*"We may be fighting"*); Crosswell, *Beetle*, 90 (*"possibly 100 to 125"*); memo, "Location of Caves in Germany," SHAEF G-2, Apr. 16, 1945, and memo, "Photographic Cover of National Redoubt," SHAEF G-2, Apr. 14, 1945, NARA RG 331, E 240B, 6th Army Group, files 452.2 and "National Redoubt," boxes 3 and 5 (*two hundred caves*); Jenkins, "The Battle of the National Redoubt," *Military Review* (Dec. 1946): 3+ (*ordered Devers's army group*); Hinsley, 613 (*First Allied Airborne Army*); LO, 422.

593 *"no less than 70 examples"*: SHAEF weekly intelligence summary no. 57, Apr. 22, 1945, Robert D. Burhans papers, HIA, box 14; "Strategy of the Campaign in Western Europe, 1944–1945," USFET General Board study no. 1, n.d., 102 (*one hundred divisions*); VW, vol. 2, 429–31 (*"fanatical resistance"*); Georg Ritter von Hengl, Apr. 25, 1946, FMS #B-459, ETHINT, vol. 24, MHI, 11 (*"run its course"*).

593 *Shortly after midnight on Friday*: Ayer, *Before the Colors Fade*, 210 (*"hot air"*); PP, 694 (*"a figment"*); diary, Apr. 11, 1945, GSP, LOC MS Div, box 3, folder 11 (*carbine by his cot*); corr, GSP to Beatrice, Apr. 17, 1945, GSP, LOC MS Div, box 13 (*"end of this life"*); corr, March 16, 1945, GSP, LOC MS Div, box 74, folder 5 (*"hot furnace"*).

593 *"War for me"*: corr, GSP to Robert Howe Fletcher, Apr. 25, 1945, GSP, LOC MS Div, box 13.

593 *Glancing at his wristwatch*: diary, Third Army chief of staff, Feb. 9, 1945, Hobart Gay papers, MHI, box 2, 866–69. International News Service broke the story at 5:47 P.M. Washington time in a terse flash: "FDR DEAD."

594 *Franklin D. Roosevelt, a man who*: Goodman, ed., *While You Were Gone*, 116; Larrabee, *Commander in Chief*, 627 (*transcendent cause*); Taylor and Taylor, eds., *The War Diaries*, 159 (*sob like a child*); Wilmot, *The Struggle for Europe*, 716–17 (*"altered decisively"*); Leahy, *I Was There*, 346 (*"How could a man"*).

594 *His passing came*: Kennedy, *Freedom from Fear*, 808; Tully, *F.D.R. My Boss*, 359 (*stamp collection*); Hassett, *Off the Record with F.D.R.*, 332–35 (*signed into law*); Bruenn, "Clinical Notes on the Illness and Death of President Franklin D. Roosevelt," *Annals of Internal Medicine* 72, no. 4 (Apr. 1, 1970): 579+; Altman, "For F.D.R. Sleuths, New Focus on an Old Spot," *NYT*, Jan. 5, 2010, D1 (*blood pressure*); Dallek, *Franklin D. Roosevelt and American Foreign Policy, 1932–1945*, 527–33; Goodwin, *No Ordinary Time*, 603, 611–12 (*"that was it"*); Reilly, *Reilly of the White House*, 234 (*poison*). The portrait artist Elizabeth Shoumatoff denied measuring Roosevelt's nose and later wrote that the president said nothing before he collapsed (Shoumatoff, *FDR's Unfinished Portrait*, 115–18; Franklin D. Roosevelt American Heritage Center, http://www.fdrheritage.org/shoumatoff.htm).

594 *J. Austin Dillon*: memo, J. Austin Dillon, n.d., Small Collections: FDRL Miscellaneous Documents: Roosevelt, Franklin D.—Health, FDR Lib.

595 *On Friday, the daily casualty list*: MacDonald, *The Mighty Endeavor*, 484; Seventh Army war diary, Apr. 13, 1945, MHI, 653 (*"mourning badges"*); Toole, *Battle Diary*, 132 (*"This is a shock"*).

Dragon Country

595 *To an American pilot*: Ryan, *The Last Battle*, 127 (*"very crust"*); *The Seventh United States Army in France and Germany*, vol. 3, 820 (*"molten mass"*); corr, Waldo Heinrichs, Jr., May 8, 1945, Heinrichs papers, MHI, box 1 (*"running to the rear"*).

595 *This was Dragon Country*: Thompson, *Men Under Fire*, 132–33; *LO*, 410 (*"Sixty-one Roadblocks"*), 386 (*Hanover's defenses*), 404–5 (*"a conglomeration"*); *The Seventh United States Army in France and Germany*, vol. 3, 822 (*wooden sticks*); Marshall, *A Ramble Through My War*, 220; Holt, *The Deceivers*, 662 (*geraniums*); Ziemke, *The U.S. Army in the Occupation of Germany, 1944–1946*, 244–47.

596 *"The shame of German defeat"*: Carpenter, *No Woman's World*, 261.

596 *"What right had they"*: Schrijvers, *The Crash of Ruin*, 146.

596 *Alfried Krupp, an industrialist*: Bourke-White, *Portrait of Myself*, 265–70 (*said to have wept*); Manchester, *The Arms of Krupp, 1587–1966*, 521, 674–81. Arrested in April, Krupp would be formally charged in August; Manchester writes that he was dry-eyed upon being detained.

596 *"Brilliant spring sunshine"*: Thompson, *Men Under Fire*, 132–33.

596 *"old men leaning on sticks"*: White, *Conquerors' Road*, 17.

596 *And yet dragons lurked*: Murray and Millett, *A War to Be Won*, 480 (*10,677 U.S. soldiers*); Lubrich, ed., *Travels in the Reich, 1933–1945*, 328 (*"plague bacteria"*); Howarth, ed., *Men of War*, 205–6; Read and Fisher, *The Fall of Berlin*, 334; *Germany IX*, 459 (*"If we lose the war"*); Friedrich, *The Fire*, 306 (*"Negro brothels"*).

597 *Some Luftwaffe pilots*: Rudolf Lusar, "The German Weapons and Secret Weapons of World War II and Their Subsequent Development," 1956, CMH, 78; Ninth AF, intelligence summary no. 130, Apr. 30, 1945, NARA RG 334, E 315, ANSCOL, box 116 (*political indoctrination*); "History of U.S. Strategic Air Force Europe vs. German Air Force," Sept. 1945, NARA RG 457, E 9002, NSA, SRH-013, 342 (*"staking your lives"*); Muller, "Losing Air Superiority: A Case Study from the Second World War," *Air & Space Power Journal* (winter 2003): 55+ (*"total commitment missions"*); Seventh Army, G-2 bulletin no. 63, May 22, 1945, NARA RG 498, ETO G-3, Col. C. Hilldebrand, VI Corps, OR, box 1458 (*several young boys*); Lubrich, ed., *Travels in the Reich, 1933–1945*, 320 (*"heartbreaking sight"*).

597 *"women and children lined the rooftops"*: Bradley, *A Soldier's Story*, 530; *LO*, 410.

597 *In Heilbronn, on the Neckar*: *LO*, 417–18; "Attack on Heilbronn," 100th ID, July 1945, Seventh Army narratives, MHI, 4, 33; Turner and Jackson, *Destination Berchtesgaden*, 160–61; Yeide and Stout, *First to the Rhine*, 357–59; Ziemke, *The U.S. Army in the Occupation of Germany, 1944–1946*, 247 (*"noticeable stench"*).

597 *"Why don't the silly bastards"*: Arthur, *Forgotten Voices of World War II*, 414; Horst Boog, "Invasion to Surrender: The Defense of Germany," in Brower, ed., *World War II in Europe: The Final Year*, 131.

597 *"Mother, you asked me"*: "Jack's Letters," March 22, March 24, and April 3, 1945, a.p., courtesy of Rick Perry.

598 *"Half the nationalities of Europe"*: Moorehead, *Eclipse*, 254–55; Gilbert, *The Day the War Ended*, 64 (*"moving frieze"*); "Civil Affairs and Military Government Organizations and Operations," n.d., NARA RG 407, E 427, USFET General Board study no. 32, 97-USF5-0.3.0 (*4.2 million*); Abraham J. Peck, "A Continent in Chaos," in *Liberation 1945*, 101 (*eleven million unmoored*).

598 *Some were on forced marches*: diary, Darrell William Coates, Apr. 1945, HIA; http://www.b24.net/pow/stalag17.htm.

599 *"Everyone is yelling"*: Vining, ed., *American Diaries of World War II*, 417–18.

599 *"Smaller wounds were covered"*: Wandrey, *Bedpan Commando*, 181–82; Moorehead, *Eclipse*, 256 (*"jeep looks like"*); "After WWII, Economist Devoted Life," obit, *WP*, July 8, 2009, B4 (*cheered wildly*).

599 *Of the shambling millions*: "Activities and Organization of COMZ," June 11, 1945, NARA

RG 498, ETO HD, admin file #89, 11; Foreign Workers Programs, Apr. 25, 1945, Radio Luxembourg collection, HIA, box 1 (*SHAEF broadcasts*).

599 *"tractable, grateful, and powerless"*: "Displaced Persons, Refugees, and Recovered Allied Military Personnel," n.d., NARA RG 407, E 427, USFET General Board study no. 35, 97-USF5-0.3.0.

599 *Freed laborers plundered houses*: Zumbro, *Battle for the Ruhr*, 329–30; "Concentration Camp Train," G-2 Periodic Report No. 304, 30th ID, Apr. 17, 1945, NARA RG 407, ETO G-3 OR (*licked flour*); Urquhart, *A Life in Peace and War*, 79, 86 (*"rampageous"* and *Hanover cellar*); Botting, *From the Ruins of the Reich*, 26.

599 *Thousands of refugees carried*: "History of Medical Service in the European Theater," tape transcript, Oct. 1962, MHI, II-69; OH, Philip Carlquist, Sept. 1, 1978, Emory University; "The Disease Potential in Germany," in OH, Albert W. Kenner, SHAEF chief medical officer, May 27, 1948, FCP, MHI; "Displaced Persons, Refugees, and Recovered Allied Military Personnel," n.d., NARA RG 407, E 427, USFET General Board study no. 35, 97-USF5-0.3.0 (*roadblocks*); Botting, *From the Ruins of the Reich*, 29 (*"Alleluia!"*).

600 *Some went barefoot*: White, *Conquerors' Road*, 100–103.

600 *"One died taking a drink"*: Leonard C. Barney, 315th Medical Bn, 90th ID, "Inmates of Concentration Camps," 1985, Columbus WWII Round Table Collection, MHI, 3–4.

600 *"It's too big"*: Leh, "World War II from One Enlisted Man's Point of View," *Proceedings of the Lehigh County Historical Society* 39 (1990): 89+.

600 *"a kind of dull satisfaction"*: Sevareid, *Not So Wild a Dream*, 504–6.

600 *"If the heavens were paper"*: Collier, *Fighting Words*, 188.

600 *Nordhausen was overrun*: OH, Col. D. B. Hardin, VII Corps, "Concentration Camp at Nordhausen," Apr. 14, 1944, NARA RG 407, ETO ML #1028, box 19152, 1–4; *LO*, 391–92 (*"Men lay"*); Kessler, *The Battle of the Ruhr Pocket*, 156–57 (*beat up a captured German scientist*); Collins, *Lightning Joe*, 324; Carpenter, *No Woman's World*, 293–95 (*"no greater shame"*).

601 *"There was no fat"*: Ingersoll, *Top Secret*, 333.

601 *At the Wöbbelin camp*: Nordyke, *All American All the Way*, 756; "Wöbbelin," Holocaust Encyclopedia, USHMM, http://www.ushmm.org/wlc/en/article.php?ModuleId=10006160; McNally, *As Ever, John*, 65–67 (*"Each body was pulled"*); Booth and Spencer, *Paratrooper*, 294 (*never failed to weep*); Stafford, *Endgame 1945*, 311 (*"defining moment"*).

601 *"We came into a smell"*: Stafford, *Endgame 1945*, 83; Hitchcock, *The Bitter Road to Freedom*, 300–302 (*"simian throng"*), 341 (*watery soup*); "Early Measures at Belsen," lecture, June 4, 1945, Royal Society of Medicine, UK NA, WO 219/3944A (*designed for eight thousand*); Thompson, *The Imperial War Museum Book of Victory in Europe*, 252–55 (*hearts, livers, and kidneys*), 264 (*"woman squatting"*); "What the Army Did at Belsen Concentration Camp," n.d., UK NA, WO 219/3944A, 3 (*"continuous carpet"*), 16–17; "Bergen-Belsen," Holocaust Encyclopedia, USHMM, http://www.ushmm.org/wlc/en/article.php?ModuleId=10005224; Collier, *Fighting Words*, 188 (*"peeping through fingers"*).

601 *The living resembled "polished skeletons"*: Stafford, *Endgame 1945*, 83; "What the Army Did at Belsen Concentration Camp," n.d., UK NA, WO 219/3944A, 20–23 (*medics tallied*); Davis, *Soldier of Democracy*, 535–36 (*"he fell dead"*); Robert H. Abzug, "The Liberation of the Concentration Camps," in *Liberation 1945*, 33–34, 43; Arthur, *Forgotten Voices of World War II*, 419–21 (*clubbed with rifle butts*).

602 *An estimated quarter-million*: Blatman, *The Death Marches*, 11–12, 278, 310–21, 332–47; Margry, "The Gardelegen Massacre," *AB*, no. 111 (2001): 2+; "Gardelegen Massacre 13 April 1945," www.scrapbookpages.com/GerhardThiele.

602 *For the U.S. Army, the camp at Buchenwald*: investigative papers, "Buchenwald KZ," Donald McClure papers, HIA, box 1; Hackett, ed., *The Buchenwald Report*, 330–33.

603 *An hour later, outriders*: Brig. Gen. Eric F. Wood et al., "Inspection of German Concentration Camp for Political Prisoners Located at Buckenwal [*sic*]," Apr. 16, 1945, Frank J. McSherry papers, MHI, box 53; Ziemke, *The U.S. Army in the Occupation of Germany*,

1944–1946, 236–38; "Civil Affairs and Military Government Organizations and Operations," n.d., NARA RG 407, E 427, USFET General Board study no. 32, 97-USF5-0.3.0 (*six hundred calories*).

603 *"They were so thin"*: Robert H. Abzug, "The Liberation of the Concentration Camps," in *Liberation 1945*, 40.

603 *An intricate, awful world*: Brig. Gen. Eric F. Wood et al., "Inspection of German Concentration Camp for Political Prisoners Located at Buckenwal [*sic*]," Apr. 16, 1945, Frank J. McSherry papers, MHI, box 53; investigative papers, "Buchenwald KZ," Donald McClure papers, HIA, box 1.

603 *The SS had murdered*: "Buchenwald," Holocaust Encyclopedia, USHMM, http://www .ushmm.org/wlc/en/article.php?ModuleId=10005198; Ziemke, *The U.S. Army in the Occupation of Germany, 1944–1946*, 236–38 (*brick ovens*).

603 *A verse in gold and black*: White, *Conquerors' Road*, 82.

603 *Patton marched the burghers*: PP, 687, 692; Edward R. Murrow, CBS radio broadcast, Apr. 15, 1945, in *Reporting World War II*, vol. 2, 681–85 (*"The stink was beyond"*).

603 *Shocking evidence of German torture*: Kimball, *Forged in War*, 278 (*Breedonck*); Ziemke, *The U.S. Army in the Occupation of Germany, 1944–1946*, 220 (*"legacy of skepticism"*); Robert H. Abzug, "The Liberation of the Concentration Camps," in *Liberation 1945*, 56 (*barely one-third*), 66; Gilbert, *The Day the War Ended*, 17.

604 *"What kind of people"*: Tapert, ed., *Lines of Battle*, 269.

604 *"Hardly any boy infantryman"*: Fussell, *The Boys' Crusade*, 157.

604 *"I've been in the Army"*: "History, 157th Inf Regt, Apr 1945," NARA RG 405, E 427, WWII Ops Reports, 345-INF (157)-0.3.

604 *Berliners received an extra allocation*: Ryan, *The Last Battle*, 409–10, 417–18 (*Karstadt*); Klemperer, *To the Bitter End*, 209 (*"We are defending Europe"*); Read and Fisher, *The Fall of Berlin*, 335 (*birthday salute*).

604 *"All transportation is at a standstill"*: Moorhouse, *Berlin at War*, 359–60, 371–72 (*"pastor shot himself"*).

605 *"Lift our banners"*: ibid., 359–60.

605 *The man himself took the passing*: Kershaw, *Hitler, 1936–45: Nemesis*, 798; "Hitler's Höllenfahrt," *Der Spiegel* (Apr. 10, 1995): 172+ (*thirty-seven steps*).

605 *Back behind three steel doors*: Fest, *Hitler*, 764–65; Read and Fisher, *The Fall of Berlin*, 340 (*"I shall fight"*); Moorhouse, *Berlin at War*, 358–59 (*"birthday atmosphere"*); Kershaw, *Hitler, 1936–45: Nemesis*, 801 (Blutrote Rosen).

605 *The U.S. Seventh Army marked the day*: Stafford, *Endgame 1945*, 27; AAR, XV Corps, June 1, 1945, Wade H. Haislip papers, HIA, box 1; *LO*, 425; Yeide and Stout, *First to the Rhine*, 359 (*two thousand last-ditch soldiers*).

606 *"alluvial fans of rubble"*: Wyant, *Sandy Patch*, 191; Taggart, ed., *History of the Third Infantry Division*, 354–62 (*"Dog-Faced Soldier"*); White, *From Fedala to Berchtesgaden*, 265–66 (*"Casablanca. Palermo"*).

606 *A quieter commemoration*: White, *From Fedala to Berchtesgaden*, 265–66; Even, *The Tenth Engineers*, 49 (*wreath*); Palmer and Zaid, eds., *The GI's Rabbi*, 173–74; Stafford, *Endgame 1945*, 28 (*"Stars and Stripes Forever"*).

"God, Where Are You?"

606 *War correspondents had begun offering odds*: Heinz, *When We Were One*, 188–89 (*"GIvans"*); *LO*, 446–48 (*welcome signs* and *recognition signals*); Forrest C. Pogue, "The Meeting with the Russians," n.d., NARA RG 407, E 427, ML #2249, box 19185, 1 (*brigands in Cossack attire*); OH, 69th ID, NARA RG 407, E 427-A, CI 136-A, box 19050, folder #137 (*grassy hummock*).

607 *East of Leipzig*: *LO*, 446–48; Ryan, *The Last Battle*, 472; OH, 69th ID, NARA RG 407, E 427-A, CI, folder #137 (*confused Strehla with Groba*).

607 *Twenty miles north and two hours later*: OH, 69th ID, NARA RG 407, E 427-A, CI, folder #137; *LO*, 455–56; Margry, "The U.S.-Soviet Link-Up," *AB*, no. 88 (1995): 1+.

607 *After a brief, unnerving riposte*: OH, William D. Robertson, 69th ID, NARA RG 407, E 427-A, CI 136-A, box 19050, folder #137; *LO*, 455–56 (*carrying four soldiers*). After the war Robertson became a neurosurgeon in California.

608 *Thursday morning brought the full, overwrought merger*: Forrest C. Pogue, "The Meeting with the Russians," n.d., NARA RG 407, E 427, ML #2249, box 19185, 2–3; narrative, Thor Smith, n.d., Thor Smith papers, HIA, box 1 (*"Iowa picnic"*); Heinz, *When We Were One*, 189–92 (*varnished shells*); Pogue, *Pogue's War*, 368–70 (*black bread and apples*).

608 *"The Russians all looked"*: Martha Gellhorn, "The Russians," *Collier's*, June 30, 1945, in *Reporting World War II*, vol. 2, 701–6; Heinz, *When We Were One*, 189–92 (*GIs traded*).

608 *"Get that woman off"*: Heinz, *When We Were One*, 189–92; Pogue, *Pogue's War*, 372–73 (*Soviet general*).

608 *An unbroken Allied line*: Biddle, *Rhetoric and Reality in Air Warfare*, 260 (*last bombing raid*); Bessel, *Germany 1945*, 112 (*met at Ketzin*).

609 *Nothing now could thwart*: Bessel, *Germany 1945*, 104–5, 405 (*two and a half million troops*); Erickson, *The Road to Berlin*, 539–41, 622 (*three hundred thousand casualties*); "Hitler's Höllenfahrt," *Der Spiegel* (Apr. 4, 1995): 170+; Beevor, *Berlin: The Downfall, 1945*, 123, 410–13 (*typhus*); Steinhoff et al., *Voices from the Third Reich*, 454–57; interview, Rosemarie Meitzner, Apr. 1995, author, Berlin; Ryan, *The Last Battle*, 494 (*lightbulbs*), 371 ("Bleib übrig"); Sebald, *On the Natural History of Destruction*, 43 (*"hilly landscape"*).

609 *In the south, the Reich*: *LO*, 454, 425–26 (*bridge over the Danube*); Ziemke, *The U.S. Army in the Occupation of Germany, 1944–1946*, 249 (*twenty-eight towns*).

609 *"We are constantly suffering"*: memo, F. E. Morgan to G-1, Feb. 10, 1945, NARA RG 331, E 1, SHAEF SGS, file 211, box 20; *LO*, 427–30; De Lattre de Tassigny, *The History of the French First Army*, 458–59; OH, JLD, Aug. 1971, Thomas E. Griess, YCHT, box 110, 26–27.

609 *General de Gaulle had other ideas*: De Gaulle, *The Complete Memoirs of Charles de Gaulle*, 860; Clayton, *Three Marshals of France*, 114–15 (*Holding a large tract*).

610 *With Deux Mètres urging him on*: *LO*, 427–30; De Lattre de Tassigny, *The History of the French First Army*, 458–64, 491 (*"merry-go-round"*); *SC*, 460–61 (*"national interest of France"*); Wyant, *Sandy Patch*, 193 (*"Penny politics"*).

610 *"The good and upright Devers"*: Salisbury-Jones, *So Full a Glory*, 197; Yeide and Stout, *First to the Rhine*, 365–68 (*seventeen thousand men*); Reuben E. Jenkins, "The Battle of the National Redoubt," n.d., Jenkins papers, MHI, box 1, 15; Willis, *The French in Germany*, 20–21; memo, JLD, Apr. 27, 1945, JLD papers, MHI (*"an absurdity"*); *LO*, 430–31; OH, JLD, Aug. 1971, Thomas E. Griess, YCHT, box 110, 26–27 (*"trying to be Napoleon"*).

610 *This opéra bouffe*: *LO*, 430–31; Seventh Army war diary, Apr. 26, 1945, MHI, 678 (*predatory French colonial troops*); Botting, *From the Ruins of the Reich*, 22–23 (*"Hens and women"*); Wyant, *Sandy Patch*, 193 (*"Situation in Stuttgart"*); memo, JLD, Apr. 27, 1945, JLD papers, MHI (*"What can you do"*).

611 *"Stuttgart is chaotic"*: De Lattre de Tassigny, *The History of the French First Army*, 491.

611 *Devers drove into the city*: diary, JLD, 6th AG, Apr. 27, 1945, MHI; *LO*, 432–33. Clinics in nearby Tübingen reported treating hundreds of rape victims, and a substantial number of women in Konstanz sought abortions for pregnancies resulting from French assaults (Bessel, *Germany 1945*, 117).

611 *"French procedure in occupying"*: Wyant, *Sandy Patch*, 193.

611 *Eisenhower now intervened*: *LO*, 432–33; Chandler, 2657–59; Yeide and Stout, *First to the Rhine*, 366.

611 *But with a war to finish*: OH, Philippe de Camas, French First Army, Oct.–Dec. 1948, Marcel Vigneras, NARA RG 319, E P-100, *RR* background files, FRC 5; Yeide and Stout, *First to the Rhine*, 365 (*execution of a few rapists*); diary, JLD, 6th AG, Apr. 27, 1945, MHI (*"much better"*).

611 *Patch's legions meanwhile pressed south*: *LO*, 427–30; Walker, *German National Socialism and the Quest for Nuclear Power, 1939–49*, 158; Rhodes, *The Making of the Atomic Bomb*, 609–10.

611 *Bickering over the French occupation zone*: Willis, *The French in Germany*, 20–21; Porch, *The Path to Victory*, 601 (*"often on the same side"*). De Gaulle would write after these disagreements, "The roses of glory cannot be without thorns"; Truman said of the French leader, "I don't like the son of a bitch" (Fenby, *The General*, 746).

611 *Ten miles northwest of Munich*: Mollo, "Dachau," *AB*, no. 27, 1980, 1+; KZ-Gedenkstätte Dachau, Stiftung Bayerische Gedenkstätten, http://www.kz-gedenkstaette-dachau.de/index-e.html (*200,000 prisoners*); Gellately, *Backing Hitler*, 217 (*170 subcamps*); corr, JLD to SHAEF, May 4 and 6, 1945, NARA RG 498, ETO SGS classified gen'l corr, file 383.6/9, box 88 (*thirteen thousand had died*).

612 *On a chilly, sunless Sunday*: "History, 157th Inf Regt, Apr 1945," NARA RG 405, E 427, WWII Ops Reports, 345-INF (157)-0.3; Robert H. Abzug, "The Liberation of the Concentration Camps," in *Liberation 1945*, 38 (*"flower beds and trees"*); Joseph M. Whitaker, asst. IG, Seventh Army, "Investigation of Alleged Mistreatment of German Guards at Dachau," June 8, 1945, NARA RG 338, box 7; "The Train Ride into Hell," 1998, Pierre C. T. Verheye papers, HIA; Whitlock, *The Rock of Anzio*, 357–64 (*"sons of bitches"*).

612 *"That's the only thing the guy owns"*: Flint Whitlock, "Liberating Dachau," in *The World War II Reader*, 368–69.

612 *Howling inmates pursued*: *The Seventh United States Army in France and Germany*, vol. 2, 832.

612 *"They tore the Germans apart"*: Garland, *Unknown Soldiers*, 393.

612 *"We stood aside and watched"*: Palmer and Zaid, eds., *The GI's Rabbi*, 178; Carroll, ed., *War Letters*, 275–77 (*sticks and rocks*); Joseph M. Whitaker, asst. IG, Seventh Army, "Investigation of Alleged Mistreatment of German Guards at Dachau," June 8, 1945, NARA RG 338, box 7 (*crushing skulls* and *battalion surgeon refused*); OH, John A. Heintges, 1974, Jack A. Pellici, SOOHP, MHI, 370 (*"strewn all over"*).

612 *At the same hour, the vanguard*: Brig. Gen. John H. Linden, 42nd ID, "Report on Surrender of Dachau Concentration Camp," May 2, 1945, and 1st Lt. William J. Cowling, III, 42nd ID, "Report on Surrender of the German Concentration Camp at Dachau," May 2, 1945, John H. Linden papers, HIA, box 1; Flint Whitlock, "Liberating Dachau," in *The World War II Reader*, 368–69; Howard Cowan, Associated Press, "32,000 Liberated from Dachau Prison Camp," Apr. 1945, John H. Linden papers, HIA, box 1 (*"amidst a roar"*).

613 *"I haven't the words"*: Eliach and Gurewitsch, eds., *The Liberators*, vol. 1, 45; Palmer and Zaid, eds., *The GI's Rabbi*, 178–83 (*dusted with DDT*); OH, Paul D. Adams, 1975, Irving Monclova and Marlin Lang, SOOHP, MHI (*"I wouldn't bother"*).

613 *The Seventh Army inspector general*: memo, DDE, "Mistreatment of Prisoners of War," July 18, 1945, NARA RG 498, ETO SGS classified gen'l corr, 383.6, box 51.

613 *At least twenty-eight SS men*: Joseph M. Whitaker, asst. IG, Seventh Army, "Investigation of Alleged Mistreatment of German Guards at Dachau," June 8, 1945, NARA RG 338, box 7; Whitlock, *The Rock of Anzio*, 388–89 (*four U.S. soldiers*); Garland, *Unknown Soldiers*, 395–97 (*Others believed*); memo, Charles D. Decker, "Report on Results of Investigation into Mistreatment of Prisoners of War by U.S. Forces," Dec. 31, 1945, NARA RG 498, ETO SGS classified gen'l corr, 383.6, box 51 (*"violation of the letter"*). The 45th Division would be transferred to Third Army; beginning in Sicily, Patton had evinced no zeal for war crimes prosecution of U.S. soldiers.

614 *"I'm on night duty"*: Wandrey, *Bedpan Commando*, 204–5.

614 *As a specially designated "Führer City"*: Stafford, *Endgame 1945*, 242; *SC*, 456 (*"Nazi beast"*); AAR, XV Corps, June 1, 1945, Wade H. Haislip papers, HIA, box 1. Commanding the 20th Armored Division in the assault on Munich was Maj. Gen. Orlando Ward, rehabilitated after being relieved by Patton of division command in Tunisia two years earlier.

614 *"Window by window" shelling*: *The Seventh United States Army in France and Germany*, vol. 2, 834–37; *LO*, 437; Kershaw, *Hitler, 1936–45: Nemesis*, 840 (*"I am ashamed"*).

614 *Three hundred miles north*: OH, Vasily Ustyugov, Apr. 1995, Fred Hiatt, Moscow, a.p. (*Iron Crosses*); Read and Fisher, *The Fall of Berlin*, 465 (*roasting an ox*); OH, Hans-Jürgen

Habenicht, Apr. 1995, author, Berlin (*excrement and urine*); Beevor, *Berlin: The Downfall, 1945*, 388–92 (*"post-mortal"*).

614 *Far below the Reich Chancellery*: Read and Fisher, *The Fall of Berlin*, 290; Kershaw, *Hitler, 1936–45: Nemesis*, 827–28; Fest, *Hitler*, 778–79.

614 *Twelve years and four months*: Kershaw, *Hitler, 1936–45: Nemesis*, 841; Erickson, *The Road to Berlin*, 609 (*"that's the end"*).

615 *Henchmen wrapped the two bodies*: Toland, *Adolf Hitler*, 890; Beevor, *Berlin: The Downfall, 1945*, 358–60 (*"chief's on fire"*); Ryan, *The Last Battle*, 498 (*"burning bacon"*).

615 *"binding for all soldiers"*: Bessell, *Germany 1945*, 121.

615 *Fifty miles due west along the Elbe*: Stenbuck, ed., *Typewriter Battalion*, 34–47; OH, Alvan C. Gillem, Jr., XIII Corps, n.d., CJR, box 44, folder 18, 5–7.

615 *Simpson agreed to accept*: Stenbuck, ed., *Typewriter Battalion*, 34–47; LO, 465; OH, Alvan C. Gillem, Jr., 1972, Eugene Miller, SOOHP, MHI, box 1, 69–70; Beevor, *Berlin: The Downfall, 1945*, 397 (*"quite a few people"*).

616 *In Italy, an offensive*: Willmott, *The Great Crusade*, 429–30; Weinberg, *A World at Arms*, 818 (*Po River*); Philip Hamburger, "Letter from Rome," May 8, 1945, in *The New Yorker Book of War Pieces*, 479; Fisher, *Cassino to the Alps*, 524; GS VI, 121 (*Army Group C*).

616 *Along the Continent's northern lip*: In the final two months of the war, Canadian troops used flamethrowers in three thousand operations (Brig. Gen. Alden H. Waitt, chemical warfare service, "Summary Report of Situation in ETO," July 5, 1945, NARA RG 337, E 16, OR, 210.684, GHQ AGF G-3, box 2).

616 *the starving Dutch had been reduced*: Hastings, *Armageddon*, 411–14; Gander, *After These Many Quests*, 315 (*"hinged-bottom coffins"*).

616 *Allied engineers also feared*: historical report, SHAEF G-5 mission in Netherlands, July 14, 1945, NARA RG 498, ETO HD, admin file #219, 4–14; "Brief Historical Outline of the Occupation of N.W. Holland by 1 Canadian Corps," n.d., NARA RG 319, 2-3.7 CB 8, SC background files; corr, Brig. Sir Geoffrey Hardy-Roberts, May 6, 1945, LHC (*"five years of repression"*).

616 *"They left like tramps"*: Gander, *After These Many Quests*, 314, 324–25.

617 *Farther east, where four British divisions*: VW, vol. 2, 316, 337–38 (*quarter of a million prisoners*), 353; Stafford, *Endgame 1945*, 280 (*"looting, drinking"*); Chandler, 2652; LO, 464 (*two hours before the Red Army*).

617 *"Welcome Americans"*: Stanhope Mason, "Reminiscences and Anecdotes of World War II," 1988, MRC FDM, 1994.126, 250; VW, vol. 2, 332 (*"situation in Czechoslovakia"*); LO, 456–58 (*between Pilzen and Karlsbad*); SC, 454.

617 *Austrian partisans seized Innsbruck*: Marshall, *A Ramble Through My War*, 259 (*Viennese orchestra*); LO, 469–71; Royce L. Thompson, "Military Surrenders in the European Theater," June 30, 1955, CMH, 2-3.7, AE.P-28, 58 (*positioning of flags*); Martin, *Blow, Bugle, Blow*, 167 (*"internal security"*).

618 *At almost the same hour, Devers*: memo, R. E. Jenkins, May 7, 1945, Reuben E. Jenkins papers, MHI, box 1; LO, 471–72.

618 *Few locales were more freighted*: David Ian Hall, review of *Hitler's Mountain*, JMH (Jan. 2009): 310+; "Obersalzburg," AB, no. 9 (1975): 1+ (*beehives*).

618 *As a gift for the Führer's fiftieth*: Beierl, *History of the Eagle's Nest*, 103; "Das Kehlsteinhaus," http://www.kehlsteinhaus.com/ (*Otis elevator*).

618 *RAF bombers on April 25*: "Obersalzburg," AB, no. 9 (1975): 1+; Osborne, "Return to the Berghof," AB, no. 60 (1988): 50+; Walden, http://www.thirdreichruins.com/obersalzberg .htm; Nicholas, *The Rape of Europa*, 320 (*Bormann's collection*); Mitchell, *Hitler's Mountain*, 120–21 (*set fire to the house*).

619 *Flames still licked*: OH, John A. Heintges, 7th Inf, 1974, Jack A. Pellici, SOOHP, MHI, 379–85; White, *From Fedala to Berchtesgaden*, 278–80; Mitchell, *Hitler's Mountain*, 127 (*"You've had Paris"*). Both French troops and U.S. paratroopers soon found a way into the town.

619 *Despite bombing, arson, and plunder*: Osborne, "Return to the Berghof," AB, no. 60 (1988): 50+; Philip Hamburger, "Letter from Berchtesgaden," June 9, 1945, in *The New*

Yorker Book of War Pieces, 497–99 (*ice cream tubs*); Mitchell, *Hitler's Mountain*, 132 (*toilet seat*); Rapport and Northwood, *Rendezvous with Destiny*, 747 (*light fixtures*); AAR, T-Force, n.d., 6th AG, G-2, Boris T. Pash papers, HIA, box 4, file 6 (*situation maps*); Strong, *Intelligence at the Top*, 291–95 ("*coat hangers*").

619 *RAF bombs had spared*: Philip Hamburger, "Letter from Berchtesgaden," June 9, 1945, in *The New Yorker Book of War Pieces*, 500–501; Beierl, *History of the Eagle's Nest*, 116, 144–48; White, *Conquerors' Road*, 61–62 ("*on the spit*"); Rapport and Northwood, *Rendezvous with Destiny*, 747 (*guides*).

619 *Göring's booty proved*: OH, John A. Heintges, 7th Inf, 1974, Jack A. Pellici, SOOHP, MHI, 394–95, 406–7; White, *From Fedala to Berchtesgaden*, 278–80 (*eighteen thousand bottles*); "The Goering Collection," OSS, Art Looting Investigation Unit, Consolidated Interrogation Report no. 2, Sept. 15, 1945, Hermann Goering papers, HIA, box 1, 171–73; Rapport and Northwood, *Rendezvous with Destiny*, 749; Nicholas, *The Rape of Europa*, 314, 344 (*$500 million*); White, *Conquerors' Road*, 74 ("*Ah, war!*").

620 *The Reichsmarschall himself*: AAR, Robert C. Stack, 36th ID, n.d., Texas MFM (*entourage*); diary, John E. Dahlquist, May 9, 1945, and scrapbook; A. I. Goldberg, Associated Press report, May 9, 1945; *Life*, May 28, 1945, 30+, all in Dahlquist papers, MHI; corr, Alexander M. Patch, Jr., Oct. 16, 1945, Patch papers, USMA Arch, box 1 (*marshal's baton*).

620 "*Well, bugger me*": Collier, *Fighting Words*, 194–95.

620 *An American major subsequently invited*: Kesselring, *The Memoirs of Field-Marshal Kesselring*, 291; Taylor, *Swords and Plowshares*, 107 ("*historical character*").

A Great Silence

621 "*The lovely colors of the countryside*": Moorehead, *Eclipse*, 259–62, 285.

621 *Tommies fished unconventionally*: Thompson, *Men Under Fire*, 148–51; Stafford, *Endgame 1945*, 11 (*hospitals*); Col. T. G. Lindsay, "Operation Overlord Plus," n.d., LHC, 66–69 (*fine maps*).

621 *At 11:30 A.M. on Thursday*: "Surrender Negotiations," n.d., UK NA, CAB 101/330, 4–5.

621 "*I have never heard of you*": Hamilton, *Monty: Final Years of the Field-Marshal, 1944–1976*, 501–2; John Keegan, "The German Surrender," in Hollinshead and Rabb, eds., *I Wish I'd Been There*, vol. 2, 307 ("*rehearsing this*").

621 *Undaunted, Friedeburg*: Moorehead, *Eclipse*, 282–84; "Surrender Negotiations," n.d., UK NA, CAB 101/330, 6 ("*usual way*"); VW, vol. 2, 339.

622 *Calling for a map*: Moorehead, *Eclipse*, 284; Hamilton, *Monty: Final Years of the Field-Marshal, 1944–1976*, 501–4 (*tongue-lashing*); Francis de Guingand, "Notes for the Chief of Staff," May 3, 1945, LHC, 2/4/2 ("*delighted to continue*"); De Guingand, *Operation Victory*, 453–55.

622 *At five P.M. on a rainy Friday*: Thompson, *Men Under Fire*, 148–51; John Keegan, "The German Surrender," in Hollinshead and Rabb, eds., *I Wish I'd Been There*, vol. 2, 311 ("*with the doings*"); Moorehead, *Eclipse*, 285–86 ("*We will go and see*").

622 *The answer was yes*: diary entry, May 7, 1945, Harold S. Frum, "The Soldier Must Write," 1984, GCM Lib (*Donuts*); Moorehead, *Montgomery*, 223 ("*a good likeness*").

622 "*It was a grey evening*": Moorehead, *Eclipse*, 286–87.

622 *Friedeburg and his comrades rose*: Hamilton, *Monty: Final Years of the Field-Marshal, 1944–1976*, 512–13.

623 *Once all German signatures*: Moorehead, *Eclipse*, 288–89; "Surrender Negotiations," n.d., UK NA, CAB 101/330, 6–7; Thompson, *Men Under Fire*, 152–53 ("*concludes*").

623 "*The tent flaps*": "German Surrenders," AB, no. 48 (1985): 1+; VW, vol. 2, 340 ("*It looks as if*").

623 *Foul weather on Saturday*: SC, 486–87; Strong, *Intelligence at the Top*, 273 (*fresh collar*); *Three Years*, 825–26 (*twenty minutes*).

623 *Smith and Major General Strong*: Crosswell, *Beetle*, 918.

623 *Smith walked down the hall*: *Three Years*, 825–28, 834; Summersby, *Eisenhower Was My Boss*, 237 ("*let-down*").

624 *"I really expected"*: Eisenhower, *Letters to Mamie*, 250.

624 *A new negotiator arrived*: Doenitz, *Memoirs*, 462–63; OH, Kenneth Strong, May 15, 1963, CJR, box 95, folder 5, 2 (*"fight the Russians"*).

624 *"You tell them"*: *Three Years*, 830–31. Dönitz's stalling was credited with allowing 1.8 million German soldiers to surrender to the Western Allies rather than the Soviets. A substantial majority of the 10 million total German prisoners-of-war ended up being held by the West (Bessel, *Germany 1945*, 124–25).

624 *"Eisenhower insists that we sign"*: Doenitz, *Memoirs*, 462–63; SC, 487 (*"Full power"*).

624 *SHAEF typists for days*: Crosswell, *Beetle*, 921–22.

624 *In the absence of firm instructions*: ibid., 916–17; Mosely, "Dismemberment of Germany," *Foreign Affairs* (Apr. 1950): 487+; OH, Philip E. Mosely, n.d., CJR, box 43, folder 10, 3–4. The diplomat Robert Murphy asserted that Smith had simply forgotten about the EAC version (*Diplomat Among Warriors*, 240–41).

624 *He opted instead for a third, abridged document*: Counsell, *Counsell's Opinion*, 149–50, 151–53 (*pecking at a typewriter*); memoir, John Counsell, n.d., CJR, box 43, folder 3, 110–16; Ziemke, *The U.S. Army in the Occupation of Germany, 1944–1946*, 257–58; Mosely, "Dismemberment of Germany," *Foreign Affairs* (Apr. 1950): 487+ (*"enabling clause"*).

625 *"Get ready, gentlemen"*: White, *Conquerors' Road*, 115.

625 *"The effect of make-believe"*: Crosswell, *Beetle*, 922. Some of the nameplates can be found in the Sidney H. Negrotto papers, MHI.

625 *Strong laid a copy*: SC, 488.

626 *Purple circles rimmed his eyes*: White, *Conquerors' Road*, 115; Summersby, *Eisenhower Was My Boss*, 240 ("Ja. Ja"); Strong, *Intelligence at the Top*, 282 (*"You will officially"*).

626 *"I suppose this calls"*: Ambrose, *Eisenhower: Soldier, General of the Army, President-Elect, 1890–1952*, vol. 1, 407.

626 *"The mission of this Allied force"*: Chandler, 2696.

626 *The sharp odors of soap*: narrative, end of war, CBH, n.d., and diary, May 7, 1945, CBH, MHI.

626 *Bradley climbed from the bed*: Bradley, *A Soldier's Story*, 554 (*"D+335"*); narrative, end of war, CBH, n.d., and diary, May 7, 1945, CBH, MHI (*"our troubles"*).

627 *"For the first time"*: "Reports by U.S. Army Ultra Representatives with Army Field Commands in the European Theater of Operations," NARA RG 457, E 9002, NSA, SRH-023, box 14; Wheeler, *The Big Red One*, 381–82 (*21,000 Purple Hearts*); Clay, *Blood and Sacrifice*, 238 (*"It's about goddamn time"*); PP, 696 (*Peace still held*); Allen, *Lucky Forward*, 394 (*"rivers in Japan"*); Codman, *Drive*, 299 (*strode from the command post*).

627 *As word spread*: Linderman, *The World Within War*, 231 (*"mad, dangerous"*); Mitchell, *Hitler's Mountain*, 135 (*"like a hailstorm"*); "Personal Diary," May 6, 1945, JMG, MHI, box 10 (*"This is it"*); Heinz, *When We Were One*, 152 (*drank a toast*).

627 *"curiously flat"*: Moorehead, *Eclipse*, 305.

627 *"I should be completely joyous"*: Christen T. Jonassen, "Letter Written on V-E Day 1945," n.d., Columbus WWII Round Table collection, MHI, box 1.

627 *"I am in a let-down mood"*: diary, JLD, May 5, 1945, MHI.

627 *"We did not know"*: Heinz, *When We Were One*, 150, 157.

627 *"Lights scintillated"*: Robert E. Walker, "With the Stonewallers," n.d., MMD, 118.

628 *Darkness enfolded*: Forrest Pogue wrote, "We knew the war in Europe was over ... because the lights came on in Pilzen and in every village near us" (*Pogue's War*, 381).

Epilogue

628 *The* Daily Mail *in London*: Gilbert, *The Day the War Ended*, 88.

628 *No matter that word of the Reims ceremony*: "Infractions of Press Censorship," telephone transcript, SHAEF and WD, May 7, 1945, 4 P.M., NARA RG 331, E 1, SGS, file 000.73, box 4 (*ticker tape*); SC, 527–28; Voss, *Reporting the War*, 193–96.

629 *But Stalin remained adamant*: Gilbert, *The Day the War Ended*, 92–98; *SC*, 491–92 (*Eisenhower dispatched*); OH, Arthur Tedder, Feb. 13, 1947, FCP, MHI (*noisy haggling*); Summersby, *Eisenhower Was My Boss*, 250–52; De Lattre de Tassigny, *The History of the French First Army*, 518; Clayton, *Three Marshals of France*, 119; author visits, Karlshorst, Nov. 1995 and Sept. 2009; *Three Years*, 836 (*"easier to start"*).

629 *Notwithstanding a BBC announcement*: Botting, *From the Ruins of the Reich*, 94; Gilbert, *The Day the War Ended*, 98 (*"Move along"*).

630 *In Paris, a celebration*: Beevor and Cooper, *Paris After the Liberation, 1944–1949*, 195–97, (*Garde Républicaine*); Helen Van Zonneveld, "A Time to Every Purpose," n.d., HIA, 401–2 ("Salut!"); Cooper, *Old Men Forget*, 352 (*all clear*); Gilbert, *The Day the War Ended*, 220–22 (*"anywhere to anywhere"*); corr, P. B. Rogers to family, May 10, 1945, Pleas B. Rogers papers, MHI (*"Battle Hymn"*); OH, Richard Collins, 1976, Donald Bowman, SOOHP, MHI, III-26 (*Avenue de Paris*).

630 *The rest of the world*: Sulzberger, *A Long Row of Candles*, 259 (*U.S. embassy*); Dobbs, *Six Months in 1945*, 203 (*tossed into the air*); Brinkley, *Washington Goes to War*, 275 (*lights bathed the Capitol*); Gilbert, *The Day the War Ended*, 293–94 (*"treacherous Japanese"*).

630 *V-E Day dawned in London*: Ziegler, *London at War, 1939–1945*, 324 (*"Wagnerian rain"*), 325 (*cymbals*), 328 (*"Not to Be Sold"*); Mollie Panter-Downes, "Letter from London," May 19, 1945, in *The New Yorker Book of War Pieces*, 472–76; Gilbert, *The Day the War Ended*, 211 (*"We want the king!"*); Lewis, *The Mammoth Book of Eyewitness World War II*, 461 (*Hitler effigy*).

631 *Early in the afternoon Churchill left*: D'Este, *Warlord*, 692–93; Pawle, *The War and Colonel Warden*, 381; Mollie Panter-Downes, "Letter from London," May 19, 1945, in *The New Yorker Book of War Pieces*, 472–76; Gilbert, *The Day the War Ended*, 199 (*"roared ourselves"*); Thompson, *I Was Churchill's Shadow*, 157–58 (*"They expect it"*).

631 *Searchlights at dusk*: Ziegler, *London at War, 1939–1945*, 327; Gilbert, *The Day the War Ended*, 211 (*"your hour"*); D'Este, *Warlord*, 692–93 (*"ancient land"*); Taylor and Taylor, eds., *The War Diaries*, 195 (*"Hope and Glory"*). Churchill would be turned from office less than two months later when his Conservatives took a drubbing at the polls; in 1951, he again became prime minister for nearly four years.

631 *By the time Japan surrendered*: Weinberg, *A World at Arms*, 894 (*Sixty million had died*); Hitchcock, *The Bitter Road to Freedom*, 131 (*one-third of them soldiers*); Snyder, "Walter Bedell Smith: Eisenhower's Chief of Staff," *Military Affairs* (Jan. 1984): 6+ (*"great and terrible"*); Rosenbaum, "Explaining Hitler," *New Yorker* (May 1, 1995): 50+ (*"genocide"*); Fussell, *Wartime*, 132, 139 (*"unmitigated misfortune"*), 268 (*"tragic and ironic"*).

632 *"a God all-powerful"*: Danchev, 689.

632 *In Europe, the Western Allies*: Battle Itinerary Study, USFET G-3, Aug. 1946, NARA RG 498, UD 583, box 4017, 5; Gerhard L. Weinberg, "D-Day: Analysis of Costs and Benefits," in Wilson, ed., *D-Day 1944*, 337.

632 *A British military maxim*: Weigley, *Eisenhower's Lieutenants*, 730; Overy, *Why the Allies Won*, 281 (*"centralized, unified"*).

632 *Allied leadership included checks*: Overy, *Why the Allies Won*, 278–81; Roberts, *Masters and Commanders*, 580–81; Biddle, "Leveraging Strength: The Pillars of American Grand Strategy in World War II," *Orbis* (winter 2011): 4+.

633 *"Our resolution to preserve"*: Overy, *Why the Allies Won*, 324; *LO*, 477–78; Mansoor, *The GI Offensive in Europe*, 4–6, 252; "Report of Activities: Army Ground Forces, World War II," Jan. 1946, NARA RG 334, E 315, ANSCOL, AGF RTC, box 150; http://www.minneapolisfed.org/ (*roughly $4 trillion*); Stephen Daggett, "Cost of Major U.S. Wars," June 29, 2010, Congressional Research Service, 2; Montgomery, "The Cost of War, Unnoticed," *WP*, May 8, 2007, D1 (*42 million*); Millett and Murray, *Military Effectiveness*, vol. 3, *The Second World War*, 47, 62; Bynell, "Logistical Planning and Operations—Europe," lecture, March 16, 1945, NARA RG 334, E 315, ANSCOL, box 207, 14 (*"digging the Panama Canal"*).

633 *"prodigy of organization"*: Weigley, *History of the United States Army*, 475; "Supply and

Maintenance on the European Continent," n.d., NARA RG 407, E 427, USFET General Board, AG WWII operations reports, 97-USF5-0.30, no. 130, 42 (*18 million tons*); "Ordnance Diary," Dec. 1, 1945, NARA RG 498, ETOUSA HD, UD 586, box 1 (*vehicles*); "Clothing and Footwear," chapter 56, PIR, Robert M. Littlejohn papers, HIA, 2 (*footwear*); "U.S. Army in WWII," 1952, CMH, cited in "Statistical Review," RefBib, MHI (*munitions plants*); "Statistical Review," RefBib, MHI, citing *Cavalry Journal*, March–Apr. 1946, 21+ (*500 million machine-gun bullets*); Goodman, ed., *While You Were Gone*, 23 ("*American taxpayer*"); Ambrose, *Eisenhower and Berlin, 1945*, 63 (*two-thirds of all ships*).

633 *The enemy was crushed by logistical brilliance*: At its peak, the war accounted for 35.8 percent of GDP (Stephen Daggett, "Cost of Major U.S. Wars," June 29, 2010, Congressional Research Service, 2); Gropman, *Mobilizing U.S. Industry in World War II*, 107 (*smaller proportion*), 133; Ellis, *Brute Force*, 348–49.

633 "*Warfare like yours is easy*": German POW survey, Dec. 7, 1944, SHAEF, Psychological Warfare Division, RG 331, E 87, 23 782.

633 *There was nothing easy*: Stoler, *Allies in War*, 227; Willmott, *The Great Crusade*, 352 ("*European supremacy*"); Larrabee, *Commander in Chief*, 631 ("*American century*"); Brower, ed., *World War II in Europe: The Final Year*, 63 ("*great soul*").

634 *The war was a potent catalyst*: Weinberg, *A World at Arms*, 915; Weinberg, "The Place of World War II in History," lecture, 1995, U.S. Air Force Academy, Colorado Spring, Colo., 11 (*GI Bill*); Kennedy, *Freedom from Fear*, 779 (*antebellum roles*); MacGregor, *Integration of the Armed Forces*, 51–53, 56; "The Utilization of Negro Infantry Platoons in White Companies," NARA RG 330, E 94, soldier surveys, report no. ETO 82, 4–12.

634 "*Glad to be home*": Reynolds, *Rich Relations*, 444.

634 *In battered Europe, enormous tasks*: Pyle, *Brave Men*, 320 ("*broken world*"); SC, 508–10 (*Norway*), 499; Margry, "The Flensburg Government," *AB*, no. 128 (2005): 2+; J. B. Churcher, "A Soldier's Story," n.d., LHC, 80–81 ("*Any word*"); SC, 512–15; "Activities and Organization of COMZ," U.S. Senate hearing, May 28, 1945, NARA RG 498, ETO HD, admin file #89, 29 (*three million strong*); Brig. Gen. Alden H. Waitt, "Summary Report of Situation in ETO," July 5, 1945, NARA RG 337, E 16, GHQ AGF G-3, OR, 210.684, box 2 (*poisonous gas munitions*).

635 "*On the continent of Europe*": Churchill, *Triumph and Tragedy*, 549–50.

635 *Part of that cleansing*: Gill, *The Journey Back from Hell*, 24; pamphlets, "The Courthouse in Nuremberg" and "The International Military Tribunal," Oberlandgericht, Nuremberg, author visit, Feb. 13, 1996; Lewis, ed., *The Mammoth Book of Eyewitness World War II*, 561–66.

635 *Individual Allied governments*: Weingartner, "Otto Skorzeny and the Laws of War," *JMH* (Apr. 1991): 207+; Tooze, *The Wages of Destruction*, 674 (*200,000 suspected culprits*); "Bergen Belsen," Holocaust Encyclopedia, USHMM, http://www.ushmm.org/wlc /en/article.php?ModuleId=10005224. Additional Bergen-Belsen defendants were tried subsequently (Margry, "Bergen-Belsen," *AB*, no. 89 [1995]: 1+).

635 *From 1945 to 1948*: James J. Weingartner, "Early War Crimes Trials," in *Liberation 1945*, 84.

635 *The path to justice often proved*: "Malmedy Massacre Investigation," Senate Armed Services Committee, Oct. 1949, 4–16, 22–32; memo, judge advocate, European Command, March 28, 1949, CMH, LAW 2–7, 1, 26–30. During Senate hearings into the Malmédy prosecutions, Senator Joseph McCarthy accused the Army of using "Gestapo tactics" (*TT*, 623).

635 *Released from Landsberg prison*: Weingartner, *Crossroads of Death*, 238–50, 262–63; "The Death of Joachim Peiper," *AB*, no. 40 (1983): 47+; Bauserman, *The Malmédy Massacre*, 32 (*slashed the hoses*).

635 *Eisenhower's avowed "number 1 plan"*: *Three Years*, 820; Wilmot, *The Struggle for Europe*, 573n ("*I owe much*").

636 "*You have completed your mission*": Pogue, *George C. Marshall*, 583; Ferrell, ed., *The Eisenhower Diaries*, 221.

636 *Ahead lay fifteen more years*: Lyon, *Eisenhower: Portrait of the Hero*, 23 *("Ike!")*; Summersby, *Eisenhower Was My Boss*, 254–59 *("almost speak")*.

636 *On Tuesday, June 12*: Miller, *Ike the Soldier*, 780; Striner, "Eisenhower's Triumph: The Guildhall Address of 1945," American Veterans Center, http://www.americanveteranscenter.org/magazine/avq/issue-vi-springsummer-2009/eisenhower%e2%80%99s-triumph-the-guildhall-address-of-1945/; Fraser, *Alanbrooke*, 468 *("I had never realized")*; http://www.eisenhower.archives.gov/education/bsa/citizenship_merit_badge/speeches _national_historical_importance/guildhall_address.pdf.

636 *Blood there had surely been*: VW, vol. 2, 407; LO, 478; "The Normandy Invasion," statistical appendix, June 10, 1945, SHAEF, Harold R. Bull papers, DDE Lib, box 1 *(12,000 Allied planes)*. Official casualty figures from various governments rarely agree.

637 *British, Canadian, Polish*: "The Operations of 21 Army Group," 1946, CARL, N-133331.

637 *French battle casualties*: SC, 544. During the occupation and liberation, more than six hundred thousand French men were killed (Aron, *France Reborn*, 464).

637 *Of all German boys*: Tooze, *The Wages of Destruction*, 672. The number of German military deaths has long remained in dispute. John Ellis puts the dead and missing at 3.25 million, a widely cited figure (Ellis, *World War II: A Statistical Survey*, 253). Another recent analysis puts the number at 5.3 million (Rüdiger Overmans, *Deutsche militärische Verluste im Zweiten Weltkrieg*, cited in http://en.wikipedia.org/wiki/World_War_II_ casualties#cite_note-R.C5.B1diger_Overmans_2000-4).

637 *Some 14 percent of the Soviet population*: Hitchcock, *The Bitter Road to Freedom*, 131; Stoler, "The Second World War in U.S. History and Memory," International Historical Congress, Oslo, Aug. 12, 2000; Hastings, *Inferno*, 427 *(killed roughly nine times more Germans)*. Seventeen hundred Soviet towns were destroyed, plus seventy thousand villages (Dobbs, *Six Months in 1945*, 225).

637 *American soldiers bore the brunt*: LO, 478; SC, 543; Hynes, *The Soldier's Tale*, 281 *("left index finger")*; Reister, ed., *Medical Statistics in World War II*, 23 *(1,700 left blind)*; Fisher, *Legacy of Heroes*, 8–10 *(18,000 amputations)*, 20 *("their stump")*; Cowdrey, *Fighting for Life*, 321 *(hospital in Michigan)*.

637 *Seventy-five thousand Americans had been listed*: VW, vol. 2, 543; Steere and Boardman, *Final Disposition of World War II Dead, 1945–51*, 120–21 *(isolated graves)*; Litoff and Smith, eds., *Since You Went Away*, 236–37 *("Darling, come to me")*; Myra Strachner Gershkoff Papers, New York State Library, manuscripts and special collections, SC 20575, http://www.nysl.nysed.gov/msscfa/sc20575.htm.

637 *No sooner had the ink dried*: Steere and Boardman, *Final Disposition of World War II Dead, 1945–51*, 178–79; L. R. Talbot, "Graves Registration in the European Theater of Operations," 1955, chapter 26, PIR, MHI. A total of seventy-eight thousand American dead were never recovered; of remains recovered, less than 4 percent could not be identified (Risch and Kieffer, *The Quartermaster Corps*, vol. 2, 404).

638 *Within weeks, seven hundred bodies*: Steere and Boardman, *Final Disposition of World War II Dead, 1945–51*, 175, 186–204, 247.

638 *Even as this search began*: L. R. Talbot, "Graves Registration in the European Theater of Operations," 1955, chapter 26, PIR, MHI; Joseph T. Layne and Glenn D. Barquest, "Margraten: U.S. Ninth Army Military Cemetery," 1994, 172nd Engineer Combat Bn, NWWIIM, 9 *(Dutch citizens)*.

638 *"I cried for the joy"*: Babcock, *War Stories*, 212; "4ID Update," vol. 5, no. 47, June 6, 2011, http://parentsofdeployed.homestead.com/2011Jun06.html.

638 *In 1947, the next of kin*: Joseph T. Layne and Glenn D. Barquest, "Margraten: U.S. Ninth Army Military Cemetery," 1994, 172nd Engineer Combat Bn, NWWIIM, 11–12. Congress appropriated $191 million for the task, which resulted in 279,869 interments overseas and at home; just under 110,000 of those remained in cemeteries abroad (Risch and Kieffer, *The Quartermaster Corps*, vol. 2, 404).

638 *In Europe the exhumations*: Joseph T. Layne and Glenn D. Barquest, "Margraten: U.S. Ninth Army Military Cemetery," 1994, 172nd Engineer Combat Bn, NWWIIM, 13.

639 *Labor strikes in the United States*: Risch and Kieffer, *The Quartermaster Corps*, vol. 2, 402; Steere and Boardman, *Final Disposition of World War II Dead, 1945–51*, 351–54 (*"tombs"*). More than one thousand additional bodies were loaded aboard *Connolly* in subsequent European ports before she crossed the Atlantic (L. R. Talbot, "Graves Registration in the European Theater of Operations," 1955, chapter 26, PIR, MHI, 42–43).

639 *Among those waiting was Henry A. Wright*: Steere and Boardman, *Final Disposition of World War II Dead, 1945–51*, 682.

639 *Thus did the fallen return*: L. R. Talbot, "Graves Registration in the European Theater of Operations," 1955, chapter 26, PIR, MHI, 42–43; Schuyler Dean Hoslett, "The Army Effects Bureau of the Kansas City Quartermaster Depot," 1946, CMH, 4-10.8 AA.

639 *Hour after hour, day after day*: Eddy, "Treasure of Our Heroes," *American Magazine* (Apr. 1944): 44+, in Schuyler Dean Hoslett, "The Army Effects Bureau of the Kansas City Quartermaster Depot," 1946, CMH, 4-10.8 AA, appendix, 268–70; "Honoring Those Fallen Who Served," Aurora (Ill.) *Beacon News*, Apr. 12, 2005, B2. Horton, in the 32nd Infantry Division, died in December 1942. After reading his final words, his mother, Odessa J. Horton, wrote, "To me the war can never be over and you may know, this letter to us is Gethsemane" (*Congressional Record*, Nov. 24, 1943, A 5114).

640 *"The times were full of certainty"*: Liebling, *Mollie & Other War Pieces*, foreword.

640 *"Never did I feel"*: Fussell, *Doing Battle*, 174.

640 *"What we had together"*: Linderman, *The World Within War*, 264.

640 *"We are certainly no smaller"*: Fauntleroy, *The General and His Daughter*, 151–52.

640 *"The anti-aircraft gunner in a raid"*: Moorehead, *Eclipse*, 305.

641 *"the living have the cause"*: White, *Conquerors' Road*, ix.

641 *"No war is really over"*: Kotlowitz, *Before Their Time*, 192; Atkinson, "What Is Lost?" *World War II* (Nov. 2009): 32+ (*By the year 2036*).

Selected Sources

Books

Abram, David, et al. *The Rough Guide to France*. New York: Rough Guides, 2007.

Abrams, Leonard N. *Our Secret Little War*. Bethesda, Md.: International Geographic Information Foundation, 1991.

Ackroyd, Peter. *London Under: The Secret History Beneath the Streets*. London: Chatto & Windus, 2011 (e-book edition).

Addison, Paul. *Churchill, the Unexpected Hero*. New York: Oxford University Press, 2005.

Airborne Forces. London: Air Ministry, 1951.

Allen, Peter. *One More River*. New York: Charles Scribner's, 1980.

Allen, Robert S. *Lucky Forward*. New York: Vanguard Press, 1947.

Alosi, John, Jr. *War Birds: A History of the 282nd Signal Pigeon Company*. Shippensburg, Pa.: S.p., 2010.

Alter, Jonathan P., and Daniel Crouch, eds. *"My Dear Moon."* S.p., 2005.

Ambrose, Stephen E. *Band of Brothers*. New York: Touchstone, 2001.

———. *Eisenhower: Soldier, General of the Army, President-Elect, 1890–1952*. Vol. 1. New York: Simon & Schuster, 1983.

———. *Eisenhower and Berlin, 1945*. New York: W. W. Norton, 1967.

———. *Pegasus Bridge*. New York: Simon & Schuster, 1985.

———. *The Supreme Commander: The War Years of General Dwight D. Eisenhower*. Garden City, N.Y.: Doubleday, 1971.

Andrus, E. C., et al., eds. *Advances in Military Medicine*. Vols. 1 and 2. Boston: Atlantic Monthly Press, 1948.

Anonymous. *A Woman in Berlin*. Trans. Philip Boehm. New York: Metropolitan Books, 2005.

Applebaum, Anne. *Iron Curtain: The Crushing of Eastern Europe, 1944–1956*. New York: Doubleday, 2012.

Appleman, Roy E., et al. *Okinawa: The Last Battle. United States Army in World War II*. Washington, D.C.: Department of the Army, 1948.

Arnold, H. H. *Global Missions*. Blue Ridge Summit, Pa.: Tab Books, 1989.

Aron, Robert. *France Reborn*. Trans. Humphrey Hare. New York: Scribner's, 1964.

Arthur, Max. *Forgotten Voices of World War II*. Guilford, Conn.: Lyons Press, 2004.

Astor, Gerald. *June 6, 1944: The Voices of D-Day*. New York: St. Martin's Press, 1994.

Atkinson, Rick. *An Army at Dawn: The War in North Africa, 1942–1943*. New York: Henry Holt, 2002.

———. *The Day of Battle: The War in Sicily and Italy, 1943–1944*. New York: Henry Holt, 2007.

Ayer, Fred, Jr. *Before the Colors Fade*. Boston: Houghton Mifflin, 1964.

Babcock, John B. *Taught to Kill*. Washington, D.C.: Potomac Books, 2005.

Babcock, Robert O. *War Stories: Utah Beach to Pleiku*. Baton Rouge, La.: Saint John's Press, 2001.

Badsey, Stephen. *Arnhem 1944: Operation "Market Garden."* London: Osprey, 1993.

Baedeker, Karl. *Belgium and Holland*. Leipzig: Karl Baedeker, 1901.

——. *Northern France*. New York: Charles Scribner's Sons, 1919.

——. *Paris and Its Environs*. New York: C. Scribner, 1937.

Baedeker's Netherlands, n.d.

Bagnulo, Aldo H., ed. *Nothing But Praise: A History of the 1321st Engineer General Service Regiment*. Alexandria, Va.: U.S. Army Corps of Engineers, 2009.

Baily, Charles M. *Faint Praise*. Hamden, Conn.: Archon, 1983.

Bair, Deirdre. *Samuel Beckett: A Biography*. New York: Harcourt Brace Jovanovich, 1978.

Baker, Carlos. *Ernest Hemingway: A Life Story*. New York: Bantam, 1970.

Baldwin, Hanson W. *Battles Lost and Won*. New York: Harper & Row, 1966.

Baldwin, Ralph B. *The Deadly Fuze*. London: Jane's Publishing, 1980.

Balkoski, Joseph. *Beyond the Beachhead*. Harrisburg, Pa.: Stackpole Books, 1989.

——. *From Beachhead to Brittany*. Mechanicsburg, Pa.: Stackpole Books, 2008.

——. *From Brittany to the Reich*. Baltimore: Old Orchard Press, 2010.

——. *Omaha Beach: D-Day, June 6, 1944*. Mechanicsburg, Pa.: Stackpole Books, 2004.

——. *Utah Beach: The Amphibious Landing and Airborne Operations on D-Day*. Mechanicsburg, Pa.: Stackpole Books, 2005.

Barnett, Corelli, ed. *Hitler's Generals*. New York: Grove Weidenfeld, 1989.

Baron, Richard, Abe Baum, and Richard Goldhurst. *Raid! The Untold Story of Patton's Secret Mission*. New York: Dell, 2000.

Bates, Charles C., and John F. Fuller. *America's Weather Warriors, 1814–1985*. College Station, Tex.: Texas A&M University Press, 1986.

Baumgarten, Harold. *Eyewitness on Omaha Beach*. Jacksonville, Fla.: Halrit Publishing, 1994.

Baumgartner, John W., et al. *The 16th Infantry, 1798–1946*. 1946.

Bauserman, John M. *The Malmédy Massacre*. Shippensburg, Pa.: White Mane Publishing, 1995.

Baxter, James Phinney, 3rd. *Scientists Against Time*. Boston: Atlantic Monthly Press, 1947.

Baynes, John. *The Forgotten Victor*. London: Brassey's, 1989.

——. *Urquhart of Arnhem*. New York: Brassey's, 1993.

Beavan, Colin. *Operation Jedburgh*. New York: Penguin, 2007.

Beck, Alfred M., et al. *The Corps of Engineers: The War Against Germany. United States Army in World War II*. Washington, D.C.: U.S. Army, 1985.

Beevor, Antony. *Berlin: The Downfall, 1945*. New York: Viking, 2002.

——. *D-Day*. London: Viking, 2009.

——. *The Second World War*. London: Weidenfeld & Nicolson, 2012.

Beevor, Antony, and Artemis Cooper. *Paris After the Liberation, 1944–1949*. New York: Penguin Books, 2004.

Beierl, Florian M. *History of the Eagle's Nest*. World War 2 Books and Video: 1998.

Belchem, David. *All in the Day's March*. London: Collins, 1978.

Belfield, Eversley, and H. Essame. *The Battle for Normandy*. London: Pan Books, 1983.

Bennett, Ralph. *Ultra in the West*. New York: Charles Scribner's Sons, 1979.

Berlin, Robert H. *U.S. Army World War II Corps Commanders*. Fort Leavenworth, Kans.: Combat Studies Institute, 1989.

Bessel, Richard. *Germany 1945*. New York: Harper Perennial, 2010.

Biddle, Tami Davis. *Rhetoric and Reality in Air Warfare*. Princeton, N.J.: Princeton University Press, 2002.

Bischof, Günter, and Anton Pelinka, eds. *Austrian Memory & National Identity*. New Brunswick, N.J.: Transaction Publishers, 1997.

Bishop, Jim. *FDR's Last Year*. New York: William Morrow, 1974.

Black, Conrad. *Franklin Delano Roosevelt: Champion of Freedom*. New York: PublicAffairs, 2003.

Black, Robert W. *Rangers in World War II*. New York: Ballantine, 1992.

Blair, Clay. *Hitler's U-Boat War*. Vol. 2, *The Hunted, 1942–1945*. New York: Random House, 1998.

————. *Ridgway's Paratroopers*. Garden City, N.Y.: Dial Press, 1985.

Bland, Larry L., ed. *George C. Marshall Interviews and Reminiscences for Forrest C. Pogue*. Lexington, Va.: George C. Marshall Research Foundation, 1991.

Blank, Ralf, et al. *Germany and the Second World War*. Vol. 9, part 1, *German Wartime Society, 1939–1945*. Oxford, U.K.: Oxford University Press, 2008.

Blatman, Daniel. *The Death Marches: The Final Phase of Nazi Genocide*. Trans. Chaya Galai. Cambridge, Mass.: Belknap Press, 2011.

Blue Spaders: The 26th Infantry Regiment, 1917–1967. Wheaton, Ill.: Cantigny First Division Foundation, 1996.

Blumenson, Martin. *The Battle of the Generals*. New York: William Morrow, 1993.

————. *Breakout and Pursuit*. United States Army in World War II. Washington, D.C.: U.S. Army, 1993.

————. *Liberation*. Alexandria, Va.: Time-Life, 1978.

————. *Patton: The Man Behind the Legend, 1885–1945*. New York: William Morrow, 1985.

————. *The Patton Papers, 1940–1945*. New York: Da Capo Press, 1996.

Blumentritt, Guenther. *Von Rundstedt: The Soldier and the Man*. Trans. Cuthbert Reavely. London: Odhams Press, 1952.

Blunt, Roscoe C., Jr. *Foot Soldier*. Cambridge, Mass.: Da Capo Press, 2002.

Boatner, Mark M., III. *The Biographical Dictionary of World War II*. Novato, Calif.: Presidio Press, 1990.

Boesch, Paul. *Road to Huertgen*. Houston: Gulf Publishing, 1962.

Bohlen, Charles E. *Witness to History, 1929–1969*. New York: W. W. Norton, 1973.

Bollinger, Martin J. *Warriors and Wizards*. Annapolis, Md.: Naval Institute Press, 2010.

Bonn, Keith E. *When the Odds Were Even*. Novato, Calif.: Presidio Press, 1994.

Boog, Horst, et al. *Germany and the Second World War*. Vol. 7. Oxford, U.K.: Clarendon Press, 2006.

Booth, T. Michael, and Duncan Spencer. *Paratrooper: The Life of Gen. James M. Gavin*. New York: Simon & Schuster, 1994.

Botting, Douglas. *From the Ruins of the Reich*. New York: Crown, 1985.

————. *The Second Front*. Alexandria, Va.: Time-Life, 1978.

Bourke-White, Margaret. *Portrait of Myself*. Boston: G. K. Hall, 1985.

Bowen, Robert M. *Fighting with the Screaming Eagles*. Mechanicsburg, Pa.: Stackpole Books, 2001.

Bradbeer, Grace. *The Land Changed Its Face: The Evacuation of Devon's South Hams, 1943–1944*. Newton Abbot, U.K.: David & Charles, 1973.

Bradley, Omar N. *A Soldier's Story*. New York: Henry Holt, 1951.

Bradley, Omar N., and Clay Blair. *A General's Life*. New York: Simon & Schuster, 1983.

Braim, Paul F. *The Will to Win: The Life of General James A. Van Fleet*. Annapolis, Md.: Naval Institute Press, 2001.

Bredin, A.E.C. *Three Assault Landings*. Aldershot, U.K.: Gale & Polden, 1946.

Brereton, Lewis H. *The Brereton Diaries*. New York: William Morrow, 1946.

Breuer, William B. *Hitler's Fortress Cherbourg: The Conquest of a Bastion*. New York: Stein and Day, 1984.

Brinkley, David. *Washington Goes to War*. New York: Ballantine, 1989.

Brower, Charles F., ed. *World War II in Europe: The Final Year*. New York: St. Martin's Press, 1998.

Brown, Anthony Cave. *Bodyguard of Lies*. New York: Harper & Row, 1975.

————. *The Last Hero: Wild Bill Donovan*. New York: Times Books, 1982.

Brown, John Mason. *Many a Watchful Night*. New York: Whittlesey House, 1945.

Bryant, Arthur. *Triumph in the West*. Garden City, N.Y.: Doubleday, 1959.

Buell, Thomas B. *Master of Seapower: A Biography of Fleet Admiral Ernest J. King*. Boston: Little, Brown, 1980.

Buffetaut, Yves. *D-Day Ships*. Annapolis, Md.: Naval Institute Press, 1994.

Buhite, Russell D. *Decisions at Yalta: An Appraisal of Summit Diplomacy.* Wilmington, Del.: Scholarly Resources, 1986.

Bullock, Alan. *Hitler: A Study in Tyranny.* New York: Harper Torchbooks, 1964.

Burgett, Donald R. *Currahee!* New York: Dell, 2000.

Burriss, T. Moffatt. *Strike and Hold.* Washington, D.C.: Brassey's, 2000.

Butcher, Harry C. *My Three Years with Eisenhower.* New York: Simon & Schuster, 1946.

By Air to Battle. London: His Majesty's Stationery Office, 1945.

Bykofsky, Joseph, and Harold Larson. *The Transportation Corps: Operations Overseas. United States Army in World War II.* Washington, D.C.: U.S. Army, 2003.

Byrnes, James F. *Speaking Frankly.* N York: Harper & Brothers, 1947.

Calder, Angus. *The People's War: Britain, 1939–1945.* New York: Pantheon, 1969.

Callahan, Raymond. *Churchill & His Generals.* Lawrence, Kans.: University Press of Kansas, 2007.

Capa, Robert. *Slightly Out of Focus.* New York: Modern Library, 1999.

Carafano, James Jay. *After D-Day: Operation Cobra and the Normandy Breakout.* Boulder, Colo.: Lynne Rienner, 2000.

Carell, Paul. *Invasion—They're Coming!* Trans. E. Osers. New York: E. P. Dutton, 1963.

Carpenter, Iris. *No Woman's World.* Boston: Houghton Mifflin, 1946.

Carroll, Andrew. *Behind the Lines.* New York: Scribner, 2005.

———, ed. *War Letters.* New York: Washington Square Press, 2002.

Carver, Michael, ed. *The War Lords: Military Commanders of the Twentieth Century.* Boston: Little, Brown, 1976.

Catton, Bruce. *A Stillness at Appomattox.* Garden City, N.Y.: Doubleday, 1953.

Cawthon, Charles R. *Other Clay.* Niwant, Colo.: University Press of Colorado, 1990.

Chalmers, W. S. *Full Cycle.* London: Hodder and Stoughton, 1959.

Chandler, Alfred D., ed. *The Papers of Dwight David Eisenhower.* Vols. 3, 4, 5. Baltimore: Johns Hopkins University Press, 1970.

Chandler, David G., and James Lawton Collins, Jr., eds. *The D-Day Encyclopedia.* New York: Simon & Schuster, 1994.

Chatterton, George. *The Wings of Pegasus.* Nashville: Battery Press, 1982.

Cherpak, Evelyn M., ed. *The Memoirs of Admiral H. Kent Hewitt.* Newport, R.I.: Naval War College Press, 2004.

Chmielewska-Szymańska, Aneta. *Życie i działalność Stanisława Sosabowskiego.* Lezno, Poland: Wydawnictwo Instytutu, 2004.

Choltitz, Dietrich v. *Soldat Unter Soldaten.* Konstanz, Germany: Europa Verlag, 1951.

Churchill, Winston S. *Closing the Ring.* Boston: Houghton Mifflin, 1951.

———. *Triumph and Tragedy.* Boston: Houghton Mifflin, 1953.

Clark, Lloyd. *Crossing the Rhine.* New York: Atlantic Monthly Press, 2008.

Clarke, Jeffrey J., and Robert Ross Smith. *Riviera to the Rhine. United States Army in World War II.* Washington, D.C.: U.S. Army, 1993.

Clay, Steven E. *Blood and Sacrifice.* Chicago: Cantigny First Division Foundation, 2001.

Clayton, Anthony. *Three Marshals of France.* London: Brassey's, 1992.

Clemens, Diane Shaver. *Yalta.* London: Oxford University Press, 1972.

Clervaux en Ardennes. Clervaux, France: Syndicat d'Initiative, 1994.

Coakley, Robert W., and Richard M. Leighton. *Global Logistics and Strategy, 1943–1945. United States Army in World War II.* Washington, D.C.: U.S. Army, 1989.

Codman, Charles R. *Drive.* Boston: Atlantic Monthly Press, 1957.

Coffey, Thomas M. *Hap.* New York: Viking Press, 1982.

Colby, John. *War from the Ground Up: The 90th Division in WWII.* Austin, Tex.: Nortex, 1991.

Cole, Hugh M. *The Ardennes: Battle of the Bulge. USAWWII.* Washington, D.C.: U.S. Army, 1993.

———. *The Lorraine Campaign. United States Army in World War II.* Washington, D.C.: U.S. Army, 1984.

Coles, Harry L., and Albert K. Weinberg. *Civil Affairs: Soldiers Become Governors. United States Army in World War II.* Washington, D.C.: U.S. Army, 1964.

Colley, David P. *Blood for Dignity*. New York: St. Martin's Press, 2003.

———. *Decision at Strasbourg*. Annapolis, Md.: Naval Institute Press, 2008.

Collier, Basil. *The Defence of the United Kingdom*. London: Her Majesty's Stationery Office, 1957.

Collier, Richard. *Fighting Words: The War Correspondents of World War Two*. New York: St. Martin's Press, 1989.

———. *The Freedom Road, 1944–45*. New York: Atheneum, 1984.

Collins, J. Lawton. *Lightning Joe*. Baton Rouge, La.: Louisiana State University Press, 1980.

Collins, Larry, and Dominique Lapierre. *Is Paris Burning?* New York: Pocket Books, 1966.

Colville, John. *Footprints in Time*. London: Collins, 1976.

———. *The Fringes of Power*. New York: W. W. Norton, 1985.

Cooper, Belton Y. *Death Traps*. New York: Ballantine, 2003.

Cooper, Duff. *Old Men Forget*. London: Rupert Hart-Davis, 1953.

Cooper, Matthew. *The German Army, 1933–1945*. Lanham, Md.: Scarborough House, 1990.

Copp, Terry. *Cinderella Army: The Canadians in Northwest Europe, 1944–1945*. Toronto: University of Toronto Press, 2006.

———, ed. *Montgomery's Scientists*. Waterloo, Ontario: Wilfrid Laurier University, 2000.

Copp, Terry, and Bill McAndrew. *Battle Exhaustion: Soldiers and Psychiatrists in the Canadian Army, 1939–1945*. Montreal: McGill-Queen's University Press, 1990.

Copp, Terry, and Robert Vogel. *Maple Leaf Route: Falaise*. Alma, Ontario: Maple Leaf Route, 1983.

Cosmas, Graham A., and Albert E. Cowdrey. *Medical Service in the European Theater of Operations. United States Army in World War II*. Washington, D.C.: U.S. Army, 1992.

Counsell, John. *Counsell's Opinion*. London: Barrie and Rockliff, 1963.

Cowdrey, Albert E. *Fighting for Life: American Military Medicine in World War II*. New York: Free Press, 1994.

Crane, Conrad C. *Bombs, Cities & Civilians: American Airpower Strategy in World War II*. Lawrence, Kans.: University Press of Kansas, 1993.

Craven, Wesley Frank, and James Lea Cate, eds. *The Army Air Forces in World War II*. Vol. 3, *Europe: ARGUMENT to V-E Day*. Chicago: University of Chicago Press, 1951.

Cray, Ed. *General of the Army*. New York: Touchstone, 1991.

Crosswell, D. K. R. *Beetle: The Life of General Walter Bedell Smith*. Lexington, Ky.: University Press of Kentucky, 2010.

Cundiff, Paul A. *45th Infantry CP*. Tampa, Fla.: S.p., 1987.

Cunningham, Viscount of Hyndhope. *A Sailor's Odyssey*. New York: E. P. Dutton, 1951.

Currey, Cecil B. *Follow Me and Die*. New York: Stein and Day, 1984.

D'Este, Carlo. *Decision in Normandy*. New York: Harper Perennial, 1983.

———. *Eisenhower: A Soldier's Life*. New York: Henry Holt, 2002.

———. *Patton: A Genius for War*. New York: HarperPerennial, 1996.

———. *Warlord: A Life of Winston Churchill at War, 1874–1945*. New York: Harper, 2008.

Daglish, Ian. *Operation Goodwood*. Barnsley, U.K.: Pen & Sword, 2004.

Dailey, Franklyn E., Jr. *Joining the War at Sea, 1939–1945*. Wilbraham, Mass.: Dailey International Publishers, 2006.

Dallek, Robert. *Franklin D. Roosevelt and American Foreign Policy, 1932–1945*. New York: Oxford University Press, 1979.

Danchev, Alex, and Daniel Todman, eds. *War Diaries, 1939–1945, Field Marshal Lord Alanbrooke*. Berkeley and Los Angeles: University of California Press, 2001.

Daniell, David Scott. *The Royal Hampshire Regiment*. Vol. 3. Aldershot, U.K.: Gale & Polden, 1955.

Davies, Norman. *No Simple Victory*. New York: Penguin, 2008.

Davis, Franklin M. *Across the Rhine*. Alexandria, Va.: Time-Life, 1980.

Davis, Kenneth S. *Soldier of Democracy*. Garden City, N.Y.: Doubleday, Doran & Co., 1945.

Davis, Richard G. *Bombing the European Axis Powers*. Maxwell Air Force Base, Ala.: Air University Press, 2006.

——. *Carl A. Spaatz and the Air War in Europe*. Washington, D.C.: Center for Air Force History, 1993.

D-Day: The Normandy Invasion in Retrospect. Lawrence, Kans.: University Press of Kansas, 1991.

De Belot, Raymond. *The Struggle for the Mediterranean, 1939–1945*. Trans. James A. Field, Jr. Princeton, N.J.: Princeton University Press, 1951.

De Gaulle, Charles. *The Complete War Memoirs of Charles de Gaulle*. New York: Simon & Schuster, 1964.

De Guingand, Francis. *Operation Victory*. New York: Scribner's Sons, 1947.

De Lattre de Tassigny, Marshal. *The History of the French First Army*. Trans. Malcolm Barnes. London: George Allen and Unwin, 1952.

De Slag om Arnhem. Oosterbeek, Netherlands: Stichting Airborne Herdenkingen, 1994.

Dear, I. C. B., ed. *The Oxford Companion to World War II*. New York: Oxford University Press, 1995.

Devlin, Gerard M. *Paratrooper!* New York: St. Martin's Press, 1979.

Dickson, Paul. *War Slang*. New York: Pocket Books, 1994.

Dilks, David, ed. *The Diaries of Sir Alexander Cadogan*. New York: G. P. Putnam's, 1972.

Dobbs, Michael. *Six Months in 1945*. New York: Knopf, 2012.

Doenitz, Karl. *Memoirs: Ten Years and Twenty Days*. Trans. R. H. Stevens. New York: Da Capo Press, 1997.

Donnison, F. S. V. *Civil Affairs and Military Government in North-West Europe*. London: Her Majesty's Stationery Office, 1961.

Doolittle, James H., with Carroll V. Glines. *I Could Never Be So Lucky Again*. New York: Bantam, 1991.

Doubler, Michael D. *Busting the Bocage*. Ft. Leavenworth, Kans.: Combat Studies Institute, 1988.

——. *Closing with the Enemy*. Lawrence, Kans.: University Press of Kansas, 1994.

Douglas-Home, Charles. *Rommel*. New York: Saturday Review Press, 1973.

Drez, Ronald J., ed. *Voices of D-Day*. Baton Rouge, La.: Louisiana State University Press, 1996.

Dupuy, R. Ernest. *St. Vith: Lion in the Way*. Nashville: Battery Press, 1986.

Durnford-Slater, John. *Commando*. London: Greenhill Books, 2002.

Eden, Anthony. *The Reckoning: The Memoirs of Anthony Eden, Earl of Avon*. Boston: Houghton Mifflin, 1965.

Edsel, Robert M., with Bret Witter. *The Monuments Men*. New York: Center Street, 2009.

Ehlers, Robert S., Jr. *Targeting the Reich: Air Intelligence and the Allied Bombing Campaigns*. Lawrence, Kans.: University Press of Kansas, 2009.

Ehrman, John. *Grand Strategy*. Vol. 5, *August 1943–September 1944*. London: Her Majesty's Stationery Office, 1956.

——. *Grand Strategy*. Vol. 6, *October 1944–August 1945*. London: Her Majesty's Stationery Office, 1956.

Eiler, Keith E. *Mobilizing America: Robert P. Patterson and the War Effort, 1940–1945*. Ithaca, N.Y.: Cornell University Press, 1997.

Eisenhower, David. *Eisenhower at War, 1943–1945*. New York: Random House, 1986.

Eisenhower, Dwight D. *Crusade in Europe*. Baltimore: Johns Hopkins University Press, 1997.

——. *Letters to Mamie*. Ed. John S. D. Eisenhower. Garden City, N.Y.: Doubleday, 1978.

Eisenhower, John S. D. *The Bitter Woods*. New York: Da Capo Press, 1995.

——. *General Ike*. New York: Free Press, 2003.

——. *Strictly Personal*. Garden City, N.Y.: Doubleday, 1974.

Eisenhower, Susan. *Mrs. Ike: Portrait of a Marriage*. Sterling, Va.: Capital Books, 2002.

Eliach, Yaffa, and Brana Gurewitsch, eds. *The Liberators*. Vol. 1. Brooklyn, N.Y.: Center for Holocaust Studies Documentation & Research, 1981.

Ellis, John. *Brute Force: Allied Strategy and Tactics in the Second World War*. New York: Viking Press, 1990.

——. *On the Front Lines*. New York: John Wiley & Sons, 1991.

——. *World War II: A Statistical Survey*. New York: Facts on File, 1995.

Ellis, L. F. *Victory in the West*. Vol. 1, *The Battle of Normandy. History of the Second World War*. London: Her Majesty's Stationery Office, 1962.

——. *Victory in the West*. Vol. 2, *The Defeat of Germany. History of the Second World War*. London: Her Majesty's Stationery Office, 1968.

——. *Welsh Guards at War*. Aldershot, U.K.: Gale & Polden, 1946.

Elstob, Peter. *Hitler's Last Offensive*. New York: Ballantine, 1973.

English, John A. *The Canadian Army and the Normandy Campaign*. New York: Praeger, 1991.

——. *Patton's Peers*. Mechanicsburg, Pa.: Stackpole Books, 2009.

Ent, Uzal W., ed. *The First Century: A History of the 28th Infantry Division*. Harrisburg, Pa.: Stackpole Books, 1979.

Erickson, John. *The Road to Berlin*. London: Cassell, 2003.

Essame, H. *The Battle for Germany*. New York: Bonanza Books, 1969.

——. *Patton: A Study in Command*. New York: Charles Scribner's Sons, 1974.

Eustis, Morton C. *War Letters of Morton Eustis to His Mother*. Washington, D.C.: Spiral Press, 1945.

Evans, Richard J. *The Third Reich at War*. New York: Penguin, 2009.

Even, Francis A. *The Tenth Engineers*. S.p., 2003.

Ewing, Joseph H. *29 Let's Go!* Washington, D.C.: Infantry Journal Press, 1948.

Fairbanks, Douglas, Jr. *A Hell of a War*. New York: St. Martin's Press, 1993.

Fane, Francis Douglas, and Don Moore. *The Naked Warriors*. Annapolis, Md.: Naval Institute Press, 1995.

Farago, Ladislas. *Patton: Ordeal and Triumph*. New York: Ivan Obolensky, 1964.

Farrington, William, ed. *Cowboy Pete: The Autobiography of Major General Charles H. Corlett*. Santa Fe, N.M.: Sleeping Fox, 1974.

Faubus, Orval Eugene. *In This Faraway Land*. Conway, Ark.: River Road Press, 1971.

Fauntleroy, Barbara Gavin. *The General and His Daughter*. New York: Fordham University Press, 2007.

Featherston, Alwyn. *Saving the Breakout*. Novato, Calif.: Presidio Press, 1993.

Feis, Herbert. *Churchill, Roosevelt, Stalin: The War They Waged and the Peace They Sought*. Princeton, N.J.: Princeton University Press, 1957.

Fenby, Jonathan. *The General: Charles de Gaulle and the France He Saved*. New York: Simon & Schuster, 2010 (e-book edition).

Fenno, Richard F., ed. *The Yalta Conference*. Boston: Heath and Co., 1955.

Ferguson, Allen R. *All's Fair: A Personal History of War and Love*. S.p., 2005.

Fergusson, Bernard. *The Watery Maze*. New York: Holt, Rinehart and Winston, 1961.

Ferrell, Robert H., ed. *The Eisenhower Diaries*. New York: W. W. Norton, 1981.

Fest, Joachim C. *Hitler*. Trans. Richard and Clara Winston. New York: Harcourt Brace, 1974.

Fisher, Craig. *Legacy of Heroes*. Rosemont, Ill.: American Academy of Orthopaedic Surgeons, 2002.

Fisher, Ernest F., Jr. *Cassino to the Alps. United States Army in World War II*. Washington, D.C.: U.S. Army, 1977.

Fitzgerald, D. J. L. *History of the Irish Guards in the Second World War*. Aldershot, U.K.: Gale & Polden, 1949.

Foot, M. R. D. *SOE in France*. Frederick, Md.: University Publications, 1984.

Forbes, Patrick. *The Grenadier Guards in the War of 1939–1945*. Vol. 1. London: Aldershot, 1949.

Foreign Relations of the United States: The Conferences at Malta and Yalta. Washington, D.C.: Government Printing Office, 1955.

Fowle, Barry W., ed. *Builders and Fighters: U.S. Army Engineers in World War II*. Ft. Belvoir, Va.: Army Corps of Engineers, 1992.

Fox, Don M. *Patton's Vanguard: The United States Army Fourth Armored Division*. Jefferson, N.C.: McFarland, 2003.

Fraser, David. *Alanbrooke*. New York: Atheneum, 1982.

――. *And We Shall Shock Them*. London: Hodder and Stoughton, 1983.

――. *Knight's Cross*. New York: HarperCollins, 1993.

Friedrich, Jörg. *The Fire: The Bombing of Germany, 1940–1945*. Trans. Allison Brown. New York: Columbia University Press, 2006.

Frost, John. *A Drop Too Many*. London: Buchan & Enright, 1982.

――. *Nearly There*. London: Leo Cooper, 1991.

Fussell, Paul. *The Boys' Crusade*. New York: Modern Library, 2003.

――. *Doing Battle: The Making of a Skeptic*. Boston: Back Bay Books, 1998.

――. *Wartime*. New York: Oxford University Press, 1989.

Gallagher, Hugh Gregory. *FDR's Splendid Deception*. New York: Dodd, Mead, 1985.

Gander, Marsland. *After These Many Quests*. London: MacDonald, 1949.

Garland, Joseph E. *Unknown Soldiers*. Rockport, Mass.: Protean Press, 2009.

Gavin, James M. *On to Berlin*. New York: Viking Press, 1978.

Gellately, Robert. *Backing Hitler*. New York: Oxford University Press, 2001.

Gellhorn, Martha. *The Face of War*. New York: Simon & Schuster, 1959.

Gilbert, Martin. *D-Day*. Hoboken, N.J.: John Wiley, 2004.

――. *The Day the War Ended*. New York: Owl Books, 2004.

――. *The Second World War*. New York: Henry Holt, 1991.

Gill, Anton. *The Journey Back from Hell: Conversations with Concentration Camp Survivors*. London: HarperCollins, 1994.

Gilmore, Donald L., ed. *U.S. Army Atlas of the European Theater in World War II*. New York: Barnes & Noble Books, 2004.

Giziowski, Richard. *The Enigma of General Blaskowitz*. London: Leo Cooper, 1997.

Goerlitz, Walter. *History of the German General Staff, 1657–1945*. New York: Praeger, 1953.

Goodman, Jack, ed. *While You Were Gone*. New York: Simon & Schuster, 1946.

Goodwin, Doris Kearns. *No Ordinary Time*. New York: Touchstone, 1995.

Goolrick, William K., and Ogden Tanner. *The Battle of the Bulge*. Alexandria, Va.: Time-Life, 1979.

Graham, Dominick, and Shelford Bidwell. *Coalitions, Politicians & Generals*. London: Brassey's, 1993.

Graham, Don. *No Name on the Bullet*. New York: Viking Press, 1986.

Granatstein, J. L. *The Generals*. Toronto: Stoddart, 1993.

Gray, J. Glenn. *The Warriors*. New York: Harcourt, Brace, 1959.

Grayling, A. C. *Among the Dead Cities*. New York: Walker, 2006.

Green, Constance McLaughlin, et al. *The Ordnance Department: Planning Munitions for War. United States Army in World War II*. Washington, D.C.: Department of the Army, 1955.

The Green Guide to Normandy. Greenville, S.C.: Michelin, n.d.

Greenfield, Kent Roberts, ed. *Command Decisions*. New York: Harcourt, Brace, 1959.

Gropman, Alan, ed. *The Big "L": American Logistics in World War II*. Washington, D.C.: National Defense University Press, 1997.

――. *Mobilizing U.S. Industry in World War II*. Washington, D.C.: National Defense University, 1996.

Groves, Leslie R. *Now It Can Be Told*. New York: Harper & Brothers, 1962.

Guérard, Albert. *France: A Short History*. New York: W. W. Norton, 1946.

Gugeler, Russell A. *Major General Orlando Ward: Life of a Leader*. Oakland, Ore.: Red Anvil Press, 2009.

Hackett, David A., ed. *The Buchenwald Report*. Boulder, Colo.: Westview Press, 1995.

Hadley, Arthur T. *Heads or Tails*. New York: Glitterati, 2007.

Hamilton, Nigel. *Master of the Battlefield: Monty's War Years, 1942–1944*. New York: McGraw-Hill, 1983.

――. *Monty: Final Years of the Field-Marshal, 1944–1976*. New York: McGraw-Hill, 1986.

Harmon, E. N. *Combat Commander*. Englewood Cliffs, N.J.: Prentice-Hall, 1970.

Harriman, W. Averell, and Elie Abel. *Special Envoy to Churchill and Stalin, 1941–1946*. New York: Random House, 1975.

Harrison, Gordon A. *Cross-Channel Attack. United States Army in World War II.* Washington, D.C.: U.S. Army, 1951.

Hart, Russell A. *Clash of Arms.* Boulder, Colo.: Lynne Rienner, 2001.

Hart-Davis, Duff, ed. *King's Counsellor.* London: Phoenix, 2007.

Hassett, William D. *Off the Record with F.D.R.* New Brunswick, N.J.: Rutgers University Press, 1958.

Hastings, Max. *Armageddon: The Battle for Germany.* New York: Vintage, 2005.

———. *Bomber Command.* New York: Dial Press, 1979.

———. *Inferno: The World at War, 1939–1945.* New York: Knopf, 2011.

———. *OVERLORD: D-Day and the Battle for Normandy.* New York: Simon & Schuster, 1984.

———. *Das Reich.* New York: Jove Book, 1984.

———. *Winston's War.* New York: Knopf, 2010.

Hechler, Ken. *The Bridge at Remagen.* Missoula, Mont.: Pictorial Histories, 1993.

———. *Hero of the Rhine: The Karl Timmermann Story.* Missoula, Mont.: Pictorial Histories Publishing, 2004.

Heefner, Wilson A. *Dogface Soldier: The Life of General Lucian K. Truscott, Jr.* Columbia, Mo.: University of Missouri Press, 2010.

Heinz, W. C. *When We Were One.* Cambridge, Mass.: Da Capo Press, 2003.

Hesketh, Roger. *Fortitude.* Woodstock, N.Y.: Overlook Press, 2000.

Hewitt, Robert L. *Workhorse of the Western Front: The Story of the 30th Infantry Division.* Washington, D.C.: Infantry Journal Press, 1946.

Higgins, Trumbull. *Soft Underbelly.* New York: Macmillan, 1968.

Hills, R. J. T. *Phantom Was There.* London: Edward Arnold, 1951.

Hinsley, F. H. *British Intelligence in the Second World War.* Abridged ed. New York: Cambridge University Press, 1993.

Hinsley, F. H., et al. *British Intelligence in the Second World War.* Vol. 3, part 1. London: Her Majesty's Stationery Office, 1984.

———. *British Intelligence in the Second World War.* Vol. 3, part 2. New York: Cambridge University Press, 2005.

Hinsley, F. H., and C. A. G. Simkins. *British Intelligence in the Second World* War. Vol. 4, *Security and Counter-Intelligence.* New York: Cambridge University Press, 1990.

Hirshson, Stanley P. *General Patton: A Soldier's Life.* New York: HarperCollins, 2002.

History of the 120th Infantry Regiment. Washington, D.C.: Infantry Journal Press, 1947.

Hitchcock, William I. *The Bitter Road to Freedom.* New York: Free Press, 2008.

Hogan, David W., Jr. *A Command Post at War: First Army Headquarters in Europe, 1943–1945.* Washington, D.C.: U.S. Army, 2000.

Hogg, Ian V. *The Biography of General George S. Patton.* New York: Gallery Books, 1982.

Holley, Irving Brinton, Jr. *Buying Aircraft: Matériel Procurement for the Army Air Forces. United States Army in World War II.* Washington, D.C.: U.S. Army, 1964.

Hollinshead, Byron, and Theodore K. Rabb, eds. *I Wish I'd Been There.* Vol. 2. New York: Doubleday, 2008.

Holt, Thaddeus. *The Deceivers.* New York: Scribner, 2004.

Holt, Tonie, and Valmai Holt. *Major & Mrs. Holt's Battlefield Guide to the Normandy Landing Beaches.* London: Leo Cooper, 2002.

Horrocks, Brian. *Corps Commander.* New York: Scribner's, 1977.

———. *A Full Life.* London: Leo Cooper, 1974.

Howard, Michael. *British Intelligence in the Second World War.* Vol. 5, *Strategic Deception.* London: Her Majesty's Stationery Office, 1990.

———. *The Mediterranean Strategy in World War II.* London: Greenhill Books, 1993.

———. *Strategic Deception in the Second World War.* New York: W. W. Norton, 1995.

Howard, Michael, and John Sparrow. *The Coldstream Guards, 1920–1946.* London: Oxford University Press, 1951.

Howarth, David. *Dawn of D-Day.* London: Greenhill Books, 2001.

Howarth, Stephen, ed. *Men of War.* New York: St. Martin's Press, 1992.

Howarth, T. E. B., ed. *Monty at Close Quarters: Recollections of the Man.* New York: Hippocrene Books, 1985.

Hoyt, Edwin P. *The Invasion Before Normandy.* New York: Stein and Day, 1985.

Huie, William Bradford. *The Execution of Private Slovik.* New York: Dell, 1970.

Hynes, Samuel. *The Soldier's Tale: Bearing Witness to Modern War.* New York: Penguin, 1998.

Ingersoll, Ralph. *Top Secret.* New York: Somerset Books, 1946.

Irving, David. *The Mare's Nest.* New York: Little, Brown, 1965.

———. *The Trail of the Fox.* New York: Thomas Congdon, 1977.

———. *The War Between the Generals.* New York: Congdon & Lattès, 1981.

Isby, David C., ed. *Fighting the Breakout.* London: Greenhill Books, 2004.

———, ed. *Fighting the Invasion.* London: Greenhill Books, 2000.

Ismay, Lord. *The Memoirs of General Lord Ismay.* New York: Viking Press, 1960.

Jackson, W. G. F. *Overlord.* Newark, Del.: University of Delaware Press, 1979.

Jackson, William. *The Mediterranean and the Middle East.* Vol. 6, *Victory in the Mediterranean,* part 2. London: Her Majesty's Stationery Office, 1986.

Jacobsen, Hans-Adolf, and Jürgen Rohwer, eds. *Decisive Battles of World War II: The German View.* Trans. Edward Fitzgerald. London: André Deutsch, 1965.

James, D. Clayton. *A Time for Giants.* New York: Franklin Watts, 1987.

James, M. E. Clifton. *The Counterfeit General Montgomery.* New York: Avon, 1954.

Jeffers, H. Paul. *Command of Honor.* New York: NAL Caliber, 2008.

———. *In the Rough Rider's Shadow.* New York: Ballantine, 2002.

Jenkins, Roy. *Churchill: A Biography.* New York: Farrar, Straus and Giroux, 2001.

Johns, Glover S., Jr. *The Clay Pigeons of St. Lo.* Harrisburg, Pa.: MSP, 1958.

Johnson, Gerden F. *History of the Twelfth Infantry Regiment in World War II.* Boston: S.p., 1947.

Jordan, Jonathan W. *Brothers, Rivals, Victors.* New York: NAL Caliber, 2011.

Jutras, Philippe. *Sainte-Mère-Église: Les Paras du 6 Juin.* Bayeux, France: Editions Heimdal, 1991.

Karig, Walter. *Battle Report: The Atlantic War.* New York: Farrar & Rinehart, 1946.

Kedward, Rod. *France and the French: A Modern History.* Woodstock, N.Y.: Overlook Press, 2006.

Keegan, John, ed. *Churchill's Generals.* New York: Grove Weidenfeld, 1991.

———. *The First World War.* New York: Knopf, 1999.

———. *Six Armies in Normandy.* New York: Penguin, 1994.

Kennedy, David M. *Freedom from Fear.* New York: Oxford University Press, 1999.

Kennedy, John. *The Business of War.* New York: Morrow, 1958.

Kennett, Lee. *G.I.: The American Soldier in World War II.* New York: Scribner's, 1987.

Kersaudy, François. *Churchill and De Gaulle.* New York: Atheneum, 1982.

Kershaw, Alex. *The Bedford Boys.* Cambridge, Mass.: Da Capo Press, 2003.

Kershaw, Ian. *Hitler, 1936–45: Nemesis.* New York: W. W. Norton, 2001.

Kershaw, Robert J. *"It Never Snows in September."* Hersham, Surrey, U.K.: Ian Allan, 2007.

Kesselring, Albrecht. *The Memoirs of Field-Marshal Kesselring.* London: Greenhill Books, 1997.

Kessler, Leo. *The Battle of the Ruhr Pocket.* Chelsea, Mich.: Scarborough House, 1990.

Kimball, Warren F., ed. *Churchill & Roosevelt: The Complete Correspondence.* Vol. 3. Princeton, N.J.: Princeton University Press, 1987.

———. *Forged in War: Roosevelt, Churchill, and the Second World War.* Chicago: Ivan R. Dee, 2003.

King, Benjamin, and Timothy J. Kutta. *Impact.* Rockville Centre, N.Y.: Sarpedon, 1998.

King, Ernest J., and Walter Muir Whitehill. *Fleet Admiral King.* New York: W. W. Norton, 1952.

Kingseed, Cole C. *From Omaha Beach to Dawson's Ridge.* Annapolis, Md.: Naval Institute Press, 2005.

————. *Old Glory Stories: American Combat Leadership in World War II*. Annapolis, Md.: Naval Institute Press, 2006.

Kingston McCloughry, E. J. *Direction of War*. New York: Praeger, 1958.

Kirkpatrick, Charles E. *An Unknown Future and a Doubtful Present: Writing the Victory Plan of 1941*. Washington, D.C.: Center of Military History, 1990.

Kleber, Brooks E., and Dale Birdsell. *The Chemical Warfare Service: Chemicals in Combat. United States Army in World War II*. Washington, D.C.: U.S. Army, 1990.

Klemperer, Victor. *To the Bitter End: The Diaries of Victor Klemperer, 1942–45*. Trans. Martin Chalmers. London: BCA, 1999.

Kluger, Steve. *Yank: The Army Weekly*. New York: St. Martin's Press, 1991.

Knickerbocker, H. R., et al. *Danger Forward*. Washington, D.C.: Society of the First Division, 1947.

Knight, Ray. *Would You Remember This?* S.p., 1992.

Koch, Oscar W., and Robert G. Hays. *G-2: Intelligence for Patton*. Philadelphia: Army Times Publishing, 1971.

Kotlowitz, Robert. *Before Their Time*. New York: Knopf, 1997.

Kuter, Laurence S. *Airman at Yalta*. New York: Duell, Sloan and Pearce, 1955.

Laffin, John. *Combat Surgeons*. Trowbridge, U.K.: Sutton, 1999.

Lamb, Richard. *Montgomery in Europe, 1943–1945*. London: Buchen & Enright, 1987.

Lankford, Nelson Douglas, ed. *OSS Against the Reich: The World War II Diaries of Colonel David K. E. Bruce*. Kent, Ohio: Kent State University Press, 1991.

Laqueur, Walter, ed. *The Second World War*. London: Sage, 1982.

Larrabee, Eric. *Commander in Chief*. New York: Harper & Row, 1987.

Lauer, Walter E. *Battle Babies: The Story of the 99th Infantry Division in World War II*. Nashville: Battery Press, 1950.

Leahy, William D. *I Was There*. New York: Whittlesey House, 1950.

Leasor, James. *The Clock with Four Hands*. New York: Reynal & Co., 1959.

Lebda, John F. *Million Miles to Go*. Victoria, British Columbia: Trafford, 2001.

Lee, Ulysses. *The Employment of Negro Troops. United States Army in World War II*. Washington, D.C.: Center of Military History, 2000.

Lefèvre, Eric. *Panzers in Normandy Then and Now*. Trans. Roy Cooke. London: Battle of Britain International, 2002.

Lerner, Daniel. *Psychological Warfare Against Nazi Germany*. Cambridge, Mass.: M.I.T. Press, 1971.

Lewin, Ronald. *Montgomery as Military Commander*. New York: Stein and Day, 1971.

————. *Rommel as Military Commander*. New York: Barnes & Noble, 1998.

————. *Ultra Goes to War*. New York: Pocket Books, 1980.

Lewis, Jon E., ed. *The Mammoth Book of Eyewitness World War II*. New York: Carroll & Graf, 2005.

Lewis, Nigel. *Exercise Tiger*. New York: Prentice Hall, 1990.

Lewis, Norman. *Naples '44*. New York: Pantheon, 1978.

Liberation 1945. Washington, D.C.: United States Holocaust Memorial Museum, 1995.

Liddell Hart, B. H. *The German Generals Talk*. New York: William Morrow, 1948.

————. *History of the Second World War*. Old Saybrook, Conn.: Konecky & Konecky, 1970.

————. *The Other Side of the Hill*. London: Cassell, 1951.

————, ed. *The Rommel Papers*. Trans. Paul Findlay. Pennington, N.J.: Collectors Reprints, 1995.

————. *The Tanks*. Vol. 2. New York: Frederick A. Praeger, 1959.

Liddle, Peter. *D-Day by Those Who Were There*. South Yorkshire, U.K.: Pen & Sword Military, 2004.

Liebling, A. J. *Mollie & Other War Pieces*. Lincoln, Neb.: University of Nebraska Press, 2004.

Lightning: The History of the 78th Infantry Division. Washington, D.C.: Infantry Journal Press, 1947.

Linderman, Gerald F. *The World Within War: America's Combat Experience in World War II*. New York: Free Press, 1997.

Litoff, Judy Barrett, and David C. Smith, eds. *Since You Went Away*. New York: Oxford University Press, 1991.

Longmate, Norman. *The G.I.'s: The Americans in Britain, 1942–1945*. New York: Scribner's, 1975.

———. *Hitler's Rockets*. Barnsley, U.K.: Frontline Books, 2009.

Love, Robert W., Jr., and John Major, eds. *The Year of D-Day: The 1944 Diary of Admiral Sir Bertram Ramsay*. Hull, U.K.: University of Hull Press, 1994.

Lubrich, Oliver, ed. *Travels in the Reich, 1933–1945*. Trans. Kenneth Northcott et al. Chicago: University of Chicago Press, 2010.

Lucas, James, and James Barker. *The Killing Ground*. London: B. T. Batsford, 1978.

Luck, Hans von. *Panzer Commander*. New York: Praeger, 1989.

Ludewig, Joachim. *Rückzug: The German Retreat from France, 1944*. Ed. David T. Zabecki. Lexington, Ky.: University Press of Kentucky, 2012.

Luther, Craig W. H. *Blood and Honor: The History of the 12th SS Panzer Division*. San Jose, Calif.: R. James Bender Publishing, 1987.

Lyall, Gavin, ed. *The War in the Air*. New York: Ballantine, 1970.

Lyon, Peter. *Eisenhower: Portrait of the Hero*. Boston: Little, Brown, 1974.

MacDonald, Charles B. *The Battle of the Huertgen Forest*. New York: Jove, 1983.

———. *The Mighty Endeavor*. New York: Oxford University Press, 1969.

———. *The Siegfried Line Campaign. United States Army in World War II*. Washington, D.C.: U.S. Army, 1993.

———. *A Time for Trumpets*. New York: Bantam, 1985.

MacDonald, Charles B., and Sidney T. Mathews. *Three Battles: Arnaville, Altuzzo, and Schmidt*. Washington, D.C.: U.S. Army, 1952.

MacGregor, Morris J., Jr. *Integration of the Armed Forces*. Washington, D.C.: U.S. Army, 1981.

Macintyre, Ben. *Double Cross*. New York: Crown, 2012.

MacKenzie, De Witt. *Men Without Guns*. Philadelphia: Blakiston, 1945.

Macksey, Kenneth. *Kesselring: The Making of the Luftwaffe*. New York: David McKay, 1978.

Macmillan, Harold. *War Diaries*. New York: St. Martin's Press, 1984.

Macmillan, Margaret. *Paris 1919*. New York: Random House, 2003.

Maczek, Stanislaw. *Od Podwody do Czolga, Wspomnienia Wojenne 1918–1945*. Edinburgh: Tomar, 1961.

Manchester, William. *The Arms of Krupp, 1587–1966*. New York: Bantam, 1970.

Mansoor, Peter R. *The GI Offensive in Europe*. Lawrence, Kans.: University Press of Kansas, 1999.

Margolian, Howard. *Conduct Unbecoming*. Toronto: University of Toronto Press, 1998.

Margry, Karel, ed. *Operation Market-Garden Then and Now*. Vols. 1 and 2. London: Battle of Britain International, 2002.

Mark, Eduard. *Aerial Interdiction in Three Wars*. Washington, D.C.: Center for Air Force History, 1994.

Markey, Michael A. *Jake: The General from West York Avenue*. York, Pa.: Historical Society of York County, 1998.

Marshall, Charles F. *A Ramble Through My War: Anzio and Other Joys*. Baton Rouge, La.: Louisiana State University Press, 1998.

Marshall, Malcolm, ed. *Proud Americans*. S.p., 1994.

Marshall, S. L. A. *Bastogne: The Story of the First Eight Days*. Washington, D.C.: U.S. Army, 2004.

———. *Battle at Best*. New York: Jove, 1989.

———. *Night Drop*. New York: Bantam, 1963.

Martin, George E. *Blow, Bugle, Blow*. Bradenton, Fla.: S.p., 1986.

Mason, John T., Jr., ed. *The Atlantic War Remembered*. Annapolis, Md.: Naval Institute Press, 1990.

Massie, Robert K. *Nicholas and Alexandra*. New York: Atheneum, 1967.

Masterman, J. C. *The Double-Cross System.* New Haven, Conn.: Yale University Press, 1972.

Matloff, Maurice. *Strategic Planning for Coalition Warfare, 1943–1944. United States Army in World War II.* Washington, D.C.: U.S. Army, 1994.

Mauldin, Bill. *The Brass Ring.* New York: W. W. Norton, 1971.

———. *Up Front.* New York: Henry Holt, 1944.

Maule, Henry. *Out of the Sand: The Epic Story of General Leclerc.* London: Odhams Books, 1966.

Mayo, Lida. *The Ordnance Department: On Beachhead and Battlefront. United States Army in World War II.* Washington, D.C.: U.S. Army, 1991.

McCullough, David. *The Greater Journey: Americans in Paris.* New York: Simon & Schuster, 2011.

McKee, Alexander. *Caen: Anvil of Victory.* New York: St. Martin's Press, 1964.

McKernon, Francis M. *Corry.* West Haven, Conn.: Easy Rudder Press, 2003.

McLean, French L. *Quiet Flows the Rhine.* Winnipeg, Manitoba: J. J. Fedorowicz, 1996.

McManus, John C. *Alamo in the Ardennes.* Hoboken, N.J.: John Wiley & Sons, 2007.

———. *The Americans at D-Day.* New York: Tom Doherty Associates, 2004.

———. *The Americans at Normandy.* New York: Forge, 2004.

———. *The Deadly Brotherhood.* Novato, Calif.: Presidio Press, 1998.

McNally, John V. *As Ever, John.* Fairfield, Conn.: Roberts Press, 1985.

Meacham, Jon. *Franklin and Winston.* New York: Random House, 2003.

Medicine Under Canvas. Kansas City, Mo.: Sosland Press, 1949.

Meet the Americans. London: Martin Secker and Warburg, 1943.

Megargee, Geoffrey P. *Inside Hitler's High Command.* Lawrence, Kans.: University Press of Kansas, 2000.

Merriam, Robert E. *Dark December.* Chicago: Ziff-Davis, 1947.

Middlebrook, Martin. *Arnhem 1944.* London: Penguin, 1995.

Middleton, Drew. *Our Share of Night.* New York: Viking Press, 1946.

Mieczkowski, Zbigniew, ed. *The Soldiers of General Maczek in World War II.* Warsaw and London: Foundation of the Commemoration of General Maczek, 2004.

Miller, Donald L. *Masters of the Air.* New York: Simon & Schuster, 2006.

Miller, Edward G. *A Dark and Bloody Ground.* College Station, Tex.: Texas A&M University Press, 1995.

Miller, Lee G. *The Story of Ernie Pyle.* New York: Viking Press, 1950.

Miller, Merle. *Ike the Soldier.* New York: Perigree, 1987.

Miller, Nathan. *F.D.R.: An Intimate History.* Lanham, Md.: Madison Books, 1991.

Miller, Robert A. *Division Commander.* Spartenburg, S.C.: Reprint Co., 1989.

Millett, Allan R., and Williamson Murray. *Military Effectiveness.* Vol. 3, *The Second World War.* Boston: Allen & Unwin, 1988.

Minott, Rodney G. *The Fortress That Never Was.* New York: Holt, Rinehart and Winston, 1964.

Mitcham, Samuel W., Jr. *Retreat to the Reich.* Westport, Conn.: Praeger, 2000.

Mitchell, Arthur H. *Hitler's Mountain.* Jefferson, N.C.: McFarland, 2006.

Mittelman, Joseph B. *Eight Stars to Victory.* Washington, D.C.: Ninth Infantry Division Association, 1948.

———, ed., *Hold Fast!* Munich: F. Bruckmann, 1945.

Mollo, Andrew. *The Armed Forces of World War II.* New York: Crown, 1981.

Montefiore, Simon Sebag. *Stalin: The Court of the Red Tsar.* New York: Knopf, 2004.

Montgomery, Brian. *A Field-Marshal in the Family.* New York: Taplinger Publishing, 1973.

Moorehead, Alan. *Eclipse.* New York: Harper & Row, 1968.

———. *Montgomery.* New York: Coward-McCann, 1946.

Moorehead, Caroline. *Gellhorn.* New York: Henry Holt, 2003.

Moorhouse, Roger. *Berlin at War.* New York: Basic Books, 2010.

Moran, Lord. *Churchill: Taken from the Diaries of Lord Moran.* Boston: Houghton Mifflin, 1966.

Morelock, J. D. *Generals of the Ardennes.* Washington, D.C.: National Defense University Press, 1994.

Morgan, Kay Summersby. *Past Forgetting*. New York: Simon & Schuster, 1976.

Morison, Samuel Eliot. *History of United States Naval Operations in World War II*. Vol. 9, *The Invasion of France and Germany, 1944–1945*. Edison, N.J.: Castle Books, 2001.

Morris, Edmund. *Colonel Roosevelt*. New York: Random House, 2010.

Morris, Sylvia Jukes. *Edith Kermit Roosevelt*. New York: Coward, McCann & Geoghegan, 1980.

Moulton, J. L. *Battle for Antwerp*. London: Ian Allan, 1978.

Moynihan, Michael, ed. *People at War, 1939–45*. Trowbridge, U.K.: David & Charles Publishers, 1989.

Muir, Malcolm, Jr., ed. *The Human Tradition in the World War II Era*. Wilmington, Del.: SR Books, 2001.

Murphy, Audie. *To Hell and Back*. New York: MJF Books, 1977.

Murphy, Robert. *Diplomat Among Warriors*. Garden City, N.Y.: Doubleday, 1964.

Murray, Williamson, and Allan R. Millett. *A War to Be Won*. Cambridge, Mass.: Belknap Press, 2001.

Nalty, Bernard C. *Strength for the Fight*. New York: Free Press, 1986.

Neiberg, Michael. *The Blood of Free Men: The Liberation of Paris, 1944*. New York: Basic Books, 2012.

Neillands, Robin. *The Battle for the Rhine*. Woodstock, N.Y.: Overlook Press, 2005.

The New Yorker Book of War Pieces. New York: Schocken Books, 1998.

Nicholas, Lynn H. *The Rape of Europa*. New York: Vintage, 1995.

Nichols, David, ed. *Ernie's War*. New York: Touchstone, 1986.

Nickell, Lawrence R. *Red Devil: Able Company Double Dynamite*. Nashville: Eggman Publishing, 1996.

Nordyke, Phil. *All American All the Way*. Minneapolis: Zenith Press, 2005.

———. *More Than Courage*. Osceola, Wis.: Zenith Press, 2005.

Norwich, John Julius. *The Middle Sea: A History of the Mediterranean*. New York: Doubleday, 2006.

Omaha Beachhead. Washington, D.C.: U.S. Army, 2001.

Orange, Vincent. *Coningham*. Washington, D.C.: Center for Air Force History, 1992.

———. *Tedder: Quietly in Command*. London: Frank Cass, 2004.

Osmont, Marie-Louise. *The Normandy Diary of Marie-Louise Osmont*. New York: Random House, 1994.

Ossad, Steven L., and Don R. Marsh. *Major General Maurice Rose*. Lanham, Md.: Taylor Trade, 2003.

Overy, Richard. *Why the Allies Won*. New York: W. W. Norton, 1997.

Palmer, Greg, and Mark S. Zaid, eds. *The GI's Rabbi: World War II Letters of David Max Eichhorn*. Lawrence, Kans.: University Press of Kansas, 2004.

Palmer, Robert R., et al. *The Procurement and Training of Ground Combat Troops. United States Army in World War II*. Washington, D.C.: U.S. Army, 1991.

Parker, Danny S., ed. *Hitler's Ardennes Offensive: The German View*. London: Greenhill Books, 1997.

Parkinson, Robert. *A Day's March Nearer Home*. New York: David McKay, 1974.

Pash, Boris T. *The Alsos Mission*. New York: Award House, 1969.

Patton, George S. *War as I Knew It*. Boston: Houghton Mifflin, 1975.

Patton, Robert H. *The Pattons*. Washington, D.C.: Brassey's, 1994.

Pawle, Gerald. *The War and Colonel Warden*. New York: Knopf, 1963.

Peckham, Howard H., and Shirley A. Snyder, eds. *Letters from Fighting Hoosiers*. Vol. 2. Bloomington, Ind.: Indiana War Commission, 1948.

Penrose, Jane, ed. *The D-Day Companion*. New Orleans: National D-Day Museum, 2003.

Perret, Geoffrey. *There's a War to Be Won*. New York: Ivy, 1997.

Persons, Benjamin S. *Relieved of Command*. Manhattan, Kans.: Sunflower University Press, 1997.

Phillips, Henry Gerard. *The Making of a Professional: Manton S. Eddy, USA*. Westport, Conn.: Greenwood Press, 2000.

Phillips, Robert H. *To Save Bastogne*. New York: Stein and Day, 1983.

Plokhy, S. M. *Yalta: The Price of Peace*. New York: Viking Press, 2010.

Pogue, Forrest C. *George C. Marshall: Organizer of Victory*. New York: Viking Press, 1973.

———. *Pogue's War*. Lexington, Ky.: University Press of Kentucky, 2006.

———. *The Supreme Command. United States Army in World War II*. Washington, D.C.: U.S. Army, 1989.

Ponomarenko, K. *Yalta: A Short Guide*. Simpheropol, USSR: Krym Publishers, 1971.

Porch, Douglas. *The Path to Victory*. New York: Farrar, Straus and Giroux, 2004.

Posner, Gerald L., and John Ware. *Mengele: The Complete Story*. London: Futura, 1987.

Powell, Geoffrey. *The Devil's Birthday*. London: Leo Cooper, 2001.

Prados, John. *Normandy Crucible*. New York: New American Library, 2011.

Price, Frank James. *Troy H. Middleton: A Biography*. Baton Rouge, La.: Louisiana State University Press, 1974.

Probert, Henry. *Bomber Harris*. London: Greenhill Books, 2001.

Pyle, Ernie. *Brave Men*. New York: Henry Holt, 1944.

Raines, Edgar F., Jr. *Eyes of Artillery*. Washington, D.C.: U.S. Army, 2000.

Randal, P. B. *A Short History of 30 Corps in the European Campaign*. 1945.

Rapport, Leonard, and Arthur Northwood, Jr. *Rendezvous with Destiny*. Old Saybrook, Conn.: Konecky & Konecky, 2001.

Rawling, Gerald. *Cinderella Operation*. London: Cassell, 1980.

Read, Anthony, and David Fisher. *The Fall of Berlin*. New York: W. W. Norton, 1993.

Reardon, Mark. J., ed. *Defending Fortress Europe: The German Seventh Army War Diary in Normandy, 6 June to 26 July 1944*. Bedford, Pa.: Aberjona Press, 2012.

———. *Victory at Mortain*. Lawrence, Kans.: University Press of Kansas, 2002.

Regan, Geoffrey. *Blue on Blue*. New York: Avon, 1995.

Reichelt, Walter E. *Phantom Nine*. Austin, Tex.: Presidial Press, 1987.

Reilly, Michael F. *Reilly of the White House*. New York: Simon & Schuster, 1947.

Reister, Frank A., ed. *Medical Statistics in World War II*. Washington, D.C.: Office of the Surgeon General, 1975.

Reitan, Earl A. *Riflemen*. Bennington, Ver.: Merriam Press, 2001.

Renehan, Edward J., Jr. *The Lion's Pride*. New York: Oxford University Press, 1998.

Reporting World War II. Vols. 1 and 2. New York: Library of America, 1995.

Reynolds, David. *In Command of History*. New York: Random House, 2005.

———. *Rich Relations*. London: Phoenix Press, 2000.

Reynolds, Harley. *How I Survived the Three First Wave Invasions*. Minneapolis: Mill City Press, 2008.

Reynolds, Michael. *The Devil's Adjutant*. New York: Sarpedon, 1998.

———. *Men of Steel: I SS Panzer Corps, the Ardennes and Eastern Front*. New York: Sarpedon, 1999.

———. *Steel Inferno: 1st SS Panzer Corps in Normandy*. New York: Sarpedon, 1997.

Reynolds, Michael. *Hemingway: The Final Years*. New York: W. W. Norton, 2000.

Rhodes, Richard. *The Making of the Atomic Bomb*. New York: Touchstone, 1988.

Richardson, Charles. *From Churchill's Secret Circle to the BBC*. London: Brassey's, 1991.

———. *Send for Freddie*. London: William Kimber, 1987.

Richler, Mordechai, ed. *Writers on World War II*. New York: Knopf, 1991.

Rickard, John Nelson. *Advance and Destroy: Patton as Commander in the Bulge*. Lexington, Ky.: University Press of Kentucky, 2011.

———. *Patton at Bay: The Lorraine Campaign, 1944*. Washington, D.C.: Brassey's, 2004.

Ridgway, Matthew B. *Soldier*. New York: Harper, 1956.

Riding, Alan. *And the Show Went On: Cultural Life in Nazi-Occupied Paris*. New York: Knopf, 2010.

Risch, Erna, and Chester L. Kieffer. *The Quartermaster Corps: Organization, Supply, and Services*. Vol. 2. *United States Army in World War II*. Washington, D.C.: Department of the Army, 1955.

Ritgen, Helmut. *Die Geschichte der Panzer-Lehr Division im Westen.* English trans. Stuttgart: Motorbuch Verlag, 1979.

Roach, Peter. *The 8:15 to War.* London: Leo Cooper, 1982.

Robb, Graham. *The Discovery of France.* New York: W. W. Norton, 2007.

Roberts, Andrew. *Masters and Commanders.* London: Allen Lane, 2008.

———. *The Storm of War.* New York: HarperCollins, 2011.

Robichon, Jacques. *The Second D-Day.* Trans. Barbara Shuey. New York: Walker & Co., 1962.

Rollyson, Carl. *Nothing Ever Happens to the Brave.* New York: St. Martin's Press, 1990.

Room, Adrian. *Placenames of the World.* Jefferson, N.C.: McFarland, 1997.

Roosevelt, Eleanor Butler. *Day Before Yesterday.* Garden City, N.Y.: Doubleday, 1959.

Roosevelt, Elliott. *As He Saw It.* New York: Duell, Sloan & Pearce, 1946.

Roskill, S. W.. *The War at Sea, 1939–1945.* Vol. 3, part 2. London: Her Majesty's Stationery Office, 1961.

———. *White Ensign: The British Navy at War, 1939–1945.* Annapolis, Md.: U.S. Naval Institute, 1960.

Roskill, Stephen. *Churchill and the Admirals.* New York: William Morrow, 1978.

Ross, William F., and Charles F. Romanus. *The Quartermaster Corps: Operations in the War Against Germany. United States Army in World War II.* Washington, D.C.: U.S. Army, 1965.

Rosse, Laurence M. H. P., and E. R. Hill. *The Story of the Guards Armoured Division.* London: Geoffrey Bles, 1956.

Rostow, W. W. *Concept and Controversy: Sixty Years of Taking Ideas to Market.* Austin: University of Texas Press, 2003.

Rottman, Gordon L. *FUBAR: American Soldier Slang of World War II.* New York: Osprey, 2007.

Ruge, Friedrich. *Rommel in Normandy.* Trans. Ursula R. Moessner. San Rafael, Calif.: Presidio Press, 1979.

Ruggero, Ed. *The First Men In.* New York: Harper, 2007.

Ruppenthal, Roland G. *Logistical Support of the Armies.* Vol. 1. *United States Army in World War II.* Washington, D.C.: U.S. Army, 1989.

———. *Logistical Support of the Armies.* Vol. 2. *United States Army in World War II.* Washington, D.C.: U.S. Army, 1995.

———. *Utah Beach to Cherbourg.* Washington, D.C.: U.S. Army, 1994.

Rush, Robert Sterling. *Hell in Hürtgen Forest.* Lawrence, Kans.: University Press of Kansas, 2001.

Ryan, Cornelius. *A Bridge Too Far.* London: Coronet, 1975.

———. *The Last Battle.* New York: Pocket Books, 1985.

———. *The Longest Day.* Greenwich, Conn.: Crest Book, 1963.

Salisbury-Jones, Guy. *So Full a Glory.* London: Weidenfeld & Nicolson, 1954.

Saunders, Hilary St. George. *Royal Air Force, 1939–1945.* Vol. 3, *The Fight Is Won.* London: Her Majesty's Stationery Office, 1954.

———. *The Red Beret.* Nashville: Battery Press, 1985.

Scannell, Vernon. *Argument of Kings.* London: Futura, 1989.

Schlaifer, Robert, ed. *Development of Aircraft Engines and Fuels.* Elsmsford, N.Y.: Maxwell Reprint, 1970.

Schorer, Avis D. *A Half Acre of Hell: A Combat Nurse in WWII.* Lakeville, Minn.: Galde Press, 2002.

Schrijvers, Peter. *The Crash of Ruin.* New York: New York University Press, 1998.

———. *The Unknown Dead: Civilians in the Battle of the Bulge.* Lexington, Ky.: University Press of Kentucky, 2005.

Schulzinger, Robert D., ed. *A Companion to American Foreign Relations.* Malden, Mass.: Blackwell, 2003.

Sebald, W. G. *On the Natural History of Destruction.* Trans. Anthea Bell. New York: Random House, 2003.

Semmes, Harry H. *Portrait of Patton.* New York: Appleton-Century-Crofts, 1955.

Settle, Mary Lee. *All the Brave Promises.* New York: Ballantine, 1980.

Sevareid, Eric. *Not So Wild a Dream.* New York: Atheneum, 1976.

Sforza, Eula Awbrey. *A Nurse Remembers.* S.p., 1991.

Shannon, Kevin, and Stephen Wright. *One Night in June.* London: Airlife, 2002.

Shephard, Ben. *A War of Nerves.* Cambridge, Mass.: Harvard University Press, 2001.

Sherry, Michael S. *In the Shadow of War.* New Haven, Conn.: Yale University Press, 1995.

Sherwood, Robert. *Roosevelt and Hopkins: An Intimate History.* New York: Harper & Brothers, 1948.

Shirer, William L. *The Rise and Fall of the Third Reich.* New York: Ballantine, 1950.

Shomon, Joseph James. *Crosses in the Wind.* New York: Stratford House, 1947.

A Short Guide to Great Britain. Washington, D.C.: War Department, 1944.

Shoumatoff, Elizabeth. *FDR's Unfinished Portrait.* Pittsburgh, Pa.: University of Pittsburgh Press, 1990.

Simpson, Harold B. *Audie Murphy, American Soldier.* Hillsboro, Tex.: Hill Junior College Press, 1975.

Simpson, Louis. *Selected Prose.* New York: Paragon House, 1989.

Sims, James. *Arnhem Spearhead.* London: Imperial War Museum, 1978.

Sixsmith, E. K. G. *Eisenhower as Military Commander.* New York: Da Capo, 1972.

Skibinski, Franciszek. *Pierwsza Pancerna.* Warsaw: Czytelnik, 1970.

Skorzeny, Otto. *Skorzeny's Special Missions.* London: Greenhill Books, 2006.

Slany, William Z. *U.S. and Allied Efforts to Recover and Restore Gold and Other Assets Stolen or Hidden by Germany During World War II.* Google eBook: 1997.

Smith, Albert H., Jr. *The Big Red One at D-Day.* Blue Bell, Pa.: Society of the First Infantry Division, 2003.

Smith, Gaddis. *American Diplomacy During the Second World War, 1941–1945.* New York: Knopf, 1985.

Smith, Hillas. *The English Channel: A Celebration of the Channel's Role in England's History.* Upton-upon-Severn, U.K.: Images Pub, 1994.

Smith, Jean Edward. *Eisenhower in War and Peace.* New York: Random House, 2012.

Snell, John L., ed. *The Meaning of Yalta.* Baton Rouge, La.: Louisiana State University Press, 1956.

Soffer, Jonathan M. *General Matthew B. Ridgway.* Westport, Conn.: Praeger, 1998.

Sorley, Lewis. *Thunderbolt: General Creighton Abrams and the Army of His Times.* New York: Simon & Schuster, 1992.

Sosabowski, Stanislaw. *Freely I Served.* Nashville: Battery Press, 1982.

———. *Najkrótszą Drogą.* London: Komitet Wydawiczy Polskich Spadochroniarzy, 1957.

Spayd, P. A. *Bayerlein.* Atglen, Pa.: Schiffer, 2003.

Spector, Ronald H. *At War at Sea.* New York: Viking Press, 2002.

Speidel, Hans. *We Defended Normandy.* Trans. Ian Colvin. London: Herbert Jenkins, 1951.

Spoto, Donald. *Blue Angel.* New York: Doubleday, 1992.

St.-Lô. Washington, D.C.: U.S. Army, 1994.

Stacey, C. P. *The Canadian Army, 1939–1945: An Official Historical Summary.* Ottawa: King's Printer, 1948.

———. *The Victory Campaign.* Vol. 3, *Official History of the Canadian Army in the Second World War.* Ottawa: Queen's Printer and Controller of Stationery, 1960.

Stafford, David. *Endgame 1945.* London: Abacus, 2008.

———. *Ten Days to D-Day: Citizens and Soldiers on the Eve of the Invasion.* New York: Little, Brown, 2004.

Stagg, J. M. *Forecast for Overlord.* New York: W. W. Norton, 1971.

Stallworthy, Jon, ed. *The Oxford Book of War Poetry.* New York: Oxford University Press, 1984.

Steere, Edward, and Thayer M. Boardman. *Final Disposition of World War II Dead, 1945–51.* Washington, D.C.: Office of the Quartermaster General, 1957.

Steidl, Franz. *Lost Battalions.* Novato, Calif.: Presidio Press, 1997.

Steinhoff, Johannes, et al. *Voices from the Third Reich.* Washington, D.C.: Regnery Gateway, 1989.

Stenbuck, Jack, ed. *Typewriter Battalion*. New York: William Morrow, 1995.

Stettinius, Edward R., Jr. *Roosevelt and the Russians: The Yalta Conference*. Garden City, N.Y.: Doubleday, 1949.

Stiles, Bert. *Serenade to the Big Bird*. New York: W. W. Norton, 1947.

Stimson, Henry L., and McGeorge Bundy. *On Active Service in Peace and War*. New York: Harper, 1947.

Stolberg: Penetrating the Westwall. 26th Infantry Regimental Association, 1999.

Stoler, Mark A. *Allies and Adversaries*. Chapel Hill, N.C.: University of North Carolina Press, 2000.

———. *Allies in War: Britain and America Against the Axis Powers, 1940–1945*. London: Hodder Arnold, 2005.

———. *George C. Marshall: Soldier-Statesman of the American Century*. New York: Twayne, 1989.

Strong, Kenneth. *Intelligence at the Top*. Garden City, N.Y.: Doubleday, 1969.

Sulzberger, C. L. *A Long Row of Candles*. New York: Macmillan, 1969.

Summersby, Kay. *Eisenhower Was My Boss*. New York: Dell, 1948.

Swiecicki, Marek. *With the Red Devils at Arnhem*. Trans. H. C. Stevens. London: MaxLove, 1945.

Sylvan, William C., and Francis G. Smith, Jr. *Normandy to Victory: The War Diary of General Courtney H. Hodges and the First U.S. Army*. Ed. John T. Greenwood. Lexington, Ky.: University Press of Kentucky, 2008.

Taggart, Donald G., ed. *History of the Third Infantry Division in World War II*. Washington, D.C.: Infantry Journal Press, 1947.

Talty, Stephan. *Agent Garbo*. Boston: Houghton Mifflin, 2012.

Tapert, Annette, ed. *Lines of Battle*. New York: Times Books, 1987.

Taurus Pursuant: A History of 11th Armoured Division. Printing and Stationery Service, British Army of the Rhine, 1945.

Taylor, Irene, and Alan Taylor, eds. *The War Diaries*. Edinburgh: Canongate, 2004.

Taylor, John M. *General Maxwell Taylor: The Sword and the Pen*. New York: Doubleday, 1989.

Taylor, Maxwell D. *Swords and Plowshares*. New York: W. W. Norton, 1972.

Tedder, Lord. *With Prejudice*. Boston: Little, Brown, 1966.

The 35th Infantry Division in World War II. Nashville: Battery Press, 1988.

Thompson, Julian. *The Imperial War Museum Book of Victory in Europe*. London: Sidgwick & Jackson, 1994.

Thompson, R. W. *Men Under Fire*. London: MacDonald, 1946.

———. *The Price of Victory*. London: Constable, 1960.

Thompson, W. H. *I Was Churchill's Shadow*. London: Christopher Johnson, 1952.

Thornton, Willis. *The Liberation of Paris*. New York: Harcourt, Brace & World, 1962.

Tillier, Alan, et al. *Paris*. London: Dorling Kindersley, 2000.

Tobin, James. *Ernie Pyle's War*. Lawrence, Kans.: University Press of Kansas, 1997.

Toland, John. *Adolf Hitler*. New York: Ballantine, 1976.

———. *Battle: The Story of the Bulge*. New York: Meridian, 1985.

———. *The Last Hundred Days*. New York: Random House, 1966.

Toole, John H. *Battle Diary*. Missoula, Mont.: Vigilante Press, 1978.

Tooze, Adam. *The Wages of Destruction*. London: Allen Lane, 2006.

Towne, Allen N. *Doctor Danger Forward*. Jefferson, N.C.: McFarland, 2000.

Toye, Richard. *Churchill's Empire*. New York: Henry Holt, 2010.

Triplet, William S. *A Colonel in the Armored Regiments*. Columbia, Mo.: University of Missouri Press, 2001.

Tripp, Miles. *The Eighth Passenger*. Ware, U.K.: Wordsworth, 2002.

Truscott, L. K., Jr. *Command Missions*. New York: E. P. Dutton, 1954.

Tucholski, Jędrzej. *Spadochronowa opowieść, czyli o żołnierzach gen. Sosabowskiego i cichociemnych*. Warszawa: Wydawnictwa Komunikacji I Łączności, 1991.

Tully, Grace. *F.D.R. My Boss*. New York: Scribner's, 1949.

Turner, John Frayn, and Robert Jackson. *Destination Berchtesgaden*. New York: Scribner's, 1975.

Twain, Mark. *The Innocents Abroad*. New York: New American Library, 1980.

Urquhart, Brian. *A Life in Peace and War*. New York: Harper & Row, 1987.

Urquhart, R. E. *Arnhem*. New York: W. W. Norton, 1958.

The U.S. Army Corps of Engineers: A History. Alexandria, Va.: Office of History, Corps of Engineers, 2008.

Van Creveld, Martin. *Supplying War*. Cambridge, U.K.: Cambridge University Press, 1977.

Verney, G. L. *The Guards Armoured Division*. London: Hutchinson, 1955.

Vian, Philip. *Action This Day*. London: Frederick Miller, 1960.

Vigneras, Marcel. *Rearming the French. United States Army in World War II*. Washington, D.C.: Department of the Army, 1957.

Vining, Donald, ed. *American Diaries of World War II*. New York: Pepys Press, 1982.

Voss, Frederick S. *Reporting the War*. Washington, D.C.: Smithsonian Institution Press, 1994.

Waddell, Steve R. *United States Army Logistics: The Normandy Campaign, 1944*. Westport, Conn.: Greenwood Press, 1994.

Waddy, John. *A Tour of the Arnhem Battlefields*. Barnsley, U.K.: Leo Cooper, 1999.

Walker, Mark. *German National Socialism and the Quest for Nuclear Power, 1939–49*. New York: Cambridge University Press, 1993.

Waller, Douglas. *Wild Bill Donovan*. New York: Free Press, 2011.

Walter Laqueur, ed. *The Second World War*. London: Sage, 1982.

Wandrey, June. *Bedpan Commando*. Elmore, Ohio: Elmore Publishing, 1989.

Warlimont, Walter. *Inside Hitler's Headquarters*. Trans. R. H. Barry. Novato, Calif.: Presidio Press, 1964.

Warner, Philip. *Horrocks*. London: Hamish Hamilton, 1984.

Watney, John. *The Enemy Within*. London: Hodder and Stoughton, 1946.

Waugh, Evelyn. *Men at Arms*. New York: Penguin, 1964.

We Bought the Eiffel Tower: The Story of the General Purchasing Agent, European Theater. Paris, 1949.

Webster, Charles, and Noble Frankland. *The Strategic Air Offensive Against Germany, 1939–1945*. Vols. 3 and 4. London: Her Majesty's Stationery Office, 1961.

Weigley, Russell F. *The American Way of War*. Bloomington, Ind.: Indiana University Press, 1977.

———. *Eisenhower's Lieutenants*. Bloomington, Ind.: Indiana University Press, 1990.

———. *History of the United States Army*. Bloomington, Ind.: Indiana University Press, 1984.

Weinberg, Gerhard L. *A World at Arms*. Cambridge, U.K.: Cambridge University Press, 1995.

Weingartner, James J. *Crossroads of Death*. Berkeley: University of California Press, 1979.

Weintraub, Stanley. *11 Days in December*. New York: Free Press, 2006.

———. *15 Stars*. New York: Free Press, 2007.

Weiss, Robert. *Fire Mission*. Shippensburg, Pa.: Burd Street Press, 2002.

Wellard, James. *The Man in a Helmet*. London: Eyre & Spottiswoode, 1947.

Wertenbaker, Charles Christian. *Invasion!* New York: D. Appleton Century Co., 1944.

Westermann, Edward B. *Flak: German Anti-Aircraft Defenses, 1914–1945*. Lawrence, Kans.: University Press of Kansas, 2001.

Westphal, Siegfried. *The German Army in the West*. London: Cassell, 1951.

Wheeler, James Scott. *The Big Red One*. Lawrence, Kans.: University Press of Kansas, 2007.

Whitaker, Denis, and Shelagh Whitaker, with Terry Copp. *Victory at Falaise*. New York: HarperCollins, 2000.

White, Nathan William. *From Fedala to Berchtesgaden*. 1974.

White, Osmar. *Conquerors' Road*. New York: Cambridge University Press, 2003.

Whitehead, Don. *"Beachhead Don."* Ed. John B. Romeiser. New York: Fordham University Press, 2004.

Whitehead, Ernest D. *World War II: An Ex-Sergeant Remembers.* Kearney, Neb.: Morris Publishing, 1996.

Whiting, Charles. *The Home Front: Germany.* Alexandria, Va.: Time-Life Books, 1982.

Whitlock, Flint. *The Rock of Anzio.* Boulder, Colo.: Westview Press, 1998.

Wieviorka, Olivier. *Normandy.* Trans. M. B. DeBevoise. Cambridge, Mass.: Belknap Press, 2008.

Willis, F. Roy. *The French in Germany.* Stanford, Calif.: Stanford University Press, 1962.

Willmott, H. P. *The Great Crusade.* New York: Free Press, 1989.

Wills, Deryk. *Put on Your Boots and Parachutes!* S.p., 1992.

Wilmot, Chester. *The Struggle for Europe.* Old Saybrook, Conn.: Konecky & Konecky, 1952.

Wilson, Theodore A., ed. *D-Day 1944.* Lawrence, Kans.: University Press of Kansas, 1994.

Wilt, Alan F. *The French Riviera Campaign of August 1944.* Carbondale, Ill.: Southern Illinois University Press, 1981.

Wiltse, Charles M., ed. *Physical Standards in World War II.* Washington, D.C.: Office of the Surgeon General, 1967.

Winton, Harold R. *Corps Commanders of the Bulge.* Lawrence, Kans.: University Press of Kansas, 2007.

Wishnevsky, Stephen T. *Courtney Hicks Hodges.* Jefferson, N.C.: McFarland, 2006.

Wood, James A., ed. *Army of the West.* Mechanicsburg, Pa.: Stackpole Books, 2007.

Woodward, David. *Ramsay at War.* London: William Kimber, 1957.

World War II Diary of Jean Gordon Peltier. S.p., 1998.

The World War II Reader. New York: ibooks, 2004.

Wright, Robert K., Jr., and John T. Greenwood. *Airborne Forces at War.* Annapolis, Md.: Naval Institute Press, 2007.

Wyant, William K. *Sandy Patch: A Biography of Lt. Gen. Alexander M. Patch.* New York: Praeger, 1991.

Yeide, Harry. *The Longest Battle.* St. Paul, Minn.: Zenith Press, 2005.

Yeide, Harry, and Mark Stout. *First to the Rhine.* St. Paul, Minn.: Zenith Press, 2007.

Yhagapov, Mikhail, and Gennady Shekurov. *Greater Yalta.* Trans. Angelia Graf. Moscow: Novisti Press Agency, 1970.

Young, Desmond. *Rommel, the Desert Fox.* New York: Harper & Row, 1950.

Young, Norwood. *Napoleon in Exile: Elba.* Philadelphia: John C. Winston, 1914.

Yung, Christopher D. *Gators of Neptune.* Annapolis, Md.: Naval Institute Press, 2006.

Zaloga, Steven J. *Armored Thunderbolt.* Mechanicsburg, Pa.: Stackpole Books, 2008.

———. *Liberation of Paris 1944.* New York: Osprey, 2008.

———. *Remagen 1945.* New York: Osprey, 2006.

Zetterling, Niklas. *Normandy 1944.*Winnipeg: J. J. Fedorowicz, 2000.

Ziegler, Philip. *London at War, 1939–1945.* New York: Knopf, 1995.

Ziemke, Earl F. *The U.S. Army in the Occupation of Germany, 1944–1946.* Washington, D.C.: U.S. Army, 1975.

Zuckerman, Solly. *From Apes to Warlords.* New York: Harper & Row, 1978.

Zumbro, Derek S. *Battle for the Ruhr.* Lawrence, Kans.: University Press of Kansas, 2006.

PERIODICALS

Adams, Henry M. "Operations of an American Military Government Detachment in the Saar, 1944–45." *Military Affairs* (autumn 1955): 121+.

Allen, Thomas B. "Untold Stories of D-Day." *National Geographic* (June 2002): 2+.

"Arnhem." *AB*, no. 2 (1973): 1+.

Atkinson, Rick. "What Is Lost?" *World War II* (Nov. 2009): 32+.

Baily, Charles M., and Jay Karamales. "The 823rd at Mortain." *Armor* (Jan.–Feb. 1992): 12+.

Barker, Thomas M. "The Ljubljana Gap Strategy." *JMH* (Jan. 1992): 57+.

"The Battle of the Bulge." *AB*, no. 4 (1974): 1+.

"The Battle of the Falaise Pocket." *AB*, no. 8 (1975): +1.

Biddle, Tami Davis. "Dresden 1945: Reality, History, and Memory." *JMH* (Apr. 2008): 413+.

——. "Leveraging Strength: The Pillars of American Grand Strategy in World War II." *Orbis* (winter 2011): 4+.

Blumenson, Martin. "Bradley-Patton: World War II's 'Odd Couple.'" *Army* (Dec. 1985): 56+.

——. "The Hammelburg Affair." *Army* (Oct. 1965): 16+.

——. "Politics and the Military in the Liberation of Paris." *Parameters* (summer 1998): 4+.

Bolger, Daniel P. "Zero Defects: Command Climate in First U.S. Army, 1944–1945." *Military Review* (May 1991): 61+.

Bradbeer, Thomas G. "General Cota and the Battle of the Hürtgen Forest." *Army History* (spring 2010): 18+.

Bradsher, Greg. "Nazi Gold: The Merkers Mine Treasure." *Prologue: Quarterly of the National Archives and Records Administration* 31, no. 7 (spring 1999): 7+.

Bruenn, Howard G. "Clinical Notes on the Illness and Death of President Franklin D. Roosevelt." *Annals of Internal Medicine* 72 (1970): 579+.

Burns, James MacGregor. "FDR: The Untold Story of His Last Year." *Saturday Evening Post* (Apr. 11, 1970): 12+.

Butler, Frederic B. "Task Force Butler." *Armored Cavalry Journal*, part 1 (Jan.–Feb. 1948): 12+, and part 2 (March–Apr. 1948): 30+.

Carr, Caleb. "The American Rommel." *MHQ* (summer 1992): 77+.

Carroll, Andrew. "A Deserter Begs Eisenhower to Spare His Life." *World War II* (Jan.–Feb. 2012): 21+.

Cawthon, Charles R. "July, 1944: St. Lô." *American Heritage* (June 1974): 4+.

——. "Pursuit: Normandy, 1944." *American Heritage* (Feb. 1978): 80+.

Clarke, Bruce C. "The Battle for St. Vith." *Armor* (Nov.–Dec. 1974): 1+.

Cochran, Alexander S., Jr. "Protecting the Ultimate Advantage." *Military History* (June 1985): 45+.

"The Crimea and Potsdam Conferences of the Leaders of the Three Great Powers." *International Affairs*. All-Union Society, Moscow (June 1965).

D'Este, Carlo. "Raw Courage." *World War II* (July–Aug. 2011): 30+.

Davies, Arthur. "Geographical Factors in the Invasion and Battle of Normandy." *Geographical Review* (Oct. 1946): 613+.

"The Death of Joachim Peiper." *AB*, no. 40 (1983): 47+.

"Destroy the Enemy." *Time* (Dec. 4, 1944).

"Doughboy's General." *Time* (May 1, 1944): 23+.

Dziuban, Stanley W. "Rhine River Flood Prediction Service." *Military Engineer* (Sept. 1945): 348+.

Eckelmeyer, Edward H., Jr. "The Story of the Self-Sealing Tank." *U.S. Naval Institute Proceedings* (Feb. 1946): 205+.

Eddy, Don. "Treasure of Our Heroes." *American Magazine* (Apr. 1944): 44+.

"The Execution of Eddie Slovik." *AB*, no. 32 (1981): 28+.

Fest, William R. "The German Ardennes Offensive: A Study in Retrograde Logistics." *Ordnance* (Feb. 1983): 51+.

Foedrowitz, Michael. "Air Raid Shelters in Hannover." *AB*, no. 124 (2004): 2+.

Fox, William T. R. "The Super-Powers Then and Now." *International Journal* (summer 1980): 417+.

Frank, Stanley. "The Glorious Collapse of the 106th." *Saturday Evening Post* (Nov. 9, 1946).

Ganz, H. Harding. "The 11th Panzers in the Defense, 1944." *Armor* (March–Apr. 1944): 26+.

——. "Patton's Relief of General Wood." *JMH* (July 1989): 257+.

——. "Questionable Objective: The Brittany Ports, 1944." *JMH* (Jan. 1995): 77+.

Gardner, W. J. R. "The Death of Admiral Ramsay." *AB*, no. 87 (1995): 44+.

Gaskill, Gordon. "Bloody Beach." *American Magazine* (Sept. 1944): 26+.

"German Surrenders." *AB*, no. 48 (1985): 1+.

Geyr, Leo Freiherr von Schweppenburg. "Reflections on the Invasion." *Military Review* (Jan. 1961): 2+.

Gurley, Franklin Louis. "Policy Versus Strategy." *JMH* (July 1994): 481+.

Hamilton, Maxwell. "Junior in Name Only." *Retired Officer* (June 1981): 28+.

Hammon, Stratton. "When the Second Lieutenant Bearded General Eisenhower." *Military Affairs* (Oct. 1983): 129+.

Hansen, C. B. "General Bradley as Seen Close Up." *New York Times Magazine* (Nov. 30, 1947): 14+.

Harris, Arthur R. "The Bigger They Are the Harder They Fall." *Field Artillery Journal* (May–June 1938): 229+ .

Hauser, Ernest O. "Shock Nurse." *Saturday Evening Post* (March 10, 1945): 12+.

Heinz, W. C. "I Took My Son to Omaha Beach." *Collier's* (June 11, 1954): 21+.

———. "The Morning They Shot the Spies." *True* (Dec. 1949): 28+.

Hewitt, H. Kent. "Planning Operation Anvil-Dragoon." *U.S. Naval Institute Proceedings* (July–Aug. 1954): 731+.

Hillson, Franklin J. "Barrage Balloons for Low-Level Air Defense." *Airpower Journal* (summer 1989), 37+.

"Hitler's Höllenfahrt." *Der Spiegel* (Apr. 10, 1995): 172+.

Hogben, Lawrence. "The Most Important Weather Forecast in the World." *London Review of Books* 16, no. 10 (May 26, 1994): 21+.

Holland, Carolsue, and Thomas Rothbart. "The Merkers and Buchenwald Treasure Troves." *AB*, no. 93 (1996): 1+.

Houghton, Norris, "That Was Yalta." *New Yorker* (May 23, 1953): 86+.

Hubler, Richard G. "He Doesn't Want to Be a Star." *Saturday Evening Post* (Apr. 18, 1953): 34+.

Hughes, Walter E. "A Bridge Enough." *World War II* (Nov./Dec. 2012): 64+.

Huntington, Tom. "Lights. Camera. War!" *America in World War II* (June 2008): 34+.

"Inside Paris." *Newsweek* (Aug. 28, 1944): 25+.

Jenkins, Reuben E. "The Battle of the National Redoubt." *Military Review* (Dec. 1946): 3+.

Kennedy, Paul. "History from the Middle: The Case of the Second World War." *JMH* (Jan. 2010): 35+.

Lasky, Melvin. "Military History Stood on Its Head." *Berlin Journal* 14 (spring 2007), American Academy of Berlin: 20+.

Leh, John, II. "World War II from One Enlisted Man's Point of View." *Proceedings of the Lehigh County Historical Society* 39 (1990): 89+.

Liebling, A. J. "Five-Star Schoolmaster." *New Yorker* (March 10, 1951): 40+.

Lilly, J. Robert. "U.S. Military Executions." *AB*, no. 90 (1995): 50+.

"The Ludendorff Railway Bridge." *AB*, no. 16 (1977): 2+.

MacDonald, Charles B. "The Neglected Ardennes." *Military Review* (Apr. 1963): 74+.

———. "Slapton Sands: The 'Cover-Up' That Never Was." *Army* 38, no. 6 (June 1998): 64+.

Mackay, E. M. "The Battle of Arnhem Bridge." *Royal Engineer Journal* (Dec. 1954): 305+.

Mallon, Thomas. "Rocket Man." *New Yorker* (Oct. 22, 2007): 170+.

"Man of the Year." *Time* (Jan. 1, 1945): cover.

"The Man Who Paved the Way." *Time* (June 12, 1944): 23+.

Margry, Karel. "The Battle for Cologne." *AB*, no. 104 (1999): 2+.

———. "Battle of the Hürtgen Forest." *AB*, no. 171 (1991): 1+.

———. "Bergen-Belsen." *AB*, no. 89 (1995): 1+.

———. "The Death of Rommel." *AB*, no. 80 (1993): 38+.

———. "The Flensburg Government." *AB*, no. 128 (2005): 2+.

———. "The Gardelegen Massacre." *AB*, no. 111 (2001): 2+.

———. "The Hammelburg Raid." *AB*, no. 91 (1996): 1+.

———. "The U.S.-Soviet Link-Up." *AB*, no. 88 (1995): 1+.

Marshall, S. L. A. "The Mobility of One Man." *IJ* (Oct. 1949): 6+.

McCreedy, Kenneth O. "Planning the Peace: Operation Eclipse and the Occupation of Germany." *JMH* (July 2001): 713+.

Middleton, Drew. "Boss of the Heavyweights." *Saturday Evening Post* (May 20, 1944): 18+.

Milner, Marc. "Stopping the Panzers." *JMH* (Apr. 2010): 491+.

"Miracle of Supply." *Time* (Sept. 25, 1944): 8+.

Mollo, Andrew. "Dachau." *AB*, no. 27 (1980): 1+.

"Monty's Wartime Caravans." *AB*, no. 20 (1978): 32+.

Moore, Rufus J. "Operation Pluto." *U.S. Naval Institute Proceedings* (June 1954): 647+.

Morton, Harold S. "The VT Fuze." *Army Ordnance* (Jan.–Feb. 1946): 43+.

Mosely, Philip E. "Dismemberment of Germany." *Foreign Affairs* (Apr. 1950): 487+.

———. "The Occupation of Germany." *Foreign Affairs* (July 1950): 580+.

Muller, Richard R. "Losing Air Superiority: A Case Study from the Second World War." *Air & Space Power Journal* (winter 2003): 55+.

"Murder, Inc." *Time* (Sept. 11, 1944): 36.

Murray, Williamson. "Needless D-Day Slaughter." *MHQ* (spring 2003): 26+.

"Normandy, 1944–1973." *AB*, no. 1 (1973): 2.

"Normandy Executions." *AB*, no. 85 (1994): 28+.

"Obersalzburg." *AB*, no. 9 (1975): 1+.

"The Old Army Game." *Time* (Jan. 1, 1945): 45.

Olsen, C. E. "Full House at Yalta." *American Heritage* (Jan. 1972): 1+.

Osborne, Jim R. "Return to the Berghof." *AB*, no. 60 (1988): 50+.

Ose, Dieter. "Rommel and Rundstedt: The 1944 Panzer Controversy." *Military Affairs* (Jan. 1986): 7+.

Pallud, Jean Paul. "The Battle of the Mons Pocket." *AB*, no. 115 (2002): 2+.

———. "The Riviera Landings." *AB*, no. 110 (2000): 2+.

"Paris." *AB*, no. 14 (1976): 11+.

"Paris Is Free!" *Time* (Sept. 4, 1944): 34+.

"Patch of Provence." *Time* (Aug. 28, 1944): 22+.

"Pegasus and the Wyvern." *Royal Engineers Journal* (March 1946): 22+.

Perloff, Marjorie. "In Love with Hiding." *Iowa Review* (2005): 82.

Persons, Howard P., Jr. "St. Lô Breakthrough." *Military Review* (Dec. 1948): 13+.

Peszke, Michael Aldred. "The Polish Parachute Brigade in World War II." *Military Affairs* (Oct. 1984): 188+.

"Pluto: Pipeline Under the Ocean." *AB*, no. 116 (2002): 2+.

Powers, Stephen T. "The Battle of Normandy: The Lingering Controversy." *JMH* (July 1992): 455+.

"Precise Puncher." *Time* (Oct. 16, 1944): cover.

"The Presidency." *Time* (May 8, 1944): 8.

Raiber, R. "The Führerhauptquartiere." *AB*, no. 19 (1977): 1+.

"Ready for V-Day?" *Time* (Sept. 4, 1944): 17.

Reed, John. "Assault on Walcheren." *AB*, no. 36 (1982): 1+.

Rely, Achiel. "Antwerp 'City of Sudden Death.'" *AB*, no. 57 (1987): 43+.

Rivette, Donald E. "The Hot Corner at Dom Bütgenbach." *IJ* (Oct. 1945): 19+.

"Rommel's Accident." *AB*, no. 8 (1975): 42+.

Rosenbaum, Ron. "Explaining Hitler." *New Yorker* (May 1, 1995): 50+.

Rosengarten, Adolph G., Jr. "With Ultra from Omaha Beach to Weimar, Germany." *Military Affairs* (Oct. 1978): 127+.

Schaffer, Richard. "American Military Ethics in World War II: The Bombing of German Civilians." *Journal of American History* (Sept. 1980): 318+.

Seaman, Jonathan O. "Reduction of the Colmar Pocket." *Military Review* (Oct. 1951): 37+.

Snyder, William P. "Walter Bedell Smith: Eisenhower's Chief of Staff." *Military Affairs* (Jan. 1984): 6+.

Sommers, Martin. "The Longest Hour in History." *Saturday Evening Post* (July 8, 1944): 22+.

Steckel, Francis C. "Morale Problems in Combat." *Army History* (summer 1994): 1+.

Stone, Thomas R. "General William Hood Simpson: Unsung Commander of U.S. Ninth Army." *Parameters* 9, no. 2 (June 1981): 44+.

Strobridge, Truman R., and Bernard C. Nalty. "From the South Pacific to the Brenner Pass: General Alexander M. Patch." *Military Review* (June 1981): 41+.

Sullivan, John J. "The Botched Air Support of Operation COBRA." *Parameters* (March 1988): 97+.

Teulings, Ad. "Structure and Logic of Industrial Development: Philips and Electronics Industry." *Social Scientist* 9, no. 4 (Nov. 1979): 3+.

"The V-Weapons." *AB*, no. 6 (1974): 2+.

Wacker, Bob. "The Voices of D-Day." *Retired Officer* (June 1994): 26+.

Weigley, Russell F. "From the Normandy Beaches to the Falaise-Argentan Pocket." *Military Review* (Sept. 1990): 45+.

Weingartner, James J. "Otto Skorzeny and the Laws of War." *JMH* (Apr. 1991): 207+.

Weiss, Robert. "Normandy: Recollections of the 'Lost Battalion' at the Battle of Mortain." *Prologue: Quarterly of the National Archives and Records Administration* (spring 1996): 44+.

Wendt, W. W. "Logistics in Retrograde Movements." *Military Review* (July 1948): 34+.

Whipple, William. "Logistical Bottleneck." *IJ* (March 1948): 6+.

Whitaker, Richard. "Task Force Baum and the Hammelburg Raid." *Armor* (Sept.–Oct. 1996): 20+.

Williams, Clifford. "Supreme Headquarters for D-Day." *AB*, no. 84 (1994): 1+.

Willoughby, John. "The Sexual Behavior of American GIs During the Early Years of the Occupation of Germany." *JMH* (Jan. 1998): 155+.

"Winston Churchill Visits the Rhine." *AB*, no. 16 (1977): 28+.

"World Battlefronts, Western Front." *Time* (Dec. 4, 1944): 1+.

Yeide, Harry. "The German View of Patton." *World War II* (March–Apr. 2012): 27+.

Yung, Christopher D. "Action This Day." *Naval History* (June 2009): 20+.

———. "The Planners' Daunting Task." *Naval History* (June 2009): 12+.

NEWSPAPERS

"After WWII, Economist Devoted Life." Obit, *Washington Post*, July 8, 2009, B4.

Altman, Lawrence K. "For F.D.R. Sleuths, New Focus on an Old Spot." *New York Times*, Jan. 5, 2010, D1.

Antrobus, Edmund. "V-2 in Antwerp." *Yank*, May 4, 1945, 6+.

Atkinson, Rick. "Ghost of a Chanteuse." *Washington Post*, May 7, 1996.

Burns, John F. "Bill Millin, Scottish D-Day Piper, Dies at 88." *New York Times*, Aug. 19, 2010, B9.

"Caen: The Big Break-Through." *Daily Mail* (U.K.), July 19, 1944, 1.

"Crashing Bomber Wipes Out Nearly All a Village's 4 to 6 Children." *Daily Express* (U.K.), Aug. 24, 1944, 3.

Crouch, Gregory. "Frederik Philips Dies at 100; Businessman Saved Dutch Jews." *New York Times*, Dec. 7, 2005.

Daley, Robert. "The Case of the SS Hero." *New York Times*, Nov. 7, 1976.

Ecker, Allan B. "G.I. Racketeers in the Paris Black Market." *Yank*, May 4, 1945, 2.

Foreman, Jonathan. "Winston Churchill, Distilled." *Wall Street Journal*, Dec. 10, 2009, D6.

"Honoring Those Fallen Who Served." Aurora (Ill.) *Beacon News*, Apr. 12, 2005, B2.

Kaufman, Leslie. "Chester Hansen, 95, a Rare Diarist of World War II." *New York Times*, Oct. 29, 2012, D8.

"Kingsway Wins at Ascot." *Times* (London), May 15, 1944.

Kissinger, Henry A. "The Age of Kennan," review of John Lewis Gaddis, *George F. Kennan: An American Life*, New York Times Book Review, Nov. 13, 2011.

Millership, Peter. "Scots Piper Dodged Bullets." Reuters, June 1, 1994.

Montgomery, Lori. "The Cost of War, Unnoticed." *Washington Post*, May 8, 2007, D1.

Moriss, Mack. "The Defense of Stavelot." *Yank*, Feb. 9, 1945, 8+.

Nappi, Rebecca. "War Hero Enriches Soul History." Spokane, Wash., *Spokesman-Review*, Aug. 14, 2004.

Pearson, Drew. "Washington Merry-Go-Round." Apr. 29, 1944.

"Plane Kills 35 Infants in School." *Daily Telegraph* (U.K.), Aug. 24, 1944, 3.

Raitberger, François. "French Remember D-Day Landings." Reuters, May 18, 1994.

Reavis, Ed. "Crossing of Rhine Remembered." *Stars and Stripes*, March 8, 1995, 1.
Roche, John P. "Eisenhower Redux." *New York Times Book Review*, June 28, 1981.
"Rommel's Death Reported." *Argus* (Melbourne, Australia), Aug. 23, 1944, 16.
Schudel, Matt. "General Witnessed History at Nazi Camp, Panama Canal." *Washington Post*, Aug. 7, 2012, B6.
Vat, Dan van der. "Field Marshal Lord Carver." Obit, *Guardian* (U.K.), Dec. 12, 2001.
"W. C. Heinz, 93, Writing Craftsman, Dies." *New York Times*, Feb. 28, 2008.
Weil, Martin. "Gen. Jacob Devers Dies; Leader in World War II." *Washington Post*, Oct. 1979.
Yardley, Jonathan. "The Fight of Their Lives, and Not Just on the Battlefield." *Washington Post*, March 6, 2009, C1.

PAPERS, LETTERS, COLLECTIONS, PERSONAL NARRATIVES, AND DIARIES

Dwight D. Eisenhower Presidential Library, Abilene, Kans.: Henry S. Aurand Papers; Harold R. Bull Papers; Harry C. Butcher Papers; A. Dayton Clark Papers; J. Lawton Collins Papers; Norman D. Cota Papers; Robert C. Davie Papers; Dwight D. Eisenhower Papers; Alvan C. Gillem, Jr., Papers; Courtney H. Hodges Papers; C. D. Jackson Papers; Thomas B. Larkin Papers; Thomas W. Mattingly Papers; Arthur Nevins Papers; Floyd S. Parks Papers; Henry B. Sayler Papers; Walter Bedell Smith Papers; Barbara Wyden Papers

Franklin D. Roosevelt Presidential Library, Hyde Park, N.Y.: Edward J. Flynn Papers; Anna Roosevelt Halsted Papers; Map Room conferences; Ross T. McIntire Papers; Franklin D. Roosevelt Papers; U.S. Secret Service records

George C. Marshall Foundation Research Library, Lexington, Va.: Harold S. Frum, "The Soldier Must Write"; George C. Marshall Papers; Frank McCarthy Collection; Royce L. Thompson Collection; Lucian K. Truscott, Jr., Papers

Hoover Institution Archives, Stanford University, Palo Alto, Calif.: Henry J. Amy Papers; Frederick L. Anderson Papers; Kingsley Andersson Papers; William Henry Baumer Papers; Heber Blankenhorn Papers; Robert D. Burhans Papers; Howard V. Canan Papers; Don E. Carleton Papers; Darrell William Coates Papers; Thomas L. Crystal, Jr., Papers; Robert T. Frederick Papers; Harold S. Frum Papers; Hermann Goering Papers; Norman D. King Papers; John H. Linden Papers; Robert M. Littlejohn Papers; Craig W. H. Luther Papers; James B. Mason Papers; Donald McClure Papers; Walter J. Muller Papers; Boris T. Pash Papers; George Smith Patton Papers; James H. Phillips Papers; Ewart G. Plank Papers; J. Milnor Roberts, Jr., Papers; Frank S. Ross Papers; Thor M. Smith Papers; Langan W. Swent Papers; Pierre C. T. Verheye Papers; Helen Van Zonneveld Papers

Imperial War Museum, London: William Steel Brownlie, "And Came Safe Home"; Christopher "Kit" Dawnay Papers; S. C. Donnison diary; Edward M. Elliott, "Combat Diary of Edward McCosh Elliott, 1944"; E. Jones Papers; K. G. Oakley, "Normandy 'D' Day 1944"; J. H. Patterson Papers; L. F. Skinner, "The Man Who Worked on Sundays"; N. T. Tangye diary; John M. Thorpe, "A Soldier's Tale, to Normandy and Beyond"

Library of Congress, Manuscript Division, Washington, D.C.: Charles E. Bohlen Papers; Wallace Carroll Papers; Ira Eaker Papers; Truman K. Gibson Papers; W. Averell Harriman Papers; H. Kent Hewitt Papers; Everett S. Hughes Papers; Ernest J. King Papers; William D. Leahy Papers; George S. Patton, Jr., Papers; Theodore Roosevelt, Jr., Papers; Carl A. Spaatz Papers; John Toland Papers; Hoyt S. Vandenberg Papers

Liddell Hart Centre for Military Archives, King's College, London: Lord Alanbrooke Papers; J. B. Churcher, "A Soldier's Story"; Francis de Guingand Papers; Geoffrey Hardy-Roberts Papers; H. L. Ismay Papers; B. H. Liddell Hart Papers; T. G. Lindsay, "Operation Overlord Plus"; J. S. W. Stone Papers; R. W. W. "Chester" Wilmot Papers

McCormick Research Center, First Division Museum, Cantigny, Ill.: Joseph T. Dawson Collection; Theodore L. Dobol Collection; Stanhope Brasfield Mason Papers

Miscellany: Jack Golden letters; Robert P. Patterson, memoir, a.p.

National World War II Museum, New Orleans, La.: Alan Anderson Papers; Cyrus C. Aydlett diary; W. Garwood Bacon Papers; Leland A. Baker Papers; John Barnes Papers; Eugene D. Brierre Papers; Dwayne Burns Papers; John Cappell Papers; Carl Cartledge Papers; Charles M. Cooke, Jr., Papers; Willard F. Coonen Papers; Ralph Eastridge Papers; Mary Ferrell Papers; P. L. Fitts Papers; Robert Fullam memoir; Robert M. Gant Papers; Robert D. Georgen Papers; Wayne M. Harris Papers; Harold L. Hoffer Papers; John Lambourne Papers; Joseph T. Layne and Glenn D. Barquest, "Margraten: U.S. Ninth Army Military Cemetery"; Archie Ross Papers; Sid Rowling Papers; William P. Shaw memoir

Naval History and Heritage Command, Washington, D.C.: H. Kent Hewitt Papers; Samuel Eliot Morison Papers

New York State Library, Albany, N.Y.: Myra Strachner Gershkoff Papers

Ohio University Library, Athens, Ohio: Cornelius J. Ryan Papers

29th Infantry Division Archives, Maryland Military Department, Fifth Regiment Armory, Baltimore, Md.: Neal Beaver, memoir; Charles Hunter Gerhardt Papers; William Puntenney, memoir; John C. Raaen, Jr., "Sir, the 5th Rangers Have Landed Intact"; Seth Shepard, "The Story of the *LCI(L) 92*"; Robert E. Walker, "With the Stonewallers"

U.S. Army Corps of Engineers, Office of History, Ft. Belvoir, Va.: William A. Carter memoirs; William M. Hoge memoirs; William E. Potter memoirs

U.S. Army Military Academy Special Collections, West Point, N.Y.: John W. Castles, Jr., Papers; Earle C. Cheek Papers; George Bryan Conrad Papers; Garrison H. Davidson Papers; Benjamin A. Dickson Papers; Charles L. Easter Papers; Audie Leon Murphy Papers; Alexander M. Patch, Jr., Papers

U.S. Army Military History Institute, Carlisle, Pa.: Robert W. Black Papers; Omar N. Bradley Papers; Richard H. Byers Papers; Hugh Cole Papers; Richard Collins Papers; Columbus World War II Roundtable Papers; John Connell Papers; Theodore J. Conway Papers; Charles H. Corlett Papers; Raymond H. Croll Papers; Donald E. Currier Papers; John E. Dahlquist Papers; Maurice Delaval Papers; Harold C. Deutsch Papers; Jacob L. Devers Papers; Benjamin A. Dickson Papers; Charles H. Donnelly Papers; Sheffield Edwards Papers; Samuel W. Forgy Papers; James M. Gavin Papers; Hobart Gay Papers; Charles Hunter Gerhardt, memoir; Alvan Cullem Gillem, Jr., Papers; Wade H. Haislip Papers; Chester B. Hansen Papers; Robert W. Hasbrouck Papers; Paul R. Hawley Papers; Waldo Heinrichs, Jr., Papers; Courtney H. Hodges Papers; Thaddeus Holt Papers; William T. Hornaday Papers; Herndon Inge, Jr., Papers; Reuben E. Jenkins Papers; Alan W. Jones Papers; Albert W. Kenner Papers; Brooks Kleber Papers; Oscar W. Koch Papers; John C. H. Lee Papers; Charles B. MacDonald Papers; S. L. A. Marshall Papers; Frank J. McSherry Papers; James E. Moore Papers; Raymond G. Moses Papers; Samuel L. Myers Papers; Sidney H. Negrotto Papers; Arthur S. Nevins Papers; Frank A. Osmanski Papers; Floyd Lavinius Parks Papers; Forrest C. Pogue Papers; Harold E. Potter Papers; D. K. Reimers, "My War"; Matthew B. Ridgway Papers; Pleas B. Rogers Papers; Charles E. Rousek Papers; Howard J. Silbar Papers; William H. Simpson Papers; Thor M. Smith Papers; William S. Triplet Papers; James A. Van Fleet Papers; Numa A. Watson Papers

Yale University Library, Manuscript and Archives: Hanson Baldwin Papers

York County Heritage Trust, York, Pa.: Jacob L. Devers Papers

Interview, Questionnaire, and Oral History Transcripts

Author interviews: Garfield Brown; Steve Bull Bear; Paul Fussell; Walter Grabowski; Hans-Jürgen Habenicht; Ralph Hauenstein; Harry W. O. Kinnard; Leonard G. Lommell; Hans von Luck; Rosemarie Meitzner; Rich Porter; Delmar Richards; Estil Robertson; James M. Wilson, Jr.

Columbia University, Oral History Research Office, New York, N.Y.: H. Kent Hewitt; Alan Goodrich Kirk

Combined Arms Research Library, Ft. Leavenworth, Kans.: J. Lawton Collins

Cornelius J. Ryan Collection, Ohio University, Athens, Ohio: William A. B. Addison; Virgil F. Carmichael; Julian A. Cook; Dwight D. Eisenhower; Theodore Finkbeiner, Jr.; James M. Gavin; Alvan C. Gillem, Jr.; Averell Harriman; John E. Hull; Harry W. O. Kinnard; Ivan S. Koniev; Albert L. Kotzebue; Anthony C. McAuliffe; Philip E. Mosely; Eddie Newbury; Paul L. Ransom; Francis L. Sampson; William H. Simpson; Robert Sink; Kenneth Strong; Robert M. Tallon; Maxwell Taylor; Reuben H. Tucker; Brian Urquhart; Giles A. M. Vandeleur; John Whiteley; Robert H. Wienecke

Dwight D. Eisenhower Presidential Library, Abilene, Kans.: Jacob L. Devers; Dwight D. Eisenhower; LeRoy Lutes; Lauris Norstad

Emory University, Fred Roberts Crawford Witness to the Holocaust Project, Atlanta, Ga.: William R. Barton; Kenneth Bowers; Philip Carlquist; Daniel Cogar

Hoover Institution Archives, Stanford University, Palo Alto, Calif.: Frederic B. Bates; Dixon M. Raymond

Library of Congress, Veterans History Project, American Folklife Center, Washington, D.C.: William Fordham; Patrick Fordney; Gale E. Garman; Ray Goad; Robert Hagopian; Roy Haserodt; Albert Hassenzahl; Joseph Hecht; Edwin Kelmel; Orus Kinney, "Nazi Smart Bombs"; George W. Knapp; Irvin Seelye

Liddell Hart Centre for Military Archives, King's College, London: Miles Dempsey, E. J. Foord Papers

National Archive, Kew, United Kingdom: Miles Dempsey

National Archives and Records Administration, College Park, Md.

"Hospital Interviews," *RG 407*: William A. Anderson; Samuel E. Belk, III; Kenneth K. Bladorn; William A. Boykin; R. H. Brown; Charles M. Bulap; W. A. Burkholder; Jack P. Carroll; Arthur B. Clark; Bernard Coggins; Lynn Compton; Gilbert R. Cook; Charles R. Crispin; Robert M. Dasbro; Joseph Dorchak; John P. Dube; Stanley G. Emert; Charles B. Freeman; R. Harwick; John Hayduchok; Francis Healy; Warren G. Holmes; David M. Hull; Anthony N. Hutchison; William L. Johnston; Stanley G. Kowlacwiski; J. N. Kreil; Kenneth E. Lay; Bernard Lipford; A. W. Loring; H. V. Lyon; P. W. J. Malloy; Donald E. Martini; Rudolph Mongrandi; Harold J. Morse; James H. Nelson; Nelson W. Noyes; Edward V. Ott; Eugene H. Pruett; Oliver E. Reed; George M. Rhodes; Robert J. Ritter; Elmer Rohmiller; Ernest Rothemberger; George R. Sedberry; Anthony R. Seymour; Ernest D. Shacklett; Warren A. Smart; R. G. Smith; Stanfield Stach; Louis L. Toth; C. A. Wollmer

Siegfried Line Campaign interviews, RG 319: R. F. Akers; Omar N. Bradley; Harold R. Bull; J. Lawton Collins; Truman C. Thorson; Walter B. Smith

National World War II Museum, New Orleans, La.: Leonard G. Lommell

Rutgers Oral History Archive of World War II, New Brunswick, N.J.: Lee Eli Barr; Edward J. Barry; Edward Bautz; Andre Beaumont; Werner Carl Berger; Robert Billian; James B. Carlaw; Andrew J. Ciampa; Russell W. Cloer; Albert Handaly; Andrew White

University of Florida, WWII Oral History Collection, Samuel F. Proctor Archive, Department of History: Glynn Markham; Bernard Mellman; William F. Roberts; Robert W. Schwaegerl

U.S. Army Corps of Engineers, Office of History, Ft. Belvoir, Va.: Garrison H. Davidson; Franklin F. Snyder

U.S. Army Military History Institute, Carlisle, Pa.

Forrest C. Pogue interviews: Field Marshal Viscount Alanbrooke; Ray W. Barker; David Belchem; C. H. Bonesteel; Omar N. Bradley; A. M. Cameron; Arthur Coningham; Robert W. Crawford; George E. Creasy; Viscount Cunningham; J. Curtis; Charles de Gaulle; Charles Miles Dempsey; B. A. Dickson; Manton Eddy; Humphrey Gale; James Gault; T. P. Gleave; A. E. Grasset; J. Hughes Hallett; Hastings L. Ismay; Alphonse Pierre Juin; Albert Kenner; J. C. H. Lee; Robert Bruce Lockhart; Kenneth R. McClaen; R. A. McClure; Alan Moorehead; Frederick E. Morgan; Bernard Paget; Viscount Portal; James M. Robb; Adolph Rosengarten, Jr.; Leslie Scarman; J. A. Sinclair; Walter Bedell Smith; Lord Tedder; Ford Trimble; C. H. H. Vulliamy; Charles A. West; J. F. M. Whiteley; Philip Wigglesworth; E. T. Williams

Miscellany: Charles L. Bolte; Omar N. Bradley; H. R. Bull; Dwight D. Eisenhower; Francis de Guingand; Hasso von Manteuffel; Bernard L. Montgomery; Walter B. Smith
Also: *Army Service Experiences Questionnaires*
Senior Officer Oral History Program: Paul D. Adams; Henry S. Aurand; Charles H. Bonesteel, III; Andrew J. Boyle; J. Lawton Collins; Richard Collins; Theodore J. Conway; William E. Depuy; William R. Desobry; George I. Forsythe; James M. Gavin; Hobart Gay; Leonard D. Heaton; John A. Heintges; Mildred Lee Hodges; John E. Hull; Brooks Kleber; Harry Lemley; S. L. A. Marshall; James E. Moore; Charles G. Patterson; Matthew B. Ridgway; J. Milnor Roberts, Jr.; William H. Simpson; Maxwell D. Taylor; James A. Van Fleet; Russell L. Vittrup; John K. Waters; James K. Woolnough
York County Heritage Trust, York, Pa.: Jacob L. Devers; Ira C. Eaker; Reuben Jenkins; Henry Cabot Lodge; Anthony McAuliffe

MISCELLANY

Allen, J. L. "Electronics Warfare." Lecture, Sept. 21, 1944, NARA RG 334, E 315, ANSCOL, L-7-44.

Amy, H. J. Lecture, Apr. 8, 1944. NY Port of Embarkation, HIA, Henry J. Amy papers, box 2.

"Between Collaboration and Resistance: French Literary Life Under Nazi Occupation." New York Public Library. Exhibition, June 2009.

Bollinger, Martin J. "Warriors and Wizards: The Development and Defeat of Radio-Controlled Bombs of the Third Reich." 2010, a.p.

Bynell, H. D. "Logistical Planning and Operations—Europe." Lecture, March 16, 1945. NARA RG 334, E 315, ANSCOL, box 207.

Cirillo, Roger. "The Allied High Command." Lecture, n.d. British Army Doctrine and Development Directorate.

———. "Ardennes-Alsace." Pamphlet, n.d., U.S. Army Campaigns of World War II. CMH, pub 72-26.

Conway, T. J. "Operation Anvil." Lecture, n.d., Norfolk, Va., Theodore J. Conway papers, MHI, box 2.

Daniel, Derrill M. "The Capture of Aachen." Lecture, n.d., Quantico, Va.

"Defense of Antwerp Against the V-1," film, 1947, http://www.archive.org/details/gov.dod.dimoc.20375.

Domes, Peter. Hammelburg Raid Reconstruction, http://taskforcebaum.de/schedule/schedule%20us.html.

Dowling, George B. Lecture, Feb. 28, 1945. NARA RG 334, E 315, ANSCOL, box 207.

Earle, Edward Mead. "Selection of Strategic Bombing Targets." Lecture, Apr. 23, 1946, NARA RG 334, E 315, ANSCOL, box 235.

"Early Measures at Belsen." Lecture, June 4, 1945, Royal Society of Medicine, UK NA, WO 219/3944A.

Foreign Workers Programs. Radio Luxembourg collection, HIA, box 1.

"4ID Update." Vol. 5, no. 47, June 6, 2011, http://parentsofdeployed.homestead.com/2011Jun06.html

"Freckleton Air Disaster of 1944," BBC News, Aug. 7, 2009, http://news.bbc.co.uk/local/lancashire/hi/people_and_places/history/newsid_8189000/8189386.stm.

"Gardelegen Massacre, 13 April 1945." www.scrapbookpages.com/GerhardThiele.

Gilland, Morris W. "Logistical Support for the Combat Zone." Lecture, 1948, Engineer Officers Advance Course, NARA RG 319, *LSA* background file, 2-3.7 CB 6.

Greear, W. H. "Operation Neptune and Landing on Coast of Southern France." Lecture, Nov. 1944, NARA RG 334, E 315, ANSCOL, box 199.

Gurley, Franklin Louis. "Policy Versus Strategy: The Defense of Strasbourg in Dec. 1944."

Trans. from *Guerres Mondiales et Conflits Contemporains*, 1992, NARA RG 319, *RR* background files FRC 5.

Hewitt, H. K. "The Navy in the European Theater of Operations in World War II." Lecture, Naval War College, Jan. 4–7, 1947.

Hickling, H., and I. L. H. Mackillop. "The OVERLORD Artificial Harbors." Lecture, Nov. 6, 1944, CARL, N-12217.

"History of Medical Service in the European Theater." Tape transcript, Oct. 1962, MHI

Howard, C. F. Lecture, Aug. 8, 1944. NARA RG 334, E 315, ANSCOL, L-6-44, H-83, box 191.

Kappes, Irwin J. "Hitler's Ultra-Secret Adlerhorst." 2003, http://www.militaryhistoryonline .com/wwii/articles/adlerhorst.aspx.

Leppert, J. L. "Communication Plans and Lessons, Europe and Africa." Lecture, Oct. 30, 1944. NARA RG 334, E 315, ANSCOL, box 199, L-7-44.

Lewis, M. L. "Landing Craft." Lecture, Sept. 18, 1944. NARA RG 334, E 315, ANSCOL, box 199.

Littlejohn, Robert M., ed., "Passing in Review." M.d., MHI

"Malmédy Massacre Investigation." U.S. Senate Armed Services Committee, Oct. 1949.

"Notes on Task Force Baum, Narrative of Capt. Baum." N.d., National World War II Museum archives, New Orleans.

Ogden, R. J. "Meteorological Services Leading to D-Day." Royal Meteorological Society, Occasional Papers on Meteorological History, July 2001.

OH video, I&R platoon, 394th Inf, 99th ID. Compiled by the National World War II Museum, New Orleans, 2008.

"The Operations of 21 Army Group." 1946, CARL, N-133331.

Pogue, Forrest C. "The Ardennes Campaign: The Impact of Intelligence." Lecture, Dec. 16, 1980, NSA Communications Analysis Association, a.p.

Quesada, E. R. "Operations of the Ninth Tactical Air Command." Lecture, May 29, 1945, NARA RG 334, E 315, ANSCOL, L-10-45.

Sibert, Edwin L. "Military Intelligence Aspects of the Period Prior to the Ardennes Counter Offensive." Jan. 2, 1947, CBM, MHI, box 6.

Signal Corps footage, http://www.criticalpast.com/video/65675070150_General-Eisenhower _Omar-Bradley_Bernard-Montgomery_World-War-II.

Stoler, Mark A. "The Second World War in U.S. History and Memory." International Historical Congress, Oslo, Aug. 12, 2000.

Striner, Richard A. "Eisenhower's Triumph: The Guildhall Address of 1945." American Veterans Center, http://www.americanveteranscenter.org/magazine/avq/issue-vi-spring summer-2009/eisenhower%e2%80%99s-triumph-the-guildhall-address-of-1945/.

Walden, Geoffrey R. http://www.thirdreichruins.com/obersalzberg.htm.

Weinberg, Gerhard L. "The Place of World War II in History." Lecture, 1995, U.S. Air Force Academy, Colorado Springs, Colo.

ACKNOWLEDGMENTS

So there. Fourteen years after I began the Liberation Trilogy, the final volume is done. It took me far longer to tell the tale of the war in the Mediterranean and in western Europe than it took Allied armies to win those campaigns. There were more of them, true enough, but I certainly had assistance from many quarters. My debt to those who helped along the way is exceeded only by my gratitude.

Publication of the first two volumes, *An Army at Dawn* and *The Day of Battle*, encouraged many veterans and their progeny, as well as others with an interest and expertise in World War II, to provide me with memoirs, oral histories, and sundry material about the campaign in western Europe for this third volume. I would like to thank:

Creighton Abrams, James Acklin, Bruce Adkinson, John Alosi, Jr., Karen Anderson, Robert C. Baldridge, Steven Barry, Charles C. Bates, Robert W. Baumer, Günter Bischof, W. H. Black, Lloyd J. Bliss, Roger N. Bollier, Marty Bollinger, Jan Bos, David R. Boyd, Spencer Bruskin, Garfield Brown, Charles F. Bryan, Jr., Steve Bull Bear, James MacGregor Burns, Harold Burson, Andrew Carroll, Ben Celano, Robert E. Coffin, Edward M. Coffman, Michael J. Corley, Jim K. Cullen, Richard G. Davis, Joe DeMarco, Leonard Nicolas DeNucci, Carlo D'Este, Henry B. Dewey, Joseph C. Doherty, Michael D. Doubler, R. K. Doughty, Gerald H. Dorman, Roger S. Durham, Walter D. Ehlers, David Eisenhower, John S. D. Eisenhower, Coy Eklund, Jan Elvin, Isaac Epps, Francis A. Even, Daniel G. Felger, Allen R. Ferguson, Andrew E. Finkel, Giovanni Finzi-Contini, Don M. Fox, Richard B. Frank, Bill Frederick, Leonard J. Fullenkamp, Johnny Gibson, John A. Gill, Linda Gilmore, Mark Good, Walter Grabowski, Walter H. Greenfield, Jr., Fred Groff III, Hans-Jürgen Habenicht, Arthur T. Hadley, Fred W. Hall, Jr., Herb H. Ham, Ralph Hauenstein, Dixon D. Hedges, Carl F. Heintze, Walter C. Heisler, Matthew Hermes, Peter C. Hesse, Shane Hinckley, Fred Hoffman, Weldon Hogie, Rick Holderbaum, Edgar Holton, Douglas Hope, Sir Michael Howard, Charles H. Hubbell,

Tim Hughes, Dennis J. Hutchinson, Dean F. Jewett, Lewis Johnston, Douglas B. Jordan, Phil Jutras, David Kahn, Dave Kanzler, William Kearney, Robert J. Kenney, Jr., Roger Keppel, Dave Kerr, Michael Ketchum, Janet Keysser, Harry W. O. Kinnard II, Sherry Klein, Todd Kleinhuizen, William A. Knowlton, Frederick J. Kroesen, Edward Latham, John Leh II, Brian M. Linn, Roy Livengood, Leonard G. Lomell, Eugene M. Long, Jr., John F. Manning, Sanford H. Margalith, Jack A. Marshall, Joseph Edgar Martin, Peter A. McGrath, Sally McGrath, Donald L. Miller, Allan R. Millett, William W. Moir, Philip Monteleoni, Virginia P. Montgomery, Dan Morgan, Henry G. Morgan, Mary Ann Moxon, Paul Gregory Nagle, Michael Carey Nason, Lovern "Jerry" Nauss, Jeff Nichols, Randy Norton, Bruce Parker, Donald G. Patton, Rick Perry, Paul A. Philcox, Henry G. Phillips, Richard Piotrowski, Mike Popowski, Rich Porter, William P. T. Preston, Jr., Sally Quinn, William W. Quinn, Russell Rains, Daniel B. Rathbun, Edward Rathje, Mark J. Reardon, Lacy Reaves, Robert A. Reisman, Delmar Richards, John K. Rieth, Joseph P. "Phil" Rivers, Estil Robertson, Eric Ross, Stan Scislowski, Robert H. Seabrook, Allan Serviss, William P. Shaw, Kevin P. Shea, Robert Sheridan II, Nathan M. Shippee, Lewis "Bob" Sorley, Arthur O. Spaulding, Douglas M. Spencer, Roger Spiller, Gregory Stejskal, Wayne Stiles, Timothy R. Stoy, Ray Stuchell, Jim Sudmeier, C. C. Taylor, Will Thornton, Louis J. Timchak, Jr., Jack W. Tipton, Laurie Campbell Toth, Charles E. Umhey, Jr., Hoyt Sanford Vandenberg, Jr., Donald C. Van Roosen, Hans von Luck, Douglas C. Waller, George Patton "Pat" Waters, Joanne Villafane, Stephen J. Weiss, Carroll Wetzel, Jr., Clark Whelton, Tanya Bruskin White, Luther George Williams, Jr., James M. Wilson, Jr., Harold R. Winton, Scott Wolf, Tom Wolfson, John Ward Yates, and David T. Zabecki.

I had the good fortune to have seven accomplished historians read all or parts of the manuscript. I thank them for their invaluable suggestions, while accepting full responsibility for any errors of fact or judgment: Tami Davis Biddle, Roger Cirillo, Timothy K. Nenninger, Mark A. Stoler, James Scott Wheeler, David T. Zabecki, and particularly Joseph Balkoski, the gifted chronicler of the battles for Normandy and beyond, who was generous enough to read the thing twice.

For a third time I gratefully acknowledge a profound debt to the hundreds of historians, memoirists, and others whose writings over the past seventy years provide the foundation for all subsequent works of scholarship. The 114-volume *U.S. Army in World War II*, the official history known as the Green Series, has been invaluable to me, as have the official British *History of the Second World War, The Army Air Forces in World War II*, and other works, ranging from short monographs and periodical articles to multivolume studies.

But the core of this narrative, like its two predecessors, derives from primary, contemporaneous sources, including diaries, letters, and unpublished manuscripts, as well as official records, after action reports, and combat interviews. I appreciate the professionalism and patience of archivists, historians, and librarians by the score in tracking down those thousands of documents. That starts at the National Archives and Records Administration in College Park, Maryland, where cumulatively I have spent many months since January 1999. I thank Richard Boylan, Timothy Mulligan, Larry McDonald, Sharon Culley, Theresa Roy, and especially my close friend Tim Nenninger, the chief of modern military records, without whom there would be no trilogy.

The U.S. Army's Military History Institute, part of the Army Heritage and Education Center at Carlisle, Pennsylvania, remains among the greatest military archives in the world and a priceless asset to anyone studying World War II. In researching this volume, I made twenty-three pilgrimages to MHI, usually for two- or three-day stretches; in all, I made sixty-nine visits while working on the trilogy. I am beholden to the entire staff, and particularly Col. Matthew Dawson, the AHEC director; Conrad C. Crane, the MHI director; Richard L. Baker, senior technical information specialist; Molly A. Bompane, curator of photography; Stephen Bye; Terry Foster; Rodney Foytik; Tom Hendrix; Clifton Hyatt; Gary Johnson; David A. Keough; Michael E. Lynch; Jessica Sheets; Melissa K. Wiford; and particularly Richard J. Sommers.

At the adjacent U.S. Army War College at Carlisle Barracks, I thank the current commandant, Maj. Gen. Anthony A. Cucolo III, and his predecessors, Lt. Gen. David H. Huntoon, Jr., and Maj. Gen. Gregg F. Martin. Also: Bohdan I. Kohutiak, the library director, and my good friend and former co-instructor, Col. (ret.) Charles D. Allen.

The U.S. Army Center of Military History at Fort McNair in Washington, D.C., once again provided expertise and a rich lode of documents. I thank Robert J. Dalessandro, the executive director and chief of military history; Richard W. Stewart, the chief historian; Frank R. Shirer, chief of the historical resources branch; David W. Hogan, Jr.; and Beth McKenzie.

I had the good fortune to twice hold media fellowships in 2008 and 2010 at the Hoover Institution on War, Revolution and Peace at Stanford University. I thank David Brady and Mandy MacCalla, as well as archivist Carol A. Leadenham and associate archivist Brad Bauer. Thanks too to George P. Shultz for his cordial encouragement.

I was an Axel Springer Berlin Prize fellow in the fall of 2009 at the

American Academy in Berlin, a marvelously nurturing institution for scholars and artists. I thank Gary Smith, the executive director, and his entire staff.

Through the University of Chicago's Jeff Metcalf Fellows Program I was lucky enough to have research assistance in the summer of 2010 from the talented, diligent Tomek Blusiewicz, then a Chicago undergraduate and now a graduate student in history at Harvard. I'm also grateful for research assistance on volume three from Ella Hoffman, Hal Libby, and Eric Goldstein, and from my children, Sarah J. Atkinson, now a surgical resident in Cincinnati, and Rush Atkinson, now a Justice Department lawyer in Washington. The knowledgeable Steve Goodell helped with photo research.

The encouragement and generous support of the Association of the United States Army has been important from the beginning of this enterprise. I particularly thank Gen. (ret.) Gordon R. Sullivan, the association president and former Army chief of staff, Lt. Gen. (ret.) Theodore G. Stroup, Jr., and Lt. Gen. (ret.) Thomas G. Rhame.

At the Franklin D. Roosevelt Presidential Library in Hyde Park, New York, I am grateful to the former director, Cynthia M. Koch, and to supervisory archivist Robert Clark. Likewise, at the Dwight D. Eisenhower Presidential Library in Abilene, Kansas, I appreciate the assistance of archivist Christopher Abrahamson.

My appreciation again goes to the George C. Marshall Research Library at the Virginia Military Academy in Lexington, Virginia: to Joanne D. Hartog, director of research and scholarly programs; Paul B. Barron, director of the library and archives; Peggy L. Dillard, assistant librarian and archivist; Brian D. Shaw, president of the George C. Marshall Foundation; and, at VMI, Gen. (ret.) J. H. Binford Peay III, the superintendent; Prof. Malcolm "Kip" Muir, Jr.; and Brig. Gen. (ret.) Charles F. Brower IV.

For a third time I thank the Colonel Robert R. McCormick Research Center at the First Division Museum in Wheaton, Illinois, a division archive without peer. I especially appreciate help from Col. (ret.) Paul H. Herbert, executive director of the Cantigny First Division Foundation, and from Eric Gillespie, director of the research center, and Andrew E. Woods, research historian. I made very good use of the D-Day Archival Collection and other 29th Infantry Division material held by the Maryland Military Historical Society at the Fifth Regiment Armory in Baltimore, Maryland. Thanks to Wayde Minami and especially Joe Balkoski.

The flourishing National World War II Museum in New Orleans has been a source of encouragement and assistance. Thanks to Gordon H. "Nick" Mueller, the president and CEO, Stephen Watson, Jeremy Collins, Lindsey Barnes, Cindy McCurdy, Tom Czekanski, Stacy Peckham, and Sam Wegner.

The Combined Arms Research Library at Ft. Leavenworth, Kansas, provided an exceptionally diverse array of materials. Thank you to Edwin B. Burgess, Rusty P. Rafferty, Kathleen M. Buker, and Elizabeth J. Merrifield.

In the Office of History for the U.S. Army Corps of Engineers at Ft. Belvoir, Virginia, I thank Michael J. Brodhead, John Lonnquest, and Matthew T. Pearcy. In the Special Collections and Archives at the U.S. Military Academy Library, West Point, New York, I thank Suzanne M. Christoff, Susan M. Lintelman, Alicia M. Mauldin-Ware, and Valerie Dutdut. Thanks too to Janis Jorgensen, the Heritage Collection manager at the U.S. Naval Institute in Annapolis, Maryland, and to John W. Greco at the Naval History and Heritage Command in Washington, D.C.

In the United Kingdom, I appreciate help from the staff of the National Archives in Kew. At the Liddell Hart Centre for Military Archives at King's College in London, I thank Kate O'Brien, Frances Pattman, Lianne Smith, and Patricia J. Methven, the director of archive services. Grateful thanks once again to Roderick Suddaby and his staff in the Department of Documents at the Imperial War Museum. In Germany, thanks to Michael Epkenhans and Markus Pöhlmann at the Militärgeschictliches Forschungsamt in Potsdam.

Thanks to Doug McCabe, in the department of archives and special collections at Ohio University Library in Athens, Ohio, home to the remarkable Cornelius Ryan Collection. I also appreciate the help of Julian M. Pleasants and Diane Fischler in using the Samuel Proctor Oral History Program, in the University of Florida history department. Likewise, I appreciate the help of Cynthia L. Tinker, project coordinator at the Center for the Study of War and Society, University of Tennessee at Knoxville.

At the York County Heritage Trust in York, Pennsylvania, Lila Fourhman-Shaull, the library and archives director, was especially generous in helping me research the papers of Jacob L. Devers. Thanks to Brig. Gen. (ret.) John W. Nicholson and Martha Sell of the American Battle Monuments Commission, and to Rena Church, director-curator of the Aurora Public Art Commission/ Grand Army of the Republic Museum in Aurora, Illinois.

Walking the ground is vital for any military historian, and I have visited most of the European battlefields described in this volume, beginning in the mid-1990s, when I served as the Berlin bureau chief of *The Washington Post*. On several occasions I had the good fortune to study the terrain, at places like the Bulge, the Hürtgen Forest, and Colmar, with professional soldiers. For this I particularly thank Gen. (ret.) Montgomery C. Meigs and Gen. Carter F. Ham, both of whom commanded the U.S.

Army in Europe, as well as two former chiefs of Army history, Maj. Gen. (ret.) William A. Stofft and Brig. Gen. (ret.) Harold Nelson, and a team of fine historians: Scott Wheeler, Andrew N. Morris, and Layne Van Arsdale.

This is the sixth book I have written with the remarkable John Sterling as my editor and close friend; collectively those books total more than 3,700 pages, and John has improved every page. At Henry Holt, and at the publisher's parent company, Macmillan, I also thank John Sargent, Steve Rubin, Maggie Richards, Pat Eisemann, Katie Kurtzman, Kenn Russell, Meryl Levavi, Emi Ikkanda, Chuck Thompson, Jason Liebman, and Muriel Jorgensen. Jolanta Benal has copyedited all three volumes of the Liberation Trilogy, making each better in ways large and small.

All sixty-eight maps in the Liberation Trilogy are the work of master cartographer Gene Thorp, who has been a delightful, innovative partner throughout this project. My friend and agent for twenty-seven years, Rafe Sagalyn, helped see me through it all.

My thanks also goes to Antony Beevor, Ben Bradlee, Tom Brokaw, Steve Coll, Leonard Downie, Jr., Glenn Frankel, Donald E. Graham, Ken Heckler, Fred Hiatt, Robert G. Kaiser, Lewis Libby, David H. Petraeus, Catherine B. Reynolds, Wayne R. Reynolds, Thomas E. Ricks, William B. Schultz, David Von Drehle, Geoffrey Wawro, Gerhard L. Weinberg, Bob Woodward, and fellow scribbler David Maraniss. Particular thanks to Sir Max Hastings and his wife, Penny, for their generous hospitality and friendship.

Grateful acknowledgment is made of permission to quote various materials: Viscount Montgomery of Alamein for extracts from the writings of his father, Field Marshal Bernard L. Montgomery; Roger Kirk for an oral history with Adm. Alan Goodrich Kirk; Virginia P. Montgomery, for extracts from an unpublished memoir by her father, Robert P. Patterson; Linda Gilmore, for extracts from a memoir by her brother, Richard Henry Byers; George Patton "Pat" Waters, for extracts from prisoner-of-war journals kept by his father, John K. Waters, and for a photograph of Lt. Col. Waters; Margot Taylor for extracts from "And Came Safe Home," a diary by her father, William Steel Brownlie; Annette Conway for an extract from the "The Man Who Worked on Sunday," by her father, L. F. Skinner; Mavis Jones for extracts from the papers of her husband, Lt. Col. E. Jones; and Dani Smith for extracts from the diary of her father, J. H. Patterson.

Also: the Trustees of the Liddell Hart Centre for Military Archives, King's College London, for material from the collections of Capt. B. H. Liddell Hart, Field Marshal Lord Alanbrooke, Maj. Gen. J. B. Churcher, Maj. Gen. Francis de Guingand, Brigadier Sir Geoffrey Hardy-Roberts, Gen. H. L. Ismay, Col. T. G. Lindsay, Brig. J. S. W. Stone, and R. W. W. "Chester" Wilmot. And thanks to the Trustees of the Imperial War Museum, London, for material from the collection of Major E. M. Elliott.

In instances where current copyright holders could not be located, or where permissions arrived too late to be noted in this edition, I will gladly include acknowledgments in future editions.

Beyond all others, and far beyond this writer's powers of expression, I thank my gorgeous wife of thirty-four years, Jane.

INDEX

Page numbers in *italics* refer to maps.

An Army at Dawn
The War in North Africa, 1942-1943

Rick Atkinson

Volume One of The Liberation Trilogy

The liberation of Europe and the destruction of the Third Reich
is a story of courage and enduring triumph, of calamity and
miscalculation. In this first volume of the Liberation Trilogy,
Rick Atkinson shows why no modern reader can understand
the ultimate victory of the Allied powers without a grasp of the
great drama that unfolded in North Africa in 1942 and 1943.

Beginning with the daring amphibious invasion in November 1942,
An Army at Dawn follows the British and American armies as
they fight the French in Morocco and Algeria, and then take on the
Germans and Italians in Tunisia. Battle by battle, an inexperienced
and sometimes poorly led army gradually becomes a superb
fighting force. Central to the tale are the extraordinary but
fallible commanders who come to dominate the battlefield:
Eisenhower, Patton, Bradley, Montgomery and Rommel.

'Every military history buff should read
An Army at Dawn' – *Sunday Telegraph*

The Day of Battle

The War in Sicily and Italy, 1943-1944

Rick Atkinson

Volume Two of The Liberation Trilogy

The Italian campaign's outcome was never certain; in fact, Roosevelt, Churchill and their military advisors engaged in heated debate about whether an invasion of the so-called soft underbelly of Europe was even a good idea. But once underway, the commitment to liberate Italy from the Nazis never wavered, despite the agonizingly high price. The battles at Salerno, Anzio, and Monte Cassino were particularly difficult and lethal, yet as the months passed, the Allied forces continued to push the Germans up the Italian peninsula. And with the liberation of Rome in June 1944, ultimate victory at last began to seem inevitable.

Drawing on an astonishing array of primary source material, written with great drama and flair, this is narrative history of the first rank.

'A triumph of narrative history, elegantly written, thick with unforgettable description and rooted in the sights and sounds of battle' – *New York Times*

To buy any of our books and to find out
more about Abacus and Little, Brown, our authors
and titles, as well as events and book clubs,
visit our website

www.littlebrown.co.uk

and follow us on Twitter

@AbacusBooks
@LittleBrownUK

To order any Abacus titles p & p free in the UK,
please contact our mail order supplier on:

+ 44 (0)1832 737525

Customers not based in the UK should contact
the same number for appropriate postage
and packing costs.